International Directory of
COMPANY
HISTORIES

International Directory of

COMPANY HISTORIES

VOLUME 105

Editor

Jay P. Pederson

ST. JAMES PRESS
A part of Gale, Cengage Learning

Detroit • New York • San Francisco • New Haven, Conn • Waterville, Maine • London

International Directory of Company Histories, Volume 105

Jay P. Pederson, Editor

Project Editor: Miranda H. Ferrara

Editorial: Virgil Burton, Donna Craft, Louise Gagné, Peggy Geeseman, Julie Gough, Linda Hall, Sonya Hill, Keith Jones, Lynn Pearce, Holly Selden, Justine Ventimiglia

Production Technology Specialist: Mike Weaver

Imaging and Multimedia: John Watkins

Composition and Electronic Prepress: Gary Leach, Evi Seoud

Manufacturing: Rhonda Dover

Product Manager: Jenai Drouillard

For product information and technology assistance, contact us at **Gale Customer Support, 1-800-877-4253.**
For permission to use material from this text or product, submit all requests online at **www.cengage.com/permissions.**
Further permissions questions can be emailed to **permissionrequest@cengage.com**

Gale
27500 Drake Rd.
Farmington Hills, MI, 48331-3535

LIBRARY OF CONGRESS CATALOG NUMBER 89-190943
ISBN-13: 978-1-55862-639-3
ISBN-10: 1-55862-639-5

This title is also available as an e-book
ISBN-13: 978-1-55862-768-0   ISBN-10: 1-55862-768-5
Contact your Gale, a part of Cengage Learning sales representative for ordering information.

BRITISH LIBRARY CATALOGUING IN PUBLICATION DATA
International directory of company histories, Vol. 105
Jay P. Pederson
33.87409

Printed in the United States of America
1 2 3 4 5 6 7 13 12 11 10 09

Contents

Preface

The St. James Press series *The International Directory of Company Histories* (*IDCH*) is intended for reference use by students, business people, librarians, historians, economists, investors, job candidates, and others who seek to learn more about the historical development of the world's most important companies. To date, *IDCH* has covered more than 10,360 companies in 105 volumes.

INCLUSION CRITERIA

Most companies chosen for inclusion in *IDCH* have achieved a minimum of US$25 million in annual sales and are leading influences in their industries or geographical locations. Companies may be publicly held, private, or nonprofit. State-owned companies that are important in their industries and that may operate much like public or private companies also are included. Wholly owned subsidiaries and divisions are profiled if they meet the requirements for inclusion. Entries on companies that have had major changes since they were last profiled may be selected for updating.

The *IDCH* series highlights 25% private and nonprofit companies, and features updated entries on approximately 35 companies per volume.

ENTRY FORMAT

Each entry begins with the company's legal name; the address of its headquarters; its telephone, toll-free, and fax numbers; and its web site. A statement of public, private, state, or parent ownership follows. A company with a legal name in both English and the language of its headquarters country is listed by the English name, with the native-language name in parentheses.

The company's founding or earliest incorporation date, the number of employees, and the most recent available sales figures follow. Sales figures are given in local currencies with equivalents in U.S. dollars. For some private companies, sales figures are estimates and indicated by the abbreviation *est.* The entry lists the exchanges on which the company's stock is traded and its ticker symbol, as well as the company's NAICS codes.

Entries generally contain a *Company Perspectives* box which provides a short summary of the company's mission, goals, and ideals; a *Key Dates* box highlighting milestones in the company's history; lists of *Principal Subsidiaries*, *Principal Divisions*, *Principal Operating Units*, *Principal Competitors*; and articles for *Further Reading*.

American spelling is used throughout *IDCH*, and the word "billion" is used in its U.S. sense of one thousand million.

SOURCES

Entries have been compiled from publicly accessible sources both in print and on the Internet such as general and academic periodicals, books, and annual reports, as well as material supplied by the companies themselves.

CUMULATIVE INDEXES

IDCH contains three indexes: the **Cumulative Index to Companies**, which provides an alphabetical index to companies profiled in the *IDCH* series, the **Index to Industries**, which allows researchers to locate companies by their principal industry, and the **Geographic Index**, which lists companies alphabetically by the country of their headquarters. The indexes are cumulative and specific instructions for using them are found immediately preceding each index.

SPECIAL TO THIS VOLUME

This volume of *IDCH* contains an entry on Morgan Motor Company, the oldest privately held automaker in the world.

SUGGESTIONS WELCOME

Comments and suggestions from users of *IDCH* on any aspect of the product as well as suggestions for companies to be included or updated are cordially invited. Please write:

The Editor
International Directory of Company Histories
St. James Press
Gale, Cengage Learning
27500 Drake Rd.
Farmington Hills, Michigan 48331-3535

St. James Press does not endorse any of the companies or products mentioned in this series. Companies appearing in the *International Directory of Company Histories* were selected without reference to their wishes and have in no way endorsed their entries.

Notes on Contributors

M. L. Cohen
Novelist, business writer, and researcher living in Paris.

Jeffrey L. Covell
Seattle-based writer.

Ed Dinger
Writer and editor based in Bronx, New York.

Paul R. Greenland
Illinois-based writer and researcher; author of two books and former senior editor of a national business magazine; contributor to *The Encyclopedia of Chicago History, The Encyclopedia of Religion,* and the *Encyclopedia of American Industries.*

Robert Halasz
Former editor in chief of *World Progress* and *Funk & Wagnalls New Encyclopedia Yearbook*; author, *The U.S. Marines* (Millbrook Press, 1993).

Frederick C. Ingram
Writer based in South Carolina.

Kathleen Peippo
Minnesota-based writer.

Nelson Rhodes
Editor, writer, and consultant in the Chicago area.

Carrie Rothburd
Writer and editor specializing in corporate profiles, academic texts, and academic journal articles.

David E. Salamie
Part-owner of InfoWorks Development Group, a reference publication development and editorial services company.

Ted Sylvester
Photographer, writer, and editor of the environmental journal *From the Ground Up.*

Mary Tradii
Michigan-based writer.

A. Woodward
Wisconsin-based writer.

List of Abbreviations

¥ Japanese yen
£ United Kingdom pound
$ United States dollar

A

AB Aktiebolag (Finland, Sweden)
AB Oy Aktiebolag Osakeyhtiot (Finland)
A.E. Anonimos Eteria (Greece)
AED Emirati dirham
AG Aktiengesellschaft (Austria, Germany, Switzerland, Liechtenstein)
aG auf Gegenseitigkeit (Austria, Germany)
A.m.b.a. Andelsselskab med begraenset ansvar (Denmark)
A.O. Anonim Ortaklari/Ortakligi (Turkey)
ApS Amparteselskab (Denmark)
ARS Argentine peso
A.S. Anonim Sirketi (Turkey)
A/S Aksjeselskap (Norway)
A/S Aktieselskab (Denmark, Sweden)
Ay Avoinyhtio (Finland)
ATS Austrian shilling
AUD Australian dollar
ApS Amparteselskab (Denmark)
Ay Avoinyhtio (Finland)

B

B.A. Buttengewone Aansprakeiijkheid (Netherlands)
BEF Belgian franc

BHD Bahraini dinar
Bhd. Berhad (Malaysia, Brunei)
BND Brunei dollar
BRL Brazilian real
B.V. Besloten Vennootschap (Belgium, Netherlands)

C

C.A. Compania Anonima (Ecuador, Venezuela)
CAD Canadian dollar
C. de R.L. Compania de Responsabilidad Limitada (Spain)
CEO Chief Executive Officer
CFO Chief Financial Officer
CHF Swiss franc
Cia. Companhia (Brazil, Portugal)
Cia. Compania (Latin America [except Brazil], Spain)
Cia. Compagnia (Italy)
Cie. Compagnie (Belgium, France, Luxembourg, Netherlands)
CIO Chief Information Officer
CLP Chilean peso
CNY Chinese yuan
Co. Company
COO Chief Operating Officer
Coop. Cooperative
COP Colombian peso
Corp. Corporation
C. por A. Compania por Acciones (Dominican Republic)
CPT Cuideachta Phoibi Theoranta

(Republic of Ireland)
CRL Companhia a Responsabilidao Limitida (Portugal, Spain)
C.V. Commanditaire Vennootschap (Netherlands, Belgium)
CZK Czech koruna

D

D&B Dunn & Bradstreet
DEM German deutsche mark
Div. Division (United States)
DKK Danish krone
DZD Algerian dinar

E

EC Exempt Company (Arab countries)
Edms. Bpk. Eiendoms Beperk (South Africa)
EEK Estonian Kroon
eG eingetragene Genossenschaft (Germany)
EGMBH Eingetragene Genossenschaft mit beschraenkter Haftung (Austria, Germany)
EGP Egyptian pound
Ek For Ekonomisk Forening (Sweden)
EP Empresa Portuguesa (Portugal)
E.P.E. Etema Pemorismenis Evthynis (Greece)
ESOP Employee Stock Options and Ownership
ESP Spanish peseta

Et(s). Etablissement(s) (Belgium, France, Luxembourg)
eV eingetragener Verein (Germany)
EUR euro

F
FIM Finnish markka
FRF French franc

G
G.I.E. Groupement d'Interet Economique (France)
gGmbH gemeinnutzige Gesellschaft mit beschraenkter Haftung (Austria, Germany, Switzerland)
G.I.E. Groupement d'Interet Economique (France)
GmbH Gesellschaft mit beschraenkter Haftung (Austria, Germany, Switzerland)
GRD Greek drachma
GWA Gewerbte Amt (Austria, Germany)

H
HB Handelsbolag (Sweden)
HF Hlutafelag (Iceland)
HKD Hong Kong dollar
HUF Hungarian forint

I
IDR Indonesian rupiah
IEP Irish pound
ILS new Israeli shekel
Inc. Incorporated (United States, Canada)
INR Indian rupee
IPO Initial Public Offering
I/S Interesentselskap (Norway)
I/S Interessentselskab (Denmark)
ISK Icelandic krona
ITL Italian lira

J
JMD Jamaican dollar
JOD Jordanian dinar

K
KB Kommanditbolag (Sweden)
KES Kenyan schilling
Kft Korlatolt Felelossegu Tarsasag (Hungary)
KG Kommanditgesellschaft (Austria, Germany, Switzerland)

KGaA Kommanditgesellschaft auf Aktien (Austria, Germany, Switzerland)
KK Kabushiki Kaisha (Japan)
KPW North Korean won
KRW South Korean won
K/S Kommanditselskab (Denmark)
K/S Kommandittselskap (Norway)
KWD Kuwaiti dinar
Ky Kommandiitiyhtio (Finland)

L
LBO Leveraged Buyout
Lda. Limitada (Spain)
L.L.C. Limited Liability Company (Arab countries, Egypt, Greece, United States)
L.L.P. Limited Liability Partnership (United States)
L.P. Limited Partnership (Canada, South Africa, United Kingdom, United States)
Ltd. Limited
Ltda. Limitada (Brazil, Portugal)
Ltee. Limitee (Canada, France)
LUF Luxembourg franc

M
mbH mit beschraenkter Haftung (Austria, Germany)
Mij. Maatschappij (Netherlands)
MUR Mauritian rupee
MXN Mexican peso
MYR Malaysian ringgit

N
N.A. National Association (United States)
NGN Nigerian naira
NLG Netherlands guilder
NOK Norwegian krone
N.V. Naamloze Vennootschap (Belgium, Netherlands)
NZD New Zealand dollar

O
OAO Otkrytoe Aktsionernoe Obshchestve (Russia)
OHG Offene Handelsgesellschaft (Austria, Germany, Switzerland)
OMR Omani rial
OOO Obschestvo s Ogranichennoi Otvetstvennostiu (Russia)
OOUR Osnova Organizacija

Udruzenog Rada (Yugoslavia)
Oy Osakeyhtî (Finland)

P
P.C. Private Corp. (United States)
PEN Peruvian Nuevo Sol
PHP Philippine peso
PKR Pakistani rupee
P/L Part Lag (Norway)
PLC Public Limited Co. (United Kingdom, Ireland)
P.L.L.C. Professional Limited Liability Corporation (United States)
PLN Polish zloty
P.T. Perusahaan/Perseroan Terbatas (Indonesia)
PTE Portuguese escudo
Pte. Private (Singapore)
Pty. Proprietary (Australia, South Africa, United Kingdom)
Pvt. Private (India, Zimbabwe)
PVBA Personen Vennootschap met Beperkte Aansprakelijkheid (Belgium)
PYG Paraguay guarani

Q
QAR Qatar riyal

R
REIT Real Estate Investment Trust
RMB Chinese renminbi
Rt Reszvenytarsasag (Hungary)
RUB Russian ruble

S
S.A. Société Anonyme (Arab countries, Belgium, France, Jordan, Luxembourg, Switzerland)
S.A. Sociedad Anónima (Latin America [except Brazil], Spain, Mexico)
S.A. Sociedades Anônimas (Brazil, Portugal)
SAA Societe Anonyme Arabienne (Arab countries)
S.A.B. de C.V. Sociedad Anónima Bursátil de Capital Variable (Mexico)
S.A.C. Sociedad Anonima Comercial (Latin America [except Brazil])
S.A.C.I. Sociedad Anonima Comercial e Industrial (Latin America [except Brazil])

S.A.C.I.y.F. Sociedad Anonima Comercial e Industrial y Financiera (Latin America [except Brazil])

S.A. de C.V. Sociedad Anonima de Capital Variable (Mexico)

SAK Societe Anonyme Kuweitienne (Arab countries)

SAL Societe Anonyme Libanaise (Arab countries)

SAO Societe Anonyme Omanienne (Arab countries)

SAQ Societe Anonyme Qatarienne (Arab countries)

SAR Saudi riyal

S.A.R.L. Sociedade Anonima de Responsabilidade Limitada (Brazil, Portugal)

S.A.R.L. Société à Responsabilité Limitée (France, Belgium, Luxembourg)

S.A.S. Societá in Accomandita Semplice (Italy)

S.A.S. Societe Anonyme Syrienne (Arab countries)

S.C. Societe en Commandite (Belgium, France, Luxembourg)

S.C.A. Societe Cooperativa Agricole (France, Italy, Luxembourg)

S.C.I. Sociedad Cooperativa Ilimitada (Spain)

S.C.L. Sociedad Cooperativa Limitada (Spain)

S.C.R.L. Societe Cooperative a Responsabilite Limitee (Belgium)

Sdn. Bhd. Sendirian Berhad (Malaysia)

SEK Swedish krona

SGD Singapore dollar

S.L. Sociedad Limitada (Latin America [except Brazil], Portugal, Spain)

S/L Salgslag (Norway)

S.N.C. Société en Nom Collectif (France)

Soc. Sociedad (Latin America [except Brazil], Spain)

Soc. Sociedade (Brazil, Portugal)

Soc. Societa (Italy)

S.p.A. Società per Azioni (Italy)

Sp. z.o.o. Spólka z ograniczona odpowiedzialnoscia (Poland)

S.R.L. Sociedad de Responsabilidad Limitada (Spain, Mexico, Latin America [except Brazil])

S.R.L. Società a Responsabilità Limitata (Italy)

S.R.O. Spolecnost s Rucenim Omezenym (Czechoslovakia

S.S.K. Sherkate Sahami Khass (Iran)

Ste. Societe (France, Belgium, Luxembourg, Switzerland)

Ste. Cve. Societe Cooperative (Belgium)

S.V. Samemwerkende Vennootschap (Belgium)

S.Z.R.L. Societe Zairoise a Responsabilite Limitee (Zaire)

T
THB Thai baht

TND Tunisian dinar

TRL Turkish lira

TWD new Taiwan dollar

U

U.A. Uitgesloten Aansporakeiijkheid (Netherlands)

u.p.a. utan personligt ansvar (Sweden)

V

VAG Verein der Arbeitgeber (Austria, Germany)

VEB Venezuelan bolivar

VERTR Vertriebs (Austria, Germany)

VND Vietnamese dong

V.O.f. Vennootschap onder firma (Netherlands)

VVAG Versicherungsverein auf Gegenseitigkeit (Austria, Germany)

W–Z

WA Wettelika Aansprakalikhaed (Netherlands)

WLL With Limited Liability (Bahrain, Kuwait, Qatar, Saudi Arabia)

YK Yugen Kaisha (Japan)

ZAO Zakrytoe Aktsionernoe Obshchestve (Russia)

ZAR South African rand

ZMK Zambian kwacha

ZWD Zimbabwean dollar

Aché Laboratórios Farmacéuticas S.A.

—■—

Rodavia Presidente Dutra Km 222.2
Guarulhos, São Paulo 07034-904
Brazil
Telephone: (55 11) 2608-6000
Toll Free: (0800) 701-6400 (in Brazil)
Fax: (55 11) 2608-6178
Web site: http://www.ache.com.br

Private Company
Incorporated: 1965
Employees: 3,000
Sales: BRL 1.5 billion ($789 million) (2007 est.)
NAICS: 325411 Medical and Botanical Manufacturing;
   325412 Pharmaceutical Preparation Manufacturing;
   325620 Toilet Preparation Manufacturing

■ ■ ■

Aché Laboratórios Farmacéuticas S.A. is the largest Brazilian manufacturer of pharmaceutical products. Besides a large number of prescription, over-the-counter, and generic medications, it produces several cosmetics for the skin. The company invests in the development of synthetic medications, both through its own research efforts and in partnership with Brazilian research centers.

GROWING MARKETER AND MANUFACTURER: 1965–89

Aché was founded in 1965 by three young residents of São Paulo: Adalmiro Dellape Baptista, Antonio Depieri, and Victor Siaulys, friends who were sales representatives

for Squibb Corporation. They wanted to make money on a venture that would enable them to use their aptitude for sales. Initially this business was called Prodoctor, but early on they bought Aché from a French doctor named Phillip Aché. Baptista assumed the presidency of the enterprise and its leadership.

The three men divided the work, with Baptista taking charge of commerce and marketing, Depieri of administration and finance, and Siaulys of production. They met only when they had to make a decision in common. One of their earliest, and long lasting, products was the decongestant Sorine; another was Tandrilax, a painkiller introduced in 1980. Originally Aché was engaged only in distribution, but by 1973, when it moved to Guarulhos, a suburb of São Paulo, the company was manufacturing drugs as well. It was specializing in products extracted from glands.

Aché acquired the Novoterápica laboratory, a subsidiary of the Italian firm Bracco S.p.A., in 1977, and opened a plant for raw materials in 1980. It gained an important supplier when, in 1982, it won the right to produce and sell products of Parke-Davis & Co. in Brazil under exclusive license. The following year it advanced to fifth place among pharmaceutical firms in terms of sales volume. The Brazilian economy was in recession, but Aché earned a profit by cutting costs and maintained its longstanding policy of financing growth out of its own resources.

In 1988 Aché created the Prodome Química e Farmacêutica joint venture in partnership with Merck Sharp & Dohme Corp. This very profitable association

---

COMPANY PERSPECTIVES

■

Mission: To make available continually, with quality, creativity, and profitability, innovative and accessible products and services that promote the health and well-being of consumers, with motivated and capable collaborators and respect for people and for the environment.

---

combined Merck's roster of medications with Aché's marketing expertise, which included visits by company representatives to almost all Brazilian physicians.

RISE TO INDUSTRY LEADERSHIP: 1990–99

In 1990 the company acquired 42 percent of Schering-Plough Produtos Farmacêuticas Ltda., the Brazilian subsidiary of this U.S.-based drug giant. In 1994 Aché became the best-earning all-Brazilian company in the pharmaceutical field. In that year and the next three it earned $350 million in profits. By 1998 Aché had assumed first place among Brazilian pharmaceutical companies in sales, a position it never relinquished. Only two European laboratories outstripped Aché in Brazilian sales that year. Of the 20 major pharmaceutical laboratories in Brazil in 1998, only two besides Aché were majority held by Brazilian capital: Prodome and Schering-Plough.

According to a pharmaceuticals industry executive, the secret of Aché's success was its 750 diligent salespeople, who visited the 115,000 doctors in all parts of Brazil, urging them to prescribe the company's foremost medications, such as Aldomet, Caladryl, Fibrtase, Moduretic, Novocilin, and Sorine. All of the sales representatives were men. It was alleged that women would have difficulty carrying around the 33 pound sample cases and visiting out-of-the way locations, traveling by night, and staying at all kinds of lodgings.

By this time, all three of Aché's three founders had passed the theoretical retirement age of 60. All had sons working for the company in 1996, when Baptista and Siaulys decided the situation would create rivalries and frustrate plans to hire and retain career professionals. Nevertheless, two sons of Depieri continued to work for the firm. The three partners formed family holdings, with equal stakes in the firm, in 1998 for themselves and their 12 children.

Aché was considered once of the best companies in Brazil to work for by the business magazine *Exame.* Although salaries were mediocre, the company offered free healthcare not only for the employee but also his or her spouse and children and even parents, siblings, and other relatives. Aché medications were, of course, free as well. Inside the plant was a gymnasium, a 150-bed nursery for workers' children, a space for children between seven and 14 to read and play, and classrooms offering free courses for youths between 15 and 18. Opportunities for advancement were based on quality of work rather than a diploma.

THE STRUGGLE FOR CONTROL: 2000–01

Harmony came to an end in 2000, the year in which Aché lost money for the first time. Brazilian pharmaceutical companies had suffered from a law adopted in 1996 that put an end to copying medications without a license from the patent holders. Like the others, Aché owed a large part of its sales to these drugs, including Sorine and the analgesic and anti-inflammatory drug Tandrilax. They were known as "similars" and sold at prices much below those of the original products.

U.S. drug manufacturers had long and loudly protested Brazil's removal in 1969 of patent protection for pharmaceutical products. In reply, the Brazilian government had maintained that its open-door policy was necessary to protect its own manufacturers from multinationals, who were said to control, in 1987, more than 70 percent of the Brazilian drug market.

The question became in what direction to proceed. In 1997 the consultant McKinsey & Company, Inc., had urged Aché to professionalize its management and form partnerships with international firms to sell new medications in Brazil and other Latin American countries. Family members, furthermore, were counseled to confine themselves to board positions. This plan was accepted by Siaulys and the Depieri brothers in 2000 over Baptista's objections. Baptista vainly opposed the sale that year of Aché's shares in Schering-Plough for $32.5 million, charging irregularities in the accounts.

The struggle for control of Aché was aired at a July 2000 extraordinary general stockholders meeting at which Baptista's son and an ally were accused of stealing and forging company documents. A new board was chosen in 2001 that included six members from outside the firm, and Baptista was replaced as president at the end of the year. By that time more than 30 judicial proceedings had consumed at least $10 million in expenses for the firm.

KEY DATES

1965: Three young sales representatives found Aché.

1983: Company has reached fifth place in sales volume in its field.

1988: Aché forms a partnership with Merck Sharp & Dohme Corp.

1997: Aché has earned $350 million in profits since 1994.

1998: Aché assumes first place in sales volume among Brazilian pharmaceutical firms.

2000: Dissension among the founders marks Aché's first money-losing year.

2005: Acquisition of Biosintética brings annual revenue to over BRL 1 billion.

2007: Aché enters the cosmetics market with a line of skin care products.

2009: Company is selling more than 200 brands in about 600 presentations.

The president resigned after eight months and was succeeded by another outsider who, like his predecessor, lacked the power to make strategic decisions. According to a former executive, McKinsey consultants assumed day-to-day management. After Aché's owners made peace in 2002, its president remained at the helm for another four years.

ACQUISITIONS AND NEW PRODUCTS: 2002–03

Although Aché returned to profitability, the Parke-Davis license was lost to Pfizer Inc. in 2002. The Prodome joint venture lapsed after the prescribed period of 15 years, and Aché sold its share. With its Guarulhos factory producing only at 60 percent of capacity, the company was studying the possibility of manufacturing generic drugs or manufacturing medications under license from another firm.

In 2003 Aché acquired, for BRL 100 million (about $32 million), the Brazilian subsidiary of ASTA Medica Gmbh, a German laboratory that was producing three drugs, including an anti-inflammatory named Flogoral. The company also entered the booming field of medications based on plant extracts rather than synthetic chemicals, using the funds normally spent to produce similars and splitting the development costs with universities and research centers interested in studying biodiversity in Brazil. In 2004 Aché registered Acheflar, an anti-inflammatory drug for chronic tendinitis and muscular pain. It was the first one based on plant extracts totally developed in Brazil.

THE BIOSINTÉTICA ACQUISITION IN 2005

Biosintética Farmacêutica Ltda., a pharmaceuticals manufacturer about half the size of Aché, was acquired in 2005 for an estimated BRL 500 million ($210 million). Founded in São Paulo in the 1950s, it was bought by a U.S. firm in 1977 but was sold in 1984 to Omilton Visconde, a Brazilian pharmaceuticals executive. Like Aché, Biosintética had to reinvent itself in the wake of the legislation that banned similars; in 1993, for example, the company's $38 million in revenues came from 25 similars.

Biosintética turned to generic drugs, products whose patents had expired. It also formed partnerships with laboratories in nine other countries because of the high cost of developing new drugs. One of these was with the Argentine firm Bio Sidus S.A. in a joint venture named Biolatina. Another was with the Israeli company Teva Pharmaceutical Industries Ltd., a major manufacturer of generic drugs. Like Aché, Biosintética was also developing new drugs in partnership with Brazilian universities, including medications derived from plant extracts. Also like Aché, it was considered a good place to work because of non-money factors such as easy access to the executives, autonomy, recognition of individuality, and the freedom to innovate.

The acquisition of Biosintética turned Aché into the biggest firm of its kind in Latin America and, for a brief period, the leader in the Brazilian market, with annual revenues exceeding BRL 1 billion (about $450 million) a year. Biosintética, strong in generics and cardiovascular, neurological, and intravenous drugs, complemented Aché's strengths in anti-inflammatories, nasal decongestants, and contraceptives. The purchase included Biosintética's São Paulo plant.

Most of the money needed for the acquisition came from two private banks, and the rest was lent from BNDES, the Brazilian development bank that was furthering a policy of consolidation in the industry so that national companies would be able to compete with the growing number of multinational firms eager to win business in a country of almost 200 million inhabitants. These multinationals were the companies that could afford to spend the large amounts needed to develop new drugs. Generic drugs were much cheaper to manufacture but yielded much less profit and yet were subject to foreign competition from Chinese and Indian firms. In 2006, 77 percent of Aché's revenues came from prescription drugs and only 11 percent from generics.

DRUGS PLUS COSMETICS: 2006–09

Aché restructured its operations in 2006 to align the company by business unit. The following year it entered the cosmetics market with the first of a line of skin care products. Aché supplemented its entry in this field by forming a partnership with BDF Nivea S.A., a subsidiary of the German firm Beiersdorf AG, to market Eucerin, a popular skin care product, in Brazil. The 10-year contract with Beiersdorf set an objective of introducing three new products a year to Brazil. Also in 2007, Aché completed the first phase of a new totally automated plant in Guarulhos.

In 2009 the company was selling more than 200 brands, in about 600 presentations. These included anti-osteoarthritis, anti-infection, respiratory, and anti-inflammatory medications, vitamins, and drugs relating to dermatology, cardiology, endocrinology, gastroenterology, oncology, and feminine health. Over-the-counter and generic drugs included Aerosol, Biofenac, Dorilax, Flagass, Flogarol, Sorine, and Transpulmim. In all, the roster consisted of 152 prescription drugs, 34 nonprescription (over-the-counter) drugs, and 78 generic drugs, plus 11 skin care cosmetic products. The company was fielding some 1,250 sales representatives.

With the departure of Eloi Bosio in 2006, the office of president was eliminated and Ricardo Mendes da Silva became the principal executive of Aché, with the title of director of operations. Victor Siaulys was chairman of the board. All but one of the seven board members belonged to the founding families.

Robert Halasz

PRINCIPAL SUBSIDIARIES

Magenta Participações S.A.

PRINCIPAL OPERATING UNITS

Development & Innovation; Generic Drugs; Industrial and Research; Non-Prescription Drugs; Prescription Drugs.

PRINCIPAL COMPETITORS

AstraZeneca do Brasil Ltda.; Sanofi-Aventis Farmacêutica Ltda.

FURTHER READING

"Biosintética," *Exame,* August 23, 2000, supplement, p. 79.

Caetano, José Roberto, "Quem disse que três é de mais?" *Exame,* January 13, 1999, pp. 28–30.

Capela De Guarulhos, Mauricio, "Aché traca plano para tomar da Pfizer a liderança do Mercado," *NoticiasFinancieras,* March 3, 2004, p. 1.

Dryden, Steve, and Linda J. Wilson, "Brazil's Patent Policy Irks U.S. Drug Makers," *Chemical Week,* September 30, 1987, pp. 15–16.

Ferraz, Eduardo, "Pílulas da discórdia," *Exame,* November 14, 2001, pp. 104–06.

———, "Tem remédio?" *Exame,* May 17, 2000, pp. 114–16.

"Foreign Drugmakers Can't Say No," *Business Latin America,* November 7, 2005, p. 5.

"Grupo Aché," *Exame,* August 25, 1999, supplement, p. 53.

Mano, Cristiane, "Hora da trégua," *Exame,* May 14, 2003, pp. 80–82.

Nascimento, Iolanda, "Aché aposta em marcado de remedio de venda livre," *NoticiasFinancieras,* July 11, 2007, p. 1.

———, "Aché compra Biosintética e se torna a maior de Pais," *Gazeta Mercantil,* October 19, 2005 (on Latin American Newsstand database).

Paduan, Roberta, "Após a supertele, o superlaboratório," *Exame,* June 18, 2008, pp. 119–21.

Pinto de Almeida, Edson, "O filhote deixou os pais para trás," *Exame Melhores e Maiores,* July 2001, pp. 184, 186.

"Por que a Aché foi a melhor," *Exame Melhores e Maiores,* September 1984, p. 218.

Adelman Travel Group

6980 North Port Washington Road
Milwaukee, Wisconsin 53217-2877
U.S.A.
Telephone: (414) 410-8300
Toll Free: (800) 248-5562
Fax: (414) 410-8309
Web site: http://www.adelmantravel.com

Private Company
Incorporated: 1985 as Adelman Travel Systems, Inc.
Employees: 298
Sales: $350 million (2007 est.)
NAICS: 561510 Travel Services

∎ ∎ ∎

Adelman Travel Group bills itself as a business travel management company, serving corporations that have a global purview. The Milwaukee, Wisconsin-based company is a pioneer in its field, initiating the idea of full-service, onsite travel centers. In addition to booking flights and hotel rooms, Adelman handles the logistics of corporate, board, and training meetings; offers incentive travel programs to reward employees; and maintains a vacation division to help employees book personal getaways. Besides serving as its corporate headquarters, the Milwaukee operation also oversees the central region of the United States, while offices in Fort Worth, Texas; Windsor, Connecticut; and Irvine, California; cover other sections of the country.

Adelman also operates five strategically located call centers. Affiliate offices are maintained in Canada, Asia, and Europe, and Adelman extends its global reach by participating in the Radius travel network, providing working relationships with travel agencies in 80 countries. The company is headed by its founder, Craig Adelman.

FOUNDER: SECOND GENERATION OF RUSSIAN IMMIGRANTS

Adelman's grandparents were Russian immigrants who came to the United States and started a dry cleaning business in Milwaukee. Adelman's father, Albert Adelman, came with his parents and quickly assimilated to the new country, becoming an accomplished tennis player and a football star at Northwestern University, good enough to be offered a contract to play for the Chicago Cardinals of the National Football League. Although Albert planned to enroll in graduate school at Harvard University and serve as an assistant football coach, he joined his father in Milwaukee to help run the struggling cleaning business for a year. He would stay in Milwaukee for the rest of his life and build a dry cleaning empire.

Craig Adelman started out in the family business as well but left after a year to pursue his own interests, most of which were connected to travel. An English major with a minor in journalism from the University of Wisconsin–River Falls, he had earned a master's degree in Shakespearian studies from Wroxton College in Bayberry, England, and then spent three years studying English literature at Jerusalem's Hebrew University. All the while, he traveled throughout Europe. Like his father, Adelman was also an excellent tennis player, another activity that led to extensive travel. He spent six months teaching English and tennis at the University of Nairobi in Kenya.

After a brief stint in the laundry business Adelman took a job as director of public relations at the University of Wisconsin–Milwaukee. Two years later he eagerly accepted a job offer from a friend who ran a travel agency to serve as an account executive. Adelman quickly learned that business travelers accounted for about 70 percent of airline business, and he began thinking of ways to better serve this core customer base, resulting in the idea of placing onsite personnel who were devoted to the travel needs of a single corporation, something that was not permitted according to government regulations. His chance to make his idea a reality came with the deregulation of the airlines in 1978, when airlines were allowed to set their own routes, among other changes. Four years later they were permitted to set their own fares, and the resulting myriad of flight possibilities and prices led to a greater need for travel agencies to book air travel.

BEGINNINGS IN FLORIDA: 1983

In 1983 Adelman struck out on his own, forming Adelman Travel Systems Inc. in Boca Raton, Florida, backed financially by his father, who became chairman of the new company, and father-in-law, Bill Kyle, a former chairman of Congoleum Corporation. Adelman quickly built the Florida business, adding five more agencies in a matter of 18 months. Because he preferred to live in Milwaukee, in 1985 he sold this business and returned to Wisconsin. In March of that year he launched a new Adelman Travel Systems in Milwaukee and quickly grew the business, so that by the autumn of the following year the company was operating a dozen satellite offices. Half of them were onsite for corporate clients, who were won over as Adelman proved that his concept worked.

Although onsite travel agents, assisted by online computers, were employed by Adelman, they were very much a part of a client's operation, a convenient way for business travelers to arrange flights and pick up tickets

and boarding passes, even at the last minute if necessary. Under the old system, travel arrangements were done by phone, and tickets had to be delivered. Adelman also served corporate clients by providing monthly itemized travel expense reports, a major inducement for some clients to sign with the agency. To further serve the needs of corporations and their employees, as well as create some diversity, Adelman added leisure travel services, making it convenient for corporate employees to book personal flights and make hotel reservations. In the late summer of 1986 Adelman opened its first office outside of Milwaukee, setting up a travel desk for Tombstone Pizza Corp. in Medford, Wisconsin.

Adelman Travel increased sales to about $20 million in 1986. While Adelman expanded, others in the travel industry struggled as falling fares resulted in lower commissions, forcing a number of agencies to merge or go out of business. Adelman soon extended its reach outside of Wisconsin, where it won over an increasing number of corporations to the idea of housing travel agents on their premises. By 1993 Adelman had 75 locations in 38 states, including satellite operations that issued tickets electronically for clients not large enough to warrant a full-time agent. Annual sales by this stage approached nearly $100 million, making Adelman one of the 50 largest travel management companies in the United States, which was served by 40,000 travel agencies, a number that was steadily dwindling.

COMMISSION CAP HAS LIMITED IMPACT: 1995

In early 1995 the major airlines imposed a cap on commissions they paid travel agents for booking domestic flights. Unlike other travel management companies that made up the shortfall by introducing a number of fees for services that had once been free, such as overnight delivery and re-ticketing, Adelman refrained and enjoyed a major growth spurt, due in large part to an increasing number of corporations downsizing, outsourcing operations, and merging with others in consolidating industries. Many downsizing companies eliminated the corporate meeting planner position, allowing Adelman to take over on a contract basis, making arrangements for conventions, sales meetings, and other corporate gatherings.

The increase in merger activity also resulted in the need for executives to not only negotiate combinations but to travel to integrate the operations in the wake of a successful merger. Moreover, Adelman served clients by negotiating on their behalf to receive discounts for the use of certain airlines, hotels, and car rental agencies. Adelman developed revenue streams outside of the corporate world as well. It signed clients from the

KEY DATES

1983: Craig Adelman starts business travel agency in Florida.
1985: Adelman returns home to Milwaukee to found Adelman Travel Systems.
1993: Sales approach $100 million mark.
1998: New headquarters opens.
2003: Two Connecticut travel companies are acquired.
2004: Acquisition of Carlson Travel Academy is completed.
2005: Wisconsin state contract leads to political controversy.
2006: Pegasus Travel is acquired.

nonprofit sector, including Make-A-Wish-Foundation and the Sierra Club. The company also pursued government contracts, placing winning bids with the Federal Bureau of Investigation, the Peace Corps, and other agencies.

NEW HEADQUARTERS OPEN: 1998

To keep pace with growth, Adelman needed new office space. In 1997 it began construction on a $2 million, 26,000-square-foot corporate headquarters building in the Milwaukee suburb of Glendale. Opened a year later it also leased space to other businesses. The extra space met the needs of the company's growing corporate business as well as its leisure travel unit and larger employee training center. The Glendale location was also important because it was situated close to Milwaukee's affluent Northshore suburbs, whose residents the expanded leisure travel unit planned to target. Shortly after the new headquarters opened, Adelman launched its Adelman Vacations division to pursue these customers, hoping to offset declining airline commissions and boost the company's then-annual revenues of $135 million.

To jump-start the division, Adelman acquired Apex Travel, a Brookfield, Wisconsin, leisure travel agency. Leisure travel was an especially important part of the business mix because unlike the airlines, vacation packagers, hotels, and cruise lines had not cut their commissions. Moreover, with the economy soaring, corporate clients were also in the market for more leisure travel services.

Like other travel management companies, Adelman had to eventually add transaction fees to cover its cost of

doing business, but as Adelman entered the new century it took advantage of the Internet to provide clients a way to reduce some of those fees. The company developed an online booking system called Sabre Business Travel Solution that allowed corporate travel clients to book airline flights, hotel rooms, and rental cars themselves, saving as much as 25 percent over the usual transaction fees. The arrangement was also advantageous to Adelman. With corporate customers handling more of their own transactions, Adelman did not need as many employees at their onsite operations.

The good economic times of the late 1990s gave way to a recession early in the first decade of the 2000s, and the travel industry was hurt further by the terrorist attacks against the United States on September 11, 2001, which caused a sudden decrease in air travel. Adelman's business remained strong, however, and the company continued to look for new opportunities. It targeted Connecticut, home to many corporations that were potential clients. To spur growth in that market, Adelman acquired a pair of established corporate travel agencies. Early in 2003 it purchased Hartford-area Professional Travel Corp., adding $20 million in annual business to Adelman's annual revenues of about $200 million. Later in 2003 the company added another $15 million in sales through the acquisition of Rifkin Travel Inc., based near New Haven, Connecticut.

Adelman completed another acquisition early in 2004 but rather than another travel agency, Adelman bought a travel school, Carlson Travel Academy in Milwaukee. One of the few travel schools licensed in Wisconsin, the academy was established in 1978 by the Carlson Travel Agency. A few years earlier the agency had sold the business to its manager. To train travel professionals, the school offered seven-week, full-day courses as well as 16-week night class courses. The addition of the academy allowed Adelman to address a shortage of trained travel consultants while also providing continuing training to existing personnel.

POLITICAL CONTROVERSY

After 20 years in business in Milwaukee, Craig Adelman received a regional Ernst & Young Entrepreneur of the Year award in 2005. A few weeks later in the fall of that year, however, he found himself and his firm tied to a political controversy involving Wisconsin's Democratic governor, James Edward "Jim" Doyle. After Adelman Travel won a contract to provide travel services to state employees, Wisconsin Republicans raised questions about contributions that Craig Adelman and others in his company made to Doyle. Making matters worse were Adelman's well-known connections to the Democratic Party: Craig Adelman's brother, Lynn Adelman, had been a longtime Democratic state senator. An investigation was launched and in January 2006 the region's U.S. attorney, Steven Biskupic, obtained an indictment from a federal grand jury charging a Wisconsin Department of Administration official, 56-year-old Georgia Thompson, with directing the travel contract to Adelman as a way to score political points with her superiors.

In light of the controversy, Governor Doyle canceled the Adelman contract shortly after Thompson's indictment. Although no one in his administration, Craig Adelman, or anyone at Adelman Travel was charged with any wrongdoing, Doyle was dogged by the matter all through the year as he sought reelection in 2006. In the end, though, he won handily, and the only one who suffered harm was Thompson, who had to stand trial for politically motivated bid-rigging, a charge that was quickly taken to court as the campaign for the governor's seat heated up. In essence, she was accused of inflating Adelman's score in the evaluation process. She maintained that she knew nothing about Adelman's contributions to the Doyle campaign and said she was not pressured in her evaluation of the companies vying for the contract, none of whom complained about the process or claimed that Adelman had received preferential treatment. Nevertheless, Thompson was found guilty and sentenced to 18 months in prison. She appealed but served almost four months before the U.S. Court of Appeals for the Seventh Circuit in April 2007 overturned the verdict, issuing an immediate ruling after just 26 minutes of oral argument, during which one judge said "the evidence is beyond thin." Thompson was immediately released from prison, a highly unusual order from an appeals court.

GROWTH AND EXPANSION

The lost revenue from the canceled Wisconsin state contract had only a minor impact on Adelman Travel, which continued to enjoy steady growth. In October 2006 the company acquired Fort Worth, Texas-based Pegasus Travel, a business travel management company with annual revenues of more than $25 million. A few weeks later Adelman launched a new Independent Contractors Program for its leisure travel business, aimed at independent travel agencies.

By 2008 Adelman was generating annual sales of about $350 million, making it the largest travel agency in Wisconsin and in the top ten nationally among travel management companies. In September 2008 changes were made to the top ranks of Adelman's leadership. Longtime CFO and COO Bob Chaiken was named president while remaining CFO, with Steve Cline taking over as COO. With a stable management team, the company was able to adjust to the changing conditions and the needs of its customers. A new proprietary reporting system was slated for release in late 2008, and as online bookings continued to increase, Adelman was developing new programs to further that trend, hoping that by 2010 the majority of its transactions would be done online. Adelman also looked to Canada and the United Kingdom as possible venues for expansion.

Ed Dinger

PRINCIPAL DIVISIONS

Adelman Meetings and Incentives Group; Adelman Travel Systems, Inc.; Adelman Vacations.

PRINCIPAL COMPETITORS

American Express Company; BCD Travel; Carlson Wagonlit Travel.

FURTHER READING

Barton, Gina, "18-Month Sentence in Travel Scandal," *Milwaukee Journal Sentinel*, September 23, 2006.

Borowski, Greg J., and Patrick Marley, "Verdict Puts Doyle on Defense," *Milwaukee Journal Sentinel*, June 14, 2006.

Brinkman, Phil, "She's a Small Fish, but Only Fish in Net," *Milwaukee Journal Sentinel*, June 5, 2006.

Callender, David, "Doyle Cancels Adelman Pact but Governor Won't Return Large Campaign Gifts," *Madison (Wis.) Capital Times*, January 30, 2006, p. A1.

Daykin, Tom, "Adelman Travel to Build Headquarters in Glendale," *Milwaukee Journal Sentinel*, August 21, 1997.

———, "Milwaukee-Based Adelman Travel Group Buys Connecticut Management Firm," *Milwaukee Journal Sentinel*, September 5, 2003.

Joshi, Pradnya, "Travel Company Reaps Benefits of Unpleasant Corporate Trends," *Milwaukee Journal Sentinel*, September 25, 1995.

Lank, Avrum D., "Still Cleaning Up: With Sheer Chutzpah, Adelman Built Formidable Empire," *Milwaukee Journal Sentinel*, January 15, 2007.

Lieffers, Jennifer, "Adelman Scrubbed Industry Career and Launched Travel Agency," *Business Journal–Milwaukee*, October 13, 1986, p. 10.

Romell, Rick, "Adelman to Expand Leisure Travel Business," *Milwaukee Journal Sentinel*, October 12, 1998, p. D3.

Walters, Steven, "Testimony Links Politics, Contract," *Milwaukee Journal Sentinel*, June 6, 2006.

Walters, Steven, and John Diedrich, "Ex-State Official Freed," *Milwaukee Journal Sentinel*, April 6, 2007.

Wooten, Bradley, "Adelman Uses Travel Academy to Train Existing, Future Agents," *Business Journal of Milwaukee*, February 25, 2005.

Albaugh, Inc.

1525 Northeast 36th Street
Ankeny, Iowa 50021-6754
U.S.A.
Telephone: (515) 964-9444
Toll Free: (800) 247-8013
Fax: (515) 964-7813
Web site: http://www.albaughinc.com

Private Company
Incorporated: 1979
Employees: 800
Sales: $1.1 billion (2007)
NAICS: 325320 Pesticide and Other Agricultural
    Chemical Manufacturing

■ ■ ■

Albaugh, Inc., is an Ankeny, Iowa-based formulator-packager of crop-protection products that avoids the expense of research and development by specializing in the production and selling of off-patent chemicals, offering a variety of herbicides, insecticides, fungicides, and plant growth regulators sold under the Agri Star and other labels. The company's portfolio of chemicals includes glyphosate; 2,4-dichlorophenoxyacetic acid (2,4-D); atrazine; bromoxynil; dicamba; and trifluralin. Manufacturing is done in St. Joseph, Missouri, at a 32-acre, 24-building site containing 522,000 square feet. Marketing in the United States is split among five regions, in which managers promote company products to distributors, relying on direct mailings and word of mouth to influence co-op and retail managers, who in turn influence the end market of farmers eager to save money by eschewing the expensive name-brand products that rely on the same active ingredients used by Albaugh products. The company also owns Agri-Estrella of Mexico and serves South America through an Argentine subsidiary, Atanor SA. Albaugh also conducts business in Europe.

The largest independent company in the industry, Albaugh is 100 percent owned by its founder, Dennis Albaugh, also an avid horseman and car collector, who put the business on the block in 2008. Listed among *Forbes* magazine's richest 400 Americans with a net worth of $3.5 billion in 2008, Albaugh maintains his home in Marco Island, Florida, where he is not subject to state income tax.

IOWA-BORN FOUNDER: 1949

Dennis Albaugh was born in 1949 on a family farm in Ankeny, Iowa, near Des Moines. Because his older brother was slated to take over the farm, which was not large enough to support a second sibling, Albaugh made alternative plans after graduation from Ankeny High School in 1968. He enrolled at Des Moines Area Community College, earning a two-year degree in agricultural business. He went to work for a local co-op, selling seeds, fertilizer, and chemicals for seven years. Albaugh then joined Thompson-Hayward Chemical Company, selling crop chemicals in central Iowa as well as Illinois and Nebraska. He was asked to transfer to Birmingham, Alabama, but rather than leave Ankeny he elected to quit his job and strike out on his own as an independent crop chemical distributor.

In 1979 Albaugh founded his start-up venture on a shoestring, setting up shop in his basement. He mortgaged his house and emptied his $2,000 savings account to buy a used truck and 1,500 gallons of weed killer intended for a customer in South Dakota. Unfortunately, his tanker leaked and after traveling 500 miles to make his delivery, Albaugh discovered that he had nothing to sell. After soothing his angry customer, he persuaded the farmer to give him a second chance and three days to make good on the delivery. Albaugh returned home, rented a more reliable truck, and arranged to purchase another 1,500 gallons of chemicals on credit from his supplier. This time he completed a successful delivery and his business survived an early scrape that could have easily ended his entrepreneurial career before it began.

ALBAUGH BECOMES A MANUFACTURER

Albaugh Inc. was hardly an overnight success, however. In the 1980s Dennis Albaugh focused on 2,4-D, which had been introduced in 1947 but had fallen out of favor in the 1970s, not because it was no longer effective but because newer products had garnered more attention in the marketplace. He bought the weed-killing chemical from Helena Chemical, making modest profits while scuffling for sales with Helena's own salespeople. Albaugh relied on Helena's Des Moines plant where 2,4-D was blended but the plant was sold to another company that planned to cease production of the chemical. In order to maintain the supply of his primary product, Albaugh was essentially forced to become a reformulator. He secured a $100,000 Small Business Administration loan to purchase Helena's mixing tanks and pumps, which he moved a short distance north to Ankeny to begin producing his own 2,4-D.

Albaugh made a living as a 2,4-D formulator in the 1980s but he was far from growing wealthy. By 1987 he was selling to 315 dealers in five states; the keys to his success were low prices and a willingness to provide the

services his competitors had dropped in recent years. A major turning point came in 1990 when one of those competitors, Agrolinz Melamin, decided to sell its plant in St. Joseph, Missouri, for the asking price of $750,000. Albaugh recognized an opportunity, and as he had done in the past, he showed a willingness to take a chance. When no bank would provide financing, he still proceeded with the purchase. Prior to closing on the deal, he took possession of the plant's inventory, which he then liquidated to raise the necessary cash. With the new plant active, he closed the Ankeny operation.

In the first year, the addition of the St. Joseph plant led to an increase in Albaugh's annual sales from $10 million to $26 million. Looking to improve his margins, Albaugh sought a better deal from Dow Chemical on the price of the 2,4-D he blended. When Dow refused, he decided to make his own raw materials and invested in the necessary equipment. Albaugh began producing his own acid, providing the leverage necessary to prompt Dow to lower their prices. Albaugh accepted the lower-priced deal and made use of his new equipment elsewhere in his operations.

CAPITALIZING ON ATANOR

Albaugh began offering other products in addition to 2,4-D, including the herbicide trifluralin, which along with other top-selling products was produced by his Argentine supplier Atanor SA. The Buenos Aires-based company maintained five plants in the country that produced 2,4-D, trifluralin, dichlorprop, and triazine. He recognized that the company was not making year-round use of its operations and believed that instead of shutting down for the winter, the plants could serve the U.S. market, which in the Northern Hemisphere was enjoying spring and summer.

Convinced he could make Atanor more profitable, Albaugh was once again willing to risk financial ruin to seize an opportunity, determined to purchase a company that with $200 million in annual revenues was four times larger than his company was. There was no shortage of obstacles. Not only was Atanor a publicly traded company, Argentina was in the midst of an economic crisis and suffering from a recession and credit crunch. Turned down by two dozen Argentine banks, Albaugh was forced once again to piece together a creative financial package to raise the $60 million needed to acquire a controlling interest in Atanor. In the United States he was able to secure $20 million by pledging his company. Albaugh then received a break when he finally found a banker in Argentina who recognized an opportunity to secure Atanor's banking business. The banker raised $30 million from three banks, and Albaugh turned to high-interest mezzanine financing to

KEY DATES

1979: Dennis Albaugh starts company.
1990: St. Joseph, Missouri, plant is acquired.
1996: Acquisition of Argentine company Atanor SA is completed.
1999: Muldur SA, another Argentine company, is acquired.
2001: Company begins selling glyphosate.
2003: Albaugh acquires remainder of Atanor stock.
2008: Albaugh puts company up for sale.

secure the final $10 million. Thus, in 1996 he was able to purchase a 51 percent controlling stake in Atanor, providing Albaugh with raw ingredients at the same cost as major chemical companies, thereby leveling the playing field.

INTRODUCTION OF AGRI STAR LABEL

Albaugh offered its products under private-label deals with major distributors who wanted to promote their names in the marketplace. In the late 1990s Albaugh introduced its own Agri Star brand, but rather than jeopardize its edge in pricing by investing in brand-awareness campaigns, the company focused on marketing to key constituents, co-op and retail managers, who in turn drove sales to farmers who were more concerned with lowering their costs of production than with the logo on a label.

Forever opportunistic, Dennis Albaugh anticipated the addition of another potentially lucrative product, glyphosate, the active ingredient in Monsanto's highly popular Roundup herbicide, which was scheduled to go off patent in September 2000. Sprayed on weeds in the ground before crops are planted, Roundup had been in use for decades because not only did it effectively kill all leafy weeds, it broke down in soil, rendering it harmless to the crops that followed. Moreover, Monsanto in the mid-1990s introduced seeds that had been genetically modified to survive Roundup, in this way allowing the crops themselves to be sprayed, opening up an even larger market for Roundup and generic glyphosate. Generic manufacturers were eager to sell glyphosate after the patent expired but first had to compensate Monsanto for a fair share of the costs Monsanto had incurred in generating safety and other information to obtain registration of the chemical with the Environmental Protection Agency (EPA). It was a requirement with

which Albaugh was well familiar, having devoted several years to working out compensation with Dow over trifluralin.

Albaugh found a way to skirt the issue of EPA certification data compensation by having Atanor in 1999 pay $22 million for the glyphosate business of another Argentine company, Muldur SA, which had its own formula for glyphosate. As a result, Albaugh possessed a good deal of leverage in his negotiations with Monsanto over data compensation, in effect threatening to import glyphosate from Argentina, a move that could drive down the price of the U.S. chemical. A deal was reached and shortly after the Roundup patent expired Albaugh began selling glyphosate, which as the world's bestselling agrochemical took the company to an entirely new level in revenues. Competition brought down the price of glyphosate from $40 a gallon to $10 over the next few years but because Albaugh was able to increase volume, becoming the second largest producer of the chemical in the United States, trailing only Monsanto, the company was able to compensate for shrinking margins. Revenues grew at a 25 to 30 percent rate each year.

TAKING ATANOR PRIVATE: 2004

While Dennis Albaugh was enjoying success in the sale of glyphosate in the United States early in the first decade of the 2000s, he was also buying out the other shareholders in Atanor to gain complete control, having borrowed another $60 million to complete the deal. In 2002 Argentina's economy collapsed as did the country's currency. Because his banks were desperate for their money, Albaugh arranged a $4 million discount for early repayment from one of his South American banks by taking out a loan in the United States. After buying out the last shareholders, Albaugh took Atanor private in 2004. The Argentine company also prospered from the sale of glyphosate in South America. In 2007, after 11 years of negotiating an approval process, Atanor began selling the herbicide in the key market of Brazil.

Albaugh also expanded its operations into Mexico. In October 2003 the company spent $10 million to acquire the plant of Cuproquim de Mexico, a company founded in 1986 to produce copper-based fungicides, copper oxychloride and hydroxide. Albaugh renamed the company Agri-Estrella S. de R.L. de C.V. According to *Forbes* in 2007, he "was having trouble getting farmers to pay their bills."

As the annual revenues of Albaugh, Inc., soared to $1.1 billion in 2007, so too did the personal wealth of Dennis Albaugh. In 2007 *Forbes* listed his net worth at $1.5 billion, an amount that grew to $3.5 billion just one year later. The former farm boy, who now spent most of the year in Florida, was able to indulge his interests. He built a 19-hole golf course in Ankeny, the extra hole intended for playoffs, and assembled an impressive collection of classic automobiles. He also became interested in horse racing through his son-in-law and formed Roll Reroll Stable to purchase racehorses. It was likely that Albaugh would soon have even more funds at his disposal to pursue his hobbies. In July 2008 he put Albaugh, Inc., up for sale, hiring UBS AG to conduct a formal auction. Whether a deal would ever be reached was uncertain but there remained every reason to expect that the crop-protection business created by Dennis Albaugh would continue to prosper.

Ed Dinger

PRINCIPAL SUBSIDIARIES

Atanor SA (Argentina); Agri-Estrella (Mexico).

PRINCIPAL COMPETITORS

KMG Chemicals, Inc.; Luxembourg-Pamo; Monsanto Company.

FURTHER READING

Burchett, Andrew, "Little Giants of Generic," *Top Producer,* November 2003.

Erman, Michael, and Euan Rocha, "Chemicals Co Albaugh Up for Sales—Sources," *Reuters,* July 30, 2008.

Lambert, Emily, "Pesticide Prince," *Forbes,* April 9, 2007, p. 68.

Miller, Matthew, and Duncan Greenburg, "Lord of Leisure," *Forbes,* October 8, 2008.

"New Ruling on Generic Pesticides," *Chemical Market Reporter,* November 9, 1998, p. 25.

Allbritton Communications Company

1000 Wilson Boulevard, Suite 2700
Arlington, Virginia 22209-3921
U.S.A.
Telephone: (703) 647-8700
Fax: (703) 236-9268

Private Company
Incorporated: 1974
Employees: 1,094
Sales: $224.1 million (2008)
NAICS: 511110 Newspaper Publishers; 515120 Television Broadcasting

■ ■ ■

A private company based in Arlington, Virginia, Allbritton Communications Company (ACC) owns and operates ten television stations, a 24-hour cable news channel, and Capitol News Company LLC. All of the stations are affiliated with the ABC network and are located in Birmingham, Alabama; Harrisburg-Lancaster-York, Lebanon, Pennsylvania; Little Rock, Arkansas; Tulsa, Oklahoma; Roanoke-Lynchburg, Virginia; Charleston, South Carolina; and Washington, D.C. WJLA in Washington, ACC's flagship station, also houses the NewsChannel 8 operation, providing 24-hour news coverage in the Washington market, as well as The Politico, a Capitol News Company operation. Available online as Politico.com or in a print version distributed free in the Washington area and available on a subscription basis elsewhere, *Politico* offers political and legislative news and opinion. When Congress is in session, *Politico* is published three times a week. During congressional recesses it becomes a weekly. Heading ACC is Chairman and Chief Executive Officer Robert L. Allbritton, son of the company's founder, Joseph L. Allbritton.

MISSISSIPPI-BORN FOUNDER: 1924

Joseph Lewis Allbritton was born in the final days of 1924 in D'Lo, Mississippi, a lumber town where his father ran the company store. Later the family moved to Houston, Texas, where his father started a chain of cafeterias, and not surprisingly the younger Allbritton's first job was washing dishes. Although he received a degree from Baylor University law school in 1949 (following a three-year stint in the U.S. Navy during World War II) and had established a law practice, Allbritton was not especially interested in being a lawyer. Rather, like many Texans, he considered law school to be the first step in a business career.

Standing five feet, three inches and known as the "Little Wrangler," Allbritton proved to be a shrewd investor in real estate, making his first million by age 30. He turned his attention to banking, founding San Jacinto Savings & Loan in 1956 and five years later purchasing a 45 percent interest in Citizens Bank and Trust. In 1970 he merged Citizens with Houston Bank and Trust and then sold it to First International Bancshares, becoming the largest shareholder in that holding company, the largest banking concern in the region at the time. Over the years, Allbritton also invested in a wide variety of other businesses, including a California chain of funeral homes (prompting wags to rename him the "Little Mortician"); a Los Angeles insurance company; a bank in Luxembourg; several hotels in London, England; as well as Washington Star Communications, Inc., publisher of the *Washington Star* afternoon newspaper, in 1974.

FORMING ALLBRITTON COMMUNICATIONS COMPANY: 1974

Allbritton paid $25 million for a 37 percent stake in Washington Star Communications and became chairman and chief executive officer of the newspaper. With the purchase of the *Star,* Allbritton formed Allbritton Communications Company (ACC) in 1974. The *Star,* founded in 1852, had once been the dominant newspaper in the capital but had been surpassed by the *Washington Post,* a morning daily. The *Star* had been losing money for several years. The saving grace for the newspaper's parent company was its other media holdings: a pair of radio stations in Washington and Lynchburg, Virginia; a radio syndicate; and three television stations in Washington, Lynchburg, and Charleston. Because of the sale, the Federal Communications Commission's rules that banned the concentration of media ownership now applied to Star Communications, and Allbritton was given three years to divest either his Washington television and radio properties or the *Star.*

Allbritton sold the radio stations as well as some small newspapers owned by Star Communications, and made some progress in turning around the *Star.* In the end, however, he decided to keep the Washington television station, whose call letters he changed to WJLA to match his initials, and sold the newspaper for $20 million to Time Inc. in 1978. Three years later the *Star* folded.

With the sale of the *Star,* Allbritton and ACC did not completely exit the newspaper field, however. In 1976 he had hired a 25-year-old newspaperman, William Dean Singleton, who had owned eight weekly newspapers but failed in his attempt to revive the *Fort Worth Press.* Singleton had asked Allbritton to back him in the purchase of the *Westfield (Massachusetts) Evening News* but Allbritton refused to participate until he

noticed that the young man, as he began to exit their luncheon meeting, wore suspenders. He called him back, saying, "Any twenty-five-year-old who wears suspenders has got to be conservative. You go up there and buy the newspaper and I'll wire 'em the money," according to Scott Sherman in the *Columbia Journalism Review* in 2003. Singleton later ran the *Star* for a year, managing to turn a profit during his stint, and after the *Star* was sold Allbritton purchased some other newspapers for Singleton to run, including three Massachusetts papers: New Jersey's the *Paterson News* and the *Hudson Dispatch* of Union City, bought in 1977; and the *Irwin (Pennsylvania) Standard Observer.* In 1981 ACC added the *Trenton Times,* acquired from The Washington Post Company.

ACQUISITION OF TELEVISION STATIONS: 1983

In addition to print properties, ACC acquired WCKN AM and FM in Kansas City, Kansas, and in 1983 added to its slate of television stations by paying about $80 million to Leake TV Inc. for a pair of ABC affiliates: KATV in Little Rock and KTUL-TV in Tulsa. ACC exited the print business later in the 1980s, following the 1983 departure of Singleton. Thwarted in his desire to become a partner in ACC, Singleton formed a new venture, MediaNews Group, Inc., with partner Richard Scudder and began acquiring newspapers in several states. ACC sold the *Trenton Times* to the Newhouse Newspaper Group in 1986. Also in that year the Paterson and Union City newspapers were sold to Garden State Newspapers Inc. The radio properties were also divested, leaving just the television stations.

In truth ACC was not a major priority for Allbritton after he sold his interest in the *Star,* which had provided the millionaire with cachet and some measure of power in the nation's capital. He regained his stature in the city in a way that was more comfortable to him, as a banker. In 1981 he took control of the venerable Riggs National Bank, which would soon advertise itself "The Most Important Bank in the Most Important City in the World." Founded in 1836, it was also known as the "Bank of Presidents," having served Abraham Lincoln, Theodore Roosevelt, and Harry Truman. The Riggs, as Allbritton called it, became his preoccupation.

In the meantime, his son, Robert Lewis Allbritton, came of age, and developed an interest in broadcasting. After earning a degree from Wesleyan College in Middleton, Connecticut, in 1992, the younger Allbritton tried his hand as a mutual funds analyst with Riggs Investment Management Co. but quit after three months to join ACC. At the time, ACC's assets, in addition to five television stations, included a syndicated

KEY DATES

1974: Joe Allbritton forms Allbritton Communications Company (ACC) and acquires control of Washington Star Company, including newspaper, radio, and television assets.
1978: ACC sells the *Washington Star.*
1983: Television stations in Little Rock, Arkansas, and Tulsa, Oklahoma, are added to the fold.
1994: Robert Allbritton is named chief operating officer.
1995: Pennsylvania television station is acquired.
1996: The television assets of two Alabama stations are acquired.
2001: Robert Allbritton is named chairman and chief executive officer.
2007: The *Politico* debuts.

program, *Working Woman,* and a consulting business, Allbritton Television Services. NewsChannel 8 was owned by a sister company, Allnewsco. In fiscal 1992 ACC posted revenues of $98.6 million.

PENNSYLVANIA STATION ACQUISITION: 1995

Robert Allbritton devoted two years to learning the television business, spending three months at all five of the ACC stations and working at virtually every job, from switchboard operator to on-air anchor. As a result, he grew familiar with all the employees of the organization. In November 1994 he became executive vice-president and chief operating officer at ACC. Allbritton looked to emphasize local news, a key revenue generator, and to acquire additional television stations. In 1995 ACC bought its first station in a dozen years, paying $113 million for WHTM-TV, a Pennsylvania station that served Harrisburg, Lancaster, Lebanon, and York.

ACC's revenues increased to $138.2 million in fiscal 1995, which ended on September 30 of that year. Two months later the company agreed to acquire another television station, WCFT-TV in Tuscaloosa, Alabama, for $20 million in a deal that closed in March 1996. ACC also had an option to purchase WNAL-TV, serving Gadsden and Birmingham, Alabama, but in early 1996 it instead added WJSU-TV (a CBS affiliate) of Anniston, Alabama, on a time brokerage agreement. The station then joined the ABC network and its tower was relocated in order to serve Birmingham and

neighboring Tuscaloosa. It was not until March 2000 that WJSU was formally acquired by ACC, which also owned a low-power television station licensed in Birmingham. WCFT, WJSU, and WBMA carried identical programming and the Nielsen ratings service considered them a single entity.

Also of importance in 1996, ACC solidified its relationship with the ABC network by signing ten-year affiliate agreements for its stations. Two years later there was press speculation that ABC was close to acquiring ACC's stations, the key property being WJLA in Washington, for which ABC had expressed interest for a number of years. Joe Allbritton had supposedly offered his stable of stations to ABC (NewsChannel 8 was not included) for $1 billion as well as stock in The Walt Disney Company, ABC's corporate parent. In the end, Disney was not willing to meet his price and the ACC properties remained intact.

ROBERT ALLBRITTON BECOMES CHAIRMAN AND CEO: 2001

In 1998, 29-year-old Robert Allbritton was named president of ACC but he would soon take on additional responsibilities for his father's business interests as well. A year later he became vice-chairman of Riggs National Corp., a clear indication that he was being groomed to succeed his father, who was well into his 70s. Further steps in the transition took place in early 2001 when Robert Allbritton was named chairman and CEO of ACC and Riggs National Corp., which had been performing poorly for many years. Matters grew only worse when in 2004 Riggs became embroiled in a money-laundering scandal involving people with connections to the terrorists responsible for the September 11, 2001, terrorist attacks on the United States, and to the former dictator of Chile, Augusto Pinochet. Neither Joe Allbritton or his son was charged with any wrongdoing but the damage to their reputations was such that they were forced to find a buyer for Riggs, which in 2005 was sold to PNC Financial Services Group Inc., thus bringing an end to the illustrious Riggs name in Washington banking circles.

While dealing with the problems surrounding Riggs, Robert Allbritton continued to run ACC. In 2002 WJLA and NewsChannel 8 combined their operations in a single location in a high-rise building in Rosslyn, Virginia, creating the largest electronic newsgathering organization in the area. The facility and the capabilities of the two units would also form a foundation for a new venture announced in 2006, a newspaper called the *Capitol Leader,* a three-day-a-week tabloid covering Capitol Hill, but in addition to politics and legislative news, the publication promised to provide such cultural coverage as restaurant and book reviews.

ACC's new venture soon included a web component anchored by a pair of *Washington Post* political reporters: John F. Harris, the *Post*'s national political editor, and reporter Jim VandeHei, who had also worked previously at the *Wall Street Journal* and *Roll Call*. The two men had pitched the idea of a web site devoted entirely to politics to the *Post* but were turned down, making them ideal candidates to join forces with Robert Allbritton. With their input, the concept developed further and in early 2007 it emerged as the *Politico*, a hybrid political newspaper–web site, which quickly snapped up top writers and editors. The *Capitol Leader*, as a result, was scrapped.

Sharing the newsroom of WJLA and NewsChannel 8, the *Politico* made its debut on January 23, 2007, one day after Hillary Rodham Clinton announced she was running for the presidency. The multiplatform entity received mixed reviews but possessed the infrastructure and financial backing of ACC that made it more than likely that the *Politico* would find its niche. While it was a feather in the cap of ACC, the television operations remained the core business and were likely to continue as such for years to come.

Ed Dinger

PRINCIPAL SUBSIDIARIES

Capitol News Company.

PRINCIPAL COMPETITORS

Gannett Co., Inc.; National Journal Group Inc.; The Economist Group Limited; NBC Universal, Inc.

FURTHER READING

"Allbritton Makes Family Tradition His Own," *Broadcasting & Cable*, November 13, 1995, p. 113.

Ellison, Sarah, "Washington Post Loses 2 Reporters to Web Venture," *Wall Street Journal*, November 21, 2006, p. B5.

Foisie, Geoffrey, "The Unveiling of Allbritton," *Broadcasting*, July 6, 1992, p. 54.

Hunter, Marjorie, "Publisher to Stay On," *New York Times*, February 4, 1978.

Kiely, Kathy, "Politico Mojo," *American Journalism Review*, February–March 2007, p. 10.

Lafayette, Jon, "Allbritton, ABC Deal May Be Near," *Electronic Media*, June 22, 1998, p. 3.

Malone, Michael, "All in at Allbritton," *Broadcasting & Cable*, October 6, 2008, p. 12.

Milk, Leslie, "Five Business Leaders Who Went After Opportunities to Get to the Top," *Washingtonian.com*, November 1, 2002.

Montgomery, David, and Kathleen Day, "Critics Say Allbritton Ruined Bank He Loved," *Washington Post*, July 17, 2004, p. A1.

O'Hara, Terence, "At Riggs, Problems Passed On with Legacy," *Washington Post*, April 18, 2004, p. A16.

Rathbun, Elizabeth, "Allbritton Takes Another Route to Birmingham," *Broadcasting & Cable*, January 8, 1996, p. 51.

Sherman, Scott, "The Evolution of Dean Singleton," *Columbia Journalism Review*, March–April 2003, p. 32.

Trigoboff, Dan, and Ken Kerschbaumer, "Making Two Newsrooms One," *Broadcasting & Cable*, June 10, 2002, p. 23.

Weaver, Warren, Jr., "A Texas Banker Buys into Washington Star News," *New York Times*, July 18, 1974.

Amil Participações S.A.

———————■———————

Av. das Americas 4200 Barra da Tijuca
Rio de Janeiro, Rio de Janeiro 22640-907
Brazil
Telephone: (55 21) 3805-1000
Toll Free: (0800) 021-2583 (in Brazil)
Fax: (55 21) 3805-1222
Web site: http://www.amilpar.com.br

Public Company
Incorporated: 1991 as Amil Participações Ltda.
Employees: 10,800
Sales: BRL 4.39 billion ($2.39 billion) (2008)
Stock Exchanges: São Paulo
Ticker Symbol: AMIL3
NAICS: 551112 Offices of Other Holding Companies;
    621491 HMO Medical Centers; 621511 Medical
    Laboratories; 621910 Ambulance Services; 622110
    General Medical and Surgical Hospitals

■ ■ ■

Amil Participações S.A. (Amil, or Amilpar) is a holding company that, through its subsidiaries, sells private healthcare plans and offers managed care, partly through its own hospitals, clinics, and laboratories. Its plans include outpatient as well as inpatient hospital services. It also provides dental services, prescription plans, and administrative assistance to hospitals and clinics. Amil is the largest group of its kind in Brazil, and its founder, Dr. Edson de Godoy Bueno, is one of Brazil's richest men. The company's focus is on expanding access to reliable health services by means of networks of hospitals, clinics, laboratories, and imaging services chosen on the basis of technological and human excellence. These services are available throughout Brazil through the National Provider Network. Amil's array of offerings includes exclusive network plans, free-choice plans, and closed-panel plans, which emphasize highly reputable doctors and the best hospitals and services.

SERVING POOR PEOPLE: 1972–77

Bueno, a young gastroenterologist, founded what became Amil in 1972. Born to poor parents in a small town in the state of São Paulo, he lost his father at the age of six, failed an elementary school grade four times, and shined shoes to bring in some money for his mother, a domestic worker. However, a physician who came to town became his inspiration. "He made me want to become a great student, so I became one," Bueno recalled to Michael T. McCue for a story in *Managed Healthcare Executive.* "I went to the same medical school he went to ... because he was everything I wanted to be."

Bueno was practicing medicine in Duque de Caixias, an impoverished suburb of Rio de Janeiro, when the small 35-bed hospital and clinic, actually a converted house, where he worked came close to bankruptcy. He assumed the debt and suddenly found he owned the hospital. In so doing, he "discovered that my vocation was to be an entrepreneur," Bueno told Melina Costu for a story on Brazilian billionaires that appeared in the business magazine *Exame.*

It was a precarious venture. Brazil guaranteed healthcare for all its citizens but did not provide sufficient funds, which resulted in services being rationed and some regions being more poorly serviced than others. About a quarter of the population had private insurance and often broke the law by lending member identification cards to others. Bueno, though, made the hospital profitable. Most of the patients were poor pregnant women, many of whom had avoided seeking prenatal care at the facility because it was at the top of a hill. He made the hospital van available in the morning hours to bring them to the entrance and ingratiated them with gestures such as offering free Coca-Cola. Since the government paid for each visit, increased traffic meant more revenue. Over the next few years Bueno bought two other hospitals in Duque de Caxias and established Empresa de Serviços Hospitalares (Esho) to manage the units.

EXPANDING AMIL'S RANGE:
1978–93

In 1978 Bueno and his close associate, Jorge Ferreira da Rocha, a cardiologist, decided to take the enterprise into managed healthcare and established Amil Assistência Médica Internacional Ltda. (or Amil, by its acronym) in Rio de Janeiro. The initial capital came from a federal fund for medical businesses, but the new company did not have any success at first persuading companies to sign on.

Bueno and Rocha then decided to spend all available funds on advertising, including television spots that highlighted an easy-to-remember telephone number ending in 1000. This number offered telephone consultation with doctors around the clock, but the main purpose of the campaign was to raise the profile of the company in the eyes of corporate executives who had never heard of Amil. By 1982 Amil had annual operating revenue of more than $5 million.

Amil entered São Paulo in 1986 and adopted a strategy of growth two years later based totally on aggregate marketing. The company made it clear that its goal was profit, not philanthropy. It brought in consultants from abroad such as Tom Peters to offer advice on raising its profile. Clients were also invited to participate. To establish and reinforce ties to doctors,

Amil offered training programs for their children and secretaries. Specialists were invited to visit U.S. hospitals.

Three of the six plans that Amil offered were tied to the company's own network. Two of them, aimed at business executives and managers, offered a free choice of hospitals and medical services. The sixth was said to be the only plan in Brazil that covered major medical risk by means of a monthly payment but outpatient visits and tests out of pocket. Enrollees received a card that entitled them to discounts in stores, boutiques, pharmacies, restaurants, and other enterprises.

Another initiative, EAT, brought Amil into foodservice in 1990. The Brazilian government had a program by which any business could issue meal vouchers to its employees and pay only one-third the cost, since the government would pay nearly one-half and the employees the rest. Intensively marketed, EAT had achieved annual revenue of $90 million a year by 1993. In that year Amil opened a chain of lunch counters in Argentina.

Only a year earlier, Amil had initiated Clube do Amilziho, which invited parents to enroll their children in a club and receive gifts for the children and a free children's magazine intended to promote good health habits. The club offered a special health plan covering the medical expenses of the children.

Rocha was responsible for the establishment of Amil Health Rescue in 1993. This program promised those living far from Brazil's big cities and able to afford it, helicopter service, linked to an ambulance on the ground that would whisk a stricken person to the emergency room of an intensive care facility. The service became the first of its kind in South America on land and air and included fully equipped mobile surgery and intensive care units with specialized medical crews to minister to patients en route to the hospital. Within a few months of the televised offer, 100,000 people had enrolled in the plan.

MULTI-COMPANY,
MULTINATIONAL GROUP:
1994–98

By 1994 Amil was the second largest Brazilian enterprise in the field of managed healthcare. It had become a group of 21 companies with annual revenues of $500 million a year. In the United States, Amil established a Delaware-based holding company called Health Visions in 1993. In practice, it was based in Pasadena, California, where Bueno bought a fast-food chain named Crocodile that did not thrive. The first operational company was Nevada Health, which began

KEY DATES

1972: Dr. Edson de Godoy Bueno founds the enterprise.
1978: Amil offers a managed care health plan in Rio de Janeiro.
1982: Amil has annual operating revenue of more than $5 million.
1986: Amil enters São Paulo, Brazil's largest city.
1990: Company begins providing foodservice through EAT.
1993: Company establishes Amil Health Rescue, which includes helicopter service.
1994: Amil has become a group of 21 companies with annual revenues of $500 million.
1999: Total Care is founded for patients with complex needs.
2000: Amil restructures its operations after costs outstrip payments.
2005: Company has purchased ten hospitals in the last five years.
2007: Amil makes its initial public offering of stock, on the Bolsa de Valores de São Paulo.
2008: Amil has 3.18 million enrolled members.

that year to sell health plans in the Las Vegas area, one of the fastest growing in the United States. Another opened in Austin, Texas, in 1995. In 1997 Amil established a Miami-based enterprise offering its customers medical care anywhere on earth.

Amil's head office was informal in the extreme, with employees wearing badges that identified them by first name only. On the other hand, however, it was characterized by an explicit personality cult, according to one reporter. Visitors received a copy of a biography of Bueno that resembled a coffee table book, with photos of the company founder on almost every page.

This reporter described Rocha as Amil's "brain." From his office in Alphaville (a gated community on the outskirts of São Paulo), he administered the rescue team and Farmalife, a network of pharmacies acquired in 1992, where enrolled members bought discounted drugs. All advertising campaigns also came under his supervision.

Amil was rated by the Brazilian business magazine *Exame* as one of the nation's best companies to work for in 1998. Although salaries and benefits were only average, the company was considered better than average in five other areas and especially favorable in terms of

career opportunities. The 75 executives, half of them women, had received intensive training in what was called the Amil School of Business Administration, a 14-month in-house program. The more than 200 courses, held one day a week, included economics, strategic planning, personal leadership, and time management.

The company established Total Care in 1999 for special medical care. Initially offered only in Rio de Janeiro, it was extended to São Paulo the following year. Total Care offered advanced diagnosis, treatment, and prevention centers for patients with complex needs. Medical Excellence, founded in 2001, established a network for services with the main objective of prolonging and preserving the lives of its clients. In 2002 Amil moved to new headquarters in Rio de Janeiro.

RESTRUCTURING, RETRENCHMENT, AND RENAISSANCE: 2000–05

During this period, however, one of economic recession in Brazil, Amil started to suffer financial setbacks. The government had begun to restrict increases in payments made to health maintenance organizations (HMOs) without controlling the costs that HMOs including Amil had to pay to its suppliers. Even the nation's biggest health insurers, such as subsidiaries of Banco Bradesco S.A. and SulAmérica S.A., lost money, while many smaller ones closed their doors.

Amil remained barely profitable, but its operations in São Paulo and Brasília fell into the red. After a restructuring in 2000, Amil dissolved ten of the 12 franchises that had opened, mostly in northern and northeastern Brazil. It also withdrew from the United States; the last operation there, Nevada Health, was sold to the Blue Cross and Blue Shield Association at the end of 2005.

Amil fought its way out of trouble by relying on its own hospitals, clinics, laboratories, and physicians to control expenses by increasing efficiency. Between 2000 and 2005 the company acquired ten hospitals in Brasília, Rio de Janeiro, and São Paulo. In 2003 it bought another HMO, Amico, from the U.S. insurer CIGNA Corporation by assuming its debts of approximately BRL 200 million ($110 million).

In 2005, benefiting from vertical integration, Amil's São Paulo operations returned to profitability for the first time in five years. To do so, it had entered new terrain by offering diagnostic services and clinical analyses. The growing number of tests ordered by physicians had grown rapidly with the advent of new technology and now accounted for about 30 percent of the costs incurred by health plans.

PUBLIC COMPANY: 2007–08

With its finances in order again, Amil made its initial public offering (IPO) of stock on the Bolsa de Valores de São Paulo in 2007, raising BRL 1.2 billion ($630 million). The company, in 2008, was active in three Brazilian states (Rio de Janeiro, São Paulo, and Paraná) and the federal district of Brasília. It had contracts with 2,962 hospitals and many thousands of laboratories, diagnostic centers, outpatient clinics, and physicians in private practice. Its 13 hospitals and 19 outpatient facilities included Hospital 9 de Julho in São Paulo, purchased in 2008. Amil had 3.18 million enrollees in 2008. As of 2007, 61.5 percent of its members were affiliated through corporate plans; 22.1 percent in individual plans; and 16.4 percent in dental plans.

Private managed healthcare in Brazil remained a competitive and fragmented field, with many players. In 2008 supplementary healthcare covered only 20 percent of the population. The ten largest companies combined held only 27 percent of this marketplace. J.P.L.S.P.E. Empreendimentos e Participações Ltda., a company presumably representing Bueno's interests, retained 79.5 percent of Amil's shares before its IPO. As J.P.L.S.P.E. Empreendimentos e Participações S.A., it held 64 percent of the shares in early 2009. Bueno remained president and chairman of the board of Amil.

Robert Halasz

PRINCIPAL SUBSIDIARIES

Amico Saúde Ltda.; Amil Assistência Médica Internacional Ltda.

PRINCIPAL COMPETITORS

Banco Bradesco S.A.; Golden Cross Assisténcia Internacional de Saúde S.A.; Intermédica Sistema de Saúde S.A.; Médial Saúde S.A.; SulAmérica Serviços Médicos S.A.

FURTHER READING

"Amil," *Exame,* August 12, 1998, supplement, p. 42.

Breitinger, Jacqueline, "Amil a 1000," *Exame,* August 26, 1998, pp. 60–64.

Goulart, Rubeny, "A Amil está a mais de mil," *Exame,* July 6, 1994, pp. 68–69.

McCue, Michael T., "South America's Comeback Kid," *Managed Healthcare Executive,* April 2003, pp. 18, 20.

Rapp, Stan, and Thomas L. Collins, *Beyond MaxiMarketing: The New Power of Caring and Daring,* New York: McGraw-Hill, 1994, ch. 12.

Salomão, Alexa, "A Amil dá um passo para trás," *Exame,* February 1, 2006, pp. 54–55.

AXA Equitable Life Insurance Company

1290 Avenue of the Americas
New York, New York 10104
U.S.A.
Telephone: (212) 554-1234
Web site: http://www.axa-equitable.com

Wholly Owned Subsidiary of AXA Financial, Inc.
Incorporated: 1859 as The Equitable Life Assurance
Society of the United States
Employees: 5,560
Total Assets: $136.26 billion (2008)
NAICS: 524113 Direct Life Insurance Carriers; 523991
Trust, Fiduciary, and Custody Activities; 524210
Insurance Agencies and Brokerages; 525110 Pension
Funds; 525190 Other Insurance Funds; 525910
Open-End Investment Funds; 525920 Trusts,
Estates, and Agency Accounts; 525990 Other
Financial Vehicles; 523999 Miscellaneous Financial
Investment Activities

∎∎∎

AXA Equitable Life Insurance Company, a leading
financial protection company, provides life insurance,
annuity, and investment products and services to more
than three million clients in the United States, Puerto
Rico, and the Virgin Islands. The company distributes
its products and services to individuals and business
owners through its retail channel, AXA Advisors, LLC;
to the financial services market through its wholesale
channel, AXA Distributors, LLC; and to corporations
and their employees through its Corporate Market

distribution channel. Long ranked among the largest
insurance companies in America, Equitable demutual-
ized in 1992 and formed a partnership with AXA
Group. The Paris-based holding company attained sole
ownership in 2000.

SURE START: 1859–98

The Equitable Life Assurance Society of the United
States was started in Manhattan in 1859 when Henry
Baldwin Hyde, an ambitious young cashier for the giant
Mutual Life Insurance Company of New York, left that
firm to found his own. Equitable's first office, rented for
$75 a month, was located at 98 Broadway.

Life insurance ran in Hyde's family; his father was
one of Mutual's top salesmen and would sell many policies for Equitable. Hyde organized his new firm as a
joint-stock company, enlisting his friends to help sell
shares. William C. Alexander, a lawyer and minor politi-
cian whom Hyde knew through their mutual association
with the First Presbyterian Church of New York, was
chosen as the firm's first president, with Hyde running
its day-to-day affairs through the office of vice-president.
Forgoing IOUs, the accepted industry practice of the
time, the 25-year-old Hyde required policyholders to
make cash payments in support of capital reserves and
growth.

Equitable got off to a good start, selling 769 policies worth a total of more than $2.6 million in its first
full year (1860). Business boomed during the Civil War,
as the ravages of armed conflict impressed upon many
the wisdom of insuring their lives. In 1865, the last year

COMPANY PERSPECTIVES

In our first 150 years, we have endured two world wars, the Great Depression, 18 recessions and a terrorist attack on our own soil. We have emerged stronger as a result of these experiences. As we look forward to our next 150 years, we will draw on both our storied history and the talent of our employees and financial professionals to make us even smarter, stronger and more focused on meeting the evolving needs of our clients.—Christopher M. "Kip" Condron, chairman and CEO

of the war, the firm had $27.6 million worth of active coverage and the industry's largest sales force. Equitable had begun selling policies overseas almost immediately after its founding. It had an agent in Southeast Asia as early as 1860, and over the next two decades it established its presence elsewhere in the Far East, Europe, the Middle East, South America, and Canada.

William C. Alexander died in 1874 and was succeeded by Hyde. Business continued to skyrocket during his active stewardship, and in 1886 Equitable surpassed Mutual to become the largest life insurance company in the world. That year, it sold $111.5 million worth of policies, giving it a total of $411.8 million of coverage in force. During those boom years, the firm could boast of having among its directors Ulysses S. Grant and financier John Jacob Astor.

The period was also marked by innovation, according to a company 150th anniversary news release. Equitable designed "an annuity for individuals that paid dividends and offered Americans in the 1860s a new method of saving for retirement." In 1881, Equitable began expediting death claim benefits, forgoing long waiting periods, a standard practice of the time.

Henry B. Hyde retired in 1898 and died the next year. He was succeeded by his close friend James W. Alexander, nephew of William C. Alexander; Hyde's son James Hazen Hyde became vice-president. Besides sharing their family affiliations with Equitable, both were men of culture and devoted Europhiles. They both spent much of their time in Paris, and, not coincidentally, the firm intensified its French operations in the first few years of the new century. Both men, however, also set into motion events that presented Equitable with its first major crisis.

REWORKED: 1905–46

It started in January 1905, when James Hyde threw a lavish coming-out party for his niece. It was covered heavily in the society pages and rumors circulated through the press that it had been paid for with company funds. The resulting controversy, aggravated by a power struggle between James Hyde and Alexander over Hyde's role in the firm, led the directors to commission an internal review of its management practices. The report, presented in May, found sloppy management and financial irregularities on the part of Equitable officers and lax oversight by its directors, and recommended immediate and radical reorganization. Given these findings, Hyde had little choice but to sell his substantial holdings in the firm. He found a buyer in financier Thomas Fortune Ryan, who persuaded the directors to elect his associate Paul Morton, who had been Secretary of the Navy under Theodore Roosevelt, as chairman. Ryan then persuaded George Westinghouse, former President Grover Cleveland, and New York Appeals Court Judge Morgan O'Brien to act as trustees and administer Ryan's share of the firm. James Hyde then left New York to live in Paris.

Paul Morton's first acts as chairman of Equitable were to secure the resignations of all of its officers, including Alexander and Hyde, and appoint himself president. His presence helped restore public confidence in Equitable, but his reign lasted only five years; he died suddenly in 1911 and was succeeded by retired judge William A. Day.

Equitable, continuing its innovative ways in the early 1900s, was counted among the first companies offering group insurance for both employees and employers. In 1911, the company implemented underwriting techniques and risk structures intended to make its products more affordable.

During Day's tenure, Equitable amended its charter and became a mutual company—that is, one in which the policyholders and not the shareholders have the right to elect its directors. Proposals for mutualization had surfaced as part of the fallout from the scandals of 1905; the idea was later taken up by J. P. Morgan, who bought Thomas Fortune Ryan's shares in 1909, and it was finally pressed home by industrialist T. Coleman du Pont, who bought the shares in turn from Morgan's estate in 1915.

World War I did not affect Equitable very much, except to inspire it to invest heavily in war bonds. The influenza epidemic of 1918, however, cost the firm about $8 million in death claims. After the war, the economic disruption in Europe, combined with generally higher mortality rates abroad and laws and tax rates that the firm considered to be onerous, inspired

KEY DATES

1859: A young insurance company cashier, Henry Baldwin Hyde, strikes out on his own to form The Equitable Life Assurance Society of the United States.

1886: With Hyde at the helm, Equitable ranks as the world's largest life insurance company.

1905: Scandal involving Hyde's son James triggers a move toward mutual structure.

1925: Business dwindles due to unfavorable conditions abroad.

1942: Equitable enters into large-scale housing development.

1959: One of the largest insurance companies in the nation, Equitable turns 100 years old.

1977: Real estate holdings top $1.3 billion.

1985: Company acquires majority interest in securities firm Donaldson, Lufkin & Jenrette.

1991: AXA Group invests $1 billion in Equitable.

1992: Equitable completes IPO with AXA as single largest shareholder.

2000: AXA Group buys outstanding minority shares of Equitable parent company, AXA Financial, Inc.

2004: Equitable officially changes its name to AXA Equitable Life Insurance Company.

2009: AXA Equitable celebrates its 150th year of operation.

Equitable to discontinue all foreign operations. The process was a drawn out one, but by 1925 the firm was maintaining only a few policies outside the United States.

The 1920s were boom years for Equitable, as they were for the nation as a whole. In 1929 the firm booked more than $2.5 billion worth of new policies and had $6.8 billion worth of coverage in force. William Day retired in 1927, citing ill health, and was succeeded by Thomas I. Parkinson, who would see Equitable through the Great Depression and World War II. During the Depression, the firm suffered a steady decline in business. It also filled its investment portfolio with government bonds, since other kinds of securities were hard to find and risky when they could be found. Because of its investments in mortgages, Equitable also came into possession of a number of farms during this time as borrowers defaulted. It sold most of these

properties during World War II, once food and land prices began to turn up again.

World War II had little effect on Equitable. As it had during World War I, the firm authorized a policy rider that restricted coverage against death in war or aviation mishaps. The sudden splurge in government borrowing that sustained the U.S. war effort and the consequent low yields to be had from government bonds did prompt a change in Equitable's investment policy. In 1942 the firm took its first plunge into large-scale housing development, building a series of apartment complexes in Brooklyn. It followed this in 1946 with another series of apartment buildings in the Bronx.

SECOND CENTURY: 1953–79

Parkinson stepped down as chief executive officer in 1953 and was succeeded by Ray D. Murphy, who was then succeeded by James F. Oates Jr., a lawyer and onetime utilities executive. In 1959 Equitable marked its centennial with a gala celebration at New York's Madison Square Garden. At the end of its first hundred years, the firm had nearly $10 billion worth of assets and $34.4 billion of insurance in force, making it one of the largest insurance companies of any kind in the nation. Ironically, James Hazen Hyde died on July 26, 1959, the 100th anniversary of Equitable. During World War II, Hyde had returned to New York, where he had been living quietly.

Under Oates's stewardship, Equitable became known during the 1960s as an insurance company with a social conscience. In 1962, the firm began a job-training program for school dropouts in New York in an attempt to address the problem of hardcore minority unemployment. The idea originated with Oates, who was serving on President John F. Kennedy's Committee on Youth Employment at the time. In 1968 Equitable pledged $160 million to an industry-wide drive to finance the rehabilitation of housing units in urban slums. The firm also invested in Columbia, Maryland, a city developed during the late 1960s on the "new town" model, an urban planning concept intended to create self-sufficient communities of manageable size.

Oates retired in 1969 and was succeeded by J. Henry Smith, who had first given thought to entering the insurance business during his senior year in college, after chatting with an Equitable salesman who had sold a policy to his father. Equitable began to diversify during Smith's tenure. In 1973 it acquired Informatics, a California-based computer systems company. The next year, it entered the field of property and casualty insurance when it acquired Houston General Insurance, Traders & General Insurance, and Associated Employers

General Agency from an insurance holding company, W.R. Berkeley. Smith retired in 1975 and was succeeded by Coy G. Eklund, and the trend toward diversification continued. In 1976 Equitable joined with Newmont Mining Company, Texasgulf, The Williams Companies, and Fluor Corporation to form a consortium that bought Peabody Coal Company from Kennecott Copper. That same year, the firm joined an industry-wide move toward investing heavily in real estate, when it acquired 17 buildings as part of the self-liquidation of Tishman Realty and Construction. In 1977 it acquired several hotels from Marriott.

Equitable was gradually metamorphosing into a fully diversified financial services company. Two developments that occurred later in the decade, however, threatened to block that progress. A minor controversy swirled around the firm in 1975 when the Department of Justice filed a conflict-of-interest suit against Eklund over his directorship of Chase Manhattan Bank, out of concern that he might be tempted to give Chase Manhattan preferential treatment in investing Equitable premiums. Eklund finally resolved the dispute in 1978 when he announced that he would not seek reelection to his bank post. In 1979 the firm was forced to lay off 550 employees because of sharply rising labor costs and increased competition from young, up-and-coming competitors. The move, which came despite a record earnings year in 1978, was a radical departure from the firm's long tradition of loyalty to its employees and dealt a serious blow to staff morale. Lower productivity, unionization, and discrimination suits all loomed.

BEYOND INSURANCE: 1980–90

To deal with these threats to its financial performance while maintaining its position as the nation's third largest life insurance company, Equitable pursued an apparently paradoxical course of divestiture on the one hand and expansion and diversification on the other. In 1980 it sold Houston General Insurance to Japanese giant Tokio Marine and Fire; it also sold its Toronto-based subsidiary Heritage Life Assurance to Unicorp Financial, a Canadian insurance holding company. In 1981 it sold Equitable General Insurance to GEICO Corporation.

Meanwhile, Equitable continued its push into real estate. In 1982 it bought Equitable Life Mortgage Realty Trust, the real estate investment trust (REIT) that it managed. Buying REITs was widely considered to be a low-cost way of acquiring large pools of property. The firm also announced plans to build a new headquarters skyscraper in Manhattan despite softening demand for office space. Equitable's real estate development activity was given additional impetus by a 1983 change in New York state insurance law allowing insurance companies to engage in almost any financial service other than banking. That year, it acquired Kravco, a Pennsylvania-based shopping center developer, and 50 percent of Continental Companies, a Miami-based hotel developer. In 1984 it bought 19 shopping centers from Iowa-based General Growth Properties.

Equitable took fullest advantage of the more liberal laws under which it could operate; in 1985, it acquired a majority interest in the prominent Wall Street securities firm Donaldson, Lufkin & Jenrette (DLJ). Under the terms of the merger, DLJ founder, Chairman, and CEO Richard H. Jenrette became vice-chairman of Equitable. Two years later, he became chairman upon the retirement of Robert F. Froehlke. Jenrette's rapid promotion reflected the increasing importance of investment and other non-insurance operations to Equitable and to insurance companies in general at a time when people were buying life insurance for investment purposes at least as much as for protection.

Equitable also continued to divest in the late 1980s. In 1987 the firm sold Equitable Life Leasing to mortgage banker Lomas & Nettleton. In 1988 it sold National Integrity Life Insurance and Integrity Life Insurance to Australia-based National Mutual Life Assurance of Australasia. Equitable had not done a sufficient job of cutting costs and improving financial performance to suit the firm's directors. John B. Carter, who succeeded Coy Eklund as CEO in 1984, retired in 1990 amid this displeasure at the relatively young age of 55, and was replaced by Richard H. Jenrette. Chief Financial Officer Glenn H. Gettier also resigned and was replaced by Thomas Kirwan, previously chief financial officer of the firm's insurance operations.

Known for decades as one of the largest life insurance companies in the nation, Equitable could describe itself in 1990 as a diversified financial services company. Besides its traditional insurance operations, Equitable was involved heavily in real estate development and, thanks to its 1985 acquisition of DLJ, in securities brokerage. Its future, though, was about to change.

NEW ERA: 1991–92

In December 1990, Equitable announced its intention to proceed with the development of a plan to demutualize. Equitable would be the first major life insurance company to explore the use of New York State's new demutualization law, which took effect in 1988, as a means of increasing its capital base. The formal demutualization plan first required approval by the Equitable board, then the approval of the New York State Insurance Department and certain classes of policyholders, a lengthy and complex process extending from a year to 18 months.

In making the announcement, Jenrette stated that the decision to seek new capital was part of a three-step program to strengthen Equitable. The first step was a reduction in Equitable's annual operating expenses by more than $150 million, a program carried out earlier in the year. The second step was to strengthen management, most notably through the addition of Joseph Melone as president. Equitable hoped that Melone's background as head of Prudential's field operations would complement Jenrette's financial background.

Paris-based AXA Groupe, S.A., the eighth largest European insurance company, invested $1 billion in The Equitable Life Assurance Society in 1991, in "the largest cash infusion ever in a U.S. insurance company," according to *Pantagraph*. "The deal will help enable Equitable to thrive in an insurance environment laced with troubled companies with bad investments in real estate and junk bonds. Equitable earnings have been battered, with its capital falling 18.4 percent to $1.69 billion in 1990." The infusion elevated Equitable's capital to $2.6 billion, "with a ratio of 6 percent of capital to liabilities vs. 4% percent before the deal." AXA Chairman Claude Bébéar and Jenrette touted the agreement as mutually beneficial. AXA, which earlier failed in a bid for a U.S. insurer, controlled 49 insurance, reinsurance, and financial companies in Europe, North America, and Asia.

Conversion to stock ownership was completed in July 1992, in a $450 million initial public offering (IPO). AXA was the principal shareholder of The Equitable Companies Incorporated, a holding company for The Equitable Life Assurance Society; Alliance Capital Management, L.P.; Donaldson, Lufkin & Jenrette, Inc.; Equitable Real Estate Investment Management, Inc.; and Equitable Capital Management Corp.

Later in 1992, Melone added CEO to his list of titles, tightening his focus on the insurance and annuity businesses. The insurance subsidiary and the four investment subsidiaries reported to holding company Chairman and CEO Jenrette, who anticipated a return to profit. The company's operations had "previously been hindered by asset writedowns and losses in its guaranteed interest contract business," Terrance Little reported in a September 1992 *PR Newswire* article.

UNDER AXA: 1996–2004

Equitable Life had more than $232 billion of individual life insurance and $33 billion of annuity contracts in force at year-end 1996. The company had 7,200 agents and 80 agency locations. In 1997, Edward D. Miller succeeded Melone as president and CEO, of both The Equitable Companies and principal subsidiary, Equitable

Life. Melone continued as chairman of Equitable Life and advanced to chairman of the Executive Committee of the holding company. Miller, a 35-year veteran in consumer financial services, had been senior vice-chairman for The Chase Manhattan Corporation.

AXA's Bébéar retired as chairman of The Equitable Companies in 1998, and was succeeded by Henri de Castries. The following year, the holding company took the AXA name. As AXA Financial, Inc., the company was repositioning "its image beyond that of an insurance company," Michael D. Moore observed for *American Banker*. The name change reflected "its move to become a broader financial services provider and adviser."

Part of the new growth strategy included the creation of AXA Advisors, LLC, targeting the growing number of affluent Americans. Among the products financial planners touted were those under the venerable Equitable Life brand. The insurance company produced 50 percent of AXA Financial's profits of $1.1 billion in 1999, according to *American Banker*.

In 2000, AXA Group moved to acquire shares not held in AXA Financial for approximately $10 billion. Also in the works was the sale of DLJ to Credit Suisse Group, in an $11.5 billion cash and stock deal. "The unusual twin multibillion-dollar deals are characteristic of the opportunism that has transformed AXA Group from a provincial French insurer to a global insurance giant in the space of three decades," Thomas Kamm wrote for the *Wall Street Journal*. Meanwhile, Alliance Capital Management was poised to acquire money manager Sanford C. Bernstein & Co. for $3.5 billion. The actions were indicative of the company's tightened focus on its core "financial protection" businesses.

Christopher M. "Kip" Condron stepped in as the new head of AXA Financial and Equitable Life in 2001, while Miller was moved to AXA Group's supervisory board. Condron, a Mellon Financial Corporation executive, brought asset management and distribution know-how to the table.

Condron advanced the strategy of building a strong financial advisory system that would in turn drive sales of products. "In addition, I've been focused on brand. Although Equitable is a wonderful insurance brand, the brand we're trying to drive forward is the AXA brand, because it is a financial-services brand. Although we will keep the Equitable name and manufacture insurance products under that name, AXA is the brand we're now focused on," Condron told *Best's Review* in 2002.

AXA Financial's product distribution system was poised, in September 2003, to receive a significant boost through a $1.5 billion agreement to acquire New York-based MONY Group Inc. "The announcement comes on the heels of a period of weak sales for many life-insurance and annuity products, particularly so-called variable products that are generally more attractive to investors during good times for the stock market. Still, sales for variable-life and -annuity products—such as those that MONY sells—have been improving in recent months," Robin Sidel reported for the *Wall Street Journal.* The deal for MONY was completed in October 2004 (Mutual Life Insurance Company of New York, to which MONY traced its roots, was the former employer of Equitable founder Henry Hyde).

Condron, meanwhile, cut 2,500 agents from the proprietary network. Those who remained, retrained to sell investment products and give financial advice, and were joined by 1,000 new agents. Also under Condron, product development and enhancement ratcheted up. New product introduction doubled for comparable 12-month periods, between mid-2002 to mid-2004. Net earnings from new life business rose 68 percent in 2003, reaching $302 million, according to *Institutional Investor International.* The Equitable Life Assurance Society of the United States officially changed its name to AXA Equitable Life Insurance Company in 2004.

NEW GAME: 2005–09

AXA Equitable had begun growing its distribution relationships with large banks, JPMorgan Chase & Co. and Wells Fargo & Co. among them, according to a June 2006 *American Banker* article. The company was also developing more of a presence with regional banks.

AXA Equitable CEO and Chairman Condron told *American Banker* the company had set the goal of doubling revenue and sales and tripling profits by 2012, via organic growth and strategic acquisitions. Tactics to drive organic growth included increasing distribution, as well as adding products and courting baby boomers. Furthermore, in 2002, the company had instituted an initiative tying compensation to earnings targets, expense levels, and new business.

During 2005, AXA Equitable expanded its overall share of new variable annuity sales, which took into account sales from all its distribution channels, to 8.01 percent, up from 7.43 percent in 2004. AXA Equitable followed just behind industry leaders TIAA-CREF, MetLife, and Hartford Life in the rankings. Traditional annuities tied guaranteed monthly payments to age. Variable annuities, on the other hand, provided more benefit options but came with higher fees.

In July 2007, AXA Equitable announced the addition of a "marketing and innovation" group to expedite the development and introduction of new products. The next January, a new distribution channel for retirement planning and products was unveiled. Corporate Markets targeted *Fortune* 1000 corporations and their employees. The company's other distribution channels served individuals (AXA Advisors) and the financial services market (AXA Distributors).

As of June 30, 2007, AXA Equitable had $862.2 billion in assets under management. Its ultimate parent company AXA Group, claimed $1.86 trillion in assets under management.

American Banker reported AXA Equitable topped the rankings in 2007, in terms of variable annuity sales growth. The company's variable annuity sales had tripled from 2001, reaching $15.5 billion. During the year, third-party sales to broker-dealers, banks, and independent financial planners climbed 26.3 percent, to $9.5 billion.

Back in 1996 the company had introduced "the first variable annuity with a 'living benefit' that offered investors the ability to receive guaranteed income for life regardless of market conditions," AXA Equitable recounted. The concept took hold in the industry.

Problems arose when the U.S. mortgage-market collapsed, and virtually the entire financial system fell into crisis. Investments across the board lost their value and credit froze. Meanwhile, companies holding variable annuity contracts faced the prospect of raising more capital to meet regulatory requirements regarding the beefed-up investment tool. "While AXA Equitable is certainly not immune from the market conditions, we do have a strong balance sheet, conservatively managed assets, disciplined risk management and adequate resources to meet customer obligations," a spokesman said in the *Wall Street Journal* in November 2008. Nevertheless, well into 2009, AXA Equitable still contended with the fallout from the economic meltdown.

Douglas Sun
Updated, Kathleen Peippo

PRINCIPAL DIVISIONS

AXA Advisors, LLC; AXA Distributors, LLC.

PRINCIPAL COMPETITORS

Allianz Life Insurance Company of North America; Genworth Financial, Inc.; Hartford Life, Inc.

FURTHER READING

"A.M. Best Revises Outlook to Negative for AXA Financial, Inc., and Its Subsidiaries," *Business Wire,* June 12, 2009.

Ackermann, Matt, "AXA Exec Talks of Growth by Deal, and Otherwise," *American Banker,* May 3, 2006, p. 8.

Amiel, Nancy M., "New President and CEO Named at The Equitable Companies and Equitable Life," *PR Newswire,* July 9, 1997.

"AXA Takes Top Spot in Variable Growth," *American Banker,* March 13, 2008.

"AXA Wielder," *Institutional Investor International,* October 2004.

Burley, R. Carlyle, *The Equitable Life Assurance Society of the United States: 1859–1964,* New York: Appleton-Century-Crofts, 1964.

"Chairman to Retire in Changes at Equitable," *New York Times,* February 20, 1998, p. D6.

Chordas, Lori, "Making His Mark," *Best's Review,* April 2002.

"Equitable Secures $1 Billion from French Insurance Group," *Pantagraph,* July 19, 1991, p. D1.

Garmhausen, Steve, "Innovation Chief at AXA Says Times Demand Post," *American Banker,* July 30, 2007.

Gjertsen, Lee Ann, "MONY CEO Under Fire for Low AXA Deal," *American Banker,* September 19, 2003, p. 9.

"In Major Branding Strategy, AXA Financial Launches AXA Advisors to Communicate Depth of Financial Services," *PR Newswire,* September 21, 1999.

Kamm, Thomas, "Wheat Faces His Biggest Challenge in Purchase of DLJ—AXA Group Is Offering to Acquire Remainder of AXA Financial," *Wall Street Journal,* August 31, 2000, p. C1.

Kraus, James R., "AXA Says Its Expansion Plans Do Not Include Bank Deals," *American Banker,* April 25, 2000, p. 1.

Little, Terrance, " Equitable Names Melone to Head Insurance Subsidiary," *PR Newswire,* September 17, 1992.

Moore, Michael, "Equitable Changes Name—to AXA—and Its Focus," *American Banker,* September 21, 1999, p. 15.

Ring, Niamh, "Mellon's Condron Tapped to Head AXA Financial," *American Banker,* May 17, 2001, p. 1.

Scism, Leslie, "Annuities Annoy Insurers' Holders," *Wall Street Journal,* November 5, 2008, p. C1.

Sidel, Robin, "AXA to Buy MONY for $1.5 Billion, Bolstering Its Presence in the U.S.," *Wall Street Journal,* September 18, 2003, C 10.

Spano, Alexander, "AXA: Retirement Web Site Isn't Just About Sales," *American Banker,* July 30, 2008.

Updegrave, Walter, "Those Annuity Ads on TV? Monkey Feather!" *Money,* March 2007.

"Why Equitable Life Looks Good but Feels Bad," *Business Week,* March 26, 1979.

Betsy Ann Candies, Inc.

322 Perry Highway
Pittsburgh, Pennsylvania 15229
U.S.A.
Telephone: (412) 931-4288
Toll Free: (888) 487-8335
Fax: (412) 931-9777
Web site: http://www.betsyann.com

Private Company
Incorporated: 1949 as Betsy Ann Candy Co.
Employees: 90
Sales: $3 million (2008 est.)
NAICS: 311330 Confectionery Manufacturing from Purchased Chocolate; 311911 Roasted Nuts and Peanut Butter Manufacturing; 445292 Confectionery and Nut Stores; 454110 Electronic Shopping and Mail-Order Houses

■ ■ ■

Betsy Ann Candies, Inc., produces boxed gift, novelty, and seasonal handmade truffles, gourmet dark and light chocolates, fudge, and other candy items, including nuts. In the first decade of the 2000s, the company was operating a factory store and about ten franchises mostly in and around Pittsburgh, Pennsylvania, but it has opted to end its retail operations in favor of selling online and via its catalog.

BESSIE HELSEL OPERATES A SMALL CANDY COMPANY: 1949–68

Bessie J. Enyeart was 27 years old when she arrived in Pittsburgh, Pennsylvania, from her childhood home in Blair County. She married Elmer J. Helsel and went to work at Korinis Confectioners on Pittsburgh's north side, first as a chocolate dipper and then as a bookkeeper and general helper. Having learned every aspect of the candy-making business, Helsel began to make candies in her kitchen for her appreciative family members and friends.

By 1949, Helsel's candy business had grown so big that she opened her first shop, called Betsy Ann Candy Co., on Pittsburgh's North Side. Customers began to flock to the store and, before long, Helsel received a contract to make candy for Joseph Horne Company, known as Joseph Horne's, and its department stores. As the business grew, Betsy Ann needed additional space and moved to a bigger shop a few blocks away in 1956. Two years later, when fire destroyed that shop, the company moved to a third location on the same avenue. There, Betsy Ann remained until the early 1960s when the shop was torn down to make room for a highway.

In 1962, Helsel bought a two-story brick and concrete office building, shop, and warehouse to house the Betsy Ann Candy shop and candy-making factory in 17,000 square feet of space. She and her husband moved into the apartment above the store and went to work for the business, as did Helsel's father.

THE PARAS FAMILY CONTINUES THE BETSY ANN TRADITION: 1968–86

When Helsel fell down a flight of stairs in 1964 at age 60, she had to cut back on her business responsibilities, and in 1968, she sold Betsy Ann Candy to Harry J. and Catherine Paras. Harry Paras was a baker with an interest and some experience in making candy. Helsel was known as a perfectionist, but also for being "very good-hearted and understanding" and "hard working," according to a former employee in a 1994 *Pittsburgh Post-Gazette* article. She continued to work with the Parases for the next year, teaching them how to make her candies. She later died in 1986.

James D. Paras, the Parases' son, joined the company after graduating college in about 1980. Brothers Dan and Robert, and James's wife, Karen, also came to work for the business. Throughout the 1970s and 1980s, the Parases continued to use Bessie Helsel's original recipes for many of their candies, and to follow her business strategy whereby the majority of the company's business derived from its longtime accounts with department stores.

However, once the major domestic department stores began to consolidate and the retail industry fell upon hard times in the mid-1980s, the company began to suffer. Betsy Ann lost much of its private-label department store business, and its growth reached a plateau. After about a decade of working with his parents, Jim became company president in 1990, overseeing retail sales, packaging design, and marketing. Dan Paras became vice-president and was more involved in candy-making. Karen Paras's main responsibility was customer service. "As I pored through everything, I realized that if we didn't start making some changes, the trends that were going on in this business were going to put us under," Paras recounted in a 1998 *Pittsburgh Post-Gazette* article.

CREATING A RETAIL BRAND

The company consulted the Family Business Institute in Pittsburgh about restructuring from a mostly wholesale to a retail-based operation, and, after two decades of maintaining the status quo at Betsy Ann Candies, the Parases began to develop the Betsy Ann concept and scope. Technically, Betsy Ann was in violation of its supply contract with Horne's in venturing into retail sales, but faced with the alternative of Betsy Ann terminating its contract by closing up shop, Horne's did not seem to mind.

The Parases focused on creating an identifiable brand when they opened two new stores, one in 1989 and one in 1991, which they called "chocolate boutiques." The stores were decorated predominantly in shades of pink, rose, and mauve. Hand-stenciled roses and bows covered the walls, and candy boxes, which looked like lace, were trimmed with pink ribbons and American Beauty roses. Store clerks wore colonial shirtwaists and aprons bedecked with ruffles. In the two new stores, the candies were displayed in mahogany Chippendale-style cases.

GROWTH THROUGH PARAS TRUFFLES AND FRANCHISES: 1992

Fulfilling Jim Paras's vision of becoming an upscale retailer of high-end chocolates, the Parases also added two lines of expensive truffles called Paras Truffles in 1992. These were marketed as European truffles and American Originals, advertised as the "first truly American truffle." The Paras Parfait Truffle, consisting of three layers of white, milk, and dark chocolate mousse filling, surrounded by dark chocolate, was originally introduced as a limited-time offer, but quickly developed a following, and, by 1994, truffle sales accounted for about half of Betsy Ann's $2 million in sales. Another 25 percent came from sales to Horne's department stores.

In 1992, the company initiated a plan to further expand through franchises and thereby build the company name, stem competition, stimulate stalled growth, and overcome the costs of expansion. The hoped-for steady flow in chocolate orders would boost production.

Franchises were designed to be turnkey operations. For a total investment of $125,000, of which $25,000 was the franchise fee, Betsy Ann provided store designing, opening promotions, initial inventory, an insurance package, and working capital. Franchises were required to be 800 to 1,200 square feet and to remain open from 9 A.M. to 9 P.M. Monday through Saturday and noon to 4 or 5 P.M. on Sunday. Franchisees were to work at least 20 hours per week in the store.

By 1995, Betsy Ann employed 85 people at peak production time and its retail stores, with the exception of the original factory store, were open year-round. In

KEY DATES

■

1949: Bessie Helsel opens Betsy Ann Candy Co. on Pittsburgh, Pennsylvania's North Side.

1956: Betsy Ann Candy Co. moves to a bigger shop a few blocks away from its original facility.

1958: Fire destroys Betsy Ann and the company moves to a third location on the same avenue.

1962: Betsy Ann Candy shop and candy-making factory purchase and move into a two-story brick and concrete office building, shop, and warehouse.

1968: Helsel sells Betsy Ann Candy to husband and wife Harry J. and Catherine Paras.

1986: Bessie Helsel dies.

1989: The Parases open their first chocolate "boutique."

1991: Company opens its second boutique, bringing its total to three stores.

1992: Company introduces two lines of upscale truffles.

1995: First Betsy Ann franchise opens.

2008: Company begins to phase out its retail operations.

1998, there were nine Betsy Ann Chocolate shops in the Pittsburgh area, five of them franchises. Over the next several years, the company added new candies and new flavors to its truffle offerings, such as macadamia coconut and double dark. It appeared on a candy episode of the Food Network program, *The Best Of,* where it was dubbed the "crown jewel of chocolate companies," and was voted one of the top three treats in Pittsburgh in 1993, 1994, and 1995 by the local *City Paper.*

MAINTAINING HANDMADE TRADITIONS

Still, the company continued to make all of its confections by hand. Using the top grade of Peters Ultra milk chocolate made by Nestlé, employees hand-poured chocolate into molds, then tapped them down several times to get rid of bubbles before putting them in coolers. Nuts were purchased raw by Betsy Ann and hand-roasted. The designs on top of the chocolates that designated the filling were also done by hand.

In fact, the only machine the company used was an enrober (used for coating various food items with chocolate) for "more control," according to Paras, and many pieces were run through several times. "We even hand chop the fresh cashews we buy from India with a special hammer to get the perfect size," Jim Paras explained in a 2002 *Pittsburgh Post-Gazette* article. "[T]o get that made-from-scratch taste, there is no better way."

The company began to make customized products as well. For a one-time tooling fee of about $200, a customer could order a personalized mold, and order (and reorder) chocolates for the regular fee of $16 a pound. Also in 2003, Betsy Ann teamed up with Gospa Missions in Evans City, Pennsylvania, to make chocolate rosary beads, "a new type of tradition that is more suited for today's lifestyles," according to Paras in the *Pittsburgh Post-Gazette* in 2003.

REMAINING SMALL

Betsy Ann's annual retail sales of $200,000 in 1988 grew to $2 million in 2001 with eight company stores and four franchise stores, including one in Cleveland. By this time, the relationship with Horne's had ended.

By 2008, the company's revenues had increased to $3 million and employees numbered 100, but Betsy Ann Candies was phasing out its retail stores in favor of fundraising and Internet sales. During the second part of the decade, small specialty stores had begun to struggle and lose in the competition with grocery stores or big-box retailers that offered the convenience of one-stop shopping. The company would continue to sell to the upscale gift market while offering a wide breadth of products and had plans to enter the fundraising market as well.

Betsy Ann had shuttered six of its stores by December 2008, and the store had returned to its department store roots as Macy's Home Store began to sell Betsy Ann items both in bulk and in bags and boxes. It was unclear exactly what next steps the company would take, but under the determined direction of the Paras family in general and Jim Paras in particular, the company aimed to continue to delight candy lovers nationwide.

Carrie Rothburd

PRINCIPAL COMPETITORS

Godiva Chocolatier, Inc.; Moonstruck Chocolate Company; Dynamic Confections, Inc.; Russell Stover Candies Inc.

FURTHER READING

Bates, Daniel, "West View Chocolate Maker Jumps into Franchising," *Small Business News: Pittsburgh,* October 1994, p. 6.

"Betsy Ann Chocolates Filled with Rich History," *Pittsburgh Post-Gazette,* March 20, 1994, p. V3.

Carpico, Maria, "Chocolatier Answers His Prayers," *Pittsburgh Post-Gazette,* October 29, 2003, p. N6.

Deasy, Deborah, "How Sweet It Is: Even the Easter Bunny Can't Outdo This West View Chocolate Maker," *Pittsburgh Tribune Review,* April 16, 1995, p. D1.

Leonard, Kim. "Sweet! Macy's to Carry Betsy Ann Chocolates," *Pittsburgh Tribune Review,* December 10, 2008.

MacKenzie, Mary Kate, "The Best of Betsy Ann: Food Network Focuses Spotlight on West View Family," *Pittsburgh Post-Gazette,* April 9, 2002, p. G14.

"The Sweet Part: Jim Paras Thinks Betsy Ann Chocolates Has Put Difficult Past Behind It," *Pittsburgh Post-Gazette,* April 12, 1998, p. C5.

Zrimsek, Andrea, "Sweet Things: Betsy Ann Chocolates Still Made by Hand," *Pittsburgh Business Times,* May 2, 2003, p. 15.

Blimpie

9311 East Via de Ventura
Scottsdale, Arizona 85258-3423
U.S.A.
Telephone: (480) 362-4800
Toll Free: (866) 452-4252
Fax: (480) 362-4812
Web site: http://www.blimpie.com

Operating Unit of Kahala Corp.
Incorporated: 1977 as International Blimpie Corporation
Sales: $270 million (2007 systemwide est.)
NAICS: 722211 Limited-Service Restaurants; 533110
   Lessors of Nonfinancial Intangible Assets (Except
   Copyrighted Works)

■ ■ ■

Blimpie is the number three submarine sandwich chain in the United States, trailing only Subway and Quiznos. The menu at the nearly 1,100 franchised Blimpie outlets across the United States features a variety of freshly sliced, deli-style sandwiches, including deli subs, hot subs, and panini-grilled subs, as well as soups, salads, and beverages. In addition to locations in malls and shopping centers, Blimpies can be found in various nontraditional sites, such as inside convenience stores, colleges, hospitals, sports arenas, and Wal-Mart stores. Founded in 1964, Blimpie was acquired in 2006 by Kahala Corp., a franchiser of a dozen quick-service restaurant chains, including Cold Stone Creamery, Great Steak & Potato Co., Samurai Sam's Teriyaki Grill, Surf City Squeeze, and Taco Time.

EARLY HISTORY

The first Blimpie sub shop was opened in Hoboken, New Jersey, in 1964 by Tony Conza, Peter DeCarlo, and Angelo Bandassare, a trio of former high school buddies. Inspired by a successful Point Pleasant, New Jersey, operation called Mike's Submarines, Conza, DeCarlo, and Bandassare speculated that a similar restaurant would do well in Hoboken. They raised $2,500 in seed capital by borrowing from friends and began serving essentially the same sandwich for which people were lining up at Mike's. The founders came up with the name for their shop while flipping through a dictionary, looking for an alternative to such typical sandwich terms as *submarine* and *hoagie,* and eventually landing on *blimp.* The original Blimpie was an instant hit, and, before long, customers began asking about starting up franchises. The first franchise was sold to a friend in western New York for $600 during the company's first year of operation.

In 1965 Bandassare left the company to start his own foodservice supply firm. Conza and DeCarlo decided to expand into New York City, beginning with a store on 55th Street in Manhattan, near Carnegie Hall. By 1967 there were ten Blimpies in the chain, four of which were owned by the company's two remaining founders. Unfortunately, Conza and DeCarlo were not experienced businessmen, and, in spite of the chain's rapid growth and good sales volume, profits were difficult to attain. To keep the company afloat, the partners sold the four stores they owned and began to concentrate primarily on franchising.

COMPANY PERSPECTIVES

Blimpie's roots can be traced back to three friends armed with an entrepreneurial spirit and a business itch to introduce what the world now knows as the beloved submarine sandwich. After months of research and planning, all the components were in place for them to begin their journey of becoming business owners, with one exception—they needed a name. With a desire to set themselves apart from their competition, they decided to call their sandwiches something other than submarines or hoagies. Hoping to find some inspiration, they paged through a dictionary until they came to the word "blimp" and a picture resembling the healthy, generous-size sandwiches they saw as their competitive edge. That was the "eureka" moment, and the Blimpie sandwich and restaurant chain was born! On April 4, 1964, the three friends opened for business in Hoboken, N.J.

Today with more than four decades of history and locations from coast to coast, the Blimpie brand continues to grow with the strength of its past propelling it forward. Though times have changed since those three friends began their journey, enjoying a meal at Blimpie is still like returning to your neighborhood deli. With fresh sliced meats and high quality ingredients, Blimpie keeps the dream of its founders alive while still setting itself apart from the competition.

By the mid-1970s, Conza felt the time was ripe to introduce Blimpie subs to the South. Partner DeCarlo, however, was against the move. This disagreement eventually led to a split between the two men. In 1976 Blimpie was divided into two separate entities, with both retaining rights to the Blimpie trademark. DeCarlo became head of a new, completely independent company, Metropolitan Blimpie, Inc., which controlled franchising rights in New York, New Jersey, and other parts of the East Coast. Conza retained control of the original company, which was incorporated in 1977 as International Blimpie Corporation. Conza, a college dropout with no business credentials other than his experience with Blimpie, remained chairman and CEO of Blimpie through January 2002.

During the late 1970s, Conza was willing to sell franchises anywhere there was an interested franchisee.

Blimpie began selling franchises both for individual stores and for whole territories. Unfortunately, many of these new franchises were rather isolated from the rest of the chain, and some of the benefits of franchise arrangements such as chainwide advertising had little effect in those locations. Although the chain was growing rapidly, several of the newer stores failed. By 1983, International Blimpie's annual revenues were approaching $1 million, and Blimpie's franchises totaled 150. Conza took the company public that year, with a modest initial over-the-counter offering of 90 cents per share.

MID-1980S: ILL-FATED DIVERSIFICATION PROGRAM

Over the next few years, Blimpie embarked on a diversification program that failed miserably. Conza began to feel that there was no future in submarine sandwiches. At the same time, he longed for the kind of respect that comes only to real restaurateurs, not fast-food moguls. In 1984 Conza opened the Border Café, a tablecloth restaurant serving southwestern cuisine on Manhattan's swanky Upper East Side. Although the Border Café did reasonably well at first, this shift in focus proved to be a major blunder. While Conza was turning his attention away from the subs that had gotten him where he was, competitor Subway, which was founded in 1965, just a year after the first Blimpie's was opened, was beginning an expansion drive that would push it far ahead of Blimpie as the world's foremost submarine sandwich chain.

To reflect his increasing concentration on non-Blimpie activities, Conza changed the name of the company to Astor Restaurant Group, Inc., in October 1986. Meanwhile, the Blimpie's chain was stagnating. The number of outlets was stalled at about 200. In Manhattan, the company's birthplace, the Blimpie name suffered severe image problems. In the early days, the company had not been particularly selective as to who could get a franchise. In addition, its early franchise contracts allowed operators quite a bit of latitude in how the restaurants were to be run. This led to a degree of uniformity among stores far below that of other national fast-food chains, not to mention a reputation for questionable sanitation standards.

After the Border Café's initial success, Conza opened two more of them in 1986, one in Woodstock, New York, and the other, with New York Yankee Dave Winfield as a partner, on the Upper West Side of Manhattan. Unfortunately, the Border Café idea turned out to be a big money loser. Although Astor brought in $4.5 million in revenues for 1987 (its largest total to that date), the company showed a net loss of $347,800 for the year. That year, only 30 new Blimpie restaurants

---

KEY DATES

1964: First Blimpie sub shop is opened in Hoboken, New Jersey, by Tony Conza, Peter DeCarlo, and Angelo Bandassare.

1965: Bandassare leaves the company.

1976: Conza and DeCarlo divide Blimpie into two separate entities, with DeCarlo keeping the locations in the Northeast and forming a new company called Metropolitan Blimpie, Inc., and Conza retaining control of the original company and the rights to the Blimpie name everywhere else.

1977: Conza incorporates the original company as International Blimpie Corporation.

1983: Company goes public.

1986: Company name is changed to Astor Restaurant Group, Inc.

1992: Company is renamed Blimpie International, Inc.

1995: The 1,000th Blimpie outlet opens.

2002: A private investor group led by Jeffrey K. Endervelt, a Blimpie subfranchisee, agrees to take Blimpie International private in a $25.7 million transaction; Endervelt replaces Conza as chairman and CEO of the firm.

2005: Endervelt resigns from his posts of chairman and CEO.

2006: Quick-service restaurant franchiser Kahala Corp. acquires Blimpie International.

2007: Kahala acquires Metropolitan Blimpie and thus reunites the two long-separated Blimpie entities.

---

were opened, and company stock was in free-fall, bottoming out as low as 15 cents per share. Gradually, Conza's interest in his core business began to return. Over the next few years, Atlanta became the company's biggest target for new Blimpie's franchises. In 1987 the company celebrated the opening of the 50th Blimpie's store in the Atlanta area by giving away 25,000 free sandwiches to customers there.

REVITALIZATION EFFORTS

By 1988 Conza had realized the error of his ways, and he quickly got out of the Tex-Mex business. Seeing the tremendous success of Subway, Conza decided to redouble his efforts in the hoagie arena. He began to ad-

dress the Blimpie problem with renewed vigor and a more systematic approach than he had used before. The first step in Conza's revitalization program was to identify four fundamental problems plaguing the business: a lack of goals, poor use of financial resources, low employee morale, and procrastination. He then met with a group of managers and drew up a list of "101 Small Improvements." Delegating to his senior staff much of the day-to-day managing he had always done himself, Conza went on the road in an attempt to open up the long-closed channels of communication between Blimpie and its franchisees.

Next, Blimpie launched a quality-control program aimed at cleaning up its 140 New York restaurants, which had long been sources of embarrassment to the chain. At the same time, Conza continued in his efforts to improve relations with franchisees, many of whom had become disgruntled over the last decade. In addition to flying to dozens of cities to meet restaurant owners, Conza formed a franchisee advisory council to keep him apprised of important issues; he launched a newsletter called *No Baloney News* and a toll-free hotline to get important information out to franchisees; and he gave franchisees more control over advertising through the formation of regional advertising co-ops.

In 1989 Blimpie began testing a new low-calorie menu in the hope of attracting a bigger share of the increasingly fat-conscious American public. The new menu, called Blimpie Lite, included a variety of tuna-, crab-, chicken-, and turkey-based items, in both salad and pita-bread sandwich form. The following year, the company launched another test: gourmet salads sold under the name Blimpie Fresherie. Blimpie also began tinkering with its prototype restaurant design around this time, incorporating the company's signature lime-green and yellow colors into a sleeker look for new outlets. By 1990 the Blimpie turnaround was well underway, with systemwide sales reaching $120 million per year.

The Blimpie chain continued to grow steadily through the early 1990s. Much of this growth was fueled by the company's area developer program, in which franchise rights were sold for an entire area to a developer, who then subfranchised those rights to individual operators. The company continued testing new products throughout this period. In 1991 Blimpie unveiled its Quick Bite menu in response to the appearance of value menus in many fast-food establishments, including archrival Subway. Items on the Quick Bite menu included three-inch hero sandwiches for 99 cents; a six-inch bacon, lettuce, and tomato sandwich for $1.59; and a veggie pocket pita sandwich, also priced at $1.59. The company also began testing pizza at a handful of locations in an effort to breathe some life into its dinner business. Conza's attempts to improve franchisee relations continued as well. The company's first annual franchisee convention was held in 1991.

OVER 1,000 UNITS

By the beginning of 1992, there were Blimpie restaurants in 27 states. That year, the chain passed the 500-unit mark and the company changed its name to Blimpie International, Inc., reflecting the renewed focus on the sub brand. In the spring of 1993, Blimpie began listing its stock on the up-and-coming NASDAQ. Around this time, the company began to sink more resources into advertising than it had in the past, doubling its marketing budget to about $2 million per year. A new advertising campaign was launched, encompassing just about every medium available, including television, radio, print, and point-of-purchase. This campaign marked the introduction of the chain's new tagline: "Simply Blimpie for fresh-sliced subs." Some of the television spots featured people on the street struggling to repeat the tongue-twisting phrase, "Simply Blimpie."

Sales throughout the Blimpie system reached $132 million by 1993, and Blimpie International earned $1 million on $12 million in revenue. By autumn of that year, the chain had grown to 670 outlets. Improved marketing support from the parent company helped reduce the rate of franchise failures from 10 percent to 3 percent. In some cases, such as in the brutally competitive Chicago market, Conza allowed franchisees to divert their 6 percent annual franchise fee to advertising.

As the 1990s continued, Blimpie came up with a new concept that accelerated the chain's growth even further. Blimpie's franchises began appearing in a variety of nontraditional locations. First it was convenience stores. As convenience store proprietors began to seek new ways to compensate for declining cigarette sales, they started turning to fast food. Blimpie's was the natural choice for many, for two main reasons: a real kitchen was not required, and startup costs were relatively low (as little as $35,000) compared with other fast-food operations. Among the early nontraditional sites for Blimpie's outlets were the Des Moines, Iowa-based Kum & Go convenience store chain; Texaco Food Marts in Mississippi; and the food court at the University of Texas. Blimpie's also became part of the first Home Depot superstore restaurant section, located in Atlanta.

In 1994 the 800th Blimpie, in Iron City, Michigan, was opened. That year, the company launched several new concepts to further its drive for nontraditional venues. The Blimpie kiosk was a movable, condensed restaurant that could fit into a 100-square-foot area. The kiosk, which could serve four types of sandwiches, drinks, and side orders, was designed for use at stadiums, fairs, and other special events. Another new idea was the movable display cart, suitable for high-traffic areas such as airports, college campuses, and concerts. Other new wrinkles included a special refrigerated case for convenience stores (Blimpie's fastest-growing market), and the Blimpie Bakery, offering a variety of baked goods aimed at boosting early morning business.

Blimpie reached two major milestones in 1995. Largely on the strength of its nontraditional location push, the chain passed the 1,000-outlet mark that year. Blimpie International also lived up to the second word in its name for the first time in company history, with the opening of a location in Stockholm, Sweden. As the 1990s continued, the company looked for more new ways to sell Blimpie sandwiches, including vending machines, outlets in supermarkets, and new types of carts and other mobile product delivery systems.

SEEKING GROWTH THROUGH NEW CONCEPTS

With the opening of new outlets in the United States slowing and with overseas growth occurring only at a very slow pace (there were only 61 overseas locations in 15 countries by 2001), Blimpie launched a new diversification effort in the late 1990s. The first such initiative came late in 1997 when the company acquired a 75 percent stake in Maui Tacos, a fast-food chain with six units in Hawaii. This concept featured traditional quick-service Mexican food, such as burritos, tacos, and quesadillas, but with a Hawaiian twist, such as meat marinated in pineapple, lime, and other Hawaiian flavorings. Under Blimpie's majority ownership, Maui Tacos was soon introduced to the mainland, and by 2001 there were 15 such units in nine states and the District of Columbia.

After almost two years of in-house development, Blimpie launched Pasta Central in 1999. Unlike Maui Tacos, Pasta Central was not a stand-alone concept but was created as a cobranding vehicle that would be coupled with Blimpie Subs & Salads. Cobranding emerged as a hot growth vehicle in the late 1990s and involved the placement of two (or more) restaurant brands within a single unit. There were a number of rationales behind cobranded units, including the idea that the additional choices that they offered customers made them more attractive to groups of people, but for Blimpie International it was the desire to increase dinner revenues that propelled the creation of Pasta Central. Because sandwiches were largely considered lunch fare, Blimpie Subs outlets made the bulk of their sales from 11 A.M. to 2 P.M. Pasta Central, by contrast, with its Italian-style pasta dishes and its pizza offerings, was designed to generate a lot of traffic during dinner, thereby making it complementary to Blimpie. In addition, Pasta Central was also created with a home meal replacement component built in: a selection of prepared refrigerated and frozen entrees and prepacked foods for preparation at home. By mid-2001 there were eight units cobranded with Blimpie and Pasta Central, with the units located in Puerto Rico, Georgia, South Carolina, Texas, and Wyoming.

A third new concept was Smoothie Island, which was launched through Maui Tacos in 1998. Smoothie Island's menu featured beverages blended with frozen yogurt and fruit. In addition to opening stand-alone units, including such nontraditional locations as airports, health clubs, and grocery stores, Blimpie also planned to cobrand Smoothie Island with the Maui Tacos and Blimpie concepts, both in dual-branding and tribranding formats. By mid-2001 there were 80 Smoothie Island units located in the United States, Puerto Rico, and four other countries.

A STRUGGLING CHAIN TAKEN PRIVATE

By the new millennium, Blimpie International was struggling. Net income had fallen steadily throughout the second half of the 1990s, dropping from the high of $4 million in fiscal 1995 to just $1.1 million in fiscal 2000. A main factor in this decline was that the subfranchiser rights to the Blimpie Subs chain had largely been sold by the mid-1990s, thus bringing a halt to what had been a steady stream of income. Another factor was that the drive to open nontraditional outlets was far from a winning strategy. Many of these units proved unprofitable, and a number of them were subsequently closed. During one 12-month period from mid-2000 to mid-2001 the company closed 155 underperforming Blimpie outlets, 70 percent of which were in nontraditional locations. The company also announced plans to close seven unprofitable company-owned Maui Tacos and Smoothie Island outlets, a move that left the firm with just five company-owned stores out of its nearly 2,000 sites. Also during 2001, the Blimpie chain began receiving a revamping that involved menu upgrades, more extensive point-of-sale merchandising, and an overhaul of the decor. One of the key changes to the menu was the addition of a line of hot grilled sandwiches that proved quite popular in market testing.

As Blimpie's struggles continued, net income having fallen below $100,000 for the fiscal year ending in June 2001, investors showed little interest in the company, and the price of the company's stock sagged. Seeing little benefit in being a publicly traded firm, Blimpie joined the growing ranks of restaurant companies fleeing the public market. In October 2001 a private investor group led by Jeffrey K. Endervelt, owner of the 44-unit Blimpie of California subfranchise, agreed to buy Blimpie International for $25.7 million. The transaction was completed in January 2002, whereupon Endervelt took over as chairman, president, and CEO, and Conza, who was a partner in the investor group, remained involved at the company but in an advisory capacity.

Attempting to play catch-up with the ever-larger hoagie behemoth Subway, Endervelt moved quickly on a number of fronts. In addition to closing underperforming units (about 120 during the fiscal year ending in June 2003), Endervelt placed a greater emphasis on making sure that franchisees were keeping their stores in compliance with company standards. Among other moves, the remodeling program launched in 2001, which had been voluntary, was made mandatory. In addition, the chain's limited marketing budget was directed away from media campaigns and toward local efforts, particularly in-store displays and targeted neighborhood marketing.

While these efforts generated some positive effects, overall trends at Blimpie remained negative. Systemwide sales, which totaled an estimated $280 million in fiscal 2004, continued to decline, although part of the fall stemmed from store closures. After shuttering nearly 200 more locations in fiscal 2004, the chain total stood at about 1,700. During 2004 the company entered into an agreement with Wal-Mart Stores, Inc., to open more than 100 Blimpie Xpress restaurants within the retail giant's stores. The menu for these units was somewhat more limited than the typical Blimpie, but did include a line of low-carbohydrate sandwiches that had recently been introduced at the full-scale outlets to cater to a diet craze then sweeping the United States.

In 2005 the changes at Blimpie were taken to a new level when the company launched an effort to reposition the brand as an upscale alternative to Subway. A new remodeling effort upgraded the decor and introduced a refreshed logo. Seeking to push the per-person check average from $5.50 to more than $6, Blimpie debuted a new line of panini-style grilled sandwiches on ciabatta bread that were priced slightly higher than the chain's existing subs. In total, the overhaul aimed to differentiate Blimpie from its chief competitors, Subway and Quiznos, by offering, as Chief Marketing Officer Mark

Mears related to the *Atlanta Business Chronicle,* "a better-quality sandwich at a quick-service price."

While Endervelt's turnaround efforts continued, the Blimpie leader came under fire from a number of the chain's area developers and subfranchisers, who accused him of receiving kickbacks from supplier contracts, misusing marketing and advertising funds, and failing to share royalties with subfranchisers. Endervelt vigorously denied these allegations, but in the fall of 2005 he resigned from his posts at Blimpie while remaining on the company board and continuing to manage the firm's Maui Tacos and Smoothie Island brands.

THE KAHALA ERA

Just a few months later, in January 2006, Blimpie International was acquired for an undisclosed sum by Kahala Corp., based in Scottsdale, Arizona. Kahala was the franchiser of nine quick-service restaurant chains, including Great Steak & Potato Co., Samurai Sam's Teriyaki Grill, Surf City Squeeze, and Taco Time. Its chains included an aggregate total of about 1,250 units. Kahala's takeover of Blimpie International did not encompass the Blimpie sister chains, including Maui Tacos and Smoothie Island. Also not a part of the deal were the 300 or so Blimpie locations on the East Coast still owned and operated separately by Metropolitan Blimpie, Inc. Following the acquisition, Blimpie's headquarters were shifted from Atlanta to Scottsdale.

Kahala worked quickly to repair relations with its area developers and franchisees. Among its initiatives in this area was the offering of incentives to franchisees to remodel stores. Kahala also placed Blimpie back on a growth path, building particularly on the nascent partnership with Wal-Mart. At the time Kahala took over Blimpie, there were about 115 Blimpies located within Wal-Marts; Kahala immediately set in place plans to open 60 more during 2006.

Another important step in Blimpie's evolution occurred in 2007. In May of that year, shortly after Kahala gained another high-profile brand through a merger with ice cream chain Cold Stone Creamery, Kahala acquired the assets of Metropolitan Blimpie, reuniting the two Blimpie companies more than 30 years after their separation. Kahala thus gained full control of the Blimpie brand, which promised to offer benefits of scale in purchasing and distribution contracts and allowed for a consolidation of marketing and training efforts. Full ownership of the brand was also expected to aid growth efforts, particularly internationally, as the previous bifurcated situation proved unappealing to overseas companies evaluating the prospect of becoming Blimpie franchisees.

During 2008, with the U.S. economy on the decline, Blimpie launched a value promotion centering on $5 footlong subs. This effort succeeded in pushing the chain's sales up 8 percent during the first month after the promotion's launch in mid-June. In 2009, as it celebrated its 45th anniversary, Blimpie continued to freshen its menu offerings, introducing pretzel bread and several new sandwiches, including a buffalo chicken and pepperoni sub on grilled ciabatta bread and a turkey bacon cheddar sub on pretzel bread. At the same time, however, it was clear that Kahala remained in turnaround mode in regard to Blimpie as the chain total dropped to fewer than 1,100 units as a culling of under-performing units apparently continued.

Robert R. Jacobson
Updated, David E. Salamie

PRINCIPAL COMPETITORS

Doctor's Associates Inc. (Subway); The Quiznos Master LLC; Arby's Restaurant Group, Inc.; Panera Bread Company; Jimmy John's Franchise, LLC; Deli Management, Inc.; Einstein Noah Restaurant Group, Inc.

FURTHER READING

Bird, Laura, "Building a Lighter, Fresher Blimpie," *Adweek's Marketing Week,* August 6, 1990, p. 23.

"Blimpie Program Helps BUILD Neighborhoods," *Nation's Restaurant News,* November 13, 2000, p. 122.

"Blimpie Seeks Financial Health in Cutting Back Company Units," *Nation's Restaurant News,* May 18, 2001, pp. 18, 40.

"Blimpie Subs Surface at Wal-Mart," *Retail Merchandiser,* March 2004, p. 10.

"Blimpie's Starts Quality Drive in Manhattan," *Nation's Restaurant News,* April 4, 1988, p. 63.

Cohen, Andrew, "'Blimpie' and 'Lite' May No Longer Be Contradictory Terms," *Wall Street Journal,* April 27, 1989, p. B5.

Conza, Tony, "My Biggest Mistake," *Inc.,* April 1999, p. 105.

———, *Success: It's a Beautiful Thing: Lessons on Life and Business from the Founder of Blimpie International,* New York: Wiley, 2000, 242 p.

Credeur, Mary Jane, "Blimpie Craves Gourmet Diners," *Atlanta Business Chronicle,* April 1, 2005.

Duecy, Erica, "Blimpie Seeks to Reposition Brand, Plans Menu, Decor Upgrades," *Nation's Restaurant News,* August 30, 2004, pp. 1, 89.

Dugan, I. Jeanne, "Half a Loaf at Blimpie," *Business Week,* August 10, 1998, pp. 43–44.

Edwards, Joe, "Astor Puts Blimpie in a Growth Mode," *Nation's Restaurant News,* November 9, 1987, p. F25.

"Endervelt Exits As Blimpie Chairman, CEO, President," *Nation's Restaurant News,* November 7, 2005, p. 80.

Farkas, David, "Sub Mission," *Chain Leader,* October 2003, pp. 43–44+.

Frumkin, Paul, "Blimpie Ramps Up Menu, Design to Recast Concept As Upscale Deli," *Nation's Restaurant News,* April 25, 2005, pp. 8, 69.

———, "Blimpie Sets Course with Concept Revamp," *Nation's Restaurant News,* August 27, 2001, pp. 1, 132.

———, "Newly Merged Kahala–Cold Stone Buys Independent Blimpie Franchisor in N.Y.," *Nation's Restaurant News,* May 28, 2007, pp. 4, 50, 53.

———, "Private Investor Group Set to Buy Blimpie for $26M," *Nation's Restaurant News,* October 22, 2001, pp. 1, 11, 71.

Gabriel, Frederick, "A Divided Blimpie Charts New Course," *Crain's New York Business,* September 15, 1997, p. 4.

Grimm, Matthew, "Blimpie Plans Winter Image Push," *Adweek's Marketing Week,* September 2, 1991, p. 7.

Hamstra, Mark, "Blimpie Goes Hawaiian, Buys Mexican Chain," *Nation's Restaurant News,* November 10, 1997, pp. 1, 143.

———, "Hawaiian-Style Mexican Hits the Mainland with Maui Tacos," *Nation's Restaurant News,* November 23, 1998, pp. 1, 108.

Hayes, Jack, "Blimpie Operators Slam Policy Shifts, Allege Kickbacks to Endervelt Regime," *Nation's Restaurant News,* October 4, 2004, pp. 5, 206–207.

Hein, Kenneth, "Blimpie Floats Challenge to Subway and Quiznos," *Brandweek,* October 4, 2004, p. 12.

———, "Blimpie Plans Fresh Look to Help Raise the Sub," *Brandweek,* March 21, 2005, p. 7.

Howard, Theresa, "Now on Deck for Blimpie: NASDAQ, New Ad Campaign," *Nation's Restaurant News,* February 22, 1993, p. 16.

"Kahala: Blimpie Deal Lifts System to 2,500 Outlets," *Nation's Restaurant News,* February 6, 2006, p. 3.

Keegan, Peter O., "Under New VP, Blimpie Int'l. Eyes Nontraditional Growth," *Nation's Restaurant News,* September 5, 1994, p. 7.

Kleinfield, N. R., "Trying to Build a Bigger Blimpie," *New York Times,* December 13, 1987, p. F4.

Littman, Margaret, "A New Way to Slice It," *Chain Leader,* July 2002, pp. 32–33.

———, "Pro Choice: Blimpie International Takes on Its Competitors by Emphasizing Its Options," *Chain Leader,* August 2005, pp. 28–29.

Lockyer, Sarah E., "Blimpie Franchisor Kahala Aims to Fix Operators' Gripes vs. Former Regime," *Nation's Restaurant News,* May 1, 2006, pp. 1, 100.

O'Dwyer, Gerard, "Blimpie Develops a Swede Tooth," *Crain's New York Business,* December 11, 1995, p. 17.

Richman, Louis S., "Rekindling the Entrepreneurial Fire," *Fortune,* February 21, 1994, p. 112.

Rigg, Cynthia, "Blimpie's Cuts Mustard with Convenience Stores," *Crain's New York Business,* October 11, 1993, p. 3.

Rogers, Monica, "Sandwich Chic: Jenn Townsend Revitalizes Blimpie with Hot, Grilled, and Ethnic Sandwiches," *Chain Leader,* October 2004, pp. 37–38+.

Sagon, Erica, "Blimpie Bought by Valley Firm," *Arizona Republic* (Phoenix), January 25, 2006, p. D1.

Stafford, Leon, "Blimpie Tinkers with Look in Tough Market," *Atlanta Journal-Constitution,* April 7, 2005, p. B1.

Touby, Laurel, "Blimpie Is Trying to Be a Hero to Franchisees Again," *Business Week,* March 22, 1993, p. 70.

Vranica, Suzanne, "Can Blimpie Heroes Defeat a Giant?" *Wall Street Journal,* May 8, 2002, p. B8.

Zimmerman, Ann, "Wal-Mart Is Serving Up Blimpie to Satisfy 'Low-Carb' Shoppers," *Wall Street Journal,* February 2, 2004, p. B3.

Zuber, Amy, "Blimpie Eyes Higher-End QSR, Opens Pasta Central," *Nation's Restaurant News,* April 19, 1999, pp. 1, 6.

Bowen Engineering Corporation

8802 North Meridian Street
Indianapolis, Indiana 46260
U.S.A.
Telephone: (317) 842-2616
Fax: (317) 841-4247
Web site: http://www.bowenenginerring.com

Private Company
Incorporated: 1967
Employees: 250
Sales: $228 million (2007 est.)
NAICS: 237990 Other Heavy and Civil Engineering
   Construction

■ ■ ■

Bowen Engineering Corporation is a full-service construction company based in Indianapolis, Indiana, its business divided among four divisions. They include the company's original focus, Public Works, the construction of wastewater and water treatment facilities; Power/ Industrial, serving the general industrial and power generation industries; Private Water, involved in water production and water treatment projects for both industrial and private utility clients; and Performance Contracting, working with municipal clients on infrastructure improvement projects. Bowen's slate of clients includes Advatech, American Electric Power, American Water Co., Black and Veatch, Tennessee Valley Authority, and Veolia Water. The company maintains regional offices in Evansville and Crown Point, Indiana; Columbus, Ohio; and Knoxville, Tennessee.

Although Bowen mostly serves Indiana, Illinois, Ohio, Kentucky, and Michigan, it has completed projects in a dozen other states, mostly in the Midwest. Owned by about 80 employees, Bowen has been ranked among the Top 25 Best Places to Work in America by the Great Place to Work Institute and the Society for Human Resource Management. The company is headed by its founder, Robert L. Bowen, who serves as chairman and chief executive officer. His son, Douglas Bowen, is the company's president.

FOUNDER, A PURDUE UNIVERSITY GRADUATE: 1962

Born in 1939, Robert Bowen was the son of a civil engineer who worked as a paving contractor; as a youth, Bowen was taught how to survey by his father. In the late 1950s the younger Bowen enrolled at Purdue University to study engineering and during summer vacations put those surveying skills to profitable use, running a survey crew for the Indiana Department of Highways in 1960 and the following year serving as survey chief for his father's survey crew. Bowen graduated from Purdue with a degree in civil engineering in 1962 and with the help of one of his professors, Frank Stubbs, took a job in California as a project manager with W.M. Lyles Construction Company, a firm that built utilities and other heavy projects.

Bowen worked at W.M. Lyles for five years, during which time he learned all aspects of the business, knowledge that he would put to use in starting his own construction company. Moreover, he became a stockholder. In 1967 Bowen returned home to Indiana to strike out on his own and cashed in his stock, raising $45,000 to launch Bowen Engineering Company. He started out in the wastewater business. His first job, awarded in 1968, was a $180,000 wastewater treatment plant in Brookston, Indiana, for which Bowen Engineering was the only bidder. Later in the year the firm landed its second contract, the Jamestown Wastewater Treatment Plant in Jamestown, Indiana. This time Bowen was one of two bidders, but the award process lasted a year and Bowen finally secured the job after the other bidder withdrew.

FIRST BRANCH OFFICE OPENS: 1971

Having established itself in the wastewater field in such fashion, Bowen Engineering opened its first branch office in 1971, located in Indianapolis. A year later the company was admitted to Associated General Contractors of Indiana. Bowen had sought admission when first starting his business but the application had been denied due to "no reputable experience." Five years later that was no longer the case. In 1972, for example, Bowen Engineering was involved in a large-scale intake structure project that crossed the Maumee River in Ft. Wayne, Indiana. The intake was 50 feet deep, 50 feet wide, and 100 feet long, and the project was flooded three times before it was successfully completed.

In 1975 Bowen Engineering moved its main office to Fishers, Indiana, located northeast of Indianapolis in Hamilton County. This period represented a rough patch for the company, which had difficulty turning a profit on its projects. Changes were made at a sewage treatment plant project in DeMotte Sewage, where a superintendent and project manager were put onsite. By having them keep closer tabs on the project, the DeMotte Sewage Treatment Plant became Bowen Engineering's only profitable job that year. Going forward, all contracts emulated this arrangement. The command structure was modified further in 1977 when the company began hiring project coordinators, who

were able to speed up project completion by simplifying project details.

After a decade in business Bowen Engineering was well established in the public sector in Indiana and continued to enjoy steady growth. To maintain its edge the company began computerizing all of its business functions in 1988 and by the start of the next decade emerged as Indiana's largest utility contractor. Bowen Engineering reached a watershed moment in its history in 1990 when it won its largest contract to that point, the $16 million Indianapolis Water Company Water Treatment Plant. The firm solidified its reputation by completing the plant ahead of schedule and under budget, thus triggering an $80,000 bonus. Moreover, the owner of the plant became the first private client of Bowen Engineering.

The company generated $50 million in construction work in 1990, but the future was uncertain because federal grants to finance treatment plants were no longer available, resulting in fewer facilities being built. Because it was clear that there was not enough work available in Indiana to keep it busy, Bowen Engineering was eager to become more involved in Illinois, where it had done some work in the past. In 1991 the company completed the Consumer Illinois Water Treatment Plant in Danville, Illinois, a project that was also important because it was the first of a number of value-engineering and design-build projects.

ILLINOIS OFFICE PLANS SCRAPPED: 1991

Bowen Engineering also made plans in 1991 to open a branch office in the twin cities of Bloomington and Normal, rather than Chicago. Not only was Illinois's economy more robust than Indiana, it was a strong union state at a time when Indiana's unions were weakening. As a union contractor that preferred union employees because of their hard work, training, and safety record, Bowen Engineering was feeling competitive pressure from nonunion contractors in its home state and believed the playing field would be more even in Illinois. The Bloomington-Normal area was also attractive because its labor unions, while strong, were known to work cooperatively with contractors. Plans for the new office had to be scrapped, however, due to the recession that cut federal funds and led to municipalities shelving public works projects. The Bloomington-Normal economy was actually doing well, but did not offer enough water treatment plant work to justify Bowen Engineering's entry into the market.

In 1993 Robert Bowen's son, Douglas Bowen, joined the company after earning a degree in business

KEY DATES

1967: Company founded is by Robert L. Bowen.
1968: First project is completed.
1975: Company opens headquarters in Fishers, Indiana.
1977: Project coordinators are hired on each job.
1990: Company obtains first private client.
1998: First major industrial project is completed.
1999: Evansville, Indiana, office opens.
2003: Company adds fuel gas desulfurization services.
2007: Robert Bowen's son, Douglas Bowen, is named president.

management from Purdue University. He would work with his father for a few years before leaving to work as a project engineer with Vitton Construction in San Jose, California. With some outside seasoning he then returned to Indiana and Bowen Engineering in 1998 to be groomed to succeed his father as the head of the company. While he was away and the economy recovered, the company opened a second office in Crown Point, Indiana, in 1996 to build water treatment plants in Crown Point and neighboring communities. The company leased offices and in 1999 erected a permanent 12,000-square-foot facility in Crown Point. Another important moment in the development of Bowen Engineering came in 1997 when the company completed the Indiana American Water Treatment Plant in Jeffersonville, Indiana, a design-build project that was budgeted for $32 million but value-engineered down to $26 million. As the firm's reputation grew, so too did its scope. In 1998, Bowen Engineering completed its first major industrial project, the Grain Processing Corporation Wastewater Treatment Plant in Washington, Indiana.

EVANSVILLE OFFICE OPENS: 1999

Bowen Engineering ended the 1990s by adding a third office, which opened in Evansville, Indiana, in 1999. As the new century dawned, the company began the process of establishing a long-term position for itself in the industry, becoming what it termed a professionally run construction company. In this regard a new president, Jed Holt, was brought in while Doug Bowen took on greater responsibility and Robert Bowen began to turn over the reins. A trained civil engineer, Holt was a 20-year veteran of the company, having joined it as a superintendent at the age of 33. He then worked his

way up through the ranks: engineer, project manager, chief estimator, safety director, and chief operating officer.

The breadth of projects in the early 2000s clearly demonstrated the stature of Bowen Engineering among engineering-construction firms. Water and wastewater treatment plant projects included the $53 million treatment plant in Lafayette, Indiana, as well as other contracts won on competitive bid in Fishers and Owensboro, Kentucky, as well as several design-build jobs in Indiana. The firm won competitive bids for underground utility projects, including a sanitary sewer sliplining job in Evansville, Indiana; a chilled water facility at the University of Illinois; and a steam tunnel in Bloomington, Indiana. Industrial projects during this time included a grain processing production facility in southern Indiana; a United Airlines maintenance facility in Indianapolis; a cement facility in Greencastle, Indiana; cement unloading facilities in Mt. Vernon, Indiana; and a campus utilities project for Lexmark International in Lexington, Kentucky. Power also became a core business. Projects included a central plant at Indiana University in Bloomington, a mass burn unit in Indianapolis, and a water intake and transmission main designed and built in Waterford, Ohio.

Annual revenues reached $120 million in 2002 and continued to climb at a steady rate, as Bowen Engineering added capabilities, such as tunneling, to drive further growth. In 2003 the company began offering fuel gas desulfurization services to gain more business in the air pollution market. Offices were also opened in Columbus, Ohio, and Knoxville, Tennessee, to cast a wider net for new business. By expanding the scope of its projects and geographic base, Bowen Engineering increased revenues to $170 million in 2006 and $228 million in 2007, of which 54 percent was generated outside of Indiana. The company planned to continue the trend of taking on more out-of-state work, estimating that within a few years revenues from jobs across North America and internationally would account for as much as 80 percent of annual revenues. Nevertheless, Bowen Engineering planned to keep its corporate headquarters in central Indiana, although it outgrew its accommodations in Fishers. Unable to find a suitable location locally, the company crossed the county line several miles away into Marion County and Indianapolis, moving into its new corporate headquarters in 2008. As an incentive for coming to Indianapolis, the company received a seven-year property tax abatement worth nearly $300,000.

Although the transition to the next generation of leadership at Bowen Engineering was well underway, the company's founder remained chairman and chief executive officer. A successful businessman, Robert Bowen and his wife devoted an increasing amount of their time and money to philanthropic endeavors. In the mid-1990s they established the Bowen Foundation to provide scholarships to minority students in Indianapolis interested in learning a trade, and took the time to meet with each candidate. In 2002 they gave $3.25 million to Purdue to help build a civil engineering research laboratory that would bear the Bowen name. They also backed the school's Science Bound program that, starting in 2002, began working in Indianapolis public schools to encourage students from eighth grade through high school to pursue careers in science and technical fields.

DOUG BOWEN BECOMES PRESIDENT: 2007

Ready to take on greater responsibilities, Doug Bowen was named president in 2007, replacing Jed Holt, who stayed on as executive vice-president. The younger Bowen expressed a modest approach to leadership, telling the *Indianapolis Business Journal* that he viewed himself as little more than a coach: "None of us are as smart as all of us. I want to be the dumbest guy in the room." He also believed that his work background was an asset as he took over day-to-day responsibility for running Bowen Engineering, explaining to the *Journal*, "I've worked as a laborer, carpenter, project manager, and contract manager. I wasn't great in any of those jobs, bit it gave me an understanding of what those people are doing. Those experiences have given me insight into how people think." With his father still involved in the company as well as other seasoned executives who owned stakes in the business, there was certainly reason

to expect that Bowen Engineering would continue to grow for years to come.

Ed Dinger

PRINCIPAL DIVISIONS

Public Works; Power/Industrial; Private Water; Performance Contracting.

PRINCIPAL COMPETITORS

F.A. Wilhelm Construction Company, Inc.; Hagerman Construction Corporation; Hunt Construction Group, Inc.

FURTHER READING

"Building a Name: Indiana's Major Commercial Construction Firms," *Indiana Business Magazine,* November 1, 2005.

Diddie, Deborah, "Bowen Engineering Corp. Expanding to Crown Point," *Post-Tribune* (Ind.), January 14, 1999, p. B1.

Fricks, Holly, "Indiana's Entrepreneurs of the Year," *Indiana Business Magazine,* September 1998, p. 12.

Katterjohn, Chris, "Forty Under 40," *Indianapolis Business Journal,* February 4, 2008, p. 4B.

Olson, Scott, "Funding a Chance at Success," *Indianapolis Business Journal,* February 7, 2005, p. 19A.

Swiech, Paul, "Bowen Engineering Not Expanding to B-N," *Pantagraph,* August 4, 1992, p. D1.

———, "Contractor May Pick Twin Cities," *Pantagraph,* May 9, 1991, p. A1.

Tiflis, Fernie Grace, "Getting 'Dirty and Messy,'" *Construction Today,* August 2007, p. 62.

Wersich, Carol, "Bowen Relocating Downtown," *Evansville Courier,* August 17, 2005, p. B8.

"Who's Who in Construction, Design & Engineering: Robert L. Bowen," *Indianapolis Business Journal,* February 4, 2002, p. 31.

Bremer Financial Corporation

2100 Bremer Tower
445 Minnesota Street
St. Paul, Minnesota 55101
U.S.A.
Telephone: (651) 227-7621
Toll Free: (800) 908-2265
Fax: (651) 312-3550
Web site: http://www.bremer.com

Private Company
Incorporated: 1943 as Otto Bremer Company
Employees: 1,800
Total Assets: $7.72 billion (2008)
NAICS: 551111 Offices of Bank Holding Companies

■ ■ ■

Bremer Financial Corporation, a bank holding company, operates under a unique ownership structure. Owned by its employees and a nonprofit foundation, it is the only entity of its type in the United States. The vision of founder Otto Bremer, a German immigrant and at one time the largest investor of bank stocks in the Midwest, continues to guide the work of the Otto Bremer Foundation. Much of the holding company's profits return to the communities it serves through foundation grants. Bremer Financial offers banking, investment, trust, and insurance services to customers in a three-state area, Minnesota, North Dakota, and Wisconsin.

BUILDING BUSINESS RELATIONSHIPS: 1886–1954

Otto Bremer and his younger brother Adolph immigrated from Germany to the United States in 1886. The Midwest, where the young men settled, had experienced a period of rapid growth: the population had exploded and business opportunities were abundant. Otto Bremer's first job was as a stock clerk for a wholesale hardware business in St. Paul, Minnesota. In 1887, he took a bookkeeping position with the National German-American Bank; he had three years of elementary banking training in Germany, according to a *Ramsey County History* article by Thomas J. Kelley. Bremer eventually became chief clerk.

A bust followed the boom days of the 1880s in the early 1890s. Banks in St. Paul's sister city of Minneapolis went under. The National German-American Bank had to suspend operations for a time. By the end of the decade, the nation was in a deep economic depression.

Otto Bremer left the National German-American Bank in 1900 to make a run for the office of city treasurer. A well-established and respected member of the community by this time, he won the election and served for five terms. (He had an unsuccessful but closely contested race for mayor in 1912.) Meanwhile, his brother Adolph was making his own headway in St. Paul's business community. One connection led to a romance as well. Adolph married Marie Schmidt, the daughter of North Star Brewery owner Jacob Schmidt, in 1896.

COMPANY PERSPECTIVES

Our Vision: To build healthy communities through partnerships. Our Mission: To nurture a culture of inclusiveness, respect, service and growth. To fulfill our vision and mission, Bremer employees strive to deliver exceptional value by providing individualized solutions to our clients' total financial services needs while ensuring a fair return to our shareholders. Our values define who we are and what we believe in.

While serving as city treasurer, Otto Bremer became a charter member of the board of directors for the American National Bank. The bank was formed in 1903 through the merging of two St. Paul banks. Bremer held 50 of the 2,000 shares of capital stock. The charter members of the board of directors, well aware of potential pitfalls, operated a conservative banking business, unlike the days of wild growth when banks and customers were extended beyond their means. Brother Adolph's responsibilities also continued to grow. When the brewery was reorganized as the Jacob Schmidt Brewing Company in 1899, he was named president. Adolph Bremer took over operating control when Schmidt died in 1910. He brought Otto in as secretary and treasurer shortly thereafter.

As Adolph gained ownership in the brewery, Otto Bremer increased his holdings in the bank, becoming a major shareholder by 1916. Adolph joined his brother on the American National Bank board of directors that year.

In 1921, Benjamin Baer, the bank's second president and an original board member, died. Otto Bremer was named chairman. He also bought much of Baer's stock and by 1924 gained controlling interest in the bank.

The brewery and its sales agencies in rural Minnesota, North Dakota, and Wisconsin provided a direct link to the Bremers and American National Bank in St. Paul. The brewery or the Bremers owned the land or buildings the sales agencies occupied, creating a starting point for further business relationships in the communities.

Otto Bremer became an adviser to local bankers, who often formed corresponding partnerships with American National. Dependent on the cyclical agricultural economy, country banks needed loans from city banks with a more diverse and therefore a more stable base of business. Otto Bremer formed a deep commitment to the rural communities, and when economic disaster struck he was there to help.

Trouble began with a ramp-up of farm production in response to the needs created by the United States' entry into World War I. Farmers began planting more acres and buying expensive machinery. Agricultural land increased in value. Farmers took out larger loans to drive the expansion. Demand collapsed following the war. Harsh weather conditions in the Midwest further hampered farmers. Loans went unpaid. A recession hit the nation in 1920, taxing city banks supporting the stressed country banks.

"Bent on maintaining the public trust in the country banks, Otto Bremer loaned them his good name and his money. Throughout the 1920s banks came into the fold of the American National Bank or the Bremer group," wrote Kelley. Eventually, Bremer had to begin borrowing against his assets to keep country banks afloat.

By 1933, he held large or controlling interests in 55 banks in Minnesota, North Dakota, Wisconsin, and Montana, apart from his holdings in American National. However, he was $8 million in debt. The backing of Adolph Bremer's shares in the Jacob Schmidt Brewing Company and a loan from the Federal Reconstruction Finance Corporation helped Otto Bremer keep his stock in American National and the country banks in the family.

Despite the one-two punch delivered by the farm recession and Great Depression, the Bremer brothers had kept control of both the brewery and the bank. When Adolph Bremer died in 1939, Otto Bremer succeed him as president of the Jacob Schmidt Brewing Company.

In 1943, he created Otto Bremer Company. The bank holding company consolidated his holdings in the country banks and would protect them from being sold to settle his estate, according to the Kelley article.

The Otto Bremer Foundation was formed the next year to make charitable grants in the communities served by the country banks. The ownership of Otto Bremer Company was transferred to the foundation in 1949. After Bremer's death in 1951, the banking chain entered an extended period of consolidation. The brewery was sold in 1954, but descendants of Adolph Bremer held stock in American National until it was sold to Milwaukee-based Firstar Corp. in 1996.

LEGACY AND TRADITION THREATENED: 1961–89

Robert J. Reardon, who joined the holding company in 1961, was named president in 1967, and the next year

KEY DATES

1886: Bremer brothers arrive in the United States.

1933: Otto Bremer holds interest in 55 banks in Minnesota, Wisconsin, North Dakota, and Montana.

1943: Otto Bremer Company is created.

1944: Otto Bremer Foundation is established.

1951: Otto Bremer dies.

1969: Tax law threatens Bremer legacy.

1983: Holding company reorganizes, and the independent banks take a common name, First American.

1989: Foundation sells part of holding company to employees.

1998: Banks take on Bremer name for the first time.

2001: Bremer Financial purchases 11 branches from Firstar Bank, its first significant purchase in Twin Cities metropolitan area.

2005: Bremer combats declining mortgage and home equity loan levels.

2007: Net income declines due to problems in home equity loan portfolio.

2008: Bremer stays solid in midst of near collapse of nation's financial system.

became a trustee of the Otto Bremer Foundation. He was dedicated to upholding Otto Bremer's tradition of commitment to the rural communities in which the banks were located. However, a year after Reardon took over leadership of the foundation, a federal tax law was passed that threatened to dismantle the Bremer legacy.

The 1969 tax law required charitable foundations to cut their ownership in for-profit enterprises to 50 percent by May 26, 1989. The law had been enacted to weed out charitable trusts being used as tax shelters for corporate profits.

"In its original form, the law presented something of a Catch-22 to the Bremer Foundation," a 1984 *American Banker* article posited. Local banks with enough capital to buy the bank holding company could not do so due to antitrust regulations. Interstate banking laws of the time blocked the sale of the company to banks outside Minnesota. Non-banking organizations were eliminated from the pool of potential buyers by federal bank holding company law. In addition, the Internal Revenue Service's interpretation of the holding company's status further complicated matters: Reardon

was able to circumvent that roadblock with the help of local congressmen. He had met with less success when he went to Congress to seek exemption from the tax law itself.

Bremer Financial began coordinating the activities among its banks beginning in 1983. A number of factors prompted the move. To begin with, the Bremer Foundation had been unable to find a solution to the 1969 tax-law dilemma, and the deadline was looming. The banking industry itself was in a period of change, thanks to deregulation. Moreover, the agricultural economy, with which the company's rural and small town banks were still closely tied, was in deep trouble once again.

To strengthen the operation, the holding company reorganized into five regional groups. One bank president within each region was designated to lead the drive for more coordination and cooperation among the member banks.

To increase diversification, Bremer Financial Services Inc. added discount brokerage and trust services. Established in 1973, the enterprise at first performed audits and credit reviews of the banks. Later bond purchasing and other financial services were introduced. The company also upped its marketing activities and established a common name: First American.

By 1985, First American banks were writing off bad loans to the tune of $21.5 million, up from $4.6 million in 1983. The severe downturn in the rural economy had also made the prospects for selling off the banks to comply with the 1969 tax law more difficult. Banks located in agriculture-dependent regions were struggling across the nation: potential buyers would be looking for bargains.

Meanwhile, Bremer Financial continued to strengthen itself internally. Data processing was centralized and standardized lending procedures were developed. Loan managers were trained to spot potential problems and intervene early.

All in all, despite challenges, Bremer Financial stayed the course. David Shern, former state banking commissioner, said in a 1987 *Minneapolis Star Tribune* article by Joe Blade, "That is one of the best-run bank holding companies in Minnesota." As it had been in Otto Bremer's day, the corporation stepped in to strengthen its banks when they encountered trouble. "That is a very clean operation. They are solid people. They run good banks," he said. Total assets were $1.6 billion, according to the Blade article.

In 1989, Bremer Foundation solved its tax law problem by selling 8 percent of the holding company to its employees and giving them majority-voting rights. The foundation retained 92 percent of the economic value of the holding company.

EYE TOWARD BIG CITY GROWTH: 1990–2001

Beginning in the early 1990s, Bremer Financial set its sights on modernization. A big investment in technology improved efficiency and cut costs. The company also upgraded banking services and moved into new business areas. Although it was late in the game, Bremer Financial began offering proprietary mutual funds in 1997.

The entry of banks into the investment management business had peaked in 1992 and declined to a trickle since then. Bremer planned to target the retirement market. The bank holding company had been selling mutual funds since the mid-1980s through a partnership with Invest Financial Corp., but established its own equity growth fund and an intermediate bond fund using $60 million of corporate trust assets.

First American opened its first Twin Cities grocery store branches in mid-1997. The bank had operated in grocery stores in other areas since 1990. The move was part of an effort to expand its presence in the metropolitan area. The company had already increased its commercial business by adding international business services.

Also in 1997, the Otto Bremer Foundation, Bremer Financial Corporation, and Bremer employees pitched in $1.5 million to help with disaster relief in the Red River Valley. Flooding in the spring of that year devastated the area bordering eastern North Dakota and northwestern Minnesota. Tim Huber, reporting for *City-Business* in August, noted that the founder "would have appreciated the relief effort." Catastrophic aid was one of the foundation's original purposes. Reminiscent of earlier days, Bremer Financial found when it entered the Fargo, North Dakota, market that the foundation's support of the region's nonprofit organizations had already prepared the ground for business relationships with many in the community.

The Bremer Foundation received the profits of the individual banks through dividends from the holding company and in turn distributed them back into the communities through charitable grants. According to the Huber article, the foundation and Bremer employees received $12.5 million in dividends in 1996.

Even though Bremer Financial had no Wall Street investors to satisfy, the corporation needed to perform well to maintain its independence. The company strived to sustain annual earnings growth of 10 percent. In 1996, it exceeded the mark. Earnings were $31.8 million, up from $27.1 million the previous year.

The seven First American banks located in the Twin Cities underwent a name change in July 1998. The holding company's remaining banks and the trust and insurance operations would take on the Bremer name toward year-end. The move marked the first time the banks themselves would wear the founder's name. The company also planned to open its first bank location in downtown St. Paul, longtime home of its corporate and foundation headquarters.

Bremer Financial projected the costs related to the name change would exceed $1 million. The company planned to emphasize Bremer's historical commitment to community in its marketing. At the time, mergers were eliminating some well-known names in Twin Cities banking. Minneapolis-based Norwest would take the name of California-based Wells Fargo, and First Bank System opted for U.S. Bank, following its purchase of Portland's U.S. Bancorp.

Norwest's assets were $96.1 billion. U.S. Bancorp's were $71 billion. Another large Minnesota-based banking concern, TCF Financial, followed well behind with $9.7 billion. Acquisitions helped Bremer Financial grow from $1.4 million in assets in 1984 to $3.2 billion in 1997.

Bremer could put its name back on a building in downtown St. Paul following the purchase of Dean Financial (a building bearing the Bremer name had been razed in the late 1990s). In addition to gaining a significant physical presence, Bremer added $312 million in assets, 11 offices, and four bank charters to its holdings in the 1999 deal. Overall, Bremer would hold 50 banking offices in Minnesota, 31 in North Dakota, and 16 in Wisconsin.

The holding company finally attained a long-sought goal when it purchased 11 branches from Firstar Bank. In addition to boosting its visibility in the metro area, the deal also eased Bremer Financial's reliance on the farm economy. The acquisition was made possible, according to a February 2001 *American Banker* article, when federal regulators told Firstar, which was about to buy U.S. Bancorp, to divest some of its Twin Cities branches to preserve competition. Gaining $769 million in deposits, Bremer Financial climbed a notch in the Twin Cities market, moving from sixth to fifth, and became the third largest holder of deposits in the state, up from fifth. The Firstar purchase was the company's ninth acquisition since 1993.

However, the deal took an unusual turn when the Department of Justice required some commercial accounts, the chairman of Firstar Bank Minnesota, and five commercial managers to be moved to Bremer. In general, deposits and branches were involved in divestitures, not specific accounts and personnel, according to a February 2001 *Star Tribune* article.

"Analysts say they were not surprised that Firstar chose a local buyer," Ben Jackson reported for *American Banker*. Stan Dardis, president and CEO, "said it also helped that the Justice Department was advocating a sale to one buyer and that Bremer has a relationship with both Firstar and U.S. Bancorp: Bremer is Firstar's largest credit card partner in Minnesota, and U.S. Bancorp provides logistical support on Bremer's network of automated teller machines."

Keeping with the tradition of building community connections, Bremer Financial formed a partnership with the Minnesota Council of Nonprofits in 2001. The council's 1,110 members, both large and small organizations, would be offered a variety of special services, including favorable interest rates on deposit accounts and certificates of deposit (CDs). About 25 percent of the state's financially active nonprofits were members of the council, according to a June 2001 *Star Tribune* article. Minnesota's nonprofit community held about $24 billion in total assets.

CHANGING CIRCUMSTANCES: 2002–05

The U.S. economy fell into a recession in the days and months following the September 11, 2001, terrorist attacks on the finance and government power centers. The inherent uncertainty of the times, plus ongoing mergers among financial institutions, prompted Bremer to create a wealth advisory services division in late 2002. People "are questioning whether they've gotten the advice they needed when they should have," Dardis told *American Banker*.

Bremer planned to merge elements of its insurance, investment, and trust departments into the new downtown Minneapolis-based private banking unit, which would offer services such as succession and estate planning. The bank strove, not only, to retain existing customers but also to draw in new small business owners and affluent retirees.

Looking toward the other end of the economic spectrum during 2003, Bremer entered into a public-private program to assist lower income employees with their housing needs. The first to participate in REAL/HELP, the bank saw the home buyer/renter assistance program as a way to retain metro area personnel, which comprised about a third of Bremer's 1,800 employees. The effort dovetailed with the Bremer Foundation's mis-

sion to serve communities in which the bank operated and with congressional banking guidelines regarding community credit needs.

Despite "a slow-growth environment," the $6 billion asset Bremer was reporting strong profits in the later half of 2004, according to a November 2004 *Star Tribune* article. The CEO's reward for the bank's success was modest, though, when compared to some compensation packages in the industry. Dardis received about $550,000 in 2003, Neal St. Anthony reported. He and Chief Operating Officer Patrick Donovan "are known as solid executives who aren't in it for the last buck on the table. There aren't multimillion-dollar paydays or hundreds of thousands of options dished out to Bremer's brass." In addition to growing the bank, the pair sought to increase philanthropy and improve employee retention.

Bremer put its stamp on a downtown St. Paul tower in 2005, acquiring naming rights and signing a ten-year lease for nearly 32,000 square feet of office space. The bank, which moved its headquarters from South St. Paul to downtown in 1991, sought to increase its visibility in the city. Another St. Paul tower had been renamed Wells Fargo Center. Bremer continued to open new metro area branches.

Looking at the industry as a whole, the year was marked by rising short-term interest rates and a corresponding softening of the housing market. Banks shifted their tactics to lure in consumers, raising ceilings on primary and secondary mortgages, financing larger portions of home prices, and allowing a larger percentage of disposable income for mortgage payments, Thomas Lee reported for the *Star Tribune* in December 2005.

Bremer's low-doc/no-doc loan volume increased by 20 percent during the year. Under these terms, homebuyers could opt for higher down payments or higher interest rates in return for the easing of asset and income verification, Lee explained. Regulators had voiced concern over such alternate mortgages and the likelihood that unqualified buyers would enter the market in greater numbers. In fact, riskier loans had been infiltrating the financial system, as bankers and brokers sought to keep origination levels up and investors, in turn, snapped them up packaged as mortgage-backed securities.

Not only had Bremer seen a flattening out of new mortgages and outright decline in refinancing, rate-sensitive home equity loans were on the skids. Bremer followed the suit of other banks, offering home equity loan rate cuts. The housing industry had been the principal driver of the U.S. economy following the

September 11, 2001, terrorist attacks against the United States.

Bremer posted record earnings in 2005, climbing to $72 million from $64.2 million in 2004. On the downside, nonperforming assets had climbed by about 24 percent year over year and the provision for loan losses was increased significantly. Furthermore, the company expected the lending and deposit markets to remain competitive, keeping a damper on net interest margins.

A CLASS ALONE: 2006–09

Bremer faced the perils of the day from a unique position. Bremer stock was divided by two classes. Employees owned 80 percent of class "A" voting shares, and the foundation owned 20 percent. The economic value of the company, though, was controlled by the foundation, with 92 percent of class "B" stock. Employees held the remaining 8 percent. A vote to sell the bank would trigger a shift of class "B" stock to voting stock. Dardis explained in the *Star Tribune:* "If there was someone who would come in and say, 'OK, we'll pay you three times book [value]for your organization' and the employees say, 'Oooh, big payout,' which is what a lot of management teams are doing nowadays—we don't have that option. We don't want that option. Thereby, it's the old deal that Bremer is not for sale. Bremer will never be for sale. You can't perpetuate community banking if you are selling the banks."

Bremer launched a new branding campaign to remind the world it was different in other ways. "We did not come to the Twin Cities to become a metropolitan bank. We are not a retail bank. We are not a TCF, we are not a US," Dardis told the *Star Tribune* in February 2006.

Bremer targeted business owners and executives of small- to mid-size businesses, $5 million to $100 million in sales, surrounding its Twin Cities branch locations. The bank emphasized its service and ability to meet the needs of businesses and business owners in ways not found through large- and mid-size competitors, including U.S. Bank, Wells Fargo, TCF Bank, and Marshall & Ilsley.

Net income climbed slightly in 2006, but Bremer reported a 5.5 percent drop the next year, to $68.1 million, "primarily due to an increased level of delinquencies and losses associated with home equity lending." The Twin Cities housing market had been problematic, with property values eroding. The bank benefited from a solid performance in its trust and insurance businesses and non-metro markets. Nevertheless, the level of nonperforming assets continued to markedly climb.

Such institutions as Citigroup, Lehman Brothers, Merrill Lynch, and Bear Stearns, on the other hand, had mortgage-related problems that threatened the country's financial system. The operations had borrowed heavily "to finance mortgage-backed bond portfolios on the secondary mortgage market," St. Anthony explained in October 2008. Short-term commercial paper (loans between financial institutions for a period ranging from a few days to a few weeks) funded some of the transactions. As the value of portfolios decayed with massive subprime loan defaults, lending came to a halt. "The losses taken by those money center banks," wrote St. Anthony, "wiped out their equity capital and left them insolvent and subject to government takeover or bankruptcy."

Bremer Banks continued to make loans and remained solvent. The community bank, covered by federal deposit insurance, derived its funds primarily through low-cost customer deposits in checking and savings accounts and in CDs.

Bremer anticipated an increase of about 6 percent in commercial loans for 2008 but had seen a decline in consumer loans as the economy continued to decay. Yet, in the midst of the uncertainty enveloping the U.S. financial system, many Americans began looking for solid institutions in which to bank. Bremer actually had begun seeing inflow in funds, according to an October 2008 *McClatchy-Tribune Business News* article. The banks' Small Business Administration–insured loans also climbed even as they decreased on a state and national level.

Earnings returned to the $72 million mark for the year. Net interest income and non-interest income, in particular insurance revenue, offset the 85.7 percent increase in loan loss provisions. Bremer ranked in the top 25 percent of its peer group in terms of profitability in 2008 and continued to be well capitalized according to regulatory requirements. Earnings were the source of its capital.

While the bank had fared well in 2008, many in the communities it served had not. In response, the bank and foundation partnered to distribute $4.2 million in charitable grants to nonprofits for direct financial assistance to "provide the helping hand that people in crisis need this winter," the company announced in January 2009.

Bremer's CEO planned to retire in April 2010, with Donovan to succeed him. A former U.S. Air Force instructor pilot, Dardis began his banking career as an agricultural loan officer in South Dakota, and served as president, CEO, and director of Metropolitan Federal Bank before joining Bremer in 1998. Donovan, who had been named executive vice-president and COO of

Bremer in 2002, was a former Wells Fargo executive and had held management positions with First Bank and Norwest.

"The succession plan we have in place is as relevant in today's rapidly-changing world as it was when we created it nearly four years ago," Dardis said in March 2009. "With a full year to implement, this thoughtful and well-planned leadership transition should be seamless for our employees, clients and communities."

The next month, Bremer joined the ranks of community banks exiting the student loan business. Earlier legislative action had driven down profitability, and the new Obama administration proposed designating the Department of Education as sole lender, *American Banker* explained.

Kathleen Peippo

PRINCIPAL COMPETITORS

Wells Fargo & Company; U.S. Bancorp; TCF Financial Corporation.

FURTHER READING

Blade, Joe, "Bremer Foundation Caught in a Bind," *Minneapolis Star Tribune,* April 5, 1987, p. 1D.

"Bremer Deepens Commitment to Region Through Agreement with Kwik Trip Convenience Stores," *Business Wire,* July 8, 2004, p. 1.

Chin, Richard, "R.J. Reardon, Social Services Booster, Dies," *St. Paul Pioneer Press,* January 24, 1995, p. 5C.

DePass, Dee, "Bremer Agrees to Buy Banks of Dean Financial," *Minneapolis Star Tribune,* January 27, 1999, p. 3D.

———, "Bremer, Nonprofit Council Form Banking Partnership," *Minneapolis Star Tribune,* June 9, 2001, p. 1D.

———, "Firstar Managers Joining Bremer," *Minneapolis Star Tribune,* February 22, 2001, p. 1D.

"A Dilemma for Minnesota's Bremer," *American Banker,* June 8, 1984, pp. 16+.

Fajt, Marissa, "First Financial, Bremer Join Student Lending Departures," *American Banker,* April 21, 2009, p. 5.

Gendler, Neal, "Employer-Assisted Housing," *Minneapolis Star Tribune,* April 19, 2003, p. 4H.

Hage, Dave, "Another Union Battle Puts Willmar in Spotlight," *Minneapolis Star Tribune,* May 3, 1987, 1D.

Huber, Tim, "First American Shops for Growth," *City Business,* June 6, 1997.

———, "Foundation Fosters Bremer Legacy," *CityBusiness,* August 8, 1997.

Hughlett, Mike, "At Last: A Bremer Bank," *St. Paul Pioneer Press,* June 25, 1998, p. 1D.

Jackson, Ben, "Bremer Making Twin Kill in Twin Cities Branch Deal," *American Banker,* February 5, 2001, p. 6.

———, "Mergers Prompt Advisory Launch at Bremer," *American Banker,* November 1, 2002, p. 5.

Kelly, Thomas J., "The American National Bank and the Bremer Brothers," *Ramsey County History,* 1988, pp. 3–13.

Lee, Thomas, "Bremer's Men of Action," *Minneapolis Star Tribune,* February 20, 2006, p. 1D.

———, "Regulators Warn of Fallout from Risky Mortgages," *Minneapolis Star Tribune,* December 2, 2005, p. 1D.

Lutton, Laura Pavlenko, "Small Banks Taking Name of Philanthropic Founder," *American Banker,* July 13, 1998, p. 7.

———, "U.S. Says Profit-Sharing Plan Short Changed Workers," *American Banker,* January 6, 1999.

St. Anthony, Neal, "At Bremer Bank, Good People Do Good Business," *Minneapolis Star Tribune,* November 30, 2004, p. 1D.

———, "Local Lenders Making Money, Loans the Old-Fashioned Way: While Big Wall Street 'Money Centers' Tumble on Bad Bets and Frozen Credit, Community Banks and Their Customers Are Doing Fine," *McClatchy-Tribune Business News,* October 14, 2008.

Sitaramiah, Gita, "Bremer Financial Gets Naming Rights for North Central Life Tower," *Knight-Ridder/Tribune Business News,* February 5, 2005.

Talley, Karen, "Fewer Banks Trying Their Luck with Proprietary Mutual Funds," *American Banker,* April 28, 1997, p. 1+.

British Airways PLC

Waterside, P.O. Box 365
Harmondsworth, Middlesex UB7 0GB
England
Telephone: (44 20) 8562 4444
Toll Free: (800) 247-9297 (U.S. only)
Fax: (44 20) 8759 4314
Web site: http://www.britishairways.com

Public Company
Founded: 1916 as Aircraft Transport & Travel Ltd.
Employees: 40,627
Sales: £8.99 billion ($14.4 billion) (2009)
Stock Exchanges: London
Ticker Symbol: BAY
NAICS: 481111 Scheduled Passenger Air Transportation; 481112 Scheduled Freight Air Transportation; 561520 Tour Operators

■ ■ ■

British Airways PLC is the United Kingdom's largest international airline, and one of the world's leading airlines. British Airways, which continues to operate primarily from its Heathrow Airport base, operates scheduled flights to more than 300 destinations around the world. Faced with increasing competitive pressure from the rise of domestic short-haul and international discount airlines, British Airways is focusing on the international premium sector in the 2000s. As part of that effort, the company operates two premium class airlines, CityFlyer and OpenSkies. The company's total fleet includes 245 aircraft. British Airways flights carry

more than 33 million passengers and more than 777,000 metric tons of cargo each year. Passenger revenues account for more than 87 percent of the company's total sales of £8.99 billion ($14 billion) in 2008, while cargo revenues added 7.5 percent. The United Kingdom accounts for more than 46 percent of the company's sales, with the United States adding 19 percent and Continental Europe adding 15.8 percent.

British Airways also serves Africa, the Middle East, India, Australasia and markets in the Far East. British Airways has long operated in partnership with a number of other international airlines, including Spain's Iberia, Australia's Qantas, and the United States' American Airlines. The company has been in negotiations to merge with Iberia since 2008, and has expressed its interest in a wider merger including Qantas and American Airlines. The company is listed on the London Stock Exchange, and is led by CEO Willie Walsh.

EARLY HISTORY: LINKING THE BRITISH EMPIRE

British Airways' earliest predecessor was Aircraft Transport & Travel, Ltd., founded in 1916. On August 25, 1919, this company inaugurated the world's first scheduled international air service with a converted de Havilland 4A day bomber leaving Hounslow (later Heathrow) Airport for London and also Le Bourget in Paris. Eight days later another company, Handley Page Transport, Ltd., started a cross-channel service between London's Cricklewood Field and both Paris and Brussels.

That same year Britain's advisory committee for civil aviation proposed plans for establishing a world airline network linking Britain with Canada, India, South Africa, Australia, and New Zealand. Because airplanes capable of crossing wide stretches of water were not yet available, the committee recommended that first priority be given to a route to India and be operated by a state-assisted private enterprise.

Progress was made quickly. Before the end of the year the British government was operating a service to Karachi and had established a network of 43 Royal Air Force (RAF) landing strips throughout Africa to the Cape of Good Hope. Meanwhile, strong competition from subsidized foreign airline companies had forced many of the private British air carriers out of business. By March 1921 all British airline companies had suspended their operations. The government intervened with a pledge to keep the British companies flying, using its own form of subsidization.

In January 1923 Parliament appointed the Civil Air Transport Subsidies Committee to form a single British international air carrier from existing companies. On March 31, 1924 Daimler Airway, British Marine Air Navigation, Instone Air Line, and Handley Page merged to become Imperial Air Transportation, Ltd.

In 1925 Imperial Airways operated a number of European routes while it surveyed a route across the Arabian desert from Cairo to Basra in present-day Iraq. The airline was faced with a number of problems on this route. The desert was featureless, making it easy to get lost. Water stops and meteorological and radio stations were difficult to maintain. Basra was a major terminal on the route to India. However, on January 7, 1927, the Persian government forbade Britain the use of its airspace, blocking all flights to India. Negotiations reopened this airspace two years later, but not before generating a demand for longer range aircraft.

Passengers flying to India flew from London via Paris to Basel, where they boarded a train for Genoa.

Next, a flying boat took them on to Alexandria, where they flew in stages to Karachi. The passage to India, previously three weeks by sea, had been reduced to one week by air.

Imperial Airways' service to Calcutta was established in July 1933, to Rangoon in September, and to Singapore in December. In January of the following year, Australia's Queensland and Northern Territories Air Service (Qantas) inaugurated a route linking Singapore with Brisbane. The passage to Australia could be completed in 12½ days.

A commercial service through Africa was opened in 1931 with flying boats linking Cairo with Mwanza on Lake Victoria. In April 1933 the route was extended to Cape Town, the trip from London taking 10½ days. An east-west trans-African route from Khartoum in the Sudan to Kano in northern Nigeria was established in February 1936. This route completed a world network that linked nearly all the countries of the British Empire.

The primary source of revenue on the network was not from transporting passengers but mail. Nevertheless, an increase in demand for more passenger seating and cargo space generated a need for larger airplanes. Britain's primary supplier of flying boats, the Short Company, developed a new model designated the C-class, with 24 seats and weighing 18 tons. Since it had an increased range and flew 145 miles per hour, it was able to simply bypass "politically difficult areas." The Short C-class went into service in October 1936. A year later Imperial Airways made its first transatlantic crossing with a flying boat equipped with extra fuel tanks. It was Pan Am, however, that first scheduled a regular transatlantic service, employing more sophisticated and updated Boeing airplanes.

WORLD WAR II AND NATIONALIZATION

Imperial Airways was formed with the intention of being Britain's "chosen instrument" for overseas air service. On its European services, however, Imperial was competing with the British Continental airline and an aggressive newcomer called British Airways, which had been created in October 1935 by the merger of three smaller airline companies. Three months later the company acquired a fleet of Lockheed 10 Electras, which were the fastest airplanes available. The competition from British Airways threatened the "chosen instrument" so much that in November 1937 a Parliamentary committee proposed the nationalization and merger of Imperial and British Airways. When the reorganization was completed on November 24, 1939, the British Overseas Airways Corporation (BOAC) was formed.

KEY DATES

1916: Predecessor Aircraft Transport & Travel Ltd. is founded.

1919: Company inaugurates the world's first scheduled international air service.

1933: Service to India and Singapore is established.

1935: British Airways is formed by the merger of three smaller airline companies.

1939: British Airways and Imperial Airways are merged and nationalized to form British Overseas Airways Corporation (BOAC).

1949: British South American Airways (BSAA) is absorbed by BOAC.

1958: First successful jet transatlantic service is completed.

1962: BOAC and Air France agree to commit funds to build a supersonic transport (SST).

1967: BOAC establishes its second around-the-world route.

1974: Company is reorganized under the "British Airways" name.

1976: British Airways and Air France simultaneously inaugurate the first SST Concordes into service.

1987: British Airways is privatized; company acquires British Caledonian (BCal).

1988: British Airways forms a marketing alliance with United Airlines that collapses two years later.

1992: British Airways purchases 44 percent of US-Air Inc.

1997: Company sells its stake in USAir Inc.

1998: "Oneworld" global alliance is launched between British Airways, American Airlines, Qantas, Canadian Airlines, and Cathay Pacific, a group that eventually grows to eight members.

2000: British Airways shuts down its Go low-cost airline.

2001: British Airways begins restructuring, cutting more than 13,000 jobs.

2005: Willie Walsh takes over as British Airways CEO.

2008: British Airways launches a new all-business premium airline, OpenSkies; company begins merger talks with Spain's Iberia Airlines.

The creation of BOAC was overshadowed by the declaration of war on Germany the previous September. The Secretary of State for Air assumed control of all British air services, including BOAC. Within a year Italy had entered the war and France had fallen. Britain's air routes through Europe had been eliminated. British flying boats, however, continued to ferry personnel and war cargo between London and West Africa with an intermediate stop at Lisbon in neutral Portugal. The air link to Khartoum maintained Britain's connection to the "Horseshoe Route," from Cape Town through East Africa, Arabia, India, and Singapore to Australia. When Malaysia and Singapore were invaded by the Japanese, BOAC and Qantas opened a nonstop service between Ceylon and Perth in western Australia. BOAC transported ball bearings from neutral Sweden using a route that was dangerously exposed to the German Luftwaffe. BOAC also operated a service for returning flight crews to North America after they delivered American- and Canadian-built aircraft to the RAF.

When the war ended, BOAC had a fleet of 160 aircraft and an aerial network that covered 54,000 miles. The South American destinations of BOAC were assigned to a new state-owned airline, British South American Airways (BSAA), in March 1946. Similarly, the European services were turned over to British European Airways (BEA) in August 1946. After the war, Britain reestablished its overseas services to the nations of its empire. Some of the nations that had recently gained their independence from Britain received advice (and often finance) from BOAC.

In order to remain competitive with the American airline companies, BOAC purchased Lockheed Constellations, the most advanced commercial aircraft of the day. They later added Boeing 377 Stratocruisers and Canadair Argonauts (modified DC-4s). BEA operated generally smaller airplanes and more frequent flights between the British Isles and Continental Europe. In 1948 it joined other Allied airline companies in the airlift to Berlin during the Soviet blockade.

FLEET STRATEGIES IN THE FIFTIES

Following a series of equipment failures at BSAA, the Civil Aviation ministry declared that the company should reemerge with BOAC. On July 30, 1949, BSAA was absorbed by BOAC. Even though its passenger load had steadily increased, BOAC accumulated a debt of £32 million in the five years from 1946 to 1951. Much of this was due to "recapitalization," or purchasing new equipment, including the British-built Handley Page Hermes and de Havilland's DH Comet 1, the world's first jetliners.

In January 1954 one of BOAC's Comets exploded near Elba in the Mediterranean. Another Comet crashed near Naples only 16 days after an investigation of the first crash was concluded. As a result, the Comet's certificate of airworthiness was withdrawn. An investigation determined that the Comet's pressurized cabin was inadequately designed to withstand low-air pressures at altitudes over 25,000 feet. When the airplane reached that altitude it simply exploded. The cabin was strengthened and the jet reintroduced in 1958 as the DH Comet 4.

The company was forced to purchase propeller-driven DC-7s to cover equipment shortages when delivery of its Britannia turboprops was delayed in 1956. When the Comet reentered service in 1958, BOAC found itself with two undesirable fleets of aircraft, which were later sold at a loss of £51 million.

South American operations were suspended in 1954 when the Comet was taken out of service. Operation of the route with shorter range aircraft was too costly. At the insistence of Argentina and Brazil, which claimed Britain had "lost interest" in South America, the routes were reopened in 1960. That same year the first of 15 Boeing 707 jetliners was delivered to BOAC.

British European Airways used a wide variety of aircraft for its operations and remained a good customer for British aircraft manufacturers. In 1964 the company accepted delivery of the first de Havilland Trident 1, a three-engine airliner capable of speeds up to 600 miles per hour. A few years later, when the company expressed an interest in purchasing a mixed fleet of Boeing 727s and 737s, it was instructed by the government to "buy British" instead. BEA complied, ordering BAC 1-11s and improved versions of the Trident.

BOAC's cargo traffic was growing at an annual rate of 27 percent. Nevertheless, a sudden and unexplained drop in passenger traffic during 1961 left many of the world's airline companies with "excess capacity," or too many empty seats to fly profitably. At the end of the fiscal year BOAC's accumulated deficit had grown to £64 million. The losses, however, were underwritten by the British government, which could not allow its flag carrier to go bankrupt.

SUPERSONIC IN 1976

BOAC and Air France agreed to commit funds to build a supersonic transport (SST) in 1962. In June the company became associated with the Cunard Steamship Company. A new company, BOAC-Cunard Ltd., was placed in charge of the transatlantic air services in an attempt to capture a larger portion of the American travel markets.

The British government published a "white paper" (a statement of government policy) that recommended a drastic reorganization of BOAC. In response, the company's chairman, Sir Matthew Slattery, and the managing director, Sir Basil Smallpiece, resigned. Britain's minister for aviation appointed Sir Giles Guthrie as the new chairman and chief executive officer. Under Guthrie BOAC suspended its unprofitable services and rescheduled its equipment purchases and debt payments. After the financial situation had improved, the company continued to purchase new equipment and expand its flight network. In April 1967 BOAC established its second around-the-world route and opened a new cargo terminal at Heathrow.

The company's sister airline, BEA, had been paying close attention to consumer marketing for vacationers. In 1967 the company created a division called BEA Airtours Ltd., offering complete travel packages to a number of vacation spots. In May 1969 BOAC opened a passage to Japan via the North Pole. The route was shortened even further when the Soviet Union granted BOAC landing rights in Moscow and a Siberian air lane to Tokyo.

On March 31, 1972, after six years of record profits, BOAC announced that it no longer owed any money to the government. Later, on July 17, following several recommendations on further reorganization of the state-owned airline companies, management of BEA and BOAC were coordinated under a new government agency called the British Airways Group. On April 1, 1974 the two companies were merged and renamed British Airways. A second reorganization of the internal management structure occurred in 1977.

The first British Airways' Concorde was introduced in 1976. Jointly manufactured by British Aerospace and the French firm Aerospatiale, the supersonic Concorde was capable of carrying 100 passengers at the speed of 1,350 miles per hour at an altitude of 55,000 feet. A seven-hour flight from New York to London was cut nearly in half the time by the Concorde. British Airways employed additional Concordes on a number of international services, most notably London-Singapore, which was temporarily suspended through 1978 due to "political difficulties."

ROAD TO PRIVATIZATION IN THE EIGHTIES

In 1980 Prime Minister Margaret Thatcher appointed Lord (John) King as the new chairman of British Airways. His stated assignment was to prepare the airline for privatization (sale to private stockholders). Lord King's first move was to adopt aggressive

"American-style" marketing and management philosophies. As a result, he initiated a massive campaign to scale down the company and reduce costs. Additional unprofitable air services were terminated, and a staff reduction (begun under Lord King's predecessor, Roy Watts) was continued. A British Airways official told *Business Week* magazine, "we had too many staff but couldn't get rid of them because of the unions." In order to use the excess labor, the company was forced to remain large. Lord King established a better relationship with labor, which had become more agreeable to layoffs and revisions of work rules. In three years the workforce was reduced from 60,000 to 38,000 without a strike.

On July 11, 1983, no fewer than 50 senior executives were fired. The company's chief executive officer, Colin Marshall, hired in their place a team of younger executives (mostly with non-airline business backgrounds). The new executive staff initiated a series of programs to improve punctuality and service at the airline, whose BA acronym stood in many customers' minds for "Bloody Awful." They hired Landor Associates, a successful San Francisco-based design firm with considerable experience with airlines, to develop an entirely new image for British Airways. The result was controversial. The British Airways coat of arms and portion of the Union Jack on the airplane's tail fin was bound to upset the more politically temperamental countries of the third world, which the company served. The familiar "Speedbird" logo, which harkened back to the days of Imperial Airways, was removed despite employee petitions to retain it.

British Airways also recognized a need to replace older airplanes in its fleet with more modern and efficient equipment. The company's Lockheed TriStars were sold to the RAF for conversion into tankers, and the BAC-111s were sold because they would violate new noise regulations. British Airways leased a number of airplanes until new purchases could be made after the privatization.

The company was plagued by its decision to retain separate European and overseas divisions. The result was a perpetuation of the previous management regimes of BEA and BOAC. To rectify this problem the operation was further divided into eight regional groups involved in three different businesses: cargo, charter, and tours. Each of the eight groups was given increased autonomy and responsibility for its business and profitability.

The Laker Airways Skytrain, an initially successful cut-rate transatlantic airline, was forced to close down due to what its chairman, Freddie Laker, claimed was a coordinated attack by a number of airlines to drive the company into bankruptcy. Laker charged the companies, which included British Airways, with violations of antitrust laws. He later settled out of court for £48 million, but in a subsequent civil suit British Airways was also required to issue travel coupons to passengers who claimed they were hurt by the collapse of Laker Airways.

Ironically, in the mid-1980s the company began advocating the deregulation of European airlines in the belief that it could compete more effectively than its rivals. Air France and Lufthansa in particular were reluctant to participate, claiming that deregulation would endanger the delicate market balance which took so many years to establish.

In 1985 British Airways was made a public limited company, but its stock was retained by the government until such time that it could be offered to the public. The privatization of British Airways (which was limited to a 51 percent sale) was delayed by a number of problems. The company's chief domestic rival, British Caledonian, opposed British Airways' privatization, claiming that the company already controlled 80 percent of the domestic market and was too large to compete against. However, British Airways' most significant obstacle to privatization involved reducing the debt that it accumulated during the 1970s, and increasing the company's profitability. In February 1987 the privatization was finally consummated when 720.2 million shares of British Airways stock were sold to the public for £1 billion ($1.47 billion).

POISED FOR INTERNATIONAL GROWTH: ACQUISITIONS AND ALLIANCES

British Caledonian, or BCal, was formed in 1970 through the merger of Caledonian Airways and British United Airways. For many years, BCal was British Airways' only large domestic competitor, fighting vigorously under the direction of Sir Adam Thompson for more favorable operating rights from the British government. When Britain's Civil Aviation Authority recommended the reallocation of British Airways routes to BCal in 1984, Lord King threatened to resign. Instead, British Airways was instructed to trade its profitable Middle East routes for some of BCal's less profitable Latin American destinations. The Middle Eastern routes became much less popular during 1986 as a result of regional tensions and falling oil prices. BCal, which had been generating a fair profit, started to lose money and was faced with bankruptcy.

In July 1987 British Airways acquired BCal for £237 million in stock. The new airline had almost 200 aircraft, and by combining British Airways' 560,000-kilometer-route structure with BCal's unduplicated 110,000-kilometer network, now formed one of the largest airline companies in the world. Several smaller independent British airline companies unsuccessfully challenged the BA/BCal merger on the grounds that the new company would dominate both London's Heathrow and Gatwick Airports, forcing them to relocate to the less accessible and underdeveloped field at Stansted.

With its dominance of the home market secure for the time being, British Airways aggressively expanded in Europe, North America, and the Pacific Rim over the next several years, aiming to become a global airline. Its first foray into the lucrative U.S. market came in 1988 when it formed a marketing alliance with United Airlines designed to feed customers from one carrier to the other and vice-versa. This partnership set the pattern for British Airways' expansion; it would not be based on forming new airlines outside England or acquiring them, but rather through strategic alliances. Nevertheless, this first partnership collapsed a little more than two years later when United became a direct competitor to British Airways once it had gained access to Heathrow in 1991, along with American Airlines. The two strongest airlines in the United States had purchased the Heathrow rights from the floundering Pan Am and TWA, immediately increasing competition in British Airways' home market.

While the alliance with United was still operating, British Airways suffered losses in Europe in 1990 and 1991 because of the Gulf crisis in the Middle East. Shortly after, in July 1991, it entered into an alliance with Aeroflot in Russia to create a new airline called Air Russia. After several false starts over the next few years, this venture never got off the ground. Additional proposed alliances failed for assorted other reasons. Officials from British Airways and KLM Royal Dutch Airlines held merger discussions in 1991 and 1992, but talks broke down over the valuation of the two firms. Later in 1992 British Airways attempted to purchase 44 percent of US Air Inc. for $750 million. American, United, and Delta Air Lines (the U.S. "Big Three") vigorously lobbied against the deal and demanded enhanced access to the British market if the deal was to be approved by the U.S. government. In December the US Air purchase was blocked.

FACING COMPETITION IN THE EARLY EIGHTIES

That same month the first in a string of alliances was struck when the airline paid £450 million for 25 percent of Qantas, the Australia-based international airline. British Airways next acquired a 49.9 percent stake in the leading French independent carrier TAT European Airlines, and later launched a start-up in Germany called Deutsche BA with 49 percent ownership.

Through these alliances, British Airways enhanced its position in the Pacific Rim and Europe. It refocused its attention across the Atlantic where it restructured an offer for a piece of USAir into a $400 million purchase of 25 percent of the company. This alliance received U.S. government approval. The government also approved a code-sharing arrangement that enabled the partners to offer their customers a seamless operation when they used both airlines to reach their destination.

While all this deal making was going on abroad, British Airways faced an embarrassing and potentially costly fight at home with Richard Branson's upstart Virgin Atlantic Airlines. Since starting operations in the early 1980s, Virgin had made some inroads against British Airways primarily by focusing on customer service, something "Bloody Awful" BA had neglected for years. Branson filed suit against British Airways in 1991 alleging that British Airways had smeared Branson and his airline and conducted "dirty tricks" such as spreading rumors about Virgin's insolvency. In 1993 the suit was settled out of court with British Airways offering a public apology and paying £500,000 to Branson and £110,000 to Virgin. The case also led to the resignation of Lord King. Second-in-command Colin Marshall took over as chairman. Further litigation followed between the two rivals, most seriously a $1 billion antitrust suit brought by Virgin in the United States. Various suits damaged British Airways' reputation and led to comments such as the following from the *Economist:* "BA now looks … like an anxious, overbearing giant trying to squash a feisty little rival."

With its Virgin difficulties continuing, British Airways' overseas partners suffered huge losses: in 1993 Qantas lost $271 million, while in 1994 TAT lost $60 million and USAir lost $350 million. The situation at USAir was so grim that British Airways declared that they would hold back an additional $450 million investment in the firm until the carrier reestablished itself in the black. The alliance continued to deteriorate and in pursuit of more promising partnerships, British Airways eventually sold its stakes in USAir in 1997.

ONEWORLD ALLIANCE IN 1998

As it approached the long-awaited 1997 deregulation of the European airline industry, British Airways was on solid ground. In the process of becoming one of the largest airlines in the world, it had also managed to remain one of the most profitable.

In mid-1996 British Airways announced plans for a broad alliance with American Airlines. Under this plan, the two carriers would coordinate schedules and pricing, code-share (sell seats) and more importantly, share profits and revenues. Together they submitted a joint application to the U.S. Department of Transportation requesting approval of the proposed venture and granting antitrust immunity. Their plan was vehemently attacked by competitors on the basis that it would permit the two airlines to monopolize cross-Atlantic traffic between Heathrow and the United States. Both airlines had, in fact, previously refused to relinquish takeoff and landing slots at Heathrow; combined, they would control 85 percent of the peak takeoff slots in the largest single aviation market in the world. Intermittent negotiations and attempts to secure antitrust immunity continued into 2001, with both airlines struggling to agree on terms more conducive to an "open skies" agreement between the two countries. Competitors United Airlines and Lufthansa had already secured antitrust immunity and had prospered from "open skies" between the United States and Germany. Air France and Delta Airlines threatened to beat British Airways and American to the punch.

Separately, the "Oneworld" alliance formed in 1998 by British Airways and a group of others eventually became one of the most successful. Officially launched in February 1999 by British Airways, American Airlines, Qantas, Canadian Airlines, and Cathay Pacific, it provided an interchangeable network for frequent fliers to claim rewards. The group eventually grew to eight members and 23 affiliates by 2001, and collectively served more than 200 million passengers in 133 countries with 566 destinations.

British Airways continued to expand its network through a combination of new routes, code-sharing agreements, and franchise partnerships with both domestic and international carriers. By 2001 it had acquired CityFlyer Express and British Regional Airlines Group, and a 9 percent stake in Spain's Iberia Airlines.

ON THE BRINK IN THE NINETIES

Starting in the mid-1990s, British Airways began investing in advanced information technologies to build a "virtual airline" to expedite ticketing, scheduling, and customer service functions. It also began outsourcing "non-core" operations that had been previously overstaffed (ground transport services, in-flight catering, and heavy-engine maintenance) to reduce costs and allow the company to refocus squarely on operating its air network. The outsourcing measures frustrated industrial relations and failed to significantly reduce employee numbers. Further, industry analysts speculated that the airline would be more vulnerable to an economic downturn because it would no longer have secondary sources of revenue to offset the accompanying downturn in air travel revenues. Not surprisingly, when the air

travel market slowed in 1998, British Airways' net profits of $330 million dropped precipitously to $34 million.

Declining profitability during the late 1990s led the airline to concentrate on the premium market for business travelers. By combining fleet and network changes, it could increase the number of business passengers, lower costs, and cater to a more profitable section of the market.

Tapped for the role of chief executive in May 2000, Rod Eddington set out to reduce exposure in unprofitable and non-core areas, selling stakes in Air Liberté and even placing its own no-frills carrier, Go (launched only in 1998), on the market. Plans to build Gatwick into a second international hub were abandoned. Instead, unprofitable routes were suspended and key long-haul routes were relocated to Heathrow. Smaller aircraft, specifically Boeing 777s, would replace the older, larger aircraft and play a major role in a new fleet strategy. With bigger business travel sections, each new aircraft could seat a greater number of premium business travelers and help cut excess capacity. It was anticipated that by 2002 more than half of British Airways' fleet would consist of Boeing 777s.

In an effort to create a more appealing environment for its premium business travelers, British Airways invested in costly product and service enhancements. These included passenger seats that expanded into six-foot flat beds for in-flight sleeping; new state-of-the-art, in-flight entertainment; and modernized airport lounges with an upscale look and feel.

RESTRUCTURING TO REMAIN COMPETITIVE

A veteran of Cathay Pacific and Ansett, Eddington improved both operations and morale. During his first year, the airline faced a number of adversities. Following a tragic Air France Concorde accident in Paris in 2000, British Airways' entire Concorde fleet was grounded. The Concorde never recovered, and by 2003, Air France and British Airways had decided to put a permanent end to the Concorde service.

Other troubles rose to hamper the company's performance. An outbreak of foot-and-mouth disease caused a serious decline in travel and tourism in England, at the beginning of the century. Rising oil prices doubled fuel prices, cutting sharply into the company's bottom line. British Airways was also forced to throw in the towel on its discount airline operations, shutting down its Go service in 2000.

Nonetheless, into early 2001, the British Airways fleet and product strategy appeared to be working. Two positive trends had emerged: premium business traffic was on the rise and costs were on the decline. Pretax profits in 2001 amounted to £145 million, a marked improvement over the previous year's £5 million. The impact of the U.S. economic slowdown remained to be determined, though, and the airline faced difficult conditions in both passenger and cargo markets. British Airways' fleet of seven Concordes was expected to return to service after a full year of safety modifications and further comfort upgrades. However, the September 11, 2001, terrorist attacks on the United States (9/11) added new levels of financial stress and uncertainty to the travel and airline industries.

European airlines found themselves on the brink of momentous change in 2001. The potential for industry-wide consolidation had begun to fuel discussions of cross-border alliances, even cross-border mergers, that would be necessary to survive the ensuing instability. British Airways was certain to take aggressive action in staking a claim. In June 2001, it resumed talks with KLM for a £5 billion merger between the two, which could create the world's third largest airline. These talks eventually broke down, however.

Chief Executive Eddington vowed to continue pressing European regulatory authorities to allow the cross-border consolidation process, declaring "[Consolidation] is a lengthy process (it took 30 years in the United States), but it is both inevitable and necessary if we're to develop our position in the long-term. And I intend that British Airways will be in the vanguard of that process."

PAYROLL CUTS

British Airways' heavy exposure to the U.S. market following 9/11 left the company particularly vulnerable to the sudden collapse in international travel. As a result, the company was forced to carry out a major restructuring effort, resulting in the elimination of more than 13,000 jobs, 25 percent of its payroll, over the next two years.

These payroll cuts came as part of CEO Eddington's announcement of a new company goal of achieving cost savings of $635 million per year. As part of that effort, the company shut down a number of its underperforming routes. This marked the beginning of the company's shift to its most profitable flights, which tended to be its long-distance international flights. The company also began increasingly to focus on developing its premium air travel business.

The company's restructuring continued into 2004. Additional payroll reductions eliminated 30 percent of the company's head office jobs, and another 15 percent

of its operational crew. This decision would come to haunt the company, as it found itself short-staffed. As a result, flight delays, baggage losses, and other problems began to tarnish the company's reputation. However, by 2005 the airline's efforts appeared to be paying off, as company profits neared $500 million on revenues of $14.7 billion.

Eddington stepped down as CEO at the end of 2005, and was replaced by Willie Walsh, who had rescued embattled Aer Lingus from bankruptcy earlier in the decade. One of Walsh's first major decisions at British Airways was to launch a new effort to crack the low-cost market, which had expanded strongly during the decade to capture an increasing proportion of European passengers. In early 2006, British Airway's completed a revamping of its CitiExpress air service, adopting many of the features of the company's low-cost rivals. The new service was then rebranded as BA Connect.

A GLOBAL AIRLINE IN 2010

The new low-cost operation remained only a minor part of British Airways' operations, however. Through the second half of the decade, the company's focus increasingly turned toward the premium air travel segment. By the later years of the first decade of the 2000s, British Airways had begun to describe itself as "one of the world's leading scheduled premium international airlines." As part of that effort, the company added a new premium business class operation, called OpenSkies. The new service, launched in June 2008, featured a fleet of Boeing 757 aircraft refitted to accommodate just 64 passengers.

The choice of name for the new service was deliberate. In 2007, the U.S. and European aviation authorities reached a new agreement liberalizing flights between their markets. The "Open Skies" agreement permitted U.S. and European airlines to operate anywhere within the United States and Europe, creating a new and highly competitive market. Faced with the certain prospect of an intensification of competition, particularly at its Heathrow base, British Airways' own OpenSkies service was meant to position the company at the high end of the airline market.

British Airways nonetheless retained its home advantage, as the company celebrated the opening of Heathrow Airport's Terminal 5 in March 2008. The opening of the new terminal, which cost more than $8.6 billion, got off to a rocky start, however, after problems in its baggage handling, parking, and security systems forced the company to cancel more than 380 flights within a two-week period. The opening of the new terminal, however, provided British Airways with a major new base of operations.

British Airways turned its attention toward what many saw as the inevitable consolidation of the international airline market, which had begun to gather momentum since the Open Skies agreement. British Airways itself stepped up as a major player in the coming consolidation, announcing, in July 2008, that it had entered talks to acquire Spanish partner Iberia. Talks between the two companies went slowly. Amid the global economic collapse that year, however, which placed new pressures on the global airline industry, the merger appeared to be making progress by June of the following year.

By then, British Airways had announced its interest in acquiring its troubled U.S. partner, American Airlines. At the same time, British Airways suggested that the fourth partner in the OneWorld alliance, Qantas, also become an affiliate of the larger company. The merger of these companies, possibly by 2010, would create the world's first global airline.

Updated, David E. Salamie; Suzanne Selvaggi;
M. L. Cohen

PRINCIPAL SUBSIDIARIES

BA & AA Holdings Limited; BA Cash Management Limited; BA Cityflyer Limited; BA European Limited; BritAir Holdings Limited; British Airways 777 Leasing Limited; British Airways Avionic Engineering Limited; British Airways Holdings Limited; British Airways Holidays Limited; British Airways Interior Engineering Limited; British Airways Leasing Limited; British Airways Maintenance Cardiff Limited; Flyline Tele Sales & Services GmbH (Germany); Speedbird Cash Management Limited; Speedbird Insurance Company Limited; The Mileage Company Limited.

PRINCIPAL DIVISIONS

Passenger; Cargo.

PRINCIPAL OPERATING UNITS

OpenSkies; CityFlyer.

PRINCIPAL COMPETITORS

Deutsche Lufthansa AG; Société Air France; American Airlines; KLM Royal Dutch Airlines; Singapore Airlines Limited; Scandinavian Airlines System; Swissair Group; Japan Airlines Company, Ltd.; UAL Corporation (United Airlines); Virgin Atlantic Airways Limited.

FURTHER READING

"After Rod," *Investors Chronicle*, January 21, 2005.

"Antitrust Implications: The British Airways-American Airlines Alliance," U.S. Senate Subcommittee on Antitrust, Business Rights, and Competition of the Committee on the Judiciary, 105th Congress, 1st Session, April 22, 1997, p. 342.

"BA Embraces No-Frills Model," *Investors Chronicle*, January 13, 2006.

"BA-Iberia Talks Gain Fresh Momentum," *Airline Business*, February 16, 2009.

Banks, Howard, *The Rise and Fall of Freddie Laker*, London: Faber, 1982, p. 155.

"British Airways Is Predator and Prey," *Investors Chronicle*, April 5, 2007.

Campbell-Smith, Duncan, *The British Airways Story: Struggle for Take-Off*, London: Hodder and Stoughton, 1986, 327 p.

Capell, Kerry, "BA's OpenSkies Flies into Headwinds," *Business Week Online*, October 30, 2008.

———, "British Airways Eyes Qantas, Iberia Tieups," *Business Week Online*, December 5, 2008.

———, "British Airways Hit by Heathrow Fiasco," *Business Week Online*, April 3, 2008.

Corke, Alison, *British Airways: The Path to Profitability*, New York: St. Martin's Press, 1986, p. 145.

Doganis, Rigas, *The Airline Business in the Twenty-First Century*, New York: Routledge, 2001, 256 p.

Done, Kevin, "BA and American Joint Venture Plan Faces Criticism," *Financial Times*, July 23, 2001, p. 14.

Done, Kevin, and Mark Odell, "BA and American Under Pressure on Joint Venture," *Financial Times*, July 30, 2001.

Dwyer, Paula, "Air Raid: British Air's Bold Global Push," *Business Week*, August 24, 1992, pp. 54–60.

Dwyer, Paula, and Keith L. Alexander, "Sky Anxiety: Faltering Partners Are Shaking British Airways' Strategy of Global Alliances," *Business Week*, March 21, 1994, p. 38.

"Fighting to Keep Aloft," *Time International*, October 8, 2001, p. 62.

Fishbein, Jennifer, "Turbulence Alert for Europe's Big Carriers," *Business Week Online*, September 13, 2007.

"Flying in Formation," *Economist*, August 2, 2008.

Gurassa, Charles, "BA Stood for Bloody Awful," *Across the Board*, January 1995, pp. 55–56.

Kindel, Stephen, "Economies of Scope," *Financial World*, September 14, 1993, pp. 42–43.

Lynn, Matthew, "Battle of the Atlantic," *Management Today*, November 1991, p. 48.

Palmer, Jay, "The British Are Coming: By Slashing Costs, Selling Comfort and Forging Alliances, British Airways Has Made Itself a Contender in the Battle to Rule the Skies," *Barron's*, December 12, 1994, pp. 29–34.

Penrose, Harald, *Wings Across the World: An Illustrated History of British Airways*, London: Cassell, 1980, p. 304.

Regnier, Pat, and Rod Eddington, "The Long Haul to Profits," *Time International*, February 25, 2002, p. 58.

Simensen, Ivar M., "BA, KLM Seen Back in Merger Talks," *Financial Times*, June 10, 2001.

Tatge, Mark, and Miriam Gottfried, "The British Are Coming!" *Forbes,* February 13, 2006, p. 51.

"Terminal," *Economist,* July 26, 2003, p. 55US.

Wada, Isae, "Going Global: BA Chief Executive Outlines Carrier's Expansion Plans," *Travel Weekly,* September 6, 1990, pp. 1–3.

"We Are Flying into Turbulence," *Economist,* March 4, 1995, pp. 64–66.

Cadbury plc

25 Berkeley Square
London, W1J 6HB
United Kingdom
Telephone: (44 20) 7409-1313
Fax: (44 20) 7830-5200
Web site: http://www.cadbury.com

Public Company
Incorporated: 1969 as Cadbury Schweppes PLC
Employees: 45,000
Sales: £5.38 billion ($9.8 billion) (2008)
Stock Exchanges: London New York
Ticker Symbols: CBRY.L CBY.N
NAICS: 311320 Chocolate and Confectionery Manufacturing from Cacao Beans; 311330 Confectionery Manufacturing from Purchased Chocolate

■ ■ ■

Cadbury plc is one of the world's leading confectionery companies. The former Cadbury Schweppes spun off its remaining U.S. beverages division (Dr Pepper Snapple Group) in 2008 in order to focus solely on its core operations producing and marketing candy, chocolate, and chewing gum. The company claims an 11 percent share of the total global confectionery market, and holds a leading position in 20 of the top 50 confectionery markets. The company claims the number one spot worldwide in the candy segment, the number two position in chewing gum, and number five in chocolate, for the second place position overall. Chocolate is the company's largest division, accounting for 46 percent of the company's £5.38 billion ($9.8 billion) in revenue in 2008. The company's chocolate brands include Cadbury, Dairy Milk, and Creme Egg. Chewing Gum is the group's fastest-growing division, and features such brands as Trident, Dentyne, Stimorol, Hollywood, Stride, Clorets, Chiclets, Bubbaloo, and Dirol. This division generates 33 percent of group revenues. Candy, the most fragmented confectionery sector, adds 21 percent of group sales. Brands in this division include Halls, The Natural Confectionery Co., Cadbury Eclairs, Maynards, Bassett's, Trebor, Sour Patch Kids, and Swedish Fish. Cadbury is listed on the London Stock Exchange and is led by CEO Todd Spitzer and Chairman Roger Carr.

THE BIRTH OF A CHOCOLATE GIANT: 1824–68

The history of Cadbury dates back to 1824, when John Cadbury opened his grocery business in Birmingham. From the start, drinking-cocoa and chocolate were his most popular products, and in 1831 he moved to larger quarters and began manufacturing his own cocoa products. In 1847 he took on his brother Benjamin as a partner. Two years later the Cadbury brothers spun off their retail operations to Richard Cadbury Barrow, a nephew, and concentrated on manufacture and wholesale distribution. In 1853 Cadbury Brothers received a royal warrant as manufacturers to Queen Victoria; the company still holds the distinction of being confectioner to the Crown.

Shortly thereafter, however, business began to decline. The two Cadbury brothers dissolved their

Cadbury is a leading global business in the exciting world of confectionery, a large, growing, brand-led industry. With an outstanding portfolio of chocolate, gum and candy brands, the largest emerging markets business and a focused and experienced team, Cadbury is committed to its long-term vision to be the world's biggest and best confectionery company.

partnership in 1860 when Benjamin left the company, and John also retired the very next year. He left the business to his sons Richard and George, who continued to struggle for several years. However, in 1866, the new Cadbury brothers introduced an improved process for pressing cocoa butter out of the cocoa bean to produce cocoa essence. This resulted in purer drinking-cocoa and plentiful cocoa butter that could be made into eating chocolate. In 1868, Cadbury Brothers began marketing its own lines of chocolate candy, reviving its fortunes and breaking the stranglehold that French confectioners had on the British market.

INNOVATION AND EXPANSION: 1879–1964

Renewed success brought with it renewed expansion. In 1879 Cadbury Brothers began constructing a new factory outside Birmingham. In 1881 the firm received its first export order from a representative in Australia, and by the middle of the decade its overseas business had expanded to New Zealand, South Africa, India, the West Indies, and both North and South America. In 1899 it incorporated as Cadbury Brothers Limited, with George Cadbury as chairman.

In 1906 Cadbury Brothers introduced a new recipe for milk chocolate, marketed under the name Cadbury Dairy Milk, which has remained a mainstay of its product line ever since. After World War I, innovations in industrial technology made the manufacture of chocolate cheap enough to price chocolate candy for a wider market, and the company accordingly retooled its factory for mass production in the late 1920s. Cadbury Brothers opened its first overseas plant in Australia in 1922, and more foreign production ventures followed from its 1919 acquisition of J.S. Fry & Sons. In 1932 Fry's Canadian plant began to manufacture Cadbury products, and the next year Cadbury Fry, now a subsidiary of Cadbury Brothers, opened a factory in

Ireland. Cadbury Brothers also began to manufacture in South Africa in 1939 and India in 1947.

Throughout the postwar years, Cadbury maintained its position as the leading chocolate manufacturer in the world's leading per-capita candy-consuming nation. ("They chew through plays and they chew through films and they chew in trains," a theater critic for the *London Daily Mail* once lamented. "They suck lollies through *Macbeth* and *Hamlet,* and they while away Tennessee Williams with the chocolates with the scrumptious centers.") In 1962 Cadbury and Cadbury Fry, along with their competitor Rowntree, accounted for 51 percent of British candy sales.

In 1964 Cadbury entered the sugar-candy business when it acquired confectioner Pascall Murray. All the while, the company remained a family business. At the time of the merger with Schweppes, its chairman had always been a direct descendant of John Cadbury and the vast majority of its stock belonged to family members or trusts.

TESTING THE WATERS: THE EARLY YEARS OF SCHWEPPES LIMITED, 1790–1851

The same cannot be said, however, for Schweppes Limited, which has not felt the guiding hand of a Schweppe for almost 200 years. The company bears the name of Jacob Schweppe, a German-born jeweler and amateur chemist who entered into a joint venture in 1790 with pharmacist Henry Gosse, engineer Jacques Paul, and his son Nicholas. Together, they formed Schweppe, Paul & Gosse, which devoted itself to producing artificial mineral water. Schweppe moved to London in 1792 to establish the company's English operations, and when the partnership dissolved the next year he retained the business for himself.

In those days, aerated water was believed to have medicinal value, and the Schweppes brand was popular because it contained a higher degree of carbonation than its competitors. In 1799 Schweppe sold a 75 percent interest in his business to three men from the island of Jersey and retired. The company, however, continued to use the Schweppe name.

In 1834 Schweppes, as it was then called, was bought by William Evill and John Kemp-Welch, whose descendants would remain associated with the company until 1950. In 1836 the company received its first royal warrant, from the Duchess of Kent and Princess Victoria, soon to become Queen Victoria. Schweppes also gained substantial prestige when it was granted a catering concession for the Great Exhibition of 1851.

KEY DATES

1790: Jacob Schweppe, Jacques Paul, and Henry Gosse join to form Schweppe, Paul & Gosse.

1792: Jacob Schweppe moves to London.

1824: John Cadbury begins selling cocoa and chocolate in Birmingham, England.

1834: William Evill and John Kemp-Welch acquire Schweppes, as the company is known.

1853: Cadbury Brothers receives royal warrant to manufacture chocolate for Queen Victoria.

1868: Cadbury Brothers introduces its first line of chocolate candy.

1897: Schweppes Limited goes public.

1899: Cadbury Brothers Limited is incorporated.

1906: Cadbury Brothers begins marketing Cadbury Dairy Milk.

1922: Cadbury Brothers opens a plant in Australia.

1969: Cadbury Limited merges with Schweppes Limited to form Cadbury Schweppes PLC.

1974: Adrian Cadbury becomes chairman of Cadbury Schweppes.

1982: Cadbury Schweppes acquires Duffy-Mott.

1986: Cadbury Schweppes acquires Canada Dry and Sunkist soft-drink lines from RJR Nabisco.

1995: Cadbury Schweppes acquires Dr Pepper/Seven Up.

1999: Cadbury Schweppes sells non-U.S. soft-drink business to Coca-Cola.

2003: Company acquires the Adams chewing gum company from Pfizer Inc., becoming the world's largest confectionery company.

2007: Cadbury Schweppes acquires Sansei Food Co. of Japan and Intergum of Turkey; announces plans to sell its beverage division.

2008: Company spins off its beverage operations as Dr. Pepper Snapple Group, which lists on the New York Stock Exchange; company then changes its name to Cadbury Plc.

2009: Cadbury announces plans to plant up to ten million cocoa trees in India per year.

DIVERSIFICATION AND INTERNATIONAL GROWTH: 1870–1969

The company began to introduce new product lines in the second half of the century. Schweppes started marketing ginger ale in the 1870s. Tonic water, its most famous product, also appeared at about this time in response to a demand from Britons returning from India who had developed a taste for the solution of quinine, sugar, and water they had drunk there as a malaria preventive. In 1885, Schweppes introduced a carbonated lemonade. Such was the company's success during the Victorian era that it went public in 1897.

In 1923 Schweppes consolidated its overseas operations into a single British-based subsidiary. This move was intended to facilitate further international expansion. During the interwar years and through World War II, however, the company's fortunes began to wane as sales went soft. It was not until Sir Frederick Hooper took over as managing director in 1948 that Schweppes regained its strength through shrewd marketing and a renewed focus on its overseas business. An integral part of that campaign for two decades was the use of Commander Edward Whitehead, who became chairman of Schweppes USA in 1952, as the company's U.S. advertising spokesman. From the early 1950s through the early 1970s, Commander Whitehead, whom *Time* once described as an "engaging walrus," ingratiated himself with Americans as he espoused his products' unique "Schweppervescence." By 1962, foreign operations accounted for one-fifth of the company's net sales.

Schweppes was forced to diversify as the demand for soft drinks and mixers at home leveled off. In 1960 it acquired three makers of jams and jellies: Hartley's, Moorhouse, and Chivers. These acquisitions required substantial reorganization, however, and did not work out very well; by 1964 only Hartley's was turning a profit for its parent company. Nonetheless, Schweppes prospered under Sir Frederick Hooper's guidance. Its annual profits increased nearly sevenfold between 1953 and 1962, from $756,000 to $4.8 million. Hooper retired in 1964 and was succeeded by Harold Watkinson, a former Conservative defense minister.

JOINING FORCES IN 1969

In 1968 Schweppes acquired Typhoo Tea to further diversify its product line and strengthen its ties to grocery retailers. However, with no growth in its domestic markets, Lord Watkinson realized that overseas expansion was the key to Schweppes' future. Unfortunately, its capital base was tiny compared with that of the U.S. conglomerates with which it would have to compete. That fall, Watkinson met with Cadbury Chairman Adrian Cadbury at a trade show and found that Cadbury had similar concerns about his own company. Schweppes and Cadbury began merger talks soon thereafter and reached an agreement in January 1969.

Technically, Schweppes came out of the merger as the surviving company. It bought out Cadbury stockholders by replacing their shares with $290 million worth of its own stock. Watkinson became chairman in the new chain of command, with Adrian Cadbury assuming the titles of deputy chairman and co-managing director. The new company, though, bore the Cadbury name in front of Schweppes', and the candy business was clearly not to be neglected. Although the two companies consolidated some of their operations, they maintained autonomy in the matter of distribution, since bottling franchisees controlled local distribution in the soft-drink business.

The 1970s were marked by further diversification and attempts to capture international markets. In 1973 Cadbury Schweppes ventured into alcoholic beverages when it acquired Courtney Wines International from LRL International. Also in 1973, Schweppes South Africa merged with Groovy Beverages. A year later, it acquired Pepsi Cola South Africa. Most of Cadbury Schweppes' moves in the early 1970s were small in scale and generally unsuccessful. It also spread itself thin at home by introducing a large number of unprofitable new products.

U.S. FOCUS FROM THE SEVENTIES

Adrian Cadbury succeeded Watkinson as chairman in 1974, and under his direction Cadbury Schweppes focused its efforts on gaining a greater share of the lucrative U.S. market. In 1978, aided by a strong pound, it acquired Peter Paul, a Connecticut-based confectioner, for $58 million. This gave Cadbury Schweppes a 10 percent share of the U.S. candy market in one swoop. In 1982 it bought Duffy-Mott, a producer of fruit juices and other fruit products, from American Brands for $60 million.

Cadbury Schweppes made several other overseas acquisitions in the early 1980s. In 1980 it increased its stake in its French subsidiary, Schweppes France, to 100 percent. In 1982 it purchased a two-thirds interest in Rioblanco, a Spanish soft-drink company that owned the Schweppes franchise in Spain. In 1984 it acquired Cottees General Foods, General Foods' Australian subsidiary and a producer of coffee products, jams, jellies, and fruit juice cordials. In Britain it ended its 32-year-old franchising agreement with PepsiCo in 1985 to become Coca-Cola's British franchisee, noting Coke's dominant position in the British market.

However, Cadbury Schweppes remained focused on the U.S. market throughout the 1980s. In 1985 it acquired Sodastream Holdings, a British company that

produced equipment for making carbonated drinks at home, as a way of trying to capture U.S. customers without competing head-on with Coke and Pepsi. Cadbury Schweppes held only 1 percent of the U.S. market in 1986, while the two native giants controlled roughly three-quarters between them.

Cadbury Schweppes nevertheless began to take on Coke and Pepsi with increasing vigor. In 1986 it bought the Canada Dry and Sunkist soft-drink lines from RJR Nabisco for $230 million. RJR Nabisco was anxious to leave the soft-drink business in the face of increased competition from Coca-Cola and Pepsi, which were growing ever larger. Pepsi had just acquired Seven Up, and Coca-Cola had agreed to buy Dr Pepper, a deal that would later fall apart. Sunkist was in danger of losing market share to Coca-Cola's new Minute Maid line and Pepsi's Slice. While RJR Nabisco was ready to get out, Cadbury Schweppes was desperate to get into the market. Buying Canada Dry and Sunkist increased its share of U.S. soft-drink sales to 5.3 percent, making it the fourth largest soft-drink company in the nation.

Cadbury Schweppes then spun off Canada Dry's Canadian operations to Coca-Cola for $90 million. It needed the cash to acquire 30 percent of Dr Pepper as part of a consortium that included the brokerage house Shearson Lehman Brothers and Dallas-based investment group Hicks & Haas. This group bought the soft-drink company from Forstmann Little & Company for $416 million.

TAKEOVER SPECULATION IN THE EIGHTIES

Cadbury Schweppes became the subject of takeover speculation in 1987 after General Cinema announced that it had acquired an 8.3 percent interest in the company. General Cinema, a soft-drink bottler that also owned the Neiman Marcus department stores and operated a large movie theater chain, said that it had bought the Cadbury Schweppes shares purely as an investment. Speculation increased later that year when General Cinema raised its stake to 18.2 percent. The next year, rumors circulated that Swiss giant Nestlé would try to acquire Cadbury Schweppes. With stock prices depressed in the wake of the October 1987 stock market crash and Cadbury Schweppes' strong financial performance, it was an attractive takeover candidate.

Amid all this uncertainty, however, Cadbury Schweppes continued to go about its business. In 1987 it acquired Chocolat Poulain, a French confectioner, from Midial for $173.1 million. In 1988 it sold its U.S. confectionery operations to Hershey Foods as a franchise, deciding that its products would benefit from

Hershey's superior distribution network in the United States. In 1989 it bought out the British confectioner Bassett Foods to rescue it from a hostile takeover by the Swedish consumer products concern Procordia. It also continued its pursuit of the U.S. soft-drink market by acquiring Crush International from Procter & Gamble for $220 million. At that point, Cadbury Schweppes controlled a 4.7 percent market share in the United States and a 15.1 percent share in Canada.

In a sense, the takeover speculation surrounding Cadbury Schweppes was a tribute to its success over the last decade. In 1979 the company announced that it would refocus on its core businesses and devote itself to cracking the U.S. marketplace. In 1986 it sold off its domestic beverage and foods division, which included the tea and jam businesses that Schweppes had acquired in the 1960s and Cadbury's popular Smash instant mashed potato product. All of its other important actions in the 1980s related to confectionery and soft drinks. These moves paid off. Cadbury Schweppes increased its share of U.S. soft-drink sales almost fivefold and improved its financial situation significantly.

Perhaps the most interesting aspect of Cadbury Schweppes was the fact that it remained a family-run business even though it had also become a major corporation. Sir Adrian Cadbury (he was knighted in 1977), the great-grandson of John Cadbury, was still chairman in 1990. His brother Dominic was appointed CEO in 1983.

COMPETING IN THE GLOBAL MARKETPLACE IN THE NINETIES

In the early 1990s, with European unification looming on the horizon, Cadbury Schweppes began to develop a new business strategy, one that would give it a chance to establish leading positions in a variety of highly competitive foreign markets. In spite of its global reach, Cadbury Schweppes still had only a niche presence in the majority of the countries where it did business; although the company had operations in numerous countries worldwide, none of its overseas holdings were substantial enough to dominate any one region. Chairman Dominic Cadbury summed up the company's dilemma in June 1993: "If you are more than national, but less than global, you are an uncomfortable animal to describe." In short, Cadbury Schweppes needed to boost its international profile.

Each of the company's core businesses presented its own unique challenges. Expanding the company's soft-drink line in Europe was, in many respects, fairly straightforward. To attain the sales volume necessary to justify building a new network of bottling plants, the company needed to find a way to increase distribution of its products in Europe. Although a number of its brands, notably Schweppes and Canada Dry, had name recognition overseas, they did not claim a commanding share of any one marketplace. The company considered establishing new operations in individual countries, but joint ventures, with which the company already had a lot of experience, seemed much more appealing in the long term. One such pact, with Apollinaris Brunnen in Germany, was forged in 1991, and showed strong sales after only its first year of operation.

FOCUSING ON THE U.S. BEVERAGE MARKET

In the United States, however, the company's strategy was radically different. Since the cola market was clearly dominated by Coke and Pepsi, Cadbury Schweppes looked for opportunity in the fruit juice and non-cola marketplaces. A number of crucial acquisitions helped put the company on the map. In August 1993 Cadbury Schweppes obtained a 20.2 percent stake in Dr Pepper/Seven Up; the following month, the company acquired A&W, the largest root beer producer in the United States, for $334 million. Although small steps, these deals helped set the stage for further growth. In 1995 the company paid $1.6 billion for the remaining stake in Dr Pepper/Seven Up, giving it a 17 percent share of the overall U.S. soft-drink market. On one hand, this number was still small compared with the shares commanded by Coke and Pepsi. Pn the other, it gave Cadbury Schweppes a full 50 percent, however, of the non-cola drink sector, a segment that was growing far more rapidly than the cola business, accounting for 35 percent of the $49 billion U.S. soft-drink industry in 1995.

There were still obstacles to overcome, though. Coke and Pepsi controlled much of the U.S. distribution and bottling systems that Cadbury Schweppes had been using for years, and for the most part the arrangement had been stable. Now that Cadbury Schweppes was jockeying for market share, however, the relationships between the companies were in danger of becoming less friendly. Less than eager to remain at the mercy of its competitors, Cadbury Schweppes began looking into the possibility of establishing its own network by striking deals with independent bottlers. Unfortunately, the independents were notoriously disorganized in the United States, and any worthwhile system would take several years, and a substantial investment, to set in place. In February 1998 the company took a preliminary step toward creating its own network when it formed American Bottling, a joint venture with two independent bottlers in the U.S. Midwest. Perhaps most significant, in mid-1999 Cadbury Schweppes sold all of its non-U.S. soft-drink holdings to Coca-Cola for $700 million, signaling its intention to devote itself full-time to the U.S. market.

The sale also infused the company with a large dose of investment capital, putting it in a position to strengthen its European confectionery business through acquisition. In the late 1990s the company also began playing with the idea of further diversification. Although the company ultimately failed in its bid to acquire Nabisco in July 2000, it would not rule out future attempts to try to enter the snack-food business.

CONFECTIONERY LEADER IN 2003

For the time being, however, Cadbury Schweppes focused on building up both its confectionery and drinks businesses. The company bought the France-based chewing gum and candy operations of Kraft Foods in 2000. That year also marked the end of the company's association with the Cadbury family, when Sir Dominic Cadbury stepped down as group chairman.

Cadbury Schweppes remained on the lookout for the next big deal. This came in 2003, when the group agreed to pay pharmaceuticals giant Pfizer $4.3 billion to acquire the Adams chewing gum company. The Adams acquisition not only added the Trident chewing gum brand to the group's brand stable, it also boosted Cadbury Schweppes to the leading position in the global confectionery market.

Also during the decade, Cadbury Schweppes responded to the rising popularity of dark chocolate, and to the increasing interest in organic products, by acquiring the organic chocolate brand Green & Black in 2005. At the same time, the company completed several extensions to its global manufacturing capacity, including a $75 million upgrade of its Bournville factory in Birmingham in 2005. The company built a new chewing gum factory in Poland the following year, while also carrying out an $18 million upgrade of its factory in Hobart, Australia. Cadbury Schweppes' infrastructure upgrades continued through the end of the decade. In 2009, for example, the company announced its intention to plant as many as ten million cocoa trees per year in India in order to ensure its supply of the increasingly rare crop.

In the meantime, Cadbury Schweppes had also attempted to build its U.S. beverages operations. In 2002, the company expanded its line with the purchase of the Squirt soft-drink brand, and the Nantucket Nectars fruit-based drinks line. The company also targeted the fast-growing health drinks category, cutting prices on its Snapple and Motts brands. In 2005, Cadbury

Schweppes also launched a line of reduced sugar drinks, in order to build on the strength of its diet drinks segment, which led the U.S. market with a 23 percent share.

CONFECTIONERY FOCUS

The company's beverages division continued to lag far behind overall leaders Coca-Cola and PepsiCo. The company's 7-Up brand, which had formerly led its category, had failed to outpace the faster-growing Sprite brand. The launch of new drink flavors, including Cherry Coke, also threatened the company's Dr Pepper brand.

The arrival of shareholder activist Nelson Peltz, who acquired a 2.98 percent stake in Cadbury Schweppes in March 2007, set the stage for the next phase in the company's history. Just two days after Peltz acquired his stake, the company announced its decision to sell off its U.S. beverages operations. The company then entered talks with a number of private equity firms, including Blackstone, KKR, and Thomas H. Lee Partners, for the sale of the beverage business, valued at as much as $16 million.

The sale quickly fell through, however, when the collapse of the global credit market made it impossible to raise funds for the purchase. Cadbury Schweppes was forced to abandon hopes for the sale. Instead, in October 2007, the company announced that it would spin off the drinks business as a separate, publicly listed company, called Dr Pepper Snapple Group. That operation was completed in May 2008.

Renamed Cadbury Plc., the newly streamlined confectionery specialist set out to boost its position in the global market. By then, the company had been outpaced by its larger rivals, Nestlé and Mars, while the market held few large-scale acquisitions prospects. Cadbury nonetheless completed a number of smaller purchases, including the $111 million purchase of Sensei Food Co. of Japan in 2007.

Also that year, the company paid $450 million to buy Intergum, based in Turkey and one of that country's leading chewing gum companies. This purchase came as part of a larger group effort to position itself at the forefront of developing markets. Confectionery sales in these markets were expected to soar in the new century as the populations in these countries became more affluent.

Updated, Steve Meyer; M. L. Cohen

PRINCIPAL SUBSIDIARIES

Cadbury Adams Brasil Industria e Comercio de Produtos Alimenticios Ltda; Cadbury Adams Canada Inc.;

Cadbury Adams Colombia SA; Cadbury Adams Distribution Mexico, SA de CV; Cadbury Adams Mexico, S de RL de CV; Cadbury Adams USA LLC; Cadbury Adams, SA (Venezuela); Cadbury España, SL; Cadbury France; Cadbury Hellas AE; Cadbury Ireland Ltd; Cadbury Portugal–Produtos de Conféitaria, Lda; Cadbury Stani Adams Argentina SA; Cadbury Switzerland Faguet & Co; Cadbury Wedel Sp. zo.o. (Poland); Camelot Group PLC (20%); Crystal Candy (Private) Ltd (Zimbabwe; 49%); Dandy A/S (Denmark); Dirol Cadbury LLC (Russia); Intergum Gida Sanayi ve Ticaret Anonim Sirketi (Turkey); Kent Gida Maddeleri Sanayii ve Ticaret Anonim Sirketi (Turkey; 95.36%); Meito Adams Company Ltd (Japan; 50%).

PRINCIPAL DIVISIONS

Candy; Chocolate; Chewing Gum.

PRINCIPAL COMPETITORS

Nestlé SA; Mars, Incorporated; Hershey Foods Corporation; Wm. Wrigley Company; Chupa Chups SA; Ferrero SpA.

FURTHER READING

Ball, James, "Cadbury Develops World's First 'Bean to Bar' Operation," *Grocer,* June 13, 2009, p. 18.

Capell, Kerry, "Building European Brands Through Social Media," *Business Week Online,* June 22, 2009.

Clews, Mary-Louise, "Speculation Mounts over Restructure at Cadbury," *Marketing Week,* July 2, 2009, p. 5.

de Jonquieres, Guy, "An Uncomfortable Animal Seeks Big Game Status," *Financial Times* (London), June 8, 1993, p. 21.

Denton, Nicholas, and Roderick Oram, "Cadbury Schweppes Set to Pay £1bn for US Drinks Group," *Financial Times* (London), January 23, 1995, p. 1.

Norton, Kate, "Cadbury's Split Cheers Investors," *Business Week Online,* March 16, 2007.

"Of Sweets and Appetites," *Economist,* May 27, 2000, p. 67.

Riley, Lisa, "Cadbury Aiming for a Bigger Share in Bagged Chocolates," *Grocer,* March 21, 2009, p. 31.

Scott, Mark, "Cadbury Schweppes: What Now?" *Business Week Online,* October 22, 2007.

———, "Cadbury's Not for Sale—Just Yet," *Business Week Online,* July 30, 2007.

———, "A New Future for Cadbury Schweppes," *Business Week Online,* April 14, 2008.

Williams, Iolo A., *The Firm of Cadbury 1831–1931,* London: Constable and Co., 1931.

Willman, John, "Cadbury Schweppes Nears $700m Deal with Coca-Cola," *Financial Times* (London), July 29, 1999, p. 27.

Caffyns PLC

Meads Road
Eastbourne, BN20 7DR
United Kingdom
Telephone: (+44 01323) 730201
Fax: (+44 01323) 739680
Web site: http://www.caffyns.co.uk

Public Company
Incorporated: 1865
Employees: 738
Sales: £158.65 million ($262.2 million) (2008)
Stock Exchanges: London
Ticker Symbol: CFYN
NAICS: 441110 New Car Dealers

■ ■ ■

Caffyns PLC is one of southeast England's leading automotive retailers. The Eastbourne-based company holds franchises for 14 major automotive makes, including Audi, Chevrolet, Chrysler, Citroën, Dodge, Ford, Jaguar, Jeep, Land Rover, Nissan, Peugeot, Skoda, Vauxhall, Volvo, and Volkswagen. The company also provides warranty services for its former Rover franchise, following that make's demise in 2005. Caffyns' sales are carried out at 24 sites throughout the Sussex and Kent regions. The company also operates three dedicated Accident Repair Centers, and three Parts Centers, also in Kent and Sussex. Caffyns provides both private and corporate leasing services, as well as financing. After-sales services include the fixed-price à la carte Flexi-Serve annual service program; and the online service organizer,

My Caffyns. The company also provides accessibility adapted automobiles for the disabled through an affiliated nonprofit entity named Motability. Caffyns has been listed on the London Stock Exchange since 1899. The Caffyn family remains the group's dominant shareholders, controlling more than 60 percent of its voting rights. Simon Caffyn is the group's chief executive officer. As a result of the disastrous economic climate in 2008, the group's revenues slipped back to £159 million for the year, resulting in a £4 million loss.

19TH-CENTURY BEGINNINGS

Born in 1842, William Morris Caffyn began an apprenticeship as an "Ironmonger, Tinman and Brazier," at his uncle's workshop in Eastbourne in 1856. By 1865, Caffyn was ready to set up his own shop, also in Eastbourne. From the start, Caffyn displayed an interest in the era's latest inventions. Among his initial products and services were the fitting of gas and water heaters. By 1871, Caffyn had also acquired a license for storing petroleum products.

Joined by sons Percy and Harry, the company branched out into home appliances, including the earliest electrical appliances in the early 1890s. This activity led the company to open its first branch store at the end of the decade. Caffyns also became a public company in 1899, although the Caffyn family maintained control of the company.

The group added electrical installation services in 1901. The growth of this activity led to the acquisition of a new location, a former butchery located near Eastbourne's Marine Parade, which became the center of

Caffyns's electricity business. The butchery, and especially its large doorway, played a role in introducing the Caffyns to what was to become the family's main business in the 20th century.

Caffyns's entry into the automotive market happened almost by chance. Shortly after the new century began, the family was approached by an early automobilist, who arrived in Eastbourne driving his Renault. The driver asked to park his car in the former butchery, which with its large doorway could easily accommodate the Renault. The Caffyns agreed, and cut away the bottom sill of the shop to allow the automobile to enter.

ADDING AUTOMOTIVE SERVICES IN THE 20TH CENTURY

While the Renault had been the first car the Caffyns had ever seen, the brothers recognized the potential of developing a business providing automobile services, such as parking, repairs, and cleaning and polishing. In 1903, therefore, the brothers bought the former butchery shop from their father for £1,800 and set up a new business, Caffyn Brothers. The following year, the company built an extension to the garage, providing accommodation for 16 cars.

The Caffyns quickly began adding to their range of services. By the end of their first year, they had begun selling automobiles. The company also added an insurance agency providing accident insurance through the General Accident Assurance Corporation. By 1906, the brothers had decided to build a new garage at Marine Parade large enough to hold 100 automobiles. The new premises also featured an in-house coach-building and repair facility for the various steam-driven, electric, and petrol-driven vehicles of the time.

In the years leading up to World War I, Caffyns's range of operations included the production of various driving accessories, such as dust covers, leather aprons, hoods, and other items needed to protect drivers from the elements. The company sold and fitted horns and lamps, and also launched a car rental business during this time.

Caffyns opened a new showroom and garage on Meads Road in 1911. That site later became the group's head office. The company also began expanding to new locations. In 1912, Caffyns acquired a cycle shop in Heathfield, which was then expanded into a full-fledged garage. The company carried out a major expansion of its Marine Parade business, doubling its size, in 1913. By 1916, the company had added a branch in Bexhill. By then, the company had also added a new "Motor Mart Showroom" on Eastbourne's Terminus Road.

INTERWAR EXPANSION

Following the war, Caffyns expanded its Eastbourne presence with the purchase of rival Eastbourne & District Motor Cab Co. in 1919. Into the next decade, Caffyns successfully competed for car dealership franchises from the increasing number of automobile and motorcycle brands. Among the company's franchises during this period were Bleriot-Whippet, Kingsbury, Phenix, and A.C., as well as Harley-Davidson, Matchless, Triumph, Sunbeam, and others. In 1927, the company gained a Rolls-Royce franchise as well.

Another rapidly growing business for the company was its trade in commercial vehicles, including delivery vans. During the 1920s, the company opened a number of dedicated Commercial Vehicle branches, including a first in Lewes in 1927, followed by a branch in Hove the following year. These openings came amid the company's wider expansion, which included the acquisition of Aitken, Grinstead & Co. in Eastebourne at the end of the decade.

By then the company had been joined by the next generation, Sydney and Edward, sons of Percy Caffyn. The new set of brothers were to play a crucial role in the company's development, building it into one of England's leading automotive dealers through the second half of the century. Car sales had come to play an increasingly important role in the company's operations. This was highlighted as the company achieved a new milestone in 1929, when the company's annual volume topped more than 1,000 automobiles.

In the meantime, Caffyns continued to put its pieces into place. The company became one of the United Kingdom's pioneers in the corporate fleet rental and leasing market. In 1934, the company established its dedicated Contract Hire and Leasing facility. The following year marked a new milestone, as Caffyns entered the Kent region for the first time, buying Tonbridge-

KEY DATES

1865: William Morris Caffyn founds an ironmonger's shop in Eastbourne, England.
1903: Sons Percy and Harry Caffyn launch garage and service station services for the nascent automobile market.
1929: Caffyns automobile sales top 1,000 vehicles for the first time.
1985: Caffyns introduces the Flexi-Serve service and maintenance program.
1992: Caffyns adds the Jeep franchise.
2005: Bankruptcy of MG Rover causes Caffyns to lose 25 percent of its business.
2009: Caffyns posts a loss for the 2009 year amid the global economic crisis.

based Chas. Baker & Co. Also in the 1930s, the company made the decision to focus its automobile dealerships exclusively on the British auto industry.

SURVIVING WORLD WAR II

Caffyns' proximity to the coast exposed it to the vagaries of war; many of the group's buildings were requisitioned for military use. Other buildings suffered extensive bombing damage. In addition, the company's staff, including Edward Caffyn, were called up for military service. Much of the group's remaining resources were turned toward the support of the country's military effort.

Nonetheless, Caffyns continued to operate, and even grow, during the war years. The company acquired several more motor dealerships, garages, and service stations, including Ryders in Eastbourne, Seaford Motor Company, and the Saltdean Service Company. These were followed in 1945 with the purchases of Maitby's, an East Kent-based coach work specialist, and Watson Ltd., located in Tonbridge.

With raw material shortages launching new construction, Caffyns completed a number of new acquisitions following the war, opening branches in Maidstone and Margate. In 1952, the company added a new branch in Lewes as well. By then, Edward Caffyn had returned from a visit to the United States and brought with him many of the ideas that were then revolutionizing the U.S. retail automobile market.

The company's rebuilding program got underway in 1954 as the British government lifted the wartime restrictions. The company made a major advance during this period when it bought another Sussex-based business, Brittains. The purchase added a number of new automobile showrooms in West Sussex, as well as the franchises for the MG, Morris, and Riley brands. The following year, Caffyns bought a new company, A.C. Sharp, based in Westerham. These purchases came ahead of the resumption of production of new cars in the British automobile industry in 1956. With the first new car sales since the war, Caffyns's revenues jumped by 25 percent in one year.

ACQUIRING SCALE IN THE SEVENTIES

The arrival of a fourth generation of Caffyns led to a restructuring of the group's shareholding. In 1961, the company added stock exchange listings for its Preference and Ordinary shares. At the same time, the company created a new class of Second Preference Shares, which were endowed with voting rights. These shares were controlled by the Caffyn family, effectively ensuring the family's control over the company. Into the next century, the Caffyn family's share of the group's voting rights topped 60 percent.

Caffyns continued its string of acquisitions through the 1960s and 1970s as the British economic boom years led to a surge in automobile ownership in the country. The company's acquisitions included the Hythe Motor Cab Company in 1963; Dover & Continental Motors, in Dover, and Jackson Bros., in Horsham, in 1964; Sussex Motors in 1966; and Chas. Hayward & Sons in 1967. Throughout this period, the company continued to add to its operations elsewhere, including the opening of a major new showroom in Eastbourne in 1965. The company, which had already been operating service stations at a number of its locations, also introduced 24-hour filling services in 1967.

In the next decade, Caffyns added East Kent Motors, based in Deal, in 1968; A&H Motors in Brighton, in 1969; Eastbourne-based Clark & Lambert and Willetts, in 1970; Ramsgate's A&B Motors in 1972; and Henlys, based in Bexhill, in 1976. Another major acquisition came in 1977, when the company acquired the Robert Walker group of garages. This purchase added sites in Hampshire, Wiltshire, and Dorset, marking the company's first expansion beyond its core Sussex and Kent regions. The acquisition also changed the complexion of the group's automotive franchise portfolio, adding Fiat and Mercedes-Benz, the first non-British brands handled by the company since the 1930s.

NEW SERVICES IN THE EIGHTIES

Caffyns decided to adopt a strategy of a diversified franchise portfolio into the 1980s. Starting in 1981, the company added Renault dealerships at three of its showrooms, Audi-Vauxhall at two sites, and Lancia at the former Rob Walker branches. At the same time, the company carried out a restructuring of its operations, adopting a new regional organization. As a result, the company closed several branches into the middle of the decade. The company also ended its longstanding dealer relationship with Rolls-Royce in 1984.

Caffyns boosted its service offering during the 1980s as well. The group revamped its leasing operations, launching Caffyns Motor Contracts, in 1984. In 1985, the company launched its innovative Flexi-Serve service program. The new system, developed by Anthony Caffyn, part of the company's fourth generation and then managing director, provided fixed-price menu-style maintenance services, backed by a three-month guarantee.

In 1986, the company began developing vehicle financing products, starting with Driveplan. This new service made leasing services available to private customers for the first time. The company also developed its Accident Repair and Parts Delivery businesses, with each expanding to three branches in the Kent and Sussex regions.

Toward the end of the decade, Caffyns looked beyond the European market, adding its first Japanese automobile franchise, for the Toyota brand, in 1987. The company also focused on expanding its luxury class portfolio, which included Jaguar, with the opening of a number of new Mercedes-Benz showrooms, including in Dorchester in 1987 and in Salisbury in 1989.

ADAPTING TO THE CHANGING MARKET

Edward Caffyn died in 1990 at the age of 86, having helped build Caffyns into one of England's leading automobile dealers. In that year, also, future CEO and fifth-generation family member Simon Caffyn joined the group. The year 1990 was also marked by the launch of the company's own credit card.

Caffyns found itself forced to adapt to the rapid changes in the European automotive market that took place during the 1990s and into the new century. The creation of the European Union in 1992 and new legislation governing environmental, health and safety, and other issues sparked a wave of mergers among the world's major automakers. One result of this trend toward large-scale, multi-brand groups was a significant reduction in the number of automobile franchises. Remaining franchises were then expected to cover a wider geographic area.

In order to respond to this new trend, Caffyns shut down a number of its own branches. At the same time, the company acquired a number of new properties, in order to build larger showrooms capable of handling several different automobile brands. By 2009, the group's operations had been pared back to just 24 locations, primarily in the Sussex and Kent regions. Nonetheless, the company had also boosted its number of franchises, totaling 15 different car makes.

Among the company's new franchises were Jeep, added in 1992; Volvo in 2001; and Daewoo in 2003. In 2005, however, Caffyns was dealt a blow with the collapse of MG Rover, which at the time accounted for 25 percent of Caffyns' total sales. The loss forced the company to sell two of its eight Rover branches, while converting the remaining six to other brands.

By 2008, Caffyns appeared to have overcome the Rover loss, posting revenue of more than £180 million ($260 million). However the company still faced rough roads. In the past decade, a number of large-scale, publicly listed automobile retail groups had sprung up, including Pendragon and Inchape. Caffyns relatively small size left it at a distinct competitive disadvantage.

In this light, the company faced a threat from within, when minority shareholder and "activist investor" Mark Bruce-Smith attempted to stage a shareholders' revolt and force the Caffyn family to sell the company in 2008. The Caffyns resisted the effort. However, the company bore the brunt of the economic collapse that hit Britain and the rest of the world that year. Caffyns' sales plummeted, dropping back to £158 million ($230 million) by the end of the year. The company's profits also tumbled into losses of nearly £4 million. Nonetheless, with more than 100 years in the British automotive market, Caffyns had weathered other storms to remain one of the country's leading regional automobile dealers.

M. L. Cohen

PRINCIPAL SUBSIDIARIES

Caffyns Properties Limited; Caffyns Wessex Limited; Fasthaven Limited.

PRINCIPAL OPERATING UNITS

Accident Repair Centers; Dealerships; Parts Centers.

PRINCIPAL COMPETITORS

Co-operative Group Ltd.; Inchcape PLC; Pendragon PLC; Arnold Clark Automobiles Ltd.; Lookers PLC; Reg Vardy Ltd.; Renault UK Ltd.; Citroën UK Ltd.; Camden Group Services Ltd.; European Motor Holdings Ltd.

FURTHER READING

Bolitho, Nigel, "Caffyns Motors On," *Investors Chronicle,* May 29, 2007.

"Caffyns Back on the Right Road," *Birmingham Post,* May 26, 2007, p. 18.

"Caffyns May Find the Road Ahead a Lot Tougher," *Independent,* November 29, 2002, p. 27.

"Caffyns Reports Full-Year Loss," *RRTNews,* May 29, 2009.

"Caffyns Says Chairman Brian Carte Quits, Names Brian Kirkenhead As Replacement," *AFX UK,* August 8, 2008.

"Deaks Give Caffyns New Energy," *Daily Mail,* June 5, 2004, p. 80.

Hopkins, Gordon, "Caffyns Minimizes MG Rover Demise," *Financial Times,* May 28, 2005, p. 5.

"Jobs Shake-up at Car Dealership," *Eastbourne Herald,* February 10, 2009.

Kavanagh, Michael, "Caffyns Sees Tough Trading," *Financial Times,* May 30, 2008, p. 20.

"Sir Edward Caffyn, Obituary," *Times* (London), June 20, 1990.

Wood, Zoe, "Blogs at Dawn As Investor Wages Web War on Car Firm," *Observer,* July 20, 2008, p. 2.

Canadian Solar Inc.

No. 199 Lushan Road
Suzhou New District
Suzhou, Jiangsu 215129
China
Telephone: (86 512) 5247-7677
Fax: (86 512) 5247-7589
Web site: http://www.csisolar.com

Public Company
Incorporated: 2001
Employees: 4,000
Sales: $709.2 million (2008)
Stock Exchanges: NASDAQ
Ticker Symbol: CSIQ
NAICS: 334413 Semiconductor and Related Device
Manufacturing

■ ■ ■

Canadian Solar Inc. (CSI), despite its name, is a Chinese firm. The company is incorporated in the Province of Ontario, Canada, but its headquarters are in Suzhou, Jiangsu Province, and all of its manufacturing and research facilities are located in the People's Republic of China. Not even a decade old, CSI is one of the leading solar power product makers in the world. Most of the firm's sales are in Europe and almost all of its profits are from solar modules, followed by solar cells and wafers. CSI's solar modules are used for all types of system applications, both on-grid and off-grid, from large-scale solar farms to commercial and residential rooftop systems. The company's specialty products include customized solar modules for GPS tracking systems, car battery chargers, and street, garden, marine, and traffic lights.

CANADIAN IN NAME ONLY

Dr. Shawn (Xiaohua) Qu, a Chinese native, founded Canadian Solar Inc., or CSI, in Ontario, Canada, in October 2001 after spending five years working for various alternative energy businesses in North America, Europe, and Asia. After obtaining a Ph.D. degree in material science from the University of Toronto in 1995, Dr. Qu focused his postdoctorate research on semiconductor optical devices and solar cells. In 1996, he joined Ontario Power Generation Corp. as a solar power research scientist.

From 1998 to 2001, Dr. Qu worked as a product engineer and manager for Ontario-based Automation Tooling Systems, and as technical vice-president of the Asia-Pacific region for its subsidiary, Photowatt International S.A., of France, where he developed extensive experience managing silicon feedstock supply sourcing.

After Dr. Qu incorporated CSI in the Toronto suburb of Markham in October 2001, he began to set up company offices and manufacturing operations in China. In November 2001, the firm created CSI Solar-tronics Co., Ltd., in Changshu, Jiangsu Province. Initially, the affiliate focused primarily on the production of specialty solar modules and products, such as customized solar modules for Carmanah Technologies Corp., which were used to power lights for London bus

COMPANY PERSPECTIVES

Founded in 2001, Canadian Solar Inc. is a vertically integrated manufacturer of solar cell, solar module and custom-designed solar application products serving customers worldwide. Canadian Solar is incorporated in Canada and conducts all of its manufacturing operations in China. Backed by years of experience and knowledge in the solar power market and the silicon industry, Canadian Solar has become a major global provider of solar power products for a wide range of applications.

stops, and solar-powered car battery chargers for Audi-Volkswagen.

ESTABLISHING A NICHE

By the end of 2001, CSI acquired its first turnkey production line for solar modules, and in March 2002 began manufacturing specialty solar modules and products with an initial annual production capacity of 3 megawatts (MW). A one-megawatt plant running continuously at full capacity can power 778 households each year, according to the U.S. Department of Energy.

In 2002, CSI landed its first solar power development project. In conjunction with the Canadian International Development Agency and the government of China, CSI began a three-year, CAD 1.8 million "Solar Electrification for Western China" project designed to bring solar power generation to rural areas of China. Also in 2002, CSI established its first production line for silicon ingots and wafers, essential supply chain items for solar cell and module production.

In August 2003, CSI created its second subsidiary, CSI Solar Technologies Inc., in Suzhou, Jiangsu Province. The affiliate was set up for research and development of solar module products, which accounted for 97.5 percent of the company's $4.1 million in revenues for 2003. At the end of the year, the company had 89 employees and a net income of $761,245.

SHIFTING GEARS

Although CSI more than tripled its sales of solar module products from 0.7 MW in 2003 to 2.2 MW in 2004, its gross margin decreased from 42.3 percent to 33.2 percent. The change reflected a significant shift in the company's product mix from specialty to standard solar modules, as well as an increase in silicon feedstock and solar cell prices.

In January 2005, the firm opened a second Suzhou facility and its third subsidiary, CSI Solar Manufacture Inc. The new factory was set up for production of standard solar modules. June 2005 marked the completion of the company's participation in the "Solar Electrification for Western China" project. Also in June, CSI was selected by Volkswagen as its main supplier of solar-powered car battery chargers.

During 2005, CSI began providing recycled silicon feedstock for Deutsche Solar, a subsidiary of Solar World Group of Germany, to turn into wafers in a toll manufacturing arrangement. CSI ended 2005 with 196 employees and a $3.8 million profit on net revenues of $18.3 million, up more than fivefold since 2003. Solar module product sales in 2005 almost doubled from 2004 to 4.1 MW due to a significant increase in sales to Germany and Spain.

PUMPING, PRIMPING, AND GOING PUBLIC

The firm incorporated its fourth subsidiary, CSI Central Solar Power Co., Ltd., or CSI Luoyang, in Luoyang City, Henan Province, in February 2006. The Luoyang factory was set up to manufacture solar modules, ingots, and wafers. CSI's fifth affiliate was incorporated in June 2006. CSI Solarchip International Co., Ltd. (later renamed CSI Cells Co., Ltd.), was established in Suzhou to produce solar cells.

In August 2006, CSI founded its sixth subsidiary in China. CSI Advanced Solar Inc., located in Changshu, was also set up to produce solar modules. As of August 2006, CSI Luoyang, CSI Solarchip, and CSI Advanced had not actually begun manufacturing operations but were awaiting capital as well as necessary operating permits.

On November 9, 2006, CSI began trading on the NASDAQ Global Exchange under the ticker symbol "CSIQ." CSI and other stockholders offered 7.7 million shares at the price of $15 a share, which represented a 28 percent stake in the company. The company netted $83.2 million, and as a result of the transaction, founder, Chairman, President, and CEO Qu reduced his stake in CSI from 65.2 percent to 50.14 percent.

THE EUROPEAN CONNECTION

In early January 2007, the firm announced a distribution and sales agreement with Amur Energy Division, of Spain, for delivery of up to $50 million of CSI's solar modules in 2007. Also in January, in an expansion of an

```
┌─────────────────────────────────────────────┐
│                                               │
│              KEY DATES                        │
│                 ■                             │
│                                               │
│  2001:  Dr. Shawn Qu incorporates Canadian    │
│         Solar; firm creates subsidiary CSI    │
│         Solartronics to produce specialty     │
│         solar modules.                        │
│  2003:  CSI Solar Technologies Inc., an R&D   │
│         subsidiary, is founded in Suzhou,     │
│         Jiangsu Province.                     │
│  2005:  Another Suzhou facility, CSI Solar    │
│         Manufacture Inc., opens to make       │
│         standard solar modules.               │
│  2006:  The firm's November IPO on the        │
│         NASDAQ nets $83.2 million; Qu         │
│         retains majority ownership.           │
│  2007:  CSI Cells Co., Ltd., created in 2006, │
│         opens Suzhou solar cell plant.        │
│  2008:  CSI Advanced Solar, formed in 2006,   │
│         begins module production at new       │
│         Changshu factory.                     │
│                                               │
└─────────────────────────────────────────────┘
```

existing relationship, Deutsche Solar agreed to supply CSI with approximately EUR 180 million of silicon wafers over a 12-year period. CSI closed the month with a sale of up to $40 million of solar modules to pro solar Solarstrom GmbH in Germany.

By the end of the first quarter of 2007, CSI had its first 25 MW solar cell production line up and running. In April, the company completed its second 25 MW manufacturing line and celebrated the grand opening of the Suzhou solar cell factory. At the same time, the firm inked a deal to obtain up to $60 million of solar cells by year's end from JA Solar Holdings Co. Ltd., of China's Hebei Province.

In May 2007, the company started building a new 250 MW module factory in Changshu. In June 2007, CSI began delivery of 31 MW of solar modules to Germany's Solar City AG as part of a $122 million contract to supply projects in Germany and Spain, most of which were scheduled for completion in 2007. With almost 90 percent of sales revenue coming from primarily Germany and Spain, and the other 10 percent from South America, the company incorporated CSI Solar Inc., in Delaware, in June 2007, and in August opened an office in Phoenix, Arizona, for an increased marketing presence in the United States.

RAMPING UP

In August 2007, the company started construction of its Luoyang silicon ingot and wafer plant, with a projected annual output capacity of 3,000 tons. In mid-November 2007, one year after going public, CSI's share price climbed 48 percent to around $16 in one week after the company reported a fivefold increase in third quarter revenue to $97.4 million from $17.8 million in 2006. The rally was helped by a November contract to sell an additional 60 MW of solar modules to German City Solar Group for a solar power station in Spain.

In late November 2007, the company agreed to buy 25 MW of solar cells from China Sunergy Co., and 22 MW from Gintech Energy Corporation, of Taiwan. By December 2007, CSI said it had four solar cell production lines operating with a total annual manufacturing capacity of 100 MW. As 2007 came to an end, the company had 2,700 employees and an annual manufacturing capacity for solar modules of 180 MW.

In January 2008, CSI more than doubled its total annual solar module production capacity to 400 MW when it opened its new Changshu solar module facility. With its own crystal and silicon wafer plant still under construction, CSI in February 2008 signed four more solar wafer supply contracts. The deals provided for 12 MW of wafers to be delivered by the summer and a long-term agreement with Jiangsu Shunda Group Corporation for more than 700 MW of wafers over an eight-year period.

SURGING SALES

As reported by the firm in March 2008, net revenues for 2007 skyrocketed 344 percent to $302.8 million, compared to $68.2 million for 2006. The report boosted CSI share price 20 percent to around $21, and temporarily reversed a 30 percent decline in company stock that started at the beginning of 2008. Company stock surged more than 28 percent to over $43 in mid-day trading on May 12, 2008, after CSI topped Wall Street estimates with a first-quarter net income of $19 million, or 61 cents a share, on revenue of $171.2 million.

In June 2008, CSI inked a five-year $500 million contract to obtain several hundred megawatts of solar cells from Neo Solar Power, of Taiwan, a supplier for the firm since March 2007. At the same time, CSI secured 5,000 metric tons of solar-grade silicon in a three-year contract with Toronto-based Timminco Ltd., also a supplier since early 2007.

In the summer of 2008, CSI rolled out e-Modules, which it touted as an advanced technology solar module. In mid-June, the firm made its first delivery of the new product to pro solar Solarstrom GmbH and Il-iotec Solar GmbH of Germany. CSI closed the month with a ten-year 800 MW wafer supply contract with LDK Solar.

EXCEEDING EXPECTATIONS

In July 2008, CSI expanded its geographic customer base, which already included Germany, Spain, the United States, South Korea, and China, with five new sales agreements for standard solar modules in Italy and the Czech Republic. Mid-July brought a 12-month 9 MW sales agreement for the company's e-Modules with Conergy USA. On July 23, CSI raised $112.7 million in a follow-on public offering of 3.5 million shares at $34 a share.

August 2008 brought another quarterly financial report that exceeded market expectations. Revenue for the second quarter rose to $212.6 million from $60.4 million a year earlier, with sales in Europe more than tripling from $57.3 million to $188.3 million. However, CSI stock, which was trading around $30 per share, fell 11 percent on the company's revised 2009 shipping outlook. August also marked the completion of the second phase of the company's solar cells production plan, which added another 150 MW of annual manufacturing capacity.

In September 2008, China-based GCL Silicon Technology Holdings Inc. agreed to supply CSI with 510 metric tons of high-purity polysilicon feedstock in 2008 and 2009 and up to 1.8 GW of wafers from 2010 to 2015. Like other solar power product companies, CSI saw its share price in September undergo a steady and significant decline due to a growing global financial crisis. The whole solar sector rebounded briefly in late September after the U.S. Senate voted to extend solar tax credits worth $18 billion for renewable energy.

In October 2008, CSI announced the completion of the first phase of its Luoyang ingot and wafer plant, with an initial annual manufacturing capacity of 60 MW. The month also brought more solar module sales to German companies: two contracts totaling 48 MW with Iliotec Solar International and another deal for 60 MW to Systaic AG.

LOWERING EXPECTATIONS

As reported by CSI on November 20, 2008, third-quarter revenue of $252 million more than doubled from the previous year. However, profits amounted to only 31 cents per share instead of the expected 54 cents, and company stock closed the day at $3.78 per share. Citing a tightened credit market and decreasing demand for solar products in Europe and the United States, the firm lowered its guidance for fourth-quarter sales to between $70 million and $85 million, far below the $270.1 million that analysts were expecting. CSI also lowered sales projections for 2008 from between $850 million and $970 million to a range of $650 million to $750 million, also far below analyst expectations of $901.9 million.

In a January 2009 visit to Los Angeles, CSI Chairman and CEO Qu said the company, along with another unnamed Chinese solar power firm, would invest RMB 3.3 billion in California over the next decade to make solar power more accessible to local residents. Dr. Qu also announced it was moving its U.S. head office and customer center to San Ramon, California. Back in Suzhou, CSI joined a partnership with DuPont, the University of Toronto, and Shanghai Jiao Tong University, and consolidated all of its research and development facilities in a new $10 million solar cell engineering technology research facility.

On February 17, 2009, the company pre-announced 2008 fourth-quarter financial results, saying that it expected to formally report revenues of $66 million to $71 million and a negative gross margin in mid-March. The news drove CSI's market value even lower, and on March 9, company stock closed at what was an all-time low of $3.

POISED FOR RECOVERY

On March 17, CSI officially posted a net loss of $50.6 million, or $1.42 a share, on revenues of only $73 million for the last quarter of 2008. Revenue from Europe fell 54 percent but sales in North America jumped to $6.4 million from $500,000, and sales in Asia more than tripled to $9.6 million. Combined, sales in North America and Asia made up 22 percent of revenue, up from only 2.7 percent a year earlier.

For fiscal 2008, the firm reported a net loss of $10 million, or 32 cents a share, on revenues of $709.2 million. CSI also revised its solar module shipping guidance for 2009 to 300 MW to 350 MW and said it expected revenue of $600 million to $800 million for the year. The firm ended 2008 with $136 million in cash, accounts receivables of $50.6 million, and a debt to equity ratio of 47 percent.

In early April 2009, CSI won a bid to supply 80,000 solar home systems for rural households in Sichuan Province. The 1.6 MW rural electrification project was initiated and financed by China's Ministry of Agriculture and the Sichuan Provincial Government. April also brought a 5 MW solar module purchase agreement from Helio Micro Utility, of Berkeley, California.

As May 2009 began, Dr. Qu told the press that CSI's shipping and revenue guidance assumed improved global economic conditions in the second half of the year. Having obtained a credit facility of $2.2 billion from three Chinese banks in late April, and with approximately 262 MW of projected 2009 module sales secured by contracts and an additional 190 MW in the near-term contract pipeline, the company appeared stable enough to tough it out and remain competitive in a very hostile economic environment.

Ted Sylvester

PRINCIPAL SUBSIDIARIES

CSI Solartronics Co., Ltd.; CSI Solar Technologies Inc.; CSI Solar Manufacture Inc.; CSI Central Solar Power Co., Ltd.; CSI Cells Co., Ltd.; CSI Advanced Solar Inc.; CSI Solar Inc. (USA).

PRINCIPAL COMPETITORS

BP Solar; Suntech Power Holdings Co., Ltd.; Renewable Energy Corporation ASA; Sharp Corporation; SunPower Corporation; LDK Solar Co., Ltd.; Trina Solar Limited; SolarWorld AG; Solarfun Power Holdings Co., Ltd.; First Solar, Inc.; Yingli Green Energy Holding Company Limited.

FURTHER READING

Alpert, Bill, "China's Solar Boom Loses Its Luster," *Barron's,* October 8, 2007, p. 22.

Ball, Yvonne, "IPO Outlook: Deals & Deal Makers: Ten IPOs from China Set Record," *Wall Street Journal,* June 11, 2007, p. C5.

Blackwell, Richard, "Profit, Sales Data Energize Canadian Solar Shares," *Globe and Mail,* May 14, 2008, p. B15.

Bogoslaw, David, "Solar Stocks Get Their Day in the Sun," *BusinessWeek Online,* January 3, 2008.

Chen, Kevin, "Gintech Energy Inks Deal with Canadian Solar," *Taipei Times,* November 28, 2007.

"CSI Launched Long Crystal & Silicon Chip Project," *China Chemical Reporter,* October 6, 2007.

Gage, Jack, "High Energy Stocks; Demand for Energy Has Made It the Hottest Industry on Wall Street," *Forbes,* June 16, 2008.

Gold, Donald H., "Once-Powerful Solar Stocks Take a Beating," *Investor's Business Daily,* July 3, 2008.

Gupta, Swagata, "Canadian Solar Wins Contract in Spain; Shares Rise," *Reuters News,* November 16, 2007.

Jennemann, Tom, "Timminco Agrees to Provide Canadian Solar with Silicon," *American Metal Market,* June 2, 2008.

Kamalakaran, Ajay, "Canadian Solar Q1 Profit Tops Estimates, Shares Soar," *Reuters News,* May 13, 2008.

"Q1 2007 Canadian Solar Inc. Earnings Conference Call—Final," *Voxant FD WIRE,* May 14, 2007.

"Sales Brighten for Solar Power Equipment Firm," *Shanghai Daily,* July 3, 2007.

Savitz, Eric J., "Prospects of Rain in Spain Make for Gloomy Solar Week," *Barron's,* July 28, 2008, p. 27.

"Solar Energy Still Seeing a Bright Future," *Shanghai Daily,* June 10, 2008.

Spencer, Jane, "China Solar Stocks Shine in U.S., but Some Could Be Overheated," *Wall Street Journal Asia,* May 23, 2007, p. 21.

Taylor, Sophie, "Canadian Solar Aims to Boost Staff by a Third," *Reuters News,* January 17, 2008.

Tracy, Tennille, "Traders Bet on Sustained Rally in Solar Cos," *Dow Jones Newswires,* March 26, 2009.

Wang, Terry, "Facing a Declining Overseas Market, Chinese PV Product Makers Need Govt Support—CSI CEO," *Interfax: China Energy Newswire,* December 12, 2008.

Canlan Ice Sports Corp.

———■———

6501 Sprott Street
Burnaby, British Columbia V5B 3B8
Canada
Telephone: (604) 736-9152
Fax: (604) 736-9170
Web site: http://www.icesports.com

Public Company
Incorporated: 1956 as Burrard Mortgage Investments Ltd.
Employees: 950
Sales: CAD 64.66 million (2008)
Stock Exchanges: Toronto
Ticker Symbol: ICE
NAICS: 713940 Fitness and Recreational Sports Centers

■ ■ ■

Canlan Ice Sports Corp. is the largest owner and operator of private-sector ice sports facilities in North America. The company owns, leases, or manages 22 facilities in the United States and Canada that house 63 full-sized ice sheets, two indoor soccer fields, and three curling surfaces. Of the 22 facilities, the company owns 11, leases five, and manages six for third-party owners. Canlan organizes and hosts tournaments, leagues, and youth camps at its facilities, enjoying its greatest success with the Adult Safe Hockey League, the largest adult recreational hockey league in North America, comprising more than 50,000 players. Other programs offered by the company include a hockey academy, a skating academy, indoor soccer leagues, and a slo-pitch softball

league. Canlan generates more than 70 percent of its revenue from ice-time rental and registration and enrollment fees collected from its leagues, tournaments, and camps. One-fifth of the company's revenue is derived from the restaurants and lounges operating within the ice facilities. Canlan collects approximately 3 percent of its revenue from stores housed within its facilities that sell hockey, skating, and soccer equipment and apparel.

ORIGINS

Canlan developed its expertise in owning and managing ice rink facilities after spending decades in the real estate business. The company was incorporated in British Columbia in 1956 under the name Burrard Mortgage Investments Ltd. The Canlan name first appeared in 1978, when Burrard Mortgage Investments adopted the corporate title of Canlan Investment Corporation. The change in strategic focus occurred 20 years later, when executives at the Vancouver, British Columbia-based company resolved to become the premier operator of recreational ice facilities in North America.

The turning point in Canlan's development occurred in July 1997, two years before it adopted Canlan Ice Sports Corp. as its corporate title. In 1997, Canlan was generating CAD 78 million in revenue, collecting CAD 43 million of the total from its real estate division. For years, the company had been involved in developing real estate in Vancouver, Seattle, Washington, and Portland, Oregon. Canlan leased commercial space and warehouses that ranged between 16,000 square feet and 75,000 square feet and it developed single-family lots, condominiums, and townhouses. Its flagship development project was the Morgan Creek Golf Course, located 45 minutes from Vancouver. The focal point of the project was an 18-hole golf course that opened in 1995. Around the golf course, Canlan was developing 514 single-family lots and 383 luxury townhouses.

The company's smaller division, responsible for CAD 29 million of the CAD 78 million collected in revenue in 1997, represented its future. The ice rink division comprised a dozen recreational facilities in Canada and the United States. Canlan owned and, in one case, managed properties in Quebec, Ontario, Manitoba, Saskatchewan, and British Columbia. The company also held interests in two facilities in the United States, a two-rink complex in Wichita, Kansas, and a two-rink complex in Stamford, Connecticut, both of which opened in late 1996. Its largest facility, the aptly named Ice Sports 8-Rinks facility in Burnaby, British Columbia, operated eight rinks in 225,000 square feet of space. The division also included programs offered by Canlan in the facilities it owned or managed, none more important than the Adult Safe Hockey League, or ASHL. The ASHL consisted of more than 1,600 teams in Canada in 1997, figuring as the most important component of the company's program offerings at its facilities.

CANLAN COMMITS TO ICE SPORTS

The decision to shutter its real estate division and to focus its resources on the acquisition, development, and operation of multi-sheet ice rink facilities meant that the company was reducing its size by more than half. It would be years before Canlan equaled the revenue volume it had recorded as a company involved in both

real estate and ice rink ownership and management. Grant Ballantyne, Canlan's future chief executive officer, explained the crucible management faced in the mid-1990s. "The company at the time needed to decide what business it was in and decided to be in the ice sports business," he said in the January–February issue of *US Business Review*. "The company wasn't as ideally suited to be in real estate development so we exited that side of the business. It was a fairly substantial cost at the time, getting rid of our investments in real estate."

Canlan ceased any new commitments related to real estate in 1997 and began divesting its existing properties, Morgan Creek included. "Canlan will sell its revenue property portfolio as opportunities arise and redeploy resources to the ice rink expansion program," the company explained in its 1997 annual filing with the Canadian Securities Administrators. The company entered a restructuring period that concluded with the appointment of Ballantyne as chief executive officer and Mike Gellard as vice-president of finance in January 2001. Frank Barker, the departing chief executive officer, announced the leadership changes in a statement published in the May 2, 2001 issue of *Market News Publishing*. "These changes reflect the company's new direction and mark the completion of a three-year program to restructure the company's finances and management. The board and I are very satisfied with the job Grant and Mike have done for the company the past few years and feel that it is time for me to step away and let the operators operate."

Ballantyne, a chartered accountant with an undergraduate degree in economics from Waterloo Lutheran University, joined Canlan in 1998. He was hired as the company's vice-president of operations, joining the company while it was in the midst of disposing of its real estate assets. Ballantyne earned a promotion to president and chief operating officer before beginning his tenure as chief executive officer.

BALLANTYNE SPEARHEADS EXPANSION

Ballantyne's singular focus as the principal executive at Canlan was to make the company the dominant competitor in the ice rink industry in North America. Expansion was achieved within months of his appointment, as Canlan increased its presence in the United States. In May 2001, the company signed a contract with the City of Danbury, Connecticut, a municipality whose efforts to build an ice rink had become an exercise in frustration. The original developer of the facility became mired in financial difficulties, leaving the two-rink project partly built. For three years, Danbury officials solicited bids to complete the project, but each

KEY DATES

1956: Canlan is incorporated under the name Burrard Mortgage Investments Ltd.

1978: Burrard Mortgage changes its name to Canlan Investment Corporation.

1997: Canlan Investments decides to exit the real estate business and focus exclusively on owning and operating ice sports facilities.

1999: Canlan Investment changes its name to Canlan Ice Sports Corp.

2001: Grant Ballantyne is named chief executive officer.

2005: Registration in the Adult Safe Hockey League reaches 40,000 players.

2008: Canlan begins managing Vineland Ice Arena in Vineland, New Jersey.

2009: Canlan begins managing the McMillen Ice Arena in Fort Wayne, Indiana.

bid was far beyond what the city was willing to pay. Canlan stepped in, offering to complete the project for $2.9 million, less than half the price of competing bids, and was awarded the contract, drawing praise from Danbury's mayor, Gene Enriquez. "On reviewing the field of eligible contractors we felt conclusively that Canlan Ice Sports displayed a level of construction expertise that stood head and shoulders above the others in the industry," he said in the May 7, 2001 issue of *Market News Publishing.*

At the same time Canlan was awarded the Danbury project, the company's management services division achieved further success in the United States. Canlan was asked to manage two facilities in the greater St. Louis, Missouri, area. The company assumed operational control over a three-rink complex in Chesterfield, Missouri, that the National Hockey League's St. Louis Blues used as a practice facility. Canlan also began managing a two-rink facility in Fairview Heights, Illinois.

Back in Canada, Canlan built on its lead as the largest owner and operator of private sector ice sports facilities in North America. In April 2002, the company signed a joint venture agreement with P.M. Bull & Company Ltd., a Vancouver-based company involved in acquiring and developing commercial properties in British Columbia and Alberta. The two companies announced they would acquire and manage a two-rink facility in Langley, British Columbia. P.M. Bull agreed

to upgrade the facility, which housed National Hockey League–sized rinks, dressing rooms, a retail shop, and centers for physiotherapy and orthotics. P.M. Bull committed to improving the ice quality at the facility and re-opening a sports bar and restaurant located on the second floor. Canlan took over management of the 90,000-square-foot property, which began operating under the name "Canlan Ice Sports—Langley Twin Rinks."

PROGRAMS CENTRAL TO SUCCESS

The addition of new facilities, either through ownership or management contacts, drove Canlan's financial growth, but Ballantyne was well aware of the vital importance the company's programming efforts played in the company's financial health. Between 2000 and 2005, the company revenues increased from CAD 39.5 million to CAD 48.7 million, growth that Ballantyne credited to the company's efforts on offering attractive programming. "The important thing was identifying the fact that our success was dependent on two key components," he said in the January–February issue of *US Business Review.* "First, we understood that the thing that makes us unique is that our key product is really the programs we operate within our facilities, and that we needed to focus our efforts on developing quality, internally owned and branded programs. We then take a proactive approach to the way we market these programs into the communities—that's our core philosophy and the reason for the growth we've seen in the last four or five years."

By 2005, Canlan offered a host of leagues, tournaments, and camps at the 20 facilities it owned or managed. The company's branded programs included the Youth Hockey League, Camp Canlan, Canlan Ice Sports Hockey Academy, and Canlan Ice Sports Skating Academy, but its flagship brand continued to be the ASHL, which comprised more than 3,000 teams and 40,000 players by 2005. As the league's organizer, Canlan made sure the games took place on time and provided timekeepers and referees. Each year, the company paid to fly players to Montreal, Vancouver, or Toronto to participate in the ASHL's national championships.

Solid revenue growth highlighted Canlan's progress during the years immediately following 2005. By 2008, a decade after the company had committed itself exclusively to ice sports, revenues reached CAD 64.6 million. During the year, the company increased its involvement in the United States, agreeing in September to manage the operation of New Jersey-based Vineland Ice Arena. "Expanding into strategic U.S. markets is a key component of our long-term growth plan," Ballantyne said in the September 30, 2008 issue of *CNW Group*. Under the terms of the lease-to-own agreement, Canlan began leasing the facility for a period of up to 52 months, at which point it would be given the option to purchase the two-rink facility.

THE CANLAN PORTFOLIO OF FACILITIES

The addition of the property in Vineland was followed in 2009 by another management contract, an agreement to take over the operation of the McMillen Ice Arena in Fort Wayne, Indiana. Canlan began managing the three-rink property in May. The McMillen Ice Arena became the third property Canlan managed in the United States—its management contracts with properties in Kansas, Missouri, and Illinois had expired. The company's third property in the United States was a two-rink complex in Monroe, Michigan, owned by the City of Monroe and managed by Canlan under a contract scheduled to expire at the end of 2010.

In Canada, Canlan maintained a far more comprehensive presence than it did in the United States. The company collected the greatest percentage of its annual revenue, 50 percent, from its six facilities in Ontario. Canlan owned the Ice Sports Etobicoke in Etobicoke, which contained four National Hockey League–sized rinks, a licensed restaurant, and a sports store. It owned the Ice Sports York in Toronto, leasing the land it occupied under a long-term land-lease agreement with York University. The facility featured five National Hockey League–sized rinks, one Olympic-sized surface, a licensed restaurant, and a retail store. The company owned Ice Sports Oakville in Oakville, containing four National Hockey League–sized rinks, a licensed restaurant, and a sports store. Canlan owned Ice Sports Scarborough in Scarborough, a facility with four National Hockey League–sized rinks, a licensed restaurant, and a sports store. The fifth company-owned facility in Ontario was Ice Sports Oshawa in Oshawa, housing two National Hockey League–sized rinks, a licensed restaurant, and a retail store. Canlan leased its sixth property in Ontario, Ice Sports Victoria Park, a two-rink complex in Toronto.

Canlan generated 26 percent of its annual revenue from its six facilities in British Columbia. The company owned only one of the properties in the province, its largest, Ice Sports 8-Rinks in Burnaby, where the company had moved its main offices after leaving Vancouver. Canlan managed the five other facilities in British Columbia. Ice Sports North Shore was a complex in North Vancouver featuring three National Hockey League–sized rinks, a licensed restaurant and lounge, and a sports store. Ice Sports Langley Twin Rinks in Langley contained two National Hockey League–sized rinks, a licensed restaurant and lounge, and a sports store. South Cariboo Recreation Centre in 100 Mile House housed one National Hockey League–sized rink, three curling surfaces, and food and beverage concession outlets. The Prospera Centre in Chilliwack contained two National Hockey League–sized rinks and food and beverage concession outlets. The Armstrong/Spallumcheen Parks & Recreation facility in Armstrong housed one rink, rodeo fairgrounds, baseball diamonds, and a swimming pool, all under Canlan's management.

The remaining 25 percent of Canlan's annual revenue was derived from its activities in Alberta, Saskatchewan, Manitoba, New Brunswick, and Quebec. Through a wholly owned subsidiary, Iceplex 2000 Ltd., Canlan owned three facilities in Saskatchewan: Ice Sports Jemini in Saskatoon, a four-rink complex; Ice Sports Agriplace in Saskatoon, a two-rink facility; and Ice Sports Regina in Regina, a two-rink complex. Each of the Saskatchewan facilities featured National Hockey League standard ice surfaces, licensed restaurants and sports stores. In Alberta, Canlan managed River Cree Twin Rinks in Enoch, a two-rink facility attached to a casino-hotel complex. In Manitoba, Canlan owned Ice Sports Winnipeg in Winnipeg, a facility housing three National Hockey League–sized rinks, one indoor soccer field, a licensed restaurant, and a sports store. In New Brunswick, Canlan managed Campbellton Memorial Civic Center, overseeing one National Hockey League–sized rink, an Olympic-sized rink, a fitness center, a swimming pool, a licensed restaurant, and a sports store. Canlan owned two facilities in Quebec: Les 4 Glaces, which housed four National Hockey League–sized rinks, a licensed restaurant, and a sports store; and Ice Sports Candiac, which contained two National Hockey League standard ice surfaces, a licensed restaurant, and a sports store.

Jeffrey L. Covell

PRINCIPAL SUBSIDIARIES

Canlan Ice Sports (USA) Corp.; Canlan Management Services Ltd.; Iceplex 2000 Ltd.; Les Quatre Glaces (1994) Inc.

PRINCIPAL DIVISIONS

Management Services.

PRINCIPAL COMPETITORS

Premier & Curzons Fitness Clubs; Comcast Spectacor, L.P.; YMCA of the USA.

FURTHER READING

"Canlan Ice Sports Corp.," *Market News Publishing*, May 2, 2001.

"Canlan Ice Sports Corp.," *Market News Publishing*, May 7, 2001.

"Canlan Ice Sports Corp.," *Market News Publishing*, April 30, 2002.

"Canlan Ice Sports Expands U.S. Operations," *CNW Group*, September 30, 2008.

Srinivasan, Kirsten, "Eye on the Puck," *US Business Review*, January–February 2005, p. 200.

Capital City Bank Group, Inc.

---

217 North Monroe Street
Tallahassee, Florida 32301
U.S.A.
Telephone: (850) 402-7000
Toll Free: (888) 671-0400
Fax: (850) 878-9150
Web site: http://www.ccbg.com

Public Company
Incorporated: 1982
Employees: 1,097
Total Assets: $2.48 billion (2008)
Stock Exchanges: NASDAQ
Ticker Symbol: CCBG
NAICS: 551111 Offices of Bank Holding Companies;
   522110 Commercial Banking

∎∎∎

Capital City Bank Group, Inc., with nearly $2.5 billion in assets, ranks as one of the largest publicly traded financial services companies based in Florida. Subsidiary Capital City Bank engages in commercial and retail banking, operating 68 locations and 80 ATMs, in its home state and in neighboring Georgia and Alabama. The bank offers a full range of services including deposit and credit, asset management, trust, mortgage banking, merchant, bank card, data processing, and securities brokerage services. The company declined an infusion of government funds intended to stabilize the industry undercut by the mortgage market collapse. Capital City

Bank Group's top executive and his brother are major shareholders.

BANKING BEGINNINGS: 1895–1975

George W. Saxon founded Capital City Bank on March 20, 1895, upon receipt of a state charter. The dry goods store-owner had been making loans to Tallahassee-area farmers for a number of years. In just over three months, the city's first bank claimed deposits of $41,000 and held resources of $84,000. It operated out of a single location and had five directors and three associates.

The bank's ties to Tallahassee continued to strengthen in the early decades of the 20th century. A $10,000 loan to the city, in 1917, established it as "the community's bank." Capital City Bank continued to grow even as other Florida banks failed during the volatile 1920s and 1930s.

The United States' entry into World War II changed countless individual lives and businesses. Godfrey Smith, the president of the start-up Industrial Bank and the son of one of the Capital City directors, was called upon to serve his country in 1941. In response, "the comptroller allowed the Bank to pay off investors, liquidate assets, and temporarily close until 1946 when hostilities ceased."

The bank, riding the wave of postwar regional growth, changed its name to Capital City First National Bank in 1963. Four years later, Capital City Second National Bank was formed under a new charter.

COMPANY PERSPECTIVES

Capital City is unique because we focus on communities where banks can make a difference—and where bankers make a difference. Our associates live in these communities. We coach softball, serve on the city council, and participate in the Rotary Club. Because we have a personal stake in the communities we serve, we are eager to support our hometown neighbors and businesses. When you walk through our doors, you can bank on knowledgeable, caring and nice associates to help you with your financial needs.

Bank director and great-grandson of the founder DuBose Ausley joined forces with Godfrey Smith in the 1970s to develop a new concept for the bank. Capital City Bank Group, formed in 1975, established a common board of directors over a number of local banks. In five years, the "Capital City family" had grown to "13 banks, 17 offices, and eight Bank N' Shop outlets."

UNDER ONE ROOF: 1982–96

Capital City Bank Group, Inc., was established in December 1982, to acquire five national banks and one state bank. The six subsequently operated as part of Florida-chartered subsidiary Capital City Bank.

William G. "Bill" Smith succeeded his father, Godfrey Smith, as president, in 1989, ending a stay with the company that spanned more than a half century. The younger Smith brought in Tom Barron, head of Second National and Industrial National Bank, "to serve alongside him." The pair faced an environment rocked by the savings and loan crisis.

By the mid-1990s, smaller healthy independent Florida community banks garnered the attention of growth-hungry institutions. With many of the larger banks and thrifts already off the market, operations such as Capital City Group started looking inviting. "Most of these banks are attractive because they have a good franchise," Samuel Beebe, vice-president of Tampa's Robert W. Baird & Co. brokerage firm, said in *American Banker.* "They don't have any terminal asset-quality problems. That's all behind them." Florida's positive demographics generated in-state mergers and acquisitions and drew out-of-state suitors, elevating the demand for, and the asking price of, banks.

Capital City Bank Group posted an earnings increase of 7.1 percent at year-end 1994, to $8.8

million. In January 1995, seven Tallahassee-area banks merged into Capital City Bank, clarifying its identity. While the consolidation enhanced marketing, it brought some initial costs that temporarily cut into earnings. Capital City Bank Group also held small-town banks in both Chiefland and Trenton, located southwest of Gainesville, and one in Branford, located northwest of Gainesville near the Suwannee River.

Capital City Bank Group expanded into the counties of Madison and Taylor, east of Tallahassee, and into Hernando and Pasco, north of Tampa, with the purchase of First Federal Bank, in 1996. The $20 million deal positioned Capital City Bank Group to capitalize on the expected migration of south Floridians north along the Gulf Coast, according to *Knight-Ridder/ Tribune Business News.*

The acquisition broadened Capital City Bank Group's service area to 11 counties extending west of Tallahassee to north of Tampa. The purchase increased Capital City's assets to nearly $1 billion and the number of banking offices to 37. Smith eyed north-central Florida counties along I-75 and along U.S. 27 and I-10 for future expansion, Fred A. Schneyer reported.

Ongoing financial industry consolidation played a role in precipitating the expansion drive. "It makes our vision of staying independent at least as secure if not more secure," Capital City Bank President Tom Barron told Schneyer. "It shows that a company of our size can marshal the resources to do this purchase." Other potential merger benefits included a bump to profits, market diversification, and increased efficiencies.

BEYOND FLORIDA: 1999–2004

In 1999, Capital City Bank Group moved into southwest Georgia with the acquisition of Grady Holding Co. of Cairo. The deal was accomplished through a "pooling of interests," according to *American Banker,* valued at $31 million. Capital City would issue 21.5 shares of its common stock for each share of the $114 million-asset Grady Holding. Subsidiary First National Bank of Grady County held market leadership in its home county.

The following year, the Florida-based bank group announced its pending entry into Alabama, through a $17.3 million stock and cash deal for First Bankshares of West Point Inc., located in Georgia. Subsidiary First National Bank of West Point operated one bank in West Point and two in Valley, Alabama, on the other side of the Chattahoochee River dividing the two states. First Bankshares held $155 million in assets.

Despite the economic downturn following the attacks of September 11, 2001, Capital City Bank Group

KEY DATES

1975: Local banks join forces under common directors.
1982: Capital City Bank Group, Inc., is incorporated in Florida.
1995: All banks assume Capital City name.
1999: Florida-based bank enters Georgia.
2000: Alabama is next on the list.
2004: Company sets earnings target of $50 million by 2010.
2007: New focus is placed on higher growth metro areas.
2008: Troubled economic conditions hurt earnings.

produced strong earnings in 2002. "Capital City's stock enjoyed its best yearly performance in the company's glorious 108-year history," Smith announced to shareholders. "I hope you don't grow to expect those kinds of returns annually, but it won't keep us from trying." Diversified economies such as those Capital City served had fared better, thus far, than more populous areas with major corporate ties, *Knight-Ridder Tribune Business News* reported.

Mortgage lending rose 13 percent during 2002, exceeding $310 million in home loans. Assets under management also increased and generated greater fee revenue. Capital City added branches during the year upon the completion of the First Bankshares acquisition. Smith benefited from the company's performance: his profitability-based bonuses increased 174 percent to $437,648. His base salary climbed 11 percent to $175,000.

Capital City Bank Group held $2.4 billion in assets at the mid-point of the decade. The company had begun seeking banks in the range of $100 million to $400 million in assets in areas adjacent to major Florida, Georgia, and Alabama markets, according to *American Banker.*

During 2004, Capital City Bank Group acquired $127 million-asset Quincy State Bank in the Florida panhandle and $390 million-asset Farmers and Merchants Bank in Dublin, Georgia. In February 2005, the financial company announced a deal to acquire $229 million-asset First Alchua Banking Corp., located in suburban Gainesville.

The banking operation posted record earnings of $29.4 million in 2004, a jump of more than 17 percent year-over-year. A goal of $50 million in earnings by

2010 was set, balanced slightly more heavily on organic growth as opposed to growth via acquisition.

"We are in predictable markets with very steady growth that are not that exciting," Smith told *American Banker* in February 2005. "If you've been to any of our Florida markets, you were probably not on vacation, but lost."

BANKING ON GROWTH: 2005–08

One of its unexciting markets, producing slow but consistent growth, was the developing area of northwest Florida. Capital City Bank Group had established itself in locales in which it could rank among the leaders, influencing service standards and pricing. It held the top spot in the Tallahassee metropolitan area, with close to 20 percent of deposits, and second place in Levy County on the northwest coast of Florida, with 34 percent of deposits, according to *American Banker.* Income from existing branches was expected to climb 7 to 9 percent per year. Some modest new branch building was planned in markets entered through acquisition.

Capital City Bank Group posted earnings of $33.3 million in 2006, but souring economic conditions factored into a decline the following year. Earnings fell to $29.7 million in 2007; the slowing housing and real estate markets were contributing factors, according to its annual report. Capital City Bank Group, nevertheless, was able to repurchase more than $1.4 million shares and pay out a dividend of more than $12 million.

To withstand the challenging circumstances, the company mitigated the effects of Federal Reserve cuts on its interest rate margins; maintained the in-flow of low-cost core deposits; and managed credit risks. The banking group also benefited from revenue diversification. Non-interest income, as a percentage of operating revenue, exceeded that of its peer group. Finally, cost controls implemented during 2006 had "paid dividends in 2007," Smith wrote in his letter to shareholders.

Capital City Bank Group altered its acquisition strategy in the light of the rapidly deteriorating economic conditions. The company "is betting regulators will shutter one or more banks in Florida or Georgia, and that it could step in and buy the failed bank's deposits and branches on the cheap," David Breitkopf explained in an August 2008 *American Banker* article. The $2.6 billion-asset operation was unlikely to be alone in that thinking.

The company had acquired more than a dozen banks, dating back to 1984, bringing in $1.6 billion in deposits. No purchases, however, had been completed since 2005.

Kim Davis, chief financial officer, told *American Banker* "the sellers' expectations were too high." Company Chairman, CEO, and President William Smith had passed on a couple with problem loan portfolios.

Capital City Bank Group, meanwhile, continued to hold a strong capital position and practiced very conservative underwriting. According to *American Banker* these qualities made it a likely candidate for Federal Deposit Insurance Corporation directed purchases. Nonetheless, the bank was not immune to the harsh economic reality, recording an uptick in delinquent loans to residential real estate developers and a corresponding downturn in earnings during the first half of the year.

GOING FORWARD

In November 2008, Capital City Bank Group chose not to increase its capital through a government bank bailout program. "While we wholeheartedly support the Treasury Department's decisive action to help alleviate the turmoil in the financial markets, our Board ultimately believed that specific to Capital City, the costs and other restrictions associated with participating in the Capital Purchase Program outweighed the potential benefits," Smith said. The company did not rule out future participation in the evolving Troubled Asset Relief Program, according to *GlobeNewswire*.

At year-end 2008, Capital City Bank Group held total deposits of about $2 billion. Shareholder's equity was about $279 million. Earnings fell to $15.2 million. Addressing the 48.7 percent decline, the annual report stated: "For the year, turbulent economic and market conditions and an associated increase in the provision for loan losses and the level of nonperforming assets significantly impacted our earnings performance."

As for the future, Capital City Bank Group planned to continue to expand through organic growth and acquisitions. A "more tactical focus" had been placed on such higher growth metro markets as Macon, Tallahas-

see, and Gainesville. Acquisitions outside Florida, Georgia, and Alabama were not on the radar. During the spring of 2009, the U.S. economic downturn showed some signs of slowing. Unemployment rates, though, continued at levels not seen for a quarter century.

Kathleen Peippo

PRINCIPAL SUBSIDIARIES

Capital City Bank; CCBG Capital Trust I; CCBG Capital Trust II; Capital City Trust Company; Capital City Banc Investments, Inc.; Capital City Services Company; First Insurance Agency of Grady County, Inc.; Southern Oaks, Inc.; FNB Financial Services, Inc.

PRINCIPAL COMPETITORS

Bank of America Corporation; SunTrust Banks Inc.; Wachovia Corporation.

FURTHER READING

Breitkopf, David, "With Failure As an Option, Bidders Opt to Hold Back," *American Banker,* August 4, 2008, p. 1.

"Capital City Bank Group, Inc. Chooses Not to Participate in the Capital Purchase Program," *Globe Newswire,* November 12, 2008.

Rhoads, Christopher, "In Florida, Some Small Banks Are Getting Hot," *American Banker,* September 12, 1994, p. 8.

Sams, Rachel, "Small-Town Approach Serves Capital City Bank Group Well," *Knight-Ridder/Tribune Business News,* April 22, 2003.

Schneyer, Fred A., "Capital City Bank Group Foresees Rising Demand in North Florida," *Knight-Ridder/Tribune Business News,* January 3, 1996.

Thompson, Laura K., "Florida Bank's Deal for Foothold in Ala.," *American Banker,* September 27, 2000, p. 6.

Thompson Osuri, Laura, "Capital City of Fla. Details Multistate Expansion Plan," *American Banker,* February 16, 2005, p. 1.

Whiteman, Louis, "In Brief: Fla. Company Entering Ga. with $31M Deal," *American Banker,* February 17, 1999, p. 8.

Catalyst Paper
Corporation

3600 Lysander Land, 2nd Floor
Richmond, British Columbia V7B 1C3
Canada
Telephone: (604) 247-4400
Fax: (604) 247-0512
Web site: http://www.catalystpaper.com

Public Company
Incorporated: 1946 as British Columbia Forest Products
   Limited
Employees: 2,711
Sales: CAD 1.84 billion ($1.51 billion) (2008)
Stock Exchanges: Toronto
Ticker Symbol: CTL
NAICS: 322121 Paper (Except Newsprint) Mills

■■■

Catalyst Paper Corporation is a major North American mechanical paper company, each year manufacturing 2.5 million tons of paper and pulp products, 38 percent of which is newsprint. Based in Richmond, British Columbia, Catalyst operates four mills in British Columbia and a recycled newsprint mill in Arizona. Catalyst's newsprint, directory paper, and lightweight coated paper are used to produce newspapers and newspaper inserts, telephone and other types of directories, magazines, catalogs, retail flyers, direct-mail pieces, and product packaging. Pulp products include printing and writing papers, containerboard, and tissue. Brand names include Electrasoft, Electrabrite, and Electracote for specialty printing papers; Catalyst for direc-tory paper; Marathon for newsprint; and Crofton Kraft for pulp products.

Most of Catalyst's products, 56 percent, are sold to the United States, followed by Asia and Australia with 17 percent, Canada with 12 percent, Latin America with 9 percent, and the remainder to Europe and other countries. Catalyst is a public company listed on the Toronto Stock Exchange. Its largest shareholder, controlling nearly 40 percent of the stock, is New York City-based Third Avenue Management, LLC.

POST–WORLD WAR II LINEAGE

Catalyst Paper traces its origins to the 1946 creation of British Columbia Forest Products Limited. This logging and sawmilling company diversified into pulp and paper products in the early 1950s. Scott Paper Company became a major investor during the decade and by fiscal 1960 British Columbia Forest Product's annual revenues topped $50 million. It would be eventually controlled by Scott, Mead Corp. and Alberta Energy Co. By 1965 the company was producing 107,000 tons of newsprint each year, making it the 20th largest producer in North America. A recession in the early 1980s led to severe losses, $61 million in 1982 and a further $32.7 million a year later, forcing the company to scrap plans to open a new sawmill and newsprint mill in Alberta, Canada, or expand a paper mill in Grand Rapids, Minnesota. Lumber prices rebounded later in the decade, due in large part to an increased number of housing starts, resulting in a soaring stock price that allowed the company to resume some expansion projects, while also making it an attractive property.

In February 1987 New Zealand conglomerate Fletcher Challenge Limited paid $381 million (CAD 506.6 million) for a 47 percent stake in British Columbia Forest Products. Because the rest of the company was owned by more than 4,000 investors, Fletcher Challenge gained effective control of the company. The deal was part of an effort by the New Zealand parent company to expand into new markets. Fletcher Challenge had been formed in 1981 through the merger of Fletcher Holdings Ltd., Challenge Corporation Ltd., and Tasman Pulp and Paper Company Ltd., in which Fletcher held a 56.5 percent interest and Challenge about 28 percent. Tasman had been created in the early 1950s when the New Zealand government urged private industry to take advantage of the country's forests to develop a paper, pulp, and newsprint industry. Fletcher answered the call, offering to build a pulp and newsprint mill. Thus, in 1952 Tasman was formed, its shares held by Fletcher, the government, and the public. The new company began producing pulp and newsprint in 1955 and expanded steadily over the ensuing decades and became one of New Zealand's largest public companies, along with Fletcher and Challenge. When the three came together the resulting conglomerate dominated the New Zealand economy, and it was soon looking to diversify into new markets. One of its targets was the Northwest of North America.

FLETCHER CHALLENGE ENTERS CANADIAN MARKET: 1993

Fletcher Challenge became involved in British Columbia in 1983 by acquiring Crown Forest Industries, which was involved in wood products, packaging, and pulp and paper products. After gaining control of British Columbia Forest Products, Fletcher Challenge combined the two companies in 1988 resulting in Fletcher Challenge Canada Limited, which had assets of $1.8 billion and combined annual sales of $2 billion. The parent company also owned operations in Chile and Brazil, making it the world's second largest manufacturer of newsprint.

Over the next decade Fletcher Challenge Canada narrowed its focus to pulp and paper and gradually shed other assets. In 1991 the company sold its 45 percent stake in Donohue St.-Felicien Inc., a forest products company, for $120 million. In 1992 the Crown Forest lumber and plywood operations were divested, to be followed by corrugated container manufacturer Crown Packaging Ltd. The sale of its majority interest in TimberWest Forest Ltd. in 1997 completed Fletch Challenge Canada's departure from the wood products business and transition to a focus on the groundwood papers market. Also in 1997, in order to raise cash to remain competitive, the company sold Grand Rapids, Minnesota-based Blandin Paper Company for $650 million. At the same time, Fletcher Challenge Canada had to contend with labor problems. Labor-management relations had been strained industry-wide in British Columbia throughout the decade, including a six-week strike at Fletcher Challenge Canada mills that began in late 1994, and in 1997 Fletcher Challenge Canada was singled out for the next round of wage and benefit contracts. Negotiations eventually broke down and in July 1997 workers struck at several of the company's mills.

FLETCHER CHALLENGE CANADA PUT UP FOR SALE: 2000

The New Zealand parent company attempted to merge some of its international assets with Fletcher Challenge Canada in 1999. The result would have been a company with assets of $3.4 billion, but minority shareholders rejected the proposal. Its bid spurned, Fletcher Challenge, looking to pay down debt, in February 2000 put up for sale its interest in Fletcher Challenge Canada and the rest of its pulp and paper assets. A number of suitors sought the properties, but in the end the Norwegian company Norske Skogindustrier ASA tendered the successful bid of $2.5 billion. Norske Skog was Norway's largest forest products group. By adding the Fletcher Challenge assets, it gained a presence in North America while achieving greater global reach, becoming the world's second largest newsprint manufacturer. Moreover, it gained the economies of scale needed to compete in the highly competitive pulp and paper industry that was fragmented and dealing with overcapacity.

In the fall of 2000 Fletcher Challenge Canada was named Norske Skog Canada Limited. The company grew further a year later by acquiring another British Columbia-based company, Pacifica Papers Inc., for $230 million, a deal completed in November 2001 that es-

KEY DATES

1946: British Columbia Forest Products Limited is formed.
1987: Fletcher Challenge Limited acquires company.
1988: British Columbia Forest Products combines with Crown Forest Industries to create Fletch Challenge Canada.
2000: Norske Skog acquires company, which becomes Norske Skog Canada.
2001: Following merger with Pacifica Papers, company is renamed NorskeCanada.
2005: Company is renamed Catalyst Paper Corporation.
2008: Snowflake Mill is acquired.

sentially doubled the company's size. NorskeCanada, as it was now known, became the largest groundwood specialty paper company on the West Coast, North America's third largest newsprint and groundwood specialty papers company, and the fourth largest producer of newsprint in North America. In addition to providing the company with financial backing, new ownership brought a fresh start to labor relations, which were not only strained because of the 1997 strike with Fletcher Challenge but also because of difficulties between labor and Pacifica Papers. In particular, Pacifica's Power River mill, according to *Canadian HR Reporter,* was regarded by union workers "as the worst mill in the worst company in the worst industry in British Columbia."

A new management team with a fresh approach helped restore relations with workers when management trimmed Powell River's workforce from 1,000 to 300 but offered transfers to other plants, buyout packages, or retraining, all the while working closely with the union in an effort to save as many jobs as possible. As a result, the two sides created a healthy atmosphere so that when it came time to negotiate a new five-year labor contract, a deal did not have to be hammered out at the 11th hour or at the end of a bitter strike or lockout, nor did the union target NorskeCanada to establish a pattern for negotiating with other British Columbia pulp and paper companies. Rather, the two sides agreed to negotiate voluntarily to reach an agreement that served the best interests for NorskeCanada and its workers without regard for the rest of the industry. Management also pledged not to ask for any concessions or "clawbacks" from previous contracts. As a result of improved rela-

tions, the two sides reached an agreement in November 2002, ten months before the old contract expired.

ACQUISITION OF DE-INKING PLANT: 2003

NorskeCanada grew further through acquisition in late 2003 when it paid $29 million in cash and another $29 million in stock to Newstech Recycling for a de-inking plant, whose primary customer had been NorskeCanada. The facility, the largest of its kind in western Canada, established a platform for a NorskeCanada recycling division, which would use old newspapers and magazines to make pulp for the manufacture of paper products. By bringing the recycling operation in-house, NorskeCanada also saved about $16 million each year.

COMPANY ADOPTS CATALYST PAPER NAME: 2005

Any savings that could be achieved took on greater importance as Canadian newsprint makers faced increasingly difficult business conditions. The price of raw materials rose as the Canadian government imposed restrictions on timber cutting, the value of the Canadian dollar also led to higher prices for necessary goods, and to exacerbate the situation further the price of energy increased, a serious problem given the large amounts of energy used by paper mills. More devastating to the industry was the collapse of the pulp and paper markets. In just one year the price of pulp fell from $700 a ton to $400. Newsprint, in the meantime, experienced a drop in demand in the United States, leading to paper prices declining about 25 percent. There was not much NorskeCanada could do to control these forces. To at least improve its marketing position, the company in the fall of 2005 changed its name to Catalyst Paper Corporation. The company was already using Catalyst as a brand name for directory papers, so that the corporate name change provided some brand building. It also created separation from Norske Skog, important because the Norwegian company was cutting its ties to the Canadian venture. In a secondary stock offering conducted in February 2006, Norske Skog sold the last of its shares in Catalyst Paper.

Catalyst Paper appeared to lack a sense of direction after being cast off by Norske Skog, devoting a good bit of effort fighting with local authorities over what it believed were excessively high industrial tax rates. Nevertheless, Catalyst drew the attention of New York's Third Avenue Management, which believed the stock was undervalued. The firm made an unsolicited offer to purchase 39 million shares, thereby giving it a 38 percent interest and effective control of the company. Catalyst's board resisted the takeover bid, imposing a shareholder rights plan, and made overtures to potential white knights to keep Catalyst out of the hands of Third Avenue Management, whose intentions they maintained were "unclear and inconsistent." Resistance proved ineffective, and in late 2006 Third Avenue Management achieved its 38 percent stake and began to exert influence on the direction of Catalyst. Early in 2007 the company's top pair of executives resigned, although they stayed on until the company held its annual meeting in March.

PURCHASE OF SNOWFLAKE MILL: 2008

To meet the challenge of difficult economic conditions, Catalyst implemented a $21.2 million restructuring program in 2007, resulting in some consolidation of operations and a large number of job cuts. Production of newsprint, the demand for which continued to fall, was also curtailed. While a number of newsprint producers had fallen by the wayside in recent years, Catalyst remained strong enough to take advantage of the industry's plight in 2008 to pay $161 million for the Snowflake Mill, a 100 percent recycled newsprint manufacturing operation located in northern Arizona. Not only did Catalyst expand outside of Canada for the first time and provide a hedge against Canadian dollar fluctuations, it established itself as the largest newsprint producer in western North America, one of five manufacturers who combined to supply 85 percent of all newsprint used in North America. With a base of operations in Arizona, Catalyst was also better positioned to serve customers on the West Coast and attract new ones.

A weakening economy, high energy prices, the rising costs of chemicals and distribution, and low demand for newsprint continued to offer challenges for Catalyst. More job cuts and production curtailments followed in 2008 and 2009. The company performed as well as could be expected under such conditions, but there was no indication that business would improve in the near future.

Ed Dinger

PRINCIPAL OPERATING UNITS

Specialty Printing Papers; Newsprint; Pulp.

PRINCIPAL COMPETITORS

AbitibiBowater Inc.; International Paper Company; NewPage Group Inc.

FURTHER READING

Brown, Tom, "New Zealand Company Lands on U.S. Shores," *Chicago Tribune,* February 27, 1989, p. 3.

"Catalyst Expands Newsprint Clout," *Pulp & Paper,* April 2008, p. 6.

"Catalyst Shutting BC Capacity to Lift Profits," *Pulp & Paper,* July 2007, p. 8.

Gilpin, Kenneth N., "Canadian Paper Maker Realigns Management," *New York Times,* September 17, 1984.

Johnson, Jim, "NorskeCanada to Buy Mill from Newstech Recycling," *Waste News,* November 24, 2003, p. 15.

Miller, Drew, "Fletcher Challenge Canada: Assets Shed; Focused on Groundwood Papers," *Pulp & Paper,* September 1997, p. 40.

Rodden, Graeme, "Surviving the 'Perfect Storm,'" *Pulp & Paper,* March 2006, p. 5.

Rosenberg, Jim, "Paper Giants," *Editor & Publisher,* April 24, 2000, p. 51.

Shenfield, Allen Ponak, "From Acrimony to Respect," *Canadian HR Reporter,* February 26, 2007, p. 10.

Willis, Andrew, "Catalyst Brass Resign amid Rift with Investor," *Globe & Mail,* January 16, 2007, p. B1.

Check Into Cash, Inc.

201 Keith Street SW, Suite 80
Cleveland, Tennessee 37311
U.S.A.
Telephone: (423) 479-2400
Toll Free: (800) 504-9101
Fax: (423) 559-1099
Web site: http://www.checkintocash.com

Private Company
Incorporated: 1993
Employees: 2,979
Sales: $356.3 million (2008 est.)
NAICS: 522291 Consumer Lending

■ ■ ■

Check Into Cash, Inc., is a private company based in Cleveland, Tennessee, that participates in what is commonly called the payday loan business, but is known in the industry as "deferred presentment services." In essence the controversial lending practice calls for a customer, who has an active checking account and proof of employment, to write a postdated check to the loan agency for an amount that covers the loan plus a fee, generally $15 to $20 per $100 received, rather than an interest charge. The agency then deposits the check, generally on the day of the customer's next paycheck.

Check Into Cash and other payday loan companies maintain that they fill a need not addressed by traditional lenders, providing consumers with quick, small loans to cover a temporary need for cash. Detractors of the practice call it legal loan sharking, predatory lending aimed at people who can least afford to cover the amount of the check when it comes due and all too often fall into the so-called refinancing trap. Unlike a pawn shop loan in which the borrower simply forfeits the item offered as a pledge and carries no further obligation, a payday loan borrower has no easy recourse and in many cases a second loan is taken out to cover the first, a "rollover" loan that creates a vicious circle for some borrowers who continue to pay fees without the wherewithal to reduce the principal of the loan. As a result, the final cost to the consumer is many times that of the original loan. As part of its adherence to the best practices in the industry, Check Into Cash limits the number of rollover loans to no more than four, depending on state law. Check Into Cash is one of the largest payday lenders in the United States, operating about 1,250 stores in some 30 states. The company also provides online lending, and many of the stores provide check cashing services and work with TaxOne to provide tax preparation services that include "Refund Anticipation Loans." Check Into Cash is owned by its founder, chairman, and chief executive officer, W. Allan Jones.

19TH-CENTURY GROWTH OF SALARY LENDING

The payday lending business has deep roots in the United States. In the late 1800s the salary lending business enjoyed rapid growth. Many of the early practitioners were "five for six" lenders whose customers borrowed $5 on Monday and repaid $6 when they received their pay on Friday or Saturday. The interest rate seemed modest in the context of a week, but at 20

COMPANY PERSPECTIVES

At Check Into Cash, we are proud of the reputation we have earned as financial service professionals in the cash advance, payday advance, and payday lending industry.

percent per week, if extended over the course of a year it amounted to more than 1,000 percent per annum. These salary lenders, primarily found in the Northeast, became known as loan sharks. Salary lending enjoyed strong growth in the late 1800s because of the emerging lower-middle class in the United States, members of which held steady jobs but were often subject to financial setbacks and lacked the means to secure bank loans. These workers had families and were unlikely to flee town, and because of the Victorian mores of the day they were eager to conceal their personal debt. Lenders could play on this quality to shame borrowers into making payments, in some cases hiring a "bawler-out," usually a loud woman who paid a visit to a workplace to deliver a pointed denunciation of a borrower's failure to meet his financial obligations. These early loan sharks did their best to extract as many payments as possible without a reduction in the principal of the loan, creating what was then known as "chain debt." Such high-cost lending became a major problem in the late 1800s and carried into the next century. To combat it, personal bankruptcy laws were liberalized and other laws addressing the illicit practices of lenders were enacted. Moreover, charitable lending institutions and mutual savings and loan organizations arose to meet the credit needs of the middle class.

While loan sharking under the auspices of organized crime persisted in the 20th century, the short-term cash loan business once again became a mainstream activity in the 1980s. According to Aaron Huckstep writing in *Fordham Journal of Corporate & Financial Law,* "The deregulation of the banking industry, the absence of traditional small loan providers and the elimination of interest rate caps set the stage for the emergence of payday lending. As banks eliminated less profitable services (such as short-term loan services), families and individuals in need of short-term cash flow were left with nowhere to turn. While the payday lending market emerged at about this time, many consider the father of 'modern' payday lending to be W. Allan Jones."

JONES LEARNS OF CASH ADVANCE CONCEPT: 1993

Raised in Cleveland, Tennessee, Jones was originally involved in the credit bureau and debt collection business. His father, W. A. Jones Jr., had founded Credit Bureau Services Inc. in Cleveland and the younger Jones joined him at the age of 20 after dropping out of Middle Tennessee State University. He then nurtured and expanded the business until it included about a dozen offices. It was while recruiting a job candidate in 1993 that he became aware of the cash advance concept. That candidate was James Eaton, who had worked with Jones's father in the credit-bureau business. After that business became more national through consolidation Eaton had turned his attention to short-term loans, opening up Check Cashing, Inc., in late 1991 and setting up shop in a former gas station in Johnson City, Tennessee, adorned with a banner that read "Check Cashing."

While Jones tried to persuade Eaton to take a job with Credit Bureau Services, their conversation was constantly interrupted by a steady stream of customers and it became apparent that not only did Eaton have no interest in a job, his store was not cashing checks in the normal sense. Instead, Eaton was advancing customers money on postdated checks that included a 20 percent fee. When Jones expressed surprise at such a high charge, Eaton supposedly countered with "Allan, it's a lot cheaper than overdrafts." Jones's interest was piqued, and a few weeks later he spent a day with Eaton as he opened a new check cashing office in Kingsport, Tennessee.

About six weeks after his initial visit with Eaton, Jones opened his first Check Into Cash store in his hometown of Cleveland, located on North Keith Street. Rather than check cashing, he positioned the transaction as a "payday advance," and from the start envisioned a national chain of outlets. His business started out slowly, however. After three days his new store had not completed a single transaction. Finally as the week came to a close an Army recruiter, who was eager to buy a bicycle for his son's birthday but whose paycheck had not arrived on time, walked out of the store with $100 in hand, leaving behind a check for $120. Business then began to pick up at a steady pace.

JONES SELLS CREDIT BUREAU SERVICES: 1998

At the end of the first year in business, Check Into Cash generated revenues of less than $80,000. The company enjoyed exponential growth, as Jones opened new stores at a rapid pace, establishing the first national payday loan chain. By the end of five years he was generating $21.4 million from more than 425 stores in 15 states, and was opening 15 new stores each month. Jones filed the necessary documents with the Securities and Exchange Commission to make Check Into Cash the first public company, but in the end elected to remain private. The venture was so successful that in 1998 he sold Credit Bureau Services, Tennessee's largest credit collection company, in order to focus on payday lending. In that same year he bought the 19.5-acre Village Shopping Mall in Cleveland and converted it into a business plaza with Check Into Cash serving as the anchor tenant.

Jones's success spawned competition, especially from traditional check-cashing agencies that were eager to find a replacement for the business lost to the rise of direct-deposit paychecks. The fast-growing industry also caught the attention of consumer advocacy groups. A lawsuit filed on behalf of 50 Tennesseans alleging illegal practices and violation of the federal Truth in Lending Act and Fair Debt Collection Act named Check Into Cash and other chains. To settle the matter, Check Into Cash agreed to make $2.2 million in payments.

Even before the Tennessee suit was settled, Jones and others in the business had taken steps to influence legislation in the state to regulate payday lending, in the process making considerable campaign contributions. According to critics, the law, passed in 1997, came under the guise of consumer protection but in reality legitimized loan sharking. Companies were allowed to lend up to $500 per customer for 31 days. A fee ceiling was set at 15 percent or $30, whichever was lower, and rollover loans were prohibited, although it was a provision that critics maintained could be easily circumvented and still provided lenders with an annual interest rate of about 800 percent. Moreover, the law did not define the fees as interest, thus exempting the transactions from truth-in-lending regulations, a boon to payday loan companies in fending off class-action lawsuits. To make it more palatable to the public, the law was passed with

a sunset provision, requiring that it be reapproved after two years. More controversy only ensued at that time, but the law was reapproved.

EXPANSION CONTINUES

By the start of the new century Check Into Cash had grown to more than 550 units in 18 states. The company also added to its service offerings by launching CIC Financial Services, LLC, to provide tax and mortgage services. Further expansion continued as Check Into Cash moved into new markets, such as Colorado in 2000. Less than two years later the chain topped 750 units, operating in 20 states. Jones was also involved in other ventures, including Jones Properties, LLC, which owned a number of historic buildings in downtown Cleveland, Tennessee; Village Barbers; a Cleveland technology center; the Bald Headed Bistro; and Jones Management Services, LLC, providing management and administrative services for his various businesses. A wealthy man, Jones also became a well-known philanthropist, supporting preservation efforts in Cleveland, building a wrestling center at his old high school, and putting his name on an aquatic center at the University of Tennessee.

While Jones received accolades for his good deeds, the source of much of his wealth was not above criticism. Other lawsuits followed, including one in Indiana in 2002 in which Check Into Cash agreed to forgive $1.6 million in unpaid customer obligations. In another state, Georgia, the payday lending industry also faced serious scrutiny. In 2004 the state adopted one of the strictest laws regulating short-term loans, forbidding lenders from charging one-time fees. Rather, they were required to employ an installment plan model. As a result, Check Into Cash closed its 24 stores in Georgia, and the other major payday loan chains followed suit.

The loss of two dozen stores did little to blunt Check Into Cash's momentum, however. In October 2004 the company opened its 1,000th unit and announced plans to expand its corporate headquarters, adding 42,000 square feet to keep pace with expansion. The new space would allow for an expanded information technology department to support the company's new Internet financial services, which was operated in conjunction with affiliate Loanbyphone.com to offer payday loans by telephone and Internet in some states.

FORCED OUT OF NORTH
CAROLINA: 2006

By the fall of 2005 the Check Into Cash chain increased to more than 1,200 centers spread across 35 states. The company and other participants in the payday loan business faced challenges unlike those of other industries, however. They were continually fighting political battles to keep states from restricting their operations or making efforts to reopen lost markets by repealing prior legislation. In North Carolina payday lending was made illegal in 2001, yet Check Into Cash and other chains continued to find loopholes to operate in the state until 2006 when they were forced by the state attorney general to leave North Carolina. In that same year payday lenders were able to delay the implementation of new regulations in New Mexico by going to court to obtain a restraining order. A year later new limitations went into effect in Oregon that imposed a 36 percent interest rate cap as well as other regulations, prompting Check Into Cash and others to exit that market as well. The industry also suffered a blow in 2007 when the U.S. Congress imposed a 36 percent interest rate limit on loans to members of the armed services, which essentially put an end to doing business with military families. Ballot initiatives in Ohio and Arizona to lift restrictions on payday lending also failed in November 2008.

A sputtering economy in 2008 spurred the use of payday loans as many middle-class consumers were overextended, and lacking any kind of financial cushion they turned to such loans as a last resort. There was clearly a need for short-term loans and companies like Check Into Cash filled it. The company also continued to diversify beyond payday lending. In 2009 it signed an agent agreement with Western Union to offer global money transfer and money order services. Whether Check Into Cash would find other services to pursue in order to transcend the stigma attached to payday lending remained an unanswered question.

Ed Dinger

PRINCIPAL SUBSIDIARIES

CIC Financial Services, LLC.

PRINCIPAL COMPETITORS

Advance America Cash Advance Centers, Inc.; CNG Financial Corp.; Dollar Financial Corp.

FURTHER READING

Brook, Daniel, "Usury Country: Welcome to the Birthplace of Payday Lending," *Harper's Magazine,* April 2008.

"Check Into Cash Plans Expansion of Facilities," *Cleveland Daily Banner,* October 2, 2004.

Christensen, Kim, "Hooked on Debt," *Los Angeles Times,* December 24, 2008, p. A1.

Foust, Dean, "Easy Money," *Business Week,* April 24, 2000, p. 107.

Hendren, John, "Exorbitant 'Payday Loans' Tide Over the Desperate," *Los Angeles Times,* January 24, 1999, p. 1.

Ho, Rodney, "Fees of Quick-Cash Chains Draw Scrutiny," *Wall Street Journal,* June 10, 1997, p. B1.

Huckstep, Aaron, "Payday Lending: Do Outrageous Prices Necessarily Mean Outrageous Profits?" *Fordham Journal of Corporate & Financial Law,* 2007, p. 203.

Peterson, Christopher, *Taming the Sharks: Toward a Cure for the High-Cost Credit Market,* Akron, Ohio: University of Akron Press, 2004, 451 p.

Teegardin, Carrie, "Payday Lenders Hope to Return," *Atlanta Journal-Constitution,* March 18, 2007, p. A1.

Wissner, Sheila, "Traveling Loan Industry's Secrecy Worries Officials," *Tennessean,* April 18, 1999, p. 1A.

Cherry Brothers LLC

—■—

1035 Mill Road
Allentown, Pennsylvania 18196
U.S.A.
Telephone: (610) 366-1606
Toll Free: (800) 333-4525
Web site: http://www.cherrydale.com

Private Company
Incorporated: 1907 as E. Cherry Sons & Co.
Employees: 200
Sales: $44 million (2008 est.)
NAICS: 311330 Confectionery Manufacturing from Purchased Chocolate; 311340 Nonchocolate Confectionery Manufacturing; 424930 Flower, Nursery Stock, and Florists' Supplies Merchant Wholesalers; 453220 Gift, Novelty, and Souvenir Stores

■ ■ ■

Cherry Brothers LLC, doing business as Cherrydale, is one of the nation's leading suppliers of fundraising programs and products to schools and organizations. Its manufacturing segment, Cherrydale Manufacturing, produces chocolate and non-chocolate confections and snack and energy bars under the Barton's, Barton's Gold, and Heavenly Dark brand names. Its fundraising segment, Cherrydale Fundraising, sells the company's candies along with brand-name licensed products made by Pepsi, Crayola, Pillsbury, McDonald's, Mikasa, and John Deere, among others. The company's manufacturing facilities are located in Allentown, Pennsylvania, and

its fulfillment centers are in Texas, Michigan, California, and New York. Cherrydale's retail business sells chocolates and confections under the Haddington Farms brand.

GROWING IN PHILADELPHIA: 1907 TO LATE FIFTIES

In 1907, Louis Cherry, an importer of nuts, confections, and gourmet foods, and his wife, Esther, founded E. Cherry Sons & Co. in Old City Philadelphia, Pennsylvania. The business originally sold Esther's handmade candies and treats, as well as coffees and teas, mostly to neighbors. Throughout the 1920s, the little candy store grew as word spread of the Cherry family's commitment to quality and customer service.

In 1932, in the midst of the Depression, Walter Cherry, the founders' son, started the company's fundraising arm. At that time, the company was the nation's largest importer of nutmegs and fruits. According to Richard Toltzis, who joined the company in 1980, in a 1996 *Morning Call* article: "He started putting our first product, cashew crunch, in vending machines. ... Then he got the idea to sell to organizations that wanted to raise funds. He found that people want to help people, particularly if it's for youth."

Throughout the 1940s, the company grew both as a retailer and in fundraising sales. Then, in the 1950s, it began to concentrate on fundraising. Various nonprofit groups, mostly churches, approached the E. Cherry Sons & Co. shop wanting to sell some of its candy items to help their group raise money. The Cherrys soon started soliciting other nonprofits, and as their mail-order "fundraising" business expanded, so did E. Cherry. In 1958, it moved from its original Old City location to a much larger building in West Philadelphia, where it remained for the next 20 years.

By 1958, the Cherrys had four stores operating in the Philadelphia area that supplied candies for fundraising to hundreds of organizations. In the early 1970s, the company entered another period of continued growth. By mid-decade, it started supplying candy and chocolate items to Miss Chocolate, a fundraising company located in New York. It was Miss Chocolate that developed the practice of rewarding the high-volume sellers of fundraising campaigns, a practice Cherrydale copied.

DEDICATED TO FUNDRAISING: EARLY EIGHTIES

By 1980, when Ross Cherry, a third-generation Cherry family member, finished college at George Washington University and joined the family company as a sales representative in the Washington, D.C., area, revenues were $4 million. In 1981, Ross Cherry went to Houston to take the fundraising business model to another part of the country. Within days of his arrival, three schools signed up to work with Cherrydale Fundraising. Soon after, Richard Toltzis, Ross's cousin and Larry Cherry, Ross's younger brother, joined the family business.

The conservatively run Cherrydale had become the national leader in selling sweets for elementary school fundraisers by 1984 and had outgrown its factory for a second time. The following year, the company closed the last of its Philadelphia candy stores, and, in 1986, with annual sales of $15 million, the company moved into a new $25 million, 400,000-square-foot facility in Pennsburg, Pennsylvania. The facility provided the surrounding area with more employment, and drew employees from as far away as Camden, New Jersey, and Allentown, Pennsylvania.

AGGRESSIVE EXPANSION UNDER NEW OWNERSHIP: 1994–99

Between 1984 and 1996, what the company described in a 1995 *Candy Industry* article as its "aggressive growth posture" led to a compounded growth rate of 20 to 25 percent each year. In 1989, Cherrydale acquired its first fundraising company, Academy Fundraisers, based in Baltimore, Maryland. In 1994, a warehouse addition almost doubled the size of its Pennsburg facility. By the mid-1990s, Cherrydale was the leading manufacturer of chocolates and confections for retail and fundraising customers and of non-food items for fundraisers.

Fourth-generation member Ross Cherry and his cousin, Richard Toltzis, took over the business in 1994. One of their first moves was to seek new investors to boost the company's capital and set it up for its next stage of growth. "In the past, all of our growth was funded internally," explained Ross Cherry in a 1995 *Candy Industry* article. "With our parents retiring, and our desire to continue building the company at historical percentage rates, we needed to bring in outside partners, both financial and professional." In 1994, Cherrydale sold a majority stake in its business to Golder, Thoma, Cressey, Rauner Inc. of Chicago and Jackson National Life Insurance Co.

The new executives also brought in outsiders for the company's top executive roles. In 1994, Gary Heine became president and chief operating officer. Explained Ross Cherry in *Candy Industry* in 1995: "The company was at a size where we could no longer be effective wearing as many hats. We could not treat this as a family business anymore."

Describing the company at the time, Toltzis assessed its strengths: "We're a formidable competitor these days. We're a full line confectioner—enrobed; molded from solid novelties to solids with inclusions; truffles, liquid-filled cherries; and starch molding from pectin jellies to case caramels to marshmallow products." The company roasted and processed its own nut meats, caramel-coated popcorns, crunch products, and trail mixes. Cherrydale's fundraising lines were equally varied; it sold cookies, cheeses, meats, calendars, kitchen accessories, stationery, gift wrappings, greeting cards, toys, and books.

It was during the mid-1990s that Cherrydale's retail business, its Haddington Farms brands, originally designed to counterbalance the seasonal nature of its fundraising efforts, began to grow at a much greater rate than the other parts of its business and became its primary focus. The increase was due to the consolidation then occurring among mass merchandisers and Cherrydale's own ability to sell at a lesser cost than many of its competitors.

KEY DATES

1907: Esther and Louis Cherry found E. Cherry Sons & Co.

1932: Walter Cherry starts the fundraising arm of the company.

1958: Company moves from its original Old City location to a building in West Philadelphia.

1980: Ross Cherry and Richard Toltzis, third-generation family members, join the company, now doing business as Cherrydale.

1985: Company closes the last of its Philadelphia stores.

1986: Company closes its manufacturing site in Philadelphia and opens a new plant in Pennsburg.

1989: Cherrydale acquires its first fundraising company, Academy Fundraisers of Baltimore, Maryland.

1994: Warehouse addition almost doubles the size of the Pennsburg facility; Ross Cherry and Richard Toltzis take charge of the business; Cherry family sells the company to an investment group; Gary Heine becomes chief executive officer.

1996: Arthur G. Murray becomes chief executive officer.

1999: Cherry family buys the company out of bankruptcy; company sells the Pennsburg plant to Hershey.

2000: Cherrydale moves to new headquarters and manufacturing plant near Allentown, Pennsylvania.

2001: Cherrydale buys Barton's from Consolidated Foods.

2006: Larry Rosen purchases majority interest in the company; Nellie Mahabir becomes the new chief executive.

Throughout the 1990s, Cherrydale expanded its sales force, and, by 1996, the company's ranks had swelled to 350 employees; it had 15,000 schools signed up and exceeded $100 million in sales mostly between September and December. During this decade, "America's Fund Raiser" developed its "Colossus," its first fundraising brochure that included not only Cherrydale's renowned chocolates and confections, but a multitude of products ranging from gift wrap to licensed brand items. Arthur G. Murray, former president and chief executive of Sunshine Biscuits, joined as chief executive, replacing Heine in 1996.

Cherrydale also purchased a pizza company and a T-shirt company during the mid-1990s as part of its strategy to keep its options open by diversifying, making both fundraising and confectionery acquisitions. According to Cherry in *Morning Call,* "[W]hen you sell variety, people buy in multiples. ... Instead of only cashew crunch, we started making other candies. When you get a family with five different tastes, some will buy chocolate-covered cherries and some will buy peanut butter cups."

CHERRYS BUY THE COMPANY OUT OF BANKRUPTCY: 1999

However, even as the company was growing and diversifying, it was on rocky ground. Cherrydale's new owners had, according to observers, mismanaged the business and the company filed for bankruptcy in March 1999, prompting Ross Cherry and Richard Toltzis suddenly to lead an investment group that repurchased the company in April. "This is something that never, ever, should have happened," Ross Cherry, co-president with Richard Toltzis, offered in a 1999 *Morning Call* article after stepping in to rescue the company in 1999. The reorganized Cherrydale, under Co-Presidents Ross Cherry and Richard Toltzis, promised publicly to make good on all its orders or get refunds to all the people who had bought its candy.

The Cherry family put several hundred thousand dollars into the business to get fundraising orders out the door. Management leased a 115,000-square-foot building for Cherrydale's headquarters and distribution near Allentown, Pennsylvania, and employed more than 100 people there beginning in 2000. It retained its distribution warehouses in Michigan and Texas and its Haddington Farms retail division, but sold its Pennsburg candy-making plant to Hershey Foods Corp. After shifting production of its original candy recipes to Consolidated Brands of Altoona, Pennsylvania, maker of Boyer's and Barton's candies, it bought equity in Consolidated Brands.

BACK IN THE BLACK: 2000

Within six months of repurchase, the company was back in the black. In 2001, it acquired Barton's from Consolidated, becoming the largest manufacturer of Kosher-for-Passover candy in the country. Cherrydale made the decision to preserve Barton's traditional recipes while updating its packaging and distribution for increased sales.

Beginning in 2004, Cherrydale began to extend its core competency by producing snack-related products, such as breakfast bars. By 2005, Cherrydale served more than 20,000 schools and organizations nationwide, filling about 12,000 orders a day during the four-month fundraising season from Labor Day until Christmas. The company also manufactured private-label confections for J.C. Penney, Costco, 1-800-FLOWERS, and Wal-Mart, among others.

By the time Larry Rosen purchased an interest in the company in 2006, the company had been enjoying double-digit gains for the preceding five years. However, it was the candy business that was supplying most of the growth; half of Cherrydale's sales came from contract manufacturing, split evenly between branded and private-label products. Rosen and his new chief executive, Nellie Mahabir, began in 2007 to expand the Barton's brand and to seek ways to build upon Cherrydale's proud legacy and the foundation that Toltzis and Cherry had laid for continued prosperity: new packaging, new products, and a state-of-the-art distribution center next to the company's manufacturing facility. From its fundraising roots in 1932, Cherrydale had helped customers raise more than $1.5 billion.

Carrie Rothburd

PRINCIPAL DIVISIONS

Cherrydale Farms Canada.

PRINCIPAL COMPETITORS

Harry London Candies, Inc.; Rocky Mountain Chocolate Factory, Inc.; See's Candies, Inc.; Chase General Corporation; Nestlé S.A.; World's Finest Chocolate Inc.; The Reader's Digest Association, Inc.; QSP, Inc.; Kathryn Beich, Inc.

FURTHER READING

Karp, Gregory, "Cherrydale Farms Rescued by Family; Plan Calls for Hershey Foods to Buy Plant in Pennsburg," *Morning Call,* April 24, 1999, p. B24.

Orenstein, Beth, "Then and Now: Family Members Return to Save Candy Business from Bankruptcy," *Eastern Pennsylvania Business Journal,* February 12, 2001, p. 4.

Pacyniak, Bernard, "From Toys to Truffles," *Candy Industry,* February 2007, p. 16.

Shope, Dan, "Candy Maker Says Investors, Expansion Are the Right Ingredients," *Morning Call,* September 8, 1996, p. D1.

Tiffany, Susan, "Cherrydale Farms: Poised for the Future," *Candy Industry,* October 1995, p. 22.

CHHJ Franchising LLC

4836 West Gandy Boulevard
Tampa, Florida 33689
U.S.A.
Telephone: (813) 489-7030
Toll Free: (800) 586-5872
Fax: (813) 839-1828
Web site: http://www.1800junkusa.com

Private Company
Incorporated: 2005
Employees: 100
Sales: $3 million (2008 est.)
NAICS: 562111 Solid Waste Collection

■ ■ ■

CHHJ Franchising LLC is the operator and franchiser of College Hunks Hauling Junk, a business that removes unwanted material for residential and commercial customers. Customers are charged according to the size of the material removed, as measured in fractions of a truckload. The company provides free estimates, and the price it charges includes labor, disposal fees, and travel time. CHHJ operates its junk-removal services in the metropolitan Washington, D.C., area and licenses the concept to franchisees who provide the service in a dozen states. Customers use a toll-free telephone number or the company's web site to schedule appointments. Franchisee candidates must have a minimum of $75,000 in liquid assets and be able to invest between $100,000 and $150,000 to establish a franchised operation.

ORIGINS

CHHJ's founders, Nick Friedman and Omar Soliman, met while they were attending high school in the storied halls and classrooms of Washington, D.C.'s prestigious Sidwell Friends School. There, at the school of choice for the children of Presidents Theodore Roosevelt, Richard Nixon, Bill Clinton, and Barack Obama, the two soon-to-be entrepreneurs formed a friendship that would endure after they left the Quaker-run academy. Friedman headed west to California, enrolling at Pomona College in Claremont. Soliman headed south to attend the University of Miami. They reunited during the summer months back in Washington, where they worked to pay for their tuition. One interval between studies, the summer before their senior years, served as the catalyst for their professional careers, a period when the idea for College Hunks Hauling Junk began to take shape.

When Friedman and Soliman returned home in mid-2003, they began working summer jobs. Friedman, pursuing an economics degree, worked as an intern at the International Monetary Fund. Soliman, studying business, began hauling junk. His mother, who owned a furniture store in the Adams Morgan neighborhood of Washington, first suggested the line of work after her son had used one of her store's cargo vans to help people move. She also came up with a name for her son's summertime business, suggesting he advertise his efforts as College Hunks Hauling Junk. Soliman enjoyed immediate success after following his mother's advice, attracting enough business to prompt Friedman to help his friend out during weekends. By the end of the summer, the pair earned roughly $10,000 from their work and returned to their respective schools to finish their education.

CONCEPT WINS A PRIZE

In the fall of 2003, thousands of miles away from Washington, Friedman and Soliman continued to receive telephone calls requesting their services as junk haulers. Both students were surprised at the continued demand for work, which began to persuade them they had stumbled upon a potentially lucrative business idea. Soliman became inspired, developing a business plan that he submitted to the University of Miami's Leigh Rothschild Entrepreneurship Competition. Financially backed by Leigh M. Rothschild, a University of Miami alumnus, the competition attracted 131 entrants, each seeking to win the grand prize of $10,000. Soliman was awarded first place, deepening his belief that College Hunks Hauling Junk represented a viable business idea.

After earning their degrees, Soliman and Friedman returned to Washington, but they did not launch a junk-hauling business immediately. Soliman began working as a marketing and sales associate for The Advisory Board Company, spending his off-hours tending to College Hunks Hauling Junk. Friedman accepted a position at a consulting company. "I created spreadsheets, [providing] economic research to billion-dollar businesses to make more billions," he said in the October 1, 2008 edition of the *New York Times*. Within six months, both Soliman and Friedman quit their jobs, using the $10,000 prize money to make College Hunks Hauling Junk a full-time, full-scale business.

THE BUSINESS IS LAUNCHED

The company began modestly, but Soliman and Friedman hatched ambitious plans for the venture from the start. The location of company headquarters was determined by where the cargo van was parked at night: at the home of Friedman's parents. There was little

evidence at first of what would develop, but Soliman and Friedman were determined to make their enterprise a nationally oriented company from the first day they left their jobs. They committed themselves to franchising the concept, embracing the least expensive route toward nationwide expansion.

Friedman, in an interview published in the July 2007 issue of *SmartCEO Magazine,* offered a glimpse into the preparations that were required to turn College Hunks Hauling Junk into CHHJ Franchising. "We really had to systemize things to be capable of growth," he explained. "For instance, we had to start writing manuals for each of the positions and write step-by-step checklists—how do you relate to the customer, how do you load the truck, how do you estimate the jobs, and things like that. It was sort of helter-skelter for a while."

The founders' business soon evolved from a two-person enterprise into a legitimate company. Their base of operations moved from Friedman's parents' home to a two-story building in an industrial park in Kensington, Maryland, just outside D.C. Soliman and Friedman began hiring employees and acquired a small fleet of trucks capable of hauling loads of refuse. To staff their company, they recruited workers from the University of Maryland and nearby community colleges, offering students $11 per hour as well as bonuses of $20 to $50 per shift if a customer called the Kensington headquarters to compliment the haulers' work. A slogan, "Let tomorrow's leaders haul your junk today!" was printed on fliers and door hangers to advertise the company's services in the greater Washington area. Soliman and Friedman began handing out business cards.

"It took us a good six months to research and figure out everything we needed to actually start operating the business," Friedman explained in his interview with *SmartCEO Magazine.* "Even after we started the business we were still figuring out things, like licenses we were supposed to have but didn't discover until we needed them. You get pulled over for a [Department of Transportation] inspection and it turns out you don't have flashers on the truck or something, something that may have been evident, but we just didn't turn that rock."

CHHJ found a receptive audience in the greater Washington area. The company attracted residential customers primarily, recording its greatest success in affluent neighborhoods where residents happily paid to have their unwanted materials carted away. CHHJ priced its service according to the size of the cargo, dividing a truckload into eighths. Customers paid $99 to have a single item removed and up to $500 for a full truckload, with extra charges applied for hauling concrete, dirt, construction materials, and certain other

KEY DATES

2003: College students Omar Soliman and Nick Friedman begin hauling junk from residences in Washington, D.C.
2005: CHHJ Franchising is formed.
2007: Company sells its first franchise.
2008: Revenues reach $3 million, a total collected from the company's operations in Washington and from the 14 franchised businesses in operation.

debris. The company promised to recycle or to donate as much of the junk as possible. CHHJ did not pick up combustibles or other hazardous waste, but the company's pickup crews were willing to clean out areas and remove refuse. Customers did not need to put their junk on the curbside. "Calling College Hunks gets the stuff out in one sweep," Friedman said in the October 1, 2008 edition of the *New York Times.*

PREPARATIONS FOR FRANCHISING BEGIN

By mid-2006, sufficient organizational and financial progress had been achieved to allow Friedman and Soliman to make the move they had planned to make from the start. Revenues for the previous 12 months reached $500,000, giving the founders enough cash to begin developing a franchising program for their concept. They hired George Palmer, a seasoned veteran with more than 30 years of experience in franchising, as director of franchise development and spent approximately $250,000 to create the tools and infrastructure to support the CHHJ program. The money was spent on establishing a call center and to develop software to allow customers to search online for CHHJ by entering their ZIP code. The founders also spent $13,000 to obtain 1-800-JUNK-USA as a toll-free telephone number.

By the end of 2006, Friedman and Soliman were marketing junk-removal service to residential and commercial customers and marketing their business model to potential franchisees. Start-up expenses for a one-territory area averaged $60,000, which included a franchise fee, a grand opening package, insurance deposits, training expenses, and other costs. Franchisees received training in how to operate their business, gleaning information for a five-day seminar at the company's "Junk University" in Tampa, Florida, and they received

marketing and operational support from CHHJ headquarters. Palmer created marketing materials designed for distinct types of customers, developing materials to attract residential customers, real estate agents, moving companies, and other potential customers.

FIRST FRANCHISE SALE: 2007

A new phase in CHHJ's development began at the start of 2007, ushering in an era that promised to see an armada of CHHJ green-and-orange-painted trucks sweep across the nation. In January 2007, the company sold its first franchise, a three-territory agreement with a central Florida resident, Faisal Ansari. "With the completion of our proprietary software, manuals, and legal documents," Soliman said in the April 24, 2007 release of the *America's Intelligence Wire,* "we plan to grow our franchise program systematically by offering streamlined operations, a central call center, and a highly marketable brand name." Friedman commented on the occasion as well, saying, "We're excited about our first franchise sale, and we look forward to making College Hunks Hauling Junk a household name throughout the country." At age 25, Soliman and Friedman became the youngest franchisers in the United States.

CHHJ began to cause a stir in 2007, a year in which the company generated $2.5 million in revenue. The American Marketing Association nominated CHHJ in five categories for the awards it bestowed annually, selecting the company as the winner in three of the categories: "Corporate Identity," "Marketing Web Site," and "Marketing Campaign on a Shoestring Budget." CHHJ spent very little on advertising, generating 40 percent of its business from referrals, fliers, and door hangers and deriving another 40 percent of its business from pay-per-click advertisements on Google. Despite its modest advertising budget, the company was gaining traction as a national competitor in its field, as its franchise operations recorded solid growth. Franchise agreements led CHHJ into Illinois, Ohio, Texas, Colorado, Michigan, Arkansas, Kentucky, North Carolina, Arizona, and California. In March 2008, the company moved its headquarters to Tampa, Florida. The company ended 2008 with 14 franchised businesses in operation and $3 million in systemwide sales. "In our minds," Soliman said in the October 1, 2008 edition of the *New York Times,* "we want to have 80 to 125 franchise partners across the country. We think we can do that within three years."

As Soliman and Friedman looked ahead, they envisioned the maturation of their fledgling enterprise. The initial success of CHHJ prompted them to start a sister company in 2008, College Foxes Packing Boxes, a business created to help residential customers prepare for moving. In assessing CHHJ's prospects, they saw robust growth in the years ahead. They expected revenues to reach $5 million by the end of 2009, $10 million by 2010, and $20 million in 2011.

Jeffrey L. Covell

PRINCIPAL COMPETITORS

RBDS Rubbish Boys Disposal Service Inc.; Waste Industries USA, Inc.; Waste Management, Inc.

FURTHER READING

Barzak, Ibrahim, "College Hunks Hauling Junk Announces First Franchise," *America's Intelligence Wire,* April 24, 2007.

Gill, Dee, "Hauling Junk (with a Touch of Class)," *New York Times,* October 1, 2008, p. L7.

McClain, Buzz, "One Man's Junk," *SmartCEO,* July 2007, p. 29.

Mui, Ylan Q., "Getting a Load of a Business Opportunity: 'College Hunks' Idea to Haul Junk Turns Profitable," *Washington Post,* August 5, 2005, p. B3.

China FAW Group Corporation

3025 Dongfeng St.
Changchun, 130011
China
Telephone: (86 431) 8590 5407
Fax: (86 431) 8761 4780
Web site: http://www.faw.com

Government-Owned Company
Founded: 1953
Employees: 132,500
Sales: $32.12 billion (2008)
NAICS: 336111 Automobile Manufacturing; 336211
    Motor Vehicle Body Manufacturing; 336399 All
    Other Motor Vehicle Parts Manufacturing

■ ■ ■

China FAW Group Corporation is one of China's largest automobile, truck, and bus manufacturers. With annual car production of over 1.5 million vehicles per year, it is among the ten largest automobile manufacturers in the world. Through its wholly owned subsidiaries and foreign joint ventures with Toyota Motor Company, Volkswagen AG, and Mazda Motor Corporation, the company offers a complete line of passenger vehicles and sport-utility vehicles (SUVs). These include small economy cars, such as the TFC, Vita, and Golf, and midsized cars, such as the Sagitar/Jetta, Audi, and FAW's own Besturn line. Luxury sedans include the Crown, Reiz, and FAW's first passenger car brand, Hongqi. Under the Jiefang brand, the company produces light-, medium-, and heavy-duty trucks, rang-

ing from one ton to 50 tons. China FAW Group produces municipal buses, luxury tourist coach buses, custom bus chassis, and mini-vehicles. Automotive parts and components are produced for domestic production, and automotive parts, vehicle kits, and complete vehicles are exported to 70 countries. With assets of $14.27 billion, China FAW Group operates production facilities in Jilin and Heilongjiang provinces in northeast China, in Tianjin city and Shandong Province in the east, in Hunan Province in the south, and Sichuan and Yunnan provinces in the southwest. The company's primary production complex at Changchun, is located in Jilin. A state-of-the-art research and development facility is located in Changchun also.

COMMUNIST GOVERNMENT ESTABLISHES CHINESE AUTO INDUSTRY

The genesis of First Automotive Works (FAW), precursor to China FAW Group Corporation, occurred in 1949, when Chairman Mao Zedong traveled to the Union of Soviet Socialist Republics (U.S.S.R.). While touring industrial facilities, Mao took particular interest in the U.S.S.R.'s truck and automobile manufacturing. He determined to establish a self-sufficient transportation manufacturing base as part of China's first five-year economic plan. The Sino-Soviet Friendship Alliance Treaty, signed in 1950, initiated cooperation in building an industrial infrastructure in China, including automobile manufacturing.

China's Ministry of Heavy Industries formed the Automobile Industry Preparatory Committee to research automobile manufacturing and prepare for industrial development. Several groups of Chinese managers and technicians traveled to the Soviet Union for training in truck production, and Soviet advisers relocated to Changchun to assist with factory construction. FAW broke ground on its first automobile factory there on July 15, 1953. Mao underscored the significance of the automotive industry to China by signing his name to the foundation stone.

Upon completion of the factory complex three years later, FAW employed many thousands of workers, including 20,000 mechanical and electrical tradespeople who built and installed production equipment. The Soviet government provided all necessary tooling and more than 80 percent of the production machinery, as well as technical support. After a trial run of truck parts manufacturing in 1955, production of the CA10 four-ton, medium-duty commercial truck, began in 1956, with annual production set at 30,000 units. Mao gave the truck the name "Jiefang," meaning liberation. Despite its similarities to World War II–era Ford truck design, the Jiefang became a symbol of China's growing industrial self-sufficiency.

FAW began producing two passenger vehicles in 1958, the Dong Feng (meaning east wind), a passenger sedan, and the Hongqi (meaning red flag), a hand-crafted luxury sedan. Intended for use by government officials, the Hongqi 72 featured a 200 horsepower engine and a fanlike grill, considered classic styling in China. The Hongqi open-top limousine, intended to carry top Chinese leaders in National Day parades, debuted in September 1958. That year FAW introduced a new truck model, the CA30 Jiefang, an all-wheel drive, four-ton truck designed for off-road uses.

IMPLEMENTATION OF CAPITALIST-STYLE MANAGEMENT TECHNIQUES

In its eagerness to modernize into an industrialized nation with social equality, China pursued government programs that resulted in delaying development of its manufacturing base. Ironically, large-scale manufacturing of passenger sedans stalled as the Chinese government attempted to speed the pace of industrial development.

Dubbed the Great Leap Forward, the program hindered industrial expansion by spreading financial and management resources too widely. However, by 1960, a strategic plan for rejuvenating the automobile industry took effect, and FAW participated in the development of Second Automobile Works in 1964, overseeing construction of 11 manufacturing units. During this time FAW designed a company logo, an oval with a number one in the center and flaglike stripes.

Development of an industrial base was one of several goals of the Chinese communist government, and social prerogatives interfered with industrialization. Between 1966 and 1972, the Cultural Revolution, an attempt to equalize bourgeois and proletarian social relations, diverted China from its path of industrial expansion. Nevertheless, in another ironic twist, FAW introduced new Hongqi limousine designs for transporting heads of state visiting China. Limousines included the CA772 armored model, introduced in 1969. In 1973, FAW began construction of the 60-ton CA390, a mammoth off-highway mining truck.

By the mid-1970s, the Chinese government realized that successful industrial development required a decentralized approach to organization management. In 1975 Deputy Premier Deng Xiaoping put forward reforms for management of state enterprises. Additional reforms implemented in 1977 and 1978 specifically aided FAW in reestablishing technological and product development. China sent a group of 20 engineers to Japan in May 1978 for instruction in the efficient manufacturing techniques developed by Toyota, Mitsubishi, Isuzu, Nissan, and Honda.

Meanwhile, FAW progressed in several other projects. At Second Automobile Works, later Dongfeng Motor Corporation, FAW added new vehicle styles and increased annual production from 30,000 to 60,000 units. In 1979, FAW began to redesign the CA10/30 medium truck to include state-of-the-art automotive technology. Research and development, testing, and related facility modernization took nine years to complete. By the time production of the CA141 five-ton truck began in 1986, FAW integrated several aspects of the Japanese model of efficiency into its manufacturing process.

Factory modernization coincided with China's transition from exclusively state-run enterprises to the capitalist style of organization. Between 1983 and 1988, FAW adopted a company culture motivated by sales and profit. China's Central Committee granted FAW rights to manage operations independent from state authority, as well as to develop its own channels for domestic and international sales. One of the primary outcomes of the changes involved rapid development of new car and

KEY DATES

1953: First Automotive Works (FAW) breaks ground on manufacturing complex in Changchun.
1956: First vehicle, a medium-duty truck, is produced under the Jiefang brand.
1958: FAW introduces a passenger and a luxury sedan under Hongqi brand.
1964: FAW launches Hongqi logo.
1975: Chinese communist government initiates reforms in industrial management.
1983: China begins transition toward sales and profit orientation in manufacturing.
1988: Pilot engineering project with Volkswagen leads to first international joint venture in car production.
1998: First joint venture with Toyota Motor Company begins production of automobiles and buses.
2003: FAW obtains license to produce Mazda cars in China; FAW-VW increase joint venture car production.
2005: Vehicle production at FAW exceeds one million units for the first time.

truck designs, including continual development of new model styles and modifications. In 1986, FAW began construction on new office and factory infrastructure to develop and build cars and light-duty trucks. To strengthen FAW's capacity to manufacture light-, medium-, and heavy-load trucks, the Central Committee merged FAW with Jilin Light Truck and Mini Vehicle Corporation in 1987.

INTERNATIONAL COOPERATION, EXPANSION OF MANUFACTURING

During the late 1980s, China and FAW took steps to ensure that its industrial production would increase. Toward that end, China pursued "international cooperation" with foreign automakers. The cooperation involved the formation of joint ventures that would bring much needed knowledge and resources to Chinese companies. The first such relationship began through a pilot engineering program with Volkswagen AG. In 1988, FAW imported 30,000 Audi 100 car kits for assembly at a jointly operated plant at Changchun. The Chinese began production of the Audi 100 1.8L sedan in 1989.

Success with the pilot program led to the formation of a joint venture with Volkswagen in 1991. The first goal of FAW-Volkswagen Automobile Company, Ltd., involved building a state-of-the-art, 150,000-unit capacity automobile factory. By late 1992, FAW-Volkswagen began full production of the Audi 100 2.6 liter V6-powered sedan. The joint venture added the Golf IV in 1995. Also, FAW purchased intellectual property rights from Volkswagen in order to redesign the Hongqi sedan for broader market appeal than the brand's original government usage. In 1998 FAW introduced a new model CA7460 Hongqi luxury sedan.

FAW took the name China First Automobile Works Group Corporation in 1992 to reflect the cluster of companies developing within its domain, including joint ventures with foreign companies. In 1997 FAW Group listed on the Shenzhen stock exchange.

FAW Group formed its first joint ventures with Toyota Motor Company during the mid-1990s. Toyota joint ventures for automotive parts manufacturing were initiated in 1995 and 1996, for constant velocity universal joints and automobile engines, respectively. Vehicle production began through Sichuan Toyota Motor Co. Ltd., in November 1998 and Tianjin FAW Toyota Motor Co. Ltd. (TFTM), in June 2000. Automotive parts joint ventures included FAW-Kelsey Hayes Automobile Chassis Systems (later a TRW organization) and United Aluminum Radiator Co. Ltd., a joint venture with Visteon. These joint ventures produced automotive parts for the Chinese market and for export to 70 countries

By 2001, FAW Group had made significant strides in developing its car and truck manufacturing bases. Leaders reported to the Party Representative Conference at the 11th annual meeting with representatives of the Central Committee. Sales income, profit, and employee income had increased significantly as car and truck production had quintupled since 1988. Cars and trucks accounted for an equal amount of production. Also, FAW reached two production milestones in 2001. The 100,000th Jiefang heavy-duty commercial truck and the three millionth medium-duty truck rolled off FAW assembly lines.

PURSUING MAJOR EXPANSION THROUGH JOINT VENTURES

FAW Group President Zhu Yangeng and Toyota Motor Corporation President Fujio Cho signed an agreement as the first step toward intensifying cooperative industrial development in China. FAW expected international cooperation with Toyota to strengthen FAW's competitive stand with Shanghai Automotive Industry Corporation (SAIC), China's leader in passenger car manufacturing. Plans involved building toward annual production of 500,000 compact cars, luxury sedans, and SUVs.

The first project established was the Sichuan FAW Toyota Motor Company, Ltd. FAW acquired an 80 percent interest in Sichuan Bus Company, in which Toyota already participated as a joint venture partner in the production of coaster-class buses.

In 2002, FAW Group acquired 51 percent ownership of Tianjin Xiali Automobile from the Tianjin Automotive Industry, then formed a joint venture with Toyota. The acquisition provided FAW with the Xiali small car brand and a base for manufacturing small cars with Toyota. The Vios, an economy car model, began production in October 2002.

Other projects with Toyota included an April 2003 agreement to transfer technology for the production of four vehicle models, including the Corolla and Crown passenger cars, plus the Land Cruiser and Land Cruiser Prado SUVs. The alliance provided FAW with new technology to improve the Hongqi luxury sedan. Sichuan FAW Toyota Motor Co. began production of the Land Cruiser 100 in 2003. Also, a joint venture with Toyota's Daihatsu led to the production of 10,000 Dario compact SUVs beginning in October 2003.

Infrastructure for car production required the formation of several joint ventures. In September 2003 FAW Toyota Motor Sales Co. was established to develop sales networks for jointly produced automobiles, buses, SUVs, as well as Daihatsu vehicles. Previously, vehicles were sold through Chinese dealerships. Sales and service offices were set up in Beijing and five Chinese cities.

To maintain an adequate supply of steel for automobile production, FAW and Baosteel, one of China's leading steel manufacturers, signed an agreement to develop a steel manufacturing base near FAW. Along with Sumitomo Corporation of Japan, the investment of $21 million involved development of steel processing technology and delivery logistics, as well as business management and automobile sales models that address the competitive atmosphere for cars and steel in China and worldwide.

In further preparation for expansion of Toyota production, another Tianjin joint venture, Toyota FAW (Tianjin) Dies Co., Ltd., (TFTD), announced plans to begin production of large automotive stamping dies in 2004. Toyota invested 90 percent of the capital in this project, rather than the usual 50 percent. TFTD produced stamping dies for three car models, eventually expanding to six car models.

In 2004 the new joint venture FAW Toyota Changchun Engine Company began manufacturing three-liter

V6 engines for the Crown luxury sedan, the latter to be produced by TFTM. Production began on the Crown car in March 2005, followed by the Reiz, manufactured along the same production line, for total production of 150,000 units. The Reiz, a sedan available in three models, was designed to compete with midpriced sedans distributed by Honda, Nissan, and Mazda. The Reiz entered production with customer preorders in October 2005.

FAW Group continued to develop operations with Volkswagen. In 2002, the FAW-Volkswagen production surpassed the 500,000 unit mark, with 207,860 cars built in 2002 alone. These included the Volkswagen Jetta (marketed as the Sagitar), Golf, and Bora models, and the Audi 4 and Audi 6 models. In July 2003 FAW-Volkswagen began construction on three new manufacturing facilities. FAW-Volkswagen No. 2 Salon Car Factory, Ltd., and FAW-Salon Car Co. added production capacity for another 100,000 cars annually, for total production of 660,000 units by FAW and Volkswagen.

In 2003 FAW obtained a license to produce Mazda6 and Mazda Premacy cars. The Mazda6 sedan sold 20,000 units during the first half of 2004, prompting FAW to expand production to 100,000 units annually. FAW and Mazda arranged to increase automotive parts procurement in order to meet new production levels. FAW Mazda Motor Sales formed in 2005 to develop a dealer sales and service network for Mazda cars.

GROWTH BRINGS PROBLEMS, NEW OPPORTUNITIES

While FAW reached a major milestone in exceeding the one million mark for annual production in 2005, the company faced financial difficulties. Its FAW-Volkswagen joint venture experienced substantial losses, and large investments in the FAW-Toyota joint ventures hindered short-term profitability. The Xiali line of car brands sold very well, but garnered small profit margins. Moreover, it became questionable whether the Hongqi brand of cars could be revived.

FAW's strategy for renewing profitability and growth involved regional and international initiatives. FAW Jilin planned to begin production of 1.3 liter and 1.5 liter engine minibuses by early 2007, and the company intended to develop new car models to increase its production base. Toward that end, FAW Jilin signed an agreement with Daihatsu to design a minicar. In September 2005, Guangzhou-based FAW Hongta Yunnan Automobile absorbed Baolong Special Vehicle Company, manufacturer of trucks, agricultural vehicles, passenger cars, and sedans. FAW planned to expand the facility, in an effort to capture market share in southern China.

FAW sought to increase its business with Russia. FAW planned to build a pickup truck assembly plant in Russia through a joint venture with Hebei Zhongxing Automobile Co. in northern China, with which FAW already exported cars. FAW contributed technology to the venture while Hebei Zhongxing contributed parts and components. After selling 1,000 minivans and light- and heavy-duty trucks in 2005, FAW intended to increase its export to 10,000 complete vehicles, including economy cars. Russia's reduction of tariffs on Chinese auto parts and kits, and increase in tariffs on complete cars, forced FAW to adjust its strategy.

FAW formed joint ventures with several automotive supply manufacturers, to produce automotive parts for domestic use and for export. Companies included Tianjin Fawer Desno Air Conditioner Co. and the Valeo Fawer Compressor, the latter of which produced air conditioner compressors. TRW Fawer Commercial Vehicle Steering Systems Co. formed in 2004, and the ArvinMerito FAW Sichuan Vehicle Brake Co. formed in 2005. Fawer Y-TEC produced chassis parts for Mazda6 cars. FAW Forging Co. formed a joint venture with India's Bhorat Forge in 2006. FAW Bhorat Forge provided heat treatment, tool and die, machining, processing, testing, and logistics for 900 different forged parts for cars and trucks. The factory produced 100,000 tons of parts annually, and the venture planned for total capacity of 200,000 tons within ten years.

In April 2006 FAW-VW drastically reduced the price of the Sports Bora, and FAW cut prices on several other vehicles. FAW increased credit available to purchase FAW Group vehicles through First Automobile Finance, a consumer credit organization able to process applications within seven days. FAW Mazda Motor Sales, Ltd., launched its automobile financing for all FAW Group vehicles, not just FAW Mazda brands, at outlets in Beijing, Shanghai, Shenzhen, and Changchun.

FAW PURSUES INDEPENDENT AUTOMOBILE DEVELOPMENT

In August 2006 FAW Car Company Ltd. introduced what the company considered its first independently developed automobile, the Besturn 301. However, the Besturn utilized the Mazda6 production platform and certain technologies from foreign automakers, such as all aluminum fuel-injection. Designed by Giorgetto Giugiaro, of Italy, the car offered luxury and style as well as performance and safety features. The Besturn line of six models competed with foreign midsized sedans, such as

the Buick Regal, Ford Mondeo, Toyota Camry, and Honda Accord. FAW priced the cars low, according to consumer preference showed in market surveys.

FAW attempted to revive its original brand vehicles, the Jiefang truck and Hongqi passenger sedans. The Jiefang J6 long-distance heavy tractor truck, which took six years to design, succeeded in reaching quality standards that made the vehicle more competitive with foreign manufacturers. FAW Group considered the J6 an important product for its growing export business to the Middle East, Asia, and North Africa. New markets included Indonesia, Argentina, Iran, Russia, and Egypt. However, FAW Group lacked the sales network and talent for significant international business development.

The Hongqi brand offered a line of HQ3 sedans, styled to compete with General Motors Cadillac, Mercedes Benz, Toyota Majesta, and Volkswagen Audi luxury sedans. Toyota sold FAW intellectual property for the platform for the HQ3 from its Majesta brand. The sedan featured aerodynamic styling, adaptive front lighting, speed-sensitive progressive variable-ratio steering, powerful V6 or V8 engine options, automatic transmission, and a navigation system.

FAW Group rebounded from its earlier difficulties as the company successfully built 1.47 million cars and sold 1.44 million in 2007, a 23.2 percent increase over 2006. Cars sold under FAW brands increased 12.8 percent, to 620,000 vehicles. Export sales increased 44 percent, to 28,800 vehicles. Vehicles produced by FAW Group's joint ventures increased 32 percent, to 816,000 vehicles. The VW Jetta was particularly successful, with 201,131 units sold in 2007. Revenue reached CNY 187.6 billion in 2007

As China became the second largest market for new car sales, FAW announced its intention to invest $1.7 billion to develop new vehicle brands and styles through 2015. SUVs, Hongqi sedans, and commercial vehicles were included in the plan. At its state-of-the-art research center in Changchun, FAW employed 1,600 engineers to support its goal. The facility featured the only vehicle testing in China for cold and semitropical weather.

FAW Mexico partner Grupo Salinas, broke ground on a $150 million car assembly plant in the state of Michoacán in late 2007. FAW offered two small cars, the Xiali and Vita, for sale through 18 dealerships in Mexico and Central America. Grupo Salinas sold 5,000 FAW cars in 2008.

FAW Group and Toyota broke ground on the sixth joint venture automobile manufacturing plant in November 2008. FAW and Toyota planned to build 100,000 Corollas annually at the facility, increasing Toyota's auto manufacturing base in China to 643,000 cars. The two companies expanded two other plants and planned to add a 120,000 capacity production line at the Guangzhou factory, jointly owned with Guangzhou Automotive, increasing that plant's capacity to 200,000 vehicles per year. These developments brought Toyota's annual production in China to just over one million cars per year.

Although production and sales continued to increase at FAW Group, the company retained the atmosphere of a state-owned entity, a situation that hindered its ability to keep pace with China's rapidly growing automobile market. The more entrepreneurial SAIC expanded at a much faster rate, succeeding FAW Group as the largest automaker in the country in 2008.

Losing market share to other Chinese automakers, FAW Group launched its own new vehicle styles, such as the Besturn B70, which sold 47,750 units in 2008, double sales of 2007. In 2009 FAW Group launched the Besturn B50 sedan, comparable to the VW Jetta and using the VW Sagitar 1.6 liter engine. FAW both competed and cooperated with Volkswagen, as FAW-Volkswagen acquired Chengdu FAW in southwestern China in March 2009, increasing the joint venture's annual production by 50,000 units.

FAW Group designed the Haima 3 Hatchback to attract younger car buyers. The second generation of Haima 3, the Haima Family and Haima Happin models, did not do well, primarily attracting customers over 40 years of age and causing distributors to reduce prices. FAW Group hoped to counter Haima's stodgy image with the Haima 3 Hatchback. The model filled the gap left by the Mazda 323 in 2006, when Mazda exited the Chinese market.

FAW Group sought to address the environmental concerns related to automotive emissions. In 2009 the company launched two new small car models, the TFC-M1 and the TFC-M2, to replace the Xiali N3 and the Weizh. FAW Group began to develop alternative energy technology, such as a 1.3 liter hybrid engine for the Besturn B7. Another project involved transforming the small Veta car model into an all-electric vehicle. Work on new buses involved hybrid and natural gas powered buses using proprietary powertrain technology. The Dalian Public Transportation Group Company ordered 150 hybrid buses and 11 natural gas buses, to be manufactured at a bus production facility expected to open in Dalian in 2010.

Mary Tradii

PRINCIPAL SUBSIDIARIES

Changchun FAW Sichuan Automobile Co. Ltd.; FAW Bus and Coach Co. Ltd.; FAW Car Co. Ltd.; FAW Jief-ang Truck Co. Ltd.; FAW-Volkswagen Automobile Co. Ltd. (50 %); Tianjin FAW Toyota Motor Co. Ltd. (50 %); Tianjin FAW Xiali Automobile Co. Ltd.

PRINCIPAL COMPETITORS

Brilliance China Automotive Holdings, Ltd.; Chang'an Motors; Dongfeng Motor Group Company Ltd.; Shanghai Automotive Industry Corporation.

FURTHER READING

"Auto Price Cuts in China," *SinoCast, LLC China Transportation Watch,* April 7, 2006.

"China Exclusive: China's Home-Grown Auto Brands Eager to Shed Low-Grade Image, Penetrate Overseas Markets," *Xinhua Economic News,* July 15, 2007.

"China FAW Boosting Auto Credit," *SinoCast China Financial Watch,* June 26, 2006.

"China FAW Group Corp.," *Automotive News,* April 27, 2009, p. S022.

"FAW Group to Attempt Toyota Marketing Model," *SinoCast, LLC China Transportation Watch,* March 23, 2007.

"The FAW Group in Acquisition Plan," *Asia Africa Intelligence Wire,* November 14, 2006.

"The FAW Group Vies for Chinese High-Grade Sedan Market," *SinoCast, LLC China Transportation Watch,* March 14, 2007.

"FAW Increases Spending on Auto Parts," *SinoCast, LLC China Transportation Watch,* June 14, 2007.

"FAW Making Jetta in SW China," *SinoCast, LLC China Transportation Watch,* July 30, 2007.

"FAW Unveils Own Brand Besturn," *SinoCast, LLC China Transportation Watch,* August 24, 2006.

"FAW-Volkswagen to Launch Audi A8L in Dec.," *SinoCast, LLC China Transportation Watch,* November 22, 2007.

"GN Plans Truck JV with FAW," *Business Daily Update,* February 10, 2009.

"Jilin Provincial Gov't Launches Policies to Support FAW," *Asia Africa Intelligence Wire,* July 13, 2005.

"Toyota, FAW Group Set Up Joint Car Sales Company in China," *KYODO News International,* October 29, 2003.

"Toyota to Challenge Japanese Rivals in China with New Hit," *SinoCast, LLC China Transportation Watch,* September 16, 2005.

"Toyota's Push into China to Rev Up Competition," *Asia Africa Intelligence Wire,* August 31, 2002.

Treece, James B., "FAW Had an Edge, Now It Struggles to Sharpen It; Old Government Ties Give It 'Guanxi' but Hinder Performance," *Automotive News Europe,* November 17, 2003, p. 20.

Chongqing Department Store Company Ltd.

2 Minquan Road
Yuzhong District
Chongqing, 400010
China
Telephone: (+86 023) 6384 3197
Fax: (+86 023) 6384 4212
Web site: http://www.cqbhdl.com.cn

Public Company
Incorporated: 1992
Employees: 8,634
Sales: CNY 6.4 billion ($936.8 million) (2008)
Stock Exchanges: Shanghai
Ticker Symbol: 600729
NAICS: 452110 Department Stores

∎∎∎

Chongqing Department Store Company Ltd. is one of the leading retail groups in the city of Chongqing (formerly known as Chungking) and in the wider Sichuan (or Szechuan) Province of China. Chongqing operates more than 22 department stores, primarily in the Chongqing metropolitan region, which includes a population of more than 14 million people. Since the turn of the century, Chongqing Department Store has been expanding beyond its core market. In 2007, for example, the company opened its first store outside of its home base, in Zunyi, in nearby Guizhou Province. The company has also targeted a number of specific markets for growth, including Chengdu, Luzhou, Panzhihua, Leshan, Jianyang, Guiyang, and Xi'an. The

company has announced plans to boost its total number of department stores past 40 by 2010. Chongqing Department Store, a state-owned publicly listed company, also operates in two other retail sectors, electronics stores and supermarkets, adding an additional 60 stores to its retail operations. Chongqing Department Store is listed on the Shanghai Stock Exchange. Its major shareholder is Chongqing General Trading (Group) Company Ltd., a diversified conglomerate that also counts among China's leading retail groups, which also owns other retail groups, including Chongqing New Century Department Store Company, among others. Chongqing Department Store Company posted total revenues of CNY 6.4 billion ($936.8 million) in 2008.

STATE-RUN RETAILER IN 1950

Chongqing became one of China's major urban centers in the middle of the 20th century. The city's location at the beginning of the Yangtze River made the city an important gateway into the western regions of China. The city's population at the time was relatively small, numbering just 250,000 into the middle of the century.

From the 1920s, the city achieved some notoriety as an outpost for organized crime, running opium and other goods to other Chinese cities. During the war between China and Japan in the 1930s, Chongqing became the headquarters for Chiang Kai-shek. Through the first half of the 1940s, it served as the capital of Free China during Chiang Kai-shek's battle against the Communists.

Chongqing therefore had the dubious honor of becoming one of the first Chinese cities to be "liberated" by the Communists in 1949. Among the new local government's first moves was the nationalization of the region's industries. This included a takeover of the retail sector, which became subject to the collective policies of the new Communist state. Local governments then established "department stores," stocked with China-produced goods. Chongqing was the first to open a department store in 1950, which became the predecessor to the future Chongqing Department Store Company.

The Western-style department store format had arrived in China after 1900, when a number of expatriate Chinese who had been living in Australia returned to China. Nonetheless, the retail format remained a somewhat limited phenomenon, particularly in China's less populated outlying regions. Even in Shanghai, the economic capital of China during the first half of the century, there were only four large-scale department stores in operation at the time of the Communist Revolution.

In the 1940s, the wave of Chinese nationalist sentiment had led many of the country's department stores to emphasize Chinese-made products. This trend culminated in the establishment of a number of department stores entirely specialized in trading Chinese goods. The state-run department stores, including the Chongqing store, that were established following the Communist takeover took up the same policy of stocking only goods produced in China.

MARKET REFORMS IN THE SEVENTIES AND EIGHTIES

State-run companies dominated China's retail sector over the next decades. Yet production levels and production quality suffered under the years of disastrous economic, agricultural, and industrial policies carried out by the Maoist regime. Department stores were required to purchase through state-run wholesale companies, which in turn were supplied by state-run manufacturers, providing little incentive to achieve basic quality standards, production efficiencies, and service

levels. Retailers also sold goods at prices fixed by the government.

As a result, shoppers at the Chongqing Department Store and others were offered little choice in the type and quality of goods. Clothing choices, for example, were often limited to the infamous drab Mao-inspired uniform of the era, and exhibited a lack of concern for style. Little choice existed either in quality levels, as high-end and higher-quality products remained unavailable to the average Chinese. On the whole, retail offerings were limited to basic and slow-moving goods, including buttons, cloth, farm equipment, and housewares with little room for luxury.

The state-run stores often dispensed with packaging altogether, and had no need to advertise. Other consumer-unfriendly retail policies of the period included a lack of dressing rooms for trying on clothing prior to a purchase. Consumers were confronted with the state-run stores' no-returns policies as well.

The new era for China's retail sector arrived with the development of the country's economic reform program in the late 1970s under Deng Xiaoping. The government began to implement a gradual shift to an economy based, at least in part, on a free-market system. Much of these early reform efforts focused on the country's heavily populated eastern region.

Into the mid-1980s, Chongqing too became designated as one of the Chinese government's proving grounds for its new economic policies. Designated as a "pathfinder on the road to modernization," Chongqing began liberalizing its retail sector by the middle of the decade. Under the new policies, competing, privately owned stores were allowed to be opened for the first time. Retailers were also given the right to purchase directly, and negotiate their own terms, from manufacturers. At the same time, retailers were also given more flexibility to set their own prices.

Chongqing Department Store and other state-run department stores helped set the tone. Into the end of the decade, the state-run stores began running lotteries, using highly sought-after appliances as incentives to attract shoppers. The state-owned retailers also launched sales promotions, promising discounts of 10 percent or more. At the same time, the state-run stores were freed to develop a wider product assortment, including higher-end goods from China's newly bustling manufacturing sector, as well as imported goods.

CHONGQING MARKET LEADER IN THE NINETIES

By 1992, the local Chongqing government had begun moving toward relinquishing control over its state-run

KEY DATES

1950: Local Chongqing (Chungking) government establishes a state-owned department store.

1992: Chongqing government incorporates Chongqing Department Store Company, affiliated with Chongqing General Trading (Group) Company Ltd.

1996: Chongqing Department Store goes public on the Shanghai Stock Exchange.

2004: Chongqing Department Store merges with Chongqing General Trading (Group) Company Ltd.

2009: Chongqing Department Store announces plans to open up to ten stores that year.

department stores. This process began with the creation of a new company, Chongqing Department Store Company, that year. The new company took over the city's largest department store, as well as a number of other stores in the Chongqing metropolitan district. In 1996, Chongqing Department Store Company went public, listing its shares on the Shanghai Stock Exchange. The company remained closely affiliated with another state-run entity, Chongqing General Trading (Group) Company Ltd., a diversified conglomerate with operations in the manufacturing and industrial sectors, as well as in the retail sector.

The Chinese economic reform policies nonetheless had other consequences for the large state-owned department stores. Most prominent among these was the introduction of a new and highly competitive environment, including the creation of a number of new Chinese-owned department store groups, as well as the entry into the mainland market of a number of foreign players, notably the United States' Wal-Mart, France's Carrefour, and the United Kingdom's Tesco, among others.

These players also became part of a shift in the retail sector toward more specialized operations, including the appearance of new Western-style supermarkets. Other specialty shops also began to emerge focusing on a single product category, such as electronics and home appliances or furniture, for example. Also during the 1990s, the Chinese market witnessed the arrival of the first hypermarkets, which combined supermarket operations with department store features, as well as a growing number of large-scale shopping malls.

Meanwhile, buoyed by the rapidly increasing consumer purchasing power in the late 1980s and through the mid-1990s, the department store sector continued its own expansion. In 1992, there were just 98 department stores in operation across the country. By 1998, that number had swollen to more than 1,000.

MARKET CHANGES

Chongqing Department Store Company responded to the changes in the market with its own expansion drive. The company began extending its department store network, opening or acquiring new sites throughout the Chongqing metropolitan district. The company also added its own specialty retail operations, targeting the supermarket and electronics retail sectors, building up a portfolio of 60 stores by 2005. The company also entered shopping mall operation with the construction of the Chongbai Hechuan Shopping Mall that same year. Chongqing Department Store Company rose to become one of China's top 25 department store companies.

The department store sector elsewhere in China began to stumble toward the end of the 1990s. This was in part because of new austerity measures put in place by the Chinese government. At the same time, consumer spending patterns had begun to shift, placing a greater emphasis on housing, education, and retirement pensions, and reducing their discretionary spending. Many of the country's department stores were forced to close, while others began merging together for strength, creating a smaller number of large-scale department store groups.

Chongqing Department Store Company enjoyed a degree of protection from these trends, in large part because of its leading status in what had become China's fastest-growing urban center. Indeed, by the early 2000s, Chongqing (including a number of outlying rural areas) claimed to be China's single largest metropolis, with a population of more than 14 million and climbing. The steady influx of people enabled the company to continue to enjoy strong growth.

EXPANDING BEYOND CHONGQING

Nonetheless, the increasing importance of Chongqing as a gateway to China's less developed western regions also attracted the attention of outside groups, both from elsewhere in China and among the multinationals. Chongqing Department Store Company recognized that it needed to become part of a larger group in order to retain its status as a market leader. In 2004, therefore the company carried out a merger with Chongqing

General Trading (Group) Company Ltd., which by then had grown into China's 14th largest department store group. The combination of the two created China's eighth largest retail chain, with revenues of more than CNY 11 billion (approximately $1.3 billion).

Following the merger, Chongqing General held approximately one-third of Chongqing Department Store, which remained a publicly listed company. The merged group then announced its intention to expand its revenues to CNY 20 billion by 2007, and again to CNY 30 billion by 2010.

Chongqing Department Store Company intended to play a leading role in that growth. Into the middle of the decade, the company adopted a new strategy of expanding beyond its core Chongqing market, adding a number of new stores throughout the Sichuan Province.

The company then targeted growth beyond Sichuan Province. In 2006, the company made its first move outside of its home region, opening a store in Zunyi, in Guizhou Province. The success of that venture led the company to develop greater ambitions. In 2007, Chongqing Department Store Company announced plans to open stores in Chengdu, Luzhou, Panzhihua, Leshan, Jianyang, Guiyang, and Xi'an through the end of the decade.

The company's growth strategy was buoyed by its strong results. In 2007, for example, the group reported revenue gains of over 14 percent in its department store division, and 33 percent and 36 percent in its supermarket and electrical appliances operations. These gains continued through 2008, despite the softening of the Chinese economy amid the global financial crisis, as the company's total revenues improved by approximately 17 percent, climbing to CNY 6.4 billion ($936.8 million). In that year, the company announced plans to open as many as ten new stores through 2009, and raise its total number of department stores from 22 to 40 by 2010. As one of the oldest of China's department store groups, Chongqing Department Store Company appeared determined to remain among the leaders in the new century.

M. L. Cohen

PRINCIPAL SUBSIDIARIES

Chongqing Department Store is a subsidiary of Chongqing General Trading (Group) Company Ltd.

PRINCIPAL DIVISIONS

General Merchandise; Supermarkets; Electronics and Appliances.

PRINCIPAL COMPETITORS

Dashang Group Company Ltd.; Beijing Wanfujing Department Store (Group) Company Ltd.; Shanghai Bailian Group Company Ltd.; Beijing Hualian Hypermarket Company Ltd.; Wuhan Zhongbai Group Company Ltd.; Beijing Jingkelong Company Ltd.; Shanghai Yuyuan Tourist Mart Company Ltd.; Chongqing Dept Store Company Ltd.; Wuhan Department Store Group Company Ltd.; Hefei Department Store Group Company Ltd.; Parkson Retail Group Ltd.

FURTHER READING

"Chongqing Becomes Leading Business Center in Western China," *Alestron*, February 1, 2001.

"Chongqing Department Store Brewing More Supermarkets," *Alestron*, September 18, 2008.

"Chongqing Department Store Expects 75% Growth in H1 Profits," *Alestron*, July 17, 2008.

"Chongqing Department Store to Buy Land for Expansion," *Alestron*, December 13, 2005.

"Chongqing's Local Retailer Prepares for External Challenge," *Alestron*, April 13, 2004.

"CPDSG to Build Largest Department Store in Chongqing," *Asia Africa Intelligence Wire*, February 5, 2004.

"Department Stores in IPO Frenzy," *SinoCast China Financial Watch*, March 22, 2007.

"Guang'an Store of Chongqing Department Store Opened," *Alestron*, July 25, 2007.

"Retailers Quickens Expansion in Sichuan 2nd-Tier Cities," *Alestron*, October 8, 2008.

"Supermarket Chains Expand Despite Tough Conditions," *Australia China Connections*, February 3, 2009.

"2008 Annual Report: Chongqing Department Store Co., Ltd.," *Xinhua Economic News*, February 26, 2009.

Cincinnati Bell Inc.

221 East Fourth Street
Cincinnati, Ohio 45202
U.S.A.
Telephone: (513) 397-9900
Toll Free: (800) 276-2384
Fax: (513) 397-5092
Web site: http://www.cincinnatibell.com

Public Company
Incorporated: 1873 as City and Suburban Telegraph Association
Employees: 3,300
Sales: $1.4 billion (2008)
Stock Exchanges: New York
Ticker Symbol: CBB
NAICS: 517110 Wired Telecommunications Carriers; 511210 Software Publishers; 518210 Data Processing, Hosting, and Related Services; 551112 Offices of Other Holding Companies

■ ■ ■

Cincinnati Bell Inc. is a regional provider of data and voice communications services, using both wireline and wireless networks. The company provides wireline voice and data services through Cincinnati Bell Telephone Company LLC, which serves customers in southwestern Ohio, northern Kentucky, and southeastern Indiana, as well as Dayton and Mason, Ohio. Cincinnati Bell's wireless business is operated through another subsidiary, Cincinnati Bell Wireless LLC, which serves customers in the same operating territory served by its wireline

subsidiary. A third business segment, technology solutions, provides outsourced telecommunications and information technology services through Cincinnati Bell Technology Solutions Inc. and GramTel Inc. The company's wireline local voice business accounts for 27 percent of its annual revenue. Its wireline data business, which includes a customer base of 233,000 digital-subscriber-line (DSL) customers, accounts for 19 percent of its annual revenue. The technology solutions segment contributes 22 percent of Cincinnati Bell's annual revenue. The company's wireless business, which provides cellular service to 550,000 subscribers, accounts for 22 percent of its annual revenue.

19TH-CENTURY ORIGINS

For the bulk of its history, Cincinnati Bell limited its operations to phone services in its home area surrounding Cincinnati. With the breakup of the U.S. telephone monopoly, however, Cincinnati Bell gained the opportunity to enter unregulated fields, and altered its corporate direction in the ensuing years to take advantage of new technologies in the computer and telecommunications fields.

The company that would become Cincinnati Bell was founded in 1873, when the City and Suburban Telegraph Association was incorporated in the State of Ohio. This company, established to provide telegraph links between the workplaces and private homes of businessmen, got its start when Cincinnati transportation executive Charles H. Kilgour hired a clerk to run errands between Kilgour's home and office, after his mobility was curtailed by an injury. When the clerk

COMPANY PERSPECTIVES

Cincinnati Bell is one of the nation's most respected and best performing local exchange and wireless providers, with a legacy of unparalleled customer service excellence and financial strength. Cincinnati Bell provides a wide range of telecommunications products and services to residential and business customers in Ohio, Kentucky and Indiana.

tired of his daily round, he suggested that a telegraph line be strung between Kilgour's residence and his place of business to allow easier communication. This was done, and soon other businessmen became intrigued by the idea. Together with Kilgour, they founded a company for the purpose of installing home telegraph lines.

By 1874 the fledgling company had issued stock to raise funds, held its first shareholders' meeting, and selected a president. In its early years the company operated at a deficit, but by mid-1877, it had installed nearly 50 private telegraph lines between homes and offices. Customers who signed up for the service were also equipped with simple telegraph instruments and code books for sending and deciphering messages in Morse code.

1877: FIRST TELEPHONE CUSTOMER

In July 1877 the managers of the City and Suburban Telegraph Association were given a demonstration of a new communication device, the telephone. First invented by Alexander Graham Bell in Boston in 1875, the telephone had been patented and exhibited to great acclaim at the Great Industrial Exposition in Philadelphia in 1876. The men assembled in Kilgour's study in Cincinnati heard the voice of a telegraph operator come to them over the wires from a post at the Mount Lookout Observatory outside of town. Excited by what they heard, the stockholders of City and Suburban decided to market the new device. They hired the person who had arranged the telephone's demonstration, James O. Shiras, as their first salesman, and assigned him the task of persuading their telegraph customers to switch to the new method, and enrolling the rest of the public as well.

By August 21, 1877, the company lined up its first telephone customer, the Cincinnati Gas & Coke

Company. Soon, a grocer followed suit, and other Cincinnati businesses signed on in short order. In the spring and summer of the following year, City and Suburban began negotiations to become the exclusive franchise holder of Bell Telephone Company in the Cincinnati area. On September 10, a contract was signed, and within a short period 18 customers had been enrolled. They paid City and Suburban $3 a month for service, which doubled to $6 in the following year. To reflect its widening role, the company changed its name to City and Suburban Telegraph Association and Telephonic Exchange.

City and Suburban's switchboard, state of the art for the day, was run by young men, who worked a foot treadle to provide the electricity necessary to ring the call bells. The telephones themselves had one hand-piece, which the operator moved from ear to mouth, and users were required to depress a button on the phone while they were using it in order to maintain the connection.

CITY AND SUBURBAN TANGLES WITH WESTERN UNION

A short while after City and Suburban introduced telephone service, a competitor in the market, Western Union, appeared and began offering its own telephone equipment, based on the inventions of Thomas Edison and others. After a yearlong nationwide struggle for the developing market, Western Union and Bell Telephone reached an agreement in late 1879 in which the former relinquished its participation in the telephone industry, and Bell promised not to compete in the telegraph business.

In May 1879 Cincinnati's first telephone book appeared, with classified listings of over 500 patrons. Shortly thereafter, the first women were employed in the job they would come to dominate, telephone operator. By the end of 1879 telephone lines reached across the Suspension Bridge over the Ohio River to Covington, Kentucky.

In addition to its geographical expansion, the company adopted technological innovations. Its switchboard, which had been designed by Thomas Watson, Alexander Graham Bell's assistant, was replaced by a Cincinnati-built Jones Switch Table. Further, small branch exchanges were built throughout the city and connected by trunk lines.

By 1889, the company served more than 1,000 customers and employed 25 people. As a result of its successful expansion, City and Suburban paid its first dividend. Three years later, the company signed its first contract with the American Telephone and Telegraph

KEY DATES

1873: Cincinnati Bell's earliest predecessor, City and Suburban Telegraph Association, is formed.

1877: Company switches its focus from telegraph to telephone.

1889: City and Suburban begins providing long-distance service.

1903: Company's name is changed to Cincinnati and Suburban Bell Telephone Company.

1941: Company installs its 100,000th telephone.

1952: Conversion to dial service is completed.

1983: Company reorganizes itself as a holding company.

1996: Federal legislation allows long-distance companies to offer local-exchange services.

1998: Cincinnati Bell launches a wireless business.

1999: Company acquires IXC Communications for $3.2 billion, which leads it to change its name to BroadWing Inc.

2003: Company divests the IXC assets and changes its name back to Cincinnati Bell.

2004: Cincinnati Bell begins offering residential telephone service in Dayton, Ohio.

2008: Company acquires eGix Inc., which provides voice and data services in 23 states.

Company (AT&T), the corporate heir to the Bell System, for long-distance service. By that time, City and Suburban's franchise had expanded to cover parts of Ohio, Kentucky, and Indiana. The company's switchboards required the efforts of 100 operators, who directed calls over 2,000 miles of telephone cable.

In 1883 and 1884, City and Suburban was challenged by a series of floods on the Ohio River, which crested at over 60 feet 13 times in just two years. As a result of these events, the company was compelled to spend over $1 million on reconstruction. Despite these setbacks, by 1885 the system had expanded to include 450 towns surrounding Cincinnati, and an ever increasing number of customers within city limits. With the introduction of electricity and electric street cars, City and Suburban encountered another problem with its network as the electric wires interfered with transmission over the phone lines, and also caused fires. The eventual solution to this problem was to consolidate the maze of overhead wires into one cable, which could be buried underground.

In the 1890s telephone installers and repairmen transported themselves by bicycle. In 1893, Cincinnati's first long-distance call was put through to the mayor of New York City. In that same year, the Bell System's patents expired, and competition returned to the telephone industry. Customers of City and Suburban were free to purchase telephone equipment and service from other firms. In order to have complete telephone service, however, subscribers needed to have one phone from each competing company installed, causing them considerable expense and annoyance at having to locate other subscriber numbers in an assortment of phonebooks. This era ended in 1906, when the mayor of Cincinnati declared that he would veto any franchise granted to competing telephone companies by the city council.

NAME CHANGE IN 1903

Six years earlier, however, City and Suburban replaced its obsolete switchboards and equipment with new facilities which eliminated the use of the magneto crank phone. In 1903 the company changed its name, becoming Cincinnati and Suburban Bell Telephone Company. In the following year, the first public coin-operated phones were installed, and in 1905 they began appearing on city streets. Cincinnati Bell entered an era of steady expansion in the early 1900s as rates for service dropped.

The government, responsible for regulating telephone service areas and rates in Ohio beginning in 1911, established a regulatory agency, the Public Utilities Commission of Ohio, in 1913. The agency provided protection from competition in exchange for Cincinnati Bell's agreement to limit its service area and set its rates as determined by the agency. Also in 1913 Cincinnati Bell moved into a new headquarters building, lending much-needed room for an additional exchange. Further expansion came in the next few years, as the company acquired Harrison Telephone Company in Indiana and Citizens Telephone Company in northern Kentucky.

When the United States entered World War I in April 1917, the economy was transformed. Cincinnati Bell lost employees to the military effort, and the company suffered from high inflation and shortages of materials. In 1918 the federal government assumed operation of all telephone companies until the signing of a peace treaty in November of that year. When the companies were put back in the hands of their owners, an enormous, pent-up demand for new service greeted them.

In July 1919 the first union of Cincinnati Bell employees was formed when the Telephone Employees

Association was voted into existence to advocate for higher wages and better working conditions. Also in that year, the company purchased one of its competitors, located in Hamilton, Ohio, after a prolonged legal battle. Shortly thereafter, Cincinnati Bell also consolidated and purchased a number of independent telephone operations in Clermont County, Ohio.

INFRASTRUCTURE IMPROVE-MENTS DURING THE TWENTIES

The 1920s were a period of strong growth and expansion for the company. By 1923, its 50th year, Cincinnati Bell's network incorporated almost 141,000 phones. Four years later the company introduced the handset telephone to replace the upright "candlestick phone," which had a separate piece to be held to the ear. In that same year, the company's first transatlantic telephone call was made by the president of Cincinnati Bell from Ohio to London.

On a slightly less grand scale, Cincinnati Bell inaugurated its own submarine cable when it laid wires across the Ohio River from Cincinnati to Covington, Kentucky, in 1928. In addition, the company launched the expensive transformation from switchboard operator service to dial service, in which calls were automatically connected by a switching machine. The company brought the ambitious activities of the decade to a close by embarking on the construction of a new 12-story headquarters building, specially designed with tiled floors and smooth concrete walls to shield sensitive dial telephone switching equipment from dust.

By 1929 Cincinnati Bell boasted a network of nearly 200,000 telephones, and assets worth $38 million. Its momentum, however, was threatened by the crash of the New York Stock Exchange in the fall of that year, which threw the country into the Great Depression. The next decade saw Cincinnati Bell's growth seriously curtailed by the country's poor economic climate. Nevertheless, some forward strides were made. A second underwater cable was laid on the bottom of Licking River in 1934. Two years later, the company announced that it would construct three new telephone exchanges in rapidly growing suburban areas.

In 1937 service to 13,000 Cincinnati Bell telephones was knocked out when the Ohio River flooded once again, spilling over its banks and cresting at 80 feet. Despite this setback, and the widespread devastation it caused within the company's service area, Cincinnati Bell continued its campaign to convert its operations to dial service, changing over two-thirds of its exchanges by the end of the decade. The year 1939 also

marked the end of the company's financial downturn when the number of its telephones in service once again began to increase. In 1941 Cincinnati Bell celebrated the installation of its 100,000th phone.

Later that year, however, this milestone was overshadowed by the involvement of the United States in World War II. Once again, the company suffered wartime shortages of manpower and materials. Within two years of the war's start, Cincinnati Bell had accumulated 10,000 unfilled orders for service. Even though the company began handing out obsolete upright phones it had stored away, it was not able to fill all demands for service. Still, in October 1946 it became the first Bell System company to clear up its wartime backlog of orders.

POSTWAR GROWTH

In the postwar years Cincinnati's economy began a rapid expansion; Cincinnati Bell grew with it. The company inaugurated service on its 300,000th telephone in 1947. Two years later, as it struggled still with shortages of material, which drove costs up, the company applied for and received its first rate increase in 23 years.

By 1952 Cincinnati Bell had attained its goal of converting its entire system to dial service. The transformation cost $30 million over the course of 23 years. In that same year the company installed its 400,000th telephone. The postwar baby boom and the rapidly growing U.S. economy caused strong expansion of company activities throughout the decade. However, stringent regulation kept profits down, and Cincinnati Bell was forced to turn to marketing efforts for the first time in the 1950s, as it tried to strengthen its bottom line. The company looked to sales of additional phones in a given household, phones in different colors, speaker phones, springy cords, shoulder rests, and other optional paraphernalia to boost revenues.

In the 1960s Cincinnati Bell continued to add new phones to its system and implement technological breakthroughs. The year 1962 marked the installation of the company's 600,000th phone, as well as the first billing of long-distance customers by the number and destination of their call. Innovations such as Touch-Tone service, wide-area switching service, and advanced electronic switching systems helped to upgrade the company's offerings. In the mid-1960s the old system of configuring telephone numbers with the first two letters of a word and five numbers was replaced by a new system which simply used seven digits. This change helped to avoid confusion in long-distance dialing.

In 1968 Cincinnati Bell suffered a strike by the Communications Workers of America; it lasted for two weeks before the company granted workers wage increases. The higher costs this brought about, as well as the expenses of implementing technological developments such as electronic switching, prompted Cincinnati Bell to request rate increases for two years running in the early 1970s, with only partial success. The company subsequently undertook a program of cost controls. This was followed by an official change in the company's name in 1971. What had been the Cincinnati and Suburban Bell Telephone Company was simplified to Cincinnati Bell Inc.

DEREGULATION IN THE EIGHTIES

Perhaps the most dramatic change in Cincinnati Bell's history came in the early 1980s, when the federal government broke up the Bell telephone monopoly. Cincinnati Bell was free to enter non-regulated industries, while retaining its local exchange business, its long-distance holdings, its directory operations, and its role as AT&T's agent for AT&T equipment and service in the Cincinnati area. Taking advantage of this opportunity, Cincinnati Bell reorganized itself as a holding company and entered the software business, forming Cincinnati Bell Information Systems, Inc., in 1983 to sell computer programs for telecommunications systems. In January 1984 the company began to repurchase the 33 percent of its stock held by AT&T, severing a financial relationship, but not the business relationship, that had lasted for more than a century. The following year Cincinnati Bell suffered a setback in its local telephone business when the company lost a court case to retain a rate hike, and was ordered to refund between $6 million and $7 million to customers, in addition to reducing its fees for service. Two years later a decision by the U.S. Supreme Court in the same matter forced a $20 million refund to customers.

ACQUISITIONS

During the mid-1980s Cincinnati Bell beefed up its holdings in other fields of operation by buying computer software companies. Acquisitions included Creative Management Systems, located in McLean, Virginia; Commtrack, a unit of Control Data Corporation; and Auxton Computer Enterprises, which Cincinnati Bell purchased for $92 million. In 1988 the company also bought Vanguard Technologies International, Inc., for $72 million. One year later Cincinnati Bell formed a joint venture with a British firm to market software in the United Kingdom, which was later dissolved.

During this time the company also invested in firms that produced testing devices for telecommunications

equipment, and accelerated efforts to expand and upgrade its telephone network with digital switching fiber-optic cables. In the late 1980s Cincinnati Bell branched out further, buying firms that specialized in telephone marketing, which allowed it to form Matrixx Marketing, Inc., a national telemarketing subsidiary. In addition, the company expanded its radio paging business with the purchase of Metro-Page of Kentucky and formed a new company, Cincinnati Bell Directory, to focus on the Yellow Pages and electronic information markets.

NEW TECHNOLOGY FORCES SWEEPING CHANGES

As Cincinnati Bell began the last decade of the 20th century, it entered an era that demanded all telecommunications companies to respond to technological advancements as profound as the invention of the telephone more than a century earlier. Remaining static was no longer an option: deregulation, the advent of the Internet, the burgeoning growth of cellular telephone service, and the incursive threat of cable companies and other entities required decisive ripostes from venerable local-exchange companies such as Cincinnati Bell. The period bridging the 20th and 21st centuries was a crucible for Cincinnati Bell, a period that would witness some of its boldest moves and see it falter and succeed. Cincinnati Bell emerged from the tumult of change as a transformed company, having survived arguably the greatest test in its history.

Deregulation in 1996 presented the first challenge of the era, as federal legislation allowed long-distance companies to offer local exchange services. Cincinnati Bell's monopoly of its local market ended in August 1997, when it signed an agreement with Time Warner Communications stipulating how Time Warner would connect with Cincinnati Bell's network and how telephone calls would be exchanged between customers of each company. Cincinnati Bell entered negotiations with five other long-distance carriers as well, striking agreements with telecommunications companies such as MCI and Sprint.

A SPINOFF AND A PUSH INTO WIRELESS IN 1998

While the company dealt with the arrival of a new breed of competitor, it implemented a major overhaul of its structure. A diversification program begun in the early 1980s had greatly increased the company's involvement in non-telephone activities. By the mid-1990s, subsidiaries Matrixx and Cincinnati Bell Information Systems

(CBIS), which provided billing and customer care services to wireless, cable television operators, and other communications providers, accounted for slightly more than half of Cincinnati Bell's annual revenues. The two companies were growing rapidly, far more robustly than the telephone side of Cincinnati Bell's business. The disparity between the two facets of the company's business prompted management to spin off its two vibrant subsidiaries so that a more accurate valuation of their worth on Wall Street could be realized. In mid-1998, Matrixx and CBIS became a separate company, Convergys Corp., a publicly traded entity with annual revenues of $1.4 billion and a payroll of 29,500 employees.

At roughly the same time Cincinnati Bell stripped itself of Matrixx and CBIS, it added a new dimension to its business. In May 1998, Cincinnati Bell Wireless was formed, a cellular telephone subsidiary created from Cincinnati Bell's purchase of an 80 percent interest in a cellular network owned by AT&T Wireless Services that served Cincinnati and Dayton.

CINCINNATI BELL EMBRACES BROADBAND AND BECOMES BROADWING

Next, Cincinnati Bell made one of the most daring moves in its history in an attempt to redefine itself for the 21st century. In 1999, management, led by CEO Richard Ellenberger, acquired IXC Communications Inc., which owned a 13,000-mile, fiber-optic network that encompassed 25 metropolitan areas. The Austin, Texas-based company, a $669 million firm, represented Cincinnati's bid to push headlong into the broadband business and to become a nationally oriented competitor in the telecommunications industry. "I think management questioned what their future was as a small, regional communications company," an industry analyst said in the October 22, 1999 edition of *Cincinnati Business Courier*. "With IXC they get a large, national footprint."

The acquisition of IXC was a transforming event. After Cincinnati Bell completed the massive $3.2 billion acquisition, it changed its name to BroadWing Inc. (the local-exchange operations retained the Cincinnati Bell name) and began investing in the acquired network, which operated under the name BroadWing Communications Services Inc. The foray into broadband proved disastrous, as excess capacity in the broadband industry made it extremely difficult for the newly named BroadWing to turn its gamble into a success. In February 2003, the broadband services unit was sold to Columbia, Maryland-based Corvis Corp. for $129 million in cash and $375 million in operating liabilities. After the sale, BroadWing Inc. changed its name back to

Cincinnati Bell Inc., but vestiges of the broadband debacle remained after the name change. Cincinnati Bell was saddled with $2.75 billion of debt after the sale of BroadWing Communications Services and posted a staggering $4.2 billion loss in 2002.

JOHN F. CASSIDY TAKES THE HELM IN 2003

To guide Cincinnati Bell toward better times, the company's board of directors turned to John F. Cassidy. The former leader of the wireless segment, Cassidy was promoted to chief operating officer of the entire company before being selected as its chief executive officer in July 2003.

In the wake of the ill-timed investment in broadband, the company relied on its local and long-distance wireline service, its wireless service, and, through its ZoomTown subsidiary, its DSL service. Encouraging progress was achieved on all fronts, as Cassidy built on the company's solid foundation. In 2004, Cincinnati Bell began offering residential telephone service in Dayton, where it already provided cellular and business telephone service. The company installed its own telephone switching equipment, staking its presence in its first major market outside its home territory of greater Cincinnati. In 2005, the company enjoyed record growth in its DSL subscriber base and reported a 38 percent increase in wireless activations, although the cost of adding the new customers prevented it from achieving any significant revenue or profit growth.

NEW SERVICES FOR THE FUTURE

As Cassidy plotted Cincinnati Bell's future course, new products and services figured prominently in his plans. At the end of 2007, he paid $18 million to purchase Carmel, Indiana-based eGix Inc., which provided bundled voice and data services to 17,000 customers in 23 states. In 2008, Cincinnati Bell began offering text-messaging capabilities to residential wireline customers via the company's "Smart Home Phone," making it the first carrier in the United States to offer text messaging as a home-phone feature. The year also saw Cassidy sign an agreement with mobile media company PlayPhone that allowed Cincinnati Wireless customers to access a library of mobile entertainment downloads via their wireless handsets. To remain competitive in the fast-changing telecommunications industry, Cassidy needed to keep Cincinnati Bell on the technological vanguard. Customers demanded sophisticated voice and data services, and with the freedom to choose from numerous providers, Cassidy had to satisfy their needs to ensure Cincinnati Bell enjoyed a profitable future.

Elizabeth Rourke
Updated, Jeffrey L. Covell

PRINCIPAL SUBSIDIARIES

Cincinnati Bell Telephone Company LLC; Cincinnati Bell Telecommunications Services LLC; Cincinnati Bell Extended Territories LLC; Cincinnati Bell Entertainment Inc.; Cincinnati Bell Wireless Company; Cincinnati Bell Wireless LLC; Cincinnati Bell Any Distance Inc.; BRCOM Inc.; Cincinnati Bell Technology Solutions Inc.; GramTel Inc.; IXC Internet Services, Inc.; Mutual Signal Holding Corporation; Mutual Signal Corporation; Mutual Signal Corporation of Michigan; MSM Assoc. Limited Partnership; Cincinnati Bell Complete Protection Inc.; MVNO Holdings LLC; CB Funding LLC; CBTS Software LLC; Cincinnati Bell Shared Services LLC; CBTS Canada Inc.; Cincinnati Bell Technology Solutions UK Limited.

PRINCIPAL COMPETITORS

AT&T Inc.; Sprint Nextel Corporation; Verizon Communications Inc.

FURTHER READING

Bohman, Jim, "Cincinnati Bell Enters Dayton, Ohio, Residential Phone Market," *Dayton Daily News,* March 2, 2004.

Carroll, Kelly, "Wireless Networks," *Telephony,* May 10, 1999.

"Cincinnati Bell Debuts Text Messaging and SpinVox for the Home Phone," *Wireless News,* November 30, 2008.

Gubbins, Ed, "Sawed Off in Cincinnati," *Wireless Review,* February 1, 2004.

Head, Lauren Lawley, "Bell Getting Wired into National Arena," *Cincinnati Business Courier,* October 22, 1999, p. 3.

Krause, Reinhardt, "High-Speed Networks," *Investor's Business Daily,* August 2, 2001, p. A4.

Lundegaard, Karen M., "New Bell CEO Has Business in His Blood," *Cincinnati Business Courier,* October 11, 1993, p. 3.

"Mini Megamerger," *Telephony,* July 26, 1999.

Olson, Scott, "Egix Buyout Sets Up Bell Battle," *Indianapolis Business Journal,* December 17, 2007, p. 3.

"PlayPhone and Cincinnati Bell Wireless Ink Content Deal," *Wireless News,* December 4, 2008.

Sangor, Elizabeth, "Eat Well or Sleep Well?" *Barron's,* October 10, 1983.

Sekhri, Rajiv, "Bell Breakup Won't Help Phone Unit," *Cincinnati Business Courier,* May 1, 1998, p. 1.

———, "Cincinnati Bell Positioning for Local Phone War," *Cincinnati Business Courier,* September 26, 1997, p. 32.

White, James A., and Paul Ingrassia, "AT&T Break-Up Gives Its Two Mavericks an Opportunity to Compete in New Fields," *Wall Street Journal,* March 10, 1982.

Costco Wholesale Corporation

———■———

999 Lake Drive
Issaquah, Washington 98027
U.S.A.
Telephone: (425) 313-8100
Fax: (425) 313-6430
Web site: http://www.costco.com

Public Company
Incorporated: 1983
Employees: 142,000
Sales: $72.48 billion (2008)
Stock Exchanges: NASDAQ (GS)
Ticker Symbol: COST
NAICS: 452910 Warehouse Clubs and Superstores

■ ■ ■

Costco Wholesale Corporation is the largest members-only wholesale club in the United States leading Wal-Mart's Sam's Club. The company operates 557 warehouse stores, 406 of which are located in 40 U.S. states and Puerto Rico. The remainder can be found in Canada, Mexico, Japan, Taiwan, Korea, and the United Kingdom. Nearly 55 million cardholders patronize Costco regularly each year. The average Costco warehouse is 141,000 square feet in size and offers, in the company's own words, "one of the largest and most exclusive product category selections to be found under a single roof."

BEGINNINGS

In September 1983 Costco's first warehouse opened in Seattle, Washington. At this time, warehouse outlets had long existed, but the concept of a wholesale club was relatively new and promising. Dubbed "buyers' clubs" and begun in 1976, these warehouses were wholesalers that required shoppers to become members and pay an annual membership fee. The membership fee helped reduce already low overhead, so that items could be sold at an average of 9 percent over cost from the manufacturer. At the time Costco was formed, membership warehouses were primarily a West Coast phenomenon.

Jeffrey H. Brotman served as chairman of Costco, and James D. Sinegal as president. While Sinegal had a background in membership warehouses and retail chains (having been mentored by Sol Price, the founder of Fed Mart and Price Club), Brotman was an executive of an oil exploration company and cofounder of a group that operated a chain of apparel stores. In 1985 Costco became a publicly owned company, and in 1993 Costco merged with Price Club to become Price/Costco, Inc. In August 1999, the company reincorporated and changed its name to Costco Wholesale Corporation.

INCREASED SALES AND NEW MARKETING CONCEPTS

During Costco's early years, the company increased the size of its shopping carts multiple times. A growing number of customers were attracted by savvy stocking practices and expanded offerings. For example, Costco was the first membership warehouse to offer an expanded fresh-food section (featuring a bakery, refrigerated produce area, fresh meats, and seafood). In 1995 customers visited an average of once every three weeks, but by 1999, they were returning every ten days. With increasing numbers of frequently returning customers, as well as the company's constant expansion into new markets with warehouses opening every year, Costco saw its earnings grow 6 percent annually from 1995 to 2000.

Costco offered three membership levels, ranging in price from $50 to $100 a year (in the United States): Business, Gold Star (individual), and Executive. Any business or store with a retail sales license qualified for a Business membership ($50 a year), allowing these customers to shop for resale or business use. Business members (numbering 5.6 million in 2008) could also buy goods for private use, and the membership included a spouse card. The member also had the option of buying up to six additional membership cards ($40 each) for associates or partners in the business.

Gold Star memberships ($50 annual fee) were available to individuals who did not own a business. These memberships included the same wholesale prices offered to business members. Annual fees were fully refunded if members were not satisfied.

The third membership level, Executive ($100 annual fee), had all the perks of the other memberships, along with additional benefits. Members could purchase additional services such as auto and homeowner insurance, long-distance services, and mortgage services, as well as health insurance and merchant credit card processing at vastly reduced rates. Executive members also received a 2 percent annual reward on most of their purchases. An additional perk for Executive and Business members was special opening hours, beyond the regular member shopping hours.

DISCOUNT-SHOPPING WAREHOUSE STRATEGY CHANGES AND EXPANDS

Costco's strategy was to offer high-quality, brand-name merchandise at prices below those of traditional wholesalers, discount retailers, and supermarkets. To achieve this, Costco bought nearly all of its merchandise at volume discounts from manufacturers, rather than

distributors, and stock was usually shipped directly to selling warehouses to minimize freight costs. The number of sales and service employees was also minimal, with about 45 percent of employees holding part-time status. Warehouses were almost entirely self-service, from finding and buying items, to loading them into a customer's vehicle.

Despite having warehouses that spanned three acres, and piles of merchandise stacked to the ceiling, Costco carried only 4,000 carefully chosen products at a time. Three-quarters of the items were such "basic" products as batteries, laundry detergent, and instant noodles. Then there were the ldquo;high-end" name-brand products, which might be stocked at Costco one day and then gone the next. With the complete lack of advertising (with expenditures largely reserved for new warehouse openings), the sudden and seemingly random appearance of ultra-cheap name-brand products kept customers returning for fear of missing a good deal. Word of mouth and savings did the rest. Striving for high volume, not high margins, kept profits high. In 1999, Costco's individual warehouses were pulling in an average of $91 million per year.

The company also developed its own line of products, released under the Costco label of Kirkland Signature. "We sell a six-pack of Kodak 200-speed film for $21.99," CEO Sinegal told *Fortune* magazine in 1999, "Then we have our own [private-label brand] for $6.99. How can you not provide that value for your customers? That doesn't mean we want to get rid of Kodak. But at some point, a vendor's going to realize that option is open. And it does create leverage for us." In 1999, roughly 12 percent of Costco's products were released under the Kirkland name.

Early on, Costco garnered trust and loyalty among its customers with an extremely generous return policy, offering a "return-anything-at-anytime" guarantee. *Fortune* magazine, profiling the "cult of Costco" in 1999, highlighted the "diamond guarantee," where Costco promised to pay a member $100 if a stone was appraised for less than double the Costco price. Such upscale items on sale in a warehouse next to stacks of printer paper or a year's supply of cat food seemed odd to many, but Costco tended to attract middle- and upper-middle-class customers, those who were "noticeably more bourgeois, ... some of the most overeducated, overemployed hoarders," according to *Fortune*.

Over the years, Costco added departments, expanding beyond the traditional discount warehouse offerings. A large majority of the stores featured a pharmacy, an optical-dispensing center, one-hour photo services, a food court, and the ever popular and inexpensive hot-dog stands. More than half offered hearing-aid centers,

KEY DATES

1983: Costco opens its first warehouse in Seattle, Washington.

1985: Costco becomes a publicly owned company.

1993: Price Club, a major wholesale club competitor, merges with Costco to form Price/Costco, Inc.

1998: The Costco.com web site is launched.

1999: Costco reincorporates and changes its name to Costco Wholesale Corporation.

2001: Costco introduces its B2B web site.

2006: Following $1.69 billion in stock repurchases over the previous year, Costco's board authorizes an additional $2 billion worth of stock repurchases.

2007: CEO Jim Sinegal indicates the company is on pace to have more than 1,000 stores by 2017.

2008: Costco announces plans to open stores in Australia during 2009.

and a handful were equipped with print shops and copy centers.

By 2001, 125 of the U.S. Costco stores also featured gas stations with cut-rate prices. The trend of selling gas at discount superstores was repeated by chains such as Wal-Mart and Sam's Club, competing with traditional gas stations, and cutting into the market. According to Reuters, these so-called hypermarkets (including Costco) contributed to an at least one-cent decline in U.S. retail gasoline profits from 1997 to 2001, from 13.6 to 12.4 cents a gallon. "Gasoline wars are becoming more frequent as a result of the growing share of these big competitors," Holly Tuminello, vice-president of the Petroleum Marketers Association of America told Reuters in July 2001. "That's because they are willing to use gasoline as a loss-leader to attract people to their other products." In 2001 the "hypermarket" gasoline sales accounted for roughly 3.5 percent of U.S. gasoline sales (or more than 12.6 million gallons a day), but that amount was expected to grow to 16 percent by 2005 as the various superstore chains continued to expand their services to meet the demand.

SURVIVING 21ST-CENTURY CHALLENGES

Following more than six consecutive years of profit-earning increases, Costco experienced an unexpected decline in earnings in the first half of 2001. Much of this was beyond the company's control, as the West Coast of the United States suffered from an energy crisis that sent energy prices skyrocketing. The state of California, where fully one-fourth of Costco's warehouses were located, experienced some of the worst of the crisis, as rolling blackouts became a concern. "Energy prices in California will certainly impact Costco more than another national retailer," David Schick, an analyst at Robinson-Humphrey, told the *New York Times* in June 2001. "It costs more to operate in California, and they have an awful lot of operations in California." The company responded to the crisis by equipping California stores with backup generators to keep refrigeration units running in case of blackouts, turning down air-conditioning, and designing new warehouses with as many skylights as building codes permitted, allowing lights to be turned off during the day.

Although the energy crisis was much to blame for the slide in profits, there were several other factors that contributed. The economy was in a slowdown, decreasing overall retail sales. Plus, the company was dramatically expanding, having opened 27 new warehouses that fiscal year (a 90 percent spending jump), bringing the total to 360 warehouses in the United States, Canada, Mexico, the United Kingdom, Korea, Taiwan, and Japan. Also, the profits could not match the year-earlier profits that were driven in large part by Y2K-related buying.

Despite the slowdown, Costco sales (in stores open at least a year) rose 5 percent in 2001, a crucial statistic in the industry. Revenue from membership fees (which had been increased the previous year) increased 23 percent, and Costco continued to maintain an impressive 86 percent renewal rate in memberships, the highest in the industry. The company had about 16 million active members and over 35 million cardholders.

In addition to its existing e-commerce web site for members, Costco.com (launched in 1998), Costco officially launched the "B2B" (business to business) portion of its online shopping web site in April 2001. This new feature allowed businesses in the United States to order products online for delivery, with some areas (Seattle, Los Angeles, and San Francisco) having the option of next-business-day local delivery from the Costco fleet.

ACCELERATED GROWTH AND EXPANSION

Midway through 2001, Costco revealed plans for 70 new stores over the next year, marking its largest expansion initiative to date. That year, the company's capital expenditures totaled $1.3 billion. A similar amount was earmarked for the 2002 fiscal year. By this time, Costco enjoyed a base of 35 million members, some 86 percent of whom renewed their membership annually.

Construction of a Bellevue, Washington-based gourmet foods store named Costco Fresh began in 2002, providing the company with an outlet for testing items before they were introduced throughout the Costco chain. In addition, a home furnishings store called Costco Home was established in Kirkland, Washington, as part of an effort to test whether or not home furnishings could be sold successfully at all of the company's stores.

In May, three new warehouses opened their doors in England. Followed by another location later that year, Costco's presence in the United Kingdom grew to 15 locations. Ultimately, the company estimated that it could have as many as 50 clubs throughout the United Kingdom. Costco ended 2001 with sales of $37.99 billion, up 11 percent from the previous year. Net income rose 16 percent, reaching $700 million.

By September 2002, Costco had established 59 new clubs over the course of two years. About 75 percent of these locations were in new markets. Moving forward, the company revealed plans to focus on expanding within markets where it already had an established presence, and also on international growth. This was evident by the addition of new warehouse clubs in England, Japan, and Puerto Rico throughout 2002.

In early 2003 Jim Sinegal revealed that, because of rising expenses, Costco had decided not to pursue its Costco Fresh concept. However, expansion continued as the company made plans to open 14 new U.S. stores, as well as a Canadian location and two other sites outside North America. In October, Costco paid approximately $95,000 in cash in order to secure Carrefour Nederland B.V.'s 20 percent stake in Costco Wholesale UK Ltd.

EXPANDED OFFERINGS

Costco continued along a path of expansion into the middle of the first decade of the 2000s, announcing plans to open 25 new stores during fiscal 2004. Late that year, the company partnered with American Express to offer two different co-branded cash-rebate credit cards.

New offerings continued into 2005. Midway through the year, Costco revealed plans to pilot self-checkout lanes in certain stores, and to unveil a new Kirkland Signature by Borghese line of cosmetic products. The company also announced plans to offer individual health insurance products to its general members in the state of California.

Costco capped off 2005 with net sales of $51.86 billion, up from $47.15 billion in 2004. On the heels of approximately $400 million in stock repurchases, the company also announced plans to buy back an additional $1 billion worth of its common stock.

Costco kicked off 2006 by piloting a drive-through car wash service at its Fourth Avenue location in Seattle. Midway through the year, the company increased its membership fees for the first time in six years. The cost of Gold Star and Business memberships increased from $45 to $50. Costco estimated this would generate an additional $75 million in annual revenues. In July, the company revealed that it had spent $1.69 billion in stock repurchases over the previous year. At that time, Costco's board authorized an additional $2 billion worth of stock repurchases.

In early 2007 Costco CEO Jim Sinegal indicated that his company was on track to have more than 1,000 stores by 2017, based on plans to open as many as 500 additional stores during the next ten to 12 years. In 2007 alone, 35 new locations were expected to open, followed by as many as 40 in 2008.

One important development in 2007 was a change to Costco's liberal return policy. Specifically, a 90-day limit was implemented for electronics items, when it was discovered that related returns were hurting the company's profits. Customers were still allowed to return items such as high-definition televisions with no questions asked, as well as no stocking fees on open boxes, within the 90-day window.

WEATHERING THE ECONOMIC STORM

In early 2008 Costco announced that it planned to open stores in Australia sometime in 2009. Despite a worsening economy, including the impact of inflation on the company's costs, Costco did everything it could to keep its prices low for members. The company ended 2008 with net sales of $72.48 billion, up from $63.09 billion in 2007.

By late 2008 commodity prices were skyrocketing, making it more difficult for Costco to keep its prices low. However, the company continued to pull out all the stops on this front. For example, in order to continue offering store-baked pies at a competitive price, Costco considered the possibility of growing its own pumpkins. Additionally, the company literally purchased hundreds of truckloads of toilet paper and paper towels from Procter & Gamble when a price increase was announced for those items.

Although it operated in a challenging economic climate as the first decade of the 2000s neared its end, Costco's prospects for continued success seemed good as the company remained committed to saving its members as much money as possible.

Carol I. Keely
Updated, Linda M. Gwilym; Paul R. Greenland

PRINCIPAL SUBSIDIARIES

Costco Canada Holdings Inc.; Costco Wholesale Canada Ltd.; Costco Wholesale Membership Inc.; NW Re Ltd. (Bermuda).

PRINCIPAL COMPETITORS

BJs Wholesale Club Inc.; SAM'S CLUB; Target Corporation.

FURTHER READING

Branch, Shelly, "Inside the Cult of Costco," *Fortune,* September 6, 1999.

"Costco July Same-Store Sales Fall 7 Percent," *Reuters,* August 6, 2009.

"Costco Plans to Raise Annual Membership Fees, Marking Its First Increase in Six Years," *Chain Store Age,* May 2006.

"Costco Reports Record Year-End Sales, Profit," *Supermarket News,* November 9, 1992.

"Costco's Artful Discounts; with Costs of Everything on the Rise, the Big-Box Retailer Gets Creative," *Business Week,* October 20, 2008.

Desjardins, Doug, "Costco CEO: Store Count Could Top 1,000 by End of Decade," *Retailing Today,* February 12, 2007.

"Expansion Costs Blamed for Costco's 13% Decline in Earnings," *New York Times,* June 1, 2001, p. C4.

"Expansion Is Charted by Costco," *MMR,* September 23, 2002.

"Gas Stations Facing Threat from Superstores," *Reuters,* July 17, 2001.

Levisohn, Ben, "Costco Gets Bitten by Inflation; the Club Store Chain Warns Earnings Will Fall Short of Estimates Because of Higher Food and Energy Costs," *Business Week Online,* July 24, 2008.

Nelson, Robert T., "Costco Profit Slides 12% As Energy Dims Earnings," *Seattle Times,* June 1, 2001, p. C1.

———, "Slowdown Trips Up Costco's Bull Run," *Seattle Times,* March 9, 2001, p. C1.

Cross Country Healthcare, Inc.

———— ■ ————

6551 Park of Commerce Boulevard, Suite 200
Boca Raton, Florida 33487-8247
U.S.A.
Telephone: (561) 998-2232
Toll Free: (800) 347-2264
Fax: (800) 768-8128
Web site: http://www.crosscountryhealthcare.com

Public Company
Incorporated: 2003
Employees: 5,893
Sales: $734.3 million (2008)
Stock Exchanges: NASDAQ
Ticker Symbol: CCRN
NAICS: 561320 Temporary Help Services; 621999 All
Other Miscellaneous Ambulatory Heath Care
Services

■ ■ ■

Cross Country Healthcare, Inc., is one of the leading providers of temporary healthcare staffing, including nurses and allied staffing, specialists, and physicians. Cross Country Staffing and related subsidiaries offer long-term and per diem nursing staff services to acute care hospitals and other healthcare facilities in the United States, Canada, Bermuda, the U.S. Virgin Islands, and the United Kingdom. Cross Country Trav-Corps is the largest traveling nurse company in the United States, and field nurses travel wherever they are needed for three-month assignments. Overall, Cross Country provides more than 5,000 full-time equivalent

nurse and allied staffing daily. Other services offered by Cross Country Healthcare include clinical trial staffing and management to biotechnology and pharmaceutical firms. Locum tenens through MDA Holdings involves temporary placement of medical doctors in hospitals or family practices. Physician specialties include radiology, anesthesiology, internal medicine, and a variety of surgical specialties. Cross Country Healthcare offers medical staff recruitment and education as well. The company holds contracts with more than 5,000 healthcare facilities and organizations.

EARLY SUCCESSES BRING OWNERSHIP CHANGES

Cross Country Healthcare was founded as Cross Country Healthcare Personnel in 1986. In 1991 it became part of the W.R. Grace & Co. conglomerate of businesses. At that time, Cross Country Healthcare employed 140 staff and nurses and generated $80 million in revenue. W.R. Grace purchased a 47 percent stake in the company for $25 million. By 1996 Cross Country Healthcare had become a leader in healthcare staffing and the largest company to provide traveling healthcare practitioners, employing more than 2,000 nurses, physical therapists, and advanced practitioners in 50 states.

The staffing agency expanded further in 1996 through the formation of a joint venture with MRA (Medical Recruiters of America), Inc., a subsidiary of Nestor Healthcare, the leading British healthcare staffing company. Working together under the Cross Country Staffing name, the two companies formed the largest temporary staffing agency serving acute care hospitals and healthcare facilities. Cross Country planned to expand its base of temporary professionals across the United States, and collaboration with a British company expanded the range to Canada, Bermuda, and the U.S. Virgin Islands, as well as to the United Kingdom. Cross Country Staffing CEO Joe Boshart expected sales to surpass $115 million during the first year of the venture.

Over the long-term, Nestor and W.R. Grace intended to sell the joint venture, and by 1999, with revenues up to $159 million, the process began. Cross Country Staffing became an independent company in 1999 as Nestor and W.R. Grace sold their interests, at 34 percent and 66 percent, respectively, to members of management and an affiliate of Charterhouse Group International, Inc., a private-equity firm.

Through Charterhouse Group's connections to Morgan Stanley Dean Witter Private Equity, the new corporation immediately expanded with the acquisition of TravCorps, a company that specialized in staffing traveling nurses. Field nurses worked at hospitals anywhere in the country for three-month terms, and TravCorps paid moving expenses to one of the 2,900 apartments leased by the company. Cross Country expected the combined operations to enable the company to better serve medical facility customers by more readily filling temporary healthcare staffing positions from 5,000 nurses. TravCorps' operations included Cejka & Company, specializing in physician and executive searches for permanent posts. Cejka served hospitals, physician practice groups, pharmaceutical companies, and insurance companies.

For a few years, the merged company operated as Cross Country TravCorps, then Cross Country, Inc., before settling on Cross Country Healthcare in 2003. During this time, Cross Country diversified its base of business to include clinical trial staffing and hospital staff management consulting. In March 2001 Cross Country acquired ClinForce, based in Raleigh, North Carolina, a temporary staffing agency specializing in clinical trial services. The $3.9 million acquisition of Jennings Ryan & Kolb in March and the $3.6 million acquisition of Gill/Basano Consulting in May gave Cross Country a foothold in management consulting.

POSITIVE OUTLOOK LEADS TO IPO

Cross Country Healthcare grew at a steady pace. Due to a shortage of nurses, the company's field staff could choose from about ten new assignments when one assignment ended. The outlook for future growth appeared positive, as the $7 billion market was expected to grow 15 to 20 percent annually over the next five years. Moreover, admissions to nursing schools did not meet the expected demand for nurses as the population aged. Hospitals benefited from the temporary staffing option by gaining the certainty of having a highly qualified nurse work for a three-month stretch. Simultaneously, the nurse shortage was a risk of the business, as 126,000 unfilled positions on any given day meant that competition for available nurses might require higher pay that could not be passed along to customers. Cross Country charged $50 an hour for temporary nurse staffing, after a 12 percent increase in 2000. That year, Cross Country reported revenue of $368 million, double 1998 revenue. The company earned a profit of $4.6 million in 2000.

Functioning with steady growth and preparing for expansion, in 2001 Cross Country announced plans for an initial public offering (IPO) of stock. At a time when healthcare companies were among the few able to pursue public funding successfully, Cross Country offered 7.8 million shares on October 25, 2001, for $17 per share. Net proceeds of $122 million paid $114 million of debt that accompanied the acquisition of TravCorps. In January 2002 Cross Country purchased NovaPro, a medical staffing firm for $7.12 million. Based in Tampa, NovaPro added to Cross Country's strength in the local Florida markets.

SHIFTING MARKET AND BUSINESS OPTIONS FOLLOW YEARS OF GROWTH

The market in temporary nurse staffing changed unexpectedly, prompting Cross Country to change its growth strategy. Cross Country experienced a decline in demand for contract nurses, because many hospitals sought alternatives to the high cost of contract staffing. Hospitals developed their own pool of temporary nurses or they expanded permanent staff by offering $10,000 hiring bonuses. In Cross Country's home market, Florida, the need for temporary staffing remained high, as hospitals experienced greater traffic during the winter

```
╔══════════════════════════════════════╗
║                                      ║
║            KEY DATES                 ║
║              ──◆──                   ║
║                                      ║
║  1986:  Cross Country Staffing Per-  ║
║         sonnel is founded.           ║
║  1991:  W.R. Grace acquires Cross    ║
║         Country Staffing.            ║
║  1996:  Joint venture with MRA, Inc.,║
║         is first step toward spinoff.║
║  1999:  Cross Country Staffing be-   ║
║         comes independent company    ║
║         and purchases TravCorps nurse║
║         staffing company.            ║
║  2003:  Company takes the name Cross ║
║         Country Healthcare.          ║
║  2006:  Cross Country begins series  ║
║         of acquisitions in clinical  ║
║         research staffing and        ║
║         management.                  ║
║  2008:  Entry into physician staffing║
║         provides stability amid      ║
║         economic turmoil.            ║
║                                      ║
╚══════════════════════════════════════╝
```

months, when the state became home to senior citizens from colder climates.

Cross Country addressed the changes in nurse staffing by seeking new clients. In November 2002, Cross Country signed a significant staffing agreement with VHA, Inc., an alliance of 2,200 community hospitals and their affiliated physicians. The three-year contract covered fixed-term and per diem nurse staffing services to VHA's 2,200 members, including international healthcare institutions.

In anticipation of an acquisition, Cross Country obtained a $200 million credit facility from Wachovia in May 2003. The "B" term loan of $125 million and a $75 million revolving loan reflected Cross Country's perceived weakness in being narrowly focused on temporary nursing staff. This lack of diversity in its income stream put the company at risk in case of regulatory or market changes. However, the credit facility funded the July acquisition of Med-Staff, a nurse staffing agency that expanded Cross Country's access to new markets. These included military hospitals and clinics, as well as hospitals requiring temporary staffing on a day-to-day basis. Cross Country paid $104 million cash for Med-Staff, with an additional $37.5 million to be paid based on 2003 earnings.

With $122 million in revenues in 2002, Med-Staff raised Cross Country to the top as the largest temporary healthcare staffing company in the nation. Moreover, the acquisition provided a counterweight to lower revenues due to a decline in healthcare medical staffing. Revenue at Cross Country declined 6 percent, but the company experienced an overall 7 percent increase in revenue, to $686.9 million, due to part-year income from Med-

Staff. Cross Country remained profitable, with $25.8 million in net earnings in 2002.

Despite the need for a diversified revenue base, Cross Country decided to divest two of its hospital consulting businesses in November 2004. Overall, Cross Country found that consulting did not combine well with the staffing side of business and the market tended to be volatile. The company received $12.25 million for the operations, which contributed $11.6 million in revenue during 2003. Cross Country planned to sell the Cejka consulting practice as well.

Cross Country's traveling nurse business continued to fare well. In January 2005, Child Health Corporation of America (CHCA) signed a two-year contract with Cross Country. CHCA acted as a clearinghouse for children's hospitals. The agreement with Cross Country provided traveling nurses for CHCA's 25 pediatric hospital clients. The contract included education and training for participating hospitals' permanent staffs as well.

In 2005 Morgan Stanley sold its 13 percent stake in Cross Country to Citigroup for $69 million. Charterhouse retained its 21.7 percent interest. The change in ownership did not affect operations at Cross Country.

CLINICAL TRIAL STAFFING PROVIDES COMPANY WITH DIVERSIFIED INCOME BASE

During late 2004 and early 2005, Cross Country continued to experience a decline in demand, as hospitals saw lower patient admissions. The company's focus turned toward diversification of its business operations. Cross Country decided to expand its range of services in clinical trial management and staffing services to the biotechnology and pharmaceutical industries. Cross Country pursued this line of operation through a series of acquisitions.

In August 2006 Cross Country acquired Metropolitan Research Associates (MRA) and Metropolitan Research Staffing Associates, of New York City, for $18.5 million. The acquisition brought with it a wide range of clinical trial management experience, including women's health, pain management, obesity, central nervous system, and infectious disease clinical trials. Also, the clinical trials staffing services along with strong market demand for such services complemented activities at ClinForce.

The acquisition of AKOS Limited, in June 2007, expanded Cross Country's range geographically. Based in the prestigious research triangle reaching from London and encompassing Cambridge and Oxford universities, AKOS provided drug safety, regulatory, and clinic trial management to clients in the United States, Canada, Europe, and Asia. In addition to its expertise in international clinical trial standards, Cross Country expected AKOS to contribute $5.5 million in annual revenue. Cross Country paid $14 million for the company, with additional payments in 2007 and 2008 based on performance.

The acquisition of Assent Consulting, based in Cupertino, California, further expanded Cross Country's contract staffing capabilities. Purchased for $19.6 million, Assent specialized in providing temporary professional staffing for clinical research, biostatistics, and drug safety. Assent would add $13.2 million to Cross Country's annual revenue base.

PHYSICIAN STAFFING PROVIDES CROSS COUNTRY WITH STABILITY

In September 2008 Cross Country entered a new area of temporary healthcare staffing when the company acquired MDA Holdings, Inc., of Norcross, Georgia, for $112.3 million. Since 1987, MDA, for Medical Doctors Associates, offered locum tenens, temporary staffing of physicians and specialists and allied staffing to healthcare institutions nationwide. Cross Country's locum tenens business included physician practices and specialties such as radiology, anesthesiology, family practice, surgical specialties, and internal medicine.

The acquisition of MDA proved to be timely for the financial stability it provided Cross Country during the financial crisis of late 2008 and the economic downturn of 2009. Cross Country experienced a sharp decline in demand for clinical trials staffing and services, as pharmaceutical companies reduced research and development expenses and biotechnology companies were unable to obtain funding. Also, hospitals cut expenses by reducing nurse staffing, considered a cost center.

In 2008, Cross Country reported $734.28 million in revenues, compared to $718.27 million the previous year. To deal with the decline in nurse staffing revenue, Cross Country initiated several cost-cutting measures. Business travel, capital expenditures, advertising, reliance on external vendors, and discretionary spending were reduced. The company was able to generate strong cash flow, allowing the company to pay down the $150 million debt incurred for the acquisition of MDA. The company ended 2007 with $33 million in debt. Due to the economic shifts, Cross Country charged $244.1 million in impairment of intangible assets, resulting in a net loss of $142.95 million compared to net income of

$24.58 million in 2007. The impairment charge stemmed from a loss in goodwill, as Boshart did not expect a recovery of nurse and allied staffing during 2009.

Mary Tradii

PRINCIPAL SUBSIDIARIES

=AKOS; Assent; Assignment America; Cejka Search; ClinForce; Cross Country Education; Cross Country Local; Cross Country TravCorps; Cross Country Staffing; MedStaff; Metropolitan Research Associates; NovaPro.

PRINCIPAL COMPETITORS

AMN Healthcare Services, Inc.; ATC Healthcare, Inc.; Medical Staffing Network Holdings, Inc.

FURTHER READING

"Cross Country Healthcare Announces Agreement to Acquire Medical Doctor Associates," *Business Wire,* July 22, 2008.

"Cross Country Healthcare Announces Definitive Agreement to Acquire Assets of Metropolitan Research Associates and Metropolitan Research Staffing Associates," *PR Newswire,* July 13, 2006.

"Cross Country Healthcare First to Deliver Complete Staffing Solutions to Arizona Healthcare Facilities Through Its Flexstaff On-Call Division," *PR Newswire,* October 9, 1995.

"Cross Country Lacks Diverse Focus," *Loan Market Week,* May 26, 2003, p. 9.

"Cross Country Staffing and TravCorps Corporation Announce Merger to Create Leading Temporary Medical Staffing Company," *PR Newswire,* November 8, 1999.

"Cross Country Staffing Selected by Child Health Corporation of America to Provide Nurse Staffing Services to CHCA's Owner Pediatric Hospitals," *Business Wire,* January 5, 2004.

Galewitz, Phil, "Investors Running to Cross Country," *Palm Beach Post,* December 27, 2001, p. 1D.

————, "Nurse Staffing Firms Must Tend Wounds; Industry Ailing As Hospitals Cut Back," *Palm Beach Post,* June 1, 2003, p. 1F.

"Grace Agrees to Sell Cross Country Staffing," *PR Newswire,* June 25, 1999.

Pounds, Marcia Heroux, "Nurse Shortage Spurs Cross Country IPO—Money Sought for Expansion and Paying Down Debt," *Fort Lauderdale (Fla.) Sun-Sentinel,* July 14, 2001, p. 12B.

Seemuth, Mike, "Morgan Cuts Holding in Cross Country Healthcare," *Broward Daily Business Review,* May 4, 2005.

"Two Leading Healthcare Staffing Firms Form Joint Venture," *Business Wire,* June 3, 1996.

Denny's Corporation

———■———

203 East Main Street
Spartanburg, South Carolina 29319-9966
U.S.A.
Telephone: (864) 597-8000
Toll Free: (800) 733-6697
Fax: (864) 597-8780
Web site: http://www.dennys.com

Public Company
Incorporated: 1979 as Trans World Corporation
Employees: 15,000
Sales: $760.27 million (2008)
Stock Exchanges: NASDAQ
Ticker Symbol: DENN
NAICS: 722110 Full-Service Restaurants

■ ■ ■

Denny's Corporation is the operator of the Denny's restaurant chain, one of the largest family-style dining chains in the United States. Denny's units typically never close, offering breakfast items, appetizers, sandwiches, dinner entrees, and desserts. Denny's operates in 49 states, the District of Columbia, two U.S. territories, and in five foreign countries. The 1,541-restaurant chain is operated primarily through franchise and licensing agreements. Franchised and licensed restaurants represent 80 percent of the Denny's units in operation. The greatest concentration of restaurants is located in California, home to 102 company-owned units and 304 franchised and licensed units. Systemwide sales, including both company-owned and franchised

and licensed restaurants, exceed $2 billion. The average size of a Denny's restaurant is 4,500 square feet, sufficient to accommodate 140 customers.

ORIGINS

Denny's predecessors emerged in the early 1990s from Trans World Corporation, which was created in 1979 as a holding company for Trans World Airlines (TWA), Hilton International hotels, and Canteen Corporation, a contract foodservice company. Later that year Trans World acquired Century 21 Real Estate and Spartan Food Systems, which owned the restaurant chain Quincy's Family Steakhouse and is the largest franchisee of Hardee's restaurants. In the mid-1980s Trans World moved to streamline its diverse operations, spinning off TWA to its shareholders and selling Century 21 to the Metropolitan Life Insurance Company.

In 1986 Trans World's profits declined sharply after its purchase of American Medical Services, a nursing home operator in poor financial shape. As a result of this acquisition, the company's stock price dropped dramatically, attracting the attention of corporate raiders, who sought to buy up the inexpensive shares of Trans World stock, take over the company, and sell its other valuable constituent parts for a profit. To ward off such hostile takeover attempts, Trans World was forced to restructure. The company's stock was liquidated on December 31, 1986, and new stock, for a company called TW Services, Inc., was issued. This new entity included the assets of Canteen, Spartan, and American Medical Systems, along with other businesses.

COMPANY PERSPECTIVES

◼

Our new vision is simple in concept, yet a great challenge for restaurants such as ours that never close. The vision recognizes each customer has certain reasonable expectations that must always be met. These include: quality food that tastes good; friendly, attentive servers who make customers feel welcome; clean, well-maintained surroundings; and prices that represent a good value. We believe these expectations must be met every time a customer enters one of our restaurants. Denny's new vision is summed up in the statement: Great Food, Great Service, Great People ... Every Time!

A FOCUS ON RESTAURANTS

The following year TW Services moved to consolidate its operations further, and it sold its hotel operations, Hilton International, to Allegis, Inc. At the same time, TW Services expanded and strengthened its restaurant operations, purchasing Denny's, a restaurant chain with 1,200 outlets, and El Pollo Loco, another chain of 70 eateries specializing in chicken. After this process of corporate restructurings, TW Services emerged as an operator of chain restaurants and other foodservices. The company's five principal food-oriented businesses included Denny's, Hardee's, Quincy's Family Steakhouse, El Pollo Loco, and Canteen Corporation.

EARLY HISTORY OF THE CANTEEN SUBSIDIARY

The oldest of TW Services' units was Canteen, founded in July 1929 by Nathaniel Leverone and two other partners. Just before the onset of the Great Depression, Leverone acquired the Chicago Automatic Canteen Corporation, the vending operations of an American Legion chapter in Chicago. The company oversaw the operations of 100 five-cent candy bar machines stationed throughout the Chicago area. In 1930 Leverone changed the name of his company to the Automatic Canteen Company of America, and he began to seek franchise operators, who would be given an exclusive contract to operate Canteen machines in different areas of the country. By 1931, 15 different franchises had been established.

Wartime shortages in the early 1940s challenged the abilities of Canteen's franchise operators. At the end of the war, however, a sharp increase in the manufacture of consumer goods proved a boon to Canteen operators, since many of their machines were located in factory lunchrooms. The company thrived throughout the 1950s, and in 1960 its operations were expanded with the purchase of Nationwide Food Service, which also provided foodservices for people in their workplace. In the mid-1960s American Canteen shortened its name to Canteen Corporation. Three years later the company was purchased by International Telephone and Telegraph (ITT). Under ITT, Canteen's operations continued to expand, as it moved into the fields of hospital and college campus foodservices. In 1973 Canteen was sold to Trans World Corporation, and over the next several years Canteen became involved in running foodservices for the National Aeronautics and Space Administration, as well as concession stands in national parks and at convention centers, sports arenas, and massive entertainment complexes.

EARLY HISTORY OF DENNY'S

The second oldest of the TW Services restaurant units was Denny's, founded as a doughnut stand in Lakewood, California, in 1953. Originally called Danny's Donuts, the shop was opened by Harold Butler, who planned to offer coffee and doughnuts 24 hours a day. By the end of its first year in operation, Butler's doughnut stand had garnered profits of $120,000. In 1954 Danny's Donuts became Danny's Coffee Shops, and Butler began expanding his operations, opening additional stores. Five years later the chain of coffee shops became Denny's restaurants, and doughnuts were phased out of the menu.

In choosing locations for his restaurants, Butler concentrated on major highway and freeway exits, where travelers would be plentiful at all hours of the day and night. The expansion of a national network of interstate highways during this time prompted increasing numbers of Americans to travel by car, and Denny's restaurants became a rapid success.

In 1967 Denny's opened its first foreign restaurant, located in Acapulco, Mexico, and eventually established additional outlets in Mexico as well as Hong Kong. In 1969, in an effort to streamline and centralize its food production, Denny's bought Delly's Food, changing the name of that concern to Proficient Food Company. This subsidiary was responsible for running warehouse and distribution operations to keep the company's restaurants supplied. Four years later Denny's opened its own food processing facility, called Portion-Trol Foods, in Mansfield, Texas. In the mid-1980s Denny's was purchased for $800 million by a group of investors in a leveraged buyout. Two years later these investors sold the company to TW Services for $843 million.

KEY DATES

1979: Trans World Corporation is formed as a holding company whose assets include Trans World Airlines, Hilton International, and the restaurant chain Quincy's Family Steakhouse.

1986: Trans World restructures, becoming TW Services, Inc.

1987: TW Services focuses on its restaurant holdings and acquires two restaurant chains, Denny's and El Pollo Loco.

1989: Investment firm Coniston Partners acquires TW Services for $1.7 billion.

1990: Company headquarters are moved from Paramus, New Jersey, to Spartanburg, South Carolina.

1993: In the midst of discrimination allegations, TW Services changes its name to Flagstar Corp.

1996: Amid staggering financial losses, Flagstar divests all nonrestaurant businesses and acquires the family-dining chains Coco's and Carrows.

1998: After declaring bankruptcy the previous year, the company emerges from Chapter 11 protection as Advantica Restaurant Group.

1999: Advantica sells its El Pollo Loco chain.

2001: Nelson J. Marchioli is named president and chief executive officer of Advantica.

2002: The Coco's and Carrows chains are sold, prompting Advantica to change its name to Denny's Corporation.

2006: After more than a decade, the company reports its first annual profit.

2007: Marchioli launches the franchise growth initiative, aimed at converting Denny's to a franchise-based business model.

2008: Of the chain's 1,541 restaurants, 80 percent are operated by franchisees.

EARLY HISTORY OF SPARTAN FOOD SYSTEMS

TW Services also owned and operated the largest franchisee of Hardee's, one of the units of Spartan Food Systems. The first Hardee's franchise was opened in October 1961 in Spartanburg, South Carolina. A second Hardee's franchise outlet was soon opened in another area of Spartanburg. This restaurant, which was a walk-up operation rather than a drive-in, was owned and run by Jerry Richardson and four other investors, who contributed a total of $20,000 and called their enterprise Spartan Investment Company.

Offering hamburgers, french fries, and beverages priced between 10 and 15 cents, the franchised Hardee's was a success, and the Spartan investors soon opened other outlets. Within five years they were running 15 different Hardee's restaurants. In 1969 the partnership changed its name to Spartan Food Systems and began to offer stock to the public. In 1976 Spartan was listed on the New York Stock Exchange for the first time.

The following year, with the money raised from this stock offering, Spartan purchased the Quincy's Family Steakhouse chain, founded in 1973 as the Western Family Steak House, a single restaurant located in Greenville, South Carolina. By 1976 nine Western Family Steak Houses were in operation, and the company's name was changed to Quincy's, in honor of cofounder Bill Brittain's grandfather. By 1978 the number of Quincy's restaurants had almost tripled, and this rate of rapid growth continued after Spartan was purchased by Trans World in 1979. Over the next five years, an additional 189 Quincy's steakhouse restaurants were opened throughout the Southeast.

TW Services also acquired El Pollo Loco, Spanish for "The Crazy Chicken," a company that got its start in Mexico in 1975. Francisco Ochoa opened a modest restaurant by the side of a road in the small town of Gusave, serving flame-broiled chicken that had been marinated with his family's recipe of fruit juices, herbs, and spices. Ochoa's operation expanded rapidly in Mexico, as 90 outlets in 20 cities were opened during the 1970s.

At the end of 1980 the company opened its first restaurant in the United States, on Alvarado Street in Los Angeles, and within three years 16 more American restaurants were established. In 1983 the Ochoa family sold its American restaurants to Denny's, retaining the El Pollo Loco Mexican operations. Under its new owner, the American El Pollo Locos were expanded to include several new outlets in California and Nevada, before being purchased by TW Services in 1987.

With a stable group of foodservice properties in place, TW Services announced in 1987 that it planned to invest $700 million in expanding and improving its operations in an effort to strengthen its presence in the foodservices industry. Toward this end the company cut back the administrative staff at Denny's headquarters and simplified the chain's menus, improving the company's profitability.

HOSTILE TAKEOVER IN LATE EIGHTIES

Before other efforts had begun to take effect, however, TW Services found itself in the midst of another corporate takeover battle in the fall of 1988. Coniston Partners, an investor group known for breaking up and selling off parts of other big corporations, sought to buy TW Services for $1.14 billion. In response, the company put in place a "poison pill" defense intended to make it extremely expensive for any outsider to buy more than 20 percent of its stock. Coniston challenged this move in court, while continuing to purchase increments of TW Services stock. By mid-December 1988, 85 percent of TW Services' stock had been purchased by Coniston, and by the middle of the following year the deal had been completed. Coniston bought TW Services for $1.7 billion. The company's new owners planned to keep its foodservices units and sell its less profitable nursing home unit.

In 1990 American Medical Services was divested, along with two other smaller units, The Rowe Corporation and the Milnot Corporation. In addition, the company consolidated the administration of all of its restaurant chains, moving the headquarters of TW Services from Paramus, New Jersey, to Spartanburg, South Carolina, where its Hardee's franchises were based. In the months following, the headquarters of Canteen was moved from Chicago to Spartanburg as was Denny's administrative staff, which transferred from Irvine, California. Only El Pollo Loco, whose restaurants were located exclusively in the western states, retained its headquarters outside the new central company facilities.

These moves were intended to help TW Services run more efficiently, to offset its high debt, and to stem its losses, which reached $67.8 million in 1990. The transfer of operations was completed in 1991, but the company still finished 1991 with losses of $67.6 million. Help for the beleaguered company came in 1992, when TW Services cut a deal with the venture capital firm Kohlberg Kravis Roberts & Company, which contributed $300 million in capital to TW Services, in return for a 47 percent stake in the company.

DENNY'S DISCRIMINATION PROBLEM IN THE EARLY NINETIES

Hope for financial improvements was offset, however, by disturbing news on another front: African American customers at Denny's restaurants in California began to complain that they had been discriminated against and denied service. Specifically, the customers alleged that some Denny's restaurants either refused adequate service or forced them to pay in advance for their meals, while white customers in the restaurants were not asked to do the same.

As the U.S. Justice Department began an investigation into Denny's, TW Services began an effort to control the public relations damage to its reputation. The company apologized to customers, made contact with civil rights groups, fired or transferred problematic employees, and implemented a cultural relations team designed to educate employees on issues of race. Negotiations with the Justice Department continued throughout 1992. In March 1993, TW Services signed a consent decree with the Justice Department that called for an end to prejudicial practices. The company agreed to initiate improved training guidelines for employees and to allow for the spot testing of Denny's restaurants for compliance with its nondiscriminatory policy.

Nevertheless, the company's legal troubles continued, as aggrieved customers pressed lawsuits. Moreover, in May 1993, six African American Secret Service agents sued Denny's, claiming that they had been denied service at a restaurant in Annapolis, Maryland. The charges received extensive media exposure, as critics charged that Denny's employees exhibited such consistent racist behavior that it constituted a part of the company's culture.

In the midst of these image problems, TW Services changed its name in June 1993. Shedding all vestiges of its past association with Trans World, the company took Flagstar as its new name. Flagstar also hired its first African American executive, a human relations administrator who vowed to tackle the problems at Denny's.

One month later, Flagstar announced an ambitious minority advancement program developed in conjunction with the NAACP. To demonstrate its good faith in its effort to stamp out racism, Flagstar announced that it would double the number of Denny's franchises owned by minorities to 107, hire 325 African American managers, and pledge $1 billion to be earmarked for goods purchased from minority-owned contractors over a seven-year period. Moreover, the company promised to maintain a policy of designating 12 percent of its purchasing budget, 10 percent of its marketing and advertising budget, and 15 percent of its legal, accounting, and consulting budget, exclusively for minority-owned firms.

FINANCIAL TROUBLE IN THE MID-NINETIES

Flagstar continued to suffer financial difficulties. Surveys showed that the customer traffic in its Denny's chain, which contributed the bulk of its revenues, was down by 7 percent. In an effort to draw more people into its restaurants, Denny's inaugurated an all-you-can-eat promotion, which had to be canceled in the summer of 1993 when it became too expensive. By the end of the year the company's losses had reached $1.7 billion, which included a $1.5 billion write-off of goodwill and other intangible assets. In addition, in January 1994, Flagstar announced that it would take a $192 million restructuring charge to close or franchise 14 percent of its restaurants, primarily Denny's outlets. The company also announced that it would embark upon a modernization program for its 1,000 company restaurants, installing new facades and menus, additional lights, and contemporary logos in facilities that, in many cases, had not been updated in 20 years.

The company's poor financial performance prompted the layoff of 300 employees in March 1994. Although the company had announced in February an 18-month program for gradual downsizing, it considerably accelerated the plan. The eliminated positions were primarily in support staff, particularly clerical, payroll, and building services.

In June 1994 Flagstar announced that it had completed the sale of the Canteen food and vending operations to London-based Compass Group PLC for $450 million. At the same time Flagstar began searching for buyers for its Volume Services and TW Recreational Services divisions. These efforts reflected the company's decision to focus on its restaurants, Flagstar's core business.

By December 1995, Flagstar had agreed to pay a total of $54 million to plaintiffs in three class-action lawsuits against Denny's. This sum represented the largest and broadest settlement ever made in such suits. With this move, the company hoped to settle 4,300 claims against it, contained in legal proceedings taking place in Maryland, Virginia, and California. At the same time, the company renewed its commitment to improving race relations at Denny's, setting up discrimination testing programs and monitoring employee behavior.

SUCCESSIVE LEADERS GRAPPLE WITH PROFOUND PROBLEMS

Flagstar CEO Jerry Richardson brokered the settlements and hired Ron Petty to take over as president of Denny's, with clear instructions to solve the chain's race relations problems. Richardson faced other problems, however, namely $2.3 billion in debt and five straight years of losses by the end of 1994. In January 1995 he was replaced as CEO by Jim Adamson. Adamson moved decisively to change the company's environment of racial discrimination. He instituted diversity training for his employees, set up management training programs to help minorities rise into executive positions, increased recruitment of minorities for both company positions and for franchise ownership, and sought minority suppliers.

The company's financial problems proved more difficult to overcome. In 1995 Flagstar lost $55 million on revenues of $2.6 billion. Struggling with a poor image and with annual interest payments of $230 million, the company had lost Wall Street's confidence; the stock price had fallen to a low of $2.88 in 1995. The company's mainstay, Denny's, had begun to recover in 1994, with revenues up 35 percent. That growth stalled in 1995 as Flagstar sold 45 company-owned restaurants to franchisees, resulting in Denny's revenues dropping from $1.55 billion in 1994 to $1.49 billion in 1995. Hardee's was also a drain in 1995, as revenues fell almost 6 percent to $660 million. Hardee's same-store sales showed a depressing decline of 8.6 percent.

Adamson tackled the company's problems on several fronts. Flagstar already had begun refocusing on its restaurant businesses; Adamson completed that task by divesting all of the company's nonrestaurant businesses by mid-1996. To offset competition at Denny's from fast-food restaurants, he lowered prices, introducing five morning meals under $2 to supplement the chain's popular $1.99 Grand Slam breakfast. In addition, Denny's added a "value" lunch menu, with meals from $2.99 to $4.99. To regain Hardee's customer base, Adamson ordered a cut in burger prices and an increase in burger size. In addition, he brought in a new president, Craig Bushey, to rejuvenate the 580-store chain.

FLAGSTAR BECOMES ADVANTICA IN 1998

In May 1996 Flagstar acquired two family dining chains, Coco's and Carrows, hoping to add more consistent performers to its stable of restaurant chains. Unable to continue under its staggering burden of debt, however, Flagstar spent 1997 reorganizing under Chapter 11 bankruptcy protection. The company finished the year with revenues of $2.61 billion, a slight increase over 1996, but reported another net loss of $134.5 million.

In January 1998, Flagstar emerged from Chapter 11 with a new name, Advantica Restaurant Group, and a debt load $1.1 billion lighter. Adamson remained CEO, but the company had a new board of directors and newly issued common stock trading over the NASDAQ. In February Advantica signed an agreement to sell its

Hardee's franchise subsidiary to CKE Restaurants, Inc. The $427 million deal comprised $381 million in cash and $46 million in debt obligations. Soon after, Advantica sold its Quincy's Family Steakhouse chain as well. Advantica planned to use the cash from the two transactions to further reduce its debt and to invest in its other restaurant chains. Not only was Advantica in a more hopeful financial position in mid-1998, it was receiving recognition for its dramatic turnaround in race relations. *Fortune* magazine named Advantica the number two best company in the country for Asians, African Americans, and Hispanics. With a rejuvenated balance sheet and image, Advantica hoped to complete a solid turnaround by the end of the decade.

ADVANTICA ENTERS THE 21ST CENTURY

Recovery proved elusive for Advantica, as the beleaguered company stumbled into the new century. The company continued to post substantial losses, recording a net loss of $381.9 million in 1999 and a $98 million loss in 2000. Clearly, further changes were needed, which prompted Adamson to continue down the divestiture path. Advantica sold the El Pollo Loco chain in 1999 and in 2000 it announced its intentions to sever ties with the Coco's and Carrows chains as well. Adamson decided to embrace a "one company, one brand" strategy and focus all the company's resources on its flagship brand, Denny's. The chain comprised 784 company-owned units and 1,032 franchised units in 2001, when Adamson retired and passed the reins of command to Nelson J. Marchioli, who had served as the president of El Pollo Loco for the previous four years.

Marchioli would serve as the company's president and chief executive officer throughout the coming decade. He began his tenure taking charge of a company hobbled by debt and reeling from a string of annual financial losses. Advantica ceased to be a $1 billion company after 2001, as revenues slipped from $1.3 billion to $948 million and continued to slip downward. The company posted an $88 million loss in 2001, another glaring blemish on a financial record that had not included an annual profit in more than a decade. Marchioli was assailed on all fronts, but his most pressing task was to implement Adamson's vision and concentrate all of Advantica's energies in one direction.

ADVANTICA BECOMES DENNY'S CORPORATION IN 2002

The Coco's and Carrows chains were operated by an Advantica subsidiary named FRD Acquisition Co. In September 2000, the company began reporting FRD as a discontinued operation, but before the company could stride forward with its sharpened focus it needed to dispense with the two chains. In early 2001, FRD declared bankruptcy, a move intended to facilitate the divestiture of the properties by forcing creditors to renegotiate the subsidiary's debt. A year passed before Advantica, which continued to post financial losses, could celebrate the disposition of Coco's and Carrows. In July 2002, the two chains were sold to its bondholders for $32.5 million, the maximum amount allowed under the provisions of FRD's declaration of bankruptcy. Immediately after the sale was completed, Advantica changed its name, becoming Denny's Corporation.

FINANCIAL TURNAROUND

Gradually, Denny's began showing signs of improvement. Restaurants were closed, a systemwide remodeling program was implemented, and the company's debt was reduced. Annual losses continued, but the losses were becoming smaller. In 2004, the company registered a $37 million loss, but during the year same-store sales were the highest in more than a decade. In 2005, the company's loss was trimmed to $7.3 million, the same year its stock, which had been delisted by the NASDAQ, was relisted as "DENN" as a result of its sustained sales growth and improvements to its restaurant operations. In 2006, the company at last turned the corner on profitability, posting a rousing $30.3 million profit.

For the years ahead, Marchioli pinned Denny's financial vitality on the growth of the company's franchised operations. Franchised units were less capital intensive than company-owned units were and they yielded higher profit margins than company-owned restaurants produced. In 2007, he introduced Denny's franchise growth initiative, which was implemented to convert Denny's to a franchise-based business model. Substantial progress was achieved within a year, as Denny's, a 66 percent franchise-operated chain in 2007, had 80 percent of units operated by franchisees in 2008, its third consecutive year of posting an annual profit. In the future, the expansion of Denny's franchised operations was expected to drive the company's financial growth and give the organization what it had long lacked: sustained financial health.

Elizabeth Rourke
Updated, Susan Windisch Brown;
Jeffrey L. Covell

PRINCIPAL SUBSIDIARIES

Denny's Holdings, Inc.; Denny's, Inc.; DFO, LLC; Denny's Realty, LLC.

PRINCIPAL COMPETITORS

Waffle House, Inc.; DineEquity, Inc.; Brinker International, Inc.

FURTHER READING

Allen, Robin Lee, "Family Feud," *Nation's Restaurant News,* June 22, 1998, pp. 130–38.

Anderson, Trevor, "Denny's Lowers Debt, Increases Sales," *Spartanburg Herald-Journal,* January 5, 2007.

Carlino, Bill, "Flagstar Cuts 300 Jobs, Steps Up Restructuring," *Nation's Restaurant News,* March 14, 1994, p. 3.

"Completing Advantica Restaurant Group's Strategy of Becoming a Single-Brand Operator, the Company Changed Its Name to Denny's Corp.," *Nation's Restaurant News Daily NewsFax,* July 15, 2002, p. 1.

"Denny's Owner to Pare Back," *Mergers & Acquisitions Journal,* April 2000, p. 34.

Deveny, Kathleen, "Do These Raiders Really Want to Start Flipping Burgers?" *Business Week,* October 10, 1988.

Fairclost, Anne, "Guess Who's Coming to Denny's," *Fortune,* August 3, 1998, pp. 108–10.

Farkas, David, "Breaking Out of a Slump: Denny's Is Getting Some Hits by Improving Service and Boasting About Breakfast," *Chain Leader,* July 2004, p. 47.

Frank, Robert, "Flagstar Loss Is $1.65 Billion on Big Charge," *Wall Street Journal,* January 25, 1994.

Hayes, Jack, "Advantica Names Marchioli New CEO," *Nation's Restaurant News,* January 15, 2001, p. 1.

Holden, Benjamin A., "Parent of Denny's Restaurants, NAACP Agree on Plan to Boost Minorities' Role," *Wall Street Journal,* July 1, 1993.

Labaton, Stephen, "Denny's Restaurants to Pay $54 Million in Race Bias Suits," *New York Times,* May 25, 1994.

"On the Griddle," *Forbes,* October 7, 1996, p. 128.

Rice, Faye, "Denny's Changes Its Spots," *Fortune,* May 13, 1996, pp. 133–38.

Ringer, Richard, "Denny's Parent Has Loss After a Large Write-Off," *New York Times,* January 25, 1994.

Serwer, Andrew E., "What to Do When Race Charges Fly," *Fortune,* July 12, 1993.

Shepherd, Lauren, "Restaurants: Denny's and IHOP Want to Reclaim Their Former Status As Kings at the Breakfast Table," *Houston Chronicle,* August 6, 2008, p. 3.

Spector, Amy, "Advantica's Coco's/Carrows Files Ch. 11 to Woo Buyers," *Nation's Restaurant News,* February 26, 2001, p. 4.

Dongfeng Motor
Corporation

Special No. 1 Dongfeng Road
Wuhan Econ and Tech Dev Zone
Wuhan, 430056
China
Telephone: (86 719) 8226 962
Fax: (86 719) 8226 845
Web site: http://www.dfmc.com.cn

Private Company
Founded: 1969 as Second Automobile Works
Employees: 120,000
Sales: $32.12 billion (2008)
NAICS: 336111 Automobile Manufacturing; 336211 Motor Vehicle Body Manufacturing; 336399 All Other Motor Vehicle Parts Manufacturing

■ ■ ■

Dongfeng Motor Corporation is the third largest vehicle manufacturer in China, producing full lines of passenger automobiles and commercial trucks as well as vehicle engines and components. In addition to building its own branded vehicles, the company operates significant joint ventures with Nissan Motor Company and PSA Peugeot Citroën. Other joint venture partners include Honda Motor Company, Kia Motors, and Renault SA. The company's truck and automobile parts production are located in Shiyan, and automobile manufacturing and research and development centers for cars and trucks are located in Wuhan, in Hubei Province. Other plants are located in Guangdong Province, Guangxi Zhuang Autonomous Region in southern China, Zhe-

jiang Province in the east, and XinJiang Uygur Autonomous Region in the northwest. Dongfeng and its joint venture subsidiaries operate retail dealership and financing services in major Chinese cities.

CHINA'S SECOND AUTOMOBILE COMPANY FORMS IN 1969

The original name of Dongfeng Motor Corporation (DFM), Second Automobile Works (SAW), reflected the creation of the company as the second automobile manufacturing concern in China. First Automobile Works (FAW; later known as China FAW Group) assisted in the development of SAW's manufacturing complex, which included hospitals, schools, dormitories, and other institutional needs of the company's employees. Its facilities were located in Shiyan, in Hubei Province of central China, where vehicle manufacturing infrastructure would be secure from foreign invasion.

Founded under Mao Zedong in 1969, SAW produced medium- and heavy-duty trucks. After several years of facility construction and manufacturing design, SAW began production of a 2.5-ton cross-country cruiser in 1975, followed by a five-ton civil vehicle in 1978. At this time, FAW contributed to the development of new vehicle styles and assisted in raising annual production. After construction delays, SAW production capacity surpassed 30,000 units when the facility in Xiangfan opened in 1983. At an adjacent facility, a joint venture with Cummins Engine Company supplied SAW with B series diesel engines for cargo trucks, allowing production to increase further. In 1986 the company reached annual production capacity of 100,000 trucks.

COMPANY PERSPECTIVES

■

Corporate Ideology: Care for every single person and vehicle. Corporate Philosophy: Learn, innovate, surpass. Corporate Spirit: Realize the value, shift the future.

SAW took the Dongfeng name, meaning "east wind," in 1992, just as it began production on light passenger cars. Through a joint venture with Peugeot Citroën SA, Dongfeng introduced the Fukang DC7140, a remake of the Citroën ZX. Early partnerships with Honda and Nissan helped Dongfeng achieve production and sales volume of 220,000 units in 1993, and profit of RMB 1.49 billion.

DFM facilitated further growth through joint venture agreements to manufacture automotive parts and components with foreign companies. A 1996 joint venture established between Delphi Saginaw Steering Systems and DFM's Shanghai Shenhui Auto Steering Gear Corporation began manufacturing rack and pinion gears for distribution to most of China's automobile companies. Also, DFM extended its partnership with Cummins Engine Company, to produce C series diesel engines, ranging from 150 to 240 horsepower. The engines powered commercial vehicles, including cargo trucks, transit buses, construction equipment, and boats. In July 1996 a DFM subsidiary, Shenlong Automobile Accessories Corporation, and Cummins began producing engine filters through the formation of joint venture Shanghai Fleetguard.

A new partnership with Honda Motor Company in 1998 involved the manufacture of automobile engines to be used in production of Honda cars produced by Guangzhou Auto Group. Sharing production facilities with Guangzhou Auto at former Guangzhou Peugeot facilities, Dongfeng Honda Engine Co. initiated production of 30,000 engines in October 1999. DFM retained rights to sell Honda automobiles produced at the factory, which reached annual capacity of 240,000 units by 2003.

ENTRY INTO WORLD TRADE ORGANIZATION FEEDS STEADY GROWTH

After experiencing fluctuations in production, sales, and profits, China's entry into the World Trade Organization (WTO) provided DFM with the structure for steady expansion through foreign joint ventures.

Through international joint ventures, DFM would gain knowledge of automobile technology and management techniques while maintaining independent operations. Development of Dongfeng brand automobiles, particularly economy cars, would expand DFM's product line and regional distribution networks would expand the company's reach into new Chinese markets. DFM established a five-year plan to reach 18 percent market share by 2005 and production of one million vehicles annually.

Ironically, one of DFM's first projects sidestepped WTO restrictions. A July 2002 memorandum of understanding between DFM, Guangzhou Auto, and Honda spurred development of an automobile factory intended to produce cars for export only. Its location in an export processing zone allowed China to circumvent WTO restrictions on exports, and it gave Honda a majority ownership in the venture.

DFM formed new joint venture agreements with existing partners. In early 2003 Honda and DFM began negotiations to produce vehicles in Wuhan. Initial production of 5,000 complete sets of upscale jeeps began at Wuhan Wantong Automobile Company while facility construction prepared the joint venture for production of 200,000 jeeps annually. New vehicles to emerge from the Dongfeng Peugeot Citroën Automobile (DPCA) joint venture included cars based on the Peugeot 206 and Peugeot 307 platforms.

With Kia Motors of Korea and Yueda Automobile Group, in China, DFM expanded on an existing partnership for the production of 400,000 vehicles per year. At a facility in Jaingsu Province in eastern China, Dongfeng Yueda Kia Motors produced the Qianlima compact sedan, with more than 26,000 units sold in the first half of 2003. The joint venture hoped to sell 50,000 cars for the year, including units of the Pride car. Expansion plans included the development of new car styles and sport-utility vehicles (SUVs).

In October 2002 DFM and Renault Trucks took steps toward the formation of a joint venture in manufacturing heavy trucks in China. Renault agreed to transfer technology for its 11-liter dCi 11 engines as negotiations for further cooperation continued. In 2004, Renault agreed to acquire a stake in Dongfeng Liuzhou Motors, as well as to contribute branding, products, and additional technology. The agreement called for annual production of 7,000 heavy trucks.

DONGFENG AND NISSAN FORM LARGEST JOINT VENTURE IN CHINA

Nissan Motor Company and DFM entered into negotiations in 2002 to form an automobile and truck

KEY DATES

1969: China forms Second Automobile Works in Hubei Province.
1975: Second Automobile Works begins production of medium-duty trucks.
1978: Production of heavy-duty trucks begins.
1986: Production capacity reaches 100,000 units annually.
1992: Renamed Dongfeng Motor Corporation (DFM), the company begins production of light automobiles.
2003: DFM forms joint venture with Nissan, the largest in China.
2005: Subsidiary Dongfeng Motor Group Corporation sells 30 percent of stock on Hong Kong exchange.
2007: DFM exceeds 2010 sales goal of one million vehicles.

manufacturing joint venture. However, differences in organizational attitudes delayed progress. For instance, defining the roles of the chief executive officer, the chairman, and the Communist Party took time to establish. Nissan reluctantly agreed to have members of the Communist Party on the board of directors, such as the official secretary to the Communist Party. However, Nissan did so because officials might be useful to the company in pursuing its initiatives.

Key points of negotiations involved Dongfeng's other operations. The social institutions and other joint venture operations with Citroën, Honda, and Kia remained with DFM. Also, Nissan required a much smaller employee base for its lean production style than the Chinese government preferred. Of its 120,000 employees, DFM transferred 74,000 workers to DFL operations in Wuhan, and Nissan pruned another 7,000 people from operations.

After resolving their differences, Dongfeng and Nissan Motor Company formed a 50-50 joint venture, Dongfeng Motor Company, Ltd. (DFL), on July 1, 2003. Under the agreement, Nissan brands would grace passenger vehicles and the Dongfeng name would cover commercial vehicles. The joint venture's headquarters and manufacturing base were located in Wuhan, a regional economic center. The move from Shiyan reflected DFM's modernized approach to business, with Nissan providing DFL with the knowledge to upgrade

and update production processes and to become responsive to the automobile market.

One of the challenges of the Nissan-Dongfeng venture involved the high demand for trucks in China and Nissan's limited knowledge in the specifics of truck manufacturing. However, Nissan drew from its connections with other truck manufacturers. Nissan sought to bring the quality of trucks up to the competitive standards required for export by closing two small production facilities, scrapping outdated equipment, and implementing efficient production processes. DFM's acquisition of an equity stake in Nissan Zhengzhou streamlined DFL's plans to build higher-priced pickup trucks and SUVs. The company introduced the Dongfeng Star light-duty truck in 2004. DFL established the Commercial Vehicle Company in Shiyan, and the Dongfeng-Vossen premium passenger bus began production in 2004. A series of heavy-duty trucks were launched in 2006, under the Tianlong name. Eventually, DFL expected to export commercial vehicles to developing countries in Africa, Asia, and Latin America.

Plans for the venture involved increasing manufacturing capacity from 60,000 to 300,000 cars during the first year. The goal included increasing sales of Nissan brand cars to 100,000 units, specifically 60,000 Bluebird and Sunny sedans, 20,000 SUVs and pickup trucks manufactured by another Nissan joint venture, and 20,000 vehicles to be imported from Japan. Production on the Sunny brand sedan began immediately with the first model rolling off the assembly line in Guangzhou a week after the joint venture agreement was signed. DFL introduced the Teana luxury sedan in 2004 and the Tiida in 2005. A network of 300 retail automobile dealerships was in operation by the end of 2005. Production on new Teana and Bluebird Sylphy models began in 2006.

DFL became the largest automobile joint venture in China, and it helped to make DFM the third largest automaker in China in 2005. The success of the Dongfeng-Nissan venture was made evident by the numerous awards earned by DFL. These included awards for the quality of its cars and trucks as well as the organization's management. With such success, DFL Chairman and CEO Miao Wei gave DFM a reputation as a maverick and risk-taker among Chinese automakers.

PUBLIC OFFERING OF STOCK BRINGS CAPITAL FOR EXPANSION

On December 8, 2005, Dongfeng Motor Group Corporation (DMGC), subsidiary of DFM, debuted on the Hong Kong stock exchange with an initial public offering (IPO) priced at HKD 1.60, or $0.22 per share.

The offering of 2.48 billion shares included 9.1 percent existing stock and 90.9 percent new shares. To attract investors, interest in DFM's joint ventures with Nissan, Honda, and Peugeot were included in the DMGC offering. The company raised HKD 3.97 billion, of which 90 percent was used to pay debt. DFM was an attractive investment as one of the major Chinese automakers. Also, its links to Nissan and Honda, which had a reputation for quality manufacturing, gave DFM an edge over its competitors. Institutional investors requested double the shares available to them.

IPO funds were applied to capital investment, as DFM sought to maintain its number three position in the rapidly expanding Chinese automobile market. DFM expanded its manufacturing capabilities and improved economies of scale. The company planned to introduce at least ten passenger cars into the market by 2008. As only 24 in every 1,000 people owned vehicles in China, DFM recognized the potential for losing market share despite overall economic growth. Moreover, the company experienced a decline in profit margins as competition resulted in lower vehicle pricing. Profit margins on commercial trucks declined from 9.6 percent to 7.7 percent and on passenger vehicles from about 23 percent to 11.6 percent.

In February 2006 Dongfeng Honda Automobile Co. completed expansion of the joint venture's Wuhan plant. Production capacity was expanded from 30,000 to 120,000 units annually. About 70 percent of parts were procured locally and all of the cars were intended to be sold in China. Dongfeng Honda began manufacturing Honda Civics in March with the aim to manufacture and sell 50,000 Honda Civics by the end of the year.

In advance of new DPCA passenger vehicles in 2006, DFM formed a financing partnership with Peugeot Citroën and Bank of China. In December 2005 the China Banking Regulatory Commission approved the formation of the Dongfeng Peugeot Auto Finance Company. The Bank of China owned a 50 percent stake and DFM and Peugeot Citroën each owned 25 percent. In July 2006 the company began offering wholesale financing to automobile dealers in Beijing, then expanded nationwide. The financing applied to Dongfeng Peugeot and Dongfeng Citroën purchases and was obtained through Bank of China's national network of offices.

DPCA released three new car models in 2006, the Peugeot 206 in March; the Citroën C-Triompe sedan, based on the C-4 hatchback, in May; and a new compact car, the Citroën C2 five-door hatchback, introduced in October. DPCA initiated construction of a new Wuhan facility to accommodate expanded production capacity, planned to reach 300,000 vehicles by 2008.

Dongfeng Nissan Auto Finance began operations in July 2007. The new organization provided wholesale financing to Nissan and Infiniti auto dealers as well as to consumers buying those brands of vehicles. Based in Shanghai, the company planned to make financing available in Beijing, Guangzhou, and Wuhan by 2010. The finance arm supported the release of new vehicle models, such as the Livina car, the Yumsun mini personal vehicle, and the Oting SUV.

DFM reached its sales goal of one million vehicles by 2010 three years early. Growth rates of 39.39 percent in 2005, 27.85 percent in 2006, and 21.89 percent in 2007 culminated in total vehicle sales of 1.13 million units in 2007. That year, DFM reported sales of RMB 12.8 billion, a 26.6 percent increase over 2006. Based on the strength of revenue from trucks and diesel engines, DFM reported a 9.5 percent increase in profits, from RMB 619.3 million in 2006 to RMB 677.8 million in 2007.

PASSENGER VEHICLES, ENVIRONMENTAL CONCERNS DOMINATING PLANS FOR THE FUTURE

DFM continued to implement plans to develop passenger cars and increase production. In September 2007, Dongfeng Passenger Vehicle Company began construction of a factory dedicated to producing medium- and high-grade sedans. DFM's expansion strategy for 2008 and 2009 involved increasing overall production from 1.11 million vehicles in 2007 to 1.61 million vehicles by 2010.

Concern for pollution and the rising cost of fuel influenced new passenger car development at DFM. The company's DPCA joint venture already produced a compact van, DFM a beach minivan, and DFL a personal mini vehicle. In 2008 Dongfeng Yu'an established a production base of 200,000 units at a new plant under construction. Also, the company purchased Hafei Automobile Group in northern China, which specialized in mini-cars. DMG planned to develop cars utilizing 1.3 liter and smaller engines. In a joint venture with Peugeot, production capacity was boosted by 100,000 units and plans were made to produce stylish, low-priced mini-cars from Peugeot.

DFM experimented with hybrid engines for all of its vehicles. Hybrid gas-electric buses were operational in Wuhan. DFM tested a one-ton, light-duty truck powered by electric storage batteries and capable of traveling 100 to 150 kilometers on each charge. TNT, an express service provider, began a trial operation of two electric trucks in May 2008. DFM developed electric hybrid sedans to be tested at a later date. In June 2009 DFM and Detroit Electric Holdings initiated negotiations to research, develop, and market pure electric vehicles in China using Detroit Electric technology.

Through its joint ventures, DFM continued to develop infrastructure for its regular passenger cars. Capitalizing on the fast-growing car market in China, Honda increased its investment in production and dealership networks. Dongfeng Honda Motor added production lines to increase capacity to 240,000 units by the end of 2008.

After Nissan and Dongfeng experienced a 100 percent increase in sales over five years, to 610,000 units in 2007, the joint venture laid plans to increase production capacity to one million vehicles by 2012. Nissan and Dongfeng forged a new cooperative agreement in July for the purpose of building 3.0 liter diesel engines at a new factory in Zhengzhou. The joint venture began construction on the factory in March 2009, with DFM holding a 51 percent interest in the project. With production at 120,000 engines per year, the venture would supply Zhengzhou Nissan Automobile Company, another DFM-Nissan joint venture, for light business vehicles.

GLOBAL FINANCIAL CRISIS IMPACTS GOALS

The global financial crisis that emerged in late 2008, prompted DFM to slow down its plans for expansion during 2009. New joint venture projects with Volvo, Hafei, and Renault were affected, and the company postponed the launch of new self-developed sedans. Overall production declined, except for Dongfeng Honda Automobile, which maintained target sales levels. DPCA decided to cut its 450,000 unit production capacity. DFM experienced slower sales of its trucks and accessories as well.

Despite dire concerns over the economic situation, DFM was on target to sell 1.3 million vehicles in 2008. Sales increased 16.12 percent over 2007, giving DFM the fastest growth of the top three Chinese automakers. Also, DFM experienced a sales increase during the first quarter of 2009 over the previous year. Sales of passenger cars rose 5.5 percent and those of commercial vehicles rose by 20.41 percent.

DFM retained its plans to introduce compact cars in 2009, presuming that government tax preferences for small cars would make the cars more attractive in uncertain economic times. In April DFM launched its "self-developed" sedan, the Fengshen S30, a four-door passenger car powered by a 1.6 liter engine. DFM applied European design concepts to the exterior and chassis, and derived transmission and engine components from PSA Peugeot Citroën and Aisin Seiki. Other activities involved DPCA's construction of a plant, where the company planned to produce about 70,000 Peugeot 407 family cars in late 2009. DPCA renewed intentions to produce the Peugeot 408 in 2010.

While the Chinese automotive market weathered the global financial crisis, the Chinese government sought to reduce potential problems by encouraging its automakers to merge. With the intention of reducing the number of companies from 14 to ten, the plan involved organizing three major companies to produce more than two million vehicles per year and four to five companies to produce about one million vehicles annually. For DFM, the Chinese government requested a cross-country merger with China FAW Group and ChangAn Automobile Group.

Mary Tradii

PRINCIPAL SUBSIDIARIES

Cummins Engine (Beijing) Co., Ltd. (50%); Dongfeng Citroën Auto Finance Company (25%); Dongfeng Honda Automobile Co., Ltd, (50%); Dongfeng Honda Engine Co. (50%); Dongfeng Motor Group Corporation, Ltd. (70%); Dongfeng Nissan Auto Finance Co. (50%); Dongfeng Peugeot Citroën Automobile Co. Ltd. (50%); Shanghai Saginaw Delphi Dongfeng Steering Gear Ltd. (50%); Zhengzhou Nissan Automobile Co., Ltd. (51%).

PRINCIPAL COMPETITORS

Beijing Automobile Group Co. Ltd; ChangAn Automobile Group Co., Ltd.; China FAW Group Corporation Ltd.; China National Heavy Duty Truck Group Co. Ltd.; Guangzhou Automobile Group Co. Ltd.; Shanghai Automotive Industry Corporation (Group).

FURTHER READING

"China Auto Industry Reshuffle Is on the Way," March 6, 2009.

"Cummins Announces Engine Venture in China; Second Major International Deal in Three Months," *Diesel Progress Engines & Drives,* September 1996, p. 86.

De Saint-Seine, Sylviane, "Dongfeng to Export Trucks; Chinese Automaker, Nissan Will Supply Africa, Asia, Latin

America," *Automotive News Europe,* January 12, 2004.

"Delphi Joins Partner to Supply Gears in China," *PR Newswire,* March 11, 1996.

"Dongfeng Honda Completes Auto Plant Expansion; Increases Annual Production Capacity to 120,000 Units," *JCN Newswires,* February 27, 2006.

"Dongfeng Motor Posted 75% Profit Rise," *SinoCast, LLC China Transportation Watch,* September 6, 2007.

"Dongfeng Motor Relocates HQ to Wuhan," *AsiaPulse News,* June 22, 2006.

"Dongfeng Peugeot Citroën Ready to Make Peugeot 407 in China," *SinoCast Daily Business Beat,* June 10, 2009.

Furukawa, Tsukasa, "Honda Driving into Chinese Market," *American Metal Market,* May 18, 1998, p. 4.

Kwong, Vicki, and Tian Ying, "Dongfeng Motor Rumbles in Debut; Optimism About Chinese Car Market Lifts Hong Kong Shares," *International Herald Tribune,* December 8, 2005, p. 19.

Mak, Fulton, "Joint Venture Carmaker to Launch Own-Brand Trucks," *Standard,* November 6, 2006.

"Miao Wei: Chairman and Chief Executive, Dongfeng Motor Corp.," *Business Week,* July 12, 2004, p. 66.

Mitchell, Tom, "Honda Plant Marks Mainland First: Joint Venture Wins Approval to Produce Cars for the Export Market," *Asia Africa Intelligence Wire,* November 14, 2002.

Treece, James B., "Nissan's China Venture Was No Slam-Dunk Deal; for Dongfeng, the Devil Was in the Details," *Automotive News,* June 16, 2003, p. 43.

"U.S./China: Detroit Electric Inks EV Deal with Dongfeng," *just-auto.com,* June 19, 2009.

Wong, Kandy, and Tim LeeMaster, "Carmakers Eye Parts Units of Foreign Giants," *South China Morning Post,* May 4, 2009.

Douglas Emmett, Inc.

—— ■ ——

808 Wilshire Boulevard, Suite 200
Santa Monica, California 90401
U.S.A.
Telephone: (310) 255-7700
Fax: (310) 255-7701
Web site: http://www.douglasemmett.com

Public Company
Incorporated: 2005
Employees: 450
Sales: $608.09 million (2008)
Stock Exchanges: New York
Ticker Symbol: DEI
NAICS: 525930 Real Estate Investment Trusts

■ ■ ■

Douglas Emmett, Inc., is a real estate investment trust involved in acquiring, leasing, and managing commercial and residential properties in Los Angeles County and Honolulu, Hawaii. The company's property holdings are concentrated in the Los Angeles submarkets of West Los Angeles, San Fernando Valley, and Tri-Cities. Douglas Emmett owns nine multifamily residential properties and 55 office properties, generating the bulk of its revenue from leasing its more than 13 million square feet of office space.

THE FOUNDERS

Douglas Emmett bore the surnames of the principal architects of its formation and development, Jon A. Douglas and Dan A. Emmett. The two real estate tycoons met during college, a decade before they joined forces and began purchasing real estate in Los Angeles County. Douglas and Emmett met north of their professional hunting grounds, in Palo Alto, where they attended Stanford University in the late 1950s and early 1960s. Douglas, whose athletic prowess rivaled his accomplishments in real estate, distinguished himself at Stanford, enjoying a high-profile collegiate career that made him a well-known figure on campus. Douglas became Stanford's first All-American athlete in tennis, placing second in both singles and doubles in the NCAA Men's Tennis Championship in 1957, the same year he was the starting quarterback for the university's football team. After earning his bachelor's degree, Douglas joined the professional tennis circuit, becoming one of the top ten players in the country between 1960 and 1962.

After his professional tennis career ended, Douglas entered the real estate business. He joined a firm named Elkins Real Estate before starting his own company, Jon Douglas Co. In the course of running his own real estate business, Douglas was reunited with Emmett, who graduated from Stanford in 1961 and earned a law degree from Harvard University in 1964. Beginning in 1971, the year Douglas Emmett recognized as its year of formation, the two Stanford alumni began acquiring, developing, and managing real estate properties. They conducted their activities through Jon Douglas Co. and affiliated companies, including Douglas, Emmett & Co., the development arm of Jon Douglas Co. and one of three companies considered as the direct predecessors to Douglas Emmett, Inc.

COMPANY PERSPECTIVES

The company utilizes the same focused business strategy that was implemented by its founding principals—managing, developing, redeveloping and acquiring multifamily and commercial real estate in high barrier-to-entry submarkets that exhibit strong economic characteristics such as population and job growth, as well as inherent supply constraints, such as limited developable land due to natural and political barriers. The company strives to capitalize on the experience of its seasoned management team to create continued value.

1991: A CHANGE IN FOCUS

For 20 years, Douglas and Emmett built a portfolio of properties, restricting their investment activities within Los Angeles County. They focused primarily on the residential real estate market during the period, acquiring and leasing multifamily properties in upscale neighborhoods. A turning point occurred during the early 1990s, when Jon Douglas ceased being actively involved in managing the Douglas Emmett predecessors and the firms shifted their focus to commercial real estate. When the pivotal change in management and strategy occurred, Jordan L. Kaplan gained prominence, emerging as an executive of influence who eventually would become president and chief executive officer of Douglas Emmett, Inc.

Kaplan replaced Douglas as Emmett's most trusted collaborator, forming a partnership that would make Douglas Emmett, Inc., a "trophy landlord," as *Real Estate Finance and Investment* described the company in a June 26, 2006 article. Kaplan joined Douglas, Emmett & Co. in 1986, the year he received his M.B.A. from the University of California, Los Angeles. Kaplan distinguished himself at the firm, cofounding Douglas Emmett Realty Advisors with Emmett in 1991. Through the company, one of the three predecessor companies that constituted Douglas Emmett, Inc., and Douglas, Emmett & Co., Kaplan and Emmett conducted the investment activity that made Douglas Emmett, Inc., a powerhouse in Los Angeles County's commercial real estate market.

Although the Douglas Emmett predecessors were involved in residential real estate, from the early 1990s forward the entities built their reputation in the commercial sector. Based in the tony Los Angeles neighborhood of Brentwood, Douglas Emmett focused on high-

rise properties located in Brentwood and other posh Los Angeles districts such as Santa Monica, Beverly Hills, Burbank, and Wilshire. They conducted their investment, leasing, and management activities on behalf of institutional investors such as the pension funds of Princeton University and Harvard University, deploying the capital provided by their backers to develop a portfolio capable of returning handsome dividends.

OFFICE PROPERTY ACQUISITIONS IN THE NINETIES

One of the first major acquisitions completed by the new iteration of Douglas Emmett was the acquisition of Studio Plaza in 1993. The company acquired the 434,000-square-foot office building for $83 million. With the property, as with all the properties the company would acquire in the years to follow, Douglas Emmett made its money by leasing the space to tenants and by selling the property later for a higher price.

The acquisition of the Studio Plaza property roughly coincided with an acquisition spree orchestrated by Douglas Emmett, one that would continue nearly unabated for the next 15 years. The company acquired three office properties in 1994, Bundy Olympic, The Gateway Building, and Village on Canon, and moved into higher gear in 1995, completing a dizzying number of transactions. Among the properties purchased during the year were: the 500,000-square-foot Nestlé USA Inc. headquarters in Glendale; the 220,000-square-foot Executive Tower office building in West Los Angeles; the 106,500-square-foot Palisades Promenade office and retail complex in Santa Monica; the 90,000-square-foot CenFed Banks office building in Brentwood; and the 65,000-square-foot Camden Medical Building in Beverly Hills. Douglas Emmett was attracting attention as one of the most active commercial property investors in the region, carving a presence in Los Angeles's most prestigious submarkets that would serve as the foundation underpinning the dominant position it enjoyed in the 21st century.

DOUGLAS EMMETT ENTERING THE NEW MILLENNIUM

Douglas Emmett, using a series of separate institutional funds to fuel its acquisitive activity, continued to add properties to its portfolio during the second half of the 1990s. The company ended the decade with the addition of one of the most coveted properties in Los Angeles County, a 21-story office tower whose prestigious address gave the property its name. Douglas Emmett paid $91 million in 1999 for the 100 Wilshire building, a 245,000-square-foot building with sweeping

KEY DATES

1971: Jon A. Douglas and Dan A. Emmett begin acquiring real estate properties in Los Angeles County.
1986: Jordan L. Kaplan joins Douglas and Emmett.
1991: Douglas Emmett Realty Advisors is formed.
2002: In the largest deal in its history, Douglas Emmett pays $355 million for the Warner Center Plaza complex.
2006: Douglas Emmett completes an initial public offering of stock.
2008: Revenues exceed $600 million, a record high.

views of Santa Monica Bay. The property, developed by entertainer Lawrence Welk in 1969 to house GTE Corp., commanded some of the highest rents in the area, drawing $4.25 per square foot per month. The acquisition of 100 Wilshire was part of $329 million invested by Douglas Emmett in 1999, making it the largest investor in Los Angles County real estate during the year. The company, after 30 years of acquisitions and a decade-long focus on purchasing office space, boasted a portfolio worth $2.5 billion with a total of ten million square feet of residential, office, and retail space. Douglas Emmett ranked as one of the largest property owners in Beverly Hills, the largest property owner on Ventura Boulevard in the San Fernando Valley, the dominant property owner along San Vicente Boulevard in Brentwood, and the largest property owner in downtown Santa Monica.

Major acquisitions continued to chart Douglas Emmett's progress as it entered the 21st century and a decade that would witness profound changes at the 300-employee, Brentwood-based firm. In 2001, the company acquired 1901 Avenue of the Stars, an office building in the center of Los Angeles's financial district. Douglas Emmett paid an estimated $155 million for the 19-story, 482,000-square-foot building. The following year, the company completed the largest acquisition in its history and the largest real estate deal in Los Angeles County in 2002, concluding a two-year-long negotiating process spearheaded by Kaplan. Douglas Emmett paid a reported $355 million for the Warner Center Plaza office tower complex, gaining control over 1.8 million square feet of space in six high-rise office buildings that defined the skyline of western San Fernando Valley. The property became the company's third major holding in the San Fernando Valley, joining Sherman Oaks Galleria

and the Nestlé USA building in Glendale, although the trio did not remain part of the company's portfolio for long. Before the end of the year, Douglas Emmett sold the Nestlé USA building for $160 million.

A rare lull in acquisitive activity followed the purchase of the Warner Center Plaza complex, a respite that stemmed from a paucity of attractive properties in the real estate market. Douglas Emmett did not make a significant purchase for roughly 18 months, ending the quiet period in 2004 with the acquisition of Beverly Hills Medical Center, Bishop Place, and Harbor Court. Late in the year, the company reached an agreement to acquire The Trillium, a property that included two office towers with 590,000 square feet of space, two retail buildings, and the land on which an adjoining Hilton hotel was situated. The deal was significant because it made Douglas Emmett the dominant property owner in San Fernando Valley, enabling the company to insulate itself from fluctuations in the real estate market because it could control lease rates. "That captures the high-rise market," a real estate broker said in the October 25, 2004 issue of the *San Fernando Valley Business Journal.* "Any tenant that wants a high-rise office will have to deal with them."

At the end of 2004, Douglas Emmett began raising capital for its seventh and largest fund. The company's previous fund, DERF 2002, had fallen short of expectations. "We didn't see very many opportunities we liked in 2003 and early 2004," a Douglas Emmett executive said in the December 6, 2004 issue of *Real Estate Finance and Investment,* and the company intended to compensate for the lull in activity. Douglas Emmett was looking to raise $300 million to strengthen its already stalwart position in Santa Monica, Century City, and Brentwood. It also wanted to increase its involvement in Hawaii, where the company had begun to stake a presence in Honolulu's central business district.

INITIAL PUBLIC OFFERING IN 2006

As Douglas Emmett set out on its next acquisition spree, rumors began to circulate in the Southern California real estate community that the company was planning to go public. Reports that one of the largest private owners of Class A office properties in the region was gearing for an initial public offering (IPO) of stock persisted throughout 2005, but months passed without a stock offering. "I think the issue is that they have a lot of institutional investors and when you're going to take something public that involves a lot of investors, it takes a very long time," an industry observer speculated in the January 23, 2006 issue of the *Los Angeles Business Journal.* "Clearly, they don't want to overemphasize how long this has taken."

Douglas Emmett filed with the U.S. Securities and Exchange Commission for an IPO in June 2006, intending to make its public debut as a real estate investment trust, or REIT, a tax designation for a corporation investing in real estate that distributes at least 90 percent of its taxable income to investors in the form of dividends. By operating as a REIT, Douglas Emmett greatly reduced the amount of corporate income tax it was required to pay. When Douglas Emmett filed for its IPO, it was bucking a trend. During the previous year, more than $10 billion in office REIT shares had disappeared from the public markets, as rivals Arden Realty, CarrAmerica, and Trizec Properties repurchased their stock and returned to private ownership. Douglas Emmett hoped the series of privatizations in the office sector would heighten demand for its IPO, enabling the company to raise a record amount of capital.

Douglas Emmett completed its IPO in October 2006, raising $1.1 billion, a new record for a REIT completing an IPO. In preparation for the conversion to public ownership, Douglas Emmett, Inc., was created to acquire Douglas, Emmett & Co., Douglas Emmett Realty Advisors, and the third predecessor company, P.L.E. Builders, Inc., a construction services company.

In the wake of the IPO, Douglas Emmett continued to add to its portfolio of properties. In 2007, the company acquired two office properties, Century Park West and Cornerstone Plaza. In 2008, it acquired seven office properties, including Honolulu Club, five buildings on Wilshire Boulevard, and Warner Corporate Center. By the end of 2008, the company owned 55 properties with 13.32 million square feet of rentable space, figures that were expected to increase in the years ahead, as one of the most aggressive players in Southern California's real estate market added to its swelling portfolio.

Jeffrey L. Covell

PRINCIPAL SUBSIDIARIES

Douglas Emmett Management, Inc.; Douglas Emmett Builders; HNLC, Inc.; Douglas Emmett Fund X REIT, Inc.; Barrington Pacific, LLC; DEG, LLC; DEG III, LLC; DEG Residential, LLC; DEGA, LLC; DEIX, LLC; Douglas Emmett Management, LLC; Douglas Emmett Management Hawaii, LLC; Westwood Place Investors, LLC.

PRINCIPAL COMPETITORS

Acadia Realty Trust; Beacon Capital Partners, LLC; Weingarten Realty Investors.

FURTHER READING

Berry, Kate, "Emmett IPO Percolates, but Will It Hit a Full Boil Soon?" *Los Angeles Business Journal,* January 23, 2006, p. 20.

Berton, Brad, "Burbank 'Media District' Tower Sales Ranks As One of Year's Biggest," *Los Angeles Business Journal,* September 6, 1993, p. 27.

———, "Douglas Emmett Lands Westside Office Property," *Los Angeles Business Journal,* March 4, 1996, p. 39.

DeCambre, Mark, "Douglas Emmett Closes In on Jumbo L.A. Office Buy," *Real Estate Finance and Investment,* July 16, 2001, p. 1.

"Douglas Emmett to Raise Largest Fund to Date," *Real Estate Finance and Investment,* December 6, 2004, p. 6.

Garcia, Shelly, "Trillium Deal Would Make Douglas Emmett Top Owner," *San Fernando Valley Business Journal,* October 25, 2004, p. 3.

Hayes, Elizabeth, "Premier Tower in Santa Monica Sold by Japanese," *Los Angeles Business Journal,* February 15, 1999, p. 1.

Holleran, Scott, "Douglas Emmett Keeps Adding to Its L.A. Portfolio," *Los Angeles Business Journal,* March 13, 2000, p. 38.

Kotsianas, Nicoletta, "Douglas Emmett Plans Record-Breaking IPO," *Real Estate Finance and Investment,* June 26, 2006, p. 1.

"Nestlé's Headquarters Goes Back on the Block," *Real Estate Finance and Investment,* September 30, 2002, p. 4.

Wilcox, Gregory J., "Los Angeles–Area Office Tower Complex Changes Ownership Again," *Daily News,* September 11, 2002.

Drinks Americas Holdings, LTD.

372 Danbury Road, Suite 163
Wilton, Connecticut 06897-2523
U.S.A.
Telephone: (203) 762-7000
Fax: (203) 762-8992
Web site: http://www.drinksamericas.com

Public Company
Incorporated: 1986 as Vicuna, Inc.
Employees: 12
Sales: $4.5 million (2008)
Stock Exchanges: Over the Counter (OTC)
Ticker Symbol: DKAM
NAICS: 312140 Distilleries

■ ■ ■

Drinks Americas Holdings, LTD., is a developer, marketer, and distributor of alcoholic and nonalcoholic beverages, focusing on iconic brands, primarily those related to celebrities. Products include Donald Trump's Trump Super Premium Vodka and Trump Premium Flavored Vodkas (orange, citron, grape, and raspberry), Willie Nelson's six-year-old Whiskey River Bourbon, Paul Newman's Own Lightly Sparkling Fruit Juice Drinks and Flavored Waters, and Kid Rock Beer. Another iconic, albeit non-celebrity, brand owned by Drinks is Rheingold beer, a historic brew of New York City. The company offers fine Italian wines under the Casa BoMargo label in association with former-policeman-turned-celebrity Bo Dietl. Other Drinks' products include Mexico's herbal-based Damiana

Liqueur and Aguila Tequila, and Panama's guarana-infused Cohete Rum.

Manufacture of Drinks' products is done on a co-packing basis with Heaven Hill Distilleries in Kentucky; American Beverage Company in St. Louis; Sake One in Oregon; F.X. Matt in Utica, New York; Interamericana de Licores in Panama; and Tequila El Viejito S.A. and Damiana S.A. in Mexico. The Netherlands' WV Wanders is responsible for producing Trump Super Premium Vodka. Through subsidiaries Drinks Global Imports LLC and Drinks International Select Wines, the company also imports superpremium wines from such countries as Australia, Chile, France, Italy, New Zealand, and Spain. A network of about 60 independent beverage distributors allows Drinks to sell its products in most of North America. The company also exports some of its products to Germany and Israel. Research and development is conducted by Wynn Starr Flavors, Inc., a Drinks' shareholder. Based in Wilton, Connecticut, Drinks is a public company, its shares trading over the counter. The company is headed by founder and CEO J. Patrick Kenny.

FOUNDER, LONGTIME SEAGRAM EXECUTIVE

Kenny was enrolled at the U.S. Military Academy at West Point but an athletic injury that warranted extended rehabilitation forced him to leave school. He later earned an undergraduate degree at Georgetown University, followed by a master's degree from New York City's St. John's University. He then went to work as a sales representative for Scott Paper Co. and moved up through the management ranks before he was recruited by Coca-Cola. He then learned the alcoholic beverage business by joining Coca-Cola's Wine Spectrum. His experience with Coke led Kenny to join Joseph E. Seagram & Sons, eventually becoming a senior vice-president and general manager. During his 22-year tenure with the company he played important roles in the creation of Seagrams Wine Cooler and nonalcoholic products. Thus, he saw firsthand the success achieved with the Seagrams Wine Cooler product by linking it with actor Bruce Willis, who served as spokesperson for the brand. From this experience, Kenny told *Beverage World* in a 2006 profile, "I realized it takes the right icon, with the right product in the right business partnership to immediately accelerate a beverage in the consumer's eye."

Shortly before Seagram was sold to Vivendi Universal in 2000, Kenny left his longtime employer to start a trademark licensing and media company, Sweet 16 Intermedia Inc., with popular singer Britney Spears. After two years the company was sold to TEENTV Inc. and Kenny was looking for a fresh opportunity and conceived of Drinks Americas. "The idea came from a combination of my time with Sweet 16 and Seagram," he explained to the *Stamford Advocate*. "I thought it would be interesting to acquire, partner with and/or develop products with companies and icon entertainers and destinations."

FORMATION OF DRINKS AMERICAS: 2002

In September 2002 Kenny and associates formed Drinks Americas, Inc., in Wilton, Connecticut, to develop, market, and distribute beverages tied to icon entertainers, sports figures, celebrities, and destinations. "We view an icon," Kenney explained to the *Advocate*, "as one that's transgenerational, who doesn't need an introduction anywhere in the world." In the following year the company introduced singer-songwriter Willie Nelson's Old Whiskey River Kentucky Straight Bourbon Whiskey, the name alluding to his song "Whiskey River." It came packaged with a guitar pick bearing his

printed signature. Another line was David Frost Wines, possessing the name of the professional golfer whose family had actually been involved in the wine business in South Africa for the past half-century. The labels of the new wines also featured LeRoy Neiman paintings of such golfing figures as Arnold Palmer and Gene Sarazen, followed a year later by an image of Jack Nicklaus. Another early product was master Hawaiian chef Roy Yamaguchi's Y Sake. In addition, Drinks reached agreements to distribute Cohete Rojo Rum, Aguila Tequila, and Norman's Wines from Australia, as well as nonalcoholic beverages: Swiss T, a line of fruit drinks using pure cane sugar imported from Switzerland, and the Barrilitos Sodas line of Hispanic flavored soft drinks. Kenny also assembled a board of advisers, which included Marvin S. Traub, the well-known New York real investor and former chief executive of Bloomingdale's.

REVERSE MERGER, GOING PUBLIC: 2005

Drinks added to its stable of brands in 2004, reaching an agreement to market Paul Newman's "Newman's Own Sparkling Lemonades and Juices." After an 18-month distribution test the product was formally launched in 2005. Also in 2004 the company began the process of becoming a public entity through a reverse merger with a shell company, Gourmet Group, Inc. It was incorporated in Nevada in 1986 as Vicuna, Inc., a vehicle designed to raise capital for an unspecified business. In 1998 it acquired a Florida company, World Seaair Corporation, and changed its name to Seaair Group, Inc. Two years later it merged with Jardine Foods, a Texas maker of southwestern hot sauces and drink mixes, and became Gourmet Group, Inc. When Jardine Foods, the sole operating entity, was sold in 2002, Gourmet Group became a dormant public corporation. Completed in March 2005, the reverse merger between Gourmet and Drinks led to Drinks' shareholders receiving about 90 percent of Gourmet's shares. Gourmet was then renamed Drinks Americas Holdings, LTD. In June 2005 shares began trading on the NASDAQ Over the Counter Bulletin Board market.

In addition to going public, Drinks made strides on a number of other fronts in 2005. A U.S. distribution deal was secured for Damiana, a Hispanic liqueur often used as a "topper" for Margaritas. Hispanics were one of Drinks' target markets, as were young urban consumers. Nevertheless, the company continued to cater to the NASCAR market through Willie Nelson's Old Whiskey River Bourbon, which was doing particularly well in Virginia, the Carolinas, and Texas, all key markets for

KEY DATES

2002: J. Patrick Kenny forms Drinks Americas, Inc.
2003: First products are introduced.
2005: Company is taken public in reverse merger.
2006: Trump Vodka is introduced.
2007: Company reaches licensing agreement with Interscope Feddeb A&M.
2008: Partnership is forged with Dr. Dre.
2009: Olifant Vodka is acquired.

bourbon. In 2005 the company looked to drive further sales of the product by adding a 1.75-liter size to complement standard 750-milliliter packages. To appeal to older, more well-heeled consumers and achieve a measure of diversity, Drinks in 2005 formed Drinks Global Imports LLC to import superpremium wines from around the world, initially Australia, France, Italy, and New Zealand.

In 2005 Drinks secured the rights to an icon of a different sort through the acquisition of the resurrected Rheingold Brewing Company. Rheingold beer was a legendary New York City beer, best known for its Miss Rheingold competitions of the 1940s, 1950s, and 1960s. Founded by the Liebmann family in Brooklyn in 1883, Rheingold Brewing drew on a German river for its name. The brewery flourished in Brooklyn until World War I brought animosity to anything German-sounding and the advent of Prohibition brought all legal alcohol sales in the United States to a halt. The brewery survived by making near beer and lemonade, and following the repeal of Prohibition Rheingold beer returned to the market and flourished, due in large measure to the Miss Rheingold competition that helped advertise the brand. The local brew was unable to compete against national brands, however, and in 1976 the brewery closed. In 1998 a member of the Liebmann family revived the Rheingold label as well as the Miss Rheingold competition, but instead of working-class consumers Rheingold catered to a younger, hipper consumer and the focus of the Miss Rheingold competition was more on attitude than bathing beauty. The initial bid to revive the brand failed to take hold, and in 2003 a second attempt was made. Drinks bought the Rheingold business at a modest price and essentially put it on the back burner, looking to reformulate the product and relaunch at a later date. In the meantime, Drinks enjoyed the benefits of the residual appeal of the

Rheingold name, licensing the brand for hats, clothing, and glassware.

INTRODUCTION OF TRUMP VODKA: 2006

Of more immediate importance to Drinks in 2005 was the development of a new superpremium vodka under the Trump banner. In 2005 a licensing agreement was reached with Trump Mark, LLC, the entity of real estate mogul Donald Trump that leveraged the brand value of the Trump name. It was Marvin Traub who brought together Trump and Kenny, the three men discussing the concept of a Trump vodka over lunch. Despite not drinking alcohol, Trump was enthusiastic about the idea of lending his name to a superpremium vodka. To produce the beverage, Drinks contracted with Wanders Distillery in Holland, which had been making vodka since 1631. The new product was introduced in the fall of 2006, carried by trendy hotel bars and some liquor stores. It also found a ready market at Trump resorts and duty-free shops where tourists viewed the vodka as an attractive souvenir. The Trump name was later added to a line of premium flavored vodkas.

More celebrity business followed in 2007. At the start of the year Drinks began importing fine Italian wines under the Casa BoMargo label in association with former law enforcement officer Bo Dietl, who became a well-known personality following the depiction of his career in the 1998 film *One Tough Cop*. His first name and that of his wife, Margo, were fused to coin the brand name of the new import line. Later in 2007 Drinks reached an agreement with Universal Music Group's Interscope Geffen A&M to develop alcoholic and nonalcoholic beverages with the label's roster of recording stars. With revenues hard hit by digital technologies that made the illegal copying of music prevalent, the music industry hoped to find alternative revenue streams. Drinks, on the other hand, hoped to launch beverages that gained instant credibility in the marketplace because of the name of the artist attached to it.

Out of the Geffen relationship came the 2008 partnership with rap impresario Dr. Dre to develop and market a portfolio of drinks. Together they developed Dr. Dre's Aftermath Cognac as well as a sparkling vodka. Cognac, an old guard drink, was enjoying a comeback as a drink of choice for rappers and their fans. It was not surprising, therefore, that Drinks arranged to import Leyrat Cognac, and also signed rappers 50 Cent and Busta Rhymes, in conjunction with Violator Management, to lend their names to new cognac and sparkling vodka products. Drinks also signed artist Kid Rock to develop a beer product.

ACQUISITION OF OLIFANT VODKA: 2009

While Drinks continued to build its business in 2008, it faced challenges as well. Positive developments included a 15-year distribution deal in Germany with Zwilichiovskij Import-Export, which initially represented Trump Vodka and Old Whiskey River Bourbon. A distribution deal of the same length was also reached with a company in Israel. A downturn in the economy, however, led to a credit crunch and Drinks like many companies found it difficult to secure sufficient working capital. To make matters worse, some key suppliers were also adversely impacted by the tight credit market. As a result, Drinks was forced to keep inventory levels to a minimum, hampering its ability to grow the business. In 2009 the company was able to arrange an adequate credit line, which was used to help launch the new Kid Rock beer. Also in 2009 Drinks acquired Olifant Vodka, produced in the Netherlands. Drinks had a number of products in the pipeline, and although it remained a penny-stock company, it held some valuable licenses and retained a great deal of potential.

Ed Dinger

PRINCIPAL SUBSIDIARIES

Drinks Americas, Inc.; Drinks Global Imports LLC.

PRINCIPAL COMPETITORS

Bacardi U.S.A., Inc.; Diageo PLC; Beam Global Spirits & Wine, Inc.

FURTHER READING

Davis, Harold, "Beer to Last All Summer Long: Kid Rock Pairs with Wilton Firm for New Beverage," *Advocate* (Stamford-Norwalk, Conn.), October 3, 2008, p. A5.

———, "Connecticut Drinks Company Teams Celebrities with Alcoholic Beverages," *Stamford Advocate*, October 15, 2003.

Juliano, Michael C., "Star-Powered Sales," *Advocate*, January 4, 2009.

Lee, Richard, "Wilton, Conn., Drinks Firm Buys Rheingold Beer Name," *Stamford Advocate*, July 6, 2005.

———, "Year-Old Wilton, Conn.-based Drinks Americas Agrees to Sell to New York Firm," *Stamford Advocate*, June 16, 2004.

Marks, Paul, "Tasting Celebrity," *Hartford Courant*, January 18, 2006, p. E1.

Mastro, Ken, "Drinks Americas Making Moves in Liquor, Beer, and Wine Markets," *Wilton Bulletin*, July 14, 2005, p. C011.

Smith, Ethan, "Interscope Cuts Deal for Celebrity Drinks," *Wall Street Journal*, June 26, 2007, p. B4.

Strzelecki, Molly V., "Drinks Americas: Serving Up Premium Beverages Nationwide," *Beverage Industry*, September 2005.

Varnon, Rob, "Drinks Americas Holds Its Liquor," *Advocate*, May 7, 2009, p. C008.

Wright, Susan, "Drinking with the Stars," *Beverage World*, December 2006, p. 62.

Duckwall-ALCO Stores, Inc.

———————■———————

401 Cottage Street
Abilene, Kansas 67410-2832
U.S.A.
Telephone: (785) 263-3350
Fax: (785) 263-7531
Web site: http://www.duckwall.com

Public Company
Founded: 1901 as The Racket Store
Incorporated: 1915 as The A. L. Duckwall Five & Dime
  Store Company
Employees: 4,200
Sales: $490.02 million (2009)
Stock Exchanges: NASDAQ
Ticker Symbol: DUCK
NAICS: 452112 Discount Department Stores; 452990
  All Other General Merchandise Stores

■ ■ ■

A regional discount retailer, Duckwall-ALCO Stores, Inc., operates more than 260 stores in a 22-state region in the central United States. Duckwall-ALCO's stores operate under two names, Duckwall and ALCO, but all of the company's retail outlets share the distinction of operating in small rural communities. Of the company's two formats, ALCO represents the dominant force. There are more than 200 ALCO stores in operation, with the average store consisting of about 20,500 square feet of selling space. Each store stocks roughly 35,000 items, including apparel and shoes, automotive supplies, candy, crafts, domestic goods, electronics, fabrics, furniture, hardware, health and beauty aids, housewares, jewelry, prerecorded music and video, seasonal items, sporting goods, stationery, and toys. The company's Duckwall variety stores, similar to the typical five-and-dime store popular during the first half of the 20th century, offer a more limited selection of merchandise in stores much smaller than a typical ALCO. There are about 60 Duckwall stores in operation. The ALCO and Duckwall stores are supported through a 350,000-square-foot distribution center in Abilene, Kansas, where the firm has been based during its entire century-plus history. Duckwall-ALCO's strategy focuses on tapping consumer demand in small rural towns with populations lower than 5,000 and in markets comprising fewer than 16,000 residents. By adhering to this strategy, the company operates in communities frequently ignored by other discount retailers.

EARLY 20TH-CENTURY ORIGINS

Duckwall-ALCO traces its roots to humble and rural beginnings, back to the first store owned by the company's entrepreneurial founder, A. L. Duckwall Sr. Duckwall laid the foundation for an enterprise that would endure for more than a century when he spent $400 in 1901 to purchase and begin managing The Racket Store, located in Abilene, Kansas. A variety merchandise store, Duckwall's first retail venture "offered a little bit of everything," according to its owner, presenting the store's farmland customers with an array of goods from which they had rarely had the luxury to choose. This premise set the theme for subsequent stores established in the following decades under the Duckwall banner. In 1915, during this expansion, A. L. Duckwall

COMPANY PERSPECTIVES

Our mission is to be the best general merchandise retailer in America, serving smaller, hometown communities. We strive every day to achieve that goal with our work ethic, quality selection of goods, competitive prices, and friendly service of bygone days. We owe much of our success to three important members of the ALCO team: our associates, our vendor partners, and our shareholders.

Our team helps us to meet our goals every day by listening to our customers and responding to their needs in our stores. Our vendor partners supply the quality goods at the affordable prices which are the keystone for our success.

We would like to say "thank you" to all of those associates, vendor partners, and shareholders who have helped us grow over the past 100 years. No matter how big we grow, we will stay committed to our basic Midwestern beliefs: hard work, family values, honesty, steady growth, and dedication to our customers.

incorporated what at the time was a seven-store business as The A. L. Duckwall Five & Dime Store Company. The company name was later changed to The A. L. Duckwall Stores Company.

The generations of leadership that followed in A. L. Duckwall's wake continued to target rural communities deprived of the diversity of merchandise to which their urban counterparts had become accustomed. In the decades following the success of The Racket Store, a steady stream of variety stores were established in rural communities, each operating under the Duckwall banner. The concept, and the series of new stores that presented the concept to eager rural customers, proved to be an encouraging success, able to surmount the economic vagaries of the first half of the 20th century and adapt to the changing consumer tastes of the years. By the end of the 1960s, after six decades of tapping rural demand for a potpourri of goods, there were 100 Duckwall variety stores situated in the Midwest, positioned in rural towns with populations ranging between 2,000 and 10,000.

The late 1960s marked a signal turning point in the business established by A. L. Duckwall Sr., a defining transition that was overseen by his son, A. L. Duckwall Jr. In 1968 the company opened its first ALCO discount store, located in Newton, Kansas. Although the opening of its first discount-oriented store did not drastically alter the heart of the company's strategic philosophy of catering to rural customers, it did represent a decided shift toward a new merchandising strategy. The success of the first ALCO store heralded the birth of a new, stronger retail breed and sounded the death knell for Duckwall's variety store concept. During the seven decades separating the beginning of the 1970s and the era in which Duckwall had opened his first store, the dynamics of operating a retail business in a rural setting had changed considerably. The modern rural customer had become accustomed to a broad selection of merchandise as large national chains moved into smaller communities. Accordingly, price became the leverage point for any retail business hoping to succeed against much larger competition. Duckwall-ALCO, operating under its new corporate name, had changed with the times. Another significant event occurred in 1972, when the company was taken public.

REVITALIZED BY ACQUISITIONS IN THE MID-EIGHTIES

By the early 1980s the number of Duckwall variety stores operated by the company, which had peaked at 100 units ten years earlier, had been winnowed down to 34. In their stead, a slew of ALCO discount stores had emerged, stores that by this point bore the burden of driving the company's financial growth. Of the roughly $200 million Duckwall-ALCO was collecting in sales during the early 1980s, the 34 Duckwall variety stores contributed a mere $10 million. A changing of the guard had taken place at the company's Abilene, Kansas, headquarters, and all hopes were pinned to the vitality of the ALCO chain. For those executives who awaited strident financial growth, however, the early 1980s were remembered as a tortuous time.

During the early 1980s Duckwall-ALCO was best known as a rurally oriented retail chain based in the birthplace of President Dwight D. Eisenhower. It was also known, and quickly disregarded by those on Wall Street, as a company suffering from anemic financial performance. In 1981, for instance, sales increased a paltry 1 percent, as profits slid precipitously by 24 percent. As one analyst noted at the time, in reference to Duckwall-ALCO's regard among investors, "It was an ignored stock for a long, long time." Caught in the grip of pernicious economic recession, Duckwall-ALCO executives were grappling to find a solution and end the trauma. Their salvation was found through an important acquisition, completed just as the company's financial standing was becoming precarious.

KEY DATES

1901: A. L. Duckwall Sr. purchases and begins managing a variety merchandise store located in Abilene, Kansas, called The Racket Store; the Duckwall banner is subsequently introduced.

1915: Having expanded to seven stores, company is incorporated as The A. L. Duckwall Five & Dime Store Company.

1968: Already operating 100 Duckwall variety stores, the company opens its first ALCO discount store, located in Newton, Kansas; company name is later changed to Duckwall-ALCO Stores, Inc.

1972: Company is taken public.

1983: Company acquires Sterling Stores Co. Inc., operator of a 48-store discount chain based in Little Rock, Arkansas.

1985: Firm is taken private via a management-led leveraged buyout.

1989: Company files for Chapter 11 bankruptcy protection.

1991: Having closed more than 50 stores, firm emerges from bankruptcy.

1994: Duckwall-ALCO is once again taken public via an initial public offering.

2008: After a major shareholder threatens a proxy fight, top management and board of directors at the company are overhauled.

In May 1983, in a deal brokered with a handshake in February, Duckwall-ALCO acquired Sterling Stores Co. Inc., the parent company of a 48-store discount chain based in Little Rock, Arkansas, that operated under the name Magic Mart. Its inclusion within Duckwall-ALCO's fold was the remedy for which company executives were searching, quickly effecting an about-turn in Duckwall-ALCO's financial performance. The Magic Mart chain, which generated $111.6 million in revenues in 1982, was credited for the robust increase in Duckwall-ALCO's financial totals, arresting what threatened to be a damaging slide and restoring to its new owner the solid financial state it historically had enjoyed. Less than two years after watching profits sink 24 percent, Duckwall-ALCO's stock price more than tripled. In 1983 sales swelled to $317 million, up nearly 50 percent from the previous year's total. The company's profits accomplished an even more dramatic

leap, nearly doubling to $8.6 million. By all measures, the company once again stood as a solid performer, piquing the interest of Wall Street and earning the respect of other similarly sized retailers competing for the business of rural consumers.

Buoyed by the resurgence realized from the Sterling/Magic Mart acquisition, Duckwall-ALCO made another move on the acquisition front a short time later. In January 1984 the company purchased four discount stores in Wichita, Kansas, operating under the David's banner. One year later Duckwall-ALCO completed another acquisition, acquiring nine stores from the Illinois-based Hornsby chain. The acquisitions were indicative of the optimism pervading Duckwall-ALCO's corporate offices, the same optimism that prompted a management-led leveraged buyout of the company in 1985. A. L. Duckwall Jr., the last member of the founding family to head the business, had decided to retire at roughly the same time an investment firm, E.F. Hutton LBO, approached Duckwall-ALCO's president, Robert Soelter, about initiating the buyout. Planning to include as many as 57 ALCO managers in the buyout group, Soelter pushed ahead with the deal, completing the purchase of the company in September 1985. At this point there were 127 ALCO discount department stores in operation in 14 states, complemented by 33 Duckwall variety stores operating in a four-state territory. The strength of the company resided in its ALCO units, which served as one-stop-shopping destinations situated in markets too small to support specialty stores.

1989 BANKRUPTCY FILING

Slightly less than three years after the management-led buyout, Soelter retired, paving the way for the promotion of Glen L. Shank, a Duckwall-ALCO employee since 1973 and merchandising vice-president for the previous eight years. To Shank, who would guide the company into the early 21st century, fell the unenviable responsibility of announcing Duckwall-ALCO's most devastating news in its nearly 90-year history. In May 1989 Duckwall-ALCO, the promising and vibrant discount retailer of the early and mid-1980s, filed for Chapter 11 bankruptcy protection, a last-ditch effort to stave off deleterious financial losses. Duckwall-ALCO's darkest hour had not arrived suddenly. Between 1986 and early 1989 the company had closed 20 stores, as poor profit performance at a number of the stores forced closures. By 1989 the piecemeal elimination of unprofitable stores was no longer an option. The financial losses racked up by dozens of stores had become too severe. Wholesale changes were desperately needed, and Shank, who barely had time to settle into his new position at Duckwall-ALCO, was the central figure responsible for devising what those sweeping changes needed to be.

The root of the problem, ironically, was the source of Duckwall-ALCO's growth during the early and mid-1980s. The three acquisitions the company had completed between May 1983 and January 1985 had done much to revitalize Duckwall-ALCO's financial health, but the absorption of the acquired stores had also created serious problems. Magic Mart, the greatest savior of the three acquisitions, also ranked as the biggest culprit, bringing the company in close competition with giant national discount chains such as Arkansas-based Wal-Mart. Prior to the acquisition of the Magic Mart chain, Duckwall-ALCO had competed directly against Wal-Mart in six of its markets; after the acquisition, Duckwall-ALCO was positioned in close proximity to Wal-Mart in 40 new markets. The results were disastrous. Duckwall-ALCO could not compete effectively against the far more financially powerful Wal-Mart, as consumers flocked to the larger stores operated by the behemoth Arkansas retailer.

By the time the company filed for Chapter 11, it had identified 52 of its worst-performing stores, units that registered $10 million in losses in 1988 alone. The stores were scattered throughout a ten-state territory and included many of the units acquired from Magic Mart, David's, and Hornsby. On May 15, 1989, all 52 of the stores were closed, stripping the company of one-third of its store count. Next began the arduous task of developing a reorganization plan, as Shank labored to find a solution that would appease creditors and enable Duckwall-ALCO to emerge from under the protective umbrella of Chapter 11. For two years the reorganization process dragged on until at last Duckwall-ALCO received approval to begin anew in 1991.

RETURN TO PROSPERITY

The road back to a healthy and promising future was a difficult course to travel, and it did not progress quickly. After Chapter 11, it took roughly two years before company officials could point to anything that suggested a return to consistent prosperity. The first solid sign arrived in 1993, when Duckwall-ALCO posted a heartening $2.3 million in earnings. The next positive development occurred in November 1994, when the company completed a successful initial public offering of stock. With the proceeds gained from the company's stock offering, it entered 1995 with the best opportunity it had seen in years for a full revival. Optimism had returned to the company's headquarters in Abilene.

As proof of the bright outlook Duckwall-ALCO officials embraced, the company announced it would open 20 stores a year as it entered 1995. Planning to open three ALCO discount stores for every two Duckwall variety stores it opened, the company was employing the

strategy it had devised to compete against larger discounters and to protect itself from the profit erosion that had signaled its near collapse in 1989. Duckwall-ALCO executives resolved to establish new stores in the smallest of rural communities, reducing its maximum population base for a store to fewer than 16,000 residents in a particular market and fewer than 5,000 residents in a targeted town. The plan placed a new emphasis on the once-forsaken Duckwall format. Further, it was a preemptive expansion strategy predicated on avoiding competition rather than meeting other regional discounters head on. By opening a store in a location that met the company's population criteria, Duckwall-ALCO established a presence that discouraged other, similarly sized discount retailers from encroachment and positioned it in markets largely ignored by heavyweights such as Wal-Mart. The operating strategy developed by A. L. Duckwall Sr. in 1901 had been fine-tuned for the 1990s.

To the relief of anxious Duckwall-ALCO executives, the strategy worked. Financial health returned to the company, with a consistency and strength that suggested a complete turnaround from the troubled late 1980s and early 1990s. Moreover, optimistic expectations for the future were buttressed by the identification of more than 100 locations that were "understored" in markets matching the company's demographic criteria. Accordingly, expansion pushed ahead as the company moved into the late 1990s and neared its centennial.

In September 1996 Duckwall-ALCO acquired 14 retail locations from New Castle, Indiana-based Val Corp., which added stores located in eastern Indiana and western Ohio. The acquired stores were remodeled as ALCO units and reopened in early 1997, accelerating the company's previously announced expansion pace. In November 1997 Duckwall-ALCO acquired 18 stores located in Texas and New Mexico from Perry Brothers, Inc., which debuted as Duckwall units in early 1998. On this note, with the pace of expansion exceeding expectations and the company's financial growth pointing to a healthy enterprise, Duckwall-ALCO prepared for the century ahead and the coming celebration of its 100th year of business.

EARLY 21ST-CENTURY DOLDRUMS

By the time of the company's centennial year, however, Duckwall-ALCO was in the midst of a new period of struggle. Between fiscal 2000 and fiscal 2004, the company managed to stay in the black, but sales flatlined. On a yearly basis, comparable-store sales were essentially flat or grew at a rate of less than 1 percent throughout this period, with the exception of fiscal

2002 when comparable-store sales rose 2.9 percent. In the summer of 2004, major shareholder Raymond French, of the hedge fund Strongbow Capital, Ltd., began pressuring Duckwall-ALCO to address its lackluster performance and even began exploring with other shareholders the possibility of a forced sale of the company.

By March 2005 a turnaround plan was in place that centered on cutting costs, upgrading the firm's technology, and expanding a test ALCO format featuring more consumable goods and fresh food. The company also began closing underperforming stores, including eight ALCO outlets and 12 Duckwalls. These initiatives occurred at a time when a search for a new CEO was underway after Shank announced plans to retire. Late in March 2005, 35-year retail veteran Bruce Dale was hired as CEO. Dale was best known for an eight-year stint as president of the framing and art supply chain Aaron Brothers, during which time he successfully turned around this division of Michaels Stores, Inc.

Dale almost immediately cut the head-office staff by 46, or about 10 percent of the total. Later, he halted the rollout of the new ALCO format in favor of the launch of a new prototype with upgraded apparel and consumer electronics offerings. Although the company's performance showed some improvement, and it embarked on a new expansion program that included the opening of the 200th ALCO store in the fall of 2007, French remained unhappy. He was particularly concerned with the firm's anemic return on equity, and threatened to launch a proxy fight to overhaul the board of directors. Only a few months later, in February 2008, Dale resigned from the company. A month after that, French's proxy fight proved unnecessary as the board chairman and another director resigned, French was appointed to the board, and French's choice for chairman, existing director Royce Winsten, was indeed named to that post. In July 2008 Lawrence J. Zigerelli was named Duckwall-ALCO president and CEO. Zigerelli had held senior positions at a number of retailers, including serving as chief executive of Levitz Furniture and as president and board member of supercenter retailer Meijer Inc. Nearly all the other senior managers at Duckwall-ALCO were replaced around this same time as well.

BRINGING DUCKWALL-ALCO INTO THE "MODERN RETAILING ERA"

The new management team quickly launched a five-pronged turnaround program designed, according to Winsten, to bring the company "into the modern era of retailing." Merchandising and marketing programs were

overhauled by bringing a number of key brands into the stores, launching improved promotions through data analysis, and successfully testing and rolling out a loyalty program. A new drive began to thoroughly expunge unnecessary costs from the company's operations. Efforts were made to keep stores better stocked and to improve in-store service. Additional funds were invested in technology not only to aid the stocking initiative but also to assist with making timely clearance markdowns and to tailor, for the first time, products and programs on a regional and demographic basis. Finally, in a follow-up to the top management shakeup, numerous changes were made to the personnel in the areas of merchandise buyers, district field managers, and store managers.

The initial costs of this revitalization effort were quite steep as the company posted a net loss of nearly $5 million for the fiscal year ending on February 1, 2009, on revenues of $490 million. In a weak economic environment, same-store sales that year dropped 5.1 percent. Some improvement was evident during the first five months of fiscal 2010 with same-store sales increasing 2.2 percent, but it was far too early to determine whether the latest overhaul at Duckwall-ALCO, one of the country's last remaining regional discounters, was destined to lead to a prolonged renaissance.

Jeffrey L. Covell
Updated, David E. Salamie

PRINCIPAL COMPETITORS

Wal-Mart Stores, Inc.; Target Corporation; Dollar General Corporation; Sears Holdings Corporation; Pamida Stores Operating Company, LLC.

FURTHER READING

Berry, Mike, "Duckwall-ALCO Marks 100 Years in Business," *Wichita (Kans.) Eagle,* April 22, 2001, p. 1B.

Davis, Mark, "Duckwall-ALCO CEO Resigns," *Kansas City (Mo.) Star,* February 23, 2008, p. C2.

———, "Duckwall-ALCO Sees 76 Percent Drop in Fourth-Quarter Earnings," *Kansas City (Mo.) Star,* April 30, 2008, p. C4.

Diennor, Richard, "Duckwall Gets OK on Disclosure," *Daily News Record,* April 10, 1991, p. 11.

"Duckwall-ALCO Inks Deal to Acquire 14 Locations," *Daily News Record,* September 19, 1996, p. 10.

Gilman, Hank, "Duckwall-ALCO: Gold in Those Small-Town Hills," *Chain Store Age—General Merchandise Edition,* March 1984, pp. 28+.

Haury, David A., "Come Back to the Five and Dime," *Kansas Heritage,* Winter 2004, pp. 16–22.

Hayes, David, "Duckwall-ALCO Appoints Retail Veteran As CEO," *Kansas City (Mo.) Star,* July 2, 2008.

Howell, Debbie, "Duckwall Feels Wrath of Outspoken Investors," *DSN Retailing Today,* September 6, 2004, pp. 5, 62.

———, "Duckwall Launches Aggressive Turnaround Plan," *DSN Retailing Today,* February 6, 2006, pp. 4, 31.

———, "Duckwall New CEO to Lead Turnaround," *DSN Retailing Today,* April 11, 2005, pp. 4, 49.

———, "Duckwall Upgrades ALCO Stores," *DSN Retailing Today,* June 18, 2001, pp. 3, 46.

———, "Troubled Duckwall-ALCO Unveils Revival Plans," *DSN Retailing Today,* March 14, 2005, pp. 5, 29.

Kelly, Mary Ellen, "ALCO Files for Chapter 11; To Close 52 Units in 10 States," *Discount Store News,* May 22, 1989, p. 2.

———, "ALCO Names Shank Prez; Fortifies Merchandising Staff," *Discount Store News,* July 4, 1988, p. 3.

Mammarella, James, "Duckwall-ALCO Bounces Back," *Discount Store News,* February 20, 1995, p. 23.

Margolies, Dan, "Duckwall-ALCO Stores' Biggest Shareholder Threatens Proxy Fight," *Kansas City (Mo.) Star,* November 21, 2007, p. C1.

"New Stores Push Up Sales, Profits," *Chain Store Age—General Merchandise Edition,* June 1984, p. 96.

"Retail Entrepreneurs of the Year: Glen L. Shank," *Chain Store Age,* December 1998, p. 70.

Schrag, Duane, "Revamping Duckwall-ALCO: New President and CEO Has No Qualms About Taking on the Big Boys," *Salina (Kans.) Journal,* December 18, 2005, p. D1.

Stafford, Diane, "Duckwall-ALCO Finds the Perfect Fit," *Kansas City (Mo.) Star,* May 15, 2007, p. G13.

"Strong Duckwall-ALCO Growth Prompts $150M Buyout Bid," *Discount Store News,* February 4, 1985.

Unruh, Tim, "Bold Moves: New CEO Takes Steps to Make Abilene-Based Retailer Competitive," *Salina (Kans.) Journal,* May 8, 2005, p. D1.

———, "Duckwall-ALCO Chief Resigns," *Salina (Kans.) Journal,* February 23, 2008, p. A1.

———, "Duckwall-ALCO Likes Small Niche: Targeting Smaller Towns, Nearly Century-Old Company Saw Steady Growth in 1990s," *Salina (Kans.) Journal,* January 3, 2000.

Voorhis, Dan, "Five-and-Dime Works for Change: Duckwall-ALCO Updates Its Strategy to Boost Profits and Compete with National Discounter," *Wichita (Kans.) Eagle,* May 22, 2005, p. 1C.

easyhome Ltd.

10239-178 Street
Edmonton, Alberta T5S 1M3
Canada
Telephone: (780) 930-3000
Fax: (780) 481-7426
Web site: http://www.easyhome.ca

Public Company
Incorporated: 1991 as RTO Enterprises Inc.
Employees: 1,425
Sales: CAD 162.49 million (2008)
Stock Exchanges: Toronto
Ticker Symbol: EH
NAICS: 442110 Furniture Stores; 443111 Household
   Appliance Stores; 443112 Radio, Television, and
   Other Electronics Stores; 443120 Computer and
   Software Stores

■ ■ ■

easyhome Ltd. is the largest rental-purchase company in
Canada and the third largest in North America. The
company operates 229 stores in Canada and the United
States that cater to credit or cash restrained customers
who sign weekly or monthly payment agreements for
merchandise. Customers have the choice of either renting the merchandise with no long-term obligation or
purchasing the merchandise. easyhome stores carry
brand-name home furnishings, appliances, and
electronics. A master franchiser, easygates LLC sells
franchises in the United States, operating in the 36
states that do not share a border with Canada.

ORIGINS

easyhome's rise to the top of its industry occurred under
the name RTO Enterprises Inc., a feat orchestrated by
RTO's founder, Gordon J. Reykdal. Building Canada's
largest rental-purchase company was an impressive ac-
complishment, but the achievement took on an added
layer of luster when Reykdal's previous experience in the
rent-to-own business was taken into consideration.
Before launching RTO, Reykdal served as president and
chief executive officer of Rentown Enterprises Inc., a
rental-purchase company that declared bankruptcy in
January 1991. Reykdal felt the sting of failure, but
before the end of the year he dusted himself off and
started anew, achieving far greater success with his
second assault on the rental-purchase market.

RTO began with one store in operation in August
1991, the meager foundation upon which the third largest rental-purchase company in North America was
built. Initially, Reykdal served as RTO's general
manager, a title he held until 1993, when he assumed
the duties of president and chief executive officer. The
year was an important one in terms of the maturation of
Reykdal's venture, marking its debut as a publicly traded
company. Reykdal chose the most expedient route
toward converting to public ownership, merging his
company with Aumo Explorations Inc., a publicly held
shell corporation, thereby making RTO a publicly
traded company. Once he had converted to public
ownership, Reykdal launched his campaign to make
RTO the dominant competitor in Canada.

COMPANY PERSPECTIVES

Everyone should be given the opportunity to enhance their home and lifestyle. We are the leader in helping people get exactly what they want for as long as they want … right now.

EXPANSION THROUGH ACQUISITIONS

Reykdal reached his objective by completing a series of acquisitions. RTO grew quickly, making its living by giving its customers the choice of renting-to-own or renting brand name home entertainment products, appliances, and household furniture. In September 1994, Reykdal completed his first major transaction, acquiring assets intimately familiar to him. He spent CAD 12.8 million for 41 Rentown stores, acquiring the retail chain that had foundered under his control three years earlier. TCF Asset Management Corporation had taken control of the stores in the midst of bankruptcy proceedings. The 41 stores, a massive addition to Reykdal's store count, generated CAD 27 million in annual sales.

Next, Reykdal set his sights on a business with ties to the United Kingdom. Granada Canada Holdings Inc., a subsidiary of U.K.-based Granada Overseas Group of Companies, entered the Canadian market in 1969 when it acquired a television sales business with one location in Toronto, Ontario. The company used the single location as a springboard for developing a chain of stores that rented home electronics products, primarily televisions. Granada expanded into Alberta and Quebec, growing into a 102-store chain before financial difficulties forced management to reduce the size of the chain to 42 stores by 1991. Further store closings followed, leaving the company with only a handful of units by the time Reykdal expressed interest in acquiring the company. In December 1995, RTO paid CAD 18 million to acquire the Granada banner, giving Reykdal assets he would use to bolster RTO's involvement in the home electronics segment of the rent-to-own market.

Acquisitions fueled RTO's financial growth, as Reykdal cobbled together a chain that stretched across Canada. RTO generated CAD 2.3 million in 1993, a total that mushroomed to CAD 28.1 million by the end of 1995. Sales nearly doubled the following year, when Reykdal acquired 11 rent-to-own stores operating under the name "North American TV Appliance and Rental." RTO paid CAD 5.2 million for the stores, which were located in pockets of eastern and central Ontario where the company did not maintain a presence. In April 1997, Reykdal filled in another hole in RTO's operating territory, purchasing a store in Cornwall, Ontario, that operated under the name "Lease Magic Plus." A much larger acquisition followed two months later, when RTO purchased Rent-A-Centre Canada Inc. for CAD 14.1 million. The deal included 29 stores that generated CAD 20 million in annual sales. In September 1997, Reykdal changed the name of the Rent-A-Centre chain, putting the stores under the "First Choice" banner.

REORGANIZATION EFFORTS BEGIN IN 1998

By the end of 1997, Reykdal presided over the largest rental-purchase chain in Canada, having eclipsed all rivals within six years. RTO, operating under various names, controlled 150 stores in 81 cities. The company maintained a presence in nine provinces, generating CAD 56 million in sales. The rapid expansion created a new, dominant retailer, but it also produced growing pains that prompted Reykdal to halt further expansion while he focused on making his new empire perform efficiently. RTO entered a period of reorganization, a three-year period that began in 1998 with the closure of 16 stores. Additional units were shuttered in the months that followed, leaving RTO with 128 stores by the end of the decade.

In the midst of the restructuring efforts, leadership changes became the dominant theme. Reykdal, who briefly flirted with the idea of returning RTO to private ownership, announced his retirement in mid-2000. Bruce Reid, the former chief executive officer of Brick Warehouse and former chairman of the Retail Council of Canada, was recruited to replace Reykdal. At roughly the same time, RTO's largest shareholder, Donald K. Johnson, was elected chairman. Reykdal expressed confidence in Reid's ability to lead the company. "The transition of my management responsibilities to my successor, Bruce Reid, has been even smoother than expected and I am confident that the company's management is in good hands," he said in the August 11, 2000 issue of *Canadian Corporate News*. "As the company's second largest shareholder, I certainly have a vested interest in the company's future success. RTO is now well positioned to enter its next stage of growth as Canada's leading rental-purchase organization."

Reid's singular focus during his brief reign of command was to continue the restructuring efforts begun in the late 1990s. Improvements were made in employee training, merchandising, and marketing programs. Seasoned industry executives were added to RTO's board of directors, its accounting policies were tailored

KEY DATES

1991: Gordon J. Reykdal forms RTO Enterprises Inc.

1993: After merging with publicly traded Aumo Explorations Inc., RTO becomes a publicly owned company.

1994: RTO acquires 41 Rentown stores.

1995: RTO acquires Granada Canada Holdings Inc.

1996: RTO acquires 11 rent-to-own stores operating under the name "North American TV Appliance and Rental."

1997: RTO acquires the 29-store Rent-A-Centre Canada Inc. chain.

2000: Reykdal retires and appoints Bruce Reid as his successor.

2001: Reid is replaced as president and chief executive officer by David Ingram.

2003: RTO changes its name to easyhome Ltd., bringing all retail locations under a single banner.

2007: easygates, LLC, is formed to sell franchises in the United States.

2008: easyhome acquires Insta-rent Inc., a 50-store, rent-to-own company.

to the accounting policies of publicly traded rent-to-own companies in the United States, and a new budgeting process was implemented. Perhaps most important, Reid instilled discipline throughout the RTO organization, which had begun to overlook the ability of its customers to meet their lease obligations. Far too frequently, store personnel were forced to devote the bulk of their time dealing with delinquent accounts instead of concentrating on new sales, which led to worrisome financial losses.

RESTRUCTURING COMPLETED IN 2001

The restructuring efforts were completed by March 2001, signaling the end of Reid's service as president and chief executive officer. "It was always my intention to relinquish my line management responsibilities once I was comfortable that the key elements of the restructuring strategy had been implemented and a suitable successor was ready to assume my responsibilities," Reid said in the May 2, 2001 issue of *Market News Publishing*. To lead RTO forward, the company's board of directors turned to David Ingram, who had been

hired as chief operating officer in December 2000. Before joining RTO, Ingram had led Rent-A-Centre's retail operations in Canada and the United States.

A NEW IDENTITY IN 2003

Once RTO regained its financial footing, Ingram could turn his attention to bringing cohesion to the fragmented chain of RTO stores. A pretax loss of CAD 9.1 million in 2000 was turned into a pretax profit of CAD 2.7 million during the first nine months of 2002, freeing Ingram to focus on RTO's identity. The company had 136 stores in operation by the end of 2002, a chain of retail units that operated under a handful of different banners. From province to province, the RTO chain was known to customers under the names First Choice, North American, Rentown, Louer Pour Acheter, and RTO Centers. At the beginning of 2003, Ingram brought order to the confusing mess he watched over, uniting all the stores under a single banner: easyhome. The new signage, implemented in January 2003, became the new corporate title for RTO in May 2003, when shareholders approved the name change to easyhome Ltd.

Financially healthy and unified under a new name, easyhome began to focus on growth. The chain grew to 161 stores by 2005, the year Ingram brokered a deal with Leon's Furniture Limited, a retailer that sold home furnishings, appliances, and electronics at 55 stores in Canada. The agreement between the two retailers allowed easyhome to offer its rental-purchase proposition at a Leon's store in Toronto. "This is a great opportunity for both Leon's and easyhome," Ingram said in the April 8, 2005 issue of *Canadian Corporate News*. "Many of our customers come to easyhome after shopping at Leon's because financial status has limited their ability to complete a transaction at their Leon's location. easyhome offers Leon's the ability to service their potential customers that are cash and credit constrained on site."

2005–07: EXPANSION OF THE CHAIN

During the next two years, easyhome celebrated a flurry of new store openings. The company had 192 stores in operation by 2007, the year Ingram launched "easydecor" as a new easyhome business. easydecor was formed to provide short-term rentals of furniture, appliances, and electronics for staging and other event needs. The new entity began cultivating relationships with real estate agents seeking to furnish properties for sale and with set designers in the film, theater, and television industries, using a distribution center in Toronto dedicated to serving its commercial clientele.

As Ingram began developing a more diverse customer base, preparations were being made to extend the easyhome banner into a vast new market. The time had come for a concerted push into the $6 billion, rent-to-own market in the United States, a major geographic leap that would be accomplished through an affiliated company. In 2007, Bud Gates, the former chairman and chief executive officer of Rent-A-Center and Thorn Americas Inc., became a master franchiser of the easyhome business model, forming easygates, LLC, to establish easyhome stores in the 36 states that did not share a border with Canada. In June 2008, Gates claimed his first success, signing a franchise agreement with two parties that called for the opening of 16 stores. "We have spent the last year building the management team and infrastructure needed to support aggressive franchise growth," Gates said in the June 10, 2008 issue of *Canadian Corporate News.* "Those efforts are now bearing fruit."

ACQUISITION OF INSTA-RENT INC. IN 2008

While Gates watched over the expansion of the easyhome chain in the United States, Ingram focused on the expansion of the chain in Canada. In August 2008, he announced a deal that harkened back to the Reykdal era of growth through acquisition, revealing his intention to acquire a competitor. His sights were set on Insta-rent Inc., a publicly traded rental-purchase company with 50 stores in Canada. In November 2008, easyhome completed the deal, paying CAD 10.2 million for Insta-rent. The month also marked the opening of easygate's first store in the United States, a franchise unit in Olathe, Kansas.

As easyhome neared its 20th anniversary, the expansion of the chain figured prominently in Ingram's future plans. The company opened 17 company-owned stores and six franchise stores in 2008, giving it a total of 229 stores by the end of the year. In 2009, Ingram planned to open between five and eight company-owned stores and between ten and 15 franchise locations, ensuring that Canada's largest rental-purchase company would maintain its lead in the years ahead.

Jeffrey L. Covell

PRINCIPAL SUBSIDIARIES

RTO Distribution Inc.; RTO Asset Management Inc.; easyfinancial Services Inc.; easyhome U.S. Ltd. (United States); easygates, LLC; Insta-rent Inc.

PRINCIPAL COMPETITORS

Aaron Rents, Inc.; Rent-A-Center, Inc.; Bestway, Inc.

FURTHER READING

"Bruce Reid to Relinquish CEO Role, Continue As a Director and Advisor on Corporate Strategy," *Market News Publishing,* May 2, 2001.

"Easygates, LLC and Easyhome Master Franchisor Announces Plans to Open First Stores," *Canadian Corporate News,* June 10, 2008.

"Easyhome Ltd. and Leon's Furniture Limited in Joint Venture to Maximize Customer Satisfaction," *Canadian Corporate News,* April 8, 2005.

"Easyhome to Launch New Staging, Events and Props Division for Furniture and Accessory Rentals," *Canadian Corporate News,* April 17, 2007.

"Insta-Rent Announces Friendly $0.50 Per Share Cash Offer by Easyhome," *CNW Group,* August 14, 2008.

"RTO Enterprises Inc.," *Canadian Corporate News,* August 11, 2000.

"RTO Enterprises Inc. Announces Approval of Name Change to Easyhome Ltd.," *Canadian Corporate News,* May 2, 2003.

"RTO Enterprises Inc. Launches Re-Branding Initiative," *Canadian Corporate News,* January 24, 2003.

EMAK Worldwide, Inc.

—■—

6330 San Vicente Boulevard
Los Angeles, California 90048
U.S.A.
Telephone: (323) 932-4300
Fax: (323) 932-4400
Web site: http://www.emak.com

Public Company
Incorporated: 1991 as Equity Marketing, Inc.
Employees: 350
Sales: $164.17 million (2007)
Stock Exchanges: Over the Counter (OTC)
Ticker Symbol: EMAK
NAICS: 541810 Advertising Agencies

■ ■ ■

EMAK Worldwide, Inc., is the parent company for a group of marketing services agencies that design and manufacture custom promotional products and provide event-marketing services. EMAK's client roster includes Burger King Corporation, Miller Brewing Company, Procter & Gamble Co., and Kraft Foods, Inc., among other high-profile customers. The company maintains offices in Los Angeles, Chicago, Amsterdam, Frankfurt, London, Paris, and Hong Kong.

ORIGINS

The principal architects of EMAK's development were Stephen P. Robeck and Donald A. Kurz, two executives who turned a division of a separate company into a leader in the marketing services industry. EMAK's roots sprang from a New York City-based company named

Marketing Equities International, a travel incentive firm that marketed free trips for airlines. The Marketing Equities division, formed in 1983, designed promotional merchandise, primarily toys, for corporate clientele. It was an aspect of Marketing Equities' business that Robeck and Kurz believed had the potential to become a thriving stand-alone business, and they pursued the idea, setting in motion the events that ultimately led to the emergence of the EMAK name.

Robeck and Kurz hatched their entrepreneurial plans while working for Marketing Equities. Robeck, a graduate of Lake Forest College, joined the firm in 1987 as chief operating officer. Kurz, who earned a bachelor's degree from Johns Hopkins University and an M.B.A. from Columbia University, joined Marketing Equities in 1990 as executive vice-president. From their respective perches, Robeck and Kurz eyed Marketing Equities' promotional toy unit with particular interest. Research revealed that the promotional and premium toys niche was the fastest growing component of the $65 billion licensing industry and sparsely populated with competitors. The lure of fast-paced growth convinced the two executives that the division could stand on its own and capitalize on the growing demand for promotional merchandise. In 1991, Robeck and Kurz engineered a leveraged buyout of the Marketing Equities' division and named the business Equity Marketing, Inc., the direct predecessor to EMAK.

EARLY GROWTH OF EQUITY MARKETING

Robeck and Kurz took control of a $15.3 million-in-sales business with 15 employees when they launched

COMPANY PERSPECTIVES

We believe in "participative marketing." Consumers no longer want to be spectators; they want to be engaged and involved. We get consumers to touch, feel, play with, and be a part of our clients' brands. Marketing for good in the space of green & sustainability, health & wellness and corporate & social responsibility. We do marketing that sells. Specifically, our agencies are experts at market research, trend-spotting, and insight-mining. Promotional marketing, integrated marketing and calendar planning, custom promotional products—designed, produced and delivered. Retail marketing, co-marketing, shopper marketing, retail design. Sponsorships, sports and entertainment marketing, word of mouth, buzz and viral campaigns.

Equity Marketing. Under Marketing Equities' last year of control, the business posted a loss of $250,000, a deficit Robeck and Kurz planned to turn into a profit by negotiating long-term licensing agreements with movie studios. "Licensing depends on a combination of mechanical skills, innovation, manufacturing, and the ability to understand and work with creative people," Robeck said in the November 1995 issue of *Chief Executive.* "One of the biggest killers is getting studio approval of a toy—it's vital to get it right the first time."

Equity Marketing was established to provide a full-range of services to corporate clientele who were spending nearly $1 billion annually for giveaway merchandise. The company aided in concept development and product design, secured licensor approval, and took responsibility for safety testing, manufacturing, and shipping promotional merchandise intended to support specific marketing campaigns. During their first years in charge, Robeck and Kurz, who shared the position of chief executive officer, signed licensing agreements with film studios such as The Walt Disney Company, Warner Bros., and 20th Century Fox, obtaining the rights to manufacture toys and figurines based on popular entertainment characters. They established a presence in Hong Kong, forming Equity Marketing Hong Kong, Ltd., to orchestrate the manufacture of the promotional merchandise in mainland China. Robeck and Kurz used the assets to court high-profile, deep-pocketed clientele, building a customer base that included The Coca-Cola Co., Pizza Hut International, and Burger King Corp.

AN EMPHASIS ON VOLUME AND SPEED

Equity Marketing enjoyed immediate success, displaying talents that separated it from traditional toy manufacturers. Such global giants as Mattel and Hasbro often spent two years developing toys and preparing for their manufacture. Equity Marketing, in contrast, had to move fast and with precision. Typically, once the company had signed a contract, it had six months to prepare for a launch and deliver millions of toys to distribution centers scattered across the United States. One of the highlights during its early years occurred in 1994, when Equity Marketing produced 30 million toys based on the film *The Lion King* for a single Burger King promotion, a campaign whose success required Equity Marketing to manufacture an additional 20 million toys to satisfy the demand for the hugely popular figurines.

STOCK OFFERING IN 1994

The year of *The Lion King* promotion marked a pivotal year in Equity Marketing's development. In 1994, the company moved its headquarters from New York City to Los Angeles, establishing its main office on Rodeo Drive in Beverly Hills. "It helped us enormously to be closer to the entertainment industry," Kurz said in the September 9, 1996 issue of the *Los Angeles Business Journal.* "It really raised our profile," he said of the move. The year also saw the company complete its initial public offering (IPO) of stock, giving it access to capital to fuel its expansion. Investors were greeted by a company that had achieved impressive growth since Robeck and Kurz had led a leveraged buyout of the Marketing Equities division. Annual sales reached $84 million in 1994, more than five times the total generated in 1991. Arguably of greater importance to Wall Street, the company was profitable, turning the $250,000 loss inherited by Robeck and Kurz into a profit of $4.6 million.

A DEPENDENCE ON BURGER KING CORP.

Equity Marketing was expanding at an admirable pace, but the company suffered from one perceived fault, a shortcoming that posed a greater threat to its reputation after it completed its IPO. Much of the company's success hinged on its business with Burger King, which accounted for 85 percent of Equity Marketing's sales in 1993, leading some Wall Street analysts to voice concerns about the company's dependence on the fast-food behemoth. Robeck and Kurz were aware of the potential for disaster if Burger King severed its ties with

KEY DATES

1983: Predecessor to EMAK is established as a division of Marketing Equities International.
1991: Stephen P. Robeck and Donald A. Kurz purchase the Marketing Equities division and rename it Equity Marketing, Inc.
1994: Equity Marketing moves its headquarters to Los Angeles and completes an initial public offering of stock.
2001: Equity Marketing launches an acquisition campaign aimed at diversifying its business.
2004: Equity Marketing changes its name to EMAK Worldwide, Inc.
2005: Kurz resigns as chief executive officer and is replaced by Jim Holbrook.
2006: Holbrook consolidates EMAK's activities into three agencies.
2008: EMAK is delisted from the NASDAQ.

their company, and they had began looking to diversify Equity Marketing's business well before the IPO. "That's been the basis of our strategy since day one," Kurz said in the September 9, 1996 issue of the *Los Angeles Business Journal.*

Aside from focusing on expanding their company's roster of clients, Robeck and Kurz delved into new business lines. In 1993, they formed a retail toy division that designed toys for major retailers such as Toys "R" Us, Wal-Mart, and Kay Bee Toys. By 1995, the retail toy division had grown into a $10.7 million business, accounting for nearly 13 percent of Equity Marketing's revenue volume. Robeck and Kurz also looked to expand the company's international business, seeing potential for robust growth in Latin America where Equity Marketing collected $11 million in sales in 1994. "We want to get Burger King well below 50 percent of overall revenues," Kurz said in the November 1995 issue of *Chief Executive,* "even while it keeps growing."

FALTERING STEPS IN THE LATE NINETIES

Robeck and Kurz served as co-chief executive officers until 1999, when Robeck assumed the duties of nonexecutive chairman and Kurz accepted full responsibility for Equity Marketing's strategic direction as the company's sole chief executive officer. The managerial realignment occurred at an important juncture in the company's development. Revenues in 1998 reached

$227 million, nearly tripling in the four years since the IPO, but the reliance on Burger King continued, with the fast-food giant accounting for 80 percent of Equity Marketing's business. Of greater concern to Kurz was the damage engendered by two failures late in the decade, the release of toys related to Sony Pictures Entertainment's *Godzilla* and Universal Studio's *Babe: Pig in the City.* The merchandise associated with the two films recorded anemic sales, crimping Equity Marketing's profits. "They stubbed their toe through no fault of their own," an analyst said in the January 11, 1999 issue of *Advertising Age.* "If you don't succeed on the silver screen, it's very hard to have merchandise jump off the shelves."

DIVERSIFICATION BEGINS IN 2001

Kurz responded to the situation by embarking on an acquisition campaign, one that was partly financed by a $25 million investment by Crown Capital Group in March 2000. In July 2001, Equity Marketing paid $12.2 million to buy Logistix Ltd., a London, England-based marketing services company that focused on supporting family-friendly brands. The purchase of Logistix added $20 million in annual revenue to Equity Marketing's business and it provided entry into Europe through contracts with clients such as Kellogg Co., Coca-Cola, and Procter & Gamble Co. One year later, in July 2002, Equity Marketing paid $10.3 million for Promotional Marketing LLC, a Chicago-based firm specializing in promotions and events. In September 2003, Kurz purchased a nearby rival, Ontario, California-based SCI Promotion Group LLC, for $9.4 million. Several months later, in January 2004, Equity Marketing paid roughly $4 million for Minneapolis, Minnesota-based Johnson Grossfield Inc., a marketing services firm that provided licensed promotional items to Doctor's Associates, Inc., the owner of the Subway sandwich chain. After completing its flurry of acquisitions, Equity Marketing changed its name, adopting EMAK Worldwide, Inc., as its corporate title in September 2004.

LEADERSHIP CHANGE IN 2005

The diversification program achieved the desired result of lessening the company's dependence on Burger King, but the addition of the new businesses exacted a toll on EMAK's financial performance. By 2005, Burger King accounted for 52 percent of the company's sales, the percentage the company had been trying to reach for more than a decade. Celebrations at company headquarters were muted, however, as the company slipped into the red because of its diversification program. Integrating the new purchases into the company's fold proved to be a difficult process, draining EMAK of its financial vitality. "Typically, when you buy a small company that was pretty entrepreneurial, it's hard to convert it to a corporate entity," an analyst explained in the April 24, 2006 issue of the *Los Angeles Business Journal.* "Each one of the acquisitions had some down time and a negative period." After recording nearly $8 million in net income in 2003, the company posted a loss of $15.6 million in 2004 and a numbing loss of $31.7 million in 2005, a disastrous year that marked the departure of Kurz. He resigned in mid-2005, leaving the stewardship of EMAK to his longtime partner, Robeck.

Robeck stepped in as interim chief executive officer while a search was conducted to find a replacement for Kurz. In November 2005, EMAK selected its candidate, Jim Holbrook. Holbrook earned his bachelor's degree from Vanderbilt University and his M.B.A. from Washington University, enabling him to launch a professional career in sales and marketing. He worked for Procter & Gamble and Ralston Purina Co. before becoming part owner of Zipatoni Co., a marketing services agency.

HOLBROOK CONSOLIDATES IN 2006

Holbrook inherited the problems associated with the diversification program begun in 2001 and sought to lend cohesion and profitability to the handful of entities under his control. "The strategy of the acquisitions was a good strategy," he said in the April 24, 2006 issue of the *Los Angeles Business Journal.* "The execution of integrating the agencies didn't go as well. So, what we are doing is completing that integration." In 2006, Holbrook consolidated EMAK's operations, organizing the purchases made between 2001 and 2004 into three agencies: Equity Marketing, Logistix, and Upshot, the new name for the business purchased in the acquisition of Promotional Marketing LLC.

Holbrook's restructuring efforts marked the beginning of EMAK's road to recovery. Sales remained static between the late 1990s and 2005, hovering in the $230 million range, and then began to decrease, slipping to $181 million in 2006 and falling to $164 million in 2007. Annual losses continued to pock the company's financial performance during the downslide, as EMAK recorded a $2.2 million loss in 2006 and a $7.4 million loss in 2007. Adding further uncertainty to the

company's prospects for a turnaround, its stock was delisted from the NASDAQ in early 2008, the same year rumors began to circulate that a Los Angeles-based investment firm, Marlin Equity Partners LLC, was interested in acquiring EMAK. The company faced serious challenges as it prepared for the future, but Holbrook and his management team were determined to set EMAK on a course toward profitability and growth.

Jeffrey L. Covell

PRINCIPAL SUBSIDIARIES

Equity Marketing Hong Kong, Ltd.; Corinthian Marketing, Inc.; Logistix Limited (UK); Johnson Grossfield, Inc.; Equity Marketing, Inc.; Upshot, Inc.; Logistix Marketing, Inc.; Logistix, Inc.; Logistix Retail, Inc.; EMAK Worldwide Service Corp.; EMAK Europe Holdings Limited (UK); EMAK Hong Kong Limited; EMAK China Limited (Hong Kong); EMAK Asia Holding Company Limited (Hong Kong); Megaprint Group Limited (UK); Megapromotions BV (Netherlands); Logistix Marketing GmbH (Germany).

PRINCIPAL COMPETITORS

Arc Worldwide; DraftFCB; Wunderman.

FURTHER READING

Brown, Rachel, "EMAK Recasting Itself amid Growing Pains, Internal Strife," *Los Angeles Business Journal,* April 24, 2006, p. 12.

Chalfant, Erin, "Correct: Emak Worldwide CEO Kurz Resigns," *America's Intelligence Wire,* May 19, 2005.

Dougherty, Conor, "Equity Marketing Secures Long-Term Deal with Burger King," *Los Angeles Business Journal,* December 16, 2002, p. 7.

Friedman, Wayne, "Saying Goodbye to Hollywood," *Advertising Age,* January 11, 1999, p. 12.

Grove, Chris, "Toying with Success," *Los Angeles Business Journal,* September 9, 1996, p. 12.

Hayes, Elizabeth, "Promotion Firm's Reliance on One Client Is a Concern," *Los Angeles Business Journal,* May 15, 2000, p. 73.

Johnson, Greg, "Equity Marketing Buying UK Rival," *Daily Deal,* August 3, 2001.

Rehak, Judith, "Equity Marketing's License to Sell," *Chief Executive,* November 1995, p. 23.

Spethmann, Betsy, "Holbrook to Head EMAK," *Promo,* November 10, 2005.

Ferrovie Dello Stato Societa Di Trasporti e Servizi S.p.A.

Piazza della Croce Rossa 1
Rome, I-00161
Italy
Telephone: (+39 06) 44101
Fax: (+39 06) 44105325
Web site: http://www.ferroviedellostato.it

Government-Owned Public Company
Incorporated: 1905
Employees: 97,000
Sales: EUR 8.1 billion ($11 billion) (2008)
NAICS: 482111 Line-Haul Railroads

■ ■ ■

Ferrovie Dello Stato Societa Di Trasporti e Servizi S.p.A., or FS, is the operator of Italy's national railway network. As such, the company oversees 9,000 trains operating on more than 16,500 kilometers of track. The company's operations include 4,500 locomotives, 10,000 passenger cars, and 50,000 freight cars. Each year, the company carries more than 500 million passengers, and transports 80 million metric tons of freight. The company is also the largest employer in Italy, with approximately 97,000 employees, including 87,000 railway workers. FS is structured into three primary divisions: Trenitalia SpA, which oversees the group's passenger rail operations; Rete Ferroviaria Italiana, the group's infrastructure division, responsible for building and maintaining the rail network; and TAV (Treno Alta Velocita), which oversees the development and operation of the country's high-speed rail network. FS completed a major restructuring of its operations in the period between 1996 and 2006, which saw its payroll slashed in half and its operating losses greatly reduced. Nonetheless, the company, which generates revenues of more than EUR 8 billion, continues to post losses in the hundreds of millions of euros each year. FS is a non-quoted public company owned by the Italian government and operated under the Ministry of Transport. Mauro Moretti is the group's managing director.

BUILDING RAILWAYS IN PRE-UNIFIED ITALY

The development and structure of Italy's railway network in the 19th century reflected the lack of unification and the multiple spheres of influence over the Italian peninsula in the pre-Resorgimenta era. The earliest Italian railway was built in the Kingdom of the Two Sicilies, by the company that had built the world's first railroad, connecting Manchester and Liverpool, in 1830. The first Italian railroad, which connected Naples and Portici over 7.6 kilometers of track, was completed in 1839 on behest of the royal court under Ferdinand II.

The Austrian-dominated Kingdom of Lombardy-Venetia began construction of its own railroad in 1840. The new line provided a 12-kilometer connection between Milan and Monza. At the same time, the kingdom launched the construction of the country's first strategic railway, between Milan and Venice. This line was important both for the commercial advantages of connecting the two cities, but also from a military standpoint.

COMPANY PERSPECTIVES

Mission and strategy: We are the largest company in the country. Every day, 87,000 rail workers help to run 9,200 trains and manage a network of almost 16,500 kilometers. In one year we carry almost 500 million passengers and about 80 million tonnes of freight. The mission: With our services and interventions to strengthen the network, contribute to the development of a major project for mobility and logistics for the country, and to the country's economic, social and cultural development.

Technological innovation and security are our strength, attested by two excellence awards at the international level. The basis of our work is attention to the quality of life of clients and workers, guidance on a project that looks to the future and respect for the environment.

Other railways made their appearances through the middle of the century. These included a 32-kilometer railway between Padua and Mestre, opened in 1842, followed by new lines connecting Milan and Treviglio, and Padua and Vincenza, in 1846. The Kingdom of Sardinia joined in, adding a line from Genoa to Milan, completed over a ten-year period in 1853. Soon after, the first railways in the Lombardy-Austria region added connections to the French and Swiss railroads. In the Papal States, railroad development had been slowed by the resistance of the Vatican; in 1846, however, work began on railroads linking Rome to Frascati and Civitavecchia. The first locomotive factory was also completed, in Genoa, ending British dominance over the country's rolling stock.

LATE 19TH-CENTURY REORGANIZATION

These railroads became important elements in the several Wars of Independence, which ultimately succeeded in uniting much of the peninsula under the Kingdom of Italy (the country was fully unified only after World War I). Into the mid-1860s, the kingdom's total network reached more than 2,000 kilometers, with another 300 kilometers under construction in the Papal States, and the first railroad built in Sicily, completed in 1863.

The various railways, many of which operated as private companies, had been built according to different

standards. The new kingdom began working to integrate the network. The country's railroad system was then placed under five regional operating but still privately held companies, in 1865. The outbreak of war again the following year had a devastating effect on the increasingly industrialized Italian economy, including the railroads. The near collapse of the kingdom's railroad sector led the government to bail out the operating companies, giving the kingdom more control over what had become a vital part of the country's industrial, economic, and political infrastructure.

Work continued on developing the Italian railway system, including the creation of a secondary rail network linking minor towns and cities. These railways were often owned and operated by smaller independent companies. The addition of the remaining Papal States to the kingdom in 1870 helped raised the country's total rail network to more than 7,000. At the same time, the government reduced the number of regional operators to just four. In 1875, the completion of a railroad between Orte and Orvieto permitted direct train routes between Florence and Rome for the first time.

By then, the first calls to unite the Italian railway network under a single company had brought down the government. However, the various rail companies struggled to maintain their financial viability. Funding new railway extensions while maintaining existing lines proved too costly for the private companies, resulting in poor service, a lack of comfort, and unsafe conditions throughout much of the country. The collapse of two of the companies, Società per le strade ferrate dell'Alta Italia (SFIA) and Società per le strade ferrate Romane (SFR), led to their takeover by the government.

FORMING A NATIONAL RAILWAY OPERATOR IN 1905

Movement toward a state-owned railroad company began in the 1880s, when the government created a new concession-based system. The country's 8,500 kilometers of railways were divided along new regional lines under three companies. While these companies remained privately held, their operations were placed under the oversight of a General Inspectorate for Railroads, which itself was part of the Ministry of Public Works. The government also provided funding for continued infrastructure development.

The new organization permitted the extension of the Italian rail network by another 2,000 kilometers over the next decade. Yet private ownership failed to correct the poor overall conditions of rail operation, and in many cases only exacerbated the problems encountered both by the companies and the customers.

KEY DATES

1839: Construction of the first railroad in the future Italy is completed between Naples and Portici.

1865: Italian railroad system is reorganized under five privately owned companies.

1905: Italian government nationalizes the country's train network, creating Ferrovie dello Stato (FS).

1970: FS launches construction of the country's first high-speed train line between Rome and Naples.

1985: FS is reincorporated as a limited liability company owned by the Italian government.

1996: Giancarlo Cimoli becomes the company's chief executive and leads a major restructuring of its operations.

2000: FS becomes a holding company for its infrastructure, passenger and freight, and high-speed train subsidiaries.

2005: Rome-Naples high-speed train line finally becomes operational.

2006: FS posts a loss of more than EUR 1.6 billion.

If a number of larger lines were able to achieve a degree of profitability, many other lines, and particularly the smaller lines, could not.

The country's rolling stock was also severely outdated. A great many of the country's locomotives were older than 30 years; similarly, the average age of passenger cars was over 30 years old, while the average age of the country's freight cars was more than 40 years. As a result, rail services continued to degrade. The lack of reliable rail services also had a severe impact on the growth of the Italian economy during this time.

At last, in the face of protest both from railway workers and the rest of the population, the Italian government was forced to act. In 1905, the government pushed through legislation nationalizing the country's railroads. The new bill was coupled with a ban on strikes by civil servants, including railroad workers. The move brought a new wave of protests, and brought down another government. Nonetheless, the new government under Fortis moved forward with the nationalization program, creating Ferrovie dello Stato (FS) in July 1905. Over the next year, the new state-owned company worked at integrating the various

railways, and by 1906 had raised the total length of track under its control past 13,000 kilometers.

THE MUSSOLINI-ERA TRAIN MYTH

The new company set out to upgrade its operations. FS launched a vast new construction program, adding nearly 570 locomotives, nearly 1,250 passenger cars, and more than 20,250 freight cars over the next year. Into the years leading up to World War I, FS doubled its rolling stock, boasting more than 5,000 locomotives, and more than 117,000 passenger and freight cars. These were then painted with the company's new FS logo, which became one of modern Italy's major symbols. In addition to expanding its rolling stock, FS also continued to extend its rail network, adding another 2,000 kilometers. The company had also begun modernizing the national network, adding electricity and modern signaling and switching equipment.

World War I destroyed most of these improvements, however. Following the war, FS was required to rebuild large portions of its rail network, as well as replace much of its rolling stock. The breakup of the Austrian Empire had also placed new regions under Italian control. FS took over the operation of the railroads in the new areas as well. However, because these railroads had been built to a different standard, FS was also required to convert these lines to its own standard.

Nonetheless, the reconstruction of the Italian railway network was well underway by the early 1920s and the fascist power grab under Benito Mussolini. The Italian railway quickly became the source of a popular myth promulgated by the Mussolini government, which declared that under the fascist regime the trains ran on time. That the claim had little basis in reality did not prevent the myth from taking hold; indeed, the myth helped to fuel the popular support for the Mussolini dictatorship.

FS did, however, continue to expand and improve the railway network through the fascist era. The company completed new direct connections between Rome and Naples, and between Florence and Bologna, helping to reduce cross-country travel times still further. In 1928, FS added a direct connection linking Milan, Turin, Rome, and Naples, as well. The company also carried out the conversion of the rail network to the 3,000-volt direct current standard. Many of the country's largest train stations, including Milano Centrale, Rome's Ostiense, and Naples's Megerllina, were also completed during this time. The company also began to increase train speeds, which topped 200 kilometers per hour (125 miles per hour) in the late

1930s. Other improvements included the addition of refrigerated freight cars.

REBUILDING FOLLOWING THE WAR

Many of these projects had been initiated before the Mussolini regime took power. In addition, despite the importance of FS to the fascist propaganda machine, the government failed to implement infrastructure improvements across the entire railway network. The main lines, and particularly the lines serving major tourist destinations, received priority. Smaller and outlying lines fell into disrepair and otherwise failed to keep pace with the modernization of the rail industry.

This resulted in faltering service by the outbreak of World War II. The lack of infrastructure improvements had other consequences, as well. At the beginning of the war, nearly all of Italy's coal imports came through its seaports. When these were cut off during the war, the country was forced to bring much needed coal in through its railroad, and particularly through the out-of-date line crossing the Italian Alps. As a result, the country's coal inputs fell sharply, hampering its industrial and military efforts.

Italy's defeat and subsequent liberation at the end of the war destroyed much of the country's railroads, including nearly all of its rolling stock. The FS was once again faced with rebuilding the country's rail network with assistance from the Marshall Plan. Work continued through the 1950s, and included substantial improvement and modernization of both the rail infrastructure and rolling stock, including the introduction of new passenger car designs. During this period and into the 1960s, electric and diesel locomotives entirely replaced steam locomotives.

The FS next played an important role in the great Italian population shift of the postwar era, as many fled the poverty of the country's southern regions for the prosperity of the more heavily industrialized northern region.

By the 1960s, the FS had largely completed its reconstruction effort. However the company, and the Italian government, had let slip by the opportunity to carry out a complete overhaul of the rail network. This resulted in continued inefficiencies that were to haunt the company into the next century. Nonetheless, by the 1960s, the upgrades completed by the company had enabled a growing number of lines to achieve train speeds of more than 200 kilometers per hour. The company also began to build interoperability partnerships with its neighboring European railroads, becoming one of the members of the Trans Europe Express service in the 1960s.

HIGH-SPEED BEGINNINGS IN THE SEVENTIES

As part of this effort, FS began developing its own high-speed train projects toward the end of the 1960s and into the 1970s. This culminated in the construction of a new direct link between Rome and Florence, including Europe's longest bridge, the 5,375-meter bridge over the Paglia river. Nonetheless the 1970s also marked the start of a new era of corruption and incompetence for the FS as the company became a political pawn for a succession of unstable governments and a growing pool of railway unions.

One result of this period was the dramatic expansion of the company's payroll. In just one three-year period in the early 1970s, the FS added more than 70,000 jobs. By the end of the 1980s, the heavily bloated company carried more than 220,000 highly unionized people on its payroll. Many of these jobs were in areas completely unrelated to railway operations, as FS carried out a wide-scale diversification, building up a list of more than 150 often money-losing subsidiaries.

At the same time, the company failed to implement much of its infrastructure improvements, in part because of an Italian government policy of granting subsidies only on a yearly basis. As a result, when funds ran out for the year, FS was forced to abandon work on its projects. Even with funding, work was able to proceed only slowly, bogged down by an increasingly burdensome Italian bureaucracy. The result was that the country's high-speed rail project lagged far behind its European counterparts. The Paglia River bridge, for example, was finally completed only in the 1990s. By then, FS had become woefully inefficient, with an under-maintained infrastructure, aging rolling stock, famously dismal service, and losses in the billions of dollars each year.

RESTRUCTURING

A first step toward the revitalization of the Italian rail system came in the mid-1980s, when the Italian government moved toward the privatization of the Italian railroad, reincorporating FS as a state-owned limited liability company. It was not until 1996, when FS's then president was caught up in a corruption scandal, that FS launched a new restructuring effort. This led to the appointment of former Edison SpA chief Giancarlo Cimoli as the company's chief executive.

Over the next decade, Cimoli carried out a sweeping restructuring of FS's operations. Despite heavy resistance, particularly from the rail workers unions, Cimoli managed to cut the company's payroll in half early in the first decade of the 2000s. Continued payroll reductions through the decade resulted in a much leaner organization of less than 90,000 workers. FS also sold off or shut down nearly all of its non-railroad related business, restoring its focus on its core operations.

These were then restructured, along the lines of many of Europe's national railroads, into distinct, independent businesses. The new operations included Rete Ferroviaria Italiana, in charge of the group's infrastructure operations; Trenitalia, which took over the operation of the group's passenger and freight business; and Treno Alta Velocita (TAV), responsible for high-speed train development. The company also carried out a refurbishment of its major train stations, the operation of which was then turned over to a private consortium led by the Benetton clothing group. Following the 2000 restructuring, FS became a holding company.

The effort appeared to pay off. High-speed train service at last launched along the Rome-Naples line in 2005. The company also managed to report a tiny operating profit into the middle of the decade. FS had also received stronger funding from the Italian government, enabling the company to step up its infrastructure development. Yet the company's passenger services, the least expensive in Europe, had become a major burden on its books, as the government refused to allow the company to make the necessary fare increases. In the meantime, Cimoli left the company in 2004, in order to try to rescue the struggling Alitalia airline.

FS's losses began to climb again into the second half of the decade. By 2006, the company's losses had topped EUR 1.6 billion. The company also began to feel the pressure from a growing number of rivals, as the deregulation of the European railway industry had opened up the market to competition for the first time. Most of this competition, however, came in the more lucrative freight sector. In some markets, FS quickly lost as much as one-third of its market share.

In response, FS, led by Mauro Moretti, announced its interest in acquiring port operations, in the interest of redeveloping itself as an integrated logistics management company, and therefore reducing its reliance on its money-losing railroad business. For the time being, however, FS continued in its struggle to improve the performance of its existing operations, not to mention its long-held reputation for poor service and fumbled development.

M. L. Cohen

PRINCIPAL SUBSIDIARIES

Italferr SpA; Rete Ferroviaria Italiana; Trenitalia S.p.A.

PRINCIPAL DIVISIONS

FS Divisione Passeggeri; FS Regionale; FS Cargo.

PRINCIPAL OPERATING UNITS

Grandi Stazioni, CentoStazioni; Sogin; Fercredit.

PRINCIPAL COMPETITORS

Deutsche Bahn AG; Vivendi S.A.; SNCF International; Compania Nationala de Cai Ferate; Financiere de l'Odet S.A.; Veolia Transport S.A.; FirstGroup PLC (FGP); SBB AG; Oesterreichische Bundesbahnen-Holding AG; N.V. Nederlandse Spoorwegen.

FURTHER READING

Bennett, Steve, "FS to Create New Infrastructure Company," *International Railway Journal,* December 2000, p. 13.

Betts, Paul, "Mr. Diesel Directs an Uphill Task," *Financial Times,* May 17, 2000, p. 19.

Briginshaw, David, "Italy's 'Miracle' Holds Lessons for Others," *Railway Age,* January 2003, p. 76.

"First New High Speed Line to Open in 2003," *International Railway Journal,* December 2000, p. 20.

"FNM Denies Rumours on Ferrovie Dello Stato Merger," *TendersInfo,* April 2, 2009.

"FS Invests Heavily in Infrastructure," *International Railway Journal,* April 2001, p. 5.

"FS Turns to Rail Specialists to Get Back on Track," *Europe Intelligence Wire,* September 26, 2006.

"Italian Railroad to Close Onboard Restaurants," *International Herald Tribune,* June 23, 2008, p. 22.

"Italian Railways Eyes Port Operations," *Lloyds List,* April 5, 2007.

"Off the Rails," *Economist,* February 14, 1998, p. 64.

"Rescue Plan Put to Government," *Railway Gazette International,* April 2007, p. 194.

Wright, Robin, "Cimoli Transported from Trains to Planes," *Financial Times,* May 10, 2004, p. 20.

——, "Tensions High Between Operators," *Financial Times,* December 12, 2008, p. 14.

First Artist Corporation PLC

———————————•———————————

3 Tenterden Street
London, W1S 1TD
United Kingdom
Telephone: (+44 207) 993-0000
Fax: (+44 203) 205-2100
Web site: http://www.firstartist.com

Public Company
Incorporated: 1986
Employees: 259
Sales: £54.1 million (2008)
Stock Exchanges: London AIM
Ticker Symbol: FAN
NAICS: 541840 Media Representatives; 541820 Public
    Relations Agencies

■ ■ ■

First Artist Corporation PLC is one of the leading sports and entertainment management companies in the world, operating businesses involved in representing and managing the interests of football (soccer) players, managers, and broadcast commentators as well as theatrical productions. First Artist also offers event management and corporate sponsorship services. The company maintains offices in Europe, North America, and Asia.

ORIGINS

The stereotype of a British football agent, a shady figure cloaked in a trench coat, surreptitiously passing out cash in brown envelopes, persisted when Jon Smith began representing football players in 1986. Smith did his best to ameliorate the seedy perception of his profession, and he did so by becoming the most prolific football agent in the world, heading a company that was publicly listed. Instead of conducting his business in the shadows, Smith offered transparency, and as such, figured as an iconoclast in the realm of football agents.

Before forming First Artist, Smith enjoyed success in a different profession. He started a company that was involved in record production and music publishing, the origination of a career path that took a turn when tragedy struck his personal life. In 1981, Smith's wife died, prompting him to sell his company for £1 million and reassess his future. "I took my money and ran to the U.S.," he said in the September 15, 2005 edition of the *Guardian*. "I loved what they did out there; sport is part of the entertainment business and I wanted to bring back that theory."

Smith formed First Artist in 1986 when he was 34 years old, basing the company in Wembley, a district in northwest London, and enlisting the help of his brother, Phil Smith. The Smith brothers established a name for themselves immediately, negotiating a deal to represent the commercial interests of the English national team. Securing the national team as its first client had a profound effect on establishing First Artist as a legitimate football agency, but the agreement paled in importance to Jon Smith's next move, his masterstroke. His second client was Diego Maradona, an Argentine midfielder extolled as the best player in the world. "It put us on the map," Smith said in the September 15, 2005 edition of the *Guardian*.

Over the course of the next 15 years, Smith built First Artist into one of the world's leading football agencies. He signed on high-profile players, managers, and television commentators and he managed the interests of the English cricket and Welsh rugby teams. He organized and promoted the speaking tours of Mikhail Gorbachev and Mother Teresa and promoted England's Golden Jubilee celebrations commemorating the end of World War II. Mainly, though, he built his company and reputation by becoming the agent of choice to football players, using his experience in the United States as inspiration for turning the sport's icons into full-fledged celebrities. "We took them out of *Shoot* (an English football magazine targeted for children) and into *Cosmo* and *Harper's*," Smith said in the December 2, 2001 edition of the *Observer*, "and tried to make them more pizzazzful."

By the beginning of the 21st century, First Artist held sway as the preeminent football agency in Europe. The company represented 175 football players, managers, and media pundits. In 2000, First Artist generated £2 million in revenue, a total collected primarily from fees related to the transfer and contract renegotiations of players, and posted £500,000 in profits. At this point, Smith was ready to make a move no other football agent had made. He announced his intention to make First Artist the first player management business to trade shares on a stock market.

PUBLIC DEBUT IN 2001

Smith wanted to expand First Artist. "The market is consolidating and there are a lot of opportunities," he said in the November 5, 2000 edition of *Sunday Business.* "Having a listing will help us raise the profile of the business and provide funding to support our growth plans." He wanted to open regional offices and expand into underdeveloped markets such as the Far East, Australia, and Eastern Europe. In March 2001, First Artist debuted on the OFEX exchange, the lowest rung within the United Kingdom's three-tier market system. The initial public offering (IPO) of stock raised £2.3 million. Within months, Smith proposed another bold move, one that would help finance the acquisition of Fimo AG, a Swiss-Italian agency that represented players from Real Madrid and Barcelona, two of the most prestigious clubs in the world. He announced plans to launch a stock offering on the Alternative Investment Market (AIM), the exchange ranking between the Official List and OFEX. In December 2001, First Artist completed the move to AIM, raising £5 million.

The addition of Fimo more than doubled the size of First Artist. The £16 million acquisition added Fimo's 200 players to First Artist's portfolio of 175 players, managers, and broadcasters, creating an agency that dominated its industry. "We're now the biggest management agency in Europe, the engine-room of the biggest market in football, which is the biggest sporting industry in the world and also the biggest entertainment industry on God's planet," Smith declared in the December 2, 2001 edition of the *Observer*. His ebullience soon faded, however, not long after football's governing body, Federation Internationale de Football Association (F.I.F.A.), issued a decree that dramatically changed the dynamics of the player representation business.

F.I.F.A. RULING PROMPTS DIVERSIFICATION

Starting in the 2002–03 football season, F.I.F.A. greatly shorted the registration period, or "transfer window," during which players could move from club to club. In England, and most other countries, transfers were allowed only between January 1 and February 2 and for several weeks during the summer, a restriction that put Smith and all other football agents in a precarious position. "It's a restriction of trade," Smith said in the December 16, 2002 edition of the *Guardian*. "I can only generate income in a third of the year—so, I'm sitting around, knowing our overheads trundle along at £300,000 pounds a month across our offices worldwide and I can only start earning money on January 1."

The imposition of football's transfer window system forced Smith to develop a new strategy for First Artist. His profitable business quickly slipped into the red: "the gravy train is over," he said in the March 14, 2003 edi-

KEY DATES

1986: Jon Smith forms First Artist.
2001: First Artist completes its initial public offering of stock.
2002: Restrictions are placed on negotiating transfers, prompting Smith to reduce First Artist's reliance on football.
2003: First Artist begins providing financial management services to its clients.
2005: First Artist enters the event management business by acquiring The Finishing Touch.
2006: First Artist acquires Dewynters Limited, an agency that promotes theatrical productions.
2008: First Artist acquires SpotCo, a New York City-based agency that promotes theatrical productions on Broadway.

tion of the *Daily Mail.* He responded by diversifying the company's business to compensate for the drop in income. In early 2003, he established a wealth management division to serve his 426 clients, offering accountancy, taxation, investment products, and mortgage and insurance services to his players, managers, and sport commentators. "We already manage everything from booking our clients' cinema tickets to arranging their flights and doing their shopping," he explained in the February 19, 2003 edition of the *Daily Telegraph.* "We have done everything apart from financial management ... it is the final piece of our jigsaw." In July 2005, he deepened his involvement in providing financial management service by acquiring ABG Financial Management, which provided financial advice to sports and media celebrities. The £3 million acquisition became a new First Artist subsidiary named Optimal Wealth Management Limited.

ACQUISITION OF THE FINISHING TOUCH: 2005

Smith developed new streams of revenue from his clients, but his most important actions in the wake of the restrictions on negotiating transfers saw him lessen First Artist's reliance on football. He began to shape First Artist into a more broadly defined company, completing acquisitions and forming divisions that created a group of First Artist companies involved in a number of different businesses. In September 2005, he purchased The Finishing Touch (Corporate Events) Limited, paying £3.3 million for the London-based

event management company. The following month, he launched an entertainment and corporate speaking division, First Artist Entertainment.

Smith's efforts to diversify First Artist's interests helped the company return to profitability by 2006, but the arrival of net income did not lessen his desire to expand his football and non-football business. Smith maintained he was committed to football (a commitment evinced by the acquisition of Scandinavia's leading football management agency in July 2006) while also demonstrating he was committed to developing First Artist's non-football capabilities. In July 2006, he paid £1.7 million for NCI Management, a London-based agency that represented sports broadcasters and journalists, using the purchase to strengthen his entertainment business. In October 2006, he formed a joint venture company, Fisher Family Office, with H.W. Fisher & Co., a chartered accountancy firm. "This joint venture," Smith said in the October 20, 2006 release of *Europe Intelligence Wire,* "will bring significant momentum to the growth of Optimal Wealth Management in what is becoming a very important industry for a lot of the operators in our market."

ACQUISITION OF DEWYNTERS LIMITED IN 2006

Smith's boldest move on the diversification front occurred at the end of 2006, a deal that injected financial vitality into his company and ensured that First Artist would not be viewed only as a football agency. In December, he acquired Dewynters Limited in a deal valued at £15.5 million. Dewynters, which generated £26 million in annual revenue, developed the advertising and promotion campaigns for an estimated 70 percent of the productions in London's West End theater district, taking responsibility for a range of tasks from designing posters to constructing web sites for immensely popular musicals such as *Les Miserables* and *Cats.* Dewynters also owned a U.S.-based subsidiary, Dewynters Advertising Inc., and London-based Newman Display Limited, which designed displays for theaters.

ROBUST FINANCIAL GROWTH

The acquisition of Dewynters did more to reduce First Artist's reliance on football than any previous attempt at diversification. By the end of 2007, the first full year Dewynters contributed to First Artist's financial totals, the company derived only 20 percent of its revenues from football. Dewynters accounted for two-thirds of the company's revenues, helping to quadruple sales during the year. As if to acknowledge the importance of

Dewynters to the company's business, First Artist moved its headquarters in September 2007, occupying new offices in London's West End.

The restrictions on negotiating transfers forced Smith's hand. Out of necessity, he diversified his business, launching an expansion program that greatly increased the stature of First Artist. The company generated £6.7 million in revenue in 2002, when F.I.F.A. imposed its restrictions. By 2008, the company's volume of business had increased exponentially, swelling to £54.1 million. Although Smith remained committed to representing football players, he also realized the financial gains to be made by expanding First Artist's operations into other businesses. Looking forward, he intended to continue to diversify and to flesh out his holdings in the entertainment and media sectors. Evidence of his interest in acquiring non-football assets was displayed in late 2008, when First Artist acquired SpotCo, a New York City-based agency that promoted Broadway shows such as *Chicago* and *Rent*. In the years ahead, further acquisitions were expected, as Smith endeavored to make First Artist the dominant player in its industry.

Jeffrey L. Covell

PRINCIPAL SUBSIDIARIES

The Finishing Touch Limited; Optimal Wealth Management Limited; First Artist Management Limited; Dewynters Limited; Dewynters Advertising Inc. (USA); Sponsorship Consulting Limited; Newman Displays Limited; First Rights Limited; First Artist Sport Limited; Promosport SRL (Italy); First Artist Scandinavia A/S (Denmark).

PRINCIPAL COMPETITORS

GPK Sports Management; International Sport Management S.R.O.; Global Services Management S.A.

FURTHER READING

Blitz, Roger, "West End Resurgence Lifts First Artist," *Financial Times,* September 18, 2007, p. 22.

"Business of Sport," *Guardian,* September 15, 2005, p. 8.

Campbell, Denis, "The Biggest Noise on Planet Football," *Observer,* December 2, 2001, p. 14.

Cave, Andrew, "First Artist to Score with Wealth Goal," *Daily Telegraph,* February 19, 2003.

Elliott, Stuart, "Top New York Theatrical Agency Is Combining with London Counterpart," *New York Times,* August 11, 2008, p. C6.

"First Artist in Wealth Management JV with H. W. Fisher," *Europe Intelligence Wire,* October 20, 2006.

"First Artist to Target Ofex," *Sunday Business,* November 5, 2000, p. 2M.

"Football Agent's Goal Is Expansion into Europe," *Express,* October 29, 2001, p. 55.

"Football Agents Hear Final Whistle," *Daily Mail,* March 14, 2003, p. 85.

Harvey, Fiona, "The Show Must Move On," *Financial Times,* May 27, 2003, p. 5.

John, Peter, "First Artist Buys ABGFM for £3M," *Financial Times,* July 23, 2005, p. 5.

Nisse, Jason, "First Artist Corners Player Market," *Independent,* March 25, 2001, p. 3.

Patten, Sally, "First Artist Corporation Hopes to Score with Asian Expansion," *Times* (London), February 25, 2002, p. 46.

White, Jim, "Interview: Jon Smith, Brown Envelopes, Bungs, Backhaulers," *Guardian,* December 16, 2002, p. 14.

First Busey Corporation

201 West Main Street
Urbana, Illinois 61801-2621
U.S.A.
Telephone: (217) 365-4513
Toll Free: (800) 672-8739
Fax: (217) 365-4879
Web site: http://www.busey.com

Public Company
Incorporated: 1980
Employees: 986
Total Assets: $4.46 billion (2008)
Stock Exchanges: NASDAQ
Ticker Symbol: BUSE
NAICS: 551111 Offices of Bank Holding Companies

■ ■ ■

First Busey Corporation is an Urbana, Illinois-based financial holding company for two banks and related subsidiaries. The flagship operation is Busey Bank, an Illinois state-chartered bank that maintains its headquarters in Champaign, Illinois. The full-service bank has 42 in-state branches as well as a location in Indianapolis and a Florida loan production office that concentrates on commercial, residential, agricultural, and consumer lending. The second bank, Busey Bank N.A., is a national bank based in Fort Myers, Florida. Other subsidiaries include Busey Wealth Management, providing trust asset management, retail brokerage, and insurance products and services; and FirsTech, Inc., a retail payment processing company with offices in Deca-

tur, Illinois, and Clayton, Missouri. With $4.46 billion in assets, First Busey is a public company listed on the NASDAQ. Longtime Chairman Douglas C. Mills is the company's largest shareholder.

POST–CIVIL WAR ORIGINS

First Busey dates its origins to 1868 when Busey Brothers and Company was formed in Urbana, Illinois, by General Samuel T. Busey, Simeon Busey, and Dr. W. R. Earhart. The Busey family came to the county when Kentucky-born Matthew Busey, a builder and contractor who turned his attention to farming and raising stock, moved his family there in 1836. The older of the two Busey brothers, Simeon as an adult became a major farmer in the area and also became involved in the organization of the First National Bank of Champaign.

The younger and more illustrious brother, General Samuel Busey, was a Civil War hero. Born in 1835, the sixth child of his parents, he was an infant when his family moved to Illinois. As a young man he became involved in merchandising but with the advent of the Civil War he sold his business, and served with the Urbana Zouaves before recruiting a regiment of the Illinois Infantry, for which he served as its commanding colonel. He led his troops in a number of important battles in the western theater of the war, and was wounded in the siege of Fort Blakeley before being mustered out of the service in August 1865 with the honorary rank of general. He returned home and farmed until deciding to starting a bank. In 1867 he enlisted his brother and Dr. Earhart as partners, and together they raised $11,000. On January 13, 1868, the bank opened its doors in Urbana as Busey Brothers and Company, with General Busey serving as its first president. Dr. Earhart's involvement was brief. A year later he sold his interest to the Busey brothers, who renamed the business Busey Brothers Bank.

A second generation of the Busey family became involved in the bank in 1875 when one of Simeon Busey's sons, 21-year-old Matthew W. Busey, became a bookkeeper. He then purchased what had been Earhart's share in 1877, and two years later bought out his father. He succeeded his uncle as president of the bank in 1888. Simeon Busey remained connected to the bank until shortly before his death in June 1901. General Busey, who was also involved in politics, served as mayor of Urbana, and from 1891 to 1893 was a member of the U.S. House of Representatives. He died in August 1909.

BANK RECEIVES STATE CHARTER: 1913

Busey Brothers Bank received its state charter in 1913 and was renamed Busey State Bank. It remained under the leadership of Matthew Busey until 1932 when he died. At the start of the year the bank avoided the fate of many banks during the Great Depression that were devastated by withdrawals by panicky depositors. In early 1932 a bank in nearby Champaign was forced to close its doors and the next morning anxious depositors lined up early outside the door of Busey State Bank and the First National Bank of Urbana. At 10:30 A.M. Busey suspended further payments. The city of Urbana then declared martial law in order to close all businesses and the town's two banks for five days. During that time major depositors were urged to sign cards pledging not to withdraw their money from the local banks "until this present period of hysteria has fully subsided." Whispering campaigns against the banks were also quashed by Urbana's Emergency Committee. With the emotions of depositors back in check, Busey State Bank reopened to normal business.

Following the death of Matthew Busey, who had served as president for 44 years, he was succeeded by his

son Paul. The following year the son-in-law of Colonel Busey, Guy A. Tawney, a philosophy professor, was named chairman of the board. Under the new leadership team, the bank received its federal charter in 1945 and adopted the name Busey First National Bank. Control of the bank eventually passed to one of Samuel Busey's granddaughters, Catherine Jane Klassen, and her husband, James Klassen.

FAMILY TIES END: 1971

In 1971 the Busey family severed its ties to the bank when the Klassens sold their interest to Douglas C. Mills. A graduate of the University of Illinois, Mills had worked as a salesman for Mead Johnson & Co. before taking a position with American National Bank in Chicago. He was just 30 when he learned from Ms. Klassen that she and her husband were interested in selling their controlling interest in Busey Bank. Recognizing an opportunity, Mills turned to Chicago attorney Howard McKee, who owned a group of 20 banks, for advice. McKee became an investor and helped Mills to broker the deal. Also playing key roles were University of Illinois accounting professor and Mills's freshman counselor, Art Wyatt, and Martin Klingel, a life underwriter, who later acquired McKee's interest in Busey. The forbearance of his wife was of further importance, given that Mills would be giving up a good job in Chicago to move to Champaign-Urbana at a time when the couple had a one-year-old son to care for and a second child on the way. Despite the obstacles, the young Mills acquired control of the bank and continued the tradition established by the Busey family.

First Busey Corporation holding company was formed in 1980, and Busey Bank began to expand beyond community banking in the mid-1980s by adding financial service planning. It soon became apparent that customers wanted more than just advice, as was soon vividly demonstrated. One of the bank's financial planners recommended that a couple, both of whom were doctors, should purchase mutual funds as part of a strategy to manage their sizable income. The customers, who were ready to invest on the spot, learned that the bank did not actually have any mutual funds to offer. They were less than pleased that they would have to take further time out from their busy schedules to buy mutual funds elsewhere. As a result of this experience, Busey established its own brokerage subsidiary to offer mutual funds and other securities so that in 1986 it was able to field a full-service investment unit.

Busey expanded geographically in the 1990s under the leadership of P. David Kuhl, a 12-year veteran of the bank who became president in 1991. A pair of branches were added through the acquisition of CSF Holdings,

```
┌─────────────────────────────────────────────┐
│                                               │
│              KEY DATES                        │
│              ───────■───────                  │
│                                               │
│   1868:  Busey Brothers and Company is founded in │
│          Urbana, Illinois.                    │
│   1913:  Busey State Bank name is adopted following │
│          state charter.                       │
│   1945:  Federal charter leads to Busey First National │
│          Bank name.                           │
│   1971:  Busey family sells interest in bank. │
│   1980:  First Busey Corporation is formed.   │
│   1994:  Busey launches first web site.       │
│   1996:  Loan production office opens in Fort Myers, │
│          Florida.                             │
│   2001:  Busey subsidiary is renamed Busey Bank │
│          Florida.                             │
│   2007:  Main Street Trust, Inc., is acquired.│
│                                               │
└─────────────────────────────────────────────┘
```

Inc., in 1992, as well as deposits from the Bloomington, Normal, and Kankakee branches of the former Olympic Federal Savings, purchased from the Resolution Trust Corporation (which was charged with selling assets from institutions that folded during the savings and loan scandal of the 1980s). The Kankakee deposits were subsequently sold, this business secondary to Busey's plan to enter the Bloomington-Normal market. Deposits were also acquired from the Urbana and St. Joseph branches of American Savings Bank. A year later, Busey acquired Eagle Bank of Champaign County and Empire Capital Corporation in Illinois. During this time, Busey also looked to generate business beyond its backyard by opening a loan production office in Indianapolis.

FIRST WEB SITE: 1994

Kohl was the driving force behind Busey's early entry into Internet banking. The company developed its first web site in 1994. In his personal life Kohl was an early adopter of technology, but more importantly he was catering to his customer base. Busey served an area with a sophisticated clientele, the community home to large hospitals and the University of Illinois. It was at the school's supercomputer center, in fact, that the first true graphic interface for the Internet, Mosaic, was developed, the foundation for Netscape and the other Web browsers to follow. Unlike banks in other markets in which customers had to be prodded to consider on-line banking, Busey's customers at the University of Illinois were eager to bank electronically and urged Busey to proceed. In December 1996 Busey became one of the first banks in the world to allow customers to conduct

transactions on the Web, such as reviewing bank statements, transferring between accounts, and paying bills. Busey also created an online merchant mall, which was soon populated by the university bookstore, an area movie theater, a florist, and a law firm. Aside from the Internet, Busey embraced a variety of other delivery channels, including telephone bill payments, automated tellers, debit cards, and supermarket branches.

In the second half of the 1990s Busey bolstered its online banking capabilities, making the web site into a virtual branch of the bank. In 1999 it added an online budgeting tool that categorized a customer's transactions to help with budgeting as well as tax preparation. An electronic bill presentment and payment system was undergoing beta testing and would be added a year later. Other changes were made to the bank as well during this period. In February 1999 trust and securities services were brought together under one unit, Busey Investment, a move intended to eliminate customer as well as employee confusion about where to turn for investment services. The new unit primarily targeted high-net-worth individuals and institutions. Also in 1999 Busey completed an acquisition, paying $26.6 million in cash for Eagle BancGroup Inc. of Bloomington, Illinois, parent of First Federal Savings and Loan Association, which had $183 million in assets and operated four branches. In addition to local growth, Busey turned to Florida for fresh opportunities. Busey Bank Florida was formed and in 1996 a loan production office was opened in Fort Myers. A second loan office in southwest Florida followed in 1999, established in downtown Naples.

"VISION 2010"

In 2000 First Busey implemented a long-term strategy called "Vision 2010," its goal to increase assets to $5 billion by 2010. Much of the growth was achieved through external means. In June 2000 First Busey Securities acquired Bloomington, Illinois-based Secord Asset Management Inc. In that same month, newly acquired First Federal changed its name to Busey Bank fsb, which in November 2001 opened Busey's second branch in Fort Myers, Florida. In November 2001, Busey Bank fsb transferred its charter to Florida and became Busey Bank Florida, while its Illinois assets were consolidated with Busey Bank. Another important acquisition followed in 2004, when Busey acquired First Capital Bank of Peoria, Illinois, in a $42 million stock deal. First Capital was a community bank that found a comfortable fit with Busey, while its new corporate parent found the alliance favorable because it was eager to do business in Peoria, where First Capital maintained three offices, as well as a branch in Pekin, Illinois.

Busey searched further for strategic acquisitions. In February 2005 it strengthened its commitment to Florida by acquiring Tarpon Coast National Bank for $35.6 million in cash and stock. The Port Charlotte, Florida-based bank brought with it $375 million in assets and offices in Murdock, Punta Gorda, Englewood, and North Port, Florida, as well as a mortgage facility in Port Charlotte City Center. Busey did not neglect Illinois, however. In September 2006 it reached an agreement on a deal that would close the following year to acquire Main Street Trust, Inc., a longtime competitor whose markets, with the exception of Decatur, Illinois, overlapped. The Main Street name had been adopted in 2004 following the merger of First National Bank of Decatur, First Trust Bank of Shelbyville, and BankIllinois. A year later Main Street grew further by adding Citizens Savings Bank of Bloomington. As a result of the Main Street acquisition, First Busey grew its banking centers to 45. To help customers adjust to the name change for the new branches, Busey launched a branding strategy later in 2007, including a new logo and fresh signage.

Following the Main Street deal, Busey sought to integrate the operations and find efficiencies wherever possible. Trimming costs became especially important given the difficult economic conditions that were to trouble the company in 2008 when it posted a net loss of $37.9 million, much of that due to heavy losses in southwest Florida. Matters grew only worse in 2009 as the nation became enveloped in a banking crisis, leading to several branch closings for Busey and the postponement of plans for opening new branches. Nevertheless, First Busey remained well-capitalized. Its core earnings had held steady, and in all likelihood the company was poised to resume its pattern of strong growth as conditions improved.

Ed Dinger

PRINCIPAL SUBSIDIARIES

Busey Bank; Busey Bank, N.A.; Busey Wealth Management, Inc.; First Busey Statutory Trust II; First Busey Statutory Trust III; First Busey Statutory Trust IV; Millennium Properties, Inc.

PRINCIPAL COMPETITORS

First Midwest Bancorp, Inc.; JPMorgan Chase & Co.; The PNC Financial Services Group, Inc.

FURTHER READING

Bloom, Jennifer Kingson, "Community Banker Hurrying onto the Internet," *American Banker,* December 17, 1996, p. 1.

Dodson, Don, "Bank to Expand in Florida," *Champaign-Urbana (Ill.) News-Gazette,* February 25, 2005, p. C8.

———, "First Busey Corp Chairman Celebrates 35 Years with Company," *Champaign-Urbana (Ill.) News-Gazette,* March 29, 2006.

"How Two Towns Saved Their Banks," *Nation's Business,* May 1932, p. 80.

Lunt, Penny, "Controlled Hustle," *ABA Banking,* January 1995, p. 40.

Monahan, Julie, "Busey Bank's Know-How Propels Mutual Fund and Securities Sales," *American Banker,* October 25, 1994, p. 6A.

———, "First Busey Securities Getting Stronger with Age," *American Banker,* August 24, 2000, p. 14A.

Stewart, J. R., *A Standard History of Champaign County Illinois,* Chicago and New York: Lewis Publishing Company, 1918.

Szoke, Anita, "First Busey Corp. Will Buy First Capital Bank," *Peoria Journal Star,* January 7, 2004, p. B5.

FirstMerit Corporation

III Cascade Plaza
Akron, Ohio 44308
U.S.A.
Telephone: (330) 996-6300
Toll Free: (888) 554-4362
Fax: (330) 384-7133
Web site: http://www.firstmerit.com

Public Company
Incorporated: 1981 as First Bancorporation of Ohio
Employees: 2,575
Total Assets: $11.1 billion (2008)
Stock Exchanges: NASDAQ
Ticker Symbol: FMER
NAICS: 551111 Offices of Bank Holding Companies;
    522110 Commercial Banking

∎∎∎

FirstMerit Corporation is a diversified financial services company. Principal subsidiary First Merit Bank, N.A. operates 158 banking offices and 172 ATMs in Ohio and Western Pennsylvania counties. The bank primarily serves northeastern Ohio and holds the top spot in some Akron area markets. Major business lines include commercial, retail, and wealth. FirstMerit also engages in services such as insurance, brokerage, and equipment lease financing through non-banking direct and indirect subsidiaries.

COMBINATION: 1981–98

First Bancorporation of Ohio formed in 1981 via the combination of First National Bank of Akron and Old Phoenix National Bank of Medina. Through the decade and into the next, the financial institution embarked on a series of acquisitions and mergers of banks and banking offices in northeastern Ohio.

In the early 1990s, two bank subsidiaries formed. One provided lease financing and related services. The other was in response to the Community Reinvestment Act, which required banks to provide financing opportunities for low-to-moderate income communities and small businesses.

The holding company made its largest purchase to date in 1995, Canton-based CIVISTA Corporation. Its Citizens Savings bank merged with First National Bank of Massillon, a 1989 First Bancorporation acquisition. Reflecting the changes brought about through the decade-spanning acquisition drive, the $5.7 billion-asset company adopted a new name, FirstMerit Corporation. Subsidiary banks would use the FirstMerit name in conjunction with their own, bringing cohesion to marketing efforts.

Loosened restrictions on interstate banking had triggered a wave of bank mergers, resulting in ever larger financial entities by the mid-1990s. FirstMerit positioned itself as an alternative to corporate giants, as a bank with a small town feel, a *Knight Ridder/Tribune Business News* article explained. Regions were headed by a local president and retained decision-making authority.

FirstMerit diversified into life insurance and financial consulting with the acquisition of Abell & As-

COMPANY PERSPECTIVES

FirstMerit is a banking institution with roots reaching more than 160 years into Northeast Ohio history. Our community commitment and financial strength shows that from generation to generation, FirstMerit has been a vital force in the lives of our communities and our customers. It is our desire to continue that record of service and excellence long into the future.

sociates, in 1997. The next year, the company completed two more bank mergers. The first was with $602 million asset CoBancorp, based in Elyria, Ohio, southwest of Cleveland, and parent to Premier Bank.

The second 1998 merger, a $256 million stock deal for Security First Corporation, increased FirstMerit's market share in six of its 11 counties of operation, according to an *American Banker* report. The deal was considered somewhat expensive, but FirstMerit expected a quick bump in earnings and growth in fee-based revenues in 1999.

The merger produced side effects for some Security First employees. Job losses came with the elimination of branches and back office operations. Although the chairman of the acquired company was not among the job seekers, he was slated to come aboard to head a new residential construction division.

ONE TOO MANY: 1999–2003

Before the Security First deal had even closed, FirstMerit moved on to another. In August 1998, it announced its intention to buy 32-branch Signal Corp. for about $470 million in stock. The $1.9 billion-asset thrift operated as Signal Bank and Summit Bank in Ohio and as First Federal Savings Bank in western Pennsylvania and owned a mobile home finance company.

"This is an excellent strategic fit," Chairman and CEO John R. Cochran said in *American Banker*. "First-Merit will increase its dominance in several key northeast Ohio communities as well as gain a strong entrance to contiguous markets." The acquisition was completed in February 1999.

Cochran, a 28-year veteran of Norwest Corp., joined FirstMerit in 1995, enticing Sid A. Bostic, First-Merit president and CEO, and three other Norwest executives to follow. Cochran quickly put his sales skills to work at FirstMerit, expecting employees to follow

suit. Training and technology helped boost the number of products sold per day and per customer.

From 1996 to 1998, net climbed 26 percent and return on assets 18 percent, but as the 20th century wound down FirstMerit had a problem to clean up. In March 1999, the $9.1 billion-asset company announced it had increased charges related to the Signal deal by 52 percent, to $79 million, *American Banker* reported. The main culprit was the prefabricated housing operation.

Manufactured home sales slipped 6.5 percent in 1999, according to the Manufactured Housing Institute. The industry suffered from excess supply and an increasing number of repossessions. The prefab unit hurt First-Merit's stock price, but accounting rules placed a two-year prohibition on the sale of a subsidiary acquired through a pooling-of-interests transaction, according to *American Banker*. FirstMerit ceased originating manufactured housing loans in 2001. Two years later, Warren Buffett's Berkshire Hathaway Inc. acquired the remaining loan portfolio.

Meanwhile, FirstMerit shareholders, by way of the First National Bank of Massillon acquisition, urged the board to consider selling or merging with another bank to drive up the lagging stock price. The company opposed the proposal. Lehman Brothers analyst Brock Vandervliet told *Crain's Cleveland Business* that the banking industry in general had been challenged by a series of interest rate hikes. The Federal Reserve's action "between June 1999 and June 2000 compressed what's commonly referred to as the 'spread income' earned from making loans," Josh Cable wrote. FirstMerit's balance sheet suffered as a result.

Net income fell from $159.8 million in 2000 to $116.3 million in 2001. Earnings rebounded in 2002 only to drop again the following year. Net charge-offs, meanwhile, doubled from 2001 to 2002, and reached $127 million in 2003.

REGROUPING: 2004–07

As 2004 progressed, FirstMerit saw improvement in its commercial lending although the consumer and small business segment lagged behind. Earlier growth had been generated through purchases: 13 between 1981 and 1999. At this point, however, the $10.5 billion-asset company was in no position to make an acquisition. On the contrary, *Inside Business*'s Sara Lepro noted low earnings placed FirstMerit in the opposite position, as a potential takeover target of some cash-rich European bank or an in-state competitor.

FirstMerit worked to strengthen itself so that would not happen. The company implemented more loan

---

KEY DATES

1981: Bank holding company First Bancorporation of Ohio is formed.

1995: Company completes its largest acquisition to date and changes its name.

1997: FirstMerit Corporation broadens its lines of business.

1999: Acquisition of Signal Corp. caps off a string of purchases.

2001: Company ceases origination of manufactured housing loans.

2003: Remaining prefab loan portfolio, acquired with Signal Corp., is sold.

2006: New CEO Paul Greig tackles FirstMerit's credit quality.

2008: Financial institution turns a profit as others in the nation falter.

2009: FirstMerit repurchases preferred stock and warrant sold to U.S. Department of Treasury.

---

generation oversight in its eight regions, especially on smaller commercial loans. Loans were limited to its market footprint. Stricter guidelines were set in place on startup lending. Net charge-offs dropped by more than half for 2004.

In addition to improving credit quality, FirstMerit continued its effort to boost revenue. Branches were built at a faster rate. More commercial and small business bankers were hired. One call center was created to handle routine tasks and another for retail marketing. The bank also went after smaller trust accounts, those overlooked by larger competitors, Ben Jackson reported for *American Banker.* Finally, FirstMerit tackled inefficiencies: linking pay to performance, implementing peak time scheduling, and using technology to reduce and also monitor employees.

Paul G. Greig succeeded John Cochran as CEO in May 2006 and put the credit quality issue at the top of his list, selling off tens of millions in troubled loans. "There really is a strong core bank, and when we get the credit completely fixed, we certainly have the opportunity to be one of the top performers in our peer group," Greig told *American Banker* in June 2007. "Credit-quality improvement is the biggest driver in improving the bank." Greig previously headed the Royal Bank of Scotland Group PLC's Charter One Financial Inc. in Illinois.

The new CEO moved FirstMerit from a geographic alignment to business-line structure and "now he meets weekly with each business head," Tim Mazzucca wrote. He improved loan oversight by adding branch managers. Previously, none of the 160 branches had one. Among the other changes Greig implemented, incentive compensation was tied to credit quality improvement.

Greig also pushed for more sales of wealth and investment services to commercial customers, according to *Crain's Cleveland Business.* In turn, he expected regional CEOs to bring in more commercial business. Branch jobs were eliminated, in response to an increased use of online, telephone, and ATM banking by customers.

RECOVERY: 2008–09

In October 2008, FirstMerit was among the nation's banks considering taking part in the Troubled Asset Relief Program (TARP). "We have been encouraged by our regulators to participate in the program," Greig said in a *McClatchy-Tribune Business News* article. The Emergency Economic Stabilization Act and its $250 billion Capital Purchase Program was intended to shore up the country's financial system, undermined by a deluge of bad investments in the mortgage market. The government hoped a capital infusion into the badly shaken banking system would get credit and loans moving again.

FirstMerit completed the sale of $125 million newly issued non-voting preferred shares of stock to the U.S. Department of Treasury on January 9, 2009. Later in the month, the company reported 2008 year-end profits of $119.5 million. Although earnings fell from $123 million the prior year, FirstMerit maintained profitability while others in the industry floundered.

Greig told shareholders at the annual meeting that FirstMerit had "dodged" four risk areas plaguing others in the industry. In addition to selling off troubled loans in 2007, the company had sold its Fannie Mae and Freddie Mac stock in early 2008, prior to their bankruptcy. The company also had reduced its residential construction portfolio before that sector collapsed and had passed altogether on subprime lending, according to *McClatchy-Tribune Business News.*

Greig's compensation for the year climbed 22 percent to $3.7 million, based on an Associated Press news service formula. The *Akron Beacon Journal* added that an employee 401(k) saving plan match had been suspended and a stock purchase plan was eliminated, as were some workers. "Greig has said the cuts were made to offset the impact of a substantial increase in the bank's Federal Deposit Insurance Corp. premium by $10 million in 2009," Betty Lin-Fisher wrote.

In the spring of 2009, FirstMerit repurchased all the preferred non-voting stock and the warrant to purchase common stock issued to the Treasury Department, as part of the Capital Purchase Program. The company had conducted its own "stress test" in conjunction with a third party, prior to opting out of the program, according to *McClatchy-Tribune Business News.* Greig said the move would reduce the related dividend expense and assure shareholders of FirstMerit's capital strength.

Kathleen Peippo

PRINCIPAL SUBSIDIARIES

FirstMerit Bank, N.A.; FirstMerit Mortgage Corporation; FirstMerit Title Agency, Ltd.; FirstMerit Community Development Corporation.

PRINCIPAL COMPETITORS

Fifth Third Bancorp; KeyCorp; PNC Financial Services Group, Inc.; U. S. Bancorp; Huntington Bancshares Incorporated.

FURTHER READING

Adams, David, "Ohio's FirstMerit Bank's Message Is, Bigger Is Not Better," *American Banker,* July 2, 1995, p. 7.

Bergquist, Erick, "Buffett Buys: Positive Signs for Pre-Fab?" *American Banker,* December 3, 2003, p. 1.

Cable, Josh, "Family of Investors Wants FirstMerit to Consider a Sale," *Crain's Cleveland Business,* March 26, 2001, p. 26.

Chase, Brett, "FirstMerit in $256M Deal for Cleveland-Area Thrift," *American Banker,* April 7, 1998, p. 28.

———, "Ohio's FirstMerit Buying Signal in 2nd In-State Deal in 4 Months," *American Banker,* August 12, 1998, p. 5.

Gjertsen, Lee Ann, "FirstMerit Expands Alliance Strategy Online," *American Banker,* August 22, 2002, p. 5.

Irwin, Gloria, "FirstMerit Shaves 221 Jobs: Bank Reduces Branch Positions Companywide As Part of Restructuring Efforts," *Akron Beacon Journal,* July 25, 2006.

Jackson, Ben, "FirstMerit: Better Underwriting Will Provide '05 Boost," *American Banker,* February 24, 2005, p. 4.

Kass, Arielle, "FirstMerit's Stress Test Impetus for TARP Payoff," *Crain's Cleveland Business,* May 4–10, 2009.

———, "A New Reality for FirstMerit," *Crain's Cleveland Business,* November 24–30, 2008.

Lepro, Sara, "Shark or Bait? How John Cochran Has FirstMerit Swimming Hard to Stay Ahead," *Inside Business,* July 2004, pp. 36+.

Lin-Fisher, Betty, "FirstMerit Dodges Housing Mess, CEO Says," *McClatchy-Tribune Business News,* April 16, 2009.

———, "FirstMerit Reports Profit, Though It's Down from '08," *Akron Beacon Journal,* April 28, 2009.

———, "FirstMerit Reports Profits in Fourth Quarter: Akron Bank's Net Income Is Down, but It's Doing Better Than Many Competitors," *Akron Beacon Journal,* January 27, 2009.

———, "FirstMerit to Return Aid: Akron Bank Says It Won't Need U.S. Funds to Bolster Capital," *McClatchy-Tribune Business News,* April 17, 2009.

———, "FirstMerit's Executives Get Raises," *Akron Beacon Journal,* March 10, 2009.

Lutton, Laura Pavlenko, "FirstMerit Takes Its Cues on Sales from Chief Exec," *American Banker,* March 30, 1999, p. 8.

Mackinnon, Jim, "FirstMerit Considers Federal Equity Stake: Government Would Invest Up to $250 Million in Bank," *McClatchy-Tribune Business News,* October 29, 2008.

Mazzucca, Tim, "A Progress Report on FirstMerit," *American Banker,* June 19, 2007, p. 1.

Padgett, Tania, "GreenPoint, FirstMerit Stock Hit by News Big Rival Would Quit Prefab Loan Business," *American Banker,* February 11, 2000, p. 1.

"Roundup: Ohio's 1st Bancorp Changes Name to FirstMerit," *American Banker,* March 6, 1995, p. 8.

Turner, Shawn A., "FirstMerit's Top Executive Turns Around Credit Quality," *Crain's Cleveland Business,* October 15, 2007, p. 3.

FISKARS

Fiskars Corporation

Mannerheimintie 14 A
P.O. Box 235
Helsinki, 00101
Finland
Telephone: (+358 9) 618 861
Fax: (+358 9) 604 053
Web site: http://www.fiskars.fi

Public Company
Founded: 1649 as Fiskars Ironworks
Employees: 4,119
Sales: $982.4 million (2008)
Stock Exchanges: NASDAQ OMX Helsinki
Ticker Symbols: FISAS (Series A); FISKS (Series K)
NAICS: 551112 Offices of Other Holding Companies;
332312 Fabricated Structural Metal Manufacturing;
326299 All Other Rubber Product Manufacturing;
326199 All Other Plastics Product Manufacturing;
332211 Cutlery and Flatware (Except Precious)
Manufacturing; 332212 Hand and Edge Tool
Manufacturing

■ ■ ■

Fiskars Corporation, headquartered in Helsinki, Finland, is one of the oldest companies in the western world, having been established as Fiskars Ironworks in 1649 and in continuous operation since then. Even during its involvement in several wars between Sweden and Russia, Fiskars gained a reputation as one of the finest iron and copperworks in the north. In the 1830s, the company expanded its knifeworks, manufactured forks and scissors, established Finland's first machine shop, and manufactured the first Finnish steam engine. After surviving the ravages of two world wars, Fiskars gradually became the world's leading manufacturer of scissors and of other cutting products for home, school, and office; produced lawn and garden accessories; and made products for craft and outdoor-recreation activities.

The company's main focus is on consumer products that represent the majority of its sales. Fiskars is organized into four main business areas. The company's Home business (45% of sales), focuses on kitchen, home, and interior design products. The Garden business (33%) offers a leading portfolio of garden cutting tools. The Outdoor business (21%) produces boats, as well as camping, fishing, hunting, and navigation equipment. Finally, Fiskars's Other business (1%) includes its Real Estate operation, which is responsible for managing the corporation's properties and related services.

INDUSTRY BACKGROUND

Finland's experience as an iron producing area dates back to the Iron Age (circa 600–800 B.C.). In the early Middle Ages, Finland was still a sparsely populated, remote country where the inhabitants farmed and also made pig iron from the ore gathered from their country's lakes and bogs. In the 12th century, Finland, which had remained relatively isolated from Western Europe, was annexed to Sweden and then began to evolve in the trading and the mining industries. During the reign of King Gustavus Vasa of Sweden-Finland, the first iron mine was opened at Ojamo in Lohja, Finland, in 1538–40. About 20 years later, the king set up a simple bar-iron shop which used ore from the Ojamo mine. Sweden had become an important exporter of iron ore to Europe.

Early in the 17th century, under the reign of King Gustavus II Adolphus, Sweden-Finland became a great power and was a major producer of iron. However, Sweden's participation in the Thirty Years' War—fought on political and religious issues among the Germans, Swedish, French and Spanish, and ending in 1648—delved deeply into the Swedish kingdom's resources. The abundance of Finland's unharnessed water power and, especially, its immense forest resources for charcoal production (charcoal was made by burning wood in kilns) made it feasible to found ironworks in that country. Furthermore, private merchants, as well as the Crown, were allowed to develop the iron trade. Between 1616 and 1649, ironworks were established in Mustio, Antskog, Bilmas, Fagervik, and Fiskars, all located in, or close to, the parish of Pohja, which became the center of the Finnish iron industry. According to the Fiskars' company history *Fiskars 1649: 350 Years of Finnish Industrial History,* "the term *ironworks* referred to industrial establishments that had received official permits for such things as pig-iron works, blast furnaces and other installations which concentrated mainly on refining iron ore and processing iron."

In 1649 Peter Thorwöste, an immigrant from Holland, acquired Antskog ironworks. He received permission to mine iron ore from the Ojamo mine and to manufacture cast iron and forged products, with the exception of cannons. Thorwöste also gained a permit to set up a blast furnace and bar hammer in Fiskars Village, in western Finland. Thus, Fiskars Iron Works came into being. Mining ore in Finland soon proved to be unprofitable; therefore iron ore was imported from the Uto mine in the Stockholm archipelago.

Among the items that Fiskars Ironworks produced were nails, wire, knives, hoes, reinforced wheels from pig iron, and cast-iron products including pots and frying pans. The finished products were sent via Pohjankuru either to Stockholm or to the southern provinces along the Gulf of Finland. Bar iron was exported to Sweden and sold at Stockholm's Iron Market. In 1656, according to *350 Years,* the Fiskars and Antskog ironworks had a workforce of 54, who were paid in cash and in goods. Employees included a master builder, a furnace supervisor, and 16 smiths. The peasants engaged by the ironworks worked 1.5 days a week.

1700–1900: FAMINE, WARS, AUTONOMY UNDER RUSSIA, NEW IDEAS

The last years of the 17th century brought famine to Sweden-Finland; the country was reduced to poverty and no longer enjoyed the unity brought about by King Gustavus Vasa. The famine claimed the lives of one-third of Finland's 500,000 inhabitants. The Russians began to ravage the Finnish coast in 1700, at the beginning of the Great Northern War that did not end until 1721. By that time, many Fiskars' workers were dead, and Sweden-Finland was no longer a powerful country. The new great power was in Russia and at St. Petersburg, the capital city. After the war, while the Finns could not finance the revival of their ironworks, wealthy men from Stockholm invested money in Finnish ironworks and recruited workers from abroad. In 1740, there were only 115 inhabitants in Fiskars Village.

As economic and cultural activity slowly revived, merchant shipping increased on the Baltic Sea and elsewhere. James Watts's invention of the steam engine offered new hope for industry, and coke could be used to replace the labor-intensive making of charcoal. Copper ore was discovered in the Orijarvi area, and Fiskars began to refine copper as well as iron. In 1783 Bengt Magnus Björkman acquired both the Fiskars and the Antskog ironworks. Fiskars' coppersmiths continued to forge artistically crafted utensils well into the 19th century.

In 1808 war broke out again between Russia and Sweden with the result that Finland was ceded to Russia and became an autonomous Grand Duchy with the status of a distinct nation. Bengt Ludvig Björkman, son of Bengt Magnus, moved to Finland and took over the management of the Fiskars, Antskog, and Doski ironworks. Problems with the availability of iron ore and with former trading relations, combined with Bengt Ludvig's option for a life of luxury, led to Fiskars being sold to Finnish Johan Jacob Julin. Fiskars had closed down its blast furnace in 1802, so what Johan Julin took over was really a copperworks rather than an ironworks.

Julin sought knowledge not only for himself but for others. He had a school built so that all children, even those who were working, could be educated. He participated in founding the first savings bank in

KEY DATES

1649: Peter Thorwöste establishes the Fiskars Ironworks.

1783: Bengt Magnus Björkman acquires Fiskars Ironworks and Finland's first copper mine at Orijarvi.

1809: Finland is ceded to Russia and granted status as a distinct nation; Bengt Ludvig Björkman, son of Bengt Magnus, takes over management of the Fiskars, Antskog, and Doski ironworks.

1822: Johan Jacob Julin buys Fiskars Ironworks and inaugurates one of the most progressive periods in the history of Finland's ironworks.

1837: Julin begins construction of Finland's first engineering workshop.

1883: Fiskars Ironworks becomes a joint-stock limited liability company and is renamed Fiskars Aktiebolag-osakeyhtio.

1917: Finland declares its independence from Russia.

1920s: Fiskars expands and modernizes.

1960: Company manufactures the first Finnish microwave oven.

1967: World's first scissors with plastic handles are introduced.

1978: Fiskars establishes scissors manufacturing in the United States.

1980: Company withdraws from the traditional iron and steel industry.

1999: Fiskars celebrates its 350th anniversary.

2004: Wartsila Corp. becomes an associated company.

2006: Subsidiary Fiskars Brands announces plans to eliminate 430 jobs in the United States, as part of a strategy to shift some production to Asia.

2009: Fiskars reveals plans to acquire Agrofin OY AB, its largest single shareholder.

Finland and created a model farm in Fiskars Village, where crop rotation was practiced. Intending to shift the emphasis from refining of iron ore to the refining of iron, he traveled extensively in Sweden and Britain to gather information on fine iron forging, among other things. A forge was completed on the upper Fiskars River rapids in 1836. Although the ironworks used most of the forge's products, household utensils were also made at the forge. Furthermore, the Fiskars forge became famous for what was considered an extraordinary achievement at that time: 90 cast-iron columns and a large waterwheel were built for the Finlayson cotton mill in Tampere in 1837. The waterwheel's diameter measured more than six feet and did not have a match in all of Europe.

In 1837 Julin began construction of Finland's first machine workshop. The following year, the workshop produced the first steamship engine for the SS *Helsingfors,* the first Finnish steamship. In 1849 Julin was elevated to the rank of nobleman.

During the winter of 1851, the SS *Majava* ("the Beaver") was built on the ice in Pohjankuru harbor from finished components transported by horse and sleigh from the Fiskars machine shop. The ship was "automatically launched," so to speak, when the ice melted in the spring. Other products of the machine workshop included the iron gate and bridge structure for the Saimaa Canal; blowers; warm air generators; and agricultural equipment (such as plows, chaff rakes, and sowing machinery).

The Industrial Revolution accelerated industrial and economic development in Europe; Fiskars' skilled workmen established the ironworks' reputation of being the finest iron and copperworks in the north. The ironworks not only expanded its manufacture of knives, forks, and scissors but also contributed to the development of Finnish agriculture. Various plows (ploughs) were imported for experiments, and then a plow especially suitable for Finnish soil was created. According to *350 Years,* "Ploughs became the ironworks' most important line of products. At the 1860 St. Petersburg exhibition, Fiskars' wooden plough won an award. By 1891 the ironworks was producing 11 different ploughs, and by the end of the century the range had been extended to 40 models. In all, over a million horse-drawn ploughs were made."

Johan Jacob von Julin died in 1853, and a guardianship administration, known as the "Ironworks Company John von Julin," was established to manage Fiskars Ironworks. However, power gradually became consolidated in the hands of Emil Lindsay von Julin. Furthermore, the company began experiencing financial problems, lacking adequate operating capital. As part of its recovery plan, Fiskars became a limited liability company, known as Fiskars Aktiebolag-osakeyhtio, with a share capital of FIM 1 million.

A railway line built between Helsinki and St. Petersburg offered additional opportunities for trade between Finland and Russia. In fact, Fiskars' continuing profitability was partly due to the fact that about half of the exports went to Russia. At the St. Petersburg's

Exhibit in 1860, Fiskars received its first recorded recognition of a product: an award for a new horse-drawn plow. During the last decades of the 1800s the company invested in additional equipment for the ironworks. For example, Fiskars acquired the Åminnefors works and began to use a Siemens-Martin furnace built in 1887, the third of its kind in Finland. In a bankruptcy sale, Fiskars bought the Åminnefors rolling mill, which had four puddling furnaces, two welding furnaces, and a brick-built outdoor kiln for drying wood. In 1894 there were 250 employees working at the ironworks; the entire community consisted of about 1,050 inhabitants.

1900–76: TWO WORLD WARS, INDEPENDENCE, STRIKES, REORGANIZATION

Initially, World War I increased orders from Russia; however, when the Bolsheviks seized power, the upheaval had strong repercussions in Finland. In December 1917 Finland issued its Declaration of Independence, and the ensuing civil war and loss of the Russian market upset its economy. To compensate, Fiskars targeted the newly independent Baltic states and tried to win a larger share of the Western Europe market. After World War I, Fiskars began to expand and to modernize its operation. The rolling mill was renovated; better steel-refining methods were developed; and Fiskars founded Finland's first metal spring factory. The company acquired the Inha ironworks in Ähtäri, Oy Ferraría Ab with its plants in Jokioinen, Loimaa, and Pero on the Karalian Isthmus, and several other companies.

In 1930, worldwide economic depression halted Fiskars' expansion. Although an upward trend soon followed, involvement in World War II made Finland pay dearly in human lives, virtually wiped out trade, and stalled production for the domestic market until 1948. The end of the war and the signing of a peace treaty with the Soviet Union helped Finland on the road to recovery. Specifically, postwar demands by the Soviet Union generated much business for the metal industry. However, in 1956, as Finnish leader Urho Kekkonen began his 26-year presidency, a general strike practically paralyzed every field of industry; inflation and devaluations would continue into the early 1990s, while a strike in 1971 led to the closing of the Fiskars plant for several weeks.

During such challenging economic times, diversification seemed imperative. Fiskars at first had a moderate degree of success with new product exports and new designs. For example, the company was one of the first in Europe to produce the microwave oven in 1965, and the company also began a foray into plastic tableware in 1962.

Also during this time, a product was introduced for which Fiskars would gain its greatest notoriety, at least in the United States. Through experiments with strip stainless steel and injection-molded plastics, Fiskars engineer Olaf Backstrom reportedly designed the world's first lightweight "classic scissors" with orange plastic handles. The design was as artistic as it was functional. The scissors were later included in the Design Collection of the Museum of Modern Art in New York and in the Philadelphia Museum of Art. A few years after their introduction in the Finnish market, the scissors were spotted by representatives from Normark, a U.S. company that had distribution rights to Rapala lures, also manufactured in Finland. Normark obtained distribution rights to market the scissors in the United States, where they would quickly find an appreciative audience.

In the early 1960s Fiskars had set out to expand by means of takeovers. However, this expansion program, too broad in scope, was eroding the company's profits, and Fiskars soon found itself in need of focus and restructure. Toward that end, Fiskars sold some of its land and, more importantly, divested its original steelmaking business, which it sold to Ovako Oy Ab, thereby safeguarding its supplies of raw materials and boosting profits.

Under the tenure of Gorman J. Ehrnrooth, chairman of the board, Fiskars completed its restructuring, with a strategy based on new products, new markets, and acquisitions based on competencies. To ensure its success as an international company, Fiskars focused on the United States, as it had the world's strongest economy and, according to *350 Years,* could provide "a foundation for internationalization, as well as a good location for expansion and also for gaining valuable experience."

1977–2000: FISKARS' CUTTING EDGE

In 1977 Fiskars established a scissors plant in Wausau, Wisconsin, and then acquired several consumer-oriented companies, such as Wallace Manufacturing Co., Gerber Legendary Blades, and Coltellerie Montana. Gradually, scissors became a profitable product line that appealed to consumers around the world. Over the next 20 years, Fiskars would come to function well as a business corporation structured in three business units—The Consumer Products Group (CPG), Inha Works Ltd., and the Real Estate Group—and made judicious acquisitions of companies that strengthened these units.

The Consumer Products Group (CPG), the largest business unit, was headquartered in Madison, Wisconsin, and managed the consumer business worldwide through offices in North America and most of the European countries, including an office and manufacturing facility in Fiskars Village. In 1996, CPG accounted for the largest share, about 89 percent, of the parent company's $461 million in revenues. This group concentrated its activities on the manufacture, sale, and distribution of three primary families of products; scissors and other housewares products; outdoor recreation products; and lawn and garden products. "We're very decentralized," CPG Vice-President Roy Prestage told Judy Newman of the *Wisconsin Business Journal.* "We keep decision-making close to the marketplace so we can respond quickly to its needs," Prestage explained. A case in point was Fiskars' Softouch Scissors, with their oversized, cushioned gray handles operated by squeezing the whole hand. The new scissors were developed when market studies showed that people with arthritis found regular scissors too painful to use. Moreover, the company applied the "whole hand" technology to a line of garden tools. "Ergonomics is what we're about," commented James Woodside, another CPG vice-president.

Fiskars bolstered CPG operations in the late 1990s with acquisitions: Aquapore Moisture Systems, Inc., which manufactured garden irrigation products; Enviro-Works, Inc., a manufacturer of portable shade structure and plastic-resin flower pots; Werga-Tools GmbH, a German distribution company in the lawn and garden products market; and Vikingate Ltd., a British company specializing in propagators and plastic flower pots. Research and development remained vital at CPG and in its new subsidiaries; Aquapore, for example, recycled automobile tires to make crushed-rubber mats, which were then used in gardens to prevent weed growth, as decorative garden stepping stones, and in rubber lawn edgings. In 1999 Fiskars acquired three additional companies that manufactured lawn and garden products: Richard Sankey & Sons Ltd., which made plastic pots similar to those made by EnviroWorks; American Designer Pottery L.P., which produced large decorative plastic pots; and Syroco Inc., a leading U.S. manufacturer of resin outdoor furniture. As a result of all these acquisitions, the Lawn and Garden Group became the largest business category in the Fiskars CPG division.

The second product group at Fiskars was represented by Inha Works, Ltd., headquartered in Ähtäri, Finland, founded in 1841, and part of Fiskars since 1917. Inha was the leading manufacturer of aluminum boats for professional and leisure use in northern Europe. The company also forged products and building components, such as hinges for the door and window industry and special-purpose radiators for humid rooms, distributed mainly to the Nordic market. Inha's principal forged products consisted of rail fasteners that were sold mainly to Finnish, Swedish, and Norwegian railways under long-term supply agreements. According to Fiskars' 1998 annual report, Inha's "customer-driven product development, innovative models, and continuous improvement of production processes strengthened the position of the "Buster" [brand name] as the leading outboard boat in Scandinavia."

The Real Estate Group, headquartered in Fiskars, managed the corporation's 15,000 hectares (37,050 acres) of real estate properties and related properties. The land holdings, situated in southwest Finland, were a valuable corporate asset that included some 100 lakes and 250 kilometers of shoreline. A 1998 agreement with the environmental authorities resulted in the designation of 100 hectares for the protection of the old-growth forest in this area. The major part (11,000 hectares) of the real estate was located in and around Fiskars Village. According to long-term plans, only environment-friendly forestry and farming were allowed; wood had to be harvested in a way that assured a good balance between the requirements of forest regeneration and the needs of the wood-processing industry. In order to preserve the Fiskars village as a lively historical industrial community, revenues from real estate operations were applied to maintenance of the buildings and surrounding landscape.

2000–05: A NEW MILLENNIUM BEGINS

Fiskars ushered in the new millennium as a strong, international enterprise based on providing innovative solutions to the needs of consumers. As its corporate vision statement intimated, the company remained "embedded in the soil of its old ironworks community" as it opened its strong business wings all over the world.

Despite its organizational strength, Fiskars' profits were hindered by recessionary conditions during the early 2000s. Business was especially sluggish in the United States. In 2001 the company's net sales fell 7 percent, totaling EUR 762 million. Net sales declined another 5 percent in 2002, as a result of a weakened U.S. dollar. However, Fiskars saw its operating profit jump 120 percent that year, reaching EUR 27.9 million.

Several noteworthy developments occurred during the early 2000s. In May 2002, Fiskars settled a patent infringement lawsuit with competitor Acme United Corp., which had violated the company's patent for easy grip scissors. Early the following year, news surfaced that

President and CEO Bertel Langenskioeld had accepted an offer to become president of Metso Corp.'s rock and mineral processing operation, Metso Minerals.

Growth continued as Fiskars approached mid-decade. In early 2004 the company's Fiskars Brands Inc. subsidiary acquired CMG, which manufactured light-emitting portable outdoor products. The deal allowed Fiskars Brands to bolster its Outdoor Recreation business. In April, the Swedish company Investor AB sold its 8.6 percent stake in Fiskars. At the same time, Fiskars increased its investment in Wartsila Corp. so that it controlled 21.2 percent of the company's shares, as well as 28.7 percent of the votes. In addition, Fiskars added Wartsila to its financial statements as an associated company.

A number of important developments unfolded at Fiskars Brands in late 2004. In September, the company sold its Syroco division, which manufactured resin-based furniture and home decorations, to Puerto Rico-based Vassallo Industries Inc. That same month, President and CEO Bill Denton announced his retirement, effective in October. Chief Operating Officer Jim Purdin was named as his replacement, presiding over an operation that included some 3,500 employees and net sales of $700 million.

Fiskars started off 2005 on a high note when Chief Information Officer Herman Nell was named one of the world's Premier 100 IT Leaders by *Computerworld* magazine from a pool of 600 nominees. Around the same time, Fiskars Brands acquired Greensboro, North Carolina-based Gingher Inc., a high-end scissors manufacturer. Another acquisition occurred in the fall when Fiskars Brands acquired the Geneva, Illinois-based folding utility knife manufacturer Superknife, bolstering its Outdoor Recreation Division and Gerber Legendary Blades business.

2006–09: ORGANIZATIONAL CHANGES

In mid-2006 Fiskars Brands announced plans to eliminate 430 jobs in the United States, as part of a strategy to shift some production to China, Taiwan, and other countries in Asia. Specifically, the company planned to shutter its plants in Wausau and Spencer, Wisconsin, which employed about 300 people. In addition, a rubber floor mat manufacturing operation in Georgia, as well as a soaker hose business in Arizona, also were targeted for closure. By this time Fiskars Brands employed a workforce of approximately 3,000 people at 25 sites worldwide.

It also was in mid-2006 that Fiskars Brands announced plans to sell its Minnesota-based Power Sentry business, which manufactured consumer electronics accessories, to Royal Philips Electronics. In September, Fiskars agreed to acquire Silva Group, a Swedish manufacturer of binoculars, compasses, and headlamps. The deal included a Silva subsidiary in the United States named The Brunton Co.

Growth continued in 2007, when Fiskars agreed to acquire the tabletop company Littala Group PLC in an estimated $313 million deal with ABN AMRO Capital. For the year, net sales totaled EUR 647 million, up from EUR 530 million in 2006. Operating profits totaled EUR 106.9 million that year, up from EUR 85.8 million in 2006.

Heading into 2008, Fiskars employed a workforce of about 4,500 people. That year, the company's sales increased again, reaching EUR 697 million. However, operating profits fell to EUR 70.9 million. In April 2009 Fiskars announced that it was acquiring Agrofin OY AB, its largest single shareholder, in a transaction that would result in the merger of both organizations. A special milestone was reached in 2009, when the company celebrated its 360th anniversary. Approaching the 21st century's second decade, Fiskars remained the oldest company in Finland, and seemed well-positioned for continued success.

Gloria A. Lemieux
Updated, Paul R. Greenland

PRINCIPAL SUBSIDIARIES

Alterra Holdings Corp. (USA); Alterra Management Services Corp. (USA); Aquapore Moisture Systems Inc. (USA); EnviroWorks Inc. (USA); Ferraria Oy Ab; Finlandia Cutlery Pvt. Ltd. (India; 24%); Fiskars (Australia) Pty Limited; Fiskars AB (Sweden); Fiskars Brands Inc. (USA); Fiskars Canada Inc.; Fiskars Consumer Europe ApS (Denmark); Fiskars Consumer Holding AB (Sweden); Fiskars Consumer Holding AS (Norway); Fiskars Consumer Holding GmbH (Germany); Fiskars Consumer Oy Ab; Fiskars Consumer Products Europe SPRL (Belgium); Fiskars Danmark A/S (Denmark); Fiskars de Mexico, S.A. de C.V.; Fiskars Deutschland GmbH (Germany); Fiskars Europe Holding GmbH (Germany); Fiskars GmbH & Co. KG (Germany); Fiskars France S.A.R.L.; Fiskars Hungary Ltd.; Fiskars India Limited (29.9%); Fiskars Montana S.r.l. (Italy); Fiskars Norge AS (Norway); Fiskars Poland Ltd.; Fiskars Servicios S.A. de C.V. (Mexico); Fiskars Sverige AB (Sweden); Fiskars UK Limited (UK); Hangon Sahko Oy (93.2%); Inha Works Ltd.; Puntomex International S.A. de C.V. (Mexico); Richard Sankey & Son Limited (UK); Royal Rubber & Manufacturing Co. (USA); Vikingate Limited (UK); Werga-Tools GmbH (Germany); ZAO Baltic Tool (Russia).

PRINCIPAL OPERATING UNITS

Americas; EMEA; Wärtsilä Corp.; Other.

PRINCIPAL COMPETITORS

Acme United Corp.; Esselte Corp.; Newell Rubbermaid Inc.

FURTHER READING

"Bill Denton, President & CEO of Fiskars Brands, Inc., Announces Retirement," *PR Newswire,* September 22, 2004.

"Board of Directors Proposes a Combination of Share Series and a Merger of Agrofin OY AB into Fiskars," Helsinki, Finland: Fiskars Corp., April 15, 2009.

"Fiskars Corporation Increases Holding in Wartsila Corporation," *Nordic Business Report,* April 1, 2004.

"Fiskars: Finland's Gateway to the World," *Focus,* January 1999.

Fiskars 1649: 350 Years of Finnish Industrial History, Pohja, Finland: Fiskars Oyj Abp, 1999, 84 p.

Hajewski, Doris, "Scissors-Maker Fiskars Will Cut 300 State Jobs: Madison Firm's Production Will Move to Asian Nations," *Milwaukee Journal Sentinel,* May 3, 2006.

Newman, Judy, "Finnish Firm Fiskars Grows with Expanded Product Line, Acquisitions," *Wisconsin State Journal,* February 27, 1997.

4imprint Group PLC

7-8 Market Place
London, W1W 8AG
United Kingdom
Telephone: (+44 020) 7299 7201
Fax: (+44 020) 7299 7209
Web site: http://www.4imprint.co.uk

Public Company
Incorporated: 1826 as Bemrose & Company
Employees: 991
Sales: £168.9 million ($214.2 million) (2008)
Stock Exchanges: London
Ticker Symbol: FOUR
NAICS: 339950 Sign Manufacturing; 541870 Advertising Material Distribution Services

■ ■ ■

4imprint Group PLC is one of the global top four producers and distributors of corporate catalogs and promotional products. 4imprint operates across three main divisions: Direct Marketing, End User, and Trade. The Direct Marketing division is the largest, accounting for 58 percent of the company's total revenues of £169 million in 2008. This division, which is primarily active through its base in Oshkosh, Wisconsin, is the U.S. leader in the production and distribution of corporate promotional catalogs, and a leading provider of Internet-based direct-marketing services as well. In 2007, 4imprint created a dedicated direct-marketing unit, based in Manchester, for its U.K. operations, which is expected to serve as a base for a European-wide rollout

in the next decade. The End User division, which accounted for 32.5 percent of group sales, is responsible for the production and distribution of corporate promotional products. This division comprises three subsidiaries, Brand Addition, the largest, based in Manchester and focused on the U.K. market; Product Plus International, based in London and Hong Kong, which focuses on the premium gifts sector; and Kreyer, based in Hagen, Germany, which works in cooperation with Brand Addition to serve the European continent. The End User division targets large corporate clients. 4imprint's smallest division is the Trade division. This division manufactures and prints promotional items, and also provides sourcing and distribution services. The division operates primarily through SPS (EU) Ltd., one of the United Kingdom's leaders in this segment. 4imprint is listed on the London Stock Exchange. The company does not have a group chief executive; instead, each division is led by its own chief executive officer, with overall direction guided by an executive chairman, Ken Minton.

RAILWAY SCHEDULES IN THE 19TH CENTURY

4imprint Group originated as a small Derby, England-based printing company founded in 1826 by William Bemrose. Then 34 years old, Bemrose had come to Derby in 1815 with his former employer, Mozleys, a printer originally from Gainsborough. The Industrial Revolution and, particularly, the construction of Britain's railway system, offered new opportunities for the printing industry. Bemrose, for example, became particularly known for the printing of railway timetables. Like many printers, Bemrose's business activities also included the retail sales of books and stationery supplies.

Soon after founding the company, Bemrose began printing the pro-Tory conservative newspaper the *Derbyshire Courier*. Bemrose apparently shared the newspaper's political convictions. In 1831, as Parliament debated a Reform bill promising universal suffrage, Bemrose displayed an anti-reform petition in his shop's window during a local demonstration in favor of the legislation. The crowd attacked Bemrose's shop, breaking its windows and destroying much of its stock.

The event did not, however, prevent Bemrose's business from becoming a success, and the Bemrose family itself became one of Derby's most prominent. The business continued to grow into the middle of the decade. During this period, Bemrose opened a second shop, on London Paternoster Row. Bemrose was also joined by his sons, Henry Howe and William Jr., during this time.

The Bemrose brothers quickly distinguished themselves as technological innovators. In 1854, the brothers received a patent for a rotary perforation machine that could be used for paper, cardboard, and other materials. By 1958, the brothers had become partners in their father's printing business, which became known as Bemrose & Sons.

INCORPORATION IN 1891

Bemrose's London operation expanded in 1867, when the company joined forces with a neighboring printer and bookseller, run by a Mr. Lothian on Amen Corner. In that year, the two shops agreed to merge, transferring Lothian's business to Bemrose's Paternoster shop. This shop then took on the name of Bemrose and Lothian. The family's Derby shop kept the Messrs. Bemrose &

Sons name. In 1891, the business formerly incorporated under that name. Henry Howe, who had also begun a career in politics, including serving as a Member of Parliament for Derby, became the company's first chairman.

While Henry Howe Sr. pursued his political career, and ultimately received a knighthood in 1897, the company came under the direction of Henry Howe Arnold Bemrose, who joined the business in 1879. In addition to running the printing company, the younger Bemrose was also an avid archeologist, publishing a number of papers and books focusing on the history of Derbyshire.

The family tradition continued into the next century, when Karl Bemrose, born in 1893, achieved the status of master printer by his early 20s. In 1914, however, Bemrose enlisted in the British army, and was reported missing two years later. His body was never found. Nonetheless, the printing company remained in the family's hands, as Arthur Bemrose died only at the age of 86 in 1940. In the meantime, his younger son, Max Bemrose, born in 1904, had joined the company in 1926.

UNIVERSAL PRINTERS IN THE TWENTIES

By then, the British printing industry had changed dramatically since the company's founding. The modern era of the printing industry, incorporating new printing technologies and capable of printing increasingly high volumes, had led to the emergence of a number of larger-scale, dedicated printing companies.

Bemrose too had recognized the need to join forces to create a larger group. In 1922, therefore, the company joined with Manchester's Natzio and Co., founded in 1848, and Alf Cook Ltd., founded in 1866, which operated in Leeds and Norbury, to form Universal Printers Ltd. Both companies, like Bemrose, had operated as family-owned companies in the north of England. However, the printing companies continued to operate in their original locations (Natzio later becoming known as Norbury Printers) making Bemrose one of the leading printers in England's northern region. As an indication of the company's stature, its operations were valued at £800,000 at its founding, a significant sum for the time.

Max Bemrose emerged as the new company's leader, ultimately becoming company chairman. Over the next few decades, the firm grew strongly, in part because of its readiness to invest in new equipment,

KEY DATES

1826: William Bemrose opens a printer's shop in Derby, England.

1854: Bemrose's sons Henry Howe and William Jr. receive a patent for a rotary perforation machine.

1891: Company is incorporated as Bemrose & Sons.

1922: Bemrose merges with two other North England printers to become Universal Printers Ltd.

1957: Universal Printers lists its shares on the London Stock Exchange.

1971: Universal Printers changes its name to Bemrose Corporation.

1993: Bemrose acquires McCleery-Cumming of Iowa.

2000: After acquiring 4imprint of Wisconsin, Bemrose sells off its printing businesses and refocuses on the promotional products sector as 4imprint Group.

2001: 4imprint acquires Adventures in Advertising (sold in 2005).

2007: 4imprint acquires Supreme, based in Blackpool, and establishes new Trade division.

2008: 4imprint completes restructuring into a three division organization.

ADDING A CATALOG PRINTING BUSINESS IN 1961

In 1961, Universal Printers grew with the acquisition of another family-owned printing company, Balding & Mansell. Based in Wisbech, Balding & Mansell represented something of a milestone for the future 4imprint Group, while the other companies in the Universal Printers group focused on the packaging sector, Balding & Mansell allowed the company to enter the publicity printing sector, including catalog printing.

The addition of Balding & Mansell enabled the company to compete for a number of high-profile contracts, such as printing the British Museum catalog of printed books in 1967. For this the company developed its own technology, which in turn helped the company win the contract to print and publish the U.S. Library of Congress National Union Catalog that year. For this job, the company created a new subsidiary, Mansell Information/Publishing Ltd. The addition of the new business ultimately helped boost the group's sales to £7.9 million by the end of 1968.

Also during the 1960s, Universal Printers had recognized the importance of the emerging self-service supermarket format and the impact it was to have on British buying habits. As a result, the company became an early adopter of printing technologies both for traditional carton containers and for new flexible packaging formats. Into the 1970s, the group's range of printed products included cigarette shells, checks and securities, playing cards, paper bags, advertising materials, calendars, and diaries.

STRUGGLES IN THE SEVENTIES

Universal Printers changed its name to Bemrose Corporation in 1971, with its headquarters in Derby. The early part of the decade appeared promising for the company, as its sales topped £10 million and it entered the decade posting its highest ever profits. The company then launched a major investment, spending £3 million in order to expand its operations into the textiles market with the incorporation of newly developing heat transfer printing methods. Toward this end, the company acquired a new factory in Derby, as well as the necessary machinery, bringing the facility online in 1973. At the same time, the group sold off non-core operations, dropping its sales back to £6.5 million.

Bemrose's timing proved unfortunate, however, as England, swept up into a new trend toward natural fabrics, shunned printed synthetic fabrics. This led to a significant drop in profits for the year. These difficulties appeared short-lived, as the company absorbed the start-up costs of the heat transfer unit, and rebuilt its

technology, and facilities. Between 1946 and 1956, for example, the company spent more than £1.3 million on modernizing and expanding its production capacity. This willingness to invest helped the company maintain a steady string of profits in the years following World War II, with annual profits of nearly £500,000 in the early 1950s.

In 1953, Universal Printers, which had operated on a partnership basis, decided to list its shares on the London Stock Exchange. The listing was taken in part because the number of family member shareholders in the company had grown over the previous decades. Through the listing, the company replaced the negotiations that had formerly marked the sale and exchange of shares among shareholders with the more streamlined process available at the stock market. The listing also enabled the company to bring in a number of prominent institutional investments from among the United Kingdom's financial and insurance industries, among others.

sales past £10 million. Nonetheless, the company struggled through much of the decade, in large part because of the shrinking economy brought on by the steep rise in oil prices in the 1970s.

Helping to offset its problems in the United Kingdom, however, was the group's drive to expand its export sales. During the second half of the decade, the company managed to raise its international revenues to more than 20 percent of its total. The company also maintained a strong investment program, adding computerized photo-typesetting equipment, developing a security printing business, based on its own production technology. The company also produced much of its own printing machinery, including new laminating machinery which began production testing in 1977.

BETTING ON THE UNITED STATES IN THE NINETIES

The successful growth of Bemrose's export business led the company to seek new international expansion. The company entered the U.S. market, setting up its Bemrose USA, or BUSA subsidiary, which focused on the advertising and promotional materials market. The company also entered a joint venture partnership there, acquiring 50 percent of Bemrose Yattendon.

Bemrose in the meantime faced down a takeover attempt, when Bunzl Corporation launched a bid to acquire control of the group in the early 1980s. Bemrose rejected Bunzl's initial bid, and received support from publishing magnate Robert Maxwell, who acquired a 12.6 percent stake in Bemrose through his British Printing and Communications Corporation. Bunzl returned with a new, higher bid, but once again failed to win support from Bemrose's shareholders, in part because the Maxwell stake had helped to raise the group's share price.

Toward the end of the decade and into the next, Bemrose began strengthening its focus on the security and promotional printing specialities in both the United States and the United Kingdom. In 1988, the company agreed to sell BUSA to Bemrose Yattendon, thereby increasing its own stake in the joint venture. This was accompanied by a purchase, in England, of Hull-based Henry Booth. That group's chief, Rodger Booth, then became CEO of Bemrose in the early 1990s.

Despite the recession, Bemrose continued to seek new growth opportunities. The group raised its U.S. profile in 1993, when it paid $27 million to acquire Iowa-based McCleery-Cumming. The purchase positioned Bemrose as the United States' second largest advertising calendar printer, adding nearly $32 million to the group's total sales of approximately $90 million.

BECOMING 4IMPRINT

Bemrose completed several more acquisitions through the 1990s, including Gerber Industries in Arizona; Lockwoods Calendars in the United Kingdom; and promotional products group Incentives Two in the United Kingdom. The company's most significant acquisition, however, came in 1996, when it acquired Oshkosh, Wisconsin's Nelson Marketing. That company, which changed its name to 4imprint in 1999, had grown into one of the leading promotional products companies in the United States.

By the end of the decade, Bemrose recognized that the promotional products sector offered stronger growth potential than its traditional printing specialties. This led the company to take the unusual move of combining all of its promotional products business under the 4imprint name in 2000. Following the restructuring, the company sold off its printing business, which was renamed Bemrose Booth. Nelson Marketing founder Dick Nelson became 4imprint's chief executive.

4imprint added a new business in 2001, when it acquired Adventures in Advertising (AIA), a franchise-based distributor of promotional products. At the same time, the company established a new Corporate Programmes division, competing for large-scale contracts with major corporations. By 2002 that unit celebrated its largest contract to that time, for $9 million with ING North America. Other major clients followed, including Brunswick Bowling & Billiards and Union Partners Corporation. By the end of the decade, the group's client list included such giants as Microsoft, Accenture, IBM, and AMEC.

THREE DIVISION STRUCTURE INTO 2010

4imprint brought in a new executive chairman, Ken Minton, who led a restructuring of the company in the second half of the decade. The company, which eliminated the group level chief executive spot, adopted a new three division structure, with each division led by its own chief executive officer. As part of the restructuring process, the company sold off AIA in 2005. The company acquired one of its main U.K. rivals, Supreme, which was then merged with the group's other UK Product Source and MT Golf subsidiaries to form its new Trade division.

In 2008, the company also took steps to extend its largest division, Direct Marketing, based on the original 4imprint business, to the United Kingdom. To this end the company established a new direct-marketing unit based in Manchester. This move came as part of the group's overall restructuring, as it braced itself for the impact of the newly emerging global economic crisis. Nonetheless, 4imprint's revenue growth remained strong for the year, climbing 14 percent to nearly £170 million. With a history stretching back more than 180 years, the former Bemrose Corporation had reinvented itself as 4imprint for the new century.

M. L. Cohen

PRINCIPAL SUBSIDIARIES

4imprint Direct Ltd.; 4imprint Inc. (USA); Broadway Incentives Ltd.; Kreyer Promotion Service GmbH; Product Plus International Ltd.; SPS (EU) Ltd.

PRINCIPAL DIVISIONS

Direct Marketing; End User; Trade.

PRINCIPAL OPERATING UNITS

Brand Addition; Product Plus International; Kreyer Promotion Service.

PRINCIPAL COMPETITORS

Encore Marketing International Inc.; Berry Network Inc.; Campaigners Inc.; Welcome Wagon International Inc; PHD Media Ltd.; Initiative Media North America; Wheel; List Syzygy Ltd.

FURTHER READING

Bolitho, Nigel, "4imprint Reorganises Ahead of Recession," *Investors Chronicle,* August 11, 2008.

"4imprint Acquires Adventures in Advertising," *Wearables Business,* February 2001, p. 22.

"4imprint Launches 'Two-Minute Takeaways,'" *Marketing Weekly News,* October 4, 2008, p. 7.

Hackett, Dennis, *The History of the Future: The Bemrose Corporation, 1826–1976,* London: Scolar Press, 1976.

Miller, Paul, "4imprint Makes an Impression with Samples," *Catalog Age,* February 2001, p. 18.

"No Stopping 4imprint," *Investors Chronicle,* August 3, 2007.

Richards, Matthew, "4imprint Sells US Business for £6.5m," *Financial Times,* July 23, 2005, p. 5.

Schuyler, David, "Making an Imprint," *Business Journal-Milwaukee,* May 19, 2000, p. 25.

Wallop, Harry, "4imprint Belts Out the Cash," *Daily Telegraph,* January 22, 2005.

FRED PERRY

Fred Perry Limited

24 West Street
London, WC2H 9NA
England
Telephone: (+44 20) 7632 2800
Fax: (+44 20) 7632 2828
Web site: http://www.fredperry.com

Wholly Owned Subsidiary of Hit Union Company Ltd.
Incorporated: 1949 as Fred Perry Sportswear Ltd.
Employees: 350
Sales: £75 million ($110 million) (2007 est.)
NAICS: 315223 Men's and Boys' Cut and Sew Shirt (Except Work Shirt) Manufacturing; 315232 Women's and Girls' Cut and Sew Blouse and Shirt Manufacturing; 315999 Other Apparel Accessories and Other Apparel Manufacturing; 316213 Men's Footwear (Except Athletic) Manufacturing; 316214 Women's Footwear (Except Athletic) Manufacturing; 424320 Men's and Boys' Clothing and Furnishings Merchant Wholesalers; 424330 Women's, Children's, and Infants' Clothing and Accessories Merchant Wholesalers; 424340 Footwear Merchant Wholesalers; 448110 Men's Clothing Stores; 448120 Women's Clothing Stores

■ ■ ■

Fred Perry Limited sells a popular niche brand of casual apparel. Its distinctive polo shirt, first introduced in 1952, was among the first athletic garments to succeed as street wear. Since 1995 Fred Perry has been a subsidiary of Hit Union Company Ltd., its former Japanese licensee.

In his 1984 autobiography, Perry acknowledged that the sportswear company was thriving decades after his Wimbledon achievements were consigned to history books. However, his name has been a perennial source of publicity even after his death in 1995, being mentioned on an annual basis as Britons awaited a homegrown Wimbledon singles champion. Perry held the title for three years in a row before turning pro in 1937 and was at one point considered the finest tennis player in the world.

Other brands muscled into tennis clothing in the Open Era (after 1968); at the same time, the Fred Perry brand was becoming an enduring favorite of Britain's youth culture. Eventually street fashion became its primary business, although the classic Fred Perry polo developed for the tennis courts has remained a mainstay of the business. In 2009 tennis-specific clothing accounted for just 5 to 7 percent of total annual sales.

AN ACTIVE LIFE

Frederick John Perry was born May 18, 1909, in Stockport, England, the son of a millworker turned Labour MP. He became a world table-tennis champion as a teenager, but turned to lawn tennis at 18 after peering at the game, and its affluent lifestyle, through the fence at a private club.

In spite of his working-class background, he succeeded in mastering a sport that was then primarily the province of the privileged classes. He won three consecutive Wimbledon championships beginning in 1934 and was considered by many to be the best player in the world, leaping onto the cover of *Time* magazine and winning each of the four Grand Slam events at least once.

Perry cut a striking figure on court. He was known for his dapper, tailored outfits (he would continue to prefer long pants after most of the sport made the transition to shorts), and for a relentless, attacking style of play.

Anxious about securing income in a day when the major tennis championships were amateurs only, he turned pro in January 1937, playing richly lucrative exhibitions throughout the United States and Europe. Five years later, Perry's playing career was cut short by an elbow injury. He left the circuit in 1942 to become a media commentator and businessman.

With his winnings, Perry was able to move to Hollywood and buy a share in the Beverly Hills Tennis Club. There he indulged his interest in movie starlets, marrying a total of four times.

INTO THE APPAREL BUSINESS

Although he maintained a high profile with his TV and radio commentary, there appeared to be little interest by equipment manufacturers in using Perry's name to sell shoes or racquets, in contrast to the situation enjoyed by later tennis stars such as Jack Kramer and Stan Smith. However, Tibby Wegner, a former soccer player from Austria, sought Perry's support in manufacturing a sweatband under his name.

After some product development, Perry agreed and the pair launched a business in 1949. Initial start-up capital was £300. The sweatbands and, later, shirts, were manufactured under contract in Leicester. Wegner focused on organizing manufacturing while Perry's job was to use his formidable connections to market the merchandise. Perry's commentating for the media and his legendary status—for decades, British tennis fans would ask, when could the country produce another Fred Perry—provided an enduring well of publicity, and the company spent very little on advertising.

THE FRED PERRY POLO DEBUTS IN 1952

Fred Perry's signature shirt, introduced in 1952, was not the first polo shirt in tennis; that honor is claimed by another classic brand, that of French champion René Lacoste, whose alligator shirts debuted some two dozen years earlier. Sartorially sophisticated, Perry boasted the superior fit of his polos. The material, brushed-cotton piqué, was among the softest and most breathable fabrics then available.

Wegner persuaded Perry not to adopt his trademark smoking pipe as the company's logo, fearing it would alienate female buyers. After considering other alternatives, including the rose, they settled upon the laurel wreath, an ancient symbol of victory. It was inspired by the ribbons bestowed upon prewar Wimbledon champions. Perry had been wearing the laurel wreath on his own clothing since winning the first of three singles titles in 1934. He successfully persuaded the All England Club to allow this usage, and the logo soon became one of the most recognizable in fashion. (According to Perry's 1984 autobiography, the logos on the first shirts were green because the model given the embroiderers was a mixed doubles award featuring that color.)

To promote the new shirts, Perry gave them to top players at Wimbledon. The company blanketed not just the players but the BBC crew who were televising the championships. This publicity coup resulted in demand so great that when Perry called on his former tennis colleagues who had moved on to retail trades, the buyer for Lillywhite's phoned his colleagues at other stores and the initial batch of 75 dozen was all sold within a half hour.

The shirts the company provided players and high-profile figures were embroidered with the recipients' initials below the laurel wreath logo, further endearing them to the bearers. They were allotted two letters per monogram, with rare exceptions such as Perry himself; President John F. Kennedy Jr.; and Billie Jean King (née Moffitt), who were accorded three-letter monograms. In another highly personal touch, the company provided monogrammed baby clothes for the top players' infants.

Part of the reasoning behind the personalization was to discourage recipients from merely reselling their items. However, before it established an international distribution network, the company did allow touring players to buy merchandise in lots and resell them overseas.

The company then began making shorts, although Fred Perry himself preferred to play in long pants, which he felt looked more professional. It naturally

KEY DATES

1934: Fred Perry wins his first of three consecutive Wimbledon singles championships; begins wearing laurel wreath logo.

1949: Tibby Wegner, a soccer player from Austria, joins Perry in launching a successful sweatband venture.

1952: Fred Perry Sportswear, Ltd., introduces its famous polo shirt at Wimbledon.

1961: Perry and Wegner sell the business to raincoat manufacturer Charles Mackintosh.

1973: Ohio-based A-T-O, Inc. (later Figgie International) acquires the firm.

1995: Japan's Hit Union Company Ltd. buys Fred Perry from Figgie International.

2009: Andy Murray wears the Fred Perry centenary kit into the semifinals of Wimbledon.

branched into other tennis apparel, such as sweaters, jackets, accessories, and skirts, and clothing for golf and other sports. Not everything Perry touched turned to gold. An early 1950s shipment of low-cut soccer shoes from Hungary was deemed a bit too early for its time.

Fred Perry's polos were worn by tennis legends such as Margaret Court, Rod Laver, and Arthur Ashe, and created an impression in popular culture far beyond the tennis court. Fred Perry's refusal to pay endorsement fees in the Open Era (after 1968, when the top tournaments began admitting professionals) reduced the brand's prominence on the tennis courts as others (Italian ones in particular) snapped up the star players with exclusive contracts.

However, by this time, British music culture, particularly the Mods, picked up on the Fred Perry polo as a means to look sharp through a weekend of partying. Such artists as Paul Weller of The Jam remained true to the look in the 1970s and 1980s, and the Britpop movement of the 1990s found it being sported by such bands as Blur, Pulp, and Oasis.

A desire to ameliorate the seasonal nature of the business resulted in a tie-in with the Charles Mackintosh raincoat company, which bought the firm from Perry and Wegner in 1961. Fred Perry himself soon returned as a spokesperson. A-T-O, Inc., a diversified conglomerate based in Willoughby, Ohio, bought Fred Perry Sportswear, Ltd., and parent Fred Perry & Paynes, Ltd., in 1973, as well as its U.S. licensee Carl Fix, Inc., of Verona, New Jersey. A-T-O was renamed

Figgie International Inc. in 1981. In 1995, Fred Perry was acquired by Hit Union Company, Ltd., of Osaka, Japan. The brand's annual global revenues were then reportedly $20 million.

In 1990 the company had hired John Flynn, a marketing executive with experience at Marks & Spencer, Levi Strauss, and Debenhams. He became managing director in 1993 and stayed to lead the company into the 21st century.

MAINTAINING A CLASSIC

Apparently content to rest on its laurels, the company did not spend much on advertising. Its first television ads did not come until 1989. By then the brand seemed to have lost its direction and standing in the fashion marketplace. It was also besieged by counterfeiters, a longstanding problem. Seeking international growth, in the 1990s Fred Perry had an unsuccessful licensing experience with a certain American licensee that had strayed from the brand's traditional athletic fit.

Fred Perry's largest markets outside the United Kingdom were Japan and Italy. It was becoming increasingly popular in Spain and Germany. In 2005, when it opened an upscale Laurel store in Berlin, Fred Perry was sold at 300 locations in Germany, compared to 125 to 150 sites in the United States. Among its company-owned stores, Authentic Shops specialized in classic designs, while the Laurel Shops focused on the higher-end pieces.

To keep the brand fresh, Fred Perry collaborated with designers such as Raf Simons, Comme des Garçons, and Stussy to bring cutting-edge looks to its signature styles. Its Laurel line catered to the affluent, while Subculture was dedicated to music-loving urban youth.

Endorsements were becoming another factor in maintaining the brand's visibility and relevance. Fred Perry had long eschewed professional endorsements, but in the 1990s it backed top 20 Swedish tennis player Magnus Gustafsson. In the 2000s it made a much larger commitment to rising Scottish star Andy Murray. By 2005 worldwide revenues were estimated between £75 and £90 million. Polo shirts accounted for one-fifth of sales, with menswear making up the bulk of the business.

COURTING THE NEXT GENERATION

Sports companies often courted promising players early in their careers, before they were widely known and could command exorbitant fees. Fred Perry's relationship with Andy Murray was a textbook example. When it signed the fast-rising Scottish tennis player on March 2, 2005, he was ranked 418th in the world. He broke into the top 100 within a few months, and reached number three in 2009. He was a sentimental favorite to return the men's singles trophy to Britain for the first time since Fred Perry himself last won it.

Andy Murray seemed a natural fit for the brand due to more than just his ranking. Still a teenager, he was known to arrive on court listening to tunes on an iPod, suggesting a connection to the hipster youth culture which made up the bulk of the company's sales. His brashness recalled something of Perry's rebellious nature. Nevertheless, as his rating grew, he was persistently wooed by larger, rival clothing brands.

CENTENARY

The year 2009, in which the 100th anniversary of Fred Perry's birth was celebrated, began with the company opening a store in New York City. The brand then claimed 3,500 points of sale worldwide. By this time, the traditional knit cotton polo was available in three dozen colors. The tennis line included versions made of synthetic wicking fabrics. Fred Perry produced a special shirt to support the 30th anniversary reunion tour of The Specials, an influential British ska band whose followers were among the brand's most devoted customers.

In the fiscal year ended March 2009, the company earned profits of £10 million on revenues of £75 million, according to the *Guardian.* The tennis business had shrunk to just a 5 to 7 percent share. Exports accounted for 60 percent of sales.

Frederick C. Ingram

PRINCIPAL OPERATING UNITS

Authentic Shops; Laurel Shops.

PRINCIPAL COMPETITORS

Lacoste S.A.; Ben Sherman Group Limited.

FURTHER READING

Beckett, Whitney, "Fred Perry Targets Growth for U.S.," *WWD,* February 21, 2007, p. 15.

Brooke, Simon, "The Classic Fred Perry Polo Shirt Endures," *Financial Times,* June 20, 2009.

Engel, Matthew, "The Last Champion," *Financial Times,* June 20, 2009.

Henderson, Jon, *The Last Champion: The Life of Fred Perry,* London: Yellow Jersey Press, 2009.

Henderson, Jon, and Denis Campbell, "Style Secret of Murray's Mint: A Shrewd Decision by the New No. 1 of British Tennis to Go with the Classic Fred Perry Label Has Sent His Earnings—As Well As Theirs—Soaring," *Observer,* February 26, 2006, p. 7.

Hoggan, Karen, "Fred Perry Looks to TV for Image Boost: Fred Perry's Debut on Television Is Out to Highlight the Brand's 'Classic' Heritage," *Marketing,* November 2, 1989.

Jefferys, Kevin, "Fred Perry and British Tennis: 'Fifty Years to Honor a Winner,'" *Sport in History,* Vol. 29, No. 1, March 2009, pp. 1–24.

Jones, Nina, "British Designers Tap into Fred Perry Archives," *Women's Wear Daily,* June 8, 2006, p. 14.

McGuinness, Damien, "Fred Perry Hits Germany," *Women's Wear Daily,* November 17, 2005, p. 10.

Newman, Paul, "Murray Has Designs on Perry's Winning Ways; Retro Kit Shows British No. 1 Is Happy to Court Comparisons with 1936 Champion," *Independent* (London), June 16, 2009, p. 52.

Owen, David, "Fred Perry's Teenage Ambassador," *Financial Times,* November 15, 2005, p. 14.

Perry, Fred, "The Sportswear Magnate," *Fred Perry: An Autobiography,* London: Hutchinson, 1984, pp. 148–159.

Thurmond, Sarah, "Resting on Its Laurel Wreath," *Tennis,* July 2009, p. 48.

Wood, Zoe, "The Man Who Bet His Shirt on Andy Murray at Wimbledon: When John Flynn Got Britain's Future Tennis No. 1 to Wear Fred Perry, He Gave New Life to a Mod Classic," *Guardian* (London), July 3, 2009, Financial Sec., p. 31.

Grupo Positivo

Av. Cándido Hartmann, 1400
Curitaba, Paraná 80710-570
Brazil
Telephone: (55 41) 3336-3838
Fax: (55 41) 3316-5135
Web site: http://www.positivo.com.br

Private Company
Founded: 1972
Employees: 4,000
Sales: BRL 2.6 billion ($1.37 billion) (2007 est.)
NAICS: 334111 Electronic Computer Manufacturing;
    511120 Periodical Publishers; 511130 Book
    Publishers; 511210 Software Publishers; 518112
    Web Search Portal; 611110 Elementary and
    Secondary Schools; 611310 Colleges, University
    and Professional Schools; 611691 Exam Preparation
    and Tutoring; 611710 Educational Support Services

■ ■ ■

Grupo Positivo calls itself Brazil's national leader in three areas: education, publishing and graphics, and information technology. Positivo Informática S.A., a public company, is Brazil's leader in the manufacture of personal computers (PCs). In addition, the group, which operates worldwide, offers the most advanced information technology solutions, develops education software, and runs education portals as well as providing teacher training and educational and technical support for partner schools.

Grupo Positivo's other activities in the field of education range from the preschool level to a university campus that offers more than 26 undergraduate courses and 40 graduate courses. It also includes foreign language instruction in English, French, and Spanish and various graduate and extension courses. A network of schools in Brazil and other countries is linked to the group's own teaching system. Two printing and publishing subsidiaries turn out a variety of textbooks, supplementary materials, children's literature, and promotional materials.

POSITIVO IN THE 20TH CENTURY

The group was founded in Curitiba, Paraná, in 1972 by eight teachers who initiated what they called Curso Positivo to prepare students for university entrance examinations. They established a small printing plant in a garage for the materials they were creating and attracted more than 3,000 students in the first year of operation. Colegio Positivo was established as a secondary school in 1976 and Colegio Positivo Jûnior for pupils ranging from kindergarten to the eighth grade in the following year.

The Positivo Teaching System was established in 1979 to serve eight outside associated institutions. A center for creating teaching materials was founded in 1983. By the end of 1985 the number of students using the system's education materials at associated schools had reached 77,000. This number increased steadily, reaching 400,000 by the end of the century, including thousands in Japan (where many Brazilians of Japanese ancestry were living and working).

Higher education was introduced in 1988 in a facility where courses were offered in foreign trade, information, rural administration, and business administration. Positivo Informática S.A. was founded in 1989 and soon began to sell its computers to schools. The Positivo foreign language center and Positivo university center were established in 1998.

POSITIVO AT THE MILLENNIUM

Grupo Positivo dominated the educational landscape of Curitiba, a city of 1.5 million, as the 20th century drew to a close. For many inhabitants, to be a student at one of the three schools was evidence of status. Its installations included gymnasiums equipped with enormous swimming pools. Besides these schools and the two preparatory Curso Positivos, the educational unit was administering five primary schools for employees of forestry companies in rural areas. The large new university center campus, which included a lake bordered by pine trees, boasted a library inspired by the New York Public Library. Some 7,000 students attended courses that included dentistry, physiotherapy, nutrition, and mechanical engineering.

Positivo Informática's catalog of 56 software titles made it the leader in this market in Brazil. A newly established web portal for continuing education had been visited by more than 300,000 people and had links to about 180 schools. Its offerings included e-mail and extracurricular programs, among other services, for students, parents, and teachers. The foreign language center was serving 22 franchised units, and an English language laboratory was selling multimedia materials to 21 schools in 17 cities.

Positivo Informática's computers were being sold throughout Brazil, with the public sector being the main customer. After presenting the low bid to the federal ministry of education, it provided 150,000 computers at a cost of about $360 each. However, the contract was canceled because the ministry felt Positivo was charging too much money.

Gráfica e Editora Posigraf S.A., the group's printing arm, began with a mimeograph machine but by 1995 was bringing in more money than the schools and courses. Besides churning out large quantities of teaching materials, it had become a major commercial publisher for outside customers. In 1998 it became Brazil's leader in the publication of books, periodicals, commercial printing, and promotions, a distinction it maintained for at least eight consecutive years. Originally called Editora Nova Didática Ltda., it was aided by Distribuidora Positivo Ltda., which distributed educational materials to over 2,000 schools.

Grupo Positivo offered its associated institutions a package of services that included teaching evaluations by a board of 35 professionals. To attract new associated institutions, Positivo had begun to invest in national marketing campaigns that included television commercials and magazine ads. Group Positivo had revenues of BRL 285 million ($156 million) in 2000. Its president was Oriovisto Guimaräes, trained as a mathematician and engineer but one of the five partners in the group and very much a businessman.

PUBLISHING ACTIVITIES: 2002–05

Grupo Positivo had four web portals by the end of 2002. In the following year it signed a seven-year contract, renewable for another seven years, to publish *Aurélio,* a popular dictionary. The group then established Editora Positivo as its publishing arm.

Positivo, in March 2004, introduced *Mini Aurélio,* which sold 220,000 copies in the first six months. Later that year it presented the third edition of *Aurélio,* revised and updated. It also introduced Baby Einstein, a line of products for very young children developed in collaboration with The Walt Disney Company. Positivo had established a partnership with Disney in 2001 to distribute educational software in Brazil. Also in 2004, Positivo introduced *Revista Aprende Brasil,* its first national publication directed at the general market. A year later, Positivo launched SABE, a learning system for the general public.

Posigraf was accounting for about 40 percent of the group's revenues. One of its main customers was the British owner of *Living Spirit,* a magazine sold in 28 countries. It was also publishing three other foreign periodicals: *Comprar,* which was aimed at Hispanics living in Miami; *Cameoline,* edited in New York; and *Asian Vibe,* edited in Atlanta. In Brazil, 560,000 students in 2,300 schools were using educational materials published by Posigraf.

COMPUTERS LEAD THE WAY: 2004–06

The group's major advance, though, was in computer sales. Positivo's PCs, which carried *Aurélio* free on compact disc, were being sold in large stores. Of the group's revenues of approximately BRL 600 million ($200 million) in 2004, Positivo Informática accounted for some 35 percent, compared to only 15 percent in 1994. In the last quarter of the year, it became the national leader in the PC market, a distinction it continued to hold. In 2005, when the company introduced a new line of computers with sharply reduced prices, its share of the group's revenues reached 55 percent.

By this time, retail accounted for 75 percent of Positivo's computer sales, as its PCs increasingly appeared in large stores. They sold for as low as BRL 1,200 ($500). The Positivo notebook, at BRL 2,990 ($1,245) was the lowest-priced on the market. About half of the components of Positivo's computers were made in Brazil and the other half imported.

Grupo Positivo was also making a bigger impact outside Brazil. One product exported to the United States was E-Block, a table with computer, software, and letter blocks for teaching English.

Positivo Informática was chosen by the 2006 edition of the Brazilian business yearbook *Exame Melhores e Maiores* as the best company in the field of technology and computation after a spectacular year in which its revenues rose to $308.7 million, an increase of about 150 percent over 2004. Sales of its computers almost quadrupled during the year, outstripping even the U.S.-based giants Dell Computer Corporation and Hewlett-Packard Company. In December 2005 alone, the company sold 60,000 PCs, half of them in big retail chains.

GRUPO POSITIVO IN 2007–08

Positivo Informática became a public company in December 2006, collecting BRL 604.1 million ($300 million) for 30 percent of its stock in its initial public offering (IPO) on the São Paulo exchange. It remained the Brazilian market leader in PCs in 2007, with 1.38 million sold, almost 15 percent of the total. Its sales in the retail market came to fully one-third of the total. The company established a computer plant in Manaus to supply northern Brazil and one in Ilhéus, Bahia, to make LCD monitors.

The year 2008 saw Positivo Informática's retail sales fall to one-quarter of the total spent on computers. One reason was that the government of São Paulo, Brazil's most populous and prosperous state, imposed a tax on computers manufactured outside the state. The company retained a major network of computer dealers in Brazil, with 6,800 points of sale. It sold 1.6 million PCs that year, of which two-thirds were desktops and one-third notebooks. Retail sales constituted nearly 74 percent, sales to governments, 20 percent, and corporate sales—a market tied to multinationals and difficult to crack—6.5 percent. The Curitiba plant began producing motherboards in 2008.

The world economic crisis took a heavy toll on Positivo Informática's shares, which in late 2008 were worth only about one-fifth the value established in the company's IPO two years earlier and one-tenth of their value at its peak in November 2007. Rumors spread that the company might be sold to Dell, Hewlett-Packard, or Lenovo Group Ltd. Dell was said to particularly prize the company because of its strong retail distribution network.

Positivo Informática was active on other fronts. In 2007 it launched what it called a unique 21st century package of products and solutions giving customers access to state-of-the-art technology in the basic education and higher learning segments, as well as the corporate area. Also that year, it established a partnership with the big mobile phone operator Vivo S.A. that offered Positivo computer owners discounted prices for cellphones.

Gráfica e Editora Posigraf was printing two million books a year. Educational products were reaching 900,000 students throughout Brazil. Universidade Positivo had received government accreditation as the nation's 86th university.

Robert Halasz

PRINCIPAL SUBSIDIARIES

Editora Positivo; Gráfica e Editora Posigraf S.A.; Positivo Informática Ltda.; Positivo Informática S.A.; Positivo Informática da Amazônia Ltda.

PRINCIPAL COMPETITORS

Editora Abril S.A.; Hewlett-Packard Brasil Ltda.; IBM Brasil Indústria de Máquinas e Serviços Ltda; Intelbras S.A.; LG Electrónica de São Paulo Ltda.; Objetivo; Semp Toshiba Informática Ltda.; Sistema Pitágoras de Ensino Sociedade Ltda.; Xerox Comércio e Indústria Ltda.

FURTHER READING

Adachi, Vanessa, "Concorrentes negociam compra da Positivo," *Valor Econômico,* December 8, 2008.

Agostini, Renata, "No encalço da Positivo," *Exame,* February 11, 2009, pp. 52–53.

Barbieri, Cristiane, "Ex-socialista comanda império no PR," *Folha de S. Paulo,* March 30, 2008.

Costa, Flávio, "Lucros além da sala de aula," *Exame,* November 10, 2004, pp. 76–77.

Freitas, Clayton, "Micro em escola turbine vendas do Grupo Positivo," *Jornal do Comércio,* February 13, 2006.

Herzog, Ana Luiza, "Notas altas," *Exame,* March 21, 2001, pp. 82–84, 86.

"Information Technology," *Latin American Monitor: Brazil Monitor,* April 2008, p. 6.

Lima, Marti, "A empresa gráfica Posaigraf imprime revista britânica," *NoticiasFinancieras,* August 19, 2004, p. 1.

———, "O grupo paranaense Positivo quer reforcar sua presence na area editorial," *NoticiasFinancieras,* September 30, 2004, p. 1.

Moura Fé, Ana Lúcia, "O show do Milhão," *Exame Melhores e Maiores,* July 2006, pp. 230–32.

Hankook Tire Company Ltd.

647-15 Yoksam 1-Dong, Gangnam-gu
Seoul, 135 723
South Korea
Telephone: (+82 02) 2222 1000
Fax: (+82 02) 2222 1100
Web site: http://www.hankooktire.co.kr

Public Company
Incorporated: 1941 as Chosun Tire Company
Employees: 14,000
Sales: KRW 4.07 trillion ($3.7 billion) (2008)
Stock Exchanges: Seoul
Ticker Symbol: 00240
NAICS: 326211 Tire Manufacturing (Except Retreading); 336399 All Other Motor Vehicle Parts Manufacturing

■ ■ ■

Hankook Tire Company Ltd. is South Korea's leading manufacturer of automobile, truck, and other tires, the leader in the Chinese market, and ranks as number seven among the top ten tire producers in the world. Founded in 1941, Hankook is also one of the world's fastest-growing tire makers, targeting a spot in the global top five in the early years of the new century. Hankook operates a global network of sales, production, and research and development (R&D) subsidiaries, and distributes its tires to more than 185 countries. The company operates technical centers in South Korea, Germany, the United States, Japan, and China. Manufacturing is carried out at plants in South Korea, China, Germany, and Hungary. International sales account for 70 percent of the group's total sales, which topped KRW 4.07 trillion ($3.7 billion) in 2008.

In South Korea, Hankook claims more than 45 percent of the total tire market, while in China, Hankook's market share tops 25 percent. The original equipment market represents a significant share of the group's total production. Hankook supplies all of the Korean truck and automobile manufacturers, as well as Chery, Geely, FAW Haima, and Shanghai Volkswagen in China, and Ford, General Motors, Volkswagen, Renault, Audi, Smart, Mitsubishi, and others, in Europe, North America, and elsewhere. The group also produces run-flat tires in partnership with France's Michelin. Hankook is strongly positioned in the replacement tire market, through its Hankook, Aurora, and Kingstar brands. Hankook is also involved in tire distribution through its T'Station network of franchised tire service centers in Korea and China, and the Tire Town wholesale and retail network and TBX truck and bus tire chain in Korea. In addition to tires, Hankook also owns auto parts producers Atlas BX (batteries) and Frixa (brakes), and the tire production machinery manufacturer Daehwa Engineering & Machinery Co., Ltd. Hankook is listed on the Seoul Stock Exchange, and the Cho family, led by Chairman Cho Yang Rae, is the group's major shareholder. Suh Seung-hwa, who joined the company in the early 1970s, is Hankook's president and CEO.

COMPANY PERSPECTIVES

Vision: We will deliver trust and value to the world. Hankook Tire strives to achieve its grand vision of becoming a global-leading company that delivers high value to the world by providing high-quality products and services to our valued customers.

FIRST KOREAN TIRE MANUFACTURER IN 1941

Hankook's roots trace back to the Japanese occupation of Korea during World War II. At the time Korea was a relatively poor, non-industrial country, with little in the way of modern infrastructure. In order to supply the vehicles of the occupying forces with tires, the Japanese company Bridgestone set up a small factory in Youngdeungpo, situated on what was then the outskirts of Seoul, in 1941. The new business, called Chosun Tire Company, began producing its first tires in 1942 and marked the effective beginning of Korea's tire manufacturing industry. Initial production remained modest, focused on reprocessing existing tires, and reaching a capacity of just 110,000 tires per year.

The Korean government took over Chosun Tire following World War II. Into the next decade, the company began developing a new brand name, Hankook. However, the outbreak of the Korean conflict and the outbreak of war between North and South Korea put an end to the factory's tire production. The need to rebuild South Korea following the end of the conflict left the Youngdeungpo factory with little resources to resume production. As a result, the company remained largely dormant for most of the 1950s.

This situation changed in the 1960s. Chosun Tire's production soon surpassed its pre-conflict levels. Yet the Korean automobile market continued to be highly undeveloped. Into the early 1970s, the country's total automobile population barely reached 250,000. As a result, Chosun quickly turned to the export market to take up its excess production. For this, the company targeted other Asian markets, starting with Thailand and Pakistan in 1962. Over the next two decades, the Middle East also became a prominent market for the company as well.

PUBLIC OFFERING IN 1968

The 1960s also marked the start of the Korean government's intensive industrialization strategy that was to transform the country into one of the Asian region's industrial and technological powerhouses. In order to take advantage of the coming boom in domestic tire demand, Chosun Tire went public in 1968, listing its shares on the Seoul Stock Exchange. At the same time, the company changed its name, becoming Hankook Tire Manufacturing.

Hankook invested heavily in R&D during the 1970s in order to build its own technological expertise. This effort led the company to launch its first radial tire in 1974. By the following year, the company launched Korea's first steel-belted radial tire as well. These products helped the company outpace the growing number of domestic rivals, including Kumho, as well as the foreign brands. Over the next decade, Hankook became the dominant tire producer in Korea, accounting for more than 45 percent of all tire sales. These included truck and bus tires as well.

South Korea's automobile population in the meantime continued to grow quickly. By 1980, the country counted more than one million automobiles. Hankook had by then responded to the growing demand with the construction of two new factories. The first, built in Incheon, was completed in 1977 and specialized in the production of tubes. The second, in Daejeon, became the group's largest plant, with an initial production capacity of 6,500 tires per day.

R&D EFFORTS IN THE EIGHTIES

Hankook had also been building up its own network of retail tire centers and distributors. In order to strengthen its supply in this market, the company acquired Korea Storage Battery, a producer of automotive batteries, in 1977. That company, later known as Atlas BX, had been founded in 1944. As part of Hankook, Atlas BX grew strongly, becoming one of the world's top ten battery manufacturers by the end of the century.

Into the late 1970s, Hankook's export sales also grew strongly. By 1980, the company's foreign sales had topped $100 million, making Hankook the leading tire exporter as well. While the Asian and Middle East markets represented most of the company's exports at the time, Hankook set its sights on building a presence in the United States. In 1981, therefore, the company set up a dedicated sales and marketing subsidiary, called HANAM, in the United States. The new subsidiary enabled Hankook to make strong inroads as an original equipment supplier to the major U.S. automakers.

Hankook also recognized that, in order to establish its presence in the United States and later in Europe, it needed to raise its quality and technology levels. To this end, the group established a new R&D center in

KEY DATES

1941: Bridgestone of Japan founds Chosun Tire Company in Seoul during Japanese occupation of Korea.
1955: Chosun develops Hankook brand name, although company remains dormant for most of the decade.
1962: Chosun begins exporting tires to Thailand, Pakistan, and other markets.
1968: Company goes public as Hankook Tire Manufacturing Corporation.
1981: Hankook launches U.S. sales subsidiary, HANAM.
1992: Hankook opens U.S.-based Technical Center in Akron, Ohio.
1996: Hankook builds its first factory in Jiaxing, China.
2002: Hankook establishes a European Distribution Center in the Netherlands.
2007: Hankook launches production at its new ultrahigh performance (UHP) tire factory in Hungary.
2009: Hankook completes new UHP tire factory in Geumsan, South Korea.

Daeduk Science Town, in Korea, which became the group's central R&D facility. In 1985, the company built its own tire test track, becoming the first Korean tire maker to incorporate testing facilities into its product development program.

These R&D efforts resulted in the launch of the group's Optimo passenger tire line in 1989. The new tire design helped establish the company among the global top-tier tire manufacturers for the first time. Into the next decade, Hankook saw the potential of developing a technology component focused on the particularities of the U.S. car driving population, where drivers tended to cover long distances at moderate speeds. As a result, long-wearing tires were a major priority. In 1992, Hankook founded a dedicated research center in the United States, the Akron Technical Center, in Akron, Ohio.

By then, the company had become one of the world's top ten tire producers. The company's total production topped 16 million tires per year. Helping to fuel the group's growth was the steady rise of automobile use in Korea. Into the early 1980s, the country counted more than five million passenger cars.

Nonetheless, exports continued to drive Hankook's growth as well. By 1992, exports represented more than 55 percent of the group's total revenues of more than $700 million. The United States had become the company's single-largest market. Hankook had also successfully expanded its presence in Europe, which had become its second largest export market into the early 1990s.

SUCCESS IN CHINA IN THE NINETIES

Hankook had continued to expand its production facilities in order to match its rising sales. The company completed a series of plant expansions at its Daejeon facility, boosting its output to 19 million tires annually by the mid-1990s. At the same time, the company launched construction of a new state-of-the-art factory in Geumsan, completing the first phase in 1997.

The new factory became part of Hankook's ambition to place itself among the global top five by the year 2000. Hankook had also taken another important step toward that goal in the mid-1990s, as it entered the mainland China market. For this, the group built a dedicated factory in Jiaxing in 1996. That plant began production in 1998. In that year, the group founded a second Chinese production subsidiary, in Jiangsu, bringing its factory online by 1999.

Where other foreign tire manufacturers had attempted, and failed, to break into the Chinese market, Hankook succeeded. The company credited its success in part to shared cultural elements between China and Korea, in particular the Korean language's use of Chinese characters. In any event, Hankook rapidly outpaced its competitors, and into the next decade dominated the market with a 25 percent share. In addition to leading the replacement tire market, the company also succeeded in placing its tires as original equipment with most of China's automakers.

Hankook continued to respond to the fast-growing automotive market in China. In 2002, the company announced plans to spend $250 million to expand its two Chinese plants through the end of the decade. This expansion was expected to raise capacity by five million tires per year by 2010.

TARGETING THE TOP FIVE

Hankook's success in China helped raise the company's market position to number seven by 2000. The company then shifted its attention to expanding its European operations, in order to gain a greater share of what remained one of the world's largest tire markets. In 2001, the company opened its new European Distribution Center, in Rotterdam, Netherlands. Two years later,

Hankook signed a partnership agreement with French tire leader Michelin to produce tires incorporating Michelin's no-flat technology.

Into the middle of the decade, Hankook launched plans to build its first European production site, focusing on the ultrahigh performance (UHP) tire segment. Construction on the Hungary-based factory began in 2006, and initial production started the following year. Final construction at the state-of-the-art facility was expected to be completed by 2010, raising total production capacity to ten million tires per year.

The new manufacturing position helped raise the company's profile in the European and U.S. automotive markets. This enabled the company to boost its standing in the original equipment market. In 2005, for example, the company signed a strategic alliance with Ford Motor Company, and the company also became the first Korean tire maker to supply General Motors automobiles. Hankook also began supplying tires for Volkswagen, and in 2006 formed a technical cooperation agreement with Audi.

Back at home, Hankook had expanded into the retail service market, establishing its own franchised chain of tire service stations, called T'Station, in 2005. The formula proved a quick success, and by 2009 the T'Station network neared 200 shops. These also included an entry into the mainland Chinese market, where the first T'Station opened in Shanghai in 2007. Hankook planned to expand its Chinese retail presence to 300 shops by 2012.

By the end of the decade, Hankook's sales had topped KRW 4.07 trillion ($3.7 billion), consolidating the company's seventh place position in the global market. Hankook's strategy continued to target breaking into the top five, raising its sales past the KRW 10 trillion level. To this end, the company launched a new $250 million expansion of its Korean manufacturing base, beginning construction of a new UHP tire factory in Geumsan. That facility, expected to be completed by 2009, was to add another five million tires per year to the group's capacity. As the world's fastest-growing tire manufacturer, Hankook appeared to have found a smooth road to achieving its strategy.

M. L. Cohen

PRINCIPAL SUBSIDIARIES

ASA Co., Ltd.; Atlas BX Co., Ltd.; Daehwa Engineering & Machinery Co., Ltd.; Frixa Co., Ltd.; Hankook Espana S.A. (Spain); Hankook France SARL; Hankook Reifen Deutschland GmbH (Germany); Hankook Tire America Corp. (USA); Hankook Tire Australia Pty., Ltd.; Hankook Tire Canada Corp.; Hankook Tire China Co., Ltd.; Hankook Tire China Headquarters; Hankook Tire Italia S.R.L. (Italy); Hankook Tire Japan Corp.; Hankook Tire Netherlands B.V.; Hankook Tyre U.K. Ltd.; Jiangsu Hankook Tire Co., Ltd. (China).

PRINCIPAL DIVISIONS

America Headquarters; China Headquarters; Europe Headquarters; Korea Headquarters; L.A.A.M. Headquarters.

PRINCIPAL OPERATING UNITS

Akron Technical Center (ATC); China Technical Center (CTC); Europe Technical Center (ETC); Japan Technical Liaison Center (JTC); Main R&D Center.

PRINCIPAL COMPETITORS

Bridgestone Corp.; Continental AG; Compagnie Generale des Etablissements Michelin S.C.A.; Goodyear Tire and Rubber Co.; Bibojee Services (Private) Ltd.; Haci Oemer Sabanci Holding A.S.; Yokohama Rubber Company Ltd.; Pirelli Tyres Nederland B.V.; Sumitomo Rubber Industries Ltd.; Pirelli and C S.p.A.; Hyosung Corp.

FURTHER READING

Anglebrandt, Gary, "Hankook Plans to Bring Fuel-Saving Tire to North America," *Automotive News*, October 20, 2008, p. 18.

Chow, Namrita, "Hankook Tire Rolls Out One-Stop Auto Service Format," *Tire Business*, August 27, 2007, p. 34.

"Hankook Achieves EPA SmartWay Certification for Truck Tires," *Refrigerated Transporter*, February 1, 2009.

"Hankook Pumps Up Environmentally Friendly Budget," *Fleet Owner*, June 11, 2008.

"Hankook Tire," *Rubber World*, August 2008, p. 6.

Kim, Hordon, "Pumping Up," *Rubber & Plastics News*, January 28, 2002, p. 6.

Noga, Edward, "Hankook Shifts Production," *European Rubber Journal*, June 1999, p. 16.

Salmon, Andrew, "Burning Rubber," *Forbes*, June 16, 2008, p. 50.

Shaw, David, "Hankook Building UHP Car Tyre Plant in Hungary," *European Rubber Journal*, January 1, 2006, p. 8.

———, "Hankook Confirms Plans to Build UHP Tyre Plant in Korea," *European Rubber Journal*, March 1, 2007, p. 9.

———, "Hankook Tire Is on a Mission," *European Rubber Journal*, November 1, 2007, p. S08.

White, Liz, "Hankook—Aiming for the Top Five," *European Rubber Journal*, January 1998, p. 28.

Hard Rock Café International, Inc.

———— ■ ————

6100 Old Park Lane
Orlando, Florida 32835
U.S.A.
Telephone: (407) 445-7625
Fax: (407) 445-9709
Web site: http://www.hardrock.com

■ ■ ■

Wholly Owned Subsidiary of Seminole Hard Rock Entertainment Inc.
Incorporated: 1977 as Hard Rock Café International PLC
Employees: 3,000
Sales: $1 billion (2009 est.)
NAICS: 722110 Full-Service Restaurants; 721110 Hotels (Except Casino Hotels) and Motels; 721120 Casino Hotels

■ ■ ■

Hard Rock Café International, Inc., has enjoyed a stellar success that eluded competitor Planet Hollywood, and spawned a slew of themed imitators including Rainforest Café and the House of Blues. Founded in London in 1971 by Isaac Tigrett and Peter Morton, who split the company and sold their interests to a succession of owners, Hard Rock International encompasses the entire Hard Rock brand that includes its extremely popular restaurants and a growing number of hotel/casino resorts popping up all over the globe. Owned by the Seminole Tribe of Florida, Hard Rock has rediscovered its identity after faltering in the late 1990s and early 2000s to become an instantly recognized brand worldwide, representing food, fun, music, and a rock memorabilia collection rumored to be worth $40 million or more.

AN INCREDIBLE CONCEPT: 1971–79

The popularity of the Hard Rock Cafés grew exponentially from the opening of the first Café on June 14, 1971, in London. Two young Americans, Isaac Tigrett and Peter Morton, who were the quintessential odd couple, borrowed money from their parents to open a quirky restaurant. They were only 22 years old at the time, and they selected Park Lane in London's fashionable Mayfair district as the site of their "Hard Rock Café." The decor and menu contrasted sharply with the lavish hotels lining posh Park Lane, where strictly enforced dress codes were the norm, and hamburgers, milk shakes, and the music of the Rolling Stones most certainly were not.

Tigrett, son of a wealthy Tennessee financier named John Burton Tigrett, had moved to England with his family at age 15, attended private school in Lugano, Switzerland, and then spent his days in London selling used Rolls-Royces to Americans. Morton came from a wealthy and venerable Chicago restaurant family, a heritage he tapped when opening The Great American Disaster, an American-style restaurant located in Chelsea, London. As a restaurateur, Morton was immediately successful, but his first venture was all but forgotten after he hooked up with Tigrett.

The excitement generated by the first Café, an opening that quickly drew queues of patrons eager to take part in the Hard Rock Café's carnival-like atmosphere, was duplicated with each additional opening of restaurants in other cities and other countries, becoming more intense as the restaurants became grander and earned the reputation as popular gathering spots for celebrities. Unfortunately, Hard Rock's growth became contentious due to disagreements between Tigrett and Morton, who had little in common other than youth and wealth.

Morton had been described as aloof, reserved, and a "business-first businessman," personality traits that initially complemented and then later butted against Tigrett's impulsiveness. A self-described "raving Marxist," Tigrett became legendary for his flamboyance and recklessness, renowned for being an eccentric figure who played the principal role in many of the titillating stories of Hard Rock Café lore. Outrageous incidents, true or not, as well as the storied sightings of celebrities added to the mystique and unpredictability of a visit to Tigrett and Morton's establishments, creating invaluable marketing material when little time or money was spent on traditional advertising.

Celebrities did indeed frequent the Café, including rock group Led Zeppelin, whose members reportedly hurled whiskey bottles against the walls. Other musicians such as Carole King wrote musical tributes, while one of Eric Clapton's guitars found its way onto the Café's wall. Pete Townshend of The Who then donated his guitar with a note that read, "Mine's as good as his." The two guitars became part of the Café's growing rock memorabilia collection, while the magnetic power of the Hard Rock to attract celebrities also pulled in such

notable personages as the Duke of Westminster and director Steven Spielberg.

Publicized reports of who did what at the Hard Rock soon led to its popularity as a destination for tourists and locals as a way to pay homage to the famous and the peculiar. Although the Hard Rock was a marketing boon, its customers lingered, dawdled, and gawked, remaining for hours to take part in the paparazzi-filled days and nights. Low customer turnover stunted profits, leading Tigrett and Morton to turn up the volume of the music. Louder music meant people talked less, ate and drank faster, and loitered less, a change that quintupled the Café's turnover rate and lifted profits. The partners also segued into merchandising during this time, offering shirts, hats, watches, and coffee mugs with the Hard Rock logo, contributing mightily to Hard Rock's bottom line.

As the restaurant became increasingly popular and successful, the relationship between Tigrett and Morton grew increasingly strained. In 1974 Tigrett made an about-face in his personal life, becoming a Hindu convert and devoted follower of spiritual leader Sai Baba. Espousing a "Love All, Serve All" tenet, he moved in with and later married Ringo Starr's ex-wife, Maureen Starkey. Tigrett's all-inclusive doctrine of love did not, however, include Morton, and the partners went their separate ways in 1979 when Morton returned to the United States.

THE END OF AN ERA: 1980–89

A protracted separation between Tigrett and Morton led to fighting over the legal rights to the Hard Rock name. Three years later, in 1982, the situation was resolved when Morton gained the rights to the Hard Rock name for all the world west of the Mississippi River, and all the world east of the Mississippi River was granted to Tigrett. There were exceptions to this demarcation line (Morton was given the rights to Chicago, and Tigrett was awarded Dallas), but from 1982 forward there would be two companies controlling the Hard Rock name and operating Hard Rock Cafés: Morton's Hard Rock America, Inc., and Tigrett's Hard Rock Café International, Inc.

Morton's Hard Rock America beat Tigrett's Hard Rock Café International to the punch when it opened the first Hard Rock in the United States in 1982. Located in Los Angeles, Morton's Hard Rock was backed financially by Hard Rock devotee Steven Spielberg, Hollywood film studio magnate Barry Diller, actor Henry Winkler, and singers Willie Nelson and John Denver, who helped Morton transport the Hard Rock concept across international borders for the first time.

KEY DATES

1971: First Hard Rock restaurant opens in London.

1977: Company is incorporated as Hard Rock Café International PLC.

1982: Founders Isaac Tigrett and Peter Morton split the company and go their separate ways.

1984: Tigrett takes his Hard Rock company public on the New York Stock Exchange.

1986: The 10th Hard Rock restaurant opens in Dallas.

1988: Tigrett sells his interest in Hard Rock International to Robert Earl.

1992: Planet Hollywood and House of Blues become rivals of Hard Rock.

1994: Rainforest Café opens its first themed restaurant.

1996: Rank Group PLC buys Hard Rock America and Hard Rock Canada.

1997: Hard Rock Live! debuts on VH1.

1998: First Hard Rock Hotel opens in Bali.

1999: The 100th Hard Rock opens in Amsterdam.

2001: Hard Rock celebrates its 30th anniversary.

2005: First Hard Rock Café opens in India.

2007: Rank Group sells Hard Rock to the Seminole Tribe of Florida.

2009: Hard Rock Hotel/Casino resorts open in Hungary and Malaysia.

Although Morton brought the concept to the United States, Tigrett was the first to realize immediate success by opening a Hard Rock in New York City with financial assistance from comedian Dan Aykroyd and actor Yul Brynner.

Critics hailed Tigrett's New York restaurant as the true Hard Rock incarnation and crowds flocked to the new venue. Inside the new restaurant Tigrett created the first guitar-shaped bar, the largest collection of rock-n-roll memorabilia, and his "God Wall," a tribute to the inspirational forces guiding people's lives, featuring, among other things, a photograph of Sai Baba, a giant Krugerrand, and an enormous Quaalude.

After the opening of the New York Hard Rock, the two former partners continued to compete. Morton opened a café in San Francisco in an old automobile showroom; Tigrett opened one in Stockholm in 1985, followed by the largest Hard Rock at the time in Dallas the following year. While Tigrett and Morton built their respective empires, others joined the fray by appropriat-

ing the Hard Rock name and independently opening ersatz Hard Rock Cafés in Amsterdam, Bombay, Bangkok, and Manila.

By the late 1980s, after nearly 20 years in existence, the Hard Rock concept had become a confusing mess. The restaurants themselves were flourishing, but behind the scenes a tempest was growing. Then Robert Earl approached Tigrett with an offer. The son of a British pop singer, Earl was several years younger than both Tigrett and Morton. He had been involved in several food industry successes and amassed an empire of 70 restaurants by the time he merged his company President Entertainments with Pleasurama PLC, a London-based leisure group, in 1987. The transaction yielded Earl $63 million.

One of the first deals Earl completed for Pleasurama was the acquisition of Tigrett's half of the Hard Rock business, which had gone public in 1984. Investors had included Drexel Burnham Lambert, which sold a chunk of the company prior to the stock market plunge in October 1987, in turn sending Tigrett's stock cascading downward. Less than a year later, in August 1988, Tigrett sold his Hard Rock holdings to Earl and Pleasurama for $100 million, ending his 17-year tenure as a Hard Rock showman.

Earl took the four Hard Rocks located in Tigrett's eastern sector and began opening new establishments. He also ended his affiliation with Pleasurama in 1989, when the leisure company was acquired by Mecca Leisure PLC.

A RENAISSANCE FOR HARD ROCK: 1990–95

After Mecca Leisure PLC acquired Pleasurama, it in turn was swallowed by Rank Organisation PLC, a British-based conglomerate, in 1990. By the time the dust had settled, there were 25 Hard Rocks dotting the globe, counting both Morton's and Earl's, the newest, largest, and most successful being the Orlando, Florida, Hard Rock, which opened in 1990 and almost immediately began serving 5,000 customers a day.

The Orlando Hard Rock belonged to Earl, as did nine more slated for construction in the coming years. Surprisingly, Tigrett and Morton found themselves agreeing on one issue: neither could abide Earl. Tigrett condemned Earl for treating the Hard Rock concept like a cash cow to be duplicated again and again until its novelty was exhausted, and Morton and Earl had become adversaries during the course of their business relationship.

Earl and Morton jointly owned Hard Rock Licensing Corporation, the company controlling the rights to

Hard Rock's lucrative trademarks. The licensing entity also served as a proving ground for both owners' divergent views as to which direction the name should be taken. A running feud between the two had begun almost as soon as Earl bought Tigrett's half of the Hard Rock empire, and as time progressed the animosity intensified.

Earl irrevocably aggravated tensions in 1991 when he opened Planet Hollywood in New York, a block away from the Hard Rock Café, with his own band of celebrity investors including film producer Keith Barish, director John Hughes, and actors Arnold Schwarzenegger and Bruce Willis. Designed by Anton Furst (who created the sets for the first *Batman* film), Planet Hollywood was to the film world what Hard Rock was to rock-n-roll, a restaurant housing memorabilia from the film industry, providing customers with an opportunity to enjoy the glamour of Hollywood. When Morton accused Earl of illegally copying the Hard Rock concept, Earl flatly denied it, commenting to *New York* magazine, "Planet Hollywood was carefully designed so there would be no accusation whatsoever of duplication. You'll find zero similarity."

By the summer of 1992 Morton filed three lawsuits against Rank Organisation and Robert Earl. Earl responded by announcing his intention to leave Rank and pursue his Planet Hollywood-related business interests, opening the door for Art Levitt to become president and CEO of Hard Rock International. Levitt, formerly of Walt Disney Company, inherited 22 Hard Rock Cafés in 13 countries, as well as competition from another musically themed eatery, House of Blues, from former insider Isaac Tigrett. Not to be outdone, Levitt expanded Hard Rock's reach into a host of exotic locations including San Juan, Miami, Mexico City, Bali, and Taipei.

In 1994 Hard Rock added four international restaurants to its roster (in Beijing, Cozumel, Kowloon, and Madrid), while stateside, the company set out to conquer the country music capital of the world in Nashville. The year also saw the debut of another themed restaurant chain, Rainforest Café, followed by 14 new Hard Rocks in 1995 as both Rainforest Café and Planet Hollywood went public. Both were initial successes and Hard Rock quaked just a bit.

THEMED RESTAURANTS HIT THEIR ZENITH: 1996–99

With competitors popping up around the globe, often within spitting distance, Hard Rock continued its aggressive expansion with 13 new restaurants in 1996. However, the biggest news of the year went to Rank

(which changed its name to Rank Group PLC), scoring a coup by acquiring Peter Morton's Hard Rock America as well as the ownership to Hard Rock Canada, owned by Nick Bitove. The Hard Rock name and brand, a formidable and lucrative force worldwide, was owned by one entity in total control of the increasingly popular trademark.

Tigrett's House of Blues chain, meanwhile, had opened a heavily touted restaurant/club in Chicago and Earl's Planet Hollywood aggressively expanded as well. Yet all was not well in the flashy industry, as the market seemed to overload on garishly themed restaurants.

By early 1997 Hard Rock actually came to mean music as the company teamed up with VH1 for *Hard Rock Live!*, a weekly television series. Each show featured performances by top names in the music industry, from the hottest new groups to legends from the annals of rock history. Aired on MTV's popular sibling VH1, *Hard Rock Live!* was a hit, spawning a concert series and record deal with Rhino Records. Stages were added to Hard Rock restaurants in Orlando and Mexico City, creating complexes for food, fun, and live rock performances.

Fresh from its flourishing television series, Hard Rock Café International leapt in three disparate directions in 1998: the first was inking a deal with the National Basketball Association to open ten basketball-themed restaurants; the second was a jump into the hospitality industry when the first Hard Rock Hotel opened in Bali in May; and the third was the debut of the company's official web site, www.hardrock.com. Revenues for 1998 reached $398 million with a net profit of $84 million from Hard Rock's more than 25 million customers.

In 1999 Peter J. Beaudrault was named president of Hard Rock Café International, the year Earl's Planet Hollywood chain filed for Chapter 11 bankruptcy. As an undisclosed number of Planet Hollywoods were closed, Hard Rock opened new eateries in Indiana, Florida, Tennessee, and Japan, bringing the tally to 104 cafés in 36 countries. Hard Rock had also signed with Full House Resorts Inc. to develop a number of U.S.-based hotels and casinos as corporate parent Rank brought in a new CEO, Mike Smith. Smith promptly put Rank's entire operation under close scrutiny, believing Hard Rock and other subsidiaries were bloated and mismanaged. Cost-cutting, mostly in the form of layoffs, followed with 500 Rank employees getting the ax, including 107 at Hard Rock.

A NEW ERA: 2000–07

Hard Rock underwent a metamorphosis in 2000, in part to shore up its sagging sales and image, and to prepare for its 30th anniversary. For only the second time, the company unleashed a major media campaign touting its rock-n-roll roots and celebrating its eclectic atmosphere as the original and best themed restaurant chain. By mid-year Hard Rock launched a redesigned web site and threw a one-day "Rockfest" in Chicago to tout its rebirth.

The hoopla had some effect but Hard Rock's revenues fell significantly in 2001 after the September 11 terrorist attacks and well into 2002. In 2003 Hard Rock renewed its exclusive beverage deal with PepsiCo, signing on for another seven years, as Beaudrault left the ailing company after four years at the helm. Rank's Mike Smith assumed his duties until Hamish Dodds, a former PepsiCo and Cabcorp executive, joined Hard Rock as president and CEO in March 2004. The year also saw the beginning of a lucrative partnership between Hard Rock and Florida's Seminole Tribe, as the two collaborated on a new hotel and casino in Tampa.

By 2005 there were about 120 Hard Rock Café restaurants in 40-plus countries and Rank Group had come to believe hotel/casino resorts were a particularly profitable venue for the brand. To secure a stronger foothold in the industry, Rank Group hired Vegas veteran Michael Soll, formerly of Caesars Entertainment, to fill a newly created vice-president of casinos position. While many Hard Rock hotels and restaurants worldwide continued to thrive, others fell victim to consumer apathy and lower-priced fare. In 2006 Rank Group announced its intention to sell Hard Rock International for a rumored $1 billion, including the chain's huge memorabilia collection with some 60,000 iconic items.

Once Hard Rock International was put on the block, Florida's Seminole Tribe, one of the company's hotel/casino partners, became a possible suitor. Despite wrangling and vocal opposition from numerous bidders and interested parties, the Seminole Tribe, which operated seven casinos in Florida (including two Hard Rock Hotel gaming resorts), acquired Hard Rock International for $965 million in early 2007. It proved to be a win-win situation: Rank Group was able to concentrate on its U.K.-based operations and the Seminoles were able to expand their gaming enterprises throughout the world with an instantly recognizable brand.

NEW OWNERSHIP: 2008 AND BEYOND

Hard Rock's fortunes steadily increased under the leadership of its new parent, Seminole Hard Rock Entertainment, Inc. In 2008 Hard Rock opened its first eatery in Bucharest, Romania, a second location in Singapore, a third restaurant in India, and reopened restaurants in Seoul, Beijing, and Kuala Lampur after renovations. Stateside the company launched its annual Ambassadors of Rock charity tour featuring an impressive roster including Eric Clapton, Sheryl Crow, and The Police, then partnered with cancer survivor Melissa Etheridge for "Pinktober" to raise funds and awareness of breast cancer throughout the month of October.

As new cafés were opened in 2009 including international sites in India, Italy, and the Czech Republic, and domestically in Dallas and Seattle, Hard Rock was busy expanding its hotel/casino holdings with new resorts planned in Hungary and Penang/Malaysia (2009); Atlanta, Palm Springs, Singapore, and Panama (2010); Dubai (2011); and Abu Dhabi (2012). While there had been vehement opposition to the Seminole Tribe's purchase of Hard Rock International, the new ownership had proven not only lucrative but a sound business decision. Within three years of acquiring the well-known brand, the Seminoles had increased its revenues from around $600 million to an estimated $1 billion annually.

As the company approached the 40-year mark, Hard Rock had once again gained the pinnacle of success and showed no signs of slowing down. Like 60-somethings Mick Jagger, Eric Clapton, and Paul McCartney, Hard Rock Café International proved itself a powerful, enduring brand and a dominant force in the industry it had helped to create.

Jeffrey L. Covell
Updated, Nelson Rhodes

PRINCIPAL OPERATING UNITS

Hard Rock Cafés; Hard Rock Hotels/Casinos; Hard Rock Entertainment.

PRINCIPAL COMPETITORS

Ark Restaurants Corporation; Bubba Gump Shrimp Company Restaurants, Inc.; Johnny Rockets Group, Inc.; Planet Hollywood International, Inc.; Rainforest Café, Inc.; HOB Entertainment Inc.

FURTHER READING

Buchthal, Kristina, "Sour Notes at Hard Rock Hotel," *Crain's Chicago Business*, September 13, 2004, p. 54.

Finkelstein, Alex, "Hard Rock Café Sues Hard Hats Café," *Orlando Business Journal*, February 7, 1992, p. 3.

Giles, Jeff, "No Fear of Frying," *Rolling Stone*, November 14, 1991, pp. 15, 18, 21.

"Hard Rock Café Plans to Open a Hotel/Casino in Las Vegas," *Travel Weekly,* June 13, 1991, p. 1.

"Hard Rock Hotel to Headline in Vegas," *Restaurant/Hotel Design International,* October 1991, p. 14.

Harris, David, "Chief Bows Out from the Hard Rock Café," *Caterer & Hotelkeeper,* February 6, 2003, p. 9.

Hayes, Jack, "Earl to Rank Leisure: Hasta la Vista Baby!" *Nation's Restaurant News,* December 14, 1992, p. 1.

"HRC's Morton Files New Suit to Block Chicago 'Knock-Off,'" *Nation's Restaurant News,* June 29, 1992, p. 2.

Hume, Scott, et al., "CH-CH-CH-Changes," *Restaurants & Institutions,* July 15, 2000, p. 17.

Jackson, Jerry, "Hard Rock Café Hires Vegas Veteran to Expand Its Global Reach in Casinos," *Orlando Sentinel* (via Knight-Ridder/Tribune Business News), February 17, 2005.

———, "Planet Hollywood Files for Bankruptcy and Closes in Miami, Lauderdale," *Orlando Sentinel,* October 11, 1999.

Jeter, Lynne W., "Tribe Lands Hard Rock Hotel, Beach Club for Resort," *Mississippi Business Journal,* February 10, 2003, p. 12.

Krueger, Jill, "Pete Beaudrault Wants to Build a Better Burger," *Orlando Business Journal,* October 22, 1999, p. 3.

Martin, Richard, "Hard Rock Hits Planet Hollywood with Copycat Suit," *Nation's Restaurant News,* March 16, 1992, p. 3.

McCoy, Kevin, "Hard Rock Acquisition Is Seminole Tribe's Latest Triumph," *USA Today,* December 8, 2006, p. 4B.

Middleton, Christopher, "The Hard Rock with a Soft Sell," *Marketing,* April 25, 1991, p. 23.

Moskowitz, Milton, *The Global Marketplace,* New York: Macmillan Publishing, 1987, pp. 248–51.

O'Conner, Amy, "The Man Who Puts the Rock in the Hard Rock Café," *Restaurants & Institutions,* February 15, 1994, p. 14.

Reisinger, Sue, "The Long Shot: How the Seminoles ... Won the Bidding War for the Hard Rock Empire," *Corporate Counsel,* April 2007, pp. 76+.

Templeman, John, "Hard Rock Café, History for Sale," *Business Week Online,* July 6, 2006.

"This Hard Rock Is Rolling," *Florida Trend,* January 1992, p. 18.

Zacharias, Beth, "Art Levitt Rolls into Hard Rock," *Orlando Business Journal,* January 11, 1993, p. 3.

Harsco Corporation

■

350 Poplar Church Road
Camp Hill, Pennsylvania 17011-2521
U.S.A.
Telephone: (717) 763-7064
Fax: (717) 763-6424
Web site: http://www.harsco.com

Public Company
Incorporated: 1956
Employees: 21,500
Sales: $3.97 billion (2008)
Stock Exchanges: New York
Ticker Symbol: HSC
NAICS: 532490 Other Commercial and Industrial Machinery and Equipment Rental and Leasing; 563930 Materials Recovery Facilities; 488210 Support Activities for Rail Transportation

■ ■ ■

Harsco Corporation is a globally active, diversified industrial services company. The firm's two largest areas of operation are infrastructure and metals. In infrastructure, Harsco serves industrial and nonresidential construction customers, selling and renting scaffolding and concrete shoring and forming equipment and offering other services, including project engineering and equipment erection and dismantling. In metals, Harsco is the world leader in onsite, outsourced services for metals industries, including raw materials handling, byproduct processing, and onsite recycling. Other company units are involved in railway track maintenance services and equipment, minerals recovery services, and the production of industrial grating, air-cooled heat exchangers, and energy-efficient boilers. Western Europe accounts for about 45 percent of Harsco's revenues; North America, 35 percent; Latin America, 6 percent; the Middle East and Africa, 6 percent; Eastern Europe, 5 percent; and the Asia-Pacific region, 3 percent.

EARLY HISTORY AND ACQUISITIONS

Harsco Corporation was formed in 1956, from the merger of Harrisburg Steel Corporation, Heckett Engineering Inc., and Precision Castings Co. With a history dating back to 1853, Harrisburg Steel, based in Harrisburg, Pennsylvania, had by the mid-20th century evolved into a well-respected producer of high-quality industrial castings, forgings, and specialized metal products. Heckett Engineering had been founded in 1939 by a Dutch immigrant, Eric Heckett, who installed the first successful large-scale metallic recovery plant in the United States at Republic Steel's South Chicago plant. At its founding, Harsco also included Taylor-Wharton, a metalworking operation involved in the production of cryogenic storage vessels and high-pressure cylinders.

Several years after the 1956 merger that created Harsco, the company began a multiyear string of acquisitions that diversified its operations. In 1964 the company entered the scaffolding field through the purchase of Patent Scaffolding Company, a leading supplier of sectional and tubular scaffolding and shoring equipment. Two years later, Harsco acquired the Irving Subway Grating Co., the first commercial steel grating company, founded in 1912. In the same year, Harsco acquired two other grating makers and combined all three as the IKG Industries division.

In 1974 Harsco acquired Patterson-Kelley Company, which had begun operating in 1880 as a producer of water heaters for commercial and industrial sites. The company was the first to develop fully packaged water heaters that could be easily installed with just a few connections. By the time it became part of the expanding Harsco empire, Patterson-Kelley ranked as a leading supplier of boilers for large buildings, such as schools, hotels, and hospitals, and also produced blenders for the pharmaceutical and food-processing industries. In 1976 Patterson-Kelley was turned into a division of Harsco. That same year, Harsco purchased Air-X-Changers, a leading international supplier of air-cooled heat exchangers used in the natural gas processing industry to protect compression systems and condition natural gas during recovery, compression, and transportation. In 1979 Harsco expanded into railway track maintenance equipment and services by purchasing Fairmont Railway Motors, a firm founded in Fairmont, Minnesota, in 1909 that was a leading supplier of tie replacement and spike-driving equipment, rail grinders, and road/rail equipment.

FURTHER ACQUISITIONS IN THE EIGHTIES

Continuing its acquisitions, Harsco in 1982 bought Astralloy-Vulcan Corp., a world leader in the supply and fabrication of high-strength and wear-resistant steels used in the mining, steel, and pulp and paper industries. The following year the company acquired Structural Composites Industries, Inc., the world's largest manufacturer of compressed gas composite cylinders and Super Tanks. Also in 1983, Harsco acquired Reed

Materials Inc., which was the first company in the United States to convert utility coal slag into granules for asphalt roofing shingles.

In 1986 Harsco acquired Easco Corp. and Borden Metal Products Co., both of which were folded into the IKG Industries division. Three years later, Harsco acquired Tamper Corporation from Toronto-based Canron Inc. Based in West Columbia, South Carolina, with additional facilities in Australia, the United Kingdom, and India, Tamper was known for its comprehensive line of automated tamping equipment for lifting, leveling, lining, and tamping track. Tamper was merged into Fairmont Railway to form Fairmont Tamper.

From 1989 to 1990 Harsco's defense business was able to stem some of its losses due to Pentagon cutbacks by supplying equipment to the U.S. Army and foreign nations. In 1989 the U.S. Army chose to purchase the M88A1E1 made by BMY-Combat Systems. The vehicle was a 139,000-pound updated version of the company's M88 recovery vehicle used to aid disabled tanks on the battlefield. With new tanks weighing 70 tons, a strong recovery vehicle was needed to tow to safety those tanks rendered inoperable in the midst of battle. In addition, the Persian Gulf War of 1990 helped spur sales for "Big Foot," a five-ton truck whose tires partially deflate for sand travel.

Harsco's acquisition activity continued in the early 1990s. In 1993 the company acquired a majority equity position in INFLEX, S.A., a manufacturer of steel cylinders for permanent and liquefied gases. INFLEX, based in Buenos Aires, Argentina, had a production facility in San Luis. Also in 1993, Harsco bought the assets of Wayne Corporation, a manufacturer of school buses. Production was subsequently transferred to a converted Harsco defense plant in Marysville, Ohio.

ENTER MULTISERV, EXIT DEFENSE

A much more significant deal, and in fact the largest acquisition Harsco had completed to that time, occurred in August 1993 when the company spent $384 million for MultiServ International N.V. The takeover of the U.K.-based MultiServ more than doubled the size of Harsco's metals reclamation business. The subsequent merger of MultiServ and Harsco's Heckett division to form Heckett MultiServ created the world leader in on-site, outsourced services to the steel and metals industry, including the reclamation of usable metals from slag and the recycling of refined scrap for steelmaking. At its formation, Heckett MultiServ was serving more than 130 steel mill locations in 28 countries. Its combined revenues totaled some $550 million.

KEY DATES

1956: Harsco Corporation is formed from the merger of Harrisburg Steel Corporation, Heckett Engineering Inc., and Precision Castings Co.

1964: Company enters the scaffolding field via the purchase of Patent Scaffolding Company.

1966: Three grating companies are acquired and form the basis for the IKG Industries division.

1974: Patterson-Kelley Company, a leading supplier of boilers for large buildings, is acquired.

1976: Harsco purchases Air-X-Changers, a leading international supplier of air-cooled heat exchangers used in the natural gas processing industry.

1979: Company expands into railway track maintenance equipment and services by purchasing Fairmont Railway Motors, later Fairmont Tamper.

1993: Harsco acquires U.K.-based MultiServ International N.V. and combines it with Heckett to form the world's largest metals reclamation business, Heckett MultiServ.

1994: Company places its defense business into a joint venture with FMC Corporation.

1997: Harsco-FMC joint venture defense unit is sold to Carlyle Group.

1999: Harsco purchases the Pandrol Jackson railway track maintenance business and merges it into the Fairmont Tamper division, which is then renamed Harsco Track Technologies.

2000: Company delves further into the scaffolding sector via the purchase of the U.K. firm SGB Group Plc.

2004: Mill services operations are consolidated into a single worldwide unit operating under the name MultiServ.

2005: Harsco acquires the German firm Hünnebeck GmbH for its global infrastructure unit.

2007: Harsco acquires Excell Minerals, Inc.

2008: Main business units are rebranded as Harsco Infrastructure, Harsco Metals, and Harsco Minerals and Rail.

At the end of 1993, Malcolm W. Gambill retired as CEO after more than six years at Harsco's helm. His successor was Derek C. Hathaway, who had previously served as president and COO. As this leadership transition was implemented, and concurrent with the major deal for MultiServ, Harsco took its first step toward exiting from the defense industry by combining its defense business with that of FMC Corporation and creating the joint venture United Defense, L.P. This venture, controlled by FMC through a 60 percent stake with Harsco holding 40 percent, was officially created in January 1994.

The offloading of the defense business into the joint venture coupled with the acquisition of MultiServ laid the foundation for Hathaway to shift Harsco's focus away from manufacturing to the service sector. By 1995 Heckett MultiServ accounted for half of Harsco's revenues. Hathaway also sought growth in another service-oriented company unit, the Fairmont Tamper railway maintenance division. Around this same time the company's scaffolding business, Patent Construction Systems, moved into the scaffolding service market for the first time. In addition, Harsco's manufacturing footprint grew smaller in 1995 when the firm abandoned its nascent move into the production of school buses. The shift to services was accompanied by a big overseas push, which was also jump-started by the MultiServ acquisition. Largely because of that purchase, the portion of revenues that Harsco generated outside the United States jumped from 17 percent in 1993 to 39 percent in 1995.

Throughout its service businesses, Harsco began aggressively pursuing long-term multimillion-dollar service contracts as a base of steady revenues. In 1995, for instance, Harsco's Fairmont Tamper division entered into a six-year, multimillion-dollar agreement with Burlington Northern and Santa Fe Railway to replace railway ties on the railroad's track and re-lay and re-anchor the track. During 1996 alone, Heckett MultiServ entered into several long-term metal-reclamation and mill-services contracts valued collectively at more than $200 million over the course of the contracts. These service operations gained even greater importance starting in August 1997 when Harsco and FMC sold United Defense to Carlyle Group for $850 million.

NEW STRING OF MAINLY SERVICE-ORIENTED ACQUISITIONS

Harsco's share of the pretax cash proceeds from the sale of United Defense amounted to $344 million, and the company quickly began plowing much of this gain into acquisitions that beefed up its core operations. In April 1998 Heckett Multiserv gained added heft with the purchase of Faber Prest Plc for around $98 million. The

U.K.-based Faber provided onsite slag-processing and materials-handling services to steel producers and generated annual sales of approximately $140 million. Harsco's Taylor-Wharton gas-containment equipment division was bolstered through the June 1998 takeover of Chemi-Trol Chemical Co. for about $46 million. Chemi-Trol, based in Gibsonburg, Ohio, specialized in steel pressure tanks for the storage of propane gas and anhydrous ammonia.

In October 1999 Harsco completed a key purchase for its Fairmont Tamper division, buying Charter plc's Pandrol Jackson railway track maintenance business for about $65 million in cash and assumed debt. After Ludington, Michigan-based Pandrol Jackson was absorbed into Fairmont Tamper, the division was renamed Harsco Track Technologies. With annual revenues of around $200 million, it ranked as the second largest railway maintenance operation in the world, although it lagged far behind the global leader, Plasser & Theurer of Austria.

In June 2000, Harsco completed another key deal, acquiring SGB Group Plc for about $272 million. The London-based SGB was one of Europe's leaders in scaffolding, formwork, shoring, and other access services and products and also had a significant presence in the Middle East and Asia. With both SGB and Patent Construction Systems in the fold, Harsco had the ability to service major construction and maintenance projects anywhere in the world. The SGB buyout also helped push the company's revenues over the $2 billion mark in 2000.

Over the next few years, Harsco suspended its acquisition activity as it concentrated on contending with the economic downturn and a particularly lengthy recession in U.S. manufacturing. Reducing the increased debt load that had been incurred in the purchase of SGB was a key initiative during this period. Strong growth did not return until 2004, when the company reported record profits of $121.2 million on record revenues of $2.5 billion. Also that year, the company consolidated its mill services operations into a single worldwide unit operating under the name MultiServ.

MAJOR 2005 DEALS

Harsco's next major acquisition occurred in November 2005 with the purchase of the German firm Hünnebeck GmbH for EUR 140 million ($164 million). As the third largest provider of highly engineered construction formwork and scaffolding services in Europe, Hünnebeck served as the third leg in Harsco's global infrastructure unit. As a follow-on to the deal for SGB, Hünnebeck provided Harsco with a presence in several

additional European countries, including Germany, Norway, Sweden, Poland, Hungary, and Italy. Hünnebeck's strength in formwork engineering and rentals was also complementary to Patent's and SGB's historically strong positions in scaffolding. During 2006, Harsco's infrastructure businesses generated more than $1 billion in revenues, or more than 31 percent of the overall company total of $3.42 billion. In December 2005, meanwhile, Harsco bought the Northern Hemisphere steel mill services operations of the Australian firm Brambles Industrial Limited for around $236 million. The acquired unit provided onsite, outsourced mill services to the steel and metals industries, with operations at 19 locations in the United Kingdom, France, the Netherlands, and the United States. Worldwide revenues for MultiServ in 2006 totaled $1.37 billion, or about 40 percent of the company total.

In a move that complemented its position as a pioneer in the reuse of slag materials from the steel and metals industries, Harsco in February 2007 acquired Pittsburgh-based Excell Minerals, Inc., for around $210 million. Excell specialized in the reclamation and recycling of high-value content mainly from steelmaking slag while also working to develop mineral-based products for commercial applications. Excell generated revenues of more than $100 million from its operations in the United States, Canada, Brazil, South Africa, and Germany.

In December 2007 Harsco focused even more keenly on service businesses by selling its gas technologies operations, which included Taylor-Wharton, to the private-equity firm Wind Point Partners for $340 million. This transaction served as a fitting capstone to the career of Hathaway, who retired as CEO at the end of 2007, having thoroughly transformed Harsco during his 14-year tenure from a mishmash of largely domestic manufacturing-oriented businesses to an internationally active company concentrating on a select array of industrial services. During 2007 services accounted for 85 percent of revenues, compared to just 28 percent in 1993. Hathaway's strong international push was just as evident given that overseas revenues increased from 17 percent of the total in 1993 to around 65 percent in 2007.

RESTRUCTURING AND REBRANDING UNDER NEW LEADER

Salvatore D. Fazzolari took the helm at the beginning of 2008, promoted from his previous position as president, treasurer, and CFO. Despite the economic turmoil that year and having to contend with declining global steel production and a lackluster construction market, Harsco still managed to generate record revenues just shy of $4 billion. Profits dropped 20 percent, however, to $240.9 million in part because of a $36.1 million restructuring charge taken in the fourth quarter to cut jobs, close facilities, and cancel some contracts. Also during 2008, Harsco made a concerted push into emerging markets, entering India, Russia, Romania, and Panama. The company late in the year introduced a new corporate logo as part of a rebranding of its three business units to emphasize the Harsco name. The Patent, SGB, and Hünnebeck businesses were unified under the Harsco Infrastructure banner; the mill services operations became known as Harsco Metals; and the company's other units, including Harsco Track Technologies, Excell Minerals, and the remaining manufacturing businesses, were housed under Harsco Minerals and Rail.

Going forward, Harsco planned to continue building its balanced array of businesses with an emphasis on international growth. Emerging markets were a particularly high priority, especially the Gulf region of the Middle East, China, and India. The company planned to pursue selected bolt-on acquisitions as another avenue of growth. Harsco hoped to also continue its consistently strong and steady history of financial performance. This company hallmark was perhaps best exemplified by the firm's string of 15 consecutive years of increased dividends through the year 2008 and the payment of its 237th consecutive quarterly cash dividend to stockholders for the second quarter of 2009.

Dorothy Kroll
Updated, David E. Salamie

PRINCIPAL SUBSIDIARIES

Harsco Track Technologies Pty. Ltd. (Australia); MultiServ Holdings Pty. Limited (Australia; 55%); Hünnebeck Austria Schalungstechnik GmbH; MultiServ Limitada (Brazil); Harsco Canada Corporation; Hünnebeck SGB ApS (Denmark); SGB Egypt for Scaffolding and Formwork S.A.E. (98.85%); Harsco France SAS; Hünnebeck France S.A.S.; MultiServ S.A.S. (France); SGB S.A.S. (France); Harsco GmbH (Germany); Hünnebeck Group GmbH (Germany); SGB Scafform Limited (Ireland); Hünnebeck Italia S.p.A. (Italy); SGB Baltics S.I.A. (Latvia; 70%); Andamios Patentados, S.A. de C.V. (Mexico); Irving, S.A. de C.V. (Mexico); Harsco Europa B.V. (Netherlands); SGB Hünnebeck Formwork (Netherlands); SGB North Europe B.V. (Netherlands); Hünnebeck Norge AS (Norway); Hünnebeck Polska Sp zoo (Poland); SGB Al Darwish United WLL (Qatar; 49%); Hünnebeck Russia OOO; MultiServ South Africa (Pty.) Limited; Hün-

nebeck Sverige A.B. (Sweden); Quebeisi SGB LLC (United Arab Emirates; 49%); Hünnebeck Middle East FZE (United Arab Emirates); Harsco (UK) Holdings Ltd.; MultiServ Holding Limited (UK); SGB Group Ltd. (UK).

PRINCIPAL DIVISIONS

SGB Group; Hünnebeck Group; Patent Construction Systems; MultiServ; Harsco Track Technologies; Excell Minerals; Reed Minerals; Air-X-Changers; IKG Industries; Patterson-Kelley.

PRINCIPAL COMPETITORS

ThyssenKrupp Safway Inc.; Edw. C. Levy Co.; Philip Services Corporation; United Scaffolding, Inc.; Brand Energy, Inc.; Plasser & Theurer.

FURTHER READING

Caliri, Lois, "Harsco Sheds Old Image for New," *Central Penn Business Journal,* June 9, 1995, p. 1.

Campanella, Frank W., "Recovery Specialist: Harsco Enjoys Strong Rebound in Diverse Industrial, Defense Products," *Barron's,* October 29, 1984, pp. 51+.

Colodny, Mark M., "Frank Carlucci Goes Hunting," *Fortune,* February 25, 1991, p. 155.

Douchat, Tom, "Harsco Doubles Size of Steel Reclamation Division," *Harrisburg (Pa.) Patriot-News,* September 1, 1993, p. B7.

———, "Harsco Evolves with Times: Hathaway Leads Company's Conversion," *Harrisburg (Pa.) Patriot-News,* May 22, 1994, p. D1.

———, "Harsco Expects to Cash In from a Buying Spree," *Harrisburg (Pa.) Patriot-News,* April 5, 1998, p. D1.

———, "Harsco, FMC Merge Units," *Harrisburg (Pa.) Patriot-News,* January 29, 1994, p. A10.

———, "Harsco Sets Strategy to Beat Defense Cuts," *Harrisburg (Pa.) Patriot-News,* February 28, 1993, p. F1.

———, "Harsco's Gambill to Step Down," *Harrisburg (Pa.) Patriot-News,* December 17, 1993, p. A1.

———, "Hathaway Developed Strategies for Harsco," *Harrisburg (Pa.) Patriot-News,* August 14, 2007, p. C1.

———, "Record Sales, Earnings Boost Harsco Stock," *Harrisburg (Pa.) Patriot-News,* February 1, 2006, p. C2.

———, "Retiring Leader Did His Share for Harsco," *Harrisburg (Pa.) Patriot-News,* April 20, 2008, p. C1.

———, "Scaffolding Firm Swallows Buyout," *Harrisburg (Pa.) Patriot-News,* June 13, 2000, p. B9.

———, "Sluggish Economy Smothers Harsco's Earnings," *Harrisburg (Pa.) Patriot-News,* February 1, 2002, p. B7.

———, "United Defense Sold to Carlyle," *Harrisburg (Pa.) Patriot-News,* August 27, 1997, p. A1.

Johnston, Phil W., "Clunk, Clang, Clatter," *Popular Science,* May 1989, p. 56.

Miller, James P., and Erle Norton, "FMC and Harsco Are Planning to Merge Most Operations in the Defense Sector," *Wall Street Journal,* December 3, 1992, p. A5.

"A Sleeping Beauty with a Suitor," *Business Week,* November 19, 1990, p. 128.

Staves, Jennifer Trent, "MultiServ Expands and Diversifies Mill Services," *Metal Bulletin Monthly,* January 2008, pp. 44–45.

Stern, Gabriella, "Harsco Seeks to Shield Itself As Defense Spending Falls," *Wall Street Journal,* July 12, 1993, p. B4.

Thompson, Richard, "Harsco Is Recharged by Scrap Metal, Hazardous Waste," *Wall Street Journal,* October 11, 1995, p. B4.

Hogg Robinson Group PLC

Global House, Victoria Street
Basingstoke, RG21 3BT
United Kingdom
Telephone: (+44 01256) 312 600
Fax: (+44 01256) 325 299
Web site: http://www.hoggrobinson.co.uk

Public Company
Incorporated: 2006
Employees: 6,206
Sales: £351.3 million ($450 million) (2009)
Stock Exchanges: London
Ticker Symbol: HRG
NAICS: 488510 Freight Transportation Arrangement;
488999 All Other Support Activities for Transportation; 561599 All Other Travel Arrangement and
Reservation Services

■ ■ ■

Hogg Robinson Group PLC (HRG) is one of the world's leading providers of corporate travel and related services. Founded in 1845 as a wine merchant, and formerly one of the United Kingdom's leading insurance brokers, HRG has refocused itself around two main divisions and five core businesses. International Corporate Travel Services is the group's largest division, with operations dating back to 1945. This division includes the Corporate Travel Management, Consulting, Events & Meetings Management, and Sports business units, and is supported by a global network of subsidiaries and affiliates in more than 100 countries. Through

this division, HRG offers a full range of travel consulting, booking, events planning, sports entertainment, and travel assistance services. The second division, Spendvision/Expense Management, based on HRG's majority control of Spendvision Holdings Ltd., provides services related to the management and oversight of corporate expenses. HRG has expanded strongly in part through the acquisition of former members of the Business Travel International partnership. The company went public in 2006, with a listing on the London Stock Exchange. David Radcliffe is the group's chief executive officer. At the end of its March 2009 fiscal year, HRG's revenues topped £351 million ($450 million).

WINE AND INSURANCE IN 1845

Hogg Robinson stemmed from the business empire founded by Augustus Robinson and his brother-in-law Francis Hogg in 1845. The Robinson family by then had long held a prominent place in England's marine insurance industry. Robinson's father, John Robinson, had been a subscriber to the Lloyd's of London marine insurance brokerage at the beginning of the 19th century. Between 1800 and 1818, John Robinson also held a position on the Lloyd's governing committee.

Augustus Robinson followed his father into the marine insurance industry. Robinson also established his own trading business. This led him into cooperation with brother-in-law Francis Hogg, who had developed a career as a wine merchant. The combination of all three businesses led to the creation of the future Hogg Robinson group.

COMPANY PERSPECTIVES

Our strategy: HRG is an international corporate services company which operates five businesses, through its regionally structured organisation, related to the logistics and cost control of travel—typically an organisation's second-largest controllable expense after salaries.

HRG uses its substantial buying, processing and analytical power to drive down costs for clients while simultaneously maximising service and security to their travellers. It aligns global systems and reach with detailed local knowledge in approximately 100 markets worldwide and combines pioneering, integrated proprietary technology with strong client relationships and personnel development.

Hogg Robinson functioned as a partnership throughout most of its first century. Following Robinson's decision to retire in 1893, the company brought in a series of new partners, including members of the Hogg and Robinson families. Insurance underwriting had emerged as the company's primary business. Nonetheless, the company continued to operate in the shipping market for quite some time. The company also established its own freight-forwarding operations.

The year 1931 marked a new milestone for the company. In that year, Hogg Robinson agreed to merge with another family-based insurance brokerage, E. Capel-Cure & Company. Like Hogg Robinson, Capel-Cure's involvement in the British marine market stemmed from the 18th century. As early as 1775, a member of Capel-Cure had been one of the original Lloyd's subscribers.

ADDING CORPORATE TRAVEL
SERVICES IN 1945

Following the merger, Hogg Robinson abandoned its partnership status and incorporated as a private limited company, Hogg Robinson & Capel-Cure Ltd. Insurance underwriting continued to be the group's main business, although the company maintained its small shipping and freight-forwarding operations through the 1960s. The Hogg family also continued to be represented in the company, with Edward Hogg holding the chairman's position into that decade.

By then, the company had expanded dramatically. From just 75 employees at the time of its merger with

Capel-Cure, Hogg Robinson developed into a major internationally operating insurance underwriter, with more than 1,000 employees. The company expansion took place especially in the years following World War II. Through the 1950s, the company built up a network of branches in England and Scotland, including offices in Birmingham, Bradford, Bristol, Glasgow, Liverpool, Manchester, and Sheffield.

Hogg Robinson also expanded overseas. The company established a number of subsidiaries, as well as developed a network of associated companies. This allowed the group to gain a presence in Canada, central Africa, and Trinidad. For its East African operations, the company created a new subsidiary based in Kenya, in 1953. That company then provided insurance underwriting services to Uganda and Tanganyika, as well as in Kenya.

The postwar period marked the debut of another new activity for Hogg Robinson. In 1945, the company had begun receiving requests from a number of its insurance clients for assistance in organizing their corporate travel needs. Hogg Robinson complied, and set up its own corporate travel department. This division was to remain comparatively small into the early 1970s.

EXPANDING THE TRAVEL WING
IN THE SEVENTIES

Hogg Robinson had gone public by then, in a process launched by investment holding company Staplegreen Insurance Holdings, which acquired all of Hogg Robinson's preferred shares in early 1963. Staplegreen, which had acquired another Lloyd's underwriter, Janson, Green Ltd., in 1962, then went public in 1963. In 1964, the company launched an offer to acquire all of the deferred shares of Hogg Robinson as well.

Staplegreen acquired a number of other insurance writers through the 1960s. These included the purchases of D'Ambrumenil, Gardner Mountain, and Rennie Ltd. in 1965. Through the latter two companies, Staplegreen also expanded its African interests, buying Hutchinson & Poole. That company, with operations in Johannesburg and Salisbury, had formerly been part of the African Finance Corporation.

Hogg Robinson & Gardner Mountain, as the company now was called, formed the major part of Staplegreen Holdings in the early 1970s. Insurance, as well as the group's Lloyd's Underwriting Agents division, continued to represent the company's primary business. Indeed, the acquisition of Gardner Mountain had reduced still further the impact of the company's freight and travel operations on the group's bottom line.

KEY DATES

1845: Brothers-in-law Francis Hogg and Augustus Robinson found a company with interests in insurance, shipping, trading, and wine.

1931: Hogg Robinson merges with insurance group Capel-Cure.

1945: Hogg Robinson launches its first corporate travel operations.

1963: Hogg Robinson is acquired by Steeplechase Insurance Holding, becoming a publicly listed company.

1972: Hogg Robinson acquires Grays International Group, becoming a major U.K. travel company.

1983: Hogg Robinson acquires Wakefield Fortune Travel, becoming the United Kingdom's third largest travel group.

1990: Hogg Robinson becomes a founding partner in Business Travel International (BTI).

1993: Company focuses its travel operations on the corporate market, then sells its insurance brokering business.

2000: Hogg Robinson becomes a private company through a management buyout.

2006: Company returns to the stock market and exits the BTI partnership.

2008: Hogg Robinson acquires majority control of expense management group Spendvision.

This situation began to change in 1972, however. In that year, the company acquired Grays International Group for £475,000. The purchase enabled Hogg Robinson to position itself as a fast-growing provider of travel services to both the corporate and consumer markets. Grays, which focused primarily on the southeast England market, added its own freight-forwarding and travel services, as well as case-making and packaging services. The purchase of Grays led to the spinoff of Staplegreen's travel business into a new subsidiary, Hogg Robinson Transport.

GAINING SCALE IN THE EIGHTIES

Hogg Robinson was one of England's leading travel groups in the mid-1970s, with 17 retail agencies in operation around the United Kingdom. A consolidation of the travel sector during the decade, a result of the economic downturn of the period, brought new opportunities for this Hogg Robinson division. In 1976, the company reached an agreement to buy Grace Travel, the U.K.-based retail travel operation of conglomerate W.R. Grace. The deal added another 24 agencies, and nearly £7 million, to Hogg Robinson's travel division.

The company's insurance operations gained an entry into the U.S. market, paying $2.5 million for a 30 percent stake in Virginia's Markel Service Inc. in 1978. Two years later, the company established an insurance joint venture with Republic Steel. Hogg Robinson also added a number of other financial sector services during this time, such as pension fund management.

The future Hogg Robinson Group began to take shape in earnest during the 1980s. The company completed a major acquisition in 1983, paying £1.8 million for Wakefield Fortune Travel. Wakefield, which had struggled with losses in the early 1980s, had been owned by privately held Holland America Line Inc. The deal added another £100 million to Hogg Robinson's rapidly growing travel revenues, which by then had grown to £150 million, boosting the company to the number three spot among U.K. travel groups. The addition of Wakefield also allowed Hogg Robinson to expand its agency network into the London, West Midlands, North West, and Yorkshire markets.

Travel assumed an increasingly prominent role in the company, helping to drive profits through the middle of the 1980s. Travel had also taken on a growing share of the group's sales. This situation was heightened when the company divested its underwriting business, in accordance with new rules governing the Lloyd's-based insurance sector. Hogg Robinson grew particularly strong in the corporate travel market. By the middle of the 1980s, the company claimed to hold the number one position in the corporate travel sector.

BTI PARTNER IN THE NINETIES

Another significant acquisition, of Exchange Travel, further raised the group's travel profile. The addition of Exchange helped boost the group's agency network by some 50 stores, enabling the company to gain ground on its rivals, which then included Thomas Cook.

The late 1980s and early 1990s saw the rise of a new era of major multinational corporations. This in turn led to new opportunities for the company, which sought to expand its travel business internationally. In order to accomplish this, the company became one of the founding shareholders in Business Travel International (BTI), a gathering of corporate travel companies from around the world.

The success of BTI, which rapidly grew into one of the world leaders in the corporate travel sector, encouraged Hogg Robinson to refocus its travel business on these operations. As a result, the company sold off its leisure travel operations, to Airtours, in 1993. The following year, the company exited the insurance sector as well, selling its insurance brokering business to Inchcape-owned Bain Clarkson Ltd.

Hogg Robinson moved to gain a larger stake in the BTI partnership. In 1995, the company acquired Swedish BTI cofounder Bennett Travel Group, gaining that company's operations in Sweden, Finland, Denmark, and Norway. Two years later, the company moved into France, buying the corporate travel operations there of another BTI partner, Kuoni. That acquisition followed an agreement among BTI's four major shareholders, which included BTI Netherlands, Kuoni, and BTI Americas, to move toward the full integration of BTI's operations. In this way, the companies expected the BTI partnership to operate as a single, global company.

BTI continued to gain scale, buying several of the smaller BTI partners, including Kuoni's corporate travel business in Italy. The company added operations in Australia, Russia, and Finland, then entered Canada, taking over a 51 percent stake in BTI partner Rider Travel. Also during the 1990s, BTI entered the event management field, buying Powerwaves in 1996. The company added a number of other corporate service operations in the later half of the decade, including Paymaster Ltd., a provider of payroll and pension administration services, in 1997.

PRIVATE AND PUBLIC AGAIN

Nonetheless, the corporate travel sector had become the core business of the group, which for the time being was known as BTI UK Hogg Robinson. The company developed ambitious expansion plans. With its share price lagging, the company decided to go private, completing a management buyout led by CEO David Radcliffe and backed by venture capital group Permira.

Hogg Robinson immediately turned toward acquisitions, entering Singapore with the purchase of ASL, another member of the BTI group. The company continued to cherry-pick the BTI partnership, buying the remaining corporate travel operations of Kuoni in December 2003. The deal gave Hogg Robinson a strong position in the Central European markets, including in Switzerland, Germany, Austria, Hungary, and Liechtenstein. Hogg Robinson laid claim to being the European leader in the business travel sector. The acquisition also gave Hogg Robinson a 50 percent stake in the BTI alliance, alongside the Netherlands's BCD

Holdings. Following the Kuoni acquisition, the company announced plans to sell its non-travel related operations.

Hogg Robinson next made its move into the United States, where it acquired New York's Sea Gate Travel Group in May 2005. The purchase, which made Hogg Robinson a direct competitor with BTI's BCD-controlled U.S. operations, launched the unraveling of the BTI partnership. This process was accelerated as Hogg Robinson continued making acquisitions in the United States, including Partnership Travel Consulting and Robustelli in 2006. The company also bought travel consultancy Ian Flint & Associates in the United Kingdom that year, as well as BTI Czech Republic and BTI Slovakia.

POSSIBLE TAKEOVER TARGET IN 2009

These moves led to an agreement between Hogg Robinson and BCD to disband the BTI partnership. As a result, Hogg Robinson rebranded all of its operations under the Hogg Robinson Group (HRG). The company then decided to go public that year, listing its stock on the London Stock Exchange.

HRG continued to grow strongly into the end of the decade. The company expanded its U.S. business with the acquisition of Executive Travel Associates in 2007. Also that year, HRG entered Belgium, buying that country's Weinberg Travel. The company had also been building up related corporate services, including a division devoted to travel for sports events and organizations. Another investment was a stake in Spendvision, which provided corporate expense management services. In 2008, the company gained a majority stake in that operation.

HRG's share price was hurt most by the global economic downturn in 2008, as its shares dropped to a low of just four pence in December 2008. This provided rival BCD with the opportunity to build its own stake in HRG. In early January, BCD revealed that it had acquired more than 19 percent of the U.K. group. The share purchase sparked speculation that the privately held Dutch group might launch a full takeover of HRG.

In the meantime, HRG responded to the economic downturn by launching a major cost-cutting effort. At the same time, the company continued to seek means of expanding its global reach. The company launched its North American Affiliates Program, signing up a number of largely regional companies, including Directravel in March 2009. Hogg Robinson looked back on a history of nearly 165 years, and a future as a major player in the global corporate travel market.

M. L. Cohen

PRINCIPAL SUBSIDIARIES

Hogg Robinson Germany GmbH and Company KG; Hogg Robinson Nigeria Ltd.; Hogg Robinson Nordic A.S.; Hogg Robinson Nordic AB; Wells Fargo Insurance Services of Michigan Inc.

PRINCIPAL DIVISIONS

International Corporate Travel Services; Spendvision/ Expense Management.

PRINCIPAL OPERATING UNITS

Corporate Travel Management; Consulting; Events & Meetings Management; Sports.

PRINCIPAL COMPETITORS

Carlson Wagonlit Travel; Thomas Cook Group plc; TUI Travel PLC; Kuoni Travel Holding Ltd.

FURTHER READING

"Belgian Agency Sold to Hogg Robinson," *Travel Weekly,* July 2, 2007, p. 6.

Carroll, David, "Hogg Robinson Rebrands," *Traveltrade,* March 22, 2006, p. 8.

"Company Watch—Hogg Robinson Group," *Airguide Business,* March 16, 2009.

Hofmann, Julian, "Hogg Robinson Clouded with Uncertainty," *Investors Chronicle,* December 2, 2008.

"Hogg Claims Top Spot in Europe," *Travel Trade Gazette UK & Ireland,* December 15, 2003, p. 5.

"Hogg Robinson Given Rough Ride," *Investors Chronicle,* June 28, 2007.

"Hogg Robinson Sells All Non-Travel Divisions," *Business Travel News,* April 18, 2005, p. 4.

"Hogg Robinson Slumps After Warning," *Investors Chronicle,* March 19, 2008.

"HRG Expands Reach in Eastern Europe," *Travel Trade Gazette UK & Ireland,* August 4, 2006, p. 4.

"HRG Facing Takeover by Dutch Shareholder," *Travel Trade Gazette UK & Ireland,* January 9, 2009, p. 5.

"HRG Gains New African Partner," *Travel Trade Gazette UK & Ireland,* May 1, 2009, p. 28.

"HRG Reveals Its Sporting Goals," *Travel Weekly,* September 15, 2006.

Kirshner, Jessica, and Amon Cohen, "Hogg Robinson Buys NY Corporate Agency," *Business Travel News,* May 16, 2005, p. 1.

"Robinson Debut Not the Whole Hogg," *Investors Chronicle,* October 13, 2006.

"Three HRG Offices Merged into One," *Travel Trade Gazette UK & Ireland,* February 29, 2008, p. 6.

Hornby PLC

———■———

Westwood
Margate, CT9 4JX
United Kingdom
Telephone: (+44 01843) 233500
Fax: (+44 01843) 233513
Web site: http://www.hornby.co.uk

Public Company
Employees: 214
Sales: £55.62 million ($79.9 million) (2008)
Stock Exchanges: London
Ticker Symbol: HRN
NAICS: 339932 Game, Toy, and Children's Vehicle
   Manufacturing; 551112 Offices of Other Holding
   Companies

■ ■ ■

Hornby PLC is a U.K.-based toy company focused on the model train, miniature car, and related categories. Hornby's stable of brands includes many of the most iconic in British and European toy history, including Hornby model train sets, Corgi and Scalextric miniature cars, Airfix model planes, and Humbrol hobby paints. Hornby is also one of the most international of European toy companies, which tend to focus on individual markets. Since 2004, Hornby has acquired several leading European brands, including Electrotren in Spain, Lima and Rivarossi in Italy, and Jouef in France. Hornby has faced withering competition, particularly from gaming consoles, and has responded in part by shifting its production entirely to China at the

beginning of the 2000s. This has enabled the company to raise the level of detail and quality in its miniatures, boosting its brands' appeal among toy collectors, as well as children. The company has also updated its own technology, notably through the launch of digital railway and racing sets introduced from 2005. Frank Martin is Hornby's chief executive officer. The company is listed on the London Stock Exchange. In 2008, Hornby's sales rose 19 percent over the previous year, to £55.69 million.

MAKING BRITISH TOY HISTORY IN 1901

Frank Hornby was an unlikely toy magnate. Born in Liverpool in 1863, Hornby initially went to work with his father as a clerk for a meat import company. While Hornby had no formal training in mechanical engineering, he enjoyed tinkering, and as a young man often devoted his spare time to the pursuit of his inventions. Among Hornby's interests were the creation of a "perpetual motion machine" and the construction of working models of submarines.

Hornby returned to his inventor's hobby after he had married and fathered two sons. As Hornby's work as a clerk often took him to Liverpool's ports, he became fascinated by the workings of the harbor cranes. Hornby began conceiving of a toy that would stimulate his children's interest in mechanical engineering as well. One evening after work, Hornby began cutting up a piece of copper, which he then perforated with regular grids of holes. Hornby then took small nuts and bolts to connect the strips together, and succeeded in building a facsimile of a harbor crane.

COMPANY PERSPECTIVES

Our strategy of building a broadly based model and hobby group with strong defensive attributes has been further strengthened by the successful and profitable integration of the Airfix and Humbrol business. The acquisition of the Corgi assets now allows us to take further advantage of our distribution network and product development skills.

Hornby quickly recognized the commercial potential for his idea. Turning to his employer for financial backing, Hornby applied for and received a patent for his invention, which he called "Improvements in Toy or Educational Devices for Children and Young People." Hornby initially dubbed the toy set "Mechanics Made Easy."

Sales of the construction kit took off only slowly, however. The company operated at a loss for its first five years. Yet Hornby soon exhibited a gift for marketing as well. Recognizing that the appeal for the new building toy would easily cross international boundaries, Hornby sought a more universal sounding name. By 1907, he had settled on the brand name "Meccano." In that year, Hornby decided to set up his own business, backed by four local investors. The company incorporated as Meccano Ltd.

Hornby began pioneering a number of new marketing techniques. Among these, Hornby launched a series of contests, offering prizes for models built using the Meccano sets. The competitions helped stimulate interest in the construction toy. Demand for Hornby's construction sets grew strongly, and by 1909 the company's site, a small workshop located above a store, had become too small. Hornby then acquired a five-acre plot and built a new factory. The company traded in its original hand presses and lathes for industrial production machinery.

Meccano became an instant international success and Hornby quickly expanded production, moving several times into ever larger factories. By the outbreak of World War I, Hornby had added an international component, establishing a factory in Berlin. This site soon became a major production center for the company, supplying the U.K. market as well as the European continent and elsewhere. Meccano's U.K. factory also expanded, and by the end of the war had grown to more than 150,000 square feet, with more than 1,200 employees.

RAILWAY TO SUCCESS IN THE TWENTIES

The Meccano brand grew into one of the world's most well-known toy brands. Part of the construction toy's appeal was its ability to inspire children's imagination, while teaching them basic construction and mechanical concepts. The Meccano building sets were so popular among the world's children of the time that many would later compare their appeal with that of the video game console to children at the dawn of the 21st century.

Hornby surprisingly enough continued manufacturing at the Berlin factory throughout the duration of World War I. The German defeat in turn offered both a setback and a new opportunity for the company. Following the war, the German government seized control of the Berlin factory.

In the United Kingdom, however, British consumers, in a wave of anti-German sentiment, began to spurn German-made products. This sentiment reached into the government, as the British Board of Trade sought to develop policies reducing the weight of German imports on the U.K. market.

Germany was especially known as one of Europe's leading centers for toy manufacturing. Prior to the war, the country's toy makers had dominated the European market in a number of toy categories, including scale model train sets. With the German toy industry faced with the need to rebuild following the war, Hornby saw an opportunity to move into the gap. By 1920, Hornby had released its own toy train sets. In that year, the company launched its first "0" gauge toy trains, which were powered by a clockwork wind-up type mechanism.

RIDING HIGH IN THE THIRTIES

The Hornby trains were considered accurate replicas of existing locomotives and rolling stock. They also incorporated Meccano nuts and bolts and other components, helping to reduce their cost of manufacture for the company. Hornby quickly became synonymous with model trains in the United Kingdom and the Hornby train set became one of the country's most popular toys. By 1925, the company had introduced its first electric-driven train set. The AC-powered set was soon replaced, in 1929, by a safer version powered by a six-volt DC transformer. The company added a die-cast line of smaller "00" trains, the Hornby Dublo, in 1938.

By the end of the 1920s, Meccano had established itself as a major name in the British toy train segment. The company also continued to build on the success of

KEY DATES

1901: Frank Hornby patents a construction toy, later called Meccano.

1907: Hornby forms Meccano Ltd.

1920: Meccano launches its first Hornby train set.

1934: Meccano rebrands its miniature car line as Meccano Dinky.

1964: Meccano is acquired by Lines Brothers and Hornby trains is merged into Tri-ang Railways.

1972: After Lines Brothers' collapse, the train division is reformed as Hornby Railways.

1986: Hornby goes public on the London Stock Exchange.

1995: Hornby begins transferring production to China.

2001: Frank Martin becomes CEO and restores Hornby's growth.

2004: Hornby acquires Lima in Italy, Jouef in France, and Electrotren in Spain.

2006: Hornby acquires Airfix airplane model kits and Humbrol hobby paints.

2008: Hornby acquires Corgi scale model cars.

the Meccano, launching production of components at a site in France. The company encouraged the growth of Meccano building clubs, and launched its own *Meccano* magazine. By 1928, the magazine had a subscriber base of 96,000. Into the 1930s Meccano club membership topped 100,000 people worldwide. Meccano's sales were so strong that during the interwar years they accounted for more than 30 percent of the United Kingdom's toy exports.

Despite having launched two successful toy brands, Frank Hornby remained on the lookout for a new toy market. Into the early 1930s, the company launched a line of miniature automobiles, a series of die-cast reproductions of popular automobiles called Modelled Miniatures. The line achieved true success when it was rolled out again in 1934 as the brand Meccano Dinky. The Dinky car quickly became another bestseller for the company, selling millions during the prewar era.

The Dinky was to be Frank Hornby's last success as a toy maker. In 1931, Hornby was elected to Parliament as a representative of Everton. However, the pressure of juggling the operation of his company with his political career proved too much for Hornby, who died in 1936.

The company was then taken over by Hornby's children.

INCREASING COMPETITION LEADING TO ACQUISITION BY LINES BROTHERS

Meccano was forced to abandon production during World War II. Production of the Hornby Dublo resumed only from 1945. During the postwar period, however, Meccano found itself under steadily increasing competitive pressures. These difficulties had begun to be felt in the years prior to World War II, as a new range of toys and characters, such as Mickey Mouse, captured children's attention.

The rise of the automobile in the years following the war also hurt Hornby's train sales. In response, the company moved to add its own model racing car unit, taking over a producer of racing car sets in the early 1950s. That company then became known as Scalextric.

The Hornby trains continued to face strong competition, in part because the company had been late in adopting the industry standard two-rail system. Hornby corrected this situation only in 1958, when it abandoned its own three-rail system. By then, however, Hornby had lost ground to its U.K. rivals, which included Tri-ang Railways, owned by rival toy company Lines Brothers.

In the meantime, the company's Meccano sales had also been hit by a major new competitor: Lego. The introduction of the iconic, plastic construction sets, which were easier to use, and appealed to both girls and boys, cut sharply into sales of Meccano sets. By the early 1960s, the company had begun losing money badly. At last, in 1964, Meccano agreed to be taken over by Lines Brothers, which paid the Hornby family £781,000. Meccano's train division became known as Tri-ang Hornby.

GOING PUBLIC IN 1986

Lines Brothers became the United Kingdom's largest toy company, holding many of the country's most iconic toy brands. In the early 1970s, however, Lines Brothers itself collapsed. From its ashes rose a new company at the beginning of 1972. Now focused entirely on toy trains, the company adopted the name Hornby Railways. The company invested in upgrading its production, raising both its standards of detail and quality, in part in order to attract the growing number of adult model train enthusiasts.

Hornby went through a series of ownership changes over the next decade, reincorporating as Hornby Hobbies in 1980. In 1986, the company went public, listing on the London Stock Exchange's Unlisted Securities Market. By then, the company remained one of the sole survivors of the once flourishing British toy industry, which had been decimated by the arrival of low-cost imports from Japan and elsewhere.

Hornby had fought back, however, launching popular series of trains based on new rolling stock designs then being adopted by the recently privatized British Railways. The company also struck gold with a license to launch a train set based on the popular Thomas the Tank Engine character starting in 1985.

MOVING TO CHINA IN THE NINETIES

Hornby chugged on through the 1990s, finding it more and more difficult to compete for attention amid shifting consumer tastes and the growing numbers of toys from low-wage Asian markets. In 1995, Hornby finally made the decision to shift part of its own production to China, a move that helped the company survive through the end of the decade.

In the meantime, the growth of the video gaming industry, as well as the appeal of more modern toys and pastimes had made Hornby's train sets seem increasingly obsolete. By 2000, the group acknowledged that it was up for sale, as then Chairman Peter Newey explained to the *Financial Times:* "I can't see any other way of satisfying the wishes of shareholders. We are close to our zero base. We either need to be part of a larger group or we need more products to sell."

Finding a buyer proved difficult for the company, however. Instead, in January 2001, the company brought in a new CEO, Frank Martin, who quickly decided to take up Newey's second option. Martin at first set to work streamlining Hornby's operations, including transferring the remainder of the group's production to China. The move not only permitted the group to cut costs, it also enabled the company to introduce far more detail and higher-quality standards into its product line, while maintaining its price levels. As a result, Hornby trains once again became sought after both by train collectors and toy collectors. The company then repeated the exercise with the Scalextric model racing car line, raising sales of this division.

INTERNATIONAL TOY GROUP

Martin targeted expansion outside of the United Kingdom. In 2004, the group acquired Spain's Electrotren and Italy's Lima, which also owned the Jouef brand in France. These companies allowed Hornby to position itself as the only multinational producer of train sets in Europe, and one of the largest model train companies in the world. These acquisitions were especially significant for the company as they enabled Hornby to maintain its revenue and profit growth amid the growing economic slowdown in the United Kingdom from the middle of the decade.

As it searched for its next acquisition, Hornby also focused on updating its technology. The company released a digitally controlled racing track under the Scalextric line in 2004. This led to the launch in 2006 of the group's first digitally controlled train sets, which allowed multiple trains to run on a single track for the first time. In that year, also, the company completed two new acquisitions, of Airfix, a maker of model airplane kits, and Humbrol, the producer of hobby paints. In this way, Hornby boosted its portfolio with two more iconic brands.

Hornby completed its next major acquisition just two years later, when it agreed to acquire another British toy icon, Corgi, the manufacturer of die-cast model cars, for £7.5 million. The acquisition not only gave Hornby control of the Corgi brand, it also gave it access to the company's back catalog of some 10,000 models. Hornby then announced plans to shift Corgi's production to China as well, where it would carry out an upgrade to the line's detail and quality standards.

The addition of Corgi helped Hornby raise its sales past £55 million by the end of 2008. The company had also succeeded in more than doubling its revenues since the beginning of the decade. As one of the sole survivors of the great era of British toy manufacturing, Hornby appeared on the right track to further growth in the future.

M. L. Cohen

PRINCIPAL SUBSIDIARIES

Hornby Hobbies Limited; Hornby America Inc. (USA); Hornby España S.A (Spain); Hornby Italia s.r.l. (Italy); Hornby France S.A.S.; Hornby Deutschland GmbH (Germany).

PRINCIPAL OPERATING UNITS

Airfix; Corgi; Electrotren; Hornby; Humbrol; Jouef; Lima; Rivarossi; Scalextric.

PRINCIPAL COMPETITORS

Sony USA Inc.; Nintendo Company Ltd.; Perfekta Enterprises Ltd.; Mattel Inc.; Namco Bandai Holdings

Inc.; Sega Sammy Holdings Inc.; Hasbro Inc.; Konami Corp.; Sammy Corp.; Springs Global Inc.; Tomy Company Ltd.

FURTHER READING

Blackwell, David, "Hornby Steams into Digital Age," *Financial Times,* January 30, 2006, p. 22.

Cave, Andrew, "Adding 00s to Hornby's Bottom Line," *Daily Telegraph,* May 31, 2008, p. 35.

Hawkes, Steve, "Lewis Hamilton Overtakes Trains in the Hornby Marshalling Yard," *Times* (London), June 7, 2008, p. 63.

"Hornby Moving Corgi up a Gear," *Yorkshire Post,* June 7, 2008.

"Hornby to Focus on Corgi Core Business," *Marketing Week,* July 31, 2008, p. 6.

Johnson, Luke, "The Model Entrepreneur," *Sunday Telegraph,* July 7, 2002.

Jones, Bernard, "Die-Cast Future," *Investors Chronicle,* June 6, 2008.

Lowe, Felix, "Hornby's Trains, Planes and Automobiles," *Daily Telegraph,* May 2, 2008.

Murden, Terry, "Full Steam Ahead As Hornby Trains Sights on Change," *Scotland on Sunday,* January 8, 2006, p. 7.

Oliphant, Will, "Corgi Boards Hornby Train," *Birmingham Mail,* May 2, 2008, p. 73.

Simpson, Richard, "The Incredible Shrinking Car," *Guardian,* April 22, 1995, p. 61.

Wearden, Graeme, "Hornby Puts Its Prices up to Combat Slump in Sterling," *Guardian,* January 28, 2009, p. 25.

Zuckerman, Laurence, "Arthur Katz, 91, the Maker of Corgi Toy Cars, Is Dead," *New York Times,* July 21, 1999.

Huddle House, Inc.

5901 Peachtree Dunwoody Road Northeast, Suite B
Atlanta, Georgia 30328-5382
U.S.A.
Telephone: (770) 325-1300
Toll Free: (800) 868-5700
Web site: http://www.huddlehouse.com

Private Company
Incorporated: 1964
Employees: 550
Sales: $232 million (2008 est.)
NAICS: 722110 Full-Service Restaurants

■ ■ ■

Huddle House, Inc., is an operator and franchiser of more than 440 family restaurants located primarily in small towns or suburbs of third- or fourth-tier cities in 16 states in the southeastern and mid-Atlantic United States as well as Missouri. The chain's largest concentration of stores is in its home state of Georgia, where about 150 Huddle House restaurants are found, including about two dozen company-owned stores. The company's distribution center is also located in Atlanta, with a second operation in development for Little Rock, Arkansas, to support further geographic expansion. Most of the units operate 24 hours a day, seven days a week. Only since 2005 have franchisees been allowed to close during slow weeknights, although they are still required to remain open 24 hours on weekends.

Huddle House, long known for its breakfast items available any time of the day, has made great strides

since the mid-1990s in developing lunch and dinner items to improve business in the other times of the day. Helping in this regard is the chain's emphasis on large portions, epitomized by a line of "Big House" sandwiches. Another factor in revitalizing a once sleepy brand has been a new building format that emulates a 1950s' diner rather than a pancake house, as well as a modernized logo and uniforms. The company has also driven growth through cobranding arrangements with convenience stores and other partners. Huddle House has been owned by private-equity company Allied Capital since 2007.

FOUNDING OF CHAIN: 1964

Huddle House was founded near Atlanta in Decatur, Georgia, in April 1964 by John Sparks when he opened a coffee shop modeled after another Georgia-based family-dining chain, Waffle House, which had been established nine years earlier. Sparks's wife is credited with supplying the new restaurant with its distinctive name. According to company lore, she was watching football on television and became fascinated by the huddle, the between-play gathering of players. The restaurant, as a result, became a place for people to congregate, to "huddle," especially after high school football games.

The new eatery and its 24-hour format proved popular and was soon followed by a second Atlanta-area restaurant bearing the Huddle House name located in Avondale Estates, the hometown of Waffle House. Like Waffle House, Sparks turned in 1966 to franchising to develop a restaurant chain employing the Huddle House

COMPANY PERSPECTIVES

Huddle House is a neighborhood diner, serving delicious meals, cooked to order. A place where hungry folks gather to enjoy good food, good friends and good hospitality. The mission statement is our customer pledge. We strive to deliver our pledge of service and quality to every customer, every meal, every day!

concept without taking on debt. Unlike Waffle House, however, Huddle House did not seek out locations along interstates to attract truckers and travelers. Rather, it settled in smaller, rural communities where it might be the only restaurant in town, appealing to blue-collar consumers, especially for breakfast, which the 60-seat freestanding restaurants served around the clock.

Huddle House enjoyed steady growth, never knowing a year of declining sales under John Sparks or under his family, following his death. The chain spread beyond the Atlanta market to other parts of Georgia and then slowly throughout the Southeast. In 1990, after 25 years in existence, Huddle House operated 165 restaurants, 15 of which were located in the Atlanta market, generating systemwide sales of $65 million. The chain continued to grow and remain profitable into the 1990s, finding little competition in the 24-hour "mini-roadhouse" family-dining niche, positioned one tier below such names as Cracker Barrel, Denny's, Perkins, and Shoney's. Nevertheless, there was little strategic thinking and the brand had grown tired under family ownership.

FAMILY SELLS CHAIN: 1994

In 1994 Huddle House was acquired for an undisclosed sum by a new management team with financial backing from Charlottesville, Virginia-based merchant bank, Quad-C Inc. A major effort was then launched to reinvigorate the Huddle House brand, the focus of which was on value and service. The chain's retooling program was manifold, affecting operations, marketing, franchising, purchasing, and distribution. In order to help modify Huddle House's image as a mere breakfast place, the chain introduced a line of Big House Platters, offering large-portion meals at a modest price. Huddle House also sought to project more of an upscale image, while not losing its loyal core customers, by introducing a branded coffee that was a major improvement over previous fare. The company also spent money on slicker

television and print ads, resulting in a greater mix of customers.

By the end of 1997 the Huddle House chain grew to 335 units, which produced systemwide revenues of nearly $150 million. About 25 of these units were part of a cobranding program, bringing Huddle House restaurants to interstate highway truck stops and fuel centers. The company was able to achieve these results despite the lack of a permanent chief executive officer for about two years. Finally in October 1998 the post was filled by one of the vice-presidents that had joined the company in 1994, Philip M. Greifeld, who as chief financial officer had played a major role in revitalizing the Huddle House brand.

In some respects Greifeld was an unusual choice to lead Huddle House, a northern-born executive running what was clearly a southern restaurant concept. Born in Long Island, he earned a degree in business economics from the State University of New York College at Oneonta and started out in retail home furnishings, forming his own company with venture-capital funds. Although the business failed, Quad-C was impressed with his skills and brought him into the Huddle House deal, installing him as chief financial officer. By the time he assumed the top post, Greifeld was well versed in the restaurant's operations.

MIDWEST EXPANSION: 1999

Under Greifeld, Huddle House looked to expand into the mid-Atlantic and midwestern states. In 1999 the chain negotiated a pair of significant development deals. The Lexington, Kentucky-based casual-dining operator Thomas & King, Inc., signed a multiyear, 70-unit development deal to open Huddle House units in the Midwest, where it was already operating Applebee's restaurants in Indiana and Ohio, both new markets for Huddle House. Thomas & King would also open Huddle House restaurants in Kentucky, where the chain was already present in a small way.

Although all of the Thomas & King units were to be freestanding, Huddle House continued to open cobranded units at interstate highway travel centers and also pursued other cobranding opportunities as a way to enter new territories. Later in 1999 an agreement was reached with Lonesome Pine Dining and Lodging Inc. to develop Huddle House restaurants adjacent to Comfort Inn hotels. Another important step Greifeld took in growing Huddle House as the decade came to a close was the introduction of a 1,600-square-foot, 62-seat prototype that featured new lighting to highlight green-and-white checkerboard interiors and wooden accents. It was a look meant to appeal to women, the

KEY DATES

1964: John Sparks opens first 24-hour Huddle House restaurant in Decatur, Georgia.
1966: Huddle House begins franchising.
1994: Huddle House is sold to Quad-C Inc.
1998: Philip M. Greifeld is named chief executive.
2005: Franchisees are given the option to close on slow weeknights.
2006: Corporate headquarters move from Decatur to Atlanta.
2007: Allied Capital Corporation acquires Huddle House.

new target customer for Huddle House now that it was attempting to cater to a broader range of diners. All told, the chain added 32 restaurants in fiscal 1999.

Strong growth continued as the new century dawned. In the summer of 2000, Huddle House entered the state of West Virginia by signing a six-year development deal with Mountaineer Restaurants to open as many as 25 restaurants in West Virginia. A few weeks earlier, when fiscal 2000 came to a close, Huddle House had added 33 new stores and topped the $150 million mark in systemwide sales. One of those new restaurants relying on the prototype was an 80-seat unit that opened in Locust Grove, Georgia, and served as a corporate training center where each year about 125 people could be taught all aspects of the business, from mopping the floors to serving as an executive. Previously, Huddle House had provided classroom training at its corporate headquarters and then dispatched management trainees for onsite training throughout the system. Not only did the new training restaurant provide a more consistent regimen, it was less expensive than the older method.

FRANCHISEES SUE COMPANY: 2002

Despite its expanding footprint, Huddle House continued to supply all of the stores from the warehouse attached to the company's Decatur headquarters. Some of the franchisees, representing about 90 restaurants, were not pleased with the arrangement and in September 2002 sued the parent company, alleging Huddle House was engaging in restraint of trade and charging more than would an independent broadline distributor. The majority of franchisees disagreed, however, and the suit never gained sufficient

momentum. To better serve the growing chain, however, plans were eventually drawn up to open a second distribution center, strategically located in Little Rock.

For many consumers, Huddle House remained a breakfast house. To change the restaurant's image, the company promoted lunch and dinner in its advertising and continued to expand the menu to help increase traffic at other times of the day. Lighter menu items were added, including new Lite House salads. These changes helped to drive sales, as did the new prototype. Stores with the new interior generated as much as 15 percent more sales than those relying on the older design. Systemwide sales increased to $190 million in fiscal 2004, produced by 375 units spread across 14 states. As the year came to a close, Huddle House also announced that it planned to open its first restaurant in Texas. During this time Huddle House also began a test program that allowed some flexibility in the chain's longstanding policy of operating 24 hours a day. After two years of study, in the fall of 2005 Huddle House provided franchisees with the option of not operating 24 hours during some of the slower-traffic weeknights, although all units were required to remain open around the clock on weekends. The belief was that the change would improve employee morale and performance, as well as enhance profits.

Sales reached $215 million in fiscal 2005. Because of Huddle House's steady expansion, the company outgrew its Decatur corporate headquarters, leading in early 2006 to a move to new quarters, 15,000 square feet in size, in Atlanta. By the start of 2007 Huddle House increased the size of the chain to 420 units in 17 states. Of that number, 123 stores had been added in the previous four years, mostly outside of the company's core southeastern market, in such states as Illinois, Missouri, Ohio, Texas, Virginia, and West Virginia. In January 2007 Huddle House was sold for $124.1 million to a unit of Allied Capital Corporation, a 50-year-old Washington, D.C.-based private-equity firm that held investments in more than 100 companies, mostly private middle-market enterprises, which combined for annual revenues of more than $12 billion.

HUDDLE HOUSE ENTERS INDIANAPOLIS: 2007

Huddle House's new owner brought with it the financial wherewithal to support the expansion plans of Greifeld, who stayed on as CEO. Huddle House was eyeing new states to enter, including Colorado, Kansas, and Oklahoma, as well as larger metropolitan areas. Later in 2007 the first Huddle House restaurants opened in Indianapolis, Indiana. Management's overarching goal was to double the size of the chain by

2015. While devoting a good deal of energy in entering new markets, Huddle House also had to make sure it fended off competition where it already operated, in particular from the quick-service chains that were also found in the smaller communities that Huddle House favored. To remain vital and build the restaurant's brand image, the chain introduced a new menu design in 2007 and a promotion to reward loyal customers that included instant prizes and a $100,000 grand prize.

Systemwide sales grew to about $225 million in fiscal 2007. To help continue the chain's momentum, Huddle House in 2008 began employing e-mail marketing and electronic brochures as a cost-effective way to reach potential franchisees. The company then added Facebook, MySpace, Twitter, and YouTube as tools to help in the recruiting effort. Systemwide sales totaled $232 million in fiscal 2008, generated by 432 units. Growth was curtailed somewhat by a deteriorating economy but Huddle House's emphasis on value helped to keep the chain healthy, and there was every reason to expect that Huddle House, with the financial backing of Allied Capital, was well positioned to enjoy strong long-term growth.

Ed Dinger

PRINCIPAL SUBSIDIARIES

Hh Holdings Inc.

PRINCIPAL COMPETITORS

Cracker Barrel Old Country Store, Inc.; Denny's Corporation; Waffle House, Inc.

FURTHER READING

Cebrzynski, Gregg, "Baker Bros., Huddle House Reach Out to Guests, New Franchisees with Inaugural E-mail Campaigns," *Nation's Restaurant News,* November 17, 2008, p. 14.

————, "Rebranded Huddle House Takes on QSR Neighbors," *Nation's Restaurant News,* August 27, 2007, p. 12.

Farkas, David, "Northern Exposure: Huddle House, a Chain of Southern Roadside Diners, Is Rolling into New Territory," *Chain Leader,* April 2004, p. 48.

Hayes, Jack, "Huddle House's New Chief Sets Aggressive Expansion Plan," *Nation's Restaurant News,* December 14, 1998, p. 8.

"Huddle House, Inc., Thomas & King Sign Major Franchise Agreement; Kentucky Multi-Unit Operator to Build 70 Huddle House Restaurants over 10 Years," *PR Newswire,* August 6, 1999, p. 7027.

"Huddle House Partnered with Allied Capital," *Franchising World,* March 2007, p. 116.

I Grandi Viaggi S.p.A.

Via della Moscova 36
Milan, I-20121
Italy
Telephone: (+39 02) 290461
Fax: (+39 02) 29046509
Web site: http://www.igrandiviaggi.it

Public Company
Incorporated: 1931
Employees: 475
Sales: EUR 100.27 million ($115 million) (2008)
Stock Exchanges: Borsa Italiana
Ticker Symbol: IGV
NAICS: 561520 Tour Operators; 561510 Travel Agencies; 721110 Hotels (Except Casino Hotels) and Motels

■ ■ ■

I Grandi Viaggi S.p.A. is one of the pioneers of Italy's travel and tourism industry, with roots as a cruise operator in the 1930s. I Grandi Viaggi, or IGV, focuses on two primary travel segments: Resorts and Tours. IGV's Tours division provides packaged tours and cruises to destinations in Europe, Africa, the Middle East, and Asia. These are conducted through the company's main brands, iGV Tour and Comitours. The company's Resort operations are conducted through IGV's own network of upscale holiday resorts and vacation clubs. The company owns and operates resort villages offering all-inclusive vacations in Kenya, Maldives, Mexico, Sardinia, Seychelles, Sicily, and Zanzibar, as well as a resort in the Italian Alps. The company's Italian villages operate through its iGV Clubs unit, while its international villages operate under the Club Vacanze brand. IGV is listed on the Borsa Italiana. The group's majority shareholder is SM International SA, which holds 53.7 percent of the company. Luigi Clementi is the company's chairman and president.

ITALIAN CRUISE PIONEER FROM THE THIRTIES

I Grandi Viaggi, the name literally means "The Great Travel," became one of the pioneers of Italy's modern tourism and travel industry when it was founded in 1931. As the company's name implies, it sought to develop travel packages on a grand scale. From the start, IGV focused on cruise operations, offering a six-week tour to India. By the following year, the company had attracted attention, and praise, from the Italian media.

Through the 1930s, IGV continued to develop cruises and tours to some of the world's most romantic destinations. Among the packages offered during this period by the company were a river cruise on the River Volga; two voyages each to South America and to the Caucasus and southern Russia; a train voyage across India; cruises to Iceland and as far north as the polar region; as well as a cruise to Ceylon. The 1936 Olympic Games in Berlin offered another important milestone for the company, which organized the travel for thousands of Italians to attend the games.

COMPANY PERSPECTIVES

Try the iGV Club experience. A new holidaying experience. A resort tailored to suit all your needs: exclusive, at one with nature, beautifully maintained and superbly organized to ensure that mind and body are fully recharged by the time you leave. An extensive range of high quality hotels with all the facilities expected at any top range resort. The choicest and most exclusive locations, trained professional babysitters, highly acclaimed chefs and top quality entertainment for all the family. This is the iGV Club experience: if you choose it you can expect the best.

The war years put an end to IGV's operations, however. The company suspended its travel services for the duration, and only resumed business again in 1947. The postwar period represented a major milestone both in IGV's growth and for the tourism and travel sector in general. The sustained economic boom, brought on by the reconstruction following the war and stimulated by the industrial expansion of the 1950s and 1960s, had a significant impact on the leisure market in general. The increasing incomes and amount of leisure time available to Italians, particularly the middle and upper classes, led to a surge in interest for travel, tourism, and vacations.

CRUISING TO SUCCESS FROM THE FIFTIES

IGV met this demand by continuing to develop unique vacations and packaged tours. Among the group's highlights during the postwar period was a travel package following the Milan-Moscow Raid. Nonetheless, IGV's major interest remained on the fast-growing cruise travel segment.

The 1950s saw the first democratization of the cruising market, which had previously been reserved for the upper classes. IGV began operating its own cruise liners during this time, with vessels including the *Galileo Galilei* and the *Guglielmo Marconi*. Into the 1960s, IGV also began offering its first cruises to the United States, aboard such ships as the *Michelangelo,* the *Oceanic,* and the *Raffaello.* By the mid-1960s, IGV operated dozens of cruises each year. In 1966, the company's cruise operations were extended again to Odessa and other points with a partnership with Compagnia di Navigazione "Morflot."

While cruising remained an important part of the company's operations, IGV nonetheless adapted to a major shift in the travel and tourism market in the 1970s. The arrival of new and larger airplanes, such as the iconic Boeing 747, meant that air travel suddenly became highly affordable.

IGV's entry into this market came at the beginning of the decade. In 1970, for example, the company operated 20 travel packages to the Osaka, Japan Expo of that year. In 1972, IGV inaugurated charter vacation services to London and Paris, with 210 flights in that year alone. By 1977, the company's charter vacation operations to these two cities topped 400 per year. By then, too, the company had begun providing charter flight tours to Africa, starting with 20 trips to Kenya in 1974.

VACATION VILLAGES IN THE EIGHTIES

By the late 1970s, IGV's operations had expanded to include more than 50,000 customers per year. The company also began exploring a new vacation sector that was to define its operations into the next century. In 1977, the company began developing its first all-inclusive vacation resort packages.

IGV's resort operations at first focused on destinations in Italy. Into the early 1980s, however, the company responded to increasing interest in foreign resorts. In 1982, the company began offering vacations at the newly opened Dickwella vacation village in Sri Lanka. This was followed in 1984 with the group's first operations in Maldives, at the Bolifushi village.

The success of these operations soon led IGV to invest directly into the vacation resort sector. In 1984, the company opened its first company-owned resort, at Blue Bay in Kenya. This was followed by the opening of an 800-bed resort in Marispica, in Sicily, in 1986. By the end of the decade, the group had moved its operations in the Maldives to a new resort village, the Halaveli.

Through the 1990s, IGV underwent a series of ownership changes. This phase began in 1989, when the group's management completed a leveraged buyout (LBO) of the company, backed by France's Paribas banking group, among others. The LBO came just ahead of a global recession, however. The economic downturn had placed the travel and tourism sector under pressure, when the outbreak of the first Persian Gulf War caused a sharp drop in the tourist market. In order to reduce the debt created by the LBO, IGV turned to venture capital group Cofisa SpA, which took control of the company in 1993.

KEY DATES

1931: I Grandi Viaggi (IGV) is founded and organizes its first cruise to India.

1947: Company restarts operations after World War II, and begins expanding its cruise operations.

1966: Company begins organizing cruises to Odessa in partnership with Compagnia di Navigazione "Morflot."

1970: IGV offers chartered flights to Osaka, Japan, then extends the chartered flight business to London, Paris, and Kenya.

1977: Company begins offering vacation village packages for the first time.

1984: IGV acquires its first vacation resort, in Kenya.

1989: IGV's management completes a leveraged buyout.

1996: Grupo Monforte acquires more than 89 percent of IGV.

1999: IGV goes public with a listing on the Borsa Italiana.

2005: IGV acquires Parmatour and its Club Vacanze and Comitours brands.

2008: IGV carries out a renovation and expansion program for a number of its villages, including the Marispica in Sicily.

REBRANDING

Cofisa maintained its ownership of the company through the middle of the decade, then sold an 89.44 percent stake to Grupo Monforte in 1996. The new owners launched a major restructuring and rebranding effort that year, culminating in the creation of the iGV Club brand in 1997.

The first IGV village to sport the new brand was Le Castella, in Calabria, acquired in 1996. The company also rebranded another property added in that year, the Bahia Maya, in Mexico. By the end of 1997, all of the company's vacation villages had adopted the iGV Club brand.

IGV's restructuring effort in the meantime had permitted the group to resume its expansion. In order to generate capital for further growth, the company went public, listing its shares on the Borsa Italiana in Milan in 1998. The offering enabled the company to acquire two more vacation villages by the end of the decade, the Baia Samuele in Sicily, and the Gressoney La Trinité in

Valle d'Aosta. At the same time, IGV moved into a new market, through a management contract to operate the Henry Morgan Club on Roatan Island in Honduras.

EXPANDING THE BRAND FAMILY

IGV continued to expand its range of vacation villages in the 2000s, while also maintaining a strong packaged tour component. The latter was rebranded as iGV Tour, reflecting the company's successful iGV Club brand.

In the year 2000, the company opened a new company-owned village, the Club Santagiusta Castiadas, in Italy's Sardinia region. By the following year, the company had also added its first operations in the Middle East and Persian Gulf regions, acquiring the contract to manage the Al Hamra Fort Dubai resort on Ras Al Khaimah beach in Dubai. The company then launched construction of a new village in Palau, in the Sardinia region. Called the Santa Clara, the new iGV Club opened for business in 2005.

That year marked a new milestone as IGV completed the EUR 47 million acquisition of rival Parmatour. The purchase gave IGV control of Parmatour's own brands, tour brokerage division Comitours, and the Club Vacanze network of vacation villages. These included five villages based in the Alps, Maldives, Seychelles, and Zanzibar. Following the acquisition, IGV sold off other parts of Parmatour's operations, including its vacation rentals division, as well as two other brands, Going, Sestante and the business travel brand Clare.

IGV next concentrated on integrating its new divisions, while streamlining its portfolio of vacation villages. In 2006, for example, the group sold off one of the former Parmatour villages, the Kuda Rah in the Maldives. In its place, the company added a new site in the Maldives, on Gangehi Island, in 2007. At the same time, the group carried out a renovation and expansion program for a number of its properties, including the Dongwe Club in Zanzibar, Le Castella Capo Rizzuto in Calabria, and, in 2008, the Marispica in Sicily. Also that year, the company completed the reconstruction of its Relais Club des Alpes, in Madonna di Campiglio, which had been destroyed by fire in 2007.

The group's restructuring and renovation effort, however, hit a bump amid the slump in the travel and tourism markets, brought on by soaring oil prices in 2007. The slide into a global economic downturn the following year added to the company's woes. By the end of the year, IGV's revenues had dropped slightly, to just over EUR 100 million ($114 million). IGV also struggled to maintain profitability. By July 2009, the group had slipped into the red, reporting operating losses for the first half of the year of EUR 4.4 million.

Despite these difficulties, I Grandi Viaggi remained one of the great names in Italian vacations.

M. L. Cohen

PRINCIPAL SUBSIDIARIES

Althaea S.p.A. (82.34%); Blue Bay Village Ltd (90%); Holiday Club Maldives Ltd Pvt.; IGV Club S.r.l.; IGV Hotels S.p.A.; IGV Resort S.r.l. (61.78%); Sampieri S.r.l. (52.41%); Vacanze Zanzibar Ltd.

PRINCIPAL DIVISIONS

Resort Operations; Tour Operations.

PRINCIPAL OPERATING UNITS

iGV Club; iGV Tour; Club Vacanze; Comitours.

PRINCIPAL COMPETITORS

TUI AG; Koc Holding A.S.; Kuoni Reisen Holding AG; MyTravel Group PLC; Francoudi and Stephanou Ltd.; IFI; IFIL; SM Investments Corp.; Valtur S.p.A.; Societa Italiana Trasporti Automobilistici; Wokita.com Tour Operator.

FURTHER READING

"Grandi Viaggi Acquires Parmatour SpA–Villages & Inter from Parmalat Finanziaria SpA," *Thomson Financial Mergers & Acquisitions,* December 16, 2005.

"Grandi Viaggi Finanziari Acquires Grandi Viaggi Through a Leveraged Buyout," *Thomson Financial Mergers & Acquisitions,* November 2, 1989.

"I Grandi Viaggi, Aggiornamento Acquisto Azioni Proprie," *Teleborsa,* July 13, 2009.

"I Grandi Viaggi, Club Vacanze al Top," *Agenzia di Viaggi,* July 22, 2008.

"I Grandi Viaggi (IGV) Completes Acquisition of Two Divisions of Parmatour," *Reuters,* December 16, 2005.

"Italian I Grandi Viaggi Widens Net Loss to EUR 4.4m H1 FY '08," *ADP News Italy,* June 30, 2009.

"Parmatour Ai Grandi Viaggi per 47 Milioni," *Il Sole 24 Ore,* September 15, 2005.

Ideal Mortgage Bankers, Ltd.

———————————————■———————————————

520 Broadhollow Road
Melville, New York 11747-3604
U.S.A.
Telephone: (631) 249-9205
Toll Free: (800) 200-5363
Web site: http://www.lendamerica.com

Private Company
Incorporated: 1986
Employees: 350
Sales: $15.2 million (2008)
NAICS: 522310 Mortgage and Nonmortgage Loan
Brokers

■ ■ ■

Doing business as Lend America, Ideal Mortgage Bankers, Ltd., is a Melville, New York-based national direct lending company licensed in 46 states. The company offers Federal Housing Authority (FHA)–insured mortgage loans as well as fixed-rate and adjustable-rate mortgages (ARMs). Lend America also provides refinancing through FHA loans and other lending options, and offers home equity loans, debt consolidation loans that can combine mortgage and credit card debt, and reverse mortgages that allow seniors to continue to live in their homes while converting equity into tax-free cash. Driving the business are infomercials, some of which emulate newscasts touting lending programs that are part of the government-backed banking bailout effort. While Michael Primeau is president of Ideal Mortgage, it is the company's chief business strategist,

Michael Ashley, who although not listed as a principal is the guiding force behind the company. Ashley also brings a checkered past, having pleaded guilty to wire fraud charges in the 1990s.

MICHAEL ASHLEY ENTERS MORTGAGE BANKING INDUSTRY: 1984

According to an interview with *Mortgage Banking* in 2009, Michael Ashley dropped out of college after one semester and went to work as a copy boy at a title company. He then became involved in mortgage banking and "in 1984 became one of the first registered mortgage brokers in the state of New York." He worked for a company run by his father, an attorney, called Liberty Mortgage Banking, Ltd., licensed in New York as a mortgage banking firm. In 1987 Liberty Mortgage was approved by the Federal Home Loan Mortgage Corporation ("Freddie Mac") to sell conventional, fixed rate, and adjustable mortgages to Freddie Mac. In November 1994 Kenneth Ashley and three business associates were indicted in federal court on charges that between March 1990 and December 1992 they devised a scheme to defraud Freddie Mac.

According to government documents, they "recruited individuals with good credit histories to pose as applicants for mortgage financing in exchange for $5,000." They then created "fraudulent mortgage loan applications to be prepared for the false borrowers and submitted to Liberty. Liberty provided mortgage loans to the false borrowers and forwarded the proceeds of the loan to entities in which [Ashley] and his associates were officers and shareholders. The loans were then sold to Freddie Mac, and payments on the loans were made by Liberty to Freddie Mac in the names of the false borrowers." The loan proceeds of several million dollars were then diverted to other Ashley enterprises, Camel Properties, Inc., which acquired residential properties for use as rental income, and 22-12 23rd Corporation, a builder of multiple family properties.

MICHAEL ASHLEY PLEADS GUILTY TO WIRE FRAUD: 1993

Michael Ashley was indicted in a case related to his father's, and in 1993 pleaded guilty to two counts of wire fraud. In October 1996 he was sentenced to five years' probation and ordered to pay Freddie Mac $30,000 in damages. Under terms of his plea bargain, however, he was permitted to seek employment in the mortgage banking and mortgage industry despite his conviction. A year later his father was convicted of conspiracy, wire fraud, conspiracy to suborn perjury, and suborning perjury, and in September 1998 was sentenced to 46 months in prison. Michael Ashley minimized the importance of his conviction in comments to *Business Week* in 2008, claiming "I was just a pawn in a chess game between my father and the government."

Michael Ashley, as allowed by his agreement with the government, reentered the mortgage business. In 1996 he went to work for Melville, New York-based Consumer Home Mortgage, a small company that generated about $80 million in FHA loans a year. Ashley became a rainmaker for the company and developed a sales team; by the end of 2001 he had built up loan volume to $500 million, generated from ten branches located on Long Island, and in Brooklyn and Queens. Along the way, Consumer Home Mortgage began handling transactions for Better Homes Depot, an Ozone Park real estate company that in 1999 became the subject of a New York City Department of Consumer Affairs investigation that led to a lawsuit and also brought Consumer Home Mortgage to the attention of Consumer Affairs. In essence, Better Homes was

accused of lining up buyers for homes in poor condition and making promises of repair that were not kept or were performed by unlicensed contractors who did not obtain the necessary permits. After pocketing its fees, the company sold the FHA-backed loans, leaving the homeowners with a substandard property and all too often a mortgage they could not afford. Many of them lost their down payments and their homes and the FHA was saddled with the loss. After Better Homes' chief lender, Madison Home Equities, was banned from doing FHA business for five years, the company turned to Consumer Home Mortgage, which began writing loans for Better Homes.

Consumer Home wrote at least 200 federally guaranteed FHA loans for Better Homes, but a high percentage of the borrowers defaulted, and the company was soon sued by several dissatisfied customers. Investigations by Long Island newspaper *Newsday* revealed that "Ashley and his wife, Mindy, and other business associates, created real estate companies that, together with Consumer Home, systematically defrauded lower-income minorities out of tens of thousands of dollars." The newspaper reported that according to public records "at least 40 low-end properties owned by Mindy Ashley were 'flipped'—that is bought and quickly sold for much higher prices to buyers," who obtained loans through Consumer Home Mortgage from FHA's 203(k) program that helped people buy and renovate distressed homes.

A real estate firm called Option To Buy was registered to Mindy Ashley that bought and sold distressed homes. She also owned another company called Patch-It that flipped properties in Queens, Brooklyn, the Bronx, and Long Island. In addition, Foreclosure Network of Floral Park, New York, owned by Ashley's friend Gary Lewis, brokered deals for Consumer Home, as did Foreclosure Resource Center, another Floral Park company, owned by Ashley's cousin Robert Levy. Another cousin, Jason Ashley, often acted as the buyer's attorney and at least some cases did not reveal a potential conflict of interest.

ASHLEY JOINS U.S. MORTGAGE CORP.: 2002

Early in 2002, Michael Ashley left Consumer Mortgage, telling *Newsday* that he was offered a job with Pine Brook, New Jersey-based U.S. Mortgage Corp. to lead its New York arm in Melville under the Lend America banner. He took with him about 50 people from Consumer Home Mortgage, including a key member of the company, Michael Primeau. Within a matter of months Consumer Home Mortgage closed all of its

```
┌─────────────────────────────────────────────┐
│                                               │
│              KEY DATES                        │
│                   ■                           │
│  ─────────────────────────────────────────   │
│                                               │
│   1986:  Ideal Mortgage Bankers, Ltd., is     │
│          founded.                             │
│   2002:  Michael Ashley and Michael Primeau   │
│          joined U.S. Mortgage Corp. to do     │
│          business in New York as Lend         │
│          America.                             │
│   2003:  Ideal Mortgage and Lend America      │
│          combine, doing business under the    │
│          Lend America name.                   │
│   2005:  Lend America renews focus on FHA     │
│          loans.                               │
│   2006:  Lend America begins airing           │
│          infomercials.                        │
│   2008:  Lend America is fined and placed on  │
│          probation for deceptive mailing.     │
│                                               │
└─────────────────────────────────────────────┘
```

branch offices and voluntarily relinquished its state mortgage license. U.S. Mortgage Corp. had been founded in Pine Brook in 1996 by Michael J. McGrath, who began his real estate career in the mid-1960s.

The notoriety generated by the *Newsday* articles led to a state Banking Department investigation that found in addition to Ashley there were three other convicted felons among the loan officers employed at Lend America. They were forced to resign but attempts to oust Ashley failed because of the agreement he had struck for pleading guilty to wire fraud charges. In July 2003 Ashley further cleared his legal entanglements by settling an outstanding lawsuit from his Consumer Home Mortgage days, agreeing to a $500,000 consent judgment with four people who bought two Brooklyn homes. He said that settlement was not an admission of guilt, however, maintaining that in light of high legal fees it was the wisest way to end the matter.

Concerning his departure from Consumer Home Mortgage, Ashley offered a different account to *Mortgage Banking* in 2009, claiming that in late 2001 it was "swallowed up by U.S. Mortgage." Moreover, he said he and Primeau "didn't like the way the merger turned out. ... So Ashley and Primeau broke away, buying another Melville-based mortgage company called Ideal Mortgage Bankers," which had been in business since 1986. U.S. Mortgage would encounter legal problems regarding the sale of loans without obtaining permission from the credit unions that owned them. The company's president, Michael J. McGrath, who succeeded his father after his death in 2004, pleaded guilty to the $139 million fraud that led to the closing of U.S. Mortgage Corp. and a lengthy prison sentence for himself.

ACQUISITION OF IDEAL MORTGAGE: 2003

Ashley and Primeau took the Lend America name with them after acquiring Ideal Mortgage in 2003 and began building a direct-to-consumer model, eliminating brokers. In early 2005 they took over the www.lendamerica.com web site address from a Florida company. In various press accounts the partners said that Lend America was heavily involved in the subprime and alternative mortgage business, but in 2005 "at the height of the mortgage boom," in the words of the *Mortgage Banking* profile, Ashley "took Lend America out of the hottest game in town to start it up again from what was then the coldest sector of the market." In September 2008, as the subprime lending crisis was unfolding, Ashley told James Comtois of *Origination News*, "we saw this market crash coming, and could see how the industry was moving. We saw lenders not verifying income, the launch of pay-option ARMs and subprime loans. No one was looking at the FHA market."

There was every indication that Lend America and its leaders had never left the FHA market, but at the very least the company cut back on conventional lending and began a national expansion effort around the start of 2005. In addition to New York and Connecticut, where Ideal Mortgage had already been involved, Lend America by February 2005 became licensed in Florida, Georgia, Texas, North Carolina, and Tennessee, altogether maintaining 25 offices. According to a cached version of the firm's web site from that same month, Lend America offered "FHA, VA, Community Home-buyer, Conventional, Jumbo, No Income Check, No Asset Check and Nonconforming products." The site also revealed an attitude not in keeping with Ashley's admonishment of lenders for not verifying income, boasting "No Income Check means ... we don't verify your income, we don't ask for a lot of paper work, we just GET THE JOB DONE! As little as 0% down allowed, less than perfect credit is accepted, reduced paperwork, no income or asset verification required."

Whether by design or not, Lend America was well positioned to take advantage of a mortgage industry crisis due to the subprime market by aggressively staking out a position in the FHA loan business. The company employed infomercials to good effect, the first airing in February 2006 at 2 A.M. Lend America also enjoyed success from a toll-free number it acquired: 1-800-FHAFIXED. Moreover, Ashley reinvented himself as "Mike Ashley," champion drag racer. His racing team, Gotham City Racing, became a valuable marketing tool for Lend America, the logo for which received increased visibility through Ashley's televised competitions.

WHOLESALE LENDING BUSINESS CLOSES: 2008

Despite many positive attributes, Lend America, like other lenders, suffered from the collapse of the housing market and in the fall of 2007, according to *Long Island Business News,* began looking for a corporate parent. Instead, in early 2008 Lend America acquired The Mortgage Zone brokerage in Hauppauge, New York. In one concession to difficult business conditions, Lend America exited the wholesale lending business in July 2008, about a year after launching the platform under the Ideal Mortgage banner. The company focused all of its attention on retail lending.

In the spring of 2008 Lend America ran afoul of the government when it mailed a flyer that too closely imitated the look of an official government document. The company blamed a vendor, claiming it was an unauthorized mailing piece. Nevertheless, in December 2008 Lend America was fined $6,500 and placed on probation for six months. In the meantime, the company held great aspirations for a new government program, HOPE for Homeowners (H4H), launched by the Bush administration in October 2008 to help homeowners with ARMs to switch over to more affordable fixed-rate mortgages. Lend America persuaded mortgage holders to provide them with the names of borrowers to find homeowners whose mortgage payments were more than 31 percent of gross income and therefore eligible for the program. Lend America would then offer them fixed-rate loans. Also to attract business, Lend America turned to infomercials under the guise of the "Mortgage Loan Network," using actors as ersatz news anchors. In essence, Lend America paid the existing mortgage holder about 65 cents on the dollar for each mortgage it reorganized, while setting up homeowners with FHA-guaranteed loans. The loans were then to be bundled into a Ginnie Mae (Government National Mortgage Association) security.

The HOPE program did not fare well in the beginning, hobbled by weak incentives and strict guidelines. After six months only 51 loans were made under the program, and of those, 50 were made by Lend America, *Forbes* reported in May 2009, but they were also being held up pending federal investigations: "The officials, who insisted on anonymity because they are not authorized to speak on the matter, declined to offer specifics except to say anything from inadequate documentation to unethical practices could be the focus of the queries." Lend America claimed to have closed on 100 H4H loans. The company also said that it had been reapproved by the U.S. Department of Housing and Urban Development as an H4H lender. The future prospects of Lend America, as a result, were somewhat murky.

Ed Dinger

PRINCIPAL SUBSIDIARIES

Lend America Inc.

PRINCIPAL COMPETITORS

Bank of America N.A.; LendingTree, LLC; Residential Capital, LLC.

FURTHER READING

Bergsman, Steve, "Gearing Up for Growth," *Mortgage Banking,* June 2009, p. 32.

Berry, Kate, "Lender's FHA Twist Puts Investors Front and Center," *American Banker,* September 12, 2008, p. 1.

Desmond, Maurna, "New Troubles for a Troubled Washington Mortgage Plan," *Forbes,* May 7, 2009.

Hawkins, Asher, "To the Rescue," *Forbes,* December 12, 2008.

Launder, William, "Idea's Pitchman Has Fast Car, Fresh Start," *American Banker,* October 10, 2006, p. 9.

Murray, Christian, "Deal Keeps Ex-Felon in Banking," *Newsday,* January 17, 2003, p. A55.

———, "'Flipping' Guaranteed Grief for Some Home Buyers?" *Newsday,* May 9, 2004, p. A38.

———, "Mortgage Executive's Ouster Sought," *Newsday,* November 10, 2002, p. A55.

———, "Question of Fraud," *Newsday,* November 4, 2002, p. A31.

Terhune, Chad, and Robert Berner, "FHA-Backed Loans: The New Subprime," *Business Week,* November 19, 2008.

Theis, Laura, "Melville-Based Lend America: Ask What Your Country Can Do for You," *Long Island Business News,* August 31, 2007.

Idealab

—■—

130 West Union Street
Pasadena, California 91103
U.S.A.
Telephone: (626) 585-6900
Fax: (626) 535-2701
Web site: http://www.idealab.com

Private Company
Incorporated: 1996
Employees: 614
Sales: $44.4 million (2008)
NAICS: 523999 Miscellaneous Financial Investment
    Activities

■ ■ ■

Idealab helps business ideas develop into companies.
The company provides capital, office space and
administrative services, technological consulting services,
financial advice, and a range of fundamental support
services to start-up enterprises. Idealab takes a minority
equity stake in the companies it helps launch, but it
plays a much larger role in the conception and development of a business concept than a conventional venture-
capital firm does. Idealab, once entirely invested in Internet businesses, oversees a portfolio of 16 companies
involved in renewable energy, robotics, and hybrid
vehicle development, as well as several web-based
businesses.

BILL GROSS

If there was a poster child of the mercurial rise and the
spectacular collapse of the dot-com industry, it was Bill
Gross. Gross personified the exuberance that propelled
the technology sector to its dizzying heights,
demonstrating an irrepressible enthusiasm for virtually
anything related to the Internet. His frenetic activity,
expressed through Idealab, led to the formation of 50
dot-com start-ups, making him a billionaire and a guru
of Internet entrepreneurialism. When the dot-com
bubble burst, his exposure in the sector gave him a
front-row seat for the carnage that ensued, as trillions of
dollars in market value evaporated with shocking speed.
Gross figured as arguably the most prominent name in
the debacle, embodying one of the most dramatic
chapters in business history.

Years before Gross embarked on his roller-coaster
ride, he established an impressive track record as an
entrepreneur. He launched his career at the age of 12.
He began selling candy to children in his neighborhood
in Encino, California, recruiting a sales force of other
children to take advantage of a price difference between
two competing retailers. With profits realized from the
venture, a preteen version of arbitrage, Gross developed
plans for constructing solar-powered devices and formed
Solar Devices at the age of 15. He sold the plans
through advertisements in *Popular Mechanics* for $4
apiece, netting $25,000 from the business. The profits
from Solar Devices paid for his first year's tuition at the
California Institute of Technology, where he founded a
company named GNP Inc. that developed advanced
loudspeaker technology. The company thrived, becom-

ing one of *Inc.* magazine's 500 largest companies in the United States in 1982.

After earning a degree in mechanical engineering, Gross and his younger brother, Larry Gross, delved into software. They devised a way to make Lotus 1-2-3, a popular spreadsheet program, obey simple commands, developing their code through GNP. Lotus Development Corp.'s founder, Mitchell Kapor, learned of the Grosses' work and he purchased GNP in 1984, paying the brothers $10 million for the company. Bill Gross's next significant achievement as an entrepreneur occurred in 1991, when he founded Knowledge Adventure, a developer of educational software. The company flourished, but by the mid-1990s he was looking for a new challenge, searching for a way to give full expression to his multitude of ideas for new business ventures. Reportedly, the epiphany that led to the formation of Idealab occurred on the set of *Casper*, a film directed by Gross's friend, Steven Spielberg.

IDEALAB TAKES SHAPE

"He's kind of a mad genius," Spielberg said of Gross, referring to his friend in the February 1997 issue of *Inc.* "His brain works like a roundhouse in a train station, spinning off ideas in seven directions at once, yet not losing its focus on any one of them." Gross wanted a way to give full voice to his creativity and never-ending business ideas, deciding that forming a company in the business of creating businesses offered him the greatest opportunity to express himself. He put his brother in charge of Knowledge Adventure in September 1995 (the company was sold for $100 million to CUC International the following year) and began the work of forming Idealab, referring to the company as an "incubator." Historically, the term *incubator* had been used to refer to nonprofit organizations, usually universities that helped nascent businesses get on their feet, but the for-profit Gross gave the term a new meaning with the formation of Idealab, creating a blueprint that was

copied repeatedly in the frenzy leading up to the burst of the dot-com bubble.

IDEALAB'S ROLE AS AN INCUBATOR

Gross's vision of Idealab defied classification, at least as definitions existed when the company was formed in 1996. His mission was to develop business ideas, hand the concepts over to entrepreneurs, and give the entrepreneurs an "Internet start-up in a box," as he said in the February 1997 issue of *Inc.* Entrepreneurs, in Gross's mind, wasted time dealing with matters apart from ensuring a business concept turned into a commercial success. After developing an idea for a business, Gross, through Idealab, recruited a chief executive officer to actualize the concept and gave the leader a template for running the business, including specifics on company structure, stock options, employee compensation and benefits, providing an open-book managerial guide. The company also provided a temporary chief financial officer to help the start-up establish itself. Idealab provided shared office space and administrative services, it took a minority equity stake and provided seed funding, it helped develop technology to form the basis of new products, and it played a substantial role in overseeing the operation of its companies. Idealab was part traditional incubator, part venture-capital firm, part think tank, and part parent company, possessing characteristics that set it apart from all others.

Gross established Idealab in Pasadena and began turning his ideas into independent companies. Initially, the company was funded by a $5 million investment from a group of Gross's supporters, Spielberg included, but eventually Gross intended to make money from the equity stakes he took in his creations. Idealab controlled between 25 percent and 49 percent of the companies it spawned, banking its financial future on the maturation of its fledgling concerns into companies that could complete an initial public offering (IPO) of stock or attract the attention of a corporate suitor. Idealab only needed to have one or two of its companies complete an IPO or be acquired, "and that will fund us basically forever," Gross said in the February 1997 issue of *Inc.*

A BUSINESS FACTORY BEGINS PRODUCING BUSINESSES

Gross sat in Idealab's headquarters and began dreaming up ideas for Internet-related companies. Idealab's floor plan, reflecting Spielberg's analogy of a locomotive roundhouse, positioned Gross in the middle of the office space, seated in a glassed-in enclosure that represented the hub of the company's operations. Like

KEY DATES

1996: Bill Gross forms Idealab in Pasadena, California.

1998: Idealab Capital Partners is formed to broaden Idealab's capabilities in providing financing.

1999: EToys, an Idealab-backed company, is valued at $7.8 billion.

2000: Idealab receives $1 billion in private equity funding the same month the technology sector begins to collapse.

2001: After trading for more than $86 per share, eToys' stock value plummets to $0.09 per share and the company declares bankruptcy.

2002: Gross begins focusing his efforts on renewable energy and robotics.

2009: Idealab's portfolio comprises 16 companies.

spokes emanating from a hub, sections of the office, each representing a new business idea, stretched out radially from Gross's circular desk, where he sat spinning like a turret of creativity. Within a year, Idealab created 23 companies.

The formation of the dot-com bubble provided a fertile climate for Idealab's first wave of companies. Companies such as CareerLink, a job-hunting web site; HomeLink, an online provider of virtual tours of homes and neighborhoods; and WeddingPlanner, which enabled users to plan weddings online, made their debut, along with dozens of other start-ups. Gross formed a separate venture-capital fund, Idealab Capital Partners, in mid-1998 to provide financing beyond seed capital and to take a bigger equity stake in the companies preparing to go public. The first Idealab company to complete an IPO was Shopping.com, which was purchased by Compaq Computer Corp. in January 1999 for $220 million. CitySearch, an online listing service for community data, was acquired by USA Network Inc.'s Ticketmaster unit and the combination completed an IPO valued at $2.8 billion in December 1998. In February 1999, another Idealab company, eToys, an online retailer of toys, filed for a $115 million IPO. A bevy of other projects that would emerge as NetZero, eWallet, CarsDirect, and GoTo.com stood in various forms of development, percolating under Gross's watchful eye.

Encouraged by success, Gross pressed forward. He proposed establishing new incubators in cities such as San Francisco, New York, Boston, and London. Idealab

Capital Partners closed its second round of funding 18 months after closing its first, enabling it to develop a portfolio worth nearly $500 million by early 2000. Of the dozens of companies created by then, seven had completed IPOs, but one company stood out from the pack, epitomizing the fantastic riches to be made in e-commerce. EToys completed its IPO in May 1999, debuting at $20 per share. The company's stock value soared to $76 per share after its first day of trading, valuing it at $7.8 billion. Idealab had made an initial investment of $200,000 in eToys, making its investment worth $1.5 billion.

IDEALAB PREPARES FOR STOCK OFFERING IN 2000

Charging ahead, Gross began preparing for Idealab's IPO in early 2000, roughly the same time he appointed his brother head of Idealab Europe. Gross wanted to complete the IPO to use Idealab stock to help make investments and complete acquisitions. "We are going public to get currency for expanding our business further," he said in the June 5, 2000 issue of *Business Week*. Yet, for a company that defied classification, gaining approval from the U.S. Securities and Exchange Commission (SEC) promised to be an uphill battle. The main obstacle blocking Idealab's debut on Wall Street was the Investment Company Act of 1940, which required a company to hold a controlling interest in approximately 60 percent of its portfolio companies, otherwise it would be deemed a mutual fund or investment company and face an exceptionally complex and lengthy approval process. Gross wanted to increase his equity stakes in his independent companies enough to secure an exemption from the SEC, and he turned to a group of investors for help. In mid-March 2000, Idealab secured $1 billion in private equity funding from investors such as Dell Computer Corp., Sumitomo Corp., and BancBoston Capital, the same week the dot-com bubble burst.

THE MARKET COLLAPSES

Between March 2000 and October 2002, publicly traded technology companies lost $5 trillion of their market value. The implosion was devastating, and it happened quickly. By April 2000, eToys, whose stock was trading at $86.25 per share six months earlier, was trading at $6 per share, well along a precipitous path toward collapse that saw its stock value plummet to $0.09 per share by February 2001, one month before it declared bankruptcy. Technology companies were canceling planned IPOs in droves by April 2000, when Idealab filed for its IPO, hoping to raise $300 million provided the SEC granted the company an exemption from the Investment Act of 1940. By June 2000, the value of the holdings in Idealab's seven publicly traded companies had plunged from $2 billion to $502 million. In October 2000, after succeeding in gaining an exemption from the SEC, Gross abandoned his plans for an IPO. "Over the past several months," he said in the October 23, 2000 issue of the *IPO Reporter*, "we have seen dramatic shifts in the market and determined that it is in the best interest of the company, its employees, and investors that we not proceed with the offering during this volatile time."

Like a Category 5 hurricane, the Internet frenzy built up a terrific force and dissipated suddenly, leaving in its wake destruction and despair. For Gross, his own despair was exacerbated by the despair of others, namely the investors who had committed $1 billion to Idealab just as the technology sector began to crumble. Under the terms of the deal struck in March 2000, Gross agreed to give the investors an increasing stake in Idealab if the company's value dropped below the price set when the investment was made. In March 2000, the value of Idealab was set at $7.7 billion, but by late 2001, the company was worth less than $1 billion, which meant the holders of Idealab's preferred stock were entitled to complete ownership of Idealab. Gross offered to buy back Idealab's preferred stock for $0.10 on the dollar, but a group of investors dismissed the offer, filing a complaint against Gross. They wanted Gross to liquidate Idealab to recoup their investment. Gross refused, leading to a $1 billion lawsuit filed by the angry investors that prevented Gross from raising new capital. After several years, the parties involved settled their differences and the lawsuit was dismissed, leaving Gross with the daunting task of rebuilding Idealab.

A CHASTENED IDEALAB EMERGES

After the epic maelstrom, Idealab emerged as a more cautious company pursuing a redefined strategy. Instead of creating one company per month, the company was helping to start one, perhaps two companies per year. A more disciplined financing mentality took hold, and Idealab held onto its investments for a longer time than previously. Gross steered away from a dependence on the Internet and began focusing on technology companies that utilized "hard" science, nurturing companies that were developing hybrid vehicles, interactive robots, and cellphones that worked without the use of cellular towers. He placed an emphasis on energy projects, incubating Energy Innovations, a solar-collector developer that pursued similar goals as he had as the 15-year-old founder of Solar Devices. "Bill is starting companies of great promise and of great interest to the

venture community," one of Idealab's investors said in the September 5, 2005 issue of *Fortune*. "His enthusiasm and passion are still contagious, but now there's a clarity that comes from having to regroup and think about the next wave of companies—and a new ability to take execution to the next level."

By the end of the decade, Idealab was looking forward, using the tumult of the times to guide it toward a stable and profitable future. In 2009, the company's portfolio of companies comprised 16 entities involved in e-commerce, renewable energy, information technology, and hybrid vehicle development. In the years ahead, the composition of Idealab's holdings would be governed by Gross, increasing at a measured pace and reflecting the vision of one of the technology industry's most prominent executives.

Jeffrey L. Covell

PRINCIPAL SUBSIDIARIES

Aptera Motors; Connexus; Cooking.com; Desktop Factory; Distributed World Power; Energy Innovations; eSolar; Evolution Robotics; Idealab Capital Partners, LLC; Infinia; Internet Brands; Partsearch Technologies; Perfect Market, Inc.; RayTracker, Inc.; Snap Technologies; XI Technologies.

PRINCIPAL COMPETITORS

Accel Partners; Internet Capital Group, Inc.; Menlo Ventures.

FURTHER READING

Brinsley, John, "Incubator Becoming Dirty Word in Net Business," *Los Angeles Business Journal*, May 8, 2000, p. 1.

"The Cloning of Idealab!" *Business Week*, July 19, 1999, p. 6.

Dunphy, Laura, "Idealab Facing Tough Sell to Investors As It Files for IPO," *Los Angeles Business Journal*, April 24, 2000, p. 6.

Fisher, Sara, "Idealab Going Bi-Coastal," *Los Angeles Business Journal*, February 7, 2000, p. 33.

———, "Idealab Keeps Feeding Web Frenzy," *Los Angeles Business Journal*, June 7, 1999, p. 1.

Groom, Nichola, "A Web Pioneer Returns to Solar Energy," *International Herald Tribune*, July 21, 2008, p. 15.

Henderson, Rick, "Idealab Investor Discusses Workings of Venture Deals," *Los Angeles Business Journal*, January 3, 2000, p. 11.

Hira, Nadira A., "Idealab Reloaded," *Fortune*, September 5, 2005, p. 143.

"Is Idealab! Running Dry?" *Business Week,* June 5, 2000, p. EB50.

Jergler, Don, "Founder of Pasadena, Calif., Internet Incubator Idealab Plans Diversification," *San Gabriel Valley Tribune,* March 19, 2002.

Kurdek, Robyn, "Idealab! Can't Figure Out IPO," *IPO Reporter,* October 23, 2000.

Meyer, Cheryl, "Idealab! Forges Ahead," *Daily Deal,* February 7, 2002.

Moriarty, George, "Idealab! Closes $363M Second Fund," *Private Equity Week,* September 13, 1999, p. 6.

"That's One Hot Incubator," *Business Week,* March 13, 2000, p. 42.

Useem, Jerry, "The Start-Up Factory," *Inc.,* February 1997, p. 40.

"When an Incubator Goes Cold," *Business Week Online,* December 21, 2001.

More Than Cool™

Igloo Products Corp.

---·---

777 **Igloo Road**
Katy, Texas 77494-2972
U.S.A.
Telephone: (713) 584-6800
Toll Free: (800) 324-2653
Fax: (713) 935-7763
Web site: http://www.igloocoolers.com

Wholly Owned Subsidiary of J.H. Whitney & Co., LLC
Founded: 1947 as Igloo Manufacturing Company
Employees: 1,150
Sales: $200 million (2008 est.)
NAICS: 326199 All Other Plastics Product Manufac-
turing

■ ■ ■

Igloo Products Corp. is the largest cooler manufacturer in the world. The firm's most recognized product is the patented "Playmate" series of personal-sized coolers, but its 500-unit product line includes full-size ice chests as well as beverage, soft-sided, patio, and thermoelectric models. Igloo products are sold via more than 250 retailers in the United States and overseas. The company's headquarters, manufacturing, and distribution operations are all located at a 1.4-million-square-foot facility in Katy, Texas, a suburb of Houston. Igloo Products, whose six-decades-plus history is rife with ownership changes, was purchased in 2008 by J.H.

Whitney & Co., LLC, a private-equity firm based in New Canaan, Connecticut.

POST–WORLD WAR II FOUNDATION

The Igloo saga begins in 1947, when several Houston investors joined forces to fill what they perceived as an important market niche. At the time, drinking water was carted to the hot, humid oilfields of the region in wooden buckets. This group of innovators developed an insulated metal container that would not only change the comfort level of thousands of oil riggers, but also broaden the beverage and menu options of picnickers for decades to come. Igloo Manufacturing Company's handmade metal coolers featured a "double-locked seam" that kept water cold and prevented leakage. By the early 1950s, Igloo had acquired the Horton and Polar King brands of metal coolers. Over the course of the decade, the company added plastic and styrene liners to its metal coolers.

Soon after merging with Production Tooling Company in 1960, Igloo took on that firm's sales and marketing operation, the John T. Everett Company. In recognition of Everett's Memphis, Tennessee, headquarters, the merged firm's name was changed to Texas Tennessee Industries (TTI) in 1961. TTI used the proceeds of its 1962 initial public offering (IPO) to fund an expansion of the Houston manufacturing plant. That same year, the company introduced a major innovation to its industry, the first all-plastic ice chest. At first, TTI limited marketing of the new product to breweries, but it soon found that sportsmen and other

COMPANY PERSPECTIVES

Igloo has built its name as the most recognized brand in coolers since originating the category in 1947. Research shows that consumers regard Igloo as the most popular cooler line in the U.S. For everyone, Igloo means quality and durability. So much so that three in every four U.S. households own at least one Igloo cooler!

consumers favored the lightweight, durable containers. TTI built on the success of this initial 48-quart plastic ice chest with the launch of a line of coolers in various sizes and colors throughout the remainder of the decade.

Early on, the firm started designing ice chests and coolers with special features geared toward particular activities. For example, the Giant Sea Chest launched in 1967 was Igloo's second all-plastic model. It offered deep-sea fishermen a 155-quart/300-pound capacity and rust-, stain-, and odor-resistance; it could even be used as an extra seat. Tailoring products to the needs of specific groups, especially boaters, would become an Igloo hallmark.

Meanwhile, TTI's ties to the brewing industry developed into a flourishing private-label business during the decade as well. By the late 1960s, the company was manufacturing a full line of ice chests and soft-sided beverage coolers labeled with cigarette, beer, soft drink, and other national brands. The containers were often used as promotional items by these firms.

Perhaps emboldened by its success, TTI embarked on a number of side ventures in the late 1960s and early 1970s. In 1967 the company formed a Container Division to manufacture plastic drums for the chemical industry. This business was divested in 1980. TTI launched Nutrifoam, a fertilizer-embedded polyurethane foam intended as a growth medium for plants, but quickly liquidated the venture. S.A.G.E., a chain of discount stores in Texas and California, was bought in 1969 and sold three years later, as was a manufacturer of exercise equipment. One of the company's longer-lived diversifications was its 1968 acquisition of Impact Extrusions, Inc., a manufacturer of thermoplastic sheet. This purchase, which represented an effort to integrate vertically, lasted for more than two decades before the parent company sold it to Pawnee Extrusions, Inc., in 1989. TTI apparently learned a lesson from its late 1960s extracurriculars; in the 1970s, it concentrated

diversification efforts on its core product line instead of new ventures.

RAPID GROWTH IN THE SEVENTIES

In acknowledgment of its lead brand's success, TTI changed its name to Igloo Corporation in 1971. The company relied on market research to direct new product development, a strategy that would continue to guide numerous innovations. Igloo patented and introduced the Playmate series of beverage coolers, featuring a "tent-top" design, that same year, adding the unique push-button lock and release to the lid in 1972. Although it could hold eighteen 12-ounce cans, this new cooler could be carried with just one hand. The line was later extended to include smaller versions, including the Little Playmate (1977) and Lunchmate (1978) models. Igloo's 1972 acquisition by The Coca-Cola Bottling Company of New York presaged an energetic expansion of the product line. New products introduced in the 1970s included: Sturdy Jug utility containers; Jerry Jug containers for gasoline and other flammable liquids; new beverage coolers and ice chests; and the Kool line of specially designed containers intended for use in cars and trucks. From 1979 to 1981, Igloo averaged four new products per year, mostly extensions of established categories.

The company backed up its products with a three-year warranty that for many years was unique to the cooler category. It also won over customers with its ready supply of replacement parts, including lids, drain plugs, hinges, and spigots. Some customers did not need a warranty; they witnessed the durability of Igloo coolers firsthand. According to a company history, the containers have survived maulings by wild animals and stayed intact in burning buildings. Playmate coolers have even played a role in life-saving transplant operations; donated containers are used in some hospitals to transport human organs for transplant operations.

An export program undertaken during the 1970s expanded Igloo's reach to Canada, Japan, and Mexico. Taking a page from its early history, the company made its first forays into international markets by selling coolers to oil companies for use on overseas projects. The effort not only increased sales but also helped to smooth out seasonal fluctuations in production.

Igloo also diversified its distribution network from a concentration in sporting goods stores to mass-merchandising chains such as Kmart and Wal-Mart. Corporate sales multiplied rapidly on the strength of its expanded product line and broadened distribution network, increasing from about $25 million in 1975 to $70.9 million by the end of the decade.

KEY DATES

1947: Igloo Manufacturing Company is founded in Houston as a producer of insulated metal water coolers.

1960: Company merges with Production Tooling Company and its Memphis, Tennessee, affiliate.

1961: Merged firm is renamed Texas Tennessee Industries (TTI).

1962: TTI conducts an initial pubic offering and introduces the first all-plastic ice chest.

1971: TTI changes its name to Igloo Corporation; company introduces the Playmate personal-sized cooler.

1972: Igloo is acquired by Coca-Cola Bottling Company of New York.

1980: Houston's Anderson, Clayton & Co. conglomerate acquires Igloo.

1986: The Quaker Oats Company takes over Anderson, Clayton.

1987: Company is taken private as Igloo Products Corp. via a management-led leveraged buyout.

1997: Brunswick Corporation acquires Igloo for $154 million.

2001: Igloo is acquired by the private investment firm Westar Capital L.L.C.; Jim Morley is named president and CEO.

2004: Company consolidates its worldwide headquarters, manufacturing, and distribution operations into a single facility in Katy, Texas.

2008: Private-equity firm J.H. Whitney & Co., LLC, purchases Igloo from Westar.

2009: Morley resigns from the company; Gary Kiedaisch is named interim president and CEO.

CHANGES IN CORPORATE OWNERSHIP IN THE EIGHTIES

Corporate ownership changed in 1980, when Houston's Anderson, Clayton & Co. conglomerate acquired Igloo for $46.6 million. Increasing advertising budgets under the new ownership helped push Igloo's sales to about $80 million by 1982. New products launched in the 1980s included Tag-Along personal-sized coolers with a shoulder strap; Igloo Ice, a long-lasting, reusable substitute for ice; and Kool Tunes, a cooler with stereo speakers. Encouraged by its parent company to diversify,

Igloo also launched a line of collapsible outdoor cooking devices in 1985. The Quaker Oats Company's purchase of Anderson, Clayton in 1986 presaged another transfer of ownership for Igloo. In 1987 the company was taken private as Igloo Products Corp. through a management-led leveraged buyout brokered by New York's Metropolitan Life Insurance Company, which continued to hold a key ownership position in Igloo through the mid-1990s.

Igloo started the 1990s by marking the sale of 15 million Playmate coolers, then launched a new product blitz. New items and line extensions included insulated cups and sport bottles for both hot and cold beverages, soft-sided lunch boxes, and "trash management systems." Fashionable new colors and ergonomic handles were also expected to spur sales. In 1991 Igloo licensed its trademark to a line of rugged footwear.

Igloo and its compatriots in the ice chest category broke out of a period of heavy promotions in the recessionary early 1990s by introducing stylish new adaptations of well-established products. Igloo's wheeled, long-handled coolers made moving an ice chest full of food and beverages much easier. The company expected to sell one million wheeled coolers in 1995 alone. Igloo also developed new technology in the early 1990s. The company patented a thermoelectric module that could keep foods cold without ice, and even make ice, or heat foods to 155°F. When teamed up with the company's ice chests and coolers, it formed the core of Igloo's "active cooling" line of containers. By 1996 Igloo's revenues were estimated at $150 million, an 87.5 percent increase over the 1982 sales of $80 million.

MAINTAINING TOP COOLER SPOT THROUGH ADDITIONAL OWNERSHIP CHANGES

Brunswick Corporation purchased the ice chest manufacturer in January 1997 for $154 million in cash. Igloo had for many years been custom-manufacturing coolers for Brunswick's boats. Upon its acquisition, Igloo became part of the parent company's growing Outdoor Recreation Group, joining previous acquirees Zebco fishing gear, Roadmaster bicycles, and Nelson/Weather-Rite tents and sleeping bags. A little more than a year after this takeover, Igloo expanded its distribution capacity in Houston to accommodate its ever growing domestic product line and its overseas forays. By this time, the company had developed a strong presence in the cooler markets of Canada, Mexico, Argentina, England, Germany, Japan, and South Korea.

Igloo's Brunswick era proved short-lived as the parent firm decided to reverse course on its diversification program, selling off its Outdoor Recreation Group in the early 2000s in piecemeal fashion. In October 2001 Westar Capital L.L.C., a private investment firm based in Costa Mesa, California, acquired Igloo for an undisclosed sum. At the time, Jim Morley was named president and CEO, replacing 15-year company leader Jonathan Godshall. Morley had a strong background in consumer products, having headed marketing and sales at the U.S. unit of Finland-based Fiskars Corporation, a producer of scissors, lawn and garden items, and other consumer products.

Under Morley's leadership, Igloo continued to churn out new products each year that helped to maintain its position as the largest producer of coolers in the world. Perhaps the most important initiative of his tenure, however, occurred in 2004 when Igloo consolidated its worldwide headquarters, manufacturing, and distribution operations into a single facility in the Houston suburb of Katy. Igloo had operated a 500,000-square-foot manufacturing and distribution facility in Katy since 1979. In the 2004 move, which was designed to create a leaner and more streamlined company, Igloo closed its manufacturing and corporate offices in Houston in favor of an expanded 1.4-million-square-foot facility at the 105-acre site in Katy. The consolidated manufacturing operation included more than 100 molding machines and 18 assembly areas. Igloo's expansion of its U.S. manufacturing platform occurred at a time when many other manufacturers were outsourcing their production to locations outside the United States.

In October 2008 Igloo changed hands again when J.H. Whitney & Co., LLC, a private-equity company based in New Canaan, Connecticut, purchased the firm from Westar Capital. Although the terms of the transaction were not disclosed, the deal was backed by $135 million in debt financing. Among the nearly two dozen companies in Whitney's investment portfolio was The North Face, an outdoor apparel producer. After taking over Igloo, Whitney named Gary Kiedaisch as the firm's new chairman. Kiedaisch was the former CEO of Igloo's chief U.S. rival, The Coleman Company, Inc. Morley continued to serve as president and CEO but then resigned in January 2009 while remaining on the company board. Kiedaisch was named interim president and CEO. At the same time, David Thornhill was brought onboard as executive vice-president of operations and products. Thornhill's previous experience included stints as a senior manager at Coleman and PlayPower, Inc., a producer of commercial playground equipment. The new leaders were expected to place an increased emphasis on developing innovative new products.

April Dougal Gasbarre
Updated, David E. Salamie

PRINCIPAL COMPETITORS

The Coleman Company, Inc.; Newell Rubbermaid Inc.

FURTHER READING

Barr, Greg, "Igloo Changes Hands Again: Private Equity Firm Wraps Up Latest Sales of Ice-Chest Maker," *Houston Business Journal,* November 7, 2008.

Bayer, Tom, "Igloo Is Taking Its Case to Consumer in Ad Drive," *Advertising Age,* June 21, 1982, p. 4.

Boisseau, Charles, "$154 Million in Cold Cash: Igloo Signs Deal with Brunswick," *Houston Chronicle,* November 20, 1996.

Darwin, Jennifer, "Brunswick Comes and Goes: Outdoor Giant Buys Igloo," *Houston Business Journal,* November 22, 1996, p. 5.

Esposito, Frank, "Equity Firm Nabs Igloo," *Plastics News,* October 20, 2008, p. 1.

"Frosty Forecasting," *Discount Store News,* August 5, 1996, p. 105.

Greer, Jim, "California Company Heads for Cooler Climes with Purchase of Houston's Igloo Products," *Houston Business Journal,* November 16, 2001, p. 2.

Hall, Christine, "Igloo Products Moves to 'burbs in Corporate Consolidation Deal," *Houston Business Journal,* April 15, 2005.

Hill, Dawn, "The Ice Chest Cometh," *HFN—The Weekly Newspaper for the Home Furnishing Network,* October 23, 1995, p. 11A.

"Igloo President, CEO Stepping Down," *Houston Chronicle,* January 15, 2009.

"Igloo Products Corp.," *Journal of Commerce and Commercial,* November 9, 1990, p. 13A.

Kaplan, David, "Igloo Sold to California Equity Firm," *Houston Chronicle,* November 15, 2001.

Levinson, Brian, "Quaker Oats Sells Igloo to Investors," *Houston Chronicle,* August 11, 1987.

"Off-Season Coolers Get Warm Reception," *Discount Store News,* August 5, 1996, pp. 103–04.

"The Plastics Producers," *HFD—The Weekly Home Furnishings Newspaper,* October 21, 1985, pp. 83–94.

Renstrom, Roger, "Igloo Sees Quick Return on Twinshot Investment," *Plastics News,* March 30, 2009, p. 4.

Stromberg, Laura A., "Igloo Plans Expansion to Keep Up with Hot Market for Coolers," *Houston Business Journal,* April 17, 1998, p. 5A.

"Thermoelectrics Chill Portable Cooler," *Design News,* January 22, 1996, p. 37.

Wessling, Jack, "Sunbelt Licensed to Make Igloo Shoes,"

Footwear News, January 21, 1991, p. 30.

Wollam, Allison, "Igloo Heats Up with Katy HQ Expansion," *Houston Business Journal,* October 22, 2004, p. A6.

International Dairy Queen, Inc.

7505 Metro Boulevard
Minneapolis, Minnesota 55439-3081
U.S.A.
Telephone: (952) 830-0200
Fax: (952) 830-0273
Web site: http://www.dairyqueen.com

Wholly Owned Subsidiary of Berkshire Hathaway, Inc.
Incorporated: 1962
Employees: 2,055
NAICS: 722211 Limited-Service Restaurants; 311520
    Ice Cream and Frozen Dessert Manufacturing;
    423440 Other Commercial Equipment Merchant
    Wholesalers; 424420 Packaged Frozen Food
    Merchant Wholesalers; 533110 Owners and Lessors
    of Other Non-Financial Assets

■ ■ ■

International Dairy Queen, Inc., licenses, services, and develops over 5,900 Dairy Queen stores in the United States, Canada, and more than 20 countries. In addition to selling its famous dairy desserts, many of the stores also sell hamburgers, chicken, hot dogs, and a variety of beverages. The company also owns Karmelkorn Shoppes, Inc., a franchiser of over 60 retail stores that sell popcorn, candy, and other items, as well as Orange Julius, a franchiser of some 420 stores which feature blended drinks made from orange juice, various fruits, and fruit flavors. In 1998 International Dairy Queen was purchased by Warren Buffett's Berkshire Hathaway Inc.

A GOOD IDEA IN SEARCH OF AN AUDIENCE: 1920–40

The founders of Dairy Queen, J. F. "Grandpa" Mc-Cullough and his son Alex, originally established the Homemade Ice Cream Company in Davenport, Iowa, in 1927. The two men sold a variety of ice cream products throughout the Quad Cities area (Moline and Rock Island, Illinois, and Bettendorf and Davenport, Iowa). In order to expand their operations, during the early 1930s the McCulloughs moved their business to Green River, Illinois, and purchased a former cheese factory in which they located their ice cream mix plant.

When the McCulloughs made ice cream at their plant in Green River, it was a complicated process. Butterfat, milk solids, sweetener, and stabilizer were first combined, then mixed, and finally put into a batch freezer where the combination was chilled, given a specific amount of air (technically called "overrun"), and flavored. The product was denser and richer than most ice creams, with less overrun. When the temperature reached 23 degrees Fahrenheit, a spigot was opened in the freezer and the soft ice cream flowed into three-gallon containers. The containers were covered with lids, frozen at minus-ten degrees Fahrenheit, and delivered to customers. When an ice cream store was ready to serve the product, the ice cream was put into a dipping cabinet and the temperature increased to five degrees Fahrenheit.

The ice cream was frozen solid, not for the pleasure and enjoyment of the customer, but for the convenience of the manufacturer and store owner. Yet the elder McCullough had known for a long time that ice cream at colder temperatures numbed the tastebuds and resulted in a much less flavorful product; soft, fresh ice cream drawn from a spigot at approximately 23 degrees Fahrenheit tasted best. He began to wonder if there was some way to dispense semi-frozen ice cream that kept its shape but soon realized that the batch freezers in use during the 1930s were unsuitable. An entirely different type of freezer was required and, moreover, every ice cream store that wished to dispense the new product would have to purchase at least one of the new freezers. Faced with these difficulties, Grandpa McCullough decided to give up the idea as impractical.

After a few years, however, Grandpa McCullough was still thinking about soft ice cream, and he convinced his son that they should find out whether or not the product would capture people's tastebuds. They asked one of their customers, Sherb Noble, if he would arrange a special offering of soft ice cream at his store in Kankakee, Illinois. With an advertisement of "All you can eat for 10 cents," the sale was held in early August 1938. Using an ordinary commercial batch freezer, the men put the soft ice cream into five gallon containers and then hand-dipped the product into 16-ounce cups. In two hours, Noble and the McCulloughs dished out over 1,600 servings. A short time later, another sale of soft ice cream was offered at Mildred's Ice Cream Shop in Moline. The response from the public was the same. With such overwhelming success, the McCulloughs began searching for the type of freezer that would make dispensing soft ice cream a reality.

The McCulloughs approached two manufacturers of dairy equipment and asked if they would be interested in designing a machine that dispensed semi-frozen dairy products into dishes or ice cream cones. The first manufacturer immediately rejected their proposal, and the second firm, Stoelting Brothers Company in Kiel, Wisconsin, thought the idea lacked potential. With nowhere else to go, the McCulloughs seemed to arrive at a dead end. However, one day while Grandpa McCullough was casually paging through the want ads in the *Chicago Tribune* he noticed an advertise-

ment for a continuous freezer that would dispense soft ice cream. The ad had been placed by Harry M. Oltz.

Oltz and the McCulloughs met in the summer of 1939. Having received the patent for his freezer in 1937, Oltz extended the production rights to his new partners, as well as rights for the exclusive use of the freezer in Illinois, Wisconsin, and all the states west of the Mississippi River. According to the agreement, Oltz kept exclusive rights to use of the freezer in all states east of the Mississippi and would receive continuous royalties based on the number of gallons of soft-serve ice cream processed through all the dispensing freezers produced under the patent. Oltz then moved to Miami, Florida, and established AR-TIK Systems, Inc., a firm that would find stores to serve soft ice cream in the eastern United States. Meanwhile, the McCulloughs returned to the Stoelting Brothers and reached an agreement with them to manufacture a soft-serve ice cream freezer for their own company.

1940: DAIRY QUEEN IS BORN

The first Dairy Queen store opened in Joliet, Illinois, on June 22, 1940. Jointly owned by the McCulloughs and Sherb Noble, the store was managed by Jim and Elliot Grace. By the end of the summer, the store had grossed $4,000, and Noble decided to buy out the McCulloughs' interest in that store. On April 1, 1941, the McCulloughs opened another store in Moline and once again contracted the Graces to manage it for them. Additional stores were opened in Aurora, Illinois, and Davenport, Iowa, and by the end of 1942 there were a total of eight Dairy Queen businesses in operation. However, with the advent of World War II, manufacturing materials used for building the freezers were reassigned to the war effort. Without new freezers, no new stores were able to open for the duration of the war.

Despite the inability of the McCulloughs to open more stores, they remained active. During the war, father and son sold rights to would-be store owners to use the Dairy Queen freezer and mix, and develop businesses in certain geographical areas of the country. Since they both suspected that the popularity of Dairy Queen would be brief, it was more sensible to the McCulloughs to sell territories outright rather than to arrange an ongoing royalty system. All profits were up front, and if the product lost its appeal there was no fear of losing any income. Unfortunately, the McCulloughs' method of contracting the development of new territories was extremely informal, sometimes scribbled on a napkin, paper sack, or daily newspaper, which led to a host of problems later on.

Impressed with the long lines at the Dairy Queen store in Moline, Harry Axene, a sales manager for a

KEY DATES

1927: J. F. McCullough and his son Alex found Homemade Ice Cream Co. in Iowa.

1938: Trial sales of soft ice cream prove a hit with the public.

1940: First Dairy Queen store opens in Joliet, Illinois; others quickly follow.

1948: Nonprofit Dairy Queen National Trade Association (DQNTA) is formed.

1955: DQNTA becomes a for-profit company (DQNTC) and relocates to St. Louis, Missouri.

1962: International Dairy Queen (IDQ) takes over DQNTC and moves to Minneapolis.

1970: Investor group headed by Bill McKinstry and Harris Cooper takes control of IDQ.

1972: IDQ stock begins trading over the counter; first Dairy Queen is opened in Japan.

1985: The Blizzard, a soft ice cream treat with other blended-in items, proves a huge success.

1998: Berkshire Hathaway, Inc., purchases IDQ for $585 million.

2000: IDQ settles antitrust lawsuit brought by its franchisees six years before.

2001: Chuck Mooty is named CEO; first DQ Grill & Chill restaurant opens in Chattanooga, Tennessee.

2004: International Dairy Queen celebrates its first full year of advertising on a national basis.

2007: Company reveals plans to open 500 franchised locations throughout China over the next five years.

2008: Chief Supply Chain Officer John P. Gainor succeeds Mooty as president and CEO.

2010: International Dairy Queen celebrates the 70th anniversary of the Dairy Queen brand, as well as the 25th anniversary of its popular Blizzard.

investors at the LeClaire Hotel in Moline. Excited about organizing a national Dairy Queen franchise system, Axene introduced the idea of selling territories based on a royalty system where territory store owners would pay Axene an initial fee plus an ongoing royalty fee for the soft-serve mix. Even though no formal organization resulted from this meeting, interest in Dairy Queen stores grew at a tremendous pace. With only eight stores in operation at the end of the war, by the end of 1946 there were 17, and by the end of 1947 there were over 100 Dairy Queen stores operating throughout the United States.

In 1948, Axene arranged for 35 store owners and territory operators to meet in Minneapolis with the purpose of establishing a national organization. In December of the same year, the first official meeting of the newly incorporated Dairy Queen National Trade Association (DQNTA) was held in Davenport, Iowa. Organized as a not-for-profit corporation, with C. R. Medd as its first president, national offices were soon established in the city. The DQNTA was created in order to standardize cones, plastic goods, and all other materials used in Dairy Queen stores, along with coordinating all the various kinds of advertising for Dairy Queen products. By the early 1950s, membership in the DQNTA had grown to nearly 900 dues-paying members.

AN EXPANDING MENU IN THE FIFTIES

There were 1,400 Dairy Queen stores open for business in 1950, and up until that time the menu was limited to sundaes and cones for immediate consumption, or pints and quarts to take home. When supermarkets began to sell ice cream at low prices and when air conditioning and television began keeping people home on sultry summer evenings, sales in Dairy Queen stores across the country began to suffer. In order to keep attracting customers, most stores responded to requests for an expanded menu. In 1949, milkshakes and malts were made available, and banana splits were added in 1951. Toppings for sundaes were expanded to include hot fudge, chocolate, strawberry, pineapple, butterscotch, and other flavors. Take-home novelty products were also introduced, including the Dilly bar, a soft-serve, chocolate-dipped confection with a wooden tongue depressor inserted for the customer to hold while eating.

During the 1950s, Dairy Queen stores were also challenged by the emergence of fast-food outlets that offered hamburgers, hot dogs, french fries, and various soft drinks. Since these outlets served full meals, they remained open the entire year; Dairy Queen stores were put at a disadvantage since they were boarded up for

farm equipment company, approached Grandpa McCullough and soon became a 50-50 partner in the mix company. He also purchased the territory rights for Illinois and Iowa at a price of $12,000. By the end of the war, Axene had purchased the remaining interest in the mix company and, more importantly, had seen the future of Dairy Queen in franchising. In November 1946, Axene organized a meeting with 26 potential most of the winter season. In order to stay competitive, store operators in different parts of the country began to offer various food products, from bowls of chili to pork fritters. However, the lack of a standardized menu brought complaints from customers, until the Brazier system of broiled burgers, hot dogs, barbecued beef, french fries, and onion rings was introduced in 1958. With the introduction of this system, the quality control and standardization of meat products helped to increase profits for store owners.

Although the DQNTA had been formed in 1948 to standardize products and services for store operators, its nonprofit status rendered it unable to enforce any of its policies. As a result, the DQNTA was reformed in 1955 and made a for-profit corporation. Renamed the Dairy Queen National Development Company, its members gave it more latitude and authority to implement uniform products, operating practices, standards, and services to all Dairy Queen stores, although it had no franchising rights. Relocating its offices to St. Louis, Missouri, the new company immediately initiated a consumer research program and lobbied for a standardized mix formula for all soft-serve products.

After years of involvement, the family members who had started Dairy Queen slowly left the company. Grandpa McCullough had retired during the late 1940s, while his son retired in 1953. Harry Oltz also retired during the late 1940s, while his son Hal continued the family's involvement with the Dairy Queen system. Harry Axene presented the idea of an automatic continuous freezer to the Dairy Queen store operators convention in 1949, but when his proposal was rejected he severed ties with the system and formed the Tastee Freeze business, which he operated on the Pacific Coast for 20 years. Only Alex's son, Hugh, remained to look after the McCullough family interests during the 1950s, and by 1960 trouble was brewing on the horizon.

LEGAL TROUBLES LEAD TO A CHANGE IN OWNERSHIP

Harry Oltz's patent on his continuous freezer expired in 1954, and a number of store operators refused to continue paying royalties. Hugh McCullough responded with a lawsuit to prove that franchisees were not only paying royalties for use of the freezer, but for use of the trade name. The dispute became even more complicated when a group of store owners who had acquired their territory and franchise rights from Harry Axene filed suit to prove that people who had purchased territory rights from Axene had the right to use the Dairy Queen name because it was Axene and not the McCulloughs who owned the rights.

As the legal battles dragged on and on in the courts, Hugh McCullough grew increasingly weary, and finally agreed to sell all his holdings and the rights to the name Dairy Queen. For $1.5 million in cash, Mc-Cullough relinquished his claim to all territory and trade name rights. Thus in March 1962, a new corporation, International Dairy Queen, was formed by a group of investors led by Burt Myers, who served as chairman of the board, and Gilbert Stein, who became president.

Headquartered in Minneapolis, management immediately created a wholly owned subsidiary, American Dairy Queen Corporation, to take care of trademarks, collect royalties, and sell store franchises. More importantly, the new management quickly cleared up all the remaining lawsuits and established undisputed ownership of the name Dairy Queen. In addition, management inaugurated a standardized food program, implemented a national advertising and marketing program, created a national training school, imposed product uniformity at over 60 percent of Dairy Queen stores, revised contracts to cover percentages of sales rather than gallons of soft-serve mix, and increased the number of employees in the national office from five to 125.

During the mid-1960s, International Dairy Queen consolidated its domestic operations by purchasing the franchising rights of Harry Oltz's AR-TIK Systems, including seven southeastern states, and by securing the development rights for territories in numerous states. The confusion over who owned territory in what state, and whether fees were outstanding or not, was due to the McCulloughs' tendency during the early years to sell territories and prospective store locations in a haphazard manner. Management's intention was to provide more effective services and standardize products by ironing out these problems. At the same time, management launched an aggressive acquisition strategy by purchasing interests in franchise operations within the recreation industry. A ski-rental firm in Denver was bought first, and was soon followed by a franchise for camping equipment.

FURTHER LEADERSHIP CHANGES AND A RETURN TO PROFITABILITY

The company's consolidation of operating territory and its acquisition strategy proved costly, and a $2 million loss was forecast for fiscal 1970. With a growing cash flow problem that made it a potential takeover target, company management decided to accept the overtures of a new investment group. Headed by men who were part of the development of National Car Rental System, Inc., the group offered $3 million in cash with $2 million in credit to provide financing for working capital and expansion needs. In return, the investors assumed both majority interest and effective control of International Dairy Queen. Bill McKinstry became executive committee chairman and chairman of the board of directors and Harris Cooper was named president.

McKinstry and Cooper's reorganization strategy had immediate effects. By discontinuing one of the company's divisions, closing 16 accounting and regional offices, and standardizing operating procedures and product lines, International Dairy Queen soon became profitable once again. In 1972, the company began trading its stock on the over-the-counter (OTC) market; during the same year, its stock price increased from $1.50 per share to $22.75.

In May 1972, the first Dairy Queen store was opened in Tokyo. While 75 stores were operating outside the United States and Canada in 1976, more than 150 stores in Barbados, Guatemala, Iceland, Japan, Panama, Puerto Rico, Trinidad, the United Arab Emirates, and Hong Kong were operating by the end of the decade.

International Dairy Queen's total revenues in 1979 amounted to $956 million; as the system celebrated its 40th anniversary in 1980 total revenues came to $1.2 billion. Within the fast-food industry, Dairy Queen ranked fifth in total sales volume behind McDonald's, Kentucky Fried Chicken, Burger King, and Wendy's; the company ranked third in total number of stores behind McDonald's and KFC. In the United States, Dairy Queen had 4,314 stores in operation, with 365 in Canada, 123 in Japan, and over 30 in eight other foreign countries.

In 1976, McKinstry was replaced as chairman by John Mooty, who worked well with President Cooper. Due to a sudden fall in stock prices during the mid-1970s, Mooty implemented a stock repurchasing plan to provide more stability for the company. By the early 1980s, International Dairy Queen had used nearly $40 million to buy back two-thirds of its outstanding shares on the stock market. At the end of the decade, the performance of the stock was widely regarded as one of the best; an individual who had invested $10,000 in Dairy Queen stock in 1980 would have a portfolio worth $470,000 in 1990.

NEW PRODUCTS AND RESTAURANT CHAINS

Under Mooty and Cooper's stewardship, International Dairy Queen had introduced both the Peanut Buster Parfait and Fudge Brownie Delight, both of which were highly successful novelty products. However, it was the introduction of the Blizzard, a concoction of soft-serve ice cream blended with candy, cookies, or fruit, that secured Dairy Queen's ranking as the number one treat chain during the 1980s. In 1985 alone, the year it was introduced, the Blizzard achieved sales of over 100 million units. Along with the success of the Dairy Queen stores, the company's purchase of Golden Skillet, a chain of fried chicken restaurants; KarmelKorn Shoppes, Inc., a 60-year-old popcorn and candy franchise; and Orange Julius, a franchise selling fruit-flavored blended drinks and various snack products, secured the parent's position as the eighth ranked fast-food chain in the United States. International Dairy Queen also purchased 60 percent of a staffing agency, Firstaff, Inc., in 1989.

As the company entered the 1990s, John Mooty remained chairman of the board of directors and Mike Sullivan had replaced Cooper as president. Slow domestic growth and international expansion continued. Within the United States, the company was developing opportunities to open stores in shopping malls, office complexes, railroad stations, airports, and other nontraditional markets. In the international arena, the company initiated development programs in Thailand, Cyprus, Kuwait, Oman, Taiwan, and Indonesia, and planned a major campaign to open stores in Western and Eastern Europe.

In 1994 a dispute with franchisees surfaced when a group of store owners filed suit against International Dairy Queen, alleging that their efforts to develop alternative sources of food and paper supplies had been thwarted by the parent company. Two years later the case was granted class-action status by a federal court.

Continuing to test new marketing concepts, in 1996 the company unveiled a new, smaller prototype store in Caledonia, Minnesota. The "1500 Series" store, only 1,500 square feet in size, had half the capacity of a typical 90-seat restaurant and a smaller kitchen area. The intent was to develop a store that was appropriate for markets of 2,500 people or less. Franchisee interest was reportedly strong. The following year the company sold its 60 percent interest in Firstaff to AccuStaff, Inc., of Florida, and also jettisoned its longtime advertising agency, Campbell Mithun Esty, replacing it with Grey Advertising of New York.

ACQUISITION BY BERKSHIRE HATHAWAY DURING LATE NINETIES

The biggest news of 1997 came in the fall, when it was announced that the company would be sold to Berkshire Hathaway Inc. of Omaha, Nebraska. Investment guru Warren Buffett controlled Berkshire, which would pay $585 million in stock and cash. Owners of Dairy Queen shares grumbled that the amount was low, but the deal was approved by voting stockholders and finalized in early 1998. The sale had been spurred by the death of Rudy Luther, a Twin Cities-based car dealer who owned 15 percent of Dairy Queen. When Luther's heirs decided to sell his stake, Buffett was approached. Having previously sought to buy the entire company, he refused to take only a portion and renewed his earlier offer, which was accepted. Buffett pledged to be a "hands off" owner, and no major management or structural changes were planned.

Grey Advertising delivered the company's biggest promotional campaign ever during the summer of 1998. A new tagline, "Meet me at DQ," and an emphasis on the chain's hometown feel were features of the $25 million push. The first television spots were scheduled to run in the United States and Canada beginning in July.

In 2000 the six-year-old lawsuit with franchisees was finally settled. International Dairy Queen agreed to contribute $5 million per year for six years to the store owners' national advertising fund, while also giving the Dairy Queen Operators' Cooperative $6 million to help ensure availability of alternate sources of food and supplies. The court-approved settlement was hailed by all sides as a fair one. At the end of the year CEO Michael Sullivan stepped down and became chairman of the board, with Chief Financial Officer Chuck Mooty taking over the top position. Mooty, age 39, was the son of John Mooty, who was named chairman emeritus.

GRILLING AND CHILLING

Moving forward, Mooty's three main goals were to continue developing the Dairy Queen brand, its geographical presence, and the people responsible for its success. By this time the company operated approximately 1,000 international locations, as well as 5,100 domestic sites. A special milestone occurred when International Dairy Queen opened its first DQ Grill & Chill restaurant, with a location in Chattanooga, Tennessee.

In early 2002 International Dairy Queen began testing irradiated meat as part of an effort to improve food safety. Specifically, the practice involved the use of electron beams to eliminate potential threats such as *Salmonella*, *Listeria*, and *E. coli*. After testing irradiated beef in two Minnesota locations, the company moved forward with plans to begin introducing the product in more of its restaurants. To support its efforts, two Minnesota warehouses were constructed for distribution purposes.

Heading into 2003, International Dairy Queen had sales of approximately $460 million. On average, consumers were spending between $4.50 and $5.00 per order. Plans were in place to begin converting existing Dairy Queen restaurants into the company's new DQ Grill & Chill concept. Midway through the year, International Dairy Queen chose Spacenet Inc. to provide broadband satellite connectivity to thousands of franchisees. The technology supported a number of operational functions, from point-of-sale payments to credit card authorization, with future applications including in-store music, digital menu board support, and in-restaurant polling. In 2004, the company celebrated its first full year of advertising on a national basis.

In early 2005 International Dairy Queen announced that Chief Concept Officer Chuck Chapman would succeed Ed Watson as chief operating officer in September. Other significant leadership changes also were announced. Jean Champagne was promoted from chief operating officer of Dairy Queen Canada to chief operating officer of the company's international business. In addition, Executive Vice-President of Marketing Michael Keller was named chief brand officer.

It also was in 2005 that plans were made to expand the company's Orange Julius chain, which then consisted of approximately 400 kiosks or outlets in the United States, as well as 130 Canadian locations. By this time Orange Julius generated sales of roughly $72 million. The brand received additional attention as part of a new co-branded International Dairy Queen concept called TreatWorks, which combined offerings from Dairy Queen with those of Orange Julius.

International Dairy Queen rounded out 2005 as the world's largest ice cream retailer. On November 16, the company opened a new store in Shanghai, China, and revealed that it would have ten stores operating in Shanghai by the year's end. By late 2006 some 90 new stores were expected to open their doors throughout China.

International Dairy Queen's DQ Grill & Chill concept continued to take off during the middle of the decade. By March 2006 the company was operating 76 restaurants in 21 states, as well as 17 Canadian locations, two in the United Arab Emirates, and two in Bahrain.

INTERNATIONAL EXPANSION

Heading into the last years of the decade, International Dairy Queen's expansion plans for Asia had become more aggressive. In November 2007 the company announced that franchisee Minor Food Group plc had plans to open the first DQ Grill & Chill in Asia during the first quarter of 2008, with a location in Thailand. In addition, International Dairy Queen indicated that it would open approximately 500 franchised locations throughout China over the next five years.

A major leadership change unfolded on July 1, 2008, when Chief Supply Chain Officer John P. Gainor succeeded Chuck Mooty as president and CEO. New product developments continued that year, as the company announced a major licensing agreement with the Girl Scouts of the USA, resulting in a new treat selection named the Girl Scouts Thin Mint Cookie Blizzard.

By mid-2009 International Dairy Queen had grown to include about 5,900 locations worldwide. Despite a faltering economy, the company saw its sales grow on a national basis via the introduction of a value menu named Sweet Deals. Moving forward, International Dairy Queen prepared to begin the 21st century's second decade by celebrating the 70th anniversary of the Dairy Queen brand, as well as the 25th anniversary of its popular Blizzard.

Thomas Derdak
Updated, Frank Uhle; Paul R. Greenland

PRINCIPAL SUBSIDIARIES

American Dairy Queen Corp.; Orange Julius of America; DQF Inc.; Golden Skillet International Inc.; Karmelkorn Shoppes Inc.; Dairy Queen of Georgia Inc.; Dairy Queen Canada Inc.; Dairy Queen Corporate Stores Inc.; Firstaff Inc. (60%).

PRINCIPAL COMPETITORS

Dunkin' Brands Inc.; McDonald's Corp.; YUM! Brands Inc.

FURTHER READING

"Dairy Queen Steps into Shanghai," *Alestron,* November 18, 2005.

"Dairy Queen Taps Gainor to Replace Retiring CEO Mooty," *Nation's Restaurant News,* May 19, 2008.

Feyder, Susan, "Auto Dealer's Death Influenced IDQ's Decision to Sell," *Minneapolis Star-Tribune,* November 22, 1997, p. 1D.

Frumkin, Paul, "Having Words with John P. Gainor: President, Chief Executive, International Dairy Queen Inc.," *Nation's Restaurant News,* May 4, 2009.

Gibson, Richard, "Buffett Is Scooping Up Dairy Queen in a Deal That Has Sent Some Investors into Meltdown," *Wall Street Journal,* November 5, 1997, p. C4.

Jitpleecheep, Pitsinee, "Minor Plans Major Dairy Queen Expansion," *Bangkok Post,* November 6, 2007.

Kalstrom, Jonathan, "Sullivan Treats Franchisees Right," *Minneapolis–St. Paul CityBusiness,* May 12, 2000, p. 29.

Kramer, Louise, "Dairy Queen Touts Hometown Feeling in $25 Mil Campaign," *Advertising Age,* June 1, 1998, p. 4.

Otis, Caroline Hall, *The Cone with the Curl on Top: The Dairy Queen Story, 1940–1980,* Minneapolis: International Dairy Queen, Inc., 1990.

Shalhoup, Mara, "Federal Anti-Trust Lawsuit Against Dairy Queen Settles in Macon, Ga.," *Macon Telegraph,* March 24, 2000.

Tellijohn, Andrew, "CEO-to-Be Has DQ in His Blood," *Minneapolis–St. Paul CityBusiness,* August 25, 2000, p. 1.

Walkup, Carolyn, "Orange Julius, Smoothie Concepts Unveil Expansion Plans," *Nation's Restaurant News,* October 17, 2005.

The J. Paul Getty Trust

1200 Getty Center Drive
Los Angeles, California 90049
U.S.A.
Telephone: (310) 440-7300
Fax: (310) 440-7722
Web site: http://www.getty.edu

Private Foundation
Incorporated: 1982 as The J. Paul Getty Museum Trust
Employees: 1,400
Total Assets: $4.2 billion
NAICS: 712110 Museums; 813211 Grantmaking
Foundations; 519120 Libraries and Archives

■ ■ ■

The J. Paul Getty Trust is a cultural and philanthropic foundation funded by much of the estate left by oil tycoon Jean Paul Getty. The Trust oversees the operation of the Los Angles-based Getty Center, which includes the J. Paul Getty Museum and three institutes, as well as the Getty Villa in Malibu, California.

THE GETTY FORTUNE

One of the world's first billionaires, Jean Paul Getty amassed his fortune in the oil business, accumulating assets that eventually fell under the control of his company, Getty Oil Company. The vast financial resources at Getty's disposal (*Fortune* magazine heralded him as the wealthiest living American in 1957) gave him the means to pursue his fascination with art and antiquities. He traveled the world and spent freely, acquiring an art collection that rivaled the holdings of the world's most prestigious museums. In 1954, he began displaying his private collection to the public, establishing a museum on his 64-acre canyon estate in Malibu, California. A decade later, Getty began developing plans for a museum to replace the Spanish-style ranch house opened in 1954, a project aimed at creating a replica of the Villa of the Papyri in Herculaneum, a Roman city buried in ash from the eruption of Mount Vesuvius in A.D. 79. The project, built farther down Getty's Malibu canyon, was completed in 1974, when the J. Paul Getty Museum opened its doors. Getty died two years later, deciding before his death to leave relatively little of his fortune to his heirs and, instead, bequeath nearly all of his riches to the J. Paul Getty Museum, which, reportedly, he had never visited.

The J. Paul Getty Museum stood to become one of the wealthiest art institutions in the world when its benefactor died. It would be years, however, until the museum received its endowment, as protracted legal battles were waged over the treasure to be had. While Getty's will was being contested, the board of directors of the J. Paul Getty Museum Trust prepared for the day when the museum would receive its endowment, mindful that the enormous sum of money would require the leadership of an astute and seasoned executive. In 1981, the board of directors approached Harold M. Williams, a corporate lawyer who had served as chairman of Norton Simon Inc., dean of management at the Graduate School of Management at the University of California, Los Angeles (UCLA), and chairman of the U.S. Securities and Exchange Commission.

COMPANY PERSPECTIVES

Through the work of the four Getty programs—the Museum, Research Institute, Conservation Institute, and Foundation—the Getty aims to further knowledge and nurture critical seeing through the growth and presentation of its collections and by advancing the understanding and preservation of the world's artistic heritage. The Getty pursues this mission with the conviction that cultural awareness, creativity, and aesthetic enjoyment are essential to a vital and civil society.

"The board said that they didn't know what this place should become," Williams said in a July 19, 1999 interview with the *Los Angeles Business Journal,* recalling his first meeting with the board of directors in 1981. "They knew they wanted it to be more than the museum, but beyond that they had no firm ideas. I told the board on the first meeting that I was going to take a year, and that I would be back in May of 1982 with a plan."

A BILLION-DOLLAR VISION

Williams became the person responsible for establishing the direction of the Trust. He left the first meeting and spent a year traveling throughout the United States and Europe, seeking to find the best way to fulfill the broadly defined mission articulated by Getty: to use the money for the museum and for the diffusion of artistic and general knowledge. Williams visited with museum directors and consultants during his travels, gathering ideas, processing them, and developing a vision of what the Trust should become. He presented a plan that included the construction of a museum, a research institute, a conservation institute, and an education institute of the arts, among other facilities. The plan represented the first draft of what would emerge as the Getty Center. As Williams's dream of a campus-like arts complex was being revealed, the Trust gained access to the funds to make Williams's goals a reality. In March 1982, the museum received its bequest, a staggering $1.2 billion.

To retain its charitable status, the Trust was required to spend at least 4.25 percent of its endowment every year; otherwise, it would have to begin paying taxes. The provision allowed for an enormous annual budget, one that grew as investments made by the Trust increased in value. When Getty died, he left $660 mil-

lion to his museum, a sum that increased to $1.2 billion by the time legal matters were resolved in 1982. By the end of 1984, the Trust's portfolio was worth $2.3 billion, and from there it increased in value for more than the next 15 years as financiers made astute investment decisions throughout the 1980s and 1990s. Although Williams could not predict the Trust's endowment would increase in value to nearly $7 billion, the plan he presented to the board of directors in 1982 eventually grew in scope to reflect the massive sum of money supporting the foundation.

THE GETTY CENTER TAKES SHAPE

Williams intended to use the Trust's resources for much more than supporting Getty's museum in Malibu. In 1983, The J. Paul Getty Museum Trust changed its name to The J. Paul Getty Trust, a name change signifying the subordinate role the museum played in future plans. The J. Paul Getty Museum became one of seven programs, or institutes, that composed the proposed Getty Center. The Getty Center for History of Art and the Humanities served as a haven for visiting scholars, providing a 200,000-book library and more than one million photographs of art and architecture that scholars could use to conduct research, write, hold seminars, and exchange ideas with each other. The Getty Conservation Institute was dedicated to saving works of art from being destroyed by improper restoration and conservation treatments and to promoting scientific research into conservation techniques, the collection and dissemination of information on conservation practices, and providing advanced training programs for qualified conservators.

The Getty Art History Information Program took on the task of creating databases of art history research, enabling scholars to cross-reference research topics electronically. The Getty Center of Education in the Arts embraced the role of promoting the teaching of art history, art criticism, and aesthetics to schoolchildren, operating under the premise that the study of art was central to the human experience and to transmitting cultural values. The Program for Art on Film, managed jointly with Metropolitan Museum in New York City, strove to enhance the quality of film and video presentations on art. The Museum Management Institute offered instruction in museum management to individuals who held management posts in museums, providing an intensive introduction to management techniques.

A project of sweeping scope, the Getty Center represented a grand vision, one that would take years to turn into reality. In 1984, architect Richard Meier was awarded the commission for the Getty Center, "the

KEY DATES

1954: J. Paul Getty opens a museum on his estate in Malibu, California, to display his art collection to the public.

1974: The J. Paul Getty Museum, a re-creation of a private house in the ancient Roman city of Herculaneum, is established.

1976: Getty dies, leaving nearly all of his estate to his museum.

1982: The J. Paul Getty Museum Trust, led by Harold M. Williams, receives its endowment of $1.2 billion.

1983: The J. Paul Getty Museum Trust changes its name to The J. Paul Getty Trust.

1984: Richard Meier is awarded the commission to design the Getty Center.

1991: Meier unveils his final design for the Getty Center.

1997: The Getty Center opens in December.

1998: Williams is replaced as president and chief executive officer of the Trust by Barry Munitz.

2005: California's attorney general's office begins investigating the possible misuse of the Trust's funds.

2006: Munitz resigns from the Trust.

2007: The Getty Center celebrates its tenth anniversary.

2009: The Trust reduces its workforce by 14 percent as its endowment loses 25 percent of its value.

commission of the century," according to the October 21, 1991 issue of *Time,* and began the daunting task of designing J. Paul Getty's gift to the art world. In late 1991, after seven years of work, Meier unveiled his final design, a six-building complex with one million square feet spread across a 24-acre site on a hilltop on the southern edge of the Santa Monica Mountains. Construction of the project, initially priced at $360 million, was scheduled to begin in early 1992 and to be completed in 1996.

As might be expected, construction of the Getty Center fell behind schedule. The project also far exceeded the initial estimate of $360 million. By 1995, the cost of the complex had increased to $600 million. By 1996, when the completion date was pushed back to

the end of 1997, the Getty Center represented a $1 billion project. Once the new opening date and new cost estimate were revealed in June 1996, Williams announced his retirement, effective January 5, 1998, 18 months before his last day leading the Trust. "The date happens to be my 70th birthday," he said in the June 12, 1996 edition of the *New York Times.* "The time just seemed right. The completion of the Getty Center next year will mark the initial vision I proposed to the trustees in May 1983, so it seems appropriate that someone else takes over from there."

LEADERSHIP CHANGE IN 1998

Williams's replacement was announced in August 1997, four months before the Getty Center opened its doors. Barry Munitz was selected by a committee to head the Trust, whose endowment had increased to $4.5 billion by the time the Getty Center opened, giving it an annual budget of $225 million, or ten times the budget of the National Gallery in London. Munitz had spent a decade leading natural resources conglomerate Maxxam Inc. and he had served as president of the University of Houston, but his most prominent position was as chancellor of California State University, the nation's largest system of public higher education, with 23 campuses, more than 330,000 students, and an annual budget of $4 billion.

Munitz took the helm and soon began making his presence felt. By the time the Getty Center opened, the seven programs delineated by Williams in the early 1980s had been reduced to five programs, excluding the museums operated by the Trust. (When the Getty Center opened, its museum became known as the J. Paul Getty Museum and the museum in Malibu was renamed the Getty Villa, which was closed for remodeling in 1997 and reopened in 2006.) From the original seven institutes, the Program for Art on Film and the Management Institute were not included in the Getty Center when it opened in December 1997. In October 1998, it was announced that the Information Institute, the digital technology program originally known as the Getty Art History Program, would be closed by mid-1999. The Trust also reported that the Education Institute, originally known as the Getty Center of Education in the Arts, could be folded into one of the Getty Center's other institutes. The Trust, in the October 6, 1998 issue of *Daily News,* characterized the moves as being part of a "re-evaluation and reorganization" process that eventually focused on four divisions: the two museums; the Getty Grant Program (renamed the Getty Foundation in 2005); the Getty Conservation Institute; and the Getty Research Institute.

The Munitz era fell far short of rivaling the lasting contributions made during his predecessor's tenure. After making his changes to the Trust's programs, Munitz had to contend with lawsuits filed by homeowner associations opposing the remodeling and expansion of the Getty Villa. The project, expected to be completed by 2002, was not finished until 2006. He also had to face the realities of the Trust's dwindling endowment. The endowment peaked at $6.1 billion in 2000 and was whittled down to $4.4 billion by 2002, as the Trust's financial managers suffered losses in the stock market. The most glaring blemish on the Munitz era emerged in 2005, when the wealthiest foundation in the United States was rocked by scandal, an embarrassing episode that found Munitz at the center of the controversy.

UNDER INVESTIGATION

In 2005, the *Los Angeles Times* published a series of articles that raised questions about the compensation and perquisites provided to Munitz, first-class air travel to his wife, and a real estate deal involving the Trust and a well-known philanthropist living in Los Angeles. California's attorney general's office intervened, requesting records disclosing the compensation and expenses paid to Munitz since he joined the Trust. An investigation was begun, spurring the Council of Foundations, the nation's leading group of foundations and charitable organizations, to demand documents for its own review of the Trust's financial practices. In December 2005, the Council of Foundations placed the Trust on a 60-day probation for failing to provide the requested documents. In February 2006, while the investigation led by Attorney General Bill Lockyer was ongoing, Munitz resigned.

After more than a year of investigating the Trust, Lockyer's office issued its report in late 2006. The report concluded that the organization's trustees wrongly allowed Munitz to spend money on travel and other expenses. California's attorney general's office decided against legal action against the Trust, but it did appoint an independent monitor to oversee the Trust's actions for a two-year period, selecting John Van de Kamp, the former attorney general of California, for the task.

A NEW ERA BEGINS

Once Lockyer issued his findings, the Trust turned its attention to naming a replacement for Munitz. In December 2006, the Trust selected James N. Wood to become its new president and chief executive officer. Wood, unlike Williams and Munitz, had spent his professional career in the arts, serving as the director of

the Art Institute of Chicago for 25 years before retiring in 2004.

Under new leadership, the Trust celebrated the tenth anniversary of the Getty Center in 2007 and looked forward to the 30th anniversary of the foundation in 2012. Although the Trust would be hard pressed to find a sympathetic ear for its financial woes, the wealthiest operating foundation in the United States was not without its financial concerns. The value of its endowment, subject to the caprices of any investment portfolio, hinged on the shrewdness of its financiers. The Trust's portfolio, which recovered in value to $6 billion in 2008, stood at $4.5 billion in March 2009. The following month, its endowment was valued at $4.2 billion, forcing the Trust to reduce its workforce by 14 percent. In the years ahead, The Trust would be forced to deal with the vagaries of the marketplace as it sought to fulfill the wishes of J. Paul Getty.

Jeffrey L. Covell

PRINCIPAL DIVISIONS

J. Paul Getty Museum; Getty Villa; Getty Research Institute; Getty Conservation Institute; Getty Foundation.

PRINCIPAL COMPETITORS

The Museum of Contemporary Art, Los Angeles; Huntington Library, Art Collections and Botanical Gardens; Los Angeles County Museum of Art.

FURTHER READING

Anderson, Kurt, "A Grand New Getty," *Time,* October 21, 1991, p. 100.

Beckett, Andy, "Welcome to Gettyworld, Ca.," *Independent,* March 16, 1997, p. 12.

Belgum, Deborah, "Getty Legal Victory Could End Villa Limbo," *Los Angeles Business Journal,* September 30, 2002, p. 1.

Cole, Benjamin Mark, "Best Laid Plans," *Los Angeles Business Journal,* October 14, 2002, p. 30.

"Getty Center Design Unveiled," *Building Design & Construction,* December 1991, p. 12.

"Getty Museum Facing 25 Percent Budget Cut," *New York Times,* March 17, 2009, p. C2.

"Getty Trust Promises to Aid State Inquiry on Spending," *Chronicle of Philanthropy,* August 18, 2005.

"Head of J. Paul Getty Trust to Retire in 1998," *New York Times,* June 12, 1996.

Kanter, Larry, "Guardian of the Getty," *Los Angeles Business Journal,* August 11, 1997, p. 31.

Kennedy, Randy, "At Getty Trust, a New Chief with Solid Art Credentials," *New York Times,* December 5, 2006, p. E1.

———, "Chairman of Getty Trust Resigns, Citing Workload," *New York Times,* August 5, 2006, p. B9.

———, "President of Getty Trust Resigns Under Pressure," *New York Times,* February 10, 2006, p. A14.

Lipman, Harvy, "California Reprimands J. Paul Getty Trust and Appoints an Independent Monitor," *Chronicle of Philanthropy,* October 12, 2006.

Norman, Geraldine, "Spectrum: The Art of Spending a Fortune," *Times* (London), August 5, 1985.

Pettersson, Edvard, "Trust Chief Led Billion-Dollar Getty Center Project," *Los Angeles Business Journal,* July 19, 1999, p. 43.

Wittenauer, Cheryl, "J. Paul Getty Trust Gets Put on Probation," *America's Intelligence Wire,* December 22, 2005.

JKH Holding Co. LLC

4995 Lacross Road, Suite 1800
North Charleston, South Carolina 29406-6561
U.S.A.
Telephone: (843) 576-2255
Toll Free: (888) 833-5156
Web site: http://www.jkharris.com

Private Company
Incorporated: 1997 as JK Harris & Co.
Employees: 450
Sales: $100 million (2008 est.)
NAICS: 541213 Tax Preparation Services

■ ■ ■

JKH Holding Co. LLC is the privately held parent company of JK Harris and Company, a leading tax representation company based in North Charleston, South Carolina. JK Harris acts as an intermediary between clients and the Internal Revenue Service (IRS) to resolve tax problems, in many cases greatly reducing the amount owed through the IRS Offer in Compromise program. With 325 offices in 43 states, the company employs a hub-and-spoke model in which local offices begin the process, then funnel the cases to regional offices housing the more experienced professionals, many of them former IRS agents, lawyers, and certified public accountants (CPAs). Although JK Harris has successfully represented many thousands of clients, it has also disappointed a significant number who claim that the company promised more than it delivered, leading to class-action lawsuits and scrutiny from the at-torneys general of numerous states. As a result, JK Harris has suffered a spate of bad publicity in the process, as have others in the tax representation field.

In addition to tax resolution services, the company through subsidiary JK Harris Advisors, LLC, provides financial planning services to individuals faced with tax liabilities. Another unit, JK Harris Small Business Services, LLC, is a contract provider of tax preparation, bookkeeping, and accounting services. Founder John K. Harris is the chairman, president, and chief executive officer of the parent company.

FOUNDER, SOUTH CAROLINA–BORN, 1953

John K. Harris was born in 1953 in Charleston, South Carolina. After graduating with a degree in history and political science from the University of South Carolina in 1976, he earned a master's degree in accounting from the same school to become a CPA, after which he went to work for an accounting firm. He would go onto become a chief financial officer at a manufacturing company, a part owner of three automobile dealerships, and an owner of a pair of construction businesses. Weary of the corporate life he returned home and established a sole-practitioner accounting firm in Charleston in 1996. Given the unlikelihood of growing a large practice, he kept an eye out for a niche operation.

Harris soon found the opportunity he was looking for when a new client discovered he had a tax liability problem caused by a small business his wife operated that had failed to pay $90,000 in payroll taxes over the course of several years. Harris worked with the IRS to resolve the matter and by way of the Offer in Compromise program was able to reduce the liability to $42,000 and set up an installment plan to pay off the debt, receiving a $3,000 fee for his efforts. Harris realized that not only was there a large market for such tax resolution services, there were few willing providers. "I found this type of tax work most CPAs and tax attorneys don't want to do," he told *Accounting Today* in a 2001 profile. "And those who do, want their money up front because they don't believe people are honest enough to pay them."

ESTABLISHING JK HARRIS: 1997

In 1997 Harris established JK Harris & Co. to serve as a tax advocate for middle-to-lower income families and small businesses. To drum up business he placed small newspaper ads, expecting that he might receive two or three calls. Instead, he received 80 inquiries over the next few days, due in large part to fortuitous timing. The U.S. Senate was conducting hearings on IRS abuse, which received extensive media coverage and prompted people to take action to deal with their lingering tax problems. The focus of his efforts were on the Offer in Compromise Program, a time-consuming and uncertain proposition. Not everyone qualified and IRS policy called for all other methods of payments to be exhausted first. Moreover, only about 20 percent of offers were accepted by the IRS. When asked by clients about their chances of receiving help through an Offer in Compromise, Harris often responded by taking a quarter and flipping it in the air. It was that kind of honesty that helped prevent clients from embracing false hope, a problem that would later plague the company as it grew larger.

Harris generated further business by placing ads in Columbia, South Carolina, and Charlotte, North Carolina, as well; but he could only handle a finite number of cases as a sole practitioner. To expand the business he developed a system that could be replicated, à la H&R Block, and began hiring people experienced in the ways of the IRS: former agency employees, accountants, and tax attorneys. He also developed his own

supporting software program, opting for a customized database case management system after evaluating off-the-shelf options.

As he grew the business geographically, Harris adopted the hub-and-spoke model and in a matter of four years he had ten regional service centers covering 42 states, each fed by about 50 local sales offices, which conducted initial interviews and gathered the documentation needed by the regional processing centers. The company charged a sliding fee based on the amount of work required. A client who had not filed tax returns for several years, for example, would need JK Harris to submit all tax returns before a compromise would even be considered by the IRS. The company received 10 percent as a retainer, and a subsidiary provided loans if necessary. The balance of the fee was then paid in installments over the next nine to 12 months. Because the Offer in Compromise program was a protracted process lasting about the same amount of time, JK Harris retained some leverage over clients who failed to meet their installment payments by simply quitting their representation with the IRS, thus jeopardizing a client's hopes of ever reaching a less expensive settlement.

ACQUISITION OF FINANCIAL RECOVERY SERVICES: 2002

Harris considered franchising his operation, as H&R Block had done, but in the end decided not to, concerned that he might lose control. He also wanted to expand the services his offices could offer and took note of how H&R Block, which was expanding into financial planning, was buying back franchises to solve the problem of franchisees not willing to participate.

Harris forfeited some of that control in his efforts to expand, however, when in October 2002 he acquired Financial Recovery Services, which became JKH Financial Recovery Systems. The Baltimore, Maryland-based company offered debt-relief services in its home state that were considered a good fit with Harris's tax resolution services. It was when the unit expanded rapidly across the country that problems arose and it became the focus of lawsuits filed against the parent company, due in large part to deceptive direct mailings. A number of other complaints that led to government investigations and lawsuits were made by Harris clients who were unable to secure reductions in their IRS obligations and charged the company with misleading them about their prospects for success.

Making matters worse were changes in the Offer in Compromise program that delayed processing. In many cases a file was outdated by the time the IRS was able to

KEY DATES

1997: John K. Harris founds company.
2002: Financial Recovery Services is acquired.
2005: Company restructures in wake of legal settlements.
2007: Class-action lawsuit is settled.
2008: Settlement is reached with multiple state attorneys general.

deal with it, thus requiring the paperwork to be redone. Some of the IRS delays were also the result of such firms as JK Harris swelling the number of Offer in Compromise requests that had to be processed by the IRS. From 1997 to 2001 the number of unresolved offers grew from about 32,000 to nearly 95,000, while the average processing time increased to 312 days.

Harris's legal problems actually began before the addition of Financial Recovery Services. In July 2000 about 20 IRS agents bearing a subpoena raided the JK Harris headquarters and removed a number of documents. "Our size and success in representing people," Harris told the *New York Times* in 2000, "has also made us a target by the I.R.S., as well as certain competitors." Although the matter remained open for years to come, no charges ever stemmed from the raid.

ATTORNEYS GENERAL BEGIN GROUP INVESTIGATION: 2004

It was on the state level that JK Harris faced the most significant legal jeopardy. A dozen attorneys general, including the attorney general in the company's home state of South Carolina, formed a working group in 2004 to investigate the growing number of complaints against the company. Two of the attorneys general, in Kansas and Connecticut, soon filed lawsuits, and six more state attorneys general would eventually join the effort.

The *Charleston Post and Courier* obtained a number of the complaints made to the Federal Trade Commission, secured through the Freedom of Information Act. Instead of receiving relief from their tax problems, according to the newspaper in a March 26, 2005, article, customers claimed that "JK Harris took their money, failed to live up to its promises and made their situations a lot worse." The company maintained it did not make unrealistic promises, only a small percentage of its customers were not satisfied, and that the people who complained were demanding their money back because

they were disappointed they had not achieved the results they wanted.

Perhaps the most egregious conduct occurred in Connecticut in late 2003 when JKH Financial Recovery Systems attempted to drum up business by acquiring a list of names from a data warehousing company that searched public records for information on people facing judgments on outstanding debts. To this mailing list the company sent letters stamped "Final Notice," informing the recipients that a judgment had been filed against them for nonpayment of debt and offering to help them resolve the matter. Many people on the list, however, had no judgments against them, leading to the suit the state filed against JK Harris.

"We're not lily-white by any means," John Harris admitted to the *Post and Courier* in a March 6, 2005, article. "I know my lawyer is going to hate me saying this … we did the best we could with the rate of growth we had, and I think we did a darn good job." He contended that in addition to growing pains, the company had to deal with the ever-changing rules of the IRS, claiming it was like "doing business with a moving target." Harris also suggested that because the tax resolution field was largely unregulated, authorities were singling out JK Harris for harsh treatment to set an example for smaller companies as an indirect way of tightening the rules.

JK Harris worked to alleviate the concerns of the attorneys general as well as settle civil cases lodged against it. At the behest of the attorneys general it stopped claiming it could settle tax debt for "pennies on the dollar," a pitch the IRS had warned was a hallmark of what it called unscrupulous promoters. The first settlement of a lawsuit filed by an attorney general, in Missouri, came in June 2005. Without admitting any wrongdoing, indeed insisting that it had not violated any laws and was settling only because it was in its best interest to not litigate the matter any further, JK Harris agreed to change its advertising and business practices as well as pay $18,118 in restitution to nine people and another $25,000 to the state of Missouri to cover attorney fees and other costs related to the lawsuit.

LAYOFFS, RESTRUCTURING: 2005

A month after the Missouri settlement, JK Harris undertook a restructuring effort that included the layoff of about 100 employees. Most of the changes came at JKH Financial Recovery Systems. No longer would the unit engage in the expensive direct mailings that had caused so many problems, although according to the parent company, the decision was based solely on economics rather than legal considerations. The marketing focus would be on cross-selling the subsidiary's debt-relief services to the tax clients of JK Harris. One stroke of good fortune in the summer of 2005 was the decision by the South Carolina attorney general to drop his investigation of JK Harris despite the state's Department of Consumer Affairs receiving about 180 complaints in the previous three years (the state-mandated time limit for keeping such records), the most complaints on any company doing business in the state during that period.

JK Harris continued to provide its services even as its lawyers worked to reconcile its legal problems. In October 2006 the company reached a settlement with the attorney general of Connecticut, agreeing to pay $100,000 to the state and repay all residents who bought debt resolution services under false pretenses because of the Final Notice mailing. A year later the company reached a $6 million settlement of a national class-action lawsuit that had been lingering for several years.

Another state settlement was reached with the Ohio attorney general in June 2008, with the company agreeing to make $1.5 million in customer refunds. According to the Ohio suit, JK Harris had charged for Offer in Compromise services without first finding out if the customer qualified for a tax reduction, and in some cases the company knew the customer was not eligible and proceeded nonetheless. A few weeks later JK Harris reached settlements with all 18 state attorneys general, a step taken because John Harris, quoted in a July 2008 *Wall Street Journal* article, said that it was time to cut its legal fees and get the matter "off the radar screen" for the good of the company as well as the industry. Going forward, as a result of the settlement, there was finally a set of guidelines on how to advertise and operate in the tax resolution field. When 2008 came to a close, JK Harris posted revenues of about $100 million. Provided with a clean slate, the company, which claimed to have served more than 225,000 clients since opening its doors in 1997, hoped to significantly improve its performance in the years to come.

Ed Dinger

PRINCIPAL SUBSIDIARIES

JK Harris and Company; JK Harris Advisors, LLC; JK Harris Small Business Services, LLC.

PRINCIPAL COMPETITORS

First Tax Service Inc.; Tax Masters; Tax Resolution Services, Co.

FURTHER READING

Barlow, Jim, "Firms Help You to Get Deals with the IRS," *Houston Chronicle,* April 30, 2000, p. 1.

Herman, Tom, "Wiping Out Your Tax Debt Gets Tougher," *Wall Street Journal,* July 23, 2008, p. D1.

Mogul, Matthew, "Former JK Harris Clients Complain to FTC," *Charleston (S.C.) Post and Courier,* March 26, 2005, p. B8.

———, "JK Harris Revamps Division, Cuts Staff," *Charleston (S.C.) Post and Courier,* July 12, 2005.

———, "JK Harris' Tax Troubles," *Charleston (S.C.) Post and Courier,* March 6, 2005, p. D1.

———, "JK Harris to Cut Jobs Nationally in Restructuring," *Charleston (S.C.) Post and Courier,* July 12, 2005.

———, "Questions Raised About JK Harris' Ability to Pay Legal Claims," *Charleston (S.C.) Post and Courier,* May 5, 2005.

———, "S.C. Attorney General Closes Probe of Tax-Resolution Firm," *Charleston (S.C.) Post and Courier,* August 26, 2005.

Russell, Roger, "Offer in Compromise Program Bogged Down in Delays, Backlogs," *Accounting Today,* April 22, 2002, p. 102.

———, "Tax Resolution for the Masses," *Accounting Today,* September 24, 2001, p. 10.

Smith, Bruce, "Nationwide Tax Resolution Company Started in South Carolina," *Associated Press,* January 16, 2005.

"Tax Company Raided by I.R.S.," *New York Times,* July 27, 2000, p. C9.

Kimberly-Clark Corporation

Kimberly-Clark
Corporation

—■—

351 Phelps Drive
Irving, Texas 75038
U.S.A.
Telephone: (972) 281-1200
Fax: (972) 281-1490
Web site: http://www.kimberly-clark.com

Public Company
Incorporated: 1880 as Kimberly & Clark Company
Employees: 53,000
Sales: $19.42 billion (2008)
Stock Exchanges: New York
Ticker Symbol: KMB
NAICS: 322291 Sanitary Paper Product Manufacturing; 339112 Surgical and Medical Instrument Manufacturing; 325620 Toilet Preparation Manufacturing; 339113 Surgical Appliance and Supplies Manufacturing; 322299 All Other Converted Paper Product Manufacturing

■ ■ ■

More than 135 years since its founding, Kimberly-Clark Corporation is one of the world's leading producers of tissue, personal care products, and healthcare products. The company sells its products in more than 150 countries and maintains manufacturing operations in 35 countries. Kimberly-Clark produces a number of leading brands in the tissues, feminine-, child-, and incontinence-care product categories including Huggies, Kotex, Depend, and Kleenex. The company also is a market leader in healthcare products such as face masks, surgical gowns, sterilization wrap, and examination gloves.

EARLY HISTORY

Kimberly, Clark & Company was founded in Neenah, Wisconsin, in 1872 as a partnership of four men: John A. Kimberly, Charles B. Clark, Frank C. Shattuck, and Kimberly's cousin, Havilah Babcock. The company began the first paper mill in Wisconsin. Its initial product was newsprint made from linen and cotton rags. Within six years, the company expanded by acquiring a majority interest in the nearby Atlas paper mill, which converted ground pulpwood into manila wrapping paper. The business was incorporated in 1880 as Kimberly & Clark Company, with John Kimberly as president. In 1889, the company constructed a large pulp- and paper-making complex on the Fox River. The community that grew up around the factory was named Kimberly, in honor of John Kimberly.

Among the company's early innovations was the paper used for rotogravure, a procedure for printing photographs with a rotary press. In 1914, researchers working with bagasse, a pulp byproduct of processed sugarcane, produced creped cellulose wadding, or tissue. During World War I, this product, called cellucotton, was used to treat wounds in place of scarce surgical cottons. At that time field nurses also discovered that cellucotton worked well as a disposable feminine napkin. The company later recognized the commercial potential of this application and, in 1920, introduced its Kotex feminine napkin.

COMPANY PERSPECTIVES

Throughout our 137-year history, Kimberly-Clark has adhered to a set of simple yet insightful values established by our founders—quality, service and fair dealing. These are the standards of performance by which our leadership and employees are measured. These values have helped establish Kimberly-Clark as a leading-edge global company that produces superior health and hygiene products used by families and professionals from all walks of life and cultures around the world.

In 1924, the company introduced another disposable tissue product, Kleenex, to replace the face towels then used for removing cold cream. A survey showed, however, that consumers preferred to use Kleenex as a disposable handkerchief, prompting the company to alter its marketing strategy entirely. Nationwide advertisements promoting Kleenex for its current use began in 1930, and sales doubled within a year. Uncomfortable marketing such personal-care items as feminine napkins, Kimberly & Clark had created a separate sales company, International Cellucotton Products, which it contracted to manufacture Kotex and Kleenex.

EXPANSION FROM TWENTIES TO SIXTIES

During the 1920s the company built a Canadian pulp mill and power plant called Spruce Falls Power and Paper Company in Kapuskasing, Ontario. In 1925 the company formed what would become Canadian Cellucotton Products Limited, for marketing cellucotton products internationally. The following year Kimberly & Clark, in partnership with the New York Times Company, added a newsprint mill to the Spruce Falls complex and expanded its pulping capacity.

The company was reorganized and reincorporated in 1928 as Kimberly-Clark Corporation. That same year, as shares of Kimberly-Clark were being traded on the New York and Chicago stock exchanges for the first time, John Kimberly died. He was 90 years old and still president at the time of his death.

In the 1930s, Kimberly-Clark concentrated on marketing its new products. During World War II, the company devoted many of its resources to the war effort. The company also contracted Margaret Buell,

creator of the cartoon strip "Little Lulu," to promote Kleenex. Buell and Little Lulu continued to promote Kleenex for Kimberly-Clark into the 1960s.

After the war, Kimberly-Clark initiated a growth program to handle revived consumer product demand. Facilities were built or acquired in Balfour, North Carolina, and Memphis, Tennessee, in 1946, and in Fullerton, California, and New Milford, Connecticut, in the late 1950s. Pulp production at Terrace Bay, Ontario, was launched in 1948, and in 1949 the company, along with a group of investors and newspaper publishers, began the large Coosa River Newsprint Company in Coosa Pines, Alabama. Kimberly-Clark acquired the Michigan-based Munising Paper Company in 1952, Neenah Paper Company in 1956, Peter J. Schweitzer, Inc. (which had mills in France and the United States) in 1957, and American Envelope Company in 1959. International Cellucotton Products Company formally merged with its parent company in 1955, as did Coosa River Newsprint Company in 1962.

Throughout the 1960s the tampon, first manufactured by Tampax, gained favor among women and ate into Kotex's market share. Kimberly-Clark turned its attention to new products. In 1968 the company introduced Kimbies, a disposable diaper with tape closures. Initial sales were strong despite competition from Procter & Gamble's Pampers. While Kimberly-Clark tended to its diverse operations, however, it failed to keep up with early disposable diaper improvements and market innovations. As a result of continued poor sales and leakage problems, Kimbies were withdrawn from the market in the mid-1970s. Competition in the infant-care product industry caused Kimberly-Clark to reevaluate the balance between its consumer products and lumber and paper products divisions.

RESTRUCTURING IN THE SEVENTIES

Darwin E. Smith, who was elected president of Kimberly-Clark in 1971, took on Procter & Gamble's challenge. Smith decided that to compete properly in consumer product markets Kimberly-Clark had to prune its coated-paper business. Within one year of taking control of the company, Smith initiated changes that included the sale or closure of six paper mills and the sale of more than 300,000 acres of prime northern California land. With cash reserves of more than $250 million, primarily from the land sale, Smith then inaugurated an aggressive research campaign. He assembled a talented research and development team by hiring specialists away from competitors. The company's advertising budget was increased substantially, and plans

KEY DATES

1872: Kimberly, Clark & Company is formed in Neenah, Wisconsin.

1880: Company incorporates as Kimberly & Clark Company.

1920: Kotex feminine napkins are introduced.

1924: Kleenex tissues debut.

1928: Company reorganizes and reincorporates as Kimberly-Clark Corporation.

1948: Kimberly-Clark launches pulp production in Ontario.

1959: Company acquires American Envelope Company.

1968: Company enters disposable diaper market with its Kimbies product.

1978: Huggies disposable diapers are introduced.

1980: Depend incontinence products are launched.

1985: Company relocates from Wisconsin to Dallas, Texas.

1995: Kimberly-Clark merges with Scott Paper Co.

1997: Company acquires Tecnol Medical Products.

1999: Company acquires Attisholz Holding and Ballard Medical Products.

2000: Kimberly-Clark acquires S-K Corporation.

2002: Thomas J. Falk is chosen to succeed Wayne R. Sanders as chairman and CEO.

2004: Kimberly-Clark announces plans to spin off its paper and Canadian pulp operations into a new public company named Neenah Paper Inc., allowing it to concentrate on marketing its health and hygiene products.

2006: Following the elimination of approximately 3,000 jobs, plans are made to cut another 3,000 jobs by the end of 2008.

2009: Company announces it will trim 1,600 salaried jobs from its global workforce, in an effort to generate annual savings of roughly $150 million.

were made for the construction of additional production facilities.

Marketing was central to Smith's strategy for growth, as Kimberly-Clark emphasized its commitment to consumer products. Research and development efforts enlarged the company's technological base from traditional cellulose fiber-forming technologies to lightweight nonwovens utilizing synthetic fabrics.

A new premium-priced diaper in an hourglass shape with refastenable tapes was introduced in 1978 under the name Huggies. By 1984, Huggies had captured 50 percent of the higher quality disposable diaper market. The sudden popularity of the product caught Kimberly-Clark by surprise, and it was forced to expand production to meet consumer demand.

DIVERSIFICATION IN THE EIGHTIES

Facial tissue and feminine-care products were also part of Kimberly-Clark's growing consumer product operations. In 1984, it was estimated that the company's Kleenex brand held 50 percent of the tissue market. A chemically treated virucidal tissue called Avert was test-marketed that same year, but the higher price and limited utility of the product prevented it from gaining widespread popularity. Aimed at healthcare institutions and at companies as a product to reduce absenteeism, Avert never really got off the ground, and in 1987 Kimberly-Clark decided not to mass market the product.

The 1980 toxic shock syndrome scare caused a slump in tampon sales. Kimberly-Clark began an aggressive advertising campaign on television for Depend incontinence products in the early 1980s. At the time, incontinence products were as unmentionable as feminine-care products had been some 60 years earlier. The promotion resulted in Depend gaining a profitable share of the incontinence products market, and it quickly became the best-selling retail incontinence brand in the United States. In an effort to broaden its position in therapeutic and healthcare products, Kimberly-Clark acquired Spenco Medical Corporation in Waco, Texas, that same year.

Although sales from primary growth operations (personal-care products) were increasing, approximately 25 percent of Kimberly-Clark's sales continued to come from the pulp, newsprint, and paper businesses. The company further diversified its operations in 1984 by converting its regularly scheduled executive air-shuttle service into a regional commercial airline. The company's foray into aviation was initiated by the purchase of a six-seat plane in 1948 to shuttle executives between company headquarters in Wisconsin and Kimberly-Clark factories around the country. With six planes in 1969, Smith, then an executive vice-president for finance, suggested that company air travel be converted from a "cost center into a profit center" by offering corporate aircraft maintenance services. K-C Aviation, as the subsidiary was called, later remodeled three DC-9s and in June 1984 initiated flight service between Appleton and Milwaukee, Wisconsin; Boston; and Dallas, Texas. The fledgling airline, operated under the name Midwest Express, got off to a rocky start with a 1985 crash in Milwaukee, planes flying 80 percent empty, and large operating losses. By 1989, however, the operation was in the black, with planes at 66 percent capacity; a $120 million expansion increased the number of destinations to 15 cities and the airline boasted a fleet of 11 DC-9s.

In 1985, stating that the state had a bad climate for business, Smith relocated Kimberly-Clark's headquarters from Wisconsin to Texas. Just before this move Kimberly-Clark was sued by Procter & Gamble, who claimed that Kimberly-Clark had unlawfully infringed on its patented disposable diaper waistband material. Huggies had increased its market share to 31 percent, upsetting Procter & Gamble's Pampers. After nearly two years of litigation, a federal grand jury ruled against Procter & Gamble. Kimberly-Clark enjoyed further successes in its ongoing diaper rivalry with Procter & Gamble later in the decade when it introduced the extremely popular Huggies Pull-Ups disposable training pants in 1989. This product extension helped Kimberly-Clark trim Procter & Gamble's market share lead, as well as propel Huggies into the number one position in the disposable diaper market.

CONTINUED GROWTH

Starting in the late 1980s, Kimberly-Clark began another diversification program (this time geographically, targeting Europe), although the company's largest international growth would come in the early and mid-1990s. To keep the company growing at a healthy pace, Smith began to increase Kimberly-Clark's presence in Europe in 1988. From that year to 1992, the company invested nearly $1 billion in European plants. Although revenues from its European operations increased steadily, the huge investments (totaling $700 million in 1993 alone) and restructuring charges that went along with them began to affect the company's profits. Net income of $435.2 million in 1991 fell to $150.1 million in 1992 before recovering slightly to $231 million in 1993.

Meanwhile, the company further reduced its commodity papers operation in 1991 when it sold Spruce Falls Power and Paper. The following year, Smith, the architect of Kimberly-Clark's restructuring and diversification efforts since 1972, retired as chairman and was succeeded by Wayne R. Sanders. The new chairman had worked his way up the ranks and had spearheaded the risky endeavor of developing Huggies Pull-Ups. The year 1992 also saw the introduction of Huggies Ultra Trim diapers.

Under Sanders's leadership, it appeared as if the company would divest itself completely of its commod-

ity papers roots. Kimberly-Clark announced in late 1994 that it would explore the sale of its North American pulp and newsprint operations. The following year, however, the company decided not to sell because pulp and newsprint prices rose so high it no longer made economic sense to do so. Kimberly-Clark did divest its cigarette papers business in mid-1995 by spinning it off into a company called Schweitzer-Maudit International Inc. after shareholders initiated a proxy fight in 1994, concerned about the potential costs of liability lawsuits against tobacco, which were then beginning to gain strength.

In 1995 Sanders engineered the deal that would usher in a new era for the company: the merger of Kimberly-Clark with Scott Paper Co. The deal was the logical culmination of Kimberly-Clark's international expansion, since Scott was globally strong and held the number one position in tissue in Europe. The $9.4 billion deal led to a 1995 charge of $1.4 billion for Kimberly-Clark to consolidate the merger, which led to the layoff of 6,000 workers and the sale of several plants. To pass antitrust muster, Kimberly-Clark had to sell the Scotties facial tissue operation, two of four tissue plants in the United States, and its Baby Fresh, Wash-a-Bye Baby, and Kid Fresh brands (which it sold to Procter & Gamble).

NEW DIRECTIONS

The merger with Scott solidified Kimberly-Clark's position as the number two player in the paper products industry and nearly doubled the company's revenues. The merger also marked a change in direction for the company from a focus on low-margin paper and pulp production to higher-profit consumer products. Realizing that its entry into the "diaper wars" with Procter & Gamble would require streamlined operations, Kimberly-Clark began to divest itself of its pulp and paper manufacturing business in late 1996. The company shut down mills in Alabama, Canada, and Spain. By the end of 1997, pulp production fell to 30 percent of the company's worldwide consumption, down from 80 percent at the beginning of that year.

The company also began to expand its line of professional healthcare products. In 1997, Kimberly-Clark acquired Tecnol Medical Products, manufacturer of half of all surgical masks used in U.S. hospitals. In 1998, the company restructured its tissue business to consolidate manufacturing operations. The restructuring resulted in the closure of mills, including those in Maine and Wisconsin, and the loss of some 5,000 jobs. In 1999, Kimberly-Clark further divested its pulp business when it sold its Southeast Timberlands, which supplied wood to many of its defunct pulp mills.

In 1999, the company expanded its tissue operations in Europe with its acquisition of the Swiss company Attisholz. The acquisition nearly tripled Kimberly-Clark's tissue sales in Germany, Switzerland, and Austria. That year, Kimberly-Clark continued its foray into medical and healthcare products by purchasing Ballard Medical Products, adding such products as respiratory suction catheters, defibrillator pads, and foam-dispensed soap to its line. That acquisition was followed later that year by the purchase of Safeskin, which gave the company the leading spot in the production of disposable surgical gloves.

The company continued its rapid expansion through acquisitions. In 2000, the company grew its Asian markets when it acquired the Taiwanese company S-K Corporation and Taiwan Scott Paper. In 2001, Kimberly-Clark bought the Italian company Linostar, the second largest diaper manufacturer in Italy. In 2000, the company achieved sales of nearly $14 billion.

Developments continued during the early 2000s. Midway through 2001, the company increased its ownership stake in Kimberly-Clark Australia, a joint venture with Melbourne, Australia-based Amcor Ltd. In June 2002 Kimberly-Clark parted with approximately $375 million to secure full ownership of the Australian operation. Around the same time, the company sold its In-Mold and Non-Label Specialty Paper business units to Yupo Corp. of America.

A major leadership change occurred in September 2002, at which time Thomas J. Falk was chosen to succeed Wayne R. Sanders as chairman and CEO in February of the following year. Chief Financial Officer John Donehower also announced plans to retire in February 2003, and Vice-President of Finance Mark Buthman was chosen to succeed him on January 1.

INTERNATIONAL GROWTH

By early 2003 roughly 1.3 billion people throughout the world used Kimberly-Clark products, many of which ranked first or second in popularity within their respective categories. In April of that year, the company furthered its international growth by acquiring International Paper's Poland-based Klucze tissue operations. It also was in 2003 that Kimberly-Clark unveiled a new business plan calling for a focus on strong-growth products such as wipes and training pants, and the improvement of struggling operations including washroom products in North America and personal care products in Europe.

Kimberly-Clark began 2004 by merging its European personal care products operations into those in North America. In addition, European and North American consumer tissue operations were combined into a new North America-based unit. As evidence of the company's continued global focus, a new unit was created to pursue opportunities in the emerging markets of Eastern Europe, Latin America, and Asia. It also was in early 2004 that Kimberly-Clark sold its wound care operations to Princeton, New Jersey-based Derma Sciences.

A major development took place in mid-2004 when Kimberly-Clark announced plans to spin off its paper and Canadian pulp operations into a new public company named Neenah Paper Inc. The spinoff, which was expected to generate approximately $215 million for the company, would allow it to concentrate on marketing its health and hygiene products.

International growth continued during the middle of the first decade of the 2000s. In early 2005 Kimberly-Clark shuttered a medical products plant in Fort Worth, Texas, and relocated production to Mexico, resulting in the loss of 350 jobs. This was followed by news in July that the company would shutter an additional 20 plants and reduce its workforce by 10 percent, as part of a continued focus on its diaper and healthcare operations, as well as emerging markets. In keeping with the strategy, the company revealed plans to invest $200 million over the course of five years to grow its business in Brazil. Kimberly-Clark rounded out the year with news that it had completed the construction of a new, $90 million production facility in Beijing, China.

In early 2006, Kimberly-Clark revealed plans to invest $120 million in Turkey over the course of five years, resulting in the creation of approximately 1,000 new jobs. At the same time, Kotex feminine hygiene products were also introduced in Turkey, via the company's Hogla-Kimberly Ltd. joint venture with Israeli Paper Mills. Progress continued during the latter part of the year, as Kimberly-Clark devoted approximately $20 million to promote the introduction of a new line of Huggies Supreme diapers, co-branded with The Walt Disney Co. Kimberly-Clark rounded out the year by establishing an Innovation Center of Excellence near Seoul, South Korea, and generating sales of $16.7 billion, up 5 percent from 2005.

ECONOMIC CHALLENGES

Kimberly-Clark continued to trim its workforce as the company headed into the latter years of the decade. After cutting approximately 3,000 jobs in 2006, plans were in place to eliminate another 3,000 jobs by the end of 2008. On the international front, construction of a new diaper factory and a paper mill were planned in

Peru, which was slated to become the company's South American hub. In addition to investing $60 million in the new facilities, Kimberly-Clark was expected to double its workforce in Peru, which would grow to 1,200 people. The company rounded out the year by naming Christian A. Brickman as its new chief strategy officer in September.

Growth continued in 2009. In April, Kimberly-Clark bolstered its professional division by revealing plans to acquire Missouri-based Jackson Products Inc., a manufacturer of work safety products. In June, the company announced that it would trim 1,600 salaried jobs from its global workforce in order to generate annual savings of roughly $150 million. Chairman and CEO Tom Falk said the eliminations were necessary for continued growth in the wake of difficult economic times.

Carol I. Keeley
Updated, David E. Salamie; Lisa Whipple;
Paul R. Greenland

PRINCIPAL SUBSIDIARIES

1194127 Ontario Inc. (Canada); Abdelia Comercial Ltda. (Brazil); Avent Inc.; Avent de Honduras S.A. de C.V.; Avent Holdings LLC; Avent, S. de R.L. (Mexico); Avent Slovakia Inc.; Avent Slovakia s.r.o.; Bacraft S.A. Indústria de Papel (Brazil); Ballard Medical Products; Ballard Medical Products (Canada) Inc.; Balmoral Participações Ltda. (Brazil); Beco Inc.; Delaware Overseas Finance Inc.; Durafab Inc.; Excell Paper Sales Co.; Excell Paper Sales LLC; Fisbra Indústria e Comércio de Produtos Higiênicos Ltda. (Brazil); Gerinconfort Indústria e Comércio de Produtos Higiênicos Ltda. (Brazil); Hakle Kimberly Deutschland GmbH (Germany); Hakle Kimberly Papiervertriebs GmbH (Austria); Hercules Global Investments (Cayman Islands); Hopewell International Insurance Ltd. (Bermuda); Housing Horizons LLC; Industrial Helvetia S.A. (Chile); Industrial Mimosa S.A. (Uruguay); K-C Advertising Inc.; K-C Equipment Finance L.P. (UK); K-C Financial Services Investment Company; K-C Guernsey I Ltd. (Isle of Guernsey); K-C Guernsey II Ltd. (Isle of Guernsey); K-C Investment Partnership (Canada); K-C Nevada Inc.; K-C Worldwide LLC; Kalayaan Land Corporation (Philippines); KC Tower Corporation; KCA Retirement Fund Pty. Limited (Australia); KCC Comercial Ltda. (Brazil); KCK Tissue (Argentina); Kimberly-Clark (Barbados) Holding Ltd.; Kimberly-Clark (Cyprus) Ltd.; Kimberly-Clark (Hong Kong) Ltd.; Kimberly-Clark (Kft) Trading Limited Liability Company (Hungary); Kimberly-Clark (Trinidad) Limited (Trinidad and Tobago); Kimberly-Clark

Argentina S.A.; Kimberly-Clark Argentina Holdings S.A.; Kimberly-Clark Asia Holdings Pte. Ltd. (Singapore); Kimberly-Clark Asia Pacific Pte. Ltd. (Singapore); Kimberly-Clark Australia Consolidated Holdings Pty. Limited; Kimberly-Clark Australia Holdings Pty. Limited; Kimberly-Clark Australia Pty. Limited; Kimberly-Clark B.V. (Netherlands); Kimberly-Clark Bahrain Holding Company S.P.C.; Kimberly-Clark Brasil Holdings Limitada (Brazil); Kimberly-Clark Brasil Indústria e Comércio de Produtos de Hygiene Ltda. (Brazil); Kimberly-Clark Canada Holdings Inc.; Kimberly-Clark Canada Inc.; Kimberly-Clark Canada Inc. Kanadischen Rechts & Company KG (Germany); Kimberly-Clark Canada International Holdings Inc.; Kimberly-Clark Canada Services Corporation; Kimberly-Clark Canada U.K. Holding Limited; Kimberly-Clark Cayman Islands Company; Kimberly-Clark Cayman Islands Finance Company; Kimberly-Clark Cayman Islands Holding Company; Kimberly-Clark Colombia Limitada; Kimberly-Clark de Centro America S.A. (El Salvador); Kimberly-Clark Denmark Holdings ApS; Kimberly-Clark do Brasil Limitada (Brazil); Kimberly-Clark Dominican Republic S.A.; Kimberly-Clark Dominicana S.A. (Dominican Republic); Kimberly-Clark Dutch Holdings B.V. (Netherlands); Kimberly-Clark Ecuador S.A.; Kimberly-Clark Europe Limited (UK); Kimberly-Clark European Investment B.V. (Netherlands); Kimberly-Clark European Services Limited (UK); Kimberly-Clark Far East Pte. Limited (Singapore); Kimberly-Clark Finance Ltd. (UK); Kimberly-Clark Financial Services Inc.; Kimberly-Clark Forestal S.A. (Spain); Kimberly-Clark Foundation Inc.; Kimberly-Clark France Operations; Kimberly-Clark Global Finance Ltd. (Bermuda); Kimberly-Clark Global Partnership L.P.; Kimberly-Clark Global Sales LLC; Kimberly-Clark GmbH (Switzerland); Kimberly-Clark Health Care Inc.; Kimberly-Clark Hellas EPE (Greece); Kimberly-Clark Holding e Representações do Brasil Ltda. (Brazil); Kimberly-Clark Holdings Limited (UK); Kimberly-Clark Holland Holdings B.V. (Netherlands); Kimberly-Clark Hygiene Products Private Ltd. (India); Kimberly-Clark Inc. (Canada); Kimberly-Clark Innovation Corporation (South Korea); Kimberly-Clark Integrated Services Corporation; Kimberly-Clark International Services Corporation; Kimberly-Clark International S.A. (Panama); Kimberly-Clark Irish Finance Corporation Ltd. (UK); Kimberly-Clark Kenko Indústria e Comércio Ltda. (Brazil); Kimberly-Clark Latin America Inc.; Kimberly-Clark Latin America Inc. y Cia, S.C. (Spain); Kimberly-Clark Latin America Investments Inc.; Kimberly-Clark Lda. (Portugal); Kimberly-Clark Limited (UK); Kimberly-Clark Luxembourg S.a.r.l.; Kimberly-Clark Luxembourg Finance S.a.r.l.; Kimberly-

Clark Luxembourg Holdings S.a.r.l.; Kimberly-Clark Manufacturing (Thailand) Limited; Kimberly-Clark Mediterranean Finance Company Ltd. (Malta); Kimberly-Clark N.V. (Belgium); Kimberly-Clark Netherlands Holdings B.V.; Kimberly-Clark North Asia Co., Ltd (South Korea); Kimberly-Clark OOO (Russia); Kimberly-Clark Pacific Finance Company (Cayman Islands); Kimberly-Clark Pacific Holdings Pty Limited (Australia); Kimberly-Clark Paper (Guangzhou) Company Limited (China); Kimberly-Clark Paper (Shanghai) Company Limited (China); Kimberly-Clark Paraguay S.A.; Kimberly-Clark Patriot Holdings Inc. (Cayman Islands); Kimberly-Clark Pennsylvania LLC; Kimberly-Clark Pension Trusts Ltd. (UK); Kimberly-Clark Personal Hygienic Products (Nanjing) Co. Ltd. (China); Kimberly-Clark Personal Hygienic Products Company Limited (China); Kimberly-Clark Philippines Inc.; Kimberly-Clark Philippines Holdings Inc.; Kimberly-Clark Products (Malaysia) Sdn. Bdh.; Kimberly-Clark Produtos Para Saúde Limitada (Brazil); Kimberly-Clark Puerto Rico Inc.; Kimberly-Clark S.A. (Poland); Kimberly-Clark S.L. (Spain); Kimberly-Clark S.N.C. (France); Kimberly-Clark S.p.A. (Italy); Kimberly-Clark s.r.l. (Italy); Kimberly-Clark s.r.o. (Czech Republic); Kimberly-Clark Sales Corporation B.V. (Netherlands); Kimberly-Clark Scandinavia ApS (Denmark); Kimberly-Clark Services Argentina S.A.; Kimberly-Clark Services Asia Pacific (Australia); Kimberly-Clark Services Inc.; Kimberly-Clark Singapore Pte. Ltd.; Kimberly-Clark Singapore Finance Ltd.; Kimberly-Clark Sp. z.o.o. (Poland); Kimberly-Clark SUD S.p.A. (Italy); Kimberly-Clark Taiwan (Cayman Islands); Kimberly-Clark Thailand Limited; Kimberly-Clark Tissue do Brasil Limitada (Brazil); Kimberly-Clark Trading (Malaysia) Sdn. Bdh.; Kimberly-Clark Treasury Asia Pacific (Australia); Kimberly-Clark Tuketim Mallari Sanayi Ve Ticaret Anonim Sirketi (Turkey); Kimberly-Clark U.K. Operations Limited; Kimberly-Clark Ukraine LLC; Kimberly-Clark Ventures LLC; Kimberly-Clark Vietnam Co. Ltd.; Kimberly-Clark West Indies Finance Company (Cayman Islands); Kimberly-Clark Worldwide Australia Holdings Pty. Limited; Kimberly-Clark Worldwide Inc.; KIMNICA S.A. (Nicaragua); KS&J Indústria e Comercio Ltda. (Brazil); La Ada de Acuna S.R.L. (Mexico); Marsbaum Participaçóes Ltda. (Brazil); MFS Holdings LLC; Microcuff GmbH (Germany); Mimo Brasil Limitada (Brazil); Mimo Uruguay S.A.; Minnetonka Limitada (Brazil); Minnetonka Overseas Investments Limited (Cayman Islands); Nueva Arizona S.A. (Argentina); Papeles Absorbentes S.A. (Guatemala); PLS Holdings LLC; P.T. Kimberly-Clark Indonesia; Ridgeway Insurance Company Limited (Bermuda); Ropers LLC; Ropers II LLC; Safeskin (B.V.I.) Limited (British Virgin Islands);

Safeskin Corporation (Malaysia) Sdn. Bhd.; Safeskin Corporation (Thailand) Limited; Safeskin Industries (Thailand) Limited; Safeskin Latex (Thailand) Limited; Safeskin Medical & Scientific (Thailand) Limited; Scott CB Holding Company; Scott S.A. (France); Scott Executive Pension Trustees Limited, United Kingdom; Scott Paper Co. Honduras S.A. de C.V.; Scott Paper Eastern China Inc.; S-K Corporation (Taiwan); Syzygy Inc.; Taiwan Scott Paper Corporation; Texans LLC; Texans II LLC; Texas Company Building, LP; Three Rivers Timber Company; Tiscorp L.P.

PRINCIPAL OPERATING UNITS

Personal Care; Consumer Tissue; Health Care; K-C Professional and Other.

PRINCIPAL COMPETITORS

Energizer Holdings Inc.; Georgia-Pacific LLC; The Procter & Gamble Co.

FURTHER READING

Avila, Larry, "Kimberly-Clark Upbeat on Global Growth Plan," *Appleton (Wis.) Post-Crescent,* March 22, 2007.

Benady, David, "Kimberly-Clark Brings in US Chief," *Marketing Week,* July 23, 1998, p. 9.

Byrne, Harlan S., "Keeping the Faith," *Barron's,* December 16, 1996, p. 15.

———, "Paper Profits," *Barron's,* January 10, 2000, p. 20.

———, "Strength Ahead?" *Barron's,* July 28, 1997, p. 13.

Byrne, John A., and Joseph Weber, "The Shredder: Did CEO Dunlap Save Scott Paper—Or Just Pretty It Up?" *Business Week,* January 15, 1996, pp. 56–61.

Case, Brendan, "Irving-Based Kimberly-Clark to Cut 1,600 Positions," *Dallas Morning News,* June 25, 2009.

Cheverton, Richard E., *The Maverick Way: Profiting from the Power of the Corporate Misfit,* La Palma, Calif.: Waypoint Books, 2000.

Cody, Harold M., "Consolidation Produces Giants Hoping for Better Performance," *Pulp & Paper,* November 2000, pp. 37–44.

Collins, Glenn, "Kimberly-Clark Plans Split of Stock and Sale of 3 Mills, Stronger Position Sought Against P. & G.," *New York Times,* February 26, 1997, p. C2.

Forest, Stephanie Anderson, and Heidi Dawley, "Pulp Fiction at Kimberly-Clark," *Business Week,* February 23, 1998, p. 90.

Forest, Stephanie Anderson, and Mark Maremont, "Kimberly-Clark's European Paper Chase," *Business Week,* March 16, 1992, pp. 94, 96.

Frankovich, Mike, "Early Intervention," *Security Management,* April 2000, pp. 22–24.

Freeman, Laurie, "Kimberly Holds Its Own Against Giants," *Advertising Age,* November 19, 1984.

Glowacki, Jeremy J., "Kimberly-Clark Corp.: Accelerates Global Expansion with Scott Merger," *Pulp & Paper,* December 1995, pp. 34–35.

Goldstein, Alan, "Learning a New Set of Rules: How Kimberly-Clark Adapted When E-Business Era Arrived," *Knight-Ridder/Tribune News Service,* January 10, 2001.

"Gulfstream Buying Kimberly-Clark Aviation Unit," *New York Times,* July 25, 1998, p. B3.

Hackney, Holt, "Kimberly-Clark: No Escaping a Messy Diaper (Business)," *Financial World,* April 27, 1993, p. 16.

Ingham, John N., ed., "Kimberly, John Alfred," in *Biographical Dictionary of American Business Leaders, Vol. II,* Westport, Conn.: Greenwood, 1983.

Kaplan-Leiseron, Eva, "The Maverick Way: Profiting from the Power of the Corporate Misfit," *Training & Development,* January 2001, p. 66.

"K-C Announces Global Restructuring," *Pulp & Paper,* January 1998, p. 23.

"K-C Spin-off Going Forward," *Nonwovens Industry,* December 2004.

"K-C Takes Cool Approach to Its Newest Operating Room Apparel," *Health Industry Today,* December 1998, pp. 4–5.

"Kimberly-Clark Acquires Tecnol," *Wall Street Journal,* December 19, 1997, p. B2.

"Kimberly-Clark Awards Options," *New York Times,* October 23, 1997, p. C26.

"Kimberly-Clark Corp.," *New York Times,* April 1, 1997, p. C4.

"The Kimberly-Clark Corp to Purchase the Safeskin Corp for 3.19 Times Revenue," *Weekly Corporate Growth Report,* November 29, 1999.

"Kimberly-Clark—Down the Pan?" *Marketing Week,* April 9, 1998, p. 3.

"Kimberly-Clark Has Plans to Restructure Operations in Europe," *Wall Street Journal,* July 7, 2000, p. A6.

"Kimberly-Clark Is Selling 460,000 Acres of Timberland," *New York Times,* June 11, 1999, p. C4.

"Kimberly-Clark Kicks in with Restructuring Plan," *PPI,* January 1998, p. 9.

"Kimberly-Clark Nothing to Sneeze At," *Des Moines Business Record,* January 13, 2003.

"Kimberly-Clark Plans to Increase Prices 5% for Huggies Diapers," *Wall Street Journal,* April 16, 1998, p. A4.

"Kimberly-Clark Revises Structure," *New York Times,* December 11, 1998, p. C2.

"Kimberly-Clark Selling Southeast Timber," *Pulp & Paper,* March 1999, p. 25.

"Kimberly-Clark Snatches Attisholz's Tissue Unit," *PPI,* June 1999, p. 15.

"Kimberly-Clark Suit Alleges Infringement of Its Diaper Patents," *Wall Street Journal,* March 21, 2000, p. B8.

"Kimberly-Clark to Acquire Tecnol for 19 Times, Earnings," *Weekly Corporate Growth Report,* September 15, 1997.

"Kimberly-Clark to Buy Italian Diaper Manufacturer," *New York Times,* January 25, 2001, p. C4.

"Kimberly-Clark to Close Pulp Mill and Cut 450 Jobs," *New York Times,* May 6, 1998, p. C3.

"Kimberly-Clark to Combine Units in Reorganization," *New York Times,* January 20, 2004.

"Kimberly-Clark to Sell Lines," *Wall Street Journal,* May 19, 1999, p. C27.

"Kimberly-Clark Will Cut Staff 15% in Europe," *Wall Street Journal,* January 29, 1996, p. B2.

"Kimberly-Clark's Deal for Ballard Expands Industry Acquisition Trend," *Health Industry Today,* February 1999, pp. 1, 4.

"Kruger Agrees to Buy Kimberly-Clark Unit for $256.8 Million," *Wall Street Journal,* March 5, 1997, p. B2.

Lenzner, Robert, "The Battle of the Bottoms," *Forbes,* March 24, 1997, pp. 98–103.

Lieber, Ronald B., "Storytelling: A New Way to Get Close to Your Customer," *Fortune,* February 3, 1997, pp. 102–08.

Murray, Matt, "Kimberly-Clark to Take Charge of $1.4 Billion," *Wall Street Journal,* December 14, 1995, pp. A3, A8.

Narisetti, Raju, "For Sanders, Getting Scott Is Only the Start," *Wall Street Journal,* December 5, 1995, pp. B1, B12.

Neff, Jack, "Kimberly-Clark Finally Reaps Boon from Scott," *Advertising Age,* November 8, 1999, p. 24.

Nelson, Emily, "Kimberly-Clark Posts 7.8% Drop in Net, Lowers Forecast for the Rest of the Year," *Wall Street Journal,* April 24, 2001, p. B8.

Parker-Pope, Tara, "Contrite, Kimberly-Clark's CEO Promises to Mop Up," *Wall Street Journal,* June 1, 1998, p. B1.

Pearson, John, "Reforms Are Bearing Fruit," *Business Week,* July 8, 1996, p. 86.

"Purchase of Added 5% Stake in Australian Venture Is Set," *Wall Street Journal,* May 8, 2001, p. A14.

Richards, Amanda, "Unite and Conquer," *Marketing,* September 18, 1997, pp. 24–25.

Sheridan, John H., "Going for Growth," *Industry Week,* June 9, 1997, pp. 32–44.

Spector, Robert, *Shared Values: A History of Kimberly-Clark,* Lyme, Conn.: Greenwich Publishing Group, 1997.

Star, Marlene Givant, "Proxy Fight at Kimberly-Clark: Investors Request Tobacco Spin-Off," *Pensions & Investments,* March 6, 1995, pp. 2, 41.

Useem, Jerry, "Most Admired: Conquering Vertical Limits," *Fortune,* February 19, 2001, pp. 84–96.

"Wayne R. Sanders," *Business Week,* January 8, 2001, p. 69.

Kimpton Hotel &
Restaurant Group, Inc.

■

222 Kearny Street, Suite 200
San Francisco, California 94108-4537
U.S.A.
Telephone: (415) 397-5572
Toll Free: (800) 546-7866
Fax: (415) 296-8031
Web site: http://www.kimptonhotels.com

Private Company
Incorporated: 1981 as Kimco Hotel & Restaurant
    Management Co.
Employees: 6,000
Sales: $600 million (2008 est.)
NAICS: 721110 Hotels (Except Casino Hotels) and
    Motels

■ ■ ■

Kimpton Hotel & Restaurant Group, Inc., is a privately held, San Francisco-based boutique hotel and restaurant operator. A pioneer in the boutique hotel field, Kimpton owns and operates more than 40 hotels in 19 cities in the United States and Canada. The company maintains two sub-brands: Monaco, fashioned in architecturally significant or historic buildings, and Palomar, found in more modern buildings, with the emphasis on luxury. Regardless of brand, every Kimpton hotel is unique, most of them designed around a theme, such as All Things Red; Art in Motion; The Elements; Fun, Fresh and in the Now; History; and Music. What they all have in common are prime locations, a sense of style, friendliness, residential lobby settings, and unusual amenities, such as in-room spa treatments, yoga mats, and Pilates television programming. Pet friendly, the hotels offer guests complimentary companion goldfish as part of its "Guppy Love" program. Kimpton hotels are also known for their daily hosted wine hours.

Another key to Kimpton's success are the chef-driven restaurants that, although attached to the hotels, maintain separate entrances as well as management. Unlike typical hotel restaurants, in many cases they rank among the top restaurants in their communities. Kimpton hotels cater especially to women travelers and the gay and lesbian community. The company is also socially responsible, spearheading an employee volunteer work program, providing financial support to a number of local and regional nonprofit organizations, and maintaining a commitment to being an eco-friendly company by conserving water and energy, recycling reusable waste, eliminating harmful toxins and pollutants, and as much as possible employing sustainable materials.

FOUNDER BORN IN KANSAS CITY, 1935

The founder of Kimpton Hotels was William Drennon "Bill" Kimpton. He was born in Kansas City, Missouri, in 1935 and moved at the age of eight to Chicago, which was followed by a relocation to the West Coast. Burdened by dyslexia as well as alcoholic parents, he was not a particularly good student yet managed to earn a degree in economics from Northwestern University. He grew up interested in hotels, due in large measure, he claimed, to an early love of playing Monopoly and handling the little red hotels used in the game. He attempted to gain acceptance to the acclaimed Cornell School of Hotel Administration but his application was rejected. Instead Kimpton became an IBM salesman in Chicago. The highlight of his tenure was an order for 30 typewriters. After becoming a self-taught business broker, he took a position with the investment banking firm of Lehman Brothers and made his mark in the 1960s by recognizing the potential for the Kentucky Fried Chicken chain, which he would help take public. He spent the next several years on the road seeking out marketable companies and capital, along the way learning firsthand the rigors of travel and life in hotel rooms.

While on business in London, Kimpton stayed at one of the city's more expensive and aloof hotels, the Hyde Park Hotel. When his work was completed and he no longer had the benefit of an expense account, he stayed a few days longer in London but moved to much less expensive accommodations, a nearby small hotel, the Wilbraham, where he was pleased to find that the staff quickly made him feel at home. It was an experience that would play a key role in how he later approached the hotel business.

Of equal importance to his development as a hotelier was his association with New York real estate magnate Harry Helmsley, whom he met in the 1970s while raising funds to build the Kapalua Bay Resort Hotel, the first luxury hotel on the Hawaiian island of Maui. Learning that Helmsley was interested in building a Manhattan hotel, what would become the Helmsley Palace Hotel, Kimpton offered to raise the $23 million the project required. He accomplished the task in 18 months and along the way received some valuable advice from Helmsley, who owned a small hotel on Central Park South that was highly profitable because it eschewed the ballrooms and banquet rooms that tied up so much overhead, as well as money-losing room service. The key, Kimpton learned, was to "sell sleep." He also realized that he could enjoy a major advantage by acquiring and renovating existing hotels rather than

investing in new structures. In this way, he could price his rooms lower than his competition.

OPENING OF FIRST KIMPTON-OWNED HOTEL: 1981

Kimpton was fired as an investment banker for continually flying first class in contradiction of company policy. By that time, however, he was weary of Wall Street and eager to strike out on his own. In 1980 he moved his family to San Francisco, where he had once lived, and fulfilled a long-cherished dream of becoming a hotelier. Kimpton raised $8 million in a limited partnership that included $500,000 from his life savings. (He also formed Kimco Hotel & Restaurant Management Co. to manage the properties acquired by his partnerships.) Kimpton then paid $6.9 million for a derelict downtown hotel, the 151-room Hotel Maurice, which mostly attracted foreign tourists, and spent $1.1 million to refurbish the property into a European-style boutique hotel. Later Kimpton would claim, "I overpaid and underdecorated."

When the Bedford was ready to open in 1981, however, Kimpton had to contend with the effects of a strong dollar that tamped down tourism and crippled his primary customer base. He managed to stay in business by cold calling corporate customers, who were attracted to his favorable pricing during tough economic conditions. To keep up occupancy, Kimpton hired a staff of cold callers who were able to build the hotel's occupancy rate to 75 percent. The Bedford soon turned profitable. Along the way it also achieved a number of firsts in the hotel industry. The hotel eatery, Café Bedford, was the first specialty chef-driven restaurant in a U.S. boutique hotel. The Bedford also offered the first fully stocked honor bar. In addition, it was at the Bedford that Kimpton began the practice of holding a complimentary wine hour for hotel guests each day.

Having learned some valuable lessons, Kimpton spent just $2.2 million to acquire his second San Francisco property, the 106-room Colonial Hotel, while investing $3.6 million in renovations. Renamed the Hotel Vintage Court, it opened in 1984, and once again his team of cold callers filled the rooms with business travelers. With an emphasis on wine it became the first of Kimpton's themed properties. A restaurant was also opened with noted Japanese chef Masataka Kobayashi, the first Kimpton restaurant to feature a star chef and one that would set a pattern for those to follow. Although housed in the same building as the hotel, the restaurant, Masa, had a separate entrance and established a separate identity and loyal following apart from the traffic generated by the hotel.

```
┌─────────────────────────────────────────┐
│                                         │
│            KEY DATES                    │
│               ■                         │
│  ─────────────────────────────          │
│  1981:  Bill Kimpton forms Kimco Hotel &│
│         Restaurant Management Co., opens first │
│         boutique hotel in San Francisco.│
│  1984:  First themed hotel opens.       │
│  1991:  Kimco opens first hotel outside of California. │
│  1994:  Company is renamed Kimpton Hotel and │
│         Restaurant Group.               │
│  1998:  First Canadian hotel is added to the fold. │
│  2001:  Bill Kimpton dies.              │
│  2005:  Investment fund is launched.    │
│                                         │
└─────────────────────────────────────────┘
```

Kimpton had found a winning formula and during the rest of the 1980s he successfully applied it in San Francisco. In 1984 he bought the Hotel Sutter, which became the 177-room Galleria Park, followed a year later by the purchase of the Hotel Victoria, resulting in the 107-room Hotel Juliana. In 1986 the Manx Hotel was converted into the 177-room Villa Florence, which would include the highly popular Kuleto's "California-Italian" restaurant. The Continental Hotel was purchased in 1987 and became the Monticello Inn. In 1988 Kimpton's small chain of boutique hotels generated revenues of $34 million. Kimco also took on the management of outside hotels as well, such as the Prescott Hotel, which would house celebrity chef Wolfgang Puck's highly popular Postrio restaurant.

ACQUISITION OF PORTLAND HOTEL: 1990

In the late 1980s Kimpton looked beyond the San Francisco market. In 1989 he raised $14 million and a year later paid $3 million for the 127-room Plaza Hotel in Portland, Oregon. He spent $11 million on renovations and renamed the property the Vintage Plaza, which opened in 1991. Also in that year, Kimco opened the Harbor Court Hotel in San Francisco, notable because it was the first of a number of adaptive reuse projects, transforming the Embarcadero YMCA into a boutique hotel.

Several other hotels were added to the Kimpton chain in the early 1990s, including properties in Seattle and Tacoma, Washington, and Los Angeles, driving annual revenues to $100 million. Along the way the chain introduced elements that would further define the personality of a Kimpton hotel. The first celebrity suites were introduced in San Francisco's Hotel Triton in 1991 when musicians Jerry Garcia and Carlos Santana

designed their own rooms. A year later the chain created its pet-friendly program, supplemented in 1993 with the Guppy Love companion goldfish program. Rowing machines and exercise bikes became available for guest rooms. "Tall Rooms" were also introduced, featuring longer beds and higher-than-average counters and showerheads.

In 1994 Kimco was renamed Kimpton Hotel and Restaurant Group. By the end of the year the company was managing 16 boutique and two midsize hotels and 25 restaurants. Kimpton added the Monaco brand in 1995 when it opened the Monaco San Francisco and Grand Café Restaurant. In the second half of the 1990s the company looked to take its boutique hotel concept beyond the West Coast to other markets. In 1998 Kimpton opened the 264-room Hotel Monaco Denver in Colorado as well as a pair of Chicago properties, the 192-room Hotel Monaco Chicago and the 483-room Hotel Allegro Chicago. A year later the 122-room Hotel Burnham was also opened in Chicago, as was the 225-room Hotel Monaco Salt Lake City in Utah. At the same time Kimpton opened new properties in existing markets, the 221-room Hotel Monaco Portland in 1996, the 189-room Hotel Monaco Seattle in 1997, and two San Francisco hotels in 1999: the 195-room Hotel Palomar and the 236-room Serrano Hotel. In addition, Kimpton went international in the late 1990s. The company began managing its first resort, the Summit Lodge in Whistler, British Columbia, Canada, and in 1999 opened the Pacific Palisades Hotel in Vancouver, British Columbia.

BILL KIMPTON DIES: 2001

By the start of the new century the Kimpton operation included 28 hotels and 29 restaurants, generating annual revenues of about $400 million. In 2000 Kimpton held talks with Marriott International about joint efforts or a possible sale of the boutique chain to the hospitality giant, but in the end nothing came of the effort and Bill Kimpton remained independent.

His health, however, began to fail and after a nine-month battle with leukemia he died at the age of 65 in March 2001. He left behind a unique hotel operation but one that was not wholly dependent on his administrative skills. One of his strong suits had been his ability to find talented people and to delegate authority. Although he played a key role inspiring the organization and always keeping the focus on the needs of hotel guests, he had established a business model and corporate spirit that could carry on without him, even through the tough times in the hospitality industry that followed the terrorist attacks against the United States on September 11, 2001, as well as the technology slump that adversely affected the company's San Francisco business.

Because of poor economic conditions, Kimpton was not able to expand at the same pace planned during its founder's final years. Nevertheless, the company opened several new properties in the early 2000s. Kimpton entered the Washington, D.C., market in 2001 by taking on the management of the 99-room Topaz Hotel and the 137-room Hotel Rouse, both owned by a real estate investment trust, LaSalle Properties. A year later two more LaSalle-owned capital properties were added, the 82-room Hotel Madera and the 178-room Hotel Helix, followed in 2003 by the 139-room Hotel George. Kimpton also owned the 183-room Hotel Monaco DC (a renovation of the former U.S. Tariff Commission building), which opened in 2003.

New properties that Kimpton opened or took on to manage in other locales included the 90-room Sky Hotel in Aspen, Colorado, in 2001; the 224-room Cypress Hotel in Cupertino, California, in 2003; the 236-room Hotel Marlowe in Cambridge, Massachusetts, and the 252-room Argonaut Hotel in San Francisco, also in 2003; and the 112-room Onyx Hotel in Boston, Massachusetts, and the 200-room 70 Park Avenue Hotel in New York City in 2004. To support the chain's growth, the company launched its first national brand campaign in late 2004, employing the theme "Every Hotel Tells a Story." A year later, Kimpton entered the San Diego market, opening the 235-room Hotel Solamar.

LAUNCH OF INVESTMENT FUND: 2005

In order to fund the expansion of the Kimpton portfolio in current as well as new markets, the parent company, Kimpton Group Holdings LLC, launched the Kimpton Hospitality Partners LP $157 million investment fund in 2005. It was intended to acquire and develop more than $450 million worth of property, much of which would be dedicated to the Palomar brand. In 2006 Kimpton added the 45-room Morrison House in Alexandria, Virginia, and the 241-room Monaco Alexandria a year later. Also in 2006, the 190-room Nine Zero Hotel opened in Boston, as did the 200-room Muse Hotel in New York City; the 204-room FireSky Resort & Spa in Scottsdale, Arizona; and the Hotel Palomar in Washington, D.C. Kimpton also entered the Dallas, Texas, market, opening the 198-room Hotel Palomar Dallas in 2006, followed by the 60-room Hotel Lumen in 2007.

The first investment fund proved so successful that Kimpton Hospitality Partners II was launched in 2008, raising $246 million, mostly from college endowments. In the meantime, other properties were added to the Kimpton portfolio and continued to open in 2009. They included hotels in Atlanta, Georgia; Miami and Vero Beach, Florida; Los Angeles; Baltimore, Maryland; and Philadelphia, Pennsylvania. Moreover, new hotels opened in the existing markets of Alexandria and Arlington, Virginia, and New York City, and both the Hotel Monaco in Washington, D.C., and Portland's Hotel Vintage Plaza were renovated. A Palomar hotel was also scheduled to open in Chicago in the spring of 2010. The boutique chain had carved out a profitable niche in the market and there was reason to believe that the concept would continue to grow for many years to come.

Ed Dinger

PRINCIPAL COMPETITORS

Morgan Hotel Group Co.; The Ritz-Carlton Hotel Company, LLC; Starwood Hotels & Resorts Worldwide, Inc.

FURTHER READING

Barry, Les, "Kimco Hotel Chief's Recipe for Success Trims the Fat on Service," *Travel Weekly,* January 14, 1988, p. 13.

Carlsen, Clifford, "Boutique Hotelier Checks into New Markets," *San Francisco Business Times,* April 16, 1993, p. 1.

Chittum, Ryan, "Kimpton Will Unveil Big Expansion," *Wall Street Journal,* June 1, 2005, p. B8.

Groves, Martha, "Hotelier Lights a Fire," *Los Angeles Times,* June 17, 1992, p. 1.

King, Paul, "Hotel-Restaurant Pioneer Kimpton Dies of Leukemia," *Nation's Restaurant News,* April 9, 2001, p. 1.

Levere, Jane L., "Bill Kimpton, 65, the Chairman of a Group of Boutique Hotels," *New York Times,* April 5, 2001, p. B9.

Liddle, Alan, "William Kimpton," *Nation's Restaurant News,* January 1995, p. 111.

Machan, Dyan, "'We Sell Sleep,'" *Forbes,* September 14, 1992, p. 421.

Parets, Robyn, "Kimpton Expands Boutique Concept," *National Real Estate Investor,* August 2005, p. 14.

Rowe, Megan, "Canny Kimpton," *Lodging Hospitality,* May 1994, p. 24.

Spielberg, Susan, "Boutique Hotel, Fine-Dining Star Kimpton Plots $450M Growth," *Nation's Restaurant News,* June 13, 2005, p. 1.

Kumho Tire Company Ltd.

————■————

Gwangsan-gu, 555 Sochon-dong
Gwangju, 506 711
South Korea
Telephone: (+82 062) 940 2114
Fax: (+82 062) 941 3161
Web site: http://www.kumhotire.co.kr

Public Company
Incorporated: 1960 as Samyang Tire Company
Employees: 5,515
Sales: KRW 2 trillion ($1.71 billion) (2008)
Stock Exchanges: Seoul
Ticker Symbol: 073240
NAICS: 326211 Tire Manufacturing (Except Retreading); 423130 Tire and Tube Merchant Wholesalers

■ ■ ■

Kumho Tire Company Ltd. is one of the top ten tire makers in the world, and the second largest in Korea, behind Hankook Tire Company. Kumho operates ten factories, in Korea, China, and Vietnam, as well as a new $225 million tire factory built in Macon, Georgia, in 2008, and a new facility under construction in China in 2009. The company expects its total capacity to grow from more than 50 million tires per year to more than 75 million per year by 2010. This expansion comes as part of Kumho's strategy to position itself among the global top five tire makers by 2015. In support of this, Kumho operates four research and development (R&D) facilities, including its Akron Technical Center in Ohio, in the United States. Kumho manufactures a full range

of automobile, light truck, truck and bus, and aircraft tires. The group is one of the leading producers of ultra-high performance (UHP) tires, and one of only two producers of Extreme Speed (X-Speed) Tires, capable of handling speeds up to 360 kilometers per hour. The company is also one of only five tire manufacturers producing run-flat tires. Kumho is listed on the Seoul Stock Exchange, but remains majority controlled by Kumho Asiana Group. Kumho Tire is led by CEO and President Sae-chul Oh, Ph.D. In 2008, the company's sales topped KRW 2 trillion ($1.7 billion).

FROM TAXIS TO TIRES IN 1960

Kumho Tire Company was founded in 1960 as an offshoot of the fast-growing Kumho bus company. Kumho had originated as a taxicab business, founded in 1946 by Park In-Chun. Park, a former police officer, started out with just two cars, Ford Deluxe sedans. The business, situated in Gwangju, was initially known as Gwangju Taxi.

Park struggled from the outset. By the early 1950s and the outbreak of the Korean War, the company had ground to a halt. Following the war and the north-south division of Korea, Park tried again. Park remained focused on the public transportation sector. However, this time Park targeted the mass transportation market, launching his first bus operations.

Park's company quickly differentiated itself from its competitors, offering South Korea's first long-distance bus routes. Park rapidly gained a major share of this market, as his competitors were unwilling to launch similar services. At the time, South Korea's roadway

KEY DATES

1960: Company is founded as Samyang Tire Company, with a factory in Kwangju, as part of the Kumho business group founded by Park In-chun in 1946.

1971: Samyang commissions a new factory in Songjung.

1976: Company goes public on the Seoul Stock Exchange.

1984: Samyang is merged into the Kumho business group.

1990: Company opens a technical center in Akron, Ohio.

1996: Company changes its name to Kumho Tire Company.

1997: Kumho completes its first factory in China, in Nanjing.

2005: Kumho begins construction of a factory in Vietnam.

2008: Kumho begins building a $225 million factory in Macon, Georgia.

infrastructure remained limited, and most of the country's national roadways had been damaged during the conflict.

The company nevertheless persevered, and by the 1960s had built up a fleet of more than 650 buses. By the end of the decade, Park's company was the largest bus operator in South Korea. With the rapid expansion of the company's fleet, Park was confronted with the shortage of replacement parts, and especially tires. South Korea's tire manufacturing industry remained in its infancy at the beginning of the 1960s, with the country relying heavily on imports.

Park recognized the opportunity to extend his business interests into the production of tires, both for buses and trucks, and for the country's small but growing fleet of private automobiles. In 1960, Park founded a new company, Samyang Tire, which ultimately grew into Kumho Tire Company.

EXPORTS IN 1965

Tire manufacturing technology remained rather limited in South Korea at the time. This meant that Samyang's initial operations were based on outdated, manual production techniques. As a result, the company's initial tire production barely topped 20 tires per day, or around 5,000 tires per year. This level contrasted sharply with Kumho Tire's capacity as it approached 2010, when the company expected its total production output to top 75 million tires per year.

Samyang quickly began expanding its product range in the early 1960s. In 1963, for example, the company became the first in Korea to begin producing tires for compact automobile models. The following year, the company extended its product offering again, with the production of inner tubes. Samyang was also boosted during this time by a partnership developed with Uniroyal in 1963, providing Samyang with much needed new technologies.

Samyang had also been expanding its production capacity. Yet South Korea's automotive population remained small through the 1960s, barely reaching a quarter of a million into the 1970s. As a result, Samyang, like its main domestic rival Hankook Tire, turned toward the export market. Samyang's first exports took place in 1965, supplying tires to Thailand. The company later extended its sales across the Asian region.

The company's export business soon gain a major new destination, however, when it was granted authorization by the U.S. Department of Transportation to supply tires to that country. The United States was then the world's single largest market for automotive tires. Among the company new products available for the United States during the second half of the 1960s were its first snow tires, launched in 1969.

GROWTH IN THE SEVENTIES

Samyang began construction of a new headquarters and production facility, the Songjung Plant, in Gwangju, in 1971. Completed in 1974, the new factory enabled the company to position itself as a leader in the South Korean market. The new plant opening came at a time of strong expansion for the country's automobile market, which quadrupled in size by the end of the decade. Samyang's production capacity was also raised by the creation, through parent company Kumho, of a synthetic rubber manufacturing plant in 1970. Kumho also added a new tire export subsidiary in 1972.

By 1976, Samyang had succeeded in claiming, if only temporarily, the leadership spot in the Korean tire industry. By then, the company's total annual output had topped one million tires. In that year, the company went public, listing its shares on the Seoul Stock Exchange. Rising demand both in Korea and from abroad led the company to extend the Songjung site, with the launch of construction of a second production facility in 1977.

Through the end of the decade, the company added to its tire range as well. The group began testing its first aircraft tires in 1976, and later became a major supplier to the Korean and other militaries, as well as commercial airlines. In 1978, Samyang debuted its first steel-belted radial tire, entering that fast-growing tire segment. Into the 1980s, the group also introduced its Rainbow tires, a range of colored tires for the passenger car market.

The company had also made impressive production gains during the decade. By 1980, Samyang's total production had topped 20 million tires since the company's founding. It took just three years for this figure to climb past the 30 million mark. In 1984, Samyang was merged into the Kumho Group, although the company did not formally change its name to Kumho Tire until 1996. Kumho Tire nonetheless became the flagship of the Kumho Group, which itself was developing into one of Korea's leading *chaebol,* or conglomerates.

CHINA ENTRY IN 1995

Kumho Tire moved its headquarters to Seoul in 1985. The 1980s marked a difficult period for the company, as it faced rising competition in the domestic tire market. This came especially strongly from longtime rival Hankook, which had begun its own growth drive during the decade. At the same time, Kumho was hit hard by the political turmoil of the era. Indeed, the company was hit by three major strikes during the decade. These in turn helped stimulate a major increase in labor costs for the company, as its payroll more than doubled between 1987 and 1991.

Nonetheless, Kumho Tire remained on the track toward growth. The company then began preparing to launch construction of a new manufacturing plant, in Koksung. Groundbreaking for the factory took place in 1987, with construction completed in 1990. This helped to raise the group's total production output past 100 million tires. Kumho Tire had also continued to invest in its technology, which enabled the group to enter the exclusive market for high performance tires. This led to the commercial debut of the group's Power Racer 60/65 high performance series in 1990. The following year, the company introduced its new generation Izen snow tire. Also in 1990, the company opened a small technical center in Akron, Ohio.

The completion of the Koksung plant provided Kumho with a major production boost. This enabled the company to claim a place among the global top ten by 1992. Like its main rivals, Kumho had also begun eyeing an entry into the mainland Chinese market. The economic reforms underway in that country had begun to transform the automotive market. The rise of a middle class there promised a major boom in automobile use.

At the same time, China had begun to position itself as the world's newest and largest low-cost manufacturing market. This factor was especially important for Kumho Tire, as soaring labor costs at home forced it to look for alternative production markets.

Kumho's own entry into China came in 1995, when the company broke ground on its first foreign factory, in Nanjing. That site was completed by 1996. Kumho Tire quickly unveiled plans for a number of new foreign facilities, announcing its intention to purchase an existing tire factory in Changchun in 1997. The company also indicated its interest in adding production facilities in India and Brazil as well.

U.S. FACTORY IN 2008

Kumho instead built an entirely new factory in China, located in Tientsin, completing construction there in 1997. The company had also been building an international R&D presence, adding a technical center in Birmingham, England, in 1998. The following year, Kumho Tire expanded its U.S. R&D presence, building a new 50,000-square-foot facility in Akron.

These investments helped the company position itself among the technological leaders in the global tire market. In 2000, for example, the company became one of just a handful of tire manufacturers to launch production of "run-flat" tires, tires that allow the driver to continue driving at reduced speeds in the event of a puncture. Kumho also invested heavily in machinery and facilities for production of UHP tires. This enabled the company to position itself among the leaders in this tire segment in the United States by the middle of the decade.

Kumho Tire developed a new strategy targeting an entry into the global top five by 2015. The importance of the U.S. market in achieving this strategy was underscored when the company announced plans to build a $225 million tire manufacturing facility, located in Macon, Georgia. Construction of the new factory got underway in 2008, and was expected to help raise the company's total annual capacity past 75 million tires by 2010.

The United States remained only part of Kumho's growth strategy. The group intended to continue to leverage its position as a major producer in China, and launched construction of a fourth factory, in Nanjing, in 2006. Around the same time, the company opened a dedicated R&D facility in Tianjin, China, in 2005.

Meanwhile, Kumho had identified another new market, Vietnam, opening a new $155 million factory there in 2008. Kumho Tire appeared on the right road toward achieving its ambition of cracking the global top five by 2015.

M. L. Cohen

PRINCIPAL SUBSIDIARIES

Kumho Tire (Changchun) Co., Inc.; Kumho Tire (Tianjin) Co., Inc.; Kumho Tire (Vietnam) Co., Ltd.; Kumho Tire Canada, Inc.; Kumho Tire China Co., Inc.; Kumho Tire Europe Gmbh; Kumho Tire France S.A.S.; Kumho Tire Japan., Inc.; Kumho Tire U.S.A., Inc.; Kumho Tyre (UK) Ltd.; Kumho Tyre Australia Pty., Ltd.; Nanjing Kumho Tire Co., Ltd.

PRINCIPAL OPERATING UNITS

Changchun plant; Gooksung plant; HQ and Gwangju plant; Namkyung plant; Pyungtaek plant; Tianjin plant; Vietnam plant.

PRINCIPAL COMPETITORS

Bridgestone Corp.; Continental AG; Compagnie Generale des Etablissements Michelin S.C.A.; Goodyear Tire and Rubber Co.; Hankook Tire Company Ltd.; Yokohama Rubber Company Ltd.; Pirelli Tyres Nederland B.V.; Sumitomo Rubber Industries Ltd.; Pirelli and C S.p.A.

FURTHER READING

Davis, Bruce, "Kumho Adds Plants in South Korea," *European Rubber Journal,* February 1, 2004, p. 3.

Dawson, Brad, "Kumho Tire Opens Akron Technical Center," *Rubber & Plastics News,* April 30, 2001, p. 3.

Hockensmith, Lisa, "Kumho Takes Aim at Fifth Spot Globally," *European Rubber Journal,* January 1, 2007, p. 8.

Kim, Hordon, "S. Korea's Kumho to Sell Its Interest in Tire Venture," *Rubber & Plastics News,* November 15, 1999, p. 3.

"Korea's Kumho Tire Idles Local Plants for 3 Days on Weak Demand," *AsiaPulse News,* April 17, 2009.

"Kumho Tire Confirms Plan to Build Factory in China," *European Rubber Journal,* November 1, 2005, p. 12.

Meyer, Bruce, "Firm Looks to Make Hay in Medium Truck Radials," *Rubber & Plastic News,* February 6, 2006, p. 10.

Shaw, David, "Kumho to Build $155m Car Tyre Plant in Vietnam," *European Rubber Journal,* May 1, 2006, p. 42.

The Liverpool Football Club and Athletic Grounds PLC

───────■───────

Anfield Road
Liverpool, L4 OTH
United Kingdom
Telephone: (+44-151) 263-2361
Fax: (+44-151) 260-8813
Web site: http://www.liverpoolfc.tv

Private Company
Incorporated: 1892 as Everton Football Club and Athletic Grounds Company Limited
Employees: 313
Sales: EUR 210.9 million (2008)
NAICS: 711211 Sports Teams and Clubs

■ ■ ■

The Liverpool Football Club and Athletic Grounds PLC owns and operates Liverpool Football Club (Liverpool F.C.) and the 45,500-seat Anfield property, the stadium in which Liverpool F.C. plays its home matches. Liverpool F.C. plays in the Barclays Premier League, the world's most watched sporting league and the world's most lucrative football (soccer) league. The Liverpool Football Club and Athletic Grounds generates its revenue from gate receipts, television contracts, cup competitions, and merchandise. Gate receipts, television revenue, and financial prizes won from cup competitions contribute nearly equally to the company's annual revenue volume, accounting for 75 percent of its annual revenue. Sponsorship payments and sales from merchandise account for the company's remaining 25 percent of annual revenue. The company is owned by

U.S. businessmen George Gillett Jr. and Thomas Hicks Sr.

SPAWNED FROM THE BELLY OF THE BEAST

Although not one of the original 12 clubs composing the English Football League during its inaugural season in 1888, Liverpool F.C. came into being because of a dispute within the ranks of one of the founding clubs, Everton F.C. Everton F.C. was formed a decade before the Football League was established, beginning as St. Domingo's F.C., a club formed by St. Domingo Methodist Church. In 1879, a year after its formation, the club changed its name to Everton F.C. and five years later began playing its matches on a pitch located between Anfield Road and Walton Breck Road, the renowned Anfield ground.

When Everton F.C. moved to its home ground, the club was led by its president, John Houlding, a brewery owner who years later was elected mayor of Liverpool. Ambitious, Houlding did not let his passion for Everton F.C. preclude his efforts to profit from his commitment, a stance that ironically led the president of Everton F.C. to create the club's archenemy, Liverpool F.C. Houlding purchased Anfield a year after Everton F.C. began playing at the ground, and he soon began charging his club rent for its use, £100 at first, but as the club began to shine on the pitch, Houlding began increasing the rent. By 1889, Everton F.C. was paying its president £250 per year to play at Anfield. In 1891, when Everton F.C. won its first league championship, Houlding wanted more. He approached Everton F.C.'s committee of directors, of which he was not a member, and pressed the committee

KEY DATES

1892: Liverpool Football Club and Athletic Grounds is formed by the president of Everton Football Club, John Houlding.

1901: Liverpool F.C. wins the First Division, its first league championship in England's uppermost league.

1954: Liverpool F.C. is relegated to the Second Division, where it remains for an eight-year period.

1959: Bill Shankly is named manager of Liverpool F.C.

1965: Club wins its first F.A. Cup.

1973: Liverpool F.C. wins its first European trophy, the UEFA Cup.

1977: The club wins the European Cup.

1985: Liverpool F.C. supporters charge Juventus supporters before the European Cup final at Heysel Stadium, resulting in 39 deaths.

1989: During Liverpool F.C.'s semifinal F.A. Cup match at Hillsborough Stadium, 96 supporters are killed.

2005: Liverpool F.C. wins its fifth European Cup.

2007: U.S. businessmen George Gillett Jr. and Thomas Hicks Sr. acquire The Liverpool Football Club and Athletic Grounds.

2009: Construction of a new stadium in Stanley Park is delayed because of the global economic crisis.

Goodison Park. In June 1892, Houlding changed the name of his new club to Liverpool Football Club and Athletic Grounds Company Limited, marking the birth of one of football's most successful clubs.

A TEAM IS BUILT FROM SCRATCH

The most vital task after the dispute was to create something out of nothing; Liverpool F.C. could not field a squad when it was formed. The club retained three former Everton F.C. players after the dispute, but it needed additional players. Houlding and the small group of Everton F.C. officials who remained at Anfield recruited 13 players from Scotland, enabling the team to begin play. The club's application to join the Football League was rejected, forcing Liverpool F.C. to join the Lancashire League, which the club dominated in its first season, thereby winning election to the Second Division of the Football League in 1893. The club adopted red as the primary color of its uniforms in 1894, distinct from the blue uniforms of Everton F.C., and earned promotion to the First Division before the end of the decade. In 1901, the club secured the first of a bevy of significant trophies, winning the First Division.

Success for Liverpool F.C., as for any of its rivals, hinged on its performance on the pitch. Winning league titles and tournaments netted the club the "hardware" that predicated its financial success. Victories kept gate receipts high, attracted the most skillful players, and, in later years, brought in corporate sponsorship agreements that accounted for a substantial percentage of a club's revenue. Victories also ensured a club did not lose its status within the English football league system, a hierarchy of leagues that used the annual rite of promotion and relegation to determine in which league a club participated. At the end of each season, the teams with the worst records exchanged places with the top performers in the league immediately below them. For a club, retaining its position within a league was of vital importance, determining its ability to keep and to attract quality players and its ability to generate revenue. Relegation, or "going down," could spell financial disaster for a club, particularly in the modern era of football, when television and sponsorship revenue played a pivotal role in a club's financial standing.

1900–50: STEADY PERFORMANCE

According to the metrics of success in football, Liverpool F.C. performed reasonably well during its first half-century of existence. The club won five First Division titles, securing the championship trophy in 1901, 1906, 1922, 1923, and 1947. One honor that eluded the club was capturing the Football Association Challenge Cup

to purchase Anfield along with a tract of adjoining land he also had purchased. The committee demurred, rejecting Houlding's proposal, resulting in a schism within Everton F.C.

Houlding's response to the committee's refusal to accept his offer left little doubt as to his willingness to negotiate. In March 1892, while Everton F.C. continued to play its matches at Anfield, Houlding formed Everton Football Club and Athletic Grounds Company Limited, intending to present his club with a fait accompli by taking over Everton F.C.'s upcoming schedule of matches, its "fixtures," and its position in the Football League. England's Football Council refused Houlding's application for his newly formed club, stipulating that it would not accept a new club with the same name as an existing club, but Everton F.C.'s committee realized it had become time to part ways. In April 1892, Everton F.C. played its last match at Anfield and moved to

(F.A. Cup), the most prestigious tournament in England. Liverpool F.C. appeared in its first F.A. Cup final in 1914, but lost the match, leading to a nearly 40-year wait before qualifying for another final. The lack of an F.A. Cup triumph aside, Liverpool F.C. could look with pride at its performance during the period. The club attracted a loyal following of supporters, known as "Kopites," derived from the Spion Kop, a stand at Anfield named after the Battle of Spion Kop in the Boer War, and except for a one-year drop to the Second Division in 1905, remained a top-flight club.

Liverpool F.C.'s second half-century on the pitch saw it establish itself as one of the most successful clubs in the world, but the period began on a sour note. When the club was relegated to the Second Division in 1905, it stormed back to top-flight football. Liverpool F.C. earned promotion at the end of its first season and stood atop the First Division the following year, securing its second championship in England's premier league. Such fortitude was absent when the club again slipped into the Second Division after finishing in 22nd place in 1954. Liverpool F.C. languished in the Second Division for eight seasons, suffering through the most depressing period in the club's first century of existence. The protracted stay in the Second Division marked the beginning of one of Liverpool F.C.'s most cherished eras, however, the arrival of the club's savior, the iconic Bill Shankly.

SHANKLY ERA BEGINS IN 1959

Shankly, who ordered his ashes to be scattered in the goalmouth at the Kop end at Anfield shortly before his death, became a Liverpool F.C. legend during his 14 seasons leading the club, leaving an indelible legacy remembered with reverence by generations of Kopites. Shankly was offered the job of Liverpool F.C.'s manager in 1951, but he declined because the club did not allow its manager to select the team for a particular match, a common practice among English clubs at the time. In 1959, when Liverpool F.C. was in its sixth season in the Second Division, the club's directors approached Shankly again, offering him full control over player selection. Shankly accepted the offer, becoming Liverpool F.C.'s manager in December 1959 and giving the club "a fanatic to whom defeat was unthinkable," as he was remembered in the February 21, 1988 edition of London's *Sunday Times*.

Shankly instilled a culture of winning at Liverpool F.C., holding sway as the charismatic, inspirational leader of a club he intended to take to the greatest heights of success. Under his watchful eye sweeping changes were made, beginning with the release of 24 players within his first year in charge. He convinced the club's directors to spend money on transfers to rebuild the squad, he changed training methods, and he pressed his players to reward the ardent Anfield supporters (the club was averaging attendance of more than 45,000 while it was in the Second Division) to give them what they wanted: a formidable, victorious force. Famously, he converted a room at Anfield where players stored their cleats, or "boots," into a tearoom for the coaching staff to discuss tactics, giving birth to Anfield's storied "Boot Room." The Boot Room discussions and Shankly's driving spirit soon led Liverpool F.C. out of the Second Division and served as the springboard for the club's success on the European stage.

Liverpool F.C. escaped the Second Division in 1962, Shankly's third season, and for the remainder of the century never finished lower than eighth place in England's uppermost league. The club won the First Division in 1964, its first top-flight championship since 1947, and secured two more First Division titles during Shankly's tenure, winning in 1966 and 1973. The club won its first European trophy, emerging as UEFA Cup winners in 1973, and it at last prevailed in its pursuit of the F.A. Cup, winning the coveted trophy in 1965 before adding a second in 1974, Shankly's last year in charge of the club.

CHAMPIONS OF EUROPE

After Shankly established a tradition of winning, his successor, a Boot Room assistant named Bob Paisley, reaped the rewards of a stalwart Liverpool F.C. side during his nine years as manager. Liverpool F.C. won an astonishing six league championships under Paisley, and the club's second UEFA Cup trophy in 1976. Arguably the most important achievement during the period was Liverpool F.C.'s rise to the top of Europe. In 1977, the club won the European Cup, beating a German club, Borussia Moenchengladbach, 3–1 to win the most prized trophy in Europe. The following year, Liverpool F.C. successfully defended its title, winning its second European Cup by beating a Belgian side, FC Bruges, 1–0.

Liverpool F.C. dominated English football during the 1980s, enjoying continued success under Paisley's replacement, Joe Fagan, and Fagan's successor, former Liverpool F.C. player Kenny Dalglish. The club finished atop the First Division after Fagan's first year in 1984, its third consecutive league championship, and it added three more league titles, winning in 1986, 1988, and 1990, giving Liverpool F.C. a total of 18 league championships. The club's domestic success also included winning the F.A. Cup in 1986 and 1989, while on the European front it added two more European Cups to its trophy case, winning in 1981 and 1984.

THE HORRORS OF HEYSEL AND HILLSBOROUGH

Liverpool F.C.'s most successful decade also included the darkest days endured by the club. In 1985, the club progressed to the final match of the European Cup, ready to defend its title from the previous year against the Italian side, Juventus, at Heysel Stadium in Brussels, Belgium. One hour before kickoff, a group of Liverpool F.C. supporters breached a fence separating them from Juventus supporters and rushed forward, causing the Italian supporters to retreat against a dilapidated retaining wall. The wall collapsed, killing 39 people, mostly Juventus supporters, and injuring roughly 600 other supporters in attendance. Disaster struck again four years later when Liverpool F.C. reached the semifinals of the F.A. Cup, pitted against Nottingham Forest F.C. in a match to be played at Hillsborough Stadium, the home ground of Sheffield Wednesday F.C. A frenzied rush to enter the stadium pressed Liverpool F.C. supporters against fencing, crushing them, and causing 96 deaths. The Heysel and Hillsborough tragedies left an indelible mark on the legacy of Liverpool F.C., scarring its history with two profoundly sad disasters. The club could never forget the events of 1985 and 1989, but it pressed forward, determined to engender far more positive memories of the years ahead.

After the wide-arcing swings of emotions during the 1980s, Liverpool F.C. lived through a relatively static existence during the 1990s. Except for winning the First Division in 1990, the only piece of hardware to be celebrated during the decade was winning the F.A. Cup in 1992.

In the first decade of the 21st century, Liverpool F.C.'s performance on the pitch began to improve. The club won the F.A. Cup in 2001 and 2006, giving it a total of seven titles in the competition. Liverpool F.C. failed to finish atop the Premier League, the new name of England's uppermost league, but it did achieve success in Europe, winning the UEFA Cup in 2001 and adding a fifth European Cup, rebranded as the Champions League, in 2005, fighting back from a three-goal deficit at halftime.

NEW OWNERS IN 2007

Shortly after the club's memorable victory in the Champions League final, Liverpool F.C. began to attract attention from corporate suitors. In December 2006, Dubai International Capital, the investment arm of the government of Dubai and its ruling family, announced it intended to buy the club, offering a reported £450 million to assume control over The Liverpool Football Club and Athletic Grounds PLC. The offer sparked competing offers, notably the £470 million bid submitted by George Gillett Jr., a U.S. businessman who owned the National Hockey League's Montreal Canadiens, and another American professional sport franchise owner, Thomas Hicks Sr., who owned Major League Baseball's Texas Rangers and the Dallas Stars, a National Hockey League team. Gillett and Hicks prevailed, taking control over the club and promising to build a new stadium for Liverpool F.C. in Stanley Park, near where Everton F.C. had established its home ground more than a century earlier.

Opposition to the American owners erupted after the sale, giving rise to protests by groups such as the "Sons of Shankly." The tension between the supporters and the new owners was not helped by the deteriorating economic conditions at the end of the decade. Gillett and Hicks had promised to begin construction of the new stadium within 60 days after the completion of the purchase, but depressed market conditions prompted Hicks and Gillett to delay their financial commitment to the project. By mid-2009, the club continued to hold back on moving forward with construction, casting a cloud of uncertainty on where Liverpool F.C. would attempt to replicate the halcyon days of the 1980s in the years ahead.

Jeffrey L. Covell

PRINCIPAL SUBSIDIARIES

LFC Properties Limited; LFC Leisure Limited; LFC Services Limited; LFC Television Limited; LFC TV Limited; LFC Limited; LFC Financial Services Limited; LFC Travel Limited; Liverpool Football Club Limited; Liverpool Limited.

PRINCIPAL COMPETITORS

Manchester United Limited; Chelsea FC PLC; Arsenal Holdings PLC.

FURTHER READING
Glick, Bryan, "A Labour of Love," *Computing*, March 22, 2007.
Jacobius, Arleen, "Hicks Has His Hands Full," *Pensions & Investments*, November 26, 2007, p. 8.
"Kick-Off Delayed Until Late 2009 at Liverpool," *Contract Journal*, September 10, 2008.
"King of the Kop," *Sunday Times*, February 21, 1988.
"News Analysis: How the Americans Wooed Liverpool," *PR Week*, February 23, 2007, p. 16.
"The Shankly Resurrection," *New Straits Times*, July 9, 2001.

Lululemon Athletica Inc.

2285 Clark Drive
Vancouver, British Columbia V5N 3G9
Canada
Telephone: (604) 732-6124
Toll Free: (877) 263-9300
Fax: (604) 874-6124
Web site: http://www.lululemon.com

Public Company
Incorporated: 1998
Employees: 2,861
Sales: $353.5 million (2008)
Stock Exchanges: NASDAQ Toronto
Ticker Symbols: LULU; LLL
NAICS: 339920 Sporting and Athletic Good Manufacturing

■ ■ ■

Lululemon Athletica Inc. is a leading manufacturer of yoga clothing and accessories. Although other sportswear manufacturers have yoga lines, Lululemon is unique in that it is almost entirely focused on yoga gear. Lululemon maintains its headquarters, as well as design and manufacturing facilities, in Vancouver, British Columbia. It also manufactures through factories elsewhere in Canada, the United States, Israel, India, China, Taiwan, and Indonesia. The company sells through its own network of company-owned retail stores. Lululemon had just over 100 retail outlets in 2009. These are located in Canada, the United States, Australia, and Hong Kong. Founded by a veteran of the

Canadian surf and snowboard clothing industry, the company seized on the yoga trend at the right moment. It was seen as one of the hottest retail stocks on the market when the company went public in 2007.

FROM SNOWBOARDING TO YOGA

Lululemon was founded by Dennis "Chip" Wilson. The yoga clothing company was his second venture into the athletic apparel business. Wilson grew up in Canada but had spent summers in California. He was a competitive swimmer and avid surfer, and frequently brought California swim trunks and shorts back to Canada, where styles were quite different. When he was still a teenager, he made approximately $100,000 working on the Alaska pipeline. This was enough money for him to buy a house, pay college tuition, and to start a business. After college he worked for an oil company, and on the side he manufactured his own small line of surfing shorts. In 1979 he incorporated as Westbeach Surf. The surfing line began to sag in popularity, but at the same time, Wilson saw that snowboarding was on the rise. He changed the company name and the product line in the early 1980s to Westbeach Snowboard.

Wilson ran Westbeach with two business partners. The company prospered initially, and found a loyal following in Japan. By the mid-1990s, the company was making some 80 percent of its sales in Japan. This meant that the company was precariously dependent on the exchange rate between the yen and the Canadian dollar. The fad status of snowboarding was also a factor. When snowboarding seemed to be declining in Japan in the late 1990s at the same time that the yen was weakening, Westbeach landed in financial difficulties. With the company on the verge of collapse, Wilson and partners sold Westbeach to the U.S. company Morrow Snowboards in November 1997.

Wilson was unclear what his next step would be. He worked briefly in the United States, then returned to Vancouver and began practicing yoga. Initially he was attracted to yoga because it helped him with his balance. In the meantime, his entrepreneur's eye noticed that the clothing most people wore to yoga classes tended to be heavy cotton. Cotton clothing lacked stretch and could grow heavy with sweat. Wilson believed he could create more comfortable clothing specifically designed for the yoga crowd. In 1998 Wilson incorporated Lululemon Athletica, and opened a store in the Kitsilano district of Vancouver. This first store was a combination yoga studio and retail space. Yoga teachers and practitioners offered their input on what worked and did not work in the clothing. The line featured fabrics, including Lululemon's own "luon," that wicked sweat away from the skin. The designs were also meant to be flattering enough that women could wear their yoga gear out for coffee or errands after class. The clothes were pricey, but incorporated many extra features, such as hidden pockets.

EARLY SUCCESS

Wilson claimed his initial goal was only to open the one Vancouver store. However, he seemed to have arrived on the market at just the right time. Yoga was rapidly increasing in popularity, and there were few competitors in the yoga apparel niche. Figures varied for how much the North American yoga apparel industry was worth overall, but the *Wall Street Journal* (August 19, 2005) estimated it at $1 billion by 2005. Yoga clothing in the late 1990s and early 2000s seemed to be following in the footsteps of workout gear in the 1980s. In that case, what started as apparel worn only in the gym became mainstream. After ten years, big name designers were producing high-end sweatpants meant for everyday wear. Lululemon began producing its flattering and comfortable yoga tops and pants at a time when more and more people were drawn to yoga, and others were drawn to the look of yoga. Other clothiers who had yoga lines

also saw this niche increase. For example, Danskin launched yoga clothes in 2001, and within four years noted that this category subsumed 20 percent of its activewear sales.

Not only did the Vancouver store flourish, but Lululemon soon licensed other stores in major Canadian cities. By 2003, the company had two stores in Vancouver as well as stores in Toronto, Calgary, and Victoria. Revenue doubled every year in these early times, and the company planned expansion into other Canadian cities. Lululemon hoped to move into major markets in California next. Founder Chip Wilson married one of the company's designers in 2002, and on their wedding day, by happy coincidence, the Kitsilano store did an astonishing $30,000 in sales. The company's Toronto store was expected to bring in only $900,000 in its first year. It surpassed the mark considerably, and did $2.9 million in sales. Everything seemed to be going right for the young company. Consumers could not get enough of Lululemon.

The company prospered in spite of doing little if any traditional marketing. New stores collaborated with area yoga teachers, asking them to try out the clothes and offer advice. Lululemon's sales associates were paid to attend yoga classes, to make sure the company stayed in touch with what yoga practitioners liked. The company also selected yoga teachers and other athletes to act as "ambassadors" for the clothing line. These people made Lululemon visible in their communities, and word of mouth helped propel the brand.

Lululemon advertised in local community newspapers rather than taking out ads in more traditional news sources. The maker of the textile Lycra, Invista, paid for lavish print ads featuring Lululemon clothing in 2003, as part of its own marketing campaign. These ads appeared in *Yoga Journal* and in Canadian home and fashion magazines. Characters on the popular television show *Desperate Housewives* also wore Lululemon, giving the brand broad mainstream visibility.

QUICK EXPANSION

With everything going right for Lululemon, the company moved rapidly to open new stores. By early 2005, the firm had 15 stores in Canada as well as three in the United States. It also opened its first outpost in Australia, and a store in Tokyo. Sales reached $60 million that year, and the company had over 300 employees. At this point, founder Wilson realized Lululemon had more potential than he knew how to handle. Consequently, he brought in a new chief executive and raised cash by selling a portion of the firm.

```
┌─────────────────────────────────────────────┐
│                                               │
│              KEY DATES                        │
│                   ■                           │
│  ─────────────────────────────────────        │
│                                               │
│  1979:  Lululemon founder Chip Wilson incorporates │
│         his first apparel company, Westbeach. │
│  1997:  Wilson sells Westbeach.               │
│  1998:  Lululemon is founded.                 │
│  2005:  Wilson sells 48 percent stake in firm and │
│         brings in new CEO Robert Meers.       │
│  2007:  Company goes public.                  │
│                                               │
└─────────────────────────────────────────────┘
```

In order to fund expansion, Wilson sold 48 percent of Lululemon in December 2005 to two venture capital firms. These were both based in Massachusetts: Advent International Corp. and Highland Capital Partners. The sale raised approximately $108 million. This gave Lululemon the capacity to roll out further stores at a quick pace. At the same time, Chip Wilson moved to the role of chairman of the board and chief designer, and brought in outside talent for day-to-day management. The new president and CEO was Robert Meers, the former CEO of Reebok International.

Meers had experience in exactly the area Lululemon needed. He had overseen expansion at Reebok from the mid-1980s to the end of the 1990s, when the sportswear brand had expanded across the globe. Reebok's revenue had grown from $13 million to $4.6 billion during Meers's tenure, and moved into markets in 120 countries. Meers was happy to repeat the experience with Lululemon. While recognizing that the brand still had lots of growth potential in Canada, Meers laid plans for new stores in major cities in the United States. He also planned to bring the brand into more Asian markets, and to debut in Europe.

By 2006, Lululemon had revenue of around $225 million. It had some 40 stores, with plans to grow to several hundred in the next few years. The company brought out a second clothing line, in its first expansion beyond yoga. This was a brand of casual clothing made from natural fibers such as hemp. It sold under the name Oqoqo (pronounced oh-ko-ko). Although Lululemon branched out, there was no hint that yoga had passed its peak. The number of American yoga practitioners had more than doubled between 2001 and 2006, and its popularity could also be seen worldwide. *Yoga Journal* was published in Europe and Asia, and chains of yoga studios were opening even in Hong Kong.

While yoga's rising star was bringing Lululemon with it, other companies began to encroach on the yoga apparel market. The California yoga apparel maker Prana was only a few years older than Lululemon. In 2005 the brand was bought by major apparel company Liz Claiborne. Other makers of athletic clothing, including Nike, Fila, and Danskin, were also coming out with yoga lines. Some smaller yoga apparel companies, such as Be Present, Inner Waves, and Marika, also had increasing visibility. Even some other clothiers not known at all for athletic wear, such as the lingerie chain Victoria's Secret and the teen apparel specialist American Eagle, jumped on the yoga wagon. Yet Lululemon, standing at the pricier end of the market, nevertheless managed to stand out.

GOING PUBLIC

The next step in bringing the brand further was to take the company public. Lululemon Athletica had its initial public offering (IPO) on the NASDAQ and the Toronto stock exchange in July 2007. Investors were excited and the offering went well. An analyst at the investment bank Credit Suisse was quoted in a profile of Lululemon in the *Economist* (December 15, 2007) saying, "This is one of the best growth stories in retail." The demographics for yoga were encouraging, and despite increasing competition, Lululemon was clearly a top brand, considered by many to be more authentic and purely yoga-oriented than yoga clothing lines brought out by other larger apparel companies. A writer for the Canadian business journal *Maclean's* (February 18, 2008) likened Lululemon's public offering to "the second coming of the Gap," referring to the blockbuster urban apparel company. Lululemon had more than just an aura of a good thing. Its financial record was stellar. Its stores sold an average of $1,400 per square foot, leading the apparel industry in Canada. It continued to double revenue, and to exceed that rate in profitability. At the IPO in July, shares of Lululemon started out at $18. By October, the share price had shot up to $60 before starting to settle.

The company got what seemed to be its first bad news in late 2007 when an unflattering story came out in the *New York Times*. The company had been selling T-shirts made partially from a seaweed-derived fiber called VitaSea. Lululemon claimed VitaSea released minerals into the wearer's skin. The *Times* story announced that independent testing had failed to find any trace of seaweed in the VitaSea shirts. Then government regulators chided Lululemon for making specific health claims about the fiber, which it had not substantiated. The company agreed to alter the labels on its VitaSea products, while trying to play down the significance of the controversy. Although its stock price did seem to fall based on the negative coverage, the company was soon able to announce profits had quadrupled for the quarter, compared to a year earlier.

Lululemon had gone public and brought in a new chief executive in order to carry out an aggressive store rollout that would double or triple its size. However, by early 2008, there were hints that the company might have to adjust its plans. Amid fears of an impending economic recession in the United States, an analyst at investment bank Goldman Sachs cut earnings estimates for the entire athletic apparel industry. A few months later, Lululemon CEO Robert Meers announced that he would retire in June. He would be replaced by Christine Day, a former Starbucks executive who had been at Lululemon only a few months.

MOVING AHEAD

Day's former company Starbucks in some ways shared a lot with Lululemon. Both companies sold at the high end of their markets, and built their reputations on being authentic, caring for the world as well as their customers, with a pronounced West Coast cultural stance. Starbucks had also gone through an immense global rollout. Day clearly understood how Starbucks' expansion had been difficult for the company as it grew away from its core product. The dilemma then with Lululemon was how to build up to several hundred stores without losing the grassroots and nontraditional feel of the brand. Day announced in mid-2008 that the company planned to have more than 250 stores worldwide by 2012. Most of the growth would be in Canada and the United States, although stores were planned as well in Asia and Europe. Day was well aware of the pitfalls of fast growth that might dilute the brand. She planned to proceed cautiously and to emphasize local community relations where new stores were established.

In any case, the global recession that hit in late 2008 caused Lululemon to rethink its fast expansion. As consumer spending tumbled, Lululemon's double-digit growth halted. For the fourth quarter of 2008, profits fell by 25 percent. Sales growth at stores that had been open at least a year fell by 8 percent. Lululemon predicted that it would see the same or worse in upcoming quarters. The company opened only six stores in 2009, down from 32 in 2008, and planned to open only another 15 in 2010. This was a firmly revised growth plan. Nonetheless, Lululemon continued to think strategically about long-term placement of the brand. It kept to its nontraditional marketing approach, and it also kept its prices mostly where they were.

Other retailers had been tempted to make significant price reductions in order to move merchandise. Lululemon's premium pricing, however, was part of the allure of the brand. Its basic yoga pants made with its signature luon fabric retailed for $100. The company felt it was wiser to keep the price there, although it marked down some other apparel items and accessories. While the gloomy retail outlook for the later years of the first decade of the 2000s forced some changes, Lululemon predicted improved profitability soon. The ultimate plan to grow to 300 stores was still in place, though it perhaps would not happen as quickly as management had once thought.

A. Woodward

PRINCIPAL COMPETITORS

Liz Claiborne, Inc.; Marika Group, Inc.; Triumph Apparel Corp.

FURTHER READING

Allan, Susan, "Om-Believable," *Ottawa Citizen,* April 12, 2003, p. E6.

Bogomolny, Laura, "Toned and Ready," *Canadian Business,* April 24–May 7, 2006, p. 59.

Gagne, Claire, "Small Shops, Big Ideas," *Marketing,* February 28, 2005, p. 11.

George, Lianne, "How Lululemon Lost Its Balance," *Maclean's,* February 18, 2008, p. 30.

Lazarus, Eve, "Stretching Its Influence," *Marketing,* November 20–November 27, 2006, p. 25.

———, "The Tao of Lululemon," *Marketing,* April 14, 2008, p. 23.

McConnon, Aili, "Lululemon's Next Workout," *Business Week,* June 9, 2008, p. 43.

Moran, Susan, "Meditate on This: Yoga Is Big Business," *New York Times,* December 28, 2006, p. C3.

Norton, Leslie P., "A Threat to a Growth Story," *Barron's,* April 14, 2008, p. M4.

Penner, Derrick, "Lululemon Fans Unfazed by Clothing Controversy," *Vancouver Sun,* November 21, 2007, p. F1.

Seipell, Tuija, "Consumer Karma," *Profit,* April/May 2003, p. 8.

Stewart, Monty, "Lululemon Boss Rides Creative Wave," *Business Edge,* May 16, 2008.

Strauss, Marina, "Lululemon's Plans for Lean Times," *Globe and Mail* (Toronto), March 28, 2009, p. B3.

Tait, Carrie, "Lululemon Won't Shrink Prices," *National Post,* June 12, 2009, p. FP 1.

Vascellaro, Jessica E., "Sexier Yoga Fashions Gain More Followers on the Street," *Wall Street Journal,* August 19, 2005, p. B1.

"Well Positioned," *Economist,* December 15, 2007, p. 77.

Marc Ecko Enterprises, Inc.

———————————————— ■ ————————————————

40 West 23rd Street
New York, New York 10010
U.S.A.
Telephone: (917) 262-1002
Web site: http://www.marceckoenterprises.com

Private Company
Founded: 1993
Employees: 1,400
Sales: $1.1 billion (2009 est.)
NAICS: 315223 Men's and Boys' Cut and Sew Shirt (Except Work Shirt) Manufacturing; 315232 Women's and Girls' Cut and Sew Bouse and Shirt Manufacturing; 315299 All Other Cut and Sew Apparel Manufacturing; 315999 Other Apparel Accessories and Other Apparel Manufacturing

■ ■ ■

Marc Ecko serves as the chairman and chief creative officer of the company bearing his name, Marc Ecko Enterprises, Inc. He is a patron saint especially to graffiti artists, known as much for his tussles with New York City authorities as for his fashion designs. The company, formed in the early 1990s, has evolved into a long-reaching fashion and lifestyle empire with merchandise available in 80 countries dotting the globe. Innovative marketing and use of a rhino logo have established an image recognized around the world, as both a fashion statement and state of mind. A fervent supporter of freedom of expression, Marc Ecko's unconventional wisdom and passion extend far beyond Ecko Enterprise's apparel and accessories to billboards, buildings, video games, television, film, and online social media including blogs, Facebook, MySpace, and YouTube.

HUMBLE BEGINNINGS: 1993–99

The precursor to Marc Ecko Enterprises, *ecko unlimited, was founded in 1993 by Marc Ecko, his twin sister Marci Tapper, and investor Seth Gerszberg, a student at Yeshiva University. Marc and Marci Milecofsky had grown up in Lakewood, New Jersey, where young Marc was called "Echo," since his parents had not known they were having twins and believed his heartbeat was an echo of his sister's. The nickname stuck and when the kids decided to start a clothing company, it was initially called Echo. Unfortunately, Echo was already trademarked, so they changed the name to "Ecko," which happened to be Marc's college sweetheart's last name.

Marc had been designing T-shirts since high school and had built a small legion of fans. After graduation he and Marci attended Rutgers University, where Marc studied pharmacy like his father while creating airbrushed T-shirts in their parents' garage. The siblings hawked the shirts wherever possible, including Marc's dorm room in New Brunswick, New Jersey, which became the company's first headquarters and warehouse.

The shirts, many custom-ordered, sold relatively well but sales were far from steady. Ecko's first celebrity endorsement came when Michael Bivens, a member of R&B/hip-hop group Bell Biv Devoe, wore some of Marc's designs. Bell Biv Devoe had scored big in the

COMPANY PERSPECTIVES

Our mission is to profoundly impact the youth culture landscape by offering diverse and dynamic brands, products and services that excite and inspire our customers.

early 1990s with their debut album, *Poison.* On the other side of the urban music spectrum was Chuck D of Public Enemy, who was also a fan and gave Ecko's designs a tougher image and street credibility. Marc quit Rutgers in 1993 to concentrate on the T-shirt business, and the rest was history in the making.

In 1996 Marc legally changed his surname to Ecko as the company scored several major promotional coups, including its first major advertising campaign and the opportunity to provide clothing for Steven Spielberg's *Jurassic Park* sequel, *The Lost World.* Seen by millions of teenagers around the world, the 1997 blockbuster gave the fledgling company a healthy boost. Sales for 1998 had reached about $15 million; however, the company wound up close to $7 million in debt. In desperate need of help, Marc Ecko Enterprises found a willing partner in the Texas-based Scope Import, Inc., a clothing wholesaler, which took a majority stake (80 percent) in the company and helped restructure operations. With backing and strategy in place, sales for 1999 reached over $35 million and the future was bright.

MAJOR GROWTH AND EXPANSION: 2000–04

Ecko's next innovation took the company's designs from the silver screen to the small screen, not network television but a television screen nonetheless, outfitting characters for an Electronic Arts video game called Knockout Kings 2000. The inspired move brought the company to the forefront of imaginative cross promotions, a fashion first that earned Ecko major exposure for its clothes and growing line of accessories including footwear, undergarments, and watches.

Never content to wait for the next salvo in the branding revolution, Ecko enlisted famed film director and producer Spike Lee to promote its apparel. Lee, an early fan of Ecko's designs, produced both a short film and runway show for New York City's "Seventh on 6th" fashion extravaganza in 2000. The year also marked several major developments, including the partners' buyout of Scope Import; an agreement with Playboy Enterprises to outfit Hugh Hefner's bunnies (a perfect

segue into women's apparel); international expansion via its first shipments to Japan; and sales almost cracking $100 million. The following year, 2001, Ecko broadened its scope even further with the acquisition of Zoo York, a hard-edged sports apparel brand worn by skateboarders, BMXers, and extreme sports enthusiasts.

In 2002 the company inked a deal with Timex to license an Ecko-branded watch collection for men, signed with Target Stores to sell a sportswear line called Physical Science, and launched a pop culture magazine called *Complex,* all of which helped propel sales to some $300 million. Next came the opening of Ecko's first retail store in Massachusetts and a partnership with hip-hop superstar 50 Cent to create and market a new men's collection, G-Unit, in 2003. Bigger news, however, was the upcoming launch of a new, higher-end menswear line. A departure from most of Ecko's more urban, sporty apparel, Marc Ecko Cut & Sew debuted in 2004 with more classically tailored menswear. A new clothing line for girls, *eckored, was also launched along with women's footwear designs under the *ecko unltd. brand.

Ecko's many brands and operations, including newly purchased outerwear manufacturer Avirex, were consolidated in 2004. The company was bringing in sales of a reported $1 billion plus annually and had over 800 employees. The new firm was christened Marc Ecko Enterprises, Inc. (MEE) and opened a new 275,000-square-foot headquarters complex in the Chelsea region of New York City. The year also marked Marc's inclusion in *Details* magazine's "Power 50" list as one of the nation's most influential men under the age of 42.

CONTROVERSY, DOLLARS, ACTIVISM: 2005–06

By 2005 Ecko's transformation from an urban fashion brand to bona fide clothing empire was complete, while Marc earned a fabled accolade of his own: He became the youngest person ever invited to join the Council of Fashion Designers, one of the fashion world's most revered organizations. Gaining the council's stamp of approval was a major achievement, legitimizing Marc's status as a designer, trendsetter, and businessman.

Further milestones in 2005 included another kind of legitimacy as a baby Indian rhinoceros at the San Diego Zoo was named Ecko. The company's rhino logo had achieved international fame and recognition, and the baby rhino's christening marked Ecko's elevation to pop culture icon, especially since Indian rhinos were known to live for up to 40 years. The company also gave back to the community with the creation of Sweat Equity Enterprises, a program for underprivileged

---

KEY DATES

1993: Marc Ecko, Seth Gerszberg, and Marci Tapper form a T-shirt company in New Jersey.
1996: Company initiates its first major advertising campaign and www.eckounltd.com is launched.
1997: Ecko clothes are featured in Steven Spielberg's *Jurassic Park: The Lost World.*
1998: Ecko brand doubles its sales from the previous year.
1999: Ecko takes on a Texas partner and outfits characters in a video game.
2000: Spike Lee and Playboy Enterprises help promote the Ecko brand.
2001: Company acquires the Zoo York action sports apparel line.
2003: Hip-hop star 50 Cent partners with Ecko to create a new clothing line, G-Unit.
2004: New headquarters opens in New York City.
2005: Marc Ecko is offered membership in the Council of Fashion Designers.
2007: Shopecko.com, is launched.
2008: Company celebrates 15 years in business.
2009: Marc Ecko receives an honorary degree from Rutgers University.

---

teenagers interested in career training. Marc later likened the program to "one part Willy Wonka and one part *The Apprentice* tweaked for high school kids," in an *Adweek* interview (April 7, 2008).

Community had become a major theme for all three founders, but Marc had become increasingly aware of issues affecting young artists, especially graffiti artists or "taggers." In the middle of the first decade of the 2000s he was involved in several legal skirmishes on behalf of teen artists. Initially, he battled the city of New York over clothing deemed "taggin' gear," often worn by street artists. The case decreed certain urban clothing brands contributed to the delinquency of minors, which Marc found preposterous. He won the battle in 2005 and answered authorities with the release of the company's first video game through a partnership with Atari, Getting Up: Contents Under Pressure, about graffiti artists.

Ecko planned to celebrate the game's release with a street party, having renowned graffiti artists decorating old subway cars. Yet New York Mayor Michael Bloomberg and Queens city council members revoked his permit stating such a gathering could devolve into vandalism (aka graffiti) and possible violence. Marc filed a lawsuit, won the case when a federal judge cited freedom of speech issues, and gained loads of publicity. The wrangling led to an anti-graffiti bill that made it illegal for 18- to 21-year-olds to possess spray paint. Marc again fought city officials and again won, making him a hero to the young and a bit of an embarrassment to older fashion industry stalwarts.

Many would say Ecko went too far with its next stunt, tagging Air Force One with the words "Still Free," creating a viral video that hit the airwaves of every major news channel. The plane, it turned out, was a replica (the Pentagon even issued statements to this effect), and the hooded graffiti artist was Marc himself. As he was quoted on his web site, "Being provocative for its own sake is useless (and annoying). But when you can be provocative and raise important issues, those are the real watershed moments." The Air Force One $1 million marketing stunt not only made the designer the Pied Piper of graffiti artists nationwide, but made him an award-winning international sensation.

ECKO MATURES: 2007 AND BEYOND

On the less controversial side came the debut of eckoTV, a new marketing tool for reaching consumers in Ecko's retail outlets, including the new 32,000-square-foot store in Times Square. Although some of eckoTV's content might have been considered a bit racy to some, it proved an effective way of generating sales with teens and twentysomethings, an audience possessing an increasing amount of disposable income. Ecko's growing entertainment division also scored two lucrative deals in 2007: the first with Human Head Studios to develop new video games and programming, and a second with Lucasfilms, Ltd., to design and sell a tie-in apparel line inspired by the new *Star Wars* movie and game. In addition, shopping for Ecko branded clothes became much easier with the debut of a full-service e-commerce site, shopecko.com.

Once again thinking outside the box, Ecko scored another marketing boost courtesy of the Food Network's hit cooking show, *Iron Chef America.* Ecko signed on to design jackets for each of the four Iron Chefs (Bobby Flay, Mario Batali, Cat Cora, and Michael Symon) featured throughout the hour-long show. Designed to showcase each chef's personality and eccentricities, the new jackets varied in style and color, winning rave reviews from the individual chefs as well as viewers. The attention helped *ecko unltd. bring in sales of more than $700 million for 2007, while MEE brought in overall revenues of more than $1.4 billion for the year.

In 2008 the company celebrated 15 years in business. Among the new product launches were a revamped designer jeans line, Ecko MFG, and a licensing deal with Parlux Fragrances, Inc., to produce a fragrance collection. The company also continued to fund outreach programs like STOKED (Successful Teens with Knowledge, Experience, and Determination) which gave teenagers the opportunity to learn and perfect board (surf, snow, and skate) sports, and supported a Jewish orphanage in Ukraine called Tikva Children's Home.

In 2009 Marc received an honorary degree from Rutgers University while he and the company prepared for the launch of Ecko Rx, an upscale Italian-styled menswear line. As Ecko Enterprises neared the end of the decade, the former garage operation had over 1,400 global employees and had garnered coast to coast recognition throughout North America and a rising worldwide presence through international subsidiaries in France, Germany, Hong Kong, Italy, and Sweden. More than 5,000 domestic specialty and department stores and 70 Ecko retail stores carried Ecko-branded merchandise, while the company's rhino was known across the globe as a symbol of life, liberty, and the pursuit of artistic expression.

Nelson Rhodes

PRINCIPAL SUBSIDIARIES

*ecko unltd.; Marc Ecko Cut & Sew; Marc Ecko Entertainment; Marc Ecko Enterprises International; Avirex Sportswear; G-Unit Clothing Company; Zoo York; Complex Media LLC; Sweat Equity Enterprises.

PRINCIPAL COMPETITORS

Abercrombie & Fitch; Diesel SpA; FUBU; Phat Fashions LLC; Roc Apparel Group LLC; Tommy Hilfiger Corporation; Zumiez Inc.

FURTHER READING

Bailey, Lee, "Marc Ecko Realigns," *WWD,* June 5, 2006, p. 17.

Butler, Elizabeth, "Graffiti Artist Tags Clothing Lines," *Crain's New York Business,* January 31, 2005, p. 20.

Carracher, Jamie, "Ecko Heard in the Ukraine," *Daily News Record,* May 31, 2004, p. 30.

Clarrissimeaux, Anne, "The Next Generation: With Impatience and Exuberance, Raw Talent and Instincts, These Exciting Young Entrepreneurs Are Setting the World on Fire," *Success,* November 2008, pp. 56+.

Cooper, Andrea, "Who Wants to Be a Billionaire," *Entrepreneur,* February 2008, pp. 66+.

Curan, Catherine, "Jersey Guy Walks the City's Hip-Hop Clothing Beat," *Crain's New York Business,* February 16, 2004, p. 4.

"Ecko Line to Be Sold at Target," *MMR,* January 14, 2002, p. 29.

Farrar, Jennifer, "Film Meets Fashion," *Houston Chronicle,* December 23, 2007, p. 4.

High, Kamau, "Marc Ecko: On Fusing High-School Hustle with Fashion," *Adweek,* April 7, 2008, p. 34.

Lubow, Arthur, "It's Going to Be Big," *Inc.,* March 2009, pp. 52+.

Meoli, Daria, "Too Fat to Break Dance," *New Jersey Monthly,* January 2005, pp. 31+.

"Power 100," *Daily News Record,* October 30, 2006, p. 23.

Robertson, Jordan, "Toe the Line Between Corporate and Cool," *Business 2.0,* November 2004, p. 86.

Schneider-Levy, Barbara, "Marc Ecko Has Transformed Himself from Graffiti Artist to Innovative Clothing and Footwear Designer," *Daily News Record,* April 2, 1999, p. 20.

Master Spas Inc.

─────■─────

6927 Lincoln Parkway
Fort Wayne, Indiana 46804-5623
U.S.A.
Telephone: (260) 436-9100
Fax: (260) 432-7935
Web site: http://www.masterspas.com

Private Company
Incorporated: 1996
Employees: 350
Sales: $51.6 million (2007)
NAICS: 339999 All Other Miscellaneous Manufacturing

■ ■ ■

A private company based in Fort Wayne, Indiana, Master Spas Inc. is a highly regarded manufacturer of portable hot tubs and luxury spas. Always in the forefront of innovation in the industry, Master Spas is responsible for the incorporation of television and stereo units into hot tubs as well as the development of a propulsion exercise system that makes spa swimming possible, essentially creating an aquatic treadmill. The company's Legend series of hot tubs is available in seven sizes, from units that can seat two or three people and house 31 water jets, to ones that offer a seating capacity of seven to eight people and include 115 jets. Master Spas' H2X series of exercise spas includes the H2X Swim Spa, nearly 17 feet in length; the slightly shorter H2X CrossTrainer Swim Spa; and the more compact H2XCrossTrainer2 Swim Spa, 12 feet in length. The shells of the hot tubs and spas are available in a variety of solid colors or natural stone appearances, and rather than wood, Master Spas units rely on long-lasting polymer skirting, again available in a wide range of colors and textures.

The company is also on the cutting edge in its choice of insulation, eschewing the usual urethane foam for Icynene, a foam that expands 100 times its initial volume to fully insulate and air-seal the underside of the units, thus eliminating cold spots and lowering energy costs. Master Spas' multistage filtration system also relies on a patented porous membrane medium. Each hot tub and spa is self-contained and does not require any special plumbing or drainage.

The company operates a 250,000-square-foot manufacturing facility as well as a five-acre distribution center in Fort Wayne. Sales are handled through a national network of about 250 dealer and contract service centers. In recent years Master Spas has also grown sales in Europe. The company is headed by its president, Robert Lauter.

JACUZZI FAMILY CREATES HOT TUB INDUSTRY

The medicinal benefits of hot swirling water were well known for many years, but it was not available for home use until the post–World War II era when the Jacuzzi family of California perfected the necessary technology. In the early 1900s seven Jacuzzi brothers emigrated from Italy to California. All trained engineers, they formed an aviation company that developed propellers and later diversified into irrigation pumps.

A member of the second generation, Candido Jacuzzi, was responsible for initiating the company's development of the hot tub. In 1948 his son Kenneth, who suffered from severe rheumatoid arthritis, was receiving hydrotherapy treatments that were conducted in a hospital pool with water agitated by a jet pump. Jacuzzi recognized that the hydrotherapy pump operated on a principle similar to the industrial pumps produced by the family company. He assigned a team of Jacuzzi engineers the task of developing a hydrotherapy pump, resulting in a portable pump that could be used in a bathtub to provide hydromassage. Called the J-300, it was marketed through surgical supply stores. The therapeutic effects of the whirlpool pump caught the attention of athletes and became common in spas across the United States.

HOT TUB INDUSTRY TAKES SHAPE: 1968

Roy Jacuzzi, a member of the third generation of the Jacuzzi family and the new head of the research division, took the pump a step further in 1968 when he decided to build the J-300 into a bathtub, resulting in the Roman Bath. It was received well enough that in 1970 Jacuzzi introduced a larger unit, the Adonis, and in 1972 a two-person bath called the Gemini. Larger models billed as spas then followed and found a ready market in California among celebrities and other well-to-do consumers who referred to the whirlpool baths simply as Jacuzzis.

Interest in hot tubs spread across the country and dozens of other companies looked to become involved in their manufacture, including Fort Wayne Pools, Inc., of Indiana. Founded in the early 1970s, the company began manufacturing low-end whirlpool spas in 1978. It was a year later that Robert Lauter got his start in the hot tub business, founding a distributorship that soon became the country's largest wholesale spa distributor. In 1988 he joined Fort Wayne Pools to head the spa division, which under his leadership enjoyed record sales and profits. After seven years he left to become vice-president of L.A. Spas in Etowah, Tennessee, enjoying equal success.

CREATION OF MASTER SPAS: 1996

In the spring of 1996 Lauter returned to Indiana to lead a buyout of the Fort Wayne Pools spa division, which was underperforming. Lauter renamed the operation Master Spas Inc. The company he acquired was housed in a 100,000-square-foot facility that employed 50 people producing low-end hot tubs that were sold under the Down East Spas, Legacy Whirlpool, Tropical Spas, and Holiday Springs Spas names to such large home centers as Home Depot, Builders Square, National Home Centers, and Home Quarters. The low-margin business was generating less than $6 million in annual revenues.

Lauter's plan was to continue to sell low-end spas to home centers while developing higher-end models to be sold through specialty retailers. The new Master Spa line was introduced to the market in early 1997. It combined the best features of the best-selling spas, packaged with a new look. To help promote its products, Master Spas then signed professional golfer Steve Jones, winner of the U.S. Open in 1996, as its spokesperson.

Master Spas was making progress in building a dealer network when it suffered a major setback in 1999. Master Spas was still very much dependent on its low-end models and its largest customer, Hechinger/Home Quarters/Builders Square declared bankruptcy. Not only did Master Spas lose 40 percent of its business in one stroke, it had to absorb $250,000 in billings it would never recover. "We decided," Lauter told *Indianapolis Business Journal* in 2003, "to focus on developing the most innovative products for our industry, help our dealers learn how to sell them and then find a way to drive consumers into their showroom."

PURSUING ITS GAME PLAN

Despite working with a limited budget Master Spas pursued its game plan and soon introduced an industry first by incorporating bio-magnetic therapy in a spa. The company also tried to cater to its customers by conducting surveys, focus groups, and dealer roundtables. Out of this effort emerged the Spa Theater System, the first luxury spa in the industry to incorporate audio and visual equipment, including pop-up flat-screen televisions and floating remote controls. The introduction of the theater system set Master Spas apart from the competition, which scrambled to catch up. Master Spas adopted the policy

KEY DATES

1978: Fort Wayne Pools begins manufacturing whirlpool spas.
1996: Robert Lauter acquires assets of Fort Wayne Pools to create Master Spas Inc.
1997: Luxury spa line is introduced.
1999: Bankruptcy of major home center customer causes setback.
2003: *Consumer Reports* lists Master Spas as Best Buy in Premium spa category.
2005: New warehouse and dealer development center opens.
2006: Spa-swimming pool is introduced.

of pursuing new products only if it could offer a dramatic improvement over what was available on the market. Otherwise, the company opted to pass.

In order to market its upscale spas, Master Spas signed a new spokesperson, soccer player Michelle Akers. Lauter's daughter played soccer at the University of Tennessee and it was while attending one of her games that Lauter noticed the parking areas were filled with expensive vehicles, owned by people, presumably "soccer moms," who had the kind of disposable income that made them potential spa customers. He also knew that Akers had used Master Spas products and as a very popular woman soccer player she would make an ideal celebrity promoter of the brand. Master Spas also helped dealers to better sell its products by providing glossy brochures and in-store displays and by developing the industry's first showroom interactive information system. Furthermore, the company drove traffic to dealer showrooms through its web site, which sent visitors promotional videos and the name of the closest dealer. It soon became the industry's most visited web site.

To keep up with growing demand, Master Spas purchased an adjacent property in the summer of 2000 to house a distribution center and customer service operation. It was subsequently expanded to 75,000 square feet. In 2001 it appeared that with the economy lapsing into recession the extra space would be unnecessary, but while the spa industry as a whole suffered a 25 percent drop in sales, Master Spas enjoyed strong sales growth. After the terrorist attacks against the United States on September 11, 2001, further damaged the economy, the company anticipated lean times ahead. On the weekend following the attacks, however, a Master

Spas dealer held a scheduled sale and surprisingly the dealer experienced a 40 percent increase over the amount of sales generated from a similar event a year earlier. Many customers indicated that instead of taking a trip, they were opting to invest in their homes and install spas. To build on that sentiment, Master Spas portrayed spas as a backyard vacation and a way to bring families together. Instead of a disappointing year, Master Spas in 2001 enjoyed a 48 percent increase in sales over the prior year, which rose to $28 million. For his efforts, Lauter was named an Ernst & Young Entrepreneur of the Year in 2002.

PRESIDENTIAL RETREAT ADDS SPA: 2003

Sales continued to grow at an impressive rate in 2002, increasing to about $42 million for the year. The company also received county permission to add another 35,000 square feet in manufacturing space. Helping to drive further sales increases in 2003 was Master Spas being listed by *Consumer Reports* as the Best Buy in the Premium category of spas the magazine reviewed. A few weeks later in 2003 the company received another boost when the White House elected to install a Master Spas unit at the presidential retreat at Camp David.

A year later the company began to exploit the benefits of product placement on television shows and movies, which proved more effective than the $1 million a year the company had been spending on cable television advertising. The value of product placement had become apparent early in 2004 when comedian Wayne Brady jumped into a spa while fully dressed during an episode of his daytime variety show, *The Wayne Brady Show.* Traffic to the company's web site spiked, leading to a concerted effort to land additional placements of Master Spas hot tubs in the media. The placements came to include a spa given away on *The Price Is Right* and appearances on *The Oprah Winfrey Show* and in the Jim Carrey movie *Fun with Dick and Jane.* A spa was also among the upgrades made to a California home on the season premiere of *Extreme Makeover: Home Edition.*

A third building was added to Master Spas' Fort Wayne complex in late 2005. The new 60,000-square-foot facility included a raw-materials warehouse and a new dealer development center and concept retail store to provide training to dealers. The company also remained in the vanguard of spa innovation in 2005 by obtaining the patent to a new filter system for spas and swimming pools. It featured a microfilter surrounding a primary filter that contained a porous membrane composed of multiple plies.

INTRODUCTION OF
SPA-SWIMMING POOL: 2006

Master Spas built on its reputation as an innovator in 2006 with the introduction of its revolutionary combination spa-swimming pool, using a patented propulsion system to create a constant stream of water to allow a person to swim in place. Not only was it suitable for exercise, it also was useful in helping people recover from back surgery and knee replacement surgery, improving circulation, relieving pressure on joints, or simply providing a soothing massage. In 2007 Master Spas made the unit's current generator available on the market, allowing any pool to become an aquatic exercise machine.

To maintain its edge, Master Spas continued to challenge conventional thinking. The company's process engineers suggested that the spas be manufactured upside down, an idea that was adopted in early 2006 following the restructuring of the manufacturing facilities. The new approach was especially useful in the plumbing process, providing easier access to a spa's underside. Another way to remain fresh was to maintain close tabs on trends in other industries. In keeping with this philosophy Master Spas hired a pair of former automobile industry veterans to offer the manufacturing perspective of another industry.

Although hot tub sales began to slump in 2004, Master Spas continued to grow, due in large measure to its ability to remain in the forefront of spa technology. In 2008 the company introduced the H2X CrossTrainer, offering improved swimming control. The company was also doing well with international sales, enjoying strong growth in Europe, Russia, and China. About 14 percent of all sales came from overseas by 2008, an amount that was expected to increase significantly in the years to come. Also boding well for Master Spas was the "graying of America." As baby boomers looked to spas to ease the aches and pains of old age, the company had good reason to expect increased sales for years to come.

Ed Dinger

PRINCIPAL COMPETITORS

Blue Falls Manufacturing Ltd.; Coast Spas Manufacturing Inc.; Sundance Spas, Inc.

FURTHER READING

Clark, Thomas, "Getting the Message," *Pool & Spa News,* March 22, 2002, p. 46.

Cole, Stacy, "Indiana's Entrepreneurs of the Year," *Indiana Business Magazine,* September 2002, p. 8.

"Ernst & Young Entrepreneur of the Year: Robert Lauter," *Business People Magazine,* July 1, 2001.

Frazier, Lynne McKenna, "Indiana's Fort Wayne Pools Inc. Sells Spa Division," *Fort Wayne (Ind.) Journal Sentinel,* April 11, 1996.

Glenn, Jenni, "Master Spas Soaking in TV Attention," *Fort Wayne (Ind.) Journal Gazette,* September 23, 2004, p. 11B.

Green, Lisa, "Celebrity Sweepstake Companies Count on Product Pitchmen to Boost Sales, Image," *Fort Wayne (Ind.) Journal Gazette,* October 2, 2000, p. 1C.

Hans, Jennifer Dawn, "Masters of the Industry," *Business People Magazine,* February 1, 2006.

Lehman, Bruce, "An International Leader: Master Spas Inc.," *Business People Magazine,* February 1, 2008.

"Master Spas," *Business People Magazine,* February 1, 1998, p. 132.

"Master Spas, Inc.," *Indianapolis Business Journal,* October 20, 2003, p. S10.

McMurry, Inc.

1010 East Missouri Avenue
Phoenix, Arizona 85014-2602
U.S.A.
Telephone: (602) 395-5850
Toll Free: (888) 626-8779
Fax: (602) 395-5853
Web site: http://www.mcmurry.com

Private Company
Founded: 1984
Employees: 185
Sales: $55 million (2009 est.)
NAICS: 541810 Advertising Agencies; 511120 Periodical Publishers

■ ■ ■

Preston V. McMurry Jr. has several claims to fame, not the least of which is McMurry, Inc., a Phoenix, Arizona-based marketing firm. McMurry is well known throughout the Phoenix-Tempe area for his communications prowess, having begun his career in the healthcare field in which he transformed *Vim & Vigor* magazine into an industry powerhouse. McMurry segued from his hospital roots in advertising to provide superior services for clients in all business sectors, both large and small. McMurry, Inc., not only creates award-winning campaigns for its growing clientele, but also publishes dozens of specialized magazines and newsletters.

PIGSKIN HERO BECOMES BUSINESSMAN

Health and fitness were always important in Preston McMurry's life. His athletic skills grew throughout his childhood in Mt. Lebanon, a suburb south of Pittsburgh, Pennsylvania. While attending Mt. Lebanon High School, McMurry distinguished himself as a star running back for the football team. When he was graduated in 1955, he was offered football scholarships at colleges and universities across the country. A fateful airport encounter sent the future entrepreneur to Ohio State University in Columbus.

Encouraged by his mother to consider Ohio State, McMurry was waiting for a flight at Pittsburgh International Airport when he ran into a gentleman named Woody Hayes. Hayes was the hot-tempered yet beloved coach of Ohio State's Buckeye football team. As a result of the encounter, McMurry attended Ohio State and played for Hayes, getting to the Rose Bowl in Pasadena, California, where the team played the University of Oregon Ducks on January 1, 1958. The Buckeyes won the game (10–7) and the title of national champions for Hayes, who was also named College Coach of the Year.

In 1960, two years after his Rose Bowl appearance, McMurry left Ohio State University armed with a bachelor's degree in social administration. With lessons learned on the Buckeyes' football field and from Hayes's fiery yet righteous determination, McMurry began looking for a career in social services that had room for creativity. He also took graduate classes at Chicago's

COMPANY PERSPECTIVES

Our mission is doing business for profit. First yours. Then ours. We do this by creating marketing communications appreciated by audiences everywhere and by providing selfless service always.

Loyola University and Franklin University in Columbus over the next few years.

By the 1970s McMurry had found his niche: public relations in the healthcare field. In 1971 while working as a public relations executive at St. Francis Hospital in Milwaukee, McMurry took on the responsibilities of updating the hospital's monthly direct-mail newsletter, *Pulse.* Inserting interesting tidbits, short articles of interest, and columns, he also added a small advertisement for the facility's walk-in clinic.

The ad created a firestorm of controversy and a surge in patients for the clinic, called VertiCare. Hospital administrators, community members, and medical staff all weighed in on what many believed was an ethical matter: "selling" or profiting from basic healthcare services. Even the Wisconsin Medical Society was involved in the matter, bringing the issue before its board of ethics. The furor and investigation lasted for more than a year and VertiCare reaped the benefits, with monthly patient visits increasing twentyfold.

In the end, St. Francis and the Wisconsin Medical Board reached an agreement to permit advertising if it met specific guidelines. For McMurry the brouhaha led to a major career milestone: Marketing and healthcare were not mutually exclusive; communication was an asset in the healthcare industry as surely as it was in any other business segment. As McMurry later commented to the *Phoenix Business Journal* in a January 13, 1992, article, the incident clearly "demonstrated marketing's power to enhance an institution's bottom-line performance."

LIVING WITH *VIM & VIGOR* IN THE EIGHTIES

Along with his public relations duties, McMurry had become involved with a number of charities and foundations, the beginning of a lifelong commitment to fundraising. He also created an eponymous company in 1984 before leaving St. Francis to become executive vice-president of Baptist Hospitals and Health Systems of Phoenix in 1985.

In his first year at Baptist, Preston created a newsletter/magazine called *Vim & Vigor.* Having learned the value of promotion from his post at St. Francis, he included advertising, albeit meeting strict guidelines, and *Vim & Vigor* soon became an industry leader in healthcare publications. Hospitals around the country contracted with Baptist for customized full-color versions of *Vim & Vigor,* tailored to meet their community's needs.

McMurry's brainchild became a full-fledged quarterly magazine, attracting thousands of subscribers and licensees. Licensing fees varied according to a sliding scale, taking into consideration the size of the client (usually calculated by the total number of beds in hospitals) and the size of their mailing list. Licensees were also given extensive reprint opportunities (at no additional cost) for their own advertising campaigns.

In 1989 McMurry realized his creation had bona fide bestseller potential and bought the publication from Baptist Hospitals. The magazine continued publication in the same manner, although it was solely under the direction of McMurry and his staff.

GROWTH AND EXPANSION IN THE NINETIES

By 1991 *Vim & Vigor* had a paid circulation of about 700,000 subscribers. Each 72-page quarterly issue contained 50 pages of health-related features and 22 customized "local" pages chosen by clients. McMurry offered licensees a wealth of information from its in-house library, boasting hundred of articles, artwork, photographs, and even ad copy. Although clients customized their 22-page portion, McMurry still thoroughly edited each edition for style and consistency.

As *Vim & Vigor* continued to grow, McMurry launched a second publication, *Health Direct,* an eight-page quarterly newsletter. *Health Direct,* like its predecessor, was licensed to hospital groups with a simpler, easy-to-read format and more specialized content. Revenues for 1991 reached about $1 million but had grown to more than $5 million for 1992 because of increased licensing for both *Vim & Vigor* and *Health Direct.*

By 1994 *Vim & Vigor*'s paid circulation had grown to more than 900,000 subscribers, while staffers began work on a Spanish-language version, *Salud y Vigor.* Created for Miami-based Cedars Medical Center with an initial circulation of 30,000, *Salud* soon tapped into the rapidly growing Hispanic population of the area and became a hit. Its success, along with the original *Vim & Vigor* helped drive revenues to a reported $7.5 million for 1994.

KEY DATES

1958: Running back Preston McMurry and the Ohio State Buckeyes win the Rose Bowl.

1960: McMurry earns a degree in social administration from Ohio State University.

1971: McMurry revitalizes *Pulse,* a hospital newsletter, proving healthcare and marketing are not mutually exclusive.

1984: McMurry founds an eponymous company in Phoenix, Arizona.

1985: *Vim & Vigor* quarterly magazine is created for Phoenix's Baptist Hospitals and Health Systems.

1989: McMurry buys the rights to *Vim & Vigor* and takes the magazine private.

1994: *Vim & Vigor* reaches a paid circulation of 900,000.

1997: *Miracles,* a magazine for the Children's Miracle Network, is launched by McMurry.

2000: Chris McMurry is promoted to CEO with father Preston remaining president and chairman.

2001: McMurry takes over *Driven,* a quarterly magazine for Mothers Against Drunk Driving.

2008: McMurry buys an interactive marketing agency, Contact Designs, based in Phoenix.

2009: Company buys its second interactive media firm, Cyrus, of Orlando, Florida.

Over the next few years McMurry created several custom publications including *Miracles,* a magazine for the Children's Miracle Network (1997) and Planned Parenthood's quarterly *Choices* (1998) for distribution at its 900 centers nationwide. The company also made an acquisition: the *SmartHealth* magazine and newsletter unit of New York-based Meigher Communications, bringing an additional network of 44 hospitals and health maintenance organizations to its custom publishing operation.

As the century neared its close McMurry revamped its flagship *Vim & Vigor* and signed agreements to produce two high-profile publications: a women's health magazine for Ohio State University Medical Centers and the *Scottsdale (Arizona) Citizen* for the city of Scottsdale. In addition came the signing of European behemoth STMicroelectronics (STM) to a multimillion-dollar advertising deal as McMurry plunged headlong into becoming a full-service media provider. Its agreement with the France-based STM included coordinating creative services and media research with STM's Milan agency, Cities Group.

A NEW ERA: 2000–05

By the dawn of the new millennium McMurry Inc. had successfully expanded its operations into a full-fledged custom publisher and advertising agency. With dozens of custom magazines and newsletters and a growing roster of advertising clients, Preston McMurry felt it was the right time to step down from day-to-day operations. In early 2000, while retaining the titles of president and chairman, Preston promoted his son Chris to chief executive officer to allow himself more time to devote to fundraising and his charitable foundations.

Chris soon proved himself adept at publishing and promotion when he was named to *Folio* magazine's Top 40, recognizing publishing professionals who "innovate, show great entrepreneurial spirit, have transformed the industry or are just plain worth watching." Outside his work duties, Chris garnered attention for other skills, such as race-car driving, Le Mans in particular, which he began to pursue in earnest by the mid-decade.

The company, meanwhile, with annual revenues approaching $30 million, had continued to expand by acquiring the New York-based *Copy Editor* magazine. Other items of note were creating *School Days,* a quarterly for school districts; taking over *Driven,* Mothers Against Drunk Driving's one-million-plus circulation magazine in 2001; signing with Reader's Digest Association to coordinate custom products; launching online newsletters; and providing an increasing array of magazines for the financial, energy, medical, municipal, and gaming industries.

By 2005 McMurry's two major business segments, publishing and advertising, were both thriving. Throughout the growth process, however, one thing remained constant: the company's reliance and insistence upon values. Founder Preston McMurry's carefully created mission statement encompassed eight core values including such moral-tinged niceties as "Do the Right Thing," "Help One Another," and "Accept Social Responsibility" but also carried such business mantras as "Exceed Expectations" and "Earn a Reasonable Profit." As Chris McMurry commented to Alison Stein Wellner of *Inc.* magazine in February 2005, "In our way of thinking, our values are guideposts for just being a decent human being."

STILL EVOLVING: 2006 AND BEYOND

In 2006 McMurry, Inc., bought Redspring Communications Inc., using it to launch a presence in Saratoga Springs, New York. The company also debuted a new quarterly periodical called *Publications Management* to track the custom publishing industry. According to its own market research released in 2007, businesses with revenues under $1 billion spent nearly 25 percent of their marketing budgets on custom magazines and newsletters, whereas bigger firms ($1 billion-plus revenues) spent far less, only about 10 percent. The best news was that of the survey's respondents, nearly 90 percent planned to increase custom print spending, which boded well for McMurry.

To provide a broader spectrum of products, in 2008 McMurry bought Contact Designs, a local firm the company had contracted with for interactive web and digital design work. Revenues for 2007 reached $45 million and both McMurrys, father and son, believed they could top $75 million before the end of the decade. Unfortunately, an economic meltdown put a crimp in their plans, forcing the company to scale back as revenues fell to about $32 million for 2008. Nonetheless, McMurry committed to the future by going "green," initiating paperless policies where possible and using eco-friendly ink and recycled paper for its many publications.

In early 2009 McMurry bought a second interactive firm, the Orlando, Florida-based Cyrus, which specialized in custom media solutions for the healthcare industry. As the decade came to a close, McMurry had ventured a long way since its founding to become a full-service media firm, far outreaching its original healthcare roots. By focusing on value and values, McMurry Inc. was an anomaly among its brethren, merging 19th-century ethics with 21st-century expertise. The mix worked, again and again, as McMurry's international client base surpassed 10,000. For Preston and Chris McMurry, the sky seemed the firm's only limit.

Nelson Rhodes

PRINCIPAL OPERATING UNITS

McMurry Publishing; McMurry Ad Group.

PRINCIPAL COMPETITORS

Dailey & Associates Advertising; Fallon Worldwide; Gavin & Gavin Advertising, Inc.; Harris Publishing; Imagination Publishing; Jeffrey Alec Communications; Oster & Associates, Inc.; TBWA Worldwide.

FURTHER READING

Farrell, Greg, "McMurry Gets SmartHealth," *Mediaweek,* July 13, 1998, p. 26.

Fattah, Hassan, "Custom Publishing Grows Up," *American Demographics,* July 1, 2002.

Fell, Jason, "Luxury Mags: Not So Recession-Proof After All?" *Folio,* April 2009, p. 13.

Gabriel, Angela, "McMurry Promotes Son," *Folio,* January 14, 2000, p. 14.

Gianatasio, David, "McMurry Buys I-Shop," *Adweek (Western Edition),* May 22, 2007.

Hindman, Harriett, "Foresight, Commitment Are Keys to Starting Business from Scratch," *Business Journal,* June 29, 1992, p. 24.

Holt, Karen Jenkins, "In the Line of Succession," *Folio,* May 1, 2003.

Judd, Erin Demith, "Local Printing Firm Gets Greener by the Page," *Glens Falls (N.Y.) Post-Star,* February 28, 2008.

Jutkins, Ray, "Marketing in the Publishing World," *Direct Marketing,* August 1997, p. 38.

Maietta, Vince, "It Was a Year of Twists for Printing, Publishing," *Phoenix Business Journal,* December 28, 1992, p. 25.

———, "Preston McMurry: Publisher Brings His Marketing Savvy to Health Care Through *Vim & Vigor,*" *Phoenix Business Journal,* January 13, 1992, p. 12.

Patz, Debby, "The Changing Face of Custom Publishing," *Folio,* April 1, 1994, p. 50.

———, "Vim & Vigor Grows Bigger," *Folio,* January 15, 1995, p. 31.

———, "Vim & Vigor's Editorial License," *Folio,* August 1, 1993, p. 53.

Robertson, Anne, "Inks Deal to Buy 'Copy Editor' Newsletter," *Phoenix Business Journal,* November 3, 2000, p. 22.

———, "McMurry Goes to School," *Phoenix Business Journal,* July 13, 2002, p. 11.

———, "McMurry Named to *Folio* 40," *Phoenix Business Journal,* April 6, 2001, p. 15.

Wellner, Alison Stein, "More Than Ever Before, Americans Are Talking About Values," *Inc.,* February 1, 2005.

Merlin Entertainments Group Ltd.

3 Market Close
Poole, BH15 1NQ
United Kingdom
Telephone: (+44 01202) 666 900
Fax: (+44 01202) 661 303
Web site: http://www.merlinentertainments.biz

Private Company
Incorporated: 1999
Employees: 8,531
Sales: £660.5 million ($917.1 million) (2008)
NAICS: 713110 Amusement and Theme Parks; 713990
    All Other Amusement and Recreation Industries

■ ■ ■

Merlin Entertainments Group Ltd. is, in terms of attendance, the world's second largest theme park and amusement venue operator. The company operates nearly 60 attractions under the Sea Life, Legoland, Dungeons, and Madame Tussauds brands, as well as the London Eye and other attractions. The company also operates several large-scale theme park resorts, including Alton Towers Resort, Thorpe Park, Chessington, and Warwick Castle in the United Kingdom; Gardaland, Italy's largest theme park; and Germany's Heide Park. The company is present in 12 countries, including the United Kingdom, Germany, Italy, Denmark, and the United States. The United Kingdom continues to represent the company's major market, generating 47 percent of group earnings. Each year the group, through

its portfolio of attractions, hosts more than 35 million visitors. While this total remains far behind industry leader Disney's 100 million visitors, Merlin targets the short-stay (two to three-hour visits) market, rather than the extended stay vacation sector. As such the company has focused its future growth on its Midway Division, which includes the Sealife, Tussauds, Dungeons, and London Eye, as well as the Legoland Discovery Centre format rolled out in 2008.

The Midway division generated 31 percent of the company's revenues of £660 million ($917 million) in 2008. The group's Theme Parks division included its Theme Park Resorts and the Legoland business units, which accounted for 45 percent and 25 percent of group sales, respectively. Merlin Entertainment is a private company owned by U.S. investment firm Blackstone Partners, which controls more than 54 percent of the company. Other major shareholders include former Tussauds owner Dubai International Capital, and Merlin's management, led by CEO Nick Varney.

FORMING AN ATTRACTION IN 1992

While Merlin Entertainment was founded only in 1999, parts of the company date as far back as the 19th century: the group's Sealife Brighton attraction, founded in 1872, was the world's oldest continually operating aquarium. However, the company's true beginnings came with the creation of a number of specialized leisure and entertainment companies in the United Kingdom in the 1980s and 1990s.

COMPANY PERSPECTIVES

Our Vision: To become the worldwide leader in branded, location based entertainment. Our Strategy: To build on our position as a high value, international, family entertainment group with strong, chainable brands and a portfolio that is naturally hedged against external factors such as weather or localised market conditions.

Among these was Vardon Plc, founded in 1992 by Nick Irens and David Hudd. Both men had already established careers in the leisure industry. Irens had been finance director at First Leisure (later Esporta), while Hudd had formerly been a director with the Kunick Leisure group. Both First Leisure and Kunick had operations spanning a wide range of leisure, entertainment, and amusement holdings. Both groups also had extended their businesses to include the operation of attractions. In Kunick's case, the company oversaw the opening of the popular London Dungeons, a theme-park type re-creation of a medieval dungeon, in 1985. For its part, First Leisure had come to control a number of Britain's aquariums, including the Brighton aquarium, which were regrouped under the Sealife brand in the 1980s.

Vardon started out in business in March 1992 with the purchase of the Dungeons franchise, which by then included a second attraction opened in York. By September of that year, the company had also negotiated the acquisition of the Sealife aquarium group, paying £9.9 million to First Leisure. In order to pay for its acquisitions, the company then went public, listing its shares on the London Stock Exchange

The public offering also provided fuel for the group's ambitious expansion plans. The company launched a £900,000 refurbishment of the London Dungeons site at the end of 1992. Vardon also announced planned to add two new Sealife centers. The first of these was in Southend, Essex. The second brought Vardon across the channel and into the Netherlands, where the company established a joint venture. The company also sought to extend the Sealife brand with the £1.8 million purchase in February 1993 of the Cornish Seal Sanctuary, located in Gweek, England. First opened in the 1950s, the seal sanctuary had been expanded in the mid-1970s to include an aquarium and other amenities. Under Vardon, the sanctuary became known as the National Seal Sanctuary.

VARDON ATTRACTIONS IN 1993

Joining the company by then was Nick Varney, then in his early 30s, who had established a career in the leisure industry as U.K. marketing director for France's Tussauds Group, which had purchased Alton Towers, the largest amusement resort in England, at the beginning of the 1990s. Varney took the reins as managing director of Vardon's newly created Vardon Attractions division, overseeing development of the Dungeons and Sealife brands, as well as the group's seal sanctuary.

Vardon Attractions continued to extend its operations through the middle of the decade, adding a new site, the New Forest Nature Quest. That attraction, however, proved short-lived, as Vardon Attractions focused especially on developing its Sealife chain, which expanded to 18 locations throughout the United Kingdom and Ireland by 1995. The company then decided to expand the Sealife brand further onto the European continent, opening aquariums in Belgium, Spain, and Germany. By 1998, the company operated 24 Sealife Centres.

By then, Vardon itself had been growing rapidly. The company added the operation of bingo halls and holiday resorts in 1993. Into the middle of the decade, however, Vardon spotted a new growth market, and began positioning itself as an operator of health clubs. The company began developing a new brand, Courtneys, competing for privatization contracts to take over the operation of formerly municipally owned and operated health club and leisure centers. By 1996, Vardon had won its bid on eight contracts. Then, in 1996, the company paid £40 million to acquire the Metropolitan Clubs chain.

MANAGEMENT BUYOUT IN 1999

This purchase was followed in 1998 with a new £50 million purchase of another major U.K. health club operator, Cannons and Harbour, that established Vardon Group among the country's largest and fastest-growing health club operators. Yet the success of the health club division had by then come to overshadow growth at Vardon Attractions. The company began seeking to spin off its attractions division as an independent company, and in 1998 Vardon began negotiations with private-equity group Apax Partners.

In 1999, Vardon announced that it had agreed to sell Vardon Attractions to a management buyout (MBO) led by Nick Varney, and backed by Apax. As part of the sale, Varney led the creation of a new company, Merlin Entertainments Group, which paid Vardon nearly £40 million ($77 million) for its Sealife Centres, the National Seal Sanctuary, and the London and York Dungeons. The company's choice of the Merlin name was inspired by the group's two core businesses. As Varney explained to *Amusement Business:* "There are two perceptions of Merlin. The first is a wonderful and amazing personality that fits our Sea Life facilities, and the second has a mischievous and darker personality, perfect for our Dungeon attractions."

Merlin began repositioning the Sealife brand in the early 2000s. The company separated the chain into two segments. Sealife Centres became the name for the group's larger aquariums, while the smaller aquariums were rebranded as Sealife Aquariums. The company then sold off the latter, in order to focus the Sealife brand entirely on developing the Sealife Centre concept.

The company also retooled the centers' concept, which developed a more environmentally aware focus. New centers took on a regional format, emphasizing the local marine environment, and providing more suitable habitats for the fish and other creatures in the aquarium. In 2002, the company operated 15 Sealife Centres in eight countries in Europe. The company then launched construction of its most ambitious Sealife Centre to date, a $25.5 million site in Oberhausen, Germany.

ACQUIRING SCALE

Merlin continued to develop operations in the environmental vein, launching a new attraction in 2004, called Earth Explorer, in Oostende, Belgium. The company hoped to extend the new format, with the opening of as many as four more Earth Explorers by 2010. At the same time, the group continued to develop its environmental commitment, adding two new marine sanctuaries to its U.K. operations.

Merlin had hoped to go public within five years of its founding. The sluggish stock market, however, forced the company to abandon these plans. Instead, Apax Partners agreed to sell its stake in the company in a secondary MBO, backed by Hermes Private Equity, for $137.75 million. Once again Varney, as company chairman and CEO, led the buyout.

That buyout became the prelude for a new private-equity deal. In May 2005, U.S.-based Blackstone Partners agreed to buyout Hermes's stake, becoming Merlin's majority shareholder. Blackstone had experience in the attractions sector, having previously backed the Six Flags amusement park group, as well as holding a 50 percent stake in the Universal Studios theme park business. At the time, Merlin's revenues topped $86 million.

Blackstone's experience and willingness to back Varney's expansion strategy helped transform the company into the second half of the decade. By August 2005, Merlin had completed its largest acquisition to date, paying $460 million to acquire the Legoland theme park group. Created in 1968 by the famed Danish toy company, the Legoland theme park business had expanded to include four locations in Denmark, England, Germany, and the United States. Following the purchase, Lego became a minority shareholder in Merlin, through Kirkbi A/S.

SHORT-STAY FOCUS FOR LONG-TERM SUCCESS

Merlin continued to seek new acquisitions as it began to position itself as Europe's leading amusement park and attractions company, and one of the world's largest as well. In 2006, the group entered Italy, buying that country's largest theme park, Gardaland. The purchase boosted the group's total attendance figures to 16 million per year, making it Europe's largest, and the number six player worldwide. By the end of the year, Merlin's revenues had skyrocketed, nearing $525 million.

The company was soon to shoot up even higher in the ranks, however. In 2007, the company announced that it had agreed to pay £1 billion ($1.9 billion) to acquire Tussauds Group, operator of the world famous Madame Tussauds wax museum chain. Tussauds owned a number of other prominent attractions, most notably the London Eye, the world's largest Ferris wheel, the Heide amusement park in Germany, and Alton Towers in England. The deal positioned Tussauds majority shareholder Dubai International Capital as a major stakeholder in Merlin, with a 20 percent share. It also enabled Merlin to secure a site to build a new Legoland in Dubai, to open in 2010.

Merlin's revenues nearly doubled in size, reaching £560 million at the end of 2007, and rose again to £660.5 million ($917 million) for 2008, despite the overall malaise in the global leisure market due to the worldwide economic collapse that was triggered that year.

Merlin's focus on short-stay, and therefore less-expensive attractions, enabled the company to maintain its head above water, as families sought lower-cost alternatives to the more expensive long-stay amusement complexes. In keeping with this strategy, Merlin launched an extension of the Legoland brand, opening the first Legoland Discovery Center in 2007, before rolling out the format to the United States in 2008. The company also began rolling out the Madame Tussauds wax museum attraction for the U.S. market. With more than 35 million visitors and a place as the world's second largest amusement attractions group, Merlin had proved the wizardry behind its name.

M. L. Cohen

PRINCIPAL SUBSIDIARIES

Alton Towers Ltd.; Gardaland S.r.l. (Italy); Heide-Park Soltau GmbH (Germany); Legoland California LLC (USA); Legoland Deutschland GmbH; Legoland Discovery Centre US Inc.; London Eye Holdings Ltd.; Merlin Entertainments Group US Inc.; Sea Life Centres Ltd.; The Tussauds Group LLC; Warwick Castle Ltd.

PRINCIPAL OPERATING UNITS

Theme Parks; Resort Theme Parks; Midway.

PRINCIPAL COMPETITORS

Telefonica S.A.; Walt Disney Co.; Anheuser-Busch Companies Inc.; NBC Universal Inc.; Viacom Inc.; Acciona S.A.; Disney-MGM Studios; Busch Entertainment Corp.; Namco Bandai Holdings Inc.; Oriental Land Company Ltd.

FURTHER READING

"Agencies Line Up for £20m Merlin Media," *Campaign,* May 22, 2009, p. 01.

"Expanding Merlin Opens New Sea-Life Centre," *Leisure Report,* October 2004, p. 11.

Koranteng, Juliana, "Merlin Entertainments Sets Course with Secondary Management Buyout," *Amusement Business,* March 8, 2004, p. 10.

Lambert, Emily, "Cheap Thrills," *Forbes,* February 16, 2009, p. 72.

Lewis, Connie, "New Legoland Attractions Another Feather in Merlin's Cap," *San Diego Business Journal,* May 11, 2009, p. 33.

"Merlin Entertainments Is UK's Fastest-Growing PE-Backed Firm," *Leisure Report,* March 2008, p. 3.

"Merlin Entertainments Restructures After Tussauds Merger Approved," *Leisure Report,* July 2007, p. 9.

"Merlin Outlines Three Key Reasons Behind Its Gardaland Purchase," *Leisure Report,* December 2006, p. 10.

"Merlin Shrugs Off Gloom with Magical Results," *Leisure Report,* August 2008, p. 4.

Norton, Kate, "No Mystery in Blackstone's Wax Museum," *Business Week Online,* March 7, 2007.

O'Brien, Tim, "United Kingdom's Vardon Attractions Sold to Current Management Team," *Amusement Business,* February 8, 1999, p. 14.

———, "Varney Maintains Vision with Marine Venues," *Amusement Business,* December 23, 2002, p. 11.

Morgan Motor Company

———————— ■ ————————

Pickersleigh Road
Malvern Link, Worcestershire WR14 2LL
United Kingdom
Telephone: (+44 01684) 573104
Fax: (+44 01684) 892295
Web site: http://www.morgan-motor.co.uk

Private Company
Incorporated: 1912
Employees: 500
NAICS: 336111 Automobile Manufacturing

■ ■ ■

Morgan Motor Company is one of the world's iconic automobile manufacturers. The Worcestershire, England-based company can also claim to be the world's oldest continuously operating automaker, having produced its first three-wheeled vehicle in 1909. Morgan continues to operate on a handcrafted basis under the control of the founding Morgan family. Morgan automobiles are traditionally made with ash wood frames, aluminum, and leather. The cars also feature some of the most powerful automotive engines available, which are produced by third-party manufacturers such as BMW, Ford, and Fiat. The company maintains limited production runs of not more than 800 vehicles per year, and sells 100 percent of its production. The waiting list for the company's automobiles, which sell for approximately $90,000 (and up to $200,000 for special editions), has averaged one year. Morgan focuses on the high-end, high-performance vehicle segment,

producing a limited range of models. Most of these are based on the company's classic designs—its Four Four (or 4/4) roadster has been in production since the 1930s—but updated to meet modern safety, performance, and environmental standards. The company also debuted a more modern design, the Aeromax, in 2000, produced in a second purpose-built facility alongside the company's original Malvern Link factory. Morgan is led by Charles Morgan, grandson of the company's founder. The company does not release financial figures.

1909: FOUNDING MOTORING HISTORY

Henry Frederick Stanley Morgan, more popularly known as H. F. S, was born in Morton Jeffries, in Herefordshire in 1881. Both Morgan's father and grandfather were vicars in the Anglican church. Morgan's interests, however, turned toward engineering, which he studied at the Crystal Palace Engineering College. Following his education, Morgan began his career as a draftsman at GWR Railway Works, based in Swindon, in 1899.

Into the next century, Morgan's attention was increasingly captivated by developments in the automotive industry. By 1906, Morgan was determined to enter this market, and in that year he left GWR to set up his own garage and repair shop. Morgan, who had married the daughter of the vicar of Malvern Link, chose that village as his business's new home.

Morgan at first operated a bus service, employing a leased 15-seat, 10 horsepower (hp) vehicle built by the Wolseley company. Morgan began offering bus service between Malvern Link and Wells, before extending the line to Gloucester. At the same time, his shop acquired the agency for the Wolseley and Darraq auto makes.

Morgan began dreaming of owning his own car. One of his first driving experiences was somewhat of a disaster, when he lost control of a rented Benz while going downhill. Repairs cost him £28, a large sum at the time. Eventually, Morgan raised enough money to purchase his first automobile, a three-wheeled Eagle Tandem.

The new vehicle inspired Morgan to develop his own automotive design. By 1909, Morgan had completed his first prototype, a three-wheeled vehicle with the single wheel at the back, powered by a 7 hp Peugeot engine. Morgan's design featured a lightweight tubular steel frame, as well as independent front suspension. The car's low weight and relatively robust engine provided it with powerful start-up speeds.

Lacking his own machine shop, Morgan turned to the local engineering school to produce a prototype of the vehicle, called the Runabout. Although at first built only as a personal vehicle for Morgan himself, the number of compliments he received for the Runabout's design encouraged Morgan to launch production of several more vehicles. Morgan also patented his design that year.

INCORPORATED IN 1912

Morgan completed two more cars by the end of 1910, displaying both at the Olympia Motor Show. Both designs had only a single seat, however, and the company generated only a small number of orders. The company went back to the drawing board, developing its first two-seater designs. In the meantime, Morgan's original Runabouts were proving the mettle, capturing the win in the 1911 London-Exeter-London Reliability Trial.

Two two-seater models were completed by the end of the year and caused a sensation at the Olympia Mo-

tor Show. The new models also captured the attention of the managing director of Harrods, who placed one of Morgan's cars in the retailer's shop window, the first and only time for an automobile. The publicity helped the company quickly build a strong order book.

Lacking his own factory, Morgan at first attempted to contract out to a number of other existing automobile manufacturers. When they refused, Morgan instead invested the down payments on his advance orders to expand his shop and purchase machine tools. In 1912, Morgan incorporated his company as Morgan Motor Company. His father served as the company's first chairman, while Morgan became its managing director. Also joining the company was Morgan's sister, Dorothy, who became a noted pilot in the era's Reliability Trials. Morgan quickly established itself as a winning force both in the racing and reliability circuits.

Production was more or less halted during World War I. Nonetheless, Morgan's design team remained active, developing the prototype for the company's four-wheeled vehicle, while also designing a four-seat version of the Runabout. While the company would not produce its first four-wheeled vehicle until the 1930s, the four-seater, initially designed for Morgan himself, was put into production as the Family Runabout following the war.

FROM THREE WHEELS TO FOUR IN THE THIRTIES

The success of the new model led the company to open a new factory in 1918 capable of producing 50 cars each week. Built on a hill outside of Malvern, the new facility's production line followed the slope of the hill. Known as the Works, the site became Morgan's permanent home. Through the 1930s, the company continued to produce the Runabout according to the basic design, while adding new amenities, such as detachable wheels, and a gearbox with three forward gears and reverse. In 1933, the group achieved new success with a three-wheeler based on a Ford 10 hp engine and featuring a flat radiator. This model, called the F Super Two-seater, went on to become the best-selling three-wheeled vehicle of all.

Despite certain advantages of the three-wheel design, such as speed, the automotive and especially the auto racing sectors turned more firmly toward four-wheeled vehicles in the 1930s. Morgan at last grew serious about developing its own four-wheeled car, debuting a prototype in 1936. The model, called the Four Four because of its four wheels and four-cylinder engine, featured a steel chassis, with an ash frame supporting aluminum panels. The combination made the Four Four

KEY DATES

1909: Henry F. S. Morgan builds a prototype of his first three-wheeled motor vehicle, called the Runabout.

1912: Morgan Motor Company is incorporated, with Morgan as managing director and his father as chairman.

1918: Morgan moves to a new factory and introduces a four-seat version of the Runabout.

1936: Morgan introduces its first production four-wheeled model, the Four Four.

1950: Morgan discontinues production of three-wheeled vehicles and introduces the Plus Four.

1966: Morgan introduces its first V8-powered model, the Plus Eight.

1984: Morgan incorporates fuel injection into the Plus Eight.

2000: Morgan introduces its first new model, the Aero 8.

2009: Morgan celebrates its 100th anniversary.

extremely robust yet light in weight, enabling the model to achieve impressive speed results.

The company followed up the original Four Four Roadster with a second model, the Four Four Drophead Coupe, in 1938. Both models were hugely successful, establishing Morgan as a leader in automotive design and performance. The success of the Four Four was such that it became the company's mainstay vehicle for decades. Indeed, the Four Four remained in near continuous production into the next century, a record for any car design.

The outbreak of World War II, however, brought a new interruption in Morgan's manufacturing operations. Only the company's service and repairs departments remained in business for the duration. The company's factory instead served the British war effort.

ENDING THREE WHEEL PRODUCTION IN THE FIFTIES

Immediately following the war, Morgan resumed production. The company's expertise in working with aluminum enabled it to overcome the scarcity of steel that continued to bog down production elsewhere in the automotive industry. As a result, Morgan became the

first in the United Kingdom to resume manufacturing following the war. Joining the company during this time was H. F. S. Morgan's son, Peter, who entered the company as a design engineer and draftsman.

While Morgan's aluminum-based three-wheeled vehicles continued to sell strongly in the United Kingdom, the company struggled to revive production of its four-wheeled model. The U.K. government at the time had introduced a policy of linking a company's steel supply with its export levels. As a result, Morgan, like other manufacturers, began developing its own export market. The company then began signing up distributors around the world.

The Four Four rapidly gained popularity abroad. Far less successful, however, were the company's three-wheeled vehicles. This led the company to announce its decision to abandon three-wheeler production in 1950. Morgan turned its attention to expanding its four-wheeled range.

In 1950, the company debuted its Plus Four model. The new sports car featured a longer, reinforced chassis and more powerful engine than the Four Four. The Plus Four established itself as a leading player in the international racing circuit. In turn, the group's racing effort allowed Morgan to make continual improvements to the car's design, such as longer suspension, larger disc brakes, and wire wheels. During the 1950s, Morgan relaunched the Four Four as well. The new "Series Two" model adapted features of the Plus Four.

FACING EMISSIONS AND SAFETY STANDARDS IN THE SEVENTIES

Morgan's vehicles continued to sell briskly through the 1960s. Automobiles continued to be handcrafted at the company's original factory, leading to significant waiting lists. Into the 1980s, for example, wait times for Morgans often stretched to as much as eight years.

Through the 1960s, Morgan made new improvements to its car models, while adding to its range. In 1966, the company extended the Plus series with the launch of the Plus Eight. This model was the company's first to feature a V8 engine, using an aluminum engine built by Rover. The new engine was also featured in models from both Rover and Rolls-Royce. Yet the Rover V8 had its longest life with Morgan, continuing to power the Plus series for more than 30 years.

During the 1960s, Morgan attempted to enter a new direction when the company launched the Plus Four Plus. The first Morgan to be fully enclosed, the model failed to inspire Morgan enthusiasts, who felt that the enclosed design did not fit with Morgan's by then iconic image. In the end, production of the Plus Four Plus lasted just two years, with only 26 vehicles being built.

Exports became the main driver of the group's sales. By the end of the 1960s, the United States alone often accounted for as much as 85 percent of the company's order book. However, Morgan, and U.S. Morgan enthusiasts, faced a new setback, when the United States adopted new emission control rules in 1971. The company's Rover engines were unable to meet the new standards. The United States had also begun developing new safety standards for the automotive market as well. The cost of adapting to the new emissions and safety requirements was too much for Morgan and the company was forced to abandon the U.S. market.

Imports nonetheless resumed in the mid-1970s, thanks to the efforts of a Morgan parts dealer based in San Francisco named Bill Fink. Over several years, Fink succeeded in adapting the Rover V8 to run on propane, which was not subjected to emissions standards, while adapting the Plus 8 to meet safety requirements as well. Fink became the sole source of Morgans for the U.S. market through the end of the century.

Morgan had more success in Europe, where all of its models met European Economic Community emissions and safety requirements by 1978. The company also maintained its record of continuously improving its models. In 1984, for example, the company added fuel injection to the Plus Eight. This was followed by expanding the design from 3.5 to 3.9 liters, enabling the company to establish new speed records in the late 1980s. By then, the third generation of the Morgan family had joined the company, when Peter's son Charles entered the company in 1985. Unlike his father and grandfather, Charles Morgan's background lay in film production and journalism, including an eight-year stint as a cameraman for the United Kingdom's Independent Television Network.

NEW MODEL FOR THE NEW MILLENNIUM

A televised visit from ICI Director Sir John Harvey Jones in 1989 became a new milestone in Morgan's development. Jones had been touring the country, advising small companies on how they could improve their manufacturing processes. At Morgan, Jones suggested the company abandon its handcrafted production methods in order to double production. The Morgan family politely, and famously, refused.

As Charles Morgan explained to *Time International,* "What he suggested would have been throwing the baby out with the bathwater." The exchange nevertheless brought renewed attention to Morgan, sparking a surge in new orders, and Jones's visit was not without its effects on the company, which recognized the benefit of adapting its production line.

One change made was to redirect the company's production line, so that cars moved downhill. The changes put into place allowed the company to boost its annual production by some 25 percent, to 600 cars. Also during the 1990s, Morgan at last adapted its models to meet U.S. safety and emissions standards, allowing the company to resume direct imports to that country.

Despite Jones's suggestion, Morgan maintained its policy of producing only a limited supply of handcrafted and highly personalized vehicles. At the same time, Morgan recognized the potential of developing an entirely new, more modern design, and using new production techniques. Toward this end, the company constructed a new purpose-built factory next door to its existing facility. By 2000, the company had unveiled its first new car design in over 30 years, the Aero 8.

Featuring a bonded aluminum chassis, a modern suspension system, and a powerful BMW V8 engine, the Aero 8 also boasted a sleeker, more aerodynamic design. Nevertheless, the Aero 8 remained true to the styling and speediness that had made Morgan an automotive icon. In 2009, Morgan celebrated its 100th anniversary as an automaker, the oldest family-owned automotive company in the world.

M. L. Cohen

PRINCIPAL COMPETITORS

Daimler AG; Ford Motor Co.; Porsche Holding Gesellschaft mbH; Volkswagen-Audi Espana S.A.

FURTHER READING

Cooney, Joyceann, "One with the Road," *License!* September 2006, p. 24.

"Family Life in the Fast Lane," *Journal* (Newcastle, U.K.), April 23, 2008, p. 41.

Griffiths, John, "Champion of a Winning Formula and Limited Supply," *Financial Times,* October 25, 2003, p. 11.

Jewett, Dale, "Morgan Motor Will Sell $95,000 Aero 8 in U.S.," *Automotive News,* January 5, 2004, p. 6.

"Morgan Digs Deep to Win Young Buyers with New Logo," *Design Week,* November 22, 2007, p. 6.

"Morgan Unveils Zero-Emission Car," *Daily Post,* March 5, 2008, p. 20.

"Morgan's 70 Years of Success with One Model," *Journal* (Newcastle, U.K.), January 7, 2006, p. 54.

Moules, Jonathan, "Morgan, a Member of the Family," *Financial Times,* August 19, 2006, p. 18.

Paternie, Patrick C., "Morgan Motors at 100," *AutoWeek,* April 20, 2009, p. 14.

Selby, Dave, "Charles Morgan," *Daily Telegraph,* August 17, 2002, p. 11.

"Traditional Skills Meet New Technology," *Metalworking Production,* March 30, 2007, p. 92.

"Tribute to Man Behind Morgan," *Birmingham Post,* September 19, 2005, p. 5.

Turner, Liz, "The Rise and Rise of Morgan," *Independent,* September 26, 2006, p. 4.

"Upholding Traditions," *Finishing,* March–April 2007, p. 28.

Ward, Daniel, "Many Hands Make Slow Work on a Fast Car," *Times* (London), January 4, 1991.

Mrchocolate.com LLC

66 Water Street
Brooklyn, New York 11201
U.S.A.
Telephone: (718) 875-9772
Fax: (718) 875-2167
Web site: http://www.mrchocolate.com

Private Company
Incorporated: 2000
Employees: 50
Sales: $10 million (2008 est.)
NAICS: 311330 Confectionery Manufacturing from Purchased Chocolate; 424450 Confectionery Merchant Wholesalers; 445292 Confectionery and Nut Stores

■ ■ ■

Mrchocolate.com LLC, doing business as Jacques Torres Chocolate, sells fine designer chocolates and candies from its five locations in New York, and retail stores in Atlantic City and Michigan. With celebrity chef Jacques Torres at the creative helm, the company specializes in innovative recipes and manufacturing techniques with a focus on products that are all-natural, fresh, and preservative-free. Having started as a small three-person operation in 2000, the company has more than 50 employees with sales topping $10 million. It has been featured in numerous national publications, including the *New York Times,* the *Washington Post,* and *Forbes* magazine.

A CHOCOLATE COMPANY BUILT ON REPUTATION FOR QUALITY: 2000

In 1998, Jacques Torres was an executive pastry chef at Le Cirque 2000 and was the winner of many culinary prizes in the U.S. and abroad. He was also a well-known celebrity chef, with his own show on the Food Network and two published cookbooks. However, he was ready to run his own business and make his fortune; thus, he began researching the food business. Eventually he settled on opening a chocolate-making company because, at 20 percent, the chocolate specialty market had high profit margins, little competition, and modest start-up costs.

Two years later, he and two partners, his sous-chef, Keitaro Goto, and his long-term girlfriend, Kris Kruid, were ready to make a go of it. In the summer of 2000, they rented a 7,000-square-foot space on the bottom floor of a 120-year-old dilapidated spring factory that had been empty for 30 years. The space was located on Brooklyn's waterfront, between the Brooklyn and Manhattan bridges; the neighborhood was filled with abandoned, graffiti-covered warehouses.

Determined to avoid asking investors for cash, Kruid and Torres invested $150,000 of their retirement savings into their new company, Jacques Torres Chocolate. The three partners kept costs low during an extensive renovation of the space by working with friends and doing everything themselves. The resulting chocolate factory and retail shop was designed to be minimal and chic, with mottled mirrors, cocoa-stained wood shelves, milky marble counters, and a copper ceiling. Because the focus of the business initially was wholesale production for restaurants, hotels, and shops, the retail side of the store was small, measuring a mere 400 square feet, while the production side was quite large, exceeding 5,000 square feet.

Although the factory was not designed to accommodate visitors, it showcased chocolate production and highlighted fresh, artisan-quality chocolates. Large picture windows both street-side and within the small store enabled passersby and customers a glimpse of its inner workings. The centerpiece of the factory featured a 40-foot-long conveyor, not unlike the one on the *I Love Lucy* episode in which Lucille Ball cannot keep up with the machine, where the newly minted fillings were coated in a drizzle of chocolate.

Well-stocked, with numerous delicacies, including peanut brittle, truffles, butter crunch sprinkled with sea salt, and pistachio marzipan diamonds, Jacques Torres Chocolate opened on December 20, 2000, just in time for the holiday shopping rush. Thanks to his reputation as a world-class, award-winning pastry chef, Torres received lots of advance publicity, and the store was an immediate success. By the end of its second day, retail customers formed a line extending outside the front door and retail sales topped $8,000. Having run out of chocolate boxes, the three partners improvised, wrapping candies in paper. Within a few months, Torres and Kruid had recouped their investment.

FOCUSING ON INNOVATION AND IN-HOUSE INGREDIENT PRODUCTION: 2001–03

With Kruid handling the books and business administration and Goto looking after chocolate ordering and output, Torres devoted his talents to product development and special projects. One of his first concerns was protecting product quality while streamlining production.

During chocolate production, tiny air bubbles form as the chocolate is blended. Trapped air creates oxidation and reduces product shelf life. Rather than using chemical additives to preserve his chocolates, Torres went to Europe in search of a solution. He came back with a French vacuum mixer, a machine normally used to blend cosmetics. The machine puts ingredients under hundreds of pounds of pressure and thereby eliminates any air. Torres discovered that, in addition to antioxidant benefits, the vacuum mixer also enhanced product taste: "Everything is very concentrated, which allows for more concentration of flavor," Torres noted in a 2002 *New York Times* article. It also creates "a nice, dense texture," he commented in a 2004 *Candy Industry* article.

Later, Torres invested in another machine used in the manufacture of cosmetics: a computerized apparatus designed to fill makeup bottles that also conveniently could squirt chocolate into molds, a previously tricky procedure. The machine enabled him to make truffles incredibly fast and with far more precision than by hand. "If the technology doesn't have a negative impact on the quality of what I'm going to do, then I'll use it," he told *Candy Industry* in 2004.

With these machines and several others on hand, Torres could create high-quality, all-natural products in-house without sacrificing his ideals: "I insist on unconditional quality in our products. ... We don't use any preservatives or any artificial ingredients. No chemicals. ... It's all about flavor, a clean label and better quality. That's the direction my business is taking, and that's a direction that others in chocolate are also going," he said in the 2004 *Candy Industry* article. With this attitude, his company was in line with the chocolate consumer's shift toward purchasing an ever higher-quality product.

Another way in which Torres's talent enhanced his product was through his specialty recipes, which included seasonal elements that often went beyond the holidays. Products in the summer showcased summer fruits such as raspberries and strawberries; in the winter coconut and citrus fruit were preferred. Notably, Torres was one of only a few chocolatiers to use real champagne in his bonbons; his Tattinger truffles became a featured product. In addition, the cocoa content of his chocolates was always very high, at least 60 percent.

Although the company began as a bare-bones, three-person start-up, it grew quickly. By Valentine's Day 2002, sales were double what they had been only one year before. By 2004, Jacques Torres Chocolate was a successful enterprise, employing 18 people, with hundreds of wholesale customers.

DIVERSIFYING AND EXPANSION: 2004–06

By 2004, the company had strong sales in three business sectors; retail revenues ranged between 25 and 30

KEY DATES

2000: Jacques Torres and his partners, Kris Kruid and Keitaro Goto, open Jacques Torres Chocolate in Brooklyn, New York.

2001: Mrchocolate.com, the company's web site, launches.

2003: Company's sales hit $1 million.

2004: Jacques Torres Chocolate and Sutton Place Group, an operator of specialty food markets and restaurants, form an exclusive retail relationship; Torres builds a combination cocoa-roasting and candy-making factory and retail store, the Jacques Torres Chocolate Haven, in SoHo, New York.

2006: Three new Jacques Torres Chocolate retail stores open in New York, Atlantic City, and Michigan; sales top $6 million.

2007: King Arthur Flour Co. and Jacques Torres team up to create a line of cookie and brownie baking mixes.

2008: Company sales jump 43 percent from 2007 to hit $10 million.

2009: Company launches its ice cream line, Jacques Torres ice cream.

percent, Internet revenues were at 26 percent, and wholesale revenues hovered around 41 percent. However, the cost of ingredients was climbing, with the most notable increase being the higher price of milk. With Torres's focus on purity of ingredients, the company's production costs had started out quite high. Initially, it absorbed the increasing costs, but keeping a rein on retail prices proved increasingly more difficult. Jacques Torres Chocolate consequently began looking for ways to expand the business's reach to maximize efficiencies and lower production costs.

The company's first strategy was to form an exclusive retail partnership with Sutton Place Group, an operator of 11 specialty foods markets and six restaurants throughout the East Coast, which would showcase nine of its products. Thanks to this new partnership, Jacques Torres's products reached a much larger consumer base. However, the second strategy for increasing profits proved to be the most lucrative because it brought the company national acclaim.

Dubbed the Chocolate Haven, Torres's mecca for chocolate lovers opened in the fall of 2004 as both a retail and wholesale production space. Located in the neighborhood known as SoHo in New York City, in 8,000 square feet of industrial space, the Haven was intended to capitalize on the burgeoning sophistication of consumers' palates and aging baby boomers' interest in the health benefits of chocolate. The concept came at the perfect time, coinciding with a nationwide focus on artisan foods.

Serious about this newest project, Torres thoroughly researched all aspects of processing cocoa beans and the production of chocolate, talking to cocoa processors and manufacturers in Europe, equipment suppliers, foodservice friends, and industry consultants. The Haven was conceived as both a sanctuary for the serious art of chocolate making and a busy hive where chocolate lovers could come and drink and eat chocolate. "We've lost our relationship with food," Torres explained in a 2009 *Forbes* article. "I wanted to bring that back."

Unlike the company's thrifty Brooklyn investment, construction costs on the Jacques Torres Chocolate Haven totaled $1.5 million. In the new store, visitors could watch the creation of sweets from, as Torres put it, "bean to bar," which meant all aspects of cocoa and chocolate production were on display, from roasting, to crushing, to liquefying, to spinning, and shaping. The windowed interior store was shaped in an oval, like a cocoa pod, and provided surrounding views of working machines in the outer factory from practically every vantage point. The store's hot chocolate bar was overseen by a statue of Quetzalcoatl, the Aztec god of cacao. Candy names were cute and playful and included "Love Potion #9" and "Wicked Fun." The Haven's atmosphere and concept positioned Jacques Torres Chocolate as one of the world's premier chocolatiers, as well as celebrated the whimsy behind Torres's talent.

A PRODUCT PARTNERSHIP, NEW RETAIL STORES, AND SAVVY MARKETING: 2006–08

In the fall of 2006, the company formed another partnership. This time it was with King Arthur Flour Company. Capitalizing on a relationship Torres had formed during a 1998 PBS cooking show, the two companies collaborated on a line of cookie and brownie baking mixes that were based on Torres's recipes. The result: Pure Bliss Fudge Brownie Mix, Mudslide Cookies, and French Kiss Cookies, which were sold in Jacques Torres Chocolate shops and online via the King Arthur web sites.

Torres's skills as a chef and chocolatier had resulted in an incredibly high-quality product that justified a high price, averaging about $50 per pound. However, what really set Jacques Torres Chocolate apart from the competition (about 20 other luxury chocolate stores were located in Manhattan, not including national luxury brands) was its reputation and solid business relationships. According to industry expert Clay Gordon, editor and publisher of chocophile.com in a 2006 *Crain's New York Business* article, "Jacques Torres is the best at public relations and marketing." His savvy helped him to achieve a goal attainable by very few chocolate boutiques: sales above $5 million. By 2006, the company had a staff of 40 and more than $6 million in annual revenues from selling approximately 50 products through three sales channels (wholesale, retail, and online).

By the end of 2006, Torres opened more retail stores in New York, Atlantic City, and Michigan. By the end of 2008, Torres had a total of five stores in New York, with three shops in Brooklyn, one in SoHo (the Chocolate Haven), and one on Amsterdam Avenue on the Upper West Side. Sales topped $10 million and Torres's ambitions were high: "I want to be New York's chocolatier," said Torres in a 2005 *Bloomberg News* article. "I have 50 more ideas for chocolates that I haven't even tried."

PLANS FOR THE FUTURE: 2009

In 2009 as a worldwide recession deepened, even Jacques Torres Chocolate felt the economic pressure. By early summer, Torres had yet to lay off any employees, although the company estimated that the sales figures would be off by about 20 percent by the end of the year. To boost revenue, Jacques Torres Chocolate launched a new ice cream line that featured five chocolate flavors. The company sold its ice cream at a retail store located next door to the flagship Brooklyn store and at an ice cream stand at the Jacques Torres Chocolate Haven store in Manhattan. Most of the other retail locations featured seasonal ice cream sandwiches. Torres's future plans included delivering ice cream via a custom-built truck decked out with a French church bell.

Torres also planned to add two additional stores on Manhattan's Upper East Side and in midtown, as well as a concept store in Dubai in 2010. The concept store would employ the design talents of Jean-Paul Loppo, who had worked on projects for Cirque du Soleil. Although plans were still sketchy and the full extent of the recession unknown, Torres, in a *Forbes* article in 2009, optimistically envisioned the Dubai store to include "chocolate fountains and trees." The hard economic times did not seem to dampen Torres's vision of a future filled with extravagant sweets that pleased chocolate lovers the world over.

Carrie Rothburd

PRINCIPAL COMPETITORS

Pure Dark; Kee's Chocolate LLC; Maribelle's Sweets Inc.; Koopers Chocolate; Sweet Town; Vosages Chocolates; Varsano's Chocolates, Inc.; Talukder N Corp.; House of Gift Inc.

FURTHER READING

Cazeneuve, Brian, "All Chocolate, No Oompa-Loompas," *New York Times,* December 22, 2004, p. F1.

Friedrick, Joanne, "King Arthur, Jacques Torres Blend Ideas on Baking Line," *Gourmet News,* March 2007, p. 21.

Morago, Greg, "Sharing the Passion for Chocolate; Jacques Torres, a French Chocolatier, Celebrates the Delicious Cocoa Bean Through His Food Show and Store," *Hartford Courant,* February 10, 2005, p. G3.

Pacyniak, Bernard, "Bridging Haute Chocolate and Entrepreneurism," *Candy Industry,* June 2004, p. 20.

Perlroth, Nicole, "Sweet Talker," *Forbes,* July 13, 2009, p. 64.

Rivkin, Victoria, "Chef Tries on Entrepreneur's Hat," *Crain's New York Business,* January 16, 2006, p. 15.

Salter, Chuck, "Like Money for Chocolate," *Fast Company,* February 2004, p. 74.

Segal, David, "Milking Chocolate; For Jacques Torres, a Sweet Career Move," *Washington Post,* November 14, 2004, p. D01.

MSWG, LLC

———■———

200 Glenridge Point Parkway, Suite 200
Atlanta, Georgia 30342
U.S.A.
Telephone: (404) 255-3250
Fax: (404) 255-4978
Web site: http://www.moes.com

Subsidiary of Focus Brands Inc.
Incorporated: 2000
Employees: 60
Sales: $4 million (2008 est.)
NAICS: 722211 Limited-Service Restaurants

■ ■ ■

MSWG, LLC, operates Moe's Southwest Grill restaurants, a chain of more than 400 franchised restaurants that serve burritos, tacos, fajitas, quesadillas, and side dishes. The food is prepared without lard, oils, or butter, offering a healthful selection of freshly prepared items. Moe's Southwest Grill operates in 34 states and in Ontario, Canada. The chain is owned by Focus Brands Inc., a franchiser that operates more than 2,200 ice cream stores, bakeries, restaurants, and cafes under the names Carvel, Cinnabon, Schlotzsky's, and Seattle's Best Coffee.

THE LURE OF FAST-CASUAL

During the first decade of the 21st century, a relatively new breed of competitor secured legitimacy in the vast, $500-billion restaurant industry. Limited-service restaurants that offered higher quality food than fast-food restaurants at prices below those charged by casual-dining restaurants began to appear in increasing numbers during the 1990s. Known variously as "premium fast-serve," "upscale quick-service," "adult fast-food," the burgeoning niche blossomed into a distinct industry segment known as "fast-casual," offering higher quality dining in a limited-service setting that tapped into robust consumer demand. Sales recorded by fast-casual operators began to mushroom, reaching $5 billion by 2002 and swelling to $12 billion by the end of the decade. Although the segment represented only a fraction of the half-trillion-dollar restaurant industry, it provided fertile ground for a host of competitors, including one of the fastest-growing fast-casual concepts, Moe's Southwest Grill.

The architects behind Moe's Southwest Grill's rapid rise in the fast-casual segment were the principals of Raving Brands Inc. An Atlanta-based franchiser, Raving Brands was founded by its chief executive officer, Martin Sprock, and its president, Daryl Dollinger. Sprock and Dollinger formed Raving Brands in 1997, starting the company to build a portfolio of brands that they would develop into chains by selling franchises.

MOE'S SOUTHWEST GRILL
CONCEPT IS CREATED

The Raving Brands founders began with Planet Smoothie Café, a chain of stores that sold energy and protein drinks. Next, Sprock planned to jump into the fast-casual fray and enter a market that was growing at roughly twice the rate of other segments in the limited-

COMPANY PERSPECTIVES

This is the story of a man who woke up one morning with a song stuck in his head. A classic tune about feeling good, sharing the love and doing your own thing. His "thing" happened to be food. Southwestern fare, with a special appreciation for the form and function of a tortilla. He experimented with fresh ingredients and had an appropriate name for each creation. He opened a restaurant, and made it known loud and clear that no matter how many times a day he had to say it, everyone who came through the door would feel welcome. And if you stuck around long enough, you'd probably hear that song that helped make a man, a legend. Welcome to Moe's.

service sector. He focused on a particular type of Southwestern cuisine, "Tex-Mex," drawing his inspiration from his travels in New Mexico, Texas, and Arizona. "I had been eating burritos in different places in the Southwest and thought a similar concept would be a good idea," he explained in the May 17, 2004 issue of *Nation's Restaurant News*. "I'd been working with healthy kinds of food items and wanted to ride that trend. I saw a bunch of Tex-Mex places spring up and thought that was a great idea, the way to go."

After failing to purchase an existing Mexican food concept in 2000, Sprock developed his own concept before the end of the year, opening the first Moe's Southwest Grill in December 2001. The flagship restaurant, located in the upscale Buckhead district of Atlanta, was company-owned, the only company-owned unit in what soon would be a chain of franchised restaurants. The restaurant served as the company's prototype unit and it also served as the headquarters for Moe's Southwest Grill. Sprock moved a desk into what had been an employee washroom and used the space as his office. "We don't need posh offices and carpeted reception areas," he said in the March 2003 issue of *Chain Leader*. "That window dressing drains the company of resources better spent supporting our franchisees."

SPROCK TAKES ON THE GIANTS

From Sprock's perspective, the success of his fledgling concept hinged on its ability to expand so it could begin chipping away at the stalwart market positions enjoyed by his rivals. The Tex-Mex niche of the fast-casual seg-

ment was dominated by large chains, each supported by the giants of the fast-food segment. Denver, Colorado-based Chipotle Mexican Grill led the way, a 320-unit chain owned by McDonald's Corporation. Wendy's International, Inc., owned the second largest competitor, the 294-unit, Thousand Oaks, California-based Baja Fresh Mexican Grill chain. Wheat Ridge, Colorado-based Qdoba Mexican Grill, a 130-restaurant chain owned by Jack in the Box Inc., ranked third. Sprock, sitting in a converted bathroom with one restaurant in operation, planned to overtake each formidable opponent, aiming for "world domination," as he said in the May 17, 2004 issue of *Nation's Restaurant News*.

Sprock developed a concept he believed could compete against the market leaders, creating a model of a Tex-Mex fast-casual restaurant that could attract both customers and franchisees. The concept tied together pop culture and healthy Tex-Mex food, incorporating a color scheme of beige, red, green, and yellow, pop music playing in the background, and a menu of selections with names such as "Triple Lindy," "Art Vandalay," "The Funk Meister," and "Homewrecker." Every customer entering the restaurant was greeted with "Welcome to Moe's!" a phrase that became a trademark of the chain set to emerge. Moe's Southwest Grill featured burritos, tacos, fajitas, and quesadillas that were made to order without lard, oils, or butter. The guacamole, salsas, and marinades were prepared twice per day. Tofu was available as a substitute for all meat dishes. The restaurants operated without using freezers or microwave ovens.

With the prototype Buckhead restaurant serving as the blueprint for expansion, Sprock began franchising the Moe's Southwest Grill concept in 2001. The franchise program estimated development costs of $250,000 per restaurant, which included a $20,000 franchise. Franchisees also were required to pay Raving Brands 5 percent of a restaurant's net sales. By the end of 2001, a chain had begun to emerge, with five locations in Atlanta open for business and an additional unit operating in Charlotte, North Carolina. Franchise development agreements in place by the end of the year called for opening seven restaurants in Atlanta, eight restaurants throughout the Southeast, and one unit in Austin, Texas.

THE CHAIN EXPANDS

Initially, Moe's Southwest Grill grew one restaurant at a time, but before long Sprock and his partners began signing multi-unit development deals, increasing the pace at which the chain expanded. By the end of 2002, systemwide sales totaled $38 million, a volume generated by more than 40 restaurants. By the beginning of 2003, Sprock had added to Raving Brands' portfolio of

KEY DATES

2000: Raving Brands Inc. opens first Moe's Southwest Grill in the Buckhead neighborhood of Atlanta, Georgia.
2001: Raving Brands begins to franchise the Moe's Southwest Grill concept.
2004: Restaurant in Knoxville, Tennessee, becomes the 100th Moe's Southwest Grill to open.
2005: The 200th restaurant opens in Bloomington, Indiana.
2006: Chain opens its first stadium and airport locations.
2007: Raving Brands sells Moe's Southwest Grill to Focus Brands Inc.
2008: Paul Damico is named president of Moe's Southwest Grill.

brands, launching PR's Coffee and Mama Fu's Asian House, but he remained committed to expanding Moe's Southwest Grill. He had yet to draw a paycheck from serving as the chain's chief executive officer and he capped his partners' salaries at $48,000, directing all the resources he could to support the growth of the chain. Plans were announced for the opening of 100 units in 2003 and another 200 units in 2004, as Sprock fought to gain ground on his much larger rivals.

Expansion occurred at a slower pace than expected, but Moe's Southwest Grill achieved great strides, nonetheless. In 2004, franchisees opened the chain's 100th restaurant, a unit located in Knoxville, Tennessee, which lifted sales well above the $100 million mark. Despite failing to meet its previously stated expansion goals, the company exuded confidence, predicting a substantial surge in growth in the immediate future. "Our conservative plan is to open 150 stores this year," a company executive said in the May 17, 2004 issue of *Nation's Restaurant News,* "and our goal by the end of 2004 is to be the third largest Fresh Mex concept, behind Chipotle and Baja Fresh. Our long-term goal is to be No. 1 by 2006. We also expect to surpass both of them this year in system-wide sales."

As the fast-casual segment recorded strong growth, Moe's Southwest Grill swept across the country, expanding geographically and opening locations in specialty venues. The chain comprised 187 restaurants by the beginning of 2005, when Raving Brands launched a service on the Moe's Southwest Grill web site that allowed customers to order and to pay for take-out orders

and catering service. The chain opened its 200th restaurant during the year, a unit located in Bloomington, Indiana, and opened its 300th restaurant in 2006, a unit in Lakeland, Florida. Systemwide sales by the end of 2006 reached an estimated $250 million, a total that included sales figures from two Moe's Southwest Grills that stood out from the pack. In 2006, the chain opened its first stadium restaurant, establishing a unit at Turner Field in Atlanta, home to Major League Baseball's Atlanta Braves. The year also saw the debut of the first Moe's Southwest Grill in an airport, a unit located at Hartsfield-Jackson International Airport in Atlanta.

After five years of franchising, Moe's Southwest Grill was breaking into the upper tier of the fast-casual segment, narrowing the gap separating it from Chipotle, Qdoba, and Baja Fresh. The opening of the stadium and airport locations represented new markets to exploit, adding to the potential prowess of the chain. However, the foray into niche markets paled in importance to an announcement made in early 2007. In March, Sprock announced plans to expand the chain into Ontario, Canada, setting the stage for Moe's Southwest Grill's first move on the international front. Sprock also suggested a possible leap to the Middle East, where several U.S.-based fast-casual concepts had enjoyed success, but before he could make his first move into a foreign market, he became ensnarled in legal difficulties.

2007: A YEAR OF CHANGE

Moe's Southwest Grill was expanding by 100 units per year and earning praise from industry publications and pundits, but a group of its franchisees was not pleased. Several weeks after Raving Brands announced the push into Canada, a group of franchisees in Georgia and Tennessee filed a lawsuit against Raving Brands and Sprock, alleging various misdeeds. The disgruntled franchisees claimed Raving Brands had not clearly indicated how money would be collected for advertising. They claimed they were forced to buy food and supplies from a company-owned distributor, which forced them to pay above-market prices for the goods. They also claimed Raving Brands intended to sell Moe's Southwest Grill, a transaction they opposed because the sale would result in the "misappropriation, misapplication, and dissipation of Moe's assets," according to the April 5, 2007 edition of the *Atlanta Journal-Constitution.* In the same article, Sprock dismissed the charges, saying, "It's very upsetting because there is obviously another agenda going on here," adding, "We have no intention of selling out."

Less than a week after Sprock said he did not intend to sell Moe's Southwest Grill, Focus Brands Inc.

announced it had signed a definitive agreement to acquire Moe's Southwest Grill. Focus Brands, also based in Atlanta, operated as the franchiser of more than 1,750 ice cream stores, bakeries, sandwich shops, and cafés in the United States, Puerto Rico, and 33 countries under the names Carvel, Cinnabon, and Schlotzsky's. The company, led by President and Chief Executive Officer Steve Romaniello, also functioned as the franchiser for Seattle's Best Coffee on military bases and in particular international markets.

FOCUS BRANDS TAKES CONTROL

The change of ownership was completed in August 2007, giving Focus Brands control over the 360 Moe's Southwest Grills in operation in 34 states. The transaction gave Focus Brands its fifth concept, lifting systemwide sales above the $1 billion mark. "We're happy to welcome Moe's into the Focus Brands family," Romaniello said in an August 30, 2007 company press release. "This is a great brand with a bright future and tremendous growth prospects, and we look forward to the exciting days ahead."

A LEADER FOR THE FUTURE

Romaniello took over leadership of Moe's Southwest Grill while he searched for the appropriate executive to lead the chain forward. Romaniello's search lasted nearly a year, ending in May 2008 when he announced Paul Damico as president of Moe's Southwest Grill. "We were looking for the sort of leader whose experience reflected a strategic and long-term approach to operations and a sound grasp of concept development," Romaniello said in the May 8, 2008 issue of *Food & Beverage Close-Up*. "Paul's extensive operational background and ability to lead people makes him ideal in this role, and we are thrilled to have him aboard." Damico joined Moe's Southwest Grill after serving as chief operating officer of SSP America, where he was in charge of operations for 42 airport properties belonging to the 170-unit restaurant concessions company.

Damico took the helm and began revamping the concept developed by Sprock. During his first months in charge, Damico began working on a new store design, one that would include a salsa bar three times the size of the existing salsa bars. He also introduced pulled pork as a new menu item and began offering buffalo chicken and a limited-time-offer selection. In terms of expansion, Damico expressed the same level of ambition as Sprock had expressed. Moe's Southwest Grill opened its 400th restaurant in August 2008, a unit in Plant City, Florida. Damico planned to open another 100 restaurants in 2009, giving the nine-year-old chain a store count capable of generating $500 million in annual sales.

Jeffrey L. Covell

PRINCIPAL COMPETITORS

Chipotle Mexican Grill, Inc.; Fresh Enterprises, Inc.; Qdoba Restaurant Corporation.

FURTHER READING

Collier, Joe Guy, "Moe's Southwest Grill President Works to Re-Energize Restaurant Group," *Atlanta Journal-Constitution*, September 9, 2008.

Crecca, Donna Hood, "The Down-and-Dirty Dozen," *Chain Leader*, March 2003, p. 72.

Elan, Elissa, "Moe's Southwest Grill," *Nation's Restaurant News*, May 17, 2004, p. 56.

"Garcia Estate Bums Out Moe's," *Restaurant Business*, February 1, 2005, p. 12.

Littman, Margaret, "By the People, for the People," *Chain Leader*, February 2007, p. 26.

McBee, Julia, "Turning Tables: Moe's Southwest Grill Branching Out," *Atlanta Journal-Constitution*, December 7, 2001, p. Q2.

"Moe's Gets Online Order, Payment Capabilities," *Nation's Restaurant News*, January 10, 2005, p. 50.

"Moe's Southwest Grill Names Brand President," *Food & Beverage Close-Up*, May 8, 2008.

Reese, Krista, "Southwestern Favorites Served with a Gimmick," *Atlanta Journal-Constitution*, July 26, 2001, p. K2.

Stafford, Leon, "Franchisees of Moe's Southwest Grill Sue Restaurant Chain," *Atlanta Journal-Constitution*, April 5, 2007.

The Neiman Marcus Group, Inc.

—■—

1618 Main Street
Dallas, Texas 75201
U.S.A.
Telephone: (214) 741-6911
Fax: (214) 573-6142
Web site: http://www.neimanmarcus.com

Wholly Owned Subsidiary of Newton Holding LLC
Incorporated: 1987
Employees: 17,500
Sales: $4.6 billion (2008)
NAICS: 452110 Department Stores; 454110 Electronic Shopping and Mail-Order Houses

■ ■ ■

The name "Neiman Marcus" is synonymous with upscale retailing in the United States, where The Neiman Marcus Group, Inc., operates two high-end retail segments, Neiman Marcus and Bergdorf Goodman. In addition to its opulent stores, the company has a thriving catalog business as well as online shopping operations. Neiman Marcus celebrated its 100-year anniversary in 2007 and continues to be the clothier and luxury accessories choice for many of the nation's well-known and most fashion-conscious shoppers.

EARLY HISTORY

From the very beginning, the founders of Neiman Marcus aimed high. The original store was opened in Dallas in 1907. Its proprietors were Herbert Marcus, his sister

Carrie, and her husband, Al Neiman. All three were working in various retail positions in the Dallas area around 1900. Frustrated by their dead-end jobs, Marcus and Neiman decided to strike out on their own. The pair moved to Atlanta in 1905 to start a sales promotion and advertising business. The venture was quite successful and they were offered a lucrative buyout deal after only two years of operation. Given the choice between $25,000 cash or the Missouri franchise of a young Coca-Cola company, the partners opted for the cash. In retrospect, the decision cost them a fortune, as Coke went on to become the top-selling soda pop brand in the world; yet the entrepreneurs acquired the seed money to launch the first Neiman Marcus store.

Neiman and Marcus returned triumphantly to Dallas in 1907 and immediately set out to open a store specializing in the finest women's clothing money could buy. The store was lavishly furnished and stocked with apparel of a quality not commonly found in Texas. Within a few weeks, the store's initial inventory, mostly acquired on a buying trip to New York by Carrie, was completely sold out. Oil-rich Texans, welcoming the opportunity to flaunt their wealth in sophisticated fashion, flocked to the new store. In spite of a nationwide financial panic set off only a few weeks after its opening, Neiman Marcus was instantly successful, and its first several years of operation were quite profitable.

In 1913 the original Neiman Marcus store, and most of its merchandise, was destroyed by a fire, the first of several in the company's history. Within about two weeks, however, the store reopened at a temporary site nearby, and construction was quickly begun on a new permanent location. With capital raised through the sale of stock to a handful of manufacturing companies, the new building was ready for business by the autumn of 1914. In its first year at the new building, Neiman Marcus recorded a profit of $40,000 on sales of $700,000, nearly twice the totals reached in its last year at the original location.

Business increased steadily over the next several years, as money from oil, cattle, and cotton continued to flow into Texas. The store maintained its commitment to extravagance, lining the aisles with the fanciest merchandise and the store's reputation soon expanded beyond Texas's borders to Hollywood, New York, and even Europe.

In 1926 Al and Carrie Neiman were divorced and Neiman's interest was bought out by the Marcus family, who remained at the top of the company's management for the next 60 years. Stanley and Edward Marcus, two of Herbert's sons, joined the company in 1926. A major expansion project was completed in 1927, following the acquisition of some property next door, nearly doubling the store's capacity. Neiman Marcus added men's clothing to its offerings with the 1928 opening of the Man's Shop. By 1929, the store's net sales had reached $3.6 million.

LOWER-PRICED MERCHANDISE: THIRTIES AND FORTIES

The onset of the Great Depression forced Neiman Marcus to shift its strategy. During the 1930s the company began to include less expensive clothing lines to keep customers whose fortunes had taken a turn for the worse. Company lore from the era tells of a barefoot teenage girl walking confidently into the store and ordering thousands of dollars worth of merchandise. Her father had just struck oil, and her first impulse was to head straight for Neiman Marcus.

By striking a balance between upper-crust fashions and more moderate apparel, Neiman Marcus was able to maintain its elite reputation while also broadening its customer base. This successful transition enabled the company to sustain its impressive growth rate and by 1938 annual sales had broken the $5 million mark. Along the way, the store's Man's Shop was expanded, first in 1934 and again in 1941.

The move to include lower-priced merchandise accelerated during the 1940s. World War II brought hundreds of high-paying defense manufacturing jobs to the Dallas area. To the female workers and the wives of their male counterparts, shopping at Neiman Marcus was like a dream come true. The Marcuses were shrewd enough to stock their store with merchandise affordable to this new wave of middle-class customers. Between 1942 and 1944, sales at Neiman Marcus grew from $6 million to $11 million. Still, the company was able to cultivate its special relationship with the super-rich, and the store took on a sort of split personality. The trend increased even further at the war's end, as more companies opened offices in Dallas and young families with junior executive salaries settled in the area.

The immediate postwar years saw many changes at Neiman Marcus. Shortly after the war, two other Marcus sons, Herbert Jr., and Lawrence, joined the company. In 1946 Neiman Marcus suffered the second major fire in its history. Despite substantial damage to both the building and its merchandise, the store was closed for only five days. Even with the loss of peak Christmas shopping days, the store recorded its best season to date. Herbert Marcus Sr., died in 1950, and Carrie Neiman died just two years later, leaving Stanley Marcus in charge of the company's operations.

STANLEY TAKES THE REINS: FIFTIES TO SEVENTIES

Stanley Marcus led the company through a period of rapid expansion during the 1950s. In 1951 a second store was opened at Preston Center in the suburbs of Dallas and a new service building was opened the following year to handle merchandise for both stores. In 1953 a major renovation project added a fifth and a sixth floor to the original Dallas store, and in 1955 Neiman Marcus opened a new store in Houston. Rather than take on the expense of a new building, the company merged an existing Houston store, Ben Wolfman's, into its operation.

The company's reputation for lavish displays grew along with its stores, as the annual Neiman Marcus Fortnight was inaugurated in 1957. The Fortnight was a presentation of fashions and culture from a particular country, held in late October and early November of each year. Another popular annual publicity stunt was

KEY DATES

1907: First Neiman Marcus store, specializing in upscale women's clothing, opens in Dallas.

1926: Stanley and Edward Marcus, two of Herbert's sons, join the company.

1928: Men's clothing is added to the store's inventory.

1951: Second Neiman Marcus store is opened in the Dallas suburban area.

1963: Stanley's son Richard joins the company as a buyer.

1968: Company merges with Broadway-Hale Stores (later Carter Hawley Hale Stores, Inc.).

1979: Richard Marcus is named chairman and CEO of Neiman Marcus.

1984: Carter Hawley fends off a takeover attempt and General Cinema Corporation steps in to buy a majority stake in the retailer.

1987: Second takeover attempt leads to spinoff of Carter Hawley's specialty store division as The Neiman Marcus Group (NMG).

1988: NMG acquires the Horchow housewares catalog operation.

1998: NMG acquires a majority stake in Gurwitch Bristow Products, LLC.

1999: Majority interest in Kate Spade LLC is acquired and NMG's immediate parent (Harcourt) reduces its overall stake to 10 percent.

2002: Stanley Marcus passes away on January 22.

2005: Company is bought by Texas Pacific Group and Warburg Pincus LLC.

2006: Neiman Marcus launches CUSP for younger shoppers and sells Kate Spade to Liz Claiborne Inc.

2007: The 39th Neiman Marcus store opens in Massachusetts.

2009: Company announces plans for new stores in Washington State, Florida, New York, and New Jersey.

launched in 1960 with the extraordinary "His and Hers" gift selection included in each Neiman Marcus Christmas catalog. His and Hers gifts over the years included such spectacular items as submarines, dirigibles, and robots.

Another generation of Marcuses came on board in 1963, when Stanley's son Richard Marcus joined the company as a buyer. The following year, fire devastated the main Dallas store, again during the peak Christmas shopping season. Once again, the store was reopened quickly, and the repair work included improvements to the store's appearance. In 1965, with the population of suburban Dallas growing by leaps and bounds, the Preston Center store was closed, and a new store, more than twice its size, was opened at NorthPark Center. Another branch was opened in nearby Fort Worth around the same time. By 1967 the company's four stores were generating annual sales of $58.5 million, and profit for that year was in excess of $2 million.

Neiman Marcus ceased being a family business in 1968 when the company was merged into Broadway-Hale Stores, Inc., a West Coast retail chain with 46 stores and revenue of $457 million. The merger enabled Neiman Marcus to expand at a much faster pace than as an independent entity. Over the next 15 years, a new store opened nearly every year. With locations in California, Florida, and several other states during the 1970s, Neiman Marcus became a coast-to-coast operation. Atlanta; St. Louis; Northbrook, Illinois; Washington, D.C.; and White Plains, New York, were among other new locations opened during this period.

Neiman's Texas strongholds were changed as well, with the Dallas service center dramatically enlarged in 1973, and a new store in Ridgmar Mall replacing the previous Fort Worth location. In 1975 Stanley Marcus became executive vice-president of Carter Hawley Hale Stores, Inc. (formerly Broadway-Hale), running its specialty store division, which included Neiman Marcus. Son Richard was named chairman and CEO of Neiman Marcus in 1979.

UPS AND DOWNS IN THE EIGHTIES

By 1980, the year Neiman Marcus opened its first store in the Northeast, annual sales were about $350 million. Over the next few years almost two dozen new stores opened nationwide, for a total of 21 stores by 1984. Not all stores were performing as well as expected, however, especially against such rivals as Bloomingdale's and Saks Fifth Avenue. Parent company Carter Hawley put the brakes on expansion, but soon had a hostile takeover bid to fight. The Limited offered $1.1 billion for the company, but Carter Hawley found a white knight in General Cinema Corporation, a company whose $1 billion in revenue came from soft-drink bottling and movie theaters. General Cinema purchased 38.6 percent of Carter Hawley and thwarted Limited's takeover plans.

Two years later, The Limited teamed up with shopping center magnate Edward DeBartolo to launch a second attempt at Carter Hawley. In response, Carter Hawley restructured its operations (completed in 1987), spinning off the specialty store division into an independent, publicly traded entity called The Neiman Marcus Group, Inc. (NMG). In exchange for its Carter Hawley stock, General Cinema was awarded a 60 percent interest in the new company, consisting of not only Neiman Marcus but exclusive New York retailer Bergdorf Goodman, and the 200-store Contempo Casuals chain.

Neiman Marcus stores contributed about three-fourths of NMG's sales and expanded its retail reach in 1988 with the purchase of Dallas-based Horchow Mail Order, a cataloger specializing in upscale home furnishings, linens, and tabletop decorative items. Seeking to return Neiman Marcus to its dominant position among upper-end specialty retailers, General Cinema tapped Allen Questrom to run NMG. The departure of Richard Marcus as chief executive ended the Neiman and Marcus reign of the family business.

LEADERSHIP WOES IN THE NINETIES

In 1993 Terry Lundgren became chairman, while remaining CEO. Gerald Sampson, formerly of May Department Stores, was named president and COO. The company recorded revenues of $1.45 billion for the year, a 12.7 percent jump over 1992, due in part to increased emphasis on big-name designer labels such as Calvin Klein, Georgio Armani, and Donna Karan. General Cinema, meantime, was renamed Harcourt General, Inc.

Neiman Marcus continued its attempts to attract new, younger customers while maintaining its commitment to meet the needs of its core upscale clientele. Toward this end, career wardrobe boutiques were added at several locations while construction began on a new Neiman Marcus in Short Hills, New Jersey, in 1994, with other stores in New Jersey and Pennsylvania planned. Another reshuffling among executives also occurred that year, as Lundgren left the company and Burton Tansky, former chairman and chief executive at Bergdorf Goodman, took the helm for the group.

In July 1995, in a move designed to focus more on the upscale Neiman Marcus and Bergdorf Goodman businesses, the money-losing Contempo Casuals chain was sold to Wet Seal, Inc. By mid-1996 the number of Neiman Marcus stores had grown to 29 and the chain had its best year ever during fiscal 1996, posting record operating earnings of $134 million on sales of $1.6 billion, the latter being a 12 percent increase over the previous year. Also in 1996 came the debut of the *Book*,

a so-called magalog that combined the selling features of a catalog with the editorial content of a magazine.

Expansion was again on the agenda in the final years of the decade. In early 1998 NMG's direct-mail operation was bolstered through the acquisition of the Chef's Catalog for $31 million in cash. Founded in 1979, the Chef's Catalog offered gourmet cookware and high-end kitchenware. Running out of the types of large markets able to support a Neiman Marcus store, the group developed a concept extension for smaller markets. Dubbed the "Galleries of Neiman Marcus," these stores initially ranged in size from 9,000 to 12,000 square feet (the average Neiman Marcus store was 141,000 square feet) and featured precious and designer jewelry, gifts, and decorative home accessories. Three Galleries stores were opened in Cleveland, Phoenix, and Seattle over the next two years.

At the same time NMG was testing its Galleries, a new source of competition emerged: designer retail outlets by such fashion plates as Ralph Lauren, Gucci, and Prada. To combat any loss of sales, NMG spent some $200 million buying into up-and-coming designers and brands sold at its stores. Additionally, the company spent $6.7 million for a 51 percent stake in Gurwitch Bristow Products, LLC, marketer of the Laura Mercier cosmetics line in late 1998; paid $33.6 million for a 56 percent interest in Kate Spade LLC, the high-end handbag and accessory firm in early 1999; and launched the company's own e-commerce web site, neimanmarcus.com, in late 1999.

Also near the end of the decade, Harcourt General ended its majority control of NMG by spinning off the bulk of its stake to its shareholders. Following the transaction, Harcourt held a 10 percent interest in the group. On the store development front, the 31st Neiman Marcus opened in Hawaii, followed by plans for two stores in Florida.

A NEW ERA

In the early 2000s the company followed through with its plans for several new stores in Florida: Palm Beach opened in 2000, Tampa in 2001, and Coral Gables and Orlando in 2002. In Texas, a replacement store was opened in Plano, as plans were unveiled for new stores in San Antonio and Atlanta. Revenues for fiscal 2001 reached $3.02 billion before falling victim to a stumbling economy and severe consumer cutbacks in the wake of the September 11, 2001, terrorist attacks on the United States.

A few months later, in January 2002, an important link to the company's past slipped away as Stanley Marcus died at age 96, having served as chairman emeritus since 1975. In April of the same year, Harcourt General sold its remaining interest in the company. By 2003, The Neiman Marcus Group was ready to embark on a new era as an independent entity. Karen Katz, who had run NMG's direct marketing operations, was promoted to president and chief executive of Neiman Marcus stores with Burt Tansky retaining the same titles for the entire Neiman Marcus Group.

The next three years ushered in major change. In late 2004 the Chef's Catalog unit was sold, followed by its credit card holdings to HSBC Bank in July 2005. Next came the announcement that private-equity firms Texas Pacific Group and Warburg Pincus LLC were buying The Neiman Marcus Group. The sale was completed in October, and the company was once again private. In 2006 two brands were shed: Gurwitch Products LLC (including the Laura Mercier cosmetics line) was sold to Alticor Inc. (parent of Amway Corporation) for just under $41 million, while Kate Spade LLC was sold to Liz Claiborne Inc. for $121 million.

Next came the introduction of a new concept store called CUSP, catering to younger fashion-conscious shoppers. The first CUSP store was opened in Virginia corresponding with a web site launch (www.cusp.com). Revenues for fiscal 2006 were a solid $4 billion as the 39th Neiman Marcus store opened in Natick, a suburb of Boston, Massachusetts.

By 2007, the year of Neiman Marcus's centennial, aggressive expansion plans were once again on the agenda as locations were selected for new stores in Los Angeles; Seattle; Long Island; Princeton, New Jersey; and Sarasota, Florida. Older stores in Atlanta and Westchester, New York, were slated for renovation along with the company's stalwart Bergdorf Goodman store on Fifth Avenue in New York City. In 2008 Neiman Marcus moved ahead with its CUSP concept, opening four additional stores as a smaller, hipper version of its esteemed retailers. Revenues continued to grow steadily, with $4.4 billion in fiscal 2007 and $4.6 billion in 2008.

The end of the decade brought widespread recession and economic woes for the retail sector. While the company initiated a round of layoffs after a poor first quarter in 2009, rather than slash prices and incorporate less quality wares into their stores, Neiman Marcus and Bergdorf Goodman stood true to their status as high-end retailers. The company was not immune, however, to offering promotions and bargains to its affluent customers, who continued to shop, albeit a little less frequently.

Neiman Marcus, a name synonymous with the finest apparel and accessories money can buy, remained a luxury retailer proud to be associated with a long line of internationally known designers including Armani, Brioni, Chanel, Gucci, Prada, David Yurman, and Ermenegildo Zegna. The company had certainly come a long way since its founding in 1907, with 42 Neiman Marcus stores in 18 states and the District of Columbia, two New York City Bergdorf Goodman stores, five CUSP locations, and 24 outlet centers to handle its demand.

Robert R. Jacobson
Updated, David E. Salamie; Nelson Rhodes

PRINCIPAL SUBSIDIARIES

Bergdorf Goodman, Inc.; CUSP, Inc.; Horchow Inc.; Neiman Marcus, Inc.

PRINCIPAL OPERATING UNITS

Specialty Retail; Neiman Marcus Direct.

PRINCIPAL COMPETITORS

Barneys New York, Inc.; Bon-Ton Stores, Inc.; Dillard's, Inc.; Macy's, Inc.; Nordstrom, Inc.; Saks Inc.; Von Maur, Inc.

FURTHER READING

"Big Deal in Big D," *Newsweek,* November 4, 1968, p. 94.

Bird, Laura, "Haute Brands: Neiman Marcus, Saks Wage Expensive Battle for Upscale Shoppers," *Wall Street Journal,* November 21, 1996, p. A1.

Chabbott, Sophia, and Jeanine Poggi, "Neiman's to Buy Rest of Spade," *WWD,* November 3, 2006, p. 2.

Deutsch, Claudia H., "Neiman-Marcus Minds the Store," *New York Times,* September 4, 1988, p. F4.

Ferry, John William, *A History of the Department Store,* New York: Macmillan, 1960, pp. 161–68.

Glain, Stephen, "Sale of the Season: The Neiman Buyout Could Be a Sign of Deals to Come," *Newsweek International,* July 25, 2005, p. 78.

Haber, Holly, "Deep in the Heart of Texans," *WWD,* July 21, 1997, p. 8.

———, "Neiman's New Chief," *WWD,* March 20, 2000, p. 1.

———, "Stanley Marcus: A Luxury Legend," *WWD,* December 11, 2003, p. 11B.

———, "Winning Big in Designer," *WWD,* October 27, 1993, pp. 8–9.

Harris, Roy J., and David Stipp, "Carter Hawley Blocks Takeover Attempt … ," *Wall Street Journal,* December 9, 1986, p. 3.

Johannes, Laura, "Harcourt General to Spin Off Stake in Neiman Marcus," *Wall Street Journal,* May 18, 1999, p. C11.

Kaufman, Leslie, "Luxury's Old Guard Battered by New Realities," *New York Times,* December 16, 2001, p. 1.

Marcus, Stanley, *Minding the Store: A Memoir,* Boston: Little Brown, 1974, 383 p.

———, *Quest for the Best,* New York: Viking Press, 1979, 227 p.

Mason, Todd, "That Neiman-Marcus Mystique Isn't Traveling Well," *Business Week,* July 8, 1985, p. 44.

"The Merchant Prince of Dallas," *Business Week,* October 21, 1967, pp. 115–18.

Moin, David, "Growing Neiman Marcus: New Owner May Be Near and Expansion a Priority," *WWD,* April 19, 2005, p. 1

———, "NM Acquires 56% of Kate Spade," *WWD,* February 5, 1999, p. 2.

———, "NM Expecting Minimal Fallout from Tarr's Abrupt Resignation," *WWD,* December 19, 1996, p. 2.

———, "NM Group Puts Vendors at Top of Shopping List," *WWD,* December 3, 1998, p. 1.

———, "The NMG Problem: Finding the Successor to CEO Burt Tansky," *WWD,* January 30, 2002, p. 1.

———, "NMG Seeking Growth," *WWD,* September 10, 2004, p. 1.

———, "Red Flag for Luxury: Saks, Neiman's Rise but Worries Set In," *WWD,* March 6, 2008, p. 1.

Moin, David, and Jeanine Poggi, "Luxury Rocks 'N Rolls: Neiman's Net Up 47% Despite Competition," *WWD,* June 8, 2007, p. 1.

Moin, David, and Sharon Edelson, "Neiman's Gold Rush: An Intensified Effort to Promote Luxe Life," *WWD,* April 10, 1996, p. 1.

Montgomery, Leland, "General Cinema: The Value of Camouflage," *Financial World,* September 1, 1992, p. 17.

"Neiman Marcus Reports a Loss," *New York Times,* March 12, 2009, p. B11.

Pace, Eric, "Stanley Marcus, the Retailer from Dallas, Is Dead at 96," *New York Times,* January 23, 2002, p. A16.

Palmeri, Christopher, "Retailer's Revenge," *Forbes,* May 3, 1999, p. 62.

Pereira, Joseph, "Neiman-Marcus Names Questrom to Head Chain," *Wall Street Journal,* August 15, 1988, p. 21.

"Revamping Bergdorf's," *WWD,* September 12, 2005, p. 1.

Rosenbloom, Stephanie, "Neiman and Saks Join Trend of Job Cuts," *New York Times,* January 16, 2009, p. B4.

Seckler, Valerie, "NM Dumps Contempo for $1 Million in Stock," *WWD,* April 4, 1995, p. 2.

Strom, Stephanie, "New Neiman Marcus Head Is Named," *New York Times,* April 22, 1994, p. D4.

Tolbert, Frank X., *Neiman-Marcus, Texas,* New York: Henry Holt and Company, 1953.

Vargo, Julie, "Neiman's at 90: Kicking Up Its Heels Texas-Style," *Daily News Record,* August 25, 1997, p. 24.

Weitzman, Jennifer, "NMG Bounces Back to Black," *WWD,* September 11, 2002, p. 2.

Williamson, Rusty, "Tansky at the Top: Named Chief Executive of Neiman's Group," *WWD,* February 21, 2001, p. 1.

⬡ NOVARTIS

Novartis AG

⸺ ■ ⸺

Lichtstrasse 35
Basel, 4056
Switzerland
Telephone: (+41 61) 324-1111
Fax: (+41 61) 324-8001
Web site: http://www.novartis.com

Public Company
Incorporated: 1996
Employees: 96,700
Sales: $41.46 billion (2008)
Stock Exchanges: Swiss New York
Ticker Symbols: NOVN (Swiss); NVS (NYSE)
NAICS: 325412 Pharmaceutical Preparation Manufacturing; 325411 Medicinal and Botanical Manufacturing; 325414 Biological Product (Except Diagnostic) Manufacturing; 339115 Ophthalmic Goods Manufacturing; 541710 Research and Development in the Physical, Engineering, and Life Sciences

■ ■ ■

Novartis AG, created via the 1996 merger of Ciba-Geigy Ltd. and Sandoz Ltd., is one of the world's leading suppliers of medicinal products. Based in Basel, Switzerland, Novartis claims to be the only company to hold leadership positions in the following four areas: brand-name patented pharmaceuticals, generic pharmaceuticals (through the Sandoz unit), human vaccines and blood-testing diagnostic products, and consumer health products. The company's Pharmaceuti-

cal Division, its largest unit, contributing about 64 percent of overall sales, researches, develops, manufactures, distributes, and sells brand-name pharmaceuticals in several therapeutic areas, including cardiovascular, metabolism, oncology, neuroscience, ophthalmics, respiratory, immunology, and infectious diseases. Novartis has more than 50 pharmaceutical products on the market, and it sells brand-name pharmaceuticals in about 140 countries around the world. Among its top sellers are the high-blood-pressure medicine Diovan, leukemia treatment Gleevac/Glivec, breast cancer drug Femara, and Zometa, a treatment for certain cancers that have spread to the bones.

On the generics side, Sandoz offers approximately 950 compounds in 130 countries; Sandoz accounts for about 18 percent of overall Novartis sales. Contributing about 4 percent of group sales is the Vaccines and Diagnostics Division, which produces influenza, meningococcal, pediatric, and travel vaccines, as well as blood-testing and molecular diagnostic products used to prevent the spread of infectious diseases. Novartis's Consumer Health Division, which generates about 14 percent of total revenues, includes over-the-counter (OTC) medicines, animal health products, and the CIBA Vision unit. In OTC products, Novartis is active in more than 45 countries, offering such products as Triaminic and TheraFlu for coughs and colds and Excedrin and Voltaren for pain relief. In animal health, the company produces medicines for both companion and farm animals in 38 countries. CIBA Vision is a world leader in the research, development, and manufacturing of contact lenses and lens care products.

COMPANY PERSPECTIVES

We want to discover, develop and successfully market innovative products to prevent and cure diseases, to ease suffering and to enhance the quality of life.

We also want to provide a shareholder return that reflects outstanding performance and to adequately reward those who invest ideas and work in our company.

Novartis spends more than $7 billion each year on pharmaceutical research and development and maintains research laboratories in Basel; Cambridge, Massachusetts; East Hanover, New Jersey; Horsham, England; and Shanghai, China. Its major production facilities are located in Switzerland, England, Ireland, France, Austria, Turkey, Singapore, and the U.S. states of Nebraska and New York. The company generates about 43 percent of its revenues in Europe, 40 percent in the Americas, and 17 percent in Asia, Africa, and Australasia.

EARLY HISTORIES OF CIBA AND GEIGY

In the early years of the 20th century, the world's strongest chemical industries were in Germany, the United States, and Switzerland. German companies, fearful of losing their leading position to rapidly advancing U.S. firms, openly colluded and coordinated business strategies. After World War I the German companies formed a cartel, the notorious IG Farben. In order to remain competitive with the Germans, the three largest Swiss chemical companies, Ciba Ltd., J.R. Geigy S.A., and Sandoz Ltd., formed a similar cartel called Interessengemeinschaft Basel (Basler IG). This trust lasted from 1918 to 1951. By 1970, however, market conditions led Ciba and Geigy to merge, forming one of the world's leading pharmaceutical and specialty chemical companies. Geigy was the older of the two companies (one family member was in the drug business as early as 1758). Through several generations, the Geigy family had married into the prosperous silk manufacturing establishment in Basel and then became established in the dye trade in 1883. Only a few years later, the Geigy family set itself apart from other dyers in Basel by embracing newly discovered synthetic dying processes.

Several years earlier, in 1859, a French silk weaver named Alexander Clavel moved to Basel, where he established a dyeworks called the Gesellschaft für Chemische Industrie im Basel, or Ciba. In 1884 Clavel abandoned silk dying for a more lucrative trade in dyestuff manufacturing. Ciba gained a reputation for Fuchsine, a reddish purple dye, and Martius yellow.

By 1900 Ciba was the largest chemical company in Switzerland. With a major alkali works located at Monthey, it was one of the only Swiss manufacturers of inorganic dyes. Ciba, however, started a limited diversification into the pharmaceutical business with the introduction of an antiseptic called Vioform. Between 1900 and 1913 net assets quadrupled while profits nearly tripled. During this period, Geigy remained steadfastly committed to organic dye production; some of the dyes were still derived from coal tar.

Early in the century both Ciba and Geigy established factories in Germany, due in part to a labor shortage in Switzerland, but also to avoid enforcement of environmental laws designed to reduce pollution in the Rhine River.

Until World War I, German chemical companies dominated the world dye trade with a 90 percent market share. Those companies, including BASF, Hoechst, and Bayer, could easily have run Swiss competitors out of business through price competition; they had proven their ability to hold back the U.S. chemical industry in its infancy. Instead, Ciba and Geigy developed practices that would permit international expansion while not provoking the Germans. Central to this strategy was the abandonment of bulk dye production (a German specialty) in favor of more expensive specialty dyes.

In time, the German companies developed a vested interest in the survival of their Swiss counterparts. Eighty percent of the raw materials used by the Swiss companies came from Germany. In eliminating Swiss competitors, the German companies would eliminate customers whose capacity they could not economically absorb. Furthermore, competition among German companies to fill a sudden void left by the Swiss could have destabilized the careful balance maintained by the cartel. As Swiss companies became acclimated to the German system, they were granted certain privileges, such as an exclusive right to export to Germany. Cooperation between Swiss and German companies also took the form of an occasional profit-sharing pool, such as the one that existed between Geigy, Bayer, and BASF for black dye.

The onset of World War I in Europe in 1914 severely upset the equilibrium that had existed between Ciba, Geigy, and their German counterparts. Unable to secure raw materials and chemical intermediaries from

KEY DATES

1859: Alexander Clavel founds silk dyeing works in Basel, Switzerland, called the Gesellschaft für Chemische Industrie im Basel, or Ciba.
1886: Kern & Sandoz is formed.
1898: Geigy is founded in Grenzach, Germany.
1911: Sandoz Chemical Company Ltd. begins operations in England.
1917: Arthur Stoll creates Pharmaceutical Department at Sandoz.
1918: Ciba, Sandoz, and Geigy form Basler IG cartel.
1929: Basler IG joins IG Farben to form Dual Cartel.
1935: Geigy begins producing insecticides.
1939: Dr. Paul Mueller discovers insecticidal properties of DDT.
1949: Geigy launches antirheumatic drug Butazolidin.
1951: Basler IG is dissolved.
1958: Sandoz launches neuroleptic drug Melleril.
1964: Sandoz forms research center in East Hanover, New Jersey.
1970: Ciba and Geigy merge to form Ciba-Geigy Ltd.
1974: Ciba-Geigy Ltd. acquires Funk Seeds International.
1980: Ciba-Geigy Ltd. forms biotechnology unit.
1987: Ciba Vision is formed.
1996: Ciba-Geigy and Sandoz merge to form Novartis AG.
1999: Novartis divests seed and crop protection holdings.
2005: Novartis's generics division, Sandoz, acquires the German firm Hexal AG.
2006: Company creates the Vaccines and Diagnostics Division after taking full control of Chiron Corporation.
2007: Novartis narrows its focus to four main areas brand-name pharmaceuticals, vaccines and diagnostic products, generics, and OTC products.
2008: Novartis purchases 25 percent stake in eyecare specialist Alcon Inc. for $10.4 billion.

German suppliers, factories in Basel were forced to suspend dye production. The Swiss later negotiated an

agreement with the British, who had been dependent on German dyes and were unprepared for their trade embargo. The British agreed to supply the Swiss with raw materials on the condition that Swiss dyes would be sold preferentially to Britain. While Swiss factories in Baden were seized by the German government, the Swiss were free to export to the lucrative (and formerly German) markets in Britain and the United States and to establish factories in France and Russia.

Ciba's profits increased dramatically, from CHF 3 million in 1913 to CHF 15 million in 1917. While the end of the war reopened world markets, it also found the industry in a severe state of overcapacity. By 1921 Ciba's profits had fallen to CHF 1 million. At this time the German companies decided to reform their cartel under the aegis of a large holding company called IG Farben. Ciba, Sandoz, and Geigy were invited to join IG Farben but, true to Swiss neutrality, elected instead to form their own cartel, Basler IG.

CARTEL-ERA CIBA AND GEIGY

Basler IG, founded in 1918, was fashioned after IG Farben. The group consisted of Ciba, Geigy, and Sandoz, virtually the entire Swiss chemical industry. The agreement mandated that all competition between the three companies would cease, technical knowledge would be freely shared, and all profits would be pooled. Ciba would receive 52 percent of the group's profits, while Geigy and Sandoz would each be entitled to 24 percent. Any sales between the companies were to be invoiced at cost, raw materials would be purchased jointly, and the manufacture of any product would be assigned to whichever company could produce it at the lowest cost.

From the cartel's inception, Geigy's weak market position was a source of tension for its partners. Geigy still produced vegetable dyes, which were gradually losing market share to organic dyestuffs. Despite Sandoz's contention that it was being forced to subsidize Geigy, Basler IG remained stable. In fact, it was considered more successful than the larger and more powerful IG Farben. All three firms invested their profits into a broader range of chemical interests, including chemicals and pharmaceuticals. By 1930 these divisions contributed more than one quarter of the group's profits. A joint venture between Sandoz and Geigy led to the establishment of the Cincinnati Chemical Works, a subsidiary that gave Basler IG a tariff-free foothold in the U.S. market.

In 1929, placing profit before independence, Basler IG joined with IG Farben to create the Dual Cartel. French dyemakers joined the group shortly afterward, forming the Tripartite Cartel. In 1932, with the addition of the British cartel Imperial Chemical Industries, the group was again renamed the Quadrapartite Cartel. This pan-European cartel existed until 1939, when World War II forced its dissolution.

Because of the secrecy characteristic of Swiss firms, little is known about Basler IG's activities during the war; the company had subsidiaries in both Allied and Axis nations. At one point, Ciba angered its partners by placing its shares in Cincinnati Chemical Works under the custody of a U.S. trust. Apparently fearing the eventual seizure of those shares by the alien property custodian, Geigy and Sandoz protested in U.S. courts but were unable to retrieve Ciba's shares.

In 1939 Dr. Paul Mueller, a researcher with Geigy, discovered the insecticidal properties of DDT. Originally thought safe enough to be sprayed directly on refugees to eradicate lice, DDT was considered a "wonder chemical." Research during the war led to the development of several ethical (prescription) drugs, including Privine, a treatment for hay fever, and Nupercaine, a spinal anesthetic used in childbirth. The companies also developed drugs for treatment of high blood pressure and heart disease.

After the war Ciba notified Geigy and Sandoz that as a result of U.S. antitrust laws, the 1918 agreement could not be respected among subsidiaries in the United States. Geigy made a similar declaration regarding U.S. assets in 1947. Two years later Sandoz again raised the issue of cross-subsidization and proposed that the cartel be dissolved. Geigy opposed the motion, but Ciba, unwilling to abandon its lucrative markets in the United States, eventually sided with Sandoz; the postwar environment no longer justified cartelization for self-protection. Basler IG was finally dissolved in 1951.

POST-CARTEL YEARS AND 1970 CREATION OF CIBA-GEIGY

Geigy's poor financial performance called into question its survivability outside the cartel. During the 1950s, however, the full market potential of DDT was realized. Suddenly profitable, Geigy expanded its market in agrichemicals by introducing a corn herbicide called triazine.

Both Ciba and Geigy grew steadily during the 1950s. Between 1950 and 1959, Ciba's sales grew from CHF 531 million to CHF 1.02 billion, and Geigy's grew from CHF 260 million to CHF 738 million. By 1960 both Ciba and Geigy were diversified manufacturers, competing directly in pharmaceuticals, dyes, plastics, textile auxiliaries, and agricultural and specialty chemicals. Each year Geigy's sales grew stronger, until in 1967 the company overtook Ciba.

Although older than Ciba by 25 years, Geigy maintained a more youthful image. While Ciba sold itself as the company "where research is the tradition," Geigy recruited engineers with the slogan, "future with Geigy." In 1970, while Ciba and Geigy personnel were quibbling over their respective talents, the leaders of both companies were discussing a possible merger.

The idea to merge was first raised when the two companies jointly established a factory at Toms River, New Jersey. With increasingly difficult conditions in export markets, particularly the United States, officials of the two companies began to explore the benefits of combining their textile and pharmaceutical research; Geigy's strength in agricultural chemicals complemented Ciba's leading position in synthetic resins and petrochemicals.

Ciba and Geigy were both in excellent financial condition. However, some of the same market conditions that had led them to form Basler IG in 1918 were once again prevalent. Competition against German companies in export markets had intensified. However, it was as a defense against emerging petrochemical industries in oil-rich Persian Gulf states that the merger was most attractive.

The largest obstacle to a merger between Ciba and Geigy was U.S. antitrust legislation. Antitrust sentiment in the United States was so strong that federal prosecutors vowed to block the merger in Switzerland if it threatened to restrain U.S. trade in any way. In order to win approval in the United States, Ciba agreed to sell its American dyeworks to Crompton & Knowles Corporation, and Geigy consented to turn over its U.S. pharmaceutical holdings to Revlon. Despite further challenges, including one from consumer advocate Ralph Nader, the merger was approved.

Mechanically, the merger consisted of a takeover of Ciba by Geigy. This was done to minimize tax penalties amounting to CHF 55 million. Geigy's chairman, Dr. van Planta, assumed the chairmanship of the new company, with Ciba's chairman, Dr. Kappeli, serving as honorary chairman.

As promised, the Ciba-Geigy merger proved "synergistic." The more profitable but less diversified Geigy benefited from Ciba's research capabilities. Ciba, on the other hand, profited from Geigy's more modern approach to marketing and management. In the United States, the company's U.S. subsidiary passed the $1 billion sales mark in 1978, and doubled that figure only six years later. The company's worldwide sales that year were CHF 17.5 billion, 30 percent of which came from U.S. operations. Despite a 14 percent drop in profits between 1978 and 1980, Ciba-Geigy maintained strong annual sales growth since 1981; profits as a percentage of sales was 8.1 percent in 1985.

In contrast to its impressive performance on the balance sheet, Ciba-Geigy suffered a few problems with its public image. In the mid-1970s a Ciba-Geigy product marketed in Africa as an ordinary analgesic produced a horrifying side effect: the loss of large pieces of flesh. In addition, its plant at Toms River discontinued production of Posgene in response to a Greenpeace campaign that warned the community of a possible accident similar in magnitude to the tragedy in Bhopal, India.

Troubles at Toms River continued; in 1982 the plant was added to the U.S. Environmental Protection Agency's (EPA) list of "Superfund" cleanup sites when more than 120 chemicals were discovered in local groundwater. Then, in 1984, investigators found a leak in the ten-mile conduit leading from Ciba's facility. The company discontinued dye, resin, and additive production at Toms River in 1986 and pleaded guilty to one charge of illegal waste disposal in March 1992. The corporation paid more than $60 million in fines and landfill and groundwater cleanup costs and agreed to make donations to New Jersey state conservation projects. The Toms River experience, combined with tightening European Community pollution regulations, helped convince Ciba-Geigy to cite the environment as one of its focuses.

Environmentalism became one of the cornerstones of Ciba's "Vision 2000" strategy, a long-term plan to balance the economic, social, and environmental objectives of the company. The company logo was shortened to just "ciba," but the formal name remained unchanged. The corporation was reorganized from functional/geographical units into 14 separate businesses with autonomous research and development, production, and marketing divisions. Ciba's businesses could be grouped into three basic areas: healthcare, agriculture, and industry.

The company considered its Pharma, Plant Protection, and Additives divisions its primary businesses. Pharma, the single largest operating unit, ranked among the world's top five pharmaceutical concerns. The corporation's leading product was Voltaren, an antirheumatic. Ciba's Pharma unit also claimed the second most popular smoking cessation patch, Habitrol (known as Nicotinell outside the United States). Habitrol encountered stiff competition in the 1990s, but was launched in France and Canada in 1992 and received OTC status in the United Kingdom and Italy that year. One problem with transdermal nicotine patch sales was that the product created a self-defeating market: if the treatment worked, patients would eventu-

ally end the therapy; if the patches were ineffective, smokers would not buy them. Ciba-Geigy purchased the Dr. R. Maag plant protection business from Hoffmann-La Roche in 1990 and achieved majority ownership of Bunting Group's plant protection business in 1992.

Ciba-Geigy's Self Medication, Diagnostics, and Ciba Vision units were recognized by the corporation as growth enterprises. Self Medication was expanded with the 1992 acquisition of Fisons' North American business, and the purchase of Triton Diagnostics buttressed the Diagnostics group. Ciba Vision's contact lenses, lens care products, and ophthalmic medicines ranked number two worldwide.

Ciba-Geigy's Seeds and Composites units were considered long-term investments. In 1990 the company announced that it had successfully inserted marker genes into corn cells that produced fertile plants and passed the new traits on to viable seeds. The company thereby entered the race to genetically engineer plants with the most attractive traits.

The core industrial businesses of Ciba-Geigy in the early 1990s included Textile Dyes, Chemicals, Pigments, Polymers, and Mettler Toledo scales. The leading market positions of these businesses allowed them to function as "cash cows" for research and development in other areas. For example, Ciba's textile dyes, additives, and Mettler Toledo units ranked number one worldwide in their respective categories.

Ciba's reorganization included the divestment of its Flame Retardants and Water Treatments Chemicals businesses, valued at approximately $100 million. The units were sold to FMC Corporation in 1992. Ciba-Geigy's sales and profits increased steadily in the late 1980s and early 1990s, exceeding CHF 22 billion in revenue and CHF 1.52 billion in profits in 1992. The majority of Ciba's sales, 36 percent, were made in European Community countries. Overall European sales comprised 43 percent of the total, while North America contributed 32 percent, Asia constituted 13 percent, and Latin America made up 7 percent.

In 1992 Ciba-Geigy was one of the five largest chemical companies in the world. While it was widely diversified within the industry, it maintained a steady emphasis on sophisticated chemicals: pharmaceuticals, plastics, pigments, or pesticides.

THE EVOLUTION OF SANDOZ

In 1886 two Swiss men, Dr. Alfred Kern and Mr. Edouard Sandoz, established a company in Basel in order to manufacture and sell synthetic dyes. Thirty years earlier the English chemist William Henry Perkin, while trying to synthesize quinine from coal tar, came up with a purple dye instead. Two years later a Frenchman used a similar process to produce a magenta dye, and a new industry was born, ending the reliance on purely animal, vegetable, or mineral dyes. The new dyes were more brilliant than the old and lasted longer. They worked better on synthetic fabrics and they allowed for the development of new dye colors. It was an industry that many recognized as potentially very profitable.

Dr. Kern was 36 when the business was formed and was well known as a chemist specializing in dyestuffs trade. The two men purchased 11,000 square meters on the west bank of the Rhine River, built a manufacturing plant, and registered their business under the name of Kern & Sandoz, beginning work on the July 1, 1886. They had ten workmen and a 15-horsepower steam engine, and a certainty that they would succeed. There were some early setbacks: The dyes they originally had intended to produce, including Auramine, Victoria Blue, and Crystal Violet, required a process originated by Kern and an old partner, but that partner would not release his patent rights; another dye, Alizarine Blue, caused a reaction kettle to explode.

The company managed not only to survive but to expand. Kern developed new dyes and Sandoz traveled extensively, searching for more customers and markets for their products. In five years, from 1887 to 1892, their production increased from 13,000 kilograms of six different types of dyes to 380,000 kilograms of 28 dyes.

In 1893 the company began to change considerably. Dr. Kern collapsed and died of heart failure and, although Sandoz tried to run the company himself, two years later he was compelled to retire from active management for health reasons. In 1895 Sandoz and Company was converted into a limited company called Chemische Fabrik vormals Sandoz (Chemical Works formerly Sandoz) with a share capital of CHF 2 million and with Edouard Sandoz as the first chairman of the board. At this point, the company was fortunate in its selection of managers and chemists to replace the founders; it was these people who, over the next 30 years, provided the company with direction and enabled it to expand. On the technical side, Arnold Steiner and Melchior Boniger developed and produced new products such as sulphur and azo dyes. Two talented sales managers, Werner Stauffacher and Georg Wagner, built a worldwide sales organization that expanded up to and even through World War I.

Although the company was fortunate in the appointment of its managers, it had many misfortunes, particularly from 1903 to 1909 (known among insiders as the "seven lean years") when serious consideration was given by members of the board to the possibility of a merger or even liquidation. Prices for manufactured goods kept falling while those for raw materials increased. There were very expensive patent litigations with competitors as well. By 1910, however, profits began to increase again, reaching CHF 500,000 in 1913, the year after the company's shares first appeared on the Basel Stock Exchange.

World War I, and Switzerland's isolation, resulted in some intriguing, and later profitable, opportunities for Sandoz. Germany prohibited all exports and, as a means to this end, blocked transit traffic so that everything from fuel to raw materials was in short supply. Wood, transported to Sandoz's plant in horse-drawn carts, was used instead of coal throughout the war. Intermediates, which had formerly been imported, were now blocked, but buyers somehow managed to get those purchased in England and the United States into Switzerland. The company's own chemists were able to produce the others. After the war, the world chemical market that had formerly been dominated by the Germans was soon open to competition.

CARTEL-ERA SANDOZ

Sandoz profited under these circumstances. It purchased the Rothaus estate in Muttenz, just in case land was needed for expansion. In 1918, to circumvent the protectionist legislation in other countries, which, in turn, inhibited Sandoz's international expansion, Sandoz, Ciba, and Geigy formed the Interessengemeinschaft Basel (Basler IG) Dyestuff Manufacturers. They used this association primarily to establish jointly owned factories in many countries, although they also pooled profits to ensure that none of the members would be forced to declare bankruptcy. The original charter of the association was for 50 years, but it was amicably dissolved after 33.

In 1911 Sandoz established its first subsidiary in England, and in 1919 established another in New York. In Switzerland the technical departments were restructured by Dr. Hermann Leeman (later president of the company from 1952 to 1963). The previous organization had been a system under which any chemist might be assigned to work simultaneously in research, manufacturing, and application. According to the restructuring, these three functions became separate departments, with the addition of a patent department.

A difficult period was again experienced during the early 1920s, when a crisis in the textile industry caused a recession in the dependent dyestuffs industry. The workforce was at first put on part-time employment, but in 1921 nearly 30 percent of the employees had to be laid off. By 1929 business had been severely affected. Partly because of the protection afforded by the association, however, and partly because of the company's lead in research and development, Sandoz was able to set up numerous subsidiaries around the world providing a protective network against the failure of any one subsidiary. More significantly, the company embarked on a program of diversification into chemical agents for use by the textile, leather, and paper industries, and later for the agricultural industry. Research in these areas produced industrial cleansers, soaps, softening agents, mercerizers, bleaches and, after World War II, fungicides, herbicides, insecticides, and rodenticides.

The most interesting part of the company's diversification program began with the establishment, under Dr. Arthur Stoll, of a pharmaceuticals department. Already well-known for his work on chlorophylls, Dr. Stoll became world famous for the development of a process for the isolation and for the discovery of the importance of ergotamine, an alkaloid of the rye fungus called ergot. The products developed from ergotamine were numerous and sold steadily, so that the pharmaceuticals department gave stability to the company's sales.

When World War II started, Sandoz Ltd., as it had been named in 1939, was financially secure with fully stocked warehouses, production sites, and sales agencies throughout the world. Transportation of supplies would not be the problem it had been during the previous war, as supplies were stocked near company plants. Fuel alone remained a problem. Leeman was credited with having advised the purchase of an old brown-coal mine. This purchase was finalized and, mining 18,000 tons of fuel for itself during the war, the company had solved its fuel problem. As soon as the war was over the Muttenz site was put to use, with a large plant for chemical and agrochemical production being built there. Little is known of Sandoz's contribution, if any, to either side's war effort, but from 1933 to 1948 company profits increased from CHF 48 million to CHF 253 million.

SANDOZ'S POSTWAR EXPANSION

The international postwar expansion did not exclude Sandoz. The company's only difficulty involved increasing production to keep pace with demand. In 1949 Dr. Stoll was promoted to managing director. New headquarters were built that altered Basel's skyline. In addition, automation was introduced in the production facilities. In 1964 annual sales surpassed CHF 1 billion for the first time. Each of the three divisions, including dyes, pharmaceuticals, and chemicals, prospered individually. The dyes division created dyes for the new

plastics, paints, and synthetic fibers now in demand, as well as the new foron dyes for polyester, and dyestuffs for mass dyeing.

The developments within the pharmaceuticals division caught the world's attention. Sandoz concentrated heavily on its recently discovered synthetic compounds for the treatment of mental illness and migraine. Most of the products developed were based on ergotamine and included such drugs as Methergin, which stopped postpartum hemorrhage, and Gynergen, which when injected early enough relieved the pain of migraine headaches. Certainly the most famous of these drugs was Delysid, also called LSD 25. In 1961 the company's *Jubilee Volume* proudly reported the drug's ability to cause "disturbances in the perception of space and time, depersonalization and color hallucinations" and that "it was destined to play a great role in experimental psychiatry." Research in the hallucinogen called mescaline, derived from the Mexican peyote cactus, and in psilocybin, derived from certain mushrooms, was also aimed at producing drugs that might be used in conjunction with psychotherapy and, in particular, psychoanalysis.

Although the use of Delysid was strictly controlled, and issued only to authorized research centers, within 15 years of its discovery in 1942 it was being produced illegally all over the United States and Europe as a "recreational drug." The consequences of a large number of people across the Western world experiencing what the *Jubilee Volume* referred to as "model psychosis" from LSD had yet to be fully understood. The company quickly curtailed its research into hallucinogens, but it would always be remembered as the company that "invented acid."

The late 1960s and early 1970s continued to be a period of growth for the company; sales doubled from CHF 1.97 billion to CHF 3.61 billion. The massive size of the company required further organizational revisions. As a result, an executive committee took over management. In 1968 the dyes and chemicals divisions were amalgamated and a new agrochemical division was created. The company's diversification also continued during this time. In 1967 a merger with Wander Limited of Berne added a nutrition department. Two years later, the takeover of Durand & Huguenin eliminated a neighboring competitor in dyes manufacturing. A hospital supply business was acquired and its activities combined, during 1976, with those of Rhone-Poulenc in a joint venture. These acquisitions and mergers were engineered by one of the few nonchemist presidents of the company, Carl Maurice Jacotett, a lawyer's son from Neuchatel who had studied theology and philosophy before going into business.

During his short presidency, from 1968 to 1976, the workforce increased from 6,345 to more than 33,000 people, making Sandoz one of the world's largest pharmaceutical companies.

The oil crisis of 1973, and the consequent rise in prices for raw materials and energy, dramatically affected Sandoz and other manufacturers, who could not possibly raise the prices of products high enough to cover costs. In 1975 a five-year recession began, which led to a review of company structure to reduce overhead and streamline organization. A steady reduction in the number of personnel and a firm control of wage increases helped to decrease losses. Continued diversification and acquisitions soon increased both equity and profit. Sandoz entered the seed business with the acquisition of the U.S. firms Rogers Brothers and Northrup King Company and the Dutch company Zaadunie B.V. Sandoz added the Swedish firm Wasa in 1982; two U.S. companies, Sodyeco and Zoecon, in 1983; and another U.S. concern, Master Builders, in 1985. Master Builders introduced Sandoz into another market, chemicals for the construction industry.

By 1975 a department of ecology and safety had been set up in Basel to establish and supervise guidelines throughout the company and its holdings. An effort to develop products with low environmental impacts was also initiated. Sandoz, however, received bad publicity for an environmental disaster at one of its Basel plants. Near the end of 1986, when the company was celebrating its centennial, a large amount of toxic chemicals spilled into the Rhine River killing fish and shore life from Switzerland through West Germany to The Netherlands. Sandoz entered 1987 with sales over CHF 8 billion, profits over CHF 500 million, and an equity of more than CHF 4.5 billion.

1996 MERGER OF CIBA-GEIGY AND SANDOZ CREATES NOVARTIS

As international drug markets continued to expand rapidly in the 1990s, pharmaceutical companies realized that multinational conglomerates, with diverse operations and worldwide resources, would dominate the future of the industry. Ciba-Geigy and Sandoz were not blind to this trend, and in early 1996 the two companies announced their intention to form a new corporation, Novartis AG. At the time it was the largest merger in history, with the combined value of the two companies exceeding $70 billion. The goal of Novartis—the name was derived from the Latin *novae artes*, or "new skills"—was to become a world leader in the field of "life sciences." With the merger, Ciba and Sandoz were creating the world's largest supplier of crop-protection products, and the second largest pharmaceutical company.

The size and scope of the deal, however, raised concern among regulatory agencies, both in Europe and the United States. Because many of the two companies' principal operations overlapped, particularly in the pharmaceutical, crop protection, and animal health sectors, the European Union (EU) launched an in-depth probe into the merger in May 1996. In July the EU approved the deal, on the condition that the companies divest a number of their animal health and agricultural chemicals interests, in addition to using the new company's considerable influence to ensure competition in the field of gene therapy. To gain Federal Trade Commission (FTC) approval in the United States, the company shed a large portion of Ciba's dominant share of the U.S. crop protection market, while providing further reassurances of competitiveness in the future gene therapy business. To this latter end, the company reached a licensing agreement with rival Rhône-Poulenc Rorer Inc. for certain gene therapy patents, and in December 1996 Novartis AG was officially incorporated. Daniel Vasella, who had headed Sandoz, was named CEO of Novartis.

The new company's focus was on biotechnology, and the wide range of applications for genetic research. The FTC projected that the market for gene therapy, while still insubstantial in the late 1990s, had the potential to reach $45 billion by 2010, and Novartis was intent on becoming a dominant player in this burgeoning industry. The future growth of the industry, however, was far more promising in the United States. Patent procedures for biotechnology inventions were complicated and expensive in the EU, with costs approaching $120,000 per patent, compared to $13,000 in the United States. Fearing that this discrepancy would inevitably drive the majority of biotech research to the United States, the European Chemical Industry Council (Cefic) issued a directive in May 1997 that called for the simplification of patenting procedures. While the EU eventually adopted many of the industry's recommendations, the effort encountered strong resistance from the public, which remained wary of genetic research in the wake of the scare over mad cow disease in the early part of the decade. To help assuage these fears, the EU passed a law in September 1997 requiring that all seed and food products carry labels stating whether or not they contained genetically modified materials.

In the midst of this controversy, Novartis was searching for ways to establish a stronger research presence in the United States. In April 1998 the company announced plans to build a research institute in San Diego dedicated to the study of human genes; a second lab, devoted to plant genetics, was announced in July. At the core of the company's human gene research was the imminent completion of the Human Genome Project; the company wanted to move beyond the mapping of genes, to devote itself to the study of how genetic material functioned. At the same time, the company's plant research remained focused on the development of genetically modified, herbicide-resistant crops. Novartis remained a worldwide leader in this field, becoming the first company to sell genetically modified white corn seeds in the United States in May 1998. In June, its Bt-11 modified corn was approved for sale by the EU.

The late 1990s witnessed a dramatic shift from Europe to the United States in the pharmaceutical industry. Part of the problem again involved more stringent regulatory policies in Europe, where pricing standards were strictly governed, and there were few incentives for innovation. The United States was also quicker to realize the massive growth potential of so-called lifestyle drugs such as Viagra and Prozac, an area where the European firms were lagging behind. In the hopes of seizing a sizable piece of the booming U.S. market, Novartis Pharmaceuticals devoted itself in the latter half of the 1990s to the development of a number of potential "blockbuster" drugs, including Zelnorm, an irritable bowel medicine, and Visudyne, a treatment for macular degeneration, the most common cause of blindness in people over 50.

Unfortunately, a series of setbacks struck the Novartis agribusiness sector in the late 1990s. The company's initial success with its genetically modified crops was hit hard by a report released in the United States in May 1999, which claimed that pollen from genetically modified corn was responsible for wiping out large populations of monarch butterflies. The EU quickly suspended approval processes for genetically modified seeds pending further investigation, and agribusiness stocks plummeted. With public skepticism over genetically modified food still a powerful force, Novartis decided to divest its agribusiness holdings in order to focus on the pharmacological and therapeutic applications of biotechnology, and in late 1999 the company's seed and crop protection operations merged with a British-Swedish company to form Syngenta AG.

PRODUCT PIPELINE SUCCESSES AND DEAL-MAKING IN THE EARLY 21ST CENTURY

A restructuring of the company's pharmaceutical operations followed in July 2000, and within the next couple of years the company launched several new drugs, including Starlix, which treated type 2 diabetes, and Femara, a breast-cancer treatment. In May 2001 Novartis gained U.S. Food and Drug Administration (FDA) approval of leukemia pill Gleevac, which took a novel approach to cancer treatment by specifically targeting the chemical signals that precipitate the alteration of normal cells into cancer cells. Gleevac was marketed outside the United States as Glivec. Early in 2002 the FDA gave the green light to Zometa, a treatment for certain cancers that have spread to the bones. Later in the decade, Gleevac/Glivec, Femara, and Zometa all ranked among Novartis's top-selling drugs. Another of the company's blockbusters during this period was the high-blood-pressure medicine Diovan. Novartis also gained FDA approval for irritable-bowel syndrome treatment Zelnorm in 2002, but the EU rejected the drug three years later. In 2007 the company was forced to remove Zelnorm from the U.S. market because of an apparent link to such risks as angina, heart attacks, and strokes.

Under Vasella's continued leadership, Novartis was active not only bringing new drugs to market but also pursuing numerous significant deals. During 2001 and 2002 the company spent nearly $5 billion to acquire about one-third of the voting shares in Swiss drug rival Roche Holding AG. Vasella pushed for a full merger of the two companies, but he was rebuffed by the founding family that still controlled Roche. Novartis nevertheless continued to hold its Roche stake. Among several other noteworthy 2002 developments, Novartis sold its food and beverage business unit as part of its planned divestment of its health food and functional food business, a divestment that was completed in 2004. As it continued to place increased emphasis on the lucrative U.S. pharmaceutical market, the company in 2002 shifted its worldwide research and development headquarters to Cambridge, Massachusetts, and the newly created Novartis Institutes for BioMedical Research. By this time, Novartis's stock was trading on the New York Stock Exchange, and the firm began reporting its results in U.S. dollars. Europe remained firmly on the company's radar, however, as was clear with the 2002 purchase of the Slovenian generic pharmaceuticals company Lek Pharmaceuticals for about $900 million. Adding Lek, a major producer and distributor of generic drugs in Central and Eastern Europe, boosted Novartis's generics sales by about 20 percent.

In May 2003 Novartis acquired a majority stake in Cambridge, Massachusetts-based Idenix Pharmaceuticals Inc., a producer of antiviral and anti-infective therapies, including drugs to treat hepatitis B and C. The following year Novartis entered into merger negotiations with Aventis, the largest French drug maker, after the latter became the object of a hostile takeover attempt from a smaller French rival, Sanofi-Synthelabo. These negotiations reportedly reached an advanced stage but abruptly ended after the French government pressured Sanofi into sweetening its takeover offer, which was then accepted by Aventis. France's market intervention thus thwarted Novartis's chance at a blockbuster deal while also creating a larger rival, Sanofi-Aventis.

Undeterred by this setback, Novartis in 2004 and 2005 completed a series of deals that turned the company into a much broader-based medicinal products company. In a February 2003, $385 million deal, the company bolstered its Consumer Health Division with the addition of the global adult medical nutrition business of Mead Johnson and Company, a subsidiary of Bristol-Myers Squibb Company. Among the acquired products were Boost, a retail nutritional drink brand, and lines of oral and tube-feeding formulas geared to the elderly. In August 2005 this division grew still larger via the $660 million purchase from Bristol-Myers of a portfolio of OTC medicines mainly marketed in the United States. Novartis thus gained such brands as headache treatment Excedrin, cold remedy Comtrex, nasal decongestant 4-Way, and Keri moisturizers.

NEW DIVISIONS, FURTHER DEALS

In 2004 Novartis resurrected the Sandoz name as it united its global generics operations under a new Sandoz Division. This division was then greatly enlarged in a string of takeovers, including the August 2004 purchase of Sabex Inc., a Canadian generics manufacturer with a leading position in generic injectables. Sandoz then moved into the ranks of one of the top two generics concerns in the world, alongside Teva Pharmaceutical Industries Limited, when it acquired Hexal AG, Germany's second largest generics company, in a EUR 5.65 billion ($6.93 billion) deal completed in June 2005. Also gained in this takeover was a 67.7 percent stake in Hexal's U.S. affiliate, Eon Labs, Inc. Novartis quickly took full control of Eon by buying out the firm's outstanding shares for about another $1 billion.

Since the mid-1990s Novartis had held a substantial minority stake in Chiron Corporation, a biotechnology firm based in Emeryville, California, that specialized in human vaccines, blood-testing products, and experimental cancer drugs. In April 2006 Novartis purchased all of the Chiron shares it did not already own for a total of around $5.7 billion. The company then created a new unit, the Vaccines and Diagnostics Division, to house all of its operations in human vaccines and blood-testing and molecular diagnostic products. The remainder of Chiron was integrated into Novartis's Pharmaceuticals Division. In July 2006 Novartis spent $606 million for NeuTec Pharma plc, a U.K. biopharmaceuticals company whose pipeline included Mycograb and Aurograb, two late-stage

compounds for the treatment of life-threatening infections. Late in the year, Novartis announced plans to create a $100 million pharmaceutical research and development center in Shanghai, China.

Novartis in 2007 narrowed its focus to four main areas—brand-name pharmaceuticals, vaccines and diagnostic products, generics, and OTC products—by selling two units to Nestlé S.A. in separate deals. In July the medical nutrition unit was sold for $2.5 billion, while the Gerber infant product business was sold in September for $5.5 billion. Also in 2007, Novartis gained regulatory approval in both the United States and Europe for Tekturna/Rasilez, the first new type of high-blood-pressure medicine in more than a decade. This drug was expected to eventually serve as a replacement for Diovan, Novartis's top-selling pharmaceutical in 2007 with sales topping $5 billion. Late in the year, Novartis launched a major streamlining effort aimed at reducing layers of management and bureaucracy and cut annual operating costs by $1.6 billion. Despite a $444 million charge taken for this restructuring, the company still managed to post record profits of $11.97 billion for the year, on revenues of $39.8 billion.

In the most significant development of 2008, Novartis obtained from Nestlé the right to acquire majority control of Alcon Inc. Headquartered in Hünenberg, Switzerland, with U.S. operations based in Fort Worth, Texas, Alcon was a world leader in eye care whose product lines included contact-lens solutions and eye drops, pharmaceuticals for eye diseases, and devices used in eye surgery. A second stage of this deal provided Novartis with the right to acquire from Nestlé, between January 2010 and July 2011, the latter's remaining 52 percent stake in Alcon for up to around $28 billion. Upon completion of this second stage, Novartis would be able to combine Alcon with its existing eye-care operations, including Ciba Vision. Also in 2008, Novartis named Joerg Reinhardt to be the firm's first chief operating officer. Reinhardt, who had headed the Vaccines and Diagnostics Division, appeared positioned to become Vasella's successor.

Among the drugs in Novartis's pipeline at this time were several more targeted cancer drugs, including Afinitor, approved by the FDA in early 2009 for patients with advanced kidney cancer, as well as two meningitis vaccines with high potential. These were among the new products that Novartis hoped would replace looming lost sales from the expiration of patents on several top-selling drugs, including Diovan, which was slated to go off-patent in 2012 and thus face generic competition. In addition to its strong pipeline, Novartis hoped to survive these patent expirations by expanding aggressively in emerging markets and further bolstering its other divisions. The Consumer Health Division was expected to receive a boost after gaining FDA approval for the launch of an OTC version of the popular heartburn remedy Prevacid. The Sandoz generics unit continued to pursue growth via acquisition as it reached an agreement in May 2009 to purchase the specialty generic injectables business of Austria's EBEWE Pharma for $1.2 billion. On the vaccine front, Novartis was busy developing vaccines for the H1N1 swine flu, which reached pandemic status in 2009, and in May of that year it had received a $289 million order for swine flu vaccine supplies from the U.S. Department of Health and Human Services, which was anticipating a bigger outbreak for the fall/winter 2009–10 flu season.

Updated, April S. Dougil; Stephen Meyer;
David E. Salamie

PRINCIPAL SUBSIDIARIES

Novartis International AG; Novartis Holding AG; Novartis Research Foundation; Novartis Pharma AG; Speedel Holding AG; Sandoz AG; Sandoz Pharmaceuticals AG; Novartis Consumer Health S.A.; Novartis Consumer Health Schweiz AG; Novartis Animal Health AG; CIBA Vision AG; Novartis Argentina S.A.; Novartis Australia Pty Ltd.; Novartis Austria GmbH; Sandoz GmbH (Austria); N.V. Novartis Pharma S.A. (Belgium); N.V. Sandoz S.A. (Belgium); Novartis International Pharmaceutical Ltd. (Bermuda); Novartis Biociências S.A. (Brazil); Sandoz do Brasil Indústria Farmacêutica Ltda. (Brazil); Novartis Pharmaceuticals Canada Inc.; Sandoz Canada Inc.; Novartis Chile S.A.; Beijing Novartis Pharma Co., Ltd. (China); Novartis Pharmaceuticals (HK) Limited (China); Suzhou Novartis Pharma Technology Co. Ltd. (China); Novartis de Colombia S.A.; Lek Zagreb d.o.o. (Croatia); Novartis s.r.o. (Czech Republic); Sandoz s.r.o. (Czech Republic); Novartis Healthcare A/S (Denmark); Sandoz A/S (Denmark); Novartis Ecuador S.A.; Novartis Pharma S.A.E. (Egypt; 99%); Novartis Finland Oy; Novartis Groupe France S.A.; Novartis Pharma S.A.S. (France); Novartis Deutschland GmbH (Germany); Novartis Pharma GmbH (Germany); Sandoz International GmbH (Germany); Hexal AG (Germany); Salutas Pharma GmbH (Germany); Novartis UK Limited; Novartis Pharmaceuticals UK Limited; Novartis Grimsby Limited (UK); Sandoz Limited (UK); Novartis (Hellas) S.A.C.I. (Greece); Novartis Hungary Healthcare Limited Liability Company; Sandoz Hungary Limited Liability Company; Novartis India Limited (51%); Sandoz Private Limited (India); PT Novartis Indonesia; Novartis Ireland Limited; Novartis Farma S.p.A. (Italy); Sandoz S.p.A. (Italy); Novartis Holding Japan K.K.; Sandoz K.K. (Japan); Novartis Investments S.à r.l. (Luxembourg); Novartis Finance S.A. (Luxembourg); Novartis Corporation (Malaysia) Sdn. Bhd.; Novartis Farmacéutica, S.A. de C.V. (Mexico); Novartis Netherlands B.V.; Sandoz B.V. (Netherlands); Novartis New Zealand Ltd.; Novartis Norge AS (Norway); Novartis Pharma (Pakistan) Limited (98%); Novartis Healthcare Philippines, Inc.; Novartis Poland Sp. z o.o.; Novartis Portugal SGPS Lda.; Ex-Lax, Inc. (Puerto Rico); CIBA Vision Puerto Rico, Inc.; Sandoz S.R.L. (Romania); Novartis Pharma LLC (Russian Federation); ZAO Sandoz (Russian Federation); Novartis Singapore Pharmaceutical Manufacturing Pte Ltd.; Novartis Asia Pacific Pharmaceuticals Pte Ltd. (Singapore); Novartis Slovakia s.r.o.; Lek Pharmaceuticals d.d. (Slovenia); Sandoz Pharmaceuticals d.d. (Slovenia); Novartis South Africa (Pty) Ltd.; Sandoz South Africa (Pty) Ltd.; Novartis Korea Ltd. (99%); Novartis Farmacéutica, S.A. (Spain); Sandoz Farmacéutica, S.A. (Spain); Novartis Sverige Participations AB (Sweden); Novartis (Taiwan) Co., Ltd.; Novartis (Thailand) Limited; Novartis Saglik, Gida ve Tarim Ürünleri Sanayi ve Ticaret A.S. (Turkey); Sandoz Ilaç Sanayi ve Ticaret A.S. (Turkey); Novartis Corporation (USA); Novartis Pharmaceuticals Corporation (USA); Idenix Pharmaceuticals, Inc. (USA); Novartis Vaccines and Diagnostics, Inc. (USA); Sandoz Inc. (USA); Eon Labs, Inc. (USA); Novartis Consumer Health, Inc. (USA); Novartis Animal Health US, Inc.; CIBA Vision Corporation; Novartis de Venezuela, S.A.

PRINCIPAL DIVISIONS

Pharmaceuticals Division; Vaccines and Diagnostics Division; Sandoz Division; Consumer Health Division.

PRINCIPAL COMPETITORS

Merck & Co., Inc.; Pfizer Inc.; Roche Holding Ltd.; Bristol-Myers Squibb Company; Sanofi-Aventis; GlaxoSmithKline plc; Bayer AG; Johnson & Johnson; Teva Pharmaceutical Industries Limited; Mylan Inc.; Ratiopharm GmbH.

FURTHER READING

Ball, Deborah, and Jeanne Whalen, "Nestlé Buys Novartis Nutrition Unit for $2.5 Billion," *Wall Street Journal,* December 15, 2006, p. A10.

Buckley, Neil, "More on Gene-Modified Food," *Financial Times,* July 25, 1997.

Capell, Kerry, "Creating a Pharma Powerhouse," *Business Week,* May 26, 2003, pp. 68–70.

Capell, Kerry, with Heidi Dawley, "Healing Novartis," *Business Week,* November 8, 1999.

Carreyrou, John, Anita Raghavan, and Gautam Naik, "Native Industry: In Face of French Resistance, Swiss Giant Enters

Takeover Fray," *Wall Street Journal,* April 23, 2004, p. A1.

Dyer, Geoff, and Haig Simonian, "Swiss Chief Who Followed the American Way," *Financial Times,* January 21, 2004, p. 12.

Enri, Paul, *The Basel Marriage: History of the Ciba-Geigy Merger,* Zurich: Neue Zurcher Zeitung, 1979, 419 p.

Fisher, Lawrence M., "Two Deals Extend the Financial Frontiers of Gene Therapy," *New York Times,* January 14, 1997.

Ford, Peter, "Wary Europe Enters Biotech Age," *Christian Science Monitor,* June 10, 1998.

Fuhrmans, Vanessa, and Jill Carroll, "FDA Clears Novel Novartis Cancer Drug," *Wall Street Journal,* May 11, 2001, p. A3.

Gebhart, Fred, "Skin Patch Makers Fight to Be No. 1 in War on Nicotine," *Drug Topics,* January 20, 1992, p. 26.

Goetzl, David, "A Bitter Pill," *Advertising Age,* August 6, 2001, p. 3.

Graham, David E., "Plant Genetics to Grow Here: Swiss Company Announces $600 Million Biotech Lab," *San Diego Union-Tribune,* July 22, 1998.

Greil, Anita, "Alcon Deal Puts Novartis in a Bind," *Wall Street Journal,* June 15, 2009, p. B2.

Greil, Anita, and Julia Mengewein, "Strong Dollar Cuts into Novartis Profit," *Wall Street Journal,* April 24, 2009, p. B4.

Hall, William, "Sandoz and Ciba to Sell Part of U.S. Business," *Financial Times,* August 29, 1996.

Hamilton, David P., "Novartis Agrees to Acquire the Rest of Chiron for $5.1 Billion," *Wall Street Journal,* November 1, 2005, p. A6.

Harris, Gardiner, and Vanessa Fuhrmans, "New Prescription: Its Rivals in Funk, Novartis Finds a Way to Thrive," *Wall Street Journal,* August 23, 2002, p. A1.

Hawthorne, Fran, "Keeping the Pipeline Full," *Chief Executive* (U.S.), July 2004, pp. 30–33.

"How Sandoz Is Building a Beachhead in the U.S.," *Chemical Week,* July 13, 1983, pp. 29+.

Hunter, David, "Ciba-Geigy: Back to the Roots for Renewed Growth," *Chemical Week,* June 21, 1989, p. 21.

Jack, Andrew, and Haig Simonian, "Cancer Drug Push at Novartis," *Financial Times,* May 21, 2009, p. 23.

Jarvis, Lisa, "Acquisitions to Put Sandoz at Top of Generics Heap," *Chemical Market Reporter,* February 28, 2005, pp. 1, 9.

Johnsen, Michael, "Headache (Medicine) Acquisition May Just Be Shot in the Arm," *Drug Store News,* August 22, 2005, pp. 85–86.

Johnson, Avery, and Anita Greil, "Pfizer, Novartis Disclose Deals in Generic Drugs," *Wall Street Journal,* May 21, 2009, p. B3.

Kher, Unmesh, "Drug Lord," *Time,* July 29, 2002, pp. B6+.

Kirschner, Elisabeth, "Ciba-Geigy and New Jersey Settle Toms River Battle," *Chemical Week,* March 11, 1992, p. 14.

Krause, Carey, "Novartis Acquires Stake in Roche for $2.75 Bn," *Chemical Market Reporter,* May 14, 2001, pp. 3, 16.

Landers, Peter, and Anita Raghavan, "Novartis Sets Stage to Take Over Roche Holding," *Wall Street Journal,* January 24, 2003, p. A3.

Langley, Alison, "Clinical Trial," *Institutional Investor,* March 2005, pp. 68–75.

Langreth, Robert, "Reviving Novartis," *Forbes,* February 5, 2001, p. 90.

Lichtenstein, William, "The Toms River Experience," *Chemical Engineering,* April 1991, p. 45.

Mathews, Anna Wilde, and Jeanne Whalen, "Novartis to Pull Irritable-Bowel Drug over Heart Risks," *Wall Street Journal,* March 31, 2007, p. A5.

McCarthy, Joseph L., "Alex Krauer: Ciba-Geigy," *Chief Executive* (U.S.), July/August 1992, p. 20.

Michaels, Adrian, "Novartis Hopes New Drugs Will Boost U.S. Sales," *Financial Times,* February 15, 2001.

———, "Setbacks a Pain but Novartis May Have a Cure," *Financial Times,* August 15, 2001.

Mirasol, Feliza, "Novartis Anti-Infectives Get Boost with NeuTec Buy," *Chemical Market Reporter,* June 19–25, 2006, p. 34.

Morris, Gregory D., "Ciba-Geigy Enters the $1.5 Billion/Year Corn Biotech Race," *Chemical Week,* September 12, 1990, p. 12.

Mullin, Rick, "Novartis Shifts Its R&D Headquarters to the U.S.," *Chemical Week,* May 15, 2002, p. 27.

"The Next Cancer Bestseller?" *Forbes,* May 11, 2009, p. 58.

"Novartis Bags Sabex for $565 MM," *Chemical Market Reporter,* June 14, 2004, p. 2.

"Novartis Secures a Key Slot in Global Generics with Lek Buy," *Chemical Market Reporter,* September 2, 2002, p. 2.

Raghavan, Anita, John Carreyrou, and Gautam Naik, "Sanofi to Swallow Aventis in a Deal Set at $65 Billion," *Wall Street Journal,* April 26, 2004, p. A1.

Shon, Melissa, "Nicotine Patch Market Takes a Fall, but Why?" *Chemical Marketing Reporter,* September 14, 1992, p. 5.

Simonian, Haig, "Novartis to Get Blood Drug in Speedel Takeover," *Financial Times,* July 11, 2008, p. 14.

Simonian, Haig, and Andrew Jack, "New Post at Novartis Paves Way for Chairman's Successor," *Financial Times,* October 21, 2008, p. 22.

Timmons, Heather, and Tom Wright, "Novartis to Buy Two Makers of Generics," *New York Times,* February 22, 2005, p. C1.

Whalen, Jeanne, "CEO Gambles on a Novartis Makeover," *Wall Street Journal,* May 20, 2008, p. B1.

———, "FDA Approves a Novel Novartis Drug," *Wall Street Journal,* June 19, 2009, pp. B1, B2.

———, "Mixing Medicines: Betting $10 Billion on Generics, Novartis Seeks to Inject Growth," *Wall Street Journal,* May 4, 2006, p. A1.

———, "Novartis Expands Generics Range for $8.4 Billion," *Wall Street Journal,* February 22, 2005, p. A1.

———, "Novartis Girds for the Day Blockbuster Loses Patent," *Wall Street Journal,* December 31, 2008, p. B1.

————, "Novartis Picks Up Eye-Care Unit," *Wall Street Journal,* April 8, 2008, p. B1.

————, "Novartis Plans Restructuring," *Wall Street Journal,* December 11, 2007, p. A21.

Whalen, Jeanne, and Goran Mijuk, "Novartis Shakes Ranks As Earnings Flag," *Wall Street Journal,* October 19, 2007, p. A14.

Wilsher, Peter, "The Feeling Grows That Going Green Is Good for Business," *Management Today,* October 1991, p. 27.

Zamiska, Nicholas, "Novartis to Establish Drug R&D Center in China," *Wall Street Journal,* November 6, 2006, p. A3.

Zeller, Christian, *Globalisierungsstrategien: Der Weg von Novartis,* Berlin: Springer, 2001, 702 p.

Orbit International Corp.

80 Cabot Court
Hauppauge, New York 11788
U.S.A.
Telephone: (631) 435-8300
Fax: (631) 435-8458
Web site: http://www.orbitintl.com

Public Company
Incorporated: 1957 as Orbit Instrument Corp.
Employees: 146
Sales: $27.36 million (2008)
Stock Exchanges: NASDAQ
Ticker Symbol: ORBT
NAICS: 334113 Computer Terminal Manufacturing;
334119 Other Computer Peripheral Equipment
Manufacturing; 334419 Other Electronic
Component Manufacturing; 335311 Power,
Distribution, and Specialty Transformer
Manufacturing; 541330 Engineering Services

∎ ∎ ∎

Orbit International Corp. manufactures displays, input devices, and other hardware and software products. It supplies a wide range of military programs, from handheld GPS receivers to display systems for tanks, ships, and aircraft. Most of its business comes from prime defense contractors, and more than 90 percent of sales come from the United States.

Founded in Long Island in 1957, the company pioneered input devices such as the trackball, while its Behlman Electronics, Inc., subsidiary was an innovator in power supplies. Orbit attempted to cushion itself against the post–Cold War slowdown in military spending by building up a sizable apparel business; however this was divested within several years.

LONG ISLAND DEFENSE INDUSTRY ORIGINS

Company founder Max Reissman grew up in New York City's Lower East Side. While in his 20s, he worked at an uncle's sewing machine repair shop, which was soon converted into an engine parts plant for Pratt & Whitney with the arrival of World War II.

Reissman took engineering in college and he remained active in Long Island's thriving defense industry after the war. In 1957 he launched Orbit Instrument Corp. with start-up capital of $63,000, raised privately. The company's specialty was making components for electronic systems used by the military.

After a few years subcontracting for Westinghouse and others, Orbit landed its biggest customer, Hughes Aircraft, becoming one of hundreds supporting the aviation and space industry behemoth. Orbit supplied trackballs, keyboards, and other input devices, as well as displays and other electronic components.

THRIVING UNDER REAGAN

Orbit grew quickly after President Ronald Reagan took office in 1981 with a mandate of boosting the nation's military might. Net sales were $6.2 million in the fiscal year ended June 30, 1981, with net income of $1.4

The Orbit name is synonymous with ultra-rugged Human-Machine Interface (HMI) devices and software solutions. By delivering leading-edge mission-critical hardware with extreme environmental and operational survivability, components in the Orbit Electronics Group have become trusted suppliers of choice for military, government and industrial programs that impose stringent standards for quality and high reliability, where downtime is not an option. Advanced technologies, proven design expertise and our diligent analysis of the relationships between human and machine interface requirements, enable the Orbit Electronics Group to deliver products that help increase user productivity, reliability and overall performance in your mission critical applications. All divisions within the Orbit Electronics Group are proven to have the vision necessary to develop, implement and sustain rugged HMI products that raise the standards for performance, reliability and economy.

million. By 1985 the company was earning $4.2 million on revenues of $20 million. Net sales reached $50 million in fiscal 1989. In addition to increased defense spending, Orbit also benefited from lower corporate tax rates toward the end of the Reagan years.

In the midst of the boom, Orbit found the need for new space. It built an office and manufacturing facility in Hauppauge, New York, in 1982, expanding it to 60,000 square feet within three years. Orbit grew to 200 employees in the mid-1980s and was having a difficult time meeting its labor demands in Long Island.

Reissman was known for working long hours, and his company gained a reputation for being well run, on time, and on budget. With a focus on custom products, it commanded superior margins to its industry cohorts. Reissman aimed to take the company to $100 million in annual sales, but the reduction in military spending that accompanied the end of the Cold War intervened. Revenues approached $97 million in 1992, but the bulk of this was from a new area of operations, the apparel business.

IN AND OUT OF SEMICONDUCTORS

At the start of the Reagan years Orbit leased a plant in Cypress, California, near its main customer and other Southern California prime contractors. Executives were seeking to reduce the company's reliance on Hughes, which accounted for roughly three-quarters of its revenues in fiscal 1985.

Seeking to diversify, in November 1985 Orbit bought another California chipmaker, Comdial Technology Corp., from leading telephone manufacturer Comdial Corp., paying $1.8 million. Renamed Orbit Semiconductor Inc., the unit was soon restored to profitability. It offered quick turnarounds on low cost, customized semiconductors. It was spun off in a $4.6 million management buyout in November 1991 when it had about 175 employees. It later went public.

Orbit International earned $1.5 million on revenues of $36.4 million in fiscal 1990. A voice-response software subsidiary, Computer Integration Associates, Inc., had been shut down in July 1989. Orbit closed its small Cypress manufacturing facility in May 1990, laying off about 40 people. A handful of employees remained to maintain a small sales and service office there.

For the fiscal year ended June 30, 1991, Orbit posted sales of $47.8 million. A net loss of $6 million resulted mainly from the winding up of its semiconductor operations.

IN AND OUT OF APPAREL

In July 1991, the company was renamed Orbit International Corp. to reflect the fact that its interests had moved beyond instruments. It was made up of three segments: Electronics, United States Apparel, and Canadian Apparel.

Orbit had bought USA Classic Inc. for $1.8 million in 1988. The contract apparel manufacturer had been formed eight years earlier by Milton Adams, an accountant with connections to the maker of Garanimals children's clothing. He continued to run the company after the acquisition.

USA Classic started by making private-label clothing for department stores but within a few years landed a deal to produce athletic clothing for men and boys under the Everlast brand. Other high-profile licenses, such as children's clothing for B.U.M. Equipment and Nautica, followed. By the time Orbit bought the company, it had annual sales of $10 million.

In December 1990 Orbit acquired, through its Canada Classique Inc. subsidiary, Rice Sportswear Ltd., a $25 million a year Winnipeg manufacturer of outwear. The deal was worth up to $8 million based on future performance. In February 1993 Orbit added Symax Garment Co. (1989) Ltd., a Vancouver outerwear

```
┌─────────────────────────────────────────┐
│                                          │
│              KEY DATES                   │
│                   ■                      │
│  ────────────────────────────────────    │
│                                          │
│  1957:  Orbit Instrument Corp. is formed in Long │
│         Island, New York.                │
│  1985:  Orbit acquires semiconductor business from │
│         Comdial Corp.                    │
│  1988:  Orbit buys New York apparel company USA │
│         Classic Inc.                     │
│  1991:  Orbit Instrument is renamed Orbit │
│         International Corp. to reflect its broadening │
│         interests.                       │
│  1992:  USA Classic Inc. subsidiary goes public; │
│         Orbit retains a 43 percent stake. │
│  1993:  As USA Classic launches the Danskin │
│         sportswear line, Orbit buys another women's │
│         apparel business, Panda Group.   │
│  1994:  USA Classic collapses due to an overly ambi- │
│         tious expansion.                 │
│  1996:  Orbit acquires Behlman Electronics, Inc., and │
│         exits the apparel business.      │
│  2005:  Orbit buys Tulip Development Laboratory │
│         and its TDL Manufacturing affiliate. │
│                                          │
└─────────────────────────────────────────┘
```

manufacturer with revenues just under $1 million a year.

As annual sales reached $55 million, USA Classic Inc. went public in November 1992, leaving Orbit with a 43 percent, noncontrolling interest. Most of the $40 million in proceeds went to pay down debt, including $18 million on a $20 million loan from Orbit.

In July 1993 Orbit bought the assets of Panda Group, a New York City designer and distributor of women's clothing under the moderately priced East-West brand. Orbit paid $17 million for the fast-growing Panda, which had posted sales of $36.6 million for 1992.

By fiscal 1993, apparel accounted for 85 percent of Orbit's revenues, observed *Women's Wear Daily*. Canadian subsidiaries included Rice Sportswear, Daniel Marcus, Ax Elle Fashions Inc., and Symax Garment Company. The U.S. segment comprised the East/West division and its East End Apparel Group Ltd. subsidiary, and Orbit's 43 percent holding in USA Classic.

This last investment, the cornerstone of Orbit's apparel operations, was about to suddenly collapse. USA Classic went bankrupt in May 1994. As *Crain's New York Business* noted, the women's clothing market was much more fickle and demanding than children's wear.

USA Classic's expensive high-fashion gamble with the Danskins brand failed to catch on at the same time as the Everlast brand foundered in its shift to discount department chains including Kmart.

TRANSITIONS

Max Reissman died in February 1995 after he had a heart attack while on vacation in Hawaii. He was succeeded as president and CEO by Dennis Sunshine, who had been with the company nearly 20 years.

Net sales rose from $58.2 million in 1995 from $57.8 million the previous year. The net loss expanded as well, though, to $22.3 million from $17 million.

Seeking growth closer to its original roots, in February 1996 Orbit bought Behlman Electronics, Inc., a manufacturer of power supplies and electronic measurement and display components with military and commercial customers. Behlman had been a pioneer of AC power supply technologies since the early 1950s.

Orbit paid $3.7 million for the Behlman assets. The seller, Astrosystems of Lake Success, New York, was a holding company also involved in industrial automation; it was liquidating itself due to what it perceived as bleak prospects for defense electronics.

Orbit lost $4.5 million in 1996 on net sales of $17 million, but its profitability was swiftly restored once it shed its clothing operations. The company posted net income of $2 million in 1997 on net sales of $17.6 million.

Orbit posted net income of $1.9 million on revenues of $16.4 million in fiscal 1998. During the year the company joined suppliers such as NEC Corp. in a venture to provide flat-panel LCD monitors for stock-trading applications.

Orbit lost $1.4 million as revenues fell 25 percent to $12.2 million in fiscal 1999. Some of the deficit was attributed to a charge connected to USA Classic-related securities litigation. To keep its shares from being delisted from the NASDAQ, the company initiated a reverse stock split in October. (The NASDAQ had previously delisted the shares for several months beginning in December 1996 due to the exchange's annual meeting requirements.)

In 2000 there was a plan to merge with Homing Inc., which produced web-based software. However, Orbit called off the deal, which could have been worth about $3.6 million, that December.

AFTER 9/11

As was the case at many defense electronics firms, Orbit's revenues grew during the U.S. military buildup following the September 11, 2001, terrorist attacks on the United States. It was unique among its Long Island counterparts, noted the *New York Daily News,* in that it maintained its manufacturing capability in-house. The company had approximately 100 employees. Revenues rose 13 percent to $16.7 million in 2002 and were $17.1 million in 2003.

In 2005 Orbit bought Tulip Development Laboratory and its TDL Manufacturing affiliate, paying $8.5 million in cash, notes, and stock. Tulip, based in Quakertown, Pennsylvania, added revenues of about $5 million a year. It had been founded in 1978 and produced displays and other electronic components.

In 2006 Orbit made the *Fortune Small Business* list of the 100 fastest-growing small companies for the second year in a row. It posted a net profit of $2.4 million on revenues of $25 million for 2006.

Revenues continued to rise. In 2008 they were $27.4 million in 2008, up from $25.9 million the previous year. Earnings rose slightly to $11.6 million. The company had increased its workforce by half in just three years, to 146 employees. Most of Orbit's revenues came from U.S. military sales, a market whose near-term future was sometimes difficult to predict.

Frederick C. Ingram

PRINCIPAL SUBSIDIARIES

Behlman Electronics, Inc.; Orbit Instrument of California, Inc.; Tulip Development Laboratory, Inc.; TDL Manufacturing, Inc.; Integrated Consulting Services, Inc. d/b/a Integrated Combat Systems, Inc.

PRINCIPAL DIVISIONS

Orbit Instrument; Tulip Development Laboratory; Integrated Combat Systems.

PRINCIPAL OPERATING UNITS

Orbit Electronics Group; Orbit Power Group.

PRINCIPAL COMPETITORS

Ducommun Incorporated; Schneider Electric.

FURTHER READING

Fiedelholtz, Sara, "Danskin Betting on a Sporting Proposition," *Women's Wear Daily,* April 28, 1993, p. 10.

Furman, Phyllis, "Star Today, Gone Tomorrow," *Crain's New York Business,* May 23, 1994, p. 1.

MacIntosh, Jeane, "Orbit Acquires Panda Group for $17M," *Women's Wear Daily,* July 14, 1993, p. 4.

O'Dell, John, "Orbit Instrument to Close Cypress Plant, Cut 40 Jobs," *Los Angeles Times,* March 17, 1990.

"Orbit Instrument Buys Block of Shares from Investor Group," *Wall Street Journal,* June 4, 1991.

Park, Emily, "Orbit International in Merger Pact with Homing Inc.," *Dow Jones News Service,* June 7, 2000.

Sherman, William, "Iraq War Possibility Spurs Business for New York City Defense Contractors," *New York Daily News,* March 16, 2003.

Sternberg, Bill, "Orbit Instrument: Profits Out of This World," *Crain's New York Business,* August 11, 1986, pp. 11, 12.

Trachtenberg, Jeffrey A., "The Up and Comers: The Rewards of Subcontracting," *Forbes,* July 30, 1984, p. 70.

Patch Products Inc.

1400 East Inman Parkway
Beloit, Wisconsin 53511
U.S.A.
Telephone: (608) 362-6896
Toll Free: (800) 524-4263
Fax: (608) 362-8178
Web site: http://www.patchproducts.com

Private Company
Incorporated: 1985
Employees: 110
Sales: $50 million (2008 est.)
NAICS: 339932 Game, Toy, and Children's Vehicle
    Manufacturing

■ ■ ■

Patch Products Inc. is a leading producer of family-oriented games. It is one of the top U.S. makers of board games, including party games, children's games, and games meant for the entire family. Patch also manufactures puzzles, card games, and foam footballs, basketballs, and other sports toys. The company made its mark in the 1990s with its very popular TriBond game. TriBond and other games achieved national distribution, were widely played on air by radio disc jockeys, and catapulted Patch to one of the top spots in the U.S. game industry. Operating out of the southern Wisconsin town of Beloit, Patch licenses and distributes its products across the United States and Canada and in overseas markets in Europe, Australia, South and Central America, and the Caribbean. Patch also runs a

subsidiary company in Smethport, Pennsylvania, the Smethport Specialty Company. Smethport makes the Lauri and Smethport brands of classic and educational toys. Patch Products is privately owned by two brothers, Fran and Bryce Patch.

FROM PRINTING GAMES TO MAKING GAMES

The company that evolved into Patch Products began as a commercial printing company in Beloit, Wisconsin. Brothers Fran and Bryce Patch opened their printing company in 1971 and slowly built their business up. One of their mainstays was printing game boards, puzzles, and stickers. They printed boards for the popular role-playing game Dungeons and Dragons. They also made sticker books for another 1980s' icon, Cabbage Patch Dolls. Then in the mid-1980s, the Patch brothers' printing company was swept up into one of the biggest board game hits since World War II, Trivial Pursuit.

The board game industry was always subject to fad hits. The public's taste in games was as hard to predict as its taste in movies, fashion, or music. Some games, like chess and checkers, have an ancient lineage and enduring popularity. In postwar America, Scrabble and Monopoly were two best-selling games that demonstrated great staying power. Other games, however, quickly came and went. Trivial Pursuit was in a different category altogether. Invented by a trio of Canadians in 1979, it had only halting sales in its first couple of years. Yet by 1984, it had brought in $325 million, and sold 20 million units. The game was so

COMPANY PERSPECTIVES

Our mission: to be a leading international toy company, recognized as such by our innovative products, stable financial foundation, high caliber of employees and commitment to those with whom we do business.

popular stores could not keep it in stock, and its maker could hardly print enough copies. The Patch brothers' printing company was one of several firms that produced Trivial Pursuit game boards. The game reinvented the family game category, and showed what tremendous selling power a good board game was capable of.

Fran and Bryce Patch changed their business focus in 1985, incorporating Patch Products, Inc. While they had previously made a good living from printing other companies' puzzles and games, the new firm went into producing their own family entertainment products. The new company came out with a branded line of PuzzlePatch puzzles, which soon grew to be distributed nationwide. Patch's own blockbuster game was still a few years in the future. This was TriBond.

TriBond owed its life to an undergraduate at Colgate University, Tim Walsh. Although Walsh eventually got a degree in biology from Colgate, he had entered college on a football scholarship, and his lifelong dream was to be a professional baseball pitcher. Somewhere along the way, Walsh and two college friends invented a board game. The object was to identify what connected three seemingly disparate things, thus the name TriBond. An example of a typical TriBond question is, what do a beehive, a rooster, and a barbershop have in common? The player might come up with the answer that all three have combs. The game clearly owed something to Trivial Pursuit. It was a game of quick thinking, using question cards. As in Trivial Pursuit, players moved plastic game pieces around a board.

LICENSING A HIT GAME

Walsh and his co-inventors believed TriBond had enormous potential, but all the major U.S. game companies had turned them down. Walsh contacted Patch in 1989, and Patch initially printed the game sets. In 1992, Patch Products licensed TriBond from the inventors, and Tim Walsh joined the company. Patch pursued a clever marketing strategy, and soon the game

had national recognition. Patch mailed copies of the game to hundreds of radio stations across the country, asking disc jockeys to use TriBond questions to quiz their listeners. For example, one Wisconsin station ran a weekly "battle of the sexes" contest, featuring questions from TriBond. In 1993, the game sold 148,000 copies. Sales at Patch Products zoomed to $5 million, double that of the previous year. By the Christmas shopping season of 1994, TriBond was in the top ten of U.S. board games. It even outsold Trivial Pursuit.

Patch managed to get the game into the major national retailers, including Wal-Mart, Target, Toys "R" Us, and Kmart. This was quite a coup, since TriBond was the only top-selling game at the time that was not owned by the dominant U.S. manufacturer, Hasbro. Hasbro by 1994 owned Milton Bradley, Parker Brothers, and other leading game brands. It was the largest toy and game company in the world, and tiny Patch was a serious competitor. The big retailers, especially Wal-Mart, could make or break a game, since they offered so much exposure. Wal-Mart originally agreed to place Tri-Bond only in its stores closest to Patch's headquarters, then allowed the game into its other stores in Wisconsin. A national rollout seemed to come grudgingly.

TriBond did particularly well, though, with its widespread radio advertising. By the crucial Christmas shopping season of 1994, Patch's TriBond was well positioned in stores across the country. The company predicted its sales would double to $10 million. To manage demand, Patch outsourced much of the printing of the games. It reserved its own facilities for handling surges. This was possibly less profitable than handling most of the printing in-house. Patch was thinking long-term, however, and did not want its own production totally tied to one game. Given the fickle nature of the game market, Patch was looking for a new hit, to keep it going after TriBond cooled off.

STEADY DEVELOPMENT AFTER TRIBOND

Patch Products aimed to become a lasting player in the game market, and it planned accordingly. It extended the TriBond product line with different versions, and also came out with several new games. By 1997, the company had estimated sales of $21 million, and it invested in a large new headquarters. Patch also significantly expanded its warehouse facilities. It brought out a version of TriBond for the Christian market, called Bible TriBond. It also experimented with a computer-based version of the board game. It produced French

```
┌─────────────────────────────────────────────┐
│                                               │
│              KEY DATES                        │
│              ─────■─────                       │
│                                               │
│   1971: Brothers Fran and Bryce Patch found   │
│         printing company.                     │
│   1985: Patch brothers incorporate Patch      │
│         Products to focus on manufacturing    │
│         puzzles and family games.             │
│   1992: Company buys rights to TriBond.       │
│   2004: TriBond brand rights are sold to      │
│         Mattel.                               │
│   2009: Founding Patch brothers retire from   │
│         CEO and president posts.              │
│                                               │
└─────────────────────────────────────────────┘
```

and Spanish versions, a kid version, and also produced an updated TriBond with new clues.

TriBond originator Tim Walsh became vice-president of Patch. He and his wife created a new word game called Blurt, which came out in 1994. Blurt was followed in 1996 by Mad Gab, and then Malarky in 1997. While coming out with these new products, Patch also extended into new markets. It began selling games in Canada in 1995. It licensed its products for sale in several other foreign countries the next year. By the late 1990s, Patch had risen to the number three spot in the adult board game market. This was an impressive achievement given the vast size of the number one player, Hasbro.

By 1998, Patch Products was estimated to hold 10 percent of the market share in adult board games. While much of the company's success was due to its first hit, TriBond, in fact about half its sales were puzzles. Patch had continued to print and sell kids' puzzles while its game business flourished. By the company's own reckoning, one out of ten U.S. households owned a Patch puzzle. Patch's puzzles were for the most part small educational puzzles, which sold relatively inexpensively at discount stores and toy stores.

The company further diversified by buying a maker of outdoor toys in 1998. This was the New York-based Just Kid'n company, which made the Zoam brand of foam balls. The toy business was extremely lopsided seasonally, with some 75 to 85 percent of sales coming in the Christmas season. Patch's move into a summertime toy line was an attempt to provide some balance. Under Patch's management, the Zoam line grew to include Light Tracker lighted balls as well. A few years later, Patch also began selling foam balls with collegiate logos on them, as part of a larger strategy to license popular cultural icons.

LICENSING STRATEGY

Over two million copies of TriBond had been sold around the world by 2000. Patch was careful, though, not to link its fate entirely to that game. Because of that game's very public success, game inventors courted Patch. It no longer had to come up with its own ideas, but could sift through games brought to it by eager entrepreneurs. A big part of any game's success was effective marketing. Thus in the first decade of the 2000s, Patch began a marketing strategy popular in the game industry and in many other industries as well, licensing popular brands to sell its products. In 2000, Patch inked licensing deals with three musical groups popular with teenagers. It secured rights to make board games using brand imagery from the groups Backstreet Boys, 'N Sync, and 98. This led to the games NSYNC Backstage Pass, Backstreet Boys Around the World, and 98 Play for Keeps.

The musical groups represented just the beginning of Patch's licensing strategy. In 2001 it put out a line of games that licensed the McDonald's restaurant brand. Over the next several years it licensed the cartoon character Rudolph the Red-Nosed Reindeer, collegiate logos for its foam balls, and then the Jeff Foxworthy comedian brand, for a game called You Might Be a Redneck If. ... Patch Products also arranged a licensing agreement with the increasingly popular NASCAR racing organization, and launched a game called Chase for the NASCAR Nextel Cup.

While pursuing these various licensing agreements, Patch also maneuvered to extend its product lines in other ways. It brought out floor puzzles early in the first decade of the 2000s, as well as traditional games such as chess, checkers, and backgammon. Patch also began producing playing cards, dice and poker chips, flash cards, and dominos. The company also came out with new family card games. With all these new products early in the 2000s, Patch needed to expand its distribution center. It opened a large new site in 2002 and expanded its sales in overseas markets as well. It began distribution in the United Kingdom and France in 2002, and by 2004 was also selling its products in Germany, Singapore, South Africa, and the Philippines.

Perhaps the company's most significant move of the early 2000s, though, was what it discontinued. Amid the flurry of new products, new licensing agreements, and new markets, Patch sold the rights to TriBond and two other games in 2004. Mattel, the other dominant game company besides Hasbro, bought the game rights to TriBond, Blurt, and Mad Gab. Financial details of the sale were not released. Patch predicted that TriBond was nearing the end of its run, and it wanted to move on.

Losing TriBond led to an abrupt 25 percent drop in sales for Patch. However, this only encouraged the company to work harder to promote its dozens of other products. Sales angled up again soon. The company's good judgment was affirmed when Mattel stopped making TriBond a few years later. Clearly the game had come to the end of its heyday, and Patch had done well to sell when it did.

MAINTAINING A FAMILY FOCUS

Near the end of the new century's opening decade, Patch Products brought out five to ten new games a year. It received about 100 game ideas a month from people such as Tim Walsh, who thought they had the next hit. With much to choose from, Patch nevertheless maintained an emphasis on games whole families could play together. These included Roll It Tic Tac Toe and Farkle and the card stacking game ShakeDown. Patch also brought out an activity set for preschoolers called Can-Do Roo, and coloring books, activity books, and new floor puzzles. It brought out a line of quiz games meant for playing in the car and a new party game called What's Yours Like? These new additions gave the company a broad swathe of family entertainment products, some targeting kids and some for kids and adults together.

Another new game was Buzzword. In some ways similar to TriBond and Blurt, Buzzword was a word game based on question cards. It could be played by all ages, although a junior version was aimed at younger players. Patch marketed Buzzword as it had TriBond and other games, by sending it to disc jockeys who might use the questions in on-air quizzes. By late 2007, Patch had gotten about 100 radio stations to play Buzzword on air. Patch also arranged to promote Buzzword through the Red Robin Gourmet Burgers chain. Red Robin had been named one of the top ten best restaurant chains for families by *Parents* magazine in 2008. Like Patch, the restaurant aimed to appeal to kids and adults alike. The restaurant put Buzzword game clues on its coasters, and also offered discount coupons for Patch products on its children's menus. Patch then in turn promoted Red Robin, inserting restaurant coupons in sets of Buzzword and Buzzword Junior.

Patch made an acquisition in 2008, extending its reach into educational toys. It acquired a venerable Pennsylvania toymaker, Smethport Specialty Company. Smethport was founded as Marvel Toy Company in 1923, and had antecedents even further back, in the 1908 Electric Toy Works. Its most enduring toy was Wooly Willy, which it introduced in 1955. This was a drawing toy, where kids could manipulate a special magnetic powder on Willy's face to give him hair. In the

1950s, this toy was sold around the world, along with other magnetic Smethport toys such as Dapper Dan. Smethport also owned a Maine educational toy manufacturer called Lauri. With the Smethport purchase, Patch acquired both the Lauri and Smethport brands. Lauri's educational toy lines gave Patch access to new markets and these complemented Patch's existing product lines well.

After founding a printing company in 1971 and working side by side for almost 40 years, Fran and Bryce Patch gave up their daily leadership positions at Patch in 2009. Both Patch brothers remained on the company's board of directors. Brian Maxwell, who had been vice-president of sales, became president of the company, taking Bryce Patch's place. The chief executive officer position, which had been held by Fran Patch, went to Bob Wann. Wann had previously been chief executive of a toy company in North Carolina, Sababa Toys.

Patch had stopped releasing sales figures in the late 1990s, although it had sometimes commented more generally on how it was doing. The traditional toy and game industry had been relatively flat, especially as children's tastes swung toward video games and consumer electronics. Patch admitted to having seen a steep sales drop after 2004, when it had sold off the rights to TriBond. Yet it also claimed to have recovered quickly from that dip. As economic hard times hit almost every sector of the U.S. economy in 2008 and 2009, Patch did not indicate how it was affected. Overall, the company seemed to have operated strategically all along. Although it owed much of its good fortune to the hit status of TriBond, the company had never depended solely on that one product. It had a balanced array of toys, puzzles, and games that it sold in a variety of retail outlets, and in markets all around the globe. It seemed safe to speculate that the company's long-range planning would see it through any momentary difficulties.

A. Woodward

PRINCIPAL SUBSIDIARIES

Smethport Specialty Company.

PRINCIPAL COMPETITORS

Hasbro, Inc.; Mattel, Inc.; Buffalo Games Inc.

FURTHER READING

Feder, Barnaby J., "Game Aims at Hasbro Monopoly," *New York Times*, September 17, 1994, p. 37.

Hajewski, Doris, "Beloit, Wis., Game Maker to Sell Three Brands to Mattel," *Milwaukee Journal Sentinel,* February 4, 2004.

———, "Company Puts Pedal to the Metal on NASCAR Game," *Milwaukee Journal Sentinel,* October 3, 2007.

———, "Game Maker Patch Products Names New CEO," *Milwaukee Journal Sentinel,* April 24, 2009.

———, "Patch Products Acquires Maker of Wooly Willy," *Milwaukee Journal Sentinel,* August 14, 2008.

Ivey, Mike, "A Roll of the Dice," *Madison (Wis.) Capital Times,* December 1, 1994, pp. 1B–2B.

Newman, Judy, "Patch Builds Success on Family-Oriented Theme," *Wisconsin State Journal,* May 7, 1998, pp. 1F–2F.

———, "Patch Products Brings Home to Work," *Wisconsin State Journal,* May 7, 1998, pp. 1F–2F.

Ostrander, Kathy, "Hunting Big Game Profits," *Wisconsin State Journal,* August 3, 1997, p. 1E.

Tanyeri, Dana, "A Little Gamey," *Restaurant Business,* November 2008, p. 16.

Publix Super Markets, Inc.

3300 Publix Corporate Parkway
Lakeland, Florida 33811-3311
U.S.A.
Telephone: (863) 688-1188
Fax: (863) 284-5532
Web site: http://www.publix.com

Private Company
Incorporated: 1930
Employees: 139,000
Sales: $23.93 billion (2008)
NAICS: 445110 Supermarkets and Other Grocery
    (Except Convenience) Stores

∎ ∎ ∎

Publix Super Markets, Inc., stands as one of the top half-dozen supermarket chains in the United States as measured by sales volume and number of stores. It is the largest employee-owned supermarket; its current and former employees own the majority of Publix's shares. The rest of the company is owned by its officers and directors, many of whom are members of the founding Jenkins family. Nearly three-quarters of the chain's more than 1,000 stores are in Florida, where Publix is the grocery leader with a commanding market share of more than 40 percent. The company also has smaller but growing presences in Georgia, South Carolina, Alabama, and Tennessee. The stores are supported through Publix's eight distribution centers, including seven in Florida and one in Georgia. A focus on customer service has been Publix's hallmark throughout its 75-plus-year history.

A COMMITMENT TO SERVICE DURING THE GREAT DEPRESSION

Publix was founded in 1930 by George W. Jenkins, the son of a rural Georgia grocer. Jenkins moved to Winter Haven, Florida, in 1927 and took a job as a stock clerk at the local Piggly Wiggly. He became the store's manager six weeks later at the age of 17. At 20, he borrowed less than $2,000 and started his own 27-by-65-foot grocery store across the street with five employees. The store earned $500 its first year, in the midst of the Great Depression. By 1935, Jenkins owned five stores.

Jenkins was one of the first in the grocery business to stress customer service and high-quality goods. While most of his competitors focused on price and productivity, the signs on the front of the Publix store read, "Where shopping is a pleasure," reflecting the firm's early belief in the importance of customer satisfaction. Jenkins also stressed employee satisfaction, promoting almost entirely from within, and giving his workers a large amount of control over the section of the store in which they worked.

In 1940 Jenkins opened his first supermarket, an 11,000-square-foot space with a paved parking lot, air conditioning, wide aisles, electric doors, and frozen food cases. The aesthetics and features of Jenkins's superstore were unusual for American grocery stores during the Great Depression, reflecting the founder's attempt to make shopping an enjoyable experience. By 1950, 22

COMPANY PERSPECTIVES

Our Mission at Publix is to be the premier quality food retailer in the world.

To that end we commit to be: Passionately focused on Customer Value; Intolerant of Waste; Dedicated to the Dignity, Value and Employment Security of our Associates; Devoted to the highest standards of stewardship for our Stockholders; and Involved as Responsible Citizens in our Communities.

Publix supermarkets were in operation, including 19 stores in central Florida and along Florida's west coast that had been purchased from the All American chain in 1945. Revenues for the chain totaled $12.1 million in 1950.

In 1949 R. William Schroter stepped in to head Publix's own one-person advertising department, employing local freelancers. The department eventually grew into the W.M. Zemp & Associates advertising firm in St. Petersburg. Publix advertised heavily in newspapers but avoided the weekly circulars used by many supermarkets.

In the early 1950s, Publix began giving out S&H Green Stamps, handing shoppers a fixed number of stamps per dollar spent, which they could then redeem for discounted merchandise. The resulting sales increase far exceeded the cost of the stamp program, and Publix quickly became the largest vendor of S&H stamps in the country. Jenkins liked the stamps because he believed that they encouraged store loyalty as well as thrifty habits. In the late 1950s, Publix began to sell stock to its employees.

STEADY GROWTH THROUGHOUT THE SIXTIES AND SEVENTIES

Publix's success in less-developed parts of Florida encouraged Jenkins to move into the lucrative, but highly competitive, Miami market in 1959. In 1963 the firm opened a warehouse to service the growing number of supermarkets it was opening there. The state of Florida itself contributed to the chain's expansion as it became one of the fastest-growing states in the country. Fueled partly by its move to Miami, Publix grew to 114 stores in 1965, with sales of $262.9 million, and 157 stores, with sales of $465.7 million in 1970. In 1974

the firm opened a 200,000-square-foot warehouse in Jacksonville to supply Publix stores between Jacksonville and Tallahassee.

Publix management kept a careful eye on lifestyle trends. By 1966, as more women began to work outside the home and more people remained single, stores shifted from one small frozen food display case to large, upright cases with glass doors. Frozen food sales continued to grow, and Publix added more freezers and devoted more attention to their stocking, keeping brand-name products together rather than sorting by food type. The firm identified and responded to food trends such as yogurt and frozen pizza earlier than most of its rivals. In setting up shelves, dairy cases, and freezers, it was careful to keep ease of shopping its top priority, while also displaying high-margin items at eye level and making certain that products were arranged in a way that facilitated quick restocking.

In the early 1970s, with a wave of discount stores taking hold in Florida, Publix opened its own discount chain called Food World. In 1976 Publix introduced in-store photofinishing, giving away a roll of film or an extra set of prints with each roll it developed. Within ten years, the firm accounted for 12 percent of the total photofinishing business in its marketing area and had 24 discount stores.

In 1979 the company reached nearly $2 billion in sales and had 234 stores and 26,000 employees. It was the 11th largest chain in national sales and had an after-tax net averaging 1.7 percent, far ahead of most of its rivals. Publix was the leading grocery chain in Daytona Beach, Palm Beach, and St. Petersburg, where it had 30.6 percent of the market. It was the second largest chain in the Miami area, with 26 percent of the market. All Publix stores were similar inside and had in-store delis and bakeries. Publix supermarkets also took advantage of technology, using the second largest number of price scanners of any business in the United States.

Publix's skilled marketing and use of up-to-date technology had contributed to its success, but so had the stability of its workforce. The firm had never experienced a strike, lockout, or layoff; it had the lowest employee turnover of any large chain. This was attributed to employment policies that included a profit-sharing plan that distributed 20 percent of net profits at each store to that store's full-time workers; a retirement plan funded by 15 percent of pretax profits; and the policy of promoting from within the company. Employees were also given more responsibility than at most large chains.

KEY DATES

1930: Publix is founded by George W. Jenkins in Winter Haven, Florida.
1940: Jenkins closes his first two stores and opens the first Publix supermarket.
1956: Publix records its first million-dollar profit; the company opens a 125,000-square-foot warehouse and headquarters in Lakeland, Florida.
1959: First Miami Publix supermarket opens.
1964: Publix opens its 100th store in Winter Haven, Florida.
1974: The chain captures $1 billion in sales.
1990: Howard M. Jenkins succeeds his father as CEO.
1992: Company ventures outside Florida for the first time, opening a store in Georgia.
1993: The first Publix store in South Carolina opens for business.
1996: Chain is expanded into Alabama.
1997: In one of the largest such settlements in U.S. history, Publix agrees to pay $81.5 million to settle a class-action sexual discrimination suit.
2001: Howard Jenkins steps aside as CEO; his cousin, Charles H. Jenkins Jr., succeeds him.
2002: Publix enters its fifth state, Tennessee.
2005: Revenues reach $20 billion.
2008: William E. (Ed) Crenshaw is named the fourth CEO in Publix history; company purchases 49 Albertson's stores in Florida.
2009: The 1,000th Publix store makes its debut.

THE MOVE TO SUPERSTORES IN THE EIGHTIES

By 1980, Publix had a strong presence throughout the state of Florida, with the exception of the panhandle. Its operations were divided into three divisions: the Jacksonville division, which covered the northern third of the state; the Miami division, which covered the eastern coast south of Brevard County; and the Lakeland division, which covered the rest of the state. The company headquarters were located in Lakeland, where a 425,000-square-foot grocery warehouse stored a three-week supply of goods.

Publix spent about 0.75 percent of sales on advertising, amounting to about $15 million in 1980. Newspaper ads accounted for 68 percent of the advertising budget, television 24 percent, and radio, which aimed to reach younger Floridians, 5 percent. In-store merchandising displays, accounting for the remainder, were highly theatrical and changed weekly. They were created by employees without direction from the Publix central office because Jenkins believed that store managers best knew what would work in their own territories.

The 1980s brought considerable change to Publix. One of the first changes was automated teller machines, which Publix began installing before many banks did. The firm was also the first supermarket chain to install bar-code scanners in every store. Jenkins had always refused to open his stores on Sunday, but in 1982, losing market share to stores that did, he relented. In 1984 Joe Blanton, who had been president for ten years, died, and was replaced by Mark Hollis. Hollis began with Publix in 1946 as a bag boy at age 12 and had worked as a stock clerk and a produce and store manager. In 1985 all but three of the discount Food Worlds were closed, unable to give workers a percentage of their store's profits and turn a profit for Publix. Sales for the entire chain in 1985 reached $3.2 billion, up from $2.8 billion in 1983, making Publix the ninth largest grocery chain by sales.

Superstores, with 30,000 square feet or more, were another 1980s innovation. After competitors successfully began to rely upon them, Publix began opening its own superstores of up to 39,000 square feet each. Most were located in shopping malls where customers could shop for goods other than food as well. In the 1980s, when Publix's competitors opened combination stores where customers could fill prescriptions in addition to buying groceries, Publix followed suit, opening its first combination store in Orlando in 1986. The 55,000-square-foot, upscale space combined a grocery store with gourmet food and deli and bakery sections, as well as hardware and toy departments and the firm's first pharmacy. The combination stores included a one-hour photo department, a counter where cameras and small electronics were sold, and an expanded cosmetics, health, and beauty aids section. The stores were intended to appeal to younger, professional, two-income families, and their sites were carefully selected with an eye on demographics. Publix quickly opened two more Publix Food & Pharmacy stores in Tampa, one in Tamarac, near Fort Lauderdale, and three more in other parts of Florida. The firm also remodeled and expanded old supermarkets and opened new ones. Publix opened 28 stores in 1986 and more than 30 in 1987, often choosing sites in advance of Florida's population explosion.

To help support these new stores, Publix doubled the size of the Lakeland warehouse to 440,000 square feet, and planned a 660,000-square-foot perishables warehouse near Fort Lauderdale. To increase flexibility in merchandising and marketing, Publix dropped S&H Green Stamps in the Lakeland and Jacksonville divisions in June 1987. In 1989 Publix again tried a new technology when it began moving toward automatic checkout lanes with machines that allowed customers to scan their own groceries, then pay a central cashier.

In January 1990, after suffering a stroke, George Jenkins retired as chairman and chief executive of Publix and became chairman emeritus. He was succeeded by his son, Howard M. Jenkins, who was 38 years old. As with many Publix executives, the younger Jenkins had begun at the retail level and worked his way up through the company's ranks. At the time of the leadership change, Publix ranked as the 21st largest retailer in the United States, with 370 stores, 60,000 employees, and profits of $128.5 million on sales of $5.38 billion. Late in 1990, it announced plans to build a 48,000-square-foot store in Kingsland, Georgia, about 80 miles south of Savannah, and plans for a second store in a Savannah shopping mall soon followed. In August 1991, with 384 stores, the firm announced that it was looking for sites in Atlanta. It opened its first store in Georgia in 1992 and began to build aggressively in and around Atlanta. By 1994, Publix had snapped up 10.1 percent of the market, trailing only Kroger and Winn-Dixie, whose market shares nonetheless dropped as a result of Publix's performance. By 1995, Publix had constructed a three-million-square-foot distribution center in Lawrenceville and a milk processing plant. Its 34 Atlanta stores, all built from the ground up, offered features unknown to its Florida counterparts, such as freshly grilled fajitas and stir-fry dishes in a 100-seat dining area. In the meantime, Publix had opened its first store in South Carolina in 1993.

A STRING OF LEGAL WOES IN THE NINETIES

Publix was named one of the top ten companies to work for in the nation by the 1993 edition of *The 100 Best Companies to Work for in America*. The timing of this honor was somewhat ironic, however, as the company was then in the throes of racial- and gender-bias charges with several groups. The chain had been picketed by the United Food and Commercial Workers union since its entry into Georgia for allegedly racial- and gender-biased employment and promotion practices. In 1992 a coalition of labor, feminist, Hispanic, and African American rights groups began threatening to boycott Publix supermarkets if the company did not place more women and minorities in management jobs by 1994. Their position was based on a survey revealing that women held fewer than 2 percent, African Americans

fewer than 3 percent, and Hispanics fewer than 4 percent of the store's top management positions. In 1993 the Equal Employment Opportunity Commission (EEOC) asked the U.S. District Court in Miami to force Publix to turn over employment data for an investigation into sex bias charges. That same year, Publix agreed to pay a $500,000 fine after the Labor Department found minors working too many hours and during prohibited times in 11 Publix stores.

The year 1994 saw temporary respite from Publix's legal woes. By 1994, stores in Georgia and South Carolina were contributing to sales growth, and sales reached $8.66 billion, up 16 percent from 1993. In 1995 Publix also introduced a smaller sized, 27,000-square-foot store in Tampa, Florida. At half the size of most new Publix supermarkets, this downscaled version of Publix's megastore offered neither a pharmacy nor health and beauty aids department, and fewer dry goods to provide space to the deli, bakery, and perishable goods sections. Instead its focus was on prepackaged deli items in response to the new consumer demand for prepared foods. The company also opened its Atlanta Division distribution facility and began to introduce full-service banks located in its stores.

Despite such advances, sluggish gains in profits and sales bespoke a difficult year for Publix. Accompanying a general downturn in retailing, sales increased only 8 percent to total almost $9.4 billion in 1994. Nevertheless, Publix added a net total of about 50 stores that year to reach the 500-store mark, and the chain was rated number two, behind Kroger, in the Atlanta market with 31 stores and 14 percent of sales. The company made *Fortune* magazine's Famous 500 and Global 500 lists in 1995 and became the seventh largest-volume supermarket chain in the nation.

The chain's legal woes were resurrected in 1995, however, when eight women sued, claiming that Publix clustered women in cashier, delicatessen, and bakery jobs and denied them promotions and equal pay to men. Late in 1995 the EEOC joined in the discrimination lawsuit, and in March 1996 a judge ruled to allow the case to proceed as a class-action suit, expanding the field of possible litigants to 120,000 current or former workers and making it the largest sex discrimination case in U.S. history. A second class-action suit was filed in Miami several months later by a firm representing women who worked in the company's administrative offices, warehouses, and plants. In addition, a former employee accused Publix of coding job applications to denote race, gender, and disabilities, and work safety inspectors targeted Publix as the Florida company with the most workers' compensation claims.

Publix's growth still continued unabated. By 1996, it had captured 18 percent of the Atlanta market, and the chain expanded into Alabama that year. Its sales for the year totaled $10 billion, an impressive 9.5 percent increase over 1995. The settlement in January 1997, however, of the first of its class-action suits for $81.5 million, the fourth largest such settlement in U.S. history, took a huge chunk out of the company's earnings. In addition, it agreed to pay a $3.5 million fine to the EEOC over accusations that it had denied blacks job opportunities.

Before the company had the chance to recover, a third high-profile class-action suit was filed. Despite the fact that the company had earlier signed an agreement with the Southern Christian Leadership Conference setting specific goals on hiring, training, and promoting more minority workers, and had opened three stores in predominantly black neighborhoods in 1996, early in 1997, a group representing 50,000 blacks, who had worked for Publix since 1993, claimed that the chain systematically denied equal hiring and promotion opportunities to blacks and created a hostile work environment for minorities. In December 2000 Publix reached an agreement to pay $10 million to settle this suit. Also in 2000, the suit involving workers at the company's administrative offices, warehouses, and plants was dismissed.

In spite of these legal travails and their attendant negative publicity, Publix remained a favorite among customers. A *Consumer Reports* article in 1997 ranked it as tied for the highest overall score in terms of shopping experience. It placed above average for checkout speed, meat, deli, and produce, and average on price. The younger Jenkins had successfully wed Publix's long-standing commitment to customer service to advances in technology. Throughout 1998 and 1999, the chain held to its practice of building 40 or more stores a year. The company was also alert to acquisition possibilities, and in 1999 it acquired nine stores in Atlanta from A&P, which had decided to pull out of that market. Publix generated profits of $462.4 million in 1999 on sales of $13.07 billion.

In mid-2000 Publix announced plans to begin testing the addition of a convenience store with gas pumps to its store parking lots. The first such unit, operating under the name Pix, was opened in early 2001 at a Publix store in Tampa. In May 2001 Howard Jenkins stepped down as chief executive while remaining company chairman. During Jenkins's 11 years at the helm, Publix's annual sales nearly tripled, from $5.3 billion to $14.6 billion, while its store count leaped from 357 to 654. It was under Jenkins's watch that the chain extended its reach beyond Florida for the first time, with

the moves into Georgia, South Carolina, and Alabama. Charles H. Jenkins Jr., a cousin of Howard Jenkins, was named the new CEO.

GROWTH AND EXPERIMENTATION UNDER CHARLES JENKINS

The new leader arrived with ambitious plans to open more than 340 stores over a five-year period. During 2002, Publix opened 76 supermarkets, while closing 19, and also expanded or remodeled another 91 units. Among the new units were the chain's first four Tennessee outlets. Publix's march into its fifth state was opportunistic. Albertson's had elected to abandon the Nashville market, and Publix swooped in to purchase seven shuttered Alberton's stores there, all of which eventually reopened under the Publix banner.

During what turned out to be a seven-year tenure at the helm, Charles Jenkins managed to lead Publix through another period of tremendous growth, despite accelerating competition from the ever-expanding supercenter behemoth Wal-Mart and numerous other players. Revenues surpassed the $20 billion mark in 2005 before reaching $23.02 billion two years later. In spite of the highly competitive environment, Publix's continued focus on customer service helped it extend its share of the Florida retail grocery market to more than one-third. Even more impressively, the company's profits grew at a faster pace than its sales during this period, more than doubling from $530.4 million in 2001 to $1.18 billion in 2007. Although Jenkins fell short of his 340-unit store-opening goal, the store count did hit 926 by the end of 2007.

Another hallmark of Jenkins's leadership stint was the tremendous experimentation displayed. One such venture, an online-grocery business launched in southern Florida in the fall of 2001, was aborted after a two-year trial, but several others endured. In 2004 the company began testing a liquor store concept, with these units located adjacent to a Publix store. The venture was successful enough that more than 70 such units were in operation by the end of 2008. Also in 2004, Publix acquired majority control of Crispers, a Florida restaurant chain featuring salads and sandwiches. In 2006 the first of several Publix stores was equipped with a Little Clinic, an in-store clinic staffed by a nurse practitioner and run by a like-named company based in Louisville, Kentucky. In addition, Publix experimented with new supermarket formats. The first Publix Sabor, a Hispanic-themed supermarket, made its debut in Kissimmee, Florida, in 2005. The company two years later ventured into the natural foods sector with the opening in Palm Beach Gardens of the first Publix GreenWise

Market, a venture that leveraged the chain's GreenWise brand, which had been introduced earlier into the organic sections of Publix's traditional stores.

In March 2008 Jenkins shifted over to the chairman's seat, clearing the way for his cousin, William E. (Ed) Crenshaw, to be promoted from president to CEO. Crenshaw assumed the reins at an inauspicious time as supermarket chains across the country struggled under the impact of the economic downturn. Growth in same-store sales at Publix, which had averaged more than 5 percent over the previous four years, totaled just 1.3 percent in 2008. A store-count increase of 67, bringing the total to 993 by year-end 2008, helped push sales up 4 percent, to $23.93 billion, but profits fell 8 percent to $1.09 billion. The increase in the store count was aided by the September 2008 purchase of 49 Albertson's stores in Florida for $498 million. The deal included four stores in Pensacola, marking Publix's debut in that Florida Panhandle market.

OVER THE 1,000-UNIT MARK IN 2009

Another milestone in the firm's nearly 80-year history was reached in February 2009 when the 1,000th Publix opened in St. Augustine, Florida. Publix earmarked $665 million for 2009 capital expenses, mainly for store openings, expected to total 40 for the year, store remodelings and upgrades, and various technological initiatives. Continued economic weakness sent same-store sales down 2.7 percent for the first half of 2009, while overall sales were up 2.4 percent.

Scott Lewis
Updated, Carrie Rothburd; David E. Salamie

PRINCIPAL SUBSIDIARIES

Publix Alabama, LLC; Publix Asset Management Company; PublixDirect, LLC; Publix Tennessee, LLC; Crispers, LLC; Lone Palm Golf Club, LLC; Morning Song, LLC; PTO, LLC; Real Sub, LLC.

PRINCIPAL COMPETITORS

Wal-Mart Stores, Inc.; Winn-Dixie Stores, Inc.; Sweetbay Supermarket; Albertsons LLC; The Kroger Company.

FURTHER READING

Albright, Mark, "Grocers Scramble, Publix Gambles," *St. Petersburg Times,* August 5, 2008, p. 1A.

————, "Magistrate: Publix Racial Bias Suit Should Widen," *St. Petersburg Times,* June 17, 1998, p. 1E.

————, "Publix Buys Rival Stores," *St. Petersburg Times,* June 10, 2008, p. 1A.

————, "Publix Changes Leaders, but Stays in the Family," *St. Petersburg Times,* September 6, 2007.

————, "Publix Faces New Bias Lawsuit," *St. Petersburg Times,* April 3, 1997, p. 1E.

————, "Publix Settles Race Bias Dispute," *St. Petersburg Times,* December 30, 2000, p. 1E.

————, "Publix to Undergo Change in Leadership," *St. Petersburg Times,* May 16, 2001, p. 1E.

————, "Suit Is Just One of Chain's Legal Woes," *St. Petersburg Times,* January 11, 1998, p. 2H.

Backman, Lisa, "Marching into Atlanta," *Tampa Tribune,* May 22, 1995, p. 8.

Blank, Christine, "Publix Debuts GreenWise Market Format," *Supermarket News,* September 24, 2007, p. 8.

————, "Publix Joins Other Florida Retailers Pumping Gasoline," *Supermarket News,* June 5, 2000, p. 99.

————, "Publix's 'Sabor' Includes New Look," *Supermarket News,* May 2, 2005, p. 8.

Bork, Robert H., Jr., "Call Him Old-Fashioned," *Forbes,* August 26, 1985, p. 66.

Carvin, Joseph W., *A Piece of the Pie: The Story of Customer Service at Publix,* Lakeland, Fla.: Publix Super Markets, Inc., 2005, 176 p.

Dietrich, Robert, Mary Ann Linsen, et al., "Publix, Where Pleasure Is Profitable," *Progressive Grocer,* September 1980.

Elson, Joel, "Publix and the New Florida Market," *Supermarket News,* April 20, 1987.

Hamstra, Mark, "Publix Plays Familiar Tune in Nashville Entry," *Supermarket News,* July 8, 2002, p. 1.

————, "Publix Streaks Toward 1,000-Unit Threshold," *Supermarket News,* February 9, 2004, p. 26.

Harris, Nicole, "Revolt at the Deli Counter," *Business Week,* April 1, 1996, p. 32.

Jacobs, Cherie, "Publix Testing Liquor Market with Locations Next to Stores," *Tampa Tribune,* February 20, 2004.

Jenkins, George W., *The Publix Story,* New York: Newcomen Society in North America, 1979, 23 p.

Lewis, Len, "Publix Domain," *Progressive Grocer,* December 1998, p. 23.

Major, Meg, "Publix: Florida's Other Magic Kingdom," *Progressive Grocer,* February 15, 2003, pp. 22–29.

Martin, Timothy W., "May I Help You? Publix Super Markets Is Finding Success Where Rivals Aren't. Its Main Weapon: Customer Service," *Wall Street Journal,* April 23, 2009, p. R4.

McTaggart, Jenny, "Miami Spice: Publix's New Hispanic Banner Blends the Best of Its Conventional Supermarket with the Authentic Flavor of the Latino Specialists," *Progressive Grocer,* September 1, 2005, pp. 38–42, 44–45.

Myerson, Allen R., "Supermarket Chain to Pay $81 Million to Settle a Bias Suit," *New York Times,* January 25, 1997, p. 1.

O'Neill, Robert E., "Publix: New Face, New Challenge," *Progressive Grocer,* January 1985, pp. 55+.

Petersen, Chris, "Friendly Aisles: Providing Attentive Customer Service Is the Key to Publix Super Markets' Success in the Southeast," *U.S. Business Review,* January 2006, pp. 160, 162.

"Publix a Pacesetter from the Start," *Mass Market Retailer,* August 8, 2005, p. 14.

"Publix Settles Suit Claiming Applications Were Coded," *St. Petersburg Times,* April 17, 1996, p. 6E.

Reinan, John, "Publix Affection," *Tampa Tribune,* December 5, 1999.

Springer, Jon, "Crenshaw to Succeed Jenkins As Publix CEO,"

Supermarket News, September 10, 2007, p. 1.

Walsh, Matt, "The Schwarzkopf Gambit," *Forbes,* November 21, 1994, pp. 170+.

Watters, Pat, *Fifty Years of Pleasure: The Illustrated History of Publix Super Markets, Inc.,* Lakeland, Fla.: Publix Super Markets, 1980, 263 p.

Zweibach, Elliot, "George Jenkins Named Chairman Emeritus at Publix," *Supermarket News,* January 8, 1990, pp. 1+.

————, "Publix Adds 49 Florida Albertsons," *Supermarket News,* June 16, 2008, p. 1.

————, "Publix' Intrepreneur," *Supermarket News,* April 20, 1987, pp. 1+.

Raytheon Company

870 Winter Street
Waltham, Massachusetts 02451
U.S.A.
Telephone: (781) 522-3000
Fax: (781) 522-3001
Web site: http://www.raytheon.com

Public Company
Incorporated: 1922 as American Appliance Company
Employees: 73,000
Sales: $23.17 billion (2008)
Stock Exchanges: New York
Ticker Symbol: RTN
NAICS: 336414 Guided Missile and Space Vehicle Manufacturing; 334511 Search, Detection, Navigation, Guidance, Aeronautical, and Nautical System and Instruments Manufacturing; 334413 Semiconductor and Related Device Manufacturing; 334419 Other Electronic Component Manufacturing; 335211 Electric Houseware and Fan Manufacturing; 336413 Other Aircraft Part and Auxiliary Equipment Manufacturing

∎ ∎ ∎

Raytheon Company is the fourth largest defense contractor in the United States and the world's largest missile builder. Raytheon's principal missiles are the Patriot, Sidewinder, and Tomahawk systems. Aside from its missile business, the company designs and produces aircraft radar systems, weapons sights and targeting systems, and communications and battle-management systems. Raytheon ranks as a leading provider of marine electronics, shipboard and sonar systems, and Global Positioning System (GPS) devices. The company relies on the U.S. government for more than 85 percent of its annual sales.

BEGINNINGS IN RADIO TUBES

Raytheon was founded in 1922 when a civil engineer named Laurence Marshall was introduced to an inventor and Harvard physicist named Charles G. Smith by Dr. Vannevar Bush. Marshall proposed a business partnership with Smith and Bush after hearing that Smith had developed a new method for noiseless home refrigeration using compressed gases and no moving parts. Marshall raised $25,000 in venture capital from investors and a former World War I comrade and incorporated the partnership in Cambridge, Massachusetts (near Bush's employer, the Massachusetts Institute of Technology), as American Appliance Company.

Marshall and Smith never developed their refrigeration technologies for the market, but instead shifted their attention to vacuum tubes and other electronic devices. In 1924 Marshall made a three-month tour of the United States to study the pattern of growth in the electronics market. Noting rapidly growing consumer demand for radios, Marshall negotiated the purchase of patents for the S-tube, a gas-filled rectifier that converted alternating current (AC) used in households to the direct current (DC) used in radio sets (ironically, the technology had been developed by Smith and Bush some years earlier while they worked for the American Research and Development Corporation). Up to that time, radios ran on an auto storage battery called the A battery and a high-voltage B battery, which were costly, cumbersome, messy, and relatively expensive to replace.

In 1925, shortly before S-tube production began, a firm in Indiana laid claim to the American Appliance company name. The partners decided to change their corporate name to Raytheon Manufacturing Company. Despite the fact that *raytheon* is Greek for "god of life," the name actually was chosen for its modern sound. By 1926, Raytheon had become a major manufacturer of tube rectifiers and generated $321,000 in profit on sales of $1 million.

Virtually all the tubes produced by Raytheon were used in radio sets whose design patents were held by RCA. In 1927 RCA altered its licensing agreements with radio manufacturers to stipulate that the radios could be built only with new rectifier tubes (called Radiotrons) manufactured by RCA. Raytheon was, in effect, denied access to its markets. The company was forced to switch to the production of radio-receiving tubes, a field in which more than 100 companies were engaged in fierce competition.

Marshall's response to operating in this difficult environment was to diversify. Raytheon acquired the Acme-Delta Company, a producer of transformers, power equipment, and electronic auto parts. Profits resulting from new products were immediately put back into research and development to improve products, particularly in industrial electronics and microwave communications.

Marshall also sought the support of the National Carbon Company (a division of Union Carbide Corp.) during this difficult period. In 1929, National Carbon took a $500,000 equity position in Raytheon and held an option to buy the remaining portion of the company for an additional $19.5 million. National Carbon knew that Raytheon rectifier tubes had originally replaced its B battery business and also was convinced that its battery distribution would do well handling replacement tubes marked Eveready-Raytheon. Although the cooperative project was unsuccessful, National Carbon's investment carried Raytheon through the Great Depression. National Carbon allowed its option to acquire Raytheon to lapse in 1938.

MOVING INTO DEFENSE CONTRACTING DURING WORLD WAR II

With world war looming in 1940, U.S. President Franklin Roosevelt and British Prime Minister Winston Churchill authorized the joint development of new radar technologies by American and British institutions. Through the Radiation Laboratory at the Massachusetts Institute of Technology, Raytheon was chosen to develop the top-secret British magnetron, a microwave radar power tube. The technology would provide the range and clearer images required for successful detection and destruction of enemy planes, submarines (when they surfaced), and German warships. The new device had more than 100 times the power of previous microwave tubes and was cited as one of the Allies' top secrets. Britain, however, needed the United States' manufacturing capacity. In June 1941 Raytheon also won a contract to deliver 100 radar systems for navy ships.

Workers produced 100 magnetrons a day until Plant Manager Percy Spencer discovered a method, using punch presses, to raise production to more than 2,500 a day. Spencer's ingenuity won Raytheon an appropriation of $2 million from the U.S. Navy for the construction of a large new factory in Waltham, Massachusetts. By the end of the war, Raytheon magnetrons accounted for about 80 percent of the one million magnetrons produced during the war. By 1944, virtually every U.S. Navy ship was equipped with Raytheon radar. The company became internationally known for its reliable marine radar. The company also offered complete radar installations, with the help of subcontractors, and developed tubes for the VT radio fuse, a device that detonated fired shells when it sensed they were near solid objects. Over the course of the war, Raytheon's sales increased 55 times, from $3 million in 1940 to $168 million in 1945.

KEY DATES

1922: American Appliance Company is founded.
1925: Company changes its name to Raytheon Manufacturing Company and begins making tubes for radios.
1940: Raytheon is chosen to develop magnetrons, a tube used in microwave radar systems, marking the company's entrance into defense technology.
1941: U.S. Navy contracts with Raytheon on the delivery of 100 ship radar systems.
1950: Raytheon's Lark missile comes to the fore when it successfully intercepts and destroys a test drone.
1965: Amana Refrigeration is acquired.
1967: Company introduces the first countertop microwave under the Amana name.
1976: Production of the Patriot missile defense system begins.
1980: Company acquires Beech Aircraft.
1993: Company acquires the corporate jet unit of British Aerospace.
1995: E-Systems Inc. is acquired.
1997: Raytheon acquires the defense businesses of Texas Instruments Inc. and Hughes Electronics Corporation; its home appliances unit is divested.
2000: Raytheon Engineers & Constructors is sold to Morrison Knudsen Corporation.
2003: Company headquarters are moved from Lexington, Massachusetts, to Waltham, Massachusetts.
2006: Raytheon Aircraft Co. is sold for $3.3 billion.
2007: Company delivers its 1,000th Tomahawk Block IV missile system to the U.S. Navy.
2009: United Arab Emirates awards Raytheon a contract for Patriot missiles valued at $3 billion.

Raytheon was fortunate to be involved in a high-growth area of defense industry. When the war ended, companies specializing in high-technology military systems suffered less from cuts in the postwar defense budget than aircraft or heavy-vehicle manufacturers, or shipbuilders. In large part as a result of the war, Raytheon emerged as a profitable and influential, but still financially vulnerable, electronics company.

During the spring of 1945 Raytheon's management formulated plans to acquire several other electronics firms. As part of a strategy to consolidate independent component manufacturers into one company, in April the company purchased Belmont Electronics for $4.6 million. Belmont, located in Chicago, was a major consumer of Raytheon tubes and was developing a television for the commercial market. That October, Raytheon acquired Russell Electric for $1.1 million and entered merger negotiations with the Submarine Signal Company. Sub-Sig, as the company was known, was founded in Boston in 1901 as a manufacturer of maritime safety equipment, including a depth sounder called the fathometer. Sub-Sig manufactured a variety of sonar equipment during the war and, like Belmont, was a major Raytheon customer. When the two companies agreed to merge on May 31, 1946, it was decided that Sub-Sig would specialize in sonar devices and that Raytheon would continue to develop new radar systems.

Despite Raytheon's strengthened position as a result of the mergers, the company faced severe competition in both the sonar and radar markets from companies such as General Electric, RCA, Westinghouse Electric, and Sperry. Belmont, which planned to bring its television to market in late 1948, suffered a crippling strike during the summer and, as a result, lost much of its projected Christmas business. Unstable price conditions the following spring created further losses from which the subsidiary was, in large part, unable to recuperate. Laurence Marshall, although a superb engineer, was generally regarded as a poor manager. His inability to effect positive changes within the company led him to resign as president in February 1948. The following December he resigned as CEO, but he remained chairman of the board until May 1950, when he resigned after failing to gain support for a proposed merger with International Telephone & Telegraph (ITT). Charles F. Adams, a former financial adviser who joined Raytheon in 1947, assumed Marshall's responsibilities.

The sudden resumption of military orders after the outbreak of the Korean War in June 1950 greatly benefited Raytheon, as Defense Department contracts enabled the company to develop new technologies with initially low profitability. That year, a "Lark" missile equipped with a Raytheon-designed guidance system made history when it intercepted and destroyed a navy drone aircraft. Raytheon's advanced research center, called Lab 16, was designed to develop the Sparrow air-to-air and Hawk surface-to-air missiles. Raytheon became a partner in Selenia, a joint venture with the Italian firms Finmeccanica and Fiat, which was established to develop new radar technologies. Raytheon's association with Selenia afforded it an opportunity to work with the Italian rocket scientist Carlo Calosi.

Raytheon's Belmont operation was re-formed in 1954, but two years later all radio and television operations were sold to the Admiral Corporation. Raytheon continued, however, to develop new appliances, such as the Radarange microwave oven. In 1956 Charles Adams hired Harold S. Geneen, a highly innovative and dynamic manager, as executive vice-president. Three years later, however, Geneen left Raytheon to become chief executive of ITT. Richard E. Krafve (who once headed the Ford Motor Company's Edsel project) enjoyed only a short tenure as Geneen's successor; he disagreed frequently with Adams and was apparently unable to gain the respect of engineers. Thomas L. Phillips, manager of the Missile Division, replaced Krafve.

In 1956 and 1957, Raytheon and Minneapolis-Honeywell jointly operated a computer company called Datamatic. Raytheon soon sold its interest to Honeywell when Datamatic failed to compete effectively against IBM. Raytheon's joint venture projects with Italian companies continued to expand, however. D. Brainerd Holmes, a former director of the U.S. manned space flight program, joined Raytheon in 1963 to manage the company's military business, reporting to Phillips.

DIVERSIFYING IN THE SIXTIES AND SEVENTIES

Raytheon's top managers began to recognize weaknesses in the company's organizational structure perhaps as early as 1962; Raytheon, they decided, had become too dependent on government contracts. Thus in 1964 Adams and Phillips, who had become chairman and president, respectively, conceived a plan that aimed to diversify the company's operations. Raytheon acquired Packard-Bell's computer operations and a number of small electronics firms. In 1965 Raytheon acquired Amana Refrigeration Company. Although Raytheon had invented the microwave oven 20 years earlier, it needed Amana to commercialize the technology. (Spencer had accidentally discovered microwave cooking in 1945 when a candy bar in his pocket melted as he stood near an operating magnetron tube; the company began selling commercial refrigerator-sized Radaranges in 1947, then five years later started selling, with limited success, expensive consumer models through a licensing deal with Tappan Stove Company.) In 1967 Raytheon helped launch a domestic revolution when it introduced the first countertop microwave under the Amana name, featuring 100 volts of power and priced at just less than $500. That same year, Caloric Corporation, a major manufacturer of gas ranges and appliances, was acquired as well. By the end of the decade, Raytheon had absorbed a number of additional companies, including E.B. Badger Co., Inc., a designer and builder of petroleum and petrochemical plants; United Engineers and Constructors, a designer and builder of power plants; textbook publisher D.C. Heath & Company; and a geological survey company called Seismograph Service Corporation.

Raytheon's association with Selenia became strained in 1967. Raytheon's directors concluded that its Italian partners were unwilling to reform the operations of Selenia and Elsi (a jointly operated electronics firm). They voted to sell Raytheon's share of the companies to its partners and end their association with Calosi. Nevertheless, the defense department in 1967 selected Raytheon as the prime contractor for the new SAM-D surface-to-air missile. Renamed the Patriot in honor of the nation's bicentennial, the missile entered full-scale production in 1976. Initially designed as a defense against high-tech aircraft, the Patriot was upgraded about ten years later with the capability to intercept and destroy short-range ballistic missiles.

The goal of reducing Raytheon's proportion of sales to the government from 85 percent to 50 percent was achieved on schedule in 1970. However, while Raytheon's sales continued to rise, profits began to lag. Intracompany discussions determined that, with the exception of D.C. Heath, Raytheon should dispense with its marginally performing educational services units. In 1972, after several relatively small acquisitions, Raytheon purchased Iowa Manufacturing Company (later called Cedarapids, Inc.), a producer of road-building equipment.

When Charles Adams retired as chair in 1975, Tom Phillips was elected the new chairman and chief executive officer. Brainerd Holmes was promoted to president. Raytheon's financial performance during the mid-1970s was impressive: from 1973 to 1978 sales and profits grew at annual rates of 15 percent and 26 percent, respectively. Acquisitions in the latter years of the decade included Switchcraft, Inc., an electronics manufacturer, and Glenwood Range and Modern Maid gas range producers. The laundry products and kitchen appliance divisions of McGraw-Edison, which included the popular Speed Queen brand name, were added in 1979. The company's retained earnings were placed in high-yielding money market accounts until needed to finance acquisitions.

In 1977 Phillips tried to acquire Falcon Seaboard, an energy resources company involved primarily in strip mining coal, but withdrew the offer when favorable terms could not be reached. Instead, Phillips entered into negotiations to acquire Beech Aircraft, a leading manufacturer of single- and twin-engine aircraft. Raytheon acquired Beech in February 1980 for $800 million. The new affiliate recorded annual losses in each of the ensuing seven years, finally turning a profit in 1988.

At this time Raytheon's business with the government consisted mainly of radar systems, solar systems, communications equipment, and the Hawk, Sparrow, Patriot, and Sidewinder missiles, all of which totaled less than 40 percent of Raytheon's sales. Raytheon was more widely exposed to commercial computer and consumer markets, but these markets had become unexpectedly competitive, leading Raytheon management to reconsider its trend of moving away from stable military contracts.

Raytheon's Data Systems division, created in 1971 through the merger of the company's information processing and display units, established a small market by manufacturing terminals for airline reservation systems. Raytheon failed, however, to integrate Data Systems effectively with a word-processing subsidiary called Lexitron, which it acquired in 1978. As the computer products market expanded, Data Systems found itself unable to compete. After mounting losses, the division was sold to Telex in 1984. In January 1986 Raytheon acquired Yeargin Construction Company, a builder of electrical and chemical plants, and the following October it acquired Stearns Catalytic World Corporation, an industrial plant maintenance company.

When Brainerd Holmes retired on May 31, 1986, as he reached the traditional retirement age of 65, he was succeeded as president by R. Gene Shelley, who himself retired in July 1989 and was replaced by Dennis J. Picard. Picard succeeded Tom Phillips as chairman and chief executive of Raytheon in 1990, and Max E. Bleck rose to president.

FOCUSING ON DEFENSE AND COMMERCIAL ELECTRONICS: NINETIES AND BEYOND

While other major defense contractors moved to convert to civilian interests in the wake of post–Cold War defense budget cuts, Raytheon planned to buttress its position within its four main business segments: defense and commercial electronics, aircraft products, energy and environmental services, and major appliances. In 1992, Picard announced a new five-year plan. Its goals included increasing foreign military sales from 20 percent to 40 percent of total defense revenues; doubling energy and environmental services' $1.7 billion in sales; doubling Beech's $1.1 billion in sales; and increasing appliance sales by 60 percent.

The versatile Patriot missile, Raytheon's single most important product in the early 1990s, was considered pivotal to an increase in the company's overseas sales.

From the end of the Gulf War until late in 1994, Raytheon received nearly $2.5 billion in orders for the missiles from overseas customers. The corporation's environmental and energy service was consolidated to form Raytheon Engineers & Constructors International Inc. (RECI), one of the world's largest engineering and construction groups, in 1993. The acquisitions of Harbert Corp., Gibbs & Hill, and key segments of EBASCO Services, Inc., that year were intended to help boost RECI's annual sales. The corporate jet unit of British Aerospace plc also was purchased that year for $387.5 million. The acquisition helped expand Beech's penetration of the business aircraft market. An extensive overhaul of the appliance segment, including downsizing, consolidation, and the 1994 acquisition of UniMac Companies, helped increase that division's sales and profits. Raytheon, meantime, exited from the publishing field with the 1995 sale of D.C. Heath to Houghton Mifflin Co. for $455 million.

EXPANDING THE DEFENSE BUSINESS

The end of the Cold War and the resulting defense budget cuts ushered in a wave of mergers and consolidations in the defense industry by the mid-1990s. Raytheon was a key participant in this trend and also worked to rationalize its defense businesses. In early 1995 the company created Raytheon Electronic Systems from the merger of its Missile Systems Division and Equipment Division. Later that year Raytheon acquired Dallas-based E-Systems Inc. for more than $2.3 billion, gaining a leading developer of military intelligence communications systems. In 1996 Raytheon added two of Chrysler Corporation's defense businesses in a deal valued at about $475 million. The Chrysler units acquired were its electrospace systems operation, which was involved in satellite communications, secure communications, and electronic warfare systems; and its airborne-technologies operation, which modified commercial aircraft for use by the armed forces and by heads of state, often equipping the planes with high-tech signal-jamming and encoding equipment. Both of these units complemented the activities of E-Systems and, therefore, were consolidated into the newly named Raytheon E-Systems.

Raytheon's appetite was not yet sated, and in fact grew in 1997, when the company acquired the defense business of Texas Instruments Inc. for $2.9 billion in July and the defense business of Hughes Electronics Corporation, a subsidiary of General Motors Corporation, for $9.5 billion in December. The Texas Instruments deal brought to Raytheon a number of complementary operations, including laser-guided weapons systems, missiles, airborne radar, night vision systems, and electronic warfare systems. The Hughes defense unit was a leading supplier of advanced defense electronics systems and services. These latest acquisitions propelled Raytheon into the top three among defense contractors and into the top position in defense electronics. They also led to a marked increase in revenues, from $12.33 billion in 1996 to $19.53 billion in 1998. Following the completion of the Hughes transaction, Raytheon consolidated its defense businesses (Raytheon Electronic Systems, Raytheon E-Systems, and the Texas Instruments and Hughes units) into a new operation called Raytheon Systems Company. In connection with this restructuring and a smaller restructuring of Raytheon Engineers & Constructors, Raytheon took a $495 million restructuring charge in 1997 for a plan that by 1999 eliminated more than 14,000 jobs from the workforce and closed about 28 facilities in the United States. In December 1997, the company also created a new subsidiary called Raytheon Systems Limited, which was based in the United Kingdom and was formed to develop products for export from that country.

DIVESTING NON-DEFENSE ASSETS

By this time it was clearly evident that Raytheon had made a marked shift in strategy, placing a greater emphasis on its defense businesses, alongside the commercial electronics applications that developed out of the defense operations. The divestment of additional noncore operations was further evidence of this trend, with the divestments also helping to hold down the company's mounting debt load, which exceeded $10 billion by the end of 1997 thanks to the defense acquisitions. In 1997 Raytheon sold its home appliance, heating, air conditioning, and commercial cooking operations to Goodman Holding Co. for $522 million. That same year, the company sold its Switchcraft and Semiconductor divisions in separate transactions totaling $183 million. Divestments continued in 1998, including the sale of the firm's commercial laundry business for $334 million. Operations consisted of the defense units, Raytheon Commercial Electronics, Raytheon Aircraft Company, and Raytheon Engineers & Constructors. In December 1998 Daniel P. Burnham, a vice-chairman of AlliedSignal, Inc., took the helm at Raytheon as president and CEO. Picard remained chairman until August 1999, when Burnham took on that title as well.

Late in 1999 Raytheon revealed that it had uncovered pervasive management and financial problems in its defense electronics operations that forced it to cut its earnings projections for the fourth quarter and all of 2000. The company was over budget or behind schedule on more than a dozen Pentagon contracts, and other projects, both in the United States and overseas, were being delayed at the contract stage itself, including several billion-dollar deals involving Patriot missiles. With earnings down, Raytheon would be unable to reduce its $9.5 billion debt as quickly as it hoped. For the year, net income stood at $404 million, less than half the $844 million figure of the previous year. Meantime, late in 1999 the company launched a further restructuring, with additional job cuts, the closure or amalgamation of ten plants, and a charge of $668 million. To flatten the organizational structure, Raytheon Systems Company was reorganized into several smaller units: Electronic Systems; Command, Control, Communication and Information Systems; Raytheon Technical Services Company; and Aircraft Integration Systems. On the positive side for 1999, Raytheon contracted with the United Kingdom to develop a $1.3 billion high-tech radar surveillance system called Airborne Stand-Off Radar. That year also saw the sale of the Cedarapids subsidiary for $170 million.

As it worked to fix the problems in its defense operations, Raytheon was awarded a few more large contracts in August 2000. The U.S. Army awarded a joint venture partnership of Raytheon and Lockheed Martin a $1.24 billion production contract on the Javelin Antitank Weapon System, which the partners first began producing in 1997. In addition, Lockheed Martin selected Raytheon for the design, development, and manufacture of three radar systems for the Theater High Altitude Area Defense System, a $4 billion missile defense system contracted for by the U.S. Army. Raytheon's portion of the project amounted to $1.3 billion. Meantime, Raytheon's ongoing series of divestitures were nearing their conclusion. In July 2000 Raytheon Engineers & Constructors was sold to Morrison Knudsen Corporation for more than $800 million. Later in the year it was reported that Raytheon Aircraft Company was being shopped around. The sale of the aircraft unit essentially would focus Raytheon exclusively on defense and commercial electronics. Once again, these further divestments were in part aimed at slashing the burdensome debt load, which had crept back up over the $10 billion mark by late 2000. Raytheon would need to rein in this debt load and clear up its other financial problems if it wished to return to or surpass the steadily, if unspectacularly, profitable years that preceded the major 1997 acquisitions.

FINANCIAL WOES

Hopes for a brighter financial future were pinned on Burnham's ability to replicate the success he produced at Allied Signal, but he failed to meet expectations. Raytheon posted a meager $138 million profit in 2000 and then slipped into the red, recording a $755 million loss in 2001 and a $640 million loss in 2002. Investors' anxiety increased at the end of 2002, when the anticipated invasion of Iraq by U.S. forces piqued expectations for a rousing display by defense contractors. Raytheon, the fourth largest defense contractor in the United States, was not among the companies benefiting from the expected increase in defense spending. Raytheon's cash flow from operations in 2002 was $424 million, a figure dwarfed by the $2.29 billion recorded by Lockheed Martin. Raytheon's shares decreased in value by 3.6 percent in 2002, while Lockheed Martin's shares increased in value from 25 percent. "I just want this company to be managed better," an analyst said in the January 29, 2003 release of the *America's Intelligence Wire,* referring to Raytheon. "I want this great defense business to shine through."

SWANSON TAKES THE HELM IN 2003

In April 2003, Burnham resigned, ending his troubled, five-year stay at the company. "He was brought in to turn the company around and it hasn't turned around," an analyst commented in the April 23, 2003 release of the *America's Intelligence Wire.* William H. Swanson, who had been promoted to the post of president in July 2002, replaced Burnham as chief executive officer. Swanson, who joined Raytheon in 1972, took charge of the company shortly before it moved its headquarters from Lexington back to Waltham.

With military campaigns underway in Afghanistan and Iraq, Raytheon enjoyed a surge in business. In December 2003, the company was awarded a $1.04 billion contract to upgrade the U.S. Navy's Cobra Judy radar system, the same month its aircraft unit secured a $360 million order for 58 business jets from NetJets Inc. Raytheon began building Tomahawk Block IV missiles in 2004, producing a weapon featuring a two-way satellite data link that enabled controllers to change targets mid-flight. By 2007, Raytheon delivered its 1,000th Tomahawk Block IV to the U.S. Navy. In 2005, the company won a $1 billion contract from the U.S. Army to develop and to demonstrate the Joint Land Attack Cruise Missile Defense Elevated Netted Sensor System (JLENS), a system that provided over-the-horizon detection and tracking of incoming cruise missiles.

SALE OF RAYTHEON AIRCRAFT: 2006

Swanson's tenure witnessed the arrival of massive defense contracts and it also saw the departure of a major business segment. In 2006, the company sold Raytheon Aircraft Co. to Hawker Beechcraft Corp., a company formed by GS Capital Partners and Onex Partners. The Wichita, Kansas-based subsidiary, which generated $2.9 billion in annual revenue by delivering 416 aircraft in 2005, was sold for $3.3 billion.

Financially, Swanson's first five years at the helm of Raytheon were far more successful than Burnham's five years in charge. From 2003 to 2008, the company's net income increased from $365 million to $1.67 billion, peaking at $2.57 billion in 2007. The company's revenue performance exhibited less vitality than its profit performance, as its annual volume rose and sank erratically, but the five-year period did see an overall increase from $18.1 billion to $23.1 billion. At the end of the decade, Raytheon continued to win large contracts for its expertise in missile production—in 2009, the United Arab Emirates awarded the company a $3 billion contract for its Patriot missile system—but it also was beginning to explore business opportunities outside the defense sector. The company was attempting to use its weapon and defense technology to create innovative products and systems for civilian use, devoting its resources to projects that used radiation to aid in toll collection efforts, radio technology to facilitate oil extraction, and software to enable companies to determine which web sites their employees visited. The years ahead would determine if Raytheon could develop a sizable non-military stream of revenue and achieve the more balanced business stance enjoyed by its larger rivals.

April Dougal Gasbarre
Updated, David E. Salamie; Jeffrey L. Covell

PRINCIPAL SUBSIDIARIES

Raytheon Technical Services Company LLC; Raytheon Systems Limited (UK); Raytheon Canada Limited; Raytheon Australia Pty. Ltd.

PRINCIPAL OPERATING UNITS

Integrated Defense Systems; Intelligence and Information Systems; Missile Systems; Network Centric Systems; Space and Airborne Systems; Technical Services.

PRINCIPAL COMPETITORS

The Boeing Company; Lockheed Martin Corporation; Northrop Grumman Corporation; General Dynamics Corporation.

FURTHER READING

Alster, Norm, "Raytheon Co.," *Investor's Business Daily*, January 23, 2009, p. A5.

Banks, Howard, "Rocket Science Isn't Easy: Among Big Defense Contractors, Raytheon Is the Best of the Breed; That Ain't Saying Much," *Forbes*, November 1, 1999, pp. 79–80.

"Billion-Dollar Contract to Be Awarded for Cruise Missile Defense," *RF Design*, January 10, 2007.

Gary, Bob, Jr., "Raytheon Flies Past U.S. Defence Bonanza," *America's Intelligence Wire*, January 29, 2003.

Gillum, Jack, "Raytheon Marks 1,000th Tomahawk Delivery: Latest Tomahawk Generation Big in Navy's Arsenal," *Arizona Daily Star*, June 14, 2008.

Hawkins, Asher, "Civilian Targets," *Forbes*, October 27, 2008, p. 101.

Hughes, David, "Raytheon Targets Growth Within Four Core Groups," *Aviation Week & Space Technology*, March 1, 1993, pp. 52–53.

Jones, Steven D., and Anne Marie Squeo, "Raytheon Expects to Post Charge for Sale of Unit for $800 Million," *Wall Street Journal*, April 17, 2000, p. B4.

Kerber, Ross, "Navy Awards Raytheon $1 Billion Contract to Upgrade Radar System," *Boston Globe*, December 19, 2003.

Lipin, Steven, and Gabriella Stern, "GM Unveils Sale of Hughes Defense Arm to Raytheon Co. in $9.5 Billion Accord," *Wall Street Journal*, January 17, 1997, p. A3.

Lipin, Steven, and Jeff Cole, "Raytheon to Acquire E-Systems for $64 a Share, or $2.3 Billion," *Wall Street Journal*, April 3, 1995, p. A3.

Michaels, Daniel, "European Missile Firm Targets Raytheon," *Wall Street Journal*, August 1, 2000, p. A18.

———, "Raytheon Searches for a Buyer for Aircraft Unit," *Wall Street Journal*, October 18, 2000, p. A4.

Patron, Edward B., "Righting Raytheon," *Financial World*, March 25, 1996, pp. 34–36.

Robinson, Edward, "Raytheon Gets Streamlined," *Fortune*, June 7, 1999, pp. 32, 36.

Schriener, Judy, "Blasting Off for Peacetime Targets," *ENR*, April 18, 1994, pp. 24–28.

Scott, Otto J., *The Creative Ordeal: The Story of Raytheon*, New York: Atheneum, 1974.

Smith, Geoffrey, "Raytheon's Strategy: Guns and Lots More Butter," *Business Week*, November 6, 1992, p. 96.

Smith, Geoffrey, and Victoria Murphy, "Reality Bites at Raytheon," *Business Week*, November 15, 1999, pp. 78, 80, 82.

Squeo, Anne Marie, "Raytheon Hits Snags on Pentagon Work," *Wall Street Journal*, October 12, 1999, p. A3.

———, "Raytheon to Take $668 Million in Charges: Firm Cites Financial Snags in Defense Electronics," *Wall Street Journal*, October 13, 1999, p. A3.

Suhrbier, Robin, "Raytheon Pushes Single Brand," *Business Marketing*, January 1994, pp. 4, 40.

Therrien, Lois, "Raytheon May Find Itself on the Defensive," *Business Week*, May 26, 1986, pp. 72+.

Turner, Lance, "Raytheon to Sell Aircraft Division for $3.3 Billion," *Arkansas Business*, December 25, 2006, p. 10.

Wilke, John R., and Jon G. Auerbach, "U.S. Puts Strings on Raytheon Purchase," *Wall Street Journal*, October 1, 1997, p. A3.

Williams, Van, "Raytheon Chief Ends Stormy Tenure," *America's Intelligence Wire*, April 23, 2003.

Recordati Industria Chimica e Farmaceutica S.p.A.

Via M Civitali 1
Milan, I-20148
Italy
Telephone: (+39 02) 487871
Fax: (+39 02) 40073747
Web site: http://www.recordati.it

Public Company
Incorporated: 1926 as Laboratorio Farmacologico Reggiano
Employees: 2,159
Sales: EUR 689.63 million ($808.4 million) (2008)
Stock Exchanges: Borsa Italiana
Ticker Symbol: REC
NAICS: 325412 Pharmaceutical Preparation Manufacturing; 325131 Inorganic Dye and Pigment Manufacturing

∎ ∎ ∎

Recordati Industria Chimica e Farmaceutica S.p.A. is a midsized, family-controlled pharmaceuticals company. Based in Milan, Italy, Recordati is involved in drug discovery, research and development, and marketing, both on a stand-alone basis as well as in partnership with other pharmaceuticals companies throughout the world. Recordati's research and development efforts focus particularly on the cardiovascular and urogenital fields. Major molecules developed by the company include lercanidipine, a calcium channel blocker marketed under the Zanidip name for use as a treatment for hypertension. The company has extended that product with the 2007 launch of Zanipress, combining lercanidipine with the ACE inhibitor enalapril. In addition to its own drug development program, Recordati holds a number of marketing partnerships, including for rupatadine, an antihistamine developed by Uriach, which received European approval in 2008.

In addition to its core therapeutic areas, Recordati develops drugs for orphan diseases, through its France-based subsidiary Orphan. Pharmaceuticals represent 95 percent of the company's revenues, which neared EUR 690 million ($808 million) in 2008. The company also produces fine chemicals. Recordati has long been present on the international market, with sales throughout Western Europe and the Americas. International sales represent more than 70 percent of the group's total revenues. France is the company's second largest market outside of Italy; Recordati has also begun a drive to expand its operations into the Eastern European markets, including Russia, the Czech Republic, and Turkey. Recordati is listed on the Borsa Italiana and is led by Chairman and CEO Giovanni Recordati. The Recordati family controls 54 percent of the company's shares.

ITALIAN DRUG COMPANY BETWEEN THE WORLD WARS

The Recordati family had long served the community of Correggio Emilia as apothecaries before developing into a producer of modern medicines. The family business dated from the early 1800s, when the family operated a small shop trading in herbal medicines and other remedies.

COMPANY PERSPECTIVES

Recordati is a European specialty pharmaceutical group dedicated to partnering, discovering and developing innovative, value-added products that improve the quality of life and help people to enjoy longer, healthier and more productive lives.

Our success as a healthcare enterprise will benefit not only the patients whose needs we meet but all our stakeholders whom we serve—our customers, our shareholders, our employees and their families.

The family's transition into a modern pharmaceuticals company began in the years following World War I, as the country's pharmaceuticals industry, devastated by the war, began its reconstruction. At the same time, the war years had witnessed the emergence of the modern pharmaceuticals industry. The discovery and isolation of the first true active molecules, such as penicillin and others, was coupled with the development of new tools, equipment, and technologies. New synthesis and mass production techniques also played a significant role in making new drugs available in larger quantities and with higher purity levels. At the same time, research and development technologies were allowing scientists to discover an ever increasing range of active components. These led to highly targeted treatments for a variety of health and medical conditions.

These factors combined to provide important opportunities for a number of new players to enter the pharmaceuticals industry. Giovanni Recordati led the family's own transformation from apothecary into modern drug producer, taking over the family business in the 1920s. In 1926, Recordati incorporated the company as Laboratorio Farmacologico Reggiano. The following year, the company released one of its most successful products, Antispasmina Colica, an anticonvulsive medicine.

The company scored two more notable successes through the 1930s. In 1930, the company began marketing a laxative, Solvobil, which remained a popular treatment into the next century. The company's interest in the cardiovascular field also stemmed from this period, with the introduction of Tefamin, in 1935. This product was marketed as a heart tonic, acting as a diuretic to help reduce blood pressure. Like Solvobil, Tefamin, as well as Antispasmina Colica, remained fixtures in the group's medicine portfolio into the 21st century.

EXPANDING IN THE FIFTIES

Recordati drug development efforts remained strong through the 1930s and the years of World War II. The company's range of products were to include such strong-selling brands as Sindrenina, Insulina Recordati, Simpamina, and Dintoina. Supporting the company's growth was its decision to begin manufacturing its own active ingredients. The Recordati family rose in prominence among Italy's pharmaceuticals community, especially as the company launched publication of its own pharmacological journal, *Issues in Pharmacotherapy,* first published in 1933. Toward the end of the decade, the company also began editing the prestigious *Folia Cardiologica,* which became the journal for the Italian Society of Cardiology.

Recordati's son Arrigo joined the company in 1951 after completing his studies. Just one year later, after his father's death from a long illness, Arrigo Recordati, then just 25 years old, took over as head of the company. Recordati became determined to expand the family company. One of his first moves was to transfer the company's operations to Milan, the Italian financial capital, opening a new headquarters, as well as research and development and manufacturing facilities there in 1953.

Until then, Recordati's pharmaceutical operations had been based on active ingredients developed by others. The new facility allowed the company to strengthen its research and development operations as well. Into the middle of the decade, the company established a dedicated biopharmaceutical research laboratory. The expansion of its research and development capacity soon brought results. In 1959, the company launched the first drug based on its own proprietary research, efloxate, a coronary vasodilator marketed as Recordil.

The new research facility also helped Recordati attract its first partnership with another drug company. In 1961, the company teamed with France's Syntex, later absorbed by Roche, to conduct research and development activities in the growing field of steroidal hormones. The partnership proved a long-lasting one, remaining in place until 2005.

GOING PUBLIC IN 1984

Recordati's own research and development activities achieved a new success soon after. In 1962, the company launched a new molecule, dimefline. This respiratory analeptic was marketed by the company under the brand name Remeflin. Also during the 1960s, the company launched production of fine chemicals used as components in the production of pharmaceuti-

KEY DATES

1926: Giovanni Recordati founds a pharmaceuticals company based on his family's apothecary and pharmacy business in Correggio Emilia, Italy; company releases its first successful product, Antispasmina Colica, the following year.

1953: Arrigo Recordati becomes head of the company, which moves to Milan and launches its own biopharmaceutical research laboratory.

1959: Company launches its first in-house developed drug, efloxate, a coronary vasodilator marketed as Recordil.

1961: Company forms a partnership with Syntex (later Roche) of France, then changes its name to Recordati.

1973: Recordati's Genurin becomes first drug developed in Italy to receive U.S. Food and Drug Administration approval.

1984: Recordati goes public on the Borsa Italiana.

1987: Recordati establishes a U.S. fine chemicals distribution subsidiary.

1995: Recordati begins European expansion with subsidiary in Spain.

1997: Recordati launches Zanidip, a successful hypertension treatment.

2000: Recordati acquires Doms Adrian and Bouchara in France, creating Bouchara Recordati.

2005: Recordati acquires proprietary pharmaceuticals operations of Merckle in Germany.

2006: Recordati enters Portugal with purchase of Grupo Jaba.

2007: Recordati buys Orphan Europe, based in France.

2008: Company establishes a presence in Russia and the Commonwealth of Independent States (CIS) with purchase of FIC of France; company acquires Turkey's Yeni Ilac.

2009: Recordati enters Czech Republic with purchase of Herbacos-Bofarma.

cal preparations. This led the company to open a new manufacturing plant in Campoverde di Aprilia. The company then changed its name, becoming Recordati Industria Chimica e Farmaceutica.

The 1970s provided new successes for Recordati. The company reached a major milestone in 1973, with the introduction of a new company-developed molecule, flavoxate, a urinary anti-spasmodic treatment. The company began marketing the new drug in Europe as Genurin. Soon after, Recordati received approval from the Food and Drug Administration (FDA) to market flavoxate in the United States, becoming the first Italian company to receive FDA authorization for an in-house developed drug. The new drug was marketed as Urispas in the United States, and soon became a global bestseller for the company. Into the 2000s, the group's flavoxate products continued to be sold in more than 60 countries.

Recordati found more success at the end of the decade, with the introduction of Antoral, an oral antiseptic based on tibezonium iodide. Developed by Recordati, the new product was launched in 1977. On the corporate side, Recordati had also begun preparations for its future public offering. In 1981, for example, the company became one of the first midsized, privately held Italian pharmaceutical companies to publish an independently audited annual report.

This move proved to be a step toward the stock exchange. In 1984, Recordati went public, listing its shares on the Borsa Italiana. The Recordati family retained its majority control of the company; into the next century, the family continued to control more than 56 percent of the company's stock.

INTERNATIONAL EXPANSION IN THE NINETIES

The company's growth continued strongly through the 1980s. The group's fine chemicals division, which initially supplied Recordati's own production needs, grew to become a major supplier to third party companies. Fine chemicals also provided the company with a foothold in the U.S. market. In 1987, the company formed a new fine chemicals marketing subsidiary, Recordati Corporation, based in Cranford, New Jersey.

Recordati's drug development program added new successes through the 1990s. These included fenticonazole, a dermatological anti-mycotic introduced as Lomexin in 1986. One of the group's most important successes came a decade later, when the company received authorization to market lercanidipine-based Zanidip in the United Kingdom. Lercanidipine, a calcium-channel blocker, had been entirely developed by Recordati and became a highly effective treatment for hypertension. Following its approval in the United Kingdom in 1996, the new drug received authorization to be marketed throughout the European Union.

The company then initiated the registration process needed to bring lercanidipine to the United States, Canada, and Japan. By 2004, the drug had received approval in nearly 70 countries. At the end of the decade, more than 90 countries had granted authorization for the drug.

Recordati had also begun to expand its international operations. In 1995, the company set up a new subsidiary in Madrid, Spain. This subsidiary quickly obtained the license to market both Recordati's proprietary products, as well as third-party pharmaceutical products in Spain. In 1999, the group boosted its Spanish operations with the purchase of a factory producing active ingredients and other pharmaceutical components.

The company also targeted an entry into France, which remained the world's fourth largest pharmaceuticals market. The group took a first step into France in 1999, when it bought Doms Adrian that year. The following year, the company took over a second French pharmaceuticals manufacturer, Bouchara. The group then merged its French operations into a single business, Bouchara Recordati. By then, Arrigo Recordati had passed away; his place at the head of the company was taken up by son Giovanni Recordati.

FOCUSING ON PHARMACEUTICALS

Recordati continued to build up its European presence into the new decade. The company added operations in Germany in 2005, buying the branded pharmaceuticals operations of Merckle GmbH. That operation was subsequently renamed Merckle Recordati. Also that year, the company established new marketing subsidiaries in the United Kingdom and Greece, as well as a manufacturing plant in Ireland. The company then entered Portugal, acquiring that country's Grupo Jaba in 2006.

These moves came as part of a reorientation of the group's activities. A shift had taken place in the active ingredients and pharmaceuticals intermediates markets, as both China and India emerged as leading suppliers. The lower-wage and lower-cost structures of these countries made it impossible for Western manufacturers to compete on pricing. As a result, Recordati decided to shut down its own intermediates production operations in 2004. The company retained only its small fine chemicals division, which accounted for just 5 percent of the group's total sales.

Instead, Recordati pinned its expansion on its strong product pipeline. The company developed a new hypertensive treatment, Zanipress (also marketed as Zanextra), a combination of lercanidipine and enalapril, an ACE inhibitor, which received European Union approval and was launched in 2007. The company held a number of other promising molecules, such as silodosin, for the treatment of benign prostate hyperplasia, and the allergy treatment rupatadine.

Also in 2007, the company added a new market area with the acquisition of France's Orphan Europe Holding, a company active in a number of European markets and focused on developing and marketing treatment for so-called orphan diseases, highly rare and often genetic disorders.

TARGETING EASTERN EUROPE FROM 2008

Recordati also made a drive to expand its operations into the Eastern European markets. This led the company to complete several acquisitions in 2008, including FIC and FIC Médical, two French companies specialized in the registration and promotion of branded pharmaceuticals in Russia and other markets in the Commonwealth of Independent States (CIS).

The company next added Turkey to its list of markets, buying that country's Yeni Ilac for EUR 48 million. This company, based in Istanbul, added both its own proprietary drug development programs, as well as a strong pharmaceutical marketing operation. By then, Recordati had also put into place a new marketing agreement with Japan's Kowa Pharmaceutical, naming Recordati as the marketer and distributor of that company's pitavastatin anti-cholesterol treatment for France, Ireland, Spain, Portugal, Greece, as well as Russia, the CIS, and Turkey.

On the flip side, the group signed a marketing agreement with Almirall, granting that Spanish company the marketing license for silodosin in Spain in April 2009. By then, Recordati had bought majority control of Herbacos-Bofarma, based in Pardubice, in the Czech Republic. With a history of more than 80 years, Recordati had grown into one of Italy's high-profile midsized and family-controlled pharmaceutical companies.

M. L. Cohen

PRINCIPAL SUBSIDIARIES

Bouchara Recordati S.A.S. (France); FIC S.A.S./FIC Medical S.A.R.L. (France); Herbacos-Bofarma (Czech Republic); Innova Pharma S.p.A.; Jaba Recordati, Bonafarma, Jabafarma (Portugal); Laboratoires Bouchara Recordati S.A.S. (France); Merckle Recordati GmbH

(Germany); Orphan Europe Holding S.A. (France); Recordati Corporation (USA); Recordati Espana S.L. (Spain); Recordati Hellas Pharmaceuticals S.A. (Greece); Recordati Ireland Ltd.; Recordati Pharmaceuticals Ltd. (UK).; Recordati S.A. (Luxembourg); Recordati S.A. (Switzerland); Yeni Ilac (Turkey).

PRINCIPAL DIVISIONS

Pharmaceuticals; Pharmaceutical Chemicals.

PRINCIPAL OPERATING UNITS

Italy; France; Germany; Orphan; Others; Spain; United Kingdom.

PRINCIPAL COMPETITORS

Edison S.p.A.; A Menarini Industrie Farmaceutiche Riunite S.R.L.; Pfizer Italia S.R.L.; Sanofi-Aventis S.p.A.; Novartis Italia Group; P and R Holding S.p.A.; Abbott S.R.L.; GlaxoSmithKline S.p.A.; Fater S.p.A.; Roche S.p.A.

FURTHER READING

Davis, Andrew, "Recordati Buying French Drug Maker," *International Herald Tribune,* October 1, 2007, p. 19.

"Herbacos-Bofarma Has a New Owner," *Chemical Business Newsbase,* April 9, 2009.

"Recordati—A Health Care Group," *Chemical Specialties,* May 2001, p. 26.

"Recordati Acquires Herbacos-Bofarma in the Czech Republic," *Chemical Business Newsbase,* January 19, 2009.

"Recordati Buys Unit of Germany's Merckle," *Pharma Marketletter,* February 7, 2005.

"Recordati Restructures Fine Chemicals Division," *Chemical Business Newsbase,* January 23, 2006.

"Recordati Signs Co-Marketing Agreement with Almirall in Spain for Silodosin," *Chemical Business Newsbase,* April 3, 2009.

"Recordati SpA Finalizes Its Acquisition of Yeni Ilac in Turkey," *Chemical Business Newsbase,* December 23, 2008.

"Recordati SpA Launches Zanextra in France," *Chemical Business Newsbase,* April 15, 2009.

"Recordati SpA Obtains European License for Pitavastatin," *Chemical Business Newsbase,* October 24, 2008.

Scott, Alex, "Recordati Purchases API Unit in Ireland," *Chemical Week,* February 19, 2003, p. 51.

———, "Recordati to Sell Its Intermediate Business," *Chemical Week,* April 21, 2004, p. 29.

The Republic of Tea, Inc.

———■———

8 Digital Drive, Suite 100
Novato, California 94949
U.S.A.
Telephone: (415) 382-3400
Toll Free: (800) 298-4832
Fax: (415) 382-3401
Web site: http://www.republicoftea.com

Private Company
Incorporated: 1992
Employees: 95
Sales: $12.0 million (2008 est.)
NAICS: 424490 Other Grocery and Related Products
    Merchant Wholesalers

■ ■ ■

The Republic of Tea, Inc., is a wholesaler and marketer of premiums teas and tea-related products, distributing its products to more than 20,000 restaurants, cafés, and retail stores in the United States. The company also publishes a catalog for mail-order purchases and it sells its product online through its web site. The Republic of Tea purchases its teas from estate gardens in India and China, favoring full-leaf teas rather than cut leaves or tea "dust." The company sells a full range of black, green, oolong, white, red, and herbal teas, as well as herbal teas, chai teas, and decaffeinated teas, marketing more than 200 varieties. The products are sold in bulk, in bags, and in bottles. The Republic of Tea also sells teapots, teacups, and other brewing and serving accessories.

CLOTHING BEFORE TEA

The Republic of Tea owed its existence to "The Minister of Progress," "The Minister of Leaves," and "The Minister of Enchantment," the corporate titles used by the company's founders, Bill Rosenzweig, Mel Ziegler, and Patricia Ziegler. Idiosyncrasies abounded throughout the company's corporate culture. Stores were referred to as "embassies," customers were referred to as "citizens," the company's receptionist was known as "The Minister of First Impressions." But along with the peculiarities came an adherence to the conventions of sound management. Beneath the eccentricities was a well-developed and well-executed business plan, an example of entrepreneurial shrewdness that marked the Zieglers' second success with a start-up venture.

Mel Ziegler was working as a writer and reporter before he entered the entrepreneurial fray. Stints as a contributing writer for several magazines during the 1970s proved to be a frustrating experience, as were his days working for the *Miami Herald* and the *San Francisco Chronicle*. The path to a more rewarding career began not long after he met his wife while making copies at the *Chronicle,* where she worked as an illustrator. Patricia Ziegler looked at the world from a visual perspective, while Mel Ziegler looked at the world from a verbal perspective, giving their partnership a complementary strength first displayed when the married couple thought of launching a Safari clothing line: the bush jackets and khakis Mel Ziegler often wore. "I would not think of starting a business unless I was its first customer," he wrote, as quoted in the October 23, 1992 edition of *Globe & Mail.* "And no matter what's been said or written to the contrary, all it takes to

COMPANY PERSPECTIVES

When we set out to form our small Republic, our not so covert mission was to create a Tea Revolution. Our purpose is to enrich people's lives through the experience of fine tea and the Sip by Sip life—a life of health, balance and well-being. From the beginning, tea has been a drink that is shared with others. Around the world, at high tea in Devonshire and age-old ceremonies in Japan, tea is brewed and taken together with friends and family in rituals of hospitality and nourishment for both body and soul. Here at our e-Embassy, you'll find many ways to get to know tea anew, through a selection that will educate, inspire and communicate the quality, benefits, values and lifestyle that is The Republic of Tea.

launch a business in which you are the first customer is to find a second customer and sell him the product."

The Zieglers looked at the market for Safari clothing and saw a business opportunity, a chance to leave the *Chronicle* and put their complementary skills to use in the business world. The idea to start a clothing business, as it also would be to start a tea business, was prompted by the perception that the product in question was being inadequately addressed by the market. "The closest thing you could get to something authentic was in the surplus world, particularly British Army surplus in those days," Mel Ziegler said in the December 2000 issue of *Reveries*. "It was magnificent. We saw the surplus and were kind of excited by it. And it fulfilled this romantic fantasy of being a writer and an artist living in Africa. We just played with it." In 1978, the Zieglers opened a store in Mill Valley, California, and published a catalog, written by Mel Ziegler and illustrated by Patricia Ziegler, under the banner "Banana Republic Travel and Safari Clothing Co."

The Banana Republic retail and catalog business became an immediate success. After five years in operation, the business grew into a five-store chain generating $10 million in annual sales. A larger clothing chain, The Gap, took notice of the Zieglers' success and acquired Banana Republic in 1983. The Zieglers remained involved with the company after the sale (Mel Ziegler served as its president) until a dispute with Gap senior management led to their resignation in 1988. From there, the couple's attention turned to tea, particularly after Mel Ziegler spent a cross-country airplane trip talking to another passenger, The Republic of Tea's future

Minister of Progress, Bill Rosenzweig.

HATCHING PLANS

The relationship that evolved between the Zieglers and Bill Rosenzweig after the catalytic airplane conversation was chronicled in exceptional detail for all to see. For two years, the Zieglers and Rosenzweig shared ideas about starting a tea company, primarily communicating via fax, which provided the text for a book published in 1992 titled *The Republic of Tea*. In one of the communiqués, excerpted in the October 23, 1992 issue of the *Globe & Mail,* Ziegler wrote to Rosenzweig: "I am mad about tea. I can't think of a commodity more inappropriately marketed in the United States. I can't think of a product that is less appreciated for its awesome history, less heralded for its stunning effects, less savored for the haunting boundlessness of its many tastes. For reasons best left to others to explain, tea, the 'cup of humanity,' civilization's oldest beverage, an ancient friend to body and mind alike, gets less respect than sweetened, artificially flavored canned bubbles in the United States and most Western countries." There was no doubting Ziegler's passion for tea, a passion he intended to express with The Republic of Tea.

THE REPUBLIC IS ESTABLISHED

The discussions among the three founders covered every conceivable aspect of starting and operating a tea company. Topics ranged from the mundane to the philosophical, revealed in the 336 pages of "The Republic of Tea." The founders decided to make their enterprise a wholesale business, thereby avoiding the hazards of operating a retail chain, and they discussed extensive possibilities for extending the brand into numerous, tea-related product lines. The vulnerabilities of competitors, principally Lipton and Celestial Seasonings, were analyzed, and various forms of packaging were discussed. All was idle banter, however, until October 1991, when the Zieglers and Rosenzweig were able to secure the commitment of an investor. Bruce Katz, the founder of Rockport Shoes, invested roughly $300,000 in the concept, giving The Republic of Tea its seed money and making Katz the company's "Minister of Big Ideas." In May 1992, The Republic of Tea became a commercial enterprise, offering full-leaf teas and a 16-page catalog featuring iron, porcelain, and wooden teapots and pitchers, trays, tea biscuits, special sugar lumps, honey, and a host of other, tea-related merchandise.

NEW OWNERSHIP IN 1994

The founders spent two years planning their company's formation, and not much longer presiding over its

KEY DATES

1992: The Republic of Tea is formed.
1994: Ronald T. Rubin acquires the company from its founders.
1996: Annual sales reach $4 million.
1999: Annual sales approach $10 million.
2005: Company sells more than 150 tea and herbal products.
2009: Company's product line expands to more than 200 items.

development. Initially based in San Rafael, California, The Republic of Tea had relocated to Novato, California, by the time its path crossed with Ronald T. Rubin, an Illinois businessman who would embrace The Republic of Tea credo and steward the company during its first two decades of existence.

Rubin was born into the beverage business. His father, Hyman Rubin, founded the Central Wholesale Liquor Co., a distribution business based in Mount Vernon, Illinois. After studying wine and winemaking at the University of California at Davis, Rubin returned to Illinois to join the family business. On his first day at Central Wholesale, Rubin's father directed him to the back of the company's warehouse, to the "dead room," an area filled with liquor that no one would buy. Rubin's task was to sell the dead stock, a chore he accomplished in two weeks by convincing American Legion and Veterans of Foreign Wars halls to use the liquor as prizes for their bingo games. "I don't think most people realize—and why should they?—the demeaning crap you have to take when you want to join the family business," Rubin said in the May 6, 2001 edition of the *St. Louis Post-Dispatch.*

Despite his bleak description of becoming a second-generation liquor distributor, Rubin remained with Central Warehouse for two decades and eventually took command of the family business. He began to move away from distributing liquor at the end of the 1980s, forming New Age Beverages in 1990. The company became a master licensee of Clearly Canadian bottled water, selling more than three million cases of the product in ten states through a network of more than 100 distributors. While New Age Beverages was establishing itself, Rubin read "The Republic of Tea," which he found inspirational, prompting him to set up a meeting with the authors. Rubin initially wanted to secure a license to distribute The Republic of Tea's bottled tea, but soon the negotiations centered on a

much bigger deal. In 1994, Rubin purchased the 80 percent interest in the company owned by the Zieglers and Katz. The following year, he purchased the 20 percent owned by Rosenzweig, giving him full ownership of the company and the title "The Minister of Bottles."

THE RON RUBIN ERA BEGINS

Rubin sold his wine and liquor business in 1994 and sold his Clearly Canadian operations the following year, enabling him to focus all his energies on The Republic of Tea. Under his control, The Republic of Tea matured and expanded, becoming a recognizable force in the alternative beverages segment. When he bought the company, it was generating an estimated $2 million in annual sales, a figure that would increase as Rubin used his expertise in distribution to bring the brand to a bigger audience. One of the first moves he made was to give the company a more logical distribution hub. During its first two years of operation, the company shipped its products by United Parcel Service from northern California, a less than ideal arrangement that took as long as two weeks for shipments to reach the East Coast. Rubin, aiming for nationwide distribution, opened a new distribution and catalog fulfillment center, establishing the facility in Nashville, Illinois, 50 miles southeast of St. Louis, Missouri, and 30 miles west of his hometown of Mount Vernon.

Rubin expanded the company's distribution at a rapid pace, but he embraced The Republic of Tea's motto of living life "sip by sip, rather than gulp by gulp." He described himself as a "zentrepreneur," one who combines capitalism with the contemplative meditations of Zen. "An entrepreneur has a business," Rubin explained in the October 2, 2001 edition of the *Belleville News-Democrat,* "and a zentrepreneur has a business and a life: taking care of yourself, exercising, giving back to society, taking care of your family." The corporate culture established by the Zieglers and Rosenzweig found an enthusiastic supporter in Rubin, ensuring that the practice of conferring quirky corporate titles to The Republic of Tea's employees continued. With the "Ministries of Smooth Operations, Goodwill, and Education" aiding The Minister of Bottles, The Republic of Tea recorded solid growth. By 1996, two years after Rubin had gained control over the company, annual sales had doubled, reaching $4 million.

DISTRIBUTION SPREADS ACROSS THE NATION

The premium teas sold by The Republic of Tea found a receptive audience in store shelves across the country.

The loose, full-leaf teas, appearing in colorful tins for $8 apiece, were sold under names such as "Tea of Conviviality," and "Romancer Enhancer." The brand was available in gourmet food stores and coffee houses, but it enjoyed its greatest exposure after Barnes & Noble agreed to stock the teas. As the massive bookstore chain expanded across the country, The Republic of Tea rode its coattails, penetrating market after market. By the end of the 1990s, annual sales hovered around $10 million, as Rubin consistently extended the company's product line and its geographic reach.

The Republic of Tea sold roughly 40 varieties of teas in the mid-1990s. A decade later, the company was selling more than 150 tea and herbal products, distributing black teas, green teas, white teas, caffeine-free herbal teas, and specialty teas. Products were marketed toward children, they were bottled and sold in bulk, and they were sold in the company's signature canisters. Distribution of teas and products had expanded, adding another major bookstore chain, Borders Books, and myriad cafés, restaurants, and stores, making the Republic of Tea brand available in more than 20,000 locations throughout the United States.

As The Republic of Tea neared its 20th anniversary, the "Ambassadors of the Republic," the company's salespeople, were enjoying the entrenched position their brand had established during the previous years. Thanks to the vision of the founders and the achievements in distribution, marketing, and product-line extension spearheaded by Rubin, The Republic of Tea was a recognized and admired brand, a distinct name that had carved a lasting place in the highly competitive beverage industry. Looking ahead, there was every expectation that the achievements of the past had set The Republic of Tea on a promising path toward the future.

Jeffrey L. Covell

PRINCIPAL COMPETITORS

Celestial Seasonings, Inc.; The Stash Tea Company; Unilever PLC.

FURTHER READING

"Be Present, not Tense," *Reveries,* December 2000.

Desloge, Rick, "Rubin Brews Bottled Tea, but Risks Landing in Jam," *St. Louis Business Journal,* August 12, 1996, p. 1A.

Gallagher, Jim, "Zentrepreneur's Business Among the Cornstalks and Cattle of Little Nashville, Ill.," *St. Louis Post-Dispatch,* May 6, 2001, p. E1.

Penson, Peta, "Success Can Be Written in the (Tea) Leaves," *Business Journal,* November 21, 1994, p. 21.

Tang, Alisa, "Owner of California-Based Tea Firm to Be Keynote Speaker at Lecture Series," *Belleville News-Democrat,* October 2, 2001.

Theodore, Sarah, "The Republic of Tea," *Beverage Industry,* March 2001, p. 38.

Todd, Heather, "A Revolution Is Brewing," *Beverage World,* August 15, 2005, p. 14.

Wente, Margaret, "Zen and the Art of Making Money," *Globe & Mail,* March 6, 1993, p. C16.

Ziegler, Mel, "Tea for Who?" *Globe & Mail,* October 23, 1992, p. 106.

Sage Products Inc.

———— ■ ————

3909 Three Oaks Road
Cary, Illinois 60013-1804
U.S.A.
Telephone: (815) 455-4700
Toll Free: (800) 323-2220
Fax: (815) 455-5599
Web site: http://www.sageproducts.com

Private Company
Founded: 1971
Employees: 595
Sales: $165 million (2009 est.)
NAICS: 339113 Surgical Appliance and Supplies
Manufacturing

■ ■ ■

Sage Products Inc. has evolved from a medical supply
company to a leader in the development of healthcare
products designed for the comfort and protection of
patients in all stages of illness. What sets Sage Products
apart from its competitors is how founders Vincent W.
Foglia and Paul F. Hills view their commitment to not
only the patients and medical facilities they serve, but
their employees as well. Repeatedly recognized as one of
the nation's best places to work by both the Great Place
to Work Institute and the National Association for Business Resources, Sage Products continues to be an innovator in the healthcare manufacturing industry.

DEVELOPING A NICHE IN THE SEVENTIES

Although the 1970s were a turbulent decade in the
United States and the world, Foglia and Hills believed it
was an optimal time to establish a new company in the
Midwest. Believing their concept would indeed mirror
its name as a "sage" business endeavor, Foglia and Hills
hoped to serve the growing needs of hospitals by providing a variety of innovative supplies. Sage Products was
incorporated in 1971, the year the computerized axial
tomography (CAT) scan was introduced. Because the
CAT scan was one of the most significant medical
breakthroughs of the decade, Sage's launch during the
same year seemed a harbinger of good fortune.

Foglia and Hills were residents of North Barrington, Illinois, a far northern suburb of Chicago in
McHenry County. Both men had medical sales
backgrounds and decided to pool their interests and
network of contacts. Their first offering under the Sage
Products name was a specimen collection kit, a simple
yet effective stand-alone device that saved healthcare
professionals both time and money. The Mid-Stream
Collection Kit was unique, easy to use, and could be
bought in bulk.

In 1973, two years after founding the company,
Foglia and Hills bought an old three-story schoolhouse
in the tiny village of Hebron, near the Illinois-
Wisconsin border. The renovated building housed Sage's
15 employees and served as its first manufacturing plant.
Through word of mouth and effective sales and marketing campaigns, Sage's collection kit became a popular

COMPANY PERSPECTIVES

Sage's core belief is prevention—that evidence-based interventions will lead to improved outcomes. This belief led to the birth of Interventional Patient Hygiene, a nursing action plan focused on fortifying patients' host defenses with evidence-based care. By promoting a return to the basics of nursing care, our advanced patient hygiene products and programs help healthcare facilities improve clinical outcomes by reducing the risk of hospital-acquired infection and skin breakdown.

item in the Chicagoland medical field. Various versions of the product and other items were added to the company's lineup and by 1976 sales had reached an impressive $1.3 million.

In 1978 Foglia and Hills hired Paul Hanifl to head the company's research and development. Hanifl spurred development in several areas, from presurgical and postsurgical supplies to disposal needs. As new products launched, Sage's client list expanded beyond its immediate area that included markets in Illinois, Wisconsin, and Indiana to encompass the entire Midwest. To keep up with the demand, Sage relocated to Cary, Illinois, a village to the east of Hebron. Although Cary was significantly larger than Hebron, it was still a sleepy burg compared to its booming neighbors Crystal Lake to the west and Lake Zurich to the east.

GROWTH IN THE EIGHTIES

The company moved to its new headquarters, including both corporate offices and manufacturing space, in 1980. Within a few years, the move to Cary had more than paid off as the town began to morph into a popular hub for business and home-building activity. In 1981 Sage experienced two major milestones: The first was the hiring of Scott Brown, who would play a pivotal role in the company's future; the second was another new product launch. Brown had been hired to be an East Coast sales representative and he soon had a much needed product to sell: the simply named Blood Needle Container, which made the disposal of used hypodermic needles both safe and effortless. The new medical waste container proved very popular with healthcare facilities and helped propel Sage's sales to $3.9 million for the year.

Another important product introduction came in 1984, as Sage segued into oral care systems with sterile, easy-to-handle dental swabs for brushing the teeth and gums of hospital patients. The softly padded swabs required no water and evolved to include a variety of textured or smooth sponge or brush surfaces, flavored or unflavored dentifrices, and oral moisturizers. As the products gained popularity with caregivers and patients, Sage gave the growing product line the name Toothette. Just two years after the debut of its first oral care swab, Sage's annual sales surged to a remarkable $18.4 million for 1986, due in large part to the Toothette branded products.

Brown was promoted to national sales manager in 1987 and over the next few years researched the company's expansion into emerging nonhospital markets such as walk-in clinics, health departments, medical supply chains, and the military. Brown also helped spearhead national and regional promotional efforts, while Hanifl and the research and development department continued to launch new products. Next up was Sage's entry into the protective clothing and equipment field with the P2 line of gowns and cabinets in 1988. The "P2" stood for "Personal Protection" and the brand soon encompassed a variety of packaged clothing items and easily installed storage products.

NEW FACILITY AND PRODUCTS: 1990–95

By the beginning of the 1990s Sage had outgrown its Cary manufacturing facility. The company moved to a new office and manufacturing plant in nearby Crystal Lake in 1991, an area served by five hospitals totaling nearly 1,200 beds, all perfect customers for Sage's growing inventory. Sales for 1991 reached $55.5 million.

Sage continued to introduce products, including additional medical waste units in 1993, as top executives Foglia and Hills looked to the future. In 1995 the two invested in 1.2 acres of real estate in Crystal Lake's Lakeview Business Center, an 80-acre business park. The same year Brown was promoted to vice-president of sales and marketing. The promotion coincided with Sage's new business strategy: to concentrate on designing and selling "interventional" hygiene products for patients. Interventional products worked exactly as their name implied, they "intervened" or prevented germs and pathogens from harming susceptible patients. Sage's new Interventional Patient Hygiene (IPH) products were sterile, individually packaged, and disposable, providing medical caregivers and patients with both convenience and peace of mind.

KEY DATES

1971: Vincent Foglia and Paul Hills form a company to sell healthcare products.

1973: Sage Products relocates to a renovated schoolhouse in Hebron, Indiana.

1980: Company moves operations a second time, to Cary, Illinois.

1981: Scott Brown joins the company as a sales rep.

1984: Sage segues into oral care products.

1991: New manufacturing facility is opened in Crystal Lake, Illinois.

1996: Comfort Bath waterless cleansing system is introduced.

1999: Sage sells three of its business units to Kendall Company, a subsidiary of Tyco International, Ltd.

2001: Company marks its 30th anniversary by moving into a new manufacturing plant in Cary.

2005: Sage is named to the best medium-sized companies list by the Great Place to Work Institute.

2007: Company reaches $150 million in sales.

2008: Sage is named one of Chicago's 101 Best and Brightest Companies to Work For by the National Association for Business Resources.

SHARPENING ITS FOCUS: 1996–2005

Sage Products celebrated 25 years in business with the launch of the new IPH line in 1996. The first IPH product was a breakthrough in waterless bathing, marketed under the Comfort Bath brand name. Comfort Bath products provided one-step cleansing and moisturizing in self-contained sterile packaging. The soft and hygienic disposable washcloths eliminated the need for basins or water for sponge baths. Comfort Bath revolutionized medical care for nonambulatory patients and soon became the leading prepackaged or basinless bathing system in the nation.

Sage agreed to sell three of its business units to the Boston-based Kendall Company, a subsidiary of Tyco International, Ltd., in 1999. Kendall's acquisition of the specimen collection and medical waste/disposal products accounted for $100 million in annual sales, about two-thirds of Sage's revenue. The purchase also included Sage's 450,000-square-foot manufacturing plant in Crystal Lake, so the company began scouting locations for a new facility to support its remaining business, the IPH products line.

Reflecting its renewed focus and commitment to hygienic cleansing and care items, Sage introduced several new items in 1999 and 2000, including the Comfort Rinse-Free Shampoo Cap, the first waterless, rinse-free shampoo and conditioner system, all within a disposable cap; Comfort Shield cleansing and moisturizing perineal care washcloths; several new Comfort Bath products for confined patients; and the Suction Toothbrush, part of the Toothette brand.

The company marked its 30th anniversary with a return to Cary by moving into a new 365,000-square-foot state-of-the-art manufacturing plant in 2001. Sage also launched another oral care product line, Q•Care Cleansing and Suctioning Systems, a step beyond its Toothette brand, for patients at risk for serious side effects related to hospital care, particularly pneumonia. In 2002 Sage branched out into nonwoven materials manufacturing to broaden its protective clothing and hygienic wipes product lines.

As new Comfort Bath products were released in 2004, the bathing kits became a symbol of hope worldwide as Sage sent millions to tsunami and hurricane disaster sites as well as U.S. soldiers in Iraq and Afghanistan. The company's next Comfort Bath innovation was the I-See-Red Skin Check Guide, designed to indicate skin changes in nonresponsive patients. The year also marked another promotion for Brown as he became Sage's senior vice-president, just before the launch of the Prevalon Pressure-Relieving Heel Protector (for preventing pressure ulcers in bedridden patients) and more P2 storage cabinets. Additionally, in 2005 Sage was named one of the best medium-sized companies to work for in America by the Great Place to Work Institute, whose list was published annually by *Fortune* magazine. Sage placed an impressive third on the national ranking of firms with 251 to 999 employees, and was the only Illinois company in the category.

NEW PRODUCTS, NEW RANGE: 2006 AND BEYOND

In 2006 Sage celebrated its 35th anniversary in style. Not only did the company achieve two major firsts: a new alcohol-free cleansing cloth made with chlorhexidine gluconate (CHG), which became the first U.S. Food and Drug Administration-approved cloth of its kind, and a new Q•Care oral rinse solution containing CHG, which became the company's first pharmaceutical product. But Sage was again named to the Great Place to Work Institute's annual ranking as one of the nation's top medium-sized companies.

In the executive suite, 2006 proved pivotal as well when Brown, who celebrated 25 years with the company, was promoted to president and chief operating officer, with Foglia retaining the titles of CEO and chairman and Hills continuing as a director of the company. In 2007 Sage was recognized by the U.S. Department of Defense and Veterans Affairs as a "Champion" of healthcare product quality along with two other medical manufacturers. The company went on to reach sales of $150 million for the year.

In 2008 and 2009 Sage continued its quest to bring innovative products to the market, providing surgical and long-term patients with the highest-quality hygienic cleansing and protective materials. As the new century's first decade came to a close, Sage had gained widespread recognition for both its products and its practices, a trend it was sure to continue beyond its fourth decade in 2010.

Nelson Rhodes

PRINCIPAL COMPETITORS

3M Health Care; Baxter International, Inc.; Bayer HealthCare AG; Covidien Ltd.; Harmac Medical Products, Inc.; Johnson & Johnson; Kimberly-Clark Health; Medline Industries, Inc.; Mölnlycke Health Care AB.

FURTHER READING

Kane, Tim, "Sage Outgrows Crystal Lake Site," *Chicago Tribune,* November 8, 1999, p. 2.

Krol, Eric, "Nearly Half of Crystal Lake Business Center Space Sold," *Arlington Heights (Ill.) Daily Herald,* November 13, 1995, p. 2.

Krone, Emily, "Cary Company's Investment Paying Off for Its Employees," *Arlington Heights (Ill.) Daily Herald,* July 20, 2005, p. 1.

———, "Donated Bath Kits Provide Comfort," *Arlington Heights (Ill.) Daily Herald,* September 8, 2005, p. 1.

"Manufacturers Recognized for Excellence in Product Data Quality by DoD," *Healthcare Purchasing News,* October 2007, p. 58.

McKernan, Jonathan, "Sage Breaks Ground for Cary Headquarters," *Arlington Heights (Ill.) Daily Herald,* April 12, 2000, p. 4.

Meyers, Gary S., "Crystal Lake Has Grown, but Retains Small-town Feel," *Chicago Sun-Times,* May 12, 1991, p. 4.

Slivinski, Krystyna, "Healthcare Products Firm's Motto Is 'Follow the Patient,'" *Chicago Tribune,* July 5, 2001, p. 6A.

Santarus, Inc.

3721 Valley Centre Drive, Fourth Floor
San Diego, California 92130
U.S.A.
Telephone: (858) 314-5700
Fax: (858) 314-5701
Web site: http://www.santarus.com

Public Company
Incorporated: 1996 as TBG Pharmaceuticals, Inc.
Employees: 345
Sales: $130.2 million (2008)
Stock Exchanges: NASDAQ
Ticker Symbol: SNTS
NAICS: 325412 Pharmaceutical Preparation
Manufacturing; 541710 Research and Development
in the Physical Sciences and Engineering Sciences

∎ ∎ ∎

Santarus, Inc., is a specialty pharmaceutical company
focused on developing and acquiring drugs to treat
primarily gastrointestinal disorders. The company sells
Zegerid, an immediate-release proton pump inhibitor
for the treatment of upper gastrointestinal conditions
such as heartburn and gastroesophageal reflux disease
(GERD). Santarus also sells Glumetza, a drug proven to
improve glycemic control in adults with type 2 diabetes.
In 2009 the company had two products undergoing
review by the U.S. Food and Drug Administration
(FDA), budesonide MMX and rifamycin SV MMX,
that treat lower gastrointestinal conditions.

THE TRAVAILS OF A PHARMACEUTICAL START-UP

Like any small, development-stage pharmaceutical
company, Santarus faced the formidable challenge of
bringing a drug to market in an industry dominated by
rivals with vast resources at their disposal. Santarus's attempt to secure a place for itself in the industry was
made all the more difficult because it failed in its first
attempt to commercialize a product.

The company was formed in December 1996 as
TBG Pharmaceuticals, Inc., but it did not commence
significant business activities until two years later. In
1998, the company chose its course, banking its future
on technology developed by Dr. William J. Sandborn, a
specialist in gastroenterology at Minnesota's Mayo
Clinic. TBG Pharmaceuticals licensed technology
developed by Sandborn to treat Crohn's disease, a
chronic inflammatory disease of the digestive system,
and changed its name to Santarus, Inc.

Once the company determined the technology it
would use to enter the pharmaceutical market, it began
the lengthy and costly process of actually entering the
market. Santarus secured $4.8 million in financing in
1998 from investment firms St. Paul Venture Capital,
Windamere Capital Ventures, and Fog City Fund and
launched the drug discovery phase of bringing its drug
candidate to market, the first major step in gaining the
nod of approval from the FDA. Once a compound was
developed and its toxicology was tested in animals and
living tissue, three phases of clinical tests were
conducted on humans to assess the efficacy, safety, and
correct dosage of the compound. After clearing Phase III

trials, a company filed a New Drug Application, or NDA, a document that typically contained 100,000 pages of data, with the FDA, initiating a review process that represented the final hurdle to be cleared before the drug candidate could be sold to the public. The FDA approval process could take longer than a decade to complete, demanding substantial financial investments be made that only rarely paid dividends to the company seeking to shepherd a compound to market. Of 5,000 compounds discovered in the preclinical stage, an average of only five candidates successfully completed the FDA approval process.

Santarus became part of the failing majority with its attempt to develop a treatment for Crohn's disease. After clearing Phase I, which determined how well a drug was tolerated in the human body, the company's drug candidate entered Phase II, a two-year process that determined the efficacy and short-term side effects of the compound. Santarus's drug candidate, the company's only hope for a stream of revenue, failed to demonstrate an ability to treat Crohn's disease. In 2001, the company decided to stop developing the technology it had licensed from Sandborn, forcing it to begin anew and find another compound to bring to market.

GERALD PROEHL TAKES COMMAND

As Santarus's efforts to commercialize a pharmaceutical product foundered, one of its executives was rising through the ranks of the company's senior management. Gerald T. Proehl joined Santarus in 1999 after spending 14 years working for Hoechst Marion Roussel, Inc., a global pharmaceutical company. At Hoechst Marion, Proehl served in various capacities related to the gastrointestinal, cardiovascular, and wound care fields, eventually earning a promotion to vice-president of global marketing. Proehl oversaw the marketing programs for Hoechst Marion's gastrointestinal products Carafate, Pentasa, and Prilosec, a proton pump inhibitor (PPI), a popular class of drugs designed to treat gastrointestinal disorders.

When Proehl joined Santarus, he was hired as the company's vice-president of marketing and business development. After less than a year, he was promoted to president and chief operating officer, the posts he held when Santarus's efforts to gain approval for its Crohn's disease treatment reached their disappointing conclusion. Proehl proposed a new strategic direction for the beleaguered company, and the company's existing investors, along with a new crop of financiers—Domain Associates, J.P. Morgan Partners, and Advent Venture Partners—supported his proposal, investing an additional $33.2 million in Santarus's future. Proehl's choice for a new niche to exploit in the pharmaceutical market greatly increased the potential financial rewards to be had, steering Santarus away from the $1 billion market for Crohn's disease and aiming it at the $20 billion market for upper gastrointestinal disorders.

A SECOND ATTEMPT

In 2001, Santarus signed its second licensing agreement, intending to begin developing drugs to treat heartburn and ulcers with PPIs. During the year, doctors in the United States wrote 73.6 million prescriptions for PPIs, a 21 percent increase from the previous year. The market was lucrative, but it also was dominated by the behemoths of the industry, including a company that would figure prominently in Santarus's bid to gain a foothold in the market, London, England-based Astra-Zeneca PLC, which owned the rights to Prilosec.

Santarus signed a licensing agreement with the University of Missouri, giving the company exclusive rights to patents relating to specific formulations of immediate-release PPIs. Proehl, who was promoted to chief executive officer in 2002, found himself working in familiar territory, overseeing the development of not only a PPI, but a PPI based on Prilosec as well. Santarus used the active ingredient in Prilosec, omeprazole, and combined it with bicarbonate of soda, creating a fast-release reformulation of an existing medicine, a compound that promised to be the first immediate-release oral PPI developed for the U.S. market.

FORMING ALLIANCES

As work began on guiding the fast-acting heartburn medicine through the FDA approval process, Proehl sought to improve Santarus's odds at reaping the rewards of the company's simple yet promising drug candidate. Small pharmaceutical companies often turned to their much larger rivals for manufacturing, marketing, and technical assistance by forming strategic partnerships or signing licensing agreements, and in June 2002 Proehl struck an alliance with Tap

KEY DATES

1996: Santarus is formed as TBG Pharmaceuticals, Inc.

1998: Company licenses technology from William J. Sandborn to develop a drug to treat Crohn's disease and changes its name to Santarus, Inc.

2001: Company's Crohn's disease treatment fails to demonstrate efficacy, leading it to sign a licensing agreement for technology to develop what will become Zegerid.

2002: Gerald T. Proehl is named chief executive officer of Santarus.

2003: Santarus files for an initial public offering of stock.

2004: Company receives regulatory approval to market Zegerid.

2006: Santarus signs a licensing agreement with Schering-Plough Healthcare Products, Inc., giving the company the rights to develop Zegerid for the over-the-counter market in the United States and Canada.

2007: Santarus signs a licensing agreement with Glaxo Group Limited, giving the company the rights to market Zegerid in 114 countries.

2008: Santarus forms a partnership with Cosmo Technologies Limited to secure the rights to develop two drugs to treat lower gastrointestinal conditions.

Pharmaceuticals Products Inc. Proehl signed a licensing agreement with Tap, giving the Lake Forest, Illinois-based giant the rights to use Santarus's drug-delivery technology in exchange for milestone payments and royalties potentially worth $100 million. Tap paid $8 million in initial fees, hoping to use the technology to develop a fast-acting version of its heartburn drug, Prevacid, which generated $6 billion in worldwide sales in 2001. The agreement essentially provided ammunition to Santarus's competitor, but Proehl needed the superior marketing capabilities of Tap to better his chances of securing the financial rewards of Santarus's immediate-release technology. "The global marketplace for proton pump inhibitors is about $12 billion," Proehl said in the December 16, 2002 issue of the *San Diego Business Journal,* "so we felt that there was enough room for us, plus one additional competitor—we're not that greedy. We thought if we could get $1.5 billion or $2 billion in sales that still leaves $10 billion for Tap."

CLEVER STRATEGY SPEEDS APPROVAL PROCESS

While Tap worked on exploiting Santarus's immediate-release technology, Santarus focused its energies on ushering its drug candidate, dubbed SAN-05, through the forbidding FDA approval process. Proehl was tactically shrewd in his approach, employing a strategy that saved Santarus considerable time and money. He used a 20-year-old, FDA provision, rule 505(b) (2) of the Federal Food, Drug, and Cosmetic Act, which spared a drug company from repeating safety studies for a modified formula of an existing drug as long as the modified formula used the same core ingredient as an approved drug. Proehl turned to AstraZeneca's Prilosec, whose core medicine, omeprazole, was the same core medicine used by SAN-05. Santarus notified AstraZeneca of its intention to use the safety data on Prilosec to get FDA approval for SAN-05, waited the prescribed 45 days for AstraZeneca to object to the move, and received no protestation.

IPO AND FDA APPROVAL

By using existing safety studies, Santarus reduced the time and money required to clear SAN-05 through the FDA approval process. In mid-2003, the drug passed through Phase III clinical trials, enabling the company to file an NDA for its heartburn medication, which was renamed Zegerid. The company intended to file the NDA within months, which moved it closer to the $50 million to $100 million the drug was expected to generate in annual sales. With its commercial debut tantalizingly close, Santarus sought to convert its prospects into capital from Wall Street, filing for an initial public offering (IPO) of stock in December 2003. The company completed its IPO in April 2004, selling six million shares at $9 per share, which raised $54 million. In June 2004, celebrations erupted at the company's San Diego headquarters: the FDA approved Zegerid to be prescribed in 20-milligram dosages in powder form. In December 2004, the FDA approved Zegerid in 40-milligram dosages.

After spending six years to develop a marketable product, Santarus had its objective in sight. In June 2004, the company signed an agreement with Patheon Inc. to manufacture Zegerid. By the fall, it was ready to dispatch 230 sales representatives to help market its first FDA-approved product. Sales representatives had a strong case to make to the country's 5,000 gastrointestinal specialists and the 100,000 primary care physicians who composed Santarus's potential customer base. Zegerid provided pain relief in 25 to 45 minutes compared to the three- to four-hour wait typical of existing drugs. "The proton pump inhibitor marketplace are all products that are delayed-release with little differentiation," Proehl said in the September 6, 2004 issue of the *San Diego Business Journal*. "We know doctors like proton pump inhibitors, but they don't like the speed of onset. We offer doctors a more rapid onset, but with similar duration of delayed release." Zegerid, in a 20-milligram version, made its official commercial debut on October 5, 2004.

TAP BACKS OUT IN 2006; NEW PARTNERSHIPS ARE FORMED

As Santarus waited expectantly for the medical industry's reaction to Zegerid, the company's relationship with Tap took center stage. In 2003, Santarus alleged Tap had reached a development milestone that should have triggered a $10 million payment to Santarus as stipulated in the licensing agreement between the two companies. Tap denied the claim, which touched off a legal dispute between the two parties. In early 2005, the dispute was resolved, with Tap agreeing to pay Santarus $10 million, but the disagreement strained the relationship. In early 2006, Tap terminated the licensing agreement without cause, returning exclusive worldwide rights for the immediate-release PPI technology to Santarus but leaving it without a powerful marketing partner.

Proehl wasted little time before ceding rights to another pharmaceutical company, hoping to use the marketing muscle of a rival to realize the financial rewards of Santarus's PPI technology. In October 2006, he signed an agreement with Schering-Plough Healthcare Products, Inc., giving the company the right to seek FDA approval for an over-the-counter (OTC) version of Zegerid that Schering-Plough could sell in the United States and Canada. Next, in November 2007, he signed a licensing agreement with Glaxo Group Limited, giving Glaxo the right to commercialize prescription and OTC Zegerid in 114 countries, excluding the United States, Canada, Europe, Australia, and Japan. The agreement also allowed Glaxo to distribute Zegerid in Puerto Rico and the U.S. Virgin Islands.

Against the backdrop of Santarus's licensing agreements, the first sales of Zegerid were being recorded. During the first nine months of 2005, the drug generated $8.7 million in sales, reflecting a tepid response from the medical community that was not entirely unexpected. Santarus, unlike its much larger brethren, did not boast a massive sales force, which limited its ability to spread the word about the benefits of Zegerid. The company also was marketing Zegerid in powder form. Capsules and swallowable tablets, by far, were the most frequently prescribed dosage for patients taking PPIs, representing more than 98 percent of the PPI

prescription market. Santarus addressed both of its shortcomings, increasing its sales force by adding 150 representatives in October 2006 and launching Zegerid in capsule form in March 2006. The company submitted an NDA for Zegerid tablets in January 2009.

ESCALATING FINANCIAL TOTALS

By 2008, ten years after the company commenced significant business activities, Santarus could point to substantial financial growth, as Zegerid and the licensing agreements related to Zegerid turned the start-up company into a fast-growing pharmaceutical concern. Revenues in 2004, the year Zegerid was introduced into the market, reached $1.3 million, more than half of which came from licensing and royalty revenue. From 2005 forward, sales of Zegerid began to account for the bulk of the company's annual revenue volume. Sales climbed to $26.5 million in 2005, $49.2 million in 2006, $94.4 million in 2007, and topped $130 million in 2008. Although the company lost money perennially, the amount of its losses was decreasing substantially. In 2004, Santarus posted a loss of $81.4 million. By 2008, the company's deficit had been reduced to $18.5 million.

NEW DRUGS FOR THE FUTURE

Further financial growth was expected when the FDA approved Zegerid tablet formulations and the OTC and international markets were penetrated by Schering-Plough and Glaxo, respectively. Proehl also filled the company's product pipeline, giving his company two drug candidates that potentially could add to its financial stature. In December 2008, he formed a partnership with Cosmo Technologies, Limited, that gave Santarus the exclusive rights to develop and to commercialize budesonide MMX and rifamycin SV MMX, two products designed to treat lower gastrointestinal conditions.

Jeffrey L. Covell

PRINCIPAL COMPETITORS

Takeda Pharmaceutical Company Limited; Novartis AG; AstraZeneca PLC; Wyeth Pharmaceuticals, Inc.; Abbott Laboratories; Tap Pharmaceuticals Inc.

FURTHER READING

Benesh, Peter, "A Tale About a Tiny Drug Maker That Outflanked a Giant (Maybe)," *Investor's Business Daily*, October 18, 2004, p. A10.

Crabtree, Penni, "S.D. Firm Loses Strong Alliance: Santarus Dropped by Prevacid Maker," *San Diego Union-Tribune,* January 10, 2006.

————, "San Diego Drug Company Santarus Prevails in Dispute with Tap," *San Diego Union-Tribune,* February 16, 2005.

————, "San Diego-based Drug Company Santarus' Anti-Bleeding Medicine Completes Trial," *San Diego Union-Tribune,* August 7, 2003.

Glynn, Matt, "Lydian Trust, Santarus Unveil IPO Plans," *America's Intelligence Wire,* December 24, 2003.

"Patheon to Provide Long-Term Manufacturing Services to Santarus Inc. for Newly Approved Rapinex Product," *Asia Africa Intelligence Wire,* June 17, 2004.

"Santarus Announces Strategic Collaboration with Cosmo for US Rights to Budesonide MMX and Rifamycin SV MMX,"

Chemical Business Newsbase, December 15, 2008.

"Santarus Announces US Launch of Zegerid Capsules," *Chemical Business Newsbase,* March 28, 2006.

"Santarus Raises $54M in Initial Public Offering," *BioWorld Week,* April 5, 2004, p. 5.

Webb, Marion, "Big Push Is on for Small Local Drug Company," *San Diego Business Journal,* September 6, 2004, p. 1.

————, "Biotech Inks Deal for Heartburn Products," *San Diego Business Journal,* July 22, 2002, p. 11.

————, "Enterprise: Biotech; Santarus Seeks a Spot in a Highly Competitive Field," *San Diego Business Journal,* December 16, 2002, p. 1.

Weeks, Katie, "Santarus May Find Relief in '08 with Sale of Rights to Heartburn Medicine," *San Diego Business Journal,* October 30, 2006, p. 12.

Sapp Bros Travel Centers, Inc.

9915 South 148th Street
Omaha, Nebraska 68138-3876
U.S.A.
Telephone: (402) 895-2121
Fax: (402) 895-2123
Web site: http://www.sappbrostruckstops.com

Private Company
Incorporated: 1988 as Sapp Bros Truck Stops, Inc.
Employees: 812
Sales: $488 million (2007 est.)
NAICS: 424710 Petroleum Bulk Stations and Terminals

■ ■ ■

A private company based in Omaha, Nebraska, Sapp Bros Travel Centers, Inc., owns and operates 16 truck stops, billed as travel centers. Known for their water towers shaped like a coffeepot, they are found mostly along Interstate 80, located as far east as Clearfield, Pennsylvania, and as far west as Salt Lake City, Utah. A handful of the travel centers are also located on Interstate 70 as well as Interstate 29, which provides a link between I-80 and I-70. In addition to fuel and service, the centers offer fast food via the A&W, Burger King, Subway, and Quiznos chains and 24-hour restaurants. Some centers offer such amenities as wireless Internet, laundry facilities, showers and saunas, theater/TV lounges, and chiropractors. Owned by the religiously observant Sapp family, the centers do not sell adult magazines or alcohol but they do delegate a good deal of authority to store managers in running the

individual units, a policy that has been a key to the chain's success.

SAPP BROTHERS BECOME BUSINESS PARTNERS: 1960

The Sapp Bros travel center chain was established by Bill, Dean, Ray, and Lee Sapp. Along with three sisters they were raised during the lean years of the Great Depression of the 1930s. Their father was a failed cattle rancher who followed government project work in southeast Nebraska, the family moving to a succession of rented farmhouses, which their mother hoped would instill a sense of farm life in the children. In the post–World War II era, the economy rebounded and the boys found work. The oldest brother, Ray, along with Bill sold insurance in Lincoln, Nebraska. Lee ran a frozen food distributorship called Snow Crop, and in 1954 he was joined by Dean. In 1960 the brothers decided to join forces to acquire the Ashland Ford dealership. Needing to borrow some money to make the purchase, they hoped that banks would look more favorably on lending to four people rather than just one. Altogether they raised $25,000, a modest amount of capital for an automobile dealership, with Ray and Dean serving as managers of the business they succeeded.

In 1966 the Sapps bought 54 acres of farmland where I-80 and Highway 50 converged in Omaha. In 1971 they decided to take advantage of the location by opening a truck stop, a move that made the land more valuable, and over the years they sold some of the property to house a motel, convenience store, and fast-food restaurants.

COMPANY PERSPECTIVES

We feel that good customer service is like a warm friendship. It's longstanding, familiar, reliable, loyal and understanding. Listening to what our customers have to say lets us better understand your needs. We're here to assist you in getting what you want or solving a problem you have, and invite you back.

The Sapp Bros Truck Stop soon had a landmark to designate its location, a giant coffeepot, the creation of which was more the result of happenstance than design. The Sapp brothers learned that they could lower their property taxes if they had the ability to pump 500 gallons of water a minute for an hour. In order to achieve that goal, they bought a 100,000-gallon water tower from the South Omaha Armour plant that was being sold for scrap. It was Bill Sapp's idea to add the handle and spout and make the water tank look like a giant coffee percolator, which would become an icon that adorned all subsequent Sapp truck stops. Bill Sapp also played the key leadership role in growing the business.

CHAIN BEGINS TO TAKE SHAPE: 1978

Sapp Bros remained a single truck stop operation until 1978 when a chain began to emerge. In that year land was purchased in Council Bluffs, Iowa, at Exit 1B of I-29, an important truck corridor. Here a new truck stop was built, followed by a truck wash and eventually a service center. To supply fuel to its truck stops, the Sapps formed a petroleum unit that was incorporated as Sapp Bros Petroleum, Inc., in 1980. As a sister company to Sapp Bros Truck Stops, it was also headed by Bill Sapp and grew through a series of acquisitions in the 1990s into a regional wholesale distributor of fuel products, lubricants, antifreeze, additives, absorbents, and propane serving Nebraska and western Iowa.

A third truck stop was added in 1983 by acquiring and remodeling an existing operation in Fremont, Nebraska, that included a restaurant and shop. The company then ventured farther west on I-80, buying land in Cheyenne, Wyoming, a natural fueling location for trucks that had filled up at Sapp's Omaha truck stop. Here a new truck stop was built in 1983 along with a restaurant, motel, and service center. A year later an existing truck stop situated between Omaha and Cheyenne on I-80 was acquired and remodeled. It included a company-operated full-service restaurant and a service center leased out to a third party.

ENTERING COLORADO MARKET: 1986

More truck stops were added to the Sapp Bros chain in the second half of the 1980s. The company opened its first I-70 facility and moved into the Colorado market in 1986 by acquiring a truck stop near Denver in Commerce City. The remodeled stop included a leased-out full-service restaurant and an adjacent truck wash. A year later another existing truck stop in Columbus, Nebraska, was acquired and remodeled. It was located on Highway 30, which looped north of I-80 from Omaha to the heart of the state and provided a natural way station for trucks serving the many meatpacking plants in Columbus as well as a number of trucking companies based in the area.

In 1988 Sapp Bros looked to the east, acquiring property in Peru, Illinois, off I-80, where a new truck stop was constructed that included a full-service restaurant and a service center. A Burger King operation was later installed in the main building as well. Sapp Bros closed the 1980s by adding three truck stops, two acquired from Pro Oil. They were both located in western Nebraska along I-80 and were especially popular with car traffic during the summer vacation season. In addition, a new facility opened in 1989 south of York, Nebraska, where Highway 81 and I-80 met. It came to include a 24-hour restaurant, laundry room, and private showers.

Also in the late 1980s a wholesale fuel operation grew out of the Cheyenne truck stop. Named S.B. Fuels of Wyoming, Inc., it developed out of the effort to make better use of a gas-tanker truck the truck stop owned that all too often was idle. The operation began delivering gasoline and diesel fuel to gas stations as well as county governments throughout Wyoming, Nebraska, and Colorado. Later it added biodiesel fuels and after about 15 years was generating more than $225 million a year in revenues.

Following a recession in the early 1990s, Sapp Bros resumed the expansion of its truck stop chain. In March 1993 the company purchased 10.5 acres of land in Salt Lake City, Utah, where the westernmost Sapp Bros truck stop opened in 1994 on the I-215 spur of I-80 that was also a link to I-70 farther south. It would contain a Burger King outlet as well as a 24-hour restaurant and a dozen private showers, television lounge, chiropractor's office, and service areas. Although it catered to many of the trucking companies based in Salt Lake City, the facility portrayed itself as a travel

KEY DATES

1971: First Sapp Bros Truck Stop opens along Interstate 80 in Omaha, Nebraska.
1978: Second truck stop opens.
1980: Sapp Bros Petroleum, Inc., is formed.
1986: First truck stop opens on Interstate 70.
1995: Ray Sapp dies.
1996: Clearfield, Pennsylvania, becomes chain's easternmost center.
2001: Nebraska City center opens.
2005: Columbus, Nebraska, travel center is relocated.

center, selling gifts and souvenirs to appeal to car traffic. It became the most prosperous facility of the entire Sapp Bros chain. The travel center concept was, in fact, an industry-wide development. Because margins on fuel sales were modest, truck stops expanded their offerings, and to support the necessary investments they had to attract car traffic as well. The industry also consolidated, resulting in large national chains, such as Pilot and Flying J. Nevertheless, regional players such as Sapp Bros remained highly competitive.

RAY SAPP DIES: 1995

In December 1995 the oldest of the Sapp brothers, Ray, died unexpectedly in his sleep at the age of 69. At the time he held the second largest number of shares, about 13 percent, in Sapp Bros Truck Stops. According to agreements between the brothers, his estate was obligated to sell back the stock to the company.

Sapp's widow, Lenora, and two of his children, Jim and Judy, disagreed with the $3.5 million price tag placed on the stock, contending that it was worth $13 million. A family rift resulted, leading Jack, the eldest son of Ray and Lenora and the manager of the Cheyenne truck stop, to take sides with his uncles instead of his immediate family. Heading the effort on the other side was Jack's brother Jim, who had earned his own business reputation by building Indy Lube Service Co. Inc. in Indianapolis, and garnering a pair of entrepreneur-of-the-year awards. Jim was also known for an assertive nature and did not hesitate to call his uncles "autocratic and dictatorial," and claim that his brother "chose his job over his family." The family's differences became so heated that in 1998 Lenora and her brother-in-law Bill Sapp argued over payments for University of Nebraska football tickets, resulting in a confrontation between Bill Sapp and his nephew Jim. According to the *Omaha World Herald,* Jim was incensed and "went over to his uncle's office days later and told him never to chastise his mother again. Bill got up from his chair and grabbed Jim, pushed him on a couch and sat on him." Bill later apologized in a letter to Lenora, claiming that "I wanted to spank him … Jim provoked me too far." The family squabble eventually led to a series of lawsuits filed in 1999 and 2000. The resolution of these issues, however, was not publicly disclosed.

In the meantime, the Sapp Bros chain of travel centers continued to grow. In 1996 it extended eastward to Clearfield, Pennsylvania, where an existing facility on I-80 was purchased and remodeled to include a restaurant, service center, and full range of other amenities. Also in 1996 the Columbus, Nebraska, travel center was remodeled. Another unit was added in 1999 when Sapp Bros bought a facility nearing completion on I-70 in Junction City, Kansas, close to Fort Riley as well as a major lake recreation area.

RELOCATION OF COLUMBUS TRAVEL CENTER: 2005

The travel center chain expanded further in the new century. In 2001 property was acquired near Nebraska City, Nebraska, and Percival, Iowa, where a link opened to allow travelers to bypass the crowded Omaha and Council Bluffs area and connect to I-70 in Kansas City. The resulting travel center offered a 24-hour restaurant and a full range of amenities. In 2005 the travel center in Columbus was moved to take advantage of a new bypass around Columbus, catering to east-west traffic on Highway 30 and north-south traffic on Highway 81. In addition to the usual offerings that catered to truckers, the new facility included a state-of-the-art touchless tunnel car wash.

In 2003 another of the Sapp brothers died when Dean Sapp succumbed to cancer and kidney failure at the age of 73. Two of the four Sapp brothers who had pooled their money to buy a car dealership remained, but they too were aging. In time they would leave several business ventures, including the Sapp Bros Travel Centers chain, a business generating about $500 million by 2008, to their heirs. It faced stiff competition from larger chains, but there was every reason to expect that Sapp Bros, even as a new generation took charge, would continue to perform well as a regional concern.

Ed Dinger

PRINCIPAL SUBSIDIARIES

Sapp Bros Truck Stops, Inc.; S.B. Fuels of Wyoming, Inc.

PRINCIPAL COMPETITORS

Flying J Inc.; Pilot Corporation; Travelcenters of America LLC.

FURTHER READING

Andrews, Greg, "Jim R. Sapp Leaves a Trail of Acrimony," *Indianapolis Business Journal,* June 11, 2001, p. 4.

Cooper, Todd, "Truck Stop Fare: Food, Fuel—and Feud Suits Fracture Family," *Omaha World Herald,* February 27, 2000, p. 1.

Dorich, Alan, "Family in Fuel," *US Business Review,* May 2007, p. 85.

Dorr, Robert, "Oldest of Sapp Brothers Dies in Sleep," *Omaha World Herald,* December 3, 1995, p. 4B.

Pate, Kelly, "Truck-Stop Rivalry Revs Up Sapp Bros.," *Denver Post,* August 23, 2001, p. C1.

Rasmussen, Jim, "Aiming to Be Kings of the Roadside," *Omaha World Herald,* October 10, 1997, p. 1.

Ruggles, Rick, "Businessman Dean Sapp's Passion Was Work," *Omaha World Herald,* November 5, 2003, p. 4B.

———, "Dean Sapp's Work Powered His Life," *Omaha World Herald,* November 6, 2004, p. 4B.

"Sapp Bros. Embroiled in Family Dispute over Millions," *Lincoln Journal Star,* February 28, 2000, p. C2.

Sjuts, Dave, "York Sapp Bros. Location Joins in Company-wide Celebration," *York (Neb.) News-Times,* August 8, 2006.

Seagate Technology

Post Office Box 309GT
Ugland House, South Church Street
George Town, Grand Cayman
Cayman Islands
Telephone: (345) 949-8066
Toll Free: (877) 271-3285
Fax: (345) 949-8032
Web site: http://www.seagate.com

Public Company
Incorporated: 1979 as Seagate Technology Inc.
Employees: 54,000
Sales: $12.7 billion (2008)
Stock Exchanges: NASDAQ
Ticker Symbol: STX
NAICS: 334112 Computer Storage Device Manufacturing; 511210 Software Publishers

■ ■ ■

Seagate Technology is the world's largest developer and manufacturer of hard drives, devices that store digitally encoded data on rotating platters or disks with magnetic surfaces. The company makes hard drives for servers, mainframe computers, desktops, notebooks, and a variety of consumer electronics devices such as digital video recorders and gaming systems. Seagate derives more than 60 percent of its revenue from sales to original equipment manufacturers (OEMs) such as Hewlett-Packard Company, Dell Inc., and International Business Machines Corporation (IBM). The company also markets its products to distributors who serve smaller OEMs, dealers, and retailers. Seagate generates 30 percent of its revenue from sales in North America, 27 percent from sales in Europe, and 43 percent from sales in Asia.

PRODUCING HARD DISKS FOR COMPUTERS: 1979–84

Seagate was established in 1979 in Scotts Valley, California, by a group of businesspeople, including Alan Shugart, who had been an engineer with Memorex for four years after spending 18 years at IBM. Seagate was his second start-up after having founded Shugart Associates, the company that made floppy disk drives a standard feature on personal computers. When Shugart Associates was sold to Xerox a year later, Shugart was forced out. Of Seagate's group of four cofounders, another significant member was Tom Mitchell. He had come from Commodore, where he had served as general manager of Commodore business machines, and had previously worked at Bendix, Fairchild Camera, and Honeywell. Shugart became president and CEO of the new company, while Mitchell started out as senior vice-president of operations.

Another cofounder was Finis Conner, who left Seagate in 1984 to form Conner Peripherals. It was Conner who approached Shugart with the idea of installing hard disks in personal computers. After competing with Seagate in hard disks for more than a decade, Conner Peripherals was acquired by Seagate in 1996.

Hard disks are made of one or more magnetic-coated aluminum platters. Data is stored on, retrieved

COMPANY PERSPECTIVES

As digital content, such as music, video, photos and games, becomes more integrated into everyday life, the idea of static data storage is becoming obsolete. In today's on-demand world, you want to access, share and secure your digital content using dynamic storage solutions that give you the freedom to do business, create and interact—anytime, anywhere. From protecting treasured family photos and personal music collections to developing next-generation consumer electronics devices and large enterprise networks, Seagate delivers advanced digital storage solutions to meet the needs of today's consumers and tomorrow's applications.

from, and erased off the rapidly rotating disk by a mechanical arm, which moves across the disk. The whole mechanism is called the disk drive, or hard drive, and the technology for the sealed unit, which is also known generically as a Winchester disk, is Seagate's basic product. Hard-disk technology allows the storage of more data than a floppy disk, and does it at a faster rate.

Unlike larger mainframe computers, personal computers were originally built with only a floppy disk drive and without hard drives. Therefore, the market was open for an independent company like Seagate to manufacture hard drives and sell them directly to computer manufacturers. They in turn would incorporate the drives into their personal computers as add-on features. Seagate's first client was IBM in 1980, just as the latter was about to introduce its personal computers, which would set the standard for the industry. Seagate's first product, a 5.25-inch hard drive, was very successful. By 1982, with sales of $40 million, Seagate had captured half of the market for small disk drives. The company went public in September 1981, with an initial public offering (IPO) of three million common shares.

Seagate made a name for itself by producing the least-expensive disk drives in the industry, largely due to Mitchell's successful efforts to procure component parts from vendors at the lowest possible prices. In 1983 Mitchell replaced Shugart as president, although the latter remained chairman and CEO. Mitchell also took on the new position of chief operating officer to direct day to day operations, while Shugart oversaw planning.

By 1984 sales had shot up to $344 million as Seagate became the world's largest producer of 5.25-inch disk drives, with three-fourths of the company's shipments going to IBM. Then in mid-1984 the computer industry entered a slump, and the average price for a wholesale ten-megabyte disk drive fell from $430 to $320 in a matter of days. A number of factors contributed to the situation, including a slowing in the growth of personal computer sales, industrywide falling prices, a glut of disk-drive competitors, and rising costs of producing the new generation of drives. Diminished growth of personal computer sales came just as the disk-drive companies were squeezing the last profits from their older product lines. These difficulties were intensified for Seagate, with its reliance on IBM's business, when that company reduced orders and began demanding lower prices. Thus, Seagate's sales for the first quarter of fiscal 1985, at $50.6 million, were half of what they had been for the last quarter of fiscal 1984. Annual sales for fiscal 1985 declined 38 percent to $215 million.

FOCUSING ON LOW-COST, EFFICIENT MANUFACTURING: 1985–91

Mitchell immediately began looking into ways of manufacturing the drives even more inexpensively. Realizing that disk drives, as a commodity product, would become subject to price pressures, he had decided to begin relocating Seagate's manufacturing operations overseas where labor costs were lower, and the pressures resulting from cutbacks forced quick implementation of the move. In July 1984, 900 of the 1,600 employees in Scotts Valley were laid off, as component production shifted to Singapore. By December most of its drives were being produced there, and plans were underway to open another plant in Thailand. In so doing, Seagate successfully followed the Japanese strategy of using less-expensive Southeast Asian labor in manufacturing, which had allowed Japanese companies to dominate the floppy disk-drive market. However, with the high value of the Japanese yen, Seagate was able to undercut the prices of Fujitsu, Hitachi, NEC, Toshiba, and others, and dominate the hard-disk market.

At the same time, Mitchell made one outlet of sales more secure by extending credit to a small but important client, CMS. The latter was buying stripped-down IBM personal computers, furnishing them with Seagate drives and selling them to retailers at bargain prices. Thus, while Seagate's revenues fell temporarily in 1984–85, the company managed to stay profitable. Seagate was faced with another problem in the fall of 1984: the replacement of its ten-megabyte drives, which

KEY DATES

1979: Seagate Technology Inc. is founded to make hard-disk drives for computers.

1981: Seagate goes public with its initial public offering.

1989: Seagate acquires Control Data's disk-drive subsidiary, Imprimis.

1996: Seagate acquires competitor Conner Peripherals; forms new subsidiary, Seagate Software, Inc.

1997-98: Seagate reports a $550 million net loss on declining sales.

1998: Cofounder Alan Shugart resigns under pressure from the company's board of directors.

2000: Seagate goes private in a $20 billion stock swap and management buyout.

2002: Seagate becomes a publicly traded company, raising $870 million.

2004: William D. Watkins is named chief executive officer.

2006: Seagate acquires rival Maxtor Corp. for $1.9 billion.

2009: Watkins is replaced as chief executive officer by Chairman Stephen Luczo amid deteriorating economic conditions.

were becoming obsolete as higher capacity drives appeared on the market. Mitchell saw an opportunity to outmaneuver a rival, Computer Memories, which was providing disks with greater memory, but less reliability, to IBM. He promised IBM a shipment of 20 prototype high-capacity, high-reliability drives by December, before Seagate had even finished designing them. Working long hours, Seagate engineers pulled it off. Although mass quantities could not be delivered by March as originally promised, IBM was satisfied and placed orders for tens of thousands of the disk drives.

Seagate also sought to diversify its clientele in order to be less vulnerable to fluctuations in demand. Seagate began marketing more to value-added resellers (VARs), dealers that package stripped-down computer components and software and resell them as specialized systems. By 1987 such dealers came to represent 47 percent of Seagate's clients, up from zero in 1983, while sales to IBM fell to 24 percent. In that year a deal was also signed to supply drives to Hewlett-Packard, among other new personal computer makers. To expand sales

internationally, Seagate set up a European headquarters in Versailles, France, in 1987.

Beginning in 1985 Seagate experienced a phenomenal rise in sales, hitting $1 billion in revenue by 1987, with a record $115.3 million in profits. This reflected the rapid growth of the market for hard drives in desktop computers. In 1984 only 15 to 20 percent of personal computers had hard drives, while this figure had reached 70 percent by 1987, according to analyst Ronald Elijah at Robertson, Colman & Stephans. As the market grew, Seagate was able to maintain its dominant share by keeping its prices down. It had reduced the costs of storing data by 95 percent since it first went into business.

However, Seagate's concentration on efficient production, while allowing technological innovation to take a back seat, made it vulnerable to the boom and bust cycles of the rapidly changing high-technology industry. In 1987 computer manufacturers started demanding the smaller 3.5-inch drives earlier than anticipated. IBM, which was purchasing 30 percent of Seagate's 5.25-inch drives, was planning to manufacture some of its own 3.5-inch drives. As a consequence, Seagate's profits declined by 39 percent during this product transition period in the second half of 1987, and profits remained low into 1988.

Seagate introduced six models of its first 3.5-inch drives that spring, although 5.25-inch drives continued to dominate its sales. The company had added 32,000 square feet to its Singapore plant, where the 3.5-inch disk drives were made. Meanwhile, it expanded operations in Thailand beyond the manufacture of components and sub-assembling to include the complete assembly process and testing of disk drives. More significantly, Seagate began investing greater amounts on research and development (R&D) in 1987, double the amount of the previous year, by issuing $250 million in debentures. The company established a new R&D facility in Boulder, Colorado, in addition to the one at its headquarters in Scotts Valley.

DECLINING HEALTH IN THE LATE EIGHTIES

The market's growth was less than anticipated, however, and revenue for fiscal 1988 declined 50 percent from the previous year, while inventories of 5.25-inch disks piled up. Seagate blamed the problem on industrywide overproduction, while Shugart moved quickly to lay off nearly 2,200 employees in Singapore and the United States. The company barely stayed in the black for fiscal 1989.

Although Seagate remained the undisputed leader in market share, ups and downs in the demand for the personal computer market were a serious concern. Thus, Seagate's next move was to gain entry into the market for the high-capacity drives used in mainframes, by purchasing Control Data's disk-drive subsidiary, Imprimis, in June 1989. In addition, the $450 million acquisition nearly doubled Seagate's sales, to $2.4 billion for fiscal 1990, larger than all its U.S. competitors—Conner Peripherals, Maxtor, Micropolis, and Quantum—combined.

Seagate also had an edge on its competitors in its ability to provide consistently lower-priced products, because the company manufactured its own disk-drive components. In plants throughout the United States and in Asia, Seagate turned out motors, precision recording heads, and other parts. While the company built many of these factories itself, key component suppliers were also acquired by Seagate. In 1987 the company purchased Integrated Power Semiconductors, Ltd., of Scotland, a longtime Seagate supplier, and Aeon, a Brea, California-based producer of substrates to make thin-film magnetic recording media.

On the other hand, Seagate continued to lag behind the competition when it came to introducing new technology. "Seagate has never been that interested in getting products out of the lab first. We wait until we've squeezed every penny of cost out of a product before we bring it to market," Shugart explained in *Forbes* in 1991. "But the product cycles are getting shorter and shorter. Now we can't afford to wait." The latest product on the market was a 2.5-inch disk drive for laptop and notebook computers. Seagate introduced the drive in November 1990, only five months behind competitor Conner Peripherals, as compared with a delay of a year for the 3.5-inch drives.

EMPHASIZING NEW PRODUCTS: 1991–97

Mitchell's emphasis on high volume manufacturing over product innovation was one of the points of contention that led him to resign under pressure from the board in September 1991. Shugart then reasserted his role in running the company by giving up his position as chairman and assuming the posts of president and chief operating officer vacated by Mitchell. Gary Filler, former vice-chairman, replaced Shugart as chairman. This change in management came on the heels of a disappointing year, with the layoff of another 1,650 workers and revenues down 42 percent.

Firmly in charge again, Shugart pursued a strategy of turning out new products as soon as they were designed. He also began focusing on higher profit margins and specific markets, contrary to Mitchell's goal of general large-volume sales. One of Shugart's first products in this regard was the 1480 disk drive introduced at the end of 1991. This 425-megabyte, 3.5-inch drive was successfully targeted at the high-end workstation and minicomputer markets, where profit margins were greater. Seagate beat the competition by introducing the product first, then continuing to outsell its rivals.

Seagate's profits rebounded beyond expectations in early 1992 as sales of lower priced, high-end personal computers took off amid vendor price wars. At the same time, Seagate also benefited from the current personal computer owner trend toward buying new higher capacity drives to run more powerful programs. The company's large market share ensured that such upswings in personal computer demand would have a definite effect on its sales.

Shugart in turn pumped those profits into more R&D and strategic investments. In early 1993 Seagate invested $65 million in a factory in Londonderry, Northern Ireland, which doubled its capacity to produce a key part used in its hard drives. In addition, Seagate acquired a 25 percent stake in the Sundisk Corporation, another manufacturer of computer data storage products, and together the two companies produced data storage systems for portable computers and other handheld electronic devices. In April of that year Seagate signed an agreement with Corning, the glass manufacturer, to provide a new glass-ceramic compound for use in disks. The new material allowed Seagate to reduce the distance between a disk and its magnetic read-write head, which enabled a higher capacity for data.

EXPANDING INTO SOFTWARE: 1993–96

Disk-drive makers hit a slump in 1993 due to rapidly declining prices. Industry leaders included Seagate, Quantum Corporation, Western Digital Corporation, Conner Peripherals, Maxtor, and Micropolis. For fiscal 1993 Seagate earned $195 million, while its competitors lost a combined $400 million.

Seagate began acquiring software companies in 1994 to establish a position in data-retrieval software. It acquired software developers Palindrome Corporation of Naperville, Illinois, for $69 million, and Crystal Computer Services Inc. of Vancouver, British Columbia, for $18.6 million. It also invested in Dragon Systems Inc. of Newton, Massachusetts. The company was investing in technologies and companies that would be significant for data management in the future. For fiscal 1994 ending June 30 Seagate reported record sales of $3.5 billion and record earnings of $225 million.

CONNER PERIPHERALS
ACQUISITION IN 1996

Seagate continued to acquire software companies in 1995, including Frye Computer Systems of Boston for $20 million, NetLabs Inc., and Network Computing Inc. In September 1995 Seagate announced it would acquire competitor Conner Peripherals in a deal valued at $1.04 billion. Conner not only manufactured disk and tape drives, it owned software subsidiary Arcada Software. After experiencing component shortages, price pressures, and significant losses, Conner agreed to a merger with Seagate. The deal was completed in February 1996. Together, Seagate and Conner accounted for about 33 percent of all hard-drive units sold in 1995, making the combined company the market-share leader ahead of Quantum Corporation.

In February 1996 Seagate officially formed a new software group, the Seagate Software Storage Management Group, by combining the operations of Palindrome Corporation and Arcada Software. The division became Seagate Software, Inc., later in 1996 and was headquartered in Arcada's home of Lake Mary, Florida. During the year Seagate continued to acquire software companies, including OnDemand Software Inc. and Calypso Software Systems. Calypso specialized in enterprise systems management software.

Despite complaints from its distributors that Seagate was forcing them to take more inventory, Seagate enjoyed the highest level of sales for high-capacity, midsize, and small disk drives, according to the annual brand preference survey conducted by *Computer Reseller News*. For fiscal 1996 Seagate reported record sales of $8.59 billion and $213 million in net income. By 1997 Seagate had evolved beyond its position as the world's largest disk drive and components manufacturer into a leading provider of technology and products that enabled people to store, access, and manage information. The company committed more than $479 million in fiscal 1997 to R&D while formally establishing Advanced Concept Labs to pursue R&D activities related to storage technologies. For fiscal 1997 sales were $8.08 billion while net income tripled to $658 million.

In August 1997 Seagate acquired Quinta Corporation, a developer of optically assisted Winchester technology designed to integrate optical, magnetic, and telecommunications technologies for use in a new generation of high-capacity disk-drive storage devices. After paying $10 million for a 20 percent interest, Seagate completed the acquisition for $230 million and was responsible for an additional $96 million based on Quinta achieving certain performance targets. Seagate also acquired Holistic Systems Ltd., which developed

software for large-scale, enterprise-wide management information and decision support systems.

In September 1997 Seagate promoted Stephen J. Luczo from executive vice-president to president and chief operating officer. Luczo joined Seagate in 1993 with a background in investment banking. Shugart remained as chairman and CEO.

FINANCIAL WOES AND CHANGE
IN MANAGEMENT: 1997–98

Seagate's financial results worsened significantly in fiscal 1998. At the end of 1997 the company laid off 1,400 workers in Ireland and told analysts its third-quarter earnings would be less than half of Wall Street's estimates. For its fiscal year ending June 30, 1998, Seagate reported a net loss of $530 million on declining revenues of $6.8 billion. The poor results were due in part to Seagate losing significant market share in the server market, which accounted for about half of the company's revenues. Weak demand for personal computers and lower disk-drive prices also impacted the company's earnings. In July Shugart was removed by the board of directors and subsequently resigned his position on the board. Luczo took over as president and chief executive officer. William Watkins was subsequently promoted to chief operating officer.

Among the problems facing the company were integrating Conner Peripherals and speeding up the time it took to bring products to market. The company's worldwide workforce had grown to 100,000 employees, of which 10,000 were cut. In addition, Luczo consolidated the company's design centers from five to three. In mid-1998 Seagate acquired Eastman Software Storage Management Group, Inc., a subsidiary of Eastman Kodak Co., for $10 million.

At the end of 1998 Seagate again led the field in small hard-disk drives, according to the *Computer Reseller News* survey, ahead of Western Digital Corporation and Maxtor Corporation. In the large disk-drive class Seagate also led, ahead of Western Digital Corporation and IBM's Storage Systems Division.

RETURNING TO PROFITABILITY:
1998–99

For fiscal 1999 ending July 2 Seagate reported revenues of $6.8 billion and net income of $1.17 billion. While revenues were flat over the previous year, the company improved its profitability in spite of price erosion on disk-drive products through extensive cost-cutting and restructuring. During the fiscal year Seagate reduced its workforce from 87,000 to 82,000, of which some

65,000 were employed in Seagate's Far East operations. By the end of 1999 the company's workforce had been reduced to about 71,500 people.

The company's software subsidiary had revenues of $293 million and more than 1,700 employees, making it one of the 50 largest software companies in the world. It was organized in two operating groups, the Information Management Group and the Network and Storage Management Group. In May 1999 the Network and Storage Management Group was sold to Veritas Software Corporation in exchange for 41.6 percent of Veritas's outstanding common stock valued at $3.1 billion.

In the latter half of 1999 Seagate decided to repurchase 50 million of its shares, about 25 percent of the stock outstanding. The previous year it had repurchased 48 million shares. Some analysts considered its stock undervalued, and there were rumors that Fujitsu and IBM were interested in acquiring the company. In December Seagate acquired XlOtech, a storage area network vendor, for $360 million in stock.

GOING PRIVATE: 2000

At the end of the first quarter of 2000 Seagate announced a complex financial deal involving Veritas Software and an investor group led by Silver Lake Partners, in which Seagate would become a privately held company. According to published reports, Seagate decided to go private to get away from the scrutiny of Wall Street investors. Under the terms of the deal, Veritas would acquire all of the Veritas Software shares held by Seagate, while the investor group would acquire Seagate's operating businesses for approximately $2 billion in cash in what was described as a management buyout. The investor group included members of Seagate's management team as well as other investors.

As a private company, Seagate would be able to better focus on strengthening its core storage business. Company executives were more comfortable with their new partners' long-term views, as opposed to Wall Street's shorter-term expectations. Seagate planned to continue to implement its advanced manufacturing technologies, seek operational efficiencies, and position the company to take advantage of increased demand for storage-related technologies and products across multiple markets.

RESTRUCTURING

Seagate's return to the private sector became a time of healing, sparing CEO Luczo from fulfilling the quarterly expectations of Wall Street while he focused on improving the company's performance. Luczo, the former

managing director at investment bank Bear Stearns, spearheaded sweeping changes. Manufacturing operations were consolidated, reducing the number of Seagate's worldwide production facilities from 27 to 11. The company also became more nimble in getting new products to market. "Prior to privatization," an industry analyst said in the October 14, 2002 edition of the *San Jose Mercury News,* "it was late to market on some products and often trailed Maxtor and Quantum, where it's now a front-runner."

While Seagate sought refuge in the private sector and became stronger, the dynamics of its industry changed. Recessive economic conditions hobbled the progress of most companies, but the hard-drive market enjoyed a boom period, as consumers demanded increasingly greater storage capacity to store their digital photographs, music, and video content. Heightened demand intensified the competitive forces at play, setting the stage for a battle for market share waged by strengthened hard-drive manufacturers. In April 2001, Seagate's rival, Maxtor, strengthened its position considerably by purchasing Quantum's hard-drive manufacturing operations, making it the largest producer in the world. In late 2002, the competitive landscape changed further when IBM sold its hard-drive business to Japanese computer giant Hitachi for $2 billion, a transaction that spawned a new formidable competitor in the industry, Hitachi Global Storage Technologies.

A RETURN TO PUBLIC OWNERSHIP IN 2002

Seagate, which had turned a $522 million loss in 2001 into a $153 million profit in 2002, intended to beat all its rivals and dominate the industry. One of its first significant moves after regaining its financial footing was to announce its return to Wall Street. Luczo hoped to raise $1 billion in the company's IPO, but when Seagate completed the offering two years and 19 days after it had last sold shares on Wall Street, the result was disappointing. Seagate raised $870 million from the sale of 72.5 million shares at $12 per share, less than it wanted but a total that represented a substantial increase in the company's market capitalization since the Silver Lake–led group had taken the company private. The buyout in 2000 valued Seagate at $1.8 billion, a valuation that leaped to $5.5 billion after the IPO.

Seagate pressed forward after the IPO, ready to turn its legacy as a pioneer in the 20th century into a story of dominance in the 21st century. In 2003, the company entered the notebook market for the first time, introducing a hard drive developed under the code name "Momentus." "For the last five years, we've been improving all areas of the business so that we can effectively address every major disk-drive market with the same success we've had in the desktop and enterprise markets," Luczo said in the July 17, 2003 release of *Asia Africa Intelligence Wire.*

By 2003, Seagate stood atop its industry, controlling 29 percent of the global market for hard drives. Revenue during the year increased from $6.1 billion to $6.5 billion, while the company's profits enjoyed an impressive increase, jumping from $153 million to $631 million. His restructuring efforts completed, Luczo handed the reins of command to his chief operating officer, William Watkins, in 2004.

MAXTOR PURCHASE: 2006

Watkins presided over robust financial growth during his term as Seagate's chief executive officer, completing the largest acquisition in the history of the company. In December 2005, Seagate announced it had reached an agreement to acquire Maxtor, a massive deal that promised to strengthen the company's manufacturing capabilities in the Far East. The acquisition, a $1.9 billion deal, was completed in May 2006. Once Maxtor's assets were integrated into Seagate's operations, impressive financial gains were recorded. Seagate generated $7.5 billion in sales in 2005, a figure that increased to $11.3 billion by 2007, eclipsing the company's record total posted 11 years earlier.

As Watkins guided the company toward its 30th anniversary, he found himself assaulted on several fronts. A pricing war was underway in the hard-drive market, squeezing profit margins. Manufacturers also faced increasing competition from flash-memory chip producers, who were making worrisome headway in the market for consumer electronics products. Of greater concern was the deteriorating economic climate late in the decade. After posting record financial totals of $12.7 billion in sales and $1.2 billion in net income at the end of the company's fiscal year in June 2008, economic conditions soured. In January 2009, Seagate announced it would cut its payroll in the United States by 10 percent and its worldwide workforce by 6 percent in response to sharply declining demand for hard drives. The reduction in personnel included the departure of Watkins, who was removed from his post as CEO. Luczo returned to the helm as Seagate faced an uncertain future amid pernicious economic conditions.

Heather Behn Hedden
Updated, David P. Bianco; Jeffrey L. Covell

PRINCIPAL SUBSIDIARIES

Seagate Technology HDD Holdings; Seagate Technology (US) Holdings, Inc.; Seagate Technology International; Evault, Inc. (USA); Quinta Corporation (USA); Seagate Technology LLC (USA); Seagate Memory Product Products (US) Corporation; Seagate Technology AB (Sweden); Seagate Technology Australia Pty. Limited; Seagate Technology GmbH; Seagate Technology (Hong Kong) Limited; Seagate Technology SAS (France); Seagate Technology Taiwan Ltd.; Seagate US LLC; Maxtor Corporation (USA); Seagate Technology International (Netherlands); Seagate Technology International (Singapore); Penang Seagate Industries (M) Sdn. Bhd. (Malaysia); Perai Seagate Storage Products Sdn. Bhd. (Malaysia); Seagate International (Johor) Sdn. Bhd. (Malaysia); Seagate Memory Products International; Seagate Singapore International Headquarters Pte. Ltd.; Seagate Technology Asia Holdings; Seagate Technology China Holding Company; Seagate Technology HDD (India) Private Limited (China); Seagate Technology (Ireland) (India); Seagate Technology (Malaysia) Holding Company; Seagate Technology (Marlow) Limited (UK); Seagate Technology Media (Ireland); Seagate Technology (Thailand) Limited.

PRINCIPAL COMPETITORS

Western Digital Corporation; Fujitsu Limited; Hitachi Global Storage Technologies; Samsung Electronics Incorporated; Toshiba Corporation; GS Magicstor Inc.

FURTHER READING

Apicella, Mario, "Seagate Strikes Back," *InfoWorld.com,* June 20, 2003.

Barker, Robert, "Seagate: Is the Tide Still Rising?" *Business Week,* July 28, 2003, p. 106.

Bliss, Jeff, "Seagate Steaming Ahead with Acquisition of Conner," *Computer Reseller News,* February 12, 1996, p. 12.

Brandt, Richard, "Seagate Goes East—and Comes Back a Winner," *Business Week,* March 16, 1987, p. 94.

Brown, Erika, "A Path Out of the Forest," *Forbes,* August 13, 2007, p. 92.

"California-Based Seagate Technology Names Three Executives," *Knight-Ridder/Tribune Business News,* August 25, 1998.

Cassidy, Padraic, "Seagate's Comeback Disappoints," *Daily Deal,* December 12, 2002.

Christinat, Joe, "Silver Lake and TPG Take Seagate Public," *Private Equity Week,* December 23, 2002, p. 1.

Cote, Michael, "Boulder, Colo.-based Computer Firm's CEO Outlines Strategy," *Knight-Ridder/Tribune Business News,* November 11, 1998.

Deagon, Brian, "Seagate IPO Fails to Drive Much Interest," *Investor's Business Daily,* December 12, 2002, p. A4.

Diaz, Sam, "Seagate Technology to Go Public Again," *San Jose Mercury News,* October 14, 2002.

"Disk Drive Makers: Back in Gear," *Business Week Online,* November 14, 2005.

"Drive Woes Continue," *Computerworld,* December 15, 1997, p. 29.

"Driven Down," *Forbes,* January 9, 1989, p. 115.

Dubashi, Jaganath, "Seagate Technology: Too Soon to Bet?" *Finance World,* July 10, 1990, pp. 19–20.

Elliott, Heidi, "An Act of Privacy," *Electronic News (1991),* April 3, 2000, p. 1.

Fisher, Lawrence M., "Seagate Trips, Industry Cringes," *New York Times,* August 23, 1988, p. Dl+.

Francis, Bob, "Disk Drive Giant Purchases Palindrome," *InfoWorld,* August 1, 1994, p. 8.

———, "Seagate Riding Success Wave," *InfoWorld,* July 18, 1994, p. 8.

Gaither, Chris, "Seagate Technology Holdings' IPO Raises $276 Million," *Boston Globe,* December 12, 2002.

Gibson, Stan, "Seagate Nets Frye for Under $20M," *PC Week,* May 15, 1995, p. 101.

Grober, Mary Beth, "The Seagate Saga," *Forbes,* May 4, 1998, p. 158.

Hostetler, Michele, "Hardwaremaker Seagate Wants the Lead in Software Game," *Business Journal,* November 14, 1994, p. 7.

———, "With Seagate-Conner Deal Pending, Quantum Still Tops," *Business Journal,* December 25, 1995, p. 4A.

Howie, Amber, "Large-Drive Sweep by Seagate," *Computer Reseller News,* December 7, 1998, p. 124.

———, "Seagate Leads in Small Drives," *Computer Reseller News,* December 7, 1998, p. 122.

Kindel, Stephen, "Maverick: How Seagate Is Winning the Disc Drive Wars Through Vertical Integration," *Financial World,* January 18, 1994, p. 44.

Kovar, Joseph F., "Hard-Drive Vendor Swims Against IPO Tide," *Computer Reseller News,* April 3, 2000, p. 94.

———, "On the Prowl: Intel, Compaq and Seagate," *Computer Reseller News,* December 13, 1999, p. 196.

Larson, Erik, "Decline in Disk-Drive Demand Puts Squeeze on Many Makers," *Wall Street Journal,* December 3, 1984, p. 4.

Lashinsky, Adam, "Scotts Valley, Calif.-based Seagate Technology, Inc. Names President," *Knight-Ridder/Tribune Business News,* September 9, 1997.

Leon, Mark, "Seagate Acquires Calypso," *InfoWorld,* May 20, 1996, p. 55.

———, "Seagate Acquires OnDemand Software," *InfoWorld,* April 15, 1996, p. 66.

———, "Seagate Vies for More of LAN Market," *InfoWorld,* February 26, 1996, p. 43.

Longwell, John, "Alan Shugart," *Computer Reseller News,* November 16, 1997, p. 89.

———, "Large-Drive Lead No Surprise," *Computer Reseller News,* December 16, 1996, p. S46.

———, "Seagate Tops in Midsize Drives," *Computer Reseller News,* December 16, 1996, p. S45.

———, "Seagate Wins Big in Drives," *Computer Reseller News,* December 16, 1996, p. S44.

Marks, Don, "Seagate Technology," *Datamation,* June 15, 1992, pp. 49–52.

McCright, John S., "Seagate, Veritas Part Company," *PC Week,* April 3, 2000, p. 14.

Moltzen, Edward F., "Seagate Acquisition of Conner on Track, Hits Homestretch," *Computer Reseller News,* November 27, 1995, p. 33.

Murphy, Chris, "Seagate Goes Private in Veritas Deal," *InformationWeek,* April 3, 2000, p. 169.

Ojo, Bolaji, "Seagate Launches Its First Hard Disk Drive for Laptops," *Asia Africa Intelligence Wire,* June 17, 2003.

Pendery, David, and Ephraim Schwartz, "Big Challenge Ahead for Seagate CEO," *InfoWorld,* July 27, 1998, p. 14.

Pereira, Pedro, "Seagate Looking to Beef up Profits with Stuffing," *Computer Reseller News,* June 17, 1996, p. 2.

Pitta, Julie, "The Survivor," *Forbes,* July 8, 1991, pp. 94–95.

Poletti, Therese, "Seagate Technology's Chief Executive Works to Improve Company's Culture," *San Jose Mercury News,* August 7, 2005.

Quinlan, Tom, "Scotts Valley, Calif.-based Disk-Drive Maker Announces More Job Cuts," *Knight-Ridder/Tribune Business News,* September 14, 1999.

Rae-Dupree, Janet, "Seagate-Conner Merger Puts New Spin on Disk Drive Business," *Knight-Ridder/Tribune Business News,* February 11, 1996.

Ricadela, Aaron, "BlackArmor: Locked and Loaded," *Business Week Online,* July 8, 2008.

Rogers, Alison, "Who's Up—and Who's Down—in the Disk Drive Wars," *Fortune,* December 27, 1993, p. 12.

Schack, Justin, "Seagate: Save and Retrieve," *Institutional Investor,* January 2003, p. 44.

Schmitt, Richard B., "Seagate Technology's Mitchell Resigns As Board Decides to Shift Management," *Wall Street Journal,* September 23, 1991, p. B8(E).

Schroeder, Erica, "Seagate Taps Client/Server Software," *PC Week,* May 23, 1994, p. 171.

"Seagate Cuts Jobs, Slashes Executive Salaries," *InformationWeek,* January 14, 2009.

"Seagate Dumps Shugart," *PC Week,* August 3, 1998, p. 43.

"Seagate Income Slips," *InformationWeek,* July 20, 1998, p. 26.

"Seagate Revs, Net Slips," *Electronic News (1991),* August 12, 1996, p. 74.

"Seagate Technology Profit Rises Fivefold," *America's Intelligence Wire,* October 18, 2005.

"Seagate to Buy Maxtor for $1.9 Billion in Stock," *eWeek,* December 21, 2005.

"Seagate's Maxtor Grab Expected to Bring Leverage," *eWeek,* December 21, 2005.

"Seagate's Watkins Sounds Off," *Business Week Online,* September 21, 2007.

Sullivan, Thomas, "Veritas Acquires Seagate Software Network and Storage Management Group," *ENT,* October 21, 1998, p. 1.

"A Surge at Seagate," *Business Week,* November 22, 1999, p. 191.

Suzukamo, Leslie Brooks, "Seagate Technology to Cut 10% of Work Force, Boots CEO," *America's Intelligence Wire,* January 13, 2009.

Vaughan, Jack, "What Goes on Those Disks, Anyway?" *Software Magazine,* July 1995, p. 26.

Woolley, Scott, "Follow-Through," *Forbes,* January 20, 2003, p. 38.

Yamada, Ken, "Once-Battered Seagate Gains in Computer Price War," *Wall Street Journal,* June 1, 1992, p. B2.

Shamrock Foods Company

3540 North 29th Avenue
Phoenix, Arizona 85009-1612
U.S.A.
Telephone: (602) 233-6400
Fax: (602) 233-2791
Web site: http://www.shamrockfoods.com; http://www.shamrockfarms.net

Private Company
Founded: 1922
Employees: 2,513
Sales: $1.56 billion (2008)
NAICS: 311511 Fluid Milk Manufacturing; 311512 Creamery Butter Manufacturing; 311513 Cheese Manufacturing; 311520 Ice Cream and Frozen Dessert Manufacturing; 424410 General Line Grocery Merchant Wholesalers; 424420 Packaged Frozen Food Merchant Wholesalers; 424430 Dairy Products (Except Dried or Canned) Merchant Wholesalers; 424460 Fish and Seafood Merchant Wholesalers; 424470 Meat and Meat Product Merchant Wholesalers; 424480 Fresh Fruit and Vegetable Merchant Wholesalers; 424490 Other Grocery and Related Product Merchant Wholesalers

■ ■ ■

Shamrock Foods Company operates one of the top ten foodservice distributors in the United States as well as a major dairy farm in the Southwest. Shamrock Foods supplies more than 16,000 items for food preparation purposes, including fresh produce, meat, seafood, eggs, and dairy products, frozen and canned foods, dried foods, condiments, and spices. Other foodservice products include coffee and tea, baked goods, cleaning supplies, paper products and carry-out disposables, and tabletop and kitchen equipment. In addition to offering the company's own Shamrock Farms dairy products, Shamrock Foods offers several foodservice brands, including Aspen Gold and Xtremeliquid butter alternatives, Bountiful Harvest frozen and canned fruits and vegetables, Chef Mark dressings, syrups, and sauces, and Cobblestone Market deli foods. Shamrock Foods also offers premium, center-of-the-plate products, such as fresh seafood under the Pierport brand and meats under the Emerald Valley Ranch and Prairie Creek brands. Shamrock Foods is a founding member of Markon, a fresh produce purchasing cooperative. The company's foodservice customers include restaurants, hotels, schools, healthcare facilities, and military installations in Arizona, southeastern California, Nevada, Colorado, Utah, Wyoming, New Mexico, western Texas, Kansas, and Nebraska. Shamrock Foods serves its customers from warehouse and distribution centers in Phoenix, Denver, and Albuquerque.

Shamrock Foods operates the largest dairy farm in the Southwest, Shamrock Farms in Stanfield, Arizona, caring for a herd of 10,000 cows. Distributed to foodservice companies and grocery stores throughout the southwestern United States, fluid milk is available in quart, half-gallon, three-quarter gallon, and one-gallon containers. Shamrock offers chemical-free, organic milk and DHA omega-3 and calcium fortified milk products as well. In addition to fluid milk, Shamrock Farms

COMPANY PERSPECTIVES

Shamrock Mission: We will treat those who touch our organization with honesty, integrity, dignity, and respect. Our goal is to be viewed as a world class organization. Our commitment to quality is to achieve Total Customer Satisfaction by meeting or exceeding our customers' requirements. We will provide our employees with the opportunity for personal, professional and financial fulfillment through continuous growth, innovation and market leadership. Shamrock Motto: We treat our customers as friends, and all associates as family.

produces a wide range of other dairy products, including ice cream.

FAMILY DAIRY FARM GROWS AND CHANGES WITH THE TIMES

Shamrock Foods grew out of a family dairy operated by W. T. and Sara Winifred McClelland, who immigrated from Ireland to the United States in 1920. Two years later, the husband and wife team purchased 20 cows and a Ford Model-T automobile and started a small dairy near Tucson. "Mr. Mac" handled the physical labor of farming and milk delivery and "Winnie" handled the bookkeeping. Winnie named the dairy farm for their Irish heritage, Shamrock Dairy.

Successfully serving a small but loyal base of customers in the Tucson area, Shamrock Dairy expanded rapidly. An early adopter of new technology, in 1926 the company instituted pasteurization, which extended the shelf life of milk, allowing the company to expand its customer base over longer distances. Homogenization began in 1938.

Rationing during World War II limited Shamrock Dairy's trade, and the company trimmed its delivery schedule to daytime delivery, every other day. However, the company expanded during the postwar boom years, allowing new industry practices to be implemented. Shamrock Dairy began using waxed-paper cartons instead of glass bottle packaging, and the company purchased its first refrigerated dairy truck in 1951. The McClellands offered their employees a retirement and profit-sharing plan beginning in 1950.

The McClelland children, Frances and Norman, joined the family business in 1946 and 1949, respectively. The two were instrumental in expanding

the family business during the economic boom years of the 1950s and 1960s. With sales of $4.5 million in 1954, Shamrock Dairy prepared for future growth and invested all of the company's profits from 30 years of business into new facilities in Phoenix.

In 1954, Shamrock Dairy made its first substantial investment in expansion with the $54,000 purchase of a ten-acre site near Chandler, convenient to both Phoenix and Tucson. Construction of a state-of-the-art processing plant and several other operating facilities on the site supported production for a growing base of customers and new product development. The company relocated its dairy herd to Chandler in 1956, and the new processing plant opened in 1957. The facility included a culture room for mass-production of sour cream, cottage cheese, and buttermilk. Shamrock began producing a line of ice cream products in 1959, including ice cream sandwiches and frozen pops, the latter in Malt Missile and Root Beer Float flavors.

SHAMROCK DAIRY DIVERSIFIES WITH FOODSERVICE DISTRIBUTION BUSINESS

Shamrock Dairy capitalized on its knowledge of food distribution to broaden its operations and geographical reach. In February 1969, the newly formed Shamrock Foods began delivering fresh foods to foodservice institutions in northern California, Oregon, and Washington. The company brought frozen foods back to customers in Arizona. Acquisitions expanded Shamrock Foods' distribution operations. The company added new dairy customers through the purchase of the retail and home milk delivery business of Foremost Dairy in Phoenix in 1969 and the acquisition of the National Commission Company in Colorado Springs in 1971. Renamed Inland National Foods, the subsidiary provided geographic reach as well as operational infrastructure. The 1975 acquisition of United Food Service furthered the company's Colorado dairy trade and solidified Shamrock's development as a foodservice distribution business. Renamed Inland United Food Service, the business added $100 million to revenues by 1980.

The early success of the foodservice distribution business gained the company recognition in the industry in 1981, when *Institutional Distribution* magazine named Inland United Foods a "Great Distributor Organization." The magazine featured the company in ten articles that discussed customer service, management and sales force training and incentive programs, purchasing and budgeting processes, and practical product mix.

KEY DATES

1922: The McClellands buy 20 cows and a Ford Model-T and begin operations as a local dairy farm and milk delivery company.

1957: Expansion of farm and dairy processing facilities prepares Shamrock for growth.

1969: Shamrock Foods is formed with initial food distribution service to the West Coast.

1975: Acquisition of United Food Service aids Shamrock's further penetration into the foodservice distribution business.

1983: Shamrock opens major warehouse and distribution center near Denver, Colorado.

1990: Shamrock acquires three foodservice distributors in Colorado, expands warehouse and distribution facilities.

1998: Shamrock introduces single-serving milk products with great success.

2001: Installation of extended shelf-life pasteurization equipment broadens market reach for single-serving milk products.

2003: State-of-the-art dairy operations open in Stanfield, Arizona.

2007: New Mexico expansion includes construction of a distribution center and a local acquisition.

Operating as Shamrock Foods, the company further developed its foodservice distribution business during the 1980s. In 1983, the company completed construction on a 3.75 million-cubic-foot warehouse and office space in Commerce City, Colorado. To accommodate consumer tastes for fresh produce, as exemplified by the proliferation of salad bars, the company acquired the Phoenix and Tucson business of Romney Produce Company in 1983. Shamrock purchased equipment and inventory of the business, which included about 60 percent fresh produce, plus fresh meat and seafood, frozen foods, groceries, and disposable goods. The business sold kitchen and tabletop equipment as well. Formation of a purchasing group in 1985 with four other foodservice distribution companies provided Shamrock with volume rates for fresh fruit and vegetables. Markon, based in Salinas, California, purchased produce directly from California farmers. Hence, the five members gained a faster more efficient procurement process than offered through existing channels.

Shamrock Foods continued to expand its foodservice operations through acquisitions and facilities expansion. In 1989, Shamrock expanded in Colorado through three acquisitions, of Jensen Foods in Brighton, Sharoff Foodservice in Colorado Springs, and Booth Fisheries Distribution Center in Denver. To support its Colorado distribution, Shamrock Foods more than doubled its warehouse space in Commerce City warehouse in 1990. A new facility in Tucson was used to store and distribute fresh produce and chicken. The company added 270,000 square feet to its Phoenix distribution center, and the original 175,000 square feet were converted to exclusive use of refrigerated goods. Shamrock Foods began offering gourmet and imported foods as well as shortening and new private-label products in 1990. That year, Shamrock Foods carried 12 percent of the market share in Phoenix and 11 percent in Colorado.

Significant changes at Shamrock Foods occurred under a third-generation McClelland at the helm when Norman's son, W. Kent McClelland, became general manager of the Colorado foodservice distribution operations in 1986. Kent brought an innovative, team-oriented management style, as he instituted participatory management and decision-making processes. Self-managed teams cultivated interdepartmental communications to improve business processes and, in turn, as to reduce costs and improve customer service. The receiving and shipping aspects of food distribution operations became organizing principles, as inbound and outbound teams emerged. Through this transition, Shamrock Foods employees determined how to address the diverse needs of their customers. Hence, the company redirected its marketing and sales efforts toward specific food tastes (Pacific Rim, Italian, Mexican, and gourmet or specialty foods) and specific markets (catering, long-term healthcare, hotel/motel, national accounts, small independent accounts, and retail customers). Also, six regional profit centers were organized with their own business plans and profit-and-loss accounting.

After successfully transforming Colorado distribution operations, Kent took his experience to Arizona as president and chief operating officer of Shamrock Foods in 1993. Employees in Arizona gained from the experience of their Colorado counterparts, and operations improved more rapidly there. In 1996 the changes at Shamrock Foods gained the company the recognition by *Institutional Distributor,* for the second time, as a Great Distributor Organization. In particular, the magazine noted the company's readiness to meet the foodservice industry trend toward diverse consumer tastes and micromarketing that anticipated and targeted specific customer needs. With annual revenues nearing the $1 billion mark, Shamrock Foods celebrated its 75 year anniversary in 1997.

UPDATING DAIRY OPERATIONS AND PRODUCTS

During the 1990s, Shamrock Foods improved and updated operations in facilities at both the foodservice and dairy farm divisions. While other dairy farmers minimized operations due to a decline in milk demand in 1990, Shamrock Farms took measures to become more efficient. The largest dairy in Arizona, Shamrock Farms reorganized to produce more revenue by maximizing the use of its fixed-cost infrastructure. This involved restructuring milking operations to increase production. Previously, the cows were lined up at an angle to be milked from the side. Shamrock switched from this herringbone setup to a parallel lineup of cows, with the milking apparatus attached from between the hind legs. Thus, using the original barn, Shamrock increased the number of cows that could be milked simultaneously from 64 to 120. Shamrock expected the new layout to increase milk production from its 5,000 cowherd to 12.7 million gallons of milk. By the end of 1991 sales from dairy operations reached $437 million. Shamrock Farms produced 40 percent of the milk processed in Arizona and delivered 500,000 cases per week to customers in Colorado, New Mexico, Wyoming, and Arizona.

Additional operational improvements and facilities upgrades involved construction of a 58,000-square-foot automated cold-storage area in Chandler to replace its existing 25,000-square-foot facility. The inclusion of computer-controlled equipment provided flexibility in handling product according to shifting day-to-day demands of the market, particularly for small inventories of specialty items. Wireless communications contributed to the ease of operations by eliminating paperwork and reducing errors. Handheld readers and scanners helped forklift operators locate product inventory in the warehouse and record the transfer of inventory to the shipping area. Automation allowed the staff to monitor inventory and maintain a system of production responsive to daily changes in demands. Implementation of such a sophisticated system provided Shamrock with the organizational infrastructure to expand its geographic range as well as its product offering. Upon implementation in August 1998, the cooler had 1,600 storage locations and could handle 500 stock-keeping units.

In 1998 Shamrock Farms introduced milk in single-serving, one-pint plastic bottles. Designed to compete with the convenience of canned soda, boxed juice, and bottled water, the package integrated a reclosable lid and

tubular shape that fit into car beverage holders. Marketed under the "mmmmilk" trademark, the plastic container looked like an old-fashioned metal milk bottle with a splash of milk on the side. The product and marketing design garnered national attention and awards, as well as significant product sales.

Other new products at this time included milk and ice cream products named for Arizona culture and institutions. In 1998, Shamrock introduced Rattle Shakes single-serving milk, in honor of the new Arizona Diamondbacks baseball team. Available at the ballpark and retail outlets in regular, chocolate, and strawberry flavors, Rattle Shakes featured a diamondback rattlesnake wearing a baseball cap with the team logo on the container. Similarly, a new line of homemade-style ice cream included the Grand Slam Sundae, developed with the Arizona Diamondbacks. Other ice cream flavors paid tribute to college football teams. The official flavor of the University of Arizona was named Wildcat Crunch, and the Arizona State University flavor was named Sun Devilicious, for the Sun Devils. Later, a line of premium ice cream took pride in Arizona's famous places. These included Grand Butter PeCanyon, for the Grand Canyon, Monumint Chip Valley, for Monument Valley in northeastern Arizona, and Tombstone Roundup, for the famous town of the infamous gunfight at the O.K. Korral.

Market development for Shamrock Farms' single-serving milk products improved with the implementation of ultrapasteurized milk processing, to extend the shelf life of milk from 23 to up to 100 days. By heating milk with steam at 280 degrees, rather than 170 degrees for conventional pasteurization, the process killed more bacteria and extended the time milk remained fresh. Extending the shelf life of milk allowed the company to expand the market for its single-serving milk to places where milk products would sit on the shelf for longer periods before purchase. These included movie theaters snack bars, vending machines, and arena food courts.

The long shelf life also extended Shamrock Farms' geographic range, as milk could be shipped longer distances and remain fresh. To prepare for expanded milk distribution, Shamrock Farms developed a new farm facility in Stanfield in 2003, featuring state-of-the-art milking and processing equipment. The company relocated its entire herd of 10,000 cows to the facility in 2003.

SHAMROCK DEVELOPS NEW MEXICO OPERATIONS

Already serving New Mexico foodservice institutions, in 2006 Shamrock Foods decided to expand its capacity to serve that market by purchasing land where a 180,000-square-foot warehouse and distribution center would be built Located west of Albuquerque, facilities on the 45-acre lot allowed the company to consolidate its New Mexico distribution within the state. Existing distribution originated in Denver for northern New Mexico and Phoenix for southern New Mexico. The new location better served southern Colorado and El Paso markets as well.

To solidify its New Mexico presence, Shamrock acquired Southwest Distributing in June 2007. Southwest Distributing added a base of customers along with a product line of cleaning supplies, nonfood items, dry goods, and beverages. Southwest Distributing managers continued to operate the company until Shamrock opened the new warehouse in the summer of 2007. At that time, employees and operations moved from Southwest Distributing's leased facility to the Shamrock payroll and new warehouse. The acquisition added 120 employees and 30 delivery trucks to Shamrock's operations.

NEW MILK PRODUCTS MEET DIVERSE CONSUMER PREFERENCES

In marketing fluid milk, Shamrock Farms continued to address consumer interests in a number of areas, such as healthy beverage alternatives to soft drinks. In the market for ultrapasteurized, single-serving milk products, Shamrock catered to children, hiring 18 children, ages six to 12, to taste-test new product flavors, such as Cookies and Cream mmmmilkshakes and Root Beer Float and Dulce de Leche mmmmilk. Success with the products led to national distribution through Subway's 21,000 restaurants beginning in 2007. Subway purchased more than 2.5 million units of single-serving milk per month, more than Wal-Mart or Bashas' grocery stores. To meet this demand, Shamrock added a 28,000-square-foot facility dedicated to high-heat pasteurization.

Prompted by consumer interest in organic foods due to concerns about sustainable farming and chemical-free food, Shamrock developed an organic dairy operation adjacent to its primary farm. The facility included milking barns, misters, and cooling fans, plus a large pasture of Sudan grass to accommodate the larger grazing area required for organic milk cows. Shamrock started with 200 calves and fed them organic feed, which had not been exposed to chemical pesticides or herbicides. Following the restrictions of organic production, no synthetic growth hormones or antibiotics were administered. Over time, Shamrock expanded the herd to accommodate its entire food distribution network.

Shamrock began selling organic milk and sour cream to several grocery store chains in 2007. As the only Arizona dairy supplying the grocers, Shamrock's contribution to the additional supply of organic milk increased sales of the product in Arizona.

Shamrock Farms developed milk products to serve diverse needs of its consumers. The company introduced a three-quarter gallon of milk for singles who could not drink a full gallon before it went sour. The Rockin' Refuel protein drink was aimed at fitness buffs for post-workout replenishment. Also, the Shamrockers brand offered low-fat flavored milk to school-age children. In 2009 the company introduced Shamrock Farms Essentials, nutritionally fortified with DHA, omega-3, and calcium. Shamrock gave away 10,000 half gallons of the milk at four Bashas' grocery stores in Arizona, and gave milk to participants of the Metro Phoenix March for Babies.

Mary Tradii

PRINCIPAL DIVISIONS

Shamrock Farms; Shamrock Foods.

PRINCIPAL COMPETITORS

Dean Foods Company; Dairy Farmers of America, Inc.; Performance Food Group Company; SYSCO Corporation, U.S. Foodservice, Inc.

FURTHER READING

Brown, Ken, "Mooove Over, Milkmen," *Business Journal—Serving Phoenix and the Valley of the Sun,* October 10, 1997, p. 15.

Casper, Carol, Caroline Perkins, and Dana Tanyeri, "A Quality Journey: 1996 Great Distributor Organization, Shamrock Foods," *ID: Voice of Foodservice Distribution,* August 1996, p. 38.

Hibbard, Cynthia, "Have You Herd? Dairy Farm Saves Money by Milking Smart," *Arizona Business Gazette,* June 21, 1991, p. 1.

Jarman, Max, "Milking the Technology," *Arizona Republic,* October 5, 2008, p. D1.

Luebke, Cathy, "Shamrock Foods Co. Wins 1990 Arizona Growth Award," *Business Journal—Serving Phoenix and the Valley of the Sun,* June 11, 1990, p. 9.

Martin, Richard, "Five Distributors Form Produce-Buying Group," *Nation's Restaurant News,* November 11, 1985, p. 1.

Mattern, Hal, "Milk Taking on Whole New Attitude: Dairy Battles Soft Drinks," *Arizona Republic,* July 3, 2001, p. D1.

Metcalf, Richard, "Shamrock Purchasing a N.M. Company," *Albuquerque Journal,* June 27, 2006.

Paterik, Stephanie, "Organic Milk? Shamrock's Got It—Arizona Dairy Taps Natural-Foods Market," *Arizona Republic,* June 14, 2007, p. D1.

Pentz, Michelle, "Moooove Over, Yogurt, for New Dairy Treats," *Albuquerque Journal,* October 30, 2000, p. 7.

Scott, Luci, "Shamrock Giveaway at Stores Will Tout New Milk," *Arizona Republic,* April 9, 2009, p. 6.

"State of the Art in Automated Warehousing," *Dairy Foods,* March 1999, p. 62.

SHONEY'S®

Shoney's North America Corp.

1717 Elm Hill Pike, Suite B-1
Nashville, Tennessee 37210-3628
U.S.A.
Telephone: (615) 391-5395
Toll Free: (877) 377-2233
Fax: (615) 231-2621
Web site: http://www.shoneys.com

Wholly Owned Subsidiary of Royal Hospitality Corp.
Incorporated: 1968 as Danner Foods Inc.
Employees: 11,000
Sales: $488 million (2008 est.)
NAICS: 722110 Full-Service Restaurants; 533110 Owners and Lessors of Other Non-Financial Assets

■ ■ ■

Headquartered in Nashville, Tennessee, Shoney's is a well-known purveyor of family fare, particularly Southern food, in the process of rebuilding itself under the guidance of Chairman and CEO David Davoudpour. The restaurant chain operates roughly 280 restaurants in 18 states. A major ownership change occurred in January 2007, when Davoudpour's Royal Hospitality Corp. acquired Shoney's. At that time, Royal Hospitality established a new subsidiary named Shoney's North America Corp., which secured all franchiser rights and trademarks associated with the Shoney's brand.

EARLY EXPANSION

The company originated with a drive-in restaurant called "Parkette" in Charleston, West Virginia. Alex Shoenbaum opened the restaurant in 1947, then acquired a Big Boy franchise in 1951. Two years later, Shoenbaum renamed the Parkette "Shoney's Big Boy." During this time, Ray Danner was building a restaurant business in central Tennessee and opened his first Big Boy franchise in 1959 in Madison, Tennessee. He incorporated his privately owned company in 1968 as Danner Foods, Inc. One year later Danner Foods became a publicly traded company.

During its affiliation with Marriott Corporation, the parent company of Big Boy restaurants, Shoney's restaurants doubled in size every four years. Based on a chain of family-style coffeehouses along the busy highways of the Southeast, Shoney's restaurants featured a friendly, uniformed waitstaff that served from a "homestyle" menu adapted to the region.

ESTABLISHING "DANNER'S WAY"

In 1972 the company dropped "Big Boy Enterprises" from its name, and Ray Danner assumed the role of chairperson and chief executive officer, while Alex Shoenbaum became a senior chairperson. Danner took an active role in Shoney's management, building the company on a foundation of hands-on, operations-oriented management. His unique style became part of the corporate culture, and his managers became "Shoneyized" or imbued with respect for efficiency and a sense of responsibility.

COMPANY PERSPECTIVES

For 60 years, Shoney's has been feeding America's families. From our humble beginnings in Charleston, West Virginia, we've expanded to include hundreds of restaurants in 18 states. We may have grown, but we're proud that Shoney's is still a "down-home" restaurant, where folks can gather to enjoy our great food and great service for a great value!

"Danner's Way," as it came to be known, promoted simplicity, customer satisfaction, constant striving for perfection, and management by example. His management team worked in shirtsleeves in order to be prepared to pitch in whenever and wherever necessary. Danner himself monitored everything from corporate staff practices to foodservice through the use of "mystery shoppers" dispatched periodically to each unit. He was also known to visit restaurants in person and to clean restrooms that did not meet his standards during his spot checks. His willingness to roll up his sleeves both proved his point and embarrassed the responsible individual, who cleaned alongside him.

Although employee standards at Shoney's were uncompromising, the rewards were enticing. The company instituted a program in which the best hourly workers could be awarded college scholarships that would help pave the road to middle and upper management positions within the company. In exchange, trainees would work nights and weekends and take college courses recommended by Shoney's. The company provided students with plenty of opportunities for advancement, maintaining five to seven manager positions for each restaurant, area manager positions for every three to four restaurants, and divisional director positions supervising ten to 20 restaurants. Furthermore, Shoney's recruited more than half of its managers internally. According to many observers, Danner's management style was the basis of Shoney's strong profits and steady growth.

NEW CHAINS IN THE SEVENTIES

Opportunities in the company were not limited to work in family-style restaurants. Danner had, in 1969, begun to market a new fast-food concept featuring batter-dipped fish and related food products for sale in a chain of Mr. D's Seafood restaurants. By 1975, when the chain's name was changed to Captain D's, over 250 units were in operation. By 1980 there were more

Captain D's than Shoney's, and by 1985 the seafood chain's sales constituted 30 percent of the company's total. Captain D's consistently outproduced its competitors, including its primary rival, Long John Silver's.

After discovering that its family restaurants located near motels earned over 30 percent more than stand-alone shops, Shoney's established Shoney's Inns, a lodging division which it paired with specialty restaurants called Fifth Quarter Steak-houses. The two enterprises complemented each other, and were managed separately. Within ten years the chain of inns had grown to 21, but two nagging problems with the venture had developed. First, the hotels did not return the high, quick profits of the foodservice operations, and second, the vastly different management requirements clashed with Shoney's (and Danner's) distinctive style. The chain was eventually sold to Gulf Coast Development, Inc., in 1991.

The Fifth Quarter concept fared better as a growth vehicle for Shoney's. In a departure from the "family" concept, the dinner houses featured prime rib and alcoholic drinks on their menu. Despite its small size, providing less than 4 percent of company revenues, the Fifth Quarter chain grew at a consistent 20 percent annually and soon operated restaurants in five southeast and midwest states.

By the end of the 1970s Shoney's began to feel the constraints of a franchising agreement that limited its growth to an 11-state territory. In 1979 the company began to phase out the "Big Boy" name in its marketing. This was Shoney's first step toward severing its 25-year tie with Marriott Corporation. Shoney's forced the break when it built a restaurant in another Marriott franchisee's territory. Although the new restaurant eliminated all vestiges of Big Boy from its signs and menus, the other franchisee sued, thereby starting the breakup process, which was accomplished in 1984.

Shoney's was able to capitalize on its increasingly identifiable name and shift its menu and image toward a healthier concept as a result of the breakup. Disenfranchisement enabled the company to distance itself from the "Big Boy" character's physical image and remove the signature double-decker hamburger from its menu.

CONTINUED EXPANSION IN THE EIGHTIES

In 1981 Danner stepped aside to make David K. Wachtel the chief executive officer of Shoney's, while he remained on the board of directors. Wachtel, a product of the Shoney's management training program, had started with the company at age 16 as a dishwasher in

KEY DATES

1947: Alex Shoenbaum opens a drive-in restaurant called "Parkette" in Charleston, West Virginia.

1951: Shoenbaum acquires a Big Boy franchise.

1953: The Parkette is renamed "Shoney's Big Boy."

1959: Ray Danner opens his first Big Boy franchise.

1968: Danner incorporates his business as Danner Foods Inc.

1969: Danner Foods becomes a publicly traded company.

1972: Company drops "Big Boy Enterprises" from its name; Ray Danner assumes the role of chairperson and CEO, while Alex Shoenbaum becomes a senior chairperson.

1984: Company severs ties with Big Boy parent Marriott Corp.

1989: The Legal Defense and Educational Fund of the National Association for the Advancement of Colored People brings a discrimination suit against the company; a defendant in the suit, Danner is accused of encouraging racial bias at Shoney's.

1993: Company purchases Danner's stock, and his connection to the company ends.

1998: Amid declining customer volume and sales, Shoney's begins selling restaurants.

2002: Shoney's becomes a private company after merging with Dallas, Texas-based Lone Star Funds in a deal involving $20 million in cash and approximately $255 million in debt.

2006: Shoney's has 282 locations, down from 1,200 in 1999.

2007: Royal Capital Corp. affiliate Royal Hospitality Corp. acquires Shoney's from Lone Star Funds; Royal Hospitality establishes a new subsidiary named Shoney's North America Corp.

2008: Ray Danner dies from a brain tumor at the age of 83.

Nashville, Tennessee, and had moved steadily through the ranks of busboy and cook to become the manager of the first Captain D's in 1969 at age 28. Wachtel immediately began to make changes in the Shoney's equation. He ended the company's 14-year franchise relationship with Heublein's Kentucky Fried Chicken for the same reason that Danner broke away from Mar-

riott Big Boy: territorial limitations that set boundaries on growth.

Soon thereafter Wachtel bought Famous Recipe, a struggling midwestern chicken chain. The Famous Recipe chain consisted of 225 stores founded by Lee Cummings, a nephew of Colonel Harland Sanders of Kentucky Fried Chicken fame. Shoney's worked to hone the Famous Recipe concept over the next few years by dropping unprofitable or mismanaged franchises, adopting a uniform "farmhouse" design, and diversifying the chain's menu. Management also gave the chain a more personal image by adding "Lee's" to the name and employing Cummings as concept spokesperson. By 1985 Lee's Famous Recipe had been "Shoneyized"; its sales rose 103 percent, and the chain spanned 23 states.

During this time Wachtel also introduced a restaurant innovation that revitalized Shoney's morning sales reports. The "all-you-can-eat" breakfast bar, brought on in 1981, reversed a ten-year decline in morning sales. By the end of the decade the breakfast bar boosted morning sales at company-owned restaurants to 25 percent of total sales.

Despite accelerated morning sales and a $3.4 million net profit made in selling Heublein and acquiring Famous Recipe, Danner and other board members and managers felt that Wachtel was expanding the company too quickly, and he resigned the position of chief executive officer after occupying it for less than one year. Danner then resumed the position of chief executive officer and spent the next seven years struggling to find a successor who would carry on his management ideals.

In 1986 he made J. Mitchel Boyd, a longtime franchisee and an originator of "Pargo's" specialty restaurants, chief executive officer and vice-chair. Boyd, his wife, Betty, and Gerry A. Brunetts had founded Pargo's, a restaurant in Manasses, Virginia, that featured such light fare as appetizers, pasta, salads, and sandwiches, and was expanded to include nine restaurants in Tennessee and Virginia. This restaurant was made a part of Shoney's specialty group when Boyd assumed his role as vice-chair at Shoney's.

In 1988 Danner engineered a $728 million recapitalization that paid shareholders a $16 per share cash dividend and paid Danner, who owned 19 percent of the stock at the time, $111 million in cash. The recapitalization was a clear sign that Danner was ready to hand Shoney's over to new management, and in 1989 he gave Boyd the chair.

It only took six months for Boyd's emphases on marketing and experimentation with menus and overall company image to clash with Danner's focus on day-to-day operations of the company. As with Wachtel, financial success did not earn Boyd any points. Leonard H. Roberts succeeded Boyd in December 1989 and served as Shoney's chief executive officer and chairperson until 1992. Roberts, known as something of a maverick in the restaurant industry, engineered Arby's Inc.'s five-year turnaround in the 1980s. However, when his relationship with Arby's Victor Posner became strained over franchisee relations, Roberts accepted the chair at Shoney's. Roberts attempted to capitalize on Shoney's organizational and management strengths, while also developing its marketing and research and development.

Roberts faced a very different task at Shoney's than the Arby's situation had demanded: He was expected to continue the financial and organizational success for which the company was known before the recapitalization. Shoney's had never had an unprofitable quarter and had in the mid-1980s been named "best managed restaurant company" in the United States by the *Wall Street Transcript*. At the same time, Roberts hoped to continue the territorial expansion that Danner and others had begun after the 1984 break from Big Boy. From 1984 to 1989, Shoney's had moved into Ohio and Florida, then Kentucky, Indiana, Texas, New Mexico, Oklahoma, and Maryland/Washington, D.C., but the 1989 recapitalization hindered Shoney's ability to invest in expansion from within.

THE 1989 RACIAL DISCRIMINATION SUIT

Roberts faced another challenge early in his career at Shoney's. In 1989 the Legal Defense and Educational Fund of the National Association for the Advancement of Colored People (NAACP) brought a discrimination suit against the company. The suit, which originated in Florida, charged that Shoney's systematically discriminated against African Americans by limiting employment opportunities and job selection, creating what it termed "a hostile, racist work environment." Shoney's signed an agreement with the Southern Christian Leadership Council (SCLC) in 1989 to invest over $90 million in minority business development, community service, and other socially responsible areas. The following year Shoney's launched an affirmative action strategy called "Workforce 2000." The program mandated equitable representation of minorities and women in Shoney's ranks. The company used some programs that were already in place, such as the scholarship program, and added recruitment programs at 48 historically black colleges and universities to enhance its affirmative action efforts.

Although the NAACP case was not settled until late 1992, and the charges of racism still haunted the company's image in the early 1990s, its efforts had met with some quantifiable success by that time: Minorities represented 30 percent of Shoney's employees. Shoney's encouragement of entrepreneurship among minority businesspeople through its Minority Franchise Development Program had increased the number of minority franchisees from two to 11 and the number of units owned and operated by minority franchisees from two to 14. The company's Minority Purchasing Program used minority suppliers for everything from children's menus to food processing; from 1989 to 1992 annual purchasing from minority suppliers increased from under $2 million to nearly $14 million.

Shoney's also sought to polish its corporate image through philanthropic and community relations efforts. These included sponsorship of the Bootstrap Scholarship Awards, which honored Middle Tennessee high school seniors who achieved academic success despite serious obstacles; support of the SCLC; and support of the Tennessee Minority Purchasing Council's Business Opportunity Fair.

Roberts began to focus on franchising, a skill he honed while managing Arby's, and his primary goals were to add 500 franchises to Shoney's roster by the end of the 1990s and to "dominate the family segment." The company added 48 franchisees in fiscal 1991, and would have to increase that per-year figure in order to reach its goal by the end of the decade. One franchising deal with Thompson Hospitality L.P., one of the largest minority-run foodservice operators in the country, helped Shoney's further penetrate metropolitan Washington, D.C., and keep its agreement with the SCLC. Shoney's financed the $17 million deal to convert 31 former Marriott Big Boy restaurants into Shoney's by the mid-1990s.

To that end, Roberts tripled the size of the company's research and development staff and made that department part of marketing rather than operations. One of research and development's primary concerns was menu development, a high priority on Roberts's list.

In the early 1990s the wisdom of the 1988 recapitalization became manifest. Shoney's stock nearly tripled from 1989 to 1991 and the company's value grew accordingly, from $273 million to $809 million. Additionally, the company made extraordinary progress on debt retirement, having exceeded its scheduled payments by $155 million and reduced the debt's maturity by 3.5 years. Declining interest rates did not hurt the company, either; interest on debt dropped from a peak of 12.5 percent to 9 percent.

A primary financial objective for the 1990s was a 20 percent annual increase in earnings, which stood to increase cash flow and enable Shoney's to retire more of its debt. As the debt was diminished, the company sought to invest more in company stores, research and development, and expand its specialty chain. In order to achieve that goal, Shoney's instituted Project 80/85, a plan to increase customer satisfaction by setting goals of 80 percent customer satisfaction in 1992 and 85 percent in 1993.

In early November 1992, Shoney's, Inc., received provisional approval of a settlement in the discrimination lawsuit filed by the NAACP in 1989. The settlement addressed possible monetary damages for applicants and employees of the company's restaurants and corporate offices between February 1985 and November 3, 1992. It was estimated that between 20,000 and 40,000 current employees, former workers, and applicants would share in the settlement. Under the settlement, Shoney's made $105 million available to pay potential claims. The company also agreed to pay $26 million of plaintiff legal expenses and $4 million in various related costs. The settlement resulted in a special charge of $77.2 million against earnings for the fourth quarter and fiscal year of 1992. The company expected that substantially all of the funds would be paid over a five-year period. The lawsuit appeared to have little impact on Shoney's stock. In fact, the company's stock price rose in the days following the announcement of the settlement.

Danner's reputation suffered in the wake of the settlement, however. A defendant in the suit, Danner was accused of encouraging racial bias at Shoney's. The company's burden in the settlement was eased when Danner contributed 83 percent of the settlement by putting up some of his Shoney's stock. In March 1993 the company purchased the remainder of Danner's stock. At the same time Shoney's announced that Danner would not stand for reelection to the company's board. Other than the legacy of his substantial contributions to the company's growth, Danner's connection to the company was ended.

CONTINUED MANAGEMENT TURMOIL IN THE NINETIES

In December 1992 Len Roberts resigned as chief executive officer and chairman of Shoney's, Inc., Taylor Henry Jr., an 18-year Shoney's veteran who played a significant role in 1988's recapitalization plan, succeeded Roberts in both positions.

Shoney's moved toward decentralization of its franchising efforts, including Project 500, leaving franchising to the individual restaurant chains. A strong cash flow helped ease the company's debt burden in

1993. By May, Shoney's total debt had been decreased by $250 million, to $518 million. The company also directed some of its cash to its remodeling budget. Set at $6.6 million in 1992, Shoney's remodeling budget was more than doubled to $15 million for both 1993 and 1994. The company hoped the investment would pay off: in the past, same-store sales grew more quickly for its remodeled restaurants.

Sales fell in the mid-1990s, and the company responded with another change in management in early 1995. President and CEO Henry resigned, to be replaced with turnaround specialist Stephen Lynn. Several other top managers also left at that time. The company also sold its private-label food division, Mike Rose Foods, and Lee's Famous Recipe Chicken.

Some of the funds for that sale went toward purchasing Shoney's largest franchisee, TPI Restaurants, in 1996. The acquisition brought an additional 176 Shoney's Restaurants and 67 Captain D's into the company fold. The same year, Shoney's signed Andy Griffith as a spokesperson for the company.

The acquisition of TPI restaurants boosted fiscal 1997 revenues to $1.2 billion, up 12 percent from 1996. However, several factors led to a net loss for the year of $35.7 million. Shoney's closed 75 underperforming units in 1997 and took an asset impairment charge of $54 million because of underperforming restaurant properties. In addition, expenses from a proxy contest came to $5.3 million.

The proxy battle was initiated in 1997 by shareholders disappointed with the company's financial performance. To help resolve the fight, Shoney's added three new directors to the board in August. One of these, J. Michael Bodnar, replaced Lynn as CEO in November 1997. The management shakeup included W. Craig Barber, who resigned as senior executive vice-president and chief financial officer. As the company's sixth CEO in a little over ten years, Bodnar faced the daunting task of providing Shoney's with the leadership it wanted and clearly needed.

DIFFICULT TIMES

Despite the change in leadership, Shoney's still struggled during the late 1990s. Customer volume and revenues continued on a downward slope. Subsequently, the company began downsizing. In October 1998 it announced plans to close 33 restaurants in northern Iowa, Nebraska, and south-central Texas. Around the same time, Shoney's announced the sale of 34 company-owned restaurants in Illinois, Ohio, Kansas, Michigan, and Missouri to Warren, Michigan-based Elias Brothers Corp., which was the franchiser of more than 600 Big Boy restaurants. Another 50 restaurants were targeted for closure during the first quarter of 1999. In all, Shoney's would decrease in size from about 1,200 restaurants in 1999 to 282 by 2006.

A NEW MILLENNIUM

Shoney's kicked off the new millennium by retaining Banc of America Securities LLC to identify options for turning the company around, including restructuring, refinancing, or putting itself up for sale. Several key changes took place in 2001. That year, Bodnar retired as CEO. Leadership fell to William M. Wilson, who was named chairman and president. Midway through the year, the company sold off Commissary Operations Inc., its distribution business. In addition, a multiyear merchant credit card processing agreement was forged with National Processing Co. By this time, locations totaled about 1,000 restaurants in 27 states.

A major development unfolded in 2002. That year, Shoney's became a private company after merging with Dallas, Texas-based Lone Star Funds in a deal involving $20 million in cash and approximately $255 million in debt.

Following the Lone Star deal, Shoney's began to make a number of improvements. Breyer's Ice Cream was chosen to supply all of the company's 350 restaurants with ice cream. In addition, S&D Coffee Inc. was tapped to supply the chain with a proprietary coffee blend. In mid-2004 Shoney's convened a Chef's Council, consisting of experts from the food industry and several vendors, in an effort to improve and modernize its menu. In addition to food trends, the council discussed issues like healthy eating. Plans were made to convene the council on an annual basis.

By 2005 Shoney's was achieving results from its relationship with comedian Jeff Foxworthy, who had become a company spokesman three years before. Foxworthy helped get consumers in the door. Once there, redesigned restaurants and improved menus did their part to convert them into repeat customers.

Moving forward, the company named Dan Dahlen as its senior vice-president of marketing. Dahlen, who helped develop the well-known "Where's the Beef?" campaign for Wendy's during the 1980s and worked on Subway's "Jared" campaign, immediately announced plans for more aggressive advertising, including an Internet strategy to reach geographic regions that were too small for the chain's television campaigns. Subsequently, Shoney's moved its $20 million advertising account to New York-based Cliff Freeman and Partners.

In late 2005 Rodger Head stepped down as president of Shoney's. Following his departure, Dan Dahlen joined Chief Financial Officer Bob Stetson and Chief Operating Officer Joe Phraner in a joint company presidency arrangement.

OWNERSHIP CHANGES

In July 2006 Lone Star Funds agreed to sell Shoney's to Brentwood, Tennessee-based Centrum Equities. The deal, however, failed to materialize when Centrum raised a number of concerns, including contract and food safety issues. Nevertheless, a new deal was soon in the works, and on January 1, 2007, Royal Capital Corp. affiliate Royal Hospitality Corp. acquired Shoney's from Lone Star Funds. Royal Hospitality subsequently established a new subsidiary named Shoney's North America Corp., which secured all franchiser rights and trademarks associated with the Shoney's brand. By this time Shoney's consisted of 52 company-owned restaurants and 230 franchisee-owned locations.

Shoney's moved forward under the leadership of Chairman and CEO David Davoudpour, a real estate developer, entrepreneur, and restaurateur who also was founder and CEO of both Royal Capital and Royal Hospitality. His latter enterprise was the largest Church's Chicken franchisee in the United States, with 112 locations in California, Arizona, and Texas.

Several key developments occurred in April 2007. Shoney's named MATCH Inc. as its new advertising agency, and Davoudpour created a new executive "dream team." In addition to Dahlen and Phraner, the team included former Wendy's executive Hannibal Myers, who was named chief development officer; former Cracker Barrel Old Country Stores executive Jim Blackstock, who was named general counsel; and former Colombian Chemicals Co. executive Stuart Hall, who was named chief financial officer. Late that year the company unveiled its first chainwide gift card program, with a scented card that smelled like strawberry pie.

On August 31, 2008, former Shoney's Chairman Ray Danner died from a brain tumor at the age of 83 in Nashville, Tennessee. The industry acknowledged his role in building Shoney's to a chain that once included 1,600 locations. Heading into the 21st century's second decade, owner David Davoudpour was committed to restoring Shoney's to its former glory with a focus on healthful food, clean restaurants, and friendly staff.

April Dougal
Updated, Susan Windisch Brown;
Paul R. Greenland

PRINCIPAL COMPETITORS

Big Boy Restaurants International LLC; Bob Evans Farms Inc.; Cracker Barrel Old Country Store Inc.; Denny's Corp.

FURTHER READING

Chaudhry, Rajan, "Shoney's Mulls Life After Debt," *Restaurants & Institutions,* May 20, 1992.

Cheney, Karen, "Cater to Kids, Please Parents," *Restaurants & Institutions,* July 8, 1992.

————, "Food Bars, Light Items Wake Up Breakfast Patrons," *Restaurants & Institutions,* June 24, 1992.

Engardio, Pete, "Shoney: Bursting Out of Its Dixie Boundaries," *Business Week,* April 15, 1985.

"Ex-Shoney's Chairman Ray Danner Sr. Dies at Age 83," *Nation's Restaurant News,* September 8, 2008.

Feldman, Rona, "Market Segment Report: Family," *Restaurant Business,* August 10, 1992.

Gibson, Richard, "A New Recipe," *Wall Street Journal,* July 13, 2009.

Gindin, Rona, "Shoney's Shows Who's Boss," *Restaurant Business,* October 10, 1985.

Hayes, Jack, "Shoney's New Owner Royal Capital Eyes Brand Revival: Struggling Family Chain Aims to Return to 'Glory Days' After Purchase from Lone Star Funds," *Nation's Restaurant News,* January 15, 2007.

Hochwarth, Patricia, "Shoney's: Pulled from the Brink of Disaster by New Ownership and a Take-Charge Leader, Shoney's Fights to Regain the Faith of Its Historically Loyal Franchisees and Customers," *Restaurant Hospitality,* February 2004.

"Insights: Shoney's Expands A.M. Bar, Forecasts Unit Growth," *Restaurant Business,* January 1, 1988.

Kochilas, Diane, "Leonard Roberts," *Restaurant Business,* May 20, 1991.

Konrad, Walecia, "Shoney's Needs a Recipe for Succession," *Business Week,* December 25, 1989.

"Leonard Roberts: Can He Put More Meat on Shoney's?" *Business Week,* October 8, 1990.

"Lone Star Funds Buys Shoney's Restaurant Chain," *New York Times,* January 25, 2002.

Raffio, Ralph, "Market Segment Report: Family," *Restaurant Business,* October 10, 1991.

Rudolph, Barbara, "Something Has to Be Wrong," *Forbes,* July 19, 1982.

"Shoney's Founder Divests His Stake," *Business Week,* March 22, 1993, p. 42.

"Shoney's Retains Financial Advisor," *Nation's Restaurant News,* March 20, 2000.

"Shoney's Shines," *Forbes,* August 2, 1993, p. 152.

"Shoney's Taps Bodnar, a Dissident Director, to Be President, Chief," *Wall Street Journal,* November 13, 1997, p. B15.

Simba Dickie Group KG

Werkstrasse 1
Fuerth, D-90765
Germany
Telephone: (+49 0911) 97 65 01
Fax: (+49 0911) 97 65 120
Web site: http://www.simbatoys.de

Private Company
Incorporated: 1982
Employees: 1,700
Sales: EUR 525 million ($700 million) (2008 est.)
NAICS: 339932 Game, Toy, and Children's Vehicle
  Manufacturing

■ ■ ■

Simba Dickie Group KG is one of Europe's leading toy companies, and one of the fastest-growing as well. The Fürth (Feurth), Germany-based company serves as a holding company for a number of major brands in Germany and elsewhere. These include Simba, the group's original business, which produces the Steffi Love dress-up doll line as well as a variety of toys across a number of categories. Dickie Spielzeug represents a line of toy cars, trucks, and other vehicles, including remote-controlled vehicles. Smoby, the leading French toy producer acquired in 2008, includes the Berchet and Ecoiffier brands. Other brands in the Simba Dickie stable include BIG, Carson, Eichhorn, Nicotoy, Noris, and Schuco. While much of the company's manufacturing is conducted through partnerships in Hong Kong and mainland China, Simba Dickie maintains an active manufacturing base in Germany and France. The company is also present on a worldwide basis through a number of subsidiaries and distributor partnerships. Simba Dickie remains a private, family-owned company controlled by cofounder and CEO Michael Sieber. Manfred Duschl serves as the group's managing director. In 2008, Simba Dickie's sales reached EUR 525 million ($700 million).

EAST GERMAN TOY MAKER IN 1946

Simba-Dickie Group was not the Sieber family's first foray into the world of toys. The family's involvement dated from before World War II, when Herbert Sieber established a woodworking shop in Wilkau-Hasslau, in the Erz Mountains. Following the war, the workshop passed to his son, Fritz, who founded his own company, SISO, for Sieber and Son. By then, too, the company found itself in the Soviet-occupied zone, soon to become East Germany.

Sieber at first began producing traditional wooden toys, such as a set of wooden soldiers inspired by *The Nutcracker*. Other toys included wooden building blocks, puppet theaters, and horse stables. Much of the company's early production was destined for the West Germany market. Before long, however, East Germany's export organization had picked up SISO's toy line and begun exporting the toys to the international market. The United States and Japan became particularly important markets for SISO. Through the 1950s, more than 90 percent of the company's output made its way outside of East Germany.

Into the mid-1950s, however, the Siebers had also begun looking for a way out of Soviet-dominated East Germany. Despite the level of prestige he enjoyed, as an important source of foreign currency, Fritz Sieber, described as a "libertarian" by his son, Michael, had been unable to accommodate Communist ideology. At the same time, the East German government's nuclear program, and the implementation of a vast uranium mining program, had forced Sieber to move his company several times in just a few years.

Sieber decided to risk an escape to the West, and in that year fled with his family, including three-year-old son Michael, to Kassel via Leipzig. There, the family was taken in by a friend. Fritz Sieber was soon able to parlay his toy-making experience into a position as marketing director with Matchbox, the U.K.-based maker of miniature cars. Matchbox was then in the process of launching its products onto the European market, from a subsidiary in Emmerich, Germany. Sieber was given credit for stimulating the popularity of miniature cars in Germany.

NEW TOY SUCCESS IN 1959

Sieber's interest once again turned to developing his own company. In 1959, he left Matchbox and moved with his family to Nuremberg, the heart of the German toy-making industry and one of the world's great toy-making capitals. There, Sieber founded a new company, again named SISO, and once again focused on producing wooden toys.

SISO quickly developed into a major German toy company. Among the company's claims to fame was its launch of the "Thor" rocket, which became the first toy to be advertised on German television. The company also developed an import operation in addition to its own manufacturing facilities, and in the 1950s became the largest importer of Italian toys into the German market. Through the 1960s, SISO also developed a strong export unit, targeting particularly the Eastern European markets, including Czechoslovakia, Poland, and Romania. By 1964, the company had moved to a new headquarters building on Nürnberger Strasse.

Michael Sieber entered the family business by the end of that decade, often traveling with his father on trips to trade fairs and other business trips. The younger Sieber went on to work for a number of toy companies in England, Italy, France, and the Netherlands, acquiring marketing and sales experience, as well as managerial experience, while also completing his studies. Sieber then rejoined the family business.

Into the mid-1970s, however, Fritz Sieber, who had earlier suffered two heart attacks, had a third heart attack. This led him to the decision to take a step back from day-to-day operations. In 1976, therefore, he agreed to sell 60 percent of SISO to a toy company based in the Netherlands.

FOUNDING SIMBA IN 1982

The partnership proved an uncomfortable one for the Siebers. By 1982, the family had decided to pull out of the partnership, agreeing to sell its minority stake. With the proceeds, Fritz and Michael Sieber founded a new company, Simba, joined by five former SISO employees. The new company set out to develop its own line of toys, focusing at first on the girls' toys segment, and particularly classic dolls.

KEY DATES

1946: Fritz Sieber founds Sieber and Son (SISO) in Wilkau-Hasslau, then part of East Germany.

1959: Having escaped from East Germany earlier in the decade, Sieber founds a new SISO in Nuremberg.

1976: Sieber sells a 60 percent stake in SISO to a toy manufacturer in the Netherlands.

1982: Sieber sells his stake in SISO and founds a new toy company, Simba, with son Michael Sieber.

1984: Simba opens an office in Hong Kong and begins sourcing production of its toys from Hong Kong and China.

1987: Simba launches the Steffi Love dress-up doll and collection, which becomes a company bestseller.

1993: Simba acquires Dickie Spielzeug, becoming Simba-Dickie.

1998: Company acquires wooden toy-maker Eichhorn.

1999: Simba-Dickie acquires the Schuco brand of automobile replicas.

2004: Simba-Dickie acquires ride-on toy brand BIG.

2008: Simba-Dickie becomes a top five toy company with the acquisition of France's Smoby.

Simba began operations during a time of profound change for the European toy industry. Increasingly, traditional toy companies had begun to face competition from the arrival of massive quantities of low-cost, often shoddily built toys arriving from Asian markets. The choice of materials, too, played a role in the changes to the industry. While plastic had long been a primary material for the toy sector, new manufacturing techniques, including injection molding, made it possible for more toys to be made out of plastic than before. As a result, companies producing traditional wood-based and metal toys claimed a shrinking share of the market.

From the start, Simba recognized the necessity for developing a low-cost manufacturing base. By 1984, the company had established its first overseas operations, opening up an office in Hong Kong. The company then began building manufacturing partnerships with local manufacturers, at first in Hong Kong, and later in mainland China. Simba also later instituted a policy of owning shares in its partner manufacturers, in order to maintain control over the quality of its toys.

Simba achieved brisk growth in the 1980s. A major milestone for the company came in 1987, with the introduction of the group's first dress-up doll, called Steffi Love. The German answer to the perennially popular Barbie doll, the development of the doll, including the first collection of ten articles of clothing, was personally supervised by Michael Sieber.

The doll proved a hit for the company. Over the next 20 years, Simba sold more than 200 million Steffi Love dolls. During this time, the company created more than 1,300 products in the Steffi line, with up to 200 items remaining current at one time. Simba also rolled out a "little sister" for Steffi, called Evi, which appealed to younger girls. Ultimately, Steffi Love alone accounted for approximately one-fifth of all the toys sold by the company.

BECOMING A GERMAN LEADER IN THE NINETIES

The 1990s marked a new period of growth for Simba, as the company launched a drive to build itself into one of Germany's leading toy companies. Acquisitions formed an important part of the group's strategy through the 1990s, as it expanded its product line to include most of the major toy segments. However, the company took an interesting approach to its acquisition policy. As Michael Sieber explained in *Yo-Yo*, the company's magazine, "Our corporate policy was never aggressive. We took over companies with problems."

The first troubled company acquired by the company was Dickie Spielzeug, a company that specialized in producing miniature and remote-controlled cars. When that company's founder, Wolfgang Sauer, died in a plane crash in 1993, his widow decided to sell the company. Following its acquisition, Simba changed its name, becoming Simba-Dickie. The acquisition of Dickie also gave the company control of the import license for the popular Japanese remote-controlled racing cars series.

Family ownership was another hallmark of most of the companies acquired by Simba-Dickie. In 1998, for example, the company took over family-owned Eichhorn (German for "squirrel"), a prominent manufacturer of traditional wooden toys. This purchase was followed by that of Schuco in 1999.

Schuco had been founded in 1912 as Schreyer und Co., in partnership with Heinrich Muller, a toy maker who created a series of popular tin toys. In 1936,

Schuco began producing tin-based miniature automobile replicas. By the 1950s, Schuco had become one of Germany's leading toy manufacturers, and also a leading international brand. Schuco ultimately went bankrupt in 1976; a new family acquired and then revived the brand in 1990, before selling out to Simba-Dickie at the end of the decade. Under Simba-Dickie, the Schuco brand grew strongly, focusing on the collector's replica segment.

JOINING THE TOP FIVE IN 2008

Simba-Dickie added a new product category in 2001, buying Noris Spiele. That company had been founded in Leipzig in 1907, before moving to Nuremberg in 1912. Noris focused on puzzles and games, growing into a leader in the segment during the postwar period.

Another popular German brand joined the Simba-Dickie stable in 2004, with the purchase of BIG, the maker of the BIG Bobby Car and other ride-on toys. That company had been thrown into crisis with the death of its founder Ernst Bettag. The acquisition of BIG not only added a new product category to Simba-Dickie's portfolio, it also gave the company a manufacturing base in Germany. This production capacity became particularly important in the second half of the decade, as rising oil prices, and rising wages, had made China less attractive as a manufacturing center.

Simba-Dickie completed another acquisition, of plush toy-maker Nicotoy, in 2006. The group's move into the international toy majors came two years later, however, as Simba-Dickie reached an agreement to acquire failing French toy leader Smoby. That company had fallen deeply into debt as a result of its own acquisition drive. The acquisition of Smoby further boosted Simba-Dickie's European manufacturing capacity, while adding more than EUR 120 million to the group's revenues. Entering 2009, Simba-Dickie had grown into one of the world's top five toy makers, with revenues of EUR 525 million. Led by Michael Sieber, the company remained committed to its family-owned status, while pursuing further growth into the future.

M. L. Cohen

PRINCIPAL SUBSIDIARIES

Big-Spielwarenfabrik Gmbh & Co. KG.; Dickie Spielzeug Gmbh & Co. KG.; Dickie Toys Hk Ltd. (Hong Kong); Dickie-Schuco Gmbh & Co. KG.; Dickie-Tamiya Modellbau Gmbh & Co. KG.; Noris Spiele Georg Reulein Gmbh & Co. KG; Simba Toys (Hong Kong) Ltd.; Simba Toys Gmbh & Co. KG.; Smoby Toys Hk Limited (Hong Kong); Smoby Toys Sas (France).

PRINCIPAL DIVISIONS

Simba Toys; Dickie Toys; BIG; Smoby Toys; Schuco; Carson; Nicotoy; Tamiya; Noris.

PRINCIPAL COMPETITORS

Sony USA Inc.; Nintendo Company Ltd.; Perfekta Enterprises Ltd.; Mattel Inc.; Namco Bandai Holdings Inc.; Sega Sammy Holdings Inc.; Hasbro Inc.; Konami Corp.; Sammy Corp.; Springs Global Inc.; Tomy Company Ltd; Hornby Plc.

FURTHER READING

"Grâce au Rachat de Smoby, l'Allemand Simba Fabrique Moins de Jouets en Chine," *CIDAL,* February 5, 2009.

Higgs, Richard, "Bidders Make Play for Smoby," *Plastic News,* February 25, 2008, p. 21.

"L'Allemand Simba Reprend Smoby," *L'Express,* March 3, 2008.

"Simba Dickie Buying Smoby," *Plastics News,* March 24, 2008, p. 21.

Simba Dickie Group, "Simba Dickie Group Enjoys a Positive Annual Result," press release, February 2009.

"Simba to Invest in Big Brand," *Europe Intelligence Wire,* November 23, 2004.

"Smoby Toys Releve la Tete," *Les Echos,* December 10, 2008.

Subilia, Anne-Sophie, "Simba-Dickie Group Asseoit Sa Position dans le Marché du Jouet," *La Gazette de Berlin,* July 2, 2009.

"Tuning into Toys," *Travel Retailer International,* November–December 2006, p. 29.

"The VISION of the Fourth Generation," *Yo-Yo, the Magazine of the Simba Dickie Group,* June 2008, p. 29.

Sisters of Charity of Leavenworth Health System

9801 Renner Boulevard, Suite 100
Lenexa, Kansas 66219
U.S.A.
Telephone: (913) 895-2800
Fax: (913) 895-2900
Web site: http://www.sclhealthsystem.org

Nonprofit Company
Incorporated: 1972
Employees: 10,770
Operating Revenues: $1.83 billion (2009)
NAICS: 622110 General Medical and Surgical Hospitals

■ ■ ■

Sisters of Charity of Leavenworth Health System owns and operates nine Catholic hospitals and four clinics in Kansas, Colorado, Montana, and California. The nine hospitals house 2,054 staffed beds and handle 145,474 patient admissions annually. Through Exempla Health Care, the organization jointly operates two additional hospitals in Colorado with Lutheran Medical Center. As a Catholic ministry, the Sisters of Charity are committed to serving the uninsured, unemployed, and poor in need of medical care. The organization's four stand-alone clinics and its in-hospital Caritas Clinics serve this population, requiring minimal co-payment based on income. Those unable to pay are not required to do so. Despite these obligations, Sisters of Charity of Leavenworth Health System operates with positive cash flow due to its excellent management and adaptation to the limited reimbursements for managed care.

NUNS TAKE HEALTHCARE TO WESTERN FRONTIER

The origins of the Sisters of Charity of Leavenworth Health System date back to the 1600s, when the Daughters of Charity religious order was founded in France by Vincent de Paul (1581–1660) and Louise de Marillac (1591–1660). The women of this religious group applied the motto, "the love of Christ impels us" to the care of the sick and the poor. In the United States, an offshoot of the original order named the Sisters of Charity served new communities on the American frontier during the 1800s; the order established many hospitals or clinics where no medical care existed.

In 1858, Bishop John Baptiste Miege S.J. called for the Sisters of Charity to take its ministry to the Kansas Territory. Mother Xavier Ross led a group of nuns to Leavenworth, where they opened the first private hospital in Kansas. Sisters of Charity of Leavenworth (SCL) completed construction of St. John Hospital of Leavenworth in 1864. Sister Joanna Bruner, the first trained nurse in Kansas, managed St. John Hospital, and she taught other nuns the skill of nursing the sick as well. Financial support for the hospital came primarily from local benefactors, special fundraising events, and occasional loans. More simply, the Sisters of Charity begged for money. They readily assisted the poor and the ill, allowing their faith to sustain trust that more funds would be provided as needed. The medical requirements were great, as a multitude of people traveled west to and through Kansas, including soldiers, prisoners, Native Indians, and wagon trains of eastern

COMPANY PERSPECTIVES

Our Mission: We will, in the spirit of the Sisters of Charity, reveal God's healing love by improving the health of the individuals and communities we serve, especially those who are poor or vulnerable.

Our Vision: SCLHS will realize its Mission through the unyielding pursuit of clinical excellence, strategic growth, and health care for all.

families. Americans fled west to avoid epidemics and the destruction of the Civil War.

SCL gained a reputation for effectively operating hospitals, and officials in other Western towns requested that the sisters assist in the establishment of hospitals. Between 1864 and 1952, the SCL established or managed 18 hospitals in Kansas and across the west to California. The first extension hospitals opened in Montana. The SCL entered Montana during the late 1860s, just after the Battle of the Big Hole, in the southwestern area of the state, where the sisters cared for the sick and the wounded. They opened medical facilities as they traveled to Helena, Deer Lodge, and Anaconda. St. James Hospital in Butte opened in 1881, to provide healthcare for the area's copper miners, and St. Vincent Hospital opened in Billings in 1899.

In 1873, Mother Xavier Ross gave nine dollars to four nuns to travel to Denver, in the Colorado Territory, where the Sisters of Charity founded St. Vincent Hospital. The facility cared primarily for women, children, the homeless, and the poor. Governor William Gilpin donated land to the Sisters of Charity for construction of a new facility. The sisters renamed the facility St. Joseph Hospital in 1876, when construction began. Further expansion occurred under the auspices of businessman John K. Mullen, who earned his fortune in flour, and Mrs. J. J. Brown, known as "the Unsinkable Molly Brown" for surviving the tragic shipwreck of the *Titanic*. A card party and an enormous citywide open market raised $10,000 for the construction of an administration building in 1899. Also, the hospital obtained state-of-the-art medical devices, a brass sterilizing machine and X-ray equipment.

SCL sent ministry nurses to other towns in the western United States. One outcome was the establishment of St. Mary's Hospital in Grand Junction, Colorado, with ten beds, in 1895. SCL expanded its ministry in Kansas when the Topeka Commercial Club donated land for a hospital in 1908. Sister Mary Ger-

maine Kramer and Mother Mary Peter Dwyer raised $40,000 for construction of the 40-bed facility. When St. Francis opened in 1909, the frugal nuns created a homelike atmosphere by making colorful quilts from scraps of fabric.

MEETING GROWING NEEDS IN EARLY 20TH CENTURY

The growth of western towns created a corresponding need for healthcare and healthcare providers. By 1915, St. Vincent Hospital in Billings had cared for more than 20,000 patients. With $250,000 in funds, construction of a larger, modern hospital began there in 1917. It finally opened in 1923, after delays caused by shortages of labor and building materials during World War I. In 1915, SCL purchased the County Hospital in Miles City, Montana, from the Presentation Sisters. The facility was renamed Holy Rosary Hospital. To meet the needs of the Grand Junction, Colorado, community SCL added a 30-bed hospital wing that also housed a classroom. SCL built a completely new 80-bed hospital facility for St. Mary's in 1934.

SCL founded Providence Hospital in Kansas City, Kansas, despite an initial absence of resources. World War I hindered fundraising. As Mother Mary Berchamans had chanted, "Providence can provide, Providence did provide; Providence will provide." Hence, faith in Divine Providence yielded the name of the medical facility, which SCL established in 1920. Providence Hospital specialized in care for handicapped children and housed an orthopedic ward. The hospital provided medical care and distributed food to the poor at no cost. Also, SCL established a school of nursing at the site. After World War II, Providence Hospital expanded to address a growing population in Kansas City. Specifically, the baby boom required the hospital to add an obstetrical unit in 1946. In 1950, the hospital expanded to accommodate 200 beds, plus 40 bassinets for newborn babies.

One of the last hospitals to be founded by SCL was the St. John's Health Center in Santa Monica, California. Founded in 1942, the hospital attended to a growing need for medical care on the Pacific Coast at the advent of World War II.

ADMINISTRATIVE CHANGES AT MID-CENTURY

During the 1950s and 1960s, a variety of factors contributed to changes in providing and paying for healthcare. New technology and medical advances, and changes in health insurance, government funding, and

KEY DATES

1864: Sisters of Charity opens the first hospital in the Kansas Territory, St. John Hospital.

1876: Sister Bruner opens St. Joseph Hospital in Denver, Colorado.

1881: First of three hospitals opens in Montana Territory.

1896: St. Mary's Hospital opens in Grand Junction, Colorado.

1920: Providence Hospital opens in Kansas City, Kansas.

1972: Changes in the healthcare funding and management lead to incorporation of the Sisters of Charity of Leavenworth Health Services Corporation.

1988: Organization opens clinics for the uninsured or underinsured in Grand Junction, Colorado, and Leavenworth and Topeka, Kansas.

1994: Governance rules are changed to accommodate growing participation of lay partners.

1998: Sisters of Charity forms Exempla Healthcare through merger with Lutheran Medical Center in Denver.

2000: Organization adopts a new name, Sisters of Charity of Leavenworth Health System (SCLHS).

2006: SCLHS embarks on several major expansion projects.

litigation all contributed to the need for a different approach to hospital administration. To determine their future course the Sisters of Charity began a process of self-examination in 1969. Their conclusions led the apostolate to refocus its commitment to healthcare in a manner befitting the new dynamics. Hence, in 1972, the Sisters of Charity of Leavenworth Health Services Corporation (SCL/HSC) filed articles of incorporation and established a new structure for hospital management.

In addition to the establishment of the umbrella corporation, which managed day-to-day coordination, each hospital incorporated separately. The elected officers of the SCL religious community took positions on the boards of the Health Services Corporation (HSC) and became corporate members of individual hospital boards of directors. Each hospital board consisted of at least 51 percent officials of the SCL. The new structure

allowed SCL hospitals to develop according to local needs while benefiting from the expertise of the central organization.

SCL HOSPITALS ACCOMMODATE VARIETY OF NEEDS IN MEDICAL CARE

Over the years, some of the hospitals founded by SCL closed or were taken over by other organizations. Nevertheless, SCL sustained a core group of facilities that expanded and improved as communities grew and medical knowledge and technology progressed. For instance, during the early 1960s, St. Joseph Hospital in Denver replaced the administration buildings and remodeled other wings added over the years. In 1972 SCL added surgery facilities, and in 1977 a radiology and cardiovascular annex.

At St. Mary's SCL added several new services and facilities. An outpatient surgery clinic opened in 1978 and oncology, intensive care, pediatrics, and prenatal units opened in a newly constructed facility in 1985. During the late 1980s, St. Mary's purchased state-of-the-art medical services and equipment that would normally require patients to take a 250-mile journey to Denver to access St. Mary's Heart Center, which opened in 1986 to provide cardiovascular heart catheterization, open-heart surgery, and postoperative care. SCL added mammography, for early breast cancer detection, in 1988, and magnetic resonance imaging (MRI) in 1989.

The rising numbers of uninsured Americans created a need for free or low-cost medical care in the United States, and SCL addressed that need by opening local clinics. SCL already operated a network of Caritas clinics within its hospitals. The Caritas clinics served primarily uninsured adults, the working poor, and the unemployed. In 1988 SCL expanded to meet the growing need for such clinics. The Marillac Clinic opened in 1988 to provide care for low- and moderate-income residents in Mesa County, in eastern Kansas. In Topeka, the Marian Clinic provided both medical and dental care. It was funded by 35 faith groups, 70 organizations, 60 businesses, and over 1,800 local citizens. Healthcare professionals volunteered their time to provide care at the clinic. The clinics provided care for uninsured people who met the benchmark of earnings at 150 percent of the federal poverty guidelines or less.

Facilities development continued at SCL hospitals. At St. Mary's Hospital, SCL successfully raised $2.5 million from the Grand Junction community to build an $8 million patient care tower. A medical office building was built on the hospital grounds in 1995. That year, St. Mary's acquired the inpatient and home health services businesses from Hilltop Rehabilitation Hospital.

At Holy Rosary, economic development in the Miles City area led to construction of a healthcare complex on a 58-acre plot. The two-year project was completed in October 1995, as physician offices and extended and acute care operations were consolidated from sites around Miles City. Development of an efficiently organized healthcare facility allowed Holy Rosary to accommodate the needs of many communities in eastern Montana. While Holy Rosary was not affiliated with SCL at this time, the organizations reestablished ties in 1997.

CHANGES IN MEDICAL MANAGEMENT EFFECT SCL OPERATIONS

During the late 1990s, SCL/HSC confronted a number of challenges. The growing need for healthcare services met with a shortage of leaders as the number of nuns declined in the last decades of the 20th century. By 1995, the group's eight hospitals in Kansas, Colorado, Montana, and California handled 100,000 patient admissions annually, with a total of 2,726 beds at the company's facilities. Skyrocketing costs led to limited reimbursements from health insurers, and the federal Balanced Budget Act of 1997 led to lower Medicare reimbursements as well. Moreover, as a Catholic institution, SCL/HSC maintained a commitment to helping the poor, and the growing number of uninsured people led to higher costs to cover care for people unable to pay.

In 1994, the HSC board adopted a new governance policy to allow stronger involvement by lay partners in the health ministry through shared leadership. This allowed the organization to maintain a high quality of top-level management as fewer sisters entered hospital administration. By 1999 only one hospital in the system was headed by a Sister of Charity. For the umbrella organization, SCL/HCS hired Bill Murray as its first lay CEO in 1998. Murray, himself a Catholic, brought 23 years experience to the position, most recently as CEO of SCL's St. Vincent Hospital in Billings, Montana. Murray's transition to full leadership as president occurred over the next year, as Sister Marie Damian Glatt transferred responsibility.

As the CEO and president, Murray faced the continuing challenge of changing cost structures in medical reimbursement. One strategy involved shifting more medical procedures to outpatient service. While this had the effect of decreasing hospital stays and lowering some medical repayment revenue, it allowed patients to get treatment more quickly. The balance occurred in treating a higher volume of patients. Also, the

change reduced hospital traffic, as most outpatient surgery was located offsite.

In Denver, SCL sought to address medical management changes in that market by merging St. Joseph Hospital with Lutheran Medical Center, a 100-year-old organization based in nearby Wheat Ridge. The two organizations formed a new entity, Exempla Healthcare, which jointly operated the two hospitals, although they each still owned their respective properties. Exempla expanded in 2004 with the opening of the 143-bed Exempla Good Samaritan Medical Center, in Lafayette, Colorado, that December.

Operating under the name Sisters of Charity of Leavenworth Health System (SCLHS) as of May 2000, the organization acted to develop Providence Medical Center during the early 2000s. Providence Hospital had left the SCL system when it merged with St. Margaret Hospital during the early 1970s. Providence–St. Margaret Health Center, which relocated to the western area of Kansas City, operated as part of the Archdiocese of Kansas until 1991.

In 1998, SCLHS purchased Bethany Medical Center in Kansas City, Kansas, and joined the facility to the Providence organization. Providence implemented several cost-saving measures. Reliant on Medicaid reimbursement and burdened with a large number of uninsured patients, Bethany Medical Center was losing money when SCLHS took over management. Providence maintained operations by taking advantage of volume rates for supplies through affiliation with large purchasing groups and by consolidating redundant health programs. Cooperative programs with Sisters of Carondelet Health reduced overlap between the two systems. Also, SCLHS tapped its own cash reserves to pay bills. Changes to restore viability at Bethany Medical included becoming an ambulatory care facility and shifting more operating procedures to outpatient care at Providence in order to reduce costs associated with acute care.

SCLHS IMPLEMENTS EXPANSION PROJECTS SYSTEMWIDE

In 2006 SCLHS moved to acquire the 50 percent interest, owned by LMC Community Foundation, when Exempla found itself unable to maintain profitability. While development of the Lafayette facility hindered Exempla's ability to borrow operating funds, SCLHS maintained a top credit rating and operated profitably. Revenues for the fiscal year ended May 31, 2006, reached $3.97 billion, yielding $185.3 million in net income. Moreover, SCLHS maintained an average operating margin of just under 10 percent. SCLHS offered $311 million to obtain 100 percent ownership of the hospitals, and it offered to invest $300 million to replace St. Joseph Hospital's 436-bed facility.

However, physicians at Exempla Lutheran Medical Center attempted to block the sale of the hospital due to differences in medical ethics. Physicians and others feared that the Catholic Church's Ethical Religious Directives would dictate certain procedures, such as abortion and tubal ligation, no longer be performed at the 543-bed hospital. A citizen's injunction temporarily halted the sale of the assets. Despite pending arbitration, Exempla St. Joseph, owned by SCLHS and jointly operated by Exempla, went forward with plans for a $1 billion renovation and expansion project intended to maintain competitiveness in the Denver metropolitan healthcare market.

At other facilities, SCLHS continued to expand and improve its facilities while maintaining excellence in cost management. In the spring of 2007, after two years of consideration, SCLHS purchased property for the construction of a health park to replace Topeka's St. Francis Health Center. The 132-acre property, where the famous Menninger Clinic once sat, would hold leased medical offices and retail buildings, as well as a new hospital. Planning for the $250 million hospital began with consideration for how to redevelop the existing hospital facilities, which opened a new cardiology center in 2004. Expansion of St. John Hospital in Leavenworth involved a new wing off the main building. Patient admissions capacity would be increased from 38 beds to about 58 beds. Departments expected to be located in the new wing included emergency, surgery, and intensive care units, and an obstetrics/gynecology department.

New initiatives at Providence Medical Center involved implementation of progressive approaches to emergency care at a new Emergency Services facility. As emergency room visits increased nearly 10 percent from 2002 to 2006, Providence intended to establish the Rapid Medical Evaluation triage at the new facility. The method involved a team approach between doctors and nurses in registering and treating patients and in providing continuing care during a patient's entire stay in the emergency center. The $17 million project more than doubled the total space for emergency care, from 10,000 to 23,000 square feet. The new facility provided more private patient care areas and a radiology suite equipped with state-of-the-art technology for quicker and more effective imaging. Four fully equipped resuscitation rooms improved Providence's ability to respond should a major disaster occur in the area. Other hospital upgrades included renovation of the intensive care unit and patient rooms. Also, Providence added a new Breast Center, as women in the surrounding communities experienced a high rate of breast cancer.

In Kansas City, a $65 million project involved construction of a new building at the St. John Medical Plaza. SCLHS planned to accommodate increased inpatient capacity, particularly to meet the demand for private rooms, emergency services, an intensive care unit, surgery and surgical patient care services, and obstetrics and gynecology.

Mary Tradii

PRINCIPAL SUBSIDIARIES

Caritas, Inc.; Exempla Healthcare (50%); Leaven Insurance Company, Ltd.

PRINCIPAL COMPETITORS

Catholic Health Initiatives; Sisters of Mercy Health System; University of Colorado Health Sciences Center.

FURTHER READING

Jaffe, Anna, "Downturn Will Further Stress Ailing Health Care Providers," *Business Journal Serving Metropolitan Kansas City*, March 9, 2001, p. 22.

———, "Mission and Money," *Business Journal Serving Metropolitan Kansas City*, March 23, 2001, p. 22.

Menninger, Bonar, "Sister's Calling; She Heads Two Hospitals During Hectic Times in Health Care," *Kansas City Business Journal*, February 3, 1995, p. 3.

SJM Holdings Ltd.

Unit 14-Unit 16, 15th Floor
China Merchants Tower
Shun Tak Centre
168-200 Connaught Road Central
Hong Kong
Telephone: (852) 3960 8000
Fax: (852) 3960 8111
Web site: http://www.sjmholdings.com

Public Company
Incorporated: 1962 as Sociedade de Turismo e Diveroes
de Macau
Employees: 19,335
Sales: HKD 27.99 billion (2008)
Stock Exchanges: Hong Kong
Ticker Symbol: 880
NAICS: 713990 All Other Amusement and Recreation
Industries

■ ■ ■

Once the dominant player in Macau (also spelled as Macao)'s casino gaming sector, SJM Holdings Ltd. remains a major force in what has become the world's largest casino market. SJM's main operating subsidiary is Sociedade de Jogos de Macau, S.A. (SJM), which itself was formed in 2001 following the loss of the casino monopoly held by Sociedade de Turismo e Diveroes de Macau (STDM) since 1962. SJM holds one of six casino concessions in Macau. The company operates 18 casinos, out of a total of 30 in Macau. SJM's operations include the historic Casino Lisboa and the company's flagship, the Grand Lisboa casino, opened in 2007, which includes the Grand Lisboa hotel complex, completed in December 2008. The company also operates four slot machine "lounges." In 2009, the company expects to open two new casinos, Oceanus, in Macau's Outer Harbour area, and L'Arc, on Macau Peninsula. In total SJM operates more than 1,400 gaming tables, especially baccarat, and more than 3,800 slot machines. SJM accommodated more than 15 million customers, primarily from Hong Kong and mainland China. Led by founder and Chairman Stanley Ho, widely credited for transforming Macau into one of the world's richest states, SJM Holdings has been listed on the Hong Kong Stock Exchange since 2008. In that year the company posted revenues of HKD 27.99 billion.

MACAU GAMBLING BACKGROUND IN THE 19TH CENTURY

Macau's history as a gambling center dates back to the middle of the 19th century. Once a major trading center for China and Japan, the Portuguese possession had found itself eclipsed following the Treaty of Nanking, which opened up Hong Kong, as well as five port cities on the Chinese mainland to foreign trade in 1842. Hong Kong especially rose to become the region's major trading and banking center. By the end of the decade, Macau's economy had gone into severe decline, while the population on the tiny 11-mile-long possession had begun a mass exodus to Hong Kong and other destinations.

In order to revive Macau's flagging economy, its Portuguese governors decided to focus on developing

COMPANY PERSPECTIVES

OUR MISSION: In 1962, Dr. Stanley Ho promised: "Our purpose is to bring a new prosperity to Macau and to improve the welfare and living standards of its citizens." History shows that Dr. Ho has made good on his promise. Today, Macau has one of the highest per-capita GDP levels in Asia and in the world.

As Macau enters a new historical era, our goal is to expand and further develop our operations, while retaining advantages of local knowledge. In doing so, we will continue to promote the sustainable prosperity of Macau, the home and origin of over 90% of our employees.

We recognize that if SJM and our shareholders are to prosper, the foundations of our prosperity must be strong, and so we continue to strengthen those foundations.

activities, including gambling, and the trade in opium and "coolies" (indentured servants), that remained banned in Hong Kong and China. While gambling had been present in one form or another since Macau came under Portugal's control in the 17th century, the new legislation created a gaming tax. Passed in 1847, the gaming laws provided an important source of revenue for Macau's government.

The first licenses for Fan Tan, a popular Chinese betting game, were given out in the early 1850s. By the end of the decade, there were more than 200 Fan Tan stalls operating in Macau's markets, streets, and other locations. In their quest for revenues, Macau's governors did not stop at gaming, but also legalized the coolie trade, as well as making the sale and use of opium legal in the territory. Often, these activities, as well as prostitution and the trade in contraband, became closely intertwined with the gambling sector. The coolie trade was later banned by the Portuguese crown, however.

Macau's position as the region's major gaming center became affirmed after the Hong Kong authorities banned gambling on the island in 1871. Similarly, the Imperial Chinese government remained hostile to gambling. As a result, Macau's gaming revenues continued to grow. By 1900, more than 70 percent of the territory's revenues came from gambling. Much of the rest was provided by taxes on the opium trade.

ORIGINS OF A MONOPOLY IN 1930

The move toward Macau's modern casino industry began in the 1930s as the Portuguese government established greater control over the gambling sector. Control of the possession's gambling activities had been taken by a handful of often interrelated groups. These groups generally focused on traditional types of gambling, although casino gambling had begun to rise in popularity in the years following World War I. In 1930, the government decided to establish a casino gaming monopoly, which was awarded to the Hou Heng Company. Led by Fok Chi Ting, Hou Heng opened its first casinos at the famed Central Hotel and at the former Victoria Cinema.

Hou Heng pioneered modern casino operations in Macau. Instead of the rudimentary furnishings of the Fan Tan stalls, Hou Heng's casinos offered more luxurious surroundings. The company's casinos also offered free cigarettes, as well as fruits and snacks to its customers, and became the first to provide entertainment, in the form of Chinese operas. In order to bring wealthy patrons from Hong Kong and the mainland, Hou Heng also provided free ferry tickets.

In 1937, the Macau government decided to extend the gaming monopoly, passing a decree that gave the monopoly control over a wider variety of game types. The casino monopoly was then transferred to a new company, Companhia Tai Heng (also spelled as Tai Xing) in 1937. Tai Heng, which was led by Fu Tak Iong, head of one of the territory's wealthiest families, and Kou Ho Neng, launched a refurbishing of the Central Hotel, which became its flagship casino and the largest in Macau. The renovated casino included Baccarat tables, which had rapidly become the most popular game in Macau.

Tai Heng's exploitation of the casino monopoly remained rather modest, however. Indeed, the company later faced criticism for having been too conservative in its operations, focusing largely on traditional Chinese betting games, and not fully exploiting the potential of its casino monopoly. The creation of the Communist state in mainland China, which reinforced that country's own anti-gaming laws, and the emergence of Hong Kong as one of the world's financial capitals, had both provided strong growth opportunities for gaming in Macau.

RAGS TO RICHES CASINO MAGNATE IN 1962

In the postwar era, however, Macao's casino industry had begun to decline. This was in large part because of

KEY DATES

1962: Sociedade de Turismo e Diveroes de Macau (STDM), led by Stanley Ho, wins the Macau casino monopoly and opens its first casino, Estoril.
1970: STDM opens its flagship Lisboa casino and hotel.
2001: STDM forms Sociedade de Jogos de Macau SA (SJM) to operate its casinos ahead of the loss of its monopoly in 2002.
2006: STDM creates a new holding company, SJM Holdings Ltd., for SJM's operations.
2008: SJM Holdings goes public with a listing on the Hong Kong Stock Exchange.

the death of Fu Tak Iong. Tai Heng suffered from a lack of direction, and by the beginning of the 1960s had shut down the hotel operations of its Central Hotel casino flagship. By then, the period of Tai Heng's original monopoly concession was coming to an end.

In 1961, the governor of Macau, Jaime Silvério Marques, declared that the territory had adopted the designation as a "permanent gaming region." This became a central part of the government's new policy to establish the territory as both a major gaming and tourism center. The government passed new legislation, now defining gaming as: "Any game with results that are unpredictably and randomly generated and won purely by one's luck."

The Macau government then canceled the remainder of Tai Heng's monopoly and announced that it was opening the concession to new bidders. Tai Heng attempted to remain in the game, launching its own bid for the new concession. In the end, however, the company lost out to a newcomer, a Hong Kong-based consortium led by Stanley Ho.

Ho represented something of a rags to riches story. Ho was born in 1921 in Hong Kong to the wealthy Ho Tung family, which had long been connected to the Jardine trading house. Yet Ho's father had gone bankrupt with the Great Depression, abandoning the family and leaving them penniless.

Ho received a scholarship to study at the University of Hong Kong, then moved to Macau at the age of 22 to take a job with a Japanese import-export company. Ho's fluency in English, Japanese, and Portuguese quickly enabled him to rise to a partnership position with that company. During World War II, Ho set up his own business smuggling luxury items between China and Macau, and famously won a reward of HKD 1 million for thwarting a pirate attack. Into the postwar period, Ho used the reward to establish his first fortune in kerosene sales and especially in the booming Hong Kong construction sector.

BUILDING A GAMING CAPITAL

Ho teamed up with several other prominent Macau and Hong Kong figures, including brother-in-law Teddy Yip and Yip Hon, who had worked for Tai Heng in the 1930s before opening his own casino in prewar Shanghai. Together, they launched a winning bid for nearly $500,000 to take over the casino monopoly. Ho and partners then founded Sociedade de Turismo e Diversoes de Macao (STDM), promising to revitalize Macau's gaming market. STDM then controlled the concession with a 50-year term.

STDM quickly fulfilled its promise, taking over the Central Hotel and expanding the casino to include a wider range of gaming tables, including roulette, blackjack, and other Western-style games. STDM then opened its first new casino, Casino Estoril, by the end of 1962. Ho, who gained sole control of the company in the 1970s, also began planning the company's first flagship location, the Lisboa casino and hotel complex, which opened in 1970 (and was later featured in the James Bond film *The Man with the Golden Gun*).

Importantly, Ho had also founded another company, Shun Tak Holdings, which modernized Macau's ferry services in the early 1960s. Shun Tak invested in a fleet of high-speed modern hydrofoils, which cut the trip from Hong Kong to Macau from four hours to less than one. Later Shun Tak added helicopter service as well.

Ho is also credited with creating Macau's VIP gaming segment. As demand for ferry services grew in the 1970s, Ho noticed the appearance of a number of scalpers who would buy ferry tickets to sell at inflated prices. Ho reached an agreement with the scalpers, allowing them to organize junkets, usually among high-rollers, and providing them with private gaming areas in his casinos. In exchange, STDM would collect a percentage of the gains in the VIP rooms. The system soon evolved into a major proportion of STDM's gaming revenues.

FACING THE LOSS OF A MONOPOLY IN 2002

Macau's casino sector took off especially strongly in the 1980s, emerging as the Asian region's gambling capital. STDM responded to the increasing demand by opening a string of casinos throughout Macau. By the late 1980s, tiny Macau, with a population of only half a million, featured among the world's wealthiest in terms of per-capita revenues, and Stanley Ho had become one of the world's richest individuals.

The Portuguese government's agreement to hand over Macau to China in 1999 set the stage for the next phase in Macau's gaming industry. The Chinese government, while allowing legalized gambling to continue, announced its intention to end the monopoly over the sector. This move was carried out in 2002, when the government tendered bids for six casino concessions.

STDM had prepared for this eventuality, regrouping its casino holdings into a new company, Sociedade de Jogos de Macau, S.A. (SJM), created in 2001. SJM successfully won its bid for one of the Macau casino concessions the following year, and the Ho family remained a dominant presence in Macau's casino industry. SJM maintained its position as the leading player on the island, while members of Ho's family also held key positions in two other casino concessions awarded by the government.

SJM started out with 11 casinos in operation. The company quickly launched plans to expand its empire ahead of the appearance of new rivals, and particularly the arrival of major foreign casino operators. By the middle of the decade, SJM had expanded its operations to include 16 casinos, as well as a number of smaller operations focused on slot machines.

FIGHTING BACK IN 2009

Inevitably, SJM lost market share, as new players, including the Sands Macao, the Wynn Macau, and others helped to expand the territory's range of casinos. By the end of the decade, more than a dozen competing casinos had opened. The result was a surge in total gaming revenues, positioning Macau as the world's leading casino market, ahead of Las Vegas, by 2006.

SJM fought back, launching construction of a new flagship hotel and casino complex, the Grand Lisboa, situated across the street from the original Lisboa. The casino portion was completed by early 2007; the complex's hotel, after facing a series of bureaucratic delays, finally opened its doors in December 2008. Also during this time, the company opened a second new casino, the Ponte 16.

In the meantime, Stanley Ho, then in his mid-80s, had recognized that in order to survive the new competitive era the group would be required to make a massive investment in new and upgraded casino operations. SJM began preparing to go public, creating a

new holding company for the purpose, SJM Holdings Ltd. This process was held up, however, by a series of lawsuits from Ho's estranged sister, Winnie. By the time SJM finally completed its initial public offering (IPO), in July 2008, the market had begun to shift amid the growing global economic collapse. As a result, the IPO raised far less than the company had originally hoped.

Undaunted, SJM continued to make progress with its expansion plans. The company launched two new casino projects, the Oceanus, located in Macau's Outer Harbour area, and L'Arc, located on Macau Peninsula. Both establishments were expected to be in operation by 2009. The company also announced plans to buy the historic Casino Lisboa site, which was still owned by STDM, and redevelop it into a HKD 12 billion casino, hotel, residential, and commercial complex. In March 2009, the company was forced to put that plan on hold, however, amid the continued economic downturn.

Nonetheless, hope appeared on the horizon that year as the Chinese government announced its intention to eliminate travel restrictions for mainland residents to Macau. Previously, residents had been limited to just four trips per year. By February 2009, the Macau city officials had reached a travel agreement with Guangdong Province. SJM, which remained the largest and financially strongest in the Macau casino market, looked forward to new growth in the territory's gaming market in the near future.

M. L. Cohen

PRINCIPAL SUBSIDIARIES

Brilliant Sky Investments Limited (British Virgin Islands); Honour State International Limited (British Virgin Islands); Nam Van Lake View Investment Limited; Pier 16–Entertainment Group Corporation Limited; Pier 16–Property Development Limited; Sociedade de Jogos de Macau, S.A.

PRINCIPAL OPERATING UNITS

Casino Grand Lisboa; VIP Gaming; Mass Market Table Gaming; Slot Machine.

PRINCIPAL COMPETITORS

Galaxy Entertainment Group Ltd.; Pico Far East Holdings Ltd.; Melco International Development Ltd.; ENM Holdings Ltd.; Sino Resources Group Ltd.; Future Bright Holdings Ltd.

FURTHER READING

Bagrov, Yuri, "Ho in $1bn Spree on Casinos," *Standard*, August 13, 2004.

Fallows, James, "Macau's Big Gamble," *Atlantic,* September 2007.

Gough, Neil, "Ho Says SJM Financially Solid, Projects on Track," *South China Morning Post,* January 20, 2009.

———, "SJM Boss Has the Skills to Deliver Counterpunch," *South China Morning Post,* September 15, 2008.

———, "SJM Scraps Plan to Redevelop Lisboa Casino," *South China Morning Post,* March 24, 2009.

———, "SJM Surges to Record Close on Positive Ratings," *South China Morning Post,* May 28, 2009.

Lau, Justine, and Tom Mitchell, "Gamble Pays Off for Ho As SJM Profit Rises 8%," *Financial Times,* September 22, 2008, p. 20.

Li, Sandy, "Ho Subsidiary Confident of Winning Macau Concession," *South China Morning Post,* February 6, 2002.

Lintner, Bertil, "Stanley Ho's Luck Turns Sour," *Far Eastern Economic Review,* May 2007.

Mitchell, Tom, "Golden Dome Opens Doors to High Rollers," *Financial Times,* February 12, 2007, p. 25.

———, "Ho to Rebuild His Gaming Image out of Lisboa's Ashes," *Financial Times,* January 16, 2008, p. 24.

"Playing a Poor Hand," *Economist,* July 4, 2008.

"SJM Holdings Lists on HKSE," *AsiaLaw,* September 2008.

"Stanley Ho: The King of Gambling," *Casinoweb,* April 26, 2009.

Toh, Han Shih, "Macau Plays Fall on Grim Outlook," *South China Morning Post,* January 20, 2009.

Wong, Gillian, "Macau's Dominant Casino Operator Says Foreign Competition 'Not Welcome,'" *America's Intelligence Wire,* June 22, 2005.

Yi Hu, Fox, "Competition in Macau Gets Too Tough for Stanley Ho," *South China Morning Post,* August 12, 2006.

The Smith & Wollensky
Restaurant Group, Inc.

120 West 45th Street
New York, New York 10036
U.S.A.
Telephone: (212) 789-8100
Fax: (212) 302-8032
Web site: http://www.smithandwollenskysteak
houses.com

Private Company
Founded: 1977 as Smith & Wollensky
Employees: 1,676
Sales: $124.8 million (2008 est.)
NAICS: 722110 Full-Service Restaurants

■ ■ ■

The Smith & Wollensky Restaurant Group, Inc., owns
and operates high-priced restaurants in New York City,
Chicago, Las Vegas, Boston, Miami Beach, Philadelphia,
and several other cities. Founded by Alan Stillman, who
originated the T.G.I. Friday's restaurant chain, the
company is best known for its Smith & Wollensky steak
house in Manhattan. Formerly operating as The New
York Restaurant Group Inc., the company adopted its
current name in 1999. In 2007 it was acquired by Nick
Valenti and Joachim Splichal, in conjunction with the
private equity firm Bunker Hill Capital, for $94.6
million.

SMITH & WOLLENSKY AND
OTHERS: 1977–89

Alan Stillman was a salesman living on Manhattan's Upper East Side in the mid-1960s. Perceiving that the
many affluent unattached young people in the neighborhood needed more places to meet and mix, he took a
lease on a rundown bar on First Avenue and 63rd Street
with $5,000 borrowed from his mother and opened
what is widely recognized as the first singles bar, which
he called T.G.I. Friday's. Stillman opened, with partners,
about a dozen other Friday's in other cities, as well as
several Manhattan restaurants with names such as
Tuesday's, Wednesday's, and Thursday's. In the mid-
1970s he sold his share of the Friday's chain, reportedly
for $1 million, to Carlson Companies, except for the
original restaurant and building, which he had
purchased. Stillman sold the original restaurant in 1987
for a reported $3.8 million.

By this time Stillman had turned to serving a more
mature, and more affluent, clientele. In 1977 he
purchased Manny Wolf's, a restaurant in a landmark
1897 building on Third Avenue at 49th Street, and
converted it into a steak house named, for reasons still
obscure, Smith & Wollensky. The restaurant was not an
instant success, and in spite of gimmicks such as slices
of roast beef offered to passersby, few people entered at
first. "We came very, very close to selling," Stillman
recalled to Pamela Kruger of the *New York Times* in
1993.

Instead, Stillman went back to the investors for
money, added a 100-seat lower-priced grill next door,
and launched an effective advertising campaign. Gael

COMPANY PERSPECTIVES

Smith & Wollensky is America's premier traditional steakhouse, committed to providing outstanding hospitality and delivering the best steaks that are U.S. D.A. Prime and dry-aged for tenderness and flavor.

Greene, the restaurant critic for *New York* who rated Smith & Wollensky last among the ten steak houses she reviewed in late 1978, conceded, "The house is often crowded. The faces are young and seem happy." By 1984 the restaurant, several times refurbished and enlarged since its opening, was worthy of inclusion in *Gourmet,* where Jay Jacobs noted, "Typically, the place is about as serene as an ordinary day in a boiler factory." He called the meats and fish "top-quality stuff ... served in massive portions, and with very few exceptions ... prepared precisely as they should be."

By 1990 Smith & Wollensky was a smashing success, perhaps "not the best steakhouse in town," wrote restaurant reviewer Bryan Miller of the *New York Times,* "but it is probably the busiest. ... Smith & Wollensky is an efficient feeding machine ... that churns out more than 700 meals daily." By this time the 380-seat restaurant was more than a steak house. Although steak and prime rib continued to be best-selling individual entrées, seafood made up 40 percent of the menu. Sales volume, including the adjoining grill, came to $17 million in 1989, with the average check for the main room at $38 for lunch and $50 for dinner.

Stillman opened two more midtown Manhattan restaurants in the early 1980s. The Post House, launched in 1980, was a steak and chop house with an American theme. Restaurant reviewer Moira Hodgson of the *New York Times* wrote, "This unpretentious yet elegant restaurant offers high quality, straightforward food in a thoroughly pleasant, relaxed atmosphere. ... This is not the fare of Puritan austerity. The proportions are enormous. ... The choices are the same at lunch and dinner, with prices identical, at expense-account level." The Manhattan Ocean Club, opened in 1984, was a high-end seafood restaurant. Reviewing it some months later for the *Times,* Marian Burros wrote that the eatery "is playing to large crowds, despite high prices and some inconsistencies."

By 1984 these three restaurants formed the New York Restaurant Group (NYRG), which in 1993 encompassed a complex series of partnerships, with Stillman as general partner and owner of 25 to 85 percent

of each restaurant. (NYRG, for example, was the operator, not owner, of Smith & Wollensky. Its owner, in 1999, was St. James Associates, in which Smith & Wollensky Operating Corp., controlled by Stillman, was a general partner.) Each of the group's nine managers had been with the company for more than a decade in 1989, and 25 of the 450 employees had shares in the enterprise. Michael Byrne, who began as a bartender, had been director of operations since 1980 and had been supervising Smith & Wollensky on a daily basis for more than ten years.

A lover of fine wines and artwork, as well as haute cuisine, Stillman's wife owned a vineyard near their Long Island oceanfront home, which had been featured on Robin Leach's television program *Lifestyles of the Rich and Famous.* The luxurious restaurants of NYRG reflected the Stillmans' epicurean tastes. Smith & Wollensky carried at least 45,000 bottles of wine. The Post House was decorated with American folk art, and the Manhattan Ocean Club displayed Stillman's collection of Pablo Picasso's pottery.

EXPANSION IN THE NINETIES

La Cité, described by NYRG as a Parisian café-style restaurant, opened in midtown Manhattan near the end of 1989. It was still struggling to make money in 1993, although Stillman had revised the menu, lowered prices, added a 70-seat grill, and shortened the name to simply Cité. Reviewing it late that year, Gael Greene approved the changes, noted a greater emphasis on meat and a longer wine list, and added, "I find it the handsomest steakhouse in town."

Park Avenue Café, characterized by the company as offering "cutting-edge new American cuisine in a café atmosphere," opened on the Upper East Side, but only a few blocks north of midtown, in 1992. It was under the direction of chef David Burke, who had been lured from River Café, his previous home, where he made a name for concoctions whimsical and even bizarre. Greene declared, "Burke's tornado of creativity is delivering mostly remarkable food," including a "swordfish chop" carved from the seldom-used collarbone and neck, house-smoked salmon atop corn blini, scallops on braised oxtail, and duck-and-chicken pie rich with wild mushrooms, asparagus, and potato in a biscuit-like crust. NYRG sold The Post House that year but continued to operate it under contract.

By 1993 Stillman was estimating that he was feeding one million people a year, with the dinner check at NYRG's five operations averaging at least $47.50 and perhaps as much as $60. Described by Kruger as "Using marketing savvy-street smarts and a Donald Trump–

sized ego," Stillman had built an organization that claimed to have annual sales of $42 million, including $19 million for Smith & Wollensky. More than $1 million a year was being spent on promotion, including full-page ads in the *Times, Forbes,* and *Fortune* and commercials on cable television. Stillman had employed at least four advertising agencies in the last five years and was fond of such publicity stunts as roasting an entire steer outside The Post House.

During twice-a-year Wine Week, beginning in 1986, his customers were offered a choice of free wines for sampling during lunch; at Cité the wine-dinner promotion was offered beginning at 8 P.M. to fill a room typically vacated by diners moving on to nearby theaters.

Park Avenue Café introduced a Chicago locale in 1994, closely duplicating the original, on the second floor of the Guest Quarters Suites hotel (later the Doubletree Guest Suites hotel). NYRG already had opened a more casual Mrs. Park's Tavern on the ground floor of the hotel. Both were later sold to Doubletree, but NYRG continued to operate them.

New York Restaurant Group, L.L.C., was formed in 1995 as a holding company for a series of partnerships and limited liability companies anchored by Stillman but involving as many as 40 investors. In early 1996 Stillman sold 23 percent of the company to Thomas H.

Lee Co., a Boston-based investment house, for an estimated $15 million. This sale wiped out the company's debt, according to Stillman, reduced the number of NYRG's investors to about ten, and provided the means for financing Stillman's plans to expand the group's operations to other cities.

In 1996 NYRG launched Maloney & Porcelli. Located close to Smith & Wollensky and named for two lawyers Stillman had hired to negotiate a liquor license, the new restaurant was essentially a steak house, although its pièce de résistance was a 2½-pound hunk of "crackling" pork shank that Corby Kummer of *New York* wrote "looks like a deflated soccer ball." The influence of Burke, corporate chef for all of the group's eateries, could be found in what Kummer called "lots of little tricks that make dinner seem like a long McDonald's birthday party for grown-ups," including "a mile-high slab of chocolate cake ... topped by a dark-chocolate crossbar supporting a big white-chocolate cow."

After what Stillman described as 16 or 17 years of trying, his Smith & Wollensky partners agreed to license the name to NYRG and allow expansion. The group then spent millions of dollars to convert a former seafood restaurant in Miami Beach into a replica of the original Smith & Wollensky. When it opened in late 1997, this branch had the largest seating capacity, 670, of any NYRG restaurant at the time. Other versions of Smith & Wollensky opened in 1998 in Chicago (overlooking the Chicago River), Las Vegas (on the Strip, with 675 seats), and New Orleans (on the site of a registered national landmark), followed by Washington, D.C., in 1999. All were owned by NYRG and were on leased property except for the New Orleans and Las Vegas sites. Appointed president of NYRG in 1998, James Dunn was in charge of opening the new restaurants. Byrne remained director of New York operations and was a limited partner in St. James Associates.

NEW YORK RESTAURANT GROUP IN 1999

New York Restaurant Group, Inc., was formed in 1997 by a merger with New York Restaurant Group, L.L.C. The cost of opening new restaurants threw this enterprise into the red, with a combined loss of almost $5.5 million from 1996 to 1998, despite the rise in revenues (for group-owned restaurants) to $52.8 million in the latter year. The long-term debt was $17.6 million. Counting restaurants operated but not owned by NYRG, sales came to $89 million. Sales of $24.7 million for the year ended June 28, 1999 made Smith & Wollensky's Manhattan site one of the highest-grossing single restaurant locations in the country.

Second place in revenues for this period, $10.3 million, belonged to Maloney & Porcelli. In third place, and first among NYRG-owned restaurants, was the Chicago Smith & Wollensky, followed by Cité, Manhattan Ocean Club, and Park Avenue Café. The Las Vegas Smith & Wollensky, although open for only the last seven months of this period, had sales of $7.9 million, the same amount as the Miami Beach Smith & Wollensky, which was open for the entire period. The average check per person in this period ranged from $73.60 at The Post House to $24.30 at Chicago's Park Avenue Café (including Mrs. Park's Tavern). NYRG was stocking 92,000 bottles of wine. Stillman held 30 percent of the company's shares and Lee held 23 percent in mid-1999.

Stillman planned to make an initial public offering (IPO) for the New York Restaurant Group, which he planned to rename, in the fall of 1999. The company issued a lengthy prospectus that reflected the complexity of its organization but postponed the offering because of lukewarm investor interest. While awaiting a new offering date, NYRG announced a venture in New York City's Plaza Hotel to create and run a new restaurant concept in the space previously taken by the Edwardian Room. It also was planning to open Smith & Wollensky units in Atlanta, Boston, and Philadelphia. A Maloney & Porcelli was scheduled to open in January 2000 in Washington, D.C.

NYRG rounded out 1999 by changing its name to The Smith & Wollensky Restaurant Group, Inc., and registering sales of $120 million, a 65 percent increase from 1998. As the company expanded, television advertising was used to promote its new locations in certain markets. By early 2001, plans were once again underway for an IPO. Smith & Wollensky revealed plans to sell five million shares on the NASDAQ, and generated $8.50 per share when the IPO was completed in May. Smith & Wollensky intended to use the proceeds to reduce its debts and add more restaurants to its chain, which included nine owned locations.

SILVER ANNIVERSARY

Smith & Wollensky celebrated its 25th anniversary in 2002. By September of the following year, the company carried a nationwide wine selection valued at $5 million, and poured an estimated 16,000 bottles during each of its Wine Week events. A major development unfolded at this time, when Smith & Wollensky announced it would stop offering foreign wines. This was a significant shift, considering the fact that when Smith & Wollensky opened its doors in 1977, some 90 of the wines it offered were imports. However, by 2002 American wines had grown to represent 65 percent of its list.

In a September 24, 2003, *New York Times* article, Alan Stillman played down suggestions that the move was a political one. "We came up with this idea long before the war in Iraq and tensions with France," he said. "We figured that we were a group of American steakhouses and that it made good sense to concentrate on American wines."

Developments continued into mid-decade. After a 20-year run, the Manhattan Ocean Club closed its doors on January 1, 2006. A new concept named Quality Meats, headed by Alan Stillman and his son, Michael, was scheduled to open in its place during the spring of that year, offering a selection of New American cuisine.

On January 12, 2007, Landry's Restaurants Inc. made an unsolicited acquisition bid for Smith & Wollensky, offering to acquire the company for approximately $64.4 million, or $7.50 per share. Led by the Houston, Texas, entrepreneur Tilman Fertitta, Landry's operated more than 300 different restaurants, including the Golden Nugget casino in Las Vegas, along with Landry's Seafood House, Chart House, Holiday Inn on the Beach, and Willie G's Seafood & Steak House. By this time, the original Smith & Wollensky location in New York remained one of the nation's largest-grossing à la carte restaurants.

Following its IPO in 2001, Smith & Wollensky's stock price had hovered around $5 per share. Word of the acquisition offer pushed the company's stock up 32 percent, to $7.45. A bidding war soon emerged when restaurateurs Nick Valenti (a longtime associate of Alan Stillman) and Joachim Splichal, in conjunction with the equity firm Bunker Hill Capital LP, offered to acquire Smith & Wollensky for $9.25 per share. Landry's responded with an offer to pay $9.75 per share, pushing the value of the deal to $84 million. Ultimately, Smith & Wollensky agreed to be acquired by Valenti and Splichal in May 2007 for $94.6 million. The deal was approved by the company's stockholders in August, and the merger was finalized on the 29th of that month.

NEW OWNERSHIP

Smith & Wollensky moved forward under the leadership of Valenti and Splichal. Following the acquisition, Stillman, who established a new business named Fourth Wall Restaurants, repurchased Park Avenue Summer and Quality Meats, and also secured management contracts for the well-known Smith & Wollensky Manhattan restaurant, as well as Maloney & Porcelli and the Post House.

Heading into 2008, Smith & Wollensky's new owners had their eyes on future expansion. Nationwide, several major metropolitan locations were being considered for Smith & Wollensky restaurants, or the company's smaller Wollensky's Grill concept. Expansion into Asia and Europe also was a possibility.

In 2004 Stillman began working with the Glide Foundation in San Francisco to host an annual luncheon at Smith & Wollensky in New York City to benefit the charity. In 2009 Zhao Danyang, winner of the charity auction and head of the Pureheart China Growth Investment Fund, parted with $2.11 million for a chance to dine with investment guru Warren Buffett at Smith & Wollensky.

Despite challenging economic times, Smith & Wollensky approached the 21st century's second decade with a strong brand name, restaurants in nine major cities, and the anticipation of its 35th anniversary in 2012.

Robert Halasz
Updated, Paul R. Greenland

PRINCIPAL COMPETITORS

Morton's Restaurant Group Inc.; Palm Management Corp.; Ruth's Hospitality Group Inc.

FURTHER READING

Agovino, Theresa, "Traveling Epicure Embarks on Bistro," *Crain's New York Business,* April 24, 1989, pp. 3, 49.

Battaglia, Andy, "David Burke," *Nation's Restaurant News,* January 1999, pp. 42, 44.

Beard, Alison, "Smith & Wollensky Tries for New IPO Restaurant Chain Hopes to Raise $50m," *Financial Times,* March 28, 2001.

"Bunker Hill Capital, Nick Valenti, and Joachim Splichal Complete the Acquisition of the Smith & Wollensky Restaurant Group," *Business Wire,* August 29, 2007.

Burros, Marian, "Down to the Sea on West 58th Street," *New York Times,* September 21, 1984, p. C20.

Frumkin, Paul, "Smith & Wollensky's $90 M Sale Marks Well-Done Power Play by Patina Group," *Nation's Restaurant News,* September 10, 2007.

———, "Stillman's NYRG Heeds Soft Market, Delays IPO," *Nation's Restaurant News,* October 11, 1999, pp. 1, 6.

Gault, Yolanda, "N.Y. Steak Man Wants More to Chew On," *Crain's New York Business,* March 29, 1993, pp. 3, 41.

Greene, Gael, "Little Chop Around the Corner," *New York,* February 4, 1992, p. 127.

———, "Prime Time: The Best Steaks in Town," *New York,* December 18, 1978, pp. 72, 76–77.

———, "Sizzling Steak Wars," *New York,* January 3, 1994, p. 29.

Hodgson, Moira, "Elegant, High-Quality New Steak House," *New York Times,* October 24, 1980, p. C20.

Jacobs, Jay, "Specialties de la Maison," *Gourmet,* September 1984, pp. 24, 26.

Kamen, Robin, "Insatiable Appetite," *Crain's New York Business,* February 12, 1996, pp. 1, 21.

Kruger, Pamela, "Selling New York on the $60 Dinner," *New York Times,* May 23, 1993, Sec. 3, p. 10.

Kummer, Corby, "Slab-Happy," *New York,* September 23, 1996, p. 103.

Miller, Bryan, "Smith & Wollensky," *New York Times,* March 30, 1990, p. C20.

Papiernik, Richard L., "NYRG Divulges Losses Linked to Expansion As IPO Awaits," *Nation's Restaurant News,* August 9, 1999, pp. 6, 111.

Prewitt, Milford, "Investment Firm Buys 25% of NY Restaurant Group," *Nation's Restaurant News,* January 8, 1996, pp. 1, 4.

Prial, Frank J., "A Red with the Steak? A White? A Blue?" *New York Times,* September 24, 2003.

———, "Restaurants That Pour Freely," *New York Times,* March 8, 1995, p. C9.

Sanders, Lisa, "New Eateries, Full Plate," *Crain's New York Business,* August 31, 1998, p. 15.

"Smith & Wollensky," *Nation's Restaurant News,* May 7, 1990, p. S25.

Strauss, Karya, "Smith & Wollensky Hits Big, NYRG Plans More Portfolio Expansions," *Nation's Restaurant News,* April 12, 1999, pp. 4, 90.

Walkup, Carolyn, "NY Restaurant Group Opens 1 Concept, Plans 2nd in Chi," *Nation's Restaurant News,* November 28, 1994, p. 7.

Snap-on Incorporated

————— ■ —————

2801 80th Street
Kenosha, Wisconsin 53143-5656
U.S.A.
Telephone: (262) 656-5200
Fax: (262) 656-5577
Web site: http://www.snapon.com

Public Company
Incorporated: 1920 as Snap-on Wrench Company
Employees: 11,500
Sales: $2.85 billion (2008)
Stock Exchanges: New York
Ticker Symbol: SNA
NAICS: 332212 Hand and Edge Tool Manufacturing;
333298 All Other Industrial Machinery
Manufacturing; 333991 Power-Driven Handtool
Manufacturing; 334515 Instruments for Measuring
and Testing Electricity and Electrical Signals

■ ■ ■

Snap-on Incorporated is one of the largest and most successful manufacturers and marketers of hand tools, power tools, tool storage equipment, diagnostic equipment and software, service and repair equipment and information products, and electronic parts catalogs in the United States. The company makes hand tools such as wrenches, sockets, pliers, ratchets, and screwdrivers; power tools such as sanders, polishers, and pneumatic (air), corded (electric), and cordless (battery) drills; and a host of other items such as wheel balancing and align-

ment equipment for cars, tool chests and cabinets for industrial and automotive storage applications, and engine and emission analyzing equipment. Snap-on markets its entire range of products through multiple channels, including franchisees, distributors, company-direct sales, and e-commerce. The company considers itself the originator of the mobile van method of marketing hand tools.

EARLY HISTORY

Snap-on Wrench Company was founded in 1920 by Joseph Johnson and William A. Seidemann. Prior to Johnson's idea for "interchangeable sockets," the socket wrenches used by mechanics were one-piece units. Professional auto mechanics quickly recognized the efficiency and flexibility that resulted from pairing many sockets with few handles. From the beginning, sales were generated by demonstrating the benefits of the novel tool sets directly to the customers. New tools were added to the line, and a catalog was published in 1923. By 1925, 165 salesmen were demonstrating and distributing Snap-on tools.

Stanton Palmer, a former factory sales representative, served as president of the corporation from 1921 until his death ten years later. At that time, Snap-on sought financial help from one of its principal creditors, Forged Steel Products Company, whose owner, William E. Myers, became Snap-on's new president. When Myers died in 1939, Johnson, the corporation's conceptual founder, became the president of both Snap-on and Forged Steel. That same year, Snap-on was taken public.

COMPANY PERSPECTIVES

To know Snap-on tools is to love Snap-on tools. The wide range of products that the Snap-on family of brands has available become the treasured objects for most every type of professional tool user. That's because employees in our company are obsessed with innovation. Never satisfied, designers, engineers, and machine operators are continuously looking for ways to improve the company's products.

The company was known at this time as Snap-on Tools, Inc., having reincorporated in the state of Delaware under that name in 1930; the firm was later renamed Snap-on Tools Corporation.

Under Johnson's leadership the sales force continued to grow. During World War II, when supplying the military's needs caused tool shortages in the civilian market, Snap-on began releasing available stock to its sales force, in an attempt to maintain goodwill with the civilian customer base. By 1945 all salesmen were carrying stock and making immediate deliveries to their customers. Shortly thereafter, Snap-on made each seller an independent businessperson in an assigned territory.

THE POSTWAR ERA OF GROWTH AND PROSPERITY

Subsidiaries in Canada and Mexico aided growth in the 1950s. The Snap-on product line also was expanded. Corporate acquisitions of specialized companies brought products that addressed the mechanic's need for increasingly complex diagnostic tune-up and maintenance equipment. During this period, Snap-on also acquired its system of branches (which had operated previously as independent outlets). Branch acquisitions permitted Snap-on greater control over the marketing and distribution systems.

Victor M. Cain became president upon Johnson's retirement in 1959. In 1965 a Snap-on branch was opened in the United Kingdom. An important patent on the "flank drive" design of wrenches was also awarded in 1965, after years of legal debate. The "flank drive" design produced wrenches with a superior grip, less likely to round the corners of 12-point fasteners under high-torque conditions.

GROWTH AND EXPANSION IN THE SEVENTIES AND EIGHTIES

Snap-on's growth was dramatic in the period that followed. Sales increased from $66.2 million in 1969 to $373.6 million in 1979, while profits increased from $6 million to $42.6 million. Norman E. Lutz became president in 1974, overseeing growth in the worldwide sales force to more than 3,000. In 1978 Lutz became chair and CEO, and Edwin C. Schindler became president. That year Snap-on stock was first listed on the New York Stock Exchange.

The early 1980s saw rapid changes in the company's management. In 1982 Lutz retired and was replaced by Schindler as chairperson, while William B. Rayburn became president; the following year Schindler died, and Rayburn became the company's chairperson and CEO. A slight decrease in both revenue and earnings in 1982 was attributed to that year's recession. Snap-on examined operations and took measures to improve profitability through reducing expenses as well as marketing more aggressively. Even in this disappointing year, however, net earnings were significant at $37.3 million on $430.5 million in net sales, or 8.7 percent of sales.

Snap-on continued to cultivate its image as the foremost supplier of well-crafted products and customer-oriented service. During the 1980s, Snap-on became the sole supplier of tools to NASA for the space shuttles. In 1984 Snap-on acquired an equity stake of approximately 34 percent in Balco, Inc., a developer of engine diagnostic and wheel service equipment. The frequency of visits to customers had increased to weekly in some cases, and the vans carried $50,000 to $200,000 of hand tools and equipment inventory. Additional services provided by dealers, such as cleaning previously purchased Snap-on tools every six months, allowed dealers to identify and recommend replacement of worn-out tools. Although Snap-on was beginning to face competition from a variety of sources, including Sears, Roebuck & Co., the Mac Tools subsidiary of Stanley Works, the Matco Tools subsidiary of Chicago Pneumatic, and various Japanese companies, Snap-on was able to maintain its premium prices because of the services it offered and the customer relationships in place.

In October 1986 *Forbes* estimated that "with its long head start and 49 percent of the market, Snap-on has as many dealers tooling about as all of its competitors combined." At this time, Snap-on was distributing two million catalogs each year. The 350-page catalogs were considered Snap-on's "most valuable single marketing tool" by Rayburn, who told *Forbes* that "our industrial people leave them with buyers, purchasing agents and requisition people. Our dealers leave them

KEY DATES

1920: Joseph Johnson and William A. Seidemann form Snap-on Wrench Company to produce and market interchangeable sockets and wrench handles.

1930: Company is reincorporated as Snap-on Tools, Inc.; company name is later changed to Snap-on Tools Corporation.

1939: Company goes public.

1978: Company's stock begins trading on the New York Stock Exchange.

1991: Robert A. Cornog is brought onboard as chairman, president, and CEO.

1994: Company is renamed Snap-on Incorporated.

1998: Major restructuring is launched.

1999: Snap-on acquires the saw and tool business of the Swedish firm Sandvik AB.

2001: Dale F. Elliott begins brief stint at the helm emphasizing operations consolidation and cost-cutting.

2004: Jack D. Michaels is named chairman and CEO.

2006: Snap-on acquires the business solutions unit of ProQuest Company.

2007: Company promotes Nicholas T. Pinchuk to president and CEO.

with shop owners and mechanics. When there is a mechanical problem, they look in the catalog for a tool that can solve it."

In 1988 Marion Gregory, the new chairperson, faced a new challenge for Snap-on. An increasing number of lawsuits were filed by former and current dealers in state courts around the United States. The claims included allegations of misrepresentation, contract violations, and causing emotional distress. In an early case, George Owens, a former dealer, claimed that he was pressured to divide his territory with another dealer. A California jury awarded $6.9 million in damages, an amount later reduced in settlement. Other lawsuits claimed misrepresentation of potential profits to dealers, automatic billing of dealers by Snap-on for certain tools provided to the dealers for promotional purposes, and pressure to extend credit.

Snap-on's general policy was to consider settlement as preferable to litigation; the company accrued or paid a total of $7.9 million, $16.6 million, and $16.2 million for litigation-related costs in 1989, 1990, and 1991,

respectively, before "determining to pursue more cases to final determination and apply a more stringent policy toward settlement," per Snap-on's 1991 annual report. Snap-on also asserted claims of its own against its insurance carriers with respect to coverage on certain dealer claims.

CHANGES UNDER CORNOG

In 1991 Robert A. Cornog, formerly the president of steel cable manufacturer Macwhyte Company, became chairman, president, and CEO of Snap-on, ending a long tradition of filling these positions from within the company. Also that year, Snap-on began to enroll all new U.S. dealers as franchisees and offered the option of applying for a franchise to existing dealers. Snap-on viewed the conversion to a franchise program as an opportunity to establish greater control over the marketing and business activities of its dealers. The program was not designed to increase revenues, and costs in new group insurance programs, stock purchase programs, and special volume-purchase discounts were expected to offset franchise fees. As an inducement to convert, Snap-on waived initial and some recurring franchise fees for existing dealers. Nonetheless, most existing dealers did not elect to apply for franchises.

Snap-on issued common stock valued at approximately $21.2 million to acquire the remaining interest in Balco, Inc., in 1991. The corporation also announced its intention to consolidate product inventories from 51 branch warehouses to four regional distribution centers. By this time, operations were conducted in subsidiaries located in Canada, the United Kingdom, Mexico, Germany, Australia, Japan, and the Netherlands. Sales in other countries accounted for 17 percent of total revenue but only 5 percent of operating income.

Net earnings, which had been down from earlier levels for three years in a row, were still $34.3 million on net revenue of $881.7 million or 8.3 percent of net revenue in 1991, despite the recession in the United States and Canada. This translated to an after-tax return on average shareholders' equity of 11.4 percent, considerably below the 18 to 23 percent level that Snap-on had enjoyed from 1983 to 1989. In response, Snap-on reorganized its management structure to allow separate accountability for its three business areas: finance, manufacturing and technology, and marketing and distribution.

As Snap-on management looked to the end of the 20th century, management recognized that the corporation would have to adjust to fundamental changes in its business to achieve the high levels of return it sought. Believing that improved automotive quality and warranty programs had caused slower repair volume growth and had shifted work to the auto dealers, Snap-on determined to develop new products and services for existing customers while reaching out to the new markets as well.

Snap-on management began to consider whether other services, such as a credit card for general use, might profitably be offered to its credit-proven customers, who were in weekly contact with Snap-on dealers. Outside sourcing of products, which accounted for 35 percent of Snap-on's manufacturing, was considered an opportunity for cost savings. International and industrial markets were seen as offering a possible means toward the growth to which Snap-on had always been accustomed. Around this same time, the company decided a name change was in order to reflect its expanding product line and wider customer base. Thus, in April 1994 shareholders approved the renaming of the firm from Snap-on Tools Corporation to Snap-on Incorporated.

In maintaining its strategy in searching for new markets, during the late 1990s management at Snap-on decided to enter into a licensing agreement with Stylus Writing Instruments to manufacture and market office products under its own brand name. Snap-on office tools, such as staples, staple removers, and tape dispensers, were marketed with the designation, "Made in the USA." In reaching the agreement, management at Stylus promised that all Snap-on office tools would be "ergonomic and durable, with unique styling and colors."

LATE-CENTURY LAUNCH OF KOBALT, RESTRUCTURING, AND MAJOR ACQUISITION

At the same time, Snap-on made an about-face and ventured into direct consumer retail sales by reaching a private-label pact with home improvement retailer Lowe's Companies, Inc. Inaugurating a private-label tool line known as Kobalt, the two companies positioned themselves to compete against Sears' Craftsman brand, Wal-Mart's Popular Mechanics, and Home Depot's Husky brand-name tool line. The expansion into retail sales was expected to increase the company's 1997 revenues of $1.7 billion by at least 5 percent. Because sales of Snap-on hand tools were estimated to increase at 1.5 percent, management considered the entry into retail sales well worth the effort and risk.

In the summer of 1998, Snap-on announced a comprehensive plan to restructure its entire operation,

including the elimination of about 1,000 jobs, to increase profitability and cut annual costs by $60 million. The plan, carried out through the end of 1999, included the closure of six manufacturing facilities and seven warehouses, the discontinuation of a number of product lines, the consolidation of some business units, and the closure of more than 40 small sales offices throughout North America and Europe. Pretax restructuring charges totaling $149.9 million led to a net loss for 1998 of $4.8 million, the first full-year red ink in Snap-on history. The results for 1998 were further undermined by difficulties with the installation of a major new back-office computer system. Snafus with the new system resulted in tens of millions of dollars in lost sales.

Snap-on significantly expanded its overseas business in September 1999 when it acquired the saw and tool business of the Swedish firm Sandvik AB for about $380 million. This business, which Snap-on renamed Bahco Group AB, manufactured handheld saws and tools for professional users at 11 plants in Sweden, Germany, Portugal, France, England, the United States, and Argentina. Some analysts were concerned about how well this business fit with Snap-on's existing operations given that only about 40 percent of Bahco's products were sold in Snap-on's core industrial and automotive markets. Instead, the majority of Bahco's sales stemmed from woodworking and landscaping tools for construction and agricultural customers. In any event, this deal increased the portion of revenues Snap-on generated outside the United States from 30 percent in 1998 to more than 37 percent in 2000. The deal also helped boost the firm's overall sales by nearly 23 percent during this same period.

SEEKING IMPROVED EARNINGS IN THE EARLY 21ST CENTURY

As part of a larger Internet initiative, Snap-on in 2000 launched a new public web site featuring an online catalog with more than 14,000 products and enabling customers to order products 24 hours a day, seven days a week. The initiative also included the introduction of a dealer sales portal that provided another avenue for interaction between dealers and their customers.

Although Snap-on had bounced back from its 1998 loss with profitable years in both 1999 and 2000, a number of shareholders had grown disenchanted with the firm's earnings and with Cornog's tenure at the helm, during which time a number of acquisitions had been completed, many for seemingly little gain. By November 2000, one major shareholder was calling for the company's sale or merger with another firm. That same month, in a development Snap-on claimed was unrelated to the investor unrest, Cornog announced his intention to retire early the following year. In April 2001 Dale F. Elliott was named president and CEO, and he added the chairmanship as well a year later. Elliott had joined Snap-on in 1995, serving as head of the diagnostics and industrial division since October 1998.

During what turned out to be a brief period at the helm, Elliott focused on consolidating Snap-on's operations and cutting costs in an attempt to boost earnings. Over the course of three and a half years, Snap-on closed or consolidated more than 50 facilities and trimmed its workforce by nearly 20 percent, to around 11,500 employees. Among the closures were plants in Carmel, Indiana, and Kenosha, Wisconsin. The Kenosha plant closed after nearly 75 years of operation, although Snap-on's headquarters remained in that town. Elliott also thoroughly overhauled the management ranks, replacing about two-thirds of Snap-on's managers.

Elliott resigned suddenly in November 2004 having failed to improve earnings, although the cost of the various restructuring efforts tended to offset any resultant gains, at least in the short run. His successor, Jack D. Michaels, was a longtime member of Snap-on's board of directors. Following the leadership change, alterations were made to the company's dealer franchisee system to make the franchisees more efficient. Snap-on also implemented improvements to its supply chain to fill orders more quickly and efficiently. In addition, the company opened its first factory in China as it continued an ongoing effort to shift some of its production to lower-cost regions. In 2007 the Johnson City, Tennessee, factory was closed. This left Snap-on with just three U.S. hand-tool plants, in Milwaukee; Elkmont, Alabama; and Elizabethton, Tennessee.

In the meantime, in November 2006, Snap-on spent approximately $522 million and assumed $19 million in debt to acquire the business solutions unit of ProQuest Company. Renamed Snap-on Business Solutions, the acquired business specialized in providing parts schematics and catalogs to automobile and power-equipment dealers. This purchase thus enabled Snap-on to provide original equipment manufacturers and their dealerships with complete parts and service technology systems.

By the end of 2007, Snap-on was clearly back on track having posted record full-year earnings of $181.2 million on best-ever sales of $2.84 billion. Late that year, Nicholas T. Pinchuk was promoted from president and COO to president and CEO, with Michaels remaining chairman. Pinchuk had joined Snap-on in June 2002 as head of its worldwide commercial and industrial unit. Pinchuk added the chairmanship to his duties in April 2009. During 2008 the company achieved another record earnings total of $236.7 million, although the deteriorating economic environment led to little growth in sales. As the economic struggles carried on into 2009, undermining in particular sales of Snap-on's bigger-ticket items, such as tool storage and under-vehicle equipment, the company remained focused on process improvement and cost-reduction initiatives. In search of avenues for growth, Snap-on was looking to emerging markets in Asia, particularly China, and eastern Europe and was in the midst of expanding its manufacturing capacity in these regions.

Marcia McDermott
Updated, Thomas Derdak; David E. Salamie

PRINCIPAL SUBSIDIARIES

Equipment Services, Inc.; IDSC Holdings LLC; Mitchell Repair Information Company, LLC; Sioux Tools, Inc.; Snap-on Business Solutions (Alison) Inc.; Snap-on Business Solutions Inc.; Snap-on Capital Corp.; Snap-on Global Holdings, Inc.; Snap-on Illinois Holdings LLC; Snap-on Illinois Services LLC; Snap-on Logistics Company; Snap-on SecureCorp, Inc.; Snap-on Tools Company LLC; Snap-on Tools International LLC; Bahco Bisov Svenska AB (Sweden); SNA Europe (Benelux) B.V. (Netherlands); OOO Bahco Tools International (Russia); Bahco Magyarország Szerszámkereskedelmi Kft. (Hungary); SNA Europe–Poland Sp zo.o; Bahco Vaerktøj A/S (Denmark); Bahco Verktøej A/S (Norway); Blackhawk, S.A. (France); Deville SA (France); Eurotools France S.A.R.L.; Eurotools Investigación (Spain); FE Bahco Tools (Belarus); Hangzhou Wanda Air Tools (China); Hofmann Japan, K.K.; Hofmann Sopron Kft (Hungary); JV Bahco Bisov (Belarus); Kapman AB (Sweden); NovGaro (Russia); Proco, S.L. (Spain); Shucheng Wanda Tools Co. Ltd. (China); SN SecureCorp Dublin Limited (Ireland); SN SecureCorp Sales Limited (UK); SNA E (Australia) Pty Ltd.; SNA E Endustriyel Mamuller Ticaret Limited Sirketi (Turkey); SNA Europe (Finland) Oy; SNA Europe (Industrias) SA (Portugal); SNA Europe (Industries) AB (Sweden); SNA Europe (Italia) SpA (Italy); SNA Europe (Services) AB (Sweden); SNA Europe (Sweden) AB; SNA Europe Industries Iberia S.A. (Spain); SNA Europe SAS (France); SNA Germany GmbH; SNA Solutions UK Ltd.; SNA-E (Argentina) S.A.; SNA-E Chile Ltda.; Snap-on (Thailand) Company Limited; Snap-on Africa (Proprietary) Limited (South Africa); Snap-on Asia Manufacturing (Kunshan) Co. Ltd. (China); Snap-on Business Solutions Limited (UK); Snap-on Business Solutions Japan Company; Snap-on Business Solutions GmbH (Germany); Snap-on Business Solutions SRL (Italy); Snap-on Business Solutions SARL (France);

Snap-on Business Solutions SA (Spain); Snap-on Credit Canada Ltd.; Snap-on do Brasil Comercio e Industria Ltda. (Brazil); Snap-on Equipment Europe Ltd. (Ireland); Snap-on Equipment France, S.A.; Snap-on Equipment GmbH (Germany); Snap-on Equipment Ltd. (UK); Snap-on Equipment S.r.l. (Italy); Snap-on Europe Holding B.V. (Netherlands); Snap-on Finance B.V. (Netherlands); Snap-on Finance UK Limited; Snap-on Holdings AB (Sweden); Snap-on Investment Limited (UK); Snap-on Tools (Australia) Pty. Ltd.; Snap-on Tools B.V. (Netherlands); Snap-on Tools China Trading (Shanghai) Co. Ltd.; Snap-on Tools Hong Kong Limited; Snap-on Tools Italia S.r.l. (Italy); Snap-on Tools Japan, K.K.; Snap-on Tools Korea Ltd.; Snap-on Tools of Canada Ltd.; Snap-on Tools Private Limited (India); Snap-on Tools Singapore Pte Ltd.; Snap-on Trading (Shanghai) Co., Ltd. (China); Snap-on U.K. Holdings Limited; Snap-on/Sun de Mexico, S.A. de C.V.; Sun Electric Austria GmbH; Snap-on Business Solutions India Private Limited; Wanda Snap-on (Zhejiang) Co., Ltd. (China); Z International SAS (France).

PRINCIPAL OPERATING UNITS

Snap-on Tools Group; Commercial and Industrial Group; Diagnostics and Information Group.

PRINCIPAL COMPETITORS

The Stanley Works; Danaher Corporation; Cornwell Quality Tools Company; Sears Brands, LLC; The Home Depot, Inc.; Lowe's Companies, Inc.; Genuine Parts Company; AutoZone, Inc.; The Pep Boys—Manny, Moe & Jack; MEDCO; Integrated Supply Network, Inc.; Ingersoll-Rand Company Limited; The Black & Decker Corporation; Makita Corporation; Atlas Copco AB; Techtronic Industries Company Limited; Newell Rubbermaid Inc.; Cooper Industries, Ltd.; W.W. Grainger, Inc.; Corghi S.p.A.; SPX Corporation; Hunter Engineering Company; Dover Corporation; Car-O-Liner AB; LexCom Informationssysteme GmbH; Infomedia Limited; Enigma, Inc.

FURTHER READING

Backmann, Dave, "Snap-on's CEO Cornog Set to Retire," *Kenosha (Wis.) News*, November 30, 2000, p. A1.

Barrett, Rick, "Snap-on Expands Business, Earnings," *Milwaukee Journal Sentinel*, October 24, 2006, p. D1.

"Coming Soon to an Office Desk Near You: Snap-on Tools," *Brandweek*, September 28, 1998, p. 5.

Content, Thomas, "Snap-on to Close Two of Four Plants," *Milwaukee Journal Sentinel*, July 22, 2003, p. 1D.

Copple, Brandon, "It's a Snap," *Forbes*, July 17, 2000, p. 85.

Doherty, Jacqueline, "Retooling Snap-on," *Barron's*, April 18, 2005, p. 18.

———, "Snap-on Retooling Succeeds," *Barron's*, May 1, 2006, p. 14.

Fanning, Deirdre, "Monkey Wrench at Snap-on Tools," *Forbes*, June 27, 1988, pp. 126+.

Gertzen, Jason, "Snap-on CEO to Retire," *Milwaukee Journal Sentinel*, November 30, 2000, p. 2D.

———, "Snap-on Names CEO As Earnings Decline," *Milwaukee Journal Sentinel*, April 25, 2001, p. 3D.

Gores, Paul, "Snap-on CEO Quits After $3^{1}/_{2}$ Years of Cutting Costs," *Milwaukee Journal Sentinel*, November 16, 2004.

Hawkins, Lee, Jr., "Shareholder Seeks Sale or Merger of Snap-on," *Milwaukee Journal Sentinel*, November 17, 2000, p. 1D.

———, "Snap-on to Buy Sandvik Saw, Tool Unit," *Milwaukee Journal Sentinel*, April 23, 1999.

Kahn, Jeremy, "Is There a Screw Loose at Snap-on? The Company Has a Killer Business and a Storied Brand Name, but CEO Robert Cornog Seems to Be Missing Some Key Tools," *Fortune*, July 24, 2000, pp. 171+.

Kerwin, Kathleen, "GM: Modular Plants Won't Be a Snap," *Business Week*, November 9, 1998, pp. 168–72.

———, "Lowe's to Compete in PL Tool Race," *Discount Store News*, November 23, 1998, p. 5.

Smith, Geoffrey N., "Snap-on Plans Restructuring," *American Metal Market*, July 6, 1998, p. 4.

———, "Snap-on's Proprietary Ingredient," *Forbes*, October 6, 1986, pp. 156+.

Wiegner, Kathleen K., "Quality Still Matters: Little Snap-on Tools Charges More Than Its Giant Competitors, yet Runs Rings Around Them," *Forbes*, August 21, 1978, pp. 114+.

Solarfun Power Holdings Co., Ltd.

666 Linyang Road
Qidong, Jiangsu Province 226200
China
Telephone: (86 21) 26022833
Fax: (86 21) 26022889
Web site: http://www.solarfun.com

Public Company
Incorporated: 2004 as Jiangsu Linyang Solarfun Co., Ltd.
Employees: 2,069
Sales: $725.4 million (2008)
Stock Exchanges: NASDAQ
Ticker Symbol: SOLF
NAICS: 334413 Semiconductor and Related Device Manufacturing

∎ ∎ ∎

Solarfun Power Holdings Co., Ltd., through its subsidiaries, is one of the top producers of solar energy products in China and a growing player in the world marketplace. From its facilities in the eastern province of Jiangsu, the firm develops, manufactures, and markets its proprietary photovoltaic (PV) modules under the "Solarfun" brand, which are made entirely from the solar cells it also produces and sells to select customers. The company sells most of its products, which include silicon ingots, to system integrators and distributors in Europe, primarily located in Germany and Spain, and to other solar power product makers in China.

ESTABLISHING A SOLAR IDENTITY

Jiangsu Linyang Solarfun Co., Ltd., or Linyang China, was created in 2004 as a subsidiary of Jiangsu Linyang Electronics Co., Ltd. Linyang China's founder, Yonghua Lu, had been chairman and general manager of Linyang Electronics since 1997. Before joining Linyang Electronics, which was incorporated as a Sino-foreign joint venture in 1995, Lu had managed specialty textile factories and computer manufacturers in Jiangsu Province.

With Lu at the helm and holding a controlling interest, Linyang Electronics, a manufacturer of electronic products for power utilities, rose to be China's leading maker of electric power meters. Lu established Linyang China's corporate headquarters and manufacturing facilities next to its parent company in Qidong City, across the Yangtze River from Shanghai, in the Linyang Industrial Park. When Linyang China commenced operations on August 27, 2004, Linyang Electronics owned 68 percent of the company's equity interests.

In January 2005, Linyang China began manufacturing and selling photovoltaic (PV) modules, or solar panels. In February, the company made its first commercial shipment of PV modules, which are made of PV cells that have been electrically interconnected and laminated in a durable and weatherproof package. In November 2005, Linyang China began manufacturing and selling PV cells, which are semiconductor devices that convert sunlight into electricity by a process known as the photovoltaic effect.

Solarfun Power Holdings Co., Ltd., manufactures both PV cells and PV modules, provides PV cell processing services to convert silicon wafers into PV cells, and supplies solar system integration services in China. The Company produces both monocrystalline and multicrystalline silicon cells and modules, and manufactures 100% of its modules with in-house produced PV cells. Solarfun sells its products both through third-party distributors and directly to system integrators. The Company was founded in 2004 and its products have been certified to TUV and UL safety and quality standards.

Initially the company made PV cells primarily to supply its own PV module production and sold only a small portion to select customers. In 2005, the company produced 5.6 megawatts (MW) of PV products (a one-megawatt plant running continuously at full capacity can power 778 households each year, according to the U.S. Department of Energy).

In 2005, net revenues from the sale of PV modules totaled $20.9 million and PV cell sales generated around $700,000. The average selling price of the company's PV modules was $3.93 per watt, while PV cells averaged $3 per watt. Around 80 percent of the firm's sales were to customers outside of China, primarily in Europe, with Germany leading the way.

RESTRUCTURING FOR IPO

In the spring of 2006, the company began expanding and restructuring in anticipation of an initial public offering (IPO) scheduled for the end of the year. On March 29, 2006, Linyang China incorporated Shanghai Linyang Solar Technology Co., Ltd., or Shanghai Linyang. The 83 percent owned subsidiary was set up to focus on designing and installing custom solar application systems using the company's proprietary "Solarfun" brand PV modules.

In April 2006, Sichuan Leshan Jiayang New Energy Co., Ltd., or Sichuan Jiayang, was established as a 55 percent owned subsidiary of Linyang China to increase the company's PV module production and capture potential system integration opportunities in western China. Sichuan Jiayang's 10 MW of PV module assembly capacity became operational in June 2006.

On May 12, Solarfun Power Holdings Co., Ltd., or Solarfun, was incorporated in the Cayman Islands as a listing vehicle. On May 17, in order to raise equity capital from investors outside of China, the firm established a holding company structure by incorporating Linyang Solar Power Investment Holding Ltd., or Linyang BVI, in the British Virgin Islands. Linyang BVI, a wholly owned subsidiary, in turn, purchased all of the equity interests in Linyang China on June 2, 2006, from Linyang Electronics and three other shareholders for $7.3 million.

EXPANDING PRODUCTION CAPACITY

Expecting an ongoing shortage of raw polysilicon and processed silicon wafers needed for PV cell production to continue in 2006 and 2007, in July 2006, Solarfun added on to a March contract with China-based Rene-Sola Co., Ltd., to obtain an additional 20.3 MW of silicon wafers, with the majority of the deliveries scheduled for 2007.

In September 2006, Solarfun opened a second PV cell production line, which doubled its annual manufacturing capacity to 60 MW. Also in September, Shanghai Linyang won the bid for the Suyuan Group 74 kilowatt on-grid application system project in Nanjing. In October, Solarfun announced that it had increased its annual PV module manufacturing capacity to 60 MW and planned to expand to 80 MW by the end of 2006. In November, Shanghai Linyang was tapped to provide a majority of the PV modules for a 1 MW solar power plant in Shanghai.

In November 2006, Solarfun entered into supply agreements with LDK Solar Co., Ltd., that called for LDK to provide 9.3 MW of silicon wafers from December 2006 to July 2007 based on a fixed price, and an additional 56.4 MW of silicon wafers from July 2007 to June 2008 based on market prices.

TAKING IT PUBLIC

On December 20, 2006, Solarfun began trading on the NASDAQ Global Exchange under the ticker symbol "SOLF." The company and other stockholders offered 12 million American Depositary Shares (ADSs), each representing five ordinary shares, at the price of $12.50 per ADS. The stock closed the first day at $11.90 and share price fell more than 20 percent in the first two sessions.

Solarfun's IPO raised $150 million, and as a result of the transaction, Chairman and CEO Lu reduced his stake in the firm from 42.9 percent to 32.2 percent. Citigroup Venture Capital reduced its equity stake from

KEY DATES

2004: Jiangsu Linyang Solarfun Co., Ltd., or Linyang China, is spun off from electronics firm.
2005: Linyang China begins to manufacture and market photovoltaic (PV) modules and cells.
2006: Firm creates two subsidiaries and a listing company ahead of stock market debut; listing company, Solarfun Power Holdings Co., Ltd., acquires Linyang China's assets in June; Solarfun stock starts trading on the NASDAQ in December.
2007: Annual revenues and PV module sales nearly triple.
2008: Company completes purchase of Yangguang Solar, its majority-owned silicon ingot maker; Global economic meltdown halts expansion plans; firm shows losses despite doubling revenues.
2009: Revenues, shipments, profits, and market value remain depressed with global recession.

20.98 percent to 13.10 percent; Good Energies Investments, a Swiss investment firm, went from 8.35 percent to 6.26 percent; and Hanfei Wang, Solarfun's director and chief operating officer, from 6.97 percent to 5.23 percent.

After the IPO, Solarfun continued to conduct all of its business through its operating subsidiary, Jiangsu Linyang Solarfun Co., Ltd., or Linyang China, and its two majority-owned subsidiaries, Shanghai Linyang and Sichuan Jiayang.

SHOWING AN EARLY PROFIT

Solarfun started 2007 by signing a three-year sales contract with UB Garanty Project S.L., of Spain, for 140 MW of PV modules. The contract was reported to be worth up to $50 million in 2007. In early March 2007, the company finished installing and began operations on its third and fourth PV cell production lines, which brought annualized PV cell production capacity up to 120 MW.

As reported by the company in March 2007, net income in 2006 grew sixfold to $13.6 million, or 48 cents per ADS, on revenues of $80.8 million. The firm noted its gross margin rose from 15.8 percent to 29.2 percent primarily due to increased PV cell production

capabilities, which allowed the company to use its own PV cells for module production.

In April 2007, Solarfun landed a three-year deal to sell 182 MW of PV modules to Ecostream International, of the Netherlands. Solarfun successfully added two more PV cell production lines in July, which kept the firm on schedule to achieve its production capacity target of 240 MW by the end of 2007. At the same time, Solarfun entered a seven-year contract to purchase over 180 MW of six-inch multicrystalline wafers from an undisclosed non-domestic supplier.

SECURING RAW MATERIALS

In August 2007, Solarfun paid $8 million for a 52 percent majority stake in Jiangsu Yangguang Solar Technology Co. Ltd., a start-up manufacturer of silicon wafers. Production of wafers at Yangguang Solar started in August and the plant was expected to be fully operational in October 2007 with an initial annual production capacity of 15 to 20 MW.

In early September 2007, the firm secured large multiyear framework commitments to supply more than 185 MW of modules to three unidentified "large and well-known customers in Europe." The firm's plans to have 240 MW of cell capacity by the end of the year remained on schedule when two more 30 MW cell lines began full-scale production in October.

In a market where polysilicon supplies and products remained tight, Solarfun cut a mid-October 2007 deal with regular supplier LDK worth $266 million for the purchase of silicon wafers at a fixed price from early 2008 through 2010. In November 2007, the company signed a $306 million, eight-year supply contract, set to start in 2009, with Hawaii-based Hoku Scientific, Inc., to buy an undisclosed yearly quantity of polysilicon.

SURGING AND FALLING

In late November 2007, company stock, which had traded in a 52-week range of $8.22 to $17.69, surged 30 percent to just over $15 when Solarfun raised its 2007 guidance after posting strong third-quarter profit gains. Early December brought another jolt to company share price when Good Energies Inc. announced plans to increase its equity stake in Solarfun from 6.3 percent to 34.34 percent. The transaction by the Swiss renewable energy investment firm included the purchase of over 66.7 million ordinary shares and 281,000 ADSs from current stockholders, as well as the acquisition of half of Chairman Lu's 32.2 percent stake. Shares soared 27 percent to $26.25 on the day of the announcement.

Illustrating the significance of securing a supply of raw materials necessary to meet its growth objectives, on January 3, 2008, Solarfun stock reached an all-time high of $40.19 in intraday trading after the firm announced that it signed three contracts with a major Korean conglomerate for purchase and delivery of wafers totaling $230 million over seven years. Mid-January brought another long-term supply contract for 140 MW of silicon wafers from Wacker Schott Solar GmbH, of Germany, and a deal for the sale of 17 MW of modules to France's EDF Energies Nouvelles.

As reported by the company in late March 2008, revenues in 2007 shot up 280 percent to $328.3 million while net income rose just 40 percent, to $20.3 million. Total PV module shipments were up 310 percent to 78.4 MW, with an average selling price of $3.74 per watt. The company predicted that its 2008 revenues would double on expected shipments of 160 MW. Solarfun stock, which had fallen significantly since the start of the year, surged 17 percent to $13.36 on the news.

TRYING TO GAIN TRACTION

In May 2008, Solarfun extended its polysilicon supply contract with Hoku from eight to ten years and increased the value of the deal to $384 million. Solarfun's meteoric growth continued in the first quarter of 2008, as reported by the company in late May. Revenue for the period totaled $171 million with a net income of $15.3 million, or 32 cents per share, double what analysts had expected.

In June 2008, Solarfun inked a long-term deal with GCL Silicon Technology Holdings Ltd. for virgin polysilicon sufficient to produce approximately 1.2 gigawatts of solar modules over eight years. The firm also entered into an agreement to purchase the remaining 48 percent equity interest in Jiangsu Yangguang Solar. The deal was financed by an August equity offering of 5.4 million ADSs with net proceeds of $71.9 million. The move allowed Solarfun to take full control over the silicon ingot production company, which was expected to expand production capacity to 200 MW by year-end 2008 and 300 MW by year-end 2009.

During the summer of 2008, Solarfun made three significant module sales deals with major European PV system providers: one with Schuco International KG for 47 MW; one with Martifer Solar Sistemas Solares SA for 30 MW; and another with Q-Cells AG for no less than 100 MW of PV modules per annum, for three years starting in 2009, using PV cells supplied by Q-Cells. The company continued capacity expansions to meet growing demand for its products and by the start of the third quarter of 2008, Solarfun had initiated production on four new cell manufacturing lines, which brought their nameplate capacity to 360 MW.

FEELING THE GLOBAL PAIN

By the start of the fourth quarter of 2008, however, Solarfun's stock and that of the rest of the solar industry began reeling from the impact of the global financial crisis, which included the collapse of the crude oil market and a worldwide tightening of credit access. Not even the extension of solar tax credits through 2016 by the U.S. Congress in early October could stem the tide. Company stock, which traded around $20 per share in late August, slid into the single digits in early October and continued its downward slide to close at $2.68 on November 20.

Third-quarter financial results, as reported by the company on December 2, 2008, showed that revenues, shipments, profits, and gross margins were all down. The company also lowered its full-year shipment guidance from the top end of 190 MW, which it projected in August, to the low end of 175 MW.

The financial picture in the last quarter of 2008 remained bleak. "In the fourth quarter, funding for solar projects remained tight, excess inventories existed in many markets, and normal seasonal factors exacerbated softer demand," Solarfun Chief Executive Officer Harold Hoskens told the press in late March 2009 after releasing company financial data. The firm posted a record loss of $61.4 million for the quarter, which included a $47.8 million charge related to inventory write-downs. Results for the full year, released at the same time, showed a loss of $41.1 million, or 16 cents per ADS, even though revenue more than doubled from 2007 to $725.4 million.

STILL TRENDING DOWNWARD

As reported in May 2009, China's eastern province of Jiangsu became the country's biggest solar cell maker. With an output of 1,418 MW in 2008, it was responsible for 70 percent of the nation's photovoltaic output. The top five producers were all U.S.-listed. Suntech Power, Trina Solar Limited, Solarfun Power, China Sunergy, and Canadian Solar Inc. reached 497 MW, 209 MW, 189MW, 111 MW, and 108 MW, respectively.

Financial results for the first quarter of 2009 were made available by the company in mid-May and showed a continuing downward trend. Revenues of $100.1 million marked a 43 percent decline from the first quarter of 2008 and a 39 percent drop from the fourth quarter of 2008. PV module shipments totaled 35.7 MW, a decrease of 11.4 percent from the first quarter of 2008, and a 25 percent decline from 47.6 MW in the fourth quarter of 2008. A net loss of $1 million was significantly less than the previous quarter but was far below the $15.8 million profit in the first quarter of 2008.

As of mid-June 2009, there was still great uncertainty about when the global recession might bottom out. Solarfun, like the rest of the solar industry and most businesses in general, was adopting an optimistic but cautious attitude, pinning hopes for a rebound on the second half of 2009. Company officials assured investors that the firm's funding needs were secure and that they still had the financial resources to compete in an uncertain environment. At the same time, they prudently put all expansion plans on hold and refrained from making specific quarterly and full-year projections. With inventories still bulging and customers drawing back on purchases, it was still too hard to say if any light was visible at the end of the tunnel, and if it was, whether it was coming from a rising sun or an oncoming train.

Ted Sylvester

PRINCIPAL SUBSIDIARIES

Shanghai Linyang Solar Technology Co., Ltd.; Sichuan Leshan Jiayang New Energy Co., Ltd.; Jiangsu Yangguang Solar Technology Co. Ltd.

PRINCIPAL COMPETITORS

BP Solar; Suntech Power Holdings Co., Ltd.; Renewable Energy Corporation ASA; Sharp Corporation; SunPower Corporation; Trina Solar Limited; SolarWorld AG; First Solar, Inc.; Yingli Green Energy Holding Company Limited.; Canadian Solar Inc.; China Sunergy Co., Ltd.; Evergreen Solar, Inc.; JA Solar Holdings Co., Ltd.

FURTHER READING

Alpert, Bill, "China's Solar Boom Loses Its Luster," *Barron's,* October 8, 2007, p. 22.

Ball, Yvonne, "IPO Outlook: Deals & Deal Makers: Ten IPOs from China Set Record," *Wall Street Journal,* June 11, 2007, p. C5.

Bogoslaw David Solar, "Stocks Get Their Day in the Sun," *BusinessWeek Online,* January 3, 2008.

Cheng, Roger, "Solarfun Lights Up After Sale of Stake," *Wall Street Journal,* December 5, 2007, p. C4.

"China's Offshore-Listed Solar Firms See 77% Market Cap Drop," *China Perspective,* November 23, 2008.

"China's Photovoltaic Industry Faces Big Potential Risks," *Xinhua Electronics News,* May 21, 2007.

Gage, Jack, "High Energy Stocks; Demand for Energy Has Made It the Hottest Industry on Wall Street," *Forbes,* June 16, 2008.

Gelsi, Steve, "IPO Market Cools Down After Year-End Sprint," *Dow Jones Business News,* December 21, 2006.

Gold, Donald H., "Once-Powerful Solar Stocks Take a Beating," *Investor's Business Daily,* July 3, 2008.

Groom, Nichola, "Solar Stocks Fall, China Subsidy Enthusiasm Wanes," *Reuters News,* March 27, 2009.

"Jiangsu Emerges As No. 1 Photovoltaic Producer," *China Perspective,* May 8, 2009.

LeeMaster, Tim, "Solarfun Looking to Raise US$162m on Nasdaq," *South China Morning Post,* December 13, 2006, p. 1.

Liang, Li, "In the Shadow of the Sun," *China Business Feature,* May 9, 2007.

Nair, Adveith, "Solarfun Q2 Beats Street; Shares Fall on Margins, Prices," *Reuters News,* August 27, 2008.

"Polysilicon Price May Drop in 2010," *China Chemical Reporter,* November 16, 2008.

Reeves, Amy, "New Issue Pipeline: Will Investors Warm Up to More Solar Power IPOs?" *Investor's Business Daily,* December 19, 2006, p. A06.

Savitz, Eric J., "Prospects of Rain in Spain Make for Gloomy Solar Week," *Barron's,* July 28, 2008, p. 27.

Spencer, Jane, "China Solar Stocks Shine in U.S., but Some Could Be Overheated," *Wall Street Journal Asia,* May 23, 2007, p. 21.

Spicy Pickle Franchising, Inc.

———■———

90 Madison Street, Suite 700
Denver, Colorado 80206
U.S.A.
Telephone: (303) 297-1902
Toll Free: (800) 711-1902
Fax: (303) 297-1903
Web site: http://www.spicypickle.com

Public Company
Incorporated: 1999 as Spicy Pickle, LLC
Employees: 29
Sales: $4.41 million (2008)
Stock Exchanges: Over the Counter (OTC)
Ticker Symbol: SPKL
NAICS: 722211 Limited-Service Restaurants

■ ■ ■

Spicy Pickle Franchising, Inc., is a franchiser of Spicy Pickle and Bread Garden Urban Café restaurants. Spicy Pickle, a 39-restaurant chain operating in 12 states, serves gourmet submarine and panini sandwiches. Bread Garden, with 12 locations in British Columbia, Canada, serves specialty coffee, breakfast, lunch, and dinner. A Spicy Pickle franchise requires an initial investment of approximately $400,000. A Bread Garden franchise requires an initial investment of approximately CAD 350,000.

THE FIRST SPICY PICKLE

Unlike some entrepreneurs who set lofty goals for themselves, Anthony S. Walker and Kevin T. Morrison expressed only modest hopes for their start-up business. "This was two guys with just a passion about food and service that wanted to open up a sandwich shop that represented us, and that was it," Walker explained in the May 2004 issue of *Chain Leader*. "We didn't sit down and say this is what we're going to do in sales. We felt that if you had the food and service that people are going to come to the place and eat on a regular basis." Their plans soon became decidedly more ambitious, but when Walker and Morrison opened their first restaurant, they treated it as a part-time endeavor.

When Walker and Morrison formed Spicy Pickle, LLC, in March 1999, the two founders tended to the company during their off-hours. Walker was employed as a chef at a posh Denver restaurant, Barolo Grill. Morrison had worked at Barolo Grill as well, part of a culinary career that also included serving as a chef at Chicago's Vinci restaurant. When he joined Walker in starting Spicy Pickle, Morrison was managing his own wholesale food distribution business, Red Tomato Specialty Produce, which he had established in Denver in 1995.

Walker and Morrison officially launched their business in August 1999, when The Spicy Pickle Sub Shop opened on Lincoln Street in the Capitol Hill neighborhood of Denver. The restaurant was located in a small, concrete building, where Walker and Morrison labored in tight surroundings without heat or air conditioning. What the restaurant lacked in amenities, it compensated for by offering its customers a wealth of menu selections. The shop offered panini and submarine sandwiches using bread delivered daily from a local specialty bakery, Fornaio, and meats from Boar's Head, a New York-based purveyor of gourmet delicatessen meats. After making their meat selections from a list that included Cajun roast beef and rosemary ham, customers could choose from an array of ingredients that included 15 toppings, 11 spreads, and nine varieties of cheese. Customers also could choose from a handful of side salads, including rotini pasta, potato salad, and coleslaw. With each sandwich order, customers received Spicy Pickle's soon-to-be signature dill pickle, which was marinated for three days in a spicy blend that included three types of chili peppers.

POISED FOR GROWTH

Spicy Pickle enjoyed immediate success. "They ran out of meat in six hours—and that was their slowest day," the *Rocky Mountain News* noted in a February 8, 2003 article, describing the bustling business recorded by Walker and Morrison in 1999. The partners collected $500,000 in sales during their first year, finding themselves occupying a burgeoning niche within the foodservice industry. The average check totaled $7.25, which put Spicy Pickle in the "fast-casual" segment of the foodservice industry, a concept that had existed since the early 1990s, but did not earn its designation as a distinct segment of the industry until 2000. "The baby boomers that grew up on fast food are now looking for more variety and more healthful choices," a restaurant consultant explained in the September 22, 2003 edition of the *Denver Post*. "And they want their food with basically the same speed, convenience, and value that they had when growing up." A $5 billion segment of the foodservice industry, the fast-casual segment would provide a fertile climate for expansion once Walker and Morrison began to plot a more ambitious future for their Lincoln Street shop.

FOUNDERS TURN TO FRANCHISING IN 2003

An affordable, upscale sandwich shop proved to be a commercial success. Walker and Morrison left their jobs and began devoting all their time to Spicy Pickle, opening two more shops in Denver in 2001. By 2002, their business was generating $2 million in annual revenues, convincing them to hatch ambitious plans for their concept. The pair decided to franchise Spicy Pickle, seeking to establish between 60 and 100 units within five years. In January 2003, they changed the name of their company to Spicy Pickle Franchising, LLC, and began touting Spicy Pickle as a brand destined for national expansion.

To help them make the enormous leap from a three-store operator to a national franchiser, Walker and Morrison recruited Marc N. Geman. Walker took on the duties of chief operating officer and Morrison accepted the title of chief culinary officer, realigning their responsibilities to make room for Geman's role as president and chief executive officer, the two posts he occupied at the beginning of 2003. In Geman, the founders gained an executive seasoned in the nuances of franchising. An attorney by training, Geman worked as an investment advisor and an executive at Bayview Technology Group before becoming president of Pretzelmaker Holdings Inc. in 1994. He built Pretzelmaker into a national franchiser of soft-pretzel outlets, taking charge of a handful of locations that he grew into a 240-store chain by 1998, when the company was sold to Mrs. Fields' Original Cookies, Inc.

At first, the company attracted customers of its Denver locations as franchisees, the first aspiring entrepreneurs who had $200,000 in credit and were willing to pay the $25,000 franchising fee. Spicy Pickle sold its first franchise in the spring of 2003 and expected to have its first out-of-state unit, a shop in San Diego, opened by the end of the year.

A BLUEPRINT FOR SUCCESS

The first three franchised units, two in Denver and a third in Fort Collins, Colorado, were considered "works in progress," according to a Spicy Pickle executive in the October 27, 2003 issue of *Crittenden's Restaurant Chain Report*. Geman and his staff were still in the process of refining the Spicy Pickle prototype, but there were characteristics that defined the small chain. The shops occupied roughly 1,500 square feet of space, equipped to seat between 30 and 50 customers. Strip malls figured as the ideal location for a Spicy Pickle, preferably next to retail tenants Starbucks, Chipotle Mexican Grill, or Jamba Juice.

KEY DATES

1999: Anthony S. Walker and Kevin T. Morrison open the first Spicy Pickle in Denver, Colorado.
2001: Two additional restaurants are opened in the Denver area.
2003: Company begins franchising the Spicy Pickle concept.
2004: Spicy Pickle shop opens in San Diego, California, the first unit located outside Colorado.
2006: Spicy Pickle completes an initial public offering of stock.
2008: Company acquires Bread Garden Urban Café, a Canadian restaurant chain.

Spicy Pickle committed itself entirely to operating as a franchiser. The two original shops were sold to franchisers, and all efforts were directed at selling franchises, which required an initial investment of roughly $400,000. Franchisees paid a franchise fee of $45,000 for their first restaurant and $20,000 for additional locations. The company made its money from the franchise fees and royalty payments. Franchisees were required to pay Spicy Pickle 5 percent of their weekly gross sales and to contribute 2 percent of the weekly volume to support national and regional marketing efforts. Additionally, franchisees were required to dedicate at least 1 percent of their weekly sales total to local advertising.

Expansion occurred at a slower pace than expected, although Geman, Walker, and Morrison set their expectations high. The goal of opening 60 to 100 units within five years, as announced in early 2003, turned into an objective, as stated in late 2003, of reaching 1,000 units in five to ten years. Spicy Pickle opened two franchise units before the end of 2003, and it failed to make its expected first step out of the state before the year was through. "It took us a year to get a lease on the location in San Diego," Geman said in the January 2005 issue of *QSR Magazine*.

STOCK OFFERING IN 2006

The opening of the San Diego store in 2004 marked the tenth shop of the all-franchise Spicy Pickle. By the time it presided over 15 units in the fall of 2006, the company was ready to make a move presumably never envisioned by Walker and Morrison when they opened

their first Spicy Pickle in 1999. In October 2006, the company filed for an initial public offering (IPO) of stock, hoping to raise $5 million by debuting on the Over the Counter (OTC) Bulletin Board. "You always have pressures," Walker said in the October 27, 2006 issue of *Fast Casual*. "If you're staying private, the pressures are you have to go out and find private money. There's pros and cons with everything. Right now, we're growing and we feel going public is the right thing to do." Spicy Pickle completed its IPO, and in its first year reporting as a publicly traded company, 2007, it recorded $1.2 million in revenue from franchise fees and royalties.

A MULTI-STATE CHAIN EMERGES

Geographically, Spicy Pickle laid the foundation for significant progress in 2008, a year that saw the company make a daring move in the face of deteriorating economic conditions. In January 2008, the company sold a multi-unit development agreement that promised the expansion of the Spicy Pickle brand into the Los Angeles market. The contract with the franchisee, an instructor at the California School of Culinary Art, called for the opening of three Spicy Pickles in Los Angeles, an agreement that was signed at roughly the same time a franchise development deal was reached that called for the opening of 12 units in San Diego. The month also saw the company sign agreements for its further penetration of the greater Chicago market. The first store in the area opened in May 2007, the first step of a plan to have between 30 and 40 stores in greater Chicago.

The franchise agreement signed in January 2008 called for the opening of five restaurants, but as the year progressed the difference between the number of stores slated to open and the number of stores in operation narrowed distressingly slowly. Spicy Pickle had signed agreements with 113 franchisees by 2008, but it only had 36 units in operation. For franchisees, securing financing was becoming increasingly difficult by the by the end of 2008, forcing Geman to search for alternative ways to generate revenue for a company that subsisted on franchise fees and royalties.

BREAD GARDEN ACQUISITION IN 2008

Geman looked north for help, setting his sights on a Canadian fast-casual company, Bread Garden Urban Café. Vancouver, British Columbia-based Bread Garden, which offered a menu of specialty coffee, pastries, lunch items, and dinner entrées, developed into a 17-restaurant chain at its height, a time when the company was owned by Spectra Group of Great Restaurants Inc. Under Spectra's ownership, the Bread Garden brand began to struggle, losing CAD 1 million annually by the time the company decided to sell the chain in 2004. Spectra sold the franchising rights for the 14-restaurant brand to Zahir Dhanani and BG Franchising Inc. for CAD 1.4 million. Dhanani closed four of the restaurants after he acquired the chain, and soon realized he did not have the experience or the personnel to expand the concept.

Geman, who presumably was familiar with Bread Garden because Spectra briefly had operated three restaurants in Denver, began negotiating with Dhanani. Several meetings were held before Geman agreed to buy the concept in October 2008, a transaction that gave him a company with CAD 6 million in sales and a new brand to franchise. Spicy Pickle began offering franchises of the Bread Garden concept, estimating an initial investment of CAD 350,000 for a 2,500-square-foot restaurant.

As Geman plotted Spicy Pickle's future course, economic conditions cast a cloud of uncertainty over the company's expansion. A constricted credit market was forcing some franchisees to back out of their franchise agreements, hobbling Spicy Pickle's efforts to build a national network of restaurants. Progress was being achieved, however, giving Geman and his management team some encouraging news to share with the company's shareholders. In January 2009, the company signed an agreement for seven franchised Spicy Pickle restaurants in San Antonio, Texas. The company also announced the opening of a Bread Garden near Vancouver that offered drive-through service, a feature that potentially could be incorporated into the Spicy Pickle chain. "We are anxious to try a drive-through location for Bread Garden Urban Cafes as it has all the features that would make this type of service compelling to customers," Geman said in the January 26, 2009 issue of *Fast Casual*. "If this works well for us it opens up a

lot of future opportunity for both Bread Garden Urban Cafes and possible Spicy Pickle restaurants."

Jeffrey L. Covell

PRINCIPAL SUBSIDIARIES

SPBG Franchising, Inc. (Canada).

PRINCIPAL COMPETITORS

The Quiznos Master LLC; Doctor's Associates Inc.; Panera Bread Company; Atlanta Bread Company International, Inc.

FURTHER READING

Brand, Rachel, "Spicy Pickle Shops to Mushroom," *Rocky Mountain News*, February 8, 2003, p. 2C.

Jacober, Marcela, "Keep Them Coming Back," *Shamrock Foods*, July–August 2004.

Korstrom, Glen, "Resilient Bread Garden Chain Set for Ambitious Expansion," *Business in Vancouver*, March 10, 2009.

"Lessons from the Little Guys," *QSR Magazine*, January 2005.

Minnick, Fred, "Spicy Pickle Files for IPO," *Fast Casual*, October 27, 2006.

Norris, Maya, "Growing with Relish," *Chain Leader*, May 2004.

"Sandwich Chain in Deal to Open 5 Stores in Suburbs," *Crain's Chicago Business*, January 8, 2008.

"Spicy Pickle Accelerates to Capture Fast-Casual Market," *Crittenden's Restaurant Chain Report*, October 27, 2003, p. 4.

"Spicy Pickle Inks Texas Franchise Agreement, Opens First Drive-Thru," *Fast Casual*, January 26, 2009.

"Spicy Pickle Opens New Location in Fort Collins," *Denver Business Journal*, February 12, 2004.

"Spicy Pickle Set to Tackle L.A.," *Fast Casual*, January 17, 2008.

Tatum, Christine, "Spicy Pickle Relishes Plan to Expand Across the Country," *Denver Post*, September 22, 2003, p. E1.

Wise, Thom, "Two Delis to Die For," *Rocky Mountain News*, October 8, 1999, p. 20D.

Stepan Company

—■—

22 West Frontage Road
Northfield, Illinois 60093
U.S.A.
Telephone: (847) 446-7500
Fax: (847) 446-2853
Web site: http://www.stepan.com

Public Company
Incorporated: 1932
Employees: 1,500
Sales: $1.7 billion (2009)
Stock Exchanges: New York Chicago
Ticker Symbols: SCL; SCLPR
NAICS: 325613 Surface Active Agent Manufacturing;
325199 All Other Basic Organic Chemical
Manufacturing; 325211 Plastics Material and Resin
Manufacturing

■ ■ ■

Few Americans have heard of Stepan Company, yet its
chemicals are used in a majority of the nation's
consumer products including detergents, cleansers,
shampoos, conditioners, toothpaste, and cosmetics.
Founded in Chicago in 1932, Stepan Company has
carved out a highly specific niche market producing and
supplying specialty and intermediate chemicals to other
companies for use in a broad range of end products.
The company's three core business segments include
surfactants, used in detergents for cleaning clothes,
carpets, floors, and fine fabrics, as well as a host of other
personal care products; polymers, used in manufacturing

plastics, refrigeration, and building materials; and
specialty products, used in a range of flavoring, food,
and pharmaceuticals. Stepan Company is headquartered
in northern Illinois with operations in Brazil, Canada,
China, Colombia, England, France, Germany, Mexico,
and the Philippines.

EARLY HISTORY: LATE 19TH CENTURY TO WORLD WAR II–ERA

Stepan Corporation was founded by Alfred Stepan Jr.,
descended from a long line of Londoners. When his
father relocated from London to the United States during the late 1890s, he began working as an office boy at
Roessler & Haslacher, a chemical firm in New York
City. When the firm was later acquired by DuPont, Alfred Sr. became a preeminent chemical research scientist
in the early part of the 20th century.

Young Alfred was destined to follow in his father's
footsteps. After graduating from the University of Notre
Dame, Stepan attended law school at Northwestern
University in Evanston, Illinois. One year of law school
was enough for the ambitious young man, however, and
he decided to plunge into the chemical business. With
$500 borrowed from his mother, Stepan went into busi-
ness as a jobber of cleaning solvents and refrigeration gas
in 1932. Giving the company his surname, he initially
worked out of a $2 dollar a month office in downtown
Chicago at Navy Pier. For three years Stepan worked as
a salesman, selling his products to companies
throughout the metropolitan area. In 1935 Stepan
switched over to chemistry, creating compounds through
the process of sulfonation.

COMPANY PERSPECTIVES

Our Path to Future Growth—Research and Development: Develop a continuous stream of higher value-added product applications; improve existing processes; and develop new processes for known products. Acquisitions: Strategic acquisitions to complement existing product lines in surfactants, polyols, and urethane systems. Globalization: Establish manufacturing locations, sales offices and product development laboratories to supply Stepan's customers in their global expansion. Strategic Alliances: Leverage Stepan's core technologies in world markets with joint ventures where it adds know-how, technology, capital and customers to complement resources of local partners with raw material suppliers, plant sites, regional know-how.

It was a short step into the specialty chemicals industry. By 1940, when the name Stepan Chemical Company had been adopted, the business had moved to space at Goose Island on the Chicago River. When the United States entered World War II in December 1941, Stepan Chemical Company was firmly established as one of the fastest-growing manufacturers of surface-acting agents for use in detergents and disinfectants, perfumes, soap, bubble bath, and pesticides. By the end of the decade, Stepan had become a leading supplier of aromatic chemicals, fragrances, and flavors used in the perfume, cosmetics, and household industries.

GROWTH AND EXPANSION: FIFTIES AND SIXTIES

During the early 1950s Stepan continued to grow, catering to manufacturers of consumer goods. In 1905 the company expanded operations into a building on South Kedzie Avenue, and four years later bought 380 acres in Millsdale, near Joliet, for a manufacturing facility. Convinced the detergent and cleaning industries were recession-proof, since hospitals and large corporate buildings would always purchase cleaning agents, Alfred and Stepan's sales force focused on building a reliable customer base in these products. They succeeded beyond expectations by carving out a niche that served nearly 2,000 customers, including almost all of the large *Fortune* 500 consumer products companies. From 1955 onward, sales skyrocketed, and Alfred poured increasingly more capital into research and development (R&D). In 1958 Stepan went public on the New York

Stock Exchange and was incorporated in Delaware. The following year, 1959, Stepan used some of its initial public offering capital to make its first acquisition: Maywood Chemical Works in Maywood, New Jersey.

The company continued its growth and profitability and moved to a new headquarters facility in Northfield, Illinois, in 1960. In 1964 Stepan entered the rich citric acid market. Rather than use sugar beets as a base, as was the norm, the company tried making citric acid from blackstrap molasses at half the price. This significant effort cost the company a great deal in manpower, capital, and tons of blackstrap molasses. By the time Stepan realized the venture would not be profitable, the company had lost more than $2.5 million in 1967, and per-share profits had declined precipitously from $1.67 in 1964 to a mere 12 cents by 1967. Incredibly, Stepan turned around immediately.

Refocusing on the production of specialty chemicals for the consumer products industry, Stepan reached an agreement with a British firm to become the exclusive manufacturer and marketer of a versatile new urethane foam and developed a chemical additive to double the life of an ordinary pair of blue jeans. Additionally, the company expanded its research facility in Maywood, New Jersey, to become one of the leaders in the field of aromatic chemicals. The turnaround was so dramatic that by the end of the decade sales amounted to over $25 million and earnings increased to an all-time high of $1.69 per share.

Alfred Stepan Jr. was not only successful in business but in his personal life as well. Although one side of his family had been deeply involved in chemistry, the other side was drawn to the arts, and a number of Stepan's ancestors had been associated with famous European opera houses before immigrating to the United States. Stepan, too, was immersed in the operatic tradition and, while a prominent businessman in Chicago during the 1950s, was asked to serve as president of the city's Lyric Opera. The Lyric Opera, through mismanagement and unanticipated misfortune, had fallen on difficult financial times. When Stepan became president, he immediately reorganized the management structure of the opera and initiated fundraisers to bring the opera house back to financial stability.

TRANSITION AND CHANGE: SEVENTIES AND EIGHTIES

In 1973 Alfred Stepan stepped aside and relinquished the day-to-day operations of the company to his son F. Quinn Stepan. The younger Stepan had been raised within the chemical industry, spending most of his school vacations working in the firm's plants and

KEY DATES

1932: Alfred Stepan Jr. forms a chemical business in downtown Chicago.

1937: Stepan moves to offices on Goose Island on the Chicago River.

1940: Firm's name is changed to Stepan Chemical Company.

1950: New manufacturing and office space is added on Kedzie Avenue in Chicago.

1958: Stepan Company goes public on the New York Stock Exchange.

1961: F. Quinn Stepan joins the company full time in sales.

1972: Company begins an acquisitions spree initiated by Quinn Stepan Sr.

1973: Alfred Stepan Jr. turns daily operations of the company to son Quinn.

1984: Quinn Stepan is named CEO and chairman as Alfred retires.

1992: F. Quinn Stepan Jr. is named director of business management.

1999: Quinn Jr. takes over the duties of president from his father.

2001: Two surfactant products lines are acquired in the United Kingdom.

2004: Company forms joint ventures in Brazil and China.

2005: Stepan Company surpasses $1 billion in sales.

2006: Quinn Jr. adds CEO to his titles; Quinn Sr. remains chairman of the board.

2008: Company forms Tiorco, LLC, a joint venture with Nalco Company.

2009: Stepan maintains steady sales and profits despite the economic downturn.

laboratories, and even taking business trips with his father. Having graduated with a degree in chemistry from the University of Notre Dame, Quinn went to work full time in 1961 selling surfactants for the company. After receiving an M.B.A. from the University of Chicago in 1963, Quinn worked in a variety of positions and was promoted to vice-president in charge of corporate development in 1967.

In 1969 he was appointed vice-president of the Industrial Chemicals Division. As head of corporate development, Quinn was instrumental in shaping the company's growth during the late 1960s and early 1970s. Under his leadership sales increased 18 percent a year since 1968 and by the end of fiscal 1973 the firm's profits had increased an impressive 30 percent over the previous year. Even more impressive was that the company's sales figures had skyrocketed from $25 million in 1968 to $65 million by 1973.

When Quinn assumed the post of president in 1973, he had already developed a strategic five-year growth plan that included acquiring numerous companies within the industry. In 1972 Stepan purchased the surfactants operation of Allied Chemical; the urethane foam systems division of Diamond Shamrock; the Presto Chemical Company, a manufacturer of gel coating, mold release agents, and pigment dispersions; and Westbrook-Marriner, a producer of lanolin. In 1973 the firm bought Armstrong Cork's urethane foam systems business. These strategic acquisitions not only increased Stepan's sales of urethane from $1.5 million to over $10 million, but the purchase of Allied Chemical's surfactants operation increased Stepan's market share significantly. Stepan's first European acquisition came in 1976 with the purchase of the Grenoble, France-based Industries Chimiques de Voreppe.

In 1984 as Quinn added the duties of chief executive and chairman of the board, his comprehensive reorganization plan for the accounting, purchasing, manufacturing, and engineering departments was getting results. By the end of fiscal 1985 the company reported record-high sales of $235 million. Approximately 70 percent of this figure was accounted for by the firm's strong presence in the surfactants market.

Stepan's growth through acquisitions strategy had not only increased revenues and manufacturing capacity, but had also expanded its market share in the specialty chemicals industry. During the mid-1980s the company once again went on an acquisitions spree to strengthen its traditional core business while diversifying into process chemicals production. In June 1985 Stepan purchased Westvaco's specialty surfactants division, estimated to be worth over $20 million. The purchase included a manufacturing facility located in Winder, Georgia, which made anionic surfactants used in industrial and agricultural products.

The purchase also enabled Stepan to enter a new market, since the facility produced defoamers for pulp and paper mills as well. Another benefit of the transaction was giving Stepan a strong presence in the Southeast, complementing the company's other regional manufacturing facilities in Illinois, California, and New Jersey. Along with the Westvaco purchase, Stepan also purchased the designs, technology, customer lists, and inventory of polyurethane coating resins and polyether polyols of Reichhold, a small firm for a variety of urethane applications. Although this agreement did not include the acquisition of any plant or equipment, it added an estimated $4 million to $5 million to Stepan's sales.

Before the close of the decade Stepan continued buying surfactant business segments from several firms including Millmaster Onyx (1986); Petrolite, based in Matamoros, Mexico (1988); and two Canadian companies, Toronto's Canada Packers and Ontario's Domtar (1989).

THE THIRD GENERATION: NINETIES

The last decade of the century was a particularly good one for the company. In 1992 the third generation of Stepans began earnestly climbing the corporate ladder of the $435 million family business. F. Quinn Stepan Jr. was named director of business management. By 1997 he had been promoted to vice-president and general manager. That year sales reached an impressive $581 million. Quinn Sr., however, had set a sales goal of $1 billion by the end of 2000. To reach this goal he decided to not only increase capacity at all Stepan manufacturing facilities, but to make a concerted attempt to expand operations both in North America and in Europe through joint ventures and acquisitions.

By 1998 international sales accounted for 16 percent of the company's $635.8 million in total revenues as the aggressive growth-through-acquisitions strategy continued. Quinn Sr. hoped to garner half of the company's sales from internal growth and the other from purchases. To this end, several acquisitions were completed. These included the remaining half of a Colombian joint venture created in 1993, Stepan Colombiana de Quimicos; U.S.-based specialty surfactant product lines from DuPont; and the anionic/cationic surfactant businesses of Boehme Filatex Canada, Inc., through its Canadian subsidiary, Stepan Canada, Inc.

R&D, always an important facet of Stepan's growth, accounted for $12 million in 1998 and increased only slightly to $13 million for 1999. Revenues for fiscal 1999 remained steady, climbing minimally to $694.7 million due mostly to a surge in the surfactant division, which grew from 1998's $493,930 to $547,359 for 1999. The biggest news of the year, however, was the ascension of Quinn Jr. to president and COO, while Quinn Sr. remained CEO and chairman of the board.

A NEW ERA

By the dawn of the new millennium Stepan Company had a workforce of nearly 1,400 worldwide and while it did not meet Quinn Sr.'s goal of $1 billion in sales by the end of 2000, the firm was nonetheless a leader in the surfactants, polymers, and specialty products industry, supplying a growing number of products to manufacturers worldwide.

In 2000 Stepan bought a surfactants manufacturing plant from Manro Performance Chemicals Ltd. near Manchester, England, then acquired Manro itself in September 2001 through its subsidiary, Stepan Europe, S.A. Another surfactant firm, Akcros Chemicals Ltd., was also purchased in 2001, while the following year brought the acquisition of several chemical businesses from the United Kingdom's Pentagon Chemical Specialties, based in Workington. As Stepan continued to expand its reach through operations, the company also increased its R&D funding from 2001's $13.7 million to $15.2 million for 2003 and $16 million in 2004. Revenues reflected the company's growth, surging from $784.9 million in 2003 to $935.8 million in 2004 with stock prices averaging $24 per share.

The year 2004 was also significant for two international milestones, buying a sulfonation manufacturing plant in Vespasiano, Brazil, and announcing a joint venture with China's Sinopec, Jinling Petrochemical Corporation. The partnership, Nanjing Stepan Jinling Chemical Company, Ltd., commenced operations in early 2005 with the completion of a new manufacturing facility in Nanjing. Fiscal 2005 also marked the realization of Quinn Sr.'s goal of hitting $1 billion in sales. Even though it came five years later than hoped, it still represented a major landmark as total revenues reached nearly $1.1 billion.

Stepan was on a roll in 2006 reaping the benefits of its strategic partnerships and increased presence throughout the world. During the year, Quinn Sr. relinquished the title of CEO to his son, retaining the title of chairman of the board. Revenues for fiscal 2006 climbed to $1.2 billion as stock prices hit an all-time high of $34 per share. In 2007 as the company marked 75 years in business, another surfactant product line (agricultural) was acquired from HallStar Company, followed by two French acquisitions from Paris-based Arkema in 2008. Stepan also increased ownership in its Chinese partnership (from 50 to 80 percent); formed a joint venture with Nalco Company, named Tiorco, LLC, to produce chemical solutions used in the crude oil and gas industry; and sold a polyurethane foam product line to Bayer MaterialScience LLC.

As the economic turmoil took its toll in late 2008 and early 2009, Stepan seemed relatively untouched. While Stepan's outlook was stable, neither Quinn took the company's continued success for granted. Cost-cutting measures were initiated and acquisitions were put under much more scrutiny to maintain Stepan's healthy balance sheet.

FUTURE OUTLOOK

As Stepan Company entered the next decade, Quinn Jr. continued to lead the family business in the manner of his father and grandfather before him, searching for niche markets to complement the company's product lines and create growth potential. Stepan had become a world leader in specialty and intermediate chemicals by knowing its industry's strengths and weaknesses, creating opportunities whenever possible, and aggressively pursuing growth through acquisitions and new product development. Quinn Stepan Sr. had set a goal of reaching $1 billion in sales in the 2000s; his son Quinn Jr. could be confident the company would reach the $2 billion mark in the 2010s.

Thomas Derdak
Updated, Nelson Rhodes

PRINCIPAL SUBSIDIARIES

Stepan Canada, Inc.; Stepan Colombiana de Quimicos (Colombia); Stepan Deutschland, GmbH; Stepan Europe, S.A.; Stepan Mexico, Inc.; Stepan Philippines, Inc.; Stepan Quimica, Ltda. (Brazil); Stepan UK Limited; Tiorco, LLC (50%); Nanjing Stepan Jinling Chemical LLC (80%).

PRINCIPAL COMPETITORS

Air Products and Chemicals, Inc.; BASF SE; Dow Chemical Company; Exxon Mobil Chemical Company; Huntsman Corporation; Koppers Holdings Inc.

FURTHER READING

"Bayer MaterialScience LLC Purchases Business from Stepan Company," *Paint & Coatings Industry,* September 2008, p. 24.

Floreno, Anthony, "Jobs & People," *Chemical Market Reporter,* March 29, 1999, p. 34.

"Fuel from Veggie Oil, Tallow," *Crain's Chicago Business,* September 27, 2004, p. 14.

"He Started on Sales Trips Early in Life," *Chemical Week,* November 14, 1973, p. 48.

Lerner, Ivan, "Specialty Chemicals Quarterly Earnings Show Difficult Times," *Chemical Market Reporter,* July 30, 2001, p. 13.

Levine, Daniel Rome, "The Secret Life of Soap," *Crain's Chicago Business,* May 15, 2006, p. 33.

Levy, Robert, "The Turnaround Specialist," *Dun's Review,* October 1968, p. 92.

Morris, Gregory, "Koppers and Stepan-Reichhold Join Aristech in Expansion Race," *Chemical Week,* October 16, 1996, p. 13.

Murphy, H. Lee, "Biofuel Boom Busts Stepan," *Crain's Chicago Business,* April 30, 2007, p. 7.

———, "Stepan Staying Optimistic As Profits Continue to Slip," *Crain's Chicago Business,* May 14, 2001, p. 52.

Podmolik, Mary Ellen, "Stepan Company, Rank: 83," *Crain's Chicago Business,* June 7, 2000, p. 79.

Seewald, Nancy, "Nalco and Stepan Form Oil Recovery Technology JV," *Chemical Week,* September 15, 2008, p. 18.

"Stepan and HallStar Swap Product Lines," *Chemical Week,* May 9, 2007, p. 6.

"Stepan Company," *Soap & Cosmetics,* February 1999, p. 66.

"Stepan Company," *Soap & Cosmetics,* May 1999, p. 54.

"Stepan Elects CEO's Son As Successor," *Chemical Week,* November 23, 2005, p. 4.

"Stepan Eyes Specialty Surfactants and Overseas Markets for Growth," *Chemical Market Reporter,* March 9, 1998, p. 5.

"Stepan to Build Polyols Plant in Chinese Joint Venture," *Chemical Market Reporter,* February 16, 2004, p. 2.

Trewhitt, Jeffrey, "Stepan Steps Out in Surfactants, Urethanes," *Chemical Week,* July 3, 1985.

Wilton, Bill, "Stepan Company," *Zacks,* May 27, 2009.

ThermoFisher
SCIENTIFIC

Thermo Fisher Scientific
Inc.

81 Wyman Street
Waltham, Massachusetts 02454-9046
U.S.A.
Telephone: (781) 622-1000
Toll Free: (800) 678-5599
Fax: (781) 622-1207
Web site: http://www.thermofisher.com

Public Company
Incorporated: 1956 as Thermo Electron Corporation
Employees: 34,500
Sales: $10.5 billion (2008)
Stock Exchanges: New York
Ticker Symbol: TMO
NAICS: 325413 In-Vitro Diagnostic Substance Manufacturing; 325414 Biological Product (Except Diagnostic) Manufacturing; 326160 Plastics Bottle Manufacturing; 327215 Glass Product Manufacturing Made of Purchased Glass; 333415 Air-Conditioning and Warm Air Heating Equipment and Commercial and Industrial Refrigeration Equipment Manufacturing; 334510 Electromedical and Electrotherapeutic Apparatus Manufacturing; 334516 Analytical Laboratory Instrument Manufacturing; 334519 Other Measuring and Controlling Device Manufacturing; 339113 Surgical Appliance and Supplies Manufacturing; 511210 Software Publishers; 541710 Research and Development in the Physical, Engineering, and Life Sciences

■ ■ ■

Thermo Fisher Scientific Inc. is a world leader in serving science. Reaching out to some 350,000 customers in about 150 countries worldwide, Thermo Fisher operates as a one-stop source for the scientific and laboratory needs of its customers within pharmaceutical and biotechnology companies, hospital and clinical diagnostic laboratories, environmental and industrial process control entities, universities, research institutions, and governmental agencies. The company serves its customers via two main brands, Thermo Scientific and Fisher Scientific. Thermo Scientific is more of a technology brand, offering customers a range of high-end analytical instruments such as mass spectrometers and chromatography devices in addition to equipment, chemistry and consumable supplies, software, and services used in laboratory settings. Fisher Scientific emphasizes convenience, offering general research customers a complete line of laboratory equipment, chemicals, supplies, and services used in healthcare, scientific research, safety settings, and education. Thermo Fisher Scientific is the product of the November 2006 merger of Thermo Electron Corporation and Fisher Scientific International Inc.

HATSOPOULOS-FOUNDED
THERMO ELECTRON

Thermo Electron Corporation was the life work of Greek immigrant George N. Hatsopoulos, whose interest in applying technology to solving problems led to the involvement of Thermo Electron in such fields as environmental monitoring instruments, alternative power generation, soil remediation, and artificial heart pumps. In addition to distinguishing himself as a

COMPANY PERSPECTIVES

Thermo Fisher Scientific Inc. (NYSE: TMO) is the world leader in serving science, enabling our customers to make the world healthier, cleaner and safer. With annual revenues of $10 billion, we have more than 30,000 employees and serve over 350,000 customers within pharmaceutical and biotech companies, hospitals and clinical diagnostic labs, universities, research institutions and government agencies, as well as environmental and industrial process control settings. Serving customers through two premier brands, Thermo Scientific and Fisher Scientific, we help solve analytical challenges from routine testing to complex research and discovery.

scientist, Hatsopoulos earned a reputation as a manager of extraordinary vision.

Hatsopoulos was born in suburban Athens in 1927 to a prosperous family of professors and politicians. He developed an interest in electronics during World War II when, upon the Nazi invasion of Greece in 1941, he constructed radios capable of tuning in Allied broadcasts, a practice punishable by imprisonment in a concentration camp. He clandestinely sold receivers to the public and supplied transmitters to the Greek underground.

Following the war, Hatsopoulos studied electrical engineering at Greece's national technical university, Athens Polytechnic, where he developed a strong interest in thermodynamics, the science of extracting energy from heat. Perceiving that Athens Polytechnic could not meet his educational needs, Hatsopoulos entered the Massachusetts Institute of Technology (MIT), where he became aware that there were practical applications of thermodynamics that had not yet been explored.

In 1956, while still a graduate student at MIT, Hatsopoulos negotiated a $50,000 loan to found Thermo Electron Corporation. The company, which was at first based in a garage and employed only his brother John, was established to lend his thermodynamics experiments legitimacy, and in turn make grants easier to obtain. Hatsopoulos's first professional endeavors were in the new field of thermionics, the science of converting heat into electricity without the aid of moving parts. Although several completed and patented mechanisms were too expensive to market commercially, his pioneering efforts placed Thermo Electron among several major corporations as a leading patent mill in the area of thermodynamics, and helped inspire nearly 30 companies, including General Electric (GE), North American Aviation, and General Dynamics, to enter the field.

The company survived for several years on research grants and metal fabrication work for other businesses, but was often forced to disregard profits in order to underbid competitors, acquire experience, and develop a reputation. Many Thermo Electron contracts focused on improving electrical generators and furnaces, and served to draw Thermo Electron into the business of industrial power generation and heating. Contracted by the U.S. government and a consortium of natural gas companies, Thermo Electron also improved industrial drying and heat-treating processes. Despite the company's status as the inventor of several new technologies, the government elected to award several subsequent contracts to larger competitors, such as GE and RCA, on the belief that the smaller organization did not have sufficient resources. In 1961 the company became the object of a takeover offer from Martin Marietta, which was interested in the application of thermionics to aerospace ventures. By this time, Thermo Electron had a staff of approximately 40 engineers and technicians, with Hatsopoulos heading the company's engineering efforts and his brother presiding over financial operations. Martin Marietta offered to purchase 51 percent of the company, retain Hatsopoulos as president, and double his salary. Hatsopoulos refused. Afterward, the government also recognized the merit of Thermo Electron, awarding it several contracts that included projects related to the space program.

In the drive to commercialize and expand, Thermo Electron began in 1963 to acquire firms whose facilities and marketing could support company breakthroughs in metallurgy and rare metals manufacturing, both of which developed from high-temperature heat conversion technology. Furthermore, in order to increase the availability of funds, Thermo Electron stock was placed on the over-the-counter market in 1967 and on the New York Stock Exchange in 1980.

UNIQUE ENTREPRENEURIAL PHILOSOPHY

Much of the company's growth was directly attributable to Hatsopoulos's unique entrepreneurial philosophy: Thermo Electron engineers were encouraged to pursue their own inventions, and concepts with potential for commercial success were allotted substantial development budgets. While some of these investments failed to yield a profit, many resulted in inventions with great practical and commercial promise. An example of the

KEY DATES

1902: In Pittsburgh, Chester G. Fisher founds Scientific Materials Company as a provider of laboratory supplies.

1926: Company is renamed Fisher Scientific Company.

1956: While a grad student at the Massachusetts Institute of Technology, George Hatsopoulos founds Thermo Electron Corporation.

1965: Fisher Scientific is taken public.

1967: Thermo Electron's stock begins trading on the over-the-counter market.

1981: Fisher Scientific is acquired by Allied Corporation.

1983: Thermo Electron adopts a new strategy centering on spinning out divisions into independent, publicly traded companies majority owned by Thermo.

1985: Fisher Scientific is part of operations spun off from Allied-Signal as The Henley Group, Inc.

1991: Through a public stock offering, Hampton, New Hampshire-based Fisher Scientific International Inc. emerges as an independent firm.

1998: Thermo Electron begins streamlining its byzantine structure; Fisher management and an investor group led by Thomas H. Lee Company complete a $1.4 billion recapitalization of Fisher Scientific that leaves them in control of 87 percent of the firm's common stock.

1999: Hatsopoulos steps down from Thermo Electron's CEO position.

2001: Thermo Electron largely completes its restructuring into a firm with a single focus: analytical instruments.

2004: Fisher Scientific acquires Apogent Technologies Inc.

2005: Thermo Electron acquires SPX Corporation's Kendro Laboratory Products division.

2006: Thermo Electron and Fisher Scientific International merge to create Thermo Fisher Scientific Inc.

established a joint venture with Thermo Electron to apply this technology to automobiles. Enthusiasm on Wall Street drove Thermo Electron's share price to nearly ten times its value a year earlier, although stock values retreated when rising gasoline prices later led Ford to abandon the project in favor of high-efficiency engine research. Remade on a much smaller scale and powered by a miniature nuclear reactor, the steam engine was subsequently used to drive an artificial heart. When tested on animals, however, the device was found to be too hazardous for public use, and effective permanent models for humans never were developed. This work, however, led to the development of a battery-powered left-ventricular assist device, which later received approval from the U.S. Food and Drug Administration (FDA) as a device to help weak hearts keep pumping for patients waiting for heart transplants.

Thermo Electron's work in heat conversion and conservation technologies led to an annual grant of more than $1 million from natural gas utilities. By 1968 this support enabled the company to develop an industrial and commercial furnace division and acquire Holcroft & Company, a furnace manufacturer based in Michigan. That same year, Thermo Electron purchased Lodding Engineering, a Massachusetts manufacturer of auxiliary equipment for the paper industry. By expanding into industrial manufacturing, Thermo Electron was better able to market its innovations, test applications of its technology, and maintain quality control. By 1970 the company had diversified into other areas of primary industrial equipment manufacturing.

Hatsopoulos demonstrated the ability to anticipate and address burgeoning public and consumer needs. Recognizing the close relationship between technology and the environment, he monitored demand for environment-oriented technologies by observing social and political events. This was best demonstrated in 1971, when Hatsopoulos predicted that ratification of the Clean Air Act would create demand for environmental monitoring devices. Consequently, Thermo Electron marketed the first instrument to detect traces of nitrogen dioxide, a common compound in automobile exhaust and smog. Later, Hatsopoulos determined that the growing dependence of the United States on foreign oil would enable oil-producing nations to use their commodity as a political weapon. Hence, he stressed the development of more efficient industrial furnaces for the paper and metals industries well before the OPEC oil embargo of 1973, making the energy-efficient products and patented designs of Thermo Electron the first on the furnace market. With this type of success, the company exceeded $100 million in annual sales by the mid-1970s. In 1981 revenues surpassed $230 million and profits neared $9 million.

latter was a modified Rankine-cycle steam engine that did not pollute. In 1968, four years after the engine project was initiated, the Ford Motor Company

Thermo Electron struggled for several years in a shrinking American capital goods market, however, because of an economic recession and a diminished market for capital-intensive equipment such as furnaces. In 1983 the company grossed only $182 million, leaving a scant $50,000 profit after the deduction of new business development expenditures and write-downs. At that point, Hatsopoulos decided that Thermo Electron must explore areas other than the capital goods market, and began searching for new industries. In a characteristic move, he doubled the company research and development budget. Additionally, he mapped out what were determined to be the major issues of the 1980s and 1990s and matched these issues with Thermo Electron's strengths. Consequently, Hatsopoulos decided to develop atmospheric-particle sensing devices capable of detecting small, well-concealed bombs and controlled substances such as cocaine. Company technologies also suited the development of a hazardous substance incinerator, which could be used to treat petroleum-contaminated soil. Other market-driven innovations included surgical monitors, generators that burned agricultural waste, equipment that recycled paper, and air conditioners that ran on natural gas.

"SPIN-OUT" STRATEGY

In a search for an improved business structure, Hatsopoulos encountered the model on which Japanese trading companies were organized. These companies, he learned, were part of huge industrial groups often including hundreds of diversified firms. Each owned a small percentage of every other company; hence, a company was owned in sum by the group. Hatsopoulos found that Japanese companies, with strong interest in mutual success, had little problem raising the funds necessary for ambitious research and development. In the United States, however, companies such as Thermo Electron were financially hamstrung by the limited backing of banks. Following the lead of the Japanese, he created several Thermo Electron subsidiaries beginning in 1983, selling between 10 and 40 percent of each company to outside shareholders. The proceeds from these so-called spin-outs were used to further research and development at Thermo Electron, and nurture other subsidiaries toward public share offerings.

By 1992 there were eight publicly traded subsidiaries, as well as one other one partially sold to outside investors. By separating these promising units from the larger corporation, Hatsopoulos found, he was better able to control costs, raise funds, and inspire a greater sense of mission. "To take a company public," he told *CFO* magazine, "the company has to have an opportunity to grow at a 30 percent compounded rate for

a long period. We must have the depth of management to run it as a public company, and we must have a need for the cash." Furthermore, none of these companies paid dividends; all shareowner profit was realized from increased share value. As a result of managerial strategies such as this, as well as product diversification, Thermo Electron showed remarkable growth, posting revenues of $615 million in 1989, $721 million in 1990, $805 million in 1991, and $949 million in 1992. Profits in 1992 totaled $61 million.

Thermo Electron remained on the same course for most of the remainder of the 1990s, spinning out additional operations and also facilitating growth in its subsidiaries in part via acquisition. Thermo Instrument Systems Inc., for instance, which specialized in environmental monitoring and analytical instruments, acquired the scientific instrument division of the U.K. firm Fisons plc for about $189 million in March 1996. The deal boosted Thermo Instrument's revenue beyond $1 billion and made it the world's second largest producer of instruments for identifying and analyzing air pollution, radioactivity, complex chemical compounds, toxic metals, and other elements. In late 1994 Thermo Electron launched a hostile takeover bid for Puritan-Bennett Corporation, a producer of respiratory medical instrumentation such as blood-gas monitors. This bid, which was eventually valued at more than $300 million, was withdrawn in December 1994, however, when the target's board refused to remove its poison-pill takeover defense.

In March 1997 Thermo Instrument broadened its operations through a $442.8 million deal for Life Sciences International PLC, a U.K.-based maker of laboratory equipment used in medical research and clinical laboratories. Life Sciences, which had operations in Europe, the United States, and Asia, produced a broad range of lab equipment, including beakers, test tubes, industrial freezers, incubators, and cell and tissue processors. This acquisition helped push Thermo Instrument's revenue up to $1.66 billion by 1998, while Thermo Electron's total for that year amounted to $3.56 billion.

RESTRUCTURING TO FOCUS ON INSTRUMENTS

Over the course of the 1990s, Thermo Electron's spin-out strategy eventually created an increasingly byzantine corporate structure with no fewer than 23 publicly traded subsidiaries by 1998. Further complexity followed from the parent company's encouragement of spin-outs from spin-outs. Thus by 1998 Thermo Instrument Systems itself had seven publicly traded subsidiaries. At the same time that operations were becoming increasingly difficult to manage, share prices at the firms began suffering as investors grew ever warier of Thermo's complexity. In August 1998 Thermo Electron began reversing course when it announced a plan to streamline its structure by reducing its number of spin-out companies from 23 to 16. By early 2000 the company had reacquired full control of four of the spin-outs. In mid-1999 company founder Hatsopoulos ended his long tenure at the helm by turning the reins over to Richard F. Syron, who had been CEO of the American Stock Exchange Inc. Syron was named chairman as well in January 2000, although Hatsopoulos retained a seat on the board of directors. Also in 1999, Thermo Instrument Systems acquired the Swedish firm Spectra-Physics AB for about $351 million. Spectra-Physics, a firm with annual revenues of about $440 million, specialized in laser-based instrumentation systems, mainly for the process-control, industrial measurement, construction, research, commercial, and government markets.

In January 2000 Thermo Electron launched a more ambitious restructuring that eventually brought its spin-out era to a close. Over the next 24 months the firm sold numerous businesses with aggregate revenues of $1.2 billion. The ultimate aim was to reduce the company to a single core business: analytical instruments used in life science, laboratory, and industrial settings. The heart of the new Thermo Electron would thus be the operations of Thermo Instrument Systems, and this subsidiary was reabsorbed into the parent company in 2000. Three other key transactions rounded out the restructuring. In February 2001 Thermo Cardiosystems Inc., producer of ventricular assist devices, was sold to Thoratec Laboratories Corporation. Thermo Fibertek Inc., a manufacturer of equipment for the pulp and paper industries, was spun off to Thermo Electron shareholders as Kadant Inc. Thermo Electron also grouped a number of manufacturers of medical products for diagnosis and monitoring into a new company called Viasys Healthcare Inc., which it then spun off to shareholders in November 2001.

Having successfully overseen the dramatic transformation of Thermo Electron, Syron stepped aside from day-to-day management of the firm in November 2002. He was at that time named executive chairman and was charged with oversight of acquisition and financing strategies. Taking the operating helm as president and CEO was Marijn E. Dekkers, who had served as president and COO since July 2000. Late in 2003 Syron left the company to head mortgage finance giant Freddie Mac. Jim P. Manzi, former chief of software maker Lotus Development Corporation, was named the new chairman.

Having emerged in 2002 as a newly focused company with annual sales of a little over $2 billion, Thermo Electron enlarged itself over the next few years through a series of acquisitions that in particular bulked up its life and laboratory sciences operations. In December 2003, for instance, the company acquired the French firm Jouan SA for about $138 million. Jouan, which had manufacturing operations in France, Denmark, Italy, the Czech Republic, and the United States, produced laboratory equipment for life sciences applications, including centrifuges, incubators, biological safety cabinets, and ultralow-temperature freezers. Life and laboratory sciences became even more of a focus for Thermo Electron in July 2004 when it sold its optical technologies unit, Spectra-Physics, to Newport Corporation for approximately $300 million. Following this divestment, the life and laboratory sciences unit generated about 70 percent of Thermo Electron's revenues, with measurement and control equipment accounting for the other 30 percent. The company continued its push into life sciences in May 2005 when it acquired SPX Corporation's Kendro Laboratory Products division for $836.6 million. Kendro, based in Asheville, North Carolina, produced such lab equipment as incubators, freezers, refrigerators, centrifuges, and heat-treat ovens. Its revenues for 2004 had totaled about $365 million. By 2005, Thermo Electron's growth drive had pushed its revenues up to $2.63 billion. In May 2006 the company reached an agreement to merge with Fisher Scientific International Inc.

FISHER'S FOUNDING AND EARLY YEARS

At the beginning of the 20th century, the United States was becoming an industrial nation. In Pittsburgh, Pennsylvania, Chester G. Fisher, a 20-year-old engineering graduate of Western University of Pennsylvania, recognized the need for a company that would supply scientific tools for the city's many industries, especially the burgeoning steel business. He bought the stockroom of the Pittsburgh Testing Laboratories, which served as Western Pennsylvania's only source of laboratory supplies. Fisher dreamed of realizing the ideal expressed by French scientist Louis Pasteur: "Take interest in these sacred dwellings which we call laboratories. There it is that humanity grows greater, stronger, better." In 1902 the young engineer founded the Scientific Materials Company, the first commercial source of equipment and reagents for the region's laboratories. In the early 1900s, laboratory work consisted mainly of simple volumetric and gravimetric analysis; because very little instrumentation was available, chemists depended primarily on their eyes for analysis. Fisher's earliest products, such as microscopes, burettes, pipettes, litmus, balances, and colorimeters, allowed for better visual analysis. These tools were state-of-the-art in those days and, although relatively crude by contemporary standards, were the foundation for Fisher Scientific International Inc.'s technical leadership in serving science.

In 1904 Chester Fisher published the 400-page *Scientific Materials Co. Catalog of Laboratory Apparatus & Supplies,* illustrated with handmade woodcuts and featuring standard laboratory supplies as well as dissecting sets encased in Moroccan leather and anatomical models of the eye, the ear, and the heart. Later this catalog evolved into the *Fisher Catalog,* the company's most famous marketing tool. This biennial product reference became the industry standard as both a buying guide and a source of product specifications and technical information. The electronic edition available on the company's web site by the late 1990s was the industry's most comprehensive source for laboratory equipment and supplies, including apparatus, instrumentation, disposable lab supplies, glassware, chemicals, safety supplies, laboratory workstations, and specialized products for biotechnological, clinical, chromatographical, and environmental applications.

When World War I cut the company off from its European suppliers, Scientific Materials set up its own research, development, and manufacturing capabilities. The company's earliest manufactured products proved to be superior to those formerly imported from Europe. For example, Scientific Materials' electric-combustion furnace and combustion train for analyzing carbon levels in steel was the first of its kind, as was the electrically heated and thermostatically controlled bacteriological incubator that replaced the erratic gas-flame German incubator.

Furthermore, when the United States entered World War I, Chester Fisher made his company the first home of the U.S. Chemical Warfare Service and rushed an entire American Expeditionary Force Research Laboratory to the front lines in France to help the Allies defend themselves against gas warfare. Another landmark event was the invention of the Fisher Burner, which Ernest Child, in his book titled *Tools of the Chemist: Their Ancestry and American Evolution,* hailed as "the most significant development in burners since the original Bunsen burner." Other early inventions included a unitized system for gas analysis and an electromagnetic instrument for rapid determinations of carbon in steel. Then, in 1925, the company transcended its regional markets by purchasing Montreal-based Scientific Supplies, Limited. In 1926 Chester Fisher renamed his company Fisher Scientific Company to differentiate it from new companies with "generic" names.

In 1940 Fisher acquired Eimer & Amend (a New York-based chemical company for which Scientific Materials had once been an agent), and took over its laboratory-supply business and manufacturing of fine chemicals. Fisher Scientific established a sound reputation for its quality chemicals. It supplied chemicals used in the U.S. government's top-secret Manhattan Project for producing the world's first atomic bomb. According to company archives, in 1947 Chester Fisher was given the Award of the American Chemical Society by its Pittsburgh Section. His contributions were summarized in this way: "The nation and much of the world owe a debt to C. G. Fisher. ... A bit of C. G. is in most of the world's steel. The aluminum wings of man carry their loads more effectively because of him. Our foods are safeguarded ... our farm soils maintained ... our hospitals work more effectively ... virtually no phase of modern life exists that has not been influenced or touched by some product of the Fisher Company." Chester Fisher served 47 years as company president before he became chairman in 1949 and was succeeded by his son Aiken W. Fisher.

INVENTIONS AND ACQUISITIONS

As a manufacturer, Fisher set a new industry standard in 1954 when it introduced volumetric packaging—the packaging of liquid chemicals based on volume rather than on weight. This method of packaging resulted in better use of storeroom space, easier ordering, and cost savings. Volumetric packaging was quickly adopted by other chemical manufacturers. As a quality supplier to the medical market, Fisher provided the reagents used by Dr. Jonas Salk to develop the polio vaccine introduced in 1955. By 1961 the incidence of polio had dropped by 95 percent. Company acquisitions continued apace with the 1957 purchase of New York-based E. Machlett & Sons, which specialized in medical apparatus and supported critical medical research, including early cancer investigations.

Then Fisher Scientific established the Instrument Division to manufacture laboratory supplies ranging from complex optical-electronic instrumentation and automatic freeze-dryers to precision-scaled atom models. In 1965 the company introduced the Differential Thermalyzer, an automatically programmed system for conducting differential thermal analysis. According to the company's web site, *Chemical and Engineering News* (the official publication of the American Chemical Society) called the product "a real price breakthrough," noting that this $950 Fisher product replaced instruments typically selling for $4,000 to $8,000. In addition, the industry magazine *Industrial Research* named the Differential Thermalyzer one of the 100 most significant new technical products of the year. Another key event was the 1962 installation of an IBM computer system to record and track inventory levels for more than 40,000 items. By June 1970 all U.S. Fisher branches were linked to this system, thereby providing immediate control of inventory information.

In 1965 Chester G. Fisher died and was succeeded by his son Aiken as chairman of Fisher Scientific; another son, Benjamin, became the company's president. Chester had seen his company grow from a regional laboratory supply company, staffed by six employees in a Pittsburgh warehouse, to a leading position in manufacturing and distribution of scientific products and supplies, with $58 million in sales and close to a million customer transactions. The company went public in 1965 and was listed on the New York Stock Exchange in 1968.

With the acquisition of Pfeiffer Glass, Inc., in 1966, Fisher added the capability of mass-producing accurate pipettes for many laboratory applications. Fisher pipettes became, and remained, the industry standard. That same year Fisher's Photometric Titralyzer helped to change the way scientists did their jobs: It could analyze 15 successive samples and print out the results. The industry journal *Industrial Research* cited the Photometric Titralyzer as one of the 100 most significant new technical products of 1966. A similar honor went to the company's 1968 Hem-alyzer, which provided printed information about a patient's hemoglobin content, as well as red and white blood-cell counts, in 96 seconds. Then, following the 1968 purchase of Massachusetts-based Jarrell-Ash Company, Fisher was able to design and manufacture sophisticated optical instrumentation, particularly in the fields of emission and atomic absorption spectroscopy.

Fisher Scientific entered the educational marketplace in 1967 with the acquisition of Stansi Scientific Company, a Chicago manufacturer and distributor of equipment for teaching science in elementary and secondary schools, colleges, and universities. Nine years later, the Nigerian Ministry of Education chose Fisher Scientific from among 40 different organizations around the world to support education programs for life and physical sciences. Fisher, chosen for its competitive prices, complete product lines, and ability to fill the total order in just nine months, sent 16 chartered cargo jets carrying nearly 100,000 pieces of teaching equipment to Nigeria. At $8.75 million, this was a record-setting order in Fisher's 74-year history. Years later, Fisher shipped a large quantity of scientific supplies to Kuwait to reequip 80 laboratories of colleges and institutes ravaged by the Persian Gulf War.

During the 1970s, *Industrial Research* magazine placed two other Fisher inventions among the top 100 most important technical products of the year: the Autotensiomat, a fully automated surface-tension-measuring instrument that could be used on most liquids; and the Model 750 AtomComp, a computer-controlled, direct-reading spectrometer that was the first commercially available instrument of this type. To ensure that its millions of instruments in the field worked at peak efficiency, in 1976 Fisher Scientific established an Instrument Service Division having 11 service centers across the nation; the division installed new equipment and trained laboratory personnel in its use.

END OF FAMILY CONTROL

For 73 years Chester Fisher's scientific company was headed by either himself or one of his sons. In 1975 Aiken retired as the company's chairman and was replaced by his brother, Benjamin Fisher. Edward Perkins became the first nonfamily member to be named president and CEO. He held that position until the company was acquired by Allied Corporation in 1981.

Over the next decade, the company operated as a subsidiary of Allied Corporation, then successor Allied-Signal Inc., and finally The Henley Group, Inc., a 1985 spinoff from Allied-Signal. In 1982 Fisher chemicals were an integral component of the in-flight battery power system for the Columbia space shuttle, which was launched for its fourth mission on June 27. Fisher provided 55-gallon drums of chemicals for the 1984 development of Nova, the world's largest and most powerful laser, housed in four rooms of the Lawrence Livermore National Laboratory in Livermore, California. To meet the growing needs of scientists in biotechnology, biochemistry, and related fields, in 1985 Fisher established a Biotechnology Division. With unique products, such as Promega molecular biologicals and Mediatech bacteriological culture media, Fisher BioTech sales grew more than 30 percent annually for the next eight years. In 1988 Fisher patented its Code-On technology, a spectacular new use of automation in molecular histopathology; during that year more than 150 Code-On units were installed in laboratories throughout North America.

WORLDWIDE EXPANSION AS NEWLY INDEPENDENT FIRM

At year-end 1991 The Henley Group sold a 57 percent interest in Fisher through a public stock offering. The public entity emerged as Fisher Scientific International Inc., based in Hampton, New Hampshire. Fisher

Scientific Company remained in Pittsburgh as an operating subsidiary. Henley President Paul M. Montrone became president and CEO of Fisher Scientific International in 1991 and chairman in 1998. David T. Della Penta became president and COO in 1998. Fisher, in 1992, became the first American producer of reagents and fine chemicals to have its facilities ISO-9000 certified by the Geneva, Switzerland-based International Standards Organization, which based certification on a common set of manufacturing, trade, and communication standards. ISO-9000 certification is the worldwide standard measurement of total quality management. Fisher won a seven-year, $150 million contract with the University of California; research centers on nine of the university's campuses were linked directly to Fisher via some 50 remote-order stations and advanced electronic data systems.

Throughout the 1990s Fisher experienced dramatic growth both nationally and internationally through strategic acquisitions and mergers, joint ventures and alliances, expansion of current lines, additions to its product portfolio, and the development of its global distribution network. For instance, the 1992 purchase of Hamilton Scientific, Inc., the premier American designer and manufacturer of laboratory workstations, led to the merger of Fisher's existing laboratory-furniture capability with Hamilton to form Fisher Hamilton Inc., the world's largest manufacturer and supplier of laboratory workstations, even providing experts for design, budgeting, and project coordination.

In 1993 and 1995 Fisher completed two major laboratory-renovation projects in Russia in collaboration with one of the company's dealers, Intertech Corporation of Atkinson, New Hampshire. In early 1997 Fisher received a $400,000 grant from the U.S. Trade and Development Agency as partial funding to conduct a feasibility study for the development of a $10 million state-of-the-art laboratory in Moscow. The laboratory, the first of its kind in Russia, was to test and certify pharmaceuticals for the Russian Federation's Ministry of Health and Medical Industry, which is similar to the FDA. Fisher worked with FDA personnel and sent a team of engineers, architects, and designers to Moscow to evaluate the proposed site of the laboratory. Both the U.S. and Russian governments were expected to provide financial support for implementation of the project.

The acquisition of the organic-chemicals business of Eastman Kodak Company and of Belgium-based, industry-leader Janssen Chimica allowed Fisher to add a strong new component to its international chemical operations by merging the two product lines to form Acros Organics. Curtin Matheson Scientific Inc., a leading supplier of diagnostic instruments, tests, and related

products acquired in October 1995, was integrated into Fisher's clinical-laboratory operations to form CMS/Fisher HealthCare. A strategic alliance with Bedford, Massachusetts-based Millipore Corporation allowed Fisher to distribute Millipore laboratory filtration products in the United States, Puerto Rico, and Canada.

The 1992 acquisition of Kühn + Bayer GmbH, a leading German provider of scientific equipment and supplies to more than 4,000 customers from central Europe to Moscow, represented Fisher's first equity investment in Europe. This company was later merged with another Fisher subsidiary, Udo Fleischhacker GmbH & Co. KG, to form Fisher Scientific GmbH, which served as an automated distribution center and sales operation in Germany. Similarly, in the Netherlands two Fisher subsidiaries were combined to form Fisher Scientific of the Netherlands B.V., and in the United Kingdom, two other Fisher subsidiaries were consolidated as Fisher Scientific U.K., Limited, the largest Fisher subsidiary in Europe. Other acquisitions included Singapore-based Fisher General Scientific Pte Ltd and Malaysia-based Fisher Scientific Holdings (M), which exported to China, India, Thailand, Vietnam, Brunei, and other Asian markets.

GLOBAL ELECTRONIC COMMERCE

Chester Fisher's company pioneered as a distributor of scientific supplies. As early as 1904 he published an illustrated catalog to facilitate ordering of the company's laboratory apparatus and supplies. In 1962 an IBM computer recorded and tracked inventory levels for some 40,000 items; by mid-1970 all the U.S. company's branches were linked to Fisher "Fastback," the industry's first real-time computer system. In 1978 Fisher installed computer terminals at its major customers' sites, enabling them to place orders directly and to receive immediate order verification printouts, as well as information on their past purchases and account status.

During the 1990s, Fisher established itself as an industry leader in electronic commerce by extending the company's historical technology in inventory management and procurement systems. Search, retrieval, order-management, and transaction-processing functions were added to Fisher's Internet site. CornerStone software allowed buyers and suppliers to create public or private web sites to support their business-to-business transactions. ProcureNet, a public mall owned and operated by Fisher, gave the general commercial community access to Fisher electronic catalogs and those of other suppliers. In 1997 the Internet & Electronic Commerce Conference, organized by The Gartner Group, recognized ProcureNet as "the first public electronic mall for business-to-business transactions" and awarded Fisher Scientific the iEC Award for the Best Internet Infrastructure.

The company's distribution network by 1997 comprised 32 locations in the United States, including a national distribution center in Somerville, New Jersey, four regional centers (New Jersey, California, Illinois, and Georgia), and 27 local facilities throughout the United States. Fisher Scientific also had two centers in Canada, and one each in Germany, France, England, Belgium, Singapore, Korea, Malaysia, Mexico, and Australia. The company distributed an average of 20,000 items every business day, with products accounting for more than 90 percent of total 1997 sales shipped to customers within 24 hours of being ordered. By year-end 1997, Fisher Scientific's sales had increased to $2.18 billion, compared with $757.7 million in 1991, the year Fisher Scientific International Inc. became a public company. Sales had increased every year since 1954, when revenues were only $2.1 million.

RECAPITALIZATION AND FURTHER DEAL-MAKING

In January 1998 Fisher management and an investor group led by Thomas H. Lee Company completed a $1.4 billion recapitalization of Fisher Scientific that left them in control of 87 percent of the firm's common stock. According to Elisabeth Kirschner's story in *Chemical and Engineering News,* this action followed an unsolicited 1997 proposal from the company's former largest shareholders, the Bass brothers of Texas, who were seeking to recapitalize or take over Fisher. In an introduction to Fisher's 1997 annual report, President Paul M. Montrone wrote that 1997 was a challenging time for the company, "which did not sustain the sales and income trends of previous years." He pointed out that continuing costs associated with consolidation and restructuring, market dynamics, and a 16-day strike against United Parcel Service (responsible for more than 60 percent of Fisher's domestic deliveries) affected results.

Following the takeover by the management and investor group, Fisher Scientific pursued additional acquisitions. Late in 1998 the company purchased control of Bioblock Scientific S.A., a leading distributor of scientific and laboratory instrumentation in France, for about $136 million. In 2000 Fisher attempted to move beyond laboratory supplies into the healthcare supplies market when it agreed to acquire PSS World

Medical Inc. in a stock swap initially valued at $840 million. A sharp decline in Fisher's stock in the weeks following the announcement of this deal, however, led the two companies to call off the merger. In November 2001 Fisher acquired closely held Cole-Parmer Instrument Company for $208.5 million. Based in Vernon Hills, Illinois, Cole-Parmer was a leading worldwide manufacturer and distributor of specialty technical instruments, appliances, equipment, and supplies serving pharmaceutical companies and biotechnology researchers. Funding for this deal was derived from a secondary stock offering conducted by the company in May 2001 that raised nearly $290 million. Early the following year, the Thomas H. Lee–led investor group conducted its own offering of Fisher stock, after which the investor group's stake was reduced to 46 percent. By the end of 2003, the investor group had sold the remainder of its shares.

In the years leading up to its merger with Thermo Electron, Fisher Scientific completed a series of deals to push deeply into the fast-growing life sciences market. In September 2003 Fisher acquired the Swedish firm Perbio Science AB for about $689 million in cash plus the assumption of $44 million in debt. Perbio specialized in the manufacture of consumable tools for protein-related research and protein-based biopharma drug production, primarily for U.S. customers. Fisher next paid $330 million for Oxoid Group Holdings Limited, a U.K.-based manufacturer of microbiological culture media and other diagnostic products used primarily to test for bacteria contamination. In April 2004 the company acquired Dharmacon, Inc., for $80 million, gaining a specialist in RNA technologies used to increase the efficiency of drug discovery efforts.

Then in August 2004, Fisher Scientific completed its largest takeover to that time, the purchase of Apogent Technologies Inc. for $2.8 billion in stock and the assumption of about $1.1 billion in debt. Apogent, based in Portsmouth, New Hampshire, manufactured laboratory and life-science products for scientific research and healthcare diagnostics. This deal was particularly significant for Fisher because it increased the company's portfolio of "proprietary" products, those it either produced itself or for which it was the exclusive distributor. Such products commanded higher profit margins. By the end of 2005, $55 million in annual cost savings had been generated in the effort to integrate the operations of Apogent into Fisher. That year, revenues totaled $5.58 billion, a 21 percent increase over the previous year. Net income more than doubled to reach $389.1 million.

2006 MEGAMERGER CREATING THERMO FISHER SCIENTIFIC

In May 2006 Thermo Electron and Fisher Scientific International agreed to merge their operations and combine the former's strength in scientific instruments with the latter's formidable position in laboratory equipment and supplies. Completed in November 2006, the deal was structured as a Thermo takeover of Fisher and involved a stock swap valued at $10.28 billion. Thermo also assumed $2.28 billion in Fisher debt. On conclusion of the deal, Thermo Electron was renamed Thermo Fisher Scientific Inc. The firm remained based in Waltham, Massachusetts, and Thermo Electron's CEO (Dekkers) and chairman (Manzi) continued on in the same positions. The combined workforce totaled more than 30,000.

In the subsequent integration, some of the operations of Fisher Scientific were shifted over to become part of a newly named Thermo Scientific brand. Under this brand, the company included most of its technology offerings, including a range of high-end analytical instruments such as mass spectrometers and chromatography devices in addition to equipment, chemistry and consumable supplies, software, and services used in laboratory settings. The Fisher Scientific brand was positioned as a convenience brand, using Fisher's strong distribution network to offer general research customers in healthcare, scientific research, safety settings, and education one-stop shopping for laboratory equipment, chemicals, supplies, and services. On its formation, Thermo Fisher Scientific derived 45 percent of its revenues from life sciences customers, 20 percent from the healthcare field, and 35 percent from the environmental, industrial, and safety sectors. About 63 percent of revenues were generated in North America, 26 percent in Europe, and 11 percent elsewhere, particularly Asia.

In 2007, the first full year following the merger, Thermo Fisher posted profits of $761.1 million on revenues of $9.75 billion. During that year and 2008, the company completed a number of smaller acquisitions while also aggressively pursuing growth overseas, particularly in fast-growing markets in Asia. By the end of 2008, Thermo Fisher was operating five facilities and had about 1,000 employees in China. The firm also launched its first Chinese-language Fisher Scientific catalog in 2008, focusing primarily on products for the life sciences, environmental, and food safety markets. Another major growth market was India, where Thermo Fisher had 20 facilities and sales offices in place by the end of 2008. After posting record profits of $988.7 million in 2008 and pushing revenues over the $10 billion mark, Thermo Fisher began feeling the effects of the global economic downturn during the first quarter of 2009 and warned of declines in both profits and revenues for the full year.

John Simley and Gloria A. Lemieux
Updated, David E. Salamie

PRINCIPAL SUBSIDIARIES

Athena Diagnostics, Inc.; Barnant Company; Barnstead Thermolyne Corporation; Capitol Vial, Inc.; Cellomics, Inc.; Chase Scientific Glass, Inc.; Clintrak Clinical Labeling Services, LLC; Cole-Parmer Instrument Company; Consolidated Technologies, Inc.; Dharmacon, Inc.; EP Scientific Products LLC; Erie Scientific Company; Fisher BioServices Inc.; Fisher Clinical Services Inc.; Fisher Hamilton L.L.C.; Fisher Scientific International Inc.; Fisher Scientific Latin America Inc.; Fisher Scientific Worldwide Inc.; Hyclone Laboratories, Inc.; LabVision Corporation; Lancaster Laboratories, Inc.; Matrix Technologies LLC; Metavac LLC; Microgenics Corporation; Molecular BioProducts Inc.; Nalge Nunc International Corporation; National Scientific Company; Naugatuck Glass Company; NeoMarkers, Inc.; NERL Diagnostics LLC; Owl Separation Systems LLC; PACTECH, LLC; Pierce Biotechnology, Inc.; Pierce Milwaukee, Inc.; Remel Inc.; Richard-Allan Scientific Company; Samco Scientific Corporation; Separation Technology, Inc.; Seradyn Inc.; Acros Organics B.V.B.A. (Belgium); Perbio Science BVBA (Belgium); Fisher Scientific Limited (Canada); Fisher Scientific Worldwide (Shanghai) Co., Ltd. (China); Thermo Fisher Scientific (Shanghai) Co., Ltd. (China); Guangzhou Fisher Scientific Company Limited (China); Fisher Scientific, spol. S.r.o (Czech Republic; 67%); Fisher BioImage ApS (Denmark); Nunc A/S (Denmark); Fisher Bioblock Scientific S.A.S. (France); Fisher Scientific GmbH (Germany); Gerhard Menzel Verwaltungs GmbH (Germany); Microm International GmbH (Germany); Novodirect GmbH (Germany); Scherf Praezision Europa GmbH (Germany); Fisher Scientific Japan, Ltd.; Nalge Nunc International K.K. (Japan); Fisher Scientific Korea Ltd.; Fisher CW Medical Sdn. Bhd. (Malaysia); Fisher Scientific (Malaysia) Sdn. Bhd.; Casa Rocas S. de R.L. de C.V. (Mexico); Fisher Emergo B.V. (Netherlands); Eutech Instruments Pte. Ltd. (Singapore); Fisher Scientific (SEA) Pte. Ltd. (Singapore); Fisher Clinical Services GmbH (Switzerland); Fisher Scientific AG (Switzerland); Abgene Limited (UK); Chromacol Limited (UK); Electrothermal Engineering Limited (UK); Fisher Clinical Services U.K. Limited; Fisher Scientific U.K., Limited; Maybridge Limited (UK); Oxoid Limited (UK).

PRINCIPAL DIVISIONS

Analytical Technologies; Laboratory Products and Services.

PRINCIPAL COMPETITORS

VWR International, LLC; Agilent Technologies, Inc.; Becton, Dickinson and Company; Beckman Coulter, Inc.; Life Technologies Corporation; Waters Corporation; PerkinElmer, Inc.

FURTHER READING

Alster, Norm, "Making the Kids Stand on Their Own," *Forbes,* October 9, 1995, pp. 49+.

Altany, David, "Newton's Son: Whether He's Spinning Out Ideas or Spinning Off Divisions, George Hatsopoulos Sits Among the Innovative Elite," *Industry Week,* April 1, 1991, pp. 30+.

Bahner, Benedict, "Lab Chemicals Market: Fisher Fuses It Further," *Chemical Marketing Reporter,* December 27, 1993, pp. 5+.

Bailey, Steve, and Steven Syre, "And Thermo Begat … No End in Sight to Offspring of Waltham Firm," *Boston Globe,* March 19, 1996, p. 41.

Baldwin, William, "Serendipity," *Forbes,* November 16, 1987, pp. 274+.

Bennett, Johanna, "Lab Partners: A Smart Merger Transforms Fisher Scientific," *Barron's,* March 29, 2004, p. MW11.

Berman, Dennis K., "Thermo, Fisher Set $10.6 Billion Pact," *Wall Street Journal,* May 8, 2006, p. A3.

Buell, Barbara, "For Thermo Electron, It's Full Steam Ahead," *Business Week,* March 3, 1986, p. 90B.

Bulkeley, William M., "Bid for Fisher Scientific Brings Back Painful Memories: Firm Seeks to Stay Independent After Ownership Shifts in 1980s Hurt Results," *Wall Street Journal,* June 12, 1997, p. B4.

———, "Henley Group Plans Spin Off of Biggest Units," *Wall Street Journal,* May 3, 1990, p. A4.

———, "Thermo Electron to Take Pretax Charge, Reacquire Stakes in Four Subsidiaries," *Wall Street Journal,* May 25, 1999, p. A4.

———, "Thermo Fisher Plans Hard Sell of Lab Solutions," *Wall Street Journal,* November 15, 2006, p. B3D.

———, "Thomas H. Lee Co. Agrees to Buy Fisher Scientific for $1.06 Billion," *Wall Street Journal,* August 8, 1997, p. B5.

Bylinsky, Gene, "Thermo Electron Corporation: From the Moon to the Steam Engine," *The Innovation Millionaires: How They Succeed,* New York: Scribner, 1976.

Child, Ernest, *Tools of the Chemist: Their Ancestry and American Evolution,* New York: Reinhold Publishing, 1940, 220 p.

Deutsch, Claudia H., "A Corporate Parent with Too Big a Family," *New York Times,* June 6, 1999, p. BU6.

———, "Mr. Fix-It Rewires a Company," *New York Times,* March 5, 2000, p. BU2.

Donlon, J. P., "Not by Technology Alone," *Chief Executive* (U. S.), April 1993, pp. 38, 42–43.

Fahey, Tom, "Fisher Scientific to Buy Wis. Firm," *Manchester (N.H.) Union Leader,* December 17, 1992.

Feder, Barnaby J., "The Spinoff Stratagem: How Thermo Electron Copes with the High Cost of Capital," *New York Times,* November 11, 1990, p. F4.

"Fisher Expects Little Change," *Manchester (N.H.) Union Leader,* January 20, 1998, p. 1.

"Fisher Scientific Venture Taps Japanese Market," *Pittsburgh Business Times,* January 8, 1996.

Forelle, Charles, "Fisher Scientific Is Buying Apogent," *Wall Street Journal,* March 18, 2004, p. A14.

Fraser, Jay, "From Financial Flop to *Fortune* 500," *EDN,* June 21, 1990, pp. 326+.

"Friendly Investors Buy Fisher Scientific for $1.4 B," *Boston Business Journal,* August 8–14, 1997, p. 3.

Glazer, Sarah, "The Fabulous Hatsopoulos Boys," *CFO,* December 1989.

"Gone Fisherin': Investor Group Pays $1.4 Billion for Fisher Scientific," *New Hampshire Business Review,* September 1–11, 1997, p. 34.

Hammonds, Keith H., "Inventor, Teacher, Economist—and That's Just for Starters," *Business Week,* December 18, 1989, pp. 81+.

Hatsopoulos, George N., "A Perpetual Idea Machine," *Daedalus,* Spring 1996, pp. 81–94.

Heuser, Stephen, "Deal Turns State into Player in Lab Tools," *Boston Globe,* May 9, 2006, p. D1.

Hussey, A. F., "Scientific Boasts Growing Stake in Laboratory Supply Field," *Barron's,* May 2, 1977, p. 41.

Jaffee, Thomas, "Fisher Redux," *Forbes,* March 2, 1992, pp. 130+.

Johannes, Laura, "Thermo Electron Plans a Divestiture of $1 Billion in Major Streamlining," *Wall Street Journal,* February 1, 2000, p. A4.

Kahalas, Harvey, and Kathleen Suchon, "Managing a Perpetual Idea Machine: Inside the Creator's Mind," *Academy of Management Executive,* May 1995, pp. 57–66.

Kirschner, Elisabeth, "Fisher Scientific Going Private," *Chemical and Engineering News,* August 18, 1997, p. 10.

Krasner, Jeffrey, "Executive Shift at Thermo Electron Seen As Cap to Restructuring," *Boston Globe,* November 26, 2002, p. D3.

———, "Thermo Electron Finds Its Focus," *Boston Globe,* April 11, 2005, p. C1.

"Lab Distributors Reposition for Profitability," *Instrument Business Outlook,* September 15, 2004, pp. 7, 11.

McLaughlin, Mark, "Businessperson of the Year," *New England Business,* December 1989, pp. 38+.

"Merger Means More Lab Supplies for More Clients," *Manufacturing Today,* November/December 2006, pp. 166–67.

Moore, Stephen D., "Fisons to Sell Most of Lab Supplies Unit to Fisher Scientific for $311.9 Million," *Wall Street Journal,* August 30, 1995, p. B2.

Reese, Jennifer, "How to Grow Big by Staying Small," *Fortune,* December 28, 1992, pp. 50+.

Richman, Tom, "The Master Entrepreneur," *Inc.,* January 1990, pp. 46+.

———, "Out of the Lab: A Bite-Size Company," *Business Month,* September 1990, pp. 96+.

Rosenberg, Ronald, "Hatsopoulos to Step Down at Thermo Electron," *Boston Globe,* March 16, 1999, p. C1.

———, "Spin Cycle Shuts Down: Major Restructuring of Thermo Electron Involves Combining Firms in Reversal of Spinout Strategy," *Boston Globe,* February 1, 2000, p. D1.

Strohl, Lydia, "Fisher Scientific Experiments with International Growth, New Products," *Pittsburgh Business Times,* May 9, 1994, pp. 12+.

Syre, Steven, and Charles Stein, "Rewriting Thermo Dynamics: With Scores of Deals, CEO Turns Sprawling Company into Leaner Model and Sees Shares Double," *Boston Globe,* May 20, 2001, p. G1.

"Thermo Fisher Scientific: A Big Deal, or Not?" *Instrument Business Outlook,* May 15, 2006, pp. 1, 11.

"The Thinking Man's CEO," *Inc.,* November 1988, pp. 28+.

Tulsi, Bernard, "Thermo Electron and Fisher Scientific Merger Gets Mixed Reaction from Industry," *Laboratory Equipment,* June 2006, pp. 1, 14–15.

Wallack, Todd, "Marinus 'Marijn' Dekkers: Thermo Fisher King," *Boston Business Journal,* December 29, 2006, pp. 3+.

———, "Slimming Down, Then Bulking Up," *Boston Globe,* May 20, 2008, p. G38.

Walsh, Kerri, "Thermo and Fisher Scientific to Merge," *Chemical Week,* May 24, 2006, p. 9.

Wilke, John R., "Innovative Ways: Thermo Electron Uses an Unusual Strategy to Create Products," *Wall Street Journal,* August 5, 1993, p. A1.

Wyatt, Edward, "Thermo Electron Plans to Sell or Shut Several Businesses," *New York Times,* May 25, 1999, p. C2.

United Technologies Corporation

One Financial Plaza
Hartford, Connecticut 06103
U.S.A.
Telephone: (860) 728-7000
Fax: (860) 565-5400
Web site: http://www.utc.com

Public Company
Incorporated: 1934 as United Aircraft Company
Employees: 223,100
Sales: $58.68 billion (2008)
Stock Exchanges: New York
Ticker Symbol: UTX
NAICS: 541710 Research and Development in the Physical, Engineering, and Life Sciences; 333415 Air-Conditioning and Warm Air Heating Equipment and Commercial and Industrial Refrigeration Equipment Manufacturing; 333921 Elevator and Moving Stairway Manufacturing; 336411 Aircraft Manufacturing; 336412 Aircraft Engine and Engine Parts Manufacturing; 336111 Automobile Manufacturing

■ ■ ■

United Technologies Corporation (UTC) is one of the largest conglomerates in the world, dividing its business into two segments: commercial and aerospace. The divisions composing its commercial business are Otis, Carrier, and UTC Fire & Security. Otis, which governs the $12.9 billion-in-sales Otis Elevator Company, designs and manufactures elevators, escalators, and moving sidewalks. Carrier, which controls Carrier Corporation, serves customers in the commercial and residential property industries, providing heating, ventilating, air conditioning, and refrigeration equipment, a $14.9 billion business. UTC Fire & Security, a $6.5 billion business, provides fire and special hazard detection and suppression systems, operating under the brands Chubb, Kidde, Onity, and Lenel. UTC's aerospace segment comprises Pratt & Whitney, Hamilton Sundstrand, and Sikorsky. Pratt & Whitney manufactures aircraft engines for the commercial, military, business jet, and general aviation markets, generating $13 billion in annual revenues. Hamilton Sundstrand, consisting of Hamilton Sundstrand Corporation, produces $6.2 billion in annual revenues by supplying advanced aerospace and industrial products such as power generation systems, flight systems, and engine control systems. Sikorsky, a $5.4 billion division, controls Sikorsky Aircraft Corporation, one of the world's largest manufacturers of military and commercial helicopters.

ORIGINS

United traces its origins to Fred Rentschler, who founded Pratt & Whitney Aircraft Company in 1925 as one of the first companies to specialize in the manufacture of engines, or "power plants," for airframe builders. Pratt & Whitney's primary customers were Bill Boeing and Chance Vought. Interested in securing a market for his company's engines, Rentschler convinced Boeing and Vought to join him in forming a new company called the United Aircraft and Transportation Company. The company was formed in 1929, and

COMPANY PERSPECTIVES

Customers have a choice and how we perform determines this. Our products are everywhere and our equipment long lived, so we set goals to exceed industry performance. Whether reducing jet engine noise or generating electricity geothermally, UTC's products bring energy efficiency and conservation to the building systems and aerospace industries. We know everything we do today can be done better tomorrow, resulting in greater value for customers and shareowners.

thereafter Pratt & Whitney, Boeing, and Vought gave exclusive priority to each other's business.

Early in its history, United Aircraft became so successful that it was soon able to purchase other important suppliers and competitors, establishing a strong monopoly. The group grew to include Boeing, Pratt & Whitney, and Vought, as well as Sikorsky, Stearman, and Northrop (airframes); Hamilton Aero Manufacturing and Standard Steel Prop (propellers); and Stout Airlines, in addition to Boeing's airline companies.

The men who led these individual divisions of United Aircraft exchanged stock in their original companies for stock in United. The strong public interest in the larger company drove the value of United Aircraft's stock up in subsequent flotations. The original shareholders quickly became very wealthy; Rentschler himself had turned a meager $253 cash investment into $35.5 million by 1929.

During this time, U.S. Postmaster William Folger Brown cited United Aircraft as the largest airline network and the most stable equipment supplier in the country. Thus, the company was assured of winning the postal service's lucrative airmail contracts before it applied for them. The company's airmail business required the manufacturing division to devote all of its resources to expansion of the airline division. Soon United Aircraft controlled nearly half of the nation's airline and aircraft business, becoming a classic example of an aeronautic monopoly.

BREAKING UP IN THE THIRTIES

In 1934, Senator Hugo Black initiated an investigation of fraud and improprieties in the aeronautics business. Bill Boeing was called to the witness stand, and subsequent interrogation exposed United Aircraft's

monopolistic business practices, eventually leading to the breakup of the huge aeronautic combine. Thereafter, Boeing sold all of his stock in his company and retired. In the reorganization of the corporation, all manufacturing interests west of the Mississippi went to Boeing Airplane in Seattle, everything east of the river went to Rentschler's United Aircraft in Hartford, and the transport services became a third independent company under the name of United Air Lines, which was based in Chicago.

Chance Vought died in 1930, and his company, along with Pratt & Whitney, Sikorsky, Ham Standard and Northrop, became part of the new United Aircraft Company. Sikorsky became a principal manufacturer of helicopters, Pratt & Whitney continued to build engines, and Vought later produced a line of airplanes including the Corsair and the Cutlass.

At the onset of World War II, business increased dramatically at United's Pratt & Whitney division. The company produced several hundred thousand engines for airplanes built by Boeing, Lockheed, McDonnell Douglas, Grumman, and Vought. Over half the engines in American planes were built by Pratt & Whitney. After the war, United Aircraft turned its attention to producing jet engines. The Pratt & Whitney subsidiary's entrance into the jet engine industry was hindered, however, as customers were constantly demanding improvements in the company's piston-driven Wasp engine. In the meantime, Pratt & Whitney's competitors, General Electric and Westinghouse, were free to devote more of their capital to the research and development of jet engines. Thus, when airframe builders started looking for jet engine suppliers, Pratt & Whitney was unprepared. Even United Aircraft's Vought division had to purchase turbo jets for its Cutlass model from Westinghouse.

POSTWAR JETS

Recognizing the gravity of the situation, United Aircraft began an ambitious program to develop a line of advanced jet engines. When the Korean War began in 1950, Pratt & Whitney was again deluged with orders. The mobilization of forces gave the company the opportunity to reestablish its strong relationship with the Navy and conduct business with its newly created Air Force.

In the early 1950s, United Aircraft experienced a conflict of interest between its airframe and engine manufacturing subsidiaries, as Vought's alternate engine suppliers, Westinghouse and General Motors' Allison division, were reluctant to do business with a company so closely associated with their competitor, Pratt &

United Aircraft continued to manufacture engines and a variety of other aircraft accessories into the 1960s. Much of its business came from Boeing, which had several Pentagon contracts and whose 700-series jets were capturing 60 percent of the commercial airliner market. When Horner retired in 1968, he was succeeded by Gwinn. While this change in leadership was of little consequence to United Aircraft, which was running smoothly, Pratt & Whitney was about to enter a period of crisis.

First, there was considerable trouble with Pratt & Whitney's engines for Boeing's 747 jumbo jet. The problem, traced to a design flaw, cost Pratt & Whitney millions of dollars in research and redevelopment. Moreover, it also cost millions of dollars for Boeing in service calls and lost sales. Commercial airline companies suffered lost revenue from canceled flights and reduced passenger capacity.

A CHANGE OF VISION IN THE SEVENTIES

By 1971, the performance of the Pratt & Whitney division had begun to depress company profits. The directors of United Aircraft acted quickly by hiring a new president, Harry Gray, who was drafted away from Litton Industries. Harry Gray was born Harry Jack Grusin in 1919. He suffered the loss of his mother at age six and was entrusted to the care of his sister in Chicago, when his father's business was ruined in the Depression. In 1936, he entered the University of Illinois at Urbana, earning a degree in journalism before serving in Europe with General Patton's Third Army infantry and artillery during World War II. After the war, he returned to Urbana, where he received a master's degree in journalism. In Chicago, Grusin went through a succession of jobs, working as a truck salesperson and as a manager of a transport company. In 1951, he changed his name to Harry Gray, according to the court record, for "no reason." He moved to California in 1954 to work for the Litton Industries conglomerate, and he spent the next 17 years at Litton working his way up the corporate ladder.

Hindered in promotion at Litton by superiors who were not due to retire for several years, Gray accepted an offer from United Aircraft. While at Litton, Gray had been invited to tour General Electric's facility in Evandale, Ohio. Litton was a trusted customer of General Electric, and consequently Gray was warmly welcomed. He was made privy to rather detailed information on GE's long-range plans. A few weeks later, officials at GE read that Gray had accepted the presidency at their competitor United Aircraft. The officials protested Gray's actions but were casually reminded that Gray had

---

KEY DATES

1929: Aircraft makers Bill Boeing and Chance Vought join forces with Pratt & Whitney.

1934: United Aircraft officially incorporates from the triumvirate's eastern manufacturing assets.

1945: Pratt & Whitney powers half of all U.S. planes built during World War II.

1954: Aircraft manufacturer Vought dissolves due to conflicts of interest with Pratt & Whitney.

1975: United Aircraft buys majority of Otis Elevator; changes name to United Technologies (UTC).

1983: UTC buys Carrier Corporation, an air conditioner manufacturer.

1991: Amid global recession, Pratt & Whitney, Otis, and Carrier post losses.

1992: Major restructuring is launched by new management.

1999: UTC sells its auto parts business and buys aerospace supplier Sundstrand Corp.

2001: UTC Power is formed as a new division.

2003: UTC acquires Chubb PLC in a $1 billion transaction.

2005: UTC acquires Kidde PLC for $3 billion and unites it with Chubb to establish a new division, UTC Fire & Security.

2008: George David steps down as chief executive officer.

2009: UTC Power's assets are absorbed by three other divisions: Pratt & Whitney, Hamilton Sundstrand, and Carrier.

Whitney. On the other hand, Pratt & Whitney's other customers, Grumman, McDonnell, and Douglas, were concerned that their airframe technology would find its way to Vought. As a result, both of United Aircraft's divisions were suffering, and, in 1954, the board of directors voted to dissolve Vought.

In 1959, Fred Rentschler died, following a long illness, at the age of 68. Commenting on Rentschler's role in developing engine technology to keep pace with that of the Soviet Union, a reporter in the *New York Times* stated: "This nation's air superiority is due in no small measure to Mr. Rentschler's vision and talents." Rentschler was succeeded as president of United Aircraft by W. P. Gwinn, while Jack Horner became chairman of the company's subsidiary Pratt & Whitney.

asked not to be informed of any plans of a "proprietary" nature during his visit to the GE plant.

One of Gray's first acts at United Aircraft was to order an investigation into and reengineering of the Pratt & Whitney engines for Boeing's 747. He then sought to reduce United Aircraft's dependence on the Pentagon and began a purchasing program in an effort to diversify the business. In 1974, United Aircraft acquired Essex International, a manufacturer of wire and cables. One year later, the company purchased a majority interest in Otis Elevator for $276 million, and, in 1978, Dynell Electronics, a builder of radar systems, was added to the company's holdings. Next came Ambac Industries, which made diesel power systems and fuel injection devices.

United Aircraft changed its name to United Technologies (UTC) in 1975 in order to emphasize the diversification of the company's business. Acquisitions continued, as UTC purchased Mostek, a maker of semiconductors, for $345 million in 1981. Two years later, the company acquired Carrier Corporation, a manufacturer of air conditioning systems. In addition, UTC purchased several smaller electronics, software, and computer firms.

Gray was reportedly known to maintain a portfolio of the 50 companies he most wanted to purchase; virtually all of his targets, including the ones he later acquired, viewed Gray's takeovers as hostile. Some of the companies that successfully resisted Gray's takeover attempts were ESB Ray-O-Vac (the battery maker), Signal (which built Mack Trucks), and Babcock and Wilcox (a manufacturer of power generating equipment).

During the 1980s, UTC operated four principal divisions: Power Products, including aircraft engines and spare parts; Flight Systems, which manufactured helicopters, electronics, propellers, instruments, and space-related products; Building Systems, encompassing the businesses of Otis and Carrier; and Industrial Products, which produced various automotive parts, electric sensors and motors, and wire and printing products. The company, through its divisions, built aircraft engines for General Dynamic's YF-16 and F-111 bomber, Grumman's F-14 Tomcat, and McDonnell Douglas's F-15 Eagle. In addition, it supplied Boeing with engines for its 700-series jetliners, AWACs, B-52 bombers, and other airplanes. McDonnell Douglas and Airbus also purchased Pratt & Whitney engines.

Gray, who aimed to provide a new direction for UTC away from aerospace and defense, proved to be one of the company's most successful presidents. He learned the business of the company's principal product, jet engines, in a very short time; upon his appointment as president of United Aircraft, sales for the year

amounted to $2 billion, and, by 1986, the company was recording $16 billion in sales. A year after he joined the company, Gray was named CEO, and soon thereafter he became chairman as well. In his 15 years at UTC, Gray completely refashioned the company. As Gray's retirement drew near, however, UTC's directors had a difficult time persuading him to relinquish power and name a successor. When a potential new leader appeared to be preparing for the role, Gray would allegedly subvert that person's power. One former UTC executive commented, "Harry equates his corporate position with his own mortality."

One welcome candidate to succeed Gray was Alexander Haig, who had served on UTC's board. However, Haig left the company after being appointed secretary of state in the Reagan administration. The members of the UTC board then created a special committee to persuade Gray to name a successor. Finally, in September 1985, Robert Danieli (formerly head of the Sikorsky division) was appointed to take over Gray's responsibilities as CEO of UTC. Nevertheless, Gray remained chairman.

GETTING RID OF GRAY IN 1986

In light of the poor performances posted by the company's various divisions, some industry analysts were beginning to question Gray's leadership. His refusal to step aside threatened the stability of UTC. With the $424 million write-off of the failed Mostek unit, many analysts began talking of a general dissolution of UTC; the divisions were worth more individually than together. These critics were silenced when Gray announced in September 1986 that he would retire and that Danieli would take his place.

Even before the official departure of Gray, Danieli had moved quickly to dismantle the company's philosophy of "growth through acquisition." Hundreds of middle-management positions were eliminated, and there was speculation that some of the less promising divisions would be sold. Danieli told the *Wall Street Journal*, "This is a new era for United Technologies. Harry Gray was brought here to grow the company. But now the company is built, the blocks are in place and growth will be a secondary objective." Danieli then had to prove that neither Gray's overstayed welcome nor his departure would affect the company adversely.

Danieli also had more pressing challenges. The U.S.S.R.'s collapse in the late 1980s revealed that it had been a much weaker military foe than previously believed. As a result, the end of the Cold War brought congressional and public pressure to cut domestic defense budgets. While some other leading defense companies moved to carve out niches in the shrinking market, UTC worked to strengthen its interests in more commercial industries.

UTC's transition was not smooth, and Pratt & Whitney suffered the most. While in 1990 Pratt & Whitney had brought in one-third of UTC's sales and an impressive two-thirds of operating profit, the subsidiary's losses from 1991 to 1993 reached $1.3 billion. Pratt & Whitney was hampered not only by defense cuts, but also by the serious downturn in the commercial airline industry, intense global competition, and a worldwide recession. Moreover, saturation of the commercial real estate market during this time caused declines in demand for elevators and air conditioners, products manufactured by UTC's Otis and Carrier subsidiaries. These companies also recorded losses for 1991. That year, UTC also faced six charges of illegal dumping against its Sikorsky Aircraft division. In the largest penalty levied under the Resource Conservation & Recovery Act up to that time, UTC agreed to pay $3 million in damages.

In 1992, Danieli brought George David, who had been instrumental in the revival of both the Otis and Carrier units, on board as UTC president. David, in turn, tapped Karl Krapek, who was called a "veteran turnaround artist" by *Financial World,* to lead the beleaguered Pratt & Whitney subsidiary. Krapek quickly reduced employment at the unit from a high of 50,000 to 40,000 by the beginning of 1993. The divisional reformation also focused on manufacturing, with the goals of shortening lead times, reducing capacity, and expediting processes. Overall employment at UTC was cut by 16,500 from 1991 to 1993.

By the end of 1993, Danieli was able to report positive results; UTC made $487 million on sales of $20.74 billion. In April 1994, after leading the corporation for nearly a decade, Danieli appointed David as the company's CEO, retaining his position as UTC's chairman. Otis's annual revenues remained in the $4.5 billion range in the early to mid-1990s, while Carrier's rose from $4.3 billion in 1992 to nearly $5 billion in 1994. During the same period, automotive sales rose from $2.4 billion to $2.7 billion. Pratt & Whitney saw commercial engine revenues fall by $800 million, to 2.9 billion. Military and space engine sales fell from $2.5 billion to $1.8 billion while general aviation sales fell by about 10 percent to $1.1 billion. During this time, the company paid $180 million for environmental remediation at more than 300 sites. Although cost-cutting improved profits by the mid-1990s, UTC continued cutting jobs.

UTC entered more than a dozen joint ventures overseas while the aerospace industry suffered a recession. The company derived a little over half of its revenues from abroad, and enjoyed strong growth in Asia in the mid-1990s, at least until the Asian financial crisis of 1997. In 1996, UTC had revenues of $1 billion in the People's Republic of China and Hong Kong.

Some technical developments seemed promising. Pratt & Whitney unveiled its most powerful engine ever in 1996. The PW4090 was rated at 90,000 pounds of thrust. (Three years later, the company tested the PW4098, rated at 98,000 pounds.) The new Odyssey system at Otis allowed elevator cars to move both vertically and horizontally.

In January 1997, Sikorsky and Boeing won a $1.7 billion contract to continue developing their RAH-66 Comanche armed reconnaissance helicopter. Sikorsky was able to maintain production levels of its Black Hawk helicopter. Pratt & Whitney engines were chosen for two new military aircraft programs, the F-22 fighter and the C-17 freighter. On the civilian side, Otis Elevator cut 2,000 jobs as sales fell in the wake of the Asian financial crisis. It also closed its Paris headquarters and most of its engineering centers.

UTC was able to save money on commodities by having its thousands of vendors bid online. These types of products accounted for about a quarter of the $14 billion the company spent on outside goods and services, according to the *Financial Times.* International revenues accounted for about 56 percent of UTC's total in the late 1990s, reaching 60 percent in 1999. Profits were rising in all divisions except UT Automotive.

RECONFIGURING FOR THE FUTURE

UTC bought Sundstrand Corp. for about $4 billion in 1999, merging it with Hamilton Standard. Sundstrand derived 60 percent of its $2 billion in annual revenues from aerospace products. On the recommendation of Goldman, Sachs & Co., UTC decided to sell its automotive parts unit in the light of growing price pressure from automakers. Lear Corporation bought the business for $2.3 billion in May 1999. Otis Elevator entered a joint venture with LG Industries in South Korea while Carrier bought out North American competitor International Comfort Products and allied with Toshiba Corporation.

Layoffs continued at Sikorsky, Carrier, Pratt & Whitney, Hamilton Sundstrand, and Otis, part of a new wave of companywide restructuring designed to reduce UTC's total workforce by 10 percent, or 15,000 jobs. However, in February 2000, a federal judge barred Pratt & Whitney from moving engine repair work out of Connecticut, saying this violated an existing union agreement. Plans to close Hamilton Sundstrand's Connecticut electronics facility also prompted complaints this was aimed at taking away about 400 jobs from the machinists' union.

The company bought Cade Industries, a Michigan aerospace supplier, in February 2000. The next month, UTC announced a new engine overhaul joint venture with KLM, the Dutch airline, which already had a relationship with Hamilton Sundstrand.

UTC ENTERS THE 21ST CENTURY

The first decade of the 21st century saw UTC record robust financial growth and David establish himself as one of the most successful chief executive officers in the history of the company. Acquisitions played a major role in UTC's phenomenal revenue growth, pushing annual revenues from $24 billion in 1999 to nearly $59 billion a decade later, as David made additions to the company's operations along seven fronts: the divisions composing the conglomerate.

A new facet of UTC's business emerged in 2001. UTC Power was formed to focus on the distributed generation market, a division that began developing interests in cooling, heating, and power systems, geothermal power systems, and fuel cells. The foundation for another new division was established two years later, when UTC acquired Chubb PLC for $1 billion. Based in London, England, Chubb ranked as a leading supplier of electronic security and fire protection products, generating $2.5 billion in annual revenues. "Most of all," David said in the June 11, 2003 issue of *PR Newswire,* "we like the overlaps in our customer populations. UTC already sells to exceptionally high numbers of buildings in the world, and Chubb's installations will both overlap with and augment this large presence. We see lots of potential for synergies among Otis, Carrier, and Chubb."

One year after Chubb was acquired, David celebrated his tenth anniversary as UTC's chief executive officer. During the decade, David increased UTC's market capitalization from $8.6 billion to more than $50 billion, a massive increase that coincided with stock returns of approximately 650 percent during the period. UTC ended 2004 with net income of $2.79 billion, an 18 percent increase from the previous year's total, and revenues of $37.45 billion, a 21 percent increase over the same period.

David had achieved considerable progress during his first decade in charge, but success did not breed complacency. He remained aggressive, spending billions of dollars to increase UTC's already towering stature. In 2005, he completed three major deals, increasing the strength of both the commercial and aerospace segments composing UTC's business. In February, he reached an agreement with The Boeing Co. to acquire the company's Rocketdyne Propulsion & Power business. The acquisition, completed in August for $700 million, included a 47-acre manufacturing facility in Canoga Park, California, where the main engines for the National Aeronautics and Space Administration's space shuttle and Apollo program were designed and built. Rocketdyne became part of Pratt & Whitney after the acquisition, integrated into the division's space propulsion unit.

FORMATION OF UTC FIRE & SECURITY: 2005

Next, David followed up on his acquisition of Chubb with the purchase of British fire-safety company Kidde PLC. He had tried to acquire the company in October 2004, but Kidde's management rejected the offer. David increased his offer by 3 percent and in April 2005 Kidde's management accepted the $3 billion offer. David also paid $400 million during the year for Lenel Systems International, a Rochester, New York-based maker of security systems and software. Lenel, Kidde, and Chubb became part of a new division created in 2005, UTC Fire & Safety, which was expected to generate more than $4 billion in revenue in 2005.

David attempted to make another addition to UTC's newest division in 2008, his last year of service as the company's chief executive officer. He set his sights on Diebold, Incorporated, an Ohio-based company that generated more than two-thirds of its nearly $3 billion in annual sales from making automated teller machines (ATMs). David wanted to integrate Diebold into UTC Fire & Safety, but Diebold rejected his $2.64 billion takeover offer. In April, a month after Diebold rebuffed his advances, David stepped down as chief executive officer, but remained UTC's chairman. David's departure as chief executive officer occurred shortly before financial results for the previous quarter were announced: UTC posted a profit of $1 billion, recording an increase in sales and profits from each of its six principal divisions.

GLOBAL ECONOMY SOURS

David passed the reins of command to UTC's chief operating officer, Louis R. Chênevert. Chênevert, who had served as president of Pratt & Whitney for seven years before becoming UTC's chief operating officer in

2006, took control of a vibrant organization set to be tested by the global economic crisis that erupted soon after his appointment. In 2009, when UTC Power's assets were absorbed by Carrier, Hamilton Sundstrand, and Pratt & Whitney, Chênevert implemented a $750 million restructuring program, hoping to insulate the company from the pernicious economic climate. "The outlook for commercial aerospace and global construction markets has continued to deteriorate since UTC's December [2008] investor meeting," Chênevert said in the March 27, 2009 issue of *Economics Week,* "and the economic recovery previously anticipated in the second half of 2009 now appears unlikely." Chênevert's somber outlook set the tone for the news that followed one month later. During the first quarter of 2009, Sikorsky, which benefited from military activity in Afghanistan and Iraq, was the only UTC business to record an increase in revenue and operating profits, a distressing result that perhaps portended the beginning of difficult times for UTC.

April Dougal Gasbarre
Updated, Frederick C. Ingram; Jeffrey L. Covell

PRINCIPAL SUBSIDIARIES

Carrier Corporation; Forney Corporation; Hamilton Sundstrand Corporation; Otis Elevator Company; Pratt & Whitney; Sikorsky Aircraft Corporation; UTC Fire & Security Corporation; UT (UK) Limited (England); United Technologies France SAS; United Technologies Luxembourg S.a.r.l.; United Technologies International Corporation–Asia Private Limited (Singapore); United Technologies Holding GmbH (Germany); United Technologies Far East Limited (Hong Kong); United Technologies Canada, Ltd.; United Technologies Australia Holdings Limited.

PRINCIPAL DIVISIONS

Carrier; Otis; Pratt & Whitney; Hamilton Sundstrand; Sikorsky; UTC Fire & Security.

PRINCIPAL COMPETITORS

The Boeing Company; General Electric Company; ThyssenKrupp AG.

FURTHER READING

"*Chief Executive* Magazine Names United Technologies' George David As 'CEO of the Year,'" *Internet Wire,* February 24, 2005.

Dawkins, Pam, "Sikorsky Gains While Rest of UTC Drops," *America's Intelligence Wire,* April 22, 2009.

"EPA Levies Record RCRA, CWA Fines," *Environment Today,* June 1991, p. 14.

Fernandez, Ronald, *Excess Profits: The Rise of United Technologies,* Reading, Mass.: Addison-Wesley, 1983.

Gershon, Eric, "UTC: Billion in Profits in David's Last Quarter at Helm," *Hartford Courant,* April 18, 2008.

Griffith, Victoria, "Otis Cuts 2,000 Jobs As Asia Crisis Bites," *Financial Times,* April 14, 1998, p. 24.

Jacobs, Karen, "United Technologies' Job Cuts Spark Labor-Board Inquiry, Action by Judge," *Wall Street Journal,* February 23, 2000, p. A6.

Ma, Peter, "Virtual Auctions Knock Down Costs," *Financial Times,* November 3, 1998, pp. 17+.

Moran, John M., "United Technologies Keeps on Rolling Up Profits," *Hartford Courant,* January 22, 2005.

———, "UTC Closes Kidde Deal; Fire-Safety Company Expands Security Unit," *Hartford Courant,* April 2, 2005.

Norman, James R., "Welcome to the Real World," *Forbes,* February 15, 1993, pp. 46–47.

"Repeat Performers," *Business Week,* January 10, 2005, p. 68.

Smart, Tim, "UTC Gets a Lift from Its Smaller Engines," *Business Week,* December 20, 1993, pp. 109–10.

Stainburn, Samantha, "Big Names Bow Out," *Government Executive,* August 1997, pp. 67–81.

Sullivan, Allanna, "United Technologies, Looking to Sell Auto-Parts Business, Talks to Buyers," *Wall Street Journal,* February 17, 1999, p. A6.

———, "United Technologies Profit Exceeds Estimates, As Revamping Is Launched," *Wall Street Journal,* July 21, 1999, p. B9.

"United Technologies Corp. Agrees to Acquire Chubb PLC in $1.0 Billion Deal That Will Add Security, Fire Protection to UTC's Commercial Building Offerings," *PR Newswire,* June 11, 2003.

"UTC Expands 2009 Restructuring to $750 Million in Response to Global Economies," *Economics Week,* March 27, 2009, p. 35.

Velocci, Anthony L., Jr., "United Technologies Restructures in Bid to Boost Profitability, Competitiveness," *Aviation Week & Space Technology,* January 27, 1992, p. 35.

Wilcox, Gregory J., "Boeing Sells Rocketdyne Unit for $700 Million," *Daily News,* February 23, 2005.

The Upper Deck
Company, LLC

5909 Sea Otter Place
Carlsbad, California 92010
U.S.A.
Telephone: (760) 929-6500
Toll Free: (800) 873-7332
Fax: (760) 929-6548
Web site: http://www.upperdeck.com

Private Company
Incorporated: 1988 as Upper Deck Co., Inc.
Employees: 400
Sales: $60.0 million (2008 est.)
NAICS: 323110 Commercial Lithographic Printing;
423920 Toy and Hobby Goods and Supplies
Merchant Wholesalers

■ ■ ■

The Upper Deck Company, LLC, is a leading competitor in the trading card and collectibles industry. Upper Deck sells autographed memorabilia and trading cards for sports such as baseball, football, basketball, hockey, and stock car racing. Internationally, the company holds licenses to produce cards for Swedish hockey, English football, Japanese baseball, Chinese football, and Philippine basketball. In the entertainment realm, trading cards and memorabilia are based on television programs, political figures, and cartoon characters. The company maintains offices in the United States and overseas, enabling worldwide distribution of its merchandise.

A NEW INDUSTRY FORCE ENTERS THE MARKET

When Paul Sumner walked into a baseball card store in 1987, the stage was set for a revolution in the trading card industry. Sumner, the vice-president of a printing company based in Orange County, California, entered the store on his son's behalf, hoping to find him a hobby, but when he left the store the inspiration for a new business filled his mind, marking one of the most significant junctures in the history of a more than century-old, $1 billion industry.

Sumner struck up a conversation with the store's owners. At the time, the trading card business was flourishing, but along with the rampant growth came a surge in fraud. Counterfeit cards were everywhere, infecting the market, as forgers attempted to cash in on the heightened demand. Sumner believed he had a solution to the problem plaguing the industry, one that called upon his expertise in the printing business. Credit card companies used a hologram to thwart duplication, a technology Sumner believed could be incorporated into the printing of a trading card. He solicited the support and financial assistance of several partners and founded Upper Deck Co., Inc., in 1988.

RICHARD MCWILLIAM TAKES THE HELM

One of the partners recruited by Sumner was another Orange County businessman, Richard McWilliam, easily the most influential person in Upper Deck's first 20 years of business. McWilliam, who would serve as Upper Deck's chief executive officer during its formative

COMPANY PERSPECTIVES

We're Upper Deck. We're not just a "trading card" company; we're a worldwide sports and entertainment company. We're a company with passion and attitude ... about sports ... about authenticity ... about quality and innovation. We thrive on fast pace, risk and things that are cutting edge. Most of all, we have pride and dedication to creating products that turn memorable moments into collectibles that people want to covet.

decades, supplied the $100,000 in seed money used to buy a card distribution license from Major League Baseball and to establish production operations in Yorba Linda, California. The company purchased its license in December 1988 and delivered its first case of baseball cards in February 1989, shipping the packs of trading card sets to a baseball card store in Tulsa, Oklahoma. When the store's proprietor, George Moore, opened the shipment, the trading card industry received a powerful injection of innovation, giving all competitors a new template to emulate.

McWilliam, an accountant by training, accepted the leadership role in Upper Deck after serving as a senior administrator at an outpatient medical center in Orange County. He, like Sumner, saw an opportunity to breathe new life into an old business. "At the time I took a look at the business, it was a pretty stale, stodgy, old industry, with the main player being Topps," McWilliam said in a May 7, 2001 interview with the *San Diego Business Journal*. "We were looking to create an innovative, strategically focused company."

McWilliam set his company apart from other competitors by marketing a product that established new standards for the industry. Instead of selling its cards in wax packages, which could be opened and resealed, Upper Deck sold its cards in foil packs as a preventive measure against fraud. Instead of using cardboard, Upper Deck printed its photographs on white paper stock, giving players' photographs a glossier look of superior quality because the color was separated. Instead of using the photographs supplied by major league teams, Upper Deck dispatched its own photographers across the country in pursuit of capturing a baseball game's superlative moment: a pitcher in the midst of a no-hitter, an infielder turning a triple play, a power hitter hitting a grand slam home run. Finally,

each Upper Deck Card featured Sumner's inspiration, a hologram printed on the back to ensure authenticity.

INSTANT SUCCESS

Upper Deck cards raised the bar on production quality when they were released into the market, and they also set a new pricing standard. Typical packs of trading cards retailed for between 25¢ and 35¢, far less than the 79¢ commanded by a pack of Upper Deck cards. If there was any concern on McWilliam's part that he may have priced Upper Deck out of the market, it was thoroughly eliminated after the delivery to George Moore's shop in February 1989. At Moore's store and other retail locations throughout the nation, the response from consumers was decisive. The company's production run was sold out midway through the year. The following year, the entire stock sold out before being distributed to retailers.

Success came quickly to Upper Deck, as the trading card industry welcomed its new rising star. Sales shot up to $40 million during the company's first year, forcing McWilliam and his management team to respond nimbly to the fast-paced growth of their enterprise. In 1991, headquarters were moved from Yorba Linda to Carlsbad, 30 miles north of San Diego, where a new 260,000-square-foot manufacturing plant was built. Meanwhile, McWilliam expanded into new product categories and new business lines. Card distribution licenses were purchased from the National Basketball Association, the National Hockey League, and the National Football League, making Upper Deck the first company in a decade to receive licenses from the four major professional leagues in the United States.

UPPER DECK'S SCOPE WIDENS IN THE NINETIES

McWilliam's ambitions stretched beyond producing cards for baseball, football, basketball, and hockey. He wanted Upper Deck to diversify into other businesses to become a sports and entertainment company, and he wasted little time before moving forward with his plans. The Upper Deck Company, LLC, became the umbrella organization for several different businesses, beginning with Upper Deck Europe. Established in 1991, Upper Deck Europe, later renamed Upper Deck International, governed the company's expansion overseas, which began with an office in Italy before spreading throughout Europe and into South America, Asia, and Latin America. In 1992, Upper Deck Authenticated was created to sell autographed memorabilia, a company that used a five-step process to guarantee the authenticity of the merchandise it sold. In 1996, McWilliam entered

KEY DATES

1988: Upper Deck is formed.

1989: The company delivers its first shipment of baseball trading cards in February.

1991: Headquarters are moved from Yorba Linda to Carlsbad, California, where a new manufacturing plant is built.

1992: Upper Deck Authenticated is created to sell autographed memorabilia.

1998: Upper Deck begins inserting pieces of game memorabilia into packs of trading cards, starting with slivers of Babe Ruth's bat.

2004: Upper Deck releases the trading card industry's most expensive pack of cards, the $500 2004 NBA Exquisite Series.

2005: Upper Deck acquires Fleer Corp., a bankrupt rival.

2007: Upper Deck attempts to acquire The Topps Company, Inc.

2008: Upper Deck begins inserting strands of hair into its card sets.

into a strategic alliance and global partnership with Bandai America, the U.S. subsidiary of Tokyo, Japan-based Bandai Co., a multibillion-dollar manufacturer of toys and children's entertainment products. The agreement called for Bandai America and Upper Deck to market and to distribute a line of sports and entertainment products, adding another facet to the multipurpose company being built by McWilliam.

McWilliam diversified and he continued to preach innovation in the company's flagship trading card business, whose activities were governed by Upper Deck Entertainment. The company issued sports cards that gave the illusion of an athlete in motion when the card was moved and it randomly inserted personally autographed cards of famous athletes in packs of cards. In 1998, Upper Deck began distributing cards that included pieces of game memorabilia, such as pieces of Babe Ruth's baseball bat and swatches of jerseys worn by the athletes who had signed exclusive agreements with Upper Deck: golf's Tiger Woods, basketball's Kobe Bryant, and baseball's Ken Griffey Jr., among numerous others. In 1999, the company introduced the industry's first digital trading card, which featured video of in-game action, photographs, and the athlete's statistics.

In 2001, under the aegis of Upper Deck Authenticated, the company began using "PenCam," a

writing device with a small video camera that captured footage of an autograph being signed, giving memorabilia collectors another safeguard against fraud. "Richard McWilliam is always four steps ahead," an industry observer said in the May 7, 2001 issue of the *San Diego Business Journal.* "He's an incredible visionary, and sets an agenda that forces his staff to move forward."

INDUSTRY LOSES ITS LUSTER

There was ample cause for celebration during Upper Deck's first decade of business, but the period also saw the company falter. Upper Deck lost $15 million after it produced a line of sports cards based on Looney Tunes cartoon figures. A poster of the "Dream Team," the U.S. men's basketball team in the 1992 Summer Olympics, failed woefully, resulting in a $6 million loss. More distressing than the occasional miscue, however, was the state of the trading card industry, the cornerstone of Upper Deck's business. Sales were plummeting, consistently and perennially, as Upper Deck evolved from an upstart into an industry leader. In 1991, the wholesale market for trading cards was valued at $1.1 billion. By 2005, the market was worth an estimated $260 million. Upper Deck, despite its exemplary innovation and aggressive expansion, felt the effects of a shrinking industry. When the company generated $263 million in sales in 1992, the volume represented a peak. In 2005, Upper Deck's sales were estimated to be $60 million.

The decline of the trading card industry was a distressing development, but it was difficult to perceive any sense of McWilliam displaying a forlorn attitude about his company's situation. Instead, he pressed ahead, taking Upper Deck in new directions and demonstrating a commitment to expansion. In 2003, Upper Deck secured a global licensing agreement with Marvel Enterprises, Inc. Under the terms of the agreement, Upper Deck created a line of trading cards and games featuring Marvel Comics characters such as the Incredible Hulk, Spider-Man, and Daredevil. McWilliam also negotiated a deal with the Nickelodeon cable network to produce a SpongeBob SquarePants trading card game, as well as an agreement with Walt Disney Co. for the rights to use cartoon characters Mickey Mouse, Donald Duck, and Goofy. In 2004, undaunted by stagnant industry conditions, McWilliam unveiled the trading card industry's most expensive pack of cards, Upper Deck's limited-edition 2004 NBA Exquisite series, which retailed for $500. One card, which included swatches of jerseys worn by LeBron James and Kobe Bryant, sold for $14,000 in a four-hour auction on eBay.

While competitors suffered from the sting of a decaying industry, McWilliam remained aggressive. In 2005, one of his principal rivals, Philadelphia, Pennsylvania-based Fleer Corp., collapsed, ending a legacy begun in 1849. McWilliam pounced on the opportunity before him, entering an auction to buy Fleer's die-cast toy business and its trading card business, which had produced its first set in 1923. He won the auction, paying $6.1 million for the venerable brand name and its assets, an acquisition that set the stage for his next move, the acquisition of The Topps Company, Inc., the 70-year-old king of the trading card industry.

UPPER DECK MAKES A BID FOR TOPPS

McWilliam made a grab for Topps after the publicly traded company was approached by other parties. In March 2007, Madison Dearborn Partners, a Chicago-based private equity firm and former Walt Disney Chairman Michael Eisner's Tornante Co., offered $9.75 per share for Topps, a $385 million deal. In May 2007, McWilliam made a better offer, proposing to pay $10.75 per share for the New York City-based company. Industry observers characterized McWilliam's $425 million offer as a preemptive strike, theorizing that he feared new management and new capital would breathe new life into Topps, which was widely considered to have stagnated during the previous decade. "Upper Deck was the upstart that challenged Topps back in the 1980s," an analyst said in the May 25, 2007 edition of the *North County Times.* "Upper Deck is saying, 'We can't afford to let someone else get their hands on it.'"

Despite the higher per-share offer submitted by McWilliam, Topps's board of directors opposed the sale of their company to Upper Deck. They urged shareholders to reject the unsolicited deal, believing that the union of the two companies would trigger antitrust concerns and lead to lengthy delays before, or if, it was approved by federal regulators. Negotiations between the two parties became contentious, as the two companies exchanged verbal jabs. In September 2007, Upper Deck withdrew its offer, claiming Topps had withheld financial information it needed to assess the deal adequately, as reported in the August 23, 2007 edition of the *San Diego Union-Tribune.* Topps fired back, claiming, in the same newspaper article, that Upper Deck's offer had been a "sham" and that McWilliam's company had engaged in "unscrupulous tactics." Before the end of the month, Madison Dearborn and Tornante Co. prevailed in their bid to acquire Topps, taking the company private concurrent with the purchase.

TWO GIANTS BRACE FOR THE FUTURE

In the wake of the failed takeover of Topps, McWilliam continued to do what he had always done: create new ways for Upper Deck to generate revenue in the trading card and collectibles market. Upper Deck controlled 35 percent of the market, having seized a significant share of the business to be had, and it was not about to cede ground to its main rival, Topps. As Upper Deck celebrated its 20th anniversary in 2008 and prepared for the years ahead, it continued to experiment with new ways to pique consumers' interest. The company's anniversary year saw the introduction of autographed cards of contestants in the hugely popular *American Idol* television program. The year also saw both Upper Deck and Topps begin inserting strands of hair into random packs of cards. Upper Deck released card sets that included the hair of George Washington and Jackie Kennedy, while Topps released card sets with the hair of Ronald Reagan and Babe Ruth; both companies purchased their samples from Connecticut hair collector John Reznikoff. In the years ahead, innovation in the trading card business promised to be a major theme, as Upper Deck and Topps battled for market supremacy.

Jeffrey L. Covell

PRINCIPAL SUBSIDIARIES

Upper Deck Entertainment; Upper Deck Authenticated; Upper Deck Digital; Upper Deck International BV.

PRINCIPAL COMPETITORS

The Topps Company, Inc.; Donruss Playoff, L.P.; Marvel Publishing.

FURTHER READING

Davies, Jennifer, "Topps Blasts Upper Deck's 'Sham' Offer," *San Diego Union-Tribune,* August 23, 2007.

Fikes, Bradley J., "Upper Deck Bids for Topps—Deal Would Unite Sports Card Icons," *North County Times,* May 25, 2007.

Freeman, Mike, "Topps Spurns Upper Deck Offer," *San Diego Union-Tribune,* July 10, 2007.

Green, Frank, "Sports Trading Card Producer Upper Deck to Acquire Fleer Name and Assets," *San Diego Union-Tribune,* July 16, 2005.

Harman, Liz, "Upper Deck Dealing Off Top of Trading Card Deck," *San Diego Business Journal,* June 20, 1994, p. 1.

Hathcock, Jim, "Baseball Card Firm Brings Jobs to Carlsbad," *San Diego Business Journal,* December 3, 1990, p. 1.

Krantz, Matt, "$425M Deal Could Merge Last 2 Baseball Card Makers," *USA Today,* May 25, 2007, p. 1B.

Lewis, Connie, "Upper Deck Scores with Stable of Superhero Cards," *San Diego Business Journal,* April 14, 2003, p. 12.

Miller, James P., "Directors at Topps Brush Back Rival's Bid," *Chicago Tribune,* July 10, 2007.

Neumeister, Larry, "Topps Claims It Caught Upper Deck Steal-ing," *America's Intelligence Wire,* April 15, 2009.

Robertson, Jordan, "Carlsbad, Calif.-based Upper Deck Unveils Special Edition Sports Cards," *San Diego Union-Tribune,* June 11, 2004.

Ward, Denise T., "Upper Deck on Top Shelf of Trading Card Industry," *San Diego Business Journal,* May 7, 2001, p. 1.

Vann's Inc.

3623 Brooks Street, Suite B
Missoula, Montana 59801-7359
U.S.A.
Telephone: (406) 541-6000
Toll Free: (800) 769-5668
Web site: http://www.vanns.com

Private Company
Incorporated: 1961
Employees: 240
Sales: $124.4 million (2008)
NAICS: 443110 Appliance, Television, and Other
Electronics Stores

■ ■ ■

Focusing on higher-end merchandise, Vann's Inc. is a Missoula, Montana-based retailer of video products, including digital cameras, flat-panel televisions, DVD and Blu-ray players, digital video recorders, VCRs, and media servers; audio products, such as home theater systems, stereo equipment, and CD players and recorders; computers and peripherals; gaming systems; and a wide range of home appliances, including air conditioners, clothes washers and dryers, dishwashers, refrigerators and freezers, wine coolers, ice makers, ranges, disposals, vacuums, cookware, and small appliances. Vann's also offers television stands, wall mounts, cables, and other accessories for computers, cameras, car audio, telephones, and other Vann's product lines.

The largest independent appliance and electronic dealer in Montana, Vann's operates six stores in the state, located in Billings, Bozeman, Kalispell, Hamilton, Helena, and Missoula, as well as an outlet store in Missoula. The flagship store in Missoula is 35,000 square feet, including a 12,000-square-foot showroom. An early adopter of the Internet, Vann's generates a large percentage of its revenues from Internet sales, relying on excellent customer service and a focus of quality merchandise to solidify a place in the online marketplace. A national distribution facility is operated in Lolo, Montana. Vann's has been 100 percent, employee-owned since 2004, another key to the retailer's success.

FOUNDER BEGINS CAREER, POST–WORLD WAR II

The man behind the Vann's name is Pete R. Vann. A fourth-generation Montanan, he was born in 1937 on a cattle ranch of several hundred acres in Geyser, Montana, located in the center of the state about 60 miles from Great Falls. He learned the rudiments of the self-reliant life, driving a team of horses by the time he was seven years of age, but in 1948 his father opted for a less isolated existence and moved the family to Missoula where he acquired a dairy farm. Vann's proximity to town provided him with a chance for work outside of farming. One of his father's milk customers owned a Missoula appliance store, and the young man took advantage of the connection to begin doing odd jobs at the store, initially cleaning up. His goal was to save enough money to afford a car by the time he entered high school. As he grew older he stocked shelves and began making deliveries for the store. He also put to good use a natural mechanical ability, honed by his

COMPANY PERSPECTIVES

Here at Vann's, we may stock our warehouses and fill our showrooms with appliances and audio and video electronics, but what we really sell are solutions. And "solutions" is really just another way of saying "customer service."

upbringing on a ranch that emphasized the need to be a jack of all trades. The store was selling automatic washers but people still wanted to keep their old models, leading to Vann becoming a repairman and a start in the appliance business.

Another popular product in the postwar era was the television set, leading to Vann becoming a service technician, replacing burned-out tubes and resistors. He considered becoming a mechanical engineer and even pursued the idea during two years at the University of Montana in Missoula, but youthful odd jobs at the appliance store had evolved into full-time work that was taking his career plans into a different direction. Vann was a personable young man, well-liked by customers, resulting in his boss making him into a salesperson. He proved to be good at sales, but perhaps too ambitious. Vann bought a truckload of televisions and secured a permit to sell them on the streets of Missoula, and took out some advertising. When the owner of the appliance store found out, Vann was summarily fired. After the owner learned that the young man had sold his entire stock of televisions over a single weekend, however, Vann was rehired and promoted from salesman to general manager.

VANN BUYS FIRST STORE: 1961

In 1961, when Vann was still in his early 20s, the store owner offered to sell the business to him so that he could focus on another appliance store he owned in Butte, Montana. The asking price was $10,000, a large amount of money for Vann, who as a 24-year-old had already been married for five years and had two daughters. Although he had no equity and no more cash than his last week's paycheck, he was determined to find a way to raise the money. Vann managed to scrape together $3,000 for a down payment and secured a loan for the rest.

With no margin for error and facing entrenched competition, Vann ran his store wearing as many hats as necessary. "We had to make it," he told the *Missoulan* in

2002. "It wasn't a choice." Not only did Vann sell the appliances and deliver them (in some cases closing the store while he delivered and installed a product), if something went wrong he served as the repairman. His wife, Patricia, also kept the books and helped him to make the key decisions in the business. Another major factor in his success was becoming a dealer of General Electric (GE) appliances, the first GE dealer in the Northwest. Personable, honest, and reliable, Vann built a loyal core of customers who brought repeat business. They followed him through several changes of address and kept him afloat even as many small independents in the area, unable to cope with changing conditions, fell by the wayside. Vann held on when a multitude of sawmills shut down in Montana in the late 1960s and crippled the economy. He held on and customers remained loyal when out-of-town appliance chains in the 1970s began opening their doors in Missoula.

HELENA STORE OPENS: 1983

While old guard appliance stores failed and newcomers came and left the market, Vann expanded beyond Missoula. He opened a store in Helena in 1983, and by the early 1990s other stores opened in Hamilton, Bozeman, and Butte, Montana. In 1995 an outlet store opened in Kalispell, Montana. Vann helped to drive sales by becoming a television pitchman, starring in a string of high-energy television commercials that he performed off the cuff.

Approaching 60 years of age, Vann in 1996 began the process of retirement and cashing in his interest in Vann's by initiating an employee stock ownership plan (ESOP) that would gradually turn over the business to its employees. A year later he bought a ranch in Montana's Bitterroot Valley and began spending an increasing amount of time there with his wife, who would also retire from her duties at Vann's. Employees gained a controlling stake in the business in 2003 and acquired complete ownership in 2004. Employees over the age of 21 who worked at least 1,000 hours were eligible to enroll in the ESOP after completing their first year of employment.

Taking over the leadership posts for Pete Vann was George L. Manlove. A University of Washington graduate, Manlove had been with Vann's since the early 1980s. He came to the retailer after spending four years with Apple Computer when that company was a start-up and enjoying explosive growth. Manlove was instrumental in setting the course for Vann's in the late 1990s, bringing to bear his experience in high technology.

KEY DATES

1961:	Pete R. Vann founds company.
1983:	Store opens in Helena, Montana.
1996:	Employee stock ownership plan is initiated.
1998:	Vann's begins selling online.
2004:	Employees complete acquisition of Vann's.
2008:	Plans laid to open distribution center to serve eastern United States.

DEBUT OF WEB SITE: 1997

In early 1997 the company took advantage of the graphic design capabilities of its in-house ad department to develop an Internet home page, originally intended to advertise Vann's products, communicate with customers, and provide technical support. The company also hoped to conduct video conferencing between its six stores. The following summer Vann's added an electronic catalog to create an e-commerce component. Not only did the Internet allow Vann's to generate revenues outside of Montana and its limited population of fewer than one million (Missoula's population, for that matter, was well under 60,000), it added to the number of products the retailer could offer. Due to limited floor space, Vann's stores had to be selective about what products it could display and promote. The enhanced web site was also a boon for the stores, which installed work stations on the sales floor where associates could find more detailed information on merchandise in answer to customer questions. Another factor in Vann's favor was a lack of state sales tax that helped to compensate for the cost of shipping. Something that was not considered but played an important role in Vann's online success was the allure and mystique of Montana itself. Buying from a retailer in remote Montana held a certain appeal for a number of customers. Another key was Vann's use of the online auction site eBay.com. By placing items up for sale, the company essentially gained free advertising that began to build excellent word-of-mouth. For these reasons, and Vann's continued emphasis on customer service, the e-commerce business began to accelerate and the company staked out a space in the new electronic marketplace at a critical time in the development of the Internet so that Vann's enjoyed prolonged growth. In response to heavy demand, the company made plans in 1999 to build a new warehouse to support Internet sales.

BILLINGS STORE OPENS: 1998

While Vann's was busy establishing an online sales unit, it did not neglect the bricks-and-mortar side of the business. In the fall of 1998 the chain opened a new 12,000-square-foot store in Billings, Montana, the company's seventh store. Although it operated close to some big-box stores, management was not overly concerned. Early in 2000 Vann's had to contend with another newcomer in 2000, Best Buy Co., the country's largest electronics chain, which was making a push into the Pacific Northwest by opening stores in Kennewick, Washington, as well as Missoula and Billings, Montana. Best Buy was generating annual revenues in the $12 billion range while Vann's was doing less than $50 million in business, but the Montana company was able to compete against Best Buy (unlike much larger Circuit City, which eventually failed) as well as Amazon and other high-volume e-commerce retailers, because it refashioned itself as a specialty retailer, eschewing commodity-driven products and focusing on midscale products and services, such as providing in-depth product information and customer education. A key decision early on in the development of the e-commerce business was offering vendor-authorized merchandise online. Initially a service to rural customers, many of whom had to travel long distances to reach a Vann's store, it proved extremely popular with other customers as well. By virtue of its early online entry Vann's became one of the first e-tailers to be approved by Panasonic and one of the few to be approved by Sony. The company was also quick to offer standard warranties and hassle-free exchanges for online products.

Another Vann's advantage was a clean balance sheet. The company had always been self-funded and was never saddled with servicing debt. Nor was it publicly owned and had to deal with the quarterly expectations of investors. Rather, as the company's employees continued to buy out Pete Vann, they became increasingly invested in the health of the company, resulting in low turnover and a greater commitment to providing the kind of customer service that gave Vann's an edge in the marketplace.

INTERNET SALES EXCEED STORE SALES: 2000

In the spring of 2000 Vann's Internet operation became its top-selling store. Because almost all of the sales were from distant customers, the company was not cannibalizing sales from its stores, which also benefited because the overall increase in volume provided greater purchasing power for the entire chain. The stores were far from neglected stepchildren, however. In the early 2000s the company invested in several renovations, in large part to better appeal to residents of lifestyle communities and upscale resort communities in Montana. Rather than general showrooms, Vann's looked to add lifestyle boutiques. In 2004, for example, the Kalispell store was remodeled to include live kitchens. The Bozeman store was relocated in 2006 and a year later a fully operational "Living Kitchen" was added to the operation. The store also invited local craftsmen and designers to participate and expand the purview of the boutique. In the spring of 2008 a new store opened in Helena, and it too featured a performance kitchen.

To keep pace with growing sales, Vann's expanded its warehouse and distribution center in Lolo in 2005. A year later annual sales topped $85 million, 42 percent of which came from online sales. To keep up with rising demand on the Internet side of the business the company looked to further expand its warehouse and distribution capabilities. In late 2008 Vann's was reported to be scouting midwestern and southeastern cities for a site to house a new receiving and distribution center to better handle the company's business east of the Mississippi. All told, sales approached $125 million in 2008. There was good reason to believe that Vann's online business would maintain growth in the years to come, and there was a chance that the Vann's concept might be taken beyond Montana's borders.

Ed Dinger

PRINCIPAL COMPETITORS

Amazon.com, Inc.; Best Buy Co., Inc.; Wal-Mart Stores, Inc.

FURTHER READING

Cervini, Lisa, "Vann's," *TWICE,* August 8, 2005.

Harrington, John, "Vann's Plans Store in Skyway Shopping Center," *Helena (Mont.) Independent Record,* September 18, 2007.

Holien, Mick, "Service Counts," *Missoulian,* September 27, 2003.

Kemmick, Ed, "Montana-Grown Electronics Company to Battle National Giants," *Billings Gazette,* August 30, 1998, p. D1.

Klosek, Nancy, "Vann's," *Dealerscope Consumer Electronics Marketplace,* August 1, 2006, p. 40.

Ludwick, Jim, "Cyber Selling: Vann's Customers Can Now Do Their Shopping Online," *Missoulian,* July 12, 1998, p. D1.

Lutley, Tom, "Vann's Online Store Tops the Chain in Sales," *Associated Press,* June 13, 2000.

"Movers and Shakers: Pete Vann," *Missoulian,* December 30, 2002.

Sinioukov, Tatyana, "'I' for Integration," *Dealerscope: The Business of CE Retailing,* December 2000, p. 26.

Vaughan Foods, Inc.

216 Northeast 12th Street
Moore, Oklahoma 73160
U.S.A.
Telephone: (405) 794-2530
Fax: (405) 891-8531
Web site: http://www.vaughanfoods.com

Public Company
Incorporated: 1989
Employees: 430
Sales: $91.85 million (2008)
Stock Exchanges: NASDAQ Boston
Ticker Symbol: FOOD
NAICS: 424480 Fresh Fruit and Vegetable Merchant
Wholesalers; 493120 Refrigerated Warehousing and
Storage; 311423 Dried and Dehydrated Food
Manufacturing

■ ■ ■

Vaughan Foods, Inc., processes and packages produce and prepared, refrigerated food, distributing its products in two dozen states stretching from Colorado in the west to Pennsylvania in the east. The company uses a fleet of company-owned refrigerated trucks that haul fresh-cut produce such as lettuce, cabbage, onions, and tomatoes to foodservice distributors, restaurants, and retail chains in 12 midwestern states that are within a 500-mile radius of its processing plant in Moore, Oklahoma. Vaughan Foods' ready-to-eat line comprises prepared salads, dips, soups, and sauces that are distributed within the company's core, 12-state market-

ing area as well as to a dozen neighboring states. The majority of the company's soups, sauces, and side dishes are made at a facility in Fort Worth, Texas.

ORIGINS

It took decades for the family business that became Vaughan Foods to assert itself as a regional competitor of note. The Vaughan Foods name first appeared in 1989, when Mark E. Vaughan incorporated Vaughan Foods, Inc., as the successor to a business his parents had established in 1961. Like his parents before him, Mark Vaughan made his living by processing fresh-cut produce and distributing the packaged goods to foodservice customers. He limited his activities to selling lettuce, tomatoes, potatoes, onions, and other vegetables throughout the 1990s and into the 21st century, never straying substantially from the type of business established by his parents until the family business celebrated its 40th anniversary.

A TURNING POINT

The turning point in Vaughan Foods' development occurred in 2002. Vaughan, presiding as president and chief executive officer, began to pine for greater profit potential from his business, a desire that prompted him to diversify and expand his product line. In 2002, he began to expand his operations by developing a more diverse line of refrigerated foods. First, he added a limited number of refrigerated prepared salads, introducing a selection of ready-to-eat salads that generated greater gross profit margins than packaged, fresh-cut

COMPANY PERSPECTIVES

We believe the future of food in this country is based upon true product freshness, customization of product, and product delivered rapidly and frequently into the market. Our model is essentially centered around a "regional" concept, which puts us close to the customer with a wide, but interrelated range of fresh food products—value-added vegetables, refrigerated deli salads, soups and stews, sauces, sandwiches, and fruit.

produce. He also expanded his fresh-cut line, the staple of the Vaughan family business for 41 years, to include more salad mixes, which were packaged to make them more attractive to the company's chain-store accounts. Both the introduction of a new product line and the product line extension led Vaughan Foods into the realm of marketing "value-added" products, products able to command a higher price from customers because the packaging and preparation added value to their worth.

As Vaughan steered his company toward greater financial possibilities, he also formed a business relationship with a food-processing executive who would play a pivotal role in Vaughan Foods' development into a prominent member of its industry. Herbert B. Grimes had more than 30 years of experience in the food-processing industry by the time his career path crossed with Vaughan Foods. In 1982, he cofounded Mrs. Giles' Country Kitchens, Inc., a company later renamed Mrs. Crockett's Country Kitchens, Inc., and acquired by Orval Kent Holding Company in 1996. Grimes stayed with the company after it became a division of Orval Kent, serving initially as the president of Mrs. Crockett's before Orval Kent's management promoted him to vice-president of sales, marketing, and research and development of the holding company. Grimes served in that capacity until Orval Kent was acquired by Sky Chefs, Inc., in 2002.

After leaving Orval Kent when it was acquired by Sky Chefs, Grimes spent the next year on a sabbatical of sorts. He made his living as a private investor, but soon his entrepreneurial inclinations were expressed again. He, along with three executives from Vaughan Foods, Mark Vaughan included, started Allison's Gourmet Kitchens, LP in 2003. The business, which counted Grimes as its president and chief executive officer,

produced a line of refrigerated, prepared salads, serving restaurant chains and foodservice accounts.

PRODUCT LINE EXPANSION DELIVERS FINANCIAL GROWTH

Vaughan Foods and Allison's Gourmet soon became intertwined, but before the two companies deepened their relationship with one another, Vaughan Foods' financial stature began to increase from the product line diversification and expansion efforts launched in 2002. The company generated $36.1 million in revenue in 2004, a volume that jumped to $44.7 million the following year and climbed to $51.2 million in 2006.

At the center of the company's operations was its production plant in Moore, where increased processing activities produced increasing annual revenue. The facility, measuring 108,000 square feet, operated continuously, processing and packaging produce and ready-to-eat salads. In the plant's refrigerated production rooms, vegetables arrived from roughly 50 suppliers located in the agricultural regions of California, Arizona, Colorado, Florida, and Mexico. Once the produce arrived at the Moore plant, the vegetables were inspected to remove damaged or spoiling produce, leaving the workers with choice selections that were subsequently cut, washed, and sanitized in chilled, chlorinated water. Next, the produce was spin-dried before being weighed and packed in sizes to meet customers' needs. The packaged produce was placed in boxes, which were put on pallets and stored in a finished goods cooler, ready for delivery.

DISTRIBUTION OPERATIONS

An integral facet of Vaughan Foods' operations was its delivery system. The company's produce, ready-to-eat salads, and salad mixes had shelf lives ranging from several days to a maximum of 45 days, which demanded a heavy investment be made in transportation infrastructure. Vaughan Foods owned a fleet of 30 trucks and 34 53-foot refrigerated trailers to deliver its products to customers. The trucks were cooled before being loaded from the company's refrigerated loading dock in Moore and dispatched on routes that served its core operating territory. Vaughan Foods delivered its products at least three times per week and on a daily basis for some large foodservice distributors, using 55 outbound routes emanating from Moore. The company's fleet served a core area of 12 states in the Midwest, an operating territory whose boundaries were determined by the shelf lives of the lettuce, cabbage, tomatoes, onions, peppers, and fruits hauled in the fleet of refrigerated trucks. The company's prepared foods that had shelf lives of more than 30 days enabled it to serve a larger area, allowing delivery service to New

1989: Vaughan Foods is incorporated.
2002: Company begins to expand its product line, diversifying into prepared salads.
2003: Allison's Gourmet Kitchens, LP is formed.
2007: Vaughan Foods completes an initial public offering of stock, which enables it to acquire Allison's Gourmet.
2008: Sales approach the $100 million mark.

Mexico and Colorado in the west, and ten additional states in the east, stretching from Pennsylvania in the north to Florida in the south.

Vaughan Foods' delivery system represented a major expense for the company, but the company's fleet of trucks and its warehousing capabilities operated as an ancillary business, providing a small yet meaningful stream of revenue. Vaughan Foods "backhauled" freight, filling its empty trucks with cargo at or near the termination points of its routes. The company also was involved in what it called its "3PL" business, or Third-Party Logistics. Vaughan Foods rented space in its warehouse and hauled the cargo of other companies which had distribution requirements similar to the routes it serviced.

From 2002 forward, Mark Vaughan was determined to increase the size and scope of his company. Expanding into prepared salads delivered measurable financial growth, but to achieve substantial gains the company needed to expand physically. By relying solely on the processing and storage facilities in Moore, he could not entertain expanding beyond the company's core, 12-state operating territory. Vaughan had national aspirations by the early years of the decade, calculating it would require five production facilities on the scale of the Moore plant to reach every part of the country. His plans were ambitious, demanding that bold moves be made. By the end of 2006, he was ready to launch the most aggressive expansion program in Vaughan Foods' history.

At the Moore plant, a 44,000-square-foot expansion project was underway that would increase production and storage capacity. Before the addition to the plant, Vaughan Foods processed approximately 1.5 million pounds of ready-to-eat salads. The chicken, tuna, bean, and pasta salads were delivered to customers at least three times per week, transported by a fleet that had grown to nearly 50 trucks. The company's fresh-cut

produce business handled 39.5 million pounds of lettuce, 13.9 million pounds of cabbage, and 7.7 million pounds of onions. The products were sold to restaurant chains, grocery and food distributors, and chain-store operators, with Wal-Mart Stores, the Texas-based grocery store chain H-E-B, and seven Sysco Food Corp. distributors ranking as the company's three largest customers.

To Vaughan Foods' processing capabilities, Vaughan planned to add the company he had cofounded, Allison's Gourmet. Allison's Gourmet acquired Wild About Foods, Inc., in June 2006, adding a facility in Fort Worth, Texas, that processed soups, stews, sauces, and side dishes. The proposed acquisition would expand Vaughan Foods' product line considerably, steering the company into numerous, value-added product categories such as Walnut Pesto Chicken and Spicy Ginger Shrimp salads as well as give it a volume producer of potato salad: Allison's produced 16 varieties of potato salad, mixing 2.9 million pounds of the side dish in 2006.

PUBLIC DEBUT IN 2007

As a way to complete the acquisition of Allison's Gourmet, Vaughan proposed a solution that his parents probably never envisioned for the business they started in 1961. Vaughan decided to take Vaughan Foods public. At the beginning of 2007, he filed for an initial public offering (IPO) of stock with the U.S. Securities and Exchange Commission. The IPO was expected to raise up to $27.8 million in proceeds, giving the company the capital to expand operations in Moore, to acquire Allison's Gourmet, and to construct a new production facility. The company proposed to sell 2.8 million shares at between $8 and $10 per share, but when the IPO was completed in June 2007, expectations did not equal reality. Vaughan Foods sold 2.15 million "units," consisting of one share and two warrants, priced at $6.50 per unit, garnering the company $13.9 million in proceeds.

Upon the completion of the IPO, Allison's Gourmet became a subsidiary of Vaughan Foods. The transaction also engendered a change in leadership, as Herbert Grimes, the head of Allison's Gourmet, became the chairman and chief executive officer of the newly constituted Vaughan Foods. Mark Vaughan took on the duties of president and chief operating officer.

POST-IPO GROWTH

The acquisition of Allison's Gourmet, a transaction intended to improve Vaughan Foods' financial performance, was discernible in Vaughan Foods' financial totals for the fiscal quarter immediately following the purchase. For its third quarter of 2007, the company recorded a 58 percent increase in revenues, as its volume swelled to $20.5 million, and it realized an encouraging turnaround in terms of operating income, turning a $312,000 loss from the previous year's third quarter into a $432,000 profit.

Vaughan Foods was beginning a new era in its history after the IPO and the purchase of Allison's Gourmet. Progress was being achieved, but much remained to be determined regarding the company's bid to become a more prominent regional competitor and its evolutionary step onto the national stage. At the end of 2007, Vaughan Foods' sales increased 31 percent to $67.2 million and its operating income recorded a $754,000 increase, turning a $285,000 loss in 2006 into a $469,000 profit. The IPO and the acquisition of Allison's Gourmet kept Vaughan Foods from celebrating a profitable year in 2007, however. Costs related to operating as a public company stripped $1 million from the company's net income and the added expenses incurred by owning Allison's Gourmet left Vaughan Foods $906,000 in the red at the end of 2007. Grimes was optimistic about the company's future, however, explaining in the March 13, 2008 release of *PrimeZone Media Network,* "2007 was a year of transformation, change, and progress. Our actions have strengthened us financially, operationally, and in our human resource assets, better positioning us for 2008 and beyond."

Jeffrey L. Covell

PRINCIPAL SUBSIDIARIES

Allison's Gourmet Kitchens, Inc.

PRINCIPAL COMPETITORS

Taylor Fresh Foods, Inc.; River Ranch Fresh Foods, LLC; Ready Pac Foods, Inc.

FURTHER READING

Mecoy, Don, "Moore Salad Processor's IPO Raises Nearly $14M with 2.15 Million Units," *Daily Oklahoman,* July 6, 2007.

———, "Salad Company Mixes in Public Shares," *Daily Oklahoman,* January 26, 2007.

"Paulson Investment Company, Inc. Completes $13.98 Million Initial Public Offering for Vaughan Foods," *Internet Wire,* June 28, 2007.

"Vaughan Foods Reports 2007 Operating Results," *PrimeZone Media Network,* March 13, 2008.

Vilter Manufacturing, LLC

5555 South Packard Avenue
Cudahy, Wisconsin 53110-2623
U.S.A.
Telephone: (414) 744-0111
Fax: (414) 744-3483
Web site: http://www.vilter.com

Subsidiary of Emerson Climate Technologies
Incorporated: 1886 as The Weisel & Vilter Manufacturing Company
Employees: 300
Sales: $57 million (2007 est.)
NAICS: 333415 Air Conditioning and Warm Air Heating Equipment and Commercial and Industrial Refrigeration Equipment Manufacturing

∎ ∎ ∎

A subsidiary of Emerson Climate Technologies, Vilter Manufacturing, LLC, is a Wisconsin-based manufacturer of compressors used for industrial refrigeration and gas compression. The company's innovative single-screw compressors are not only highly reliable but are also quieter and less expensive to run than comparable compressors on the market. In addition, Vilter offers twin-screw and reciprocating compressors, condensers, heat exchangers, computer control systems, and packaged systems that include onsite installation. The company also offers parts, service, and training. Vilter industrial refrigeration products are used in a variety of markets, including beverage, dairy, food processing, pharmaceuticals, meat and poultry, seafood, micro-

electronics, cold storage, and ice rinks and arenas. Gas compression applications include vapor recovery, flare gas recovery, coal bed methane recovery, landfill gas recovery, gas gathering, Bio-gas, and Digester gas. Vilter products are sold through a global network of distributors.

19TH-CENTURY ROOTS

Vilter Manufacturing was founded as a Milwaukee machine shop in 1867 by 31-year-old Peter Weisel, who immigrated from Germany at 17 years of age. The Vilter family became involved a few years later, perhaps as early as 1870, when Ernst Vilter, another native of Germany, joined the company in 1866. He became Weisel's partner, and in 1879 purchased a half-interest in the business, which became known as Weisel & Vilter. Initially the company's primary work, aside from general jobbing, was to supply slide-valve steam engines to area industry, such as the ice houses used by the local brewing companies, including the Pabst Brewery, Schlitz Brewery, and Blatz Brewery. It was a natural progression for the shop to develop air compressors to provide refrigeration to these area brewers as well as ice plants and packing houses. Beginning in 1882 the company began manufacturing steam-driven horizontal double-acting compressors. It also produced other equipment needed by brewers, such as automatic feed power corkers.

Weisel & Vilter was still a small shop when Vilter's stepsons, Theodore O. Vilter and William O. Vilter, joined the company. His wife, Elise Meiners Oltmanns, another German native, had married Christian Oltmanns, a farmer, who later died. His widow then came to the United States with her children and married Vilter in Milwaukee in 1869, and her sons adopted his last name, keeping "Oltmanns" as their middle name. Ernst and Elise Vilter then had a son of their own, Emil Vilter, who would later join his half-brothers in business.

INCORPORATION: 1886

The first of the Vilter brothers to join the company was Theodore, the eldest of the three. He started out as an apprentice in 1874, working three months without pay before being sent on the road as a regular employee to erect machines. He later became foreman and bought an interest in the business. The next brother to join Weisel & Vilter was William Vilter, who was hired as a bookkeeper-correspondent in 1882 after gaining business experience with a hardware firm and real estate company. In June 1886 the Vilter brothers, along with their father, Weisel, and engineer Edward Goes incorporated the company as The Weisel & Vilter Manufacturing Company. Ernst Vilter died in 1888 and a year later 18-year-old Emil Vilter followed the family lead and became an apprentice machinist and later turned his attention to sales and engineering, in the process becoming familiar with all aspects of the business.

There was not an especially large demand for refrigeration equipment until 1890 when the country's natural ice crop failed and the advantages of manufactured ice and refrigeration became all too apparent. Demand soared for all sizes of Weisel & Vilter compressors, creating a turning point for the company, which began to focus on the refrigeration industry. In addition to compressors and refrigerating machines, Weisel & Vilter developed a raw water plate ice plant.

In October 1892 Weisel & Vilter suffered a setback when a fire that began in a Union Oil Company plant in Milwaukee spread out of control, engulfing almost all of Milwaukee's third ward, including the Weisel & Vilter plant, which was completely destroyed. The company managed to raise the necessary funds and build an even larger plant than the one it had lost. The new plant became operational in March 1893, around

the time that Peter Weisel sold out to his partners. After having made a business trip to Los Angeles around 1890, he found the climate so attractive that he decided to retire to California, where he would live until his passing in 1906. After he left the company, the stockholders voted to change the company's name to The Vilter Manufacturing Company. William Vilter remained treasurer, a position he had assumed following his father's death, and Theodore Vilter was named president.

For the remainder of the 1800s, what drove Vilter's growth was the construction of distilled water can ice plants, which were capable of producing large quantities of ice. New size machines were added as well as automatic controls. In the new century the trend continued. In 1910 Vilter installed a massive loading dock pre-cooling plant for the Santa Fe Railroad, capable of chilling 150 carloads of fruit each day as well as producing 225 tons of ice that was then used to maintain temperatures of 40 to 45 degrees Fahrenheit. Around 1913 Vilter played an important role in Milwaukee's first air conditioning installations, supplying the equipment needed to service the Old Badger Room in the Wisconsin Hotel. In the meantime, Vilter continued to produce steam engines, meeting the demand for more economical steam engines by developing a poppet valve engine.

THEODORE VILTER DIES: 1919

During World War I, Vilter aided the United States' war effort by supplying the military with ice plant and refrigeration equipment to keep beef and other provisions cold. Although German-born, or perhaps because he was German-born, Theodore Vilter became an ardent supporter of the United States and its allies, tirelessly championing Red Cross campaigns and Liberty Bond sales. Some friends and families maintained that his exertions in this regard impaired his health. In any event Theodore Vilter's health failed and after several months of struggle he died in September 1919. His brother Emil succeeded him as president of the company.

Vilter Manufacturing continued to make advances in the refrigeration field in the 1920s. Among other developments, the company received a patent on unit coolers. The first of these units was installed in a small Milwaukee butcher shop in 1926. With the stock market crash of 1929 that ushered in the Great Depression of the 1930s, Vilter was essentially forced to remain in the forefront of refrigeration technology as a way to generate sales in a period of severe belt-tightening. To meet the "quick freezing" needs of meatpackers, who were seeking a room that could hold a temperature of −50 degrees Fahrenheit, Vilter was the only company to

KEY DATES

1867: Peter Weisel opens machine shop in Milwaukee.
1886: Company incorporates as The Weisel & Vilter Manufacturing Company.
1893: After Weisel's retirement, company is renamed The Vilter Manufacturing Company.
1945: Vilter family sells interest in company.
1961: Company is taken public.
1988: Employee stock ownership trust is created.
1996: Vilter moves to Cudahy, Wisconsin.
2005: J.P. Kotts & Co. acquires company.
2009: Vilter becomes part of Emerson Climate Technologies.

accept the challenge and succeed. In 1931 the company introduced a rotary compressor, and a year later unveiled one of the world's first self-contained ice makers.

Later in the 1930s war began to envelop the world and, even before the United States was swept up into the conflict in late 1941, Vilter was serving the needs of the military. As it had done during World War I, the company provided essential refrigeration equipment, but it also became involved in munitions, receiving a contract in 1940 to manufacture 105 millimeter Howitzers. The first of the cannons were delivered several months before the December 7, 1941 attack on Pearl Harbor by Japanese naval forces that precipitated the United States' entry into World War II. A new facility was opened by Vilter to concentrate on the production of howitzers without jeopardizing the production capacity of the company's equally valuable refrigeration equipment.

VILTER FAMILY SELLS INTEREST: 1945

World War II was also a period of transition for Vilter. In October 1940 Emil Vilter died, and four years later the last of the Vilter brothers, William, passed away as well. Taking over as president was a descendant of Edward Goes, but the new generation of ownership was not as committed to the business as their predecessors had been and soon put their stock up for sale. Due to the surge in business caused by the war, the company had accumulated a good deal of cash, which the company's owners drew out, about $1.3 million, by selling back their interest in the company through a nonprofit stock company known as Foundation, Inc.

Thus, by May 1945 the net worth of Vilter Manufacturing was reduced to little more than $500,000, while its bank loans and income tax claims totaled $2.26 million. Controlled by a non-stock corporation, Vilter Manufacturing was essentially owner-less, organized so that profits were either reinvested into the business or donated to charity. A board of directors elected for life was charged with hiring the officers. It had as much in common with a church as it did a corporation.

With the company abandoned by the Vilter family and the other stockholders, Vilter Manufacturing was on the verge of dissolution. Playing a key role in keeping it alive was a young Chicago attorney named Albert A. Silverman. Born in Denmark in 1908, he earned his law degree from Chicago's Loyola Law School and came to Milwaukee in 1944 in the employ of a bank. A year later he was asked to evaluate the state of Vilter Manufacturing, which by this time was given little hope for survival. Silverman joined the company as a vice-president in July 1945. Vilter owed the U.S. government more than $1 million and the company attempted to claim that as a nonstock company it was not obligated to pay income taxes. When that attempt failed, Silverman persuaded the government to convert the tax obligation into a mortgage.

Granted some breathing room by erasing the tax burden, Vilter was able to carry on. Five years later the company had paid off the mortgage plus interest and all other debts. Silverman was also president, having taken over the post in 1949. The company did not ratchet up sales to solve its fiscal problems. Rather, sales held steady at around $3 million a year, but costs were better controlled and employees who had been demoralized and had gone on strike for more than half a year in 1945 were more productive than ever.

Despite its organizational problems during this period, Vilter Manufacturing continued to maintain its technological edge. In 1945 the company developed the VMC 440 reciprocating compressor, which would remain a refrigeration industry standard a half-century later. Vilter also continued to pursue multi-cylinder ammonia and halocarbon compressors. In 1947 the company installed its first ammonia machine. Five years later Vilter unveiled a 1200 RPM halocarbon 440 VMC compressor that boasted greater capacity than 900 RPM machines.

TAKEN PUBLIC: 1961

Vilter employees lacked a pension plan, but that shortcoming was rectified in 1958 when the company established a profit sharing retirement plan. A more significant change took place three years later when in

September 1961 the company made a public stock offering as Vilter Foundation sold its entire holdings of 60,000 shares of common stock, which consisted of 30,000 shares of common stock represented by trust certificates, and another 30,000 shares of $5 par value common stock. Of the 30,000 shares represented by trust certificates, 10,000 shares were offered to the employee profit sharing retirement plan and the rest were offered publicly, fetching $8 a share. The first stockholders' meeting of the new public company was held in May 1962, during which the amount of authorized common stock was increased to 500,000 shares.

Vilter stock was an attractive buy for investors given the company's excellent postwar growth. Because of strong sales in California, Arizona, and Nevada, the company opened a Los Angeles office to better serve the region. The company also looked to the north, in 1964 signing a distributorship agreement with the Canadian firm J.H. Lock & Sons, Ltd., of Toronto. To better serve the Florida market, Vilter in 1967 acquired Miami-based distributor W.L. Filbert, Inc. To keep pace with growing demand for its products, Vilter broke ground on a new facility in the spring of 1969. What was intended to house an expanded evaporative condenser department became instead a new shipping and receiving facility.

In 1971 Vilter came close to merging with The Trane Company, but two months of talks failed to bear fruit and Vilter carried on as an independent company. In 1972 the Vilter International Corporation was formed to take over international sales. Also during the 1970s the company acquired adjacent land in Milwaukee to accommodate future expansions, and at the end of the decade opened its first regional parts depot in Los Angeles.

Vilter expanded through acquisition in the early 1980s through the addition of a Milwaukee company, Advanced Engineering Corporation, maker of galvanized and stainless steel fan coil cooling units. It then operated as a Vilter subsidiary under the name Gebhardt Industrial Refrigeration, Inc. Vilter also grew through a licensing agreement. In 1983 the company acquired the North American rights to a patented single rotor design of a Dutch company, Monovis, B.V., for the manufacture of a single rotor screw compressor intended for industrial, air conditioning, and heat transfer applications.

FORMATION OF EMPLOYEE STOCK OWNERSHIP TRUST: 1988

In 1988 an employee stock ownership trust was created to purchase Vilter. Silverman along with E. J. Kocher owned 64 percent of the stock. By this time 80 years of age, Silverman relinquished the presidency in 1988 but retook the post just a year later. Finally in 1992 he was ready to turn over the reins, succeeded as president by Paul Szymaszek. At the end of the year Silverman also retired as chairman and chief executive officer. He left a company generating annual sales of $40 million to $44 million, one that had never experienced a loss since his arrival. Silverman lived until late 2001, passing away at the age of 93.

In the early 1990s Vilter began manufacturing gas compressors for Dresser Rand Group Inc., the success of which established Vilter in the gas compression market and led to more product development in this area. In the meantime, the company began looking for a new home, its 80-year-old facility having long since grown outdated. Moreover, the operations had in time expanded to 18 buildings spread across 17 acres, becoming inefficient. After an extended search, the company opted to relocate to Cudahy, Wisconsin, completing the move in 1996.

After decades of consistent profits under Silverman, Vilter began losing money in the mid-1990s, leading to cost-cutting measures. In 1999 the new Cudahy facility was sold and leased back in a move to reduce debt. A year later the company began to trim its workforce, and in October of that year Szymaszek resigned. He was replaced as president by Ronald Prebish, an attorney and operating partner with DCI Holding, an Illinois private-equity firm. He took over a company that had grown sales but had become "top heavy." To make the job even more challenging, the manufacturing sector slumped as the economy lapsed into recession. Further job cuts resulted and Prebish initiated an effort to streamline the company's production process. One crucial advantage he had was Vilter's technology, which remained in the vanguard of the industry. In 2000, for example, the company introduced the VMS Mini Screw Compressor as well as the Vilter Vission micro-controller, offered through a partnership with Logic Technologies. Prebish was, thus, able to quickly turn around Vilter, which returned to profitability in 2003 on sales of $42 million while also making important capital investments, such as a new computer infrastructure.

COMPANY SOLD IN 2005 AND 2009

Revitalized, Vilter became an attractive property after recording another profit on sales of $43.5 million in 2004. In 2005 the New Orleans private-equity firm of J.P. Kotts & Co. acquired the shares of the Vilter Employees Stock Ownership Trust to become majority owner. Sales continued to grow, and in June 2009 Vilter was acquired by Emerson Climate Technologies, a subsidiary of St. Louis-based Emerson Electric Co. Vilter became part of its new parent company's Refrigeration Division, where the company would continue its legacy in the compression sector.

Ed Dinger

PRINCIPAL DIVISIONS

Industrial Refrigeration; Gas Compression.

PRINCIPAL COMPETITORS

Alfa Laval Inc.; Carrier Corporation; Ingersoll-Rand plc.

FURTHER READING

Barrett, Rick, "Silverman Saved Vilter, 400 Jobs," *Milwaukee Journal Sentinel,* December 25, 2001, p. 4.

Bednarek, David I., "Vilter Will Move into Cudahy Plant," *Milwaukee Journal,* July 28, 1994, p. 8C.

Daykin, Tom, "Vilter Head Resigns," *Milwaukee Journal Sentinel,* November 10, 2000, p. 2.

Doherty, Chuck, "Silverman Retires As Vilter Chairman," *Milwaukee Sentinel,* July 30, 1992, p. 2.

"Emerson Acquires Vilter Manufacturing," *Air Conditioning, Heating & Refrigeration News,* June 15, 2009, p. 6.

History of Milwaukee City and County, Chicago and Milwaukee: The S.J. Clarke Publishing Company, 1922.

Milwaukee: A Half Century's Progress, 1846–1896, Milwaukee: Consolidated Illustrating Co., 1896.

Rovito, Rich, "Private Equity Firm Buys Vilter Manufacturing," *Business Journal Serving Greater Milwaukee,* February 7, 2005.

———, "Turnaround Expert Leads Vilter Rebound, Improves Profits, Adds Jobs," *Business Journal Serving Greater Milwaukee,* June 28, 2004.

Usher, Ellis Baker, *Wisconsin: Its Story and Biography: 1848–1913,* Chicago and New York: The Lewis Publishing Company, 1914.

"Vilter Booster: Special 125th Anniversary Issue on the History of Vilter Manufacturing Corporation, 1867–1992," Milwaukee: Vilter Manufacturing Company, 1992.

Viterra Inc.

2625 Victoria Avenue
Regina, Saskatchewan S4T 7T9
Canada
Telephone: (306) 569-4411
Fax: (306) 569-4708
Web site: http://www.viterra.ca

Public Company
Incorporated: 1906 as Grain Growers' Grain Company
Employees: 3,320
Sales: CAD 6.77 billion (2008)
Stock Exchanges: Toronto
Ticker Symbol: VT
NAICS: 493130 Farm Product Storage Facilities; 311211 Flour Milling; 325312 Phosphatic Fertilizer Manufacturing; 423820 Farm and Garden Machinery and Equipment Merchant Wholesalers; 488320 Marine Cargo Handling

∎ ∎ ∎

Viterra Inc. ranks as the largest grain handler in Canada, controlling more than 42 percent of the market. Viterra is a vertically integrated operation involved in the handling, manufacture, processing, and marketing of agricultural products. The company operates a network of more than 250 retail locations in Canada that sell bulk fertilizer, bagged seed, crop protection products, and agricultural equipment. It ranks as a leading fertilizer distributor and as the largest industrial oat miller in the world. Viterra manufactures and sells livestock feed. At the heart of the company is its network of grain elevators and crop processing facilities. Viterra owns 86 grain handling facilities in Manitoba, Saskatchewan, Alberta, and British Columbia, boasting a storage capacity of 1.6 million metric tons. Port terminals in British Columbia and Ontario enable Viterra to serve customers in more than 50 countries.

PREDECESSOR ENTITIES

At the beginning of the 20th century, frustration and anger flared across the Canadian prairies. Wheat farmers in Alberta, Saskatchewan, and Manitoba shared a sense of helplessness, unable to secure what they deemed a fair price for their crop. Various solutions were sought, but the farmers' most enduring response to their predicament was to take collective action. Individually, they were powerless, forced to accept whatever price grain handling, processing, and marketing entities demanded. By banding together and pooling their resources, however, the farmers were able to gain greater control over their destiny. They formed their own grain handling, processing, and marketing entities, creating numerous cooperative organizations such as the Territorial Grain Growers Association, the Saskatchewan Cooperative Elevator Company, United Grain Growers, Alberta Wheat Pool, Manitoba Pool Elevators, and the Farmers Union of Canada, among others. A century later, the Viterra corporate banner was unveiled, a new name for what represented an amalgamation of several of the cooperative movement's earliest and most influential organizations.

Viterra could trace its origins to the Grain Growers' Grain Company, a cooperative established by a group of

COMPANY PERSPECTIVES

Amid the economic and geopolitical uncertainty of today's world, Viterra is in an enviable position to meet the increasing food requirements of a growing global population. Worldwide demand for agricultural commodities—and the inputs and services needed to produce them—remains strong. As Canada's premier agribusiness, Viterra has earned a reputation for quality and excellence. We are a dominant competitor in these growing businesses and possess the most modern and efficient operating assets in an industry with high barriers to entry. We have built the financial strength required to advance our strategies and take advantage of opportunities for growth. There is a palpable sense of confidence throughout the organization that we are right where we need to be—in the right industry, with the right assets, at the right time.

farmers in Sintaluta, Saskatchewan, in 1906. The Grain Growers' Grain Company, which became United Grain Growers Ltd. (UGG) in 1917, was the first of several principal components composing Viterra. Alberta Wheat Pool followed next in 1923, one year before the formation of Manitoba Pool Elevators. More than 60 years later, in 1998, Alberta Wheat Pool and Manitoba Pool Elevators merged, forming Agricore Cooperative Ltd. The merger marked the birth of the Agricore name, which would remain in existence until the emergence of Viterra a decade later.

AGRICORE COOPERATIVE AND UGG MERGE IN 2001

The union of Alberta Wheat Pool and Manitoba Pool Elevators was part of a trend of consolidation within western Canada's grain handling system. Cooperatives, much like the farmers who originally had formed them, were banding together to strengthen their stance, propelled by either financial distress or to realize the benefits of combining two organizations into one. Both factors played a part in the 2001 merger of Agricore Cooperative and UGG, which created Agricore United Ltd., a company that constituted one half of what became Viterra.

The merger between UGG and Agricore Cooperative essentially was a takeover led by UGG. Agricore Cooperative was awash in debt and under pressure from its bankers, having overspent on constructing new grain

elevators during the 1990s. The lenders agreed to delay imposing potentially crippling measures against Agricore Cooperative if it agreed to merge with UGG, a union announced in April 2001 that promised to create one of the country's largest agribusinesses. After the merger, which was completed in November 2001, the newly constituted Agricore United controlled 172 grain elevators with a combined storage capacity of 1.86 million metric tons. The company also maintained export terminals in Vancouver, British Columbia; Thunder Bay, Ontario; and Prince Rupert, British Columbia. Agricore United also inherited UGG's diversified holdings, which had been developed during the previous decades. UGG ranked as one of the largest publishers of farm magazines in Canada, producing *Canola Guide, Grain-News,* and *Canadian Cattlemen,* among numerous other periodical titles. UGG also marketed livestock feed through subsidiaries Unifeed and Hart Feeds and advanced swine genetics through Unipork Genetics.

AGRICORE UNITED EXPANDS

The Agricore name fared better after the 2001 merger. UGG's chief executive officer, Brian Hayward, became the chief executive of Agricore United, which established its headquarters in Winnipeg, Manitoba. Under Hayward's stewardship, expansion became the dominant theme. The periodicals business, operating as Agricore United's Farm Business Communications division, was sold in 2003 to Vancouver-based Glacier Ventures International Corp. for CAD 14.4 million, but aside from the divestiture, the company added to its assets, operating from a position of strength.

Following the sale of the Farm Business Communications division, Agricore United furthered its commitment to a joint venture company formed with James Richardson International Ltd., Canada's largest, privately owned agribusiness. In 1998, Agricore Cooperative and James Richardson had formed Prairie Mountain Agri Ltd., a Roblin, Manitoba-based company. In May 2004, Agricore United announced an agreement to acquire James Richardson's interest in the joint venture company, which provided crop production services and grain handling at an elevator capable of loading 50 railcars in 12 hours.

In 2006, Hayward completed two transactions in what would prove to be his last year leading Agricore United. In February, he reached an agreement to acquire another joint venture company, Lloydminster Joint Venture, the operator of a terminal in Lloydminster, a city straddling the border between Saskatchewan and Manitoba. The terminal had opened in 1994 as a joint venture between Saskatchewan Wheat Pool and Alberta Wheat Pool. Agricore United inherited a 50 percent

KEY DATES

1998: Alberta Wheat Pool and Manitoba Pool Elevators merge, creating Agricore Cooperative Ltd.
2001: Agricore Cooperative and United Grain Growers Ltd. merge, creating Agricore United Ltd.
2004: Agricore United acquires Prairie Mountain Agri Ltd.
2006: Agricore United acquires Hi-Pro Feeds, an operator of manufacturing facilities in Texas and New Mexico that produces livestock feed.
2007: Saskatchewan Wheat Pool acquires Agricore United, creating Viterra.
2008: Revenues reach CAD 6.77 billion.

interest in the CAD 5.8 million project and acquired Saskatchewan's 50 percent interest in the transaction announced in February. A much larger acquisition followed in August, when Agricore United purchased the assets of Friona, Texas-based Hi-Pro Feeds, a nearly CAD 40 million transaction. The purchase gave Agricore United four livestock-feed-manufacturing facilities in Texas and New Mexico, positioning the company in a region that ranked as one of the fastest-growing dairy markets in the United States.

AGRICORE UNITED IS PURSUED BY CORPORATE SUITORS

At roughly the same time Hayward was negotiating the final particulars of the Hi-Pro acquisition, he was forced to turn his attention away from further expansion and deal with an aggressive suitor. Saskatchewan Wheat Pool, a cooperative that developed alongside Alberta Wheat Pool and Manitoba Pool Elevators, wanted to purchase Agricore United. Saskatchewan Wheat Pool, like Agricore Cooperative, suffered severely from the elevator construction binge of the 1990s, but it restructured in 2003, emerging strong and on the prowl.

Hayward and Agricore United's board of directors were opposed to the marriage with Saskatchewan Wheat Pool, considering the offer unsolicited and unwanted. Saskatchewan Wheat Pool was not the only company casting covetous eyes Agricore United's way, as the era of consolidation within the industry continued unabated. James Richardson also offered to buy Agricore United, which Hayward greeted with decidedly more enthusiasm than the Saskatchewan Wheat Pool offer. In

February 2007, Agricore United urged its shareholders to approve the merger with James Richardson, creating a scenario that went as far as engendering a new name—Richardson Agricore Ltd.—that would control Canada's greatest annual grain shipments, estimated to exceed 14 million metric tons.

A PROPOSED UNION OF AGRICORE UNITED AND JAMES RICHARDSON

The proposed combination of the two companies promised to create a powerhouse in Canada's agribusiness industry. James Richardson's largest market for grain handling and storage existed in Saskatchewan, an ideal complement to Agricore United's strong presence in Alberta and Manitoba. The transaction also included a James Richardson subsidiary, Canbra Foods Ltd., that ranked as Canada's largest, fully integrated canola oil processor. Curt Vossen, president of James Richardson, was selected to become chief executive officer of Richardson Agricore, paving the way for a merger that was expected to spark far fewer concerns from Canada's Competition Bureau than a merger between Agricore United and Saskatchewan Wheat Pool. "This transaction delivers significantly greater value to Agricore United shareholders than the hostile takeover bid being put forward by Saskatchewan Wheat Pool," Hayward said in the February 26, 2007 issue of *Feedstuffs*. "Not only does it provide significantly more cash, but the offer also poses a lot less risk."

SASKATCHEWAN WHEAT POOL REDOUBLES ITS EFFORTS

Rebuffed, Saskatchewan Wheat Pool was not willing to give up on its aims of taking over Agricore United. At the end of March 2007, the company announced it intended to revise its offer. Agricore United's board of directors urged shareholders to take no action. To assuage the Competition Bureau, Saskatchewan Wheat Pool announced it was seeking to sell nine grain handling and marketing facilities and a terminal in Vancouver, and quickly signed an agreement with U.S.-based Cargill Ltd. to divest the assets. When the revised offer was submitted in mid-April 2007, a CAD 842 million deal, the response from Agricore United took a decided turn. After reviewing the offer, Agricore United's board of directors changed their stance, saying the new proposal represented a superior offer to the bid submitted by James Richardson. In May 2007, Saskatchewan Wheat Pool and Agricore United agreed to merge, giving Saskatchewan Wheat Pool's president and chief executive officer, Mayo Schmidt, a moment to celebrate. "We are very pleased with the support we have received from AU shareholders in the tendering process," he said in the May 29, 2007 issue of *Canadian Corporate News*. "Together, the Pool and AU can now move forward with confidence and focus on the opportunities that lie ahead for Canada's agribusiness leader."

In June 2007, the deal was completed. Agricore United became a wholly owned subsidiary of Saskatchewan Wheat Pool. Hayward retired and Schmidt assumed the responsibilities of leading the new, combined company. In Schmidt, the company took guidance from a proven winner. After spearheading ConAgra Foods, Inc.'s expansion into Canada, Schmidt joined Saskatchewan Wheat Pool in 2000, when the company was mired in financial difficulties, hobbled by debt much like Agricore Cooperative before it merged with UGG. Schmidt led the financial restructuring effort in 2003 that put Saskatchewan Wheat Pool on the road to recovery, turning debt into equity and injecting the vitality that enabled the company to pursue Agricore United.

A NEW IDENTITY FOR THE FUTURE

Before the end of 2007, Schmidt gave the Saskatchewan Wheat Pool-Agricore United combination a new identity. In August, the company adopted the name Viterra, a corporate title intended to represent "Life from the Land." "Viterra is a solutions-oriented company with energy and commitment to deliver on our promises and exceed customers' expectations," Schmidt said in the September 10, 2007 issue of *Feedstuffs*. "Our new business name and branding reflects our position in Canada as the leading agribusiness and our enhanced status in the global marketplace. Viterra speaks to vitality, growth, and to the land that is essential to our business."

Viterra stood as a giant in Canada and an influential force globally. With annual revenues exceeding CAD 4 billion, Viterra controlled more than 100 grain handling and marketing facilities in Canada and operated an agricultural-products retail network with 276 locations. The company's holdings included ownership of Western Co-operative Fertilizers Ltd., a leading fertilizer distributor, and Can-Oat Milling, the largest industrial oat miller in the world. Further, Agricore United's acquisition of Hi-Pro gave Viterra its Livestock Services business, which operated feed manufacturing plants in western Canada, Texas, and New Mexico. "Going forward," Schmidt said in the September 10, 2007 issue of *Feedstuffs*, "our overarching goal as a leader in Canadian agriculture is to become a processor and manufacturer of quality products, utilizing our grain and agri-products asset base and expertise to support value-added opportunities."

Jeffrey L. Covell

PRINCIPAL SUBSIDIARIES

Xcan Far East Ltd. (Japan); 614429 Alberta Inc.; 6116477 Canada Inc.; 1369570 Alberta Ltd.; 1403795 Alberta Ltd.; Canadian Pool Agencies Limited; Pool Insurance Company; Agricore United Holdings Inc.

PRINCIPAL COMPETITORS

Cargill Limited; Parrish & Heimbecker Limited; Maple Leaf Foods Inc.; Ridley Canada Limited; Federated Co-operatives Limited.

FURTHER READING

"Agricore Closes Hi-Pro Acquisition," *Feedstuffs*, August 21, 2006, p. 6.

"Agricore United Acquires Full Ownership of Prairie Mountain Agri Ltd.," *Canadian Corporate News*, May 10, 2004.

"Agricore United Acquires Lloydminster Joint Venture from Saskatchewan Wheat Pool," *Canadian Corporate News*, February 3, 2006.

"Agricore United and Saskatchewan Wheat Pool Announce Shareholder Approval and Leadership Appointments," *Canadian Corporate News*, June 13, 2007.

"Agricore United Board Determines That Revised Saskatchewan Wheat Pool Offer Is a Superior Proposal," *Canadian Corporate News*, April 13, 2007.

"Agricore United Completes Sale of Farm Business Communications Division," *Canadian Corporate News*, October 9, 2003.

"Agricore United Marks Century of Service," *Canadian Corporate News*, January 31, 2006.

"Agricore United Officially Launched," *Canadian Corporate News*, November 1, 2001.

Byfield, Mike, "Business Analysis; Agricore Has Gone Bust," *Report Newsmagazine*, September 10, 2001.

Fatka, Jacqui, "Agricore Welcomes Richardson Merger," *Feedstuffs*, February 26, 2007, p. 6.

———, "SaskPool Looks to Sell Elevators," *Feedstuffs*, April 9, 2007, p. 24.

"Pool Succeeds in Bid for Agricore United," *Canadian Corporate News*, May 29, 2007.

Quigley, Leo, "Canada's UGG, Agricore Announce Plans to Merge," *Feedstuffs*, August 6, 2001, p. 6.

"SaskPool, Agricore Become Viterra," *Feedstuffs*, September 10, 2007, p. 24.

"SWP Reaches Deal to Acquire Agricore United," *Resource News International*, May 9, 2007.

Walter E. Smithe
Furniture, Inc.

—■—

1251 West Thorndale Avenue
Itasca, Illinois 60143-1149
U.S.A.
Telephone: (630) 285-8000
Toll Free: (800) 948-4263 (1-800-With-An-E)
Fax: (630) 285-8022
Web site: http://www.smithe.com

Private Company
Founded: 1945
Employees: 525
Sales: $120 million (2009 est.)
NAICS: 337122 Nonupholstered Wood Household
    Furniture Manufacturing

■ ■ ■

The Smithe brothers—Walt, Tim, and Mark—are as famous around the Chicagoland area for their wacky commercials as they are for the company founded by their grandfather in 1945. Walter E. Smithe Furniture, Inc., is a staple in upper-middle and upper-class homes throughout the Midwest, and has furnished businesses as well as dwellings. Oprah Winfrey and Martha Stewart have touted their furnishings, but quirky commercials aside, the Smithe brothers run the family business with a serious caveat passed down to each generation, putting customers first by always delivering quality over quantity. The Smithes seek to exceed client expectations and deliver on their company's well known slogan, "You dream it. We build it."

A NEW CONCEPT: FORTIES TO SIXTIES

The end of World War II ushered in a time of unprecedented growth and prosperity for Americans, as soldiers returned home and began what became known as the baby boom. It was a buoyant time for men and women in all walks of life and two Chicago gentlemen, Walter E. Smithe and William Shanahan, believed it was the perfect time to open a new business. Pooling their talents and resources, Smithe and Shanahan created Tone Appliances and Furniture, a new store on the corner of Belmont Avenue in 1945. The small establishment catered to area homeowners by selling a variety of appliances and furniture items at moderate prices.

Smithe and Shanahan enjoyed success and decided to change the company's name to reflect their ownership. "Smithe and Shanahan" was born and became a fixture on Chicago's growing northwest side. It turned out, however, that appliances and furniture were not Bill Shanahan's destiny, so he sold his half of the business to Walter's brother, Charles Smithe. From this point forward, the company became a family-owned and operated firm with two very simple guiding principles: treat your employees and your clients well, a proud tradition carried forward for the next seven decades.

The 1950s marked the debut of a newfangled device called the television, which soon swept the nation. As television sets became the centerpiece of most living or family rooms, Smithe and Shanahan began to offer them alongside other staple products including stoves, refrigerators, and sofas. The company also segued into another kitchen essential, wooden cabinetry in various styles and stains.

The next decade brought many changes to the United States and the world at large. At Walter E. Smithe, the 1960s ushered in a second generation as Walter II joined the company. Walter II had served in the armed forces where he learned computer skills, a field still in its infancy. He went on to gain invaluable experience at two behemoths of American ingenuity, General Electric Corporation and IBM. He was also busy raising the third generation of Smithes with his wife, Florence. Their first few children were born and raised in Des Plaines, but as the family continued to expand, they moved north to a bigger home in Park Ridge.

Walter II helped modernize the family business and was credited with many firsts, including the addition of custom upholstery services. The company was reportedly the first furniture retailer in the Chicagoland area to offer its growing clientele fabric choices in varying thicknesses, weaves, colors, and patterns to customize their home décor.

SMITHE WITH AN "E": SEVENTIES THROUGH NINETIES

In the 1970s, while the country was still embroiled in Vietnam amid increasing protests over the war, Walter E. Smithe represented an oasis of comfort. Representing "home" despite the turmoil of the decade, the appliance and furniture retailer gave many clients what they needed most, a venue to create their dream home. Walter II had taken the reins of the company as the third generation and first of his seven Smithe children, Walter III (known as Walt), came on board. Although Walt's first job as a paperboy in Park Ridge was not exactly a precursor to furniture sales, he had worked for his father and grandfather on and off over the years, running errands and sweeping floors of the business bearing his name.

As Walt learned the ropes, the company discontinued its appliance sales to concentrate on what had become the core of the business: home furnishings. By focusing on a primary market segment, Walter E. Smithe was better prepared to stand up to the area's

increasing competition including new rival Wickes Furniture, formed in 1971 and based in nearby Wheeling, Illinois; Harlem Furniture, which had been in the Chicagoland area since 1912; Wisconsin-based Ashley Furniture; and John M. Smyth Homemakers, with a familiar-sounding name.

To gain recognition and distinguish itself from the similarly named John M. Smyth (pronounced with a long *I*), Walter E. Smithe began to spend more money on marketing through television, radio, and print ads. The rivalry between the companies prompted one of Walter E. Smithe's most popular advertising campaigns, differentiating the two businesses with the tagline, "Smithe With An E."

By the 1980s two more Smithe boys—Tim, four years younger than Walt, and Mark, one year younger than Tim—had joined the family business. The boys also had four younger sisters and two joined the company for stints in merchandising and buying. Both, however, later left to pursue other interests, leaving the three brothers to mind the store.

KITSCH AND QUALITY: 2000–05

By the early 2000s Walter E. Smithe was a highly successful business run by three brothers and their semiretired father. The boys each held the title of vice-president while Walter II remained at the top, close to handing off his duties to Walt as president and general manager. In the meantime, however, Walt was in charge of merchandising and accounting; Tim handled marketing and sales; and Mark served as the company's general counsel and managed warehouse/distribution duties.

By this time the company had a dozen stores and an army of highly trained designers, each tutored in interior design concepts at the aptly named Smithe University. These designers visited homeowners throughout the region and were part and parcel of the company's significant growth, earning it national recognition as other furniture retailers fell victim to a soft economy. One such casualty was Heilig-Meyers, which declared bankruptcy in 2000 and sold its handful of John M. Smyth Homemakers stores (which later closed in 2005).

In 2002 Walter E. Smithe's sales had reached around $70 million when Chicago's reigning businesswoman, Oprah Winfrey, promoted the company on her show. She touted the family's passion for furniture as a prime example of what a business needed to survive and thrive in the 2000s. Other major developments included a new kind of television commercial hitting the air in 2002, ads using the goofy camaraderie of the Smithe brothers. Originally inspired by the outtakes of

KEY DATES

1945: Walter E. Smithe and Bill Shanahan form Tone Appliances and Furniture in Chicago.

1960s: Walter Jr. joins the company after stints at IBM and General Electric.

1970s: Third generation comes on board as Walter III (known as Walt) joins the business.

1980s: Tim and Mark Smithe begin working at the company alongside their brother and father.

1995: Company celebrates its 50th anniversary.

2002: Oprah Winfrey promotes the company on her show; Smithe brothers begin airing goofy TV ads.

2004: Company invests in high-end Drexel Heritage furniture.

2006: Smithe brothers pull an April Fool's joke, renaming Wrigley Field "Walter E. Smithefield."

2007: Smithe commercial earns an Emmy for Chicago director Bill O'Neil.

2008: Smithe ad spoofing the *Sex and the City* movie scores big with Chicagoland viewers.

2009: Company owns and operates 13 area stores, including two dedicated to Drexel Heritage.

2010: Company celebrates its 65th year in business.

traditional Walter E. Smithe commercials, new skits featured the offbeat humor and antics of the brothers, their sibling rivalries, favorite sports teams, and spoofs of cartoons, music videos, or movies.

Whether viewers loved or hated the ads, the commercials put Walt, Tim, and Mark on the map, making the boys water-cooler fodder like the latest episode of *Friends.* The brothers became so famous, in fact, that hearth and home diva Martha Stewart wanted to meet them. Stewart visited Chicago in late 2005, appeared in a commercial, and signed with the company to develop a line of accessories. By the end of the year Walter E. Smithe had sales of around $100 million, 13 area stores (including one dedicated to Drexel Heritage furniture), over 500 employees, and a growing legion of television fans.

FAMILY VALUES: 2006 AND BEYOND

In early 2006 the Smithe trio appeared as themselves in a Kentucky Fried Chicken commercial for a Chicago ad

agency, then followed it several weeks later with an audacious April Fool's commercial where they renamed the Windy City's beloved Wrigley Field baseball park, Walter E. Smithefield. In the commercial, directed by their longtime collaborator Bill O'Neil, the brothers joked about replacing the field's storied ivy-covered walls with video screens and give away front row seats, which were then auctioned off for charity.

In 2007 more Cubs tickets were available as part of a *Field of Dreams* spoof, and a parody of Citibank's identity theft commercials won director Bill O'Neil an Emmy. The brothers went all out with the release of the *Sex and the City* movie in 2008 by first spoofing the film, Tim's idea, then giving away scores of movie tickets from each of their stores. Although some termed their folksy commercials "annoying," they nonetheless kept the Smithe name in the news. Furniture may not have been the subject of the increasingly well known ads, but any publicity or word of mouth, positive or negative, had proven very good for business.

While Walter E. Smithe survived the economy's downturn in late 2008 by offering customers a variety of products and furnishings, including forays into Drexel Heritage and Frank Lloyd Wright–inspired designs, another longtime area retailer, Wickes Furniture, filed for bankruptcy and liquidated its assets. Others followed, but Walter E. Smithe was able to maintain its loyal customer base. The company also marked another milestone as a fourth-generation Smithe, one of Walt's daughters, joined the firm.

The financial difficulties of 2008 and 2009 weeded out underperformers in many markets, allowing a Darwinian succession for the 2010s. Walter E. Smithe's longevity, written over almost seven decades of highs and lows, seemed ensured, not only because of the company's quality products and written lifetime warranty, but because Walt, Tim, and Mark Smithe had become local TV icons. Consumers all over Chicagoland eagerly awaited their next zany television ad or pop culture parody, while others received personal visits from the brothers, who frequently rode along on deliveries.

Nelson Rhodes

PRINCIPAL COMPETITORS

Ashley Furniture Industries, Inc.; Ethan Allen, Interiors, Inc.; Furniture Brands International, Inc.; Harlem Furniture; Klaussner Furniture Industries, Inc.; Plunkett Furniture; Toms-Price Company.

FURTHER READING

Curry, Sheree R., "Trying Harder So Clients Can Relax," *Television Week,* June 7, 2004, p. 14.

Donovan, Deborah, "Smithes and the City," *Daily Herald,* May 15, 2008, Sec. 4, p. 1.

Hageman, William, "Sibling Revelry," *Chicago Tribune,* April 28, 2005, p. 2.

Lazare, Lewis, "Banks, Williams, Go Deep with Smithes at Wrigley," *Chicago Sun-Times,* July 23, 2007.

———, "Smithes Have Fun at the Old Ball Park," *Chicago Sun-Times,* April 5, 2006.

Sotonoff, Jamie, "That's F-A-M-E with an E," *Arlington Heights (Ill.) Daily Herald,* May 27, 2004, p. S1.

Thomas, Paulette, "Funds for the Whole Family," *Crain's Chicago Business,* October 11, 2004, p. 40.

Velez, Carmen, "Designing the Perfect Work Environment," *Today's Chicago Woman,* April 2002.

Ward, John L., and Laurel S. Sorenson, "Promote, Celebrate Your Family Ties," *Nation's Business,* February 1989, pp. 16+.

Yerak, Becky, "Homemakers' 130-Year Run Almost Done," *Chicago Tribune,* August 30, 2005.

Wegmans

Wegmans Food Markets, Inc.

1500 Brooks Avenue
Rochester, New York 14603-0844
U.S.A.
Telephone: (585) 328-2550
Toll Free: (800) 934-6267
Fax: (585) 464-4664
Web site: http://www.wegmans.com

Private Company
Incorporated: 1931
Employees: 37,000
Sales: $4.8 billion (2008)
NAICS: 445110 Supermarkets and Other Grocery
(Except Convenience) Stores

■ ■ ■

Wegmans Food Markets, Inc., is a privately held, family-run corporation that operates a regional supermarket chain of more than 70 Wegmans stores. Known for its innovative approach to grocery retailing, Wegmans is consistently cited as one of the nation's top retailers and best places to work. With headquarters in Rochester, New York, Wegmans operates primarily in New York State and Pennsylvania, but also has operations in New Jersey, Virginia, and Maryland.

STARTING SMALL IN 1916

Wegmans was founded as Rochester Fruit and Vegetable Company in 1916, a small food store run out of the front of the Wegman family's house in Rochester. After

six years of selling groceries from home, brothers Walter and John Wegman moved their enterprise to a small, full-scale grocery store featuring canned goods, produce, a bakery, and even a cafeteria.

The two brothers became known as innovators in the grocery business, and in the early 1930s, they opened a self-service grocery, a new concept that would revolutionize food shopping. The new store was incorporated in 1931 as Wegmans Food Markets, Inc. The Wegmans store became a successful operation as well as a tourist attraction, featuring self-service and several other innovations, including vaporized water spray for vegetables and fruits, refrigerated food display windows, homemade candy, and a cafeteria that seated 300 people.

In 1950, Robert Wegman, son and nephew of the founders, became president of Wegmans, and the company began to invest in businesses that would enhance its central focus. Wegman acquired an egg farm and developed an onsite meat-processing center and a central bakery. He also formed Wegmans Enterprises, Inc., to handle real estate development, leasing, and property management for the company. In 1969 he was named chairman and CEO of Wegmans, and the company expanded outside of Monroe County, building stores in Syracuse, New York.

BROADENING WEGMANS' SCOPE
IN THE SEVENTIES

The 1970s brought new 40,000-square-foot stores that were intended to incorporate the "mall in a store" concept. These new stores included gift cards, floral

COMPANY PERSPECTIVES

At Wegmans, we believe that good people, working toward a common goal, can accomplish anything they set out to do. In this spirit, we set our goal to be the very best at serving the needs of our customers. Every action we take should be made with this in mind. We also believe that we can achieve our goal only if we fulfill the needs of our own people. To our customers and our people we pledge continuous improvement, and we make the commitment: "Every day you get our best."

products, and pharmaceutical departments and were open 24 hours. Wegmans also became only the third chain in the country to use electronic cash registers, installing an optical scanner system in a Rochester store in 1972.

In 1973, Robert Wegman capitalized on the growing demand for do-it-yourself home improvement products, opening his Home Improvement Center next to one of the company's Rochester groceries. The following year, Wegmans purchased Bilt-Rite Chase-Pitkin, Inc., a retail operation that sold lumber, hardware, millwork, garden and landscape materials, and building supplies. Wegmans soon began expanding this chain, building Chase-Pitkin stores next to existing Wegmans stores. Robert Wegman's son Danny assumed the presidency of Wegmans in 1976.

The company began carrying its own store brand items in 1979, and the line became so popular that by the early 1990s, Wegmans was carrying 1,000 items under its own brand name, including a line of soda. In 1983 Wegmans became one of the first chains to install automated teller machines (ATMs) connected to local banks. The ATMs were profitable for the store because Wegmans owned the machines and charged fees to the bank for providing all the front-line services, including replenishing cash and receipt forms. Other developments included the 1986 establishment of the Wegmans Federal Credit Union for company employees. Four years later, the company opened one of the first child care services offered by a private company with its Wegmans Child Development Center in the town of Greece, New York.

CIVIC CONTRIBUTIONS

Wegmans prided itself on its contributions to the communities in which it operated, noting its donations of damaged packaged goods and perishables to local food banks as well as its sponsorship of local events, donations of food to charitable activities, and contributions to community projects. Wegmans had been nationally recognized several times throughout its history.

In 1987, *Fortune* magazine named Wegmans the best U.S. supermarket in terms of customer service. In 1991, Wegmans' Work-Scholarship program was awarded a "Points of Light Award" by President George H. W. Bush. The company, one of only two supermarket businesses, was also listed in the 1993 publication of the 100 Best Companies to Work For in America. Wegmans' entry in this list was based on the company's child and development center, medical and vacation benefits for part-time workers, scholarship program and Work-Scholarship Connection, job security, and opportunities for promotion.

Wegmans received the American Business Press "Points of Light" award for its community service through its Work-Scholarship Connection program. Started in 1987, the program helped mostly 14- and 15-year-old children at risk of dropping out of school. The store gave these participating students part-time jobs and assigned a mentor to each of them. The mentor, an adult coworker, helped the student on the job and with schoolwork. Students who stayed on the job and stayed in school to graduate from high school also earned a $5,000 college scholarship to the school of his or her choice.

Nevertheless, Wegmans had its share of controversy and critics. The company came under attack from consumer groups as well as the New York State Attorney General's office for its alleged refusal to adhere to the state's item pricing laws. Wegmans' violations of state item pricing laws dated back to 1986, but the company argued that item pricing increased consumer costs because of the expense of pricing each item. Wegmans continued to stand by its electronic scanner pricing, claiming it was more accurate than price stickers and refused to pay fines levied against it for violations of the unit pricing regulations. Wegmans won the attorney general's lawsuit, and the item pricing law in question subsequently expired in 1991.

Wegmans also faced protests from environmental groups when it launched a campaign to decrease paper bag use in favor of plastic. Environmentalists claimed that Wegmans was misleading the public with its claim that plastic bags were better for the environment than paper bags. The critics argued that for Wegmans the main issue was cost: paper bags cost $41 per thousand while plastic cost $18.50 per thousand. According to Wegmans, however, paper bags did not disintegrate in modern dumps any more quickly than plastic, and

KEY DATES

1916: Wegman family establishes Rochester Fruit and Vegetable Company.
1931: Wegmans is incorporated.
1949: Stores are converted to self-service format.
1974: Company acquires Bilt-Rite Chase-Pitkin building and garden supply stores.
1999: First New Jersey store is opened.
2005: Danny Wegman succeeds Robert Wegman as CEO; Danny Wegman's daughter, Colleen, is promoted to president; company announces plans to shutter its home improvement businesses.
2006: Chairman Robert Wegman dies at age 87.
2007: Plans for a $28 million, 38,000-square-foot central kitchen/culinary innovation center in Chili, New York, are announced; Wegmans sells its egg farm in Walcott, New York, to Kreher's Poultry Farms.
2008: Company announces plans to stop selling tobacco products.

production of plastic was more energy and resource efficient. Wegmans finally responded to protests by letting each customer decide how he or she wanted purchases bagged. Furthermore, the company established bins for customers to deposit plastic bags for recycling, as part of a trial program with Mobil Chemical Company for recycling plastic. Wegmans also began using paper bags made from recycled paper.

By 1993, the largest Wegmans stores were 120,000 square feet, three times the size of the "mall-in-a-store" facilities established 20 years earlier. New Wegmans superstores included cafés with Chinese food, pizza and pasta bars, as well as cappuccino and coffee bars. Wegmans promoted itself as a strong advocate of health and nutrition, launching a series of bulletins called "Strive for Five," prepared by a registered dietician and featuring information and recipes for fruits and vegetables. Furthermore, in the early 1990s, Wegmans launched a line of diet foods, called "Just Help Yourself," featuring frozen, prepackaged meals comparable to those offered by diet centers.

EXPANSION BEYOND NEW YORK

In 1993 Wegmans opened its first store outside of New York State, choosing nearby Erie, Pennsylvania. Over the next five years the chain would move eastward, adding five more stores, the last of which was located in Allentown, Pennsylvania. Wegmans appeared as if it was poised to enter the affluent suburbs of Philadelphia. Instead, the chain moved into the New Jersey market, opening a store in West Windsor Township just south of Princeton in 1999. The following year, the chain opened a store in Bridgewater, New Jersey. It also announced plans for a third unit to be located in the upscale Monmouth County bedroom community of Manalapan, an hour-and-a-half south of Manhattan. Monmouth and Ocean counties, with their populations in excess of one million and annual household income of more than $48,000, appeared to be the perfect market in which to spread the Wegmans' concept.

During the 1990s Wegmans replaced older stores with new facilities and constantly adjusted its offerings in accordance with customer feedback. Wkids Fun Center opened in stores to provide supervised child care while parents shopped. The chain added to its list of private-label products, offering phone cards, packaged bread, cereal, frozen family meals, as well as vitamins, minerals, and herbs. Wegmans was especially responsive to the baby boomer market that was becoming more health conscious, bolstering not only its offering of product lines but health-related books, magazines, and yoga videos as well. Wegmans also introduced sushi bars to many of the Market Cafes in its stores. In 1999 it opened a highly popular French patisserie in its flagship store, created in large measure by President Danny Wegman's daughter, Nicole.

Wegmans and its efforts were recognized by major publications. In 1998 it was ranked number 16 by *Fortune* magazine as one of the 100 Best Companies to Work For in America. While the industry average employee turnover rate was 16.7 percent a year, Wegmans' turnover was only 9 percent. The company would continue to make the top employer list through 2001. According to customers, in a 2000 *Consumer Reports* survey of supermarket chains, Wegmans ranked second.

However, Wegmans suffered some setbacks in the 1990s. Because of competition from home improvement chains such as Home Depot, the Buffalo-area Chase-Pitkin stores were closed. Wegmans endured a public relations embarrassment in 1997 when it, along with several manufacturers, were sued by the New York State Attorney General's office for colluding to eliminate manufacturers' coupons in upstate New York, where coupons are more heavily used than in other regions of the country, at great expense to both retailers and manufacturers. Without admitting guilt, Wegmans agreed to settle by paying $500,000.

A NEW MILLENNIUM

Wegmans, with its loyal base of customers and unique blend of ambiance, products, and services, had been somewhat immune to competition. Loathe to become so large a chain that management could not keep close tabs on individual stores, Wegmans faced a number of challenges. Mergers in the supermarket industry were creating superchains that commanded tremendous benefits from their economies of scale. Furthermore, grocery products were becoming increasingly more available at drugstore chains and such big-box discounters as Kmart and Target, which were opening supercenters that included full lines of groceries. In late 2000, the trade journal *Supermarket News* suggested that Wegmans might be an acquisition target for Kroger or Safeway, or even part of a three-way merger between Virginia-based Ukrop's Supermarkets and North Carolina-based Harris Teeter. Wegmans dismissed all such speculation, intent on remaining independent.

During the early 2000s, Wegmans continued to use advanced technology to manage its operations. In 2002 the company began using technology from Phoenix, Arizona-based Intesource, a supplier of tools for procurement and online reverse auctions. The two companies expanded their relationship late the following year.

Developments continued at Wegmans heading into mid-decade. In early 2004 the company opened a store in Sterling, Virginia, and revealed plans to construct a 50,000-square-foot meat-processing plant in Chili, New York. With a target completion date of fall 2006, the new facility would support geographic expansion. As the company continued to grow, employee satisfaction remained a key differential for Wegmans, with turnover ranging between 6 and 7 percent, compared to an industry average rate of 47 percent.

A major leadership change unfolded in January 2005 when Danny Wegman succeeded Robert Wegman as CEO of the $3.4 billion enterprise. Danny Wegman's daughter, Colleen, who had been appointed senior vice-president of merchandising in 2002, was promoted to president. Robert Wegman remained chairman. In addition to the leadership transition, Wegmans ranked first on *Fortune*'s annual 100 Best Companies to Work For ranking.

Another important development in 2005 took place in October, when the company announced plans to shutter its home improvement businesses, starting with the Syracuse, New York-based Great Northern Chase-Pitkin store, as well as the Big Flats, New York-based location in 2006. Ultimately, 12 additional locations would eventually close their doors.

In April 2006, the supermarket industry mourned the loss of Chairman Robert Wegman, who died at age 87. Remarkably, the elder Wegman had continued to work a full schedule and visit the company's stores until shortly before his death.

CONTINUING GROWTH

Moving forward, the company continued to prosper under Danny Wegman's leadership. Plans for a new Maryland store were announced in May 2006. Wegmans ushered in 2007 by announcing plans to build a $28 million, 38,000-square-foot central kitchen/culinary innovation center in Chili, New York. The facility, situated near the company's distribution center, was intended to develop unique new products. Several months later, Wegmans announced plans to close all of its in-store video rental departments, which were being replaced with automated kiosks from Redbox Automated Retail.

By mid-2007 Wegmans had plans to open 11 new stores in New York, New Jersey, Virginia, Maryland, and Pennsylvania. The company rounded out the year by selling its egg farm in Walcott, New York. After 40 years of ownership, the company decided to sell the operation to Clarence, New York-based Kreher's Poultry Farms. Following the sale, Wegmans planned to continue buying its private-label eggs from Kreher's.

Developments continued into the closing years of the decade. Wegmans kicked off 2008 by announcing plans to stop selling tobacco products, despite their profitability. CEO Danny Wegman cited the negative health impact of tobacco as the reason for the company's decision. Around the same time, *Fortune* named Wegmans to its 100 Best Companies to Work For list for the 11th consecutive year.

By 2009, virtually every sector of the economy was struggling. However, Wegmans continued to grow, announcing plans to open a new store in Abingdon, Maryland. Other new stores also were planned in that state, including locations in Columbia, Germantown, Frederick, Landover, and Crofton. To help its customers save money, and also retain market share, Wegmans expanded its pharmaceutical savings program in early 2009, slashing the cost of approximately 390 generic drugs. In addition, the company began advertising $6 meals, which included an entrée and two sides, in its prepared food departments.

Moving toward the 21st century's second decade, Wegmans retained its foothold as a privately held supermarket leader. Backed by more than 37,000 highly satisfied employees, the company seemed positioned for continued growth and success.

Wendy J. Stein
Updated, Ed Dinger; Paul R. Greenland

PRINCIPAL COMPETITORS

Giant Food Stores LLC; TOPS Markets LLC; Wal-Mart Stores Inc.

FURTHER READING

"Executive Changes: Wegmans Names Two from Family As CEO, President," *Supermarket News,* January 31, 2005.

Garry, Michael, "13. Danny Wegman; CEO, Wegmans Food Markets," *Supermarket News,* July 25, 2005.

Khermouch, Gerry, "Wegmans Builds Its Local Base with Private Label," *Brandweek,* March 8, 1993, p. 23.

Linstedt, Sharon, "Supermarkets Brace for a Good, Old-Fashioned Food Fight," *Buffalo News,* January 28, 2001, p. P50.

———, "Wegmans May Get Buyout Offer Journal Says," *Buffalo News,* September 21, 2000, p. El.

———, "Wegmans, Tops Rated Among Nation's Best Supermarkets," *Buffalo News,* August 18, 2000, p. C7.

Narisetti, Raju, "P&G Settles with New York over Coupons—Firm, Nine Others Agree to Provide $4.2 Million in Cents-Off Squabble," *Wall Street Journal,* September 10, 1997, p. A4.

"News Watch (Wegmans Food Markets Inc. to Stop Selling Tobacco Products)," *Supermarket News,* January 14, 2008.

"Robert Wegman, 87, Leader in Supermarket Innovations," *New York Times,* April 22, 2006.

Uttal, Bro, Bill Saporito, and Monci Jo Williams, "Companies That Serve You Best," *Fortune,* December 7, 1987, p. 98.

"Wegmans to Close Home Centers," *Drug Store News,* October 24, 2005.

"A Winning Day at the White House," *Supermarket Business,* November 1991, p. 9.

Whataburger Restaurants LP

300 Concord Plaza Drive
San Antonio, Texas 78216
U.S.A.
Telephone: (210) 476-6000
Web site: http://www.whataburger.com

Private Company
Incorporated: 1950
Employees: 15,500
Sales: $1 billion (2009 est.)
NAICS: 533110 Owners and Lessors of Other Non-Financial Assets; 722110 Full-Service Restaurants

■ ■ ■

Whataburger Restaurants LP is a hamburger chain with about 700 locations in Texas and nine other states. The company owns approximately 85 percent of its restaurants, and the remainder are owned by franchisees. Most locations are open around the clock, and serve breakfast items in addition to hamburgers and other fast-food fare.

EARLY GROWTH: 1950–89

Whataburger traces its roots back to August 8, 1950, when Paul Burton and a former bush pilot named Harmon A. Dobson opened a wooden hamburger stand in Corpus Christi, Texas. In addition to co-owning Whataburger, Dobson also spent time drilling for oil and making diamond runs to South America.

Dobson ultimately decided to focus on the hamburger business and bought out Burton. In exchange for full ownership in Whataburger, Burton reportedly walked away with Dobson's yellow Plymouth convertible and certain franchisee rights.

Priced at 25 cents, the operation's flagship product was given the name Whataburger, in honor of the desired customer response following consumption. Realizing the importance of presentation, Dobson made arrangements with the Rainbo Bread Co. to develop special five-inch buns, which were an inch larger than standard buns. In addition to Whataburgers, Dobson and Burton sold chips and cold drinks.

From the very beginning, the new business relied on creative marketing strategies to generate new customers. Dobson put his pilot skills to work and used his Piper Super Cub plane for promotional purposes. While towing a Whataburger banner in the air and sounding a duck-like airhorn, Dobson dropped flyers and coupons in an effort to entice prospective diners.

In 1967 the company suffered a loss when Dobson was killed in a plane crash. Following this tragic event, Dobson's wife, Grace W. Dobson, took charge of Whataburger.

Another leadership change took place in 1974, when a University of Missouri graduate named Jim Peterson was named company president. Prior to joining Whataburger, Peterson had spent his career building shopping malls and supermarkets and serving as president of a Lincoln, Nebraska-based family restaurant chain named Food Host USA.

With Peterson at the helm, Whataburger experienced explosive growth throughout the 1970s. Expansion continued into the 1980s. By 1985 the

COMPANY PERSPECTIVES
■

Way back in 1950, an adventurous and determined entrepreneur named Harmon Dobson opened up the world's first Whataburger on Ayers Street in Corpus Christi, Texas. He had a simple goal, to serve a burger so big that it took two hands to hold and so good that with one bite customers would say, "What a burger!" He succeeded on both accounts and turned that one little burger stand into a legend known throughout Texas and the South.

company was operating restaurants in Arizona, Alabama, Florida, New Mexico, and Texas. That year, sales exceeded $200 million. Following four years of development, the Whatachicken sandwich was introduced at all locations in December, allowing the company to reach more female customers.

However, as Whataburger began to shift its focus away from successful core products, sales fell for six straight years. In the midst of this situation, it became difficult to properly maintain all of the chain's physical locations. Making matters worse were declining employee morale and growing tensions between Whataburger and its franchisees.

By mid-1986 Whataburger had grown to include 240 company-owned restaurants and 140 franchised locations. Two years later, the company introduced a Spanish-language television commercial in the Houston market featuring baseball player Jose Cruz. The ad, which was subtitled in English, was developed by the advertising agency Eisaman, Johns & Laws Inc., which had been handling marketing and advertising for Whataburger since the beginning of the decade.

NEW LEADERSHIP: 1990–94

In 1990 Whataburger switched agencies and moved its roughly $5 million advertising budget to Dallas-based The Richards Group. Two years later, plans were made to install ReMACS' Quick Service Restaurant software, then used by such leading establishments as Hard Rock Cafés, Red Robin International, and EuroDisney, in all of its restaurants. The implementation process began with 60 locations, and completion was expected to take up to three years.

Another important leadership change unfolded in 1993, when Jim Peterson stepped down as CEO of Whataburger, ending a career that spanned two decades.

Thomas Dobson, son of cofounder Harmon Dobson, was named president and CEO. Under his leadership, sweeping changes were implemented in an effort to boost franchisee satisfaction, employee morale, and sales.

One major step was the replacement of many senior executives. Meetings were then held with managers of company-owned stores, resulting in 1,600 suggestions for improvement. In addition, Dobson worked to mend relations with franchisees, who were threatening to sue the company over their share of rebates that the company had been collecting from vendors on sales from both company-owned and franchised locations.

Whataburger ultimately reached settlements with all franchisees in late 1994. Improving matters was the formation of a purchasing council, comprising corporate representatives and three franchisees. A marketing council also was established, providing franchisees with a formal means to share their ideas.

Other changes included new advertising campaigns in order to connect with a younger market, stronger in-store marketing tactics, as well as the consideration of new exterior designs for restaurant locations. For example, several new locations were constructed with white brick and blue trim, as opposed to the chain's established look of brown brick and orange trim. Efforts also were implemented to speed up service.

In December 1993, creative differences led to the severing of ties between Whataburger and its advertising agency, The Richards Group. By this time the company's advertising budget totaled approximately $8 million. By early 1994 Whataburger ranked as the nation's 11th largest burger chain, with sales of approximately $342 million.

In April 1994 the company moved its advertising account to the Dallas-based agency Marketing Continuum. A new advertising campaign soon emerged. Whataburger's "What-cha Waitin' For?" campaign featured real customers, including local firefighters, to promote items such as its jalapeno burger via television and radio.

CONTINUED GROWTH: 1995–99

Dobson's efforts to improve conditions at Whataburger were successful. In 1995 sales increased to $400 million, a 10 percent increase from the previous year. In 1996, the company's chain grew to include some 522 locations.

Whataburger's growth did not go unnoticed by industry observers. NRN Research included the company on its list of 1995's ten leading fast-service sandwich chains by sales growth. At 4.71 percent,

Whataburger's sales growth was only slightly behind White Castle (6.09 percent) and McDonald's (6.45 percent).

A major development unfolded in 1996 when friends Paul K. Cohen and Paul Thomas acquired 41 Whataburger restaurants in Arizona and revealed plans to open 50 additional locations. The deal was the largest in Whataburger's history. Cohen already had an established relationship with Whataburger, operating 23 locations in El Paso.

As Whataburger headed into the late 1990s, its growth was furthered by continued creative advertising. By this time the company had selected Square One as its advertising agency. In October 1997 Whataburger introduced a campaign in which people fantasized about the contents of their own Whataburger commercial. For the year, sales totaled $550 million, and the company's advertising expenditures totaled $5.4 million.

A new product introduction occurred in mid-1998, when Whataburger unveiled its Thick & Hearty Burger, which was offered in both quarter-pound and half-pound varieties and included Nabisco's A.1. Thick & Hearty Steak Sauce. In tandem with the new product, which was offered for a limited time, the company partnered with Nabisco to develop co-promotions.

In mid-1999 Whataburger introduced a new advertising campaign leading up to its 50th anniversary in 2000. The campaign featured stories from customers about their first time eating at Whataburger.

Whataburger capped off the 1990s with several developments. Plans were made to introduce a line of branded children's clothing named Whatakids, as well as an e-commerce operation called Whatastore. In addition, the company opened a two-story, 6,100-square-foot flagship restaurant in 1999 named Whataburger by the Bay in downtown Corpus Christi.

A NEW MILLENNIUM: 2000–03

Following the dawn of the new millennium, Whataburger celebrated 50 years of operations in August 2000. By that time the company's chain had grown to include some 560 locations.

Several major leadership changes occurred in December 2000. At that time President and CEO Dobson was named chairman and CEO. His mother, Grace Dobson, transitioned from the role of chairwoman to chair emeritus. Tim Taft, who had served as senior vice-president and chief operating officer, was promoted to the role of president and chief operating officer.

At the time of the announcement, Tom Dobson commented on his family's involvement with the company over the previous half-century in a December 19, 2000 *Business Wire* release. "We are successful because we have maintained the fundamental principles that my father set forth 50 years ago and that my mother has carried forward," he said. "And that is to serve our customers a fresh, made-to-order meal in a family atmosphere at a fair price. We never set out to be the biggest hamburger chain. We just want to be the best."

Recognition continued in 2001. In April, the 77th Texas Legislature named Whataburger as an official Texas Treasure. Later that year, the company assumed operations of 39 Arizona restaurants that had been owned by Paul Cohen and Paul Thomas's business, Arizona Fast Foods LLC, which had filed for bankruptcy.

By 2002 Whataburger was generating about $1.25 million annually from each of its company-owned restaurants. By this time the company had devoted roughly $100 million to remodel many of its locations.

During the early 2000s, Whataburger continued to put considerable energy toward the enhancement of franchiser-franchisee relations and the betterment of work-life conditions for its employees. One example of this was the establishment of the Family First Foundation. Funded by small donations from employees, the foundation provided assistance to employees in need. Whataburger also created an academy focused on leadership development for its restaurant managers.

Whataburger's sales reached $614 million in 2001 and swelled to $693 million the following year. The company continued to focus on growth in 2002, securing a syndicated loan totaling about $90 million that would allow it to open up to 25 new company-owned locations per year and upgrade its technology.

A major development unfolded in late 2002 when businessman Gregory L. Feste and a number of professional athletes agreed to build 28 Whataburger locations in Jacksonville, Florida, through FesteCapital Partnerships. Midway through 2003 Whataburger signed an additional agreement with another one of Feste's businesses, Festecapital Franchise Management, to develop 99 new locations throughout 19 counties in central Florida. Whataburger rounded out the year by hiring fast-food industry veteran Sandee Pritchard as its chief people officer.

EXPANSION AND CHANGE: 2004–09

Developments continued in 2004, when Whataburger acquired Whataco Inc., its largest franchisee, thereby securing 92 restaurants in Mexico, Louisiana, New Mexico, Oklahoma, and Texas. Following the deal, more than half of all Whataburger restaurants were company-owned. Another major leadership change occurred midway through the year when Wendy Beck succeeded 24-year Whataburger veteran Mike McClellan as chief financial officer.

By 2005 Whataburger had grown to 350 company-owned restaurants and 250 franchised locations. Operations were located in Texas, Arizona, Alabama, New Mexico, Louisiana, Oklahoma, Mexico, and Florida. That year, sales totaled approximately $650 million.

At this time the company began building three new prototype restaurants in its hometown of Corpus Christi, including a design with a double-lane drive-through that outsized its traditional restaurants by approximately 800 square feet.

The last half of the decade was peppered with more leadership changes. In early 2005 Tim Taft resigned as president and chief operating officer. Following this development, Chief Development Officer Preston Atkinson was promoted to chief operating officer, and Chairman and CEO Tom Dobson assumed the additional responsibilities of president. Taft eventually was named president and CEO of Pizza Inn Inc.

After once again expanding its base of company-owned locations by acquiring 13 restaurants from four franchisees in central and northern Texas, Whataburger contended with more leadership changes in late 2005. In September, Chief People Officer Sandee Pritchard left the company to accept a similar role with Donato's Pizzeria Corp.

Leadership changes continued during the latter years of the decade. In early 2007 a new president was finally named when Chief Operating Officer Atkinson assumed that additional position. Whataburger was operating 700 restaurants by this time.

Another major development occurred in December 2008 when, after operating in the same town for 58 years, Whataburger revealed plans to relocate its headquarters from Corpus Christi to San Antonio.

Whataburger ushered in 2009 by naming Karen Bird as its new chief information officer. In March, the company revealed that it had purchased a new headquarters facility in San Antonio. Located at 300 Concord Plaza Drive, the new facility spanned 140,000 square feet. Plans were made to begin occupying the facility in June, and to complete the move by the summer's end. Of the 250 people employed at the existing headquarters facility in Corpus Christi, some 60 percent indicated they would relocate to San Antonio.

From its humble beginnings as a wooden hamburger stand, Whataburger had expanded its operations to ten states over the course of six decades. As the company headed into the 21st century's second decade, its prospects for continued success seemed strong.

Paul R. Greenland

PRINCIPAL COMPETITORS

Burger King Holdings Inc.; McDonald's Corporation; Sonic Corp.

FURTHER READING

Doss, Lori, "Whataburger: Renewed Unity and Focus Turn 52-Year-Old Chain into Texas Treasure," *Nation's Restaurant News*, May 13, 2002.

Long, Dolores, "Jim L. Peterson," *Restaurant Business,* May 1, 1986.

Nichols, Don, "What a Comeback," *Restaurant Business,* August 10, 1996.

Ruggless, Ron, "Party On: Whataburger Chain Celebrates 50th Anniversary," *Nation's Restaurant News,* August 7, 2000.

"Whataburger Promotes Atkinson to President," *Nation's Restaurant News,* February 19, 2007.

"Whataburger: Taft Exits As Prexy; Dobson Takes Over," *Nation's Restaurant News,* February 7, 2005.

"Whataburger's Dobson Family Announces Changes at the Top," *Business Wire,* December 19, 2000.

W WOODWARD

Woodward Governor Company

1000 East Drake Road
Fort Collins, Colorado 80525-1824
U.S.A.
Telephone: (970) 482-5811
Fax: (970) 498-3058
Web site: http://www.woodward.com

Public Company
Incorporated: 1902
Employees: 5,823
Sales: $1.26 billion (2008)
Stock Exchanges: NASDAQ
Ticker Symbol: WGOV
NAICS: 333995 Fluid Power Cylinder and Actuator Manufacturing; 333996 Fluid Power Pump and Motor Manufacturing; 334519 Other Measuring and Controlling Device Manufacturing; 335314 Relay and Industrial Control Manufacturing; 335999 All Other Miscellaneous Electrical Equipment and Component Manufacturing; 336412 Aircraft Engine and Engine Parts Manufacturing; 336413 Other Aircraft Parts and Auxiliary Equipment Manufacturing

∎ ∎ ∎

Woodward Governor Company is the world's oldest and one of the largest manufacturers of energy control systems and components for industrial and aircraft engines, turbines, and other power equipment. Examples of the company's products include ignition systems, fuel injection systems, integrated fuel systems, and power management controls. The main markets served by the company are power generation, transportation, process industries (such as the processing of oil and gas, petrochemicals, paper, and sugar), and aerospace. The bulk of Woodward's sales are to original equipment manufacturers (OEMs), with General Electric Company accounting for nearly one-third of overall revenues. Other customers include Caterpillar Inc., Honeywell Inc., MAN AG, Pratt & Whitney, and Rolls-Royce plc. The company operates eight plants in the United States, two each in the United Kingdom and Germany, and one each in the Netherlands and Japan.

FIRST PRODUCT: WATERWHEEL GOVERNOR

The company that would become Woodward Governor Company was founded in 1870 by Amos W. Woodward. Woodward was descended from the Woodward family that helped settle Watertown, Massachusetts, in the 1630s. Born in 1829 in Winthrop, Maine, Woodward attended Kents Hill Academy for only one term. In that short time, however, he mastered higher mathematics and physics and was considered by many to be a genius. Woodward eventually went to work in a factory in Worcester, Massachusetts, before migrating to the Midwest, specifically Rockford, Illinois, in 1856. An inveterate tinkerer and inventor, Woodward managed to earn a modest salary by selling his innovations. He also held various mechanic jobs. It was through one of those positions, in fact, that he became intrigued with a major dilemma of the day: how to control the speed at which waterwheels turned.

COMPANY PERSPECTIVES

Demand for fuel-efficient, low-emission, high performance energy drives our business. At Woodward we integrate our technologies into fuel, combustion, fluid, actuation, and electronic control systems.

Leading original equipment manufacturers use Woodward systems and components for controlling engines, turbines, and associated equipment in the aerospace, power and process industries, and transportation markets. We are focused on accurately and precisely controlling energy by integrating our components into systems that improve the emissions performance, reliability, and fuel efficiency of our customers' products, helping ensure a better environment.

Woodward solved the problem by designing a mechanism, the mechanical noncompensating water-wheel governor, in 1869. He received a patent for the device in 1870 and started a company to manufacture the governors. Despite the usefulness of Woodward's invention, the new company struggled. Besides lacking capital, Woodward also lacked the desire to build a profitable business. Like many other inventors, he was more interested in developing new ideas. Fortunately, his son Elmer Woodward had a greater knack for business. Elmer had started working in his father's shop as a boy and had, like his father, shown himself to be gifted in math and physics. On one occasion, for example, Elmer devised a contraption that automatically controlled the cutting speed and feeder of a machine that he was operating. Elmer was caught reading a book while the machine worked away.

Elmer Woodward's desire for learning stemmed from what he considered a poor formal education. To make up for the deficiency, he spent years studying technical books after dinner until midnight. As he got older, he became increasingly involved in the company's business affairs. It was then that the enterprise began to prosper. In 1891 the business had three employees and was selling about $8,000 worth of governors annually. During the 1890s, though, the company grew and even expanded into a larger manufacturing facility. At the same time that he was helping to run the business, Elmer Woodward, like his father, continued to invent. Importantly, in 1898, when he was 36 years old, Elmer received a patent for a governor that was an improve-

ment over the one his father had designed. The breakthrough device gave the company an important advantage in the burgeoning market for governors needed to control new hydroelectric generators.

In 1902 Amos and Elmer Woodward incorporated as Woodward Governor Company. By that time they were employing 25 men at their Rockford manufacturing facility. As the hydroelectric power market surged during the 1910s and 1920s, so did Woodward Governor's sales. The company also expanded overseas into Europe, Japan, New Zealand, and elsewhere throughout the world. Indeed, by the 1920s the company was making more than 35 percent of its sales to foreign buyers. In 1910 Woodward Governor moved its operations to a new five-story plant. Elmer Woodward continued to tweak and improve the company's governors in an effort to meet new needs in the marketplace, helping the company's revenues to climb. Amos Woodward died in 1919, a few years short of his 90th birthday, and his son continued to lead Woodward throughout the 1920s. Early in 1929, when he was 67 years old, Elmer Woodward hired son-in-law Irl Martin to take over day-to-day operations, while he continued to design new products and make pivotal contributions to the company well into his 70s.

By 1929, Woodward Governor was employing 50 workers and had established itself as a leader in the design and manufacture of prime mover controls (prime movers are machines that convert either heat or hydraulic energy into mechanical or electrical energy); that year, the firm posted net income of $65,000 on sales of $318,000. Unfortunately, the company's fortunes were about to change for reasons outside of its control. The stock market crash of 1929 quashed demand for Woodward's waterwheel and hydropower governors. Martin was faced with a crisis, his handling of which would demonstrate his legendary management abilities and philosophies. Rather than lay off staff, Martin called all of the workers together and offered them a choice: either fill existing orders and hope for more, or keep everyone on the payroll at 20 hours per week and at a cut in pay until business improved. The workers elected to scale back hours and pay. Until the crisis was over, Elmer Woodward paid much of their wages out of his own pocket, a practice that was, and still is, almost unheard of in any kind of corporation. It was later discovered that Woodward had borrowed against his own life insurance to meet the payroll.

EXPANDING THE PRODUCT LINE

The company's shipments began to pick up in 1932 and 1933, although the company was still lagging. Woodward and Martin realized that the company would

KEY DATES

1870: Amos W. Woodward receives a patent for the mechanical noncompensating waterwheel governor and soon begins selling the devices, marking the beginning of Rockford, Illinois-based A.W. Woodward Company.

1902: Company is incorporated as Woodward Governor Company, with Amos's son Elmer Woodward largely in charge of the firm.

1929: Elmer Woodward's son-in-law Irl Martin takes over day-to-day operations.

1930s: Company expands into controls for diesel engines and airplane propellers.

1940: Woodward Governor goes public.

1946: Martin institutes the Corporate Partnership management scheme.

1955: Company builds first factory outside Rockford, in Fort Collins, Colorado.

1976: Calvin C. Covert succeeds Martin as chairman and CEO.

1994: Company posts its first loss since 1940.

1995: John Halbrook takes over as chairman and CEO following Covert's death.

1997: Company stock is moved from OTC trading to the NASDAQ.

1998: Fuel Systems Textron, Inc., is acquired and renamed Woodward FST, Inc.

2000: Company receives a five-year, $500 million contract from GE Power Systems.

2005: Thomas Gendron is named president and CEO.

2007: Woodward's headquarters are shifted to Fort Collins, Colorado.

2008: Company acquires MPC Products Corporation, which forms basis for new airframe systems business segment.

2009: Airframe systems business is bolstered via purchase of HR Textron.

be forced to find new sources of revenue to supplant lost demand. To that end, Woodward began developing a governor to control diesel engines that were being used at the time as auxiliary systems in hydroelectric plants. Under his supervision, the company perfected a governor for diesel engines in 1933 that would become the core of the company's product line for several years. The pivotal breakthrough provided an important boost to the company's sagging bottom line. In fact, Woodward Governor's elated workers were soon making up for lost time with 60-hour weeks. Unfortunately, the federal government, concerned with underemployment, forced the company to cut them back to 40 hours. Martin feared that the company would be unable to meet demand, but their workers, realizing the urgency of the situation, continued to work 60 hours per week at only 40 hours of pay.

Woodward Governor introduced another major product breakthrough in 1934: a governor that could control the pitch of an airplane propeller. An aviation company had approached the company about creating such a control, and several of the company's younger members had gone to work to design the contraption. Unable to solve the problem, they eventually called on 73-year-old Elmer Woodward to finish the job. Within several months his team delivered a perfected governor that would give Woodward Governor a much needed entry into the aviation industry.

Although sales surged during the mid-1930s as a result of the new innovations and reached $1.4 million by 1939, exceeding the $1 million mark for the first time, the company's equipment and facilities had depreciated by the end of the decade. Rather than borrow the cash to renew the plant, Martin again called the employees together. They all agreed that everyone in the company should forgo a pay raise in order to pay cash for new equipment. Thus, Woodward Governor emerged from the Great Depression with a broader product line, new equipment, little debt, and a family-like bond between labor and management that would distinguish the company in U.S. industry. This bond also led the company to undertake a recapitalization in 1940 that greatly increased the number of shares of common stock, enabling employees to become stockholders in the company; coupled with the recapitalization was an initial public offering (IPO) of the company stock, which also took place in 1940.

Much of Woodward Governor's success in the 1930s, and even over the next several decades, was attributable to Martin's unique management techniques. In the 1930s, for example, Martin realized that some of his skilled machinists and mechanics were not producing as much as he believed they could. He believed the problem was psychological and was attributable to the workers' poor self-image. To solve the problem, he instituted a dress code that included a tie and smock, and began requiring that all employees remain neatly shaven. The workers also agreed to begin keeping their work areas extremely clean and neat. Worker productivity improved greatly and, according to Martin, the workers began to realize the true value of their contribution to the company and society. Among Martin's other management innovations was aptitude testing, which was used to help determine where a worker would perform most effectively and happily. He also introduced a cutting-edge health insurance program that focused on personal preventive medicine.

On December 31, 1940, 78-year-old Elmer Woodward, or "Pops" as he had come to be called, worked a full day, returned home, and then died of a heart attack. His exemplary service to the company spanned 64 years. Among other attributes, the soft-spoken Elmer was known for treating everyone as his equal, regardless of position or stature, as well as for earning the respect of all those who knew him. Irl Martin assumed complete leadership of the company after Elmer's death, just as Woodward Governor was entering the greatest growth phase in its history. Indeed, World War II placed huge demands on the company's production facilities as orders for its advanced propeller controls boomed; the advantage that the controls offered was that they reduced vibration in airplanes and ships by synchronizing and phasing the propellers of two or more engines.

Woodward Governor continued to innovate during the war, introducing, for example, the first aircraft turbine control in 1943, and sales skyrocketed. Amazingly, the company's ranks swelled from just 50 in 1935 to more than 1,600 during the war's peak. The explosive growth virtually changed the face of the company, which had moved its operations into a large new factory at the very start of the war. Again, Martin consulted his workers about the new facility and they all agreed to forgo some compensation to build it. The facility was completely state-of-the-art and designed with worker productivity and satisfaction in mind. The plant became much less crowded after the war, when the workforce shrank to a more manageable 500. Although demand faded during that period, sales growth resumed in the wake of the postwar economic boom of the 1950s and 1960s.

INSTITUTING THE CORPORATE PARTNERSHIP IN 1946

In 1946 Martin instituted what would become one of his most noted management schemes: the Corporate Partnership. This plan led to a number of innovative management solutions. For example, Martin was concerned about the problem of determining equitable pay rates for everyone in the company, including himself. After much thought, he decided to present a solution to the employees. Under the new system, every employee, or "member," would receive no more and no less than ten times that of the least valuable category of worker. In addition, a bonus system was put in place. At the end of each year, workers and management would rank everyone in their department according to a given set of criteria. The rankings were combined and every employee then received a ranking within the entire company. That rank was used to determine an employee's percentage of the aggregate annual bonus.

During the mid-1950s Woodward expanded its product line to include main fuel controls for aircraft gas turbines and electronic analog controls. Among the recognized innovations during the 1950s and 1960s were: the electrical cabinet actuator in 1957, the first truly electric governor in 1960, fuel valves for aerodrive turbines in 1962, control for turboprop engines in 1964, and a unique new electronic control system in 1965. As demand for the company's products increased, Martin expanded the company. In 1955 Woodward built a new factory in Fort Collins, Colorado. Subsequently, Martin oversaw the installation of production facilities throughout the world in the Netherlands, England, Japan, and Australia. By the late 1960s, Woodward was generating annual revenues of about $70 million.

Although the 65-year-old Martin officially retired from the presidency in 1960, he remained as chairman of the board and led Woodward into the 1970s. The company continued to introduce new products during the early 1970s and to strengthen its Corporate Partnership program. In fact, Martin became a sought-after speaker in the Midwest by groups wanting to hear about his unique management philosophy. Unfortunately, Martin's health began deteriorating in 1975. He resigned in March 1976 and died on April 22 after 55 years of service to Woodward Governor Company.

THRIVING UNDER COVERT'S LEADERSHIP: 1976–89

Martin was succeeded by Calvin C. Covert. Covert had joined the company in 1942, going to work in the lowly "snagging" room, where he shaved rough spots off castings. "One day Mr. Martin came out and said, 'Sonny boy, you made,'" Covert recalled in the January 1988 *Rockford Magazine*. Covert continued, "I said, 'made what.' And he said, 'I gave you one of the dirtiest jobs. Now what the hell do you want to do?'" That began Covert's rise up the corporate ladder. By the time he took the helm in 1976, he had been working in top management for most of his career. Under his direction, Woodward continued to create new products and to refine its management techniques. Major new products in the 1970s included an eight-bit microprocessor synchronizer and a digital synchronizer for aircraft. Covert also stepped up Woodward's international expansion in 1977 with a new plant in Brazil.

The company thrived under Covert's leadership. It experienced a downturn in its important turbine division in the early 1980s, but by the mid-1980s its sales were approaching the $200 million mark. During the mid-1990s the company whipped its internal operations into shape and stepped up its growth pace. Indeed, $100 invested in Woodward in 1976 would have grown to nearly $1,500 by 1988. That growth was largely the result of an economic upswing and increased demand from defense and aerospace industries during the mid- and late 1980s. Woodward's sales leapt 13 percent in 1987 to $275 million as net earnings rose 37 percent to $24 million. By the end of the decade, moreover, the company was generating more than $300 million in revenues annually.

Although Woodward Governor Company was helped by strong markets during much of the 1980s, its success was also attributed to its proven management style, which was getting increased attention within U.S. industry as a result of the firm's ability to compete with companies from Japan and other countries. As it turned out, Woodward had long been practicing management techniques (such as employee empowerment and performance-based incentives) that were emerging as major trends in the 1980s. For example, the company's president received only $247,000 in total salary and bonuses in 1986, in keeping with the company rule of not making more than ten times the amount of the lowest job category. Likewise, new Woodward employees were brought into the company by way of a solemn ceremony; other employees attended, and even joined in prayer, as the new employees were inducted into the Woodward "family." Finally, while Woodward's workers received only about 80 to 90 percent of the salary of their U.S. industrial counterparts, their bonuses consistently placed them well above the national average in compensation.

SETBACK IN THE EARLY NINETIES

Woodward entered the 1990s with record sales and profits; revenues hit $362 million in 1991. Unfortunately, waning defense and aerospace markets were beginning to take their toll on the company's bottom line. Woodward had been trying to reduce its dependence on the aircraft market since the mid-1980s, when over 60 percent of sales were attributable to that sector. By the early 1990s, however, the company was still getting more than 50 percent of its revenues from the aircraft market and was scurrying to beef up its activity in other sectors. Similarly, the company had seen the percentage of its sales attributable to defense markets fall from 20 percent in 1990 to less than 15

percent by 1993. To make up for the shortfall, Woodward began concentrating on its industrial controls division, its only major segment other than aircraft controls.

Sagging key markets hurt Woodward Governor Company in 1993 and 1994. Sales slipped to $333 million in 1994, and the company posted its first loss since 1940. By that time, John Halbrook had been brought onboard as president and chief executive. Under his leadership, the company instituted aggressive cost-cutting measures in 1994 that resulted in a $24 million restructuring charge, which pinched its net earnings. The charge also forced the company to cut its aircraft division workforce by 20 percent, resulting in one of the biggest layoffs ever conducted by the organization. The restructuring also included the closing of a plant in Stevens Point, Wisconsin. Covert passed away in December 1994 at the age of 70, and Halbrook assumed his position as chairman, announcing his commitment to continue cutting costs and improving the company's market stance.

Despite setbacks going into the mid-1990s, Woodward continued to research and introduce new products. It brought out innovative new digital controls in 1992 and 1993, for example, and had several advanced devices for both aircraft and industrial markets under development. Acquisitions were also completed, including the purchase of HSC Controls of Buffalo, New York, which made electromechanical devices for integrated control systems, especially for aircraft engines; and a small maker of fuel injection nozzles based in Kelbra, Germany, which became part of Woodward Governor Germany GmbH. In 1995, the year of Woodward Governor Company's 125th anniversary, the company bounced back, posting net income of $11.9 million on revenues of $379.7 million.

The results for 1995 ushered in a period of heightened growth for Woodward, growth that was fueled by continual expansion of the product line, strategic acquisitions, and alliance formation. In July 1996 the company acquired Deltec Fuel Systems Holding B.V., a Netherlands firm specializing in fuel control systems for natural gas engines. The purchase was part of a company push to grab a share of the burgeoning market for natural gas engines. In October 1996 Woodward and Mountain View, California-based Catalytica, Inc., created a joint venture called GENXON Power Systems, LLC, to market an aftermarket emission control system for industrial gas turbines.

A TURN TO MORE AGGRESSIVE MANAGEMENT

Early in 1997 Woodward executed a four-for-one split of its stock. The increased liquidity set the stage for the company to take what many observers considered to be a long overdue move: listing the stock on the NASDAQ. The move brought a heightened awareness to both the stock and the company because the company's shares had previously traded only via over-the-counter "pink sheets," a trading area usually used only for small start-up companies. The move to the NASDAQ, along with the company's increasing emphasis on acquisitions and alliances, highlighted a shift from the more conservative management style of the past to a much more aggressive approach.

The bold new approach was more than evident in the June 1998 acquisition of Fuel Systems Textron, Inc., from Textron Inc. for $174.8 million, by far the largest acquisition in company history. Based in Zeeland, Michigan, Fuel Systems Textron produced fuel injection nozzles, spray manifolds, and fuel metering and distribution valves for gas turbine engines used in both aircraft and industrial applications. The acquired company, which had revenues of $82 million in 1997, was subsequently renamed Woodward FST, Inc. The acquisition resulted in a substantial increase in revenues for the 1999 fiscal year, with revenues surging from $490.5 million to $596.9 million. Meantime, the company also acquired Baker Electrical Products, Inc., of Memphis, Michigan, in May 1998, gaining a supplier of electromagnetic coils for antilock braking systems; and formed an alliance with Lockheed Martin Control Systems to create a company called AESYS that was charged with creating fuel delivery systems for aircraft engine OEMs.

In June 2000 Woodward received the largest single contract in its history, a five-year deal with GE Power Systems valued at more than $500 million. GE Power Systems was a unit of General Electric Company, which had long been Woodward's largest customer. Under the contract, the company would supply GE Power Systems with fuel and combustion control systems and components for GE's array of industrial gas turbines for the power generation, oil and gas processing, and marine markets. At the time, power generation was considered a particularly key market as growing demand for power was leading to utilities building new generating plants. Woodward also completed one acquisition during 2000: Hoeflich Controls, Inc., a maker of ignition systems for industrial gas engines, purchased in November.

In June 2001 the company acquired the Bryce diesel fuel injection business of Delphi Automotive Systems, which included a plant in Cheltenham, England. For the fiscal year ending in September 2001, Woodward posted record profits of $53.1 million on record sales of $678.8 million. Hoping to get in on the ground floor of a potentially burgeoning new sector, the company announced in December 2001 that it was entering the market for fuel-cell control systems.

Acquisitions continued in 2002. In March the company bolstered its power generation sector by acquiring Leonhard-Reglerbau, which produced monitoring devices for power generation equipment at its plant in Stuttgart, Germany. The company had 1991 sales of $13 million. Also acquired in March 2002 was Nolff's Carburetion, Inc., a private company based in Romulus, Michigan, that produced fuel management systems for small industrial engines that use cleaner-burning fuels such as propane and natural gas. That same month, Woodward entered into a joint venture with MotoTron, a subsidiary of Brunswick Corporation that had developed electronic controls technology for pleasure boat engines. Woodward in April 2002 struck a seven-year, $350 million deal with GE Aircraft Engines to supply fuel delivery systems for engines used in regional and single-aisle aircraft. One month later, the company joined forces with one of its chief competitors, Hamilton Sundstrand Corporation, to establish a joint venture in China to repair jet engine parts, including fuel controls.

DOWNTURN, THEN ANOTHER SURGE

Many of Woodward Governor Company's initiatives at the beginning of the century were aimed at bolstering the firm's industrial controls operations, thereby continuing the drive to lessen dependence on the aircraft market. By 2002 industrial controls were generating about 60 percent of overall revenues. This trend became particularly important with the slump in the airline and aircraft industries that followed in the wake of the September 11, 2001, terrorist attacks on the United States. The benefits of this diversification, however, failed to materialize initially when the broader economic downturn eventually undermined Woodward's business in the power generation and industrial markets. Sales were essentially flat during fiscal 2002, while profits fell 17 percent to $45.2 million. Results for the following year were even more disappointing as revenues slumped 16 percent to $586.7 million and profits plunged more than 70 percent to just $12.3 million.

In the fall of 2002 Thomas Gendron was named president and COO of Woodward, having previously headed the firm's industrial controls division. Halbrook remained chairman and CEO. Via two acquisitions completed in 2003, Woodward became a leader in the small, high-speed industrial engine market. The company spent a total of about $58 million for Niles, Illinois-based Synchro-Start Products, Inc., a producer of actuators, solenoids, and controls for industrial engines and equipment; and Barber-Colman Dyna Products, which specialized in controls for off-highway diesel and gas engines and mobile industrial equipment. The latter company was purchased from London-based Invensys plc.

Improvements in most of its core markets enabled Woodward to bounce back strongly in fiscal 2004, when revenues surged 21 percent to $709.8 million and net income more than doubled. Also of note that year was the company's strong growth in Asia, where about 12 percent of sales had originated. The key market in that region was China, where Woodward over the previous two years had acquired a plant in Suzhou, where parts for small engines were produced, and built a new factory in Tianjin for the manufacturing of components for large industrial turbines.

In July 2005 Halbrook turned over the firm's day-to-day operations to Gendron, who was named president and CEO. Halbrook, who remained chairman, was credited with thoroughly modernizing Woodward during his tenure not only in terms of his more aggressive approach to growth but also in the area of company culture. The firm had shifted from a more inward-looking stance to a stronger focus on customers and their needs, while Halbrook also eliminated many of the conservative workplace rules that had been in effect for decades, including the strict dress code instituted in the 1930s.

A series of important developments occurred under Gendron's watch as well. In October 2006 Woodward purchased the German firm SEG Schaltanlagen-Elektronik-Geräte GmbH & Co. KG, which bolstered the company's offerings in the power generation sector. Particularly noteworthy at a time of rapid growth in windpower was SEG's inverter technology, which was a key component enabling power from large windmills to be transmitted onto a power grid. At the beginning of 2007, Woodward shifted its headquarters from Rockford, Illinois, to Fort Collins, Colorado, where the firm's industrial controls division had long been based. The company's large workforce at its Illinois plants, which focused on aircraft components, were unaffected by this shift. Woodward continued its strong rebound from the difficulties it encountered earlier in the decade with record profits of $98.2 million for fiscal 2007 on record revenues of $1.04 billion, the first time over the $1 billion mark.

MAJOR ACQUISITIONS IN 2008 AND 2009 IN AIRFRAME SYSTEMS

Late in 2007 Woodward launched a restructuring to better align its operating segments with its markets and customers. Its operations were rearranged into three segments focusing on turbine systems, engine systems, and electrical power systems. In January 2008 Gendron took on the additional role of chairman. Then in October of that year, the company consummated its largest acquisition to that point, the $383 million purchase of MPC Products Corporation. Based in Skokie, Illinois, MPC was a leading manufacturer of high-performance electromechanical motion control systems, mainly for aerospace applications. MPC, which generated $195 million in revenues for 2007, formed the basis for the new airframe systems business segment.

Revenues for fiscal 2008, which did not include sales from MPC, jumped more than 20 percent to $1.25 billion thanks largely to increased global demand for energy efficiency and emissions reduction technologies. In April 2009 Woodward completed another major acquisition, purchasing the HR Textron business from Textron Inc. for around $365 million. The acquired unit, which specialized in mission-critical actuation systems and controls for weapons, aircraft, turbine engines, and combat vehicles, was integrated into the airframe systems unit. Although sales for fiscal 2009 were likely to rise because of the acquisitions of MPC and HR Textron, profits appeared certain to fall not only because of the impact of the economic downturn but also because of restructuring costs that Woodward incurred to carry out a workforce reduction implemented in response to the downturn.

Dave Mote
Updated, David E. Salamie

PRINCIPAL SUBSIDIARIES

Baker Electrical Products, Inc.; Woodward FST, Inc.; Woodward Controls, Inc.; Woodward International, Inc.; Woodward (Tianjin) Controls Company Limited (China); Woodward Governor de Mexico S.A. de C.V.; Woodward Governor France S.A.R.L.; Woodward Governor Germany GmbH; Woodward Governor GmbH (Switzerland); Woodward Governor India Private Limited; Woodward Governor Nederland B.V. (Netherlands); Woodward Governor (Japan) Ltd.; Woodward Governor Poland Sp.Zo.o; Woodward Regulateur (Quebec), Inc. (Canada); Woodward GmbH (Germany); Woodward Controls (Suzhou) Co., Ltd. (China); Woodward Controls International Trading (Shanghai) Co. Ltd. (China); SEG Verwaltungsgesellschaft GmbH (Germany); Woodward SEG Lima S.A.C. (Peru); Woodward Comércio de Sistemas de Controle e Proteção Eléctrica Ltda. (Brazil); Woodward SEG GmbH & Co. KG (Germany); Woodward Controls and Solutions (Thailand) Ltd.; Woodward Hong Kong

Limited (China); MPC Products Corporation; Techni-Core, Inc.; MPC Export Corporation (British Virgin Islands); MPC Products Europe, SAS (France); MotoTron Corporation; WGC LLC; SEG Power Solutions GmbH (Germany); Woodward CIS Limited Liability Company (Russia).

PRINCIPAL OPERATING UNITS

Airframe Systems; Electrical Power Systems; Engine Systems; Turbine Systems.

PRINCIPAL COMPETITORS

Hamilton Sundstrand Corporation; Parker Hannifin Corporation; Westinghouse Air Brake Technologies Corporation.

FURTHER READING

Anason, Dean, "This Isn't the Place to Rest," *Atlanta Business Chronicle,* May 26, 1995, p. 1B.

Braun, Georgette, "Smaller Is More for Woodward," *Rockford Register Star,* March 19, 2002, p. 1B.

———, "Two Local Firms to Team Up in China," *Rockford Register Star,* May 23, 2002, p. 1B.

———, "Woodward Buy Boosts Power Unit," *Rockford Register Star,* March 7, 2002, p. 2C.

———, "Woodward Inks $350 Million Engine Deal with GE," *Rockford Register Star,* April 3, 2002, p. 1B.

Bremner, Brian, "Caught in Crunch: Growth Crimps Woodward Governor," *Crain's Chicago Business,* January 25, 1988, p. 20.

Ferrier, Pat, "Slowdown Makes Times Tough for Woodward," *Fort Collins Coloradoan,* January 22, 2003.

Gary, Alex, "Woodward Governor to Triple Shares," *Rockford Register Star,* January 26, 2006, p. 1D.

———, "Woodward Looks at Wind, Acquisition to Fuel Growth," *Rockford Register Star,* November 15, 2006, p. 1B.

———, "Woodward to Pay $5M in Bias Suit," *Rockford Register Star,* October 6, 2006, p. 1B.

A Gentleman Named Woodward, Rockford, Ill.: Woodward Governor Company, 1974.

Hodge, Bob, *The Woodward Way: A History of the Woodward Governor Company, Rockford, Illinois, USA, 1870–1995,* Rockford, Ill.: Woodward Governor Company, 1997, 224 p.

Knapp, Kevin, "Surging Power Demand Gives Turbine Parts Maker a Boost," *Crain's Chicago Business,* September 18, 2000, p. 47.

Knowles, Francine, "Woodward Governor Split Powers Stock," *Chicago Sun-Times,* November 22, 1996, p. 49.

McGough, Robert, "How to Win the Class Struggle," *Forbes,* November 3, 1986, pp. 153+.

Murphy, H. Lee, "Move to Big Leagues Ignites Woodward Governor's Stock," *Crain's Chicago Business,* January 27, 1997, p. 12.

———, "Shrinking Markets Put Squeeze on Woodward," *Crain's Chicago Business,* January 24, 1994, p. 19.

———, "Woodward Governor Heads West," *Crain's Chicago Business,* February 5, 2007, p. 24.

Osbourne, Randy, "An Officer and a Gentleman," *Rockford Magazine,* January 1988.

Osenga, Mike, "Woodward Buys Synchro-Start," *Diesel Progress North American Edition,* July 2003, pp. 35–36.

Palmer, Ann Therese, "Cost Controls Key for Woodward Governor," *Crain's Chicago Business,* February 6, 1995, p. 24.

Pride, Jackie, "Woodward Eliminates 200 Jobs," *Wausau Daily Herald,* April 2, 1993.

Reuteman, Rob, "It's Big Debut for Little-Known Woodward Governor," *Rocky Mountain News,* April 26, 2008.

Schaper, Bob, "Taking a Long View at Woodward," *Rockford Register Star,* August 15, 2005, p. 3D.

———, "Woodward Sees Easy Transition: Resigning Woodward CEO to Stay with Firm," *Rockford Register Star,* February 2, 2005, p. 1A.

Spivak, Cary, "Woodward Shifts Facilities to Handle Product Demand," *Crain's Chicago Business,* January 27, 1986, p. 18.

Weingarten, Paul, "Woodward's Way," *Chicago Tribune Magazine,* July 29, 1984.

Working Title Films Ltd.

76 Oxford Street, Oxford House
London, W1N 9FD
United Kingdom
Telephone: (+44-20) 7307-3000
Fax: (+44-20) 7307-3001
Web site: http://www.workingtitlefilms.com

Subsidiary of Universal Pictures International
Incorporated: 1984
Employees: 40
NAICS: 512110 Motion Picture and Video Production

■ ■ ■

Working Title Films Ltd. is one of the best-known and certainly most successful British film production companies. The company is also one of the most internationally acclaimed, having produced such global hits as *Four Weddings and a Funeral, Bean, Fargo, Billy Elliot, Notting Hill,* and *O Brother Where Art Thou?* The company's long string of hits has enabled the company to gross more than $4.3 billion at the box office since 1992. A significant feature of Working Title's success has been its ability to produce hits across multiple genres. Romantic comedy, particularly as scripted by writer Richard Curtis and often featuring actor Hugh Grant, remains a major film category for the company, however. Working Title has also produced most of the films by the Coen brothers, starting with *The Hudsucker Proxy* and continuing through 2008's *Burn After Reading.* While Working Title's focus has shifted toward mid-budget features, costing $25 million and more to

produce, the company operates a subsidiary, WT2, which concentrates on quirkier, low-budget independent films.

Another important part of Working Title Films' success has been its relationship with Universal Pictures, which owns two-thirds of the company and provides financing and global distribution for its film projects. The company also has a production and distribution agreement in place with France's CanalPlus. The driving force behind the company has been founder Tim Bevan, who launched the company in 1984, and business partner Eric Fellner, who joined Bevan in 1992. Their working relationship, often described as "symbiotic," has permitted Working Title Films to maintain an extraordinary degree of independence, despite the group's presence within the Hollywood system.

INDEPENDENT ORIGINS IN THE EIGHTIES

Working Title Films was the brainchild of Tim Bevan, who was born in New Zealand to British parents. Bevan came to England to complete his studies in the mid-1970s, then found work as a production runner in New Zealand. Bevan then completed an apprenticeship with New Zealand's National Film Unit.

At the beginning of the 1980s, however, Bevan returned to England, where he launched his own company, Aldabra. At first Bevan focused on producing music videos. Bevan quickly built a strong portfolio, producing videos for such noted groups as Simple Minds and Frankie Goes to Hollywood. It was during this period, too, that Bevan met rival producer Eric

KEY DATES

1984: Music video producer Tim Bevan founds a film production company, Working Title Films, and has his first success with *My Beautiful Laundrette.*

1992: Bevan is joined by partner Eric Fellner, as Working Title becomes part of Polygram Film Entertainment.

1994: Working Title celebrates its first international hit with *Four Weddings and a Funeral.*

1999: Polygram is acquired by Universal, which then acquires two-thirds of Working Title; Working Title launches a dedicated low-budget film subsidiary, WT2.

2002: Working Title enters Australia with plans to release up to five films per year.

2009: Working Title announces its decision to exit the Australian market.

Fellner. Among Fellner's credits were music videos for Elton John and U2. Bevan and Fellner's rivalry was intense at times. As Fellner recalled to *W:* "I probably wanted him off the f---ing planet so I could do my stuff. But we became friends, and it was because of that we teamed up in Working Title."

Both Bevan and Fellner transitioned toward producing films toward the middle of the decade. Fellner's entry into the business came with the production of the enigmatic film *Sid and Nancy,* which recounted the story of Sid Vicious, former bass player with the Sex Pistols. Another noted film produced by Fellner was *A Kiss Before Dying.* Bevan in the meantime, had decided to set up his own production company, called Working Title Films, in 1984. Joining Bevan was filmmaker Sarah Radclyffe.

Soon after, Bevan came into contact with Stephen Frears, who had been shopping around the script to his first movie. As Frears recounted to *Variety:* "It's over 10 years since I gave Tim (Bevan)—who'd never produced a film—a script and said: 'Here, you'd better do this.' It was *My Beautiful Laundrette.* I asked him recently how old he'd been at the time. Twenty-four, he said. I said I must have been drunk."

In any event, *My Beautiful Laundrette* became a smash hit in England and attracted significant attention overseas as well, while also launching Frears's own career as a writer and director. Released in 1985, *My Beautiful Laundrette* had cost $800,000 to produce, and grossed

$3 million at the box office. Importantly, the film also received an Oscar nomination for best original screenplay.

UNDER THE POLYGRAM UMBRELLA IN 1992

Over the next several years, Bevan and Radclyffe worked with a number of other noted directors, including Derek Jarman (*Caravaggio*), Terry Jones (*Personal Services*), David Leland (*Wish You Were Here,* launching the career of Emily Lloyd), the 1987 Frears's film *Sammy and Rosie Get Laid,* and *A World Apart,* starring Barbara Hershey. Early financing for the company came from the independent U.K. television broadcaster, Channel 4, among others. Bevan spent much of the company's early years balancing his producer duties with a continual quest for financing. As Bevan explained to *Variety:* "We never had any money and we never made any money."

By then, Bevan and Radclyffe had been joined by Graham Bradstreet, an accountant, who orchestrated Working Title's association with Polygram, the U.K. record company. Polygram, then led by Michael Kuhn, had been seeking to enter into the film distribution business as well. Kuhn recognized Working Title's strong potential, and agreed to take a 49 percent stake in Working Title in 1988. The two companies then launched an international sales operation, called Manifesto.

Working Title's entry into the corporate world of international film production rested uneasily with both Bradstreet and Radclyffe, who left the company in 1990 and 1991, respectively. Bevan then turned to former rival and now friend Eric Zellner to join him as a partner at Working Title.

Bevan and Zellner quickly proved to have highly complementary working styles and methods. The partners also received full confidence from Kuhn, who convinced Polygram's board to establish Polygram Filmed Entertainment (PFE) as a dedicated film production and distribution company. PFE then acquired full control of Working Title.

Bevan and Fellner found themselves faced with the need to adjust to Working Title's new financial position. As Bevan explained to *Variety,* "Things became more focused and more disciplined over a period of 18 months. We together learned what it meant to have much greater resources, to have development money, production money and the distribution structure relatively on tap. We had to get used to the fact that we didn't have to go trundling around the world trying to sell our movies, but that we had to focus on developing a decent slate and running an efficient company."

The company put into place a lean organizational structure, with just over 40 employees in total. The group then began developing its production style, although initially the group struggled with adapting to working on larger-budget projects. The early 1990s saw Working Title complete such features as *Robin Hood,* starring Patrick Bergin and Uma Thurman, which grossed a respectable $23 million worldwide. The company also launched its relationship with actor and director Tim Robbins, producing 1992's *Bob Roberts,* which grossed $8 million. Another success for the company was *Posse,* directed by Mario Van Peebles, which grossed $20 million in 1993.

FOUR WEDDINGS TO SUCCESS IN 1994

Working Title nonetheless had its share of flops. Its relationship with Robbins provided an introduction to Joel and Ethan Coen, who were then at the beginning of one of the most original careers in late 20th century Hollywood history. Working Title's first film with the Coen brothers, 1994's *The Hudsucker Proxy,* failed to stimulate audience enthusiasm, generating just $15 million at the box office, despite a budget of $25 million.

The year continued badly for the company, as another big budget international release, *Romeo Is Bleeding,* similarly failed to find an audience. By then, too, Working Title had taken the back seat to other, more visible PFE production companies, and especially Interscope, which had produced the hits *Three Men and a Baby* and *Cocktail,* and Egg Productions, set up by actress Jodie Foster. Working Title was more generally recognized, as Bevan acknowledged to *Variety,* as "a crappy arthouse label."

Nonetheless, Kuhn continued to provide Working Title, and more specifically, the team of Bevan and Fellner, with PFE's full support. The company's next project in 1994 was a low-budget romantic comedy by first-time writer Richard Curtis, and directed by Mike Newell called *Four Weddings and a Funeral.* The very British film had initially been intended for the U.K. market. Yet Bevan and Fellner, fearful that the film would be torn apart by British film critics, instead decided to release it to a small number of screens, backed by a lavish promotional campaign in order to give the $4.5 million movie the aura of a big-budget film, in the United States. The result far surpassed their initial expectations, as *Four Weddings and a Funeral* went on to gross more than $260 million worldwide. The film also generated new Oscar nominations for best picture and best original screenplay, and the Golden Globe award for best actor for Hugh Grant, among others.

PART OF UNIVERSAL IN 1999

Working Title found itself transformed into the United Kingdom's leading film production company. The company continued to develop new hits through the middle of the decade, including *French Kiss,* directed by Lawrence Kasdan for $40 million in 1995, which grossed $100 million worldwide; *Dead Man Walking,* directed by Tim Robbins, which grossed $95 million on a budget of $11 million, and gained the Oscar for best actress for Susan Sarandon. The company also scored new success with the Coen brothers, with the 1996 release of *Fargo.* That film received the Oscar for best actress and best original screenplay that year, while grossing $55 million.

Working Title closed out the decade with two new international blockbusters. The first came in 1997, with the release of *Bean,* starring Rowan Atkinson, which grossed $235 million on a budget of just $15 million. This success was followed up two years later with a new Richard Curtis film, *Notting Hill,* starring Hugh Grant and Julia Roberts, which grossed more than $360 million.

The year 1999 also marked Working Title's entry into the Universal Pictures International group (UPI), which had absorbed PFE that year. Following that acquisition, Working Title agreed to join UPI, which then acquired two-thirds of the British company. At the same time, Working Title entered into a new global distribution agreement with UPI as well as France's Canal Plus, which agreed to finance 50 percent of Working Title's production requirements.

The new financial backing, and global distribution reach, provided Working Title with even greater financial stability to pursue its somewhat eclectic film production program. These included a new international hit, *Bridget Jones's Diary,* written and directed by Richard Curtis. That hit movie became the first British film to hit the number one spot in both the U.S. and U.K. box offices simultaneously.

Despite the company's growing success, and growing budgets, Working Title was determined to remain true to its roots in the low-budget, independent film arena. Recognizing that its larger budget films had come to dominate the company's attention, in 1999, Working Title decided to set up a dedicated low-budget subsidiary, Working Title 2, or WT2. The new unit quickly booked its own success with the international hit film *Billy Elliot* and the popular British comedy *Shaun of the Dead,* both in 2001, followed by *Ali G Indahouse* in 2002.

PULLING OUT OF AUSTRALIA IN 2009

Working Title attempted to replicate its U.S. and U.K. success with an entry into Australia in 2002. The company hoped to produce up to five films per year for that market. In the end, the company managed to turn out just two films in seven years, including one direct-to-DVD release. By 2009, the company decided to pull the plug on its Australian office.

Fortunately for Working Title, its core business continued to turn in strong performances. By 2009, the company had grossed more than $4.3 billion since 1992. Importantly, more than $3 billion of that total had been generated since 1999. The company continued to add new hit titles to its roster, including new Curtis films (*Love Actually*, the sequel to Bridget Jones, and *The Boat That Rocked*). The company also displayed its diversity, adding such titles as *Frost/Nixon*, *United 93*, *The Bourne Ultimatum*, *Mr. Bean's Holiday*, *Nanny McPhee*, as well as several new Coen films.

By the end of the decade, Working Title Films had clearly established itself as the leading British film producer. In 2007, the company also renewed its partnership with Universal, signing a new seven-year production contract. Bevan and Fellner continued the fruitful partnership, enjoying their status, as Stephen Frears described it to *W* as: "the most powerful people, ever, in British film."

M. L. Cohen

PRINCIPAL SUBSIDIARIES

Working Title 2 Films Ltd.

PRINCIPAL OPERATING UNITS

Working Title Films; WT2.

PRINCIPAL COMPETITORS

Warner Communications Inc.; Mediaset SpA; Dream-Works L.L.C.; Carlton Communications PLC; Lucasfilm Ltd.; Pathe SAS Maxell Europe Ltd.; Miramax Pictures Inc.; Aardman Animations Ltd.; Industrial Light and Magic (Division of Lucasfilm Ltd.); Dream-Works Interactive.

FURTHER READING

Boland, Michaela, "Oz Expansion Isn't Working," *Variety*, February 23, 2009, p. 3.

Conti, Samantha, "The Hit Men," *W*, November 2005, p. 242.

Dawtrey, Adam, "The Rolling Cornerstones," *Variety*, October 23, 2006, p. A1.

——, "Working Title's Edge Aimed at Big Budgets," *Variety*, February 17, 1997, p. 9.

Dunkley, Cathey, "Uni, Canal Plus to Partner," *Hollywood Reporter*, May 11, 1999, p. 94.

Higgins, Charlotte, "The Producers," *Guardian*, April 16, 2005.

Jenkins, David, "The Producers: Working Boys," *W*, February 2009, p. 100.

Kemp, Stuart, "UK Duo Working Like a Charm," *Hollywood Reporter*, May 14, 2002, p. 10.

Power, Carla, "The Hitmakers," *Newsweek International*, October 16, 2000, p. 66.

Thompson, Anne, and Stuart Kempt, "Uni Retains Working Title," *Hollywood Reporter*, January 16, 2007, p. 2.

"Tim Bevan and Eric Fellner," *Business Week*, June 11, 2001, p. 32.

Zeitchik, Steven, "Working Title Books Rights to McMafia," *Hollywood Reporter*, April 14, 2009, p. 3.

Zpizza International Inc.

19712 MacArthur Boulevard, Suite 210
Irvine, California 92612
U.S.A.
Telephone: (949) 719-3800
Fax: (949) 721-4053
Web site: http://www.zpizza.com

Private Company
Incorporated: 1986
Employees: 60
Sales: $3.8 million (2008)
NAICS: 722211 Limited-Service Restaurants

■ ■ ■

Zpizza International Inc. is a predominantly franchised chain of pizza restaurants with nearly 100 units in operation. From its base in Southern California, the chain has expanded into a dozen states stretching from coast to coast. The chain also has expanded internationally, establishing restaurants in Mexico and Saudi Arabia. Each Zpizza restaurant offers dine-in, take-out, and catering service, and a menu laden with healthful selections. The chain uses organic ingredients and offers upscale pizza combinations that feature unconventional selections such as chipotle pesto sauce, Gorgonzola cheese, shiitake mushrooms, and truffle oil. The chain also serves sandwiches, salads, and pasta entrées. Every Zpizza franchisee operates more than one restaurant, paying a $30,000 franchiser's fee for the first location and $10,000 for each additional location. The total investment required to operate a franchise ranges between $250,000 and $349,000. Zpizza units are between 1,100 square feet and 1,500 square feet and capable of seating 30 customers. The company is led by Dan Rowe and Chris Bright, the principal executives and founders of Fransmart, which develops restaurant concepts into franchised chains.

ORIGINS

International expansion was never the intention of Sid Faranof when he founded Zpizza, nor was it his aim to create a chain of restaurants to blanket the nation. Mainly, he wanted to put into practice what he had learned at a holistic teaching center in Big Sur, California. A self-described bohemian, Faranof wanted to provide a healthful version of a staple of the American diet, a pizza made and topped with fresh, low-fat, and organic ingredients.

Faranof opened his first pizza restaurant in Laguna Beach, California, in 1986. He started the business with Susie Megrov, a French woman whose pronunciation of the word "the" gave the business its name. The definite article rolled off Megrov's tongue sounding like the letter "z," giving the founders' Zpizza restaurant its distinctive name. Megrov also advocated using fresh herbs and ingredients, which, coupled with Faranof's desire to use lower-fat ingredients such as part-skim mozzarella cheese, gave Zpizza its distinctive concept.

For roughly 15 years, Zpizza reflected the original vision of its founders. The restaurant served healthful pizzas to Laguna Beach residents. The massive leap from a one-restaurant business into a company bent on expanding throughout the United States and into

COMPANY PERSPECTIVES

Zpizza was founded in the art colony of Laguna Beach, California, where creativity and craftsmanship have flourished for almost a century. So it comes as no surprise that our critically acclaimed pizza is a true Laguna original. A passion for great food is why we start with dough made from premium Montana winter-wheat flour prepared fresh every day, hand-thrown and fire-baked until uniquely crisp. Our zest for quality continues when the toppings go on. We combine select ingredients using award-winning skim mozzarella from Wisconsin, certified organic tomato sauce, MSG-free pepperoni, additive-free sausage, and fresh produce. Our gourmet salads and sandwiches are just as delicious. We hope you enjoy our authentic and unique recipes as much as we enjoy making them for you.

foreign markets occurred in 1999, the year Dan Rowe and Chris Bright took an ownership stake in Zpizza.

THE FOUNDATION OF A FRANCHISER

Rowe and Bright injected a passion for growth into Zpizza, believing Faranof had developed a concept with the potential to secure a sizable share of a relatively new segment of the foodservice industry, the "fast-casual" segment. Fast-casual operators targeted customers who wanted better food than the offerings typically served at a fast-food restaurant, but at a price below the average check of a casual-dining restaurant. Fast-casual ranked between the fast-food segment and the casual-dining segment, becoming an increasingly popular type of restaurant during the 1990s. Rowe and Bright perceived Zpizza as a perfect fit for the fast-casual segment, a vehicle they could use to grab a share of the nearly $5 billion in receipts the fast-casual segment was collecting annually.

Realizing the commercial potential of foodservice chains is what Rowe and Bright did for a living. They headed a company whose name, Franchise Development Co., broadcast its mission. Although the name of the company was changed to Fransmart in 2001, its purpose remained the same: to develop restaurant concepts into national chains by selling franchises. Before taking on Zpizza as a franchise candidate, Rowe and Bright built franchise territories for Chesapeake Bagel Bakery and

Qdoba Mexican Grill, the latter a concept they transformed from one unit into a 100-unit chain that Jack in the Box Inc. acquired for $45 million.

1999–2002: CREATING A FRANCHISING PROGRAM

Rowe, a computer software specialist, and Bright, an accountant trained in business valuation, assumed managerial control over Zpizza in 1999. Faranof remained with the company, serving in a creative capacity by developing menu ideas, but Rowe and Bright were in charge of the company's day-to-day operations and dictated its long-term strategy. Their overriding objective was to franchise Faranof's concept, but Rowe and Bright did not begin courting prospective franchisees immediately. They spent three years developing a franchising program and refining the prototype Zpizza unit, one that could be replicated. They built four company-owned restaurants to test their theories and worked on streamlining systems so every aspect of running a Zpizza unit became standardized. "It was a real endeavor to compartmentalize every concept," Bright explained in the January–February 2007 issue of *Food & Drink*. "We really took a scientific approach to analyze the real estate and to evaluate the best customer model to determine the quality of the population within each area."

FRANCHISING BEGINS IN 2002

By 2002, Rowe and Bright were ready to roll out their national franchising program. A Zpizza restaurant, averaging 1,100 square feet, cost between $100,000 and $150,000 to build and to franchise, requiring an initial investment of between $40,000 and $50,000 from the franchisee. The company preferred multi-unit development agreements, seeking franchisees willing to commit to opening at least four Zpizza units. As part of its franchising program, Zpizza researched the most viable location for each franchise and created consumer profiles by interviewing area residents. Franchisees also benefited from a distribution network cobbled together by Fransmart. Because specialty and organic ingredients defined the Zpizza concept, only small, "boutique" food distributors could supply the chain, which required Rowe and Bright to form a partnership with distribution giant Sysco Corp. Through Sysco's help, a national distribution network was established to ship specialty and organic products to franchisee locations from coast to coast.

THE ZPIZZA MENU

Once in operation a franchisee took command of what promised to be a popular dining destination. All locations offered dine-in, take-out, and catering service, a comprehensive approach systematized by Fransmart. At the heart of a Zpizza franchise was its menu, which featured ingredients and selections tailored to those seeking a healthy diet. The pizza dough was made from 100 percent, certified organic wheat, hand thrown, and baked in a stone oven. Aside from the traditional tomato sauce, which was 100 percent certified organic, customers could choose from basil pesto, barbecue, roasted garlic, Thai peanut, and chipotle pesto. For those customers wanting something other than Wisconsin skim mozzarella, a half-dozen cheese selections were offered, including feta, Gorgonzola, ricotta, and soy. A total of ten meat choices were available, ranging from monosodium glutamate-free pepperoni, lime chicken, and additive-free sausage. Vegetables constituted the largest category on the menu, a cornucopia that included nearly two dozen selections such as serrano chilies, shiitake mushrooms, truffle oil, roasted eggplant, and zucchini.

GEOGRAPHIC EXPANSION

The launch of the franchising program in 2002 soon turned Zpizza into a genuine chain of restaurants. There were 16 units in operation by the time the first out-of-state Zpizza was established in Reno, Nevada, in November 2002. At the time, the company was in the midst of negotiations with franchisees that would extend the presence of the concept into Sacramento, California, and markets in Arizona. In August 2003, the company announced it would enter the Phoenix, Arizona, market through a new franchise agreement, which lifted the chain's store count to 20.

During the next three years, Zpizza broadened its geographic reach, finding willing entrepreneurs in a handful of states to open new units. By the fall of 2006, there were 40 restaurants in operation serving customers in Southern California, Nevada, Colorado, Kansas, North Carolina, Virginia, and Vermont. By the beginning of 2007, there were 54 locations open for business, with the company expecting to add another 36 units by the end of the year.

ZPIZZA GOES OVERSEAS

Zpizza's seventh year of franchising saw remarkable achievements on the expansion front and the onset of a global financial crisis. The company entered 2008 with nearly 80 restaurants in operation and an additional 300 units under development. The chain was expanding rapidly, and a deal signed at the beginning of the year set the stage for even greater growth, as Zpizza made a leap overseas. In January, the company signed its first international franchise deal, reaching an agreement with a franchisee to open 34 units in the Middle East. The breakthrough announcement, launching the Zpizza concept on a 7,500-mile journey, was followed by another international pact. In March, the company closed a multi-unit franchise agreement with Scream Solutions that called for the establishment of 20 Zpizza units in Mexico. "Not only is Zpizza expanding at a repaid pace here in the United States," Bright said in a March 13, 2008 company press release, "but we are also making great strides in new regions of the world. This is our second master franchise deal outside the United States and we are thrilled to be growing with reputable and experienced master developers."

ECONOMIC CONDITIONS PORTEND DIFFICULTIES

As preparations were being made to open Zpizza units in Mexico City and Riyadh, Saudi Arabia, economic conditions began to sour, threatening to stunt the company's expansion plans. By the fall of 2008, securing financing was becoming increasingly difficult, as the credit market tightened in response to a global financial crisis. For Zpizza, the inability of its franchisees to secure financing jeopardized the development agreements it had for more than 300 units. Industry analysts predicted some franchised chains would begin offering waivers on development agreements, recognizing that the commitments made by franchisees could not be fulfilled without loans from lenders. "The eye of the needle is getting smaller and smaller for those needing external funding," an investment adviser said in the November 1, 2008 issue of *Chain Leader*.

Despite the uncertain times, Zpizza recorded progress as it entered the last year of the decade. In

December 2008, the chain's first unit in Hawaii opened, the first of ten units scheduled to open in the state. On the international front, the company's development deals were beginning to bear fruit. The first unit in Mexico City opened its doors at the start of the year, followed by the opening of a Zpizza on Tahliya Street in Riyadh in February 2009. The Saudi Arabian restaurant flourished from its opening day, posting sales during its first month that were twice the total averaged by the chain. "Our early acceptance of our Zpizza in Riyadh is very exciting," Bright said in the February 24, 2009 issue of *Chain Leader.* "We've borrowed so many ingredients and elements from the Middle East and other parts of the Mediterranean that we're extremely pleased to see such a positive response. I'm glad to see that our first unit is up and running and doing well. ... This is our first Middle East effort and there is more to come!"

Much about Zpizza's success remained to be determined in the years ahead. Surviving the crucible of the global financial crisis was the first order of business, a crisis that represented a major impediment to the chain's expansion. By 2009, Zpizza had development deals in place to establish 400 restaurants in the United States, Mexico, and the Middle East. Turning those deals into operating units stood as the company's greatest challenge.

Jeffrey L. Covell

PRINCIPAL COMPETITORS

California Pizza Kitchen, Inc.; Chipotle Mexican Grill, Inc.; Pizza Fusion.

FURTHER READING

Cruz, Sherri, "Zpizza Creator Overseeing 300 Franchise Stores Opening Soon," *Orange County Business Journal,* April 20, 2009.

Farkas, David, "Restaurant Chains Sing Borrowing Blues," *Chain Leader,* November 1, 2008.

"International Expansion: Zpizza Opens in Saudi Arabia," *Chain Leader,* February 24, 2009.

Knudson, Brooke, "Piece of the Pie," *Food & Drink,* January–February 2007, p. 46.

"Orange County Pizza Chain Moves North," *East Bay Business Times,* October 9, 2006.

Spector, Amy, "Zpizza Eyes Larger Slice of Segment with Franchising Deals," *Nation's Restaurant News,* July 28, 2003, p. 12.

"Zpizza," *Nation's Restaurant News Daily NewsFax,* November 6, 2002, p. 1.

"Zpizza Franchisor Inks Offshore Deal for Middle East," *Nation's Restaurant News,* January 7, 2008, p. 22.

"Zpizza Signs Franchise Deal to Enter Phoenix," *Nation's Restaurant News,* September 15, 2003, p. 62.

Cumulative Index to Companies

Listings in this index are arranged in alphabetical order under the company name. Company names beginning with a letter or proper name such as Eli Lilly & Co. will be found under the first letter of the company name. Definite articles (The, Le, La) are ignored for alphabetical purposes as are forms of incorporation that precede the company name (AB, NV). Company names printed in **bold** *type have full, historical essays on the page numbers appearing in bold. Updates to entries that appeared in earlier volumes are signified by the notation* **(upd.)**. *This index is cumulative with volume numbers printed in bold type.*

A

Aggregate Industries plc, 36 20–22

Aggreko Plc, 45 10–13

Agilent Technologies Inc., 38 20–23; 93 28–32 (upd.)

Agilysys Inc., 76 7–11 (upd.)

Agnico-Eagle Mines Limited, 71 11–14

Agora S.A. Group, 77 5–8

AGRANA *see* Südzucker AG.

Agri Beef Company, 81 5–9

Agria Corporation, 101 9–13

Agrigenetics, Inc. *see* Mycogen Corp.

Agrium Inc., 73 21–23

AgustaWestland N.V., 75 18–20

Agway, Inc., 7 17–18; 21 17–19 (upd.) *see also* Cargill Inc.

AHL Services, Inc., 27 20–23

Ahlstrom Corporation, 53 22–25

Ahmanson *see* H.F. Ahmanson & Co.

AHMSA *see* Altos Hornos de México, S.A. de C.V.

Ahold *see* Koninklijke Ahold NV.

AHP *see* American Home Products Corp.

AICPA *see* The American Institute of Certified Public Accountants.

AIG *see* American International Group, Inc.

AIMCO *see* Apartment Investment and Management Co.

Ainsworth Lumber Co. Ltd., 99 18–22

Air & Water Technologies Corporation, 6 441–42 *see also* Aqua Alliance Inc.

Air Berlin GmbH & Co. Luftverkehrs KG, 71 15–17

Air Canada, 6 60–62; 23 9–12 (upd.); 59 17–22 (upd.)

Air China, 46 9–11

Air Express International Corporation, 13 19–20

Air France *see* Societe Air France.

Air-India Limited, 6 63–64; 27 24–26 (upd.)

Air Jamaica Limited, 54 3–6

Air Liquide *see* L'Air Liquide SA.

Air Mauritius Ltd., 63 17–19

Air Methods Corporation, 53 26–29

Air Midwest, Inc. *see* Mesa Air Group, Inc.

Air New Zealand Limited, 14 10–12; 38 24–27 (upd.)

Air Pacific Ltd., 70 7–9

Air Partner PLC, 93 33–36

Air Products and Chemicals, Inc., I 297–99; 10 31–33 (upd.); 74 6–9 (upd.)

Air Sahara Limited, 65 14–16

Air T, Inc., 86 6–9

Air Wisconsin Airlines Corporation, 55 10–12

Air Zimbabwe (Private) Limited, 91 5–8

AirAsia Berhad, 93 37–40

Airborne Freight Corporation, 6 345–47; 34 15–18 (upd.) *see also* DHL Worldwide Network S.A./N.V.

Airborne Systems Group, 89 39–42

Airbus Industrie *see* G.I.E. Airbus Industrie.

Airgas, Inc., 54 7–10

Airguard Industries, Inc. *see* CLARCOR Inc.

Airlink Pty Ltd *see* Qantas Airways Ltd.

Airstream *see* Thor Industries, Inc.

AirTouch Communications, 11 10–12 *see also* Vodafone Group PLC.

Airtours Plc, 27 27–29, 90, 92

AirTran Holdings, Inc., 22 21–23

Aisin Seiki Co., Ltd., III 415–16; 48 3–5 (upd.)

Aitchison & Colegrave *see* Bradford & Bingley PLC.

Aiwa Co., Ltd., 30 18–20

Ajegroup S.A., 92 1–4

Ajinomoto Co., Inc., II 463–64; 28 9–11 (upd.)

AK Steel Holding Corporation, 19 8–9; 41 3–6 (upd.)

Akamai Technologies, Inc., 71 18–21

Akbank TAS, 79 18–21

Akeena Solar, Inc., 103 6–10

Akerys S.A., 90 17–20

AKG Acoustics GmbH, 62 3–6

Akin, Gump, Strauss, Hauer & Feld, L.L.P., 33 23–25

Akorn, Inc., 32 22–24

Akro-Mills Inc. *see* Myers Industries, Inc.

Aktiebolaget SKF, III 622–25; 38 28–33 (upd.); 89 401–09 (upd.)

Akzo Nobel N.V., 13 21–23; 41 7–10 (upd.)

Al Habtoor Group L.L.C., 87 9–12

Al-Tawfeek Co. For Investment Funds Ltd. *see* Dallah Albaraka Group.

Alabama Farmers Cooperative, Inc., 63 20–22

Alabama National BanCorporation, 75 21–23

Aladdin Knowledge Systems Ltd., 101 14–17

Alain Afflelou SA, 53 30–32

Alain Manoukian *see* Groupe Alain Manoukian.

Alamo Group Inc., 32 25–28

Alamo Rent A Car, 6 348–50; 24 9–12 (upd.); 84 5–11 (upd.)

ALARIS Medical Systems, Inc., 65 17–20

Alascom, Inc. *see* AT&T Corp.

Alaska Air Group, Inc., 6 65–67; 29 11–14 (upd.)

Alaska Communications Systems Group, Inc., 89 43–46

Alaska Railroad Corporation, 60 6–9

Alba-Waldensian, Inc., 30 21–23 *see also* E.I. du Pont de Nemours and Co.

Albany International Corporation, 8 12–14; 51 11–14 (upd.)

Albany Molecular Research, Inc., 77 9–12

Albaugh, Inc., 105 9–12

Albemarle Corporation, 59 23–25

Alberici Corporation, 76 12–14

The Albert Fisher Group plc, 41 11–13

Albert Heijn NV *see* Koninklijke Ahold N.V. (Royal Ahold).

Alberta Energy Company Ltd., 16 10–12; 43 3–6 (upd.)

Alberto-Culver Company, 8 15–17; 36 23–27 (upd.); 91 9–15 (upd.)

Albert's Organics, Inc. *see* United Natural Foods, Inc.

Albertson's, Inc., II 601–03; 7 19–22 (upd.); 30 24–28 (upd.); 65 21–26 (upd.)

Alcan Aluminium Limited, IV 9–13; 31 7–12 (upd.)

Alcatel S.A., 9 9–11; 36 28–31 (upd.)

Alco Health Services Corporation, III 9–10 *see also* AmeriSource Health Corp.

Alco Standard Corporation, I 412–13

Alcoa Inc., 56 7–11 (upd.)

Alderwoods Group, Inc., 68 11–15 (upd.)

Aldi Einkauf GmbH & Co. OHG, 13 24–26; 86 10–14 (upd.)

Aldila Inc., 46 12–14

Aldus Corporation, 10 34–36 *see also* Adobe Systems Inc.

Alès Groupe, 81 10–13

Alex Lee Inc., 18 6–9; 44 10–14 (upd.)

Alexander & Alexander Services Inc., 10 37–39 *see also* Aon Corp.

Alexander & Baldwin, Inc., 10 40–42; 40 14–19 (upd.)

Alexander's, Inc., 45 14–16

Alexandra plc, 88 5–8

Alexandria Real Estate Equities, Inc., 101 18–22

Alfa Corporation, 60 10–12

Alfa Group, 99 23–26

Alfa-Laval AB, III 417–21; 64 13–18 (upd.)

Alfa Romeo, 13 27–29; 36 32–35 (upd.)

Alfa, S.A. de C.V., 19 10–12

Alfesca hf, 82 1–4

Alfred A. Knopf, Inc. *see* Random House, Inc.

Alfred Dunhill Limited *see* Vendôme Luxury Group plc.

Alfred Kärcher GmbH & Co KG, 94 9–14

Alfred Ritter GmbH & Co. KG, 58 3–7

Alga *see* BRIO AB.

Algar S/A Empreendimentos e Participações, 103 11–14

Algemene Bank Nederland N.V., II 183–84

Algerian Saudi Leasing Holding Co. *see* Dallah Albaraka Group.

Algo Group Inc., 24 13–15

Alico, Inc., 63 23–25

Alienware Corporation, 81 14–17

Align Technology, Inc., 94 15–18

Alimentation Couche-Tard Inc., 77 13–16

Alitalia–Linee Aeree Italiane, S.p.A., 6 68–69; 29 15–17 (upd.); 97 21–27 (upd.)

Aljazeera Satellite Channel, 79 22–25

All American Communications Inc., 20 3–7

The All England Lawn Tennis & Croquet Club, 54 11–13

Autostrada Torino-Milano S.p.A., 101
47–50

Autotote Corporation, 20 47–49 *see also*
Scientific Games Corp.

AutoTrader.com, L.L.C., 91 31–34

AutoZone, Inc., 9 52–54; 31 35–38
(upd.)

Auvil Fruit Company, Inc., 95 32–35

AVA AG (Allgemeine
Handelsgesellschaft der Verbraucher
AG), 33 53–56

Avado Brands, Inc., 31 39–42

Avalon Correctional Services, Inc., 75
40–43

AvalonBay Communities, Inc., 58
11–13

Avantium Technologies BV, 79 46–49

Avaya Inc., 104 22–25

Avco Financial Services Inc., 13 63–65
see also Citigroup Inc.

Avecia Group PLC, 63 49–51

Aveda Corporation, 24 55–57

Avedis Zildjian Co., 38 66–68

Avendt Group, Inc. *see* Marmon Group,
Inc.

Aventine Renewable Energy Holdings,
Inc., 89 83–86

Avery Dennison Corporation, IV
251–54; 17 27–31 (upd.); 49 34–40
(upd.)

Aviacionny Nauchno-Tehnicheskii
Komplex im. A.N. Tupoleva, 24
58–60

Aviacsa *see* Consorcio Aviacsa, S.A. de
C.V.

Aviall, Inc., 73 42–45

Avianca Aerovías Nacionales de
Colombia SA, 36 52–55

Aviation Sales Company, 41 37–39

Avid Technology Inc., 38 69–73

Avionics Specialties Inc. *see* Aerosonic
Corp.

Avions Marcel Dassault-Breguet
Aviation, I 44–46 *see also* Groupe
Dassault Aviation SA.

Avis Group Holdings, Inc., 6 356–58;
22 54–57 (upd.); 75 44–49 (upd.)

Avista Corporation, 69 48–50 (upd.)

Aviva PLC, 50 65–68 (upd.)

Avnet Inc., 9 55–57

Avocent Corporation, 65 56–58

Avon Products, Inc., III 15–16; 19
26–29 (upd.); 46 43–46 (upd.)

Avondale Industries, Inc., 7 39–41; 41
40–43 (upd.)

AVTOVAZ Joint Stock Company, 65
59–62

AVX Corporation, 67 41–43

AWA *see* America West Holdings Corp.

AWB Ltd., 56 25–27

Awrey Bakeries, Inc., 56 28–30

AXA Colonia Konzern AG, III 210–12;
49 41–45 (upd.)

AXA Equitable Life Insurance
Company, 105 21–27 (upd.)

Axcan Pharma Inc., 85 25–28

Axcelis Technologies, Inc., 95 36–39

Axel Johnson Group, I 553–55

Axel Springer Verlag AG, IV 589–91; 20
50–53 (upd.)

Axsys Technologies, Inc., 93 65–68

Aydin Corp., 19 30–32

Aynsley China Ltd. *see* Belleek Pottery
Ltd.

Azcon Corporation, 23 34–36

Azelis Group, 100 44–47

Azerbaijan Airlines, 77 46–49

Azienda Generale Italiana Petroli *see* ENI
S.p.A.

Aztar Corporation, 13 66–68; 71 41–45
(upd.)

AZZ Incorporated, 93 69–72

B

B&G Foods, Inc., 40 51–54

B&J Music Ltd. *see* Kaman Music Corp.

B&Q plc *see* Kingfisher plc.

B.A.T. Industries PLC, 22 70–73 (upd.)
see also Brown and Williamson Tobacco
Corporation

B. Dalton Bookseller Inc., 25 29–31 *see
also* Barnes & Noble, Inc.

B.F. Goodrich Co. *see* The BFGoodrich
Co.

B.J. Alan Co., Inc., 67 44–46

The B. Manischewitz Company, LLC,
31 43–46

B.R. Guest Inc., 87 43–46

B.W. Rogers Company, 94 49–52

B/E Aerospace, Inc., 30 72–74

BA *see* British Airways plc.

BAA plc, 10 121–23; 33 57–61 (upd.)

Baan Company, 25 32–34

Babbage's, Inc., 10 124–25 *see also*
GameStop Corp.

The Babcock & Wilcox Company, 82
26–30

Babcock International Group PLC, 69
51–54

Babolat VS, S.A., 97 63–66

Baby Lock USA *see* Tacony Corp.

Baby Superstore, Inc., 15 32–34 *see also*
Toys 'R Us, Inc.

Bacardi & Company Ltd., 18 39–42; 82
31–36 (upd.)

Baccarat, 24 61–63

Bachman's Inc., 22 58–60

Bachoco *see* Industrias Bachoco, S.A. de
C.V.

Back Bay Restaurant Group, Inc., 20
54–56; 102 34–38 (upd.)

Back Yard Burgers, Inc., 45 33–36

Backus y Johnston *see* Unión de
Cervecerias Peruanas Backus y Johnston
S.A.A.

Bad Boy Worldwide Entertainment
Group, 58 14–17

Badger Meter, Inc., 22 61–65

Badger Paper Mills, Inc., 15 35–37

Badger State Ethanol, LLC, 83 33–37

BAE Systems Ship Repair, 73 46–48

Bahamas Air Holdings Ltd., 66 24–26

Bahlsen GmbH & Co. KG, 44 38–41

Baidu.com Inc., 95 40–43

Bailey Nurseries, Inc., 57 59–61

Bain & Company, 55 41–43

Baird & Warner Holding Company, 87
47–50

Bairnco Corporation, 28 42–45

Bajaj Auto Limited, 39 36–38

Baker *see* Michael Baker Corp.

Baker and Botts, L.L.P., 28 46–49

Baker & Daniels LLP, 88 17–20

Baker & Hostetler LLP, 40 55–58

Baker & McKenzie, 10 126–28; 42
17–20 (upd.)

Baker & Taylor Corporation, 16 45–47;
43 59–62 (upd.)

Baker Hughes Incorporated, III 428–29;
22 66–69 (upd.); 57 62–66 (upd.)

Bakkavör Group hf., 91 35–39

Balance Bar Company, 32 70–72

Balchem Corporation, 42 21–23

Baldor Electric Company, 21 42–44; 97
63–67 (upd.)

Baldwin & Lyons, Inc., 51 37–39

Baldwin Piano & Organ Company, 18
43–46 *see also* Gibson Guitar Corp.

Baldwin Richardson Foods Company,
100 48–52

Baldwin Technology Company, Inc., 25
35–39

Balfour Beatty Construction Ltd., 36
56–60 (upd.)

Ball Corporation, I 597–98; 10 129–31
(upd.); 78 25–29 (upd.)

Ball Horticultural Company, 78 30–33

Ballantine Books *see* Random House, Inc.

Ballantyne of Omaha, Inc., 27 56–58

Ballard Medical Products, 21 45–48 *see
also* Kimberly-Clark Corp.

Ballard Power Systems Inc., 73 49–52

Ballistic Recovery Systems, Inc., 87
51–54

Bally Manufacturing Corporation, III
430–32

Bally Total Fitness Corporation, 25
40–42; 94 53–57 (upd.)

Balmac International, Inc., 94 58–61

Bâloise-Holding, 40 59–62

Baltek Corporation, 34 59–61

Baltika Brewery Joint Stock Company,
65 63–66

Baltimore & Ohio Railroad *see* CSX
Corp.

Baltimore Aircoil Company, Inc., 66
27–29

Baltimore Gas and Electric Company, V
552–54; 25 43–46 (upd.)

Baltimore Orioles L.P., 66 30–33

Baltimore Technologies Plc, 42 24–26

The Bama Companies, Inc., 80 13–16

Banamex *see* Grupo Financiero Banamex
S.A.

Banana Republic Inc., 25 47–49 *see also*
Gap, Inc.

Banc One Corporation, 10 132–34 *see
also* JPMorgan Chase & Co.

Banca Commerciale Italiana SpA, II
191–93

Banca Fideuram SpA, 63 52–54

Banca Intesa SpA, 65 67–70

Banca Monte dei Paschi di Siena SpA,
65 71–73

Fisher Scientific International Inc., 24 162–66 *see also* Thermo Fisher Scientific Inc.

Fishman & Tobin Inc., 102 124–27

Fisk Corporation, 72 132–34

Fiskars Corporation, 33 161–64; 105 180–86 (upd.)

Fisons plc, 9 224–27; 23 194–97 (upd.)

5 & Diner Franchise Corporation, 72 135–37

Five Guys Enterprises, LLC, 99 169–172

FKI Plc, 57 141–44

Flagstar Companies, Inc., 10 301–03 *see also* Advantica Restaurant Group, Inc.

Flanders Corporation, 65 149–51

Flanigan's Enterprises, Inc., 60 128–30

Flatiron Construction Corporation, 92 119–22

Fleer Corporation, 15 167–69

FleetBoston Financial Corporation, 9 228–30; 36 206–14 (upd.)

Fleetwood Enterprises, Inc., III 484–85; 22 205–08 (upd.); 81 159–64 (upd.)

Fleming Companies, Inc., II 624–25; 17 178–81 (upd.)

Fletcher Challenge Ltd., IV 278–80; 19 153–57 (upd.)

Fleury Michon S.A., 39 159–61

Flexsteel Industries Inc., 15 170–72; 41 159–62 (upd.)

Flextronics International Ltd., 38 186–89

Flight Options, LLC, 75 144–46

FlightSafety International, Inc., 9 231–33; 29 189–92 (upd.)

Flint Ink Corporation, 13 227–29; 41 163–66 (upd.)

FLIR Systems, Inc., 69 170–73

Flo *see* Groupe Flo S.A.

Floc'h & Marchand, 80 119–21

Florida Crystals Inc., 35 176–78

Florida East Coast Industries, Inc., 59 184–86

Florida Gaming Corporation, 47 130–33

Florida Progress Corp., V 621–22; 23 198–200 (upd.) *see also* Progress Energy, Inc.

Florida Public Utilities Company, 69 174–76

Florida Rock Industries, Inc., 46 195–97 *see also* Patriot Transportation Holding, Inc.

Florida's Natural Growers, 45 160–62

Florists' Transworld Delivery, Inc., 28 136–38 *see also* FTD Group, Inc.

Florsheim Shoe Group Inc., 9 234–36; 31 209–12 (upd.)

Flotek Industries Inc., 93 217–20

Flour City International, Inc., 44 181–83

Flow International Corporation, 56 132–34

Flowers Industries, Inc., 12 170–71; 35 179–82 (upd.) *see also* Keebler Foods Co.

Flowserve Corporation, 33 165–68; 77 146–51 (upd.)

FLSmidth & Co. A/S, 72 138–40

Fluke Corporation, 15 173–75

Fluor Corporation, I 569–71; 8 190–93 (upd.); 34 164–69 (upd.)

Fluxys SA, 101 188–91

FlyBE *see* Jersey European Airways (UK) Ltd.

Flying Boat, Inc. (Chalk's Ocean Airways), 56 135–37

Flying J Inc., 19 158–60

Flying Pigeon Bicycle Co. *see* Tianjin Flying Pigeon Bicycle Co., Ltd.

FMC Corp., I 442–44; 11 133–35 (upd.); 89 220–27 (upd.)

FMR Corp., 8 194–96; 32 195–200 (upd.)

FNAC, 21 224–26

FNMA *see* Federal National Mortgage Association.

Foamex International Inc., 17 182–85

Focus Features, 78 118–22

Fokker *see* N.V. Koninklijke Nederlandse Vliegtuigenfabriek Fokker.

Foley & Lardner, 28 139–42

Follett Corporation, 12 172–74; 39 162–65 (upd.)

Fonterra Co-Operative Group Ltd., 58 125–27

Food Circus Super Markets, Inc., 88 92–96

The Food Emporium, 64 125–27

Food For The Poor, Inc., 77 152–55

Food Lion LLC, II 626–27; 15 176–78 (upd.); 66 112–15 (upd.)

Foodarama Supermarkets, Inc., 28 143–45 *see also* Wakefern Food Corp.

FoodBrands America, Inc., 23 201–04 *see also* Doskocil Companies, Inc.; Tyson Foods, Inc.

Foodmaker, Inc., 14 194–96 *see also* Jack in the Box Inc.

Foot Locker, Inc., 68 157–62 (upd.)

Foot Petals L.L.C., 95 151–54

Foote, Cone & Belding Worldwide, I 12–15; 66 116–20 (upd.)

Footstar, Incorporated, 24 167–69 *see also* Foot Locker, Inc.

Forbes Inc., 30 199–201; 82 115–20 (upd.)

Force Protection Inc., 95 155–58

The Ford Foundation, 34 170–72

Ford Gum & Machine Company, Inc., 102 128–31

Ford Motor Company, I 164–68; 11 136–40 (upd.); 36 215–21 (upd.); 64 128–34 (upd.)

Ford Motor Company, S.A. de C.V., 20 219–21

FORE Systems, Inc., 25 161–63 *see also* Telefonaktiebolaget LM Ericsson.

Foremost Farms USA Cooperative, 98 116–20

FöreningsSparbanken AB, 69 177–80

Forest City Enterprises, Inc., 16 209–11; 52 128–31 (upd.)

Forest Laboratories, Inc., 11 141–43; 52 132–36 (upd.)

Forest Oil Corporation, 19 161–63; 91 182–87 (upd.)

Forever 21, Inc., 84 127–129

Forever Living Products International Inc., 17 186–88

FormFactor, Inc., 85 128–31

Formica Corporation, 13 230–32

Formosa Plastics Corporation, 14 197–99; 58 128–31 (upd.)

Forrester Research, Inc., 54 113–15

Forstmann Little & Co., 38 190–92

Fort Howard Corporation, 8 197–99 *see also* Fort James Corp.

Fort James Corporation, 22 209–12 (upd.) *see also* Georgia-Pacific Corp.

Fortis, Inc., 15 179–82; 47 134–37 (upd.); 50 4–6

Fortum Corporation, 30 202–07 (upd.) *see also* Neste Oil Corp.

Fortune Brands, Inc., 29 193–97 (upd.); 68 163–67 (upd.)

Fortunoff Fine Jewelry and Silverware Inc., 26 144–46

Forward Air Corporation, 75 147–49

Forward Industries, Inc., 86 152–55

The Forzani Group Ltd., 79 172–76

Fossil, Inc., 17 189–91

Foster Poultry Farms, 32 201–04

Foster Wheeler Corporation, 6 145–47; 23 205–08 (upd.); 76 152–56 (upd.)

FosterGrant, Inc., 60 131–34

Foster's Group Limited, 7 182–84; 21 227–30 (upd.); 50 199–203 (upd.)

Foundation Health Corporation, 12 175–77

Fountain Powerboats Industries, Inc., 28 146–48

Four Seasons Hotels Inc., 9 237–38; 29 198–200 (upd.)

Four Winns Boats LLC, 96 124–27

4imprint Group PLC, 105 187–91

4Kids Entertainment Inc., 59 187–89

Fourth Financial Corporation, 11 144–46

Fox Entertainment Group, Inc., 43 173–76

Fox Family Worldwide, Inc., 24 170–72 *see also* ABC Family Worldwide, Inc.

Fox, Inc. *see* Twentieth Century Fox Film Corp.

Foxboro Company, 13 233–35

FoxHollow Technologies, Inc., 85 132–35

FoxMeyer Health Corporation, 16 212–14 *see also* McKesson Corp.

Fox's Pizza Den, Inc., 98 121–24

Foxworth-Galbraith Lumber Company, 91 188–91

FPL Group, Inc., V 623–25; 49 143–46 (upd.)

Framatome SA, 19 164–67 aee also Alcatel S.A.; AREVA.

France Telecom S.A., V 291–93; 21 231–34 (upd.); 99 173–179 (upd.)

Francotyp-Postalia Holding AG, 92 123–27

Gannett Company, Inc., IV 612–13; 7 190–92 (upd.); 30 215–17 (upd.); 66 135–38 (upd.)
Gano Excel Enterprise Sdn. Bhd., 89 228–31
Gantos, Inc., 17 199–201
Ganz, 98 141–44
GAP *see* Grupo Aeroportuario del Pacífico, S.A. de C.V.
The Gap, Inc., V 60–62; 18 191–94 (upd.); 55 153–57 (upd.)
Garan, Inc., 16 231–33; 64 140–43 (upd.)
The Garden Company Ltd., 82 125–28
Garden Fresh Restaurant Corporation, 31 213–15
Garden Ridge Corporation, 27 163–65
Gardenburger, Inc., 33 169–71; 76 160–63 (upd.)
Gardner Denver, Inc., 49 158–60
Garmin Ltd., 60 135–37
Garst Seed Company, Inc., 86 156–59
Gart Sports Company, 24 173–75 *see also* Sports Authority, Inc.
Gartner, Inc., 21 235–37; 94 209–13 (upd.)
Garuda Indonesia, 6 90–91; 58 138–41 (upd.)
Gas Natural SDG S.A., 69 190–93
GASS *see* Grupo Ángeles Servicios de Salud, S.A. de C.V.
Gasunie *see* N.V. Nederlandse Gasunie.
Gate Gourmet International AG, 70 97–100
GateHouse Media, Inc., 91 196–99
The Gates Corporation, 9 241–43
Gateway Corporation Ltd., II 628–30 *see also* Somerfield plc.
Gateway, Inc., 10 307–09; 27 166–69 (upd.); 63 153–58 (upd.)
The Gatorade Company, 82 129–32
Gatti's Pizza, Inc. *see* Mr. Gatti's, LP.
GATX, 6 394–96; 25 168–71 (upd.)
Gaumont S.A., 25 172–75; 91 200–05 (upd.)
Gaylord Bros., Inc., 100 178–81
Gaylord Container Corporation, 8 203–05
Gaylord Entertainment Company, 11 152–54; 36 226–29 (upd.)
Gaz de France, V 626–28; 40 191–95 (upd.)
Gazprom *see* OAO Gazprom.
GBC *see* General Binding Corp.
GC Companies, Inc., 25 176–78 *see also* AMC Entertainment Inc.
GE *see* General Electric Co.
GE Aircraft Engines, 9 244–46
GE Capital Aviation Services, 36 230–33
GEA AG, 27 170–74
GEAC Computer Corporation Ltd., 43 181–85
Geberit AG, 49 161–64
Gecina SA, 42 151–53
Gedney *see* M.A. Gedney Co.
Geek Squad Inc., 102 138–41
Geerlings & Wade, Inc., 45 166–68

Geest Plc, 38 200–02 *see also* Bakkavör Group hf.
Gefco SA, 54 126–28
Geffen Records Inc., 26 150–52
GEHE AG, 27 175–78
Gehl Company, 19 172–74
GEICO Corporation, 10 310–12; 40 196–99 (upd.)
Geiger Bros., 60 138–41
Gelita AG, 74 114–18
GEMA (Gesellschaft für musikalische Aufführungs- und mechanische Vervielfältigungsrechte), 70 101–05
Gemini Sound Products Corporation, 58 142–44
Gemplus International S.A., 64 144–47
Gen-Probe Incorporated, 79 185–88
Gencor Ltd., IV 90–93; 22 233–37 (upd.) *see also* Gold Fields Ltd.
GenCorp Inc., 9 247–49
Genentech, Inc., I 637–38; 8 209–11 (upd.); 32 211–15 (upd.); 75 154–58 (upd.)
General Accident plc, III 256–57 *see also* Aviva PLC.
General Atomics, 57 151–54
General Bearing Corporation, 45 169–71
General Binding Corporation, 10 313–14; 73 159–62 (upd.)
General Cable Corporation, 40 200–03
The General Chemical Group Inc., 37 157–60
General Cigar Holdings, Inc., 66 139–42 (upd.)
General Cinema Corporation, I 245–46 *see also* GC Companies, Inc.
General DataComm Industries, Inc., 14 200–02
General Dynamics Corporation, I 57–60; 10 315–18 (upd.); 40 204–10 (upd.); 88 105–13 (upd.)
General Electric Company, II 27–31; 12 193–97 (upd.); 34 183–90 (upd.); 63 159–68 (upd.)
General Electric Company, PLC, II 24–26 *see also* Marconi plc.
General Employment Enterprises, Inc., 87 172–175
General Growth Properties, Inc., 57 155–57
General Host Corporation, 12 198–200
General Housewares Corporation, 16 234–36
General Instrument Corporation, 10 319–21 *see also* Motorola, Inc.
General Maritime Corporation, 59 197–99
General Mills, Inc., II 501–03; 10 322–24 (upd.); 36 234–39 (upd.); 85 141–49 (upd.)
General Motors Corporation, I 171–73; 10 325–27 (upd.); 36 240–44 (upd.); 64 148–53 (upd.)
General Nutrition Companies, Inc., 11 155–57; 29 210–14 (upd.) *see also* GNC Corp.

General Public Utilities Corporation, V 629–31 *see also* GPU, Inc.
General Re Corporation, III 258–59; 24 176–78 (upd.)
General Sekiyu K.K., IV 431–33 *see also* TonenGeneral Sekiyu K.K.
General Signal Corporation, 9 250–52 *see also* SPX Corp.
General Tire, Inc., 8 212–14
Generale Bank, II 294–95 *see also* Fortis, Inc.
Générale des Eaux Group, V 632–34 *see* Vivendi Universal S.A.
Generali *see* Assicurazioni Generali.
Genesco Inc., 17 202–06; 84 143–149 (upd.)
Genesee & Wyoming Inc., 27 179–81
Genesis Health Ventures, Inc., 18 195–97 *see also* NeighborCare,Inc.
Genesis Microchip Inc., 82 133–37
Genesys Telecommunications Laboratories Inc., 103 184–87
Genetics Institute, Inc., 8 215–18
Geneva Steel, 7 193–95
Genmar Holdings, Inc., 45 172–75
Genovese Drug Stores, Inc., 18 198–200
Genoyer *see* Groupe Genoyer.
GenRad, Inc., 24 179–83
Gentex Corporation, 26 153–57
Genting Bhd., 65 152–55
Gentiva Health Services, Inc., 79 189–92
Genuardi's Family Markets, Inc., 35 190–92
Genuine Parts Company, 9 253–55; 45 176–79 (upd.)
Genzyme Corporation, 13 239–42; 38 203–07 (upd.); 77 164–70 (upd.)
geobra Brandstätter GmbH & Co. KG, 48 183–86
Geodis S.A., 67 187–90
The Geon Company, 11 158–61
GeoResources, Inc., 101 196–99
Georg Fischer AG Schaffhausen, 61 106–09
George A. Hormel and Company, II 504–06 *see also* Hormel Foods Corp.
The George F. Cram Company, Inc., 55 158–60
George P. Johnson Company, 60 142–44
George S. May International Company, 55 161–63
George W. Park Seed Company, Inc., 98 145–48
George Weston Ltd., II 631–32; 36 245–48 (upd.); 88 114–19 (upd.)
George Wimpey plc, 12 201–03; 51 135–38 (upd.)
Georgia Gulf Corporation, 9 256–58; 61 110–13 (upd.)
Georgia-Pacific LLC, IV 281–83; 9 259–62 (upd.); 47 145–51 (upd.); 101 200–09 (upd.)
Geotek Communications Inc., 21 238–40
Gerald Stevens, Inc., 37 161–63

Highmark Inc., **27** 208–11
Highsmith Inc., **60** 167–70
Highveld Steel and Vanadium Corporation Limited, **59** 224–27
Hikma Pharmaceuticals Ltd., **102** 166–70
Hilb, Rogal & Hobbs Company, **77** 191–94
Hildebrandt International, **29** 235–38
Hilding Anders AB, **102** 171–74
Hill's Pet Nutrition, Inc., **27** 212–14
Hillenbrand Industries, Inc., **10** 349–51; **75** 188–92 (upd.)
Hillerich & Bradsby Company, Inc., **51** 161–64
The Hillhaven Corporation, **14** 241–43 *see also* Vencor, Inc.
Hills Industries Ltd., **104** 200–04
Hills Stores Company, **13** 260–61
Hillsdown Holdings, PLC, **II** 513–14; **24** 218–21 (upd.)
Hilmar Cheese Company, Inc., **98** 193–96
Hilo Hattie *see* Pomare Ltd.
Hilti AG, **53** 167–69
Hilton Group plc, **III** 91–93; **19** 205–08 (upd.); **62** 176–79 (upd.); **49** 191–95 (upd.)
Hindustan Lever Limited, **79** 198–201
Hines Horticulture, Inc., **49** 196–98
Hino Motors, Ltd., **7** 219–21; **21** 271–74 (upd.)
HiPP GmbH & Co. Vertrieb KG, **88** 183–88
Hiram Walker Resources Ltd., **I** 262–64
Hispanic Broadcasting Corporation, **35** 219–22
HIT Entertainment PLC, **40** 250–52
Hitachi, Ltd., **I** 454–55; **12** 237–39 (upd.); **40** 253–57 (upd.)
Hitachi Metals, Ltd., **IV** 101–02
Hitachi Zosen Corporation, **III** 513–14; **53** 170–73 (upd.)
Hitchiner Manufacturing Co., Inc., **23** 267–70
Hite Brewery Company Ltd., **97** 204–07
HMI Industries, Inc., **17** 233–35
HMV Group plc, **59** 228–30
HNI Corporation, **74** 148–52 (upd.)
Ho-Chunk Inc., **61** 125–28
HOB Entertainment, Inc., **37** 191–94
Hobby Lobby Stores Inc., **80** 139–42
Hobie Cat Company, **94** 236–39
Hochtief AG, **33** 194–97; **88** 189–94 (upd.)
The Hockey Company, **34** 215–18; **70** 124–26 (upd.)
Hodes *see* Bernard Hodes Group Inc.
Hodgson Mill, Inc., **88** 195–98
Hoechst AG, **I** 346–48; **18** 234–37 (upd.)
Hoechst Celanese Corporation, **13** 262–65
Hoenig Group Inc., **41** 207–09
Hoesch AG, **IV** 103–06
Hoffman Corporation, **78** 158–12

Hoffmann-La Roche & Co *see* F. Hoffmann-La Roche & Co.
Hogan & Hartson L.L.P., **44** 220–23
Hogg Robinson Group PLC, **105** 216–20
Hohner *see* Matth. Hohner AG.
HOK Group, Inc., **59** 231–33
Hokkaido Electric Power Company Inc. (HEPCO), **V** 635–37; **58** 160–63 (upd.)
Hokuriku Electric Power Company, **V** 638–40
Holberg Industries, Inc., **36** 266–69
Holden Ltd., **62** 180–83
Holderbank Financière Glaris Ltd., **III** 701–02 *see also* Holnam Inc
N.V. Holdingmaatschappij De Telegraaf, **23** 271–73 *see also* Telegraaf Media Groep N.V.
Holiday Inns, Inc., **III** 94–95 *see also* Promus Companies, Inc.
Holiday Retirement Corp., **87** 221–223
Holiday RV Superstores, Incorporated, **26** 192–95
Holidaybreak plc, **96** 182–86
Holland & Knight LLP, **60** 171–74
Holland Burgerville USA, **44** 224–26
The Holland Group, Inc., **82** 174–77
Hollander Home Fashions Corp., **67** 207–09
Holley Performance Products Inc., **52** 157–60
Hollinger International Inc., **24** 222–25; **62** 184–88 (upd.)
Holly Corporation, **12** 240–42
Hollywood Casino Corporation, **21** 275–77
Hollywood Entertainment Corporation, **25** 208–10
Hollywood Media Corporation, **58** 164–68
Hollywood Park, Inc., **20** 297–300
Holme Roberts & Owen LLP, **28** 196–99
Holmen AB, **52** 161–65 (upd.)
Holnam Inc., **8** 258–60; **39** 217–20 (upd.)
Holophane Corporation, **19** 209–12
Holson Burnes Group, Inc., **14** 244–45
Holt and Bugbee Company, **66** 189–91
Holt's Cigar Holdings, Inc., **42** 176–78
Holtzbrinck *see* Verlagsgruppe Georg von Holtzbrinck.
Homasote Company, **72** 178–81
Home Box Office Inc., **7** 222–24; **23** 274–77 (upd.); **76** 178–82 (upd.)
The Home Depot, Inc., **V** 75–76; **18** 238–40 (upd.); **97** 208–13 (upd.)
Home Hardware Stores Ltd., **62** 189–91
Home Inns & Hotels Management Inc., **95** 195–95
Home Insurance Company, **III** 262–64
Home Interiors & Gifts, Inc., **55** 202–04
Home Product Center plc, **104** 205–08
Home Products International, Inc., **55** 205–07

Home Properties of New York, Inc., **42** 179–81
Home Retail Group plc, **91** 242–46
Home Shopping Network, Inc., **V** 77–78; **25** 211–15 (upd.) *see also* HSN.
HomeBase, Inc., **33** 198–201 (upd.)
Homestake Mining Company, **12** 243–45; **38** 229–32 (upd.)
Hometown Auto Retailers, Inc., **44** 227–29
HomeVestors of America, Inc., **77** 195–98
Homex *see* Desarrolladora Homex, S.A. de C.V.
Hon Hai Precision Industry Co., Ltd., **59** 234–36
HON Industries Inc., **13** 266–69 *see* HNI Corp.
Honda Motor Company Ltd., **I** 174–76; **10** 352–54 (upd.); **29** 239–42 (upd.); **96** 187–93 (upd.)
Honeywell Inc., **II** 40–43; **12** 246–49 (upd.); **50** 231–35 (upd.)
Hong Kong and China Gas Company Ltd., **73** 177–79
Hong Kong Dragon Airlines Ltd., **66** 192–94
Hong Kong Telecommunications Ltd., **6** 319–21 *see also* Cable & Wireless HKT.
Hongkong and Shanghai Banking Corporation Limited, **II** 296–99 *see also* HSBC Holdings plc.
Hongkong Electric Holdings Ltd., **6** 498–500; **23** 278–81 (upd.)
Hongkong Land Holdings Ltd., **IV** 699–701; **47** 175–78 (upd.)
Honshu Paper Co., Ltd., **IV** 284–85 *see also* Oji Paper Co., Ltd.
Hoogovens *see* Koninklijke Nederlandsche Hoogovens en Staalfabricken NV.
Hooker Furniture Corporation, **80** 143–46
Hooper Holmes, Inc., **22** 264–67
Hooters of America, Inc., **18** 241–43; **69** 211–14 (upd.)
The Hoover Company, **12** 250–52; **40** 258–62 (upd.)
HOP, LLC, **80** 147–50
Hops Restaurant Bar and Brewery, **46** 233–36
Hopson Development Holdings Ltd., **87** 224–227
Horace Mann Educators Corporation, **22** 268–70; **90** 237–40 (upd.)
Horizon Food Group, Inc., **100** 225–28
Horizon Lines, Inc., **98** 197–200
Horizon Organic Holding Corporation, **37** 195–99
Hormel Foods Corporation, **18** 244–47 (upd.); **54** 164–69 (upd.)
Hornbach Holding AG, **98** 201–07
Hornbeck Offshore Services, Inc., **101** 246–49
Hornby PLC, **105** 221–25
Horsehead Industries, Inc., **51** 165–67

J. Crew Group, Inc., 12 280–82; 34 231–34 (upd.); 88 203–08

J.D. Edwards & Company, 14 268–70 *see also* Oracle Corp.

J.D. Power and Associates, 32 297–301

J. D'Addario & Company, Inc., 48 230–33

J.F. Shea Co., Inc., 55 234–36

J.H. Findorff and Son, Inc., 60 175–78

J.I. Case Company, 10 377–81 *see also* CNH Global N.V.

J.J. Darboven GmbH & Co. KG, 96 208–12

J.J. Keller & Associates, Inc., 81 2180–21

The J. Jill Group, Inc., 35 239–41; 90 249–53 (upd.)

J.L. Hammett Company, 72 196–99

J Lauritzen A/S, 90 254–57

J. Lohr Winery Corporation, 99 229–232

The J. M. Smucker Company, 11 210–12; 87 258–265 (upd.)

J.M. Voith AG, 33 222–25

J.P. Morgan Chase & Co., II 329–32; 30 261–65 (upd.); 38 253–59 (upd.)

J.R. Simplot Company, 16 287–89; 60 179–82 (upd.)

J Sainsbury plc, II 657–59; 13 282–84 (upd.); 38 260–65 (upd.); 95 212–20 (upd.)

J. W. Pepper and Son Inc., 86 220–23

J. Walter Thompson Co. *see* JWT Group Inc.

j2 Global Communications, Inc., 75 219–21

Jabil Circuit, Inc., 36 298–301; 88 209–14

Jack B. Kelley, Inc., 102 184–87

Jack Henry and Associates, Inc., 17 262–65; 94 258–63 (upd.)

Jack in the Box Inc., 89 265–71 (upd.)

Jack Morton Worldwide, 88 215–18

Jack Schwartz Shoes, Inc., 18 266–68

Jackpot Enterprises Inc., 21 298–300

Jackson Hewitt, Inc., 48 234–36

Jackson National Life Insurance Company, 8 276–77

Jacmar Companies, 87 266–269

Jaco Electronics, Inc., 30 255–57

Jacob Leinenkugel Brewing Company, 28 209–11

Jacobs Engineering Group Inc., 6 148–50; 26 220–23 (upd.)

Jacobs Suchard (AG), II 520–22 *see also* Kraft Jacobs Suchard AG.

Jacobson Stores Inc., 21 301–03

Jacor Communications, Inc., 23 292–95

Jacques Torres Chocolate *see* Mrchocolate.com LLC.

Jacques Whitford, 92 184–87

Jacquot *see* Établissements Jacquot and Cie S.A.S.

Jacuzzi Brands Inc., 23 296–98; 76 204–07 (upd.)

JAFCO Co. Ltd., 79 221–24

Jaguar Cars, Ltd., 13 285–87

Jaiprakash Associates Limited, 101 269–72

JAKKS Pacific, Inc., 52 191–94

JAL *see* Japan Airlines Company, Ltd.

Jalate Inc., 25 245–47

Jamba Juice Company, 47 199–202

James Avery Craftsman, Inc., 76 208–10

James Beattie plc, 43 242–44

James Hardie Industries N.V., 56 174–76

James Original Coney Island Inc., 84 197–200

James Purdey & Sons Limited, 87 270–275

James River Corporation of Virginia, IV 289–91 *see also* Fort James Corp.

Jani-King International, Inc., 85 191–94

JanSport, Inc., 70 134–36

Janssen Pharmaceutica N.V., 80 164–67

Janus Capital Group Inc., 57 192–94

Japan Airlines Company, Ltd., I 104–06; 32 288–92 (upd.)

Japan Broadcasting Corporation, 7 248–50

Japan Leasing Corporation, 8 278–80

Japan Pulp and Paper Company Limited, IV 292–93

Japan Tobacco Inc., V 403–04; 46 257–60 (upd.)

Jarden Corporation, 93 255–61 (upd.)

Jardine Cycle & Carriage Ltd., 73 193–95

Jardine Matheson Holdings Limited, I 468–71; 20 309–14 (upd.); 93 262–71 (upd.)

Jarvis plc, 39 237–39

Jason Incorporated, 23 299–301

Jay Jacobs, Inc., 15 243–45

Jayco Inc., 13 288–90

Jaypee Group *see* Jaiprakash Associates Ltd.

Jays Foods, Inc., 90 258–61

Jazz Basketball Investors, Inc., 55 237–39

Jazzercise, Inc., 45 212–14

JB Oxford Holdings, Inc., 32 293–96

JBS S.A., 100 233–36

JCDecaux S.A., 76 211–13

JD Wetherspoon plc, 30 258–60

JDA Software Group, Inc., 101 273–76

JDS Uniphase Corporation, 34 235–37

JE Dunn Construction Group, Inc., 85 195–98

The Jean Coutu Group (PJC) Inc., 46 261–65

Jean-Georges Enterprises L.L.C., 75 209–11

Jeanneau *see* Chantiers Jeanneau S.A.

Jefferies Group, Inc., 25 248–51

Jefferson-Pilot Corporation, 11 213–15; 29 253–56 (upd.)

Jefferson Properties, Inc. *see* JPI.

Jefferson Smurfit Group plc, IV 294–96; 19 224–27 (upd.); 49 224–29 (upd.) *see also* Smurfit-Stone Container Corp.

Jel Sert Company, 90 262–65

Jeld-Wen, Inc., 45 215–17

Jelly Belly Candy Company, 76 214–16

Jenkens & Gilchrist, P.C., 65 180–82

Jennie-O Turkey Store, Inc., 76 217–19

Jennifer Convertibles, Inc., 31 274–76

Jenny Craig, Inc., 10 382–84; 29 257–60 (upd.); 92 188–93 (upd.)

Jenoptik AG, 33 218–21

Jeppesen Sanderson, Inc., 92 194–97

Jerónimo Martins SGPS S.A., 96 213–16

Jerry's Famous Deli Inc., 24 243–45

Jersey European Airways (UK) Ltd., 61 144–46

Jersey Mike's Franchise Systems, Inc., 83 223–226

Jervis B. Webb Company, 24 246–49

Jet Airways (India) Private Limited, 65 183–85

JetBlue Airways Corporation, 44 248–50

Jetro Cash & Carry Enterprises Inc., 38 266–68

Jewett-Cameron Trading Company, Ltd., 89 272–76

JFE Shoji Holdings Inc., 88 219–22

JG Industries, Inc., 15 240–42

Jillian's Entertainment Holdings, Inc., 40 273–75

Jim Beam Brands Worldwide, Inc., 14 271–73; 58 194–96 (upd.)

The Jim Henson Company, 23 302–04

The Jim Pattison Group, 37 219–22

Jimmy Carter Work Project *see* Habitat for Humanity International.

Jimmy John's Enterprises, Inc., 103 227–30

Jitney-Jungle Stores of America, Inc., 27 245–48

JJB Sports plc, 32 302–04

JKH Holding Co. LLC, 105 260–63

JLA Credit *see* Japan Leasing Corp.

JLG Industries, Inc., 52 195–97

JLL *see* Jones Lang LaSalle Inc.

JLM Couture, Inc., 64 206–08

JM Smith Corporation, 100 237–40

JMB Realty Corporation, IV 702–03 *see also* Amfac/JMB Hawaii L.L.C.

Jo-Ann Stores, Inc., 72 200–03 (upd.)

Jockey International, Inc., 12 283–85; 34 238–42 (upd.); 77 217–23 (upd.)

Joe's Sports & Outdoor, 98 218–22 (upd.)

The Joffrey Ballet of Chicago, 52 198–202

Johanna Foods, Inc., 104 221–24

John B. Sanfilippo & Son, Inc., 14 274–76; 101 277–81 (upd.)

John Brown plc, I 572–74

The John D. and Catherine T. MacArthur Foundation, 34 243–46

John D. Brush Company Inc., 94 264–67

The John David Group plc, 90 266–69

John Deere *see* Deere & Co.

John Dewar & Sons, Ltd., 82 182–86

John Fairfax Holdings Limited, 7 251–54 *see also* Fairfax Media Ltd.

John Frieda Professional Hair Care Inc., 70 137–39
John H. Harland Company, 17 266–69
John Hancock Financial Services, Inc., III 265–68; 42 193–98 (upd.)
John Laing plc, I 575–76; 51 171–73 (upd.) *see also* Laing O'Rourke PLC.
John Lewis Partnership plc, V 93–95; 42 199–203 (upd.); 99 233–240 (upd.)
John Menzies plc, 39 240–43
The John Nuveen Company, 21 304–065
John Paul Mitchell Systems, 24 250–52
John Q. Hammons Hotels, Inc., 24 253–55
John W. Danforth Company, 48 237–39
John Wiley & Sons, Inc., 17 270–72; 65 186–90 (upd.)
Johnny Rockets Group, Inc., 31 277–81; 76 220–24 (upd.)
Johns Manville Corporation, 64 209–14 (upd.)
Johnson *see* Axel Johnson Group.
Johnson & Higgins, 14 277–80 *see also* Marsh & McLennan Companies, Inc.
Johnson & Johnson, III 35–37; 8 281–83 (upd.); 36 302–07 (upd.); 75 212–18 (upd.)
Johnson Controls, Inc., III 534–37; 26 227–32 (upd.); 59 248–54 (upd.)
Johnson Matthey PLC, IV 117–20; 16 290–94 (upd.); 49 230–35 (upd.)
Johnson Outdoors Inc., 84 201–205 (upd.)
Johnson Publishing Company, Inc., 28 212–14; 72 204–07 (upd.)
Johnson Wax *see* S.C. Johnson & Son, Inc.
Johnson Worldwide Associates, Inc., 28 215–17 *see also* Johnson Outdoors Inc.
Johnsonville Sausage L.L.C., 63 216–19
Johnston Industries, Inc., 15 246–48
Johnston Press plc, 35 242–44
Johnstown America Industries, Inc., 23 305–07
Jolly Hotels *see* Compagnia Italiana dei Jolly Hotels S.p.A.
Jones Apparel Group, Inc., 11 216–18; 39 244–47 (upd.)
Jones, Day, Reavis & Pogue, 33 226–29
Jones Intercable, Inc., 21 307–09
Jones Knowledge Group, Inc., 97 244–48
Jones Lang LaSalle Incorporated, 49 236–38
Jones Medical Industries, Inc., 24 256–58
Jones Soda Co., 69 218–21
Jongleurs Comedy Club *see* Regent Inns plc.
Jordache Enterprises, Inc., 23 308–10
The Jordan Company LP, 70 140–42
Jordan Industries, Inc., 36 308–10
Jordan-Kitt Music Inc., 86 224–27
Jordano's, Inc., 102 188–91

Jos. A. Bank Clothiers, Inc., 31 282–85; 104 225–30 (upd.)
José de Mello SGPS S.A., 96 217–20
Joseph T. Ryerson & Son, Inc., 15 249–51 *see also* Ryerson Tull, Inc.
Jostens, Inc., 7 255–57; 25 252–55 (upd.); 73 196–200 (upd.)
Jotun A/S, 80 168–71
JOULÉ Inc., 58 197–200
Journal Communications, Inc., 86 228–32
Journal Register Company, 29 261–63
Joy Global Inc., 104 231–38 (upd.)
JPI, 49 239–41
JPMorgan Chase & Co., 91 273–84 (upd.)
JPS Textile Group, Inc., 28 218–20
JSC MMC Norilsk Nickel, 48 300–02
JSP Corporation, 74 161–64
JTH Tax Inc., 103 231–34
The Judge Group, Inc., 51 174–76
Jugos del Valle, S.A. de C.V., 85 199–202
Juicy Couture, Inc., 80 172–74
Jujo Paper Co., Ltd., IV 297–98
Julius Baer Holding AG, 52 203–05
Julius Blüthner Pianofortefabrik GmbH, 78 185–88
Julius Meinl International AG, 53 177–80
Jumbo S.A., 96 221–24
Jumeirah Group, 83 227–230
Jungheinrich AG, 96 225–30
Juniper Networks, Inc., 43 251–55
Juno Lighting, Inc., 30 266–68
Juno Online Services, Inc., 38 269–72 *see also* United Online, Inc.
Jupitermedia Corporation, 75 222–24
Jurys Doyle Hotel Group plc, 64 215–17
JUSCO Co., Ltd., V 96–99 *see also* AEON Co., Ltd.
Just Bagels Manufacturing, Inc., 94 268–71
Just Born, Inc., 32 305–07
Just For Feet, Inc., 19 228–30
Justin Industries, Inc., 19 231–33 *see also* Berkshire Hathaway Inc.
Juventus F.C. S.p.A, 53 181–83
JVC *see* Victor Company of Japan, Ltd.
JWP Inc., 9 300–02 *see also* EMCOR Group Inc.
JWT Group Inc., I 19–21 *see also* WPP Group plc.
Jysk Holding A/S, 100 241–44

K

K-Swiss Inc., 33 243–45; 89 277–81 (upd.)
K-tel International, Inc., 21 325–28
K&B Inc., 12 286–88
K & G Men's Center, Inc., 21 310–12
K.A. Rasmussen AS, 99 241–244
K2 Inc., 16 295–98; 84 206–211 (upd.)
Kadant Inc., 96 231–34 (upd.)
Kaiser Aluminum Corporation, IV 121–23; 84 212–217 (upd.)

Kaiser Foundation Health Plan, Inc., 53 184–86
Kajima Corporation, I 577–78; 51 177–79 (upd.)
Kal Kan Foods, Inc., 22 298–300
Kaman Corporation, 12 289–92; 42 204–08 (upd.)
Kaman Music Corporation, 68 205–07
Kampgrounds of America, Inc., 33 230–33
Kamps AG, 44 251–54
Kana Software, Inc., 51 180–83
Kanebo, Ltd., 53 187–91
Kanematsu Corporation, IV 442–44; 24 259–62 (upd.); 102 192–95 (upd.)
The Kansai Electric Power Company, Inc., V 645–48; 62 196–200 (upd.)
Kansai Paint Company Ltd., 80 175–78
Kansallis-Osake-Pankki, II 302–03
Kansas City Power & Light Company, 6 510–12 *see also* Great Plains Energy Inc.
Kansas City Southern Industries, Inc., 6 400–02; 26 233–36 (upd.)
The Kansas City Southern Railway Company, 92 198–202
Kao Corporation, III 38–39; 20 315–17 (upd.); 79 225–30 (upd.)
Kaplan, Inc., 42 209–12; 90 270–75 (upd.)
Kar Nut Products Company, 86 233–36
Karan Co. *see* Donna Karan Co.
Karl Kani Infinity, Inc., 49 242–45
Karlsberg Brauerei GmbH & Co KG, 41 220–23
Karmann *see* Wilhelm Karmann GmbH.
Karstadt Aktiengesellschaft, V 100–02; 19 234–37 (upd.)
Karstadt Quelle AG, 57 195–201 (upd.)
Karsten Manufacturing Corporation, 51 184–86
Kash n' Karry Food Stores, Inc., 20 318–20 *see also* Sweetbay Supermarket
Kashi Company, 89 282–85
Kasper A.S.L., Ltd., 40 276–79
kate spade LLC, 68 208–11
Katokichi Company Ltd., 82 187–90
Katy Industries Inc., I 472–74; 51 187–90 (upd.)
Katz Communications, Inc., 6 32–34 *see also* Clear Channel Communications, Inc.
Katz Media Group, Inc., 35 245–48
Kaufhof Warenhaus AG, V 103–05; 23 311–14 (upd.)
Kaufman and Broad Home Corporation, 8 284–86 *see also* KB Home.
Kaufring AG, 35 249–52
Kawai Musical Instruments Manufacturing Co.,Ltd., 78 189–92
Kawasaki Heavy Industries, Ltd., III 538–40; 63 220–23 (upd.)
Kawasaki Kisen Kaisha, Ltd., V 457–60; 56 177–81 (upd.)
Kawasaki Steel Corporation, IV 124–25
Kay-Bee Toy Stores, 15 252–53 *see also* KB Toys.

Mt. Olive Pickle Company, Inc., 44 293–95
MTA *see* Metropolitan Transportation Authority.
MTC *see* Management and Training Corp.
MTel *see* Mobile Telecommunications Technologies Corp.
MTG *see* Modern Times Group AB.
MTI Enterprises Inc., 102 279–82
MTR Foods Ltd., 55 271–73
MTR Gaming Group, Inc., 75 265–67
MTS *see* Mobile TeleSystems.
MTS Inc., 37 261–64
Mueller Industries, Inc., 7 359–61; 52 256–60 (upd.)
Mueller Sports Medicine, Inc., 102 283–86
Mulberry Group PLC, 71 237–39
Mullen Advertising Inc., 51 259–61
Multi-Color Corporation, 53 234–36
Multimedia Games, Inc., 41 272–76
Multimedia, Inc., 11 330–32
Munich Re (Münchener Rückversicherungs-Gesellschaft Aktiengesellschaft in München), III 299–301; 46 303–07 (upd.)
Munir Sukhtian Group, 104 340–44
Murdock Madaus Schwabe, 26 315–19
Murphy Family Farms Inc., 22 366–68 *see also* Smithfield Foods, Inc.
Murphy Oil Corporation, 7 362–64; 32 338–41 (upd.); 95 283–89 (upd.)
Murphy's Pizza *see* Papa Murphy's International, Inc.
The Musco Family Olive Co., 91 334–37
Musco Lighting, 83 276–279
Musgrave Group Plc, 57 254–57
Music Corporation of America *see* MCA Inc.
Musicland Stores Corporation, 9 360–62; 38 313–17 (upd.)
Mutual Benefit Life Insurance Company, III 302–04
Mutual Life Insurance Company of New York, III 305–07
The Mutual of Omaha Companies, 98 248–52
Muzak, Inc., 18 353–56
MWA *see* Modern Woodmen of America.
MWH Preservation Limited Partnership, 65 245–48
MWI Veterinary Supply, Inc., 80 265–68
Mycogen Corporation, 21 385–87 *see also* Dow Chemical Co.
Myers Industries, Inc., 19 277–79; 96 293–97 (upd.)
Mylan Laboratories Inc., I 656–57; 20 380–82 (upd.); 59 304–08 (upd.)
MYOB Ltd., 86 286–90
Myriad Genetics, Inc., 95 290–95
Myriad Restaurant Group, Inc., 87 328–331
MySpace.com *see* Intermix Media, Inc.

N

N.F. Smith & Associates LP, 70 199–202
N M Rothschild & Sons Limited, 39 293–95
N.V. *see under first word of company name*
Naamloze Vennootschap tot Exploitatie van het Café Krasnapolsky *see* Grand Hotel Krasnapolsky N.V.
Nabisco Brands, Inc., II 542–44 *see also* RJR Nabisco.
Nabisco Foods Group, 7 365–68 (upd.) *see also* Kraft Foods Inc.
Nabors Industries Ltd., 9 363–65; 91 338–44 (upd.)
NACCO Industries, Inc., 7 369–71; 78 232–36 (upd.)
Nadro S.A. de C.V., 86 291–94
Naf Naf SA, 44 296–98
Nagasakiya Co., Ltd., V 149–51; 69 259–62 (upd.)
Nagase & Co., Ltd., 8 376–78; 61 226–30 (upd.)
NAI *see* Natural Alternatives International, Inc.; Network Associates, Inc.
Nalco Holding Company, I 373–75; 12 346–48 (upd.); 89 324–30 (upd.)
Nam Tai Electronics, Inc., 61 231–34
Nantucket Allserve, Inc., 22 369–71
Napster, Inc., 69 263–66
Narodowy Bank Polski, 100 297–300
NAS *see* National Audubon Society.
NASCAR *see* National Association for Stock Car Auto Racing.
NASD, 54 242–46 (upd.)
The NASDAQ Stock Market, Inc., 92 256–60
Nash Finch Company, 8 379–81; 23 356–58 (upd.); 65 249–53 (upd.)
Nashua Corporation, 8 382–84
Naspers Ltd., 66 230–32
Nastech Pharmaceutical Company Inc., 79 259–62
Nathan's Famous, Inc., 29 342–44
National Amusements Inc., 28 295–97
National Aquarium in Baltimore, Inc., 74 198–200
National Association for Stock Car Auto Racing, 32 342–44
National Association of Securities Dealers, Inc., 10 416–18 *see also* NASD.
National Audubon Society, 26 320–23
National Auto Credit, Inc., 16 379–81
National Bank of Canada, 85 291–94
National Bank of Greece, 41 277–79
The National Bank of South Carolina, 76 278–80
National Bank of Ukraine, 102 287–90
National Beverage Corporation, 26 324–26; 88 267–71 (upd.)
National Broadcasting Company, Inc., II 151–53; 6 164–66 (upd.); 28 298–301 (upd.) *see also* General Electric Co.
National Can Corp., I 607–08

National Car Rental System, Inc., 10 419–20 *see also* Republic Industries, Inc.
Nationa CineMedia, Inc., 103 266–70
National City Corporation, 15 313–16; 97 294–302 (upd.)
National Collegiate Athletic Association, 96 298–302
National Convenience Stores Incorporated, 7 372–75
National Discount Brokers Group, Inc., 28 302–04 *see also* Deutsche Bank A.G.
National Distillers and Chemical Corporation, I 376–78 *see also* Quantum Chemical Corp.
National Educational Music Co. Ltd., 47 256–58
National Enquirer see American Media, Inc.
National Envelope Corporation, 32 345–47
National Equipment Services, Inc., 57 258–60
National Express Group PLC, 50 340–42
National Financial Partners Corp., 65 254–56
National Football League, 29 345–47 *see also* NFL.
National Frozen Foods Corporation, 94 319–22
National Fuel Gas Company, 6 526–28; 95 296–300 (upd.)
National Geographic Society, 9 366–68; 30 332–35 (upd.); 79 263–69 (upd.)
National Grape Co-operative Association, Inc., 20 383–85
National Grid USA, 51 262–66 (upd.)
National Gypsum Company, 10 421–24
National Health Laboratories Incorporated, 11 333–35 *see also* Laboratory Corporation of America Holdings.
National Heritage Academies, Inc., 60 211–13
National Hockey League, 35 300–03
National Home Centers, Inc., 44 299–301
National Instruments Corporation, 22 372–74
National Intergroup, Inc., V 152–53 *see also* FoxMeyer Health Corp.
National Iranian Oil Company, IV 466–68; 61 235–38 (upd.)
National Jewish Health, 101 356–61
National Journal Group Inc., 67 256–58
National Media Corporation, 27 336–40
National Medical Enterprises, Inc., III 87–88 *see also* Tenet Healthcare Corp.
National Medical Health Card Systems, Inc., 79 270–73
National Oil Corporation, 66 233–37 (upd.)
National Oilwell, Inc., 54 247–50
National Organization for Women, Inc., 55 274–76

Orion Pictures Corporation, 6 167–70 *see also* Metro-Goldwyn-Mayer Inc.

ORIX Corporation, II 442–43; 44 324–26 (upd.); 104 354–58 (upd.)

Orkin, Inc., 104 359–62

Orkla ASA, 18 394–98; 82 259–64 (upd.)

Orleans Homebuilders, Inc., 62 260–62

Ormat Technologies, Inc., 87 353–358

Ormet Corporation, 82 265–68

Orrick, Herrington and Sutcliffe LLP, 76 299–301

Orszagos Takarekpenztar es Kereskedelmi Bank Rt. (OTP Bank), 78 288–91

Orthodontic Centers of America, Inc., 35 323–26

Orthofix International NV, 72 260–62

The Orvis Company, Inc., 28 336–39

Oryx Energy Company, 7 413–15

Osaka Gas Company, Ltd., V 679–81; 60 233–36 (upd.)

Oscar Mayer Foods Corp., 12 370–72 *see also* Kraft Foods Inc.

Oshawa Group Limited, II 649–50

OshKosh B'Gosh, Inc., 9 393–95; 42 266–70 (upd.)

Oshkosh Corporation, 7 416–18; 98 279–84 (upd.)

Oshman's Sporting Goods, Inc., 17 368–70 *see also* Gart Sports Co.

OSI Restaurant Partners, Inc., 88 286–91 (upd.)

Osmonics, Inc., 18 399–401

Osram GmbH, 86 312–16

Österreichische Bundesbahnen GmbH, 6 418–20

Österreichische Elektrizitätswirtschafts-AG, 85 307–10

Österreichische Post- und Telegraphenverwaltung, V 314–17

O'Sullivan Industries Holdings, Inc., 34 313–15

Otari Inc., 89 341–44

Otis Elevator Company, Inc., 13 384–86; 39 311–15 (upd.)

Otis Spunkmeyer, Inc., 28 340–42

Otor S.A., 77 326–29

OTP Bank *see* Orszagos Takarekpenztar es Kereskedelmi Bank Rt.

OTR Express, Inc., 25 368–70

Ottakar's plc, 64 302–04

Ottaway Newspapers, Inc., 15 335–37

Otter Tail Power Company, 18 402–05

Otto Bremer Foundation *see* Bremer Financial Corp.

Otto Fuchs KG, 100 310–14

Otto Versand GmbH & Co., V 159–61; 15 338–40 (upd.); 34 324–28 (upd.)

Outback Steakhouse, Inc., 12 373–75; 34 329–32 (upd.) *see also* OSI Restaurant Partners, Inc.

Outboard Marine Corporation, III 597–600; 20 409–12 (upd.) *see also* Bombardier Inc.

Outdoor Research, Incorporated, 67 288–90

Outdoor Systems, Inc., 25 371–73 *see also* Infinity Broadcasting Corp.

Outlook Group Corporation, 37 294–96

Outokumpu Oyj, 38 335–37

Outrigger Enterprises, Inc., 67 291–93

Overhead Door Corporation, 70 213–16

Overhill Corporation, 51 279–81

Overland Storage Inc., 100 315–20

Overnite Corporation, 14 371–73; 58 262–65 (upd.)

Overseas Shipholding Group, Inc., 11 376–77

Overstock.com, Inc., 75 307–09

Owens & Minor, Inc., 16 398–401; 68 282–85 (upd.)

Owens Corning, III 720–23; 20 413–17 (upd.); 98 285–91 (upd.)

Owens-Illinois, Inc., I 609–11; 26 350–53 (upd.); 85 311–18 (upd.)

Owosso Corporation, 29 366–68

Oxfam GB, 87 359–362

Oxford Health Plans, Inc., 16 402–04

Oxford Industries, Inc., 8 406–08; 84 290–296 (upd.)

P

P&C Foods Inc., 8 409–11

P & F Industries, Inc., 45 327–29

P&G *see* Procter & Gamble Co.

P.C. Richard & Son Corp., 23 372–74

P.F. Chang's China Bistro, Inc., 37 297–99; 86 317–21 (upd.)

P.H. Glatfelter Company, 8 412–14; 30 349–52 (upd.); 83 291–297 (upd.)

P.W. Minor and Son, Inc., 100 321–24

PACCAR Inc., I 185–86; 26 354–56 (upd.)

Pacer International, Inc., 54 274–76

Pacer Technology, 40 347–49

Pacific Basin Shipping Ltd., 86 322–26

Pacific Clay Products Inc., 88 292–95

Pacific Coast Building Products, Inc., 94 338–41

Pacific Coast Feather Company, 67 294–96

Pacific Coast Restaurants, Inc., 90 318–21

Pacific Dunlop Limited, 10 444–46 *see also* Ansell Ltd.

Pacific Enterprises, V 682–84 *see also* Sempra Energy.

Pacific Ethanol, Inc., 81 269–72

Pacific Gas and Electric Company, V 685–87 *see also* PG&E Corp.

Pacific Internet Limited, 87 363–366

Pacific Mutual Holding Company, 98 292–96

Pacific Sunwear of California, Inc., 28 343–45; 104 363–67 (upd.)

Pacific Telecom, Inc., 6 325–28

Pacific Telesis Group, V 318–20 *see also* SBC Communications.

PacifiCare Health Systems, Inc., 11 378–80

PacifiCorp, Inc., V 688–90; 26 357–60 (upd.)

Packaging Corporation of America, 12 376–78; 51 282–85 (upd.)

Packard Bell Electronics, Inc., 13 387–89

Packeteer, Inc., 81 273–76

Paddock Publications, Inc., 53 263–65

Paddy Power plc, 98 297–300

PagesJaunes Groupe SA, 79 306–09

Paging Network Inc., 11 381–83

Pagnossin S.p.A., 73 248–50

PaineWebber Group Inc., II 444–46; 22 404–07 (upd.) *see also* UBS AG.

Pakistan International Airlines Corporation, 46 323–26

Pakistan State Oil Company Ltd., 81 277–80

PAL *see* Philippine Airlines, Inc.

Palace Sports & Entertainment, Inc., 97 320–25

Palfinger AG, 100 325–28

PALIC *see* Pan-American Life Insurance Co.

Pall Corporation, 9 396–98; 72 263–66 (upd.)

Palm Harbor Homes, Inc., 39 316–18

Palm, Inc., 36 355–57; 75 310–14 (upd.)

Palm Management Corporation, 71 265–68

Palmer & Cay, Inc., 69 285–87

Palmer Candy Company, 80 277–81

Palmer Co. *see* R. M. Palmer Co.

Paloma Industries Ltd., 71 269–71

Palomar Medical Technologies, Inc., 22 408–10

Pamida Holdings Corporation, 15 341–43

The Pampered Chef Ltd., 18 406–08; 78 292–96 (upd.)

Pamplin Corp. *see* R.B. Pamplin Corp.

Pan-American Life Insurance Company, 48 311–13

Pan American World Airways, Inc., I 115–16; 12 379–81 (upd.)

Panalpina World Transport (Holding) Ltd., 47 286–88

Panamerican Beverages, Inc., 47 289–91; 54 74

PanAmSat Corporation, 46 327–29

Panattoni Development Company, Inc., 99 327–330

Panavision Inc., 24 372–74

Pancho's Mexican Buffet, Inc., 46 330–32

Panda Restaurant Group, Inc., 35 327–29; 97 326–30 (upd.)

Panera Bread Company, 44 327–29

Panhandle Eastern Corporation, V 691–92 *see also* CMS Energy Corp.

Pantone Inc., 53 266–69

The Pantry, Inc., 36 358–60

Panzani, 84 297–300

Papa Gino's Holdings Corporation, Inc., 86 327–30

Papa John's International, Inc., 15 344–46; 71 272–76 (upd.)

Papa Murphy's International, Inc., 54 277–79

Papeteries de Lancey, 23 366–68

Papetti's Hygrade Egg Products, Inc., 39 319–21

Pappas Restaurants, Inc., 76 302–04

Par Pharmaceutical Companies, Inc., 65 286–88

The Paradies Shops, Inc., 88 296–99

Paradise Music & Entertainment, Inc., 42 271–74

Paradores de Turismo de Espana S.A., 73 251–53

Parallel Petroleum Corporation, 101 400–03

Parametric Technology Corp., 16 405–07

Paramount Pictures Corporation, II 154–56; 94 342–47 (upd.)

Paramount Resources Ltd., 87 367–370

PAREXEL International Corporation, 84 301–304

Parfums Givenchy S.A., 100 329–32

Paribas *see* BNP Paribas Group.

Paris Corporation, 22 411–13

Parisian, Inc., 14 374–76 *see also* Belk, Inc.

Park Corp., 22 414–16

Park-Ohio Holdings Corp., 17 371–73; 85 319–23 (upd.)

Parker Drilling Company, 28 346–48

Parker-Hannifin Corporation, III 601–03; 24 375–78 (upd.); 99 331–337 (upd.)

Parlex Corporation, 61 279–81

Parmalat Finanziaria SpA, 50 343–46

Parque Arauco S.A., 72 267–69

Parras *see* Compañia Industrial de Parras, S.A. de C.V. (CIPSA).

Parsons Brinckerhoff Inc., 34 333–36; 104 368–72 (upd.)

The Parsons Corporation, 8 415–17; 56 263–67 (upd.)

PartnerRe Ltd., 83 298–301

Partouche SA *see* Groupe Partouche SA.

Party City Corporation, 54 280–82

Patch Products Inc., 105 340–44

Pathé SA, 29 369–71 *see also* Chargeurs International.

Pathmark Stores, Inc., 23 369–71; 101 404–08 (upd.)

Patina Oil & Gas Corporation, 24 379–81

Patrick Cudahy Inc., 102 321–25

Patrick Industries, Inc., 30 342–45

Patriot Transportation Holding, Inc., 91 371–74

Patterson Dental Co., 19 289–91

Patterson-UTI Energy, Inc., 55 293–95

Patton Boggs LLP, 71 277–79

Paul Harris Stores, Inc., 18 409–12

Paul, Hastings, Janofsky & Walker LLP, 27 357–59

Paul Mueller Company, 65 289–91

Paul Reed Smith Guitar Company, 89 345–48

The Paul Revere Corporation, 12 382–83

Paul-Son Gaming Corporation, 66 249–51

Paul, Weiss, Rifkind, Wharton & Garrison, 47 292–94

Paulaner Brauerei GmbH & Co. KG, 35 330–33

Paxson Communications Corporation, 33 322–26

Pay 'N Pak Stores, Inc., 9 399–401

Paychex, Inc., 15 347–49; 46 333–36 (upd.)

Payless Cashways, Inc., 11 384–86; 44 330–33 (upd.)

Payless ShoeSource, Inc., 18 413–15; 69 288–92 (upd.)

PayPal Inc., 58 266–69

PBL *see* Publishing and Broadcasting Ltd.

PBS *see* Public Broadcasting Stations.

The PBSJ Corporation, 82 269–73

PC Connection, Inc., 37 300–04

PCA *see* Packaging Corporation of America.

PCA International, Inc., 62 263–65

PCC *see* Companhia Suzano de Papel e Celulose S.A.

PCC Natural Markets, 94 348–51

PCL Construction Group Inc., 50 347–49

PCM Uitgevers NV, 53 270–73

PCS *see* Potash Corp. of Saskatchewan Inc.

PDI, Inc., 52 272–75

PDL BioPharma, Inc., 90 322–25

PDO *see* Petroleum Development Oman.

PDQ Food Stores Inc., 79 310–13

PDS Gaming Corporation, 44 334–37

PDVSA *see* Petróleos de Venezuela S.A.

Peabody Energy Corporation, 10 447–49; 45 330–33 (upd.)

Peabody Holding Company, Inc., IV 169–72

Peace Arch Entertainment Group Inc., 51 286–88

The Peak Technologies Group, Inc., 14 377–80

Peapod, Inc., 30 346–48

Pearl Musical Instrument Company, 78 297–300

Pearle Vision, Inc., 13 390–92

Pearson plc, IV 657–59; 46 337–41 (upd.); 103 320–26 (upd.)

Peavey Electronics Corporation, 16 408–10; 94 352–56 (upd.)

Pechiney S.A., IV 173–75; 45 334–37 (upd.)

PECO Energy Company, 11 387–90 *see also* Exelon Corp.

Pediatric Services of America, Inc., 31 356–58

Pediatrix Medical Group, Inc., 61 282–85

Peebles Inc., 16 411–13; 43 296–99 (upd.)

Peek & Cloppenburg KG, 46 342–45

Peet's Coffee & Tea, Inc., 38 338–40; 100 333–37 (upd.)

Peg Perego SpA, 88 300–03

Pegasus Solutions, Inc., 75 315–18

Pei Cobb Freed & Partners Architects LLP, 57 280–82

Pelican Products, Inc., 86 331–34

Pelikan Holding AG, 92 296–300

Pella Corporation, 12 384–86; 39 322–25 (upd.); 89 349–53 (upd.)

Pemco Aviation Group Inc., 54 283–86

PEMEX *see* Petróleos Mexicanos.

Penaflor S.A., 66 252–54

Penauille Polyservices SA, 49 318–21

Pendleton Grain Growers Inc., 64 305–08

Pendleton Woolen Mills, Inc., 42 275–78

Penford Corporation, 55 296–99

Pengrowth Energy Trust, 95 323–26

The Penguin Group, 100 338–42

The Peninsular and Oriental Steam Navigation Company, V 490–93; 38 341–46 (upd.)

Peninsular and Oriental Steam Navigation Company (Bovis Division), I 588–89 *see also* DP World.

Penn Engineering & Manufacturing Corp., 28 349–51

Penn National Gaming, Inc., 33 327–29

Penn Traffic Company, 13 393–95

Penn Virginia Corporation, 85 324–27

Penney's *see* J.C. Penney Company, Inc.

Pennington Seed Inc., 98 301–04

Pennon Group Plc, 45 338–41

Pennsylvania Blue Shield, III 325–27 *see also* Highmark Inc.

Pennsylvania Power & Light Company, V 693–94

Pennwalt Corporation, I 382–84

PennWell Corporation, 55 300–03

Pennzoil-Quaker State Company, IV 488–90; 20 418–22 (upd.); 50 350–55 (upd.)

Penske Corporation, V 494–95; 19 292–94 (upd.); 84 305–309 (upd.)

Pentair, Inc., 7 419–21; 26 361–64 (upd.); 81 281–87 (upd.)

Pentax Corporation, 78 301–05

Pentech International, Inc., 29 372–74

The Pentland Group plc, 20 423–25; 100 343–47 (upd.)

Penton Media, Inc., 27 360–62

Penzeys Spices, Inc., 79 314–16

People Express Airlines Inc., I 117–18

Peoples Energy Corporation, 6 543–44

PeopleSoft Inc., 14 381–83; 33 330–33 (upd.) *see also* Oracle Corp.

The Pep Boys—Manny, Moe & Jack, 11 391–93; 36 361–64 (upd.); 81 288–94 (upd.)

PEPCO *see* Potomac Electric Power Co.

Pepper *see* J. W. Pepper and Son Inc.

Pepper Hamilton LLP, 43 300–03

Pepperidge Farm, Incorporated, 81 295–300

The Pepsi Bottling Group, Inc., 40 350–53

PepsiAmericas, Inc., 67 297–300 (upd.)

PepsiCo, Inc., I 276–79; 10 450–54 (upd.); 38 347–54 (upd.); 93 333–44 (upd.)

Premcor Inc., 37 309–11

Premier Industrial Corporation, 9
419–21

Premier Parks, Inc., 27 382–84 *see also*
Six Flags, Inc.

Premiere Radio Networks, Inc., 102
335–38

Premium Standard Farms, Inc., 30
353–55

PremiumWear, Inc., 30 356–59

Preserver Group, Inc., 44 354–56

President Casinos, Inc., 22 438–40

Pressman Toy Corporation, 56 280–82

Presstek, Inc., 33 345–48

Preston Corporation, 6 421–23

Preussag AG, 17 378–82; 42 279–83
(upd.)

PreussenElektra Aktiengesellschaft, V
698–700 *see also* E.On AG.

PRG-Schultz International, Inc., 73
264–67

Price Communications Corporation, 42
284–86

The Price Company, V 162–64 *see also*
Costco Wholesale Corp.

Price Pfister, Inc., 70 236–39

Price Waterhouse LLP, 9 422–24 *see also*
PricewaterhouseCoopers

PriceCostco, Inc., 14 393–95 *see also*
Costco Wholesale Corp.

Priceline.com Incorporated, 57 296–99

PriceSmart, Inc., 71 287–90

PricewaterhouseCoopers, 29 389–94
(upd.)

PRIDE Enterprises *see* Prison
Rehabilitative Industries and Diversified
Enterprises, Inc.

Pride International, Inc., 78 319–23

Primark Corp., 13 416–18 *see also*
Thomson Corp.

Prime Hospitality Corporation, 52
280–83

Primedex Health Systems, Inc., 25
382–85

Primedia Inc., 22 441–43

Primerica Corporation, I 612–14

Prince Sports Group, Inc., 15 368–70

Princes Ltd., 76 312–14

Princess Cruise Lines, 22 444–46

The Princeton Review, Inc., 42 287–90

Principal Mutual Life Insurance
Company, III 328–30

Printpack, Inc., 68 293–96

Printrak, A Motorola Company, 44
357–59

Printronix, Inc., 18 434–36

Prison Rehabilitative Industries and
Diversified Enterprises, Inc. (PRIDE),
53 277–79

Pro-Build Holdings Inc., 95 344–48
(upd.)

The Procter & Gamble Company, III
50–53; 8 431–35 (upd.); 26 380–85
(upd.); 67 304–11 (upd.)

Prodigy Communications Corporation,
34 360–62

Prodware S.A., 102 339–42

Proeza S.A. de C.V., 82 288–91

Professional Bull Riders Inc., 55
310–12

The Professional Golfers' Association of
America, 41 318–21

Proffitt's, Inc., 19 323–25 *see also* Belk,
Inc.

Programmer's Paradise, Inc., 81 324–27

Progress Energy, Inc., 74 249–52

Progress Software Corporation, 15
371–74

Progressive Corporation, 11 405–07; 29
395–98 (upd.)

Progressive Enterprises Ltd., 96 339–42

ProLogis, 57 300–02

Promus Companies, Inc., 9 425–27 *see
also* Hilton Hotels Corp.

ProSiebenSat.1 Media AG, 54 295–98

Proskauer Rose LLP, 47 308–10

Protection One, Inc., 32 372–75

Provell Inc., 58 276–79 (upd.)

Providence Health System, 90 343–47

The Providence Journal Company, 28
367–69; 30 15

The Providence Service Corporation, 64
309–12

Provident Bankshares Corporation, 85
340–43

Provident Life and Accident Insurance
Company of America, III 331–33 *see
also* UnumProvident Corp.

Providian Financial Corporation, 52
284–90 (upd.)

Provigo Inc., II 651–53; 51 301–04
(upd.)

Provimi S.A., 80 292–95

PRS *see* Paul Reed Smith Guitar Co.

Prudential Financial Inc., III 337–41;
30 360–64 (upd.); 82 292–98 (upd.)

Prudential plc, III 334–36; 48 325–29
(upd.)

PSA Peugeot Citroen S.A., 28 370–74
(upd.); 54 126

PSF *see* Premium Standard Farms, Inc.

PSI Resources, 6 555–57

Psion PLC, 45 346–49

Psychemedics Corporation, 89 358–61

Psychiatric Solutions, Inc., 68 297–300

PT Astra International Tbk, 56 283–86

PT Bank Buana Indonesia Tbk, 60
240–42

PT Gudang Garam Tbk, 103 339–42

PT Indosat Tbk, 93 354–57

PT Semen Gresik Tbk, 103 343–46

PTT Public Company Ltd., 56 287–90

Pubco Corporation, 17 383–85

Public Service Company of Colorado, 6
558–60

Public Service Company of New
Hampshire, 21 408–12; 55 313–18
(upd.)

Public Service Company of New
Mexico, 6 561–64 *see also* PNM
Resources Inc.

Public Service Enterprise Group Inc., V
701–03; 44 360–63 (upd.)

Public Storage, Inc., 21 52 291–93

Publicis Groupe, 19 329–32; 77 346–50
(upd.)

Publishers Clearing House, 23 393–95;
64 313–16 (upd.)

Publishers Group, Inc., 35 357–59

Publishing and Broadcasting Limited,
54 299–302

Publix Super Markets, Inc., 7 440–42;
31 371–74 (upd.); 105 345–51 (upd.)

Puck Lazaroff Inc. *see* The Wolfgang Puck
Food Company, Inc.

Pueblo Xtra International, Inc., 47
311–13

Puerto Rico Electric Power Authority,
47 314–16

Puget Sound Energy Inc., 6 565–67; 50
365–68 (upd.)

Puig Beauty and Fashion Group S.L.,
60 243–46

Pulaski Furniture Corporation, 33
349–52; 80 296–99 (upd.)

Pulitzer Inc., 15 375–77; 58 280–83
(upd.)

Pulsar Internacional S.A., 21 413–15

Pulte Homes, Inc., 8 436–38; 42
291–94 (upd.)

Puma AG Rudolf Dassler Sport, 35
360–63

Pumpkin Masters, Inc., 48 330–32

Punch International N.V., 66 258–60

Punch Taverns plc, 70 240–42

Puratos S.A./NV, 92 315–18

Pure World, Inc., 72 285–87

Purina Mills, Inc., 32 376–79

Puritan-Bennett Corporation, 13
419–21

Purolator Products Company, 21
416–18; 74 253–56 (upd.)

Putt-Putt Golf Courses of America, Inc.,
23 396–98

PVC Container Corporation, 67 312–14

PW Eagle, Inc., 48 333–36

PWA Group, IV 323–25 *see also* Svenska
Cellulosa.

Pyramid Breweries Inc., 33 353–55; 102
343–47 (upd.)

Pyramid Companies, 54 303–05

PZ Cussons plc, 72 288–90

Q

Q.E.P. Co., Inc., 65 292–94

Qantas Airways Ltd., 6 109–13; 24
396–401 (upd.); 68 301–07 (upd.)

Qatar Airways Company Q.C.S.C., 87
404–407

Qatar National Bank SAQ, 87 408–411

Qatar Petroleum, IV 524–26; 98
324–28 (upd.)

Qatar Telecom QSA, 87 412–415

Qdoba Restaurant Corporation, 93
358–62

Qiagen N.V., 39 333–35

QLT Inc., 71 291–94

QRS Music Technologies, Inc., 95
349–53

QSC Audio Products, Inc., 56 291–93

QSS Group, Inc., 100 358–61

Quad/Graphics, Inc., 19 333–36

Quaker Chemical Corp., 91 388–91

Quaker Fabric Corp., 19 337–39

Rite Aid Corporation, V 174–76; 19 354–57 (upd.); 63 331–37 (upd.)

Ritter Sport *see* Alfred Ritter GmbH & Co. KG.

Ritter's Frozen Custard *see* RFC Franchising LLC.

Ritz Camera Centers, 34 375–77

The Ritz-Carlton Hotel Company, L.L.C., 9 455–57; 29 403–06 (upd.); 71 311–16 (upd.)

Ritz-Craft Corporation of Pennsylvania Inc., 94 365–68

Riunione Adriatica di Sicurtà SpA, III 345–48

Riva Fire *see* Gruppo Riva Fire SpA.

The Rival Company, 19 358–60

River Oaks Furniture, Inc., 43 314–16

River Ranch Fresh Foods LLC, 88 322–25

Riverbed Technology, Inc., 101 428–31

Riverwood International Corporation, 11 420–23; 48 340–44 (upd.) *see also* Graphic Packaging Holding Co.

Riviana Foods, 27 388–91

Riviera Holdings Corporation, 75 340–43

Riviera Tool Company, 89 373–76

RJR Nabisco Holdings Corp., V 408–10 *see also* R.J Reynolds Tobacco Holdings Inc., Nabisco Brands, Inc.; R.J. Reynolds Industries, Inc.

RM Auctions, Inc., 88 326–29

RMC Group p.l.c., III 737–40; 34 378–83 (upd.)

RMH Teleservices, Inc., 42 322–24

Roadhouse Grill, Inc., 22 464–66

Roadmaster Industries, Inc., 16 430–33

Roadway Express, Inc., V 502–03; 25 395–98 (upd.)

Roanoke Electric Steel Corporation, 45 368–70

Robbins & Myers Inc., 15 388–90

Roberds Inc., 19 361–63

Robert Bosch GmbH, I 392–93; 16 434–37 (upd.); 43 317–21 (upd.)

Robert Half International Inc., 18 461–63; 70 281–84 (upd.)

Robert Mondavi Corporation, 15 391–94; 50 386–90 (upd.)

Robert Talbott Inc., 88 330–33

Robert W. Baird & Co. Incorporated, 67 328–30

Robert Wood Johnson Foundation, 35 375–78

Robertet SA, 39 347–49

Roberts Dairy Company, 103 364–67

Roberts Pharmaceutical Corporation, 16 438–40

Robertson-Ceco Corporation, 19 364–66

Robins, Kaplan, Miller & Ciresi L.L.P., 89 377–81

Robinson Helicopter Company, 51 315–17

ROC *see* Royal Olympic Cruise Lines Inc.

Rocawear Apparel LLC, 77 355–58

Roche Biomedical Laboratories, Inc., 11 424–26 *see also* Laboratory Corporation of America Holdings.

Roche Bioscience, 14 403–06 (upd.)

Rochester Gas And Electric Corporation, 6 571–73

Rochester Telephone Corporation, 6 332–34

Röchling Gruppe, 94 369–74

Rock Bottom Restaurants, Inc., 25 399–401; 68 320–23 (upd.)

Rock-It Cargo USA, Inc., 86 339–42

Rock of Ages Corporation, 37 329–32

Rock-Tenn Company, 13 441–43; 59 347–51 (upd.)

The Rockefeller Foundation, 34 384–87

Rockefeller Group International Inc., 58 303–06

Rockford Corporation, 43 322–25

Rockford Products Corporation, 55 323–25

RockShox, Inc., 26 412–14

Rockwell Automation, Inc., 43 326–31 (upd.); 103 368–76 (upd.)

Rockwell International Corporation, I 78–80; 11 427–30 (upd.)

Rockwell Medical Technologies, Inc., 88 334–37

Rocky Brands, Inc., 26 415–18; 102 357–62 (upd.)

Rocky Mountain Chocolate Factory, Inc., 73 280–82

Rodale, Inc., 23 415–17; 47 336–39 (upd.)

Rodamco N.V., 26 419–21

Rodda Paint Company, 98 329–32

Rodriguez Group S.A., 90 357–60

ROFIN-SINAR Technologies Inc, 81 345–48

Rogers Communications Inc., 30 388–92 (upd.) *see also* Maclean Hunter Publishing Ltd.

Rogers Corporation, 61 310–13; 80 313–17 (upd.)

Rohde & Schwarz GmbH & Co. KG, 39 350–53

Röhm and Haas Company, I 391–93; 26 422–26 (upd.); 77 359–66 (upd.)

ROHN Industries, Inc., 22 467–69

Rohr Incorporated, 9 458–60 *see also* Goodrich Corp.

Roland Berger & Partner GmbH, 37 333–36

Roland Corporation, 38 389–91

Roland Murten A.G., 7 452–53

Rolex *see* Montres Rolex S.A.

Roll International Corporation, 37 337–39

Rollerblade, Inc., 15 395–98; 34 388–92 (upd.)

Rollins, Inc., 11 431–34; 104 397–403 (upd.)

Rolls-Royce Allison, 29 407–09 (upd.)

Rolls-Royce Group PLC, 67 331–36 (upd.)

Rolls-Royce Motors Ltd., I 194–96

Rolls-Royce plc, I 81–83; 7 454–57 (upd.); 21 433–37 (upd.)

Rolta India Ltd., 90 361–64

Roly Poly Franchise Systems LLC, 83 326–328

Romacorp, Inc., 58 307–11

Roman Meal Company, 84 331–334

Ron Tonkin Chevrolet Company, 55 326–28

RONA, Inc., 73 283–86

Ronco Corporation, 15 399–401; 80 318–23 (upd.)

Ronson PLC, 49 337–39

Rooms To Go Inc., 28 389–92

Rooney Brothers Co., 25 402–04

Roosevelt Hospital *see* Continuum Health Partners, Inc.

Roots Canada Ltd., 42 325–27

Roper Industries, Inc., 15 402–04; 50 391–95 (upd.)

Ropes & Gray, 40 377–80

Rorer Group, I 666–68

Rosauers Supermarkets, Inc., 90 365–68

Rose Acre Farms, Inc., 60 255–57

Rose Art Industries, 58 312–14

Roseburg Forest Products Company, 58 315–17

Rosemount Inc., 15 405–08 *see also* Emerson.

Rosenbluth International Inc., 14 407–09 *see also* American Express Co.

Rose's Stores, Inc., 13 444–46

Rosetta Stone Inc., 93 375–79

Ross Stores, Inc., 17 408–10; 43 332–35 (upd.); 101 432–37 (upd.)

Rossignol Ski Company, Inc. *see* Skis Rossignol S.A.

Rossmann *see* Dirk Rossmann GmbH.

Rostelecom Joint Stock Co., 99 374–377

Rostvertol plc, 62 308–10

Rosy Blue N.V., 84 335–338

Rotary International, 31 395–97

Rothmans UK Holdings Limited, V 411–13; 19 367–70 (upd.)

Roto-Rooter, Inc., 15 409–11; 61 314–19 (upd.)

Rotork plc, 46 361–64

The Rottlund Company, Inc., 28 393–95

Rouge Steel Company, 8 448–50

Rougier *see* Groupe Rougier, SA.

Roularta Media Group NV, 48 345–47

Rounder Records Corporation, 79 357–61

Roundy's Inc., 14 410–12; 58 318–21 (upd.)

The Rouse Company, 15 412–15; 63 338–41 (upd.)

Roussel Uclaf, I 669–70; 8 451–53 (upd.)

Rover Group Ltd., 7 458–60; 21 441–44 (upd.)

Rowan Companies, Inc., 43 336–39

Rowntree Mackintosh PLC, II 568–70 *see also* Nestlé S.A.

The Rowohlt Verlag GmbH, 96 356–61

Roy Anderson Corporation, 75 344–46

Roy F. Weston, Inc., 33 369–72

Southwest Airlines Co., 6 119–21; 24 452–55 (upd.); 71 343–47 (upd.)

Southwest Gas Corporation, 19 410–12

Southwest Water Company, 47 370–73

Southwestern Bell Corporation, V 328–30 see also SBC Communications Inc.

Southwestern Electric Power Co., 21 468–70

Southwestern Public Service Company, 6 579–81

Southwire Company, Inc., 8 478–80; 23 444–47 (upd.)

Souza Cruz S.A., 65 322–24

Sovereign Bancorp, Inc., 103 392–95

Sovran Self Storage, Inc., 66 299–301

SP Alpargatas see Sao Paulo Alpargatas S.A.

Spacehab, Inc., 37 364–66

Spacelabs Medical, Inc., 71 348–50

Spaghetti Warehouse, Inc., 25 436–38

Spago see The Wolfgang Puck Food Company, Inc.

Spangler Candy Company, 44 392–95

Spanish Broadcasting System, Inc., 41 383–86

Spansion Inc., 80 352–55

Spanx, Inc., 89 423–27

Spar Aerospace Limited, 32 435–37

Spar Handelsgesellschaft mbH, 35 398–401; 103 396–400 (upd.)

Spark Networks, Inc., 91 437–40

Spartan Motors Inc., 14 457–59

Spartan Stores Inc., 8 481–82; 66 302–05 (upd.)

Spartech Corporation, 19 413–15; 76 329–32 (upd.)

Sparton Corporation, 18 492–95

Spear & Jackson, Inc., 73 320–23

Spear, Leeds & Kellogg, 66 306–09

Spec's Music, Inc., 19 416–18 see also Camelot Music, Inc.

Special Olympics, Inc., 93 410–14

Specialist Computer Holdings Ltd., 80 356–59

Specialized Bicycle Components Inc., 50 445–48

Specialty Coatings Inc., 8 483–84

Specialty Equipment Companies, Inc., 25 439–42

Specialty Products & Insulation Co., 59 381–83

Specsavers Optical Group Ltd., 104 428–31

Spector Photo Group N.V., 82 344–47

Spectrum Control, Inc., 67 355–57

Spectrum Organic Products, Inc., 68 346–49

Spee-Dee Delivery Service, Inc., 93 415–18

SpeeDee Oil Change and Tune-Up, 25 443–47

Speedway Motorsports, Inc., 32 438–41

Speedy Hire plc, 84 376–379

Speidel Inc., 96 404–07

Speizman Industries, Inc., 44 396–98

Spelling Entertainment, 14 460–62; 35 402–04 (upd.)

Spencer Stuart and Associates, Inc., 14 463–65 see also SSI (U.S.), Inc.

Sperian Protection S.A., 104 432–36

Spherion Corporation, 52 316–18

Spicy Pickle Franchising, Inc., 105 434–37

Spie see Amec Spie S.A.

Spiegel, Inc., 10 489–91; 27 427–31 (upd.)

SPIEGEL-Verlag Rudolf Augstein GmbH & Co. KG, 44 399–402

Spin Master, Ltd., 61 335–38

Spinnaker Exploration Company, 72 334–36

Spirax-Sarco Engineering plc, 59 384–86

Spirit Airlines, Inc., 31 419–21

Sport Chalet, Inc., 16 454–56; 94 402–06 (upd.)

Sport Supply Group, Inc., 23 448–50

Sportmart, Inc., 15 469–71 see also Gart Sports Co.

Sports & Recreation, Inc., 17 453–55

The Sports Authority, Inc., 16 457–59; 43 385–88 (upd.)

The Sports Club Company, 25 448–51

The Sportsman's Guide, Inc., 36 443–46

Springs Global US, Inc., V 378–79; 19 419–22 (upd.); 90 378–83 (upd.)

Sprint Communications Company, L.P., 9 478–80 see also Sprint Corporation; US Sprint Communications.

Sprint Corporation, 46 373–76 (upd.)

SPS Technologies, Inc., 30 428–30

SPSS Inc., 64 360–63

SPX Corporation, 10 492–95; 47 374–79 (upd.); 103 401–09 (upd.)

Spyglass Entertainment Group, LLC, 91 441–44

SQM see Sociedad Química y Minera de Chile S.A.

Square D, 90 384–89

Square Enix Holdings Co., Ltd., 101 454–57

Squibb Corporation, I 695–97 see also Bristol-Myers Squibb Co.

SR Teleperformance S.A., 86 365–68

SRA International, Inc., 77 400–03

SRAM Corporation, 65 325–27

SRC Holdings Corporation, 67 358–60

SRI International, Inc., 57 333–36

SSA see Stevedoring Services of America Inc.

SSAB Svenskt Stål AB, 89 428–31

Ssangyong Cement Industrial Co., Ltd., III 747–50; 61 339–43 (upd.)

SSI (U.S.), Inc., 103 410–14 (upd.)

SSL International plc, 49 378–81

SSOE Inc., 76 333–35

St Ives plc, 34 393–95

St. see under Saint

St. James's Place Capital, plc, 71 324–26

The St. Joe Company, 31 422–25; 98 368–73 (upd.)

St. Joe Paper Company, 8 485–88

St. John Knits, Inc., 14 466–68

St. Jude Medical, Inc., 11 458–61; 43 347–52 (upd.); 97 350–58 (upd.)

St. Louis Music, Inc., 48 351–54

St. Luke's-Roosevelt Hospital Center see Continuum Health Partners, Inc.

St. Mary Land & Exploration Company, 63 345–47

St. Paul Bank for Cooperatives, 8 489–90

The St. Paul Travelers Companies, Inc., III 355–57; 22 492–95 (upd.); 79 362–69 (upd.)

STAAR Surgical Company, 57 337–39

The Stabler Companies Inc., 78 352–55

Stage Stores, Inc., 24 456–59; 82 348–52 (upd.)

Stagecoach Group plc, 30 431–33; 104 437–41 (upd.)

Stanadyne Automotive Corporation, 37 367–70

StanCorp Financial Group, Inc., 56 345–48

Standard Candy Company Inc., 86 369–72

Standard Chartered plc, II 357–59; 48 371–74 (upd.)

Standard Commercial Corporation, 13 490–92; 62 333–37 (upd.)

Standard Federal Bank, 9 481–83

Standard Life Assurance Company, III 358–61

Standard Microsystems Corporation, 11 462–64

Standard Motor Products, Inc., 40 414–17

Standard Pacific Corporation, 52 319–22

The Standard Register Company, 15 472–74; 93 419–25 (upd.)

Standex International Corporation, 17 456–59; 44 403–06 (upd.)

Stanhome Inc., 15 475–78

Stanley Furniture Company, Inc., 34 412–14

Stanley Leisure plc, 66 310–12

The Stanley Works, III 626–29; 20 476–80 (upd.); 79 383–91 (upd.)

Staple Cotton Cooperative Association (Staplcotn), 86 373–77

Staples, Inc., 10 496–98; 55 351–56 (upd.)

Star Banc Corporation, 11 465–67 see also Firstar Corp.

Star of the West Milling Co., 95 386–89

Starbucks Corporation, 13 493–94; 34 415–19 (upd.); 77 404–10 (upd.)

Starcraft Corporation, 30 434–36; 66 313–16 (upd.)

StarHub Ltd., 77 411–14

Starkey Laboratories, Inc., 52 323–25

Starrett see L.S. Starrett Co.

Starrett Corporation, 21 471–74

StarTek, Inc., 79 392–95

Starter Corp., 12 457–458

Starwood Hotels & Resorts Worldwide, Inc., 54 345–48

Starz LLC, 91 445–50

The Stash Tea Company, 50 449–52

United Retail Group Inc., 33 426–28
United Road Services, Inc., 69 360–62
United Service Organizations, 60 308–11
United States Cellular Corporation, 9 527–29 *see also* U.S. Cellular Corp.
United States Filter Corporation, 20 501–04 *see also* Siemens AG.
United States Health Care Systems, Inc. *see* U.S. Healthcare, Inc.
United States Pipe and Foundry Company, 62 377–80
United States Playing Card Company, 62 381–84
United States Postal Service, 14 517–20; 34 470–75 (upd.)
United States Shoe Corporation, V 207–08
United States Steel Corporation, 50 500–04 (upd.)
United States Surgical Corporation, 10 533–35; 34 476–80 (upd.)
United Stationers Inc., 14 521–23
United Talent Agency, Inc., 80 392–96
United Technologies Automotive Inc., 15 513–15
United Technologies Corporation, I 84–86; 10 536–38 (upd.); 34 481–85 (upd.); 105 455–61 (upd.)
United Telecommunications, Inc., V 344–47 *see also* Sprint Corp.
United Utilities PLC, 52 372–75 (upd.)
United Video Satellite Group, 18 535–37 *see also* TV Guide, Inc.
United Water Resources, Inc., 40 447–50; 45 277
United Way of America, 36 485–88
UnitedHealth Group Incorporated, 103 476–84 (upd.)
Unitika Ltd., V 387–89; 53 341–44 (upd.)
Unitil Corporation, 37 403–06
Unitog Co., 19 457–60 *see also* Cintas Corp.
Unitrin Inc., 16 503–05; 78 427–31 (upd.)
Univar Corporation, 9 530–32
Universal Compression, Inc., 59 402–04
Universal Corporation, V 417–18; 48 403–06 (upd.)
Universal Electronics Inc., 39 405–08
Universal Foods Corporation, 7 546–48 *see also* Sensient Technologies Corp.
Universal Forest Products, Inc., 10 539–40; 59 405–09 (upd.)
Universal Health Services, Inc., 6 191–93
Universal International, Inc., 25 510–11
Universal Manufacturing Company, 88 423–26
Universal Security Instruments, Inc., 96 434–37
Universal Stainless & Alloy Products, Inc., 75 386–88
Universal Studios, Inc., 33 429–33; 100 423–29 (upd.)
Universal Technical Institute, Inc., 81 396–99

The University of Chicago Press, 79 451–55
University of Phoenix *see* Apollo Group, Inc.
Univision Communications Inc., 24 515–18; 83 434–439 (upd.)
UNM *see* United News & Media plc.
Uno Restaurant Holdings Corporation, 18 538–40; 70 334–37 (upd.)
Unocal Corporation, IV 569–71; 24 519–23 (upd.); 71 378–84 (upd.)
UNUM Corp., 13 538–40
UnumProvident Corporation, 52 376–83 (upd.)
Uny Co., Ltd., V 209–10; 49 425–28 (upd.)
UOB *see* United Overseas Bank Ltd.
UPC *see* United Pan-Europe Communications NV.
UPI *see* United Press International.
Upjohn Company, I 707–09; 8 547–49 (upd.) *see also* Pharmacia & Upjohn Inc.; Pfizer Inc.
UPM-Kymmene Corporation, 19 461–65; 50 505–11 (upd.)
The Upper Deck Company, LLC, 105 462–66
UPS *see* United Parcel Service, Inc.
Uralita S.A., 96 438–41
Urban Engineers, Inc., 102 435–38
Urban Outfitters, Inc., 14 524–26; 74 367–70 (upd.)
Urbi Desarrollos Urbanos, S.A. de C.V., 81 400–03
Urbium PLC, 75 389–91
URS Corporation, 45 420–23; 80 397–400 (upd.)
URSI *see* United Road Services, Inc.
US *see also* U.S.
US Airways Group, Inc., I 131–32; 6 131–32 (upd.); 28 506–09 (upd.); 52 384–88 (upd.)
US 1 Industries, Inc., 89 475–78
USA Interactive, Inc., 47 418–22 (upd.)
USA Mobility Inc., 97 437–40 (upd.)
USA Truck, Inc., 42 410–13
USAA, 10 541–43; 62 385–88 (upd.)
USANA, Inc., 29 491–93
USCC *see* United States Cellular Corp.
USF&G Corporation, III 395–98 *see also* The St. Paul Companies.
USG Corporation, III 762–64; 26 507–10 (upd.); 81 404–10 (upd.)
Ushio Inc., 91 496–99
Usinas Siderúrgicas de Minas Gerais S.A., 77 454–57
Usinger's Famous Sausage *see* Fred Usinger Inc.
Usinor SA, IV 226–28; 42 414–17 (upd.)
USO *see* United Service Organizations.
USPS *see* United States Postal Service.
USSC *see* United States Surgical Corp.
UST Inc., 9 533–35; 50 512–17 (upd.)
USX Corporation, IV 572–74; 7 549–52 (upd.) *see also* United States Steel Corp.
Utah Medical Products, Inc., 36 496–99

Utah Power and Light Company, 27 483–86 *see also* PacifiCorp.
UTG Inc., 100 430–33
Utilicorp United Inc., 6 592–94 *see also* Aquilla, Inc.
UTStarcom, Inc., 77 458–61
UTV *see* Ulster Television PLC.
Utz Quality Foods, Inc., 72 358–60
UUNET, 38 468–72
Uwajimaya, Inc., 60 312–14
Uzbekistan Airways National Air Company, 99 470–473

V

V&S Vin & Sprit AB, 91 504–11 (upd.)
VA TECH ELIN EBG GmbH, 49 429–31
Vail Resorts, Inc., 11 543–46; 43 435–39 (upd.)
Vaillant GmbH, 44 436–39
Vaisala Oyj, 104 459–63
Valassis Communications, Inc., 8 550–51; 37 407–10 (upd.); 76 364–67 (upd.)
Valeo, 23 492–94; 66 350–53 (upd.)
Valero Energy Corporation, 7 553–55; 71 385–90 (upd.)
Valhi, Inc., 19 466–68; 94 431–35 (upd.)
Vallen Corporation, 45 424–26
Valley Media Inc., 35 430–33
Valley National Gases, Inc., 85 434–37
Valley Proteins, Inc., 91 500–03
ValleyCrest Companies, 81 411–14 (upd.)
Vallourec SA, 54 391–94
Valmet Oy, III 647–49 *see also* Metso Corp.
Valmont Industries, Inc., 19 469–72
Valora Holding AG, 98 425–28
Valorem S.A., 88 427–30
Valores Industriales S.A., 19 473–75
The Valspar Corporation, 8 552–54; 32 483–86 (upd.); 77 462–68 (upd.)
Value City Department Stores, Inc., 38 473–75 *see also* Retail Ventures, Inc.
Value Line, Inc., 16 506–08; 73 358–61 (upd.)
Value Merchants Inc., 13 541–43
ValueClick, Inc., 49 432–34
ValueVision International, Inc., 22 534–36
Valve Corporation, 101 483–86
Van Camp Seafood Company, Inc., 7 556–57 *see also* Chicken of the Sea International.
Van de Velde S.A./NV, 102 439–43
Van Hool S.A./NV, 96 442–45
Van Houtte Inc., 39 409–11
Van Lanschot NV, 79 456–59
Van Leer N.V. *see* Royal Packaging Industries Van Leer N.V.; Greif Inc.
Vance Publishing Corporation, 64 398–401
Vanderbilt University Medical Center, 99 474–477
The Vanguard Group, Inc., 14 530–32; 34 486–89 (upd.)

Index to Industries

Accounting

American Institute of Certified Public Accountants (AICPA), 44
Andersen, 29 (upd.); 68 (upd.)
Automatic Data Processing, Inc., III; 9 (upd.); 47 (upd.)
BDO Seidman LLP, 96
BKD LLP, 96
CROSSMARK, 79
Deloitte Touche Tohmatsu International, 9; 29 (upd.)
Ernst & Young, 9; 29 (upd.)
FTI Consulting, Inc., 77
Grant Thornton International, 57
Huron Consulting Group Inc., 87
JKH Holding Co. LLC, 105
KPMG International, 33 (upd.)
L.S. Starrett Co., 13
McLane Company, Inc., 13
NCO Group, Inc., 42
Paychex, Inc., 15; 46 (upd.)
PKF International 78
Plante & Moran, LLP, 71
PRG-Schultz International, Inc., 73
PricewaterhouseCoopers, 9; 29 (upd.)
Resources Connection, Inc., 81
Robert Wood Johnson Foundation, 35
RSM McGladrey Business Services Inc., 98
Saffery Champness, 80
Sanders\Wingo, 99
Schenck Business Solutions, 88
StarTek, Inc., 79
Travelzoo Inc., 79
Univision Communications Inc., 24; 83 (upd.)

Advertising & Other Business Services

ABM Industries Incorporated, 25 (upd.)
Abt Associates Inc., 95
AchieveGlobal Inc., 90
Ackerley Communications, Inc., 9
ACNielsen Corporation, 13; 38 (upd.)
Acosta Sales and Marketing Company, Inc., 77
Acsys, Inc., 44
Adecco S.A., 36 (upd.)
Adelman Travel Group, 105
Adia S.A., 6
Administaff, Inc., 52
The Advertising Council, Inc., 76
The Advisory Board Company, 80
Advo, Inc., 6; 53 (upd.)
Aegis Group plc, 6
Affiliated Computer Services, Inc., 61
AHL Services, Inc., 27
Allegis Group, Inc., 95
Alloy, Inc., 55
Amdocs Ltd., 47
American Building Maintenance Industries, Inc., 6
American Library Association, 86
The American Society of Composers, Authors and Publishers (ASCAP), 29
Amey Plc, 47
Analysts International Corporation, 36
aQuantive, Inc., 81
The Arbitron Company, 38
Ariba, Inc., 57
Armor Holdings, Inc., 27
Asatsu-DK Inc., 82
Ashtead Group plc, 34
The Associated Press, 13
Avalon Correctional Services, Inc., 75

Bain & Company, 55
Barrett Business Services, Inc., 16
Barton Protective Services Inc., 53
Bates Worldwide, Inc., 14; 33 (upd.)
Bearings, Inc., 13
Berlitz International, Inc., 13
Bernard Hodes Group Inc., 86
Bernstein-Rein, 92
Big Flower Press Holdings, Inc., 21
Billing Concepts, Inc., 26; 72 (upd.)
Billing Services Group Ltd., 102
The BISYS Group, Inc., 73
Booz Allen Hamilton Inc., 10; 101 (upd.)
Boron, LePore & Associates, Inc., 45
The Boston Consulting Group, 58
Bozell Worldwide Inc., 25
BrandPartners Group, Inc., 58
Bright Horizons Family Solutions, Inc., 31
Broadcast Music Inc., 23; 90 (upd.)
Buck Consultants, Inc., 55
Bureau Veritas SA, 55
Burke, Inc., 88
Burns International Services Corporation, 13; 41 (upd.)
Cambridge Technology Partners, Inc., 36
Campbell-Ewald Advertising, 86
Campbell-Mithun-Esty, Inc., 16
Cannon Design, 63
Capario, 104
Capita Group PLC, 69
Cardtronics, Inc., 93
Career Education Corporation, 45
Carmichael Lynch Inc., 28
Cash Systems, Inc., 93
Cazenove Group plc, 72
CCC Information Services Group Inc., 74
CDI Corporation, 6; 54 (upd.)
Cegedim S.A., 104
Central Parking System, 18; 104 (upd.)

Aerospace

Airlines

Malév Plc, 24
Malaysian Airlines System Berhad, 6; 29
    (upd.); 97 (upd.)
Mesa Air Group, Inc., 11; 32 (upd.); 77
    (upd.)
Mesaba Holdings, Inc., 28
Middle East Airlines - Air Liban S.A.L.,
    79
Midway Airlines Corporation, 33
Midwest Air Group, Inc., 35; 85 (upd.)
MN Airlines LLC, 104
NetJets Inc., 96 (upd.)
Northwest Airlines Corporation, I; 6
    (upd.); 26 (upd.); 74 (upd.)
Offshore Logistics, Inc., 37
Pakistan International Airlines
    Corporation, 46
Pan American World Airways, Inc., I; 12
    (upd.)
Panalpina World Transport (Holding)
    Ltd., 47
People Express Airlines, Inc., I
Petroleum Helicopters, Inc., 35
PHI, Inc., 80 (upd.)
Philippine Airlines, Inc., 6; 23 (upd.)
Pinnacle Airlines Corp., 73
Preussag AG, 42 (upd.)
Qantas Airways Ltd., 6; 24 (upd.); 68
    (upd.)
Qatar Airways Company Q.C.S.C., 87
Reno Air Inc., 23
Royal Brunei Airlines Sdn Bhd, 99
Royal Nepal Airline Corporation, 41
Ryanair Holdings plc, 35
SAA (Pty) Ltd., 28
Sabena S.A./N.V., 33
The SAS Group, 34 (upd.)
Saudi Arabian Airlines, 6; 27 (upd.)
Scandinavian Airlines System, I
Sikorsky Aircraft Corporation, 24; 104
    (upd.)
Singapore Airlines Limited, 6; 27 (upd.);
    83 (upd.)
SkyWest, Inc., 25
Société d'Exploitation AOM Air Liberté
    SA (AirLib), 53
Société Luxembourgeoise de Navigation
    Aérienne S.A., 64
Société Tunisienne de l'Air-Tunisair, 49
Southwest Airlines Co., 6; 24 (upd.); 71
    (upd.)
Spirit Airlines, Inc., 31
Sterling European Airlines A/S, 70
Sun Country Airlines, 30
Swiss Air Transport Company, Ltd., I
Swiss International Air Lines Ltd., 48
TAM Linhas Aéreas S.A., 68
TAME (Transportes Aéreos Militares
    Ecuatorianos), 100
TAP—Air Portugal Transportes Aéreos
    Portugueses S.A., 46
TAROM S.A., 64
Texas Air Corporation, I
Thai Airways International Public
    Company Limited, 6; 27 (upd.)
Tower Air, Inc., 28
Trans World Airlines, Inc., I; 12 (upd.);
    35 (upd.)

TransBrasil S/A Linhas Aéreas, 31
Transportes Aereos Portugueses, S.A., 6
Turkish Airlines Inc. (Türk Hava Yollari
    A.O.), 72
TV Guide, Inc., 43 (upd.)
UAL Corporation, 34 (upd.)
United Airlines, I; 6 (upd.)
US Airways Group, Inc., I; 6 (upd.); 28
    (upd.); 52 (upd.)
VARIG S.A. (Viação Aérea
    Rio-Grandense), 6; 29 (upd.)
Virgin Group Ltd., 12; 32 (upd.); 89
    (upd.)
Volga-Dnepr Group, 82
Vueling Airlines S.A., 97
WestJet Airlines Ltd., 38
Uzbekistan Airways National Air
    Company, 99

Automotive

AB Volvo, I; 7 (upd.); 26 (upd.); 67
    (upd.)
Accubuilt, Inc., 74
Adam Opel AG, 7; 21 (upd.); 61 (upd.)
ADESA, Inc., 71
Advance Auto Parts, Inc., 57
Aftermarket Technology Corp., 83
Aisin Seiki Co., Ltd., 48 (upd.)
Alamo Rent A Car, Inc., 6; 24 (upd.); 84
    (upd.)
Alfa Romeo, 13; 36 (upd.)
Alvis Plc, 47
America's Car-Mart, Inc., 64
American Motors Corporation, I
Amerigon Incorporated, 97
Applied Power Inc., 32 (upd.)
Arnold Clark Automobiles Ltd., 60
ArvinMeritor, Inc., 8; 54 (upd.)
Asbury Automotive Group Inc., 60
ASC, Inc., 55
Autobacs Seven Company Ltd., 76
Autocam Corporation, 51
Autoliv, Inc., 65
Automobiles Citroen, 7
Automobili Lamborghini Holding S.p.A.,
    13; 34 (upd.); 91 (upd.)
AutoNation, Inc., 50
AutoTrader.com, L.L.C., 91
AVTOVAZ Joint Stock Company, 65
Bajaj Auto Limited, 39
Bayerische Motoren Werke AG, I; 11
    (upd.); 38 (upd.)
Belron International Ltd., 76
Bendix Corporation, I
Blue Bird Corporation, 35
Bombardier Inc., 42 (upd.)
BorgWarner Inc., 14; 32 (upd.); 85 (upd.)
The Budd Company, 8
Bugatti Automobiles S.A.S., 94
Caffyns PLC, 105
Canadian Tire Corporation, Limited, 71
    (upd.)
CarMax, Inc., 55
CARQUEST Corporation, 29
Caterpillar Inc., 63 (upd.)
Checker Motors Corp., 89
China Automotive Systems Inc., 87
China FAW Group Corporation, 105

Chrysler Corporation, I; 11 (upd.)
Commercial Vehicle Group, Inc., 81
CNH Global N.V., 38 (upd.); 99 (upd.)
Consorcio G Grupo Dina, S.A. de C.V.,
    36
Crown Equipment Corporation, 15; 93
    (upd.)
CSK Auto Corporation, 38
Cummins Engine Company, Inc., I; 12
    (upd.); 40 (upd.)
Custom Chrome, Inc., 16
Daihatsu Motor Company, Ltd., 7; 21
    (upd.)
Daimler-Benz A.G., I; 15 (upd.)
DaimlerChrysler AG, 34 (upd.); 64 (upd.)
Dana Holding Corporation, I; 10 (upd.);
    99 (upd.)
Danaher Corporation, 77 (upd.)
Deere & Company, 42 (upd.)
Delphi Automotive Systems Corporation,
    45
D'Ieteren S.A./NV, 98
Directed Electronics, Inc., 87
Discount Tire Company Inc., 84
Don Massey Cadillac, Inc., 37
Donaldson Company, Inc., 49 (upd.)
Dongfeng Motor Corporation, 105
Douglas & Lomason Company, 16
Dräxlmaier Group, 90
DriveTime Automotive Group Inc., 68
    (upd.)
Ducati Motor Holding SpA, 30; 86 (upd.)
Eaton Corporation, I; 10 (upd.); 67
    (upd.)
Echlin Inc., I; 11 (upd.)
Edelbrock Corporation, 37
Europcar Groupe S.A., 104
Faurecia S.A., 70
Federal-Mogul Corporation, I; 10 (upd.);
    26 (upd.)
Ferrara Fire Apparatus, Inc., 84
Ferrari S.p.A., 13; 36 (upd.)
Fiat SpA, I; 11 (upd.); 50 (upd.)
FinishMaster, Inc., 24
Force Protection Inc., 95
Ford Motor Company, I; 11 (upd.); 36
    (upd.); 64 (upd.)
Ford Motor Company, S.A. de C.V., 20
Fruehauf Corporation, I
General Motors Corporation, I; 10 (upd.);
    36 (upd.); 64 (upd.)
Gentex Corporation, 26
Genuine Parts Company, 9; 45 (upd.)
GKN plc, III; 38 (upd.); 89 (upd.)
Group 1 Automotive, Inc., 52
Groupe Henri Heuliez S.A., 100
Grupo Ficosa International, 90
Guardian Industries Corp., 87
Harley-Davidson Inc., 7; 25 (upd.)
Hastings Manufacturing Company, 56
Hayes Lemmerz International, Inc., 27
Hendrick Motorsports, Inc., 89
The Hertz Corporation, 9; 33 (upd.); 101
    (upd.)
Hino Motors, Ltd., 7; 21 (upd.)
Holden Ltd., 62
Holley Performance Products Inc., 52
Hometown Auto Retailers, Inc., 44

Beverages

Conglomerates

Construction

Containers

Drugs & Pharmaceuticals

Electrical & Electronics

Engineering & Management Services

VA TECH ELIN EBG GmbH, 49
VECO International, Inc., 7
Vinci, 43
Volkert and Associates, Inc., 98
The Weir Group PLC, 85
Willbros Group, Inc., 56
WS Atkins Plc, 45

Entertainment & Leisure

A&E Television Networks, 32
Aardman Animations Ltd., 61
ABC Family Worldwide, Inc., 52
Academy of Television Arts & Sciences,
   Inc., 55
Acclaim Entertainment Inc., 24
Activision, Inc., 32; 89 (upd.)
Adelman Travel Group, 105
AEI Music Network Inc., 35
Affinity Group Holding Inc., 56
Airtours Plc, 27
Alaska Railroad Corporation, 60
All American Communications Inc., 20
The All England Lawn Tennis & Croquet
   Club, 54
Allgemeiner Deutscher Automobil-Club
   e.V., 100
Alliance Entertainment Corp., 17
Alternative Tentacles Records, 66
Alvin Ailey Dance Foundation, Inc., 52
Amblin Entertainment, 21
AMC Entertainment Inc., 12; 35 (upd.)
American Golf Corporation, 45
American Gramaphone LLC, 52
American Kennel Club, Inc., 74
American Skiing Company, 28
Ameristar Casinos, Inc., 33; 69 (upd.)
AMF Bowling, Inc., 40
Anaheim Angels Baseball Club, Inc., 53
Anchor Gaming, 24
AOL Time Warner Inc., 57 (upd.)
Applause Inc., 24
Apple Corps Ltd., 87
Aprilia SpA, 17
Arena Leisure Plc, 99
Argosy Gaming Company, 21
Aristocrat Leisure Limited, 54
Arsenal Holdings PLC, 79
The Art Institute of Chicago, 29
The Arthur C. Clarke Foundation, 92
Artisan Entertainment Inc., 32 (upd.)
Asahi National Broadcasting Company,
   Ltd., 9
Aspen Skiing Company, 15
Aston Villa plc, 41
The Athletics Investment Group, 62
Atlanta National League Baseball Club,
   Inc., 43
The Atlantic Group, 23
Autotote Corporation, 20
Aztar Corporation, 13
Bad Boy Worldwide Entertainment
   Group, 58
Baker & Taylor Corporation, 16; 43
   (upd.)
Bally Total Fitness Holding Corp., 25
Baltimore Orioles L.P., 66
Barden Companies, Inc., 76
The Baseball Club of Seattle, LP, 50

The Basketball Club of Seattle, LLC, 50
Beggars Group Ltd., 99
Bertelsmann A.G., IV; 15 (upd.); 43
   (upd.); 91 (upd.)
Bertucci's Inc., 16
Big Idea Productions, Inc., 49
BigBen Interactive S.A., 72
BioWare Corporation, 81
Blockbuster Inc., 9; 31 (upd.); 76 (upd.)
Boca Resorts, Inc., 37
Bonneville International Corporation, 29
Booth Creek Ski Holdings, Inc., 31
Boston Celtics Limited Partnership, 14
Boston Professional Hockey Association
   Inc., 39
The Boston Symphony Orchestra Inc., 93
The Boy Scouts of America, 34
Boyne USA Resorts, 71
Brillstein-Grey Entertainment, 80
British Broadcasting Corporation Ltd., 7;
   21 (upd.); 89 (upd.)
The British Film Institute, 80
The British Museum, 71
British Sky Broadcasting Group plc, 20;
   60 (upd.)
Brunswick Corporation, III; 22 (upd.); 77
   (upd.)
Busch Entertainment Corporation, 73
Cablevision Systems Corporation, 7
California Sports, Inc., 56
Callaway Golf Company, 45 (upd.)
Canlan Ice Sports Corp., 105
Canterbury Park Holding Corporation, 42
Capcom Company Ltd., 83
Capital Cities/ABC Inc., II
Capitol Records, Inc., 90
Carlson Companies, Inc., 6; 22 (upd.); 87
   (upd.)
Carlson Wagonlit Travel, 55
Carmike Cinemas, Inc., 14; 37 (upd.); 74
   (upd.)
The Carnegie Hall Corporation, 101
Carnival Corporation, 6; 27 (upd.); 78
   (upd.)
Carrere Group S.A., 104
The Carsey-Werner Company, L.L.C., 37
CBS Inc., II; 6 (upd.)
Cedar Fair Entertainment Company, 22;
   98 (upd.)
Central European Media Enterprises Ltd.,
   61
Central Independent Television, 7; 23
   (upd.)
Century Casinos, Inc., 53
Century Theatres, Inc., 31
Championship Auto Racing Teams, Inc.,
   37
Channel Four Television Corporation, 93
Chello Zone Ltd., 93
Chelsea Ltd., 102
Chelsea Piers Management Inc., 86
Chicago Bears Football Club, Inc., 33
Chicago National League Ball Club, Inc.,
   66
Chris-Craft Corporation, 9, 31 (upd.); 80
   (upd.)
Chrysalis Group plc, 40
Churchill Downs Incorporated, 29

Cinar Corporation, 40
Cinemark Holdings, Inc., 95
Cinemas de la República, S.A. de C.V., 83
Cineplex Odeon Corporation, 6; 23
   (upd.)
Cinram International, Inc., 43
Cirque du Soleil Inc., 29; 98 (upd.)
CKX, Inc., 102
Classic Vacation Group, Inc., 46
Cleveland Indians Baseball Company, Inc.,
   37
Club Méditerranée S.A., 6; 21 (upd.); 91
   (upd.)
ClubCorp, Inc., 33
CMG Worldwide, Inc., 89
Colonial Williamsburg Foundation, 53
Colorado Baseball Management, Inc., 72
Columbia Pictures Entertainment, Inc., II
Columbia TriStar Motion Pictures
   Companies, 12 (upd.)
Comcast Corporation, 7
Compagnie des Alpes, 48
Confluence Holdings Corporation, 76
Continental Cablevision, Inc., 7
Corporación Interamericana de
   Entretenimiento, S.A. de C.V., 83
Corporation for Public Broadcasting, 14;
   89 (upd.)
Cox Enterprises, Inc., IV; 22 (upd.); 67
   (upd.)
Cranium, Inc., 69
Crown Media Holdings, Inc., 45
Cruise America Inc., 21
Cunard Line Ltd., 23
Cyan Worlds Inc., 101
Dallas Cowboys Football Club, Ltd., 33
Dave & Buster's, Inc., 33; 104 (upd.)
Death Row Records, 27
Deluxe Entertainment Services Group,
   Inc., 100
Denver Nuggets, 51
The Detroit Lions, Inc., 55
The Detroit Pistons Basketball Company,
   41
Detroit Red Wings, 74
Detroit Tigers Baseball Club, Inc., 46
Deutsche Fussball Bund e.V., 98
dick clark productions, inc., 16
DIRECTV, Inc., 38; 75 (upd.)
Dover Downs Entertainment, Inc., 43
DreamWorks SKG, 43
Dualstar Entertainment Group LLC, 76
E! Entertainment Television Inc., 17
edel music AG, 44
Educational Broadcasting Corporation, 48
Edwards Theatres Circuit, Inc., 31
Egmont Group, 93
Electronic Arts Inc., 10; 85 (upd.)
Elektra Entertainment Group, 64
Elsinore Corporation, 48
Elvis Presley Enterprises, Inc., 61
Empire Resorts, Inc., 72
Endemol Entertainment Holding NV, 46
Entertainment Distribution Company, 89
Equity Marketing, Inc., 26
ESPN, Inc., 56
Esporta plc, 35
Euro Disney S.C.A., 20; 58 (upd.)

Financial Services: Banks

Metris Companies Inc., 56
Morgan Grenfell Group PLC, II
Morgan Stanley Dean Witter &
 Company, II; 16 (upd.); 33 (upd.)
Mountain States Mortgage Centers, Inc.,
 29
NASD, 54 (upd.)
The NASDAQ Stock Market, Inc., 92
National Association of Securities Dealers,
 Inc., 10
National Auto Credit, Inc., 16
National Discount Brokers Group, Inc.,
 28
National Financial Partners Corp., 65
Navy Federal Credit Union, 33
Neuberger Berman Inc., 57
New Street Capital Inc., 8
New York Stock Exchange, Inc., 9; 39
 (upd.)
The Nikko Securities Company Limited,
 II; 9 (upd.)
Nippon Shinpan Co., Ltd., II; 61 (upd.)
Nomura Securities Company, Limited, II;
 9 (upd.)
Norwich & Peterborough Building
 Society, 55
NovaStar Financial, Inc., 91
Oaktree Capital Management, LLC, 71
Old Mutual PLC, 61
Ontario Teachers' Pension Plan, 61
Onyx Acceptance Corporation, 59
ORIX Corporation, II; 44 (upd.); 104
 (upd.)
PaineWebber Group Inc., II; 22 (upd.)
PayPal Inc., 58
The Pew Charitable Trusts, 35
Piper Jaffray Companies Inc., 22
Pitney Bowes Inc., 47 (upd.)
Providian Financial Corporation, 52
 (upd.)
Prudential Financial Inc., III; 30 (upd.);
 82 (upd.)
The Quick & Reilly Group, Inc., 20
Quicken Loans, Inc., 93
Rathbone Brothers plc, 70
Raymond James Financial Inc., 69
Resource America, Inc., 42
Robert W. Baird & Co. Incorporated, 67
Ryan Beck & Co., Inc., 66
Safeguard Scientifics, Inc., 10
St. James's Place Capital, plc, 71
Salomon Inc., II; 13 (upd.)
Sanders Morris Harris Group Inc., 70
Sanlam Ltd., 68
SBC Warburg, 14
Schroders plc, 42
Scottrade, Inc., 85
SEI Investments Company, 96
Shearson Lehman Brothers Holdings Inc.,
 II; 9 (upd.)
Siebert Financial Corp., 32
Skipton Building Society, 80
SLM Holding Corp., 25 (upd.)
Smith Barney Inc., 15
Soros Fund Management LLC, 28
Spear, Leeds & Kellogg, 66
State Street Boston Corporation, 8
Stephens Inc., 92

Student Loan Marketing Association, II
Sun Life Financial Inc., 85
T. Rowe Price Associates, Inc., 11; 34
 (upd.)
Teachers Insurance and Annuity
 Association-College Retirement Equities
 Fund, 45 (upd.)
Texas Pacific Group Inc., 36
3i Group PLC, 73
Total System Services, Inc., 18
TradeStation Group, Inc., 83
Trilon Financial Corporation, II
United Jewish Communities, 33
The Vanguard Group, Inc., 14; 34 (upd.)
VeriFone Holdings, Inc., 18; 76 (upd.)
Viel & Cie, 76
Visa Inc., 9; 26 (upd.); 104 (upd.)
Wachovia Corporation, 12; 46 (upd.)
Waddell & Reed, Inc., 22
Washington Federal, Inc., 17
Waterhouse Investor Services, Inc., 18
Watson Wyatt Worldwide, 42
Western Union Financial Services, Inc., 54
WFS Financial Inc., 70
Working Assets Funding Service, 43
World Acceptance Corporation, 57
Yamaichi Securities Company, Limited, II
The Ziegler Companies, Inc., 24; 63
 (upd.)
Zurich Financial Services, 42 (upd.); 93
 (upd.)

Food Products

A. Duda & Sons, Inc., 88
A. Moksel AG, 59
Adecoagro LLC, 101
Agri Beef Company, 81
Agway, Inc., 7
Ajinomoto Co., Inc., II; 28 (upd.)
Alabama Farmers Cooperative, Inc., 63
The Albert Fisher Group plc, 41
Alberto-Culver Company, 8; 36 (upd.); 91
 (upd.)
Alfred Ritter GmbH & Co. KG, 58
Alfesca hf, 82
Allen Brothers, Inc., 101
Allen Canning Company, 76
Alpine Confections, Inc., 71
Alpine Lace Brands, Inc., 18
American Crystal Sugar Company, 11; 32
 (upd.)
American Foods Group, 43
American Italian Pasta Company, 27; 76
 (upd.)
American Licorice Company, 86
American Maize-Products Co., 14
American Pop Corn Company, 59
American Rice, Inc., 33
Amfac/JMB Hawaii L.L.C., 24 (upd.)
Amy's Kitchen Inc., 76
Annie's Homegrown, Inc., 59
Archer-Daniels-Midland Company, 32
 (upd.)
Archway Cookies, Inc., 29
Arcor S.A.I.C., 66
Arla Foods amba, 48
Arnott's Ltd., 66
Artisan Confections Company, 103

Asher's Chocolates, Inc., 103
Associated British Foods plc, II; 13 (upd.);
 41 (upd.)
Associated Milk Producers, Inc., 11; 48
 (upd.)
Atkinson Candy Company, 87
Atlantic Premium Brands, Ltd., 57
August Storck KG, 66
Aurora Foods Inc., 32
Auvil Fruit Company, Inc., 95
Awrey Bakeries, Inc., 56
B&G Foods, Inc., 40
The B. Manischewitz Company, LLC, 31
Bahlsen GmbH & Co. KG, 44
Bakkavör Group hf., 91
Balance Bar Company, 32
Baldwin Richardson Foods Company, 100
Baltek Corporation, 34
The Bama Companies, Inc., 80
Bar-S Foods Company, 76
Barbara's Bakery Inc., 88
Barilla G. e R. Fratelli S.p.A., 17; 50
 (upd.)
Barry Callebaut AG, 71 (upd.)
Baxters Food Group Ltd., 99
Bear Creek Corporation, 38
Beatrice Company, II
Beech-Nut Nutrition Corporation, 21; 51
 (upd.)
Beer Nuts, Inc., 86
Bel/Kaukauna USA, 76
Bellisio Foods, Inc., 95
Ben & Jerry's Homemade, Inc., 10; 35
 (upd.); 80 (upd.)
Berkeley Farms, Inc., 46
Bernard Matthews Ltd., 89
Besnier SA, 19
Best Kosher Foods Corporation, 82
Bestfoods, 22 (upd.)
Betsy Ann Candies, Inc., 105
Better Made Snack Foods, Inc., 90
Bettys & Taylors of Harrogate Ltd., 72
Birds Eye Foods, Inc., 69 (upd.)
Blue Bell Creameries L.P., 30
Blue Diamond Growers, 28
Bob's Red Mill Natural Foods, Inc., 63
Bobs Candies, Inc., 70
Bolton Group B.V., 86
Bonduelle SA, 51
Bongrain S.A., 25; 102 (upd.)
Booker PLC, 13; 31 (upd.)
Borden, Inc., II; 22 (upd.)
Boyd Coffee Company, 53
Brach and Brock Confections, Inc., 15
Brake Bros plc, 45
Bridgford Foods Corporation, 27
Brigham's Inc., 72
Brioche Pasquier S.A., 58
British Sugar plc, 84
Brossard S.A., 102
Brothers Gourmet Coffees, Inc., 20
Broughton Foods Co., 17
Brown & Haley, 23
Bruce Foods Corporation, 39
Bruegger's Corporation, 63
Bruster's Real Ice Cream, Inc., 80
BSN Groupe S.A., II
Bumble Bee Seafoods L.L.C., 64

Health & Personal Care Products

Hotels

Information Technology

Manatron, Inc., 86
ManTech International Corporation, 97
MAPICS, Inc., 55
Maryville Data Systems Inc., 96
Match.com, LP, 87
The MathWorks, Inc., 80
Maxtor Corporation, 10
Mead Data Central, Inc., 10
Mecklermedia Corporation, 24
MEDecision, Inc., 95
Media Sciences International, Inc., 104
Medical Information Technology Inc., 64
Mentor Graphics Corporation, 11
Mercury Interactive Corporation, 59
Merge Healthcare, 85
Merisel, Inc., 12
Metatec International, Inc., 47
Metavante Corporation, 100
Metro Information Services, Inc., 36
Micro Warehouse, Inc., 16
Micron Technology, Inc., 11; 29 (upd.)
Micros Systems, Inc., 18
Microsoft Corporation, 6; 27 (upd.); 63
    (upd.)
MicroStrategy Incorporated, 87
Misys plc, 45; 46
MITRE Corporation, 26
MIVA, Inc., 83
Moldflow Corporation, 73
Morningstar Inc., 68
The Motley Fool, Inc., 40
National Research Corporation, 87
National Semiconductor Corporation, 6
National TechTeam, Inc., 41
National Weather Service, 91
Navarre Corporation, 24
NAVTEQ Corporation, 69
NCR Corporation, III; 6 (upd.); 30
    (upd.); 90 (upd.)
NetCracker Technology Corporation, 98
Netezza Corporation, 69
NetIQ Corporation, 79
Netscape Communications Corporation,
    15; 35 (upd.)
Network Appliance, Inc., 58
Network Associates, Inc., 25
Nextel Communications, Inc., 10
NFO Worldwide, Inc., 24
NICE Systems Ltd., 83
Nichols Research Corporation, 18
Nimbus CD International, Inc., 20
Nixdorf Computer AG, III
Noah Education Holdings Ltd., 97
Novell, Inc., 6; 23 (upd.)
NVIDIA Corporation, 54
Océ N.V., 24; 91 (upd.)
OCLC Online Computer Library Center,
    Inc., 96
Odetics Inc., 14
Onyx Software Corporation, 53
Open Text Corporation, 79
Openwave Systems Inc., 95
Opsware Inc., 49
Oracle Corporation, 6; 24 (upd.); 67
    (upd.)
Orbitz, Inc., 61
Overland Storage Inc., 100
Packard Bell Electronics, Inc., 13

Packeteer, Inc., 81
Parametric Technology Corp., 16
PC Connection, Inc., 37
Pegasus Solutions, Inc., 75
PeopleSoft Inc., 14; 33 (upd.)
Perot Systems Corporation, 29
Phillips International Inc. 78
Pitney Bowes Inc., III
PLATINUM Technology, Inc., 14
Policy Management Systems Corporation,
    11
Policy Studies, Inc., 62
Portal Software, Inc., 47
Primark Corp., 13
The Princeton Review, Inc., 42
Printrak, A Motorola Company, 44
Printronix, Inc., 18
Prodigy Communications Corporation, 34
Prodware S.A., 102
Programmer's Paradise, Inc., 81
Progress Software Corporation, 15
Psion PLC, 45
QSS Group, Inc., 100
Quality Systems, Inc., 81
Quantum Corporation, 10; 62 (upd.)
Quark, Inc., 36
Quicken Loans, Inc., 93
Racal-Datacom Inc., 11
Radiant Systems Inc., 104
Razorfish, Inc., 37
RCM Technologies, Inc., 34
RealNetworks, Inc., 53
Red Hat, Inc., 45
Remedy Corporation, 58
Renaissance Learning, Inc., 39; 100 (upd.)
The Reynolds and Reynolds Company, 50
Ricoh Company, Ltd., III
Riverbed Technology, Inc., 101
Rocky Mountain Chocolate Factory, Inc.,
    73
Rolta India Ltd., 90
RSA Security Inc., 46
RWD Technologies, Inc., 76
SABRE Group Holdings, Inc., 26
SafeNet Inc., 101
The Sage Group, 43
salesforce.com, Inc., 79
The Santa Cruz Operation, Inc., 38
SAP AG, 16; 43 (upd.)
SAS Institute Inc., 10; 78 (upd.)
Satyam Computer Services Ltd., 85
SBS Technologies, Inc., 25
SCB Computer Technology, Inc., 29
Schawk, Inc., 24
Scientific Learning Corporation, 95
The SCO Group Inc., 78
SDL PLC, 67
Seagate Technology, 8; 34 (upd.); 105
    (upd.)
Siebel Systems, Inc., 38
Sierra On-Line, Inc., 15; 41 (upd.)
SilverPlatter Information Inc., 23
SINA Corporation, 69
SkillSoft Public Limited Company, 81
SmartForce PLC, 43
Softbank Corp., 13; 38 (upd.); 77 (upd.)
Sonic Solutions, Inc., 81
SonicWALL, Inc., 87

Spark Networks, Inc., 91
Specialist Computer Holdings Ltd., 80
SPSS Inc., 64
Square Enix Holdings Co., Ltd., 101
SRA International, Inc., 77
Standard Microsystems Corporation, 11
STC PLC, III
Steria SA, 49
Sterling Software, Inc., 11
Storage Technology Corporation, 6
Stratus Computer, Inc., 10
Sun Microsystems, Inc., 7; 30 (upd.); 91
    (upd.)
SunGard Data Systems Inc., 11
Sybase, Inc., 10; 27 (upd.)
Sykes Enterprises, Inc., 45
Symantec Corporation, 10; 82 (upd.)
Symbol Technologies, Inc., 15
Synchronoss Technologies, Inc., 95
SYNNEX Corporation, 73
Synopsys, Inc., 11; 69 (upd.)
Syntel, Inc., 92
System Software Associates, Inc., 10
Systems & Computer Technology Corp.,
    19
T-Online International AG, 61
TALX Corporation, 92
Tandem Computers, Inc., 6
TechTarget, Inc., 99
TenFold Corporation, 35
Terra Lycos, Inc., 43
Terremark Worldwide, Inc., 99
The Thomson Corporation, 34 (upd.); 77
    (upd.)
ThoughtWorks Inc., 90
3Com Corporation, 11; 34 (upd.)
The 3DO Company, 43
TIBCO Software Inc., 79
Timberline Software Corporation, 15
TomTom N.V., 81
TradeStation Group, Inc., 83
Traffix, Inc., 61
Transaction Systems Architects, Inc., 29;
    82 (upd.)
Transiciel SA, 48
Trend Micro Inc., 97
Triple P N.V., 26
Tripwire, Inc., 97
The TriZetto Group, Inc., 83
Tucows Inc. 78
Ubi Soft Entertainment S.A., 41
Unica Corporation, 77
Unilog SA, 42
Unisys Corporation, III; 6 (upd.); 36
    (upd.)
United Business Media plc, 52 (upd.)
United Internet AG, 99
United Online, Inc., 71 (upd.)
United Press International, Inc., 73 (upd.)
UUNET, 38
VASCO Data Security International, Inc.,
    79
Verbatim Corporation, 14
Veridian Corporation, 54
VeriFone Holdings, Inc., 18; 76 (upd.)
Verint Systems Inc., 73
VeriSign, Inc., 47
Veritas Software Corporation, 45

Insurance

Manufacturing

Zindart Ltd., 60
Zippo Manufacturing Company, 18; 71 (upd.)
Zodiac S.A., 36
Zygo Corporation, 42

Materials

AK Steel Holding Corporation, 19
American Biltrite Inc., 16
American Colloid Co., 13
American Standard Inc., III
Ameriwood Industries International Corp., 17
Anhui Conch Cement Company Limited, 99
Apasco S.A. de C.V., 51
Apogee Enterprises, Inc., 8
Asahi Glass Company, Limited, III
Asbury Carbons, Inc., 68
Bairnco Corporation, 28
Bayou Steel Corporation, 31
Berry Plastics Group Inc., 21; 98 (upd.)
Blessings Corp., 19
Blue Circle Industries PLC, III
Bodycote International PLC, 63
Boral Limited, III; 43 (upd.); 103 (upd.)
British Vita plc, 9; 33 (upd.)
Brush Engineered Materials Inc., 67
Bryce Corporation, 100
California Steel Industries, Inc., 67
Callanan Industries, Inc., 60
Cameron & Barkley Company, 28
Carborundum Company, 15
Carl Zeiss AG, III; 34 (upd.); 91 (upd.)
Carlisle Companies Inc., 8; 82 (upd.)
Carter Holt Harvey Ltd., 70
Cementos Argos S.A., 91
Cemex SA de CV, 20
Century Aluminum Company, 52
CertainTeed Corporation, 35
Chargeurs International, 6; 21 (upd.)
Chemfab Corporation, 35
Cimentos de Portugal SGPS S.A. (Cimpor), 76
Cold Spring Granite Company Inc., 16; 67 (upd.)
Columbia Forest Products Inc. 78
Compagnie de Saint-Gobain S.A., III; 16 (upd.)
Cookson Group plc, III; 44 (upd.)
Corning Inc., III; 44 (upd.); 90 (upd.)
CSR Limited, III; 28 (upd.); 85 (upd.)
Dal-Tile International Inc., 22
The David J. Joseph Company, 14; 76 (upd.)
The Dexter Corporation, 12 (upd.)
Dicken Masch Plastics LLC, 90
Dyckerhoff AG, 35
Dynamic Materials Corporation, 81
Dyson Group PLC, 71
ECC Group plc, III
Edw. C. Levy Co., 42
84 Lumber Company, 9; 39 (upd.)
ElkCorp, 52
Empire Resources, Inc., 81
English China Clays Ltd., 15 (upd.); 40 (upd.)
Envirodyne Industries, Inc., 17

EP Henry Corporation, 104
Feldmuhle Nobel A.G., III
Fibreboard Corporation, 16
Filtrona plc, 88
Florida Rock Industries, Inc., 46
Foamex International Inc., 17
Formica Corporation, 13
GAF Corporation, 22 (upd.)
The Geon Company, 11
Giant Cement Holding, Inc., 23
Gibraltar Steel Corporation, 37
Granite Rock Company, 26
GreenMan Technologies Inc., 99
Groupe Sidel S.A., 21
Harbison-Walker Refractories Company, 24
Harrisons & Crosfield plc, III
Heidelberger Zement AG, 31
Hexcel Corporation, 28
Holderbank Financière Glaris Ltd., III
Holnam Inc., 39 (upd.)
Holt and Bugbee Company, 66
Homasote Company, 72
Howmet Corp., 12
Huttig Building Products, Inc., 73
Ibstock Brick Ltd., 14; 37 (upd.)
Imerys S.A., 40 (upd.)
Imperial Industries, Inc., 81
Internacional de Ceramica, S.A. de C.V., 53
International Shipbreaking Ltd. L.L.C., 67
Jaiprakash Associates Limited, 101
Joseph T. Ryerson & Son, Inc., 15
Knauf Gips KG, 100
La Seda de Barcelona S.A., 100
Lafarge Coppée S.A., III
Lafarge Corporation, 28
Lehigh Portland Cement Company, 23
Loma Negra C.I.A.S.A., 95
Lyman-Richey Corporation, 96
Manville Corporation, III; 7 (upd.)
Material Sciences Corporation, 63
Matsushita Electric Works, Ltd., III; 7 (upd.)
McJunkin Corporation, 63
Medusa Corporation, 24
Mitsubishi Materials Corporation, III
Nevamar Company, 82
Nippon Sheet Glass Company, Limited, III
North Pacific Group, Inc., 61
Nuplex Industries Ltd., 92
OmniSource Corporation, 14
Onoda Cement Co., Ltd., III
Otor S.A., 77
Owens-Corning Fiberglass Corporation, III
Pacific Clay Products Inc., 88
Pilkington Group Limited, III; 34 (upd.); 87 (upd.)
Pioneer International Limited, III
PolyOne Corporation, 87 (upd.)
PPG Industries, Inc., III; 22 (upd.); 81 (upd.)
PT Semen Gresik Tbk, 103
Redland plc, III
Rinker Group Ltd., 65
RMC Group p.l.c., III

Rock of Ages Corporation, 37
Rogers Corporation, 80 (upd.)
Royal Group Technologies Limited, 73
The Rugby Group plc, 31
Scholle Corporation, 96
Schuff Steel Company, 26
Sekisui Chemical Co., Ltd., III; 72 (upd.)
Severstal Joint Stock Company, 65
Shaw Industries, 9
The Sherwin-Williams Company, III; 13 (upd.); 89 (upd.)
The Siam Cement Public Company Limited, 56
SIG plc, 71
Simplex Technologies Inc., 21
Siskin Steel & Supply Company, 70
Solutia Inc., 52
Sommer-Allibert S.A., 19
Southdown, Inc., 14
Spartech Corporation, 19; 76 (upd.)
Ssangyong Cement Industrial Co., Ltd., III; 61 (upd.)
Steel Technologies Inc., 63
Sun Distributors L.P., 12
Symyx Technologies, Inc., 77
Tarmac Limited, III, 28 (upd.); 95 (upd.)
Tergal Industries S.A.S., 102
Tilcon-Connecticut Inc., 80
TOTO LTD., III; 28 (upd.)
Toyo Sash Co., Ltd., III
Tuscarora Inc., 29
U.S. Aggregates, Inc., 42
Ube Industries, Ltd., III
United States Steel Corporation, 50 (upd.)
USG Corporation, III; 26 (upd.); 81 (upd.)
Usinas Siderúrgicas de Minas Gerais S.A., 77
Vicat S.A., 70
voestalpine AG, 57 (upd.)
Vulcan Materials Company, 7; 52 (upd.)
Wacker-Chemie GmbH, 35
Walter Industries, Inc., III
Waxman Industries, Inc., 9
Weber et Broutin France, 66
Wienerberger AG, 70
Wolseley plc, 64
ZERO Corporation, 17; 88 (upd.)
Zoltek Companies, Inc., 37

Mining & Metals

A.M. Castle & Co., 25
Acindar Industria Argentina de Aceros S.A., 87
African Rainbow Minerals Ltd., 97
Aggregate Industries plc, 36
Agnico-Eagle Mines Limited, 71
Aktiebolaget SKF, III; 38 (upd.); 89 (upd.)
Alcan Aluminium Limited, IV; 31 (upd.)
Alcoa Inc., 56 (upd.)
Alleghany Corporation, 10
Allegheny Ludlum Corporation, 8
Alliance Resource Partners, L.P., 81
Alrosa Company Ltd., 62
Altos Hornos de México, S.A. de C.V., 42
Aluminum Company of America, IV; 20 (upd.)

Potash Corporation of Saskatchewan Inc., 18; 101 (upd.)
Quanex Corporation, 13; 62 (upd.)
RAG AG, 35; 60 (upd.)
Reliance Steel & Aluminum Co., 19
Republic Engineered Steels, Inc., 7; 26 (upd.)
Reynolds Metals Company, IV
Rio Tinto PLC, 19 (upd.); 50 (upd.)
RMC Group p.l.c., 34 (upd.)
Roanoke Electric Steel Corporation, 45
Rouge Steel Company, 8
The RTZ Corporation PLC, IV
Ruhrkohle AG, IV
Ryerson Tull, Inc., 40 (upd.)
Saarberg-Konzern, IV
Salzgitter AG, IV; 101 (upd.)
Sandvik AB, IV
Saudi Basic Industries Corporation (SABIC), 58
Schmolz + Bickenbach AG, 104
Schnitzer Steel Industries, Inc., 19
Severstal Joint Stock Company, 65
Shanghai Baosteel Group Corporation, 71
Siderar S.A.I.C., 66
Silver Wheaton Corp., 95
Smorgon Steel Group Ltd., 62
Southern Peru Copper Corporation, 40
Southwire Company, Inc., 8; 23 (upd.)
SSAB Svenskt Stål AB, 89
Steel Authority of India Ltd., IV
Stelco Inc., IV
Stillwater Mining Company, 47
Sumitomo Corporation, I; 11 (upd.); 102 (upd.)
Sumitomo Metal Industries Ltd., IV; 82 (upd.)
Sumitomo Metal Mining Co., Ltd., IV
Tata Iron & Steel Co. Ltd., IV; 44 (upd.)
Teck Corporation, 27
Tenaris SA, 63
Texas Industries, Inc., 8
ThyssenKrupp AG, IV; 28 (upd.); 87 (upd.)
The Timken Company, 8; 42 (upd.)
Titanium Metals Corporation, 21
Tomen Corporation, IV
Total Fina Elf S.A., 50 (upd.)
Třinecké Železárny A.S., 92
U.S. Borax, Inc., 42
U.S. Silica Company, 104
Ugine S.A., 20
NV Umicore SA, 47
Universal Stainless & Alloy Products, Inc., 75
Uralita S.A., 96
Usinor SA, IV; 42 (upd.)
Usinor Sacilor, IV
VIAG Aktiengesellschaft, IV
Voest-Alpine Stahl AG, IV
Volcan Compañia Minera S.A.A., 92
Vulcan Materials Company, 52 (upd.)
Wah Chang, 82
Walter Industries, Inc., 22 (upd.)
Weirton Steel Corporation, IV; 26 (upd.)
Westmoreland Coal Company, 7
Wheeling-Pittsburgh Corp., 7
WHX Corporation, 98

WMC, Limited, 43
Worthington Industries, Inc., 7; 21 (upd.)
Xstrata PLC, 73
Zambia Industrial and Mining Corporation Ltd., IV
Zinifex Ltd., 85

Paper & Forestry

AbitibiBowater Inc., IV; 25 (upd.); 99 (upd.)
Albany International Corporation, 51 (upd.)
Amcor Ltd, IV; 19 (upd.); 78 (upd.)
American Greetings Corporation, 59 (upd.)
American Pad & Paper Company, 20
Aracruz Celulose S.A., 57
Arjo Wiggins Appleton p.l.c., 34
Asplundh Tree Expert Co.,20; 59 (upd.)
Avery Dennison Corporation, IV
Badger Paper Mills, Inc., 15
Beckett Papers, 23
Bemis Company, Inc., 8; 91 (upd.)
Billerud AB, 100
Blue Heron Paper Company, 90
Bohemia, Inc., 13
Boise Cascade Holdings, L.L.C.,, IV; 8 (upd.); 32 (upd.); 95 (upd.)
Bowater PLC, IV
Bunzl plc, IV
Canfor Corporation, 42
Caraustar Industries, Inc., 19; 44 (upd.)
Carter Lumber Company, 45
Cascades Inc., 71
Catalyst Paper Corporation, 105
Central National-Gottesman Inc., 95
Champion International Corporation, IV; 20 (upd.)
Chesapeake Corporation, 8; 30 (upd.); 93 (upd.)
The Collins Companies Inc., 102
Consolidated Papers, Inc., 8; 36 (upd.)
Crane & Co., Inc., 26; 103 (upd.)
Crown Vantage Inc., 29
CSS Industries, Inc., 35
Daio Paper Corporation, IV; 84 (upd.)
Daishowa Paper Manufacturing Co., Ltd., IV; 57 (upd.)
Deltic Timber Corporation, 46
Dillard Paper Company, 11
Doman Industries Limited, 59
Domtar Corporation, IV; 89 (upd.)
DS Smith Plc, 61
Empresas CMPC S.A., 70
Enso-Gutzeit Oy, IV
Esselte Pendaflex Corporation, 11
Exacompta Clairefontaine S.A., 102
Federal Paper Board Company, Inc., 8
FiberMark, Inc., 37
Fletcher Challenge Ltd., IV
Fort Howard Corporation, 8
Fort James Corporation, 22 (upd.)
Georgia-Pacific LLC, IV; 9 (upd.); 47 (upd.); 101 (upd.)
Gould Paper Corporation, 82
Graphic Packaging Holding Company, 96 (upd.)
Groupe Rougier SA, 21

Grupo Portucel Soporcel, 60
Guilbert S.A., 42
Hampton Affiliates, Inc., 77
Holmen AB, 52 (upd.)
Honshu Paper Co., Ltd., IV
International Paper Company, IV; 15 (upd.); 47 (upd.); 97 (upd.)
James River Corporation of Virginia, IV
Japan Pulp and Paper Company Limited, IV
Jefferson Smurfit Group plc, IV; 49 (upd.)
Jujo Paper Co., Ltd., IV
Kadant Inc., 96 (upd.)
Kimberly-Clark Corporation, III; 16 (upd.); 43 (upd.); 105 (upd.)
Kimberly-Clark de México, S.A. de C.V., 54
Klabin S.A., 73
Koninklijke Houthandel G Wijma & Zonen BV, 96
Kruger Inc., 17; 103 (upd.)
Kymmene Corporation, IV
Longview Fibre Company, 8; 37 (upd.)
Louisiana-Pacific Corporation, IV; 31 (upd.)
M-real Oyj, 56 (upd.)
MacMillan Bloedel Limited, IV
Matussière et Forest SA, 58
The Mead Corporation, IV; 19 (upd.)
MeadWestvaco Corporation, 76 (upd.)
Mercer International Inc., 64
Metsa-Serla Oy, IV
Metso Corporation, 30 (upd.); 85 (upd.)
Miquel y Costas Miquel S.A., 68
Mo och Domsjö AB, IV
Monadnock Paper Mills, Inc., 21
Mosinee Paper Corporation, 15
Nashua Corporation, 8
National Envelope Corporation, 32
NCH Corporation, 8
The Newark Group, Inc., 102
Norske Skogindustrier ASA, 63
Nuqul Group of Companies, 102
Oji Paper Co., Ltd., IV
P.H. Glatfelter Company, 8; 30 (upd.); 83 (upd.)
Packaging Corporation of America, 12
Papeteries de Lancey, 23
Plum Creek Timber Company, Inc., 43
Pope & Talbot, Inc., 12; 61 (upd.)
Pope Resources LP, 74
Potlatch Corporation, 8; 34 (upd.); 87 (upd.)
PWA Group, IV
Rayonier Inc., 24
Rengo Co., Ltd., IV
Reno de Medici S.p.A., 41
Rexam PLC, 32 (upd.); 85 (upd.)
Riverwood International Corporation, 11; 48 (upd.)
Rock-Tenn Company, 13; 59 (upd.)
Rogers Corporation, 61
The St. Joe Company, 8; 98 (upd.)
Sanyo-Kokusaku Pulp Co., Ltd., IV
Sappi Limited, 49
Schneidersöhne Deutschland GmbH & Co. KG, 100
Schweitzer-Mauduit International, Inc., 52

Personal Services

Petroleum

Publishing & Printing

Real Estate

Colonial Properties Trust, 65
The Corcoran Group, Inc., 58
The Corky McMillin Companies, 98
CoStar Group, Inc., 73
Cousins Properties Incorporated, 65
CSX Corporation 79 (upd.)
Cushman & Wakefield, Inc., 86
Del Webb Corporation, 14
Desarrolladora Homex, S.A. de C.V., 87
Developers Diversified Realty
    Corporation, 69
Douglas Emmett, Inc., 105
Draper and Kramer Inc., 96
Duke Realty Corporation, 57
Ducks Unlimited, Inc., 87
EastGroup Properties, Inc., 67
The Edward J. DeBartolo Corporation, 8
Enterprise Inns plc, 59
Equity Office Properties Trust, 54
Equity Residential, 49
Erickson Retirement Communities, 57
Fairfield Communities, Inc., 36
First Industrial Realty Trust, Inc., 65
Forest City Enterprises, Inc., 16; 52
    (upd.)
Gale International Llc, 93
Gecina SA, 42
General Growth Properties, Inc., 57
GMH Communities Trust, 87
Great White Shark Enterprises, Inc., 89
Griffin Land & Nurseries, Inc., 43
Grubb & Ellis Company, 21; 98 (upd.)
Guangzhou R&F Properties Co., Ltd., 95
The Haminerson Property Investment and
    Development Corporation plc, IV
Hammerson plc, 40
Hang Lung Group Ltd., 104
Harbert Corporation, 14
Helmsley Enterprises, Inc., 39 (upd.)
Henderson Land Development Company
    Ltd., 70
Home Properties of New York, Inc., 42
HomeVestors of America, Inc., 77
Hongkong Land Holdings Limited, IV;
    47 (upd.)
Holiday Retirement Corp., 87
Hopson Development Holdings Ltd., 87
Hovnanian Enterprises, Inc., 29; 89 (upd.)
Hyatt Corporation, 16 (upd.)
ILX Resorts Incorporated, 65
IRSA Inversiones y Representaciones S.A.,
    63
J.F. Shea Co., Inc., 55
Jardine Cycle & Carriage Ltd., 73
JMB Realty Corporation, IV
Jones Lang LaSalle Incorporated, 49
JPI, 49
Kaufman and Broad Home Corporation,
    8
Kennedy-Wilson, Inc., 60
Kerry Properties Limited, 22
Kimco Realty Corporation, 11
The Koll Company, 8
Land Securities PLC, IV; 49 (upd.)
Lefrak Organization Inc., 26
Lend Lease Corporation Limited, IV; 17
    (upd.); 52 (upd.)
Liberty Property Trust, 57

Lincoln Property Company, 8; 54 (upd.)
The Loewen Group Inc., 40 (upd.)
The Long & Foster Companies, Inc., 85
The Macerich Company, 57
Mack-Cali Realty Corporation, 42
Macklowe Properties, Inc., 95
Manufactured Home Communities, Inc.,
    22
Maui Land & Pineapple Company, Inc.,
    29; 100 (upd.)
Maxco Inc., 17
Meditrust, 11
Melvin Simon and Associates, Inc., 8
MEPC plc, IV
Meritage Corporation, 26
Mid-America Apartment Communities,
    Inc., 85
The Middleton Doll Company, 53
The Mills Corporation, 77
Mitsubishi Estate Company, Limited, IV;
    61 (upd.)
Mitsui Real Estate Development Co.,
    Ltd., IV
Morguard Corporation, 85
The Nature Conservancy, 28
New Plan Realty Trust, 11
New World Development Company Ltd.,
    IV
Newhall Land and Farming Company, 14
Nexity S.A., 66
NRT Incorporated, 61
Olympia & York Developments Ltd., IV;
    9 (upd.)
Panattoni Development Company, Inc.,
    99
Park Corp., 22
Parque Arauco S.A., 72
Perini Corporation, 8
Pope Resources LP, 74
Post Properties, Inc., 26
Potlatch Corporation, 8; 34 (upd.); 87
    (upd.)
ProLogis, 57
Public Storage, Inc., 52
Railtrack Group PLC, 50
RE/MAX International, Inc., 59
Reading International Inc., 70
Reckson Associates Realty Corp., 47
Regency Centers Corporation, 71
Rockefeller Group International Inc., 58
Rodamco N.V., 26
The Rouse Company, 15; 63 (upd.)
The St. Joe Company, 8; 98 (upd.)
Sapporo Holdings Limited, I; 13 (upd.);
    36 (upd.); 97 (upd.)
Shubert Organization Inc., 24
The Sierra Club, 28
Silverstein Properties, Inc., 47
Simco S.A., 37
SL Green Realty Corporation, 44
Slough Estates PLC, IV; 50 (upd.)
Sovran Self Storage, Inc., 66
Starrett Corporation, 21
The Staubach Company, 62
Storage USA, Inc., 21
Sumitomo Realty & Development Co.,
    Ltd., IV
Sun Communities Inc., 46

Sunterra Corporation, 75
Tanger Factory Outlet Centers, Inc., 49
Tarragon Realty Investors, Inc., 45
Taubman Centers, Inc., 75
Taylor Woodrow plc, 38 (upd.)
Technical Olympic USA, Inc., 75
Tejon Ranch Company, 35
Tishman Speyer Properties, L.P., 47
Tokyu Land Corporation, IV
Trammell Crow Company, 8; 57 (upd.)
Trendwest Resorts, Inc., 33
Tridel Enterprises Inc., 9
Trizec Corporation Ltd., 10
The Trump Organization, 23; 64 (upd.)
Unibail SA, 40
United Dominion Realty Trust, Inc., 52
Vistana, Inc., 22
Vornado Realty Trust, 20
W.P. Carey & Co. LLC, 49
Weingarten Realty Investors, 95
William Lyon Homes, 59
Woodbridge Holdings Corporation, 99

Retail & Wholesale

A-Mark Financial Corporation, 71
A.C. Moore Arts & Crafts, Inc., 30
A.S. Watson & Company Ltd., 84
A.T. Cross Company, 49 (upd.)
Aaron Rents, Inc., 14; 35 (upd.)
Abatix Corp., 57
ABC Appliance, Inc., 10
ABC Carpet & Home Co. Inc., 26
Abercrombie & Fitch Company, 15; 75
    (upd.)
Academy Sports & Outdoors, 27
Ace Hardware Corporation, 12; 35 (upd.)
Action Performance Companies, Inc., 27
Adams Childrenswear Ltd., 95
ADESA, Inc., 71
Adolfo Dominguez S.A., 72
AEON Co., Ltd., 68 (upd.)
Aéropostale, Inc., 89
After Hours Formalwear Inc., 60
Alabama Farmers Cooperative, Inc., 63
Alain Afflelou SA, 53
Alba-Waldensian, Inc., 30
Alberto-Culver Company, 8; 36 (upd.); 91
    (upd.)
Albertson's, Inc., 65 (upd.)
Alimentation Couche-Tard Inc., 77
Alldays plc, 49
Allders plc, 37
Alliance Boots plc (updates Boots Group
    PLC), 83 (upd.)
Allou Health & Beauty Care, Inc., 28
Almacenes Exito S.A., 89
Alpha Airports Group PLC, 77
Alrosa Company Ltd., 62
Alticor Inc., 71 (upd.)
AMAG Group, 102
Amazon.com, Inc., 25; 56 (upd.)
AMCON Distributing Company, 99
AMERCO, 67 (upd.)
American Coin Merchandising, Inc., 28;
    74 (upd.)
American Eagle Outfitters, Inc., 24; 55
    (upd.)
American Furniture Company, Inc., 21

Mediacom Communications Corporation, 69
Mercury Communications, Ltd., 7
Metrocall, Inc., 41
Metromedia Companies, 14
Métropole Télévision, 33
Métropole Télévision S.A., 76 (upd.)
MFS Communications Company, Inc., 11
Michigan Bell Telephone Co., 14
MIH Limited, 31
MITRE Corporation, 26
Mobile Telecommunications Technologies Corp., 18
Mobile TeleSystems OJSC, 59
Modern Times Group AB, 36
The Montana Power Company, 44 (upd.)
Motorola, Inc., II; 11 (upd.); 34 (upd.); 93 (upd.)
Multimedia, Inc., 11
National Broadcasting Company, Inc., 28 (upd.)
National Grid USA, 51 (upd.)
National Weather Service, 91
NCR Corporation, III; 6 (upd.); 30 (upd.); 90 (upd.)
NetCom Systems AB, 26
NeuStar, Inc., 81
Nevada Bell Telephone Company, 14
New Valley Corporation, 17
Newcom Group, 104
Nexans SA, 54
Nexstar Broadcasting Group, Inc., 73
Nextel Communications, Inc., 27 (upd.)
Nippon Telegraph and Telephone Corporation, V; 51 (upd.)
Nokia Corporation, 77 (upd.)
Norstan, Inc., 16
Nortel Networks Corporation, 36 (upd.)
Northern Telecom Limited, V
NTL Inc., 65
NTN Buzztime, Inc., 86
NYNEX Corporation, V
Octel Messaging, 14; 41 (upd.)
Ohio Bell Telephone Company, 14
Olivetti S.p.A., 34 (upd.)
Orange S.A., 84
Österreichische Post- und Telegraphenverwaltung, V
Pacific Internet Limited, 87
Pacific Telecom, Inc., 6
Pacific Telesis Group, V
Paging Network Inc., 11
PanAmSat Corporation, 46
Paxson Communications Corporation, 33
Petry Media Corporation, 102
The Phoenix Media/Communications Group, 91
PictureTel Corp., 10; 27 (upd.)
Portugal Telecom SGPS S.A., 69
Posti- ja Telelaitos, 6
Premiere Radio Networks, Inc., 102
Price Communications Corporation, 42
ProSiebenSat.1 Media AG, 54
Publishing and Broadcasting Limited, 54
Qatar Telecom QSA, 87
QUALCOMM Incorporated, 20; 47 (upd.)
QVC Network Inc., 9

Qwest Communications International, Inc., 37
RCN Corporation, 70
Regent Communications, Inc., 87
Research in Motion Ltd., 54
RMH Teleservices, Inc., 42
Rochester Telephone Corporation, 6
Rogers Communications Inc., 30 (upd.)
Rostelecom Joint Stock Co., 99
Royal KPN N.V., 30
Rural Cellular Corporation, 43
Saga Communications, Inc., 27
Salem Communications Corporation, 97
Sawtek Inc., 43 (upd.)
SBC Communications Inc., 32 (upd.)
Schweizerische Post-, Telefon- und Telegrafen-Betriebe, V
Scientific-Atlanta, Inc., 6; 45 (upd.)
Seat Pagine Gialle S.p.A., 47
Securicor Plc, 45
Shenandoah Telecommunications Company, 89
Sinclair Broadcast Group, Inc., 25
Sirius Satellite Radio, Inc., 69
Sirti S.p.A., 76
Società Finanziaria Telefonica per Azioni, V
Softbank Corporation, 77 (upd.)
Sonera Corporation, 50
Southern New England Telecommunications Corporation, 6
Southwestern Bell Corporation, V
Spanish Broadcasting System, Inc., 41
Spelling Entertainment, 35 (upd.)
Sprint Corporation, 9; 46 (upd.)
StarHub Ltd., 77
StrataCom, Inc., 16
Swedish Telecom, V
Swisscom AG, 58
Sycamore Networks, Inc., 45
Syniverse Holdings Inc., 97
SynOptics Communications, Inc., 10
T-Netix, Inc., 46
Talk America Holdings, Inc., 70
TDC A/S, 63
Tekelec, 83
Telcordia Technologies, Inc., 59
Tele Norte Leste Participações S.A., 80
Telecom Argentina S.A., 63
Telecom Australia, 6
Telecom Corporation of New Zealand Limited, 54
Telecom Eireann, 7
Telecom Italia Mobile S.p.A., 63
Telecom Italia S.p.A., 43
Telefonaktiebolaget LM Ericsson, V; 46 (upd.)
Telefónica de Argentina S.A., 61
Telefónica S.A., V; 46 (upd.)
Telefonos de Mexico S.A. de C.V., 14; 63 (upd.)
Telekom Malaysia Bhd, 76
Telekomunikacja Polska SA, 50
Telenor ASA, 69
Telephone and Data Systems, Inc., 9
Télévision Française 1, 23
TeliaSonera AB, 57 (upd.)
Tellabs, Inc., 11; 40 (upd.)

Telstra Corporation Limited, 50
Terremark Worldwide, Inc., 99
Thomas Crosbie Holdings Limited, 81
Tiscali SpA, 48
The Titan Corporation, 36
Tollgrade Communications, Inc., 44
TV Azteca, S.A. de C.V., 39
U.S. Satellite Broadcasting Company, Inc., 20
U S West, Inc., V; 25 (upd.)
U.S. Cellular Corporation, 9; 31 (upd.); 88 (upd.)
UFA TV & Film Produktion GmbH, 80
United Pan-Europe Communications NV, 47
United Telecommunications, Inc., V
United Video Satellite Group, 18
Univision Communications Inc., 24; 83 (upd.)
USA Interactive, Inc., 47 (upd.)
USA Mobility Inc., 97 (upd.)
UTStarcom, Inc., 77
Verizon Communications Inc. 43 (upd.); 78 (upd.)
ViaSat, Inc., 54
Vivendi Universal S.A., 46 (upd.)
Vodafone Group Plc, 11; 36 (upd.); 75 (upd.)
Vonage Holdings Corp., 81
The Walt Disney Company, II; 6 (upd.); 30 (upd.); 63 (upd.)
Wanadoo S.A., 75
Watkins-Johnson Company, 15
The Weather Channel Companies, 52
West Corporation, 42
Western Union Financial Services, Inc., 54
Western Wireless Corporation, 36
Westwood One, Inc., 23
Williams Communications Group, Inc., 34
The Williams Companies, Inc., 31 (upd.)
Wipro Limited, 43
Wisconsin Bell, Inc., 14
Working Assets Funding Service, 43
Worldwide Pants Inc., 97
XM Satellite Radio Holdings, Inc., 69
Young Broadcasting Inc., 40
Zain, 102
Zed Group, 93
Zoom Technologies, Inc., 53 (upd.)

Textiles & Apparel

Abercrombie & Fitch Company, 35 (upd.); 75 (upd.)
Adams Childrenswear Ltd., 95
adidas Group AG, 14; 33 (upd.); 75 (upd.)
Adolfo Dominguez S.A., 72
Aéropostale, Inc., 89
Alba-Waldensian, Inc., 30
Albany International Corp., 8
Alexandra plc, 88
Algo Group Inc., 24
Alpargatas S.A.I.C., 87
American & Efird, Inc., 82
American Apparel, Inc., 90
American Safety Razor Company, 20
Amoskeag Company, 8

Tobacco

Transport Services

Odfjell SE, 101
Odyssey Marine Exploration, Inc., 91
Oglebay Norton Company, 17
Old Dominion Freight Line, Inc., 57
OMI Corporation, 59
The Oppenheimer Group, 76
Oshkosh Corporation, 7; 98 (upd.)
Österreichische Bundesbahnen GmbH, 6
OTR Express, Inc., 25
Overnite Corporation, 14; 58 (upd.)
Overseas Shipholding Group, Inc., 11
Pacer International, Inc., 54
Pacific Basin Shipping Ltd., 86
Patriot Transportation Holding, Inc., 91
The Peninsular and Oriental Steam
    Navigation Company, V; 38 (upd.)
Penske Corporation, V; 19 (upd.); 84
    (upd.)
PHH Arval, V; 53 (upd.)
Pilot Air Freight Corp., 67
Plantation Pipe Line Company, 68
PODS Enterprises Inc., 103
Polar Air Cargo Inc., 60
The Port Authority of New York and New
    Jersey, 48
Port Imperial Ferry Corporation, 70
Post Office Group, V
Preston Corporation, 6
RailTex, Inc., 20
Railtrack Group PLC, 50
REpower Systems AG, 101
Réseau Ferré de France, 66
Roadway Express, Inc., V; 25 (upd.)
Rock-It Cargo USA, Inc., 86
Royal Olympic Cruise Lines Inc., 52
Royal Vopak NV, 41
Russian Railways Joint Stock Co., 93
Ryder System, Inc., V; 24 (upd.)
Saia, Inc., 98
Santa Fe Pacific Corporation, V
Schenker-Rhenus AG, 6
Schneider National, Inc., 36; 77 (upd.)
Seaboard Corporation, 36; 85 (upd.)
SEACOR Holdings Inc., 83
Securicor Plc, 45
Seibu Railway Company Ltd., V; 74
    (upd.)
Seino Transportation Company, Ltd., 6
Simon Transportation Services Inc., 27
Smithway Motor Xpress Corporation, 39
Société Nationale des Chemins de Fer
    Français, V; 57 (upd.)
Société Norbert Dentressangle S.A., 67
Southern Pacific Transportation Company,
    V
Spee-Dee Delivery Service, Inc., 93
Stagecoach Group plc, 30; 104 (upd.)
Stelmar Shipping Ltd., 52
Stevedoring Services of America Inc., 28
Stinnes AG, 8; 59 (upd.)
Stolt-Nielsen S.A., 42
Sunoco, Inc., 28 (upd.); 83 (upd.)
Swift Transportation Co., Inc., 42
The Swiss Federal Railways
    (Schweizerische Bundesbahnen), V
Swissport International Ltd., 70
Teekay Shipping Corporation, 25; 82
    (upd.)

Tibbett & Britten Group plc, 32
Tidewater Inc., 11; 37 (upd.)
TNT Freightways Corporation, 14
TNT Post Group N.V., V; 27 (upd.); 30
    (upd.)
Tobu Railway Company Ltd., 6; 98
    (upd.)
Tokyu Corporation, V
Totem Resources Corporation, 9
TPG N.V., 64 (upd.)
Trailer Bridge, Inc., 41
Transnet Ltd., 6
Transport Corporation of America, Inc.,
    49
Trico Marine Services, Inc., 89
Tsakos Energy Navigation Ltd., 91
TTX Company, 6; 66 (upd.)
U.S. Delivery Systems, Inc., 22
Union Pacific Corporation, V; 28 (upd.);
    79 (upd.)
United Parcel Service of America Inc., V;
    17 (upd.)
United Parcel Service, Inc., 63
United Road Services, Inc., 69
United States Postal Service, 14; 34 (upd.)
US 1 Industries, Inc., 89
USA Truck, Inc., 42
Velocity Express Corporation, 49
Werner Enterprises, Inc., 26
Wheels Inc., 96
Wincanton plc, 52
Wisconsin Central Transportation
    Corporation, 24
Wright Express Corporation, 80
Yamato Transport Co. Ltd., V; 49 (upd.)
Yellow Corporation, 14; 45 (upd.)
Yellow Freight System, Inc. of Delaware,
    V
YRC Worldwide Inc., 90 (upd.)

Utilities

AES Corporation, 10; 13 (upd.); 53
    (upd.)
Aggreko Plc, 45
Air & Water Technologies Corporation, 6
Alberta Energy Company Ltd., 16; 43
    (upd.)
Allegheny Energy, Inc., V; 38 (upd.)
Ameren Corporation, 60 (upd.)
American Electric Power Company, Inc.,
    V; 45 (upd.)
American States Water Company, 46
American Water Works Company, Inc., 6;
    38 (upd.)
Aquarion Company, 84
Aquila, Inc., 50 (upd.)
Arkla, Inc., V
Associated Natural Gas Corporation, 11
Atlanta Gas Light Company, 6; 23 (upd.)
Atlantic Energy, Inc., 6
Atmos Energy Corporation, 43
Avista Corporation, 69 (upd.)
Baltimore Gas and Electric Company, V;
    25 (upd.)
Basin Electric Power Cooperative, 103
Bay State Gas Company, 38
Bayernwerk AG, V; 23 (upd.)
Berlinwasser Holding AG, 90

Bewag AG, 39
Big Rivers Electric Corporation, 11
Black Hills Corporation, 20
Bonneville Power Administration, 50
Boston Edison Company, 12
Bouygues S.A., I; 24 (upd.); 97 (upd.)
British Energy Plc, 49
British Gas plc, V
British Nuclear Fuels plc, 6
Brooklyn Union Gas, 6
California Water Service Group, 79
Calpine Corporation, 36
Canadian Utilities Limited, 13; 56 (upd.)
Cap Rock Energy Corporation, 46
Carolina Power & Light Company, V; 23
    (upd.)
Cascade Natural Gas Corporation, 9
Cascal N.V., 103
Centerior Energy Corporation, V
Central and South West Corporation, V
Central Hudson Gas and Electricity
    Corporation, 6
Central Maine Power, 6
Central Vermont Public Service
    Corporation, 54
Centrica plc, 29 (upd.)
ČEZ a. s., 97
Chesapeake Utilities Corporation, 56
China Shenhua Energy Company
    Limited, 83
Chubu Electric Power Company, Inc., V;
    46 (upd.)
Chugoku Electric Power Company Inc.,
    V; 53 (upd.)
Cincinnati Gas & Electric Company, 6
CIPSCO Inc., 6
Citizens Utilities Company, 7
City Public Service, 6
Cleco Corporation, 37
CMS Energy Corporation, V, 14 (upd.);
    100 (upd.)
The Coastal Corporation, 31 (upd.)
Cogentrix Energy, Inc., 10
The Coleman Company, Inc., 9
The Columbia Gas System, Inc., V; 16
    (upd.)
Commonwealth Edison Company, V
Commonwealth Energy System, 14
Companhia Energética de Minas Gerais
    S.A. CEMIG, 65
Compañia de Minas Buenaventura S.A.A.,
    93
Connecticut Light and Power Co., 13
Consolidated Edison, Inc., V; 45 (upd.)
Consolidated Natural Gas Company, V;
    19 (upd.)
Consumers Power Co., 14
Consumers Water Company, 14
Consumers' Gas Company Ltd., 6
Covanta Energy Corporation, 64 (upd.)
Dalkia Holding, 66
Destec Energy, Inc., 12
The Detroit Edison Company, V
Dominion Resources, Inc., V; 54 (upd.)
DPL Inc., 6; 96 (upd.)
DQE, Inc., 6
DTE Energy Company, 20 (upd.)
Duke Energy Corporation, V; 27 (upd.)

Waste Services

Geographic Index

Sweden

Switzerland

SCP Pool Corporation, 39
Screen Actors Guild, 72
The Scripps Research Institute, 76
Sea Ray Boats Inc., 96
Seaboard Corporation, 36; 85 (upd.)
SeaChange International, Inc. 79
SEACOR Holdings Inc., 83
Seagate Technology, Inc., 8; 34 (upd.)
Seagull Energy Corporation, 11
Sealaska Corporation, 60
Sealed Air Corporation, 14; 57 (upd.)
Sealed Power Corporation, I
Sealright Co., Inc., 17
Sealy Inc., 12
Seaman Furniture Company, Inc., 32
Sean John Clothing, Inc., 70
Sears, Roebuck and Co., V; 18 (upd.); 56 (upd.)
Seattle City Light, 50
Seattle FilmWorks, Inc., 20
Seattle First National Bank Inc., 8
Seattle Lighting Fixture Company, 92
Seattle Pacific Industries, Inc., 92
Seattle Seahawks, Inc., 92
Seattle Times Company, 15
Seaway Food Town, Inc., 15
Sebastiani Vineyards, Inc., 28
The Second City, Inc., 88
Second Harvest, 29
Security Capital Corporation, 17
Security Pacific Corporation, II
SED International Holdings, Inc., 43
See's Candies, Inc., 30
Sega of America, Inc., 10
Segway LLC, 48
SEI Investments Company, 96
Seigle's Home and Building Centers, Inc., 41
Seitel, Inc., 47
Select Comfort Corporation, 34
Select Medical Corporation, 65
Selee Corporation, 88
The Selmer Company, Inc., 19
SEMCO Energy, Inc., 44
Seminis, Inc., 29
Semitool, Inc., 18; 79 (upd.)
Sempra Energy, 25 (upd.)
Semtech Corporation, 32
Seneca Foods Corporation, 17; 60 (upd.)
Senomyx, Inc., 83
Sensient Technologies Corporation, 52 (upd.)
Sensormatic Electronics Corp., 11
Sensory Science Corporation, 37
Sepracor Inc., 45
Sequa Corporation, 13; 54 (upd.)
Serologicals Corporation, 63
Serta, Inc., 28
Servco Pacific Inc., 96
Service America Corp., 7
Service Corporation International, 6; 51 (upd.)
Service Merchandise Company, Inc., V; 19 (upd.)
The ServiceMaster Company, 6; 23 (upd.); 68 (upd.)
Servidyne Inc., 100 (upd.)
Servpro Industries, Inc., 85

7-11, Inc., 32 (upd.)
Sevenson Environmental Services, Inc., 42
Seventh Generation, Inc., 73
Seyfarth Shaw LLP, 93
SFX Entertainment, Inc., 36
SGI, 29 (upd.)
Shakespeare Company, 22
Shaklee Corporation, 12; 39 (upd.)
Shamrock Foods Company, 105
Shared Medical Systems Corporation, 14
The Sharper Image Corporation, 10; 62 (upd.)
The Shaw Group, Inc., 50
Shaw Industries, Inc., 9; 40 (upd.)
Shaw's Supermarkets, Inc., 56
Shawmut National Corporation, 13
Sheaffer Pen Corporation, 82
Shearer's Foods, Inc., 72
Shearman & Sterling, 32
Shearson Lehman Brothers Holdings Inc., II; 9 (upd.)
Shedd Aquarium Society, 73
Sheetz, Inc., 85
Shelby Williams Industries, Inc., 14
Sheldahl Inc., 23
Shell Oil Company, IV; 14 (upd.); 41 (upd.)
Shell Vacations LLC, 102
Sheller-Globe Corporation, I
Shells Seafood Restaurants, Inc., 43
Shenandoah Telecommunications Company, 89
Sheplers, Inc., 96
The Sheridan Group, Inc., 86
The Sherwin-Williams Company, III; 13 (upd.); 89 (upd.)
Sherwood Brands, Inc., 53
Shoe Carnival Inc., 14; 72 (upd.)
Shoe Pavilion, Inc., 84
Shoney's North America Corp., 7; 23 (upd.); 105 (upd.)
ShopKo Stores Inc., 21; 58 (upd.)
Shoppers Food Warehouse Corporation, 66
Shorewood Packaging Corporation, 28
ShowBiz Pizza Time, Inc., 13
Showboat, Inc., 19
Showtime Networks Inc. 78
Shriners Hospitals for Children, 69
Shubert Organization Inc., 24
Shuffle Master Inc., 51
Shure Inc., 60
Shurgard Storage Centers, Inc., 52
Shutterfly, Inc., 98
Sidley Austin Brown & Wood, 40
Sidney Frank Importing Co., Inc., 69
Siebel Systems, Inc., 38
Siebert Financial Corp., 32
Siegel & Gale, 64
The Sierra Club, 28
Sierra Health Services, Inc., 15
Sierra Nevada Brewing Company, 70
Sierra On-Line, Inc., 15; 41 (upd.)
Sierra Pacific Industries, 22; 90 (upd.)
SIFCO Industries, Inc., 41
Sigma-Aldrich Corporation, I; 36 (upd.); 93 (upd.)

Signet Banking Corporation, 11; 104 (upd.)
Sikorsky Aircraft Corporation, 24
Silhouette Brands, Inc., 55
Silicon Graphics Incorporated, 9
Silver Lake Cookie Company Inc., 95
SilverPlatter Information Inc., 23
Silverstar Holdings, Ltd., 99
Silverstein Properties, Inc., 47
Simmons Company, 47
Simon & Schuster Inc., IV; 19 (upd.); 100 (upd.)
Simon Property Group Inc., 27; 84 (upd.)
Simon Transportation Services Inc., 27
Simplex Technologies Inc., 21
Simplicity Manufacturing, Inc., 64
Simpson Investment Company, 17
Simpson Thacher & Bartlett, 39
Simula, Inc., 41
Sinclair Broadcast Group, Inc., 25
Sine Qua Non, 99
The Singing Machine Company, Inc., 60
Sir Speedy, Inc., 16
Sirius Satellite Radio, Inc., 69
Siskin Steel & Supply Company, 70
Sisters of Charity of Leavenworth Health System, 105
Six Flags, Inc., 17; 54 (upd.)
SJW Corporation, 70
Skadden, Arps, Slate, Meagher & Flom, 18
Skechers U.S.A. Inc., 31; 88 (upd.)
Skeeter Products Inc., 96
Skidmore, Owings & Merrill LLP, 13; 69 (upd.)
skinnyCorp, LLC, 97
Skyline Chili, Inc., 62
Skyline Corporation, 30
SkyMall, Inc., 26
SkyWest, Inc., 25
Skyy Spirits LLC 78
SL Green Realty Corporation, 44
SL Industries, Inc., 77
Sleepy's Inc., 32
SLI, Inc., 48
Slim-Fast Foods Company, 18; 66 (upd.)
SLM Holding Corp., 25 (upd.)
Small Planet Foods, Inc., 89
Smart & Final LLC, 16; 94 (upd.)
Smart Balance, Inc., 100
SMART Modular Technologies, Inc., 86
SmartForce PLC, 43
Smead Manufacturing Co., 17
Smith & Hawken, Ltd., 68
Smith & Wesson Corp., 30; 73 (upd.)
Smith Barney Inc., 15
Smith Corona Corp., 13
Smith International, Inc., 15; 59 (upd.)
The Smith & Wollensky Restaurant Group, Inc., 105
Smith's Food & Drug Centers, Inc., 8; 57 (upd.)
Smith-Midland Corporation, 56
Smithfield Foods, Inc., 7; 43 (upd.)
SmithKline Beckman Corporation, I
Smithsonian Institution, 27
Smithway Motor Xpress Corporation, 39

Empresas Polar SA, 55 (upd.)
Petróleos de Venezuela S.A., IV; 74 (upd.)

Vietnam

Lam Son Sugar Joint Stock Corporation
(Lasuco), 60

Virgin Islands

Little Switzerland, Inc., 60

Wales

Hyder plc, 34
Iceland Group plc, 33
Kwik Save Group plc, 11

Zambia

Zambia Industrial and Mining
Corporation Ltd., IV

Zimbabwe

Air Zimbabwe (Private) Limited, 91